A STUDY OF
HISTORY

A STUDY OF HISTORY

BY

ARNOLD J. TOYNBEE

Hon. D.Litt. Oxon. and Birmingham
Hon. LL.D. Princeton, F.B.A.

*Director of Studies in the Royal Institute
of International Affairs
Research Professor of International History
in the University of London
(both on the Sir Daniel Stevenson Foundation)*

'Except the Lord build the house,
their labour is but lost that build it.
'Except the Lord keep the city,
the watchman waketh but in vain.'
Ps. cxxvii. 1–2

VOLUME V

*Issued under the auspices of the Royal Institute
of International Affairs*

OXFORD   UNIVERSITY   PRESS
LONDON   NEW YORK   TORONTO

Oxford University Press, Amen House, London E.C. 4

EDINBURGH GLASGOW NEW YORK TORONTO MELBOURNE
WELLINGTON BOMBAY CALCUTTA MADRAS CAPE TOWN

Geoffrey Cumberlege, Publisher to the University

FIRST EDITION 1939
SECOND IMPRESSION 1940
THIRD IMPRESSION 1946
FOURTH IMPRESSION 1948

PRINTED IN GREAT BRITAIN
BY JARROLD AND SONS, LTD., THE EMPIRE PRESS
NORWICH

CONTENTS

V. THE DISINTEGRATIONS OF CIVILIZATIONS

V
THE DISINTEGRATIONS OF CIVILIZATIONS

A. THE PROBLEM OF THE DISINTEGRATIONS OF CIVILIZATIONS

IN passing from the breakdowns of civilizations to their disintegrations we have once more to run the gauntlet of a question which has already confronted us, at an earlier point in this Study, when we were passing from the geneses of civilizations to their growths.[1] At that point we found ourselves constrained to pause in order to consider whether we were setting ourselves a genuine problem. If we had previously probed as far as we were able to probe into the geneses of civilizations, had we not thereby already won the right to take their growths for granted, on the assumption that growth must follow birth as automatically and as inevitably as day follows dawn? Now that, in the later part of our Study at which we have since arrived, we have again reached our Pillars of Hercules in probing, this time, into the problem of breakdowns, can we not be content to dismiss the problem of disintegrations, which occupies the next place in our plan of inquiry, as a mere formality, on the assumption that disintegration must follow breakdown as surely as night follows evening?

Perhaps the best way to deal with this question that confronts us now will be to remind ourselves of how we dealt with the analogous question that has presented itself to us before. In this previous case we found that our impulse to dismiss a problem summarily on the strength of an abstract argument *a priori* was checked—as soon as we took our customary precaution of exploring the ground empirically—by an immediate discovery of concrete evidence which showed, in the mere fact of its palpable existence, that our problem was not an empty formality after all. The problem of the growths of civilizations was found to be raised in practical terms by the enigmatic but substantial presence, in the historical landscape, of five arrested civilizations,[2] every one of which had failed to grow in spite of having succeeded—unlike the four abortive civilizations[3]—in coming to birth. If we follow this clue in applying our well-tried empirical method once again, we

[1] See Part III. A, vol. iii, p. 1, above.
[2] The Polynesian, the Eskimo, the Nomadic, the 'Osmanli, and the Spartan (see Part III. A, in vol. iii, above).
[3] The abortive Far Eastern Christian, Far Western Christian, and Scandinavian civilizations, and an abortive Syriac Civilization (see Part II. D (vii), in vol. ii, above).

shall find that our present problem of the disintegrations of civilizations is likewise substantiated by certain palpable matters of fact which have already come under our observation. The set of civilizations that have been arrested after their birth, before they have had time to begin to grow, has its analogue in another set of civilizations that have been petrified after their breakdown before they have had time to complete the downward course that runs through disintegration to dissolution.

The classic example of a petrified civilization is presented by a phase in the history of the Egyptiac Society which we have already had occasion to consider in several different contexts.[1] We have noticed that, after the Egyptiac Society had broken down under the intolerable burden that was imposed upon it by the Pyramid-Builders, and after it had then duly passed through the first and the second into the third of three phases of disintegration—a 'Time of Troubles' and a universal state and an interregnum—this apparently moribund Egyptiac Society then departed unexpectedly and abruptly, at a moment when it was on the verge of completing its life-course, from what we may provisionally regard as the standard pattern of the disintegration-process if we take for our norm the Hellenic case in which these three phases of disintegration first came to our notice.[2] At the point where the disintegration of the Hellenic Society reached what might be thought to be its natural termination—that is to say, at the point where this disintegration culminated in dissolution—the Egyptiac Society passionately refused to pass away and emulated the legendary *tour de force* of its own historic King Mycerinus[3] by rebelling against the execution of the death-sentence which it had lawfully incurred and successfully doubling the period of grace which Fate had allotted to it. When we take the time-measure of the survival of the Egyptiac Society from the moment of its galvanic reaction against the Hyksos invaders in the first quarter of the sixteenth century B.C.[4] down to the eventual obliteration of the last traces of a distinctive Egyptiac style of culture in the fifth century of the Christian Era, we find that this span of 2,000 years is at least as long as the combined span of the birth, growth, breakdown, and almost completed disintegration of the Egyptiac Civilization—reckoning back from the date of its passionate reassertion of itself in the sixteenth century B.C. to its first emergence above

---

[1] See I. C (ii), vol. i, pp. 136–46; III. C (i) (*d*), vol. iii, pp. 212–15; IV. C (ii) (*b*) 2, vol. iv, pp. 84–6; IV. C (iii) (*c*) 2 (β), vol. iv, pp. 408–14 and 418–23, above.
[2] See I. C (i) (*a*), vol. i, pp. 52–62, above.
[3] See Herodotus, Book II, chaps. 129–34, for the legend of King Mycerinus (Menkaure) of the Fourth Dynasty of the Egyptiac United Kingdom. (The legend has been cited in this Study already in IV. C (iii) (*c*) 2 (β), vol. iv, p. 409, above.)
[4] See I. C (ii), vol. i, p. 144, above.

the primitive level at some unknown date in the fourth millennium B.C. Thus the Egyptiac Society did actually succeed—in spite of having broken down and gone into disintegration—in surviving for double the term of its natural expectation of life; but this unnatural longevity was bought at a price; for the life of the Egyptiac Society during this second aeon of existence which it had wrested from Fate was a kind of life-in-death. During those two supernumerary millennia a civilization whose career during the two preceding millennia had been so full of movement and of meaning—and this during its fall as well as during its rise— lingered on, on a level with the arrested civilizations and indeed with the primitive societies, as one of 'the peoples that have no history'. In fact, it survived by becoming petrified.[1]

This extraordinary case of petrifaction which confronts us in Egyptiac history is perhaps sufficient in itself to dispose of the assumption that the breakdown of a civilization must inevitably be followed by a process of disintegration that runs straight out into dissolution in the Hellenic way. But the Egyptiac example of petrifaction does not stand alone. If we turn to the history of the main body of the Far Eastern Civilization in China, in which the moment of breakdown may be equated with the break-up of the T'ang Empire in the last quarter of the ninth century of the Christian Era,[2] we can trace the consequent process of disintegration duly following the normal course through a 'Time of Troubles' into a universal state—only to be pulled up in the universal state stage by a reaction of the same unexpected and abrupt and passionate kind as the Egyptiac Society's reaction in the interregnum following the Egyptiac universal state's disappearance. The Southern Chinese revolt, under the leadership of the founder of the Ming Dynasty, Hung Wu,[3] against a Far Eastern universal state that had been established by the barbarian Mongols, is strongly reminiscent of the Theban revolt, under the leadership of the founder of the Eighteenth Dynasty, Amosis, against the 'successor-state' which had been erected on part of the derelict domain of the defunct Egyptiac universal state (the so-called 'Middle Empire') by the barbarian Hyksos.[4] And

[1] For Ikhnaton's abortive act of creation, which was the exception that proved the rule of life-in-death during the Egyptiac aeon of petrifaction, see I. C (ii), vol. i, pp. 145–6, above, and V. C (i) (d) 6 (δ), Annex, in the present volume, pp. 695–6, below.

[2] See IV. C (ii) (b) 2, vol. iv, p. 86, above.

[3] For the Ming Dynasty see II. D (v), vol. ii, pp. 121–2, and IV. C (ii) (b) 2, vol. iv, p. 87, above.

[4] The common vein of convulsive fanaticism in the Chinese Anti-Mongol reaction and in the Theban Anti-Hyksos reaction may be accounted for by a characteristic which the Mongols and the Hyksos displayed in common. Neither of these intruding barbarian war-bands was unadulteratedly barbarian. Each of them had already acquired the tincture of a civilization which was different from the civilization towards which they were now playing the part of an external proletariat. The Hyksos had been

there has been a corresponding similarity in the sequel. For, like the Egyptiac Society, the Far Eastern Society in China has prolonged its existence in a petrified form instead of passing expeditiously through disintegration to dissolution by way of a universal state running out into an interregnum.

It is true that the survival of the Far Eastern Society in China in its petrified state cannot yet compare in duration with the period for which the Egyptiac Society contrived to survive in the same condition. So far, less than six centuries have elapsed since Hung Wu drove the Mongols out beyond the Great Wall in A.D. 1368; and at the present moment it looks as though the Far Eastern Society were fast losing its identity through being merged in 'the Great Society' of a Westernized World. The Egyptiac parallel suggests, however, that these present appearances in China may be deceptive; for if we take the expulsion of the Mongols from China in A.D. 1368 as having its Egyptiac counterpart in the expulsion of the Hyksos from Egypt *circa* 1580 B.C., we find that the year A.D. 1938, in which this volume went to press, is represented in the annals of Egyptiac history by some year in the neighbourhood of 1010 B.C.; and any open-eyed and candid-minded observer, either foreign or native, of the state of the Egyptiac Society in the latter decades of the eleventh century B.C. would almost certainly have taken then as pessimistic a view of the Egyptiac Society's expectation of life as we are apt to take now of the prospects of the Far Eastern Society in China. In spite of that, the Egyptiac Society actually continued to survive—weathering one storm after another in its state of quite incurable yet almost invincible decrepitude—for a further period of nearly 1,500 more years. And, on this showing, we may well hesitate to pronounce that, in our day, a petrified Far Eastern Society in China is within sight of extinction.[1]

Thus, in the last phase of Chinese as well as Egyptiac history, we have an empirical proof that the breakdown of a civilization is not necessarily followed by a disintegration that runs out straight

---

infected with the Sumeric Civilization (see I. C (ii), vol. i, p. 139, footnote 1, above) and the Mongols with the Abortive Far Eastern Christian Civilization (see II. D (v), vol. ii, p. 122, footnote 2; II. D (vi), vol. ii, pp. 237–8; II. D (vii), Annex VIII, vol. ii, pp. 449–51, above). This touch of an alien civilization in the social 'make-up' of the Hyksos and the Mongols is perhaps the common element which accounts for the exceptionally fanatical reaction which they evoked from their Egyptiac and Far Eastern victims. (On this question see further V. C (i) (c) 4, pp. 348–53, below.)

[1] So far from there being any certainty that the end of the Far Eastern Civilization in China was at hand in the year A.D. 1938, it seemed possible that this petrified society might be galvanized into a fresh lease of life-in-death by the extreme pressure of the Westernization which was now being applied to China through Japanese as well as through European and American channels. The galvanic effect, both upon the Far Eastern and upon the Egyptiac Society, of successive impacts of alien bodies social has been touched upon already in IV. C (ii) (b) 3, vol. iv, pp. 116–18, above.

into dissolution. And there is a possibility that these two clear cases of the phenomenon of petrifaction may be reinforced by no less than nine others, if we eventually decide that ten of the twenty-one civilizations which we provisionally identified in the first part of this Study are not, after all, independent societies existing in their own right, but are simply the 'dead trunks' of other trees which we have already counted in our list.[1] On this reckoning the Far Eastern Society itself would have to be regarded as being simply the 'dead trunk' of the Sinic Society; and this would apply to the offshoot of the Far Eastern Society in Korea and Japan, as well as to its main body in China. Similarly the Orthodox Christian Society, both in its Near Eastern main body and in its Russian offshoot, would figure as the 'dead trunk' of the Hellenic Society; and the Iranic and Arabic societies would assume the same role in Syriac history, the Mexic and Yucatec societies in Mayan history, the Hindu Society in Indic history, and the Babylonic Society in Sumeric history. If we take separate account of each of the two limbs of any bifurcating stem this procedure would bring our number of petrified civilizations up to eleven, namely:[2]

The Egyptiac *inde ab Amosi.*
The Sinic in its Far Eastern epilogue in China.
The Sinic in its Far Eastern epilogue in Korea and Japan.
The Hellenic in its Orthodox Christian epilogue in the Near East.
The Hellenic in its Orthodox Christian epilogue in Russia.
The Syriac in its Iranic epilogue.
The Syriac in its Arabic epilogue.
The Mayan in its Mexic epilogue.
The Mayan in its Yucatec epilogue.
The Indic in its Hindu epilogue.
The Sumeric in its Babylonic epilogue.

Moreover, in the history of the Sinic Society in its Far Eastern epilogue in China, we should have one example of something which might aptly, though perhaps rather quaintly, be described as a kind of social biscuit, in which the process of petrifaction had been undergone twice over: first, when the Sinic Society became petrified in the shape of the Far Eastern Society after the interregnum (*circa* A.D. 175–475) following the break-up of the universal state of the Han Dynasty; and for the second time when the Chinese branch of this petrified form of the Sinic Society became petrified to a still higher degree through that process of reaction

[1] This question has been raised in I. C (ii), vol. i, pp. 133–46, above.
[2] Compare this catalogue with those in I. C (ii), vol. i, pp. 131–3, above.

against the Mongol universal state which resulted in the establishment of the Ming Dynasty in A.D. 1368.

Perhaps we shall be wise to dispense with these reinforcements; for we have already discovered that we cannot actually disqualify our ten contested civilizations without exposing ourselves to serious difficulties. For example, if we decide to regard the Orthodox Christian Society as being merely a 'dead trunk' of the Hellenic Civilization, then we cannot refuse—without falling into an unwarrantable inconsistency—to regard our own Western Society in the same light, since the Western and Orthodox Christian societies are sister growths whose relation to the Hellenic Society is manifestly identical, whatever the relation may prove to be. Yet it would be as repugnant to our common sense to dismiss our own Western history as a mere epilogue to Hellenic history, and to decline to see in it the history of an independent society existing in its own right,[1] as conversely it would seem unreasonable to us to

---

[1] In the table of affinities that has been adopted in this Study the Hellenic and the Western Civilization appear as two separate and independent societies which are connected with one another by the relation for which we have coined the name 'Apparentation-and-Affiliation'. A closer kinship between these two civilizations, in virtue of a common quality which distinguishes the pair of them from all others, is suggested in the following passage of a letter which the writer of this Study has received from Dr. Edwyn Bevan:

'You see the process of history rather as a continual repetition of civilizations, running courses in many respects analogous, whereas it looks to me much more like a single process of unique stages. At least that seems to me the case with our European or "Western" Civilization, though, of course, I allow that civilizations like the Chinese or Indian are separate movements which may now be debouching into a common stream (as Polybius says the history of the Mediterranean peoples did in the third century B.C.) but which have hitherto run alongside of our "Western" Civilization. We should both, no doubt, allow that any bit of the historical process has both certain unique characteristics and also certain characteristics common to other bits of the process; but, while your attention and interest is directed mainly to the common characteristics, it is the uniqueness which impresses me.

'For instance, to begin at the end, the present condition of the World seems to me something like which nothing has ever been before, since Homo Sapiens was on the planet. And behind our modern world in time is the ancient Greco-Roman Civilization, the "Hellenic Civilization", as you call it, which I see, not simply as a civilization, but as the unique beginning of something new in the history of Mankind. Never before the Greek culture came into being, never in parts of the globe outside the sphere of that culture, can we see a civilization of the same rationalist character. (I admit it is a question of degree: all Mankind are rationalist up to a point.) That started a particular section of Mankind on a new track. Yet rationalist civilization in its first embodiment came to grief and was overrun by primitive barbarians. Then, when it had gradually worked its way up again through the barbarian mass, it got a fresh embodiment in our modern "Western" Civilization. That is to say, rationalist civilization is to-day making only its second try, and it seems to me hazardous to found any large generalizations about "civilizations", when, in regard to the particular kind of civilization in which we are primarily interested, you have only two examples. I see the movement of rationalist civilization in human history as it might be a battalion's assault on a fortress. The first attack is brought to a standstill and then thrown back by the coming in of an alien body of troops; but, that alien body having been disposed of, the attack is made again under conditions markedly different. No doubt, as one studied the first attack and the second attack, one would see analogous points in them: they would both go over the same ground, and meet some of the same obstacles. But the whole process containing the two attacks would be a single process, a single élan spirituel in two efforts.'

The writer of this Study has to confess that, on this important point, he finds himself unable to agree with a scholar for whose judgement he has a deep respect. To the present writer's eye the common element of rationalism which may be discernible in

erect the epilogue of Egyptiac history, in the aeon of petrifaction inaugurated by the establishment of the Eighteenth Dynasty, into the history of a distinct civilization claiming to be as independent of the Egyptiac as our Western Civilization appears in our eyes to be independent of the Hellenic. In this dilemma we shall probably still prefer to retain our original list of twenty-one distinct civilizations that have succeeded in passing from birth into growth, instead of attempting to reduce the number to ten.[1] On the other hand we shall be on sure ground in seeking reinforcements for our two undoubted specimens of petrifaction—the Egyptiac *post* 1580 B.C. and the Far Eastern in China *post* A.D. 1368—in our existing collection of fossils. Though we may not be warranted in labelling the Hindu Civilization as a petrified form of the Indic, or again the Iranic and Arabic civilizations as petrified forms of the Syriac, we need not doubt that we have discovered

the Hellenic and the Western Civilization is not so distinctive a quality as to mark this pair of societies off from all other representatives of the species. The Hellenic Society may have had a bent for rationalism—as the Western Society may have had one for machinery or the Indic Society one for religion (see III. C (iii), vol. iii, pp. 377–90, above). But the *floruit* of this Hellenic flower was as brief as it was brilliant (see IV. C (iii) (c) 2 (α), vol. iv, pp. 269–74, above, and V. C (i) (d) 6 (δ), pp. 545–68, below); and while it is, of course, true that there has been a renaissance of the Hellenic culture in the bosom of an 'affiliated' Western Society, and no less true that this Hellenic renaissance has tended to play an ever larger part in our Western life in the course of our Western history up to date, it would be begging the question (see I. B (iii), vol. i, p. 34, above) of what the essential character of the Western Civilization may be if we were simply to take it for granted that this is represented by just those elements in our Western life that can be traced to a Hellenic source. If we were to regard the Christian element in our Western culture as being the essence of it, then our reversion to Hellenism might be taken (as is suggested in Part VII, below) to be, not a fulfilment of the potentialities of Western Christendom, but an aberration from the proper path of Western growth—in fact, a false step which it may or may not be possible now to retrieve. In the present writer's view 'a unique beginning of something new in the history of Mankind' is to be seen, if anywhere, not in the flowering of a brilliant rationalism in the springtime of Hellenic history, but in the discovery—or revelation—of a new conception of God, and of Man's relation to God, which was made in the last phase of the dissolution of the Sumeric Society (if that is indeed the date and the provenance of Abraham), and which, ever since then, has gone on gathering light through a series of epiphanies of which the culmination has been Christianity. This view, which is put forward in Part VII, below, is not at variance with that of Mr. Bevan, as he has communicated it to the writer of this Study in a later letter in the same correspondence:

'I see I didn't make my view quite clear in one respect. I should hardly say that the significant central thread of History is the rise of Rationalism: I should say, rather, with you that the central thread is the preparation for the Kingdom of God and its partial coming. . . . I don't think that Rationalism is enough. It enables men to get hold better of the pattern of the Physical World, and by so doing gives them a much greater command of the physical means for accomplishing their ends; but it does not tell them what their ends ought to be. That is where the Kingdom of God comes in. . . . By "Civilization" I don't mean a right development of the whole spirit of Man or a right adjustment of human relations. I mean only an organization of society on rational principles for the attaining of certain ends, good ends or bad ends. . . . The word [Civilization] is ambiguous. You really want a different word for the kind of civilization which implies high moral and spiritual values and the kind which is simply scientific organization. . . . You may say: "A state in which the higher values of the human spirit are suppressed cannot be called 'Civilization'." Then you must find some word to distinguish such a state from an "uncivilized" condition in the sense of Primitive Barbarism. Might we say "Satanic"?'

[1] These ten civilizations which would then remain on our list would be the Egyptiac, Sinic, Hellenic, Syriac, Mayan, Indic, and Sumeric, together with the Hittite, the Minoan, and the Andean.

what are unmistakably fossilized fragments of the Indic Civiliza-
tion in the Jains of India, the Hinayanian Buddhists of Ceylon,
Burma, and Siam, and the Lamaistic Mahayanian Buddhists of
Tibet and Mongolia, and similar fossilized fragments of the
Syriac Civilization in the Parsees and the Jews and the Nestorians
and the Monophysites.[1]

In any case, however cautiously and conservatively we may feel
it wise to interpret the findings of the empirical survey that we
have just been attempting to make, the evidence seems amply
sufficient to demonstrate that the disintegration of broken-down
civilizations is not an automatic and inevitable process that can
simply be taken for granted. Even when disintegration has set in
it does not necessarily run straight out into dissolution; and, though
this may still prove to be the normal course of events, the cases of
departure from the norm, by way of petrifaction or fossilization,
are numerous enough and striking enough to raise the question of
the reasons why the declines and falls of civilizations should sometimes have this alternative denouement. Our classic example of
disintegration running straight out into dissolution has been the
latter end of the history of the Hellenic Civilization; yet, as an
eminent modern Western historian has pointed out, this society
which eventually made way for two fresh representatives of the
species was at one stage all but overtaken by the petrifaction which
has been the Far Eastern Civilization's fate:

'The spirit of the two most famous nations of Antiquity was remarkably exclusive. . . . The fact seems to be that the Greeks admired only
themselves, and that the Romans admired only themselves and the
Greeks. . . . The effect was narrowness and sameness of thought. Their
minds, if we may so express ourselves, bred in and in, and were accordingly cursed with barrenness and degeneracy. . . . The vast despotism of the Caesars, gradually effacing all national peculiarities and
assimilating the remotest provinces of the Empire to each other, aug-
mented the evil. At the close of the third century after Christ the
prospects of Mankind [sic] were fearfully dreary. . . . That great community was then in danger of experiencing a calamity far more terrible
than any of the quick, inflammatory, destroying maladies to which
nations are liable—a tottering, drivelling, paralytic longevity, the immortality of the Struldbrugs, a Chinese civilisation. It would be easy
to indicate many points of resemblance between the subjects of Diocletian and the people of that Celestial Empire where, during many
centuries, nothing has been learned or unlearned; where government,
where education, where the whole system of life, is a ceremony; where
knowledge forgets to increase and multiply, and, like the talent buried

[1] For the identification of these Indic and Syriac fossils see I. B (iii), vol. i, p. 35,
and I. C (i) (b), vol. i, pp. 90–2, above.

in the earth or the pound wrapped up in the napkin, experiences neither waste nor augmentation. The torpor was broken by two great revolutions, the one moral, the other political, the one from within, the other from without.'[1]

This merciful release for which, on Macaulay's showing, the Hellenic Society in the Imperial Age was indebted to the Church and the Barbarians, is a relatively happy ending which cannot be taken for granted. So long as life persists it is always possible that, instead of being cut off sharp by Clotho's beneficently ruthless shears, it may stiffen, by imperceptible degrees, into the paralysis of life-in-death; and the possibility that this may be the destiny of the Western Civilization[2] haunts the mind of at least one distinguished Western historian of the present generation.

'I do not think the danger before us is anarchy, but despotism, the loss of spiritual freedom, the totalitarian state, perhaps a universal world totalitarian state. As a consequence of strife between nations or classes there might be local and temporary anarchy, a passing phase. Anarchy is essentially weak, and in an anarchic world any firmly organized group with rational organisation and scientific knowledge could spread its dominion over the rest. And, as an alternative to anarchy, the World would welcome the despotic state. Then the World might enter upon a period of spiritual "petrifaction", a terrible order which for the higher activities of the human spirit would be death. The petrifaction of the Roman Empire and the petrifaction of China would appear less rigid, because [in our case] the ruling group would have much greater scientific means of power. (Do you know Macaulay's essay on "History"? He argues that the barbarian invasions were a blessing in the long run because they broke up the petrifaction. "It cost Europe a thousand years of barbarism to escape the fate of China."[3] There would be no barbarian races to break up a future world totalitarian state.)

'It seems to me possible that in such a totalitarian state, while philosophy and poetry would languish, scientific research might go on with continuous fresh discoveries. Greek science did not find the Ptolemaic realm an uncongenial environment, and I think, generally speaking, natural science may flourish under a despotism. It is to the interest of the ruling group to encourage what may increase their means of power. That, not anarchy, is, for me, the nightmare ahead, if we do not find a way of ending our present fraternal strife. But there *is* the Christian Church there, a factor to be reckoned with. It may have to undergo martyrdom in the future world-state, but, as it compelled the Roman world-state in the end to make at any rate formal submission to Christ,

---

[1] Macaulay, Lord: 'History', in *Miscellaneous Writings* (London 1860, Longmans, Green, 2 vols.), vol. i, pp. 263-7.
[2] This possibility has been touched upon in this Study already in IV. C (iii) (b) 4, vol. iv, p. 179, above.
[3] Macaulay, op. cit., vol. i, p. 268.—A.J.T.

it might again, by the way of martyrdom, conquer the scientific rationalist world-state of the future.'[1]

These reflections show that the disintegrations of civilizations present a genuine problem which demands consideration.[2]

[1] Dr. Edwyn Bevan, in the second of the two letters to the writer of this Study that have been quoted above.

[2] In this respect the history of Man in process of civilization runs true to the larger movement of the history of Life on this planet.

'The present condition of the Earth reveals to us an assemblage of differing forms of life. These different forms . . . are not all of the same age, they have existed for longer or shorter periods of time; some have persisted practically unchanged from the earliest observable geological formations, others are of relatively recent origin. A just view of the facts demands recognition, therefore, of the phenomenon of modification or change, in relation to the forms of life' (Teggart, F. J.: Theory of History (New Haven 1925, Yale University Press), p. 144).

B. THE NATURE OF THE DISINTEGRATIONS OF CIVILIZATIONS

LIKE the phenomenon of petrifaction, which compels us to study the problem of the disintegrations of civilizations, the different phenomena which reveal the nature of these disintegrations have already come to our notice incidentally. We have encountered them, for instance, in the history of the Hellenic Society, in our examination of the effects of the impact of the Solonian Economic Revolution upon the domestic politics of the Hellenic city-states[1] and upon the international politics of the Hellenic World.[2] We have met with other illustrations in the history of the Egyptiac Society, in our examination of a failure to throw off, before it was too late, the social incubus of a deified kingship, and a subsequent failure to avoid exploitation at the hands of a series of other social parasites: litterati and priests and professional soldiers.[3]

These passages of history bring to light certain likenesses and certain differences between the nature of the disintegrations of civilizations and the nature of their growths.

In studying the growths of civilizations we found[4] that they could be analysed into successions of performances of the drama of Challenge-and-Response, and that the reason why one performance followed another was because each of the responses was not only successful in answering the particular challenge by which it had been evoked, but was also instrumental in provoking a fresh challenge, which arose each time out of the new situation which the successful response had brought about. Thus the essence of the nature of the growths of civilizations proved to be an *élan* which carried the challenged party through the equilibrium of an effective response into an overbalance which declared itself in the presentation of a new challenge; and it was this element of overbalance that converted the single act of Challenge-and-Response, which we had detected in the geneses of civilizations, into the repetitive, recurrent rhythm which the concept of growth implies. This repetitiveness or recurrency is likewise implied in the concept of disintegration, which resembles the concept of growth in signifying a process and not a mere single act; and we duly discern a corresponding rhythm in those illustrations of the

---

[1] In IV. C (iii) (b) 9, vol. iv, pp. 200–6, above.
[2] In IV. C (iii) (b) 10, vol. iv, pp. 206–14; and also in IV. C (iii) (c) 2 (β), vol. iv, pp. 304–15, above.
[3] In IV. C (iii) (c) 2 (β), vol. iv, pp. 408–14 and 418–23, above.
[4] In Part III. B, vol. iii, pp. 113–27, above.

nature of the disintegrations of civilizations that have already come under our eye.

In each individual performance of the drama of Challenge-and-Response we have, of course, here to write failure for success and to change the plus sign into a minus; but the successive defeats through which the process of disintegration works itself out do nevertheless resemble the successive victories which build up the process of growth inasmuch as they, too, constitute a continuous series in which each performance leads on to the next. For example, in the history of the international politics of the Hellenic World, from the time when the Solonian economic revolution first confronted the Hellenic Society with the task of establishing a political world order, we can see that the failure of the Athenian attempt to solve the problem by means of the Delian League led on to Philip of Macedon's attempt to solve it by means of the Corinthian League, and Philip's failure to Augustus's attempt to solve it by means of a *Pax Romana* upheld by a Principate. Similarly, in the history of the Egyptiac Society's struggle with the problem of social incubuses, we can see that the failure to throw off the incubus of a deified kingship led on to a progressive complication of the unsolved problem as the litteratus and the priest and the professional soldier successively mounted, behind the king, upon the peasant-packhorse's back. In this matter of recurrency in rhythm the nature of the disintegrations of civilizations unmistakably resembles the nature of their growths. On the other hand our examples have already brought out a point of diversity which is no less striking or important than the point of likeness.

In a repetition of performances of the drama of Challenge-and-Response, where the outcome is a process of growth, the fact that the successive performances constitute a series, in which each performance is a consequence of its predecessor, does not mean that the play is staged each time with exactly the same plot. So far from that, we find that in the growth-process a particular challenge is never presented more than once, and indeed, *ex hypothesi*, could not be presented for a second time, since, *ex hypothesi*, so long as growth is being maintained, each successive challenge in the series is being successfully met or, in other words, disposed of as a living issue and relegated to the archives of the Recording Angel as another chapter of past history. By contrast, we can see that, in a series in which the outcome of each successive encounter is not victory but defeat, the unanswered challenge can never be disposed of and is therefore bound to present itself again and again until it either receives some tardy and imperfect answer or else brings about the destruction of a society which has shown itself inveterately incapable of responding to it effectively.[1] Thus, in the disintegrations of civilizations, the perpetual variety which gives light and life to their growths is replaced by a merciless uniformity;[2] and intensification, instead of diversification, is the form of change which now relieves the monotony of the series of performances. At each performance, now, the challenge is the same as it has been at every performance that has gone before since the tragic performance which witnessed the original break-down; but, after each successive failure to respond to it, the old unanswered challenge presents itself ever more insistently and in an ever more formidable shape, until at last it quite dominates and obsesses and overwhelms the unhappy souls that are being progressively defeated by it.

Thus the disintegration of a civilization, like its growth, is a cumulative as well as a continuous process. At the same time, when we are dealing with disintegration, there might seem, at first sight, to be no necessity to deny ourselves the use of the convenient spatial metaphor of 'direction', which we hesitated to apply when we were attempting to comprehend the nature of growth.[3] The direction in which disintegration runs might seem to be only too clear. Does not the disintegration of a civilization run to a defeat which brings with it the alternative penalties of an extinction without reprieve and a petrifaction which is no true mercy, since it is bound to end in dissolution sooner or later and amounts, for however long it may last, to nothing but a meaning-less and savourless life-in-death?

This view of the nature of the disintegrations of civilizations may convey a part of the truth. It may be true, as far as it goes, to say that, when once a civilization has broken down—or, at any rate, if and when an original breakdown has been confirmed by a certain number of failures to retrieve the lost position—then the broken-down civilization is (in mythological language) remorse-lessly condemned to eventual destruction or (in scientific language) mechanically dispatched to the same grim goal on a travelling belt of interlocking cause and effect that can be neither reversed nor broken nor checked. In so far as this is true, the last word on the disintegration of a civilization would seem to be the sublime and chilling Lucretian *Concede: necessest*.[4] But it would hardly be wise to concur in this famous verdict without being sure that our judge-ment has been formed in the light of the whole truth, as far as it may be possible for us to comprehend it. The Solonian *Respice*

---

[1] On this see further V. C (ii) (*b*), vol. vi, pp. 280–1, below.
[2] See V. C (iii), vol. vi, pp. 321–6, below.
[3] See Part III. B, vol. iii, pp. 124–7, above.
[4] Lucretius: *De Rerum Natura*, Book III, l. 962.

finem,[1] if it hits the mark at all, is presumably pertinent to all cases; and, until we have seen the end of an individual or a society, to pronounce an absolute verdict of either happiness or unhappiness may be equally premature. 'Whom the Lord loveth he chasteneth'[2] may be as near to the ultimate truth as the dictum, attributed to Solon by Herodotus, that 'to many people God has given a glimpse of happiness in order to destroy them root and branch'.[3] The 'son' whom we now see being 'scourged' may be found, in a later act, to be 'received'[4] after he has passed through his appointed ordeal. We cannot say our last word about the nature of the disintegrations of civilizations till we have studied the process of disintegration from beginning to end, and this in its inward experiences as well as in its outward manifestations.

---

[1] For the parable of Solon and Croesus see IV. C (iii) (c) 1, vol. iv, pp. 251–2, above.

[2] Hebrews xii. 6, quoted already in I. C (iii) (b), vol. i, p. 169, footnote 1, and in II. C (ii) (b) 1, vol. i, p. 298, above.

[3] Herodotus, Book I, chap. 32, quoted in IV. C (iii) (c) 1, vol. iv, p. 251, above.

[4] Hebrews xii. 6.

C. THE PROCESS OF THE DISINTEGRATIONS OF CIVILIZATIONS

(I) THE CRITERION OF DISINTEGRATION

(a) A LINE OF APPROACH

IN our study of the process of the growths of civilizations we began by looking for a criterion of growth[1] before we attempted to make an analysis of the process;[2] and in studying now the analogous process of the disintegrations of civilizations we may take our cue from the analogy[3] by applying the same plan of operations *mutatis mutandis*. One welcome difference in our procedure will be that we shall find ourselves absolved, this time, from retracing all the steps of our previous inquiry; for this inquiry has already led us to the conclusion that the criterion of growth is not to be found in an increasing command over the environment, either human or physical,[4] while conversely a loss of command over the environment of either kind has not proved to be the cause of the breakdowns of civilizations.[5] An empirical survey has left us doubtful whether there is any ascertainable correlation at all between the historical variations in the degree of a society's control over its environment and the historical change in the fortunes of a society whose growth is cut short by a breakdown running into a disintegration. And the evidence, so far as it goes, suggests that, if some correlation did prove to exist, we should find that an increase in command over the environment was a concomitant of breakdown and disintegration and not of growth.[6]

It looks, in fact, as though the internal struggles within the bosom of a society which bring the society's breakdown about, and which become more and more violent as its consequent disintegration proceeds, were actually more effective than the activities of genesis and growth in promoting the extension of the society's command both over the life of other living societies and over the inanimate forces of Physical Nature. In the downward course of a broken-down civilization's career there may be truth in the Ionian philosopher Heracleitus's saying that 'War is the father of all things'.[7] The sinister concentration of the society's dwind-

---

[1] In III. C (i), vol. iii, above.   [2] In III. C (ii), vol. iii, above.

[3] For the analogy between the nature of the disintegrations of civilizations and the nature of their growths see Part V. B, above.

[4] See III. C (i) (*a*) and (*b*), vol. iii, above.   [5] See IV. C (ii), vol. iv, above.

[6] See III. C (i) (*a*), vol. iii, pp. 139–54, and III. C (i) (*b*), vol. iii, *passim*, as well as IV. C (ii), vol. iv, above.

[7] Heracleitus, fragment 45. It may be noted that, in the life-time of Heracleitus (*vivebat circa* 500 B.C.), Ionia, which had been the cradle of a creative minority in the first chapter of the growth of the Hellenic Society (See III. C (ii) (*b*), vol. iii, pp. 338–9, above), was already verging towards her decline, though the Hellenic Society as a whole was at that time still in vigorous growth.

ling powers upon the absorbing business of fratricidal warfare may generate a military prowess that will place the neighbouring societies at the war-obsessed society's mercy, and may strike out a military technique that will serve as a key to the acquisition of a far-reaching technical mastery over the Material World. Since the vulgar estimates of human prosperity are reckoned in terms of power and wealth, it thus often happens that the opening chapters in the history of a society's tragic decline are popularly hailed as the culminating chapters of a magnificent growth; and this ironic misconception may even persist for centuries. Sooner or later, however, disillusionment is bound to follow; for a society that has become incurably divided against itself is almost certain to 'put back into the business' of war the greater part of those additional resources, human and material, which the same business has incidentally brought into its hands.

For instance, we see the money-power and man-power which had been won for the Hellenic Society through Alexander's conquest of the Achaemenian Empire being poured into the civil wars between Alexander's successors. The power of the same two kinds which was subsequently swept together into Roman hands through the establishment of Rome's military supremacy over the Hellenic World was almost as quickly expended in the Roman civil wars that preceded the establishment of the *Pax Augusta*. The first charge on the spoils taken by the Spanish *conquistadores* from the Aztecs and the Incas was the provision of the sinews of war for fratricidal struggles between the demoralized parvenu masters of a New World, while the residue that reached the coffers of these adventurers' lawful sovereign in Spain was blown from the cannon's mouth on the battlefields of sixteenth-century and seventeenth-century Europe.[1] Finally, in this same Western Society in our own generation, we have seen all the human and material resources of a Westernized and industrialized world being mobilized to feed the furnaces of Moloch in which *Homo Occidentalis* has made a holocaust of his own children in our great Western civil war of A.D. 1914–18.

Thus the increasing command over the environment which an ironic or malicious or retributive Providence is apt to bestow upon a society in disintegration only serves, in the end, to put a greater driving-power into the suicidally demented society's chosen work of self-destruction; and the story turns out to be a simple illustration of the theme that 'the wages of Sin is Death'.[2] Our criterion

---

[1] The historical 'law' exemplified in the self-destruction of the Macedonian and Castilian *conquistadores* has been examined in IV. C (iii) (c) 3 (α), vol. iv, pp. 484–6, above.

[2] Romans vi. 23.

for the process of the disintegration of a civilization has to be sought elsewhere; and the clue is given to us in the spectacle of that division and discord within the bosom of a society to which an increase in its command over the environment can so often be traced back. This is only what we should expect; for we have found already[1] that the ultimate criterion and the fundamental cause of the breakdowns of civilizations is an outbreak of internal discord through which they forfeit their faculty for self-determination.

The social schisms in which this discord partially reveals itself rend the broken-down society in two different dimensions simultaneously. There are 'vertical' schisms between geographically segregated communities and 'horizontal' schisms between geographically intermingled but socially segregated classes.

In the 'vertical' type of schism the articulation of the society into a number of parochial states gives rise to an internecine warfare on a crescendo note between these nominal members of one and the same body social; and this warfare exhausts the energies of the society before it brings itself to an end through a 'knock-out blow' in which a single surviving state is left staggering, half-dead, among the corpses of its fellow combatants. In an empirical survey of a considerable range we have seen how frequently the fatal discord takes this 'vertical' form of destructive warfare between states. Indeed, in no less than fourteen out of the sixteen cases[2] in which we can pronounce with assurance that a broken-down civilization has brought the breakdown upon itself, we have found that a reckless indulgence in the crime of inter-state warfare has been the main line of suicidal activity.[3] At the same time we may observe that this 'vertical' kind of schism is perhaps not the most characteristic manifestation of the discord by which the breakdowns of civilizations are brought about; for the articulation of a society into parochial communities is, after all, a phenomenon which is common to the whole genus 'Human Societies', and is not peculiar to the species 'Civilizations'. This 'vertical' articulation is part of the heritage which civilizations have derived from societies of the primitive species. The so-called 'civilized' state is merely an imposing, 'high-powered' version of the primitive

---

[1] In IV. C (iii) (a), vol. iv, pp. 119–33, above.
[2] For these sixteen cases see IV. C (ii) (b), *passim*, vol. iv, especially p. 115, above.
[3] The two exceptional cases are the Egyptiac and the Iranic. The breakdown of the Egyptiac Civilization seems to have been due mainly to the idolization of an institution (a deified kingship), and the breakdown of the Iranic Civilization mainly to a religious schism (a recrudescence of the long dormant conflict between Sunnah and Shi'ah). The militant outbreak of Shi'ism in the Iranic World was, of course, followed by fratricidal warfare between the Safawis and the 'Osmanlis (see I. C (i) (b), Annex I, in vol. i, above). For the incubus of the Pharaonic Crown see IV. C (iii) (c) 2 (β), vol. iv, pp. 408–14, above.

tribe; and, while the internecine warfare between states in the bosom of a civilization is vastly more destructive than the feeble and desultory warfare between tribes in the bosom of a primitive society, this method of suicide is merely an abuse of a potential instrument of self-destruction which is within the reach of any society of either species. On the other hand the 'horizontal' schism of a society along lines of class is not only peculiar to civilizations but is also a phenomenon which first appears at the moment of their breakdowns and which is a distinctive mark of the phases of breakdown and disintegration, by contrast with its absence during the phases of genesis and growth.[1]

We have come across this 'horizontal' kind of schism already in several different contexts in earlier parts of this Study.

We encountered it first when we were exploring the extension of our own Western Society backwards in the Time-dimension. We found ourselves led back to the Christian Church and to a number of barbarian war-bands which had come into collision with the Church in Western Europe inside the northern frontiers of the Roman Empire; and we observed that each of these two institutions—the war-bands and the Church—had been created by a social group which was not, itself, an articulation of our own Western body social and which could only be described in terms of another society, antecedent to ours, which we have labelled 'the Hellenic'. We found that we had to describe the creators of the Christian Church as 'the internal proletariat' and the creators of the barbarian war-bands as the 'external proletariat' of this Hellenic Society.[2]

At a later point in our inquiry[3] we made use of the three institutions upon which we had thus accidentally stumbled—that is to say, the Roman Empire and the barbarian war-bands and the Christian Church—as tokens of a relation which we had found

---

[1] This is not, of course, to say that either in a primitive society or in a civilization in its growth-stage horizontal lines of social articulation are unknown. So far from that, it is manifest that the structure of both these kinds of society is often highly hierarchical; and some of the hierarchical distinctions to which they are prone are also of a genealogical order which opposes a formidable barrier to the transit of individuals or families from one rank in the hierarchy to another. Even, however, where the gulfs between ranks cannot easily be crossed on bridges of intermarriage or adoption, this 'racial' cleavage in a primitive society or in a growing civilization is not apt to produce a moral schism, because the different ranks which are divided in 'race' are apt to be united morally by a common consciousness of having reciprocal functions to perform which are all indispensable for the welfare, and even perhaps for the preservation, of a society which is one and indivisible. (An example of this unity in diversity is the social relation between knights and villeins which was the ideal—though not always the practice— of our own medieval Western feudal system.) The other chief 'horizontal' line of division in primitive societies is the distinction between different age-classes; and this hierarchy of ages is sometimes elaborately articulated and graded; but an age-class is, of course, in its very nature, a form of 'horizontal' division which is transcended inevitably through the passage of Time.

[2] See I. B (iv), vol. i, pp. 40–3, above.

[3] In I. C (i), vol. i, above.

subsisting between the Hellenic Society and our own Western Society, and which we had labelled 'Apparentation-and-Affiliation'. Our immediate purpose at that stage was to discover, by the test of these tokens, whether there were other known instances of this relation between two civilizations which we had come across so far in a single example; and our ulterior purpose was to identify as many representatives as possible of the species of society which we have labelled 'Civilizations'. In order, however, to employ our three tokens with better effect, we found ourselves led to examine and define them more closely; and this inquiry led on, in its turn, to a subsidiary inquiry[1] into the respective origins and natures, and into the mutual relations, of the different social groups to which our three institutions severally owed their existence in the Hellenic World in which we had come across them.

We found that 'the internal proletariat' of the Hellenic Society, which was the creator of the Christian Church, and its 'external proletariat', which was the creator of the barbarian war-bands, had each arisen through an act of secession from the Hellenic body social during a 'Time of Troubles' in which the Hellenic Society itself was manifestly no longer creative but was already in decline; and, pushing our inquiry another stage back, we further found that these secessions of an internal and an external 'proletariat' had been provoked by an antecedent change in the character of the ruling element in the Hellenic body social. A 'creative minority' which had once evoked a voluntary allegiance from the uncreative mass, in virtue of the gift of charm which is the privilege of creativity, had now given place to a 'dominant minority' which found itself unable to exert the charm because it was destitute of the creative power. This uninspired minority, into whose hands the heritage of leadership had thus passed, could not bring itself to surrender a position of authority and eminence that it lacked the genius to earn; and, rather than climb down from the saddle, it set itself to keep its seat by force. This policy of sheer repression on 'the dominant minority's' part—a policy which was as impracticable as it was wrong-headed—was the grievance which had estranged the 'proletariat' to the point of revolt. The secessions which had eventually resulted in the creation of the barbarian war-bands and of the Christian Church were reactions to the sting of 'the dominant minority's' whip and to the prick of its spurs. Yet this defeat of its own intentions—through the disruption of a society which it was attempting, however perversely, to hold together—is not the only achievement of 'the dominant minority' that came to our notice in this context. If the barbarian

[1] In I. C (i) (a), vol. i, pp. 52–62, above.

war-bands and the Christian Church are the Hellenic 'proletariat's' handiwork, the Hellenic 'dominant minority' has also left a monument of itself in the shape of the Roman Empire; and the Empire not only took shape earlier than either the Church or the warbands: its mighty presence in the world in which these 'proletarian' institutions grew up was a factor in the growth of both of them which cannot be left out of account. This universal state in which the Hellenic 'dominant minority' encased itself was like the carapace of a giant tortoise; and while the Church was reared under its shadow—partly profiting by the protection of this borrowed shield, and partly fighting for life against the crushing pressure of its weight—the barbarians trained their war-bands by sharpening their claws on the tortoise-shell's outer face.

Finally, at a third point in the course of this Study,[1] we tried to obtain a clearer view of the nexus of cause and effect between the loss of a leading minority's gift for creation and the loss of its faculty for attracting the majority by charm without having to think of resorting to force. And here we put our finger upon the Creative Minority's expedient of social drill—as a short-cut for bringing the uncreative mass into line—in which we had already[2] found the weak spot in the relation between minority and majority in the growth-stage. On this showing, the estrangement between minority and majority which eventually comes to a head in the secession of the Proletariat is a consequence of the breaking of a link which, even in the growth-phase, has only been maintained by playing upon a well-drilled faculty of mimesis; the leaders' failure to continue to play upon this faculty in the rank-and-file is a consequence of the same leaders' failure to reply to a particular challenge by making a creative response; and it is no longer surprising to find that the link inevitably snaps when the leaders' creativity gives out, considering that, even in the growth-stage of the society's history, this link of mimesis has always been precarious by reason of a treacherous duality—the revenge of an unwilling slave—which is part of the nature of any mechanical device.[3]

These are the threads of inquiry into the 'horizontal' kind of schism in a broken-down society that are already in our hands; and perhaps the most promising way of attempting to pursue our inquiry farther will be to draw these threads together and then spin out the strand.

Our first step[4] will be to take a closer and wider survey of the three fractions—Dominant Minority and Internal and External

---

[1] In IV. C (iii) (a), vol. iv, pp. 123–4 and 131–2, above. Compare II₁. C (ii) (b), vol. iii, p. 374.   [2] In III. C (ii) (a), vol. iii, pp. 245–8, above.
[3] For the mechanicalness of mimesis see IV. C (iii) (a), vol. iv, pp. 119–33, above.
[4] In V. C (i) (c), pp. 35–376, below.

Proletariats—into which a broken-down society splits when a 'horizontal' schism rends its fabric. So far we have only had occasion to glance at the Hellenic examples; but, since we have found[1] that the respective institutional products of the Dominant Minority and the two divisions of the Proletariat—the institutions of universal state and universal church and barbarian war-bands —are not peculiar to the Hellenic Society but can also be identified in the histories of a number of other societies in their later phases there is a presumption that each of these other societies, likewise, has split into fractions corresponding to the three which, as creators of the three institutions aforesaid, have already come to our attention in the history of the Hellenic Society in its decline. Our second step[2] will be to turn—as we turned at a certain point[3] in our study of the process of growth—from the Macrocosm to the Microcosm; for, after studying the 'horizontal' schism in the fabric of a disintegrating society under its outward aspect of an increasing discord in the body social, we shall find ourselves moved to re-study it under the complementary inward aspect of an increasing distraction in the soul. Both these lines of search for a criterion of disintegration will lead us to the, at first sight, paradoxical dis-covery that the process of disintegration works out, at least in part, to a result which is logically incompatible with its nature—works out, that is to say, to a 'recurrence of birth' or 'palingenesia'.[4] And this paradox will command our attention[5] before we address our-selves to an analysis of disintegration by examining, first the rela-tion between disintegrating civilizations and the individual human beings who are 'members' of them,[6] and then the interaction be-tween these individuals through which the process of disintegration works itself out.[7] Thereafter, when we are in a position to view the whole course of the process in retrospect,[8] we shall find, as indeed we might expect, that the qualitative change which it brings with it is exactly opposite in character to that which is the outcome of growth. In a previous part of this Study[9] we have seen that in the process of growth the several growing civilizations become differ-entiated from one another. We shall now find that, conversely, the qualitative effect of the disintegration-process is standardization.

This tendency towards standardization is the more remarkable when we consider the extent of the diversity which it has to over-

---

[1] In I. C (i) (b), vol. i, above.
[2] In V. C (i) (d), in the present volume, pp. 376–568, and in vol. vi, pp. 1–168, below.
[3] Between III. C (i) (b) and III. C (i) (c), in vol. iii, above.
[4] For alternative possible meanings of the word 'palingenesia' see p. 27, footnote 2, below.
[5] In V. C (i) (e), vol. vi, pp. 169–75, below.
[6] In V. C (ii) (a), vol. vi, pp. 175–278, below.
[7] In V. C (ii) (b), vol. vi, pp. 278–321, below.
[8] In V. C (iii), vol. vi, pp. 321–6, below.
[9] In III. C (iii), vol. iii, above.

come. The broken-down civilizations bring with them, when they enter upon their disintegration, the extremely diverse dispositions —a bent towards Art or towards Clockwork, or whatever the bent may be—that they have severally acquired during their growth. And they are also further differentiated from one another in a second sense by the fact that their breakdowns overtake them at widely different ages. The Syriac Civilization, for example, broke down, *post mortem Salamonis, circa* 937 B.C.,[1] at a date which was probably less than two hundred years removed from the date of the original emergence of this civilization out of the post-Minoan interregnum. On the other hand the sister Hellenic Civilization, which emerged out of the same interregnum coevally, did not break down for another five hundred years, if we are right in equating its breakdown with the outbreak of the great Atheno-Peloponnesian War in 431 B.C.[2] Again, the Orthodox Christian Civilization broke down upon the outbreak of the great Bulgaro-Roman War in A.D. 977,[3] while in this case the sister civilization, which is our own civilization of the West, unquestionably went on growing for several centuries longer and—for all that we know—may not have broken down even yet,[4] at an age when the breakdown of the Orthodox Christian Civilization is now little less than a thousand years behind us in the past.[5] If sister civilizations can run to such different lengths of growth-span as we find in these two examples, it is manifest that the growths of civilizations are not predestined to any uniform duration; and indeed we have failed to find any convincing reason *a priori* why a civilization that has successfully come to birth, and has avoided the danger of becoming arrested in infancy, should not be able to go on growing *in saecula saeculorum*.[6] These considerations make it clear that the differences between growing civilizations are extensive and profound. Nevertheless, in the history of a civilization that has been overtaken by the catastrophe of breaking down, we shall find that, as its subsequent disintegration proceeds, the process tends to conform to a standard pattern. A 'horizontal' schism regularly splits the disintegrating society into the same three fractions—Dominant Minority and Internal and External Proletariats—and these three separate social groups which the schism has brought into

---

[1] See IV. C (ii) (*b*) 1, vol. iv, pp. 67–8, above.
[2] See IV. C (ii) (*b*) 1, vol. iv, p. 62, above.
[3] See IV. C (ii) (*b*) 1, vol. iv, p. 72, above.
[4] For a tentative diagnosis of the symptoms see V. C (ii) (*b*), vol. vi, pp. 312–21, and also Part XII, below.
[5] Even if the Western Civilization were to prove, in retrospect, to have broken down upon the outbreak of the Wars of Religion in the sixteenth century, its growth-span would be longer, even so, than the growth-span of the sister Orthodox Christian Society by a tale of little less than 600 years.
[6] This problem has been discussed in IV. C (i), vol. iv, above.

existence then regularly create the three institutions—universal state and universal church and barbarian war-bands—that are severally their characteristic handiwork.

We shall have to notice these institutions, as well as their respective creators, if our study of the disintegrations of civilizations is to be comprehensive. But, we shall find it convenient, so far as it may prove possible, to study the institutions for their own sakes in separate parts of the book[1]—partly because an attempt to complete our examination of them in the present part would heavily overload it, but also for the stronger reason that these three institutions that are apt to arise in the course of the disintegration of a civilization are something more than mere products of the disintegration-process. Our early encounters with them in this Study[2] have shown us that they may also play a role in the relations between one civilization and another; and when we examine the universal churches we shall find ourselves led to raise the question whether churches can really be comprehended in their entirety in the framework of the histories of civilizations, within which they make their first historical appearance, or whether we have not to regard them as representatives of another species of society which is at least as distinct from the species 'Civilizations' as the civilizations are distinct from the primitive societies.

This may prove to be one of the most momentous questions that a study of history, within our present range of vision, can suggest to us; but the question lies near the farther end of the line of inquiry which we have just been sketching out. We must begin by returning to our starting-point, which is the 'horizontal' schism of a broken-down society into the three fractions that we have labelled the Dominant Minority and the Internal and External Proletariats.

(b) THE MOVEMENT OF SCHISM-AND-PALINGENESIA

In an anticipatory attempt[3] to picture to ourselves the progressive estrangement of the Proletariat from the Dominant Minority in the Hellenic World, in the course of the decline of the Hellenic Civilization, we helped ourselves out by quoting a brilliant and penetrating passage from a famous work of a nineteenth-century French philosopher, de Gobineau.[4] We may fitly cap this quotation now by another from the *Summa Philosophiae*

---

[1] In parts VI, VII, and VIII, below.
[2] In I. B (iv), vol. i, pp. 40–3; I. C (i) (a), vol. i, pp. 55–7; and Part II. A, vol. i, pp. 187–8, above.
[3] In I. C (i) (a), vol. i, p. 54, above.
[4] De Gobineau, le Comte J. A.: *Essai sur l'Inégalité des Races Humaines*, vol. i, pp. 93–4.

of de Gobineau's countryman of an older generation, Saint-Simon,[1] for in this passage the social schism that follows the transition from an 'organic period' (i.e. an age of growth) to a 'critical period' (i.e. an age of disintegration)[2] is delineated in general terms and not merely with reference to the Hellenic instance.

'Aux époques organiques le but de l'activité sociale est nettement défini; tous les efforts . . . sont consacrés à l'accomplissement de ce but, vers lequel les hommes sont continuellement dirigés, dans le cours entier de leur vie, par l'éducation et la législation. Les relations générales étant fixées, les relations individuelles, modelées sur elles, le sont également; l'objet que la société se propose d'atteindre est révélé à tous les cœurs, à toutes les intelligences; il devient facile d'apprécier les capacités les plus propres à favoriser sa tendance, et les véritables supériorités se trouvent naturellement alors en possession du pouvoir; il y a légitimité, souveraineté, autorité, dans l'acception réelle de ces mots. L'harmonie règne dans les rapports sociaux. . . .

'Les époques critiques offrent un spectacle diamétralement opposé. On aperçoit, il est vrai, à leur début, un concert d'activité, déterminé par le besoin généralement éprouvé de détruire; mais la divergence ne tarde pas à éclater et à devenir complète, de toutes parts l'anarchie se manifeste, et bientôt chacun n'est plus occupé qu'à s'approprier quelques débris de l'édifice qui s'écroule et se disperse, jusqu'à ce qu'il soit réduit en poussière. Alors le but de l'activité sociale est complètement ignoré, l'incertitude des relations générales passe dans les relations privées; les véritables capacités ne sont plus et ne peuvent plus être appréciées; la légitimité du pouvoir est contestée à ceux qui l'exercent; les gouvernants et les gouvernés sont en guerre; une guerre semblable s'établit entre les intérêts particuliers, qui ont acquis chaque jour une prédominance plus marquée sur l'intérêt général.'[3]

This Saint-Simonian sketch of the social strife that accompanies the disintegration of any civilization has been almost effaced in the minds of Posterity by that tremendous picture of the class-war which has been painted—in colours borrowed from the apocalyptic visions of a repudiated religious tradition—by another Western philosopher of a later generation: the German Jew Karl Marx (*vivebat* A.D. 1818–83). The extraordinary impression which the Marxian materialist apocalypse has made upon so many millions of minds—and this often at second or third hand, and at levels of intellectual culture at which the Master's *ipsissima verba* would be unintelligible—is, of course, due in part to the political militancy, as well as to the philosophical impressiveness, of the Marxian

[1] De Gobineau *vivebat* A.D. 1816–1882; Saint-Simon *vivebat* A.D. 1760–1825.
[2] For these two technical terms of Saint-Simon's philosophy see I. C (iii) (*b*), vol. i, p. 154, footnote 4, and Part II. B, vol. i, pp. 199–200, above.
[3] Bazard, 'Exposition de la Doctrine Saint-Simonienne' in *Œuvres de Saint-Simon et d'Enfantin*, vol. xli (Paris 1877, Leroux), pp. 171–4.

diagram; for, while this 'blue-print' is the kernel of a general philosophy of history, it is also a revolutionary call to arms in which the industrial proletariat of our latter-day Western World is incited to secede from a 'capitalist' dominant minority and is invited to carry this act of secession to its logical conclusion by shaking off physically an odious and intolerable yoke against which it is assumed already to have risen in spiritual revolt. Whether the invention and the vogue of this Marxian formula of the class-war are to be taken as signs that the civilization of our Western World, in which this portent has now appeared, has its feet already set upon the path of disintegration, is a question which will occupy us in a later part of this Study[1] when we come to look into the prospects of this Western Civilization of ours. In this place we have cited Marx for other reasons: first, because he is the classic exponent of the doctrine of the class-war for our world in our age; and, second, because his formula conforms to the traditional Zoroastrian and Jewish and Christian apocalyptic pattern in unveiling, beyond a violent climax, the vision of a gentle finale.

According to the Communist prophet's intuition of the operations of his familiar goddess Historical Materialism or Determinism or Necessity, the class-war is bound to issue in a victorious proletarian revolution; but this bloody culmination of the struggle will also be the end of it; for the victory of the Proletariat will be decisive and definitive and 'the Dictatorship of the Proletariat', by which the fruits of the victory are to be safeguarded and harvested during the post-revolutionary period, is not to be a permanent institution. A time is to come when a new society that has been classless from birth will be old enough and strong enough to dispense with 'the Dictatorship of the Proletariat'—as, in the Gospel story, the paralytic who has been miraculously healed by Jesus demonstrates the reality of the cure by obeying the Master's command to take up his bed and walk.[2] Indeed, in its final—and permanent—acme of well-being the New Society of the Marxian Millennium will be able to cast away not only 'the Dictatorship of the Proletariat' but also every other institutional crutch, including the State itself; for in that Marxian earthly paradise to come 'they neither marry nor are given in marriage, but are as the angels which are in Heaven'.[3]

The interest of the Marxian eschatology for our present inquiry lies in the surprising yet unquestionable fact that this lingering political shadow of a vanished religious belief does accurately

[1] In Part XII, below.
[2] Matt. ix. 1–8 = Mark ii. 1–12 = Luke v. 18–26 = John v. 1–16.
[3] Mark xii. 25.

V   B

plot out the actual course which the class-war, or 'horizontal' schism, in a broken-down society is apt to follow as a matter of historical fact that can be ascertained from an empirical survey of the histories of societies in disintegration. History duly reveals to us in the phenomenon of disintegration a movement that runs through War to Peace; through Yang to Yin;[1] and through an apparently wanton and savage destruction of precious things, created in the Past by Time and Toil and Love, to fresh works of creation that seem to owe their special quality to the devouring glow of the flame in which they have been forged.

The schism in itself is a product of two negative movements, each of which is inspired by an evil passion. First the Dominant Minority attempts to hold by force—against all right and reason—a position of inherited privilege which it has ceased to merit; and then the Proletariat repays injustice with resentment, fear with hate, and violence with violence when it executes its act of secession. Yet the whole movement ends in positive acts of creation—and this on the part of all the actors in the tragedy of disintegration. The Dominant Minority creates a universal state, the Internal Proletariat a universal church, and even the External Proletariat a bevy of barbarian war-bands.

These three achievements are, no doubt, extremely unequal in the respective degrees of the creativity that they manifest. We have noticed at an earlier point[2] that the universal church, alone of the three, has a prospect in the Future as well as a footing in the Past, while the universal state and the war-bands belong to the Past exclusively. And it hardly needs to be pointed out that, of the two backward-looking institutions, the barbarian war-bands are poor affairs indeed compared with the universal state. By creating a universal state the Dominant Minority performs the worthy feat of checking, for a time, the process of social disintegration which its own past action has precipitated, and thus enabling the temporarily reprieved society to enjoy a brief 'Indian Summer'.[3] In creating barbarian war-bands the External Proletariat has merely sharpened its predatory beak and claws in preparation for a carrion-crow's feast upon a dead civilization's carcass. Nevertheless there is a gleam of creativeness to be discerned, even here, in the contrast that strikes our eye if we compare the war-bands that were led by Theodoric the Ostrogoth to Rome, or by Muʿā-wīyah the Umayyad to Damascus, with the hordes of Cimbri and

---

[1] For the alternating forces or phases in the rhythm of the Universe which Sinic philosophers have called Yin and Yang, see Part II. B, vol. i, pp. 201–4, above.
[2] In I. C (i) (a), vol. i, pp. 56–62, above.
[3] For this phenomenon of 'Indian Summers' in the penultimate stage of the disintegrations of civilizations see IV. C (ii) (b) 1, vol. iv, pp. 56–76, above.

Teutones that had flooded across the Alps at the turn of the second and the last century B.C., or with the hordes of Ituraeans that had silted up, at about the same date, out of the North Arabian Desert against the eastern flanks of Hermon and Antilibanus.[1]

Thus the social schism that is the outward criterion of the disintegration of a broken-down society is not just a schism and nothing more. When we grasp the movement as a whole, from beginning to end, we find that we have to describe it as Schism-and-Palingenesia[2] if we wish to give it a title that does it justice. And, considering that a secession is manifestly a particular manner of withdrawal, we may classify the specific double movement of

---

[1] For the difference in degree of barbarity between different representatives of the Hellenic external proletariat see further V. C (i) (c) 3, pp. 223–7, below.

[2] 'Palingenesia' is a Greek word (παλιγγενεσία) which occurs twice in the New Testament—in Matt. xix. 28 and in Titus iii. 5—and which in both these passages is translated by the English word 'regeneration' in the Authorized Version. This compound abstract substantive noun is derived from the verbal phrase πάλιν γίγνεσθαι, which is used by Plato, in a passage (Timæus, 23 B) that has been quoted in IV. C (i), vol. iv, pp. 24–5, above, to describe the fresh start which has to be made periodically by Human Society in Hellas and elsewhere, in contrast to an allegedly unbroken continuity of Civilization in the Egyptiac World. The substantive was perhaps coined out of the verbal phrase in order to serve as a technical term in the vocabulary of the Stoic philosophy (see Dey, J.: Παλιγγενεσία (Münster i. W. 1937, Aschendorff), pp. 6–13 and 25), which needed a special word to describe the opening of each round of an endlessly and unvaryingly repeated cyclic movement of the Universe. (For this theory of cycles, which is not peculiar to Stoicism, see IV. C (i), vol. iv, pp. 23–38, above.) There is a clear case of this Stoic usage of the word from a Stoic hand in Marcus Aurelius Antoninus: Meditations, Book XI, chap. 1, and there are nine examples of it in the Anti-Stoic treatise De Aeternitate Mundi which is traditionally attributed to the Jewish philosopher Philo of Alexandria (Dey, op. cit., pp. 8–11). Somewhat later the word seems to have been either borrowed or independently invented for the description of the transmigration of souls in those schools of Hellenic thought into which this doctrine entered (Dey, op. cit., pp. 13–24, 25, and 32). Thereafter the currency of the word spread from the metaphysical to the mundane sphere on the one hand and to the religious sphere on the other. In the mundane sphere παλιγγενεσία had made its way, by the last century B.C., into the non-technical vocabulary of cultivated circles, and in this environment at this time it was used in a variety of contexts which provide us with our earliest extant historical evidence for its employment (see Dey, op. cit., pp. 25–30 and 32–3). For example, Josephus uses it (in The Antiquities of the Jewish People, Book XI, sec. 3, chap. 9, § 66) in the sense of a political risorgimento (the return to Judaea from the Babylonish Captivity), and Cicero (Ad Atticum, vi. 6) in the sense of a personal reinstatement into a temporarily forfeited political position (Cicero's amnesty and return from banishment). In the religious sphere, outside the Christian field, the only worships in which the presence of the concept of παλιγγενεσία can be traced with any certainty are the Hermetic variety of Gnosticism, the so-called 'Mithras Liturgy', and the personal religion of Philo of Alexandria, in so far as this can be reconstructed from his surviving literary works (Dey, op. cit., pp. 36–128 and 132). In the Epistle to Titus the word παλιγγενεσία is used to describe the spiritual effect, upon the Soul, of the Christian rite of Baptism; in the Gospel according to Saint Matthew it is used to describe the social effect of the inauguration of the Kingdom of the Messiah.

The literal meaning of 'palingenesia' is 'a recurrence of birth' or, more vaguely, 'a recurrence of coming into existence' (Dey, op. cit., pp. 23 and 33); and in either variant of this meaning there is an element of ambiguity; for the recurrence might refer exclusively to the event of birth (or of coming into existence) or alternatively its reference might extend to the nature of the thing born (or brought into existence); and while in the latter use the word 'palingenesia' would mean a repetitive re-birth of something that has been born before, in the former use it would mean an unprecedented new birth of something that is now being born for the first time. The Stoic and Orphico-Pythagorean origins of the term indicate (see Dey, op. cit., pp. 7, 23–4, 33, and 125) that, as a matter of history, the use of the word in the sense of 'repetitive re-birth' was the original one. For an application of it in the other possible use, in which it figures in the New Testament, see V. C (i) (e), vol. vi, pp. 169–75, below.

Schism-and-Palingenesia as one version of the generic double
movement of Withdrawal-and Return.[1]

Schism-and-Palingenesia certainly runs true to the type of
Withdrawal-and-Return in so far as the second beat of the movement is the significant feature in it. The happiness of the palingenesia is not only a reparation for the foregoing agony of the
schism; it is also the point of the schism, or, in frankly teleological
language, its purpose. And in fact we find that, when once the
schism has occurred, nothing but frustration results from a closing
of the breach before the due palingenesia has been accomplished.
A case in point is the 'union sacrée' between the dominant
minority of the Egyptiac Society and its internal proletariat
against the external proletariat as represented by the Hyksos;[2]
for it was this reconciliation at the eleventh hour that prolonged
the existence of the Egyptiac Society—in a petrified state of life-
in-death[3]—for two thousand years beyond the date when the process of disintegration would otherwise have reached its natural
term in dissolution. And this life-in-death was not merely an
unprofitable burden to the moribund Egyptiac Society itself: it
was also a fatal blight upon the growth of the living Osirian Church[4]
which had been created by the Egyptiac internal proletariat; for
the 'union sacrée' between internal proletariat and dominant
minority took the form of an amalgamation of the living worship
of Osiris with the dead worship of the official Egyptiac Pantheon;
and this artificial act of syncretism killed the religion of the internal

[1] For this movement of Withdrawal-and-Return see III. C (ii) (b), in vol. iii,
above.
[2] For this Egyptiac 'union sacrée' and its historical consequences see I. C (ii),
vol. i, pp. 144–6, and Part V. A, pp. 2–3, with the references on p. 2, footnote 1, above.
[3] For this phenomenon of petrifaction see Part V. A, above.
[4] The word 'church' is used here, and throughout this Study, to mean no more than
the collectivity of the devotees of a certain worship. A collectivity of this kind may
be united solely by the inward-spiritual bond of their common worship of the same
divinity, or alternatively this inward unity may find an outward expression in some
kind of social organization. The classic example of an organized church is, of course,
the Primitive Christian Church; and this feature of the life of the original Christian
community has been preserved not only in the Western Catholic Church but also, on
a smaller scale and on a looser rein, in many of the other branches into which the
Christian Church has ramified in the course of its history. Another example of a highly
organized church is the Egyptiac Church which was established, under the presidency
of the Chief Priest of Amon-Re of Thebes, by the Pharaoh Thothmes III in the restoration period of Egyptiac history, after the expulsion of the Hyksos (see I. C (ii), vol. ii,
p. 145, footnote 5, and IV. C (iii) (c) 2 (β), vol. iv, p. 421, above, and V. C (i) (d) 6
(δ), in the present volume, p. 530, and V. C (i) (d) 6 (δ), Annex, pp. 653–4 and 695, below).
On the other hand the Osirian Church (see V. C (i) (c) 2, pp. 150–2, below), its offshoot
the Isiac Church in the post-Alexandrine Hellenic World (see V. C (i) (c) 2, p. 81,
below), and likewise the Orphic Church (see I. C (i) (b), vol. i, pp. 95–100, above,
and V. C (i) (c) 2, in the present volume, pp. 84–7, below), are examples of churches
of the unorganized kind. For the distinction between these two types of church see
further, for the Isiac Church, Nock, A. D.: Conversion (Oxford 1933, Clarendon Press),
pp. 135–6 and 147; for the Orphic Church, Boulanger, A.: Orphée (Paris 1925, Rieder),
p. 50, and Fracassini, U.: Il Misticismo Greco e il Cristianesimo (Città di Castello 1922,
'Il Solco'), pp. 83–5. The structure of the Orphic and Isiac churches was 'congrega-
tional' rather than 'hierarchical'.

proletariat without availing to bring the religion of the dominant minority back to life.

The unfortunate outcome of this Egyptiac 'union sacrée' suggests that this exceptional sequel to a social schism is one of those exceptions that prove a rule; and we may take the broken rule to be that a new birth, rather than a healing of the breach, is the one possible happy ending of a schism, besides being the normal ending of this particular variation on the movement of Withdrawal-and-Return.

We shall hardly be permitted, however, to take our interpretation of Schism-and-Palingenesia in terms of Withdrawal-and-Return for granted without being challenged to account for one feature in Schism-and-Palingenesia which, at first sight, might look as though it were quite incompatible with the nature of Withdrawal-and-Return as this is displayed in the process of growth. We have seen that civilizations owe their growth to the withdrawal and return of a minority—the Creative Minority which withdraws in order to find a response to some challenge that is confronting the whole society, and then returns in order to persuade an uncreative majority to follow it along the path which it has opened up. On the other hand, in the movement of Schism-and-Palingenesia that manifests itself in the process of disintegration, it would seem, at first sight, to be a majority that withdraws in the Secession of the Proletariat, while a minority—'the Dominant Minority'—now remains stolidly stationary. Is not this an exact inversion of the minority's and the majority's respective roles? And does not this mean that, after all, the movement of Schism-and-Palingenesia is of a different order from the movement of Withdrawal-and-Return, instead of being—as we had thought—a variation upon a theme with which we are already familiar?

Our best approach to this question will be to consider one difference, of which we have not yet taken note, between the Dominant Minority in a disintegrating civilization and the Creative Minority to which a growing civilization owes its growth.

In the succession of victorious responses to challenges in which the process of growth consists, the Creative Minority to whose enterprise and energy and resoluteness the victory is due is apt to be recruited from different individuals, with different social heritages and different ideas and ideals, at each successive performance of the drama.[1] This is the rule in a growing society even where the powers of government, in the widest sense of the word,

---

[1] This point has been touched upon, by anticipation, in III. C (ii) (b), vol. iii, p. 375, footnote 1, above.

are the hereditary monopoly of a close aristocracy of birth;[1] for in such circumstances the rule operates within these social limits no less surely than it operates throughout the society in cases where the whole of the society is enfranchised. In an aristocratically governed society that is in process of growth, we find one group of aristocratic families playing the part of Creative Minority in response to one challenge, and a different group in response to the next; and, if eventually the society is confronted with some challenge which is not successfully met by any group at all within the closed aristocratic circle, the aristocracy's failure does not necessarily bring the society's growth to an end; for the new challenge may still evoke a victoriously creative response from some minority in a stratum of the society that has hitherto been given no opportunity of playing a leading part in the society's affairs; and thus the series of challenges and responses, as it lengthens, may give occasion for the enfranchisement of one social stratum after another. In the history of the Hellenic Society, for example, we have seen how the old agrarian aristocracy was eventually worsted by the Malthusian problem when this was presented in a new form in the sixth century B.C. owing to the success of hostile neighbours in bringing the sheer extensive expansion of the Hellenic Society to a halt; and in the case of Attica (for which our historical record of this age happens to be less meagre than it is for other parts of Hellas) we have observed how the problem was solved nevertheless by the new-fangled class of merchants which made its appearance at Athens in the person of Solon, and how the consequences of the Solonian 'bourgeois' revolution led on in time to the enfranchisement of a new urban working class, side by side with the new urban bourgeoisie.[2] In the history of our own Western Society, in the so-called 'medieval' chapter of its growth, we can see another instance of the rise of successive creative minorities, outside the circle of a hereditary aristocracy, in the enfranchisement first of a bourgeoisie, and then of an urban working class, in the bodies politic of the North Italian city-states.

This tendency in a growing society for the Creative Minority to be recruited on each successive occasion from a new source can be accounted for by the combined operation of two distinct causes, one positive and the other negative. The positive cause is to be found in a fact which has already come to our notice.[3] A con-

---

[1] The nature of the 'horizontal' lines of social cleavage in growing societies has been touched upon already in V. C (i) (a), p. 18, footnote 1, above.
[2] For the Attic version of this particular performance of the drama of Challenge-and-Response in the history of the Hellenic Society see I. B (ii), vol. i, pp. 24–5; II. D (ii), vol. ii, pp. 37–42; Part III. B, vol. iii, p. 122; III. C (i) (a), vol. iii, pp. 139–40; III. C (i) (d), vol. iii, p. 197; III. C (ii) (b), vol. iii, p. 273, above.
[3] In Part V. B, above.

tinuance of growth implies that, in each successive round of
Challenge-and-Response, the challenge which is presented is a new
one (since *ex hypothesi*, if growth is still being maintained, the last
challenge has been victoriously met and, in being met, has been
disposed of). But if the challenge, each time, is new, it is only to
be expected that this new challenge will be met, each time, by a
newly recruited minority which can bring some hitherto unutilized
talent into play in wrestling with a hitherto unfamiliar problem.
The tendency for a new creative minority to be called up, in each
successive emergency, by the operation of this positive factor will
be accentuated by the effect of a negative factor which we have
found to be a potent cause of the breakdowns of civilizations. We
have seen in that context[1] that the gift of creativity is subject to
its own peculiar nemesis; and that a minority which has demonstrated its creative power by responding to one challenge victoriously is likely to inhibit itself from repeating its exploit—that is
to say, from responding, later on, to a different challenge with equal
success—by succumbing to one or other of the two diverse temptations with which every successful creative minority or individual
is beset: the temptation to rest on one's oars and the antithetical
temptation to kick over the traces and run amok.

For this combination of reasons the Creative Minority in a
growing society is apt to be perpetually changing—and this not
simply in its personnel, but more profoundly, by far, in its ideas
and its ideals. By contrast, the Dominant Minority in a disintegrating society tends to degenerate into a close corporation
whose ideas and ideals have the legendary rigidity of the unchanging 'laws of the Medes and Persians'—and this even when its
personnel is radically re-cast through the admission of *novi
homines* to some share in the corporation's jealously guarded
privileges.[2]

---

[1] In IV. C (iii) (*c*), vol. iv, above.

[2] The personnel of the Dominant Minority does frequently change almost completely
in its physical composition in the course of the Dominant Minority's career between
the original breakdown and the final dissolution of the disintegrating society; for the
Dominant Minority is violently self-destructive, and it would be likely to annihilate
itself long before it had come to the end of its brief turn on the stage if its strength
were not perpetually recruited by infusions of fresh blood. The Dominant Minority does
its best—or worst—to destroy itself by indulging in dissensions in its own ranks in the
midst of its truceless warfare with the Proletariat. Its members exterminate one another in
civil wars within the bosom of a single commonwealth as well as in wars between state and
state; and at the same time they sap their own vitality by running to extremes of luxurious-
ness and vice and of sluggishness and frenzy. The new blood—'viscera magnarum domu-
um dominique futuri' (Juvenal: *Satires*, III, l. 72; quoted again in V. C (i) (*c*) 2, p. 67,
below)—which keeps the Dominant Minority alive is drawn in ever larger draughts from ever
more alien sources. For example, the Roman senatorial class which represented the dominant minority of the Hellenic Society in the penultimate phase of its disintegration—
between the convulsions in the third century of the Christian Era and the death-throes
in the fifth and sixth centuries—would perhaps not have been able to trace more than
a tincture in its blood back to the veins of the Roman senatorial class of the Republican
Era, with which it was officially identical. The families which were the representatives

This social and mental and spiritual fixity that is characteristic of dominant minorities, in contrast to creative minorities, and that persists through one round after another of the series of unsuccessful responses that constitutes the disintegration-process, can be accounted for by the fact that in the disintegration of a civilization, in contrast to its growth, the challenge that is presented in each successive bout of Challenge-and-Response is always, now, the same.[1] The unanswered challenge recurs again and again, and the discomfited minority keeps the field in order to invite and incur as many successive defeats at the hands of an adversary whom it can neither overcome nor elude. The discomfiture, each time, is a foregone conclusion, since the minority which has become merely dominant has ceased, *ex hypothesi*, to be creative. The defensive posture which it substitutes for a creative activity may be either indolent or recalcitrant; but, whether it is insanely defying the lightning or inertly resting on its oars, in either posture the Dominant Minority is refusing to hand over to other aspirants the protagonist's role which it has already proved itself incompetent to play.

These postures that remain rigidly the same, through one bout after another of a losing battle, are the marks of the Dominant Minority in a disintegrating civilization. The contrast to the fluidity and versatility of the successive creative minorities in a growing civilization is extreme. The creative minorities are in perpetual flux because they are successive incarnations of the diverse forms in which the creative spirit manifests itself in response to challenges which are never the same twice running. The Dominant Minority stands stiff, like the pillar of salt into which Lot's wife was transformed as the penalty for looking back upon the abandoned Cities of the Plain instead of turning her face

---

of this class at the turn of the fourth and fifth centuries of the Christian Era were probably descended in the physical sense almost entirely from *ci-devant* members of the internal and external proletariats; from Orientals and barbarians who had acquired the Roman citizenship, or even from slaves who had purchased their freedom. Indeed, in terms of 'Race' there was almost certainly a much greater infusion of new blood into the Roman senatorial class in its decadence as a dominant minority than the aristocracies of the Roman Republic or the Macedonian Kingdom or the Athenian City-State had ever received in their prime when they were still furnishing creative minorities for a growing civilization. In physical race it is the Creative Minority of the springtime, rather than the Dominant Minority of the decadence, that is able to boast of its 'purity'. At first sight this will seem paradoxical; but on a closer view it will be seen to confirm our previous conclusion (reached in II. C (ii) (a) 1, vol. i, above) that Race counts for very little in human affairs. The telling factors are the ideas and the ideals. The Dominant Minority remains, from first to last, the rigid and static corporation that we have described, because the *novi homines* who change its racial composition are only allowed to bring in their new blood on condition of accepting the old tradition of the body into which they are being initiated. Conversely, an aristocracy in a society in the growth-stage may keep itself racially 'pure' without ceasing to throw up one creative minority after another so long as its members forbear to steel their souls against the influence of the spirit that bloweth where it listeth.

[1] On this point see Part V. B, above.

resolutely towards the mountain in which she might have found a happier habitation.

In so far as it takes this stand, the Dominant Minority condemns itself, in advance, to have no further part or lot in the work of creation; but in making its 'great refusal' it impoverishes no one but itself. By disqualifying itself from serving as an instrument, it does not bring the work to an end; for, while this civilization is falling and that civilization is rising, the work of creation still goes on. It not only goes on; it also continues to be performed through that action of Challenge-and-Response and Withdrawal-and-Return with which we have become familiar in our analysis of the process of growth. When the growth of a civilization is cut short by a breakdown, and the would-be creative minority that has stiffened into a dominant minority begins to repeat an ineffective gesture which never varies at each onset of an unanswered challenge which never ceases to recur, this monotonous celebration of the tragedy of defeat is not the only drama that is played upon the broken-down civilization's social stage. During the disintegration of a civilization two separate plays with different plots are being performed simultaneously side by side. While an unchanging dominant minority is perpetually rehearsing its own defeat, fresh challenges are perpetually evoking fresh creative responses from newly recruited minorities which proclaim their own creative power by rising, each time, to the occasion.

These ever-changing new creative minorities stand in no fixed relation to the Dominant Minority which persists in holding the floor side by side with them for as long as it retains the strength to remain upon its feet. They are not bound *a priori* to be recruited entirely outside its ranks,[1] any more than they are bound to coincide with the Dominant Minority in their membership, either wholly or in part. Manifestly the chances are in favour of their being recruited from among outsiders, since *ex hypothesi* the Dominant Minority has placed itself in a rigid posture which is inimical to creativity; yet the creative spirit does not wholly depart from the souls of the Dominant Minority before it has performed through them at least two mighty works: the creation of a school of philosophy which prepares the way for a universal church—filling some of the valleys and bringing some of the mountains low[2] in the spiritual wilderness of a society in disintegration—and the creation of a universal state as a material framework within which a universal church can flower in its tender infancy. Both these

---

[1] For the recruitment of leaders of the Internal Proletariat from the ranks of the Dominant Minority see V. C (ii) (a), vol. vi, pp. 236–41, below.

[2] Luke iii. 4–5.

things are the work of creative minorities and creative individuals who arise among the members of the Dominant Minority; but at the same time they are only a part of the work of creation that is being accomplished during the age of disintegration in the disintegrating society's ambit; for at the same time another creative minority's handiwork can be discerned in the creation of a universal church, and another's, again, in the creation of a bevy of barbarian war-bands.

We have now found our answer to the question whether the movement of Schism-and-Palingenesia, as we see it in the process of disintegration, does not differ from the movement of With-drawal-and-Return, as we have seen this in the process of growth, in the point that in Schism-and-Palingenesia it is a majority that withdraws from a minority. We can see now that the answer to our question is, after all, in the negative. In Schism-and-Palin-genesia it is still a minority that withdraws—and this, as before, for the purpose of finding a creative response to a challenge. But in a disintegrating civilization the uncreative mass, from which the Creative Minority distinguishes itself, is differently constituted from the uncreative mass of a civilization that is still in growth. Instead of consisting wholly of an impressionable rank-and-file whom the Creative Minority, when it returns, can induce to follow its lead by playing upon the faculty of mimesis, the uncreative mass now also consists in part of a Dominant Minority which is almost entirely intractable to the new creative minority's influence. What we are watching in the Secession of the Proletariat is thus not really the withdrawal of a majority from a minority. It is the performance of the Creative Minority's familiar work in the familiar way, but in the teeth of another minority of a different order—a recalcitrant minority which is persisting in a hopeless attempt to dominate a situation in which it does not any longer command the initiative. The secession which is thus accomplished by a creative minority under these special difficulties only appears to be the work of a majority because the Creative Minority attracts to itself, as usual, the mimesis of the uncreative mass apart from the fraction of this mass which is now stubbornly resisting this attraction because it has cast itself for the Dominant Minority's role. As usual, 'the floating vote' is given to the Creative Minority every time, while the Dominant Minority attracts no mimesis to itself and can do no more than withhold its own support from its creative rival. It is only this negative power of making 'the great refusal' that distinguishes the Dominant Minority from the rest of the uncreative mass;[1] and this distinction is not fundamental. The

[1] A classic illustration of this is afforded by the contrast between the status and the

most significant, though not the most conspicuous, line of division is still that which divides the whole of the uncreative mass from the Creative Minority in each successive round of Challenge-and-Response.

That the Secession of the Proletariat should thus prove, after all, to be the work of a minority and not of a majority is only what we might have expected. For an act of secession is manifestly an act that requires the exercise of initiative and courage and imagination in a high degree; and these are not the virtues of sheep without a shepherd. This point is illustrated by the historic 'Secessions of the Plebs' in the history of the Roman Republic—in allusion to which our own term 'Secession of the Proletariat' has been coined. It is notorious that in the earlier bouts of the conflict between Plebeians and Patricians the Plebs strove in vain to break its economic and political chains. It was only gradually that the challenge of oppression evoked the latent powers of leadership in a minority of the Plebeian mass; and it was this creative minority —an inchoate 'Plebeian aristocracy', to describe it through a contradiction in terms—that conceived and executed the plan of secession as a stratagem for bringing the oppressive Patricians to their knees. If this minority had not taken the lead, the rank-and file of the Plebeians would assuredly never have struck out for themselves the master-stroke of first escaping from the pen in which their oppressors fancied that they held them corralled, and then turning at bay in the security of the open wilderness.

(c) SCHISM IN THE BODY SOCIAL

1. *Dominant Minorities*

Our preliminary inquiry into the movement of Schism-and-Palingenesia has incidentally brought out the fact that no one of the several fractions into which a disintegrating society is apt to split—neither the Dominant Minority nor the Proletariat, Internal or External—is all of one homogeneous êthos in the spirit that animates its members.

We can now see that there is an element of variety even in the Dominant Minority, notwithstanding the fact that a certain fixity and uniformity of êthos is this Dominant Minority's characteristic mark. The Dominant Minority may perform prodigies of sterilization in converting to its own barren *esprit de corps* the *novi homines* whom it is continually drafting into its repeatedly self-decimated

state of mind of the French *noblesse* on the eve of the Revolution (see the quotation from de Tocqueville in IV. C (iii) (c) 2 (γ), Annex, vol. iv, p. 638, footnote 6, above). In the France of that generation the aristocracy had stamped itself unmistakably as a dominant minority, whereas in the England of the same generation the aristocracy had not yet ceased to be creative.

ranks; yet, for all its perversity, it cannot prevent itself from putting forth the creative power and activity that are revealed in the creation of a universal state and of a school of philosophy. And accordingly we find that even the Dominant Minority is apt to include a certain number of members who depart very strikingly from the characteristic type of the closed corporation to which they belong.

In the Dominant Minority this characteristic type displays two variants—one passive and the other active—which have both come to our notice already in an extreme form in our study of the arrested civilizations.[1] The passive variant resembles the Nomad who has conquered a sedentary population and who is ruthlessly exploiting his conquest in a *Raubwirtschaft* which is as reckless, and therefore as self-destructive, as it is immoral. The active variant resembles the 'Osmanli or the Spartiate who takes sufficient thought for the morrow to forgo the immediate delight of enjoying what he has won, in order to dedicate himself to the grim task of holding his prize by main force. In the dominant minority of the Hellenic Society in disintegration the nearest approach to the Avar or the Hyksos *in partibus agricolarum* is to be seen in the Roman knighted man of business (*vir equestris*) who fleeced the conquered populations in the second and the last century B.C. by farming the collection, or financing the payment, of their taxes; or in the Roman aristocrat (*vir senatorius*) who, according to his opportunities, played ducks and drakes with the wealth and happiness of a province as a Verres or of a continent as a Lucullus or of a world as a Nero. The nearest approach, in the same social milieu, to a Spartiate 'Peer' or to an Ottoman *qul* is to be seen in a Rupilius stamping out the embers of the Sicilian slave-revolt of 135–131 B.C.;[2] or in a Crassus planting an avenue of agony—six thousand crosses with a captured follower of the insurgent gladiator Spartacus nailed alive on each—along the whole length of the Great

---

[1] In Part III. A, vol. iii, above.
[2] In justice to the Roman name it should be mentioned that in this first of the two Sicilian slave-wars neither Rupilius nor any other Roman was the villain of the piece. The monster who provoked the outbreak was not a Roman citizen but a native Sicilian slave-owner, Dâmophilus of Enna, whose home city-state was politically a subject community. (For a vivid picture of Dâmophilus see Diodorus of Agyrium: *A Library of Universal History*, fragments of Books XXXIV–XXXV, chap. 2, §§ 34–7, quoted in V. C (i) (c) 2, p. 72, footnote 2, below.) The role here played by Dâmophilus points the fact that the criterion of membership in the Hellenic dominant minority, in the sense in which we are using the term, was not political citizenship but social class and, above all, economic 'pull'. This dominant minority included many oppressors who did not possess the Roman franchise; and conversely there were many Roman citizens in Dâmophilus's generation (e.g. the common soldiers in the Roman forces that put down the slave-revolt which Dâmophilus had provoked) who had sunk into being members of the proletariat—as is testified by the words and deeds of Tiberius Gracchus. (For the saying attributed to Tiberius Gracchus see IV. C (iii) (c) 3 (β), vol. iv, p. 508, above, and V. C (i) (c) 2, pp. 70–1, and V. C (ii) (a), Annex II, vol. vi, p. 381, with Table VIII, logion (α), p. 414, below.)

South Road from Rome to Capua;¹ or in a Titus sowing the site
of Jerusalem with salt.

This pair of types—the wastrel and the hangman—that are
characteristic of the members of a dominant minority in power,
has its necessary historical complement in a third type which must
evidently have been on the scene in a previous act of the play: and
that is the conqueror who has originally won the loot which the
hangman is trying to guard and the wastrel is trying to dissipate.
This third type, again, can be illustrated by conspicuous examples
from Hellenic history. In the disintegration of the Hellenic
Civilization the conqueror can first be seen at work in those internecine wars between sovereign states which raged with ever greater
violence until the Roman 'knock-out blow' imposed a peace of
exhaustion. This conqueror in the fratricidal warfare within the
bosom of the Dominant Minority was incarnate in a Philip selling
the Olynthians into slavery; in an Alexander crushing Thebes;
in a Mummius razing Corinth; in a Sulla devastating Samnium;²
and in the successive victor-victims of a century of Roman civil
wars in which the last round ended in the overthrow of Mark
Antony by Augustus. In another field we see the conqueror turning these arms that have been exercised in fratricidal warfare to
the conquest of aliens:³ both alien civilizations and alien primitive
societies. The outstanding Hellenic example of the conqueror of
alien civilizations is Alexander the Great (though his greatness lies,
as we shall see,⁴ in a vision of unity through reconciliation which
is seldom granted to those who draw the sword to cut the Gordian
Knot). The Hellenic conquerors of primitive societies are represented by the long series of consuls and pro-consuls who imposed
the Roman yoke upon the necks of all the barbarians of Western
Europe and North-West Africa from the Ligurians in the Appennines to the Brigantes in the Plain of York, and from the Kabyles
in the Aures to the Dacians in Transylvania: a Publius Cornelius
Scipio rewarding the Boii for laying down their arms in 191 B.C.
by confiscating half their land to provide allotments for Roman
colonists;⁵ a Marcus Claudius Marcellus expelling the peaceful
Gallic settlers from Venetia in 183 B.C.;⁶ a Publius Cornelius
Cethegus and a Marcus Baebius Tamphilus deporting 40,000

¹ Appian of Alexandria: *Studies in Roman History*: 'The Civil Wars', Book I, chap.
120.
² Strabo: *Geographica*, Book V, chap. 11, pp. 249–50, cited already in IV. C (iii) (c) 2
(β), vol. iv, p. 391, above.
³ For this explanation (so far as it goes) of the geographical expansion of disintegrating civilizations see III. C (i) (a), vol. iii, p. 150, and V. C (i) (a), in the present
volume, pp. 15–16, above.
⁴ In V. C (i) (d) 7, vol. vi, pp. 6–10, and V. C (ii) (a), vol. vi, p. 254,
below.
⁵ Livy, Book XXXVI, chap. 39.   ⁶ Idem, Book XXXIX, chap. 54.

Apuani from the Appennines to the Abruzzi in 180 B.C.;[1] a Quintus Petillius Spurinus annihilating in 176 B.C. the desperate defenders of Mounts Letus and Balista;[2] a Marius leading a Jugurtha in chains; a Caesar mastering a Vercingetorix.

The sheer conqueror is an even more destructive and repellent representative of the Dominant Minority than the wastrel and the hangman who enter into his heritage; yet these are not the only three types that the Hellenic dominant minority has to show. This close corporation which disgraced itself by producing the Roman conquerors and wastrels and hangmen lived on to become the fertile recruiting-ground of those innumerable and mostly anonymous Roman soldiers and civil servants who partly atoned for the misdeeds of their predatory equestrian and senatorial predecessors by creating and preserving the Hellenic universal state and so making it possible for a moribund society to bask for a moment in the clear pale sunshine of an 'Indian Summer'.[3] These later and nobler representatives of the Hellenic dominant minority are to be seen at their fine flower, on the eve of the first sharp winter frost, in the figures of an Arrian and a Pertinax and a Dio Cassius,[4] while the moral power of the altruistic tradition of social

---

[1] Livy, Book XL, chap. 38. Later in the same year 7,000 more Apuani were deported to the Abruzzi—in this case by sea—by Quintus Fulvius Flaccus (idem, Book XL, chap. 41).

[2] Idem, Book XLI, chap. 18.

[3] See IV. C (ii) (b) 1, vol. iv, pp. 58–61, above.

[4] While some of the most gifted natures and attractive personalities in the goodly company of Roman Imperial public servants are to be found among its representatives at the turn of the second and third centuries of the Christian Era—more than two hundred years after the organization of the service by Augustus—it is noteworthy that the sense of moral responsibility to which Augustus gave a classic institutional expression can be traced back among the Roman governing class to the dark days of the first generation after the Hannibalic War. In the dealings of the Roman Government with the primitive peoples in its path the victory of the policy of humanity over the policy of extermination was won as early as 173–172 B.C. (see V. C (i) (c) 1, Annex, below). The record of Roman dealings with communities which were Rome's equals or superiors in cultivation is much blacker; yet the prosecution and conviction of Verres in 70 B.C., which was made immortal by Cicero's oratory, had been anticipated, by more than a hundred years, in the proceedings which were taken against Marcus Fulvius Nobilior, one of the consuls of 189 B.C., for his treatment of the Greek city-state of Ambracia during his year of office. The story is told by Livy (Book XXXVIII, chaps. 3–9, 43–4; Book XXXIX, chaps. 4–5, 22). Ambracia, being an ally of the Aetolian Confederacy, with which Rome was at war, stood a siege from Fulvius's army but capitulated unconditionally, before being taken by storm, when the Aetolian Government opened negotiations for peace. Thereupon the Ambraciots 'gave' the consul a gold crown of 150 pounds' weight, and the city was stripped by him of all the works of art—bronzes, marbles, and canvases (Hellenicè 'boards')—for which it was famous. Two years later an Ambraciot deputation appeared before the Roman Senate and accused Fulvius of having perpetrated against their city an enormity which was indisputably perpetrated against the Ligurian Statelli in 173 B.C. by Marcus Popillius Laenas. The Ambraciots declared that the Roman commander had made an unprovoked attack on them when they were showing themselves entirely amenable to the Roman Government's will, and that he had then despoiled them as a punishment for the crime of having exercised the right of self-defence. In response to this plea the Senate resolved that restitution should be made to the Ambraciots of their political and economic sovereignty as well as of their confiscated property, and that Ambracia should not be treated as a city that had been taken by storm (a merciful ruling, since, according to Roman customary law, a conquered community was condemned in perpetuity to put up with a much worse status

duty which this long line of great public servants had marvellously built up out of a poisonous heritage of moral nihilism is to be seen at its strongest in its hold upon natures which were intrinsically violent and self-seeking. One of the most impressive surviving testimonies to the spirit with which the public servants of the Hellenic universal state were imbued is to be found in the last words which are attributed to the Emperor Lucius Septimius Severus.[1]

Moreover the Roman public servant is neither the only nor the earliest epiphany of the Hellenic dominant minority in an altruistic role. In the age of the Severi, when the reign of the Stoic Emperor Marcus was an accomplished fact of Roman history, and when a school of Stoic jurists was translating the Stoic êthos into terms of Roman Law, it was manifest that the miracle of converting the Roman wolf into a Platonic watch-dog had been the work of Greek philosophy. The high-minded philosopher thus reveals himself as another altruistic representative of the Hellenic dominant minority whose existence and influence are attested and presupposed by the eventual emergence of the dutiful public servant. If the Roman administrator was an altruistic agent of the Hellenic dominant minority's practical ability, the Greek philosopher was a still nobler exponent of its intellectual power; and the golden chain of creative Greek philosophers, which ends with Plotinus (*vivebat circa* A.D. 203–62) in the generation that lived to see the Roman public service collapse, had begun with Socrates (*vivebat circa* 470–399 B.C.) in a generation that was already grown up in 431 B.C., when the Hellenic Civilization broke down.[2] To retrieve, or at any rate to mitigate, the tragic consequences of that breakdown was the Greek philosopher's, as well as the Roman administrator's, life-work; and the philosopher's labours produced

than that of a community which had accepted Rome's political supremacy by treaty). This was a notable judgement; but the outcome was more dubious, and the precedent created was therefore less effective, than in the parallel case of Popillius. On the one hand the Senate's action against Fulvius seems to have been determined not only by the merits of the case but also in part by the intervention of one of the consuls of the year who was moved by personal motives. On the other hand the moral effect of the judgement was partly undone by the Senate's subsequent action in allowing Fulvius (though this only after a hot debate) to celebrate a triumph in which the stolen works of art from Ambracia figured among the paraded spoils, and to follow this up by spending a considerable part of the gold which he had extorted from the Ambraciots on an elaborate show for the entertainment of the Roman proletariat

[1] 'Ultima verba eius dicuntur haec fuisse: "Turbatam rem publicam ubique accepi, pacatam etiam Britannis relinquo, senex ac pedibus aeger firmum imperium Antoninis meis relinquens ac boni erunt, imbecillum si mali." iussit deinde signum tribuno dari "Laboremus", quia Pertinax, quando in imperium adscitus est, signum dederat "Militemus".'—'Severus', chap. 23, in the so-called *Historia Augusta*. These words, if authentic, were uttered by Severus at York, within sixteen miles of the place where these lines were being written.

[2] Greek philosophy may be said to have been born in the hour in which Socrates abandoned his youthful studies of Physical Science in order to concentrate his mind upon the Soul (see the passage from Plato's *Phaedo*, 96–7, which has been quoted in III. C (i) (c), vol. iii, pp. 186–7, above).

a more valuable and more durable result than the administrator's, just because they were less closely woven into the material texture of the disintegrating society's life. While the Roman adminis- trators built a Hellenic universal state, the philosophers endowed Posterity with a κτῆμα εἰς ἀεί[1] in the Academy and the Peripatus, the Stoa and the Garden, the Cynic's freedom of the highways and hedges, and the Neoplatonist's unearthly Land of Heart's Desire.

If we now extend our survey from the field of Hellenic history to the histories of other civilizations that have broken down and gone into disintegration, we shall find that the noble streak of altruism which relieves the sombre record of the Hellenic dominant minority is not a peculiar grace of the Hellenic Civilization. The types that we have now identified in the dominant minority of the Hellenic Society in disintegration all reappear elsewhere.

If we look for wastrels to match the Roman plunderers of a conquered Hellenic World in the age preceding the establishment of the *Pax Augusta*, we shall find them in the war-lords, lay and ecclesiastic, who ground the faces of the Japanese peasantry in the age preceding the foundation of the Tokugawa Shogunate. We shall find their like again, in the Arabic World, in the Mamlūks who ground the faces of the Egyptian peasantry more outrageously in their military decadence than in an earlier age when they were performing a certain public service in return for their feudal dues.[2] And our own Western history in its latter days furnishes a long gallery of portraits which are unmistakable examples of the same type: from the flauntingly predatory princes of the sixteenth and seventeenth centuries—a Rodolfo Gonzaga of Castiglione and a Henry VIII of England and a Louis XIV of France—who had shaken off the moral discipline of the medieval Church,[3] to the more discreetly predatory plutocrats of the nineteenth and twen- tieth centuries, who have put the princes in irons in order to usurp for their own bourgeois profit the adventurer's self-conferred privilege of playing the game of *Raubwirtschaft* with the whole World for their oyster.

Similarly, if we look for hangmen to match a Crassus and a Titus, we shall find them in the Assyrian war-lords, from Tiglath- Pileser III to Asshurbanipal, as they wrestle ever more savagely with their self-imposed *tour de force* of holding down a conquered

---

[1] Thucydides, Book I, chap. 22.
[2] For the Egyptian Mamlūks see Part III. A, vol. iii, pp. 30-1; and IV. C (iii) (c) 3 (α), vol. iv, pp. 447-61, above.
[3] For the revolt of the local secular princes against the moral authority of the Catholic Church in the Western World at the beginning of the Modern Age, and for the princes' seizure and exploitation of the instruments and methods of public administration which the Papal Curia had invented, see IV. C (iii) (c) 3 (β), vol. iv, pp. 534-5 and 539-40, above.

Syria with one hand and a conquered Babylonia with the other, with no hand left free for retaining their hold upon Egypt.[1] We shall find other representatives of the hangman type in the Tsars —an Ivan the Terrible and a Peter the Great and a Nicholas I— who have had recourse to all the weapons in the armoury of political repression in order to keep the yoke of a universal state upon the shoulders of a restive nobility and a ground-down peasantry and a thwarted intelligentsia. And the hangman type, like the wastrel type, presents itself in our own Western World as well. It is unmistakably represented by the sinister figures of sixteenth-century German princes hanging and burning alive their rebellious Anabaptist peasants[2] (with the approbation of a Martin Luther!). And the same type reappears as plainly in the figures of these princes' latter-day National-Socialist supplanters, who, at the moment when these words were being written, were attempting to break the spirit of Jews, Marxians, Liberals, Pacifists, Christians, and Prussian officers by employing our twentieth-century methods of barbarism in pursuit of a sixteenth-century aim. Nor is this savagery a mere local German departure from a milder Western norm; for the English observer, writing smugly in his study, will find his pen refusing to obey his fingers if he begins to thank God that he and his kinsfolk are not as men are on the Continent. If he is tempted to offer the Pharisee's thanksgiving, his conscience will rise up to remind him of the English-speaking peoples' responsibility for the crime of Negro Slavery,[3] and of those English penal laws[4]—repealed scarcely a century ago—under which an English labourer convicted of a petty theft might be sentenced by an English magistrate to deportation for life if he were lucky enough to escape the gallows.

If we want an example of the wastrel and the hangman combined in one person, we shall find it in the Egyptiac World in the Pyramid-Builder[5] whose hold over his subject peasantry was so complete that he could wear them out for the gratification of his own megalomania without having to fear that his victims would rebel under the lash.

We can also add portraits from the histories of other disintegrating civilizations to our gallery of Hellenic conquerors.

The fratricidal warfare within the bosom of the dominant minority of the Hellenic Society which ended in the delivery of

---

[1] For this phase of Assyrian history see IV. C (iii) (c) 3 (α), vol. iv, pp. 476–84, above.
[2] For the Anabaptists see V. C (i) (c) 2, pp. 167 and 169–72, below.
[3] See IV. C (iii) (b) 2, vol. iv, above.
[4] See IV. C (iii) (c) 2 (γ), Annex, vol. iv, p. 638, above.
[5] See III. C (i) (d), vol. iii, pp. 212–15, and IV. C (iii) (c) 2 (β), vol. iv, pp. 408–10 above.

a Roman 'knock-out blow' has its analogue in the Sinic World in the struggle between the contending states which ended in the triumph of Ts'in,[1] and in the Far Eastern Society in Japan in that Ishmaelitish warfare of all against all which required three successive Caesars—a Nobunaga and a Hideyoshi and an Ieyasu— to bring it to a close.[2] The disintegration of the Babylonic and Iranic civilizations was carried to its consummation by a duel between two sister Powers: Assyria and Babylonia in the one case,[3] and the 'Osmanlis and the Safawis in the other.[4] In Orthodox Christendom the duel between the East Roman Empire and Bulgaria in the tenth century of the Christian Era opened the way for the Frankish and Turkish inroads of the century following.[5] And in the Syriac and Hindu worlds a similar orgy of fratricidal warfare likewise opened the way for the Assyrian inroads into Syria[6] and for the Turkish inroads into Hindustan.[7] In Central America the forcible incorporation of the Yucatec Society into the Mexic Society seems to have been one of the penalties of the fratricidal 'War of Mayapan' in which a Yucatec dominant minority had enlisted Mexic mercenaries to help it in the suicidal work of tearing itself to pieces;[8] and it is certain that it was the war between the Aztecs and the Tlaxcalecs that afterwards condemned the Mexic Society itself to become the prey of the Spanish conquistadores.[9]

In the abortive cosmos of city-states which tried and failed, in the second chapter of our Western history, to convert a feudal society, within which it had arisen, to its own way of life, this failure can be traced everywhere—in Italy and in Flanders, in Swabia and in the Rhineland—to the internecine strife between the patriciates of one city-state and another.[10] In consequence of this failure our Western Society discarded the city-state and fell back, as we have seen, upon the old-fashioned kingdom-state, with its feudal heritage, when it was groping after a new standard unit of parochial civic organization at the beginning of the third chapter of our Western history. And, when we remind ourselves of that curious check and throwback with which the political history of this third chapter began, we are led to ask ourselves whether by making this fresh start the princes and oligarchies and

---

[1] I. C (i) (b), vol. i, p. 89; IV. C (ii) (b) 1, vol. iv, pp. 65–6, above.
[2] IV. C (ii) (b) 2, vol. iv, p. 94, above, and V. C (ii) (a), vol. vi, pp. 186, 188, and 191, below.
[3] IV. C (iii) (c) 3 (α), vol. iv, pp. 476–84, above.
[4] I. C (i) (b), Annex I, vol. i, pp. 377–400, above.
[5] IV. C (iii) (c) 2 (β), vol. iv, pp. 384–404, above.
[6] IV. C (ii) (b) 1, vol. iv, pp. 67–8, above.
[7] IV. C (ii) (b) 2, vol. iv, pp. 99–100, above.
[8] I. C (i) (b), vol. i, pp. 123–4; IV. C (ii) (b) 2, vol. iv, pp. 105–6, above.
[9] I. C (i) (b), vol. i, p. 120, and IV. C (ii) (b) 2, vol. iv, p. 105, above.
[10] See III. C (ii) (b), vol. iii, pp. 341–50, especially pp. 348–9, above.

democracies of our latter-day Western kingdom-states and national
states have succeeded—while this third chapter in our Western
history has been running its course and finally passing into a
fourth[1]—in avoiding the fratricidal warfare through which the
fair promise of the medieval Western city-states was blighted, in
an earlier chapter of the same story, by the perverse pugnacity of
the city-state patriciates. Unhappily the answer to this fateful
question is emphatically in the negative.[2]

As soon as the modern political map of our Western World
began to take shape, the masters of the new-model states made
haste to engage in fratricidal warfare on the larger scale which
their ampler resources made possible for them. The contest for
hegemony between the Hapsburgs and the Bourbons, which inaugurated the Modern Age of our Western history, has been
followed by the wars of Philip II and the wars of Louis XIV and
the Revolutionary and Napoleonic Wars of A.D. 1792–1815; our
own 'Post-Modern' Age has been inaugurated by the General War
of 1914–18; and every one of these major conflicts has brought
with it a crop of minor wars—some preceding it as its overture,
and others following it as its sequel.[3] The life of our Western
Society has been as grievously infested by the plague of War during .
these last four centuries as in any earlier age; and we have already
observed[4] how this social evil, in persisting, has been keyed up to
an unprecedented intensity by a new 'drive' that has been put into
it since the invention of Democracy and Industrialism, until the
former 'sport of kings' has become the absorbing business of whole
nations: *la Guerre Totale*. If a furore of fratricidal warfare within
the bosom of a society is presumptive evidence that a dominant
minority has come on to the scene, we must confess that, to judge
by the recent course of our Western history, our Western Society,
in its present fourth chapter, has arrived at the stage upon which
the Hellenic Society entered after the opening of the third chapter
of Hellenic history *post Alexandrum*.

Nor has the dominant minority of the disintegrating Hellenic
Civilization been unique in begetting conquerors who turn their
arms against aliens.

For example, there are other disintegrating civilizations, besides
the Hellenic, that can show their Alexanders (though these non-

---

[1] For the transition from the third to the fourth chapter of our Western history in
the last quarter of the nineteenth century of the Christian Era see Part I. A, vol. i,
ad init.
[2] See IV. C (iii) (*b*) 3, vol. iv, pp. 141–55, above, and V. C (ii) (*b*), vol. vi, pp. 312–21,
below.
[3] For the rhythm that can be discerned in the recurrences of wars in the histories
of civilizations see V. C (ii) (*b*), vol. vi, and Part XI, below.
[4] In IV. C (iii) (*b*) 3, vol. iv, above.

Hellenic Alexanders are apt to be mere men of blood unredeemed by the spiritual vision of Alexander the Great). The Sumeric Society can display a string of them: Lugalzaggisi, Sargon, Naramsin.[1] The Egyptiac Society can show the militarists of 'the New Empire'—a Thothmes I and a Thothmes III and a Ramses II—who conquered and re-conquered the domain of an abortive Syriac Civilization[2] from Gaza to the Euphrates. In the disintegration of the main body of the Orthodox Christian Society the 'Osmanlis had no sooner completed their work of establishing a universal state in which a *Pax Ottomanica* was imposed upon the whole of Orthodox Christendom apart from Russia[3] than they sought new worlds to conquer, both east and west. Selīm I was consciously following in the footsteps of Alexander when he marched against the Persians; and, though his Janissaries insisted on turning back at Tabrīz instead of allowing themselves to be led, like Alexander's Macedonians, to the banks of the Beas,[4] Selīm did successfully repeat Alexander's exploit of conquering Egypt;[5] and his successor Suleymān the Magnificent attempted the superhuman feat of mastering the Safawī Empire with òne hand and Western Christendom with the other. The disintegration of the Far Eastern Civilization in Japan produced a counterpart of Suleymān in Hideyoshi, who had scarcely completed Nobunaga's work in the Japanese Isles before he recklessly diverted an exhausted society's last energies to grandiose schemes of conquest on the Continent —only to be foiled in Korea without ever coming within range of China. The same megalomania was displayed by the Muscovite makers of the Orthodox Christian universal state in Russia when they attempted to expand their dominions simultaneously at the expense of Western Christendom in the Balticum and Finland and Poland and at the expense of the Iranic World in the Caucasus and Central Asia. This insatiable appetite for territory in potentates who are already gorged, and who cannot digest the resources of the vast tracts which they have inherited, is an example of that mania for sheer magnitude which we have already recognized[6] as a pathological effort to find some alternative means of self-expression in lieu of a lost creative power. Again, the Iranic Society threw up, in the course of its disintegration, a Nādir Shāh[7] (*dominabatur* A.D. 1736–47) whose career looks like nothing so

---

[1] See I. C (i) (*b*), vol. i, p. 109; IV. C (ii) (*b*) 1, vol. iv, p. 64, above.
[2] For this abortive Syriac Civilization see II. D (vii), vol. ii, pp. 388–91, above.
[3] For this *Pax Ottomanica* see Part III. A, vol. iii, pp. 26–7, above.
[4] See I. C (i) (*b*), Annex I, in vol. i, pp. 385–6, above.
[5] I. C (i) (*b*), Annex I, in vol. i, p. 388; IV. C (iii) (*c*) 2 (γ), vol. iv, pp. 450–2, above.
[6] In I. C (i) (*a*), vol. iii, pp. 153–4, above.
[7] See I. C (i) (*b*), Annex I, vol. i, p. 399, above, and V. C (i) (*d*) 6 (δ), Annex, vol. v, pp. 679–80, below.

much as a caricature of Alexander's as we watch this parvenu Avshār soldier of fortune ramping up and down the famous Macedonian's historic South West Asian stage—now showing his flag for a moment at Baghdad, and now rushing off to plunder Delhi—until suddenly we see him, to our astonishment, being enlightened by a gleam of the genuine Alexandrine vision of reconciliation and unity, and courting—in his daring effort to bring back the Shī'ah to the Sunnah—the assassination that swiftly overtakes him.[1]

These non-Hellenic counterparts of Alexander the Great can be matched by corresponding counterparts of the Roman conquerors of the West European and North-West African barbarians. There is a Roman touch in the conquest of Nubia by the Caesars of the Egyptiac universal state—an Amenemhat I (*imperabat circa* 2000–1971 B.C.) and a Senwosret III (*imperabat circa* 1887–1850 B.C.)[2]—and likewise in the conquest of Yunnan by the Mongol makers of the Far Eastern universal state in the main body of the Far Eastern Society on the Asiatic Continent, while in the insular offshoot of the Far Eastern Society in Japan the subjugation of the primitive Ainu in an age when the Japanese war-lords were strenuously engaged in rending one another[3] is as astonishing a feat as the Roman subjugation of Gaul and Numidia in the age of the Roman civil wars.

If we turn in conclusion, as before, to the history of our own Western World in its Modern and its 'Post-Modern' Age, we shall find, here too, the counterparts of a Caesar in Gaul and a Marius in Numidia and an Alexander in Asia—and this in an arena that expands over the whole surface of the planet. Alexander's overrunning of the Syriac and Egyptiac and Babylonic and Indic worlds of his day has been rivalled in the Spanish conquest of the Mexic and Andean worlds and the British conquest of the Hindu World and the Dutch conquest of Indonesia and the French conquest of the Maghrib. The Roman conquests of barbarians have been rivalled in the Portuguese colonization of Brazil, in the French and British colonization of North America between the Rio Grande and the Arctic Circle,[4] and in the opening up of the

---

[1] See Browne, E. G.: *A Literary History of Persia*, vol. iv (Cambridge 1928, University Press), pp. 135–8, and Lockhart, L.: *Nadir Shah* (London 1938, Luzac).

[2] For this first Egyptiac conquest of Nubia by the Theban Emperors of the Eleventh and Twelfth Dynasties see II. D (v), vol. ii, p. 115, above. For the role played by the so-called 'Middle Empire' as an Egyptiac universal state see I. C (ii), vol. i, p. 137. Senwosret III has commemorated the hardness of his heart in the inscription on the frontier-stele which he erected at Samnah in the sixteenth year of his reign (English translation in Hall, H. R.: *The Ancient History of the Near East* (London 1913, Methuen), pp. 161–2). [3] See II. D (v), vol. ii, p. 159, above.

[4] For the victory of the Western Civilization over the Mexic Civilization in the race for winning the prize of North America see II. C (ii) (a) 2, vol. i, p. 265, footnote 1, above.

whole interior of Tropical Africa, between the Kalahari Desert and the Sahara, by a simultaneous converging movement of French and Belgian and German and English and Afrikander pioneers.

In sheer geographical range this Western expansion in the last four centuries dwarfs the combined achievements of the Romans and the Macedonians; but the Hellenic conquerors of alien worlds need not fear to measure themselves against their Western counterparts when the comparison is extended from the physical to the spiritual dimension. If the British Rāj in India has succeeded in becoming as humane as the Seleucid régime in Babylonia, on the other hand the Dutch rule in Java is infected with the same taint of commercial exploitation that blights the memory of the Ptolemaic rule in Egypt, while the atrocities committed by the Spanish *conquistadores* in Mexico and Peru surpass the misdeeds of the Roman army which pillaged Asia Minor in 189–188 B.C. Nor, when he turns to consider the treatment of primitive peoples, can the Western historian congratulate himself very heartily upon the fact that the behaviour of the French colonists in Canada towards the local Red Indians can bear comparison with the best practice of the Romans in their dealings with European and African peoples on the same low level of culture; for unhappily this clean French page in the history of our modern Western colonization is an exceptional leaf in the Recording Angel's book. The lion's share of North America has fallen in the end to the French Canadians' English-speaking rivals;[1] and, although the French have played one of the leading parts in the subsequent opening up of Africa, and have partially maintained on the Senegal in the nineteenth and twentieth centuries the noble reputation which they first earned on the St. Lawrence in the seventeenth and eighteenth centuries,[2] the Western conquest of Africa has not, as we have seen, been by any means an exclusively French achievement. When we turn from the single French page to the record of the Belgians in the Congo and of the English-speaking peoples in North America and Kenya, we have to blush at passages which are almost without parallel in the history of Roman imperialism. The Romans did not exterminate the primitive inhabitants of Transappennine Europe,[3] as the primitive inhabitants of North America have been exterminated by the English-speaking settlers of the United States.[4]

[1] For this victory of the English-speaking colonists in the struggle between the Western competitors for the acquisition of North America see II. C (ii) (a) 1, vol. i, p. 211, and II. D (ii), vol. ii, pp. 65–73, above.
[2] See II. C (ii) (a) 1, vol. i, p. 225, above.
[3] See V. C (i) (c) 1, Annex, pp. 569–74, below.
[4] For the vein of ruthlessness in the modern English method of overseas settlement see II. C (ii) (a) 1, Annex, in vol. i, above. For the fate of the Red Indians in the United States see II. C (ii) (a) 1, vol. i, pp. 212 and 214, and II. D (vii), vol. ii, p. 277, footnote 2, above.

Nor, when they reduced the conquered native populations to the status of hewers of wood and drawers of water,[1] did the privileged citizens of a Roman colonial city-state attempt to segregate themselves from their fallāhīn by an impassable barrier of caste like the gulf of race-feeling that divides the English-speaking settlers in Kenya Colony from their Indian fellow immigrants and from their Bantu native labour force. When we remind ourselves of the historical fact that, in spite of this more liberal attitude and êthos, these Roman colonies *in partibus barbarorum* degenerated into parasitic growths which were eventually swept away by a proletarian revolution,[2] we shall find ourselves wondering what expectation of life there may be for a modern Western colonial enterprise like Kenya Colony, where a community of about 18,000 White immigrants is striving to-day to dominate about 55,000 Indian and Arab immigrants and 3,200,000 Black African 'Natives' in order to subordinate their welfare to the White minority's interests.

It is now manifest that our own Western Society, as well as the other non-Hellenic societies, can furnish us with examples of three social types—the conqueror, the wastrel, and the hangman—of which we identified our first specimens among the members of the dominant minority of the Hellenic Society in its disintegration. Happily, however, the comparison works out for good as well as for evil; for we have also seen that the Hellenic dominant minority displays a wide range of spiritual variety beyond the narrow limits of these three repulsive types; and the figures that are blazoned on the brighter side of a Hellenic shield can likewise be matched by examples from the membership of the other civilizations.

For instance, the Roman public servant, as he shows himself at his best over a span of two and a half centuries in Augustus's minister Agrippa (*vivebat* 63–12 B.C.) or in Severus's minister Dio Cassius (*vivebat circa* A.D. 155–235), has his worthy counterpart in the Hindu World to-day in 'the Indian Civilian': a child of the British Rāj who has been aptly named, since it is India's need of civic salvation that has called him into existence, while the standard of service which he has set before himself is not a racial idiosyncrasy of the European founders of this Indian institution, but is a spiritual ideal which can captivate and convert and inspire any human soul, irrespective of the shape or colour of its bodily tenement. The medium through which the tradition of the Indian Civil Service is transmitted is not the physical heritage of racial kinship but the spiritual communion of *esprit de corps*; and

[1] See Part III. A, vol. iii, pp. 98–9, above.
[2] Ibid., pp. 99–100, above.

it is a recognition of this truth that has nerved British statesmanship in our generation to undertake the task of transferring the
responsibility for the government of India from English to Indian
shoulders. An Englishman of little faith, who finds himself doubt-
ing whether this hazardous enterprise can ever be brought to a
successful issue, may take heart from the reflection that in the
history of the Roman Civil Service the spiritual force of *esprit de
corps* did prove equal to the demand that was made upon it when
the responsibility for the government of the Hellenic universal
state was handed on from an Italian Agrippa or Agricola to an
Asiatic Arrian or Dio.

The fact remains, however, that the genesis of the Indian Civil
Service is to be found in the labours of Europeans who have been
bred in the tradition of Western Christendom; and, while this historical fact may not reveal the whole truth about the Indian Civil
Service itself, or foreshadow its ultimate destiny as an Indian institution, it may still serve to remind us that our own Western Society,
in its Modern and its 'Post-Modern' Age, has displayed other types
in its governing class besides those of the war-lord and the despot
and the capitalist. In England in the sixteenth century of the
Christian Era this governing class brought forth not only a Henry
VIII to play the tyrant's part, but also a Saint Thomas More to
lay down his life rather than lend his countenance to the tyrant's
policy. In the same century in Lombardy 'the poisoned field'
which produced a weed after its own kind in the person of Rodolfo
Gonzaga at the same time gave birth to a saint in Rodolfo's brother
Aluigi.[1] In the seventeenth century in France the parasitic *noblesse*
from which Louis XIV recruited his corrupt and extravagant court
was also the recruiting-ground for the high-minded religious community of Port Royal. Nor are we dependent, for proving our
point, upon a more or less capricious selection of individual illustrations. The truth is more convincingly demonstrated by a
general change of aim and êthos which has declared itself unmistakably in the lives of the states of our modern Western World
in the course of the last hundred years. It is true that these states
have not put off the Old Adam. They are still the expressions and
instruments of a lawless will to power—a power of evil which, in
our generation, is threatening to bring our society to irretrievable
disaster. At the same time we can see that they have latterly begun
to assume a second aspect which is so alien from the other that
ultimately the two must assuredly prove to be mutually incom-

---

[1] See the brilliant picture in *The Vocation of Aloysius Gonzaga* (London 1929,
Sheed and Ward), by Father C. C. Martindale, S.J., of the identic social environment
in which these two brothers grew up to lead two lives which were as different from
each other as any two lives could well be.

patible. While continuing to be used as instruments of an immoral violence, these states are now also beginning to be used simultaneously as a means to social welfare. Even in the most old-fashioned communities of our twentieth-century Western World the traditional military state and police-state is now concerning itself to some extent with the promotion of health and education and employment. Nor is the modern Western State only shifting its balance of activity in practice; it is also laying more and more emphasis upon the novel aspect of its functions; and the public pose is perhaps even more significant than the underlying reality; for in thus seeking to present itself to its subjects in the guise of a ministering angel or a fairy godmother, instead of parading as a strong man armed or as a beast of prey, the modern Western State is implicitly concurring in a moral condemnation of its own blood-stained past. In this changing picture of the Western State we can discern at least a partial change of heart in our modern Western governing class; and this change is clearly analogous to the change that came over the Roman governing class in and after the generation of Augustus.[1]

Our own society is not, however, unique in furnishing us with counterparts of the Roman civil service. The Confucian litterati who administered the Sinic universal state under the Han Dynasty (*imperabant* 202 B.C.–A.D. 221) attained a standard of service and acquired an *esprit de corps* that place them on a moral level with the Roman civil servants of the first and second centuries of the Christian Era in the Hellenic World and with the English civil servants of the nineteenth and twentieth centuries in Europe and India. Even the *chinovniks* who administered the Orthodox Christian universal state in Russia for two centuries, from the reign of Peter the Great (*imperabat* A.D. 1682–1725) to the reign of Nicholas II (*imperabat* A.D. 1894–1917), and who became a byword, at home as well as in the West, for their incompetence and corruption, may be let off more lightly by the verdict of History when their record can be compared with that of the régime which has now taken their place. On this showing, Posterity will perhaps pronounce that, after all, this Petrine Russian officialdom did not acquit itself so discreditably in wrestling with the gigantic dual task of maintaining the Muscovite Empire as a going concern and at the same time transforming it into a new-fangled polity on the

---

[1] For an illuminating use of this analogy to illustrate the change of heart in the modern Western governing class in England towards the middle of the nineteenth century—a change which here found its practical expression in the passage of the Factory Acts and in the establishment of the Home Civil Service—see J. L. and Barbara Hammond: *The Rise of Modern Industry* (London 1925, Methuen), chap 15 especially pp. 255-7.

Western pattern.[1] In the main body of Orthodox Christendom
the Slave-Household of the Ottoman Pādishāh, which has likewise
become a byword for its repression of the *raʿīyeh*, will also perhaps
come to be remembered as an institution which performed at least
one signal service for the Orthodox Christian Society in imposing
upon it, even by main force, that *Pax Ottomanica* which gave a
self-tormented world a brief spell of quiet between two weary ages
of anarchy.[2] In the Far Eastern Society in Japan the feudal daim-
yos and their henchmen the Samurai, who preyed upon Society,
in preying upon one another, during the four centuries preceding
the establishment of the Tokugawa Shogunate, survived to redeem
their own past by lending themselves to Ieyasu's constructive work
of converting a feudal anarchy into a feudal order; and at the
opening of the next chapter of Japanese history they rose to a
height of self-abnegation which was almost sublime when they
voluntarily divested themselves of their ancestors' harshly won
and tightly held privileges because they were convinced that this
supreme sacrifice was required of them in order to enable Japan
to hold her own in the environment of a Westernized World from
which she could no longer hold aloof.

This vein of nobility which reveals itself to a discriminating eye
in the Japanese Samurai and in the Ottoman *qullar* is the notorious
virtue of two other ruling minorities: the Incas who were the
masters of the Andean universal state, and the Persian grandees
who governed a Syriac universal state as vicegerents of an Achaemenid King of Kings. The nobility of the *orejones* and the *megis-
tânes* is vouched for by the testimony of alien conquerors who
supplanted them and reigned in their stead and put on record,
from first-hand acquaintance, the only accounts of them that we
possess (for both these ruling minorities were singularly dumb,
considering the importance and the eminence of their historic
roles). This testimony is unimpeachable where it gives a good
report, since the alien usurpers had two strong incentives to
blacken their predecessors' memory. They would be prone to

---

[1] Since this sentence was written, there have been indications that the reputation of
the Imperial Russian *chinovniks* may be destined to be rehabilitated by the piety of
their Communist successors in office! *The Manchester Guardian* of the 16th September,
1937, contains an account of a text-book of Russian history, produced under the direction of a Professor Shestakov, which is reported to have been officially commended as
approaching, more nearly than any one of forty-five competing pieces of work, to
Stalin's idea of what such a text-book ought to be. The merit of Professor Shestakov's
work, from Stalin's point of view, appears (according to the *Izvestiya* of the 24th
August, 1937) to have lain, among other things, in the fact that, in this Communist
presentation of Russian history, the Tsars Ivan III and Ivan the Terrible and Peter
the Great are given their meed of praise as empire-builders who laid the foundations
of the U.S.S.R.

[2] See Part III. A, vol. iii, pp. 26–7, and IV. C (ii) (b) 1, vol. iv, p. 70, above, and
V. C (ii) (a), vol. vi, pp. 190–1, below.

depreciate the military prowess of warriors whom they had easily beaten at their own game, and they would be tempted to vilify the moral character of rulers whom they had wrongfully despoiled of their empire.[1] With these considerations in mind, we may believe without hesitation any good that the Spaniards tell us of the Incas, or the Greeks of the Persians; and in both records the good report conspicuously predominates over the bad.

In the Greek portrait of the Persians Herodotus's famous thumbnail sketch of the Persian boys' education—'they train them from the age of five to the age of twenty to do three things, and three things only: to ride and to shoot and to speak the truth'[2]— is not discredited by the companion picture that is presented to us of these same Persians in their manhood. There is the Herodotean tale of Xerxes' suite in the storm at sea doing obeisance to their Imperial Master and then leaping overboard to their deaths in order to save the Pādishāh's life by lightening the vessel in which the discomfited Achaemenian war-lord was fleeing from Europe to Asia after his defeat at Salamis.[3] And there is the less tragic incident, of which Xenophon was an eye-witness, when the grandees on the staff of Cyrus the Younger responded with the same unhesitating promptness to the summons of their master to sacrifice—on this occasion not their lives but their hardly less precious finery. The spectacle of these Persian nobles in their gorgeous raiment eagerly plunging into the mud in order to put their shoulders to the wheels of the baggage wagons made a deep impression on the mind of the Greek observer, as any reader of his narrative can tell.[4] But the most impressive of all Greek testimonies to Persian virtues is that of Alexander the Great, who showed by grave acts, and not just by easy words, how highly he thought of the Persians after he had made their acquaintance. He had no sooner come to know these Persians by the searching test of their reaction to an overwhelming disaster than he took a decision which was not only bound to offend his own Macedonians

---

[1] For the influence of these motives on the minds of the Spanish historians of the Incas see Baudin, L.: *L'Empire Socialiste des Inka* (Paris 1928, Institut d'Ethnologie), p. 4. On the other hand, one of the most influential of these historians, Garcilaso de la Vega, shows a bias—which has to be discounted—in favour of the Incas owing to the pride that he took in the Inca blood that ran in his own veins. (His mother was a niece of the Emperor Huayna Capac.) For a less favourable interpretation of the record of the Incas as a ruling minority see Cunow, H.: *Geschichte und Kultur des Inkareiches* (Amsterdam 1937, Elsevier,) pp. 34, 35–6, 41, 42, 46–7, 48, 49–50. The author draws attention to the vigour and obstinacy of the resistance which the Incas encountered at every stage of their progressive conquest of their empire, and he finds no reason for believing that the conquered peoples ever became reconciled to the Incas' rule. This judgement, however, seems to be exceptional, and it is modified by Cunow himself when he comes down to details (see, for example, op. cit., pp. 88–9, for the moderation of the *corvées* which the Incas imposed on their subjects).

[2] Herodotus, Book I, chap. 136.

[3] Herodotus, Book VIII, chap. 118.

[4] See Xenophon: *Expeditio Cyri*, Book I, chap. 5, §§ 7–8.

but was the surest way of outraging their feelings that he could have hit upon if this had been his deliberate aim. He decided to take the Persians into partnership in the government of an empire which the Macedonians' prowess had wrested, only yesterday, out of the Persians' hands; and he put this policy into execution with characteristic thoroughness. He took a Persian grandee's daughter to wife; he bribed or browbeat his Macedonian officers into following his example; and he drafted Persian recruits into his Macedonian regiments. A people who could evoke this extraordinary tribute from the leader of their hereditary enemies—and this on the morrow of their own utter military defeat—must have been transparently endowed with the classic virtues of 'a ruling race'.[1]

We have now managed to marshal a considerable array of evidence for the capacity of dominant minorities to produce an admirable governing class; and this evidence is borne out by the catalogue of the universal states that have been created by the dominant minorities of disintegrating civilizations; for the establishment and maintenance of a universal state presupposes the existence of a governing class with a high standard of conduct, a strong *esprit de corps*, and a persistent tradition.

In the course of previous inquiries[2] we have found incidentally that, out of twenty civilizations which have unquestionably broken down,[3] no less than fifteen have passed through a universal state on their road from breakdown towards dissolution. We have identified a Hellenic universal state in the Roman Empire;[4] an Andean in the Empire of the Incas;[5] a Sinic in the Empire of the Ts'in and Han dynasties;[6] a Minoan in 'the thalassocracy of Minos';[7] a Sumeric in the Empire of Sumer and Akkad;[8] a Babylonic in the Neo-Babylonian Empire of Nabopolassar and Nebuchadnezzar;[9] a Mayan in 'the Old Empire' of the Mayas;[10] an Egyptiac in 'the Middle Empire' of the Eleventh and Twelfth Dynasties;[11] a Syriac in the Achaemenian Empire;[12] an Indic in

---

[1] For the effect of Alexander's discovery of the Persians' true character in leading the Macedonian man of genius to his greater discovery of the unity of Mankind see V. C (i) (d) 7, vol. vi, p. 9, below.

[2] In I. C (i) (b), vol. i, and IV. C (ii), vol. iv, above.

[3] These twenty include all those, with the single uncertain exception of our own Western Civilization, that have not either miscarried before birth or become arrested immediately after it.

[4] I. C (i) (a), vol. i, pp. 52-3; IV. C (ii) (b) 1, vol. iv, p. 61, above.

[5] I. C (i) (b), vol. i, pp. 120-2; IV. C (ii) (b) 2, vol. iv, p. 103, above.

[6] I. C (i) (b), vol. i, p. 89; IV. C (ii) (b) 1, vol. iv, p. 65, above.

[7] I. C (i) (b), vol. i, pp. 93-4; IV. C (ii) (b) 1, vol. iv, p. 64, above.

[8] I. C (i) (b), vol. i, p. 106; IV. C (ii) (b) 1, vol. iv, pp. 63-4, above.

[9] I. C (i) (b), vol. i, p. 119; IV. C (ii) (b) 2, vol. iv, p. 100, above.

[10] I. C (i) (b), vol. i, pp. 125-7; IV. C (ii) (b) 2, vol. iv, p. 108, above.

[11] I. C (ii), vol. i, p. 137; IV. C (ii) (b) 2, vol. iv, p. 85, above.

[12] I. C (i) (b), vol. i, pp. 75-6; IV. C (ii) (b) 1, vol. iv, p. 67, above.

the Empire of the Mauryas;[1] a Hindu in the Timurid Empire of
Akbar and Awrangzīb.[2] We have distinguished a Russian Ortho-
dox Christian universal state in the Muscovite 'Empire of All the
Russias',[3] and another Orthodox Christian universal state, em-
bracing the main body of Orthodox Christendom, in the Ottoman
Empire;[4] and in the Far Eastern World we have met with a corre-
sponding pair: the Tokugawa Shogunate in Japan[5] and the Mongol
Empire in China.[6]

We have also observed that a number of these universal states
have been prolonged (to their natural term) or restored (after a
lapse) or reintegrated (after an interval of alien intrusion) by other
hands than those which originally created them. The Empire of
the Incas was taken over forcibly by the Spaniards and prolonged
in the Spanish Viceroyalty of Peru.[7] The Empire of Sumer and
Akkad was restored by the First Dynasty of Babylon in the reign
of Hammurabi.[8] The Neo-Babylonian Empire was engulfed in
the Achaemenian Empire,[9] and this in its turn was taken over
forcibly by Alexander, and was prolonged by Alexander's Seleucid
successors, before it was eventually broken up by Roman and
Parthian hammer-strokes and was subsequently reintegrated by
the labours of the Umayyads and 'Abbasids after the complete and
final expulsion of the Hellenic intruders from the Syriac Society's
domain.[10] The Egyptiac 'Middle Empire' of the Eleventh and
Twelfth Dynasties was re-established, after a very much shorter
breach of continuity, in 'the New Empire' of the Eighteenth and
Nineteenth Dynasties.[11] The Empire of the Mauryas was partially
taken over and prolonged by Hellenic conquerors from Bactria,
and by these Greek empire-builders' Kushan successors, and was
eventually reintegrated by the Guptas, who stand to the Mauryas
as the 'Abbasids stand to the Achaemenidae.[12] The Timurid Empire of Akbar and Awrangzīb was restored—in more solid masonry
and also, perhaps, on a sounder architectural plan—in the British
Rāj.[13] The Mongol Empire over China was re-established, to all

---

[1] I. C (i) (b), vol. i, p. 86; IV. C (ii) (b) 1, vol. iv, p. 66, above.
[2] IV. C (ii) (b) 2, vol. iv, p. 97, above.
[3] IV. C (ii) (b) 2, vol. iv, p. 88, above.
[4] Part III. A, vol. iii, pp. 26–7; IV. C (ii) (b) 1, vol. iv, p. 70, above.
[5] IV. C (ii) (b) 2, vol. iv, p. 88, above.
[6] IV. C (ii) (b) 2, vol. iv, p. 87, above.
[7] IV. C (ii) (b) 2, vol. iv, pp. 80 and 103, above.
[8] I. C (i) (b), vol. i, p. 106; IV. C (ii) (b) 1, vol. iv, pp. 63–4, above.
[9] I. C (i) (b), vol. i, p. 119, above.
[10] I. C (i) (b), vol. i, pp. 72–7, above. It is noteworthy that this final reversal of
Alexander's feat of imposing Hellenism upon the Syriac World by force of arms was
followed by a voluntary reception of Hellenic culture on the part of the Syriac Society in
the 'Abbasid Age. This cultural contact between the Syriac and Hellenic societies at this
stage of their intercourse is examined in Part IX, below.
[11] I. C (ii), vol. i, pp. 138–9, above.
[12] I. C (i) (b), vol. i, pp. 84–6; IV. C (ii) (b) 1, vol. iv, p. 66, above.
[13] IV. C (ii) (b) 2, vol. iv, pp. 96–7, above.

Chinese intents and purposes, in the Manchu Empire,[1] which stands to it as the Egyptiac 'New Empire' stands to the Egyptiac 'Middle Empire'.

It will be observed that—as might have been expected *a priori* —these works of rehabilitation have been performed, more often than not, by new arrivals on the scene who have been culturally alien from the original builders. The Spaniards, for example, were wholly alien from the Incas; the Achaemenidae from the Babylonians; the Macedonians from the Achaemenidae; the Greek and Kushan invaders of India from the Mauryas; and the British from the Timurids (as well as from the Hindus). Even the Amorite Hammurabi, though he was the sixth of his line to reign in Babylon, was probably looked askance at, as a not yet completely reclaimed barbarian, by his Akkadian subjects and *a fortiori* by their Sumerian fellow citizens of that 'Empire of the Four Quarters' which actually owed its restoration to Hammurabi's prowess and statesmanship. And this was certainly the attitude of the Chinese to the Manchus from beginning to end of the Manchu régime, in spite of the Manchus' almost complete freedom from that tincture of an alien civilization which had evoked in Chinese hearts a fanatical hatred against the Manchus' predecessors, the Mongols.[2]

We shall even find several further examples of alien handiwork among those universal states which were 'original work' and were not restorations of some older building. For example, the Timurid Turks, who made the first essay in providing the disintegrating Hindu Society with a universal state, were children of the Iranic Society and, by this token, were just as alien from the Hindu World as are their British successors. The 'Osmanlis, who gave the main body of Orthodox Christendom the only universal state that it has ever known, were the Timurids' cultural as well as racial brethren. The Mongols, who gave the main body of the Far Eastern Society its first universal state, were decidedly more alien in culture from their Chinese subjects than were the Manchus who afterwards repeated the Mongols' feat.[3]

Of the other original creators of universal states, a majority— which includes the Romans, the Incas, the Achaemenidae, the Ts'in, the Theban Dynasties, the Muscovites, and the Tokugawas —were Powers which had qualified for the role of empire-builders

[1] IV. C (ii) (*b*) 2, vol. iv, p. 87, above.
[2] For the cultural relation of the Manchus to the Chinese and to the Mongols respectively see Part III. A, vol. iii, pp. 16, 19, and 31, footnote 1, above, and V. C (i) (*c*) 3, in the present volume, pp. 309–10, and V. C (i) (*c*) 4, pp. 348–51, below.
[3] For the tinge of Far Eastern Christian culture in the social 'make-up' of the Mongols see II. D (vi), vol. ii, pp. 237–8, and II. D (vii), Annex VIII, vol. ii, above, and V. C (i) (*c*) 4, in the present volume, p. 348, below.

by serving an apprenticeship as wardens of the marches;[1] and these frontiersmen on an imperial throne have often been viewed by their more cultivated but less capable subjects in the interior with the eyes of a Sumerian litteratus looking down his nose at a Hammurabi. This, as we know from their own written testimony, was the attitude of Greek men-of-letters towards Roman statesmen and administrators as late as the Age of the Antonines, when these Romans were actually practising, with an effectiveness that no Greek had ever approached, that benevolent 'Hellenic superintendence' ('Ελληνικὴ ἐπιμέλεια) which, five hundred years before, had been so earnestly commended to King Philip by Isocrates.[2]

In so far as the universal states of which we have made this summary survey[3] prove to have been the work of alien hands, they cannot, of course, be taken as evidence of creative power in any fraction of the disintegrating society on whose ground they have been set up. It would, however, be hypercritical to stigmatize the frontiersmen empire-builders as aliens simply because the people of the interior have affected to regard them as such. If we examine more closely the Hellenic case in point, we shall probably come to the conclusion that the Greek rhetor's sensitiveness to the barbarism of the Roman official was not an entirely genuine feeling, but was partly the expression of a self-defensive mental attitude—a refusal to face the humiliating fact that the converted barbarian had proved himself, by Isocrates' own test, to be a better Hellene than the Greek himself.[4] It would, indeed, be a paradox to maintain that the Romans were no true representatives of the Hellenic

---

[1] For 'the stimulus of pressures' which has so often given 'marches' an ascendancy over 'interiors' see II. D (v), vol. ii, above.

[2] Φημὶ γὰρ χρῆναί σε τοὺς μὲν Ἕλληνας εὐεργετεῖν, Μακεδόνων δὲ βασιλεύειν, τῶν δὲ Βαρβάρων ὡς πλείστων ἄρχειν· ἢν γὰρ ταῦτα πράττῃς, ἅπαντές σοι χάριν ἕξουσιν, οἱ μὲν Ἕλληνες ὑπὲρ ὧν ἂν εὖ πάσχωσι, Μακεδόνες δ' ἢν βασιλικῶς ἀλλὰ μὴ τυραννικῶς αὐτῶν ἐπιστατῇς, τὸ δὲ τῶν ἄλλων γένος ἢν διὰ σὲ Βαρβαρικῆς δεσποτείας ἀπαλλαγέντες Ἑλληνικῆς ἐπιμελείας τύχωσιν.—Isocrates: Philippus.

[3] A complete table of the universal states that come within the purview of the present Study will be found at the end of V. C (iii), in vol. vi, p. 327, below.

[4] In an earlier chapter of the story of the Greeks' encounter with the Romans—at a stage in which the Romans were still engaged in wrecking the Hellenic Society that they were afterwards to reconstruct—the Greek pretence that the Romans were barbarians had proved impossible to keep up:

'It is said that when Pyrrhus caught his first bird's eye view, from an observation post, of the Roman army in formation, he remarked that he could see nothing barbarous about the barbarians' order of battle; and similar confessions were extorted from Greeks who were making their first acquaintance with Titus [Quinctius Flamininus]. They had had it from the Macedonians that a fellow in command of a barbarian host was on the war-path, conquering and enslaving as he came; and now they found themselves in the presence of a young man of gracious mien who was a Greek in speech and accent and was ambitious to deserve true honour. Of course they were extraordinarily charmed, and, when they left his presence to go off to their respective homes, they turned the tide of public feeling in Titus's favour—bringing tidings of him as a leader who had come to conduct the Greeks into the promised land of freedom.'— Plutarch: Life of Titus Quinctius Flamininus, chap. 5. The fourth-century Greek scholar Heracleides Ponticus hit the mark when, in the earliest mention of Rome in extant Greek literature, he described her as 'a Hellenic city' (see V. C (i) (c) 3, p. 212, footnote 3, below).

dominant minority, or the Thebans of the Egyptiac. And, even if we leave the borderline cases on one side, there are a number of instances still left in which there can be no dispute over the claim of the creators of a universal state to be representatives of the dominant minority of the society in whose domain the state has been established. Among these unquestionable exponents of a dominant minority's political creative power we may cite the Han Dynasty and 'Minos', the dynasty of Ur and the Neo-Babylonians, the Mauryas and the Guptas.

Is this political capacity the only kind of creative power that is a common attribute of dominant minorities? The question presents itself because in our analysis of the various types of character and activity in the Hellenic dominant minority we found that the creative type was not, in this case, confined to the political field. It was represented not only by the Roman public servant but also by the Greek philosopher;[1] and, if we now repeat the procedure, which we have been following so far, of surveying the lives of the other civilizations in their disintegration in order to learn whether the Hellenic phenomena reappear in them, we shall see that the Greek philosopher, as well as the Roman public servant, has his non-Hellenic counterparts. While we have found about ten disintegrating civilizations, besides the Hellenic, in which the Dominant Minority can be credited with the creative achievement of having established a universal state, we can find at least three, besides the Hellenic, in which the Dominant Minority has also thought out a philosophy.

In the history of the Babylonic Society, for example, the terrible eighth century B.C., which saw the beginning of the Hundred Years' War between Babylonia and Assyria,[2] seems also to have seen a sudden great advance in astronomical knowledge.[3] In this age Babylonic men of science discovered that the rhythm of cyclic recurrence, which had been patent, from time immemorial, in the alternations of Night and Day and in the waxing and waning of the Moon and in the Solar Cycle of the Year, was also discernible on a vaster scale in the secular motions of a heavenly host which included the planets. These stars which were traditionally named 'the wanderers' *par excellence*, in allusion to their apparently erratic courses, now proved to be bound by as strict a discipline as the Sun or the Moon or 'the fixed stars' of the Firmament in the Cosmic Cycle of a *Magnus Annus*;[4] and this exciting Babylonic discovery

[1] See pp. 39–40, above.
[2] See IV. C (iii) (c) 3 (α), vol. iv, pp. 476–80, above.
[3] See Meyer, E.: *Geschichte des Altertums*, vol. i, part (ii), third edition (Stuttgart and Berlin 1913, Cotta), pp. 191–5; vol. iii, first edition (Stuttgart 1901, Cotta), pp. 132–4.
[4] See IV. C (i), vol. iv, pp. 23–4 and 37, above.

of a hitherto unsuspected application of a familiar law of Physical Nature had much the same effect as our recent Western scientific discoveries have had upon the discoverers' conception of the Universe.

The never broken and never varying order that had thus been found to reign in all the known movements of the stellar cosmos was now assumed to govern the Universe as a whole: material and spiritual, inanimate and animate.[1] If an eclipse of the Sun or a transit of Venus could be dated with certainty to some precise moment hundreds of years back in the past, or predicted with equal certainty as bound to occur at some precise moment in an equally remote future, then was it not reasonable to suppose that human affairs were just as rigidly fixed and just as accurately calculable? And since the cosmic discipline implied that all these members of the Universe that moved in so perfect a unison were 'in sympathy'—*en rapport*—with each other, was it unreasonable to assume that the newly revealed pattern of the movements of the stars was a key to the riddle of human fortunes, so that the observer who held this astronomical clue in his hands would be able to forecast his neighbour's destinies if once he knew the date and moment of his birth? Reasonable or not, these assumptions were eagerly made; and thus a sensational scientific discovery gave birth to a fallacious philosophy of Determinism which has captivated the intellect of one civilization after another and is not quite discredited yet after a run of nearly 2,700 years.

The seductiveness of Astrology lies in its pretension to combine a theory which explains the whole *machina mundi* with a practice that will enable Tom, Dick, and Harry to spot the Derby Winner here and now. Thanks to this twofold attraction the Babylonic philosophy was able to survive the extinction of the Babylonic Civilization in the last century B.C.;[2] and the Chaldean *mathematicus* who imposed upon a prostrate Hellenic Society[3] was represented until yesterday by the Court Astrologer at Peking and the Munejjim Bāshȳ at Istanbol.

We have dwelt on this Babylonic philosophy of Determinism because it has a greater affinity than any of the Hellenic philosophies

[1] For the belief in a rule of Fate, which is one of the intellectual expressions of a sense of drift that is itself one of the symptoms of a schism in the Soul, see V. C (i) (*d*) 4, pp. 412–31, below.
[2] For the incorporation of Astrology into Mithraism see V. C (i) (*d*) 6 (δ), p. 540, below.
[3] See Wendland, P.: *Die Hellenistisch-Römische Kultur*, 2nd and 3rd editions (Tübingen 1912, Mohr), pp. 132–3, and Tarn, W. W.: *The Greeks in Bactria and India* (Cambridge 1938, University Press), pp. 59–60. In taking over Astrology from its Babylonic fathers in and after the 2nd century B.C. the Hellenes put their own imprint upon it, as is witnessed by the fact that, in India at the present day, some of the current technical terms of the practitioners of this pseudo-science are etymologically of Greek origin.

have with the still perhaps rather callow philosophical speculations of our own Western World in its present Cartesian Age. On the other hand there are counterparts of almost all the Hellenic schools of thought in the philosophies of the Indic and the Sinic World. The dominant minority of a disintegrating Indic Civilization brought forth the Jainism of Mahavira, the Primitive Buddhism of Siddhārtha Gautama,[1] the transfigured Buddhism of the Mahāyāna[2] (which differs from its acknowledged original at least as profoundly as Neoplatonism differs from the philosophy of Socrates), and the diverse Buddhistic philosophies that are part of the mental apparatus of a post-Buddhaic Hinduism. The dominant minority of a disintegrating Sinic Civilization brought forth the moralized ritualism and ritualized morality of Confucius and the paradoxical wisdom of the Tao which is ascribed to the legendary genius of Lao-tse.[3]

2. Internal Proletariats

A Hellenic Prototype.

When we pass from dominant minorities to proletariats, a closer examination of the facts will confirm, here too, our first impression that within each of the fractions of a disintegrating society there is a certain diversity of type. We shall also find, however, that, in the range of this spiritual diversity, the internal and the external proletariats are at opposite poles. While the external proletariats have a gamut which is narrower than that of the dominant minorities, the gamut of the internal proletariats is very much wider. Let us reconnoitre the wider field first.

If we wish to enter upon our survey of internal proletariats by our now customary way of approach—that is, by taking the Hellenic instance first as our standard of comparison—and if we also wish to follow the genesis of the Hellenic internal proletariat from the beginning of the embryo stage, we cannot begin better than by quoting a passage from Thucydides in which the historian of the breakdown of the Hellenic Society describes the consequent social schism in its earliest phase, as it showed itself first in Corcyra.[4]

[1] See I. C (i) (*b*), vol. i, p. 87, above, and V. C (i) (*c*) 2, in the present volume, pp. 131–2, below.
[2] See I. B (iii), vol. i, p. 35; II. D (vi), Annex, vol. ii, p. 405, footnote 1; IV. C (ii) (*b*) 1, vol. iv, p. 65, above; and V. C (i) (*c*) 2, in the present volume, pp. 133–46, below.
[3] See I. C (i) (*b*), vol. i, p. 89, and III. C (i) (*c*), vol. iii, pp. 187–9, above, and V. C (i) (*c*) 2, in the present volume, pp. 146–7, below.
[4] For the whole story of these Corcyraean faction-fights (*gerebantur* 427–425 B.C.) during the first phase of the Atheno-Peloponnesian War of 431–404 B.C. see Thucydides, Book III, chaps. 70–85, and Book IV, chaps. 46–8. The story has already been cited in IV. C (ii) (*b*) 1, vol. iv, p. 63, and IV. C (iii) (*b*) 9, vol. iv, p. 204, above.

'Such was the savagery of the class-war (*stasis*) at Corcyra as it developed, and it made the deeper impression through being the first of its kind—though eventually the upheaval spread through almost the whole of the Hellenic World. In every country there were struggles between the leaders of the Proletariat and the reactionaries in their efforts to procure the intervention of the Athenians and the Lacedaemonians respectively. In peace-time they would have had neither the opportunity nor the desire to call in the foreigner; but now there was the War; and it was easy for any revolutionary spirits in either camp to procure an alliance entailing the discomfiture of their opponents and a corresponding reinforcement of their own faction. This access of class-war brought one calamity after another upon the countries of Hellas—calamities that occur and will continue to occur so long as Human Nature remains what it is, though they may be aggravated or mitigated or modified by successive changes of circumstance. Under the favourable conditions of peace-time both countries and individuals display a sweeter reasonableness, because their hands are not forced by the logic of events; but War eats away the margins of ordinary life and, in most characters, adjusts the temperament to the new environment by its brutal training. So the countries of Hellas became infected with the class-war, and the sensation made by each successive outbreak had a cumulative effect upon the next.'[1]

Having thus put his finger on the war-spirit as the demoralizing spiritual force which shattered the Hellenic Society's moral solidarity, Thucydides goes on to make a brilliant analysis, which is at the same time an overwhelming indictment, of the demonic impulses of evil which were thus let loose in men's souls like the swarm of evil sprites that poured out of Pandora's wantonly opened box.

'It was a competition of ingenuity in the elaboration of intrigue and in the refinement of reprisals. The customary meaning of words was arbitrarily distorted to cover the conduct of those who employed them. Reckless irresponsibility was treated as courageous loyalty, cautious reserve as cowardice masked under a high-sounding name, restraint as a cloak for poor-spiritedness, and the policy of reason as a policy of *laissez faire*. A frenzied fanaticism was the popular ideal of conduct, while intrigue that took no risks was regarded as a legitimate method of self-defence. Violence of feeling was a warrant of honesty, deprecation of violence a signal for suspicion. Success in intrigue was the test of intelligence and the detection of intrigue a testimonial to superior cleverness, while anyone who so shaped his policy as to dispense with such methods was pilloried as a nihilist towards his own group and a weakling in face of their opponents. In short, approbation was reserved for those who forestalled their enemies in striking a blow or who implanted that suggestion in minds which had not previously conceived

[1] Thucydides, Book III, chap. 82.

it. The ties of party actually became closer than those of kinship,[1] because partisans were readier than kinsmen to throw themselves into an
adventure at a moment's notice, and the associations in question were
formed, not to secure the benefits of established institutions, but to
gain illegitimate advantages by violating them. Complicity in crime
was a more effective sanction for loyalty to engagements than a solemn
oath. A fair offer from opponents was received as a signal for practical
precautions by the dominant party of the moment, instead of evoking
any generous response. The exaction of reprisals was valued more
highly than an immunity from wrongs demanding them. The rare
covenants of reconciliation were only entered into on either side as a
momentary last resort and only observed so long as no alternative resource presented itself. Any one who spied a weak spot in his adversary's armour and had the nerve to seize his opportunity took more
satisfaction in obtaining his revenge by treachery than in obtaining it
in fair fight, the dominating considerations being the elimination of
risk and the added halo of intellectual brilliance investing the triumphs
of perfidy. . . .

'The cause of this whole phenomenon was the thirst for power
arising from the predatory and competitive impulses—impulses which
engender conflict, from which passion is engendered in its turn. In all
the countries of Hellas the party leaders invented high-sounding catch-
words and posed as the champions of political equality for the masses
or of moderate conservatism, in order to make spoils out of the public
interest which they served with their lips. In their unscrupulous struggle to gain the upper hand over one another they hesitated at nothing
and surpassed themselves in the prosecution of their vendettas. So far
from attempting to act within the bounds of moral right and national
interest, they recognized no limitations on either side except the caprice
of the moment. They did not shrink from bringing themselves
into power by verdicts immorally obtained against their opponents, if
not by naked force, in order to satiate their momentary rancour. In
fact, Religion had lost its hold upon either party, and they relied upon
their powers of misrepresentation to retrieve their good name whenever
they had occasion to perpetrate an invidious action. Meanwhile the
moderate elements in every country were preyed upon by the extremists
of both camps, partly for their refusal to take sides and partly out of
resentment at the prospect of their survival.

'Thus the class-war plunged the Hellenic Society into every kind of
moral evil.'[2]

This spiritual débâcle which followed the outbreak of the
Atheno-Peloponnesian War in 431 B.C. continued unchecked
during the century of warfare and revolution which was the aftermath of the great catastrophe, and the first social effect was to

---

[1] Compare Matt. x. 21 and 34–7 = Luke xii. 51–3, xiv. 25–7, and xxi. 16–17
(quoting Micah vii. 6); Matt. xii. 46–50 = Mark iii. 31–5 = Luke viii. 19–21.
—A.J.T.
[2] Thucydides, Book III, chaps. 82–3.

produce a large and ever larger floating population of 'stateless' exiles. During the growth of the Hellenic Civilization the experience of being thus uprooted from one's native social setting had been as rare to meet in Hellas as it had been dreadful to contemplate. Yet the surviving monuments of the Hellenic literature of that age testify clearly that this dreaded experience was foreknown to be the penalty for fratricide. It is one of the maxims of the Homeric Nestor's legendary wisdom that 'outcast, outlawed, outhomed is he who is in love with the lacerating warfare that rends the bosom of the People';[1] and an Athenian poet who was in his prime in the generation before the catastrophe of 431 B.C., and who was only just spared by Death from seeing his country brought low after twenty-seven years of demoralizing conflict, has written a stanza that is a judgement on his own civilization—and on ours.

> The craft of his engines hath passed his dream,
>   In haste to the good or the evil goal.
> One holdeth his city's law supreme
>   And the oath of God in his inmost soul;
> High-citied he: citiless the other
>   Who striveth, grasping at things of naught,
> On the road forbidden. From him be hidden
>   The fire that comforts and the light of thought.[2]

Sophocles himself lived to see Hellas smitten with this curse; and, within a hundred years of the date at which these foreboding lines were written,[3] the Hellenic World was swarming with homeless exiles.[4] The evil was not overcome by Alexander's greathearted attempt to induce the reigning faction of the moment in each city-state to allow its ejected opponents to return in peace to their hearths and homes;[5] and the fire made fresh fuel for itself; for the one thing that the exiles found for their hands to do was to

---

[1] Ἀφρήτωρ, ἀθέμιστος, ἀνέστιός ἐστιν ἐκεῖνος ὃς πολέμου ἔραται ἐπιδημίου ὀκρυόεντος.— Iliad, Book IX, ll. 63–4. In their present context these lines refer to the war between the Achaeans and the Trojans, and not to a civil war in the technical sense. This reference points the truth that all warfare is, 'in the last analysis', fratricidal.

[2] Sophocles: Antigone, ll. 365–75, translated by Gilbert Murray.

[3] The Antigone appears to have been written in 440 B.C.

[4] The state of Hellas in this age is luridly illustrated by the following anecdote, in Xenophon's Hellenica (Book VII. chap. 4, § 3), of an incident which appears to have occurred in the autumn of 366 B.C.:

'On his way back from Athens, [where he had been carrying out a diplomatic mission], Lycomedes [of Mantinea] met his death by a most extraordinary accident. Finding any number of ships at his disposal, he picked out the ship that took his fancy, contracted to have himself put on shore at whatever point he himself might designate, and selected for his landing-place the exact spot where the exiles [from his own country] happened to be encamped. So Lycomedes met his death in this way; but that did not prevent the alliance which he had been negotiating from being concluded.'

The tacit equation between meeting one's exiles and meeting one's death is more eloquent than words could be.

[5] For Alexander's vision of ὁμόνοια see V. C (i) (d) 7, vol. vi, pp. 6–10, and V. C (ii) (a), vol. vi, p. 254, below.

enlist as mercenary soldiers;[1] and this glut of military man-power
put fresh 'drive' into the wars by which new exiles—and thereby
more mercenaries—were being created. This vicious circle of evil
cause and effect first inflamed the fratricidal warfare in the bosom
of Hellas itself, and then discharged the men of war who had been
trained in this Hellenic school of arms to wreck the *Pax Achaemenia*—first by tempting ambitious provincial governors to break
all the tabus of Persian loyalty by hiring this Hellenic weapon for
use against the Pādishāh; then by giving Alexander of Macedon
the means of successfully accomplishing the subversive feat which
the traitor-satraps had lacked the nerve to carry through; and
finally by enabling Alexander's Macedonian successors to keep
three continents in turmoil for forty years in their struggle over
their master's stolen heritage.

The effect of these direct moral ravages of the war-spirit in
Hellas in uprooting her children was powerfully reinforced by the
operation of disruptive economic forces which the wars let loose.

For example, the wars of Alexander and his successors in South-
Western Asia gave military employment to one swarm of homeless
Greeks at the cost of uprooting another. For the mercenaries were
paid by putting into circulation the bullion which had been accumulating for two centuries in the Achaemenian treasuries; and this
sudden vast increase in the volume of currency in circulation
worked havoc among those peasants and artisans in the Greek
cities who had been spared by the flail of political strife. Prices
soared without any immediate corresponding rise in wages,[2] and
this financial revolution reduced to pauperism an element in the
body social which had hitherto enjoyed a modest competence and
a relative security.

The same effect of pauperization was produced again, a hundred
years later, by the economic consequences of the Hannibalic War
in Italy,[3] where the peasantry were uprooted from the land, first by
the direct devastation that was wrought by Hannibal's soldiery,
and then by the ever longer terms of Roman military service which
the Italian peasantry had to serve—and this not only in the main
Italian war-zone, but in Transappennine and Transmarine 'side-
shows'. These distant campaigns in the Po Basin, in the Iberian
Peninsula, in Greece and in the East did not come to an end when

[1] For the melancholy history of this mercenary military service in a disintegrating
Hellenic Society see Parke, H. W.: *Greek Mercenary Soldiers* (Oxford 1933, Clarendon
Press); and Griffith, G. T.: *The Mercenaries of the Hellenistic World* (Cambridge 1935,
University Press).

[2] For this indirectly but potently subversive economic effect of Alexander's conquest
of South-Western Asia see Tarn, W. W.: 'The Social Question in the Third Century'
in *The Hellenistic Age* (Cambridge 1923, University Press).

[3] See III. C (i) (*b*), vol. iii, pp. 170-1, and IV. C (iii) (*c*) 3 (*β*), vol. iv, pp. 507-8, above.

Hannibal evacuated Italy or when Carthage sued for peace, but remorselessly continued to increase in range and scale and to demand ever larger drafts of Italian peasant soldiers. Under this tribulation the pauperized descendants of an Italian peasantry that had been uprooted against its will by the call of conscript military service had no resource left but to make a profession out of the career which had been imposed on their ancestors as a *corvée*; and, during the century of revolution and civil war which began in 133 B.C. with the tribunate of Tiberius Gracchus and which only ended in 31 B.C. with the Battle of Actium, 'the new poor' took their toll out of the spoils of the conquests that had been won at their grandfathers' cost by taking mercenary service under the rival war-lords who were now contending for the mastery of the new Roman Empire—as the mastery of the old Achaemenian Empire had been previously contended for, with Greek mercenary arms, by the rival successors of Alexander.

In this cruel process of 'deracination' we cannot doubt that we are watching the genesis of the Hellenic internal proletariat—and this notwithstanding the fact that, at any rate in the earlier generations, the victims of the process were *ci-devant* aristocrats as often as not. For proletarianism is a state of feeling rather than a matter of outward circumstance. When we first introduced the term 'Proletariat' into this Study, we defined it,[1] for our purpose, as a 'social element or group which in some way is "in" but not "of" any given society at any given stage of such society's history'; and this definition covers the exiled Spartiate Clearchus and the other aristocratic captains of Cyrus the Younger's Greek mercenary force whose antecedents Xenophon has sketched for us in his account of their adventure,[2] as well as the meanest of the unemployed Greek and Italian labourers who enlisted as mercenaries under the standard of a Ptolemy[3] or a Marius. The true hall-mark of the proletarian is neither poverty nor humble birth but a consciousness—and the resentment which this consciousness inspires —of being disinherited from his ancestral place in Society and being unwanted in a community which is his rightful home; and this subjective proletarianism is not incompatible with the possession of material assets. The homeward-bound survivors of the Ten Thousand, whose home-sickness made them indignantly reject their leader Xenophon's prudent suggestion that they should close with Fortune's offer and should settle down to found a new

---

[1] In I. B (iv), vol. i, p. 41, above.
[2] See Xenophon: *Expeditio Cyri*, Book I, chap. 1, §§ 9-11, and chap. 2, §§ 1-3, and Book II, chap. 6. Cf. Book VI, chap. 4, § 8.
[3] See Theocritus: *Dramatic Dialogues*, Number 14: 'All for Love of Cynisca'—a poem which must have been commissioned by the Ptolemaic Government to serve the purpose of our twentieth-century Western recruiting-posters.

Greek city-state on an ideal Asiatic site,[1] were desolated to find how unwelcome their reappearance was to their brethren at home in Hellas; and their soreness at this social rebuff was not healed by an offer of temporary economic security in the shape of a new contract for their employment as mercenary troops—this time in the Lacedaemonian service. The same iron must have entered far more deeply into the souls of the survivors of those other Greek mercenaries in a later generation who were massacred, as dangerous drones, by their Macedonian comrades-in-arms when, on the news of Alexander's death, the hirelings deserted their posts in his up-country garrisons and started on the long trek back towards Hellas. It is more surprising, and therefore more significant, to find the same consciousness of being not wanted, the same sense of grievance, and the same restlessness persisting in the souls of the time-expired veterans of Roman revolutionary armies—from Sulla's army to Octavian's—who had been fitted out with new homes and lands, and organized into new civic communities, at the cost of uprooting an equal number of innocent free-holders and contented tillers of the soil through ruthless and reckless measures of un-provoked expropriation.

Thus the Hellenic internal proletariat was recruited first of all from the free citizens, and even from the aristocrats, of the dis-integrating Hellenic bodies politic; and these first recruits had been disinherited in the first instance by being robbed of a spiritual birthright; but of course their spiritual impoverishment was often accompanied, and was almost always followed, by a pauperization on the material plane; and they were soon reinforced by recruits from other sources who were material as well as spiritual pro-letarians from the start. The numbers of the Hellenic internal proletariat were vastly swollen by the aggression of Hellenic arms —made expert in the school of fratricidal warfare—at the expense of alien societies of both the primitive and the 'civilized' species. The conquests of Alexander and his successors swept the whole of the Syriac, Egyptiac, and Babylonic societies, and a consider-able part of the Indic Society,[2] into the Hellenic dominant minority's net, while the later conquests of the Romans swept in half the barbarians of Europe and North-West Africa.[3]

These involuntary alien reinforcements of the Hellenic internal proletariat were perhaps at first more fortunate than their fellow-proletarians of native Hellenic origin in one respect. Though they were morally disinherited and materially despoiled, they were not

---

[1] Xenophon: *Expeditio Cyri*, Book VI, chap. 4, § 1–chap. 5, § 4.
[2] For the partial conquest of the Indic World by the Greek princes of Bactria in and after the second decade of the second century B.C. see I. C (i) (*b*), vol. i, p. 86, above.
[3] See III. C (i) (*a*), vol. iii, pp. 140 and 149, above.

yet physically uprooted; and a majority of them permanently escaped this fate and managed just to keep alive—like the Abbé Siéyès during the Terror of a modern revolution in the West—until they tasted, at last, their long-deferred revenge when they shook off the worn-out shackles of the Hellenic dominant minority nearly a thousand years after Alexander's passage of the Hellespont.[1] Their fortunes varied, however, according to the particular degree to which their respective Hellenic oppressors were minded to turn the screw.

In Asia the Seleucids were content (till they fell upon evil days after Antiochus the Great's disastrous encounter with the Romans)[2] to take a financial toll from their Oriental subjects for supplying the Royal Exchequer and for endowing newly founded city-states of the Hellenic pattern.[3] Like the barbarian proletarians in Europe and North-West Africa who were similarly 'attributed' to the Roman colonial urban foundations of a rather later age, the Oriental proletarians under the Seleucid régime thus escaped comparatively lightly. In Egypt, on the other hand, the local tradition of 'the servile state', with its currency of some 2,500 years since the Age of the Pyramid-Builders,[4] had acquired a momentum to which the Hellenic conquerors readily yielded; and here we see the Ptolemies, and their heirs the Roman Emperors,[5] prostituting their Hellenic abilities to the prevailing Egyptiac spirit, and making their 'Hellenic superintendence' a curse instead of a boon for its Egyptian recipients, by skilfully monopolizing, for the benefit of an alien Crown, the profits of all the agricultural and industrial production of the country. At the same time a Ptolemaic Egyptian peasant or factory-hand who had travelled westward and caught a glimpse of the contemporary state of the native population in the continental African dominions of Carthage would have come home thanking Isis that she had preserved her Egyptian

[1] For the final and complete undoing of Alexander's work of conquest by the equally rapid and sensational counter-conquests of the Primitive Muslim Arabs see I. C (i) (b), vol. i, pp. 75–6, above.

[2] In the Romano-Seleucid War of 192–188 B.C. For the effect of Roman pressure on the Seleucid Government in aggravating the Seleucid Government's own pressure upon its Oriental subjects see V. C (i) (d) 9 (β), vol. vi, pp. 103–5, especially p. 105, footnote 8, below.

[3] For these foundations see Part III. A, vol. iii, pp. 98–100, and IV. C (iii) (c) 2 (β), vol. iv, pp. 311–13, above.

[4] See III. C (i) (d), vol. iii, pp. 212–15; and IV. C (iii) (c) 2 (β), vol. iv, pp. 408–13 and 418–23, above.

[5] The Roman Imperial Government gradually relaxed the centralized system of administrative control which it had inherited from the Ptolemies, and devolved upon Egyptian local authorities the responsibility for performing the thankless task of milking the Egyptian milch cow for the Imperial Exchequer's benefit. This policy—which was prompted by slackness and inefficiency rather than by enlightenment or benevolence—had the paradoxical result that, in Egypt alone among all the provinces of the Hellenic universal state, municipal self-government gained ground in an age when elsewhere it was losing ground to bureaucratic centralization (see Jones, A. H. M.: *The Cities of the Eastern Roman Provinces* (Oxford 1937, Clarendon Press), pp. 316–50).

servant from a worse than Egyptian fate; for, though the Egyptian worker might be robbed scientifically and systematically, like the domestic bee, of almost all the hard-won fruits of his labour, he at least remained in some sense personally free, whereas the Berber subject of Carthage was a hide-bound serf. Yet this serf, in his turn, must have thanked his stars when his conscript military service under his Carthaginian masters' flag brought him face to face with the slave-gangs on the plantations of Sicily. For the lure of the virgin western markets for wine and oil, which had led the Carthaginians to turn the conquered native inhabitants of their continental African hinterland into plantation-serfs, had simultaneously led the Agrigentines to extract the same profit from their own war-devastated and war-depopulated insular domain by stocking it with plantation slaves; and this West-Mediterranean economic régime of plantations worked with an imported slave-labour-force—a social evil of which we first catch sight in Greek Sicily in 480 B.C.—was extended, on a vaster scale and with a second string in the shape of slave-shepherded stock-breeding, to the devastated areas of Roman Italy after the Hannibalic War.[1]

During the last two centuries B.C. the uprooted Italian peasant-proprietors were progressively supplanted by rootless slave-hoe-men and slave-herdsmen. The wastage of this servile economic man-power on the Italian plantations and ranches was perhaps as heavy as the wastage of the nominally free military man-power of the Italian peasantry in its distant theatres of war, while the profits of the wholesale wine, oil, meat, wool, and leather production which was carried on at this human—or inhuman—cost were great enough to bear the capital charge of perpetually having to replace the human raw material (in contrast to the unprofitable-ness of the old-fashioned peasant proprietor's subsistence-farming, which could now no longer be made to pay, even when the state came to the peasants' aid by offering them opportunities of exchanging their ancestral holdings on the south side of the Appennines for new and larger plots carved out of the confiscated lands of conquered and evicted Gauls and Ligurians).[2] In consequence this age saw all the populations within range of the Mediterranean coast—both western barbarians and cultivated Orientals—being lawlessly laid under contribution in order to supply the demands of an insatiable Italian slave-labour-market.

We now see that the internal proletariat of the disintegrating Hellenic Society was composed of three distinct elements: disinherited and uprooted members of the Hellenic Society's own

---

[1] See III. C (i) (b), vol. iii, pp. 168–71, and IV. C (iii) (c) 3 (β), vol. iv, pp. 507–8, above.   [2] See V. C (i) (c) 1, Annex, pp. 569–74, below.

native body social; partially disinherited members of alien civilizations or of primitive societies who were conquered and exploited
without being torn up by the roots; and doubly disinherited conscripts from these subject populations who were not only uprooted
but were also enslaved and deported in order to be worked to
death on distant plantations and ranches without any hope of ever
seeing their homes or their kinsfolk again.[1] The sufferings of these
three sets of victims were as various as their origins were diverse,
but these differences were transcended by their overwhelming
common experience of being robbed of their social heritage and
being turned into exploited outcasts; and the confluence of these
diverse streams of human misery into a single slough is celebrated
in the famous lines in which the *colluvies gentium*[2]—Greeks, Orientals, and barbarians—in the slums of Rome is satirically described
by a Roman poet whose pen was perhaps envenomed by a dread
lest one day he himself might fall into the abyss and be swallowed
up in this all-engulfing proletariat, like so many other *ci-devant*
members of a Hellenic dominant minority.

> Non possum ferre, Quirites,
> Graecam urbem—quamvis quota portio faecis Achaei?
> iampridem Syrus in Tiberim defluxit Orontes
> et linguam et mores et cum tibicine chordas
> obliquas necnon gentilia tympana secum
> vexit et ad Circum iussas prostare puellas.
> ite, quibus grata est picta lupa barbara mitra.
> rusticus ille tuus sumit trechedipna, Quirine,
> et ceromatico fert niceteria collo.
> hic alta Sicyone, ast hic Amydone relicta,
> hic Andro, ille Samo, hic Trallibus aut Alabandis,
> Esquilias dictumque petunt a vimine collem—
> viscera magnarum domuum dominique futuri.
> ingenium velox, audacia perdita, sermo
> promptus et Isaeo torrentior: ede, quid illum
> esse putes? quemvis hominem secum attulit ad nos.
> grammaticus, rhetor, geometres, pictor, aliptes,
> augur, schoenobates, medicus, magus—omnia novit
> Graeculus esuriens: in coelum miseris, ibit.
> in summa non Maurus erat, nec Sarmata nec Thrax
> qui sumpsit pennas, mediis sed natus Athenis.[3]

It is not the conquered barbarian nor even the Hellenized Oriental
but the disinherited Hellene himself who is the most sordid representative of the Hellenic internal proletariat.

[1] For the fate of these slave-deportees, and their diverse reactions to the oppression
which they suffered at the hands of the Hellenic dominant minority, see II. D (vi),
vol. ii, pp. 213–16, above.
[2] Livy, Book IV, chap. 2, § 5.
[3] Juvenal: *Satires*, No. III, ll. 60–80.

When we come to examine how these targets of satire and victims of injustice reacted to their fate, we shall not be surprised to find that one of their reactions was an explosion of savagery which surpassed in violence the cold-blooded cruelty of those conquerors, wastrels, and hangmen who first provoked them to revolt and then repressed them. It is only natural that the victims of a wanton and intolerable oppression should display a hotter passion in seeking revenge for injuries received than has been displayed by the aggressor in inflicting these injuries without provocation; and a uniform note of passion rings through a pandemonium of desperate proletarian outbreaks.

We catch this note in a series of Egyptian insurrections against the Ptolemaic régime of exploitation—an outbreak which began at the turn of the third and second centuries B.C., as soon as the Egyptian fallāhīn had acquired a stock of arms and *esprit de corps* and self-confidence as a result of the Ptolemaic Government's signal blunder of conscripting the natives into their army, alongside of the Macedonian colonists and the Greek mercenaries, in order to beat off a Seleucid invasion.[1] We hear the same note again in the more celebrated, and more momentous, series of Jewish insurrections against a Seleucid and a Roman policy of Hellenization[2]—an outbreak which began when Judas Maccabaeus took up arms against Antiochus Epiphanes in 166 B.C., and which was not quelled by the destruction of Jerusalem in the Great Romano-Jewish War of A.D. 66–70, but burst out again among the Jewish Diasporà in Cyrene and Egypt and Cyprus in A.D. 115–17,[3] and among the Palestinian Jews in a last forlorn hope under the leadership of Bar Kōkabā in A.D. 132–5. It needed hardihood enough for the Palestinian Jews to defy the Seleucid Power in the twenty-fourth year after the Battle of Magnesia; for the loss of prestige which the Seleucid Monarchy had sustained through that defeat at Roman hands had hardly yet come to be felt in Asia Major, east of Taurus, and the latest local Seleucid feat of arms

[1] The newly conscripted native Egyptian phalangites in the Ptolemaic army won—and knew that they had won—the Battle of Raphia for Ptolemy IV Philopator against Antiochus III the Great in 217 B.C. For the part that may have been played by these Egyptian phalangites' mercenary comrades-in-arms in the evolution of the 'ideology' of the Hellenic internal proletariat see V. C (ii) (a), Annex II, vol. vi, pp. 496–500, below. See further Milne, J. G.: 'Egyptian Nationalism under Greek and Roman Rule' in *The Journal of Egyptian Archaeology*, vol. xiv, parts iii and iv (1928).
[2] For this lapse of Judaism into militancy see also IV. C (iii) (b) 12, vol. iv, pp. 224–5, above, and V. C (i) (d) 6 (δ), Annex, in the present volume, pp. 657–9, and V. C (i) (d) 9 (γ), vol. vi, pp. 120–3, below.
[3] An account of this insurrection of the Jewish Diasporà in these three Roman provinces that had once constituted the Ptolemaic Empire will be found in Bell, M. I.: *Juden und Griechen im Römischen Alexandreia* (Leipzig 1927, Hinrichs), pp. 36–40. Both the insurrection of A.D. 115–17 among the Diasporà and the insurrection of A.D. 132–5 in Palestine are dealt with in Lagrange, M.-J.: *Le Messianisme chez les Juifs* (Paris 1909, Gabalda), pp. 305–23.

in Coele Syria had been the triumphant conquest of the province from the Ptolemies in 198 B.C. In the second century before Christ the Maccabees' boldness was rewarded by a temporary military success; but nothing short of an invincible hatred was needed to nerve their successors, three hundred years later, to take up arms for a second and a third time against the omnipotence of Rome, when their first attempt to measure their strength against the Hellenic universal state had drawn upon them Titus's shattering blow. The same reckless fury also moved the semi-Hellenized and highly sophisticated natives of Western Asia Minor to expose themselves to Roman vengeance twice over: first in 132 B.C., when they joined the standard of the Attalid prince Aristonicus[1] upon hearing the appalling news that the last Attalus had bequeathed his kingdom to the Roman People; and for the second time in 88 B.C., when the cities opened their gates to Rome's rebel client-king Mithradates of Pontus, and the citizens took the opportunity to massacre the whole of the Italian business community—to a total, it was estimated, of 80,000 souls[2]—as a tardy revenge for the Roman filibustering expedition which had plundered Asia Minor, without provocation, just a hundred years before.

The rising of Aristonicus is the connecting link between the outbreaks of the subject Oriental peoples in the conquered provinces and the outbreaks of the imported slaves and the pauperized freemen in the homelands of the Hellenic Society. For slaves and 'mean freemen'[3] fought side by side in Aristonicus's rebel band;[4] and his rising was perhaps inspired by the news of the slave-revolt which had let loose the first of the two great slave-wars in Sicily (*gerebantur circa* 135–131 B.C. *et circa* 104–100 B.C.).[5] These two Sicilian outbreaks were perhaps the largest in scale and the longest-drawn-out of the slave-revolts on the western plantations and ranches of the Hellenic World in the Post-Hannibalic Age,[6] but they were neither the first nor the last of their kind, nor perhaps even the most savage. The series began, in the first decade after

---

[1] See IV. C (iii) (*c*) 3 (β), vol. iv, p. 507, above; and the present chapter and volume, pp. 179–80; V. C (i) (*d*) 6 (δ), Annex, p. 692, footnote 2; and V. C (i) (*d*) 11, Annex I, vol. vi, p. 351, below.
[2] Compare the similar wholesale massacre of the Italian business community in the East Roman Empire in A.D. 1183.
[3] The phrase may be coined on the pertinent analogy of the 'Mean Whites' in the Southern States of the North American Union.
[4] Strabo: *Geographica*, Book XIV, chap. 38, p. 646.
[5] 'As the news' of the outbreak of the first Sicilian slave-war 'spread, slave-revolts flared up everywhere. At Rome a hundred and fifty persons entered into a conspiracy, in Attica over a thousand, and others in Delos and elsewhere.'—Diodorus of Agyrium: *A Library of Universal History*, fragments of Books XXXIV–XXXV, chap. 2, § 19. Delos, which was the principal slave-market of the Hellenic World in the second century B.C., was of course on the threshold of the Attalid Kingdom in Western Asia Minor, which was the theatre of Aristonicus's tragic adventure.
[6] See III. C (i) (*d*), vol. iii, pp. 198–9, and IV. C (iii) (*c*) 3 (β), vol. iv, pp. 507–8, above.

the temporary restoration of peace between Rome and Carthage in
201 B.C., with an abortive conspiracy of the slaves of the Carthaginian hostages at Setia in 198 B.C.[1] and a rapidly suppressed
slave-rising in Etruria in 196.[2] It was continued in a formidable
insurrection of the slave-herdsmen in Apulia in 185;[3] and, after
a temporary shifting of the scene to Sicily, the climax was reached
in the desperate exploit of the runaway Thracian gladiator Spartacus, who ranged up and down the length of the Italian Peninsula
—defying the Roman wolf in his very lair—from 73 to 71 B.C.

While in Asia Minor, under Aristonicus's banner, the slaves and
the 'mean freemen' made common cause, in Sicily these two wings
of the local proletarian forces each went its separate way; and, of
the two, it was not the Sicilian slaves, but the Sicilian paupers, who
were the more revengeful and the more destructive.

'When Sicily was overtaken by these overwhelming disasters [in the
first of the two slave-wars], the Free-Born Proletariat, so far from sym-
pathizing with the victims [i.e. with the murdered slave-owners],
actually exulted over them out of resentment at the existing inequalities
of wealth and condition. This long-standing resentment was transformed from a painful into a gratifying emotion at the spectacle of
magnificence reduced to the level of the misery upon which it had
previously looked down with disdain. The most serious feature was
that, whereas the [slave] insurgents, who took long and rational views,
refrained from burning the farms or injuring the property and the
stocks of agricultural produce which they found in them, and did not
molest persons devoting their energies to work on the land, the social
resentment of the Free Proletariat was, by contrast, so profound that they
offered their services against the slaves simply as a pretext for going out
into the country and not only pillaging property but burning farms.'[4]

The rancorous resentment against the Hellenic dominant minority which found this ugly vent was not confined to 'mean free'
proletarians who were outside the pale of the Roman body politic.
Their Roman fellow proletarians who were not only freemen, but
were actually citizens of the city-state which was now politically
omnipotent in the Hellenic World, were in the still more ironical
position of being called 'the lords of the World' without having
'a single clod of earth to call their own', while for them the precious Roman citizenship, which gave their wealthy fellow citizens
an invaluable economic 'pull', carried nothing with it but an
obligation to 'go to the wars and sacrifice their lives for the sake
of other men's wealth and luxury'.[5] Thus the lot of a 'mean free'

[1] Livy, Book XXXII, chap. 26.   [2] Livy, Book XXXIII, chap. 36.
[3] Livy, Book XXXIX, chap. 29.
[4] Diodorus of Agyrium: *A Library of Universal History*, fragments of Books XXXIV–
XXXV, chap. 2, § 48.
[5] Tiberius Gracchus, quoted by Plutarch in his *Lives of the Gracchi*, chap. 9 (see

pauper who had lost his freehold and had sunk to the position of
a casual labourer on the land or an unemployed slum-dweller in
the city was still less tolerable for a *togatus* than it was for a citizen
of Centuripae or Pergamum; and the Roman pauper's feelings
were proportionately bitter. The savagery with which the Roman
citizen-proletariat turned and rent the Roman plutocracy in the
civil wars, and particularly in the paroxysm of 91–82 B.C., was quite
equal to the savagery of a Judas Maccabaeus or a Spartacus; and
the most Satanic of all the dark figures that stand out in sinister
silhouette against the glare of a world in flames are the Roman
revolutionary leaders who had been flung headlong, by some unusually violent turn of Fortune's wheel, out of the *Ordo Senatorius*
itself: a Sertorius and a Sextus Pompeius, a Marius and a Catilina.[1]

In the desperate outbreaks of which we have given this summary
catalogue, the Hellenic internal proletariat displayed a spirit like
that of the Lacedaemonian underworld which hungered 'to eat' its
Spartiate masters 'alive',[2] or like that of the Ottoman *ra'īyeh* on
Laconian ground who did succeed in wreaking their vengeance
upon their Turkish masters in A.D. 1821, when they massacred
every man, woman, and child of the dominant community in the
captured fortress of Mistrà. In this spirit the outraged slaves of
Dâmophilus repaid the monster in his own coin when at last they
had him in their power; the Marians anticipated the worst excesses
of the Sullans; and the ferocity of the Jewish Zealots[3] was a match
for the implacability of the Roman laws of war. In fact, in these
orgies of ferocious violence the Hellenic internal proletariat went
to the same lengths, in the same direction, as their oppressors the
conquerors, wastrels, and hangmen in the Hellenic dominant
minority; and this Shiva-like epiphany of the Proletariat, appalling
though it may be, is not surprising, when we remind ourselves of
the provocation to which it was a retort. It is, however, both

IV. C (iii) (c) 3 (β), vol. iv, p. 508, above, and V. C (i) (c) 1, Annex, in the present
volume, p. 36, footnote 2, and V. C (ii) (a), Annex II, vol. vi, p. 381, Table VIII,
logion (α), p. 414, below).
[1] See V. C (ii) (a), vol. vi, pp. 236–41, below.
[2] Xenophon: *Hellenica*, Book III, chap. 3, § 11, quoted in Part III. A, Annex III,
vol. iii, p. 456, above.
[3] Among the Jewish contingent in the Hellenic internal proletariat this spirit of
unslaked vengefulness found expression for itself in a special genre of literature: the
Apocalypse. This genre was in vogue for nearly three centuries, if the critics are right in
dating the composition of the Book of Daniel *circa* 166–164 B.C. and that of the Revelation
of Saint John the Divine *circa* A.D. 93–5. Fragments of an Egyptiac apocalypse, closely
corresponding to the Jewish Book of Daniel in both content and construction, have
now been discovered by our modern Western archaeologists. This Egyptiac work seems,
like its Jewish counterpart, to have been composed immediately after the local outbreak
of the militant Anti-Hellenic revolt of the Proletariat, and, as we have noticed on p. 68,
above, this broke out in Egypt some fifty years earlier than in Judaea. It is thus chronologically possible that the Book of Daniel may have been a Jewish copy of an Egyptiac
prototype (see Meyer, E.: *Ursprung und Anfänge des Christentums*, vol. ii (Stuttgart and
Berlin 1921, Cotta), pp. 187–8).

astonishing and admirable to find that this was not the only
response which was evoked from the Hellenic internal proletariat
by the tremendous challenge to which it was subjected. There was
also an antiphonal response which was at the opposite extreme of
the spiritual gamut; and at this other extremity the internal proletariat not merely attained, but rose far above, the spiritual level
which was reached by the altruists in the dominant minority—
spurred though these altruists were by pricks of conscience which
the proletarians had no occasion to feel, and equipped though they
also were with intellectual resources that were quite beyond the
proletarians' ken.

We find, in fact, that the outbreaks of violence which we have
been recording hitherto were seldom or never the only reactions
of the momentary victims to the momentary ordeal. While some
of the victims were usually moved to respond to oppression by
resorting to force on their own part, there were usually others who
met force not by counter-force but by gentleness.[1] Even the frenzied slaves of the monster Dâmophilus had at least the humanity
to refrain, in the flood-tide of their vengeance, from returning evil
for good—as they showed by the pains that they took to save Dâmophilus's tender-hearted daughter when they were dragging to their
deaths the tormenter himself and his equally inhuman wife.[2] In
the semi-legendary Jewish recollections of the ordeal which the
Palestinian Jewry had to meet in resisting Antiochus Epiphanes'
policy of Hellenizing them by force, the passive resistance, under
torture and unto death, of the old scribe Eleazer and of the Seven
Brethren and their Mother[3] precedes, in the narrative, the militant
resistance of the mighty man of valour Judas Maccabaeus.[4] In the
story of the Passion of Jesus the leader's injunction to his companions—'he that hath no sword, let him sell his garment and buy
one'[5]—is immediately followed by his 'it is enough' when two

---

[1] For the ambiguity of this term as it is used in this chapter see V. C (i) (c) 2, Annex
III, pp. 588–90, below.

[2] '[Dâmophilus and his wife Megallis] had a young unmarried daughter of a particularly unspoiled and humane disposition, who invariably did her utmost to intercede
for slaves sentenced by her parents to floggings, and to relieve those in chains. Her
goodness had won her an intense and universal affection, and on this terrible occasion
the gratitude which she had earned enlisted on her behalf the better feelings of her
former protégés. No one ventured to lay a violent hand upon her, and her honour was
scrupulously respected by all concerned. The most efficient members of the band . . .
were detailed to escort her to some relatives at Catana. . . . This was a demonstration
that the treatment meted out to the others was not the expression of any innate barbarity
in the slaves, but was simply retribution for the wrongs which had previously been
inflicted upon them.'—Diodorus of Agyrium: *A Library of Universal History*, fragments
of Books XXXIV–XXXV, chap. 2, §§ 39 and 13.

[3] In Eduard Meyer's view (*Ursprung und Anfänge des Christentums*, vol. ii (Stuttgart
and Berlin 1921, Cotta), p. 161, footnote 2, the latter of these two stories is fabulous
but the former substantially historical.

[4] 2 Maccabees, chaps. vi–vii, in contrast with the remainder of the book.

[5] Luke xxii. 36.

swords only are forthcoming among all the twelve;[1] and this perfunctory call to arms is finally stultified by the leader's own deliberate refusal to fight when he is on the point of being arrested. At that crucial moment, 'when they which were about him saw what would follow, they said unto him: "Lord, shall we smite with the sword?" And one of them smote the servant of the High Priest and cut off his right ear. And Jesus answered and said: "Suffer ye thus far." And he touched his ear and healed him.'[2] In the next chapter of the same story the behaviour of Jesus's Apostles, who boldly and obstinately refuse to obey the injunction not to preach, yet offer no physical resistance to the arm of the law, makes a deep impression upon the famous doctor Gamaliel, whose keen eye instantly perceives the striking contrast which the Apostles' behaviour presents to the conventional militancy of the contemporary epigoni of Judas Maccabaeus.

'Ye men of Israel, take heed to yourselves what ye intend to do as touching these men. For before these days rose up Theudas, boasting himself to be somebody, to whom a number of men, about four hundred, joined themselves—who were slain, and all, as many as obeyed him, were scattered and brought to naught. After this man rose up Judas of Galilee, in the days of the taxing, and drew away much people after him. He also perished; and all, even as many as obeyed him, were dispersed. And now I say unto you: Refrain from these men and let them alone. For if this counsel or this work be of men, it will come to naught; but if it be of God, ye cannot overthrow it—lest haply ye be found even to fight against God.'[3]

Here are two responses to an identic challenge which are not only different but are actually contradictory and incompatible. The gentle response is as genuine an expression of the Proletariat's will to secede as the violent response is; for the gentle martyrs who are commemorated in the Second Book of Maccabees are the spiritual progenitors of the Pharisees, and the Pharisees are 'they who separate themselves'[4]—a self-conferred title which would trans-

---

[1] Luke xxii. 38. For the origin of this incident see V. C (ii) (a), Annex II, vol. vi, p. 528, below.

[2] Luke xxii. 49-51. See V. C (ii) (a), Annex II, vol. vi, pp. 392 and 527-8, below.

[3] Acts v. 35-9. For the movement of which this Theudas and Judas were representatives, see Lagrange, M.-J.: *Le Messianisme chez les Juifs* (Paris 1909, Gabalda), pp. 10-27; Meyer, E.: *Ursprung und Anfänge des Christentums*, vol. ii (Stuttgart and Berlin 1921, Cotta), pp. 402-6; von Gall, A.: *Βασιλεία τοῦ Θεοῦ* (Heidelberg 1926, Winter), pp. 375-6. As a matter of history, Theudas' insurrection was not precedent to Judas', but was subsequent both to it and to the date (*circa* A.D. 30) at which, in the Acts of the Apostles, Gamaliel's speech is represented as having been delivered.

[4] The Greek word Φαρισαῖοι represents the Aramaic 'Perishaye'. According to Meyer, E.: *Ursprung und Anfänge des Christentums*, vol. ii (Stuttgart and Berlin 1921, Cotta), p. 284, the most probable explanation of the name is that 'it sprang from some particular political occasion, in fact from the events of the year 163 B.C., in which the Pharisees did separate themselves from their previous allies, the followers of Judas [Maccabaeus]. In etymology and history alike, the Pharisees are reminiscent of the Kharijites, i.e. "the Withdrawers", who, in the civil war between 'Alī and Mu'āwiyah, renounced their allegiance to 'Alī and withdrew from his camp, because their religious

late itself into 'secessionists' or 'schismatics' in the official language
of an Antiochus and a Titus—or indeed of a Jannaeus and a Herod.
Here are two alternative ways of shaking the dust of the agora and
the arena off the puritan's feet; but both ways cannot be followed
at once; and in the history of the Oriental proletariat of the Hellenic World from the second century B.C. onwards we see Violence
and Gentleness striving for the mastery of souls, until Violence
annihilates itself and leaves Gentleness alone in the field.[1]

The issue was raised at the outset; for the gentle way which was
taken by the protomartyrs of 167 B.C. was swiftly abandoned by
the impetuous Hasmonaean; and this proletarian 'strong man
armed's' immediate material success—tawdry and ephemeral
though it was—so dazzled Posterity that Jesus's most intimate
companions were scandalized at their Master's own predictions of
his fate, and were prostrated when these predictions came true.
At the first warning, Peter[2] began to rebuke him—'saying: "Be it
far from thee, Lord. This shall not be unto thee"'[3]—and at the hour
of decision the same Apostle was so demoralized by the order to
put up his sword again into his place, after he had just struck the
first and last physical blow in the conflict, that he actually perpetrated the thrice repeated denial of his Master which, a few hours
before, he had indignantly scouted, as something quite incredible,
when he had been warned that this was how he would behave.
'Though I should die with thee, yet will I not deny thee'; and
'likewise also said all the disciples'.[4] Yet, as soon as Jesus ordered
Peter to sheathe his sword, 'then all the disciples forsook him, and
fled'.[5] The way of Gentleness seemed to be confuted once for all
in the crucified Jesus—'unto the Jews a stumbling-block, unto the
Greeks foolishness'[6]—yet a few months after the Crucifixion
Gamaliel was already taking note of the executed leader's miraculously rallied disciples as men who might prove to have God on
their side; and a few years later Gamaliel's own disciple Paul was
preaching a crucified Christ.

This vastly painful but infinitely fruitful conversion of the first
generation of Christians[7] from the way of Violence to the way of

scruples made them reject both the two opposing claimants as criminals from whom
they wished to keep the cause of Islam clear and uncontaminated'. For the subsequent
conflicts between the Pharisees and the Hasmonaeans see Meyer, op. cit., vol. cit.,
pp. 306–11.
    [1] See V. C (i) (c) 2, Annex III, pp. 588–90, below.
    [2] Peter's slow conversion from the way of Violence to the way of Gentleness is dis-
cussed further in V. C (i) (d) 1, pp. 392–3, below.
    [3] Matt. xvi. 21–6; xvii. 22–3; xx. 17–28, with the corresponding passages in the
other two Synoptic Gospels.   [4] Matt. xxvi. 35.   [5] Matt. xxvi. 56.
    [6] 1 Cor. i. 23 (see V. C (i) (d) 11, vol. vi, pp. 150 seqq., below).
    [7] The earliest direct evidence for this conversion is to be found in the canonical
epistles of the New Testament. For the relevant passages, exhorting slaves to obey
their masters and subjects to obey their rulers, see V. C (i) (c) 2, Annex III, p. 590, below.

Gentleness had to be purchased at the price of a shattering blow to their material hopes; and what was done for Jesus's followers by the Crucifixion was done for Orthodox Jewry by the destruction of Jerusalem in A.D. 70. By that time Christianity had spread beyond the bounds of Palestine so far and wide among the internal proletariat of the Hellenic World that the infant church was in no danger of being overwhelmed by the annihilating catastrophe which now overtook its homeland. In A.D. 70 the Jewish Christian Church in Jerusalem was already eclipsed by the Greek Christian Church in Antioch, the former capital of the Hellenizing Seleucids. But the warning, placed in Jesus's mouth in the Synoptic Gospels,[1] that the Christians in Judaea should flee into the mountains when they saw 'the abomination of desolation'—Hellenic paganism in arms—reappearing on the Palestinian horizon, was spontaneously and unwittingly obeyed by at least one orthodox Jewish doctor.

Before the net of the Roman circumvallation finally closed in upon the devoted Holy City, Rabbi Johanan ben Zakkai independently took the momentous decision to break with the tradition of militancy which Judas Maccabaeus had inaugurated. Eluding the vigilance of the Jewish Zealots, he slipped across no-man's-land and prevailed upon the Roman High Command to let him through in order that he might quietly continue his teaching out of earshot of the battle; and, when the tidings of the inevitable catastrophe eventually reached him in the Hellenized Philistine township of Jabneh,[2] where he had reassembled his school, and the disciple who brought the bad news exclaimed in anguish: 'Woe to us, because the place is destroyed where they make propitiation for the sins of Israel', the master answered: 'My son, let it not grieve thee; we have yet one propitiation equal to it, and what is that but the bestowal of kindnesses?—even as it is written "I desired kindness and not sacrifice".'[3] In act and word Johanan ben Zakkai was proclaiming his conversion from the way of Violence to the way of Gentleness; and through this conversion he became the founder of a new Jewry which has survived—albeit only as a fossil[4]— in all manner of alien and inclement environments down to the present day, and which shows no signs of succumbing to its present tribulations. The secret of this latter-day Jewry's extraordinary survival power lies in its persistent cultivation of the êthos which Johanan ben Zakkai has bequeathed to it. After the lessons of

---

[1] Matt. xxiv. 15–28 = Mark xiii. 14–23 = Luke xxi. 20–4.
[2] *Hellenicè* Jamnia.
[3] Burkitt, F. C.: *Jewish and Christian Apocalypses* (London 1914, Milford), p. 8, footnote 1, and Lagrange, M.-J.: *Le Messianisme chez les Juifs* (Paris 1909, Gabalda), p. 302, both quoting from *Aboth di R. Nathan*, ch. 4.
[4] For Jewry as a fossil see I. B (iii), vol. i, p. 35; I. C (i) (*b*), vol. i, pp. 90–2; II. D (vii), vol. ii, pp. 285–6, above.

A.D. 70 and 135[1] a new school of Judaism renounced 'the notion that the Kingdom of God was an external state of things which was just upon the point of being manifested'.[2] With the signal but solitary exception of the Book of Daniel, the apocalyptic writings in which the Jewish way of Violence had found literary expression since the days of Antiochus Epiphanes were now ejected from the canon of the Law and the Prophets;[3] and the contrary principle of abstaining from all attempts to promote the fulfilment of God's will in This World by the work of human hands has become so fast ingrained in the Jewish tradition that the strictly orthodox *Agudath Israel* at this day look askance at the Zionist movement and are holding rigidly aloof from any participation in the work of building up a material Jewish 'national home' under a British mandate in post-war Palestine.[4]

If this change of heart in Orthodox Jewry since the destruction of Jerusalem in A.D. 70 has enabled Jewry to survive as a fossil, the corresponding change of heart in the companions of Jesus after the Crucifixion has opened the way to greater triumphs for the Christian Church. The Christians had come unscathed out of the local catastrophe which the militancy of the Jewish Zealots had brought upon Jewry; and, although the Christian Faith was soon officially proclaimed a *religio non licita*, the Imperial Government's standing policy during the first two centuries of the Christian Era was not to force the issue.[5] Accordingly, during this 'Indian Summer' of the Hellenic Civilization's decline, the persecutions which the Christians had to suffer were intermittent and sporadic; and the Church was not summoned to drink the cup, or to be baptized with the baptism, of its Founder and Master[6] till the third century, when the whole Hellenic World relapsed into the Ishmaelitish state of anarchy that had afflicted it during the last two centuries B.C.,[7] and when a Decius and a Valerian and a Diocletian set out to deal with an oecumenical Christian Church[8] as an Antiochus Epiphanes had dealt in the second century B.C. with the local Jewish community in Judaea. To this challenge the Christian Church responded in the gentle way of Eleazer and the Seven

---

[1] The failure of Bar Kōkabā (see p. 68, above) confirmed the victory of Johanan ben Zakkai's school (von Gall, A.: Βασιλεία τοῦ Θεοῦ (Heidelberg 1926, Winter), pp. 279–80).
[2] Burkitt, op. cit., p. 12. See further the present Study, V. C (i) (d) 9 (γ), vol. vi, pp. 124–9, below. [3] Burkitt, op. cit., p. 9.
[4] For the *Agudath Israel* see Leonard Stein in Toynbee, A. J.: *Survey of International Affairs, 1925*, vol. i (London 1927, Milford), pp. 376–7. For the deeper difference of attitude that underlies the superficial agreement between the *Agudath Israel* and the school of Johanan ben Zakkai on the negative point of Non-Violence, see Annex III to the present chapter, pp. 588–9, and V. C (i) (d) 9 (γ), vol. vi, pp. 127–8, below.
[5] For the variations in the application of the Roman Government's policy towards the Christian Church in this age see V. C (i) (d) 6 (α), in the present volume, pp. 456–7, and V. C (ii) (a), vol. vi, pp. 201–2, below. [6] Matt. xx. 22.
[7] See IV. C (i), vol. iv, p. 8, footnote 2, above, and V. C (ii) (a), vol. vi, pp. 205–6, and V. C (ii) (b), vol. vi, p. 291, below. [8] See V. C (i) (d) 3, pp. 407–9, below.

Brethren, and not in the violent way of Judas the Hammer; and its reward was the conversion of the Hellenic dominant minority. In the next ordeal, which came at the turn of the fourth and fifth centuries when the converted Roman Empire broke up, the Church responded once again in its traditional fashion; and this time its reward was the conversion of the barbarian war-bands with whom it found itself face to face in the fallen Empire's dere-lict Western provinces.[1] In an age in which the hollow futility of the secular *Fasti Triumphales* engraved in stone on the Capitol was being mercilessly exposed by the ultimate military and poli-tical bankruptcy of the Roman body politic, the Church was given the opportunity to celebrate some of the most astonishing of the triumphs of Christian Gentleness. Through this power which worked so mightily upon the men of violence, just because it was of a different order from the force which they exercised and understood, we see a Pope Leo turning back an Attila from his march on Rome when he had already reached the banks of the Mincio from the banks of the Danube and had demonstrated upon Rome's daughter Aquileia the atrocities which he intended to inflict upon Rome herself. We see a Saint Severinus coming to the rescue of Upper Danubian provinces that had been deserted by the Imperial Army and the Imperial Civil Service, and going about his Master's business—defenceless, intrepid, and unscathed —*inter gladios barbarorum*: making Gibuld king of the Alemanni tremble in his presence as he had never trembled in battle; deterring Fera king of the Rugians from carrying into captivity the refugees of Lauriacum; and giving his blessing to the young Odovacer.[2] And we hear the voice of a Saint Remi answering a Clovis' request for baptism with his 'Mitis depone colla, Sicamber'.[3]

Thus in the spiritual history of the Hellenic internal proletariat we see the two incompatible spirits of Violence and Gentleness

---

[1] See I. B (iv), vol. i, pp. 40–1, above. This victory of the Christian Church over the barbarian war-bands during the post-Hellenic interregnum was not won in every part of the field. While in the Western provinces the barbarian intruders were duly con-verted from the Arianism and the paganism that they had brought in with them (see V. C (i) (c) 3, pp. 227–33, below), the outcome, as we have seen, was different in the Greek and Oriental provinces. In the Greek provinces the barbarians were successfully kept at bay, first by a prolongation of the Empire's life and afterwards by its artificial resuscitation; and the Church was then turned into a department of state by the civil power of the East Roman *Imperium Redivivum* (see IV. C (iii) (c) 2 (β), vol. iv, pp. 346–53, with Annex II, above). In the Oriental provinces the Catholic Christianity which overcame the Arian heresy of the Goths and Lombards in the West was over-come by the Muhammadan heresy of the Arabs, because the 'successor-state' of the Roman Empire in these provinces, which had been established by the Primitive Muslim Arab barbarian invaders, was quickly called upon to play the quite different role of re-establishing the social unity of the Syriac World within the political framework of a 're-integrated' Syriac universal state which took up the interrupted work of the Achae-menian Empire (see I. C (i) (b), vol. i, pp. 73–8, above).

[2] Eugippius: *Vita Sancti Severini*, chaps. 1, 19, 31, and 7.

[3] Gregory of Tours: *Historia Ecclesiastica Francorum*, Book II, chap. 31.

perpetually struggling with one another, and Gentleness,[1] with the aid of Experience (πάθει μάθος),[2] gradually and painfully gaining the upper hand.

As soon as we grasp the plot of this 'post-classical' Hellenic drama, we see that it is not played exclusively on the proletarian stage; for there are at any rate hints of it in the spiritual history of the Hellenic dominant minority as well. The contrast between an Eleazer the Scribe and a Judas the Hammer, or between a Jesus who dies on the Cross and a contemporary Theudas and Judas who perish with the sword, has its analogue in the contrast between the gentle King Agis and the violent King Cleomenes in the third century B.C. at Sparta, or between the gentle Tribune Tiberius Gracchus and the violent Tribune Gaius Gracchus[3] in the second century B.C. at Rome. The recalcitrance of Peter against Jesus's superhuman resignation to the prospect of being wrongfully put to death is anticipated, in the generation of the breakdown at Athens, in Crito's attempt—less brusque in manner than Peter's but not less naïve in essence—to persuade Socrates to allow himself to be smuggled out of the prison where he is lying under a death-sentence that he has not deserved. Again, the victory of Gentleness over Violence in the souls of a Peter and a Paul and a Johanan ben Zakkai has its parallels in the vision of an Alexander[4] and in the clemency of a Caesar[5] and in the penitence of an Augustus.[6]

These eight famous representatives of the Hellenic dominant minority whose names have just been called to mind by the analogies which they present, in their actions and in their êthos, with as many famous representatives of the Hellenic internal proletariat, include, in the Athenian Socrates, the father of all the schools of Hellenic philosophy,[7] and, in the Roman Augustus, the founder

---

[1] See V. C (i) (c) 2, Annex III, pp. 588–90, below.

[2] Aeschylus: *Agamemnon*, line 177, quoted in I. C (iii) (b), vol. i, p. 169, footnote 1; II. C (ii) (b) 1, vol. i, p. 298; IV. C (iii) (b) 11, vol. iv, p. 218; and IV. C (iii) (c) 3 (β), vol. iv, p. 584, above; and in V. C (i) (d) 4, in the present volume, p. 416, footnote 3, and V. C (ii) (a), vol. vi, p. 275, below.

[3] In the extant portrait of Gaius Gracchus there are some incongruous traits which testify to a different presentation in which Gaius, instead of serving as a violent foil to a gentle hero in the person of his brother Tiberius, was himself cast for the gentle part, and was provided with a violent foil in the person of Marcus Fulvius Flaccus. Conversely, in the extant portrait of Jesus, there are traces of a different presentation in which he was cast for the violent part and not for the gentle one (see V. C (ii) (a), Annex II, vol. vi, p. 378, below).

[4] See V. C (i) (d) 7, vol. vi, pp. 6–10, and V. C (ii) (a), vol. vi, p. 254, below.

[5] Caesar's tardy clemency could not, of course, repair the damage that had previously been inflicted upon a miserable world by his pertinacious and devastating ambition. For the toll taken by Caesar's militarism in Gaul see Conway, R. S.: *Makers of Europe* (Cambridge, Mass. 1931, Harvard University Press), pp. 15–16; for the toll taken by it in the civil war between Caesar and the Roman Republicans see the present study, V. C (i) (a), vol. vi, pp. 186–7, below.

[6] See V. C (i) (d) 5, p. 435, V. C (i) (d) 6 (δ), Annex, p. 648, and V. C (ii) (a), vol. vi, p. 187, below.

[7] Philosophy in contrast to Physical Science—a study which had been pursued in

of the Hellenic universal state. These two great creative works of the Hellenic dominant minority are monuments, as we have seen,[1] of the labours of the altruists whom this minority bred at the opposite extreme of the spiritual gamut from its conquerors and wastrels and hangmen. If it is true, as we have suggested, that the Hellenic internal proletariat not only matched the destructiveness of these three villainous dominant types with its own proletarian brood of rebels and avengers, but also, at the opposite extreme, rose far above the spiritual level of the altruists, then we must look for signs of this higher attainment in the shape of proletarian creative works which correspond to the schools of philosophy and to the universal state but surpass these in fruitfulness as well as in sublimity; and we shall not look for these signs in vain; for the things that we are seeking stare us in the face. Among the works of the Internal Proletariat the counterparts of the philosophies are 'higher religions',[2] while the counterpart of the universal state is a universal church.[3]

Hellas since the days of Thales, more than a century before Socrates' time, and which had been consciously and deliberately abandoned by Socrates himself in his youth (see III. C (i) (c), vol. iii. pp. 186–7, and V. C (i) (c) 1, in the present volume, p. 39, footnote 2, above.   [1] In V. C (i) (c) 1, pp. 38–40, above.

[2] The religions which arise, during the disintegrations of civilizations, within the bosoms of internal proletariats constitute a distinct species within the genus; and some specific name has to be found to distinguish them from the primitive religions which hold the field, not only in the primitive societies, but also in those civilizations which—like the Hellenic Civilization itself—are not affiliated to an antecedent civilization through an internal proletariat, but are either affiliated through an external proletariat or else are derived from some primitive society direct, through a mutation (for the alternative ways in which a civilization may arise, see I. C (ii), vol. i, and Part II. A, vol. i, above). In contrast to the primitive religions, it seems legitimate to distinguish the religions discovered by internal proletariats as 'higher religions'; for a primitive religion is merely one expression, among many, of the corporate life of some local human community, whereas a 'higher religion' is the worship of a Godhead that is conceived of as transcending the whole of human life as well as the whole of the Material Universe. Our term, however, would probably be contested, as question-begging, by the devotees of Shinto in contemporary Japan and of the 'Nordic' Neo-paganism in contemporary Germany, who would agree with one another in holding that the tribe is the tribesman's spiritual absolute, and that therefore the worship of the tribe is the highest form of religion that a human being can have. This is, perhaps, the most crucial question that our Western Society will have to answer in our generation. (The difference between the two kinds of religion here in question has been pointed out by Monsieur Henri Bergson in Les Deux Sources de la Morale et de la Religion (Paris 1932, Alcan), p. 198: 'La première forme de la religion avait été infra-intellectuelle . . .; la seconde fut supra-intellectuelle. C'est en les opposant tout de suite l'une à l'autre qu'on les comprendrait le mieux'.)

[3] Of course this analogy, like all analogies, reveals no more than a likeness-in-difference. The 'higher religions' do resemble the philosophies in being attempts to find a new way of spiritual life to replace a lost or ruined spiritual heritage; and universal churches do resemble universal states in being social institutions that are constructed in order to gather together under the common shelter of a single roof the scattered children of a society that is far gone on the road from breakdown towards dissolution. There is also, up to a point, an analogy in the relation between each of the two ways of life and the respective social institution that goes with it; for, if the Catholic Church is inconceivable without Christianity, it would also not be difficult to show that Augustus could never have founded the Roman Empire if Socrates and Plato and Antisthenes and Zeno and Epicurus had not previously inoculated with their philosophies the souls of that dominant minority from which Augustus eventually recruited his public servants. At this point, however, the analogy gives out; for this relation between Greek philosophies and the Roman Empire was, in spite of its importance, imperfect. The Roman

In the Hellenic case in point the universal church was the Catholic Christian Church (which became the official church of the Hellenic universal state in the course of the fourth century of the Christian Era);[1] and the victorious 'higher religion' was the Christianity which the Catholic Church embodied. But while there was not—and could not be—more than one church that won its way to universality in the single social field of the Hellenic World, the victorious religion was victor over a bevy of discomfited competitors.

The direct opponent of Christianity was the primitive tribal religion of the Hellenic Society in its latest guise: the idolatrous worship of the Hellenic universal state in the personality of a Divus Caesar or in the abstraction of a Dea Roma.[2] It was the Church's gentle but intransigent refusal to allow its own members to practise this idolatry, even in a merely formal and perfunctory way, that drew upon it a series of official persecutions and finally compelled the Roman Imperial Government to capitulate to a spiritual power which it had failed to coerce.[3] But, though this primitive state-religion of the Roman Empire was maintained and imposed with the whole strength of the Imperial Government's right arm, it had little hold over human hearts.[4] The conventional respect for it which the Roman magistrate commanded the Christian to show by the performance of an outward ritual act was the beginning and end of this state-religion. There was nothing more in it than this

Empire was not created by Augustus, *de toutes pièces*, for the express purpose of embodying his *Pax Augusta*. It was an historic 'going concern' which he had to take as he found it and to adapt as best he could to his own ends; and the Augustan adaptation was a *tour de force*, for this Roman Empire which was turned by Augustus into an instrument of Peace was actually the child of War: the offspring of 'knock-out blows' which one of the five Great Powers of a post-Alexandrine Hellenic World had dealt to the other four. The reason why the *Pax Augusta* eventually broke down was because the Empire was never quite purged of its original sin of Militarism (see V. C (ii) (*a*), vol. vi, pp. 197-8, below). The dutiful civil servants and soldiers who kept the Empire in being as an instrument of the Augustan Peace were the heirs of those conquerors and wastrels and hangmen who had cleared the ground for it by razing a multitude of older and finer buildings; and these ancestors' criminal impulses sometimes broke out again, disconcertingly and disastrously, in the souls of their contrite successors. The spiritual union between Greek philosophy and Roman imperialism was never complete—not even when the Imperial throne was occupied by a Marcus or a Julian. The measure of the unresolved discord is given by the manifest spiritual discomfort of each of these two philosopher-kings. This unsatisfactory relation between Stoicism or Neoplatonism, as the case may be, and the Roman Empire is utterly different from the relation between Christianity and the Church; for, although the Church may actually never yet have expressed Christianity to perfection, there is at least no inherent impediment here to the attainment of a perfect harmony, since the Church has been called into existence for this purpose and for no other.

[1] The official establishment of the Catholic Church in the Roman Empire was a gradual process, which was begun by Constantine the Great (*imperabat* A.D. 306-37) and was completed by Theodosius the Great (*imperabat* A.D. 378-95), after an Arian interlude under Constantius II (*imperabat* A.D. 337-61) and a pagan reaction under Julian (*imperabat* A.D. 361-3).

[2] See I. C (iii) (*e*), Annex, vol. i, p. 443, above, and V. C (i) (*d*) 6 (δ), Annex, in the present volume, pp. 648-50, below.

[3] See IV. C (iii) (*c*) 2 (β), vol. iv, pp. 347-9, above.

[4] See V. C (i) (*d*) 6 (δ), Annex, vol. vi, pp. 648-50, below.

for those non-Christian citizens of the Empire who performed as
a matter of course what was demanded and who could not understand why the Christian insisted upon sacrificing his life rather
than comply with a trivial custom. The rivals of Christianity
which were formidable in themselves—through a native power of
attraction which needed no backing of coercive political force—
were neither this state-worship nor any other form of primitive
religion, but a number of rival 'higher religions' which sprang, like
Christianity itself, from the Hellenic internal proletariat.[1]

We can conjure these rival 'higher religions' up by reminding
ourselves of the various sources from which the Oriental contingent in the Hellenic internal proletariat was derived. The Christian religion was a contribution from a submerged Oriental people
of Syriac antecedents: the Jewish community whose home was in
Coele Syria. Syria, however, as we have seen, was only a fraction
of the Syriac World in its ultimate extension. We have observed
in other contexts how, as an accidental consequence of its breakdown and disintegration, the Syriac World eventually came to
embrace Iran.[2] Did the Iranian as well as the Syrian wing of a
thus expanded Syriac Society contribute a 'higher religion' to the
Hellenic internal proletariat? The question is answered in the
affirmative in the rise and spread of Mithraism, which was an
Iranian-born counterpart of a Syrian-born Christianity. This
Mithraism was not only Christianity's next of kin: it was also perhaps the most potent of all the 'higher religions' with which Christianity had to compete. The weaker competitors were all alike
non-Syriac,[3] though they were diverse in genius and in origin.
The worship of Isis was contributed[4] by the submerged northern
half of the Egyptiac World.[5] The worship of the Anatolian Great
Mother Cybele may perhaps be regarded as a contribution from
a Hittite Society which by this time had long been extinct on every
plane of social activity except the religious[6] (though, if we set ourselves in earnest to trace the Great Mother back to her ultimate

[1] See II. D (vi), vol. ii, pp. 215–16, above.
[2] See I. C (i) (b), vol. i, pp. 79–82; II. D (v), vol. ii, pp. 137–8; III. C (i) (a), vol. iii,
pp. 140–1, above.
[3] For the question whether Manichaeism—which was another Syriac 'higher religion'
of partly Iranian origin—has to be reckoned among the competitors of Christianity
for the conquest of the Hellenic World, or whether, on the other hand, it has to be
classed with Nestorianism and Monophysitism as one of several alternative attempts
to purge a Syro-Hellenic religious syncretism of its Hellenic alloy, see the present
chapter, p. 127, footnote 4, with Annex I, pp. 575–80, below.
[4] Isis proved strong enough to insist upon being given legal domicile in Rome, in
spite of a strenuous and long-sustained resistance on the part of the public authorities,
in the course of the half-century ending in 43 B.C. (Seeck, O.: *Geschichte des Untergangs
der Antiken Welt*, 2nd edition, vol. iii (Stuttgart 1921, Metzler), pp. 125–6).
[5] For the permanent political partition of the Egyptiac World, from the seventh century B.C. onwards, at the line of the First Cataract, see II. D (v), vol. ii, pp. 116–17, above.
[6] For the Hittite Society and its early death see I. C (i) (b), vol. i, pp. 110–15, and
IV. C (ii) (b) 2, vol. iv, pp. 108–12, above.

origins, we shall find her originally at home in the Sumeric World under the name of Ishtar,[1] before ever she established herself as Cybele at Pessinus[2] or as the Dea Syra at Hierapolis or as the Mother Earth of remote Teutonic-speaking worshippers at her grove on a Holy Island in the North Sea or the Baltic[3]).

A Minoan Lacuna and some Hittite Vestiges.

Having now studied the genesis of one internal proletariat, and taken an inventory of its works,[4] in the concrete example that is

[1] See I. C (i) (b), vol. i, p. 112, footnote 2, above.

[2] For the translation, in 204 B.C., from Pessinus to Rome, of the black stone in which the numen of the Pessinuntine Cybele was lodged, see Livy, Book XXIX, chaps. 10, 11, and 14, and the present Study, V. C (i) (d) 6 (δ), Annex, pp. 685–8, below.

[3] For a description of this distant emanation of the worship of Cybele-Ishtar see Tacitus: Germania, chap. 40. For the radiation of the worship of Ishtar from a Sumeric centre see the present chapter of this Study, pp. 147–52, below.

[4] The reader will have noticed that the worship of the Sun has not been mentioned in our catalogue of 'higher religions' arising in the bosom of the Hellenic internal proletariat, while the worships of Cybele, Isis, and Mithra, as well as Christianity, have been included. The omission has been deliberate; for the revolutionary cult of Ἥλιος ἐλευθέριος, which can be detected in the romance of Iambulus and in the émeute of Aristonicus (see the present chapter, pp. 69 and 179–80, and V. C (i) (d) 6 (δ), Annex, p. 692, footnote 2; and V. C (i) (d) 11, Annex, vol. vi, p. 351, below), seems to have been stamped out in the repression of the internal proletariat's abortive attempts to make a social revolution in the last phase of the Hellenic 'Time of Troubles', while the would-be conservative cult of Sol Invictus that is so prominent in the religious history of the Hellenic World in the third century of the Christian Era was not one of those popular religions that the internal proletariat discovered for itself. It was in a different category from the other Oriental 'higher religions', and in the same category as the Oriental philosophy of Astral Determinism (see V. C (i) (c) 1, pp. 56–7, above), by reason of the facts that it was an abstract and artificial religion; that its discoverers and devotees were members of the dominant minority; and that it was propagated from above downwards and not from below upwards. This was the nature and history of the Sun-worship that was affected by Aurelian and by Constantius Chlorus—and also by Constantius's son Constantine the Great until he abandoned Sol for Christ (see Baynes, N. H.: Constantine the Great and the Christian Church (London 1929, Milford), pp. 8 and 95–103). This Hellenic Imperial cult of Sol Invictus in the latter part of the third century of the Christian Era is strictly analogous to the Egyptian Imperial cult of the Solar Disk which was invented by Ikhnaton (and the parallel is an admirable illustration of that uniformity of human nature which sometimes produces surprisingly similar results in similar situations where there can be no suspicion of any connecting link of historical tradition). The third-century Roman Emperors—convinced, by the harrowing experience of their generation, that political institutions required spiritual sanctions and that 'philosophy' was 'not enough'—were now attempting to reinforce the official Caesar-worship, which was coeval with the Empire itself, and the unofficial Stoic philosophy, on which their own immediate predecessors in the second century had managed to live, with a semi-official Solar religion which was (they fondly hoped) to become a religious link between the dominant minority of the Hellenic World and a now once again militantly hostile proletariat. This artificial religious policy failed—as it was bound to fail—because it had nothing substantial to offer to either of the two parties to whom it was addressed. For the dominant minority Sol Invictus could not provide the 'spiritual vitamins' (if the phrase may be allowed) which Zeno had failed to give them, while for the proletariat the offer of Sol Invictus in place of Magna Mater or Isis or Mithras or Christ was the offer of a stone for bread. In a later chapter of this Study (V. C (i) (d) 6 (δ), Annex, pp. 649–50 and 691–4, below) we shall observe that the fiasco of the cult of Sol Invictus, like the fiasco of Atonism, is an example of a general 'law' to the effect that, while a 'higher religion' can be discovered by an internal proletariat and be communicated by it to a dominant minority, an attempt to reverse the direction of the movement condemns this spiritual commerce to sterility and frustration.

The cult of Sol Invictus must, of course, be distinguished from an entirely different form of Sun-worship which a third-century Roman Emperor of an earlier generation had attempted to thrust upon his subjects by an abuse of political power that presents a sharp contrast to the tact and moderation of his successors who were advocates of Sol Invictus. This other Solar religion was the historic local Sun-worship of the Syrian

offered by the history of the disintegration of the Hellenic Civilization, let us do again what we have done in our foregoing study of dominant minorities. Let us test, by making a survey, whether the phenomena which have thus presented themselves in a single case are unique and therefore of little account or regular and therefore significant. Have the disintegrations of other civilizations besides the Hellenic been accompanied by the Secession of an Internal Proletariat? If they have, has this Internal Proletariat been recruited, in these other cases too, from the same three sources: that is to say, from disinherited members of the Dominant Minority and from partially disinherited alien subject peoples and from doubly disinherited subject-alien deportees? Again, do we find such other internal proletariats responding to an identic challenge of oppression in the two alternative and contrary ways—the violent and the gentle[1]—which we have learnt to distinguish in our study of the Hellenic example? And, if the gentle way has been followed by oppressed proletarians in other cases as well, has it led, here too, to the birth of 'higher religions' and to the establishment of universal churches?

In attempting to give a comprehensive answer to this set of questions, we shall find ourselves hampered by the fact that, *ex hypothesi*, the Secession of the Internal Proletariat takes place in the obscurity of an underworld, and that the history of its genesis and of its early growth is apt to be ignored and left unrecorded by the cultivated men-of-letters in the Dominant Minority, while the nascent Proletariat itself is ill equipped for keeping its own records at this momentous early stage of its career.[2] Thus we often find ourselves in the dark about a proletariat's history until this proletariat bursts out of the subterranean twilight in which it has been born into the broad daylight which plays upon the surface of social life; and the very fact that it has risen to the surface means that a proletariat is already near, or at, its prime by the time when it thus comes into view. This difficulty besets us even when we

---

city of Emesa (a duplicate of the more famous neighbouring Sun-worship of Heliopolis-Ba'lbak) which was momentarily given precedence over all other worships in the Roman Empire by the whim of Varius Avitus Bassianus—the hereditary High Priest and namesake of this Syrian divinity Elagabalus—during his short tenure of the Imperial throne under the impudently assumed name of Marcus Aurelius Antoninus (*imperabat* A.D. 218–22). For the contrast between the respective worships of the Sun as Elagabalus and as Sol Invictus, see Wissowa, G.: *Religion und Kultus der Römer*, 2nd edition (Munich 1912, Beck), pp. 365–8. The Emesan form of Sun-worship might perhaps claim to be a proletarian religion, but it certainly could not claim to be a 'higher' one. All the same, Aurelian, in the course of his campaign against Zenobia in A.D. 272, did visit the shrine of Elagabalus at Emesa, make offerings and dedicate temples to the god, and hold himself indebted to Elagabalus for the victory of Roman over Palmyrene arms (Homo, L.: *Essai sur le Règne de l'Empereur Aurélien (270–75)* (Paris 1904, Fontemoing), p. 101).
    [1] See V. C (i) (c) 2, Annex III, pp. 588–90, below.
    [2] For the transmuting effect of the waters of the stream of 'Folk-Memory' see V. C (ii) (a), Annex II, vol. vi, pp. 438–64, below.

are dealing with a disintegrating civilization which, like the Hellenic, has bequeathed to us a legacy of literature; and it still haunts us when we are able not merely to spell this literature out but also to recapture the living thoughts and feelings which the dead words were framed to express. The difficulty is accentuated when we have to depend upon mere fragments of literatures that have been recovered by the modern Western archaeologist's spade without there being any sensitive link of continuous tradition between our lives and those of these long-buried and quite forgotten writers. *Inter enim iectast vitai pausa*[1]—and this breach of vital continuity will baffle us in grappling with the Egyptiac and Sumeric and Hittite and Babylonic civilizations, notwithstanding the marvellous ingenuity of our scholars in deciphering their scripts. We shall find ourselves baffled still more cruelly by scripts which we have not yet succeeded in puzzling out, and which, for all we know, may be so rudimentary that, even if we could read the riddle, we should merely have gained a knowledge of statistics without having come any nearer to being initiated into the writers' ideas; and this is our predicament when we gaze at the Minoan 'linear script'[2] and at the Mayan pictograms and at the knotted cords of an Andean *quipu*. In trying conclusions with civilizations as elusive as these, we may be driven to confess that we are not only entirely unable to trace the genesis and growth of an internal proletariat, but that we cannot even guess at the existence or non-existence of such a thing by inference from the presence or absence of the Internal Proletariat's characteristic works, since in some of these cases we shall find that we cannot even say whether there is a trace, or no trace at all, of a 'higher religion' and a universal church.

Did a universal church, or anything like it, take shape during the disintegration of the Mayan or the disintegration of the Minoan Civilization? In the Mayan case we have had to be content with an inconclusively negative answer.[3] In the Minoan case our eye has been caught by the tantalizing glimmer of a possibility that the vestiges of something which might be called a Minoan universal church may be preserved among the heterogeneous constituents of the historic Orphic Church which makes its appearance in Hellenic history from the sixth century B.C. onwards.[4] We cannot, however, be positively certain that any of the practices and beliefs of Orphism, as we know these from Hellenic literature and inscriptions,

---

[1] Lucretius: *De Rerum Natura*, Book III, ll. 860–1.
[2] See V. C (i) (d) 6 (γ), p. 491, footnote 3, below.
[3] See I. C (i) (b), vol. i, p. 127, above.
[4] On this question see I. C (i) (b), vol. i, pp. 95–100, above. M. P. Nilsson (*Minoan-Mycenaean Religion and its Survival in Greek Religion* (London 1927, Milford), p. 512) inclines to the view 'that Crete actively contributed to the religious revival in the Archaic Age' of Hellenic history.

derive from any of the practices and beliefs of the Minoan religion, as we have to reconstruct these by inference from such Minoan material evidence—in the shape of ecclesiastical furniture and frescoes and vase-paintings depicting religious subjects—as the accidents of archaeological discovery have placed in our hands. So far from bearing indubitable testimony to the existence of a Minoan 'higher religion' and universal church, the appearance of Orphism on the Hellenic scene in the sixth century B.C. may, for all that we know, be more correctly interpreted as presumptive evidence that a Minoan 'higher religion' never came to birth. The existence of such a thing is not conclusively proved by the presence in Orphism of Cretan elements such as the myth of 'the Cretan Dionysus' (the child-god who is wickedly slain and whose slayers are the source of Man's original sin, while the sacrament of eating his body is the key to Man's salvation). On the other hand there are undoubtedly other elements in Orphism which are strongly reminiscent of contemporary Syriac religion and Indic philosophy.

Like Yahweh, and unlike Zeus, the Orphic God Phanes is a creator;[1] and the Orphic personified abstraction 'Ageless Time' (Χρόνος Ἀγήραος) has his double in the Zoroastrian 'Endless Time' (Zrvān Akarana)—the likeness extending to the grotesquely monstrous details of the visual form in which this strange divinity is presented.[2] There is an equally unmistakable Indic flavour about the Orphic doctrines that the Universe is an egg;[3] that the body is a tomb (σῶμα σῆμα) in which a soul is imprisoned as a punishment for sin that has been committed in previous incarnations;[4] that the punishment is recurrent in a cycle of rebirths from which the soul can never escape so long as there is any debit-balance against it in an account of sin and punishment which runs on through successive births and deaths; but that there does exist a way of escape which brings 'release from the circle and relief from evil'.[5] The Orphic theology pictures the purified soul, which has obtained its release from the circle at last, as being permitted forthwith for the first time to drink a draught from the Lake of Memory,[6] in reward for its virtue and in token that its labours are at an end; and this

---

[1] Guthrie, W. K. C.: *Orpheus and Greek Tradition* (London 1935, Methuen), p. 106.
[2] Ibid., pp. 86–7, and Boulanger, A.: *Orphée* (Paris 1925, Rieder), p. 55. In Guthrie's opinion (op. cit., pp. 76–8), which is followed here, the Orphic scriptures in which this grotesque figure is described give us a substantially authentic account of the original Orphism of the sixth century B.C. On the other hand Boulanger (op. cit., pp. 53–9) contends that these scriptures reflect an Alexandrian Neo-Orphism of the second century B.C. and after, and that this differs *toto coelo* from the sixth-century original.
[3] For the vogue of this idea in the Indic Mythology see Thomas, E. J.: *The History of Buddhist Thought* (London 1933, Kegan Paul), p. 87.
[4] Guthrie, op. cit., pp. 156–8.   [5] Ibid., pp. 165–71.
[6] Ibid., p. 177.

picture will remind us of Siddhārtha Gautama's legendary experience of recollecting all his previous incarnations at the moment when he attains the enlightenment of Buddhahood.[1]

These Indic and Syriac features in Orphism are unmistakable, and the resemblances are too close to be dismissed as accidental. We have therefore to see in Orphism a 'syncretistic' religion; and we have also to take into consideration the probability that this intricate texture of Orphism is not the undesigned product of Time and Chance. It bears on its face the signs of being the deliberate artifice of a small band of creative individuals[2] who wove it, at one weaving, from a variety of materials that they picked out as apt for their purpose.[3] The result of these theological labours was a 'book religion' in which right belief was accounted more important than correctly performed ritual;[4] and, in the light of all this, we shall probably come to the conclusion that it is a rather far-fetched explanation to interpret Orphism as an effort to preserve or recapture a Minoan religious tradition which had survived the post-Minoan interregnum and had not been quite trampled out of all recognition by the barbarous Achaean usurpers of the derelict Minoan heritage.

It seems more natural to see in Orphism an effort to fill a fearful spiritual void which desolated the heart of an adolescent Hellenism just because no higher religious heritage had been transmitted to the Hellenes from their Minoan predecessors.[5] We can well imagine that a sensitive Hellenic soul might become suddenly and painfully conscious of this void in the sixth century B.C.—partly because by that time the Hellenic Civilization had risen high enough above an Achaean barbarism to look down upon Olympus with mingled feelings of horror and contempt, and partly because at that very moment the political union, under the *Pax Achaemenia*, of all South-Western Asia, from the Hellenic coast of Ionia to the

---

[1] If the Orphic Lake of Memory is the source of Socrates' theory of *anamnesis*, then we can perhaps trace back one runnel of the stream of Hellenic philosophy to an Indic fountain-head.

[2] Guthrie, op. cit., pp. 107, 120, 123. For the untoward effects of this apparently artificial origin upon the subsequent fortunes of Orphism see the present Study, V. C (i) (d) 6 (δ), Annex, pp. 697–8, below. On the other hand, Boulanger (op. cit., p. 45) submits that 'ce serait méconnaître complètement [la] nature [de l'orphisme] que de s'imaginer qu'il a pu sortir tout armé du cerveau d'un initiateur de génie. Il n'y a pas à l'origine de ce mouvement, comme à l'origine du pythagorisme, une puissante personnalité.' The uncertainty of our knowledge of Orphism is illustrated by the direct contradiction between this judgement of Boulanger's and that of Nilsson on the same point. In Nilsson's view (op. cit., p. 511) 'Orphism is a speculative religion created by a religious genius, at least in its most vital doctrines'.

[3] Guthrie, op. cit., pp. 106, 110, 116, 194–5.

[4] Ibid., pp. 155, 204, 213.

[5] For the intellectual precocity which, in the abortive Scandinavian as well as in the primitive Hellenic culture, was perhaps the consolation prize for the lack of a 'higher religion' in the new nascent civilization's social heritage, see II. D (vii), vol. ii, pp. 355–7, above.

Indic borderland in the Panjab, had suddenly opened the treasure-house of Syriac religion and Indic philosophy to any Hellene who cared to enter in and help himself to these spiritual riches.[1] This explanation of the origin of Orphism seems, on the whole, to be the more convincing of the two alternatives; and, on this showing, we shall have to confess that, after all, we have no knowledge at all of a Minoan universal church and therefore none, *a fortiori*, of a Minoan internal proletariat.[2]

We know next to nothing, again, about the internal proletariat of the Hittite Civilization, which perished, as we have seen, at an unusually tender age.[3] We can only say that the wreckage of the Hittite Society which survived the great catastrophe at the beginning of the twelfth century B.C. seems gradually to have been assimilated by the Hellenic Society in part and in part by the Syriac, so that we must look to the histories of these two alien societies for any vestiges of the Hittite body social. We have already caught a doubtful glimpse of a Hittite dominant minority in the shapes of prince-prelates presiding over Anatolian temple-

[1] 'Il n'est pas invraisemblable que, par l'intermédiaire de l'Iran, l'Ionie ait pu connaître la doctrine hindoue de la migration des âmes et lui emprunter les formules que l'orphisme a rendues célèbres' (Boulanger, op. cit., p. 45). A hint of the active circulation and collision of ideas which was taking place within the Achaemenian Empire by the end of the sixth century B.C. is given to us in the Herodotean story—legendary though this may be in itself—of how Darius the Great (*imperabat* 522–486 B.C.) amused himself by confronting the Greeks at his Court with the Indians and provoking each of the two parties in turn to express their horror at the other party's customary method of disposing of their parents' corpses. For their mutual edification, what each party said about the other's custom was translated into the latter party's language by the Court interpreters (Herodotus, Book III, chap. 38). Compare the theological disputation at the Court of the Mongol Khāqān Mangū at Qaraqorum in A.D. 1254, as described in chapter 51 of the journal of a Flemish friar of the Franciscan Order, William of Rubruck (English translation in Komroff, M.: *Contemporaries of Marco Polo* (London 1928, Cape)). For the similar appetite of the Emperor Akbar for the comparative study of Religion see V. C (i) (*d*) 6 (δ), Annex, pp. 699–704, below.

[2] If Orphism is not the creation of a Minoan internal proletariat, it cannot strictly be described as a proletarian product, since the religious experience of the Syriac internal proletariat, upon which it appears to draw, has been drawn upon at second hand, while its Hellenic creators can hardly be counted as members of a Hellenic internal proletariat which, *ex hypothesi*, cannot have come into existence until after the breakdown of the Hellenic Society about a hundred years later (assuming that this breakdown is to be equated with the outbreak of the Peloponnesian War). The self-conscious, academic, bookish element in Orphism is certainly alien from the proletarian religious êthos as we know it in the classical examples. At the same time it is interesting to find the reviewer of Mr. Guthrie's book in *The Journal of Hellenic Studies* (vol. lv, part 2 (1935), p. 260) recommending 'the addition of one important point' to Mr. Guthrie's account of the Orphic religion:

'Orphism was a creation of the lower orders of Greek Society. Hence, among other things, its patronage by the House of Peisistratus, in accordance with the usual tyrants' policy of favouring the unprivileged classes. Probably, if all facts were known, we should find that Pythagoreanism was its aristocratic, and therefore more philosophic and reasoned, counterpart—much though that system, at least in its more popular forms, undoubtedly owed to beliefs and practices of a comparatively primitive type.'

If this is the truth, then Pythagoreanism stands to Orphism as the post-Socratic schools of Hellenic philosophy, from Platonism to Neoplatonism inclusive, stand to the worships of Cybele and Isis and to Mithraism, Christianity, and the Mahāyāna.

[3] For the early death of the Hittite Civilization see I. C (i) (*b*), vol. i, pp. 93 and 114; IV. C (ii) (*b*) 2, vol. iv, pp. 108–12, above.

states[1] and oligarchies governing Etruscan city-states[2] during the last millennium B.C. The Etruscan aristocracy—whose Hittite origin seems probable, though unproven—undoubtedly gained admittance into the ranks of the Hellenic dominant minority; and we may perhaps espy the vestiges of a Hittite internal proletariat in the Cappadocian temple-serfs.[3] Such vestiges, however, must remain unauthenticated unless and until our historical evidence increases; and, even if they did prove to be authentic, they would still remain mere curiosities of history. For every piece of Hittite flotsam and jetsam which may have risen to the surface of an alien civilization in a distant age,[4] we may be certain that a thousand pieces were for ever submerged.

Changes of Masters.

In this respect the history of the Hittite wreckage, obscure though it is, throws a glimmer of light upon the common fate of all civilizations which have undergone in their disintegration the Hittite experience of being devoured by some alien civilization or civilizations before the disintegration-process has run its full normal course from breakdown to dissolution. Since we have come to suspect expansion of being a symptom of disintegration,[5] we may assume, as a working hypothesis, that a society which is successfully expanding at a disintegrating neighbour's expense is itself likely to be already in disintegration, and is therefore probably divided already against itself into a dominant minority and a proletariat of its own. In such circumstances the alien elements which the aggressive society devours will be assimilated either to its internal proletariat or to its dominant minority; and the pro-

[1] For these temple communities, which were economic 'estates' and political 'states' at the same time, see IV. C (iii) (c) 2 (β), vol. iv, p. 422, footnote 3, and IV. C (iii) (c) 3 (a), vol. iv, p. 471, above.

[2] For the probable Hittite origin of the Etruscans see I. C (i) (b), vol. i, pp. 114–15, with Annex II, 2; II. D (iii), vol. ii, pp. 85–6; and IV. C (ii) (b) 2, vol. iv, p. 109, footnote 2, above.

[3] 'À la fin de chaque guerre, le roi hittite ramène des pays conquis un butin d'hommes, de bétail et d'objets précieux. Les déportés ainsi transplantés en Hatti sont en majeure partie répartis dans les villes, dans les districts à repeupler, dans les propriétés des temples, avec un statut spécial et des droits limités; d'autres sont incorporés dans l'armée; d'autres, enfin, réduits en esclavage au profit des seigneurs et des guerriers' (Delaporte, L.: Les Hittites (Paris 1936, Renaissance du Livre), p. 184).

[4] If we are right in regarding Etruria as a Hellenized transmarine asylum of a prematurely shattered Hittite Society, we may perhaps espy a second Etruria in the Taman Peninsula which faces the Crimea across the Straits of Kerch:
'The temples on the Taman Peninsula, as we learn from an inscription of Roman date, were organized like those in Asia Minor, especially those in Pontus, Cappadocia and Armenia: a college of priests or priestesses with a grand priest or priestess at its head; vast domains belonging to the goddess; and serfs working for the goddess and for the priests' (Rostovtzeff, M.: Iranians and Greeks in South Russia (Oxford 1922, Clarendon Press), p. 73. Cf. op. cit., pp. 161–2).

[5] The evidence for this view that expansion and disintegration are correlated with one another is discussed in III. C (i) (a), vol. iii, and in IV. C (ii) (b), passim, vol. iv, above, and again in Part IX, below.

letariat is likely to be the receptacle for the majority of these alien
recruits, since in conflicts of culture, as in physical warfare, the
conquered are seldom admitted to share in the conqueror's privileges.

This *a priori* probability can be tested in the case of our own
Western Civilization, which by now has swallowed—and in some
degree digested and assimilated—at least eight alien societies: the
Mexic, the Andean, the Hindu, the Iranic, the Russian Orthodox
Christian, the Japanese Far Eastern, and the main bodies of the
Far Eastern and Orthodox Christian societies in China and in the
Near East. The number of victims rises from eight to ten if we
reckon in the Yucatec and Arabic societies, which their Mexic and
Iranic neighbours had respectively succeeded in devouring on their
own account before these two gorged beasts of prey were preyed
upon in their turn and disappeared down our Western Society's
all-devouring throat.[1] Out of all these multitudes of alien souls
that have thus been incorporated into the Western body social in
the Modern Age, what elements have found their way into the
dominant minority of our modern Western World? Apart from
Cortez's Tlaxcalec allies in Mexico, whose treaty-rights to equality
with the new masters of the Mexic World were respected by the
Spanish Crown till its own rule in Mexico came to an end in A.D.
1821, we cannot call to mind more than two drafts of alien recruits
which the Western dominant minority has admitted into its own
ranks. These two are the governing class of a Muscovite Empire
which sought and obtained admission to the comity of Western
states at the close of the seventeenth century, and the governing
class of a Japanese Empire which followed this Russian example
in the third quarter of the nineteenth century. Both these contingents of *novi homines* have been weak in numbers; and the Russian
contingent has already proved weak in social stamina as well, for
in our generation it has been swept out of existence by a shattering
revolution. When we look into the present social condition of a
more recently Westernized Japan, we shall find ourselves wondering whether the Westernized masters of Japan, who are still in the
saddle to-day, may not be destined to-morrow to follow in Russian
footsteps for a second time by going through the Russian experience
of A.D. 1917. If we do live to see a Westernized Japanese governing class share a Westernized Russian governing class's fate, then

---

[1] At our first encounter in this Study with the Iranic Civilization (in I. C (i) (*b*),
vol. i, pp. 67–70) and with the Mexic Civilization (in I. C (i) (*b*), vol. i, pp. 119 and
123–4) we happened to come across both of them at a stage at which they had already
devoured their respective sister civilizations; and accordingly, at first view, we had in
either case the illusory vision of a single civilization—the 'Islamic' and the 'Central
American'—in a field in which the presence of a pair of civilizations—the 'Iranic' and
'Arabic' and the 'Mexic' and 'Yucatec'—was revealed by further analysis.

we shall have seen the whole 'man-power' of ten disintegrating civilizations absorbed—with all previous social distinctions now confounded and effaced—into the gigantically swollen internal proletariat of the single civilization of the West.

The fate which has overtaken these ten victims of Western expansion in our own age, as well as the Hittite Society before them, suggests that it is not at all unusual for a disintegrating civilization to be devoured by a neighbour before its disintegration is complete. And this is, indeed, what we should expect *a priori*; for, while on the one hand the process of disintegration may be favourable to expansion, it is evident that on the other hand it may also expose a society to becoming the target and victim of attack instead of being the aggressor and the profiteer. A 'house divided against itself shall not stand';[1] and while it may be capable of burying the adjacent buildings under its own ruins if it is left alone to collapse, it will be quickly demolished by the house-breaker if he comes upon the scene and decides to anticipate the leisurely work of Time. A dominant minority is particularly vulnerable to assault from an alien power because it is itself already an alien power in the eyes of its subjects. A moral alienation from the Dominant Minority is the essence of what we mean by the 'Secession' of the Proletariat. What motive has the Proletariat for sacrificing itself, at its momentary master's call, in order to save his mastery for him and thereby condemn itself to remaining in servitude to this particular master instead of allowing his place to be taken by another who may perhaps turn out to have a lighter hand? And even if the Proletariat does prefer its present master—out of fear of the unknown or out of inertia or even out of positive regard for him—is it likely that its servitude will have left it with the spirit and initiative to assert its will, even within this narrowly restricted field of a choice between two alternative yokes?

A test case is the behaviour of the internal proletariat in the Andean universal state when the Spanish *conquistadores* suddenly broke in and challenged the Incas to stand and deliver. The *orejones* were perhaps the most amiable and able dominant minority that any disintegrating society has ever produced; and it seems almost an abuse of words to employ the term 'Proletariat' at all in reference to the conscientiously tended flock of these genuine 'shepherds of the people'.[2] The docile beneficiaries of a paternal

---

[1] Matt. xii. 25.

[2] Both the moral and the technical eminence of the Incas as a dominant minority are revealed in the care which they took to avoid the social evil of 'deracination' (which is one of the most effective efficient causes of an internal proletariat, to judge by the Hellenic example). The Incas were at pains to spare the established local institutions in the conquered territories—although they had absolute power, *de facto* as well as *de jure*, to alter them (Baudin, L.: *L'Empire Socialiste des Inka* (Paris 1928, Institut

Pax Incaica felt an unqualified veneration for the Incas, and would perhaps even have loved them if they had ever ventured to adopt such a sacrilegiously familiar attitude. Even in the more recently conquered subject communities there seems to have been little discontent and no eagerness for an opportunity to shake off the Grand Inca's rule. The routine of obedience had been so thoroughly inculcated into the people that 'the machine went on working by itself after the mechanic was dead, and we have Ondegardo's testimony for the fact that, after the Spanish conquest, the Indians persisted in the cultivation of the Inca's lands and in the delivery of the crops to the Imperial granaries'.[1] Yet the Inca's submissive subjects were far indeed from being 'a very present help in trouble'[2] when the Inca, with Pizarro's fangs in his throat, was in desperate need of their loyal and valiant service. We have, no doubt, to allow for the fact that at the moment when the Spaniards appeared on their horizon the mental attitude of the Inca's

d'Ethnologie), p. 62); and it was their policy to leave the hereditary local chiefs (*kuraka*) in office as members of the Incaic official hierarchy (Baudin, op. cit., pp. 119-20); but their anxiety to avoid the evil of 'deracination' is most evident in their methods of redistributing the population of their dominions. While such redistribution was carried out in the Incaic Empire on the grand scale, the cases in which the exchange of populations was made for the political purpose of severing a recalcitrant people's links with its home and its past seem to have been exceptional. Apart from those members of the dominant minority who were planted in the conquered territories as garrisons or supervisors, the great majority of the deportees (*mitimaes*) seem to have been transplanted for economic reasons: either in order to adjust the relative local density or sparseness of population to the relative local scarcity or abundance of the means of subsistence, or else in order to bring some particular kind of human skill—agricultural or industrial—to places where there was a shortage of it and where a larger supply could be employed with economic advantage. These 'economic', as contrasted with the 'political', deportees 'were granted privileges designed to facilitate their resettlement and in particular they were given long terms of exemption from all taxation. They remained under the authority of their own chiefs, and were exempt from the rule of the chiefs of the territory where they were planted. Moreover their fellow-Indians from their home-country used to come and help them at harvest-time and sowing-time.' In some cases the deportees were charged with the duty of keeping their home-country supplied with food and raw materials (e.g. lama-wool); and it became one of the administrative practices of the Imperial Government to couple districts together in pairs—e.g. a cold highland district and a warm lowland district, which might perhaps be a long distance apart—in order that they might make up one another's deficiencies by an exchange of produce. When transfers of population were made between the two districts in a pair of this kind, the deportees had, of necessity, to be exposed to a climate which was different from that to which they were accustomed. On the other hand, when a loyal population was exchanged for a disaffected population as a political measure, care was taken that the loyalists should only be sent to districts where the climate was the same as that of their homes (Baudin, op. cit., pp. 131-6; compare Joyce, T. A.: *South American Archaeology* (London 1912, Lee Warner), p. 105; Markham, Sir Clements: *The Incas of Peru* (London 1910, Smith Elder), pp. 164-5; Cunow, H.: *Geschichte und Kultur des Inkareiches* (Amsterdam 1937, Elsevier), pp. 58-60).

It will be seen that this scientifically and humanely managed 'internal colonization' in the Incaic Empire was something totally different, both in spirit and in effect, from the Assyrian deportations or from the Roman or modern Western slave-trade. The only people in the Incaic Empire who were both uprooted and enslaved were the *yanakuna*, and these domestic slaves of the Imperial Household, who originated in a band of traitors that had been reprieved from a sentence of death, eventually acquired the powers and privileges of the Ottoman Pādishāh's *qullar* (Baudin, op. cit., pp. 75-7; Cunow, op. cit., pp. 94-5).

[1] Baudin, L.: *L'Empire Socialiste des Inka* (Paris 1928, Institut d'Ethnologie), p. 25.
[2] Psalm xlvi. 1.

subjects was confused, and their allegiance divided, by the unprecedented, and therefore profoundly shocking, public calamity of the civil war between Huascar and Atahualpa.[1] This was not, however, the governing factor in the situation. The fundamental cause of the Inca's undoing is to be found in that very belief in his divinity and invincibility which had built his Empire up, and kept it in being, so long as no alien assailant had appeared above the horizon. When these human sheep saw their demigod helplessly defeated, deposed, insulted, and injured, it never occurred to them that they might help him effectively themselves. They were only conscious that their universe had been turned upside-down; and the shock was prostrating and paralysing.[2] Atahualpa's partisans looked on in horror-stricken passivity while their master was put to death, and the usurper's opponents delivered themselves tamely into his brutal murderers' hands.[3]

[1] 'On fait grand état du peu de résistance offerte par les Péruviens aux Espagnols, mais . . . à cette époque les Indiens étaient en pleine guerre civile; ceux du Pérou, dont le souverain légitime Huaskar avait été détrôné par le bâtard Atahualpa, regardaient les blancs comme des sauveurs, leur savaient gré d'avoir fait prisonnier cet usurpateur, et leur faisaient fête. Ce sont des Indiens de Cuzco qui ont marché sous les ordres des Espagnols contre les Indiens de Quito. En somme, l'arrivée des blancs n'a été qu'un épisode dans la grande lutte entre les Inka et les Kara. . . . Si les Espagnols étaient arrivés quelques années plus tôt, au moment où régnait Huayna-Kapak, ils n'auraient pas aussi facilement conquis le Pérou. . . . Ajoutons que, sans l'aide des Indiens de Cuzco, jamais les Espagnols n'auraient pu, avec les faibles effectifs dont ils disposaient, soumettre le royaume de Quito.'—Baudin, L.: *L'Empire Socialiste des Inka* (Paris 1928, Institut d'Ethnologie), p. 209.
It will be seen that Pizarro, like Cortez, was one of Fortune's spoilt children. Indeed, his arrival in the Andean World at the moment of the civil war between Huascar and Atahualpa was a far more extraordinary stroke of luck than Cortez's arrival in the Mexic World at the moment of the war between the two city-states of Tenochtitlan and Tlaxcala; for in the Mexic World in its 'Time of Troubles' international warfare was perennial, whereas in the Andean World in its universal state civil warfare was an unheard-of lapse from an established *Pax Incaica*.
[2] 'Enfin et surtout, en raison même de la centralisation excessive du pouvoir au Pérou, la perte du chef aboutissait à l'anéantissement de l'armée. L'extraordinaire discipline qui régnait dans l'Empire, chez les civils comme chez les militaires, avait à tel point détruit l'esprit d'initiative individuelle que les hommes, n'osaient ou même ne savaient plus agir quand ils n'étaient pas commandés. La preuve en est que les Indiens de l'ancien royaume de Quito, soumis pendant moins de temps que les Péruviens à la puissance de l'Inka, résistèrent vaillamment aux Espagnols. . . . Les Indiens n'étaient point des lâches, mais ils avaient été pendant si longtemps condamnés à une obéissance passive qu'ils n'étaient braves que lorsqu'ils recevaient l'ordre de l'être.'—Baudin, L., op. cit., pp. 209–10.
[3] The moral paralysis of the Inca's subjects in face of the Spanish aggressors must not, of course, be exaggerated. The recently subjected population of the *ci-devant* Kingdom of Quito did put up a stout resistance, as is pointed out in the passage quoted from a French authority in the preceding footnote. 'Quant à la débâcle de l'armée d'Atahualpa, dès que celui-ci fut pris par les Espagnols, elle s'explique fort bien. Il y eut d'abord une véritable trahison, car le souverain péruvien recevait les étrangers en amis, sans avoir tenté de les arrêter dans les défilés de la Cordillère, ce qui lui eût été extrêmement facile. . . . Les Péruviens eux-mêmes, quand ils se rendirent compte que les Espagnols détruisaient leurs institutions et dilapidaient leurs biens, trouvèrent parmi eux des chefs énergiques et peu s'en fallut que les blancs ne fussent chassés du plateau.'—Baudin, op. cit., pp. 209–10.
The heroic resistance which was kept up by the Inca 'Die-Hards' in the fastnesses of the Vilcapampa Mountains for some thirty years after the entry of the Spanish *conquistadores* into Cuzco is touched upon, in another context, in V. C (ii) (*a*), vol. vi, p. 213, below.

The last state into which the Andean internal proletariat has sunk since its exchange of indigenous for alien masters has been described at first hand by a practised nineteenth-century English observer:

'The sudden fall of a whole race is an event so rare in history that one seeks for explanations. It may be that not only the royal Inca family, but nearly the whole ruling class, was destroyed in war, leaving only the peasants who had already been serfs under their native sovereigns. But one is disposed to believe that the tremendous catastrophes which befel them, in the destruction at once of their dynasty, their empire, and their religion by fierce conquerors, incomparably superior in energy and knowledge, completely broke not only the spirit of the nation but the self-respect of the individuals who composed it. They were already a docile and submissive people, and now under a new tyranny, far harsher than that of rulers of their own blood, they sank into hopeless apathy and ceased even to remember what their forefathers had been. The intensity of their devotion to their sovereign and their deity made them helpless when both were overthrown, leaving them nothing to turn to, nothing to strive for. . . . The Peruvian subjects of the Incas had reached a state of advancement which, though much below that of the ancient Egyptians and Babylonians, was remarkable when one considers that their isolation deprived them of the enormous benefit of contact with other progressive peoples. . . . The impact of Spanish invasion not only shattered their own rudimentary civilization to pieces, but so took all the heart and spirit out of them that they have made practically no advances during four centuries, and have profited hardly at all by the Western Civilization of their masters.'[1]

If this is how the subjects of so good a master as the Inca behaved when this master was being violently and unjustly robbed of his kingdom, we shall not be surprised to see other proletariats accepting or welcoming the overthrow of dominant minorities that have been oppressive in policy or alien in origin or odious on both these accounts at once. We have observed in other contexts[2] how readily the exploited peasantry of East Central Anatolia, who had been saddled with the burden of the East Roman Government's imperialism, 'turned Turk' upon the advent of the Saljūq Muslim invaders in the eleventh century of the Christian Era. A fortiori in India, from the morrow of the death of Awrangzīb to the eve of the Indian Mutiny, the Hindu ra'īyeh looked on as harassed yet nevertheless passive and indifferent spectators while the alien Mughal Rāj was crumbling away and the likewise alien British Rāj was being erected on its derelict site. We discern the same indifference

---

[1] Bryce, James: South America: Observations and Impressions (London 1912, Macmillan), pp. 114–15 and 481–2.
[2] In IV. C (ii) (b) 1, vol. iv, pp. 74–5, and IV. C (iii) (c) 2 (β), vol. iv, pp. 398–9, above.

in the passivity with which the Egyptians accepted the substitution of an alien Macedonian for an alien Achaemenian régime in 332 B.C., ten years after the Achaemenian reconquest[1] had put an end to an interlude of national independence in Egypt and had thereby banished from the field of practical politics the only political prospect that could awaken any enthusiasm in Egyptian hearts.[2]

The Babylonians' attitude towards the contest for imperial dominion between their alien Achaemenian masters and the alien Macedonian competitors of the Achaemenidae was more positive than the Egyptians' attitude and was to that extent still more conducive to a change of alien régime. The Babylonians did not merely accept Alexander with a cynical resignation as just another Darius in Hellenic costume: they welcomed him with open arms as a liberator—in the spirit in which, some two hundred years earlier, Darius's predecessor Cyrus had likewise been welcomed in Babylonia by Jewish deportees[3] to whom the yoke of the Neo-Babylonian Empire of Nebuchadnezzar and Belshazzar had been as grievous as the yoke of the Achaemenian Empire was afterwards felt to be by the dethroned descendants of the Jews' Babylonian oppressors when these oppressors were condemned, by the turn of Fortune's wheel, to receive for themselves the measure which they had formerly meted out to others.[4] For the Jewish victims of a Babylonian dominant minority in the sixth century B.C. and for the Babylonian victims of a Persian dominant minority in the fourth century B.C. the change of alien masters almost wore the appearance of a 'dayspring from on high' which had come 'to give light to them that sit in darkness and in the shadow of death'.[5]

These examples make it evident that, whatever the spirit may be in which a subject population greets a change of masters—whether it naïvely proclaims the dawn of a new era or mutters 'plus ça change plus c'est la même chose'[6] with a sceptical shrug of the shoulders—the eviction and replacement of one dominant minority by another can very easily take place in any society that has once come to be divided against itself by that schism between Dominant Minority and Proletariat which is a symptom and a

[1] For the reconquest of Egypt in 343–2 B.C. by Artaxerxes Ochus see V. C (i) (c) 3, p. 245, footnote 4; V. C (ii) (a), vol. vi, p. 207; V. C (ii) (b), vol. vi, p. 302; and V. C (ii) (a), Annex II, vol. vi, p. 442, below.

[2] In the mental realm of 'folk-lore' the Egyptians seem to have reconciled themselves to living under the Macedonian régime by transmuting Alexander the Great into an Egyptian national hero (see V. C (ii) (a), Annex II, vol. vi, pp. 441–4, below).

[3] For the Jewish attitude towards Cyrus see 2 Chron. xxxvi. 22–3; Ezra i. 1–4; Isa. xliv. 28, and xlv. 1–4.

[4] For the Babylonians' attitude towards the Achaemenian régime see further the present chapter, p. 123, with footnote 2; V. C (i) (c) 4, pp. 347–8; and V. C (ii) (a), Annex II, vol. vi, p. 442, below.

[5] Luke i. 78–9.

[6] Karr, Alphonse: Les Guêpes, January 1849.

penalty of social disintegration. We have dwelt on this point because it is another obstacle with which we have to cope in our survey of internal proletariats. For if a disintegrating civilization is apt to have its term of independence curtailed through being eaten up by some neighbour, we are evidently likely to be baffled, in attempting to follow out the history of this or that internal proletariat, by finding our specimen suddenly incorporated into an alien body social before it has had time to bring forth its own particular fruits. This heavy mortality among disintegrating civilizations may perhaps provide the social anatomist with richer materials for study when he essays to dissect some great voracious shark—a monster such as our own Western Society has come to be in its latter days—which has swept together into its insatiable belly the half-digested remains of a shoal of smaller fry; but, by the same token, the dissection of the shark-society's victims is manifestly bound to be an inordinately difficult business if we can only recover their mortal remains in this half-masticated condition. In such adverse circumstances we must be content if we can identify an organ or trace the development of a function here and there when we are dealing with disintegrating societies whose careers have been thus cut short.

The Japanese Internal Proletariat.

Some clear tokens of the secession of an internal proletariat can be discerned in the history of the disintegration of the Far Eastern Society in Japan, which had run through its 'Time of Troubles' and entered into its universal state before the Western Society swallowed it up.

If we are looking, for instance, for counterparts of those citizens of the Hellenic city-states who were uprooted by the series of wars and revolutions which began in 431 B.C., and who found a disastrous outlet and livelihood as mercenary soldiers, we shall observe an exact parallel in the *ronin*, or masterless unemployed men-at-arms, who were thrown off, during the Japanese 'Time of Troubles', by a feudal anarchy. The parallel extends to details; for Hideyoshi's abortive attempt to conquer Korea and China, like Alexander's successful conquest of South-Western Asia and Egypt, may be interpreted as an expedient for turning these formidable vagrants' arms against an alien body social. Again, the *Eta* or pariahs who survive as outcasts in the Japanese Society of the present day may be accounted for as a still unassimilated remnant of the Ainu barbarians of the Main Island of the Japanese archipelago, who, during the 'Time of Troubles', were forcibly incorporated into the Japanese internal proletariat by the arms of the wardens of the North-Eastern marches,[1] as the barbarians of North-Western Europe and North-Western Africa were incorporated by Roman arms into the Hellenic internal proletariat during the corresponding phase of the disintegration of the Hellenic Society. In the third place we can discern Japanese equivalents of those 'higher religions'—Christianity and Mithraism and the worships of Isis and Cybele—in which the Hellenic internal proletariat sought and found its final and most effective response to the challenge of the tribulations which it had to endure at the hands of a dominant minority.

In the history of the disintegration of the Far Eastern Society in Japan the corresponding religions[2] were Jōdo ('Pure Land'), which was founded in A.D. 1175 by Hōnen Shonin (*vivebat* A.D. 1133–1212); the Jōdo Shinshū ('True Sect of Jōdo'), which was founded by Hōnen's disciple Shinran (*vivebat* A.D. 1173–1262); the Hokke ('Lotus Sect'), which was founded by Nichiren (*vivebat* A.D. 1222–82); and the Zen, which was an adaptation of the Chinese Ch'an[3] and was introduced from China into Japan by Eisai (*vivebat* A.D. 1141–1215) and Dōgen (*vivebat* A.D. 1200–53). It will be seen that, if we have been right in dating the breakdown of the Far Eastern Civilization in Japan *circa* A.D. 1156–85,[4] the founders of these four religions all belong either to the generation which came of age at the moment when the Japanese 'Time of Troubles' set in, or else to one or other of the two generations immediately following; and we have positive evidence that *post hoc* does signify *propter hoc* in this case. On the one side the founders themselves were conscious of having been born into a 'Time of Troubles'. Already in the Heian Age, which was the autumn of the exotic Far Eastern culture's brief *floruit* on Japanese soil, the Amidist Mahayanian theologian Genshin (*vivebat* A.D. 942–1017) had declared that 'the fateful days' had 'arrived';[5] and Nichiren believed himself to be living in the Age of Mappō ('the Destruction of the Law').[6] On

---

[1] The Japanese 'Time of Troubles' was inaugurated and precipitated by this conquest and incorporation of the barbarians in the no-man's-land beyond the north-eastern marches (see II. D (v), vol. ii, pp. 158–9; III. C (i) (*a*), vol. iii, pp. 144–5; and IV. C (ii) (*b*) 2, vol. iv, p. 94, above; and V. C (i) (*c*) 3, in the present volume, p. 208, below).

[2] See Murdoch, J.: *History of Japan*, vol. i (London 1910, Kegan Paul), pp. 439 and 477–8.

[3] This Chinese name Ch'an is derived from a Sanskrit word Dhyāna, meaning 'meditation'; but there appears to be no evidence that the special theory and discipline that were held and practised in China under this name were not an original product of the Far Eastern genius. (On this point see Sansom, G. B.: *Japan, A Short Cultural History* (London 1932, Cresset Press), p. 329, and Eliot, Sir Ch.: *Japanese Buddhism* (London 1935, Arnold), p. 285.)

[4] See IV. C (ii) (*b*) 2, vol. iv, p. 94, above.

[5] Anesaki, M.: *History of Japanese Religion* (London 1930, Kegan Paul), p. 170.

[6] Nichiren articulated the history of Buddhism into three millennia running from the Buddha's death (which, in the Far East, was reckoned to have occurred in 947 B.C.): first the Age of Shōbō ('the True Law' of the Hīnayāna); second the Age of Zōbō

the other side the ground-down peasants and the Spartanly disciplined soldiers to whom the founders of the new religions were addressing themselves were hungry for spiritual food. 'Many minds are turning to religion' is the opening phrase of a tract[1] which Nichiren published in A.D. 1260; and this diagnosis was borne out by the multitude of the converts which each of these new religions won within its founder's lifetime.

These religions of the Japanese internal proletariat resemble those of the Hellenic internal proletariat in being of alien inspiration. All four are variations on the theme of the Mahāyāna; three of the four (i.e. all but Nichiren's creed) had been conceived in the main body of the Far Eastern World, on the continent, before they were adopted and adapted by Japanese apostles for Japanese use; and the two apostles who transplanted the Zen both started operations by making a pilgrimage to China to study their subject in its native setting, in accordance with a precedent which had been set by earlier Japanese divines who had sought to acclimatize other schools of the Mahāyāna in Japan at the time of the original reception of the Far Eastern Civilization. When we compare them, however, with these predecessors of theirs in 'the Nara and Kyoto Period' of Japanese history, we shall find that the characteristic note of the great religious geniuses of 'the Kamakura Period'[2] is not their receptiveness but rather their vein of originality. In the forms in which it had been introduced into Japan in that earlier age, the Mahāyāna, like the Far Eastern Civilization itself, had been a hothouse plant which had never struck root in Japanese soil or acclimatized itself to the Japanese air. While it had nominally been accepted by all the Emperor's subjects *en masse*, it had never been seriously practised, and indeed never properly comprehended, outside a narrow circle round the Imperial Court; and the people at large had gone on walking in the ways of the primitive paganism of the Japanese 'Times of Ignorance'.[3] This paganism, however, no longer sufficed to satisfy the common people's spiritual needs when the glass-house which had hitherto sheltered the exotic culture collapsed in ruins, and when this cultural catastrophe spread social devastation far and wide. In its disastrous downfall the Far Eastern Civilization in Japan at last made an impact upon the masses whose life it had scarcely succeeded in affecting during its

('the Image Law' of the Mahāyāna); third (beginning *circa* A.D. 1053) the Age of Mappō ('the Destruction of the Law'). See Eliot, Sir Ch.: *Japanese Buddhism* (London 1935, Arnold), pp. 277–8 and 424–5.

[1] Quoted in Eliot, op. cit., p. 276.
[2] For this periodization of Japanese history see II. D (v), vol. ii, pp. 158–9, above.
[3] At this stage the Japanese paganism was accommodated to the Mahāyāna by the formal identification of this or that Japanese *numen* with this or that Bodhisattva (see V. C (i) (d) 6 (δ), p. 528, footnote 2, below).

brief age of artificial and precarious prosperity. The onset of a 'Time of Troubles' turned these masses into a proletariat in sore need of spiritual salvation; and the founders of the four new Japanese religions rose to the height of this critical occasion by offering their people the spiritual bread of the Mahāyāna in forms plain enough for them to manage to digest it.

This provision of a simplified Mahāyāna as a substitute for a primitive paganism was the essence of these Japanese apostles' work; and in consequence that work presents itself in diverse aspects, which differ almost to the point of being mutually contradictory, according to the standards by which we appraise it. If we compare these apostles' teachings—and this is the more apposite comparison—with the primitive paganism which, in fact though not in theory, had continued to be the religion of the common people in Japan until these simple forms of Buddhism were brought within their reach—then we shall see Jōdo and Jōdo Shinshū and Hokke and Zen as so many new 'higher religions'. On the other hand, if we compare them with the sophisticated forms of the Mahāyāna that had been cultivated in Japan by a small *élite* since the sixth century of the Christian Era, and *a fortiori* with the Chinese originals of these Japanese copies, then we shall see in the new Japanese religious mass-movements of 'the Kamakura Age' not a notable advance from paganism but a lamentable relapse, in the religious field, into the barbarism which was at this time unquestionably regaining the upper hand over the exotic Far Eastern culture in other departments of Japanese life. This second view is not untrue, but it is neither the whole truth nor, perhaps, the most significant part of it.

If the work of the Japanese apostles of 'the Kamakura Age' was in one sense an *œuvre de vulgarisation*, this was at least the deliberate act of noblemen and scholars who were not, themselves, either vulgar or ignorant. Hōnen was the son of a provincial official of the Imperial Government; Shinran and Dōgen were the sons of blue-blooded dignataries of the Imperial Court; and even Nichiren's father, who was a fisherman in a then outlandish eastern province, was said to have been a man of good family who had been banished to this obscure corner in punishment for some political offence. Again, Hōnen, Shinran, Nichiren, and Eisai all spent years of study in the famous monastry of the 'high-brow' Tendai sect on Mount Hiei, overhanging the old Imperial capital of Kyoto, before they ventured to formulate and proclaim new personal messages of their own. What moved them all to break away from an esoteric tradition, and to address themselves to the people at large in terms which simple minds could understand, was a realization, through their own experience and intuition, that the exotic Chinese forms of Buddhism which were cultivated on Hieizan could no more avail to satisfy a down-trodden Japanese peasant's soul than the exotic Chinese system of government which was practised at Kyoto could avail to keep the Japanese country-side in order. The anarchy let loose by the breakdown of an arti-ficial régime which had never been suitable to Japanese social conditions had been brought home to Hōnen as an eight-years-old child by a poignant personal experience[1] which became the starting-point of his spiritual career. The boy's father, when dying of a mortal wound received in an attack on their home by a band of brigands, had adjured his son to forgo the vendetta which was laid upon him by the conventional code of his class, and to become a monk instead. After duly mastering the traditional lore and practice of the Tendai school of the Mahāyāna, Hōnen eventually 'demonstrated his zeal by abandoning all his former attainments and devoting himself exclusively to faith in the grace of the Buddha'.[2] Hōnen and his fellow apostles had a deep feeling for the sufferings of their generation, and they strove to find a way of salvation that would be open to all Mankind.

This eagerness to reach and help all sorts and conditions of people is the key to almost every aspect of these Japanese prophets' preaching and practice. Hōnen, Shinran, and Nichiren all threw open the gates of salvation to women by teaching that they too, as well as the other sex, were capable of ultimately attaining Buddha-hood.[3] In the Zen school the principal difference between Eisai and his successor, Dōgen, is to be found not in their doctrine or in their practice but in the public to which they respectively addressed themselves. While Eisai's 'influence was limited to monks and nobles, . . . Dōgen made every effort to avoid contact with men of high rank'.[4] The Zen, which in China had been cultivated by recluses, became in Japan (like Mithraism in the Roman Empire) the religion of the soldiers. And in the Japan of 'the Kamakura Age' the soldiers, peasants, and women, between them, vastly out-numbered the courtiers, monks, and scholars.

In addressing themselves to this immense and unsophisticated public, the new teachers adopted the appropriate technique and tactics. For instance, they wrote (those of them who did write) not in Classical Chinese, but in the Japanese vernacular, and they conveyed this in a comparatively simple script.[5] (The Zen School were not troubled by any literary problem, since they eschewed

---

[1] Recounted in Anesaki, op. cit., pp. 171–2; Eliot, op. cit., p. 261.
[2] Anesaki, op. cit., p. 171.
[3] Sansom, G. B.: *Japan, A Short Cultural History* (London 1932, Cresset Press), p. 327.
[4] Anesaki, op. cit., p. 207.   [5] Sansom, op. cit., p. 320.

all scriptures and put their whole trust in austerity and intuition.)
Again, while both Hōnen and Shinran sat in Kyoto and waited for
disciples to find their way to them—until the Government forced
both these sedentary apostles into the mission-field by banishing
them to distant provinces[1]—Nichiren started his ministry by
making a round of missionary journeys, and when he reverted to
stability he planted himself, with a man of action's eye, not in the
old Imperial capital at Kyoto, from which the power had now
departed, but in the neighbourhood of Kamakura, which was the
head-quarters of the new military régime of the Minamoto Shogunate and the Hōjō Regency. From this point of vantage Nichiren
propagated his doctrine by popular preaching in public places.
Eisai and Dōgen each in turn settled in Kyoto after coming home
from China and each in turn left Kyoto after having given it a trial.
Eisai finally gravitated, like Nichiren, to Kamakura, while Dōgen
founded a monastery in the province of Echizen.

It was not enough, however, for these preachers of salvation for
all Mankind to put themselves into contact with their public in
print or in person. If they were to make certain of being 'understanded of the people', their doctrine itself must be brought within
the people's mental range; and, while the Zen school differed from
the rest in making the pursuit of salvation strenuous, they all
agreed in depreciating the value of sheer intellect.

The theory of the Zen was that the enlightenment which was
its aim could not be attained either through reading scripture or
through listening to a teacher, but only through introspection; and
this introspection could not arrive at its goal—which was the
attainment of enlightenment in a sudden flash of intuition—
except through an ascetic spiritual self-discipline. In this indispensable preparatory training the aspirant after the enlightenment
of the Zen was thrown almost entirely upon his own spiritual
resources; and it was only by hints and nudges that his spiritual
director could help him to grope his way through the darkness
towards the light.[2] This way of salvation attracted 'simple soldiers'
because it was at once morally difficult and intellectually easy.[3]
The schools which appealed to a civilian public—to 'the man in
the street' and to the woman in the paddy field—were concerned

---

[1] Hōnen and Shinran both eventually returned to Kyoto in order to die there, but
Shinran had spent more than twenty years in the provinces in the interval, though his sentence of banishment had been revoked after he had passed four years in compulsory exile.
[2] The attitude of the master towards the pupil in the Zen school of Buddhism would
appear to resemble very closely that which Plato has described as being his in a passage
(Plato's Letters, No. 7, 341 B–E) quoted in III. C (ii) (a), vol. iii, p. 245, above.
[3] The Zen was, in fact, a way of transferring the soldier's activity from the Macrocosm to the Microcosm without changing its êthos (see Murdoch, op. cit., vol. i, pp.
484–5). In the Kwanto the Zen Buddhist clergy followed the path of secularization
to the length of abandoning celibacy (Murdoch, op. cit., vol. i, pp. 482–3).

to make salvation easy in the intellectual and in the moral sense alike; and these schools all found their clue in salvation by faith.

For the Jōdo and the Jōdo Shinshū the subject of this faith was the Bodhisattva Amida (i.e. Amitabha)[1]; for the Hokke—which in this respect stood at the opposite pole from the Zen—the object was not a person but a scripture: the Lotus Sutra from which this school derived its name. Already, before the breakdown, Genshin had proclaimed that

'We, the weak and vicious people of the "Latter Days", could not be saved but by invoking the name of the Lord Amida.'[2]

And this message of salvation by faith in Amida was taken by Hōnen as his principal theme.

'There may be millions of people who would practice [Buddhist] discipline and train themselves in the way of perfection, and yet in these latter days of the Law there will be none who will attain the ideal perfection. Consider that it is now an age full of depravities. The only way available is the Gateway to the Land of Purity.[3] . . . There shall be no distinction, no regard to male or female, good or bad, exalted or lowly; none shall fail to be in His Land of Purity after having called, with complete desire, on Amida.'[4]

This concern to make salvation easy almost at all costs—in reaction against the esoteric note of Japanese Buddhism in a preceding age which had ended so disastrously—produced not altogether happy results. Nichiren, who attacked the Jōdo vehemently, nevertheless agreed with Hōnen in virtually reducing the believer's whole duty to the repetition of a spell which was supposed to enshrine the quintessence of the object of faith by invoking that object's name. Hōnen's formula was *Namu Amida Butsu* (abbreviated to *Nembutsu*), meaning 'Adoration to the Buddha of Infinite Life and Light';[5] Nichiren's was *Namu Myōhō-Renge-Kyō*, meaning 'Adoration to the Lotus of Perfect Truth'; and it was for him 'not a mere oral utterance but a real embodiment of the truths revealed in that book.[6] . . . To utter the "Sacred Title" was, according to Nichiren, the method of at once elevating oneself to the highest enlightenment of Buddhahood.'[7] This expedient

---

[1] Eliot, op. cit., pp. 392–3, draws a parallel between the attitude of the Shinshū towards Amida and that of the Hindu Shaivas and Vaishnavas towards Shiva and Vishnu. The Shinshū can, of course, be traced back to the same Indic proletarian origins as the worships of the two Hindu deities. For the Jōdo conception of Amida's Paradise see V. C (i) (d) 11, vol. vi, p. 164, footnote 3, below.

[2] Quoted by Anesaki in op. cit., p. 170.

[3] Quoted, from Hōnen's tract *Senchaku-shū*, by Anesaki in op. cit., p. 171.

[4] Quoted, from Hōnen's *Catechism in Twelve Articles*, by Anesaki in op. cit., p. 174.

[5] Anesaki, op. cit., p. 173.

[6] The Lotus Sutra lends itself to this treatment, since its twenty-first chapter is devoted to spells (see V. C (i) (d) 6 (δ), p. 556, footnote 2, below).—A.J.T.

[7] Anesaki, op. cit., pp. 192–3.

promised to bring salvation within all men's reach at the price of transmuting a sublime philosophy into a rudimentary kind of magic.[1] And this intellectual retrogression had its moral counterpart in a relaxation of the rules of conduct. Shinran, who deprecated Hōnen's insistence upon the value of 'vain repetitions', was led to differ on this point from his master not because he was intellectually sceptical about the efficacy of 'spell-binding', but because he suspected such magical 'works' of being symptoms of a lack of faith in the all-sufficing grace of Amida. On the same ground Shinran deprecated 'any scruple about sins or depravities'; and—regarding celibacy, in this light, as 'a sign of lack of absolute trust in Buddha's grace'—he practised what he preached by discarding his monkish habit and tonsure, marrying a wife, and begetting children, 'in order to "give a living testimony" . . . that the secular life of common people was no obstacle to salvation'.[2]

While the Jōdo, Jōdo Shinshū, and Hokke schools were thus all at one in seeking, at almost any price, to make salvation morally as well as intellectually easy, they were by no means uniform in their êthos; and in this aspect they display our now familiar contrast between the gentle and the violent reaction of an internal proletariat, the gentleness of the Japanese soul being incarnate in Hōnen, and its violence in Nichiren. Hōnen 'was a man of meek temper and responsive heart, and in this respect he represented the heritage from the culture of the preceding age, while he was a typical pioneer of the new age in his aspiration for the salvation of all'.[3] On the other hand, 'Nichiren's religion represented in many respects the robust spirit of Eastern Japan which had always been in revolt against the ritualism and sentimentalism of the aristocratic Buddhists of Miyako [Kyoto]', and 'his appeal found an easy acceptance among the virile warrior classes[4] and the earnest peasants of the eastern provinces'.[5] Nichiren denounced Hōnen in unmeasured terms[6] as a heretic and a decadent. In a 'Treatise on the Establishment of Righteousness and the Peace of the Country' (Risshō Ankoku Ron) which he presented to the Hōjō Regent at Kamakura in A.D. 1260[7] he laid it down that killing

---

[1] For an analogous transmutation of Hellenic philosophy in the third to fifth centuries of the Christian Era, and of Sinic philosophy in the age of the Han, see V. C (i) (d) 6 (δ), pp. 553–68, below.
[2] Anesaki, op. cit., pp. 182–4.
[3] Ibid., p. 171; cf. Eliot, op. cit., pp. 266–7.
[4] It is noteworthy that, while the Zen religion appealed to soldiers at least as strongly as Nichiren's, the Zen was nevertheless free (except for the eccentric Fukeshū or Komusō variant of it, which became fashionable among rōnin and outlaws: see Eliot, op. cit., p. 285) from that vein of violence which was characteristic of Nichiren's personality, conduct, teaching, and school.—A.J.T.
[5] Anesaki, op. cit., p. 204.
[6] See the passage quoted in Eliot, op. cit., p. 277.
[7] See p. 97, footnote 1, above.

heretics was no murder, and that it was the duty of the Government to extirpate heresy with the sword.[1] And he condemned as heretical every Japanese school of the Mahāyāna except his own. While waiting (as it proved, in vain) for the Government at Kamakura to comply with his demand that the Hokke should be erected into the exclusively authorized and officially established religion of Japan, Nichiren intervened in the tumultuous politics of his world and age with all the vigour and self-assurance of the Prophets of Israel and Judah in the Babylonic 'Time of Troubles'.[2] He prophesied correctly, eight years before the menace became imminent, that Japan would be invaded by the Mongols, and incorrectly,[3] when Qubilay's envoys duly arrived to demand the payment of tribute, that Japan would succumb to the formidable invader unless the Government adopted the prophet's own creed as the national religion.[4]

In view of this attitude and behaviour, it is not surprising that Nichiren should have been perpetually at loggerheads with the public authorities and that on one occasion he should have come within an ace of losing his head. It may seem more remarkable at first sight that the exponents of Zen and of Amidism, including the gentle Hōnen himself, should likewise have suffered persecution. The truth perhaps is that the gentle as well as the violent prophets who arose in Japan in 'the Kamakura Age' were suspect of being subversive in effect, even if not in intention, in virtue of that deep concern for the salvation of Mankind in the mass which was the common, and the dominant, feature of all four schools alike. And, during the hundred years running from the outbreak of the War of Onin in A.D. 1467 to the assumption of dictatorial powers *de facto* by Nobunaga in A.D. 1568, the atrocity of the age[5] drove the Jōdo Shinshū as well as the Hokke into militancy.[6]

The Russian and the Arabic Internal Proletariat.

In the disintegration of the Orthodox Christian Society in Russia we can watch the recruitment of an internal proletariat from three different sources. One contingent was furnished by the children of the household in the persons of those Russian religious sectaries and political recalcitrants who were expelled or deported to the fringes of an expanding Russian Orthodox Christendom.[7] A second constituent element was provided by the children of alien civilizations—Western Christians in the Balticum

---

[1] Eliot, loc. cit. [2] See the present chapter, p. 120, below.
[3] For the failure of Qubilay's attempts to conquer Japan see IV. C (ii) (*b*) 2, vol. iv, pp. 93–4, above. [4] See Eliot, op. cit., pp. 278 and 280.
[5] This century seems to have been the nadir of the Japanese 'Time of Troubles' (see V. C (ii) (*b*), vol. vi, pp. 304–5, below).
[6] Sansom, op. cit., pp. 366–9. [7] See II. D (vi), vol. ii, p. 222, above.

and Lithuania and Poland and Finland; Iranic Muslims in the
Caucasus and Transoxania—who were incorporated by conquest.
If our analogy is to hold, the third ingredient in the Russian
internal proletariat should consist of broken-in barbarians; and
this ingredient was in fact supplied by the primitive peoples of the
Arctic zone—Samoyeds and Lapps and Uralian Finns; Tungus
and Yakuts and Palaearctics—and by the corralled Nomads of the
Great Eurasian Steppe.[1] Thus the three elements with which we
have become familiar in the Hellenic case all duly contributed to
the formation of the Russian internal proletariat; and we can watch
this proletariat making its first essays in the two alternative reactions to oppression. The violent way is exemplified in the
peasant revolts under the Cossack leadership of Stenka Razin
(A.D. 1667–71) and Pugachev (A.D. 1773–4); the gentle way in an
accentuation, among certain Russian sects, of the vein of quietism
that runs through Orthodox Christianity. That, however, is as far
as we can follow the spontaneous development of an internal proletariat in the disintegration of the Russian Orthodox Christendom;
for at that point in her history Russia sought and obtained admission to membership in the Western Society, and the remaining
acts of the Russian tragedy have been played out, to order, on a
wider stage, as incidents in a Western drama.

   This same process of Westernization has overtaken the formation of an internal proletariat of the Arabic Society out of the
primitive societies of Tropical Africa—and this at a still earlier
stage. We catch a glimpse of Moroccan matchlockmen anticipating
in the last decade of the sixteenth century of the Christian Era the
nineteenth-century French and English conquest of the Sudan.[2]
And we catch another glimpse of 'Umānī and Zanzibarese Arabs
emulating in East Africa in the nineteenth century the atrocities
which were practised in West Africa during the three preceding
centuries by European slave-traders. But these Arabic exploits
were a mere prelude to the great African tragedy which is being
played in our day; and although, as we watch the present first act
of this tremendous drama, we cannot yet guess how the fifth act
will turn out, we do already know who are the principal dramatis
personae, and we can certify that the Arabic stage-villain of the
curtain-raiser is now no longer on the boards. The African play,
like the Russian play, has been worked into our Western plot; and
it is as a member of our all-embracing Western internal proletariat

---

[1] For this Russian feat of corralling the Eurasian Nomads see Part III. A, vol. iii,
pp. 18–19, above, and V. C (i) (c) 3, in the present volume, pp. 313–15, below.
[2] Using the term 'Sudan' in its proper comprehensive sense to include the whole
borderland between Tropical Africa and the Afrasian Steppe in all its breadth, from
the western escarpment of the Abyssinian Plateau to the debouchure of the Senegal
River into the Atlantic.

that the African Negro will have to say his lines and to do his business in his native continent as well as in North America.[1]

Internal Proletariats under Alien Universal States.

A curious spectacle is offered by one group of disintegrating civilizations in which, after the indigenous dominant minority has been annihilated or dethroned, the course of outward events still proceeds on normal lines—as though we were watching the dismantled hulk of a derelict society being carried along by some kind of social momentum on a course that had been set by the navigator before the ship's officers shot each other down and the sailors furled the sails and unstepped the masts and a passing pirate placed a prize-crew on board. We have already taken note of three societies—the Hindu, the Far Eastern in China, and the Orthodox Christian in the Near East—which have all duly passed through a universal state on the road from breakdown towards dissolution, but have each received this universal state as a gift—or an imposition—from alien hands instead of constructing it for themselves.[2] Iranic hands have supplied one universal state to the main body of Orthodox Christendom in the shape of the Ottoman Empire, and another to the Hindu World in the shape of the Timurid Empire which was staked out by Bābur and built up by Akbar. British hands have since reconstructed this jerry-built Mughal Rāj in India from the foundations. In China it has been the Mongols —uncouth Nomads faintly tinged with a dilution of the Far Eastern Christian culture[3]—that have played the Ottoman or Mughal part, while the work of reconstruction on a firmer basis, which the British have attempted in India, has been attempted in China by the Manchus.

When a disintegrating society is thus compelled to invite—or admit—some alien architect to furnish it with its universal state, it is confessing that its own indigenous dominant minority has become totally incompetent and sterile; and the inevitable penalty for this premature senility is a humiliating disfranchisement. The alien who comes in to do a dominant minority's work very naturally arrogates to himself a dominant minority's prerogative; and in an alien-built universal state the whole of the indigenous dominant minority is thus degraded to the ranks of the internal proletariat. The Mongol or Manchu Khāqān and the Ottoman Pādishāh and

---

[1] For the religious response of the African Negro to the challenge of being conscripted into the internal proletariat of the Western Civilization through being enslaved and transported to the American side of the Atlantic see II. D (vi), vol. ii, pp. 218–20, above.

[2] For the hostility that is apt to be aroused by alien builders of universal states see further V. C (i) (c) 4, pp. 347–51, below.

[3] See II. D (vi), vol. ii, pp. 237–8, and II. D (vii), Annex VIII, vol. ii, above, and V. C (i) (c) 4, in the present volume, pp. 348–51, below.

the Mughal or British Qaysar-i-Hind may still find it convenient
to employ the services of the Chinese litteratus or the Greek
Phanariot[1] or the Hindu Brahman as the case may be; yet although,
in the servant's role, the dispossessed master may still extort our
admiration by his doggedness in clinging to a remnant of his
former power or by his flexibility in adapting himself to the discomfort of his present *peripeteia*, he cannot hide the fact that he
is degraded in his soul as well as in his status. It is evident that
in a social situation like this, where a *ci-devant* dominant minority
has become confounded in a common abasement with an internal
proletariat upon which it has once looked down with disdain, we
are unlikely to find the process of disintegration working itself out
to the end on genuinely normal lines under the hollow shell of an
outward normality that has been preserved by the intervention
of alien hands; and, if the normal symptoms can be detected at all,
we shall not be surprised if they are faint and transitory and rudimentary.

In the internal proletariat of the Hindu Society in our own
generation we can discern the now familiar twofold proletarian
reaction in a contrast between the murders committed by a militant school of Bengali revolutionaries and a Non-Violence preached
by the Gujerati mahatma Gandhi;[2] and we can infer a longer past
history of proletarian fermentation from the presence of a number
of religious movements and organizations in which the same two
contrary veins of Violence and Gentleness are likewise both represented. In Sikhism we see a formidable hailstone that has con-
gealed out of the etherial speculations of Kabīr (*vivebat saeculo
quintodecimo aevi Christiani*);[3] and this warlike proletarian syncretism of Hinduism and Islam has its antithesis in the Brahmō Samāj,
a sect in which Hinduism has been compounded with a nineteenth-
century Liberal Protestant Christianity by the rarefied spirit of
Ram Mohan Roy (*vivebat* A.D. 1772–1833).[4]

[1] For the Phanariots see II. D (vi), vol. ii, pp. 222–8, above.

[2] It is interesting that in the India of our day the protagonist of Gentleness should
be a Gujerati and the protagonists of Violence Bengalis, considering that there is a
much stronger vein of enterprise and efficiency in the provincial êthos of Gujerat
than in that of Bengal. For the present contrast in êthos between Bengal and the
Bombay Presidency see II. D (v), vol. ii, pp. 127–33, above. For the nature of Mr.
Gandhi's creed and tactic of Satyagraha see further V. C (i) (*c*) 2, Annex III, pp. 588–
9, below.

[3] For the relation between Sikhism and the religion of Kabīr see Macauliffe, M. A.:
The Sikh Religion (Oxford 1909, Clarendon Press, 6 vols.) and V. C (i) (*d*) 6 (δ),
p. 537, footnote 3, below. For the progressive militarization of the Sikh fraternity by
the sixth Sikh Guru, Har Govind, and the tenth Sikh Guru, Govind Singh, and for
the effect of this metamorphosis on the fortunes of the Sikh religion see Macauliffe,
M. A.: 'How the Sikhs became a Militant Race' in *Supplement to the Journal of the
United Service Institution of India*, vol. xxxii, July 1903, No. 152, pp. 330–58, and
V. C (i) (*d*) 6 (δ), Annex, pp. 665–8, below.

[4] See Farquhar, J. N.: *Modern Religious Movements in India* (New York 1919,
Macmillan), chap. ii. 1.

In the internal proletariat of the Far Eastern Society in China under the Manchu régime we can see in the T'aip'ing movement, which dominated the Chinese social stage in the middle of the nineteenth century of the Christian Era, a work of the internal proletariat which is analogous to the Brahmō Samāj in one respect and to Sikhism in another: to the Brahmō Samāj in being a compound between an indigenous tradition and an exotic distillation of Protestant Christianity;[1] to Sikhism in crystallizing into a militant political force.

In the internal proletariat of the main body of Orthodox Christendom the 'Zealot' revolution at Salonica in the fifth decade of the fourteenth century of the Christian Era[2] gives us a glimpse of a violent proletarian reaction at the darkest hour of the Orthodox Christian 'Time of Troubles'—in the last generation before the Orthodox Christian Society was dragooned into a universal state by the drastic discipline of an Ottoman conquest. A vast subsequent addition to the numbers of the internal proletariat was perhaps the heaviest part of the price which Orthodox Christendom had to pay for receiving from alien hands a social service which it could not do without and yet could not provide for itself.

This addition was supplied from all the three sources which we have learnt to distinguish in the Hellenic case. In the first place the *ci-devant* Orthodox Christian dominant minority whom the 'Osmanlis displaced—that is to say, the epigoni of the old ruling class in the battered fragments of the former East Roman and Bulgarian Empires—were unceremoniously degraded to the proletarian ranks as their due historical penalty for having grossly abused their trust by bringing Orthodox Christendom to its ruin through a rake's progress of fratricidal warfare between the two leading states of the Orthodox Christian World.[3] Under Otto-

---

[1] The T'aip'ing movement was, no doubt, a crude and fantastic affair by comparison with the Brahmō Samāj—as was, indeed, to be expected in view of the difference between the respective founders. While Ram Mohan Roy was a highly cultivated man who was in close personal relations with the contemporary Protestant Christian missionaries in Bengal and had a deep understanding of the genius and êthos of both the two religions which he was seeking to blend, Hung Hsiu-ch'uan was the Confucian equivalent of a Bengali 'failed B.A.'—that is to say, an unsuccessful candidate for the degree of litteratus—and he had heard no more than a distant and distorted echo of the exotic Western religion which fired his imagination and stimulated his will to act. His source of enlightenment was a set of Protestant Christian tracts compiled by a Chinese convert, and his first mission-field and base of operations was the secluded province of Kwangsi (see Meadows, T. T.: *The Chinese and their Rebellions* (London 1856, Smith Elder), chaps. 6–8 and 19; and Fitzgerald, C. P.: *China, A Short Cultural History* (London 1935, Cresset Press), chap. 29). The movement was named after a Sinic movement, of similar character, which broke out *circa* A.D. 184 and inaugurated the break-up of the Han Empire (as the nineteenth-century T'aip'ing movement was intended to break up the Manchu Empire). Meadows (op. cit., p. 439, footnote) draws a parallel between Hung Hsiu-ch'uan's Neo-T'aip'ing movement and Swedenborgianism.   [2] See IV. C (iii) (c) 2 (β), vol. iv, p. 359, above.

[3] For the great Bulgaro-Roman War of A.D. 977–1019 and its fatal consequences see IV. C (ii) (b) 1, vol. iv, pp. 72–6, and IV. C (iii) (c) 2 (β), vol. iv, pp. 390–404, above.

man rule all the elements of the indigenous Orthodox Christian body social—intolerable grandees and exasperated peasantry alike—were confounded in a common proletarian subjection. At the same time this indigenous Orthodox Christian nucleus of an internal proletariat was enlarged both by the conquest of populations of alien culture and by the importation of slaves; and both those methods of making forcible additions to their proletarian man-power were practised by the 'Osmanlis from the latter part of the fourteenth to the latter part of the seventeenth century of the Christian Era on a scale which rivalled the Hellenic practice from the generation of Alexander the Great to the generation of Julius Caesar.[1]

In their conquests the Ottoman Pādishāhs followed the lead, but far surpassed the range, of the native militarists whom the internecine Bulgaro-Roman struggle had carried into power in the East Roman Empire in and after the tenth century. The offensive warfare which Romanus Lecapenus and Nicephorus Phocas and John Tzimisces had opened against an expiring Syriac Society on a front which eventually came to extend from the shores of Lake Van to the coasts of Tunisia[2] was resumed by Selīm I and

---

[1] While the Ottoman and Hellenic practices of enslavement are comparable, the purpose behind the practice was not the same in the two cases; and, if we take purpose into account, as we ought to take it, in any attempt that we may make to pass a comparative moral judgement, we shall find reason to condemn the Ottoman dominant minority in the Orthodox Christian World of the fourteenth to seventeenth centuries of the Christian Era less severely than the Macedonian and Roman dominant minority in the Hellenic World of the last four centuries B.C. The purpose of the Macedonian and Roman conquerors and wastrels and hangmen began and ended with their quest for docile 'man-power' to exploit. The 'Osmanlis, whose avidity for docile 'man-power' was equally strong, did at least have in view a more reputable ultimate objective. They wanted this supply of docile 'man-power' in order to distil out of it, by a careful and elaborate system of education and selection, an *élite* which was to replenish the ranks of the ruling corporation itself. We have had occasion to study the recruitment and training of the Ottoman Pādishāh's slave-household already in another context (in Part III. A, vol. iii, pp. 31–44, above). The essence of this Ottoman system in its prime was that the Dominant Minority was recruited from the Internal Proletariat wholly and exclusively. The members of the ruling corporation were slaves who remained slaves even when they were occupying the highest posts in the civil and military administration of the Empire; and the slave's career was the sole avenue of entry, whether the slave-aspirant for office had originally been a Western Christian renegade or deserter or prisoner of war or a Russian Christian victim of the Krim Tatar slave-raiders or a tribute-child conscripted by the Ottoman Government itself from its own Greek or Jugoslav Christian subjects. This Ottoman system of recruiting the Dominant Minority from the Internal Proletariat is a particularly clear illustration of the truth—which is also true for all other disintegrating societies, as well as for the main body of Orthodox Christendom—that the barrier between Dominant Minority and Proletariat is the penalty of a moral schism and is not the expression of any difference of birth or race. The Ottoman Pādishāh's slave-household, which served as the dominant minority of Orthodox Christendom during its universal state, was of precisely the same race as the *ra'īyeh* or 'human cattle' which it acquired and tended in order to recruit itself from this stock. The Ottoman ruling corporation had been replenished by adoption as well as by natural increase ever since the first generation after its original settlement in Sultān Önü in the thirteenth century of the Christian Era; and in the generation of Mehmed the Conqueror—not to come down so far as Suleymān the Magnificent—there can hardly have been a drop of the immigrant Eurasian Nomad blood to be found still coursing in any 'Osmanli's veins (see II. D (vi), vol. ii, pp. 228–9, above).

[2] See IV. C (iii) (c) 2 (β), vol. iv, pp. 399–404, above.

Suleymān the Magnificent against the nascent Iranic and Arabic societies and was then carried up the escarpment of the Iranian Plateau on the east, and down to the coasts of the Indian Ocean on the south, and as far as the borders of Morocco on the west.[1] The still more wanton offensive warfare with Hungary in which the Comneni had indulged[2] at a later stage in the East Roman Empire's decline was also resumed by Suleymān the Magnificent and was carried by him up to the gates of Vienna. The impious Ottoman assaults upon the 'Osmanlis' own parent Iranic Society proved abortive; but the simultaneous attacks upon the other two societies which were likewise neighbours of the Ottoman Empire resulted in a vast addition of Arabic Muslim and Western Christian subject populations to the Orthodox Christian internal proletariat. These recruits, who were acquired through an Ottoman conquest of their native countries, were mostly permitted to serve the conquerors as hewers of wood and drawers of water without being uprooted from their homes; but there was also a constant stream of other recruits, from territories beyond the frontiers of the Ottoman dominions, who were plucked out of their native environment—either, against their wills, as prisoners of war and victims of slave-raids, or, by their own act, as deserters and renegades—in order to swell still further the already vastly swollen numbers of the internal proletariat of Orthodox Christendom under the Ottoman régime.[3]

Both the scale and the effects of this recruitment from abroad are revealed in the testimony of an experienced and skilful English observer who was resident in Turkey during the latter part of the seventeenth century, that is to say at a time when the recruitment from this source was on the point of coming to an end and may therefore be presumed to have dwindled already by comparison with its volume in the age of Suleymān the Magnificent or in the still further past age of Mehmed the Conqueror. In a book published in London in A.D. 1668 Sir Paul Rycaut describes[4] how, in his day, the population of the Ottoman Empire was still being recruited by imports of slaves from the hinterland of the Black Sea Steppe; and these imports were also still on the grand scale; for the minimum estimate of the average numbers of the annual contingent imported through the single port of Constantinople is

[1] For the extent, and the limitations, of these Ottoman conquests see I. C (i) (b), Annex I, in vol. i, pp. 384–400, and II. D (vii), Annex VII, in vol. ii, pp. 444–5, above.
[2] See IV. C (iii) (c) 2 (β), vol. iv, p. 403, footnote 3, above.
[3] For these recruits from beyond the Ottoman frontiers see Part III. A, vol. iii, p. 35, above.
[4] Rycaut, Sir Paul: The Present State of the Ottoman Empire (London 1668, Starkey and Brome), pp. 80–2. Rycaut was particularly well placed for making his observations, since he served first as English consul at Smyrna and afterwards as secretary to the English Embassy in Constantinople.

placed by Rycaut as high as 20,000. The English observer then goes on to discuss the spiritual effect of this physical deracination.

'The greatest part, being women and children, with easie perswasions and fair promises become Turks; the men, being ignorant and generally of the Russian or Muscovite nation (who are reported not to be over-devout or of famed constancy and perseverance in religion), . . . renounce all interest in the Christian faith.'

In this ready renunciation of their own religious heritage these Russian slave-immigrants into Ottoman Rumelia might seem to compare unfavourably with those Oriental slave-immigrants into Roman Italy who still clung, in exile and adversity, to the worship of Cybele or Isis. It appears, however, from a later passage in the same work, that although these Russians may have drunk rather recklessly of the waters of Lethe, the draught did not altogether overcome them after all.

'We might proceed to recite as many sects as there are towns or schools in the Empire, in every one of which some pragmatical preacher or other have always started a new opinion which can never want disciples. And certainly the diversity of opinion in Turk[e]y is almost infinite, and more numerous then in England or other parts of Christendom, though commonly not proceeding from the same malice nor laid with the same design to the prejudice of the State. The reason of this variety amongst the Turks I attribute to the many religions which voluntarily, and for interest or by force, have entered into the Mahometan superstition—many of which being Grecians, and instructed in the arts and sciences with which that empire once flourished, which was the mine and treasury of philosophy and learning, did afterwards mix with their new religions (not being wholy satisfyed with the Alchoran) certain traditions and opinions of the ancient philosophers. And several other nations—as Russians, Muscovites, Circassians and the like—retaining some few remembrances of their first notions and principles, make a farther addition to this ill-compounded medley.'[1]

Here was a spiritual field which had been admirably prepared, by the thorough work of a trenchant Ottoman ploughshare, to receive and foster the seed of a 'higher religion' and perhaps to bring to harvest a universal church; and the golden opportunity was not neglected by would-be sowers—as we have already observed in another context[2] where we have had occasion to take note of the rudiments of new religious growths which made their appearance in Orthodox Christendom under the *Pax Ottomanica*. As early as the second decade of the fifteenth century of the Christian Era, when the Ottoman Empire had only just been established

[1] Rycaut, op. cit., p. 135.   [2] In IV. C (ii) (b) 1, vol. iv, pp. 68–9, above.

and had not yet been rounded off by the occupation of Constantinople, Sheykh Bedr-ed-Dīn of Simāv was propagating in the Ottoman dominions on both sides of the Straits a syncretism between Islam and Christianity which reminds us of the Islamic-Hindu syncretism of Kabīr or the Christian-Hindu syncretism of Ram Mohan Roy or the Christian-Taoist syncretism of Hung Hsiu-ch'uan; and at the turn of the fifteenth and sixteenth centuries the Anatolian provinces of the Empire were being impregnated with Imāmī Shi'ism by the missionaries of the Safawis.[1] Like Bedr-ed-Dīn in A.D. 1416,[2] the Safawī propagandist Shāh Qūlī blighted his own prospects in A.D. 1511 by impatiently turning from a gentle to a violent course and thereby bringing down upon himself the full weight of the Ottoman Power.[3] These early violent sowers of new seed in Orthodox Christian soil were promptly crushed and their seed was trampled into the ground; but the quiet and gradual propagation of esoterically heterodox faiths, under a parade of conformity with the Sunnah, struck deeper and spread wider during the later centuries of the Ottoman Peace; and, if at the turn of the eighteenth and nineteenth centuries the process of Westernization had not followed so hard at the heels of the break-up of the Ottoman Empire, we may conjecture that, by the present day, the Bektāshī movement might have won for itself, throughout the Near East, the position which it has actually succeeded in attaining in Albania.[4]

The Ottoman Peace (*durabat circa* A.D. 1372–1774)[5] did at least

---

[1] See I. C (i) (b), Annex I, vol. i, pp. 365–8, above, and V. C (i) (d) 6 (δ), Annex, in the present volume, pp. 662–5, below.

[2] The parallel is not quite exact, since Bedr-ed-Dīn only took to violence after his hand had been forced. The Sheykh had resigned himself to a compulsory retirement, on a pension, at Isnik, after having been deposed by Sultan Mehmed I from the high office of Qādi'l-'Asker of Rumili, which he had held from A.D. 1410 to 1413. In A.D. 1416, however, Sheykh Bedr-ed-Dīn's lieutenant Mustafā Börklüje rose in insurrection in the natural fortress of the Qāraburun Peninsula (on the Anatolian mainland, facing the Island of Chios). On receiving the news, Bedr-ed-Din made his way from Isnik via Sinope to Wallachia and thence invaded the Ottoman territory of Deli Orman (in North-Western Bulgaria, between Ruschuk and Varna). In both places the insurrections were crushed by the Ottoman Government with the utmost energy and ferocity (see Babinger, Fr.: 'Schejch Bedr-ed-Din' in *Der Islam*, vols. xi and xii). It is one of the curiosities of history that the scene of Mustafā's insurrection on Qāraburun in A.D. 1416 should have been within sight of the scene of Aristonicus's at Leucae, just across the Gulf of Smyrna, in 132 B.C. (see p. 69, above); for there is an unmistakable kinship between the two movements. According to Sheykh Bedr-ed-Dīn's contemporary, the Orthodox Christian historian Michael Ducas (chap. 21), the two main planks in the Sheykh's platform were a fraternization between Muslims and Christians and a communism in everything except wives. One is reminded of Aristonicus's common call to freemen and slaves, and of his attempt to establish, in real life, the Communist Utopia of Iambulus (see V. C (i) (d) 11, Annex I, vol. vi, p. 351, below).

[3] See I. C (i) (b), Annex I, vol. i, pp. 365 and 382–3, above.

[4] For the state of the Bektāshī movement in the latter part of the seventeenth century of the Christian Era see Rycaut, op. cit., Book II, chaps. 12 and 19, and also the present Study, IV. C (ii) (b) 1, vol. iv, pp. 68–9, above, and V. C (i) (c) 3, in the present volume, p. 295, below.

[5] See Part III. A, vol. iii, pp. 26–7, and IV. C (ii) (b) 1, vol. iv, p. 68, above, and V. C (ii) (b), vol. vi, pp. 298–300, below.

last long enough for the religious ferment which attracted Rycaut's attention in the second quarter of the seventeenth century to brew up out of the *colluvies gentium*[1] that had been collected and confounded in an Ottoman sump, like the ingredients of a cocktail in a shaker, by the cumulative operation of slave-raids and wars of conquest which had been at work, by Rycaut's day, for more than three centuries. The Mongol Peace (*durabat circa* 1280–1351)[2] was too brief to give time for the troubling of the waters in this case to produce its normal after-effects. The foregoing Mongol ravages, however, surpassed the Ottoman ravages in material scale in the measure of the difference in physical magnitude between the main body of the Far Eastern Society and the main body of Orthodox Christendom. While the alien Ottoman builders of an Orthodox Christian universal state ranged beyond the proper bounds of the society on which they were imposing their peace as far afield as Hungary and Azerbaijan and the Yaman and Algeria, the alien Mongol builders of a Far Eastern universal state likewise pushed their raids as far as Hungary in a westerly direction, while eastward they subjugated Korea and southward invaded Burma. From all quarters of the immense tract of European and Asiatic territory that was comprised within these extreme limits, the Mongol stockmen 'lifted' droves of human cattle from their native pastures and herded them together in human cattle-pens which they had hastily constructed in the heart of the Eurasian Steppe. The multiplicity and variety of the diverse cultures which were thus forced into an involuntary intercourse with one another as a result of this titanic Mongol 'round-up' might have produced a social and spiritual ferment of unexampled energy if the Mongol Peace had not fallen short of the Ottoman Peace in its Time-span as signally as it surpassed it in its spacial extension.

In the event the *Pax Mongolica* collapsed, after its ephemeral heyday, as suddenly and unexpectedly as it had sprung into existence; and, upon its collapse, the *colluvies gentium* which had been swept together at Saray-on-Volga and at Qaraqorum-on-Orkhon and at Peking-within-the-Wall either dispersed and evaporated or was absorbed and assimilated or was segregated and sterilized without having been given the time to fulfil its 'manifest destiny' of 'making history'. The sensational history which might have been made in 'the Cauldron of the North',[3] if Time and Chance had been auspicious, will leap, however, to

---

[1] Livy, Book IV, chap. 2, § 5.
[2] See II. D (v), vol. ii, p. 121; Part III. A, vol. iii, p. 25; Part III. A, Annex II, vol. ii, pp. 416–17, above; and V. C (i) (c) 4, in the present volume, pp. 348–51, and Table I, attached to V. C (iii), vol. vi, p. 327, below.
[3] Jer. i. 13; Ezek. xi. 3 and 7, and xxiv. 1–14.

the eye of any reader of the surviving narratives of those Western observers who visited the head-quarters of the Mongol Khāqān and broke their long journey at the camps of his vassal-princes in the outlying appanages of the Mongol Empire on the morrow of its establishment.[1] For a moment of time in the thirteenth century of the Christian Era Saray and Qaraqorum and Peking bade fair to become as potent 'melting-pots' as a nineteenth-century New York or as a Rome whose dilution of the Tiber with the Orontes has been immortalized in famous lines of Juvenal that have already been quoted.[2] The fact is attested by the following passages from the pen of a Flemish friar of the Franciscan order who made his adventurous journey to Qaraqorum and back in A.D. 1253–5.

'There is a fair or market following the court of Bātū at all times; but it was so far distant from us that we could not reach it. We were constrained to walk on foot for want of horses. At length certain Hungarians, who had once been clerks, found us, and one of them could sing many songs without book, and was looked upon by other Hungarians as a priest, and was sent to funerals of his deceased countrymen. There was another of them also well instructed in grammar; for he could understand the meaning of everything that we spoke, but could not answer. These Hungarians were a great comfort to us, bringing us *cosmos* [qumyz] to drink, and sometimes flesh to eat. . . .

'Upon a certain day a Cuman accompanying us saluted us in Latin, saying *Salvete, domini*. Wondering at this, and saluting him in return, I demanded of him who had taught him that kind of salutation. He said that he was baptized in Hungary by our friars, and that from them he had learned it. . . .

'I inquired . . . of the city of Talas, where there lived certain Teutons . . . of whom Friar Andrew made mention.[3] Concerning these men, I also inquired very diligently in the courts of Sartak and Bātū, but I could get no information of them . . . till I had come to the court of Mangū Khan. And there I was informed that Mangū Khan had removed them out of the jurisdiction of Bātū, for the space of a month's journey from Talas, eastward, to a certain village called Bulaq, where they are set to dig gold and to make armour. . . .

'A few days later we entered upon those alps where the Qāra Qitay people were wont to inhabit. . . . And there we found a certain village where there were Saracens, speaking the Persian language, though they dwelt a huge distance from Persia. . . .

[At Qaraqorum, where the Khāqān Mangū held his court,] 'we

---

[1] The principal documents, apart from Marco Polo's well-known and frequently published book, will be found in Beazley, C. R.: *The Texts and Versions of John de Plano Carpini and William de Rubruquis* (London 1903, Hakluyt Society), and Komroff, M.: *Contemporaries of Marco Polo* (London 1928, Cape).
[2] On p. 67, above.
[3] This Friar Andrew had visited the court of the Mongol Khāqān in the reign of Kuyuk Khan (*imperabat* A.D. 1246–8).—A.J.T.

went to a large house that we found cold and without a supply of fuel. We were still without food, and it was night. . . . A woman of Metz in Lorraine, called Paquette, and who had been a prisoner in Hungary, found us out and prepared for us a feast of the best she could. She belonged to the court of that lady who was Christian and of whom I have already spoken; she told us of the unheard-of misery she had suffered before coming to the court. But she was fairly well off, for she had a young Russian husband who made her the mother of three little children, and he was a carpenter, which is a good position among the Tatars. Among other things, she told us that there was in Qaraqorum a goldsmith named William, originally from Paris. His family name was Buchier, the name of his father Laurant Buchier. She believed, too, that he had a brother who lived on the Grand Pont and who was called Roger Buchier. . . .

'On Palm Sunday [A.D. 1254] we were at Qaraqorum. . . . The mass said, evening approached, and Master William took us with him to his home for supper, in great joy. His wife was the daughter of one Larraine, and born in Hungary. She spoke French and Cuman well. We met there another European named Basil, the son of an Englishman and born in Hungary, and who spoke the same languages.'[1]

These fellow Western Christians with whom the Flemish Friar William fell in at Qaraqorum and on his journey thither were only one of many contingents of *déracinés* whom the Mongol raiders had carried away captive to the mushroom-capital of an embryonic Far Eastern universal state. Among the new recruits who were thus forcibly levied and conscripted into a Far Eastern proletariat there were also Orthodox Christian Alans and Russians; there were Muslim Turks and Iranians and Monophysite Christian Armenians from an aged Syriac World to which the Mongol invaders had dealt a *coup de grâce*;[2] there were Lamaist Mahayanian Buddhists from Tibet; there were Catholic Mahayanian Buddhists and Taoists and Confucians from China; and there were the Manichaeans and the Nestorian Christians who were already long since at home in the oases of the Eurasian Steppe[3] before Chingis Khan started on his career of conquest. In the course of his anabasis Friar William was not only consoled and fortified by meeting co-religionists: he was also stimulated or exasperated, according to the circumstances, by encounters with representatives of the competing faiths. At an early stage in his journey, on Whitsun Eve, 1253, he was approached by

[1] *Itinerarium Fratris Willielmi de Rubruquis* [Rubruck], *de Ordine Fratrum Minorum, Galli, Anno Gratiae 1253, ad Partes Orientales*, English translation by Komroff, M., in *Contemporaries of Marco Polo* (London 1928, Cape), pp. 120–1, 126–7, 149–50, 172.
[2] See I. C (i) (*b*), vol. i, p. 72; II. D (vii), Annex VIII, vol. ii, pp. 449–52; IV. C (ii) (*b*) 1, vol. iv, p. 67, above.
[3] For the infiltration of Manichaeism and Nestorian Christianity from the Syriac World into the Far East see II. D (vi), vol. ii, pp. 237–8; II. D (vii), vol. ii, p. 375; II. D (vii), Annex VIII, vol. ii, pp. 449–50, above.

some Alan adherents of the Orthodox Church who besought this passing Western priest for instruction in Christian doctrine and observance.[1] On Whitsunday itself he was approached by a Muslim whom he instructed and all but converted.[2] He found Bātū Khan's son Sartak under the influence of Nestorian counsellors, and suspected the prince of being a crypto-Nestorian himself.[3] When he arrived at Bātū's own court, he raised a laugh among the courtiers by boldly adjuring their master to embrace the Catholic Faith.[4] In his passage through Uighuristan he visited a Buddhist temple and entered into a theological disputation with the monks.[5] After his arrival at Qaraqorum the first trace of Christianity upon which he stumbled was a chapel served by an Armenian monk;[6] and thereafter he found 'a swarm of Christians—Hungarians, Alans, Ruthenians, Georgians, Armenians'[7]—in the Khāqān's capital. When Mangū Khan granted Friar William an audience, the missionary preached the Catholic Faith to the Khāqān as boldly as he had preached it to Mangū's cousin Bātū; and Mangū responded by arranging for the holding of a theological disputation.[8] His secretaries first took down in writing depositions from the friar and his Nestorian and pagan competitors, and thereafter the three parties were called upon to defend their respective theses by word of mouth before a board of examiners consisting of one pagan, one Muslim, and one Christian. In a subsequent interview Mangū expounded his own religious beliefs in a latitudinarian vein which the Mongol Emperor's Catholic interlocutor interpreted as a confession of agnosticism.[9]

It will be seen that, at this early stage in the history of the universal state which was being imposed on the Far Eastern World by Mongol arms, the competition between the diverse religions of the *déracinés* from all quarters of the Earth who were then being thrown into a Far Eastern 'melting-pot' was already exciting the curiosity of the Mongol master of this enormous empire. And on this showing we may surmise that, if the

---

[1] *The Journal of Friar William of Rubruck*, chap. 13 (Komroff, pp. 98–9).
[2] 'He . . . said that he desired to be baptized. But, when we prepared ourselves for baptizing him, he suddenly mounted on horseback, saying that he would go home and consult with his wife what were best to be done. On the next day he told us that he could in no case receive baptism, because then he could drink no more qumyz.'—Rubruck, op. cit., chap. 14 (Komroff, p. 99.)
[3] Ibid., chaps. 17 and 18 (ibid., pp. 106–11).
[4] Ibid., op. cit., chap. 21 (ibid., p. 118).
[5] Ibid., op. cit., chap. 27 (ibid., pp. 130–2).
[6] Ibid., op. cit., chap. 31 (ibid., pp. 143–4).
[7] Ibid., op. cit., chap. 48 (ibid., p. 174).
[8] Ibid., op. cit., chap. 51 (ibid., pp. 183–92).
[9] 'The [Armenian] monk told me that the Khan believes only the Christians, but that he wants everybody to pray for him. The monk lied, for the Khan believes in no one, as you shall soon learn.'—Ibid., op. cit., chap. 37 (ibid., p. 153).

Pax Mongolica had lasted, some notable religious experiences and discoveries would have followed. As it was, the Mongol khans and hordes of the several branches of the House of Chingis did all eventually exchange their own primitive paganism for one or other of the 'higher religions' of the peoples, west of the Great Wall, who were temporarily engulfed in the Far Eastern internal proletariat as a result of the Mongol conquests. Mangū Khan's own brother and successor Qubilay Khan (*imperabat* A.D. 1257-94) was attracted by his Tibetan subjects' Lamaistic Maha-yanian Buddhism; and this was the religion to which his successors were tardily converted some two hundred years after their expulsion from China.[1] Their cousins in the appanages of Chagha-tāy and Jūjī were converted to the orthodox Sunnī form of Islam,[2] and so, in the end, were the Il-Khans of Iran and 'Irāq, after they had tried, as alternatives, both Nestorianism and the Shī'ah.[3] On the other hand the Mongol Empire broke down and broke up before any of these alien faiths had gained any deep or lasting hold upon the mass of the Far Eastern internal proletariat in Intramural China.

The tincture of Western Christianity which was introduced into the Far East under a Mongol aegis by a series of pioneer-missionaries—from Friar John of Pian di Carpini, who made his journey to Kuyuk Khan's court in A.D. 1245-7, to Friar Odoric of Pordenone, who visited Peking in the third decade of the fourteenth century—had evaporated without leaving a trace by the time when Saint Francis Xavier inaugurated the second attempt to convert China to Catholicism; Nestorianism and Mani-chaeism seem to have been absorbed into the Chinese tradition without making any visible mark on it; and even Islam, though it did succeed in gaining a permanent foothold in China thanks to the opportunities which it temporarily enjoyed there under the Mongol régime, remained segregated in the far north-western provinces of Kansu and Shensi and in the new far southern province of Yunnan which was carved out of a barbarian no-man's-land by Mongol military enterprise. The Muslim element which survives down to this day in the Chinese population of these three provinces is the most substantial monument, in China, of the short-lived and abortive alien universal state which the Mongols once provided for a disintegrating Far Eastern Society. Yet, although this exotic community has contrived to hold its

---

[1] See Part III. A, Annex II, vol. iii, p. 451, footnote 1, and IV. C (iii) (*c*) 3 (α), vol. iv, p. 497, above.
[2] See II. D (v), vol. ii, p. 145, above.
[3] See I. C (i) (*b*), Annex I, vol. i, pp. 363-4, and II. D (vii), Annex VIII, vol. ii, p. 451.

ground on the fringes of China, it has remained, even there, a peculiar people; and on Chinese ground there has been no fruitful union between Islam and any indigenous religion or philosophy. The student of the morphology of Religion will search in vain for any Chinese counterpart of the Indian syncretisms between Islam and Hinduism or the Near Eastern syncretisms between Islam and Christianity. To find a Chinese analogue of Kabirism and Sikhism and Bedreddinism and Bektashism the observer must travel far afield in both Time and Space. He must skip the Ming interlude between the Mongol and the Manchu régime, and must then shift the focus of his attention from the hinterland of Peking in the thirteenth century to the hinterland of Canton in the nineteenth century, if he wishes to catch a glimpse of a dynamic impact of alien religious ideas upon the native Chinese tradition. As we have seen above,[1] it was in Kwangsi in the middle of the nineteenth century, when the Manchu régime, in its turn, was verging towards its fall, that some casual grains of Protestant Christianity, mingling with the traditional Chinese *Weltanschauung* in the soul of a Hung Hsiu-ch'uan, produced the explosive mixture which discharged itself in the militant movement of the 'T'aip'ing'.

The Babylonic and the Syriac Internal Proletariat.

If we now pass to the Babylonic World, we shall find that the ferment of religious experience and discovery in the souls of a sorely tried internal proletariat was as active in South-Western Asia under the Assyrian terror of the eighth and seventh centuries B.C. as it was, round the Hellenized shores of the Mediterranean Basin, under a Roman terror which set in with the outbreak of the Hannibalic War and did not give way to a Roman Peace until after the Battle of Actium.

Through the agency of Assyrian arms the disintegrating Babylonic Society expanded geographically in two directions, as the disintegrating Orthodox Christian Society expanded through the prowess of the East Roman militarists[2] and their successors the 'Osmanlis, and the disintegrating Hellenic Society through the conquests of alien ground that were made by the Macedonians and the Romans. Eastward, beyond the Zagros, in Iran, the Assyrians anticipated the Romans' exploits in Europe beyond the Appennines by subjugating a host of primitive societies; westward, beyond the Euphrates, they anticipated the Macedonians' exploits on the Asiatic side of the Dardanelles by subjugating

[1] On p. 107.
[2] See IV. C (iii) (c) 2 (β), vol. iv, pp. 399–403 and p. 403, footnote 3, above.

more than one alien civilization; and the two alien civilizations—the Syriac and the Egyptiac—which were thus forcibly incorporated, for the moment, into the Babylonic internal proletariat were actually identical with two of the four which were afterwards temporarily incorporated into the Hellenic internal proletariat *post Alexandrum*. Nor were these alien victims of Babylonic militarism simply conquered without being uprooted. The classic examples of the forcible deportation of a conquered population are the transplantation of the Israelites by the Assyrian war-lord Sargon to the opposite frontiers of an expanding Babylonic World in the recently subjugated barbarian country on the western fringes of Iran, and the transplantation of the Jews by the Neo-Babylonian war-lord Nebuchadnezzar to the heart of the Babylonic World in Babylonia itself.

The compulsory exchange of populations was the sovereign device of Babylonic imperialism for breaking the spirit of conquered peoples and, above all, destroying their political *esprit de corps*; and the atrocity was by no means exclusively inflicted upon aliens and barbarians. In their own fratricidal warfare the dominant Powers of the Babylonic World did not scruple to mete out the same treatment to one another; and the Samaritan community[1]—of which a few hundred representatives can be seen, still living under the shadow of Mount Gerizim, in the present mandated territory of Palestine—is a monument of the transplantation to Syria, by Assyrian hands, of deportees from several cities of Babylonia, including the metropolis itself. The Assyrian Government's intention was to wipe out the national consciousness of the proudest and most venerable of the four sister nations[2] in the Babylonic body social, and at the same time to fill a vacuum which had been left in the recently conquered territories in Syria after the transplantation of a number of the native Israelites to Media;[3] but in the end it was the Babylonians with their Median allies, and not the Assyrians, who emerged victorious from the Assyro-Babylonian Hundred-and-Forty Years' War;[4] and at that stage it was both impossible and unnecessary for the Babylonians to deal with the Assyrians as the Assyrians had

---

[1] See Gaster, M.: *The Samaritans* (Oxford 1923, University Press).

[2] See I. C (i) (*b*), vol. i, p. 116, and II. D (v), vol. ii, pp. 135 and 137, above.

[3] The Assyrians seem not to have deported entire populations *en masse*, but to have contented themselves with carrying away captive certain selected classes—the political-minded or the skilful-handed—while the peasantry were left, helpless and leaderless, on their ancestral lands. Both the Israelites who were planted in the cities of the Medes and the Babylonians who were planted in the cities of Israel were probably minorities; and the survival of an Israelitish peasantry in the countryside of Samaria would account for the eventual victory of the indigenous Syriac over the intrusive Babylonic element in the Samaritan religion (see p. 125, footnote 1, below).

[4] For this devastating war and its outcome see IV. C (iii) (*c*) 3 (α), vol. iv, pp. 476–84, above.

dealt with them; for by that time there were no more Assyrians left to deal with. By intercalating recurrent domestic revolutions between their perpetual foreign wars, the Assyrians had achieved the extraordinary feat of annihilating themselves;[1] and, apart from a miserable remnant of squatters who continued to preserve the Assyrian name on the site of the city of Asshur itself,[2] perhaps the only survivors of the Assyrian nation were the offspring of Assyrian garrisons in the former provinces of the Assyrian Empire who purchased their survival at the price of losing their political identity and being absorbed into the surrounding native population. In the Assyrian homeland itself the Assyrian nation was being supplanted by its Syriac victims even before the collapse of the Assyrian state, as is attested by the progress of the conquered peoples' Aramaic language at the expense of the conquerors' Akkadian.[3]

It will be seen that the *furor Assyriacus* did not spend itself before it had brought into existence a Babylonic internal proletariat which bore a singularly close resemblance to the Hellenic internal proletariat in its origin and composition and experience; and the two trees brought forth similar fruits. While the later incorporation of the Syriac Society into the Hellenic internal proletariat was to bear fruit at the beginning of the Christian Era in the birth of Christianity out of Judaism, the earlier incorporation of the same Syriac Society into the Babylonic internal proletariat bore fruit in and after the eighth century B.C. in the birth of Judaism itself out of the primitive religion of one of the parochial communities into which the Syriac Society had come to be articulated.[4]

---

[1] See IV. C (iii) (*c*) 3 (α), vol. iv, pp. 480–2, above.   [2] Ibid., p. 470, above.
[3] For this victory of Aramaic over Akkadian see I. C (i) (*b*), vol. i, p. 79, and IV. C (iii) (*c*) 3 (α), vol. iv, p. 484, above, and V. C (i) (*d*) 6 (γ), in the present volume, pp. 487–91 and 499, footnote 5, below.
[4] For the nature of the primitive religion of Israel see IV. C (iii) (*c*) 2 (α), vol. iv, p. 262, above, and V. C (i) (*d*) 7, vol. vi, pp. 39–49, below. It will be seen that, while Judaism and Christianity appear to be 'philosophically contemporary and equivalent' (in the sense in which these terms have been used in I. C (iii) (*c*) and (*d*), vol. i, above) in so far as they can be regarded simply as products of the disintegration of two societies of the species which we have called 'civilizations', there is another angle of vision from which they present themselves in the quite different aspect of successive stages in a single 'ascending' process of spiritual enlightenment. In this picture Christianity stands, not side by side with Judaism, but on its shoulders, while they both tower above the primitive religion of Israel. Nor is the enlightenment of the Prophets of Israel and Judah in and after the eighth century B.C. the only intervening stage of which we have a record or a hint in the chronological and spiritual interval between the primitive worship of Yahweh and the epiphany of Christ. Before and below the Prophets, the Biblical tradition presents us with a Moses, and before and below Moses with an Abraham. These dim figures are regarded by one school of modern Western 'higher critics' as mere creatures of a primitive mythopoeic imagination, and by another school as at least partially authentic historical persons who have left their marks upon 'folk memory'. The student of history will observe that the tradition places both Abraham and Moses in the same historical setting as the Prophets and as Christ, if history is regarded as a conspectus of the rises and falls of civilizations. While Christ made his

The genesis of this 'higher religion' of Judaism among the submerged Syriac elements in the Babylonic internal proletariat has left an incomparably full and clear record of itself in the books of the pre-Exilic Prophets of Israel and Judah; and in these living and breathing memorials of a tremendous spiritual travail the burning question is the issue—already familiar to us from the Hellenic case—between the gentle and the violent way of facing an internal proletariat's ordeal. Moreover, Gentleness eventually prevailed over Violence in this case likewise; for the 'Time of Troubles', as it reached and passed its climax, delivered a series of hammer-stroke lessons which taught even the 'Die-Hards' in the tribe of Judah the futility of attempting to repay Violence in its own kind. The new 'higher religion' which was born in eighth-century Syria, in Syriac communities which were then still being pounded on their native threshing-floor by an As-syrian flail, was brought to maturity in sixth-century and fifth-century Babylonia among the uprooted and deported descendants of one of these battered Syriac peoples.

Like the Oriental slave-deportees in Roman Italy, the Jewish exiles in Nebuchadnezzar's Babylon were proof against the facile adaptability of the Russian slave-deportees in Ottoman Rumelia.[1] These uprooted Syriac members of the Babylonic internal proletariat were no chameleons.

'If I forget thee, O Jerusalem, may my right hand forget her cunning.
'If I do not remember thee, let my tongue cleave to the roof of my mouth.'[2]

Yet the memory of their home which these exiles cherished in a strange land was not just a negative imprint: it was a positive act of inspired imaginative creation. In the unearthly light of this vision seen through a mist of tears the fallen fastness became transfigured into a holy city built on a rock against which the gates of Hell should not prevail.[3] And the captives who refused to indulge their captors' whim by singing them one of the songs of Sion, and stubbornly hanged up their harps on the willows[4] by Euphrates' stream, were at that very moment composing an inaudible new melody on the invisible instrument of their hearts.

appearance in This World just after the close of a Hellenic 'Time of Troubles' and the Prophets made theirs in the midst of a Babylonic 'Time of Troubles', the epiphany of Moses is traditionally associated with the decadence of 'the New Empire' of Egypt, which was a restoration of the Egyptiac universal state, and the epiphany of Abraham with the last days of the Sumeric universal state, after its short-lived reconstruction by the energetic hands of Hammurabi. This relation between recurrent break-downs and disintegrations of civilizations and an apparently progressive process of religious enlightenment is examined further in Part VII, below.
[1] See the present chapter, p. 110, above.
[2] Ps. cxxxvii. 5–6.   [3] Matt. xvi. 18.   [4] Ps. cxxxvii. 1.

'By the waters of Babylon we sat down and wept when we remembered thee, O Sion';

and, in that weeping, the enlightenment of Jewry was accomplished.

It is evident that, in the successive religious reactions of Syriac conscripts in the ranks of an alien internal proletariat, the parallel between Babylonic and Hellenic history is very close; but the response evoked from the internal proletariat by the Babylonic dominant minority's challenge was the richer of the two in so far as it came not only from those victims who were members of an alien civilization but from the barbarian victims as well. Whereas the European and North-West African barbarians who were forcibly incorporated into the Hellenic internal proletariat by Roman arms made no religious discoveries of their own, but simply accepted the seed that was sown among them by their fellow proletarians of Oriental origin, the Iranian barbarians who were passed under the Assyrian harrow begot a native prophet in the person of Zarathustra, the founder of Zoroastrianism. The date of Zarathustra is a matter of dispute among modern Western scholars, and by the same token they are unable to tell us whether his religious discovery was an independent response to the common challenge of Assyrian militarism which was presented to Iranians and Syrians simultaneously, or whether his voice was only an echo of the cry of Israelite prophets who had been marooned in 'the cities of the Medes'.[1] It is evident, however, that, whatever the original relations between these two 'higher religions' may have been, Zoroastrianism and Judaism met on equal terms in their maturity and that, in their spiritual commerce during the Achaemenian and the Macedonian Age, the Iranian religion gave the Syrian religion at least as much inspiration as it received from it.[2] The spiritual power that was thus displayed by Zoroastrianism in the second chapter of its history is presumptive evidence that the new 'higher religion' of the barbarian wing of the Babylonic internal proletariat was a powerful spiritual force from the beginning.[3]

[1] This question has been touched upon already in I. C (i) (b), vol. i, p. 81, above. See further Pettazzone, R.: La Religione di Zarathustra (Bologna 1920, Zanichelli), pp. 82–4. It may be noted in this connexion that the human adversaries who are equated in the Gāthās with the Powers of Evil are not the Assyrians but the Eurasian Nomads, who swept out of the Steppe on to the Iranian and Anatolian plateaux in the seventh century B.C. (see II. D (v), vol. ii, pp. 136–7 and 138–9, and Part III. A, Annex II, vol. iii, p. 410, above).

[2] See von Gall, A.: Βασιλεία τοῦ Θεοῦ (Heidelberg 1926, Winter), passim, and Meyer, E.: Ursprung und Anfänge des Christentums, vol. ii (Stuttgart and Berlin 1921, Cotta), pp. 95–120, 179, and 190–204, as well as the present study, V. C (i) (d) 6 (δ), in the present volume, p. 536; V. C (i) (d) 7, vol. vi, pp. 43–4; V. C (i) (d) 9 (γ), vol. vi, p. 126, footnote 5, and p. 129, footnote 2; and V. C (i) (d) 11, vol. vi, p. 163, footnote 1, below.

[3] For the remarkable vein of intellectual abstraction which appears to have been one of the original features of Zarathustra's system see V. C (i) (d) 7, vol. vi, p. 43, footnote 4, below.

At any rate, when the Babylonic 'Time of Troubles' was brought to an end by the overthrow and annihilation of Assyria, and the Babylonic World passed on into a universal state in the shape of the Neo-Babylonian Empire, it looked as though Judaism and Zoroastrianism—the new faiths of the Syrian and Iranian wings of the Babylonic internal proletariat—would compete with one another for the privilege of establishing a universal church within the political framework that was now being provided by the Babylonic dominant minority—as, in the disintegration of the Hellenic body social, Christianity and Mithraism and the worships of Isis and Cybele did compete with the weapons of the spirit in the arena of the Roman Empire. At this juncture, however, the course of history was abruptly changed by a sudden and dramatic reversal in the relations between the apparently victorious Babylonic and the apparently vanquished Syriac Society.

This *peripeteia* was the retribution for the unusual deadliness of the injury which the Babylonic dominant minority had inflicted upon itself, during the Babylonic 'Time of Troubles', as well as upon the alien societies within striking distance. Out of the four national states—Babylonia, Assyria, Elam, and Urartu— into which the Babylonic body social had been articulated, one— Assyria—had been annihilated and two others—Elam and Urartu —had been prostrated and overwhelmed by the beginning of the sixth century B.C.; and the sole survivor—Babylonia—who was left to establish the Babylonic universal state, was suffering too severely from the shock of the Assyro-Babylonian Hundred-and-Forty Years' War to be capable of executing this heavy task single-handed. Babylonia could never have carried the long duel with her far more powerful Assyrian sister to a victorious conclusion if the Iranian barbarians had not lent her their formidably decisive aid;[1] and, while the Neo-Babylonian Empire was attempting to serve as a Babylonic universal state, it was living all the time under the shadow of a Median peril. This peril might perhaps have been exorcized, or at any rate mitigated, if the menacing barbarians had been converted to the Babylonic Civilization; but, as we have seen, the Iranians were actually converted to the Syriac Civilization instead;[2] and therewith, for Nabonidus and Belshazzar, the menace of a barbarian avalanche was merged in the still more terrible menace of a Syriac encircle-

[1] In this respect Babylonia's victory over Assyria with the aid of Median arms at the close of the seventh century B.C. may be compared with France's victory in A.D. 1918 over Germany with the aid of the English-speaking Powers. In A.D. 1938 it looked as though the same historical drama might be re-acted by China, Japan, and the Soviet Union.

[2] See I. C (i) (*b*), vol. i, pp. 79–81; II. D (v), vol. ii, pp. 137–8; IV. C (iii) (*c*) 3 (α), vol. iv, p. 471, above.

ment. The blow fell; the roles were reversed; the Achaemenian Empire supplanted the Neo-Babylonian Empire as the political framework within which the two rising religions of Judaism and Zoroastrianism were to propagate themselves; and the Achaemenian Empire was a Syriac and not a Babylonic universal state; for it was an empire in which the Babylonians found themselves a subject and aggrieved instead of a ruling and self-satisfied community,[1] while the new Iranian masters of South-Western Asia allowed the Babylonians' Jewish victims to return from exile to their Syrian fatherland and took the Babylonians' Phoenician vassals into an honourable partnership in the management of an empire which dwarfed Nebuchadnezzar's.[2]

[1] See the present chapter, p. 94, above, and V. C (i) (c) 4, in the present volume, p. 347, and V. C (ii) (a), Annex II, vol. vi, p. 442, below.

[2] Under the Achaemenian régime the four Phoenician city-states—Sidon, Tyre, Byblus, Aradus—each not only enjoyed their own local autonomy, but were actually allowed by the Achaemenian Imperial Government to reign respectively over four miniature *imperia in imperio*. The island city-state of Aradus was mistress on the mainland of a territory which included Marathus and Mariamme and extended eastward from the coast into the interior right up to the Orontes. On Sidon the Achaemenidae bestowed the Plain of Sharon, including Dora and Joppa, while Tyre bore rule over Ascalon and over some city, unidentified, on the coast of the Bay of Acre. Gaza and Ashdod seem to have been the only two Philistine cities that escaped 'mediatization' (to use the corresponding technical term in the constitutional vocabulary of the Holy Roman Empire) and that continued to depend directly upon the Achaemenian Pādishāh instead of being subordinated to one or other of the four Phoenician imperial cities (see Jones, A. H. M.: *The Cities of the Eastern Roman Provinces* (Oxford 1937, Clarendon Press), pp. 234–5). In the fourth century B.C. the Phoenician city-states were federated with one another—the seat of the federal institutions being at Tripolis (Jones, op. cit., pp. 231–2; Meyer, E.: *Geschichte des Altertums*, vol. iii (Stuttgart 1901, Cotta), pp. 138–40). On the other hand the general Achaemenian policy of studied respect for pre-existing local institutions—political, legal, and religious—was eventually defeated in Babylonia by the irreconcilable hostility of the Babylonians to an alien dominion, however moderately exercised and discreetly veiled. Whereas Cyrus had been careful to have himself installed as legitimate King of Babylon, in so far as legitimacy could be conferred by a strict observance of the traditional ceremonies of investiture (see Meyer, op. cit., vol. iii, p. 129), Xerxes followed Sennacherib's example in deliberately refraining from 'taking the hands of Bel' on New Year's Day, 484 B.C. The revolt of Babylonia in the autumn of the same year was the last act of Babylonian recalcitrance with which the Achaemenian Government had to contend, for it was suppressed with such severity that, for the next hundred and fifty years, Babylonia lay sullenly passive under the Achaemenian yoke, until Alexander entered Babylon as a liberator and raised the temple of Bel from its ruins (Meyer, op. cit., pp. 129–32; cf. the present chapter of the present Study, p. 94, above, as well as V. C (i) (c) 4, pp. 347–8, and V. C (ii) (a), Annex II, vol. vi, p. 442, below). The overthrow of the Achaemenian Empire by Macedonian arms brought with it a reversal of fortune for Phoenicia as well as for Babylonia. Before Alexander had been welcomed as a liberator by Babylon he had taken Tyre by storm and had put her to the sack in reprisal for her obstinate loyalty to the lost cause of the last Darius. Thereafter, under a Seleucid régime which continued to treat Babylonia with Alexander's considerateness (see Tarn, W. W.: *The Greeks in Bactria and India* (Cambridge 1938, University Press), pp. 56–7), the Phoenicians suffered further reverses. For example, in 259 B.C., when the Aradian monarchy was replaced by republican institutions in the imperial city itself, the Aradian empire on the mainland was simultaneously broken up into city-state republics each depending directly upon the Seleucid Government. When the Seleucid Empire itself broke up at the turn of the second and the last century B.C., Aradus recovered her dominion over Marathus and some other fragments of her former continental empire (Jones, op. cit., pp. 239–40), but in 38 B.C. these possessions were taken away from her again, and this time once for all, by Marcus Antonius (Jones, op. cit., pp. 261–2). These blows were not offset by the spread of Phoenician, at the heels of Greek, traders eastward, overland, into 'Upper Asia' (see Tarn, op. cit., p. 10).

The transformation of the Achaemenian Empire from a semi-Babylonic into a wholly

In a world in which the turn of Fortune's wheel had thus put down the Babylonians from their seat and had exalted Zoroaster's Achaemenian converts and the Jews' Phoenician cousins, the triumph of Judaism[1] and Zoroastrianism might have been expected to be more certain and more rapid than it would have been if Belshazzar's Kingdom had not been given to the Medes and Persians.[2] But Fortune intervened again to give another unexpected

Syriac universal state can be followed in the history of the Achaemenian Government's official scripts and languages. For inscriptions on stone the Babylonic cuneiform script was employed, and every inscription was trilingual—the three languages in which it was inscribed being those of the three official capitals: Elamite for Susa, Medo-Persian for Ecbatana, and Assyro-Babylonian for Babylon (Meyer, op. cit., p. 28). For the conveyance of the Medo-Persian language a special simplified version of the cuneiform script was devised. Under the later Achaemenids, however, there was a noticeable increase in the faultiness of the rendering of the cuneiform script, and this suggests that it had come by then to be an anachronism which was being perpetuated officially after it had been abandoned in ordinary life (Meyer, op. cit., p. 48). *Pari passu* with this decay of the cuneiform script there was an increase in the vogue of the Aramaic script and language. Under the Achaemenian régime Aramaic was the official provincial language for all the western provinces of the Empire—including Egypt and Anatolia, where it was not indigenous as a vernacular (Meyer, op. cit., pp. 47-8, and idem: *Der Papyrusfund von Elephantine* (Leipzig 1912, Hinrichs), p. 17; the present Study, V. C (i) (d) 6 (γ), p. 499, below). The Persian language itself was already being written in Aramaic characters on papyrus before the end of the Achaemenian Age (Meyer, *Papyrusfund*, p. 17).

[1] Eduard Meyer has gone so far as to declare that 'Judaism is a creation of the Persian Empire' (*Der Papyrusfund von Elephantine*, p. 96).

[2] The propagation of these would-be universal religions among the population of the Achaemenian Empire must also have been facilitated by the fact that—mild and even benevolent though the Achaemenian êthos was by contrast with the Assyrian (Meyer, op. cit., pp. 44-5)—the Assyrian practice of uprooting and transplanting was not altogether abandoned under the Achaemenian régime. For example, the Great King colonized the formidably torrid islands in the Persian Gulf by planting them with deportees who were officially known as *les déracinés* (οἱ ἀνάσπαστοί); and these appear to have been Iranians, to judge by the type of equipment and armament that is ascribed to them in the catalogue of Xerxes' expeditionary force (compare Herodotus, Book III, chap. 93, with Book VII, chap. 80). Apart from these presumably disloyal members of the dominant minority in the Achaemenian Empire, the principal victims of the deportation-policy appear to have been the recalcitrant members of the Greek subject population. Darius the Great's general Otanes 'netted' the island of Samos and swept it bare of all inhabitants (Herodotus, Book III, chap. 149); and other commanders of the same emperor's forces carried away captive to Susa the people of the Greek city of Barca in Libya (Herodotus, Book IV, chap. 204), of the Greek city of Miletus in Ionia (Herodotus, Book VI, chap. 20), and of the Greek city of Eretria in Eubœa (Herodotus, Book VI, chap. 119). These four cases of severity were perhaps exceptional; for we are expressly informed by the Greek historian—who would not go out of his way to present the Achaemenian régime in an unduly favourable light—that Otanes was acting, under provocation, in contravention of Darius's orders that the Samians were neither to be massacred nor to be enslaved (Herodotus, Book III, chap. 147), while, as for the deported Eretrians, Darius is recorded to have taken pity on them when he had them in his power and to have settled them comfortably on an estate of his own in Elam (Herodotus, Book VI, chap. 119). The Milesian deportees were settled at the mouth of the River Tigris (Book VI, chap. 20), and the Barcaeans in Bactria (Book IV, chap. 204). These indications suggest that the favourable picture of the Achaemenidae which has been painted for us in the Jewish tradition is on the whole true to life. The Greeks themselves are, as we have noticed already (in V. C (i) (c) 1, pp. 50-2, above), the most impressive of the witnesses in the Persians' favour. It is noteworthy, however, that—to judge by a passing remark of Plato's—the Greeks appear to have assumed that, if they had succumbed to Xerxes, it would have been their fate to have been swallowed up in the Syriac internal proletariat:

'If the common determination of the Athenians and the Lacedaemonians had not rescued Hellas from the doom of servitude which was impending over her, by this time the various Hellenic races would have become almost completely confounded with one another—and likewise the non-Hellenic with the Hellenes, and *vice versa*—to judge by the appalling present condition of the populations under the Persian yoke, which

turn to the course of events. She now delivered the Kingdom of the Medes and Persians into the hands of a Macedonian conqueror; a violent intrusion of the Hellenic Society upon the Syriac World broke the Syriac universal state in pieces long before its role was played out; and therewith the two 'higher religions' which had been converting men's souls under the Achaemenian aegis[1] were driven into the disastrous aberration of exchanging their proper religious function for a political role.[2] Each on its own ground, they became champions of the Syriac Civilization in its secular struggle against the Hellenism that had intruded

have been quite disintegrated by being interlarded and kneaded up together' (Plato: *Leges*: 692E–693A).

[1] We have little information about the spread of Judaism and Zoroastrianism among the population of the Achaemenian Empire before the Achaemenian régime was overthrown by Alexander; but by inference from the rather less fragmentary evidence relating to the subsequent age of the Hellenic ascendancy we can gather that Zoroastrianism found a welcome in Anatolia (particularly in Cappadocia: see Meyer, E.: *Geschichte des Altertums*, vol. iii (Stuttgart 1901, Cotta), pp. 128–9) and Judaism in the region that had once been Assyria (particularly in Adiabene). The uprooted Babylonians who were transplanted by the Assyrian war-lord Sargon to the territory which had once been the Kingdom of Israel became converted to a bastard form of the religion of Israel. The picturesque story in the Second Book of Kings (chap. xvii, vv. 24–41) is manifestly tinged with legend and tainted with the Jews' notorious anti-Samaritan prejudice; yet its account of the genesis of the Samaritan religion as a syncretism between the worship which the deportees found in their new home and the worships which they brought with them from their old homes is borne out by the evidence of Aramaic papyri, dating from the sixth and fifth centuries B.C., which have been discovered at Elephantinê by our modern Western archaeologists and which relate to the affairs—including the religious life—of a Jewish military colony in this frontier-fortress of the Achaemenian Empire; for the Judaism of this colony had in it a strong tincture of Babylonic polytheism; and this tincture is most easily accounted for on the hypothesis that the colony was of mixed Jewish and Samaritan origin (see van Hoonacker, A.: *Une Communauté Judéo-Araméenne à Éléphantine, en Égypte, aux vi^e et ve siècles av. J.-C.* (London 1915, Milford), especially pp. 73–85). The Biblical story may thus be taken to be true in essence—and true not only of the Samaritans themselves but of hundreds of other communities of exiles whose history has not been preserved even in the literature of their enemies. As time went on, the new Israelitish elements in the religion of the Babylonian settlers in Samaria must have gained the upper hand over the ancestral worships which the settlers had brought in with them; for the Samaritan religion, as we know it to-day, has the appearance of being a rudimentary or a degenerate form of Judaism, with no conspicuous traces of Babylonic accretions. (A possible explanation of this victory of an indigenous over an imported religion in Samaria has been suggested on p. 118, footnote 3, above.) After the reorganization, on an ecclesiastical basis, of the repatriated Jewish community at Jerusalem, the *ci-devant* Babylonic community at Samaria seem to have adopted the Torah from their little-loved neighbours in Palestine under the direction of some renegade Hierosolymitan priests (see Meyer, E.: *Geschichte des Altertums*, vol. iii (Stuttgart 1901, Cotta), p. 214; according to the same scholar, *Der Papyrusfund von Elephantine* (Leipzig 1912, Hinrichs), pp. 80–1, the Samaritans accepted Ezra's reform in all particulars save the centring of the worship of Yahweh upon Jerusalem, for which the Samaritans substituted their own Mount Gerizim). If this has been the history of the Samaritan religion, it gives us a glimpse, in one local instance, of the general process of assimilation through which the whole of the Babylonic body social, with the single exception of the outlying city-state of Harran, was absorbed into the Syriac body social before the beginning of the Christian Era. The strange survival of the Babylonic culture in Harran down to the age of the 'Abbasid Caliphate has been mentioned in another context already (in IV. C (ii) (b) 2, vol. iv, p. 101, footnote 1, above). The cause of this survival seems to have been the tenacity of the Babylonic outpost at Harran in clinging to an ancestral worship—a tenacity which contrasts very sharply with the pliancy of the Babylonic exiles at Samaria in capitulating to the god whom they found in the land to which they had been transplanted.

[2] For a general discussion of the relations between 'higher religions' and political potentates see V. C (i) (d) 6 (δ), Annex, below.

upon the Syriac domain.[1] Judaism, in its advanced position west
of the Euphrates, was inevitably cast for the part of 'forlorn hope',
and it duly broke itself against the overwhelmingly greater material power of Rome in the Romano-Jewish wars of A.D. 66–70 and
115–17 and 132–5.[2] Zoroastrianism, in its fastness east of Zagros,
took up the struggle in the third century of the Christian Era
under less desperately unequal conditions. In the Sasanian
Monarchy Zoroastrianism found a more potent weapon for an
anti-Hellenic 'crusade' than Judaism had been able to forge out
of the petty principality of the Maccabees; and the Sasanidae
gradually wore down the strength of the Roman Empire in a four-
hundred-years-long struggle which culminated in the two great
Romano-Persian wars of A.D. 572–91 and A.D. 603–28. This strategy
of attrition, however, was even more destructive to the Zoroastrian Church Militant than it was to the Hellenic adversary;
and in the end Zoroastrianism had to pay as heavily as Jewry for
having lent itself to a political enterprise.[3] At the present day the
Parsees, like the Jews, survive as a mére 'Diasporà'; and the petrified
religion which still so potently holds the scattered members of
either community together has lost its message for Mankind and
has hardened into a 'fossil'[4] of the extinct Syriac Society in the particular phase of disintegration in which that society happened to
find itself at the moment when it was smitten by the impact of
Hellenism in the fourth century B.C.[5]

This impact of an alien cultural force did not merely divert
the 'higher religions' of the Syriac internal proletariat into political
paths: it also split them into fragments, as the stones of a cathedral
are splintered by the explosion of a shell, or as a beam of light is
diffracted when it is intercepted by a prism. After the transformation of Judaism and Zoroastrianism into instruments of Syriac

[1] See I. C (i) (b), vol. i, pp. 90–1; II. D (v), vol. ii, p. 203; II. D (vi), vol. ii, pp.
234–6; II. D (vii), vol. ii, pp. 285–6 and 374; IV. C (iii) (b) 12, vol. iv, p. 225, and
IV. C (iii) (c) 2 (α), vol. iv, pp. 262–3, above, as well as V. C (i) (d) 6 (δ), Annex,
pp. 657–61, and V. C (i) (d) 9 (γ), vol. vi, pp. 120–3, below.
[2] See the present chapter, p. 68, above.
[3] There was, of course, a native vein of militancy in a religion which conceived of
the Universe as a battlefield in a cosmic war between opposing forces of Light and
Darkness; but in the Achaemenian Age the Achaemenian emperors refrained from
using their political power for the forcible propagation of a religion to which the
Imperial House itself had become converted. (For this Achaemenian tolerance see
further V. C (i) (d) 6 (δ), Annex, pp. 704–5, below.)
[4] For these and other 'fossils' of extinct civilizations see I. B (iii), vol. i, p. 35;
I. C (i) (b), vol. i, pp. 90–2; II. D (vi), vol. ii, pp. 234–9, above.
[5] This unfortunate change in the éthos of both Judaism and Zoroastrianism is revealed in the pathological exaggeration, in both religions in their petrified state, of the
elements of ritual and legal observance (for the Jewish case, see IV. C (iii) (c) 2 (α),
vol. iv, pp. 262–3, and IV. C (iii) (c) 2 (γ), Annex, vol. iv, p. 638, above). The
change might be described with equal truth in another way by saying that, in their
petrified state, Judaism and Zoroastrianism had each partially relapsed from the level
of the 'higher religions' towards the lower level of the primitive tribal religions from
which both these faiths had originally sprung.

political opposition to a Hellenic dominant minority, the Syriac religious genius took refuge among those elements in the Syriac population under Hellenic ascendancy which were reacting to the challenge in the gentle and not in the violent way; and, in giving birth to Christianity and Mithraism as its contributions to the spiritual travail of a Hellenic internal proletariat,[1] Syriac religion found new expressions for a spirit and an outlook which Judaism and Zoroastrianism had repudiated.[2] In the next chapter after that, we see the still half-submerged Syriac Society seeking to recapture, for its own benefit, some of the virtue that had gone out of Syriac into Hellenic souls in the preaching of Christianity to the Gentiles. Nestorianism and Monophysitism were alternative attempts to purge a Syro-Hellenic religious syncretism of its Hellenic alloy;[3] and the Nestorian and Monophysite 'Diasporàs' survive to-day as 'fossils' of an extinct Syriac Society as it was when it was making this second abortive attempt to cast the spirit of Hellenism out.[4]

Two successive failures, however, did not reduce the Syriac opponents of Hellenism to the apathy of despair; a third attempt followed, which was crowned with success; and this final political

---

[1] 'A dying Roman Society was fascinated by the worships of Isis, Serapis, Horus, and Mithras: worships which, once upon a time, a then just dawning soul in the East had conceived as the first dreamy, anxious expression of its existence and had filled with a new inner meaning.'—Spengler, O.: Der Untergang des Abendlandes, vol. i (Munich 1920, Beck), p. 155.

[2] In Mithraism, as in Zoroastrianism (see p. 126, footnote 3, above), there was, of course, a vein of militancy, and this no doubt accounts for the appeal which Mithraism (like Zen Buddhism) is known to have made to soldiers. The historic achievement of Mithraism was not, however, to inspire Iranian knights (as these were inspired by Zoroastrianism in the Sasanian Age) to bear arms in anti-Hellenic crusades. The soldier-converts of the Mithraic Church Militant were Roman legionaries whose professional duty was to hold the Iranian adversaries of Hellenism at bay. Thus, while Zoroastrianism failed to eject by force of arms the Hellenic intruders upon the former domain of the Achaemenian Empire, Mithraism succeeded in captivating Hellenism for an Iranian religion by making a spiritual conquest of Roman soldiers' hearts. On this showing, the spread of Mithraism in the Roman Army, no less than the spread of Christianity among the civilian population of the Roman Empire, is to be interpreted as a triumph of what Mr. Gandhi would call 'soul force'.

[3] See II. D (vii), vol. ii, pp. 286–7, and IV. C (iii) (c) 2 (β), vol. iv, pp. 325–6, above. On the surface the Nestorian and Monophysite heresies were, like Catholic Orthodoxy, part of a dialectical endeavour to express Christian theological tenets in terms of Greek philosophy; and, in the minds of the heresiarchs themselves, this was, no doubt, the very essence of their life-work, and not just a superficial and deceptive aspect of it. They can neither have intended nor foreseen the subsequent conversion of their own abstruse theologico-philosophical propositions into the popular slogans of an Oriental revolt against the ascendancy of Hellenism. The abiding potency of this ascendancy in the fifth century of the Christian Era, some eight hundred years after the date of its first establishment by the arms of Alexander, is attested by the facts that, even as late as this, the Oriental reaction against Hellenism had still to confine itself, west of the Euphrates, to a cultural field of conflict, and that, even on this ground, it found itself constrained to pay homage to the Hellenism which it was combating by fighting its intellectual battle with weapons of Hellenic make. It is no wonder that these weapons proved unavailing for the incongruous purpose which, faute de mieux, their Oriental wielders were attempting to make them serve.

[4] For the possible role of Manichaeism in this chapter of Syriac history see V. C (i) (c) 2, Annex I, on pp. 575–80, below.

triumph of the Syriac Society over Hellenism was achieved through the instrumentality of yet another religion of Syriac origin. Islam had originally been preached to the Arabian external proletariat of the Roman Empire by a prophet whose soul had been stirred by the Syriac religious influences of Judaism and Nestorianism and Monophysitism.[1] The barbarian prophet's energies had then been diverted from a painfully abortive religious mission to a triumphantly successful political career;[2] and the political unity which Muhammad and his caliphs or temporal successors succeeded in imposing upon the Arabs enabled these barbarians to conquer the Oriental provinces of the Roman Empire with one hand and the whole of the Sasanian Empire with the other, and thereby to complete the undoing of the political work of Alexander the Great by reuniting the Syriac World and re-establishing the Syriac universal state which had been first established by the Achaemenidae.[3] Within the framework of the Arab Caliphate, Islam won the prize of which Judaism and Zoroastrianism had been cheated, when it was almost within their grasp, by the distracting military intervention of Alexander. Before the Arab Caliphate broke up, Islam had become the universal church of the Syriac internal proletariat.[4]

This victory of Islam in the Syriac World resembled the victory of Christianity in the Hellenic World in being vigorously contested and hardly won; but the adversaries were not quite the same and the battle was fought with different weapons. Whereas Christianity found its most formidable opponent in the Roman Imperial Government, the Arab Caliphate was Islam's creature, friend, and ally.[5] On the other hand the rival religious move-

---

[1] See III. C (ii) (b), vol. iii, pp. 276–8, with Annex II, above. It will be seen that there is a close parallelism between the genesis of Islam and the genesis of Zoroastrianism. Both religions came to birth in a barbarian environment; and the barbarian prophets who conceived them were probably both acting under Syriac religious influences (if we are right in our conjecture that Zarathustra may have been influenced by a contact with the Israelite deportees in Iran, as Muhammad was undoubtedly influenced by his contact with the Jewish and Christian 'Diasporàs' in Arabia).

[2] See III. C (ii) (b), Annex II, in vol. iii, above.

[3] For this 're-integration' or 'resumption' of the Syriac universal state by the Umayyads and 'Abbasids see I. C (i) (b), vol. i, pp. 72–7, above.

[4] Islam succeeded where Zoroastrianism and Judaism had failed, in spite of the fact that Islam had fallen, in its turn, into the Zoroastrian and Jewish churches' error of 'going into politics'. The date of the Hijrah, which marks the moment when Muhammad abandoned Gentleness for Violence and exchanged the prophet's for the statesman's career, has been rightly taken by later generations of Muslims as the initial date for the Islamic Era, on the ground that the Hijrah made, instead of marring, Islam's fortune. For a possible explanation of this apparent paradox see V. C (i) (d) 6 (δ), Annex, pp. 673–8, below.

[5] The Caliphate was the friend of Islam under the Umayyad régime and its ally under the 'Abbasid régime which replaced the Umayyad régime in A.D. 750. The Umayyads, of course, as well as the 'Abbasids, were officially Muslims; but the Umayyads' Islam was perfunctory (the fervour of 'Umar II (imperabat A.D. 717–20) being the exception that proves the rule), and they never dreamed of forcing Islam upon the non-Muslim 'People of the Book' who constituted an overwhelming majority

ments with which the Sunnah had to contend resorted to a physical violence which was not employed by the rivals of Christianity, any more than it was by Christianity itself, in the competition between 'higher religions' in the Roman Empire.

When we peer into the depths of the Syriac underworld in the age of the Sasanian Empire and in the succeeding age of the Arab Caliphate, we behold a spectacle which recalls the dreadful picture of the Hellenic underworld in the last two centuries B.C. The seething cauldron is never quiet, and it boils over periodically in a militant revolt that is apt to be religious in form but economic or political in substance. The Communist prophet Mazdak who set himself to captivate or capture the Sasanian body politic in the fifth century of the Christian Era[1] reminds us of Aristonicus of Pergamum preaching his 'City of the Sun'. The Sicilian slave-wars of 135–131 and 104–100 B.C. have an almost exact analogue in the 'Irāqī slave-war of A.D. 869–83, in which the African Negro slave-gangs on the plantations in the neighbourhood of Basrah defied the 'Abbasid Power as the Roman Power was defied by the Syrian slave-gangs on the plantations round Enna.[2] And in the outbreaks of the Khārijīs and Carmathians and Ismā'īlīs (or 'Assassins') we seem to see the Zealots and Sicarii of the militant age of Jewish history being recalled to life. The story of a social

---

of their subjects. In this matter their policy was that of the Achaemenidae, who were Zoroastrians themselves yet never used their political power as an instrument of Zoroastrian religious propaganda. On the other hand the policy of the 'Abbasids towards Islam was rather more like that of the Sasanidae towards Zoroastrianism; for, though the charter which was conferred upon 'the People of the Book' by the Islamic *Shari'ah* inhibited the 'Abbasids from going to the Sasanian length of imposing their own dynastic religion upon their subjects by main force, the 'Abbasids did follow the example of the Sasanidae in making their state into an instrument of their religion and their religion into a pillar of their state. For a further examination of the respective policies of these four dynasties towards the religions to which they severally paid their private allegiance, see V. C (i) (d) 6 (δ), Annex, pp. 704–5 (for the Achaemenidae), pp. 659–61 (for the Sasanidae), pp. 675–7 and 704 (for the Umayyads), pp. 678 and 706 (for the 'Abbasids).

[1] See Christensen, A.: *Le Règne du Roi Kawadh I et le Communisme Mazdakite* (Copenhagen 1925, Lunos), and eundem: *L'Iran sous les Sassanides* (Copenhagen 1936, Levin & Munksgaard), chap. 7.

[2] For an account of this revolt of African Negro slaves in 'Irāq in the ninth century of the Christian Era see Nöldeke, Th.: 'A Servile War in the East' in *Sketches from Eastern History*, English translation (London and Edinburgh 1892, Black). The Zanj, as these Negroes were called, were employed by *entrepreneurs* on the heavy work of digging away the nitrous top-layer of the soil on the flats east of Basrah and laying bare, for cultivation, the fertile layer of soil that was to be found below. There were no personal relations between these slaves and their masters; and the slaves were both ill used and exasperated. When they rose, they were joined by the free rural, but not by the free urban, proletariat. Like the Syrian slave-insurgents in Sicily, these African slave-insurgents in 'Irāq had the constructive idea of establishing a state, and their leader 'Ali b. Muhammad (who was either a North Persian from Verzenīn near Tihrān, or else an 'Abd-al-Qaysī Arab from Bahrayn) founded a city, on the Shatt-al-'Arab below Basrah, which he named Mukhtārah. At different moments in the course of their operations the rebels captured Obolla, 'Abbādān, Ahwāz, Basrah, and Wāsit, and, even when the Baghdad Government managed to concentrate its forces against them, they held out stubbornly in their swamp-fastnesses. The war, which began in A.D. 869, was only brought to an end in A.D. 883 by the capture of Mukhtārah itself.

convulsion which begins as a religious or even as a philosophical movement and ends in a political *emeute* recurs again and again; and the fleeting, futile figures of a Theudas and a Judas of Galilee, as they are conjured up before our mind's eye by Gamaliel's contemptuous phrases,[1] are matched in the 'Abbasid Age by the figures of al-Muqanna', 'the Veiled Prophet' of Khurāsān, and Bābak al-Khurramī.[2] Indeed, in the history of the Syriac underworld from the time of the suppression of Mazdak by the Sasanian King Kawādh (Qubādh) I *circa* A.D. 528–9 down to the time of the smoking out of the Assassins' eyrie on Alamūt by the Mongol warlord Hulāgū *circa* A.D. 1255, the prophets of violence are legion; but the rest of their acts, and the evil that they did, are they not written in *The Book of Religious and Philosophical Sects* by the hand of the omniscient Shahrastānī?[3]

From the first generation of Islam onwards the sufferings and resentments of the disinherited and outcast masses of the Syriac internal proletariat were projected upon the figures of a martyred 'Alī and his martyred sons, whose spiritual stature increased as they passed out of history into legend; and from that time onwards a majority of the upheavals were manifestations in diverse forms of a single Protean Shī'ah.[4] The author of the Zanj revolt declared himself to be of 'Alid lineage;[5] and the violent expression of Shī'ism reached its acme in the fighting fraternity of the Carmathians and the murdering fraternity of the Assassins. It is interesting to observe that in the Shī'ah, as in Jewry, the shattering defeat of the militant movements—at the hands of powers which were overwhelmingly stronger than the insurgent proletarians in the physical force in which the insurgents had put their trust—was followed by a revulsion from Violence towards Gentleness. The trade-guild brotherhoods in which the Shī'ah embodied itself from the twelfth

---

[1] Acts v. 36–7, quoted on p. 73, above.

[2] For these and other similar upheavals in the Syriac underworld of the eighth and ninth centuries of the Christian Era see Browne, E. G.: *A Literary History of Persia*, vol. i (London 1908, Fisher Unwin), chap. 9.

[3] Shahrastānī, Muhammad al-: كتاب الملل والنحل edited by Cureton, W.: reprint (Leipzig 1923 Harrassowitz).

[4] For the history of the Shī'ah from the beginning down to the generation of Shāh Ismā'īl see I. C (i) (*b*), Annex I, vol. i, pp. 353–66 and 400–2, above.

[5] Compare the 'Alid pretensions of the Idrīsī and the Fātimī dynasties of Ifriqīyah. To claim 'Alid descent was equivalent to claiming a hereditary spiritual grace or even divinity; and the establishment of this religious pretension was of immense political value, since the credulous might be induced to risk their lives in following a prophet in a 'forlorn hope' which they would have regarded as quite desperate if it had been presented to them as a nakedly political enterprise. The Prophet Muhammad himself owed his political success in large measure to the confidence which his prophetical pretensions inspired in his followers' hearts as well as in his own self; and the Apamean slave Eunus, who instigated and led the slave-revolt at Enna which precipitated the first of the Sicilian slave-wars, prepared the ground by attempting to create a reputation for himself as a psychic 'medium' (see V. C (i) (*d*) 7, vol. vi, p. 34, footnote 5, and V. C (ii) (*a*), Annex II, vol. vi, p. 383, below).

to the fifteenth century of the Christian Era bore as little resemblance to the Carmathian war-bands or to the Ismāʻīlī *camorra* as was borne by the latter-day Jewish rabbinical schools to the Jewish Church Militant of a Judas Maccabaeus or a Simon bar Kōkabā.[1]

The Indic and the Sinic Internal Proletariat.

The disintegrating Syriac Society's experience of having its course interrupted by a brusque and violent intrusion of Hellenism befell the Indic Society likewise;[2] and it is interesting to examine how far, in this case, an identic challenge evoked a similar response.

At the time when the Indic and Hellenic societies made their first preliminary contact—as a result of Alexander's successful destruction of the Achaemenian Empire and his abortive raid into the Indus Valley—the Indic Society was already so far advanced along the road of disintegration that it was on the point of entering upon its universal state,[3] and the Indic dominant minority had long since reacted to the ordeal by creating the two philosophical schools of Jainism and Buddhism.[4] There is no evidence, however, that the Indic internal proletariat had yet discovered any 'higher religions' corresponding to the Zoroastrianism and the Judaism which were in the act of converting the Syriac World at the moment of Alexander's advent.

The first of the transactions that took place between the Indic philosophers and the remarkable alien society which had suddenly loomed up above their western horizon was an attempt, on the Indic philosophers' part, to convert their new neighbours to their own way of life. The Buddhist philosopher-king Açoka, who occupied the throne of the Indic universal state from 273 to 232 B.C., has bequeathed to us, among his inscriptions, a record of the philosophic missions which he sent, *circa* 259 B.C., to the realms of five of the Epigoni; and a hundred years later, after the first Indic universal state had broken up and the intrusion of Hellenism upon the Indic World had begun—nearly a century and a half after the crossing of the Dardanelles by Alexander of Macedon—with the crossing of the Hindu Kush by Demetrius of Bactria *post* 190 B.C.,[5] the 'gymnosophists' were given an opportunity of

[1] For this metamorphosis of the Shīʻah see the note by Professor H. A. R. Gibb in I. C (i) (*b*), Annex I, vol. i, pp. 400–2, above. See further Gibb, H. A. R., and Bowen, H.: *Islamic Society and the West*, vol. i, chap. xiv: 'The Dervishes', for the transition from a 'Thisworldly' violence to an 'Otherworldly' non-violence that accompanied the replacement of the Bāṭinīs by the Sūfīs.

[2] See I. C (i) (*b*), vol. i, pp. 84–8, above.

[3] Alexander's raid on the fringes of the Indic World took place in 327–325 B.C.; Chandragupta established the Indic universal state in 323–322 B.C.

[4] See V. C (i) (*c*) 1, p. 58, above.

[5] On this question of date see I. C (i) (*b*), vol. i, p. 86, above. Tarn, W. W.: *The Greeks in Bactria and India* (Cambridge 1938, University Press), p. 133, dates Demetrius's crossing of the Hindu Kush *circa* 183–182 B.C.

preaching to a Hellenic war-lord on their own ground, in the heart of the Indic World itself, when the flood tide of the Hellenic military invasion left Demetrius's lieutenant and successor Menander high and dry between Indus and Ganges.

This Indic philosophical propaganda had a promising field in the Hellenic Society of the age; for the Hellenic, like the Indic, Civilization was in disintegration; and Buddhism offered—for any dominant minority that was sick in soul and was conscious of its sickness—a spiritual remedy which was more radical and more courageous than the existing native Hellenic philosophical systems of Platonism and Cynicism and Epicureanism and Stoicism. A disciple of any of these Hellenic schools would have found himself at home in the spiritual climate of Buddhism;[1] and, while he would have felt himself to be in the presence of a spirit which was a match for his own in its intellectual power of penetrating to the heart of things, he would have recognized that the Indic was superior to the Hellenic philosophy in its moral power of acting up to its formidable convictions.[2] Of the five Hellenic princes to whose countries Acoka dispatched his philosophic missionaries, at least one—Antigonus Gonatas—was an admirer of Zeno[3] who might have been fired with a deeper admiration for the still more austere and masterly genius of Siddhārtha Gautama. The results of Açoka's mission to the Hellenes are, however, unknown, and this negative evidence suggests that they cannot have been very striking, while it would be rash to infer that Buddhism made a serious impression upon Menander[4] from the fact that this Hellenic intruder's name has been taken in vain by a Buddhist man-of-letters as a label for one of the characters in an imaginary philosophical dialogue.[5] We can only say that, as a philosophy, Buddhism had and saw, but missed, a chance of captivating the Hellenic dominant minority and driving the native schools of Hellenic philosophy off the field before the lists were entered by any proletarian-born religion. This, of course, was not the end of the story; for, in spite of having lost this golden opportunity, Buddhism did eventually take by storm the outlying, yet extensive and important, province of the post-Alexandrine Hellenic World which was occupied by the Greek

[1] For evidence of this see V. C (i) (d) 10, passim, vol. vi, pp. 132–48, and the passage quoted from Mr. Edwyn Bevan in V. C (i) (d) 11, vol. vi, pp. 151–52, below.
[2] See further V. C (i) (d) 10, vol. vi, p. 140, below.
[3] See V. C (ii) (a), vol. vi, p. 249, below.
[4] In the opinion of W. W. Tarn: The Greeks in Bactria and India (Cambridge 1938, University Press), p. 269, it would be 'quite unsafe to call' Menander 'a Buddhist even in the limited sense in which Antigonus Gonatas, the nearest analogy, is sometimes called a Stoic'.
[5] The Milindapañha or Questions of Menander. Tarn (in op. cit., Excursus, pp. 414–36) brings forward reasons for supposing that this Pāli work may have been at least partly inspired by a Greek original.

Kingdom of Bactria and its Eurasian Nomad 'successor-states', and
which embraced a conquered Indic territory in the Basin of the
Indus and Ganges as well as a conquered Syriac territory in the
Basin of the Oxus and Jaxartes.[1] But Buddhism did not make this
triumphant spiritual counter-conquest until it had undergone an
extraordinary metamorphosis[2] through which the old philosophy
of Siddhārtha Gautama became transformed into the new religion
of the Mahāyāna.[3]

'The Mahāyāna is a truly new religion, so radically different from
Early Buddhism that it exhibits as many points of contact with later
Brahmanical religions as with its own predecessor. . . . It never has
been fully realized what a radical revolution had transformed the

---

[1] For the political unification of these Indic and Syriac territories under the Hellenic
rule of Bactrian Greek war-lords see II. D (vii), vol. ii, pp. 371–2, above. This unification under the rule of the Euthydemid Greek dynasty was short lived; for the conqueror
Demetrius does not seem to have crossed the Hindu Kush before 183 B.C. or to have
occupied the fallen Mauryan Empire's capital at Pataliputra before about 175 B.C.,
and the fatal division of the Greek Power in the Far East, through the invasion of the
Euthydemid Empire by the Seleucid legitimist claimant Eucratides, seems to have
occurred not later than 168 B.C. (Tarn, W. W.: *The Greeks in Bactria and India* (Cambridge 1938, University Press), pp. 132–3). The still vast but no longer united Greek
dominions east of Khurāsān were then soon overrun by Nomad invaders from the
Eurasian Steppe (see V. C (i) (c) 3, pp. 239–40, with Annex II, below). In or shortly before
130 B.C. the Yuechi occupied the Upper Oxus and Jaxartes Basin (Sogdiana and
Bactria) up to the line of the Hindu Kush; and, when the Sakas and Parsians who
invaded Parthia in 129 B.C. were beaten by the Suren between 124 and 115 B.C., the
Parsians compensated themselves by ousting the Greeks, some time before 87 B.C.,
from Côphênê (round the head-waters of the Hilmand and Kābul rivers) and the Sakas
by ousting them from Patalênê (the Indus Delta), Surāshtra (Kathiāwār and Gujerāt),
Taxila (the Western Panjab), Gandhāra (the Lower Kābul Valley), and the Paropamisadae (the Upper Kābul Valley) between *circa* 110 and *circa* 60 B.C. Thereafter
the last Greek principalities in the Kābul Valley and in the Eastern Panjab were extinguished by the Parsian masters of Côphênê *circa* 30 B.C., and then in A.D. 19 this Parsian
Empire, together with the remnants of the Saka Empire in Sind and Surāshtra, was
conquered by the Parthian Suren Gondophares. It was, however, not the eastern
wing of the Parthians but one of the five war-bands of the Yuechi that achieved a lasting
reunification of the dominions which Demetrius the son of Euthydemus had held
together between 175 and 168 B.C. The Kushans united all the five Yuechi principalities in Bactria and Sogdiana under their own sovereignty and at the same time made
conquests in the Indic World which were almost, if not quite, as wide as those of
Demetrius himself; and they presented themselves to their subjects as the extinct Greek
princes' legitimate heirs. As early as about 50 B.C. the Kushan chief Miaos seems to
have lent the Greek prince Hermaeus, in the Paropamisadae, military assistance against
the Parsians of Côphênê, and to have been given a Greek princess in marriage as part
of his reward (Tarn, op. cit., pp. 342–3); and it was Miaos' descendant Kadphises I
(*regnabat post* A.D. 25–A.D. 50) who united the Yuechi under Kushan rule and began
the Kushan conquest of India (ibid., p. 338). There is numismatic evidence
(examined ibid., pp. 503–7) which seems to show that Kadphises I Kushan made
the most of his descent from Hermaeus's family in order to win the sympathies
of the Greek and Philhellene elements in the population of the Paropamisadae when he
was contending with a Parthian antagonist for the possession of this Indic country.
The Sakas, as well as the Kushans, were successors of the Greeks in India in the sense
that they took over, unchanged, their Greek predecessors' institutions: e.g. their
administrative system, their coinage, and their calendar (ibid. pp. 241–3, 300, 323, 358–
9). 'The Sakas simply stepped into the shoes of the Greeks; Indian writers regularly
classed them with the Yavanas, and regarded them, as they regarded the Yavanas,
as imperfect Kshatriyas' (p. 323).
[2] A clear account of this, in small compass, will be found in Eliot, Sir Ch.: *Japanese
Buddhism* (London 1935, Arnold), pp. 74–87.
[3] Seven distinctive notes of the Mahāyāna are set out in Eliot, Sir Ch.: *Hinduism
and Buddhism* (London 1921, Arnold, 3 vols.), vol. ii, p. 6.

Buddhist Church when the new spirit—which, however, was for a long time lurking in it—arrived at full eclosion in the first centuries A.D. When we see an atheistic, soul-denying philosophic teaching of a path to personal final deliverance, consisting in an absolute extinction of life[1] and a simple worship of the memory of its human founder— when we see it superseded by a magnificent High Church with a Supreme God, surrounded by a numerous pantheon and a host of saints: a religion highly devotional,[2] highly ceremonious and clerical, with an ideal of universal salvation of all living creatures, a salvation by the divine grace of Buddhas and Bodhisattvas, a salvation not in annihilation but in eternal life—we are fully justified in maintaining that the history of religions has scarcely witnessed such a break between new and old within the pale of what nevertheless continues to claim common descent from the same religious founder.'[3]

The transformed Buddhism which, in the shape of the Mahā-yāna, was now invading the far eastern extremity of a vastly ex-panded Hellenic World was, in fact, an Indic 'higher religion' of the same type as the Syriac and Egyptiac and Hittite 'higher religions'—Christianity and Mithraism and the worships of Isis and Cybele—that were invading the heart of the Hellenic World in the same age. Like these other alien competitors for the conversion of Hellenic souls, the Mahāyāna made itself doubly attractive to its public by combining a comfortable conformity to the externals of the Hellenic culture with the offer of an inward spiritual treasure which was the great thing lacking in the native Hellenic heritage and which was therefore desirable in Hellenic eyes just in virtue of being exotic.[4] On the one hand the Mahāyāna seized upon the mediocre version of Hellenic art which was current in the outlying Kingdom of Bactria and its barbarian 'successor-states', and drew from this unpromising source[5] the inspiration for one of the most sublime and creative schools of art that have yet been produced by the co-operation of the religious with the aesthetic faculty of the Human Spirit.[6] On the other hand the Mahāyāna offered to a

[1] A more precise account of the Primitive Buddhist conception of *Nirvāna*, from the same pen, will be found in V. C (i) (*d*) 10, vol. vi, pp. 142–3, below. The view that Siddhārtha Gautama conceived of *Nirvāna* as a negation of existence, and that he also denied the existence of God and of the Self, is challenged by Sir S. Radhakrishnan in *Gautama the Buddha* (London 1938, Milford), pp. 31–50.—A.J.T.

[2] For this new vein of emotion, which was not to be found either in the primitive Buddhist philosophy or in the primitive Aryan paganism, see further pp. 135–6, below.—A.J.T.

[3] Stcherbatsky, Th.: *The Conception of Buddhist Nirvana* (Leningrad 1927, Academy of Sciences of the U.S.S.R.), p. 36.   [4] See the present chapter, pp. 86–7, above.

[5] There was, of course, one brilliant exception to the mediocrity of this Far Eastern Greek art, and that was its coinage.

[6] This resurrection of Hellenic art through the religious power of the Mahāyāna has been noticed, by anticipation, in III C (i) (*a*), vol. iii, p. 131, and III. C (ii) (*a*), vol. iii, p. 247, footnote 2, above. 'The art of Gandhāra was born of Buddhist piety utilizing Yavana technique' (Tarn, op. cit., p. 393, following Grousset). See further the present Study, V. C (i) (*c*) 3, in the present volume, p. 196, and V. C (i) (*d*) 6 (*β*), p. 481, below.

Hellenic convert the un-Hellenic religious experience of an intimate personal relation between the worshipper and his god:[1] a relation of mutual love in which the worshipper's devotion (*bhakti*)[2] was a response to the god's loving-kindness towards his devotee.

What was the origin of this personal religion which was both the distinctive trait of the Mahāyāna and the secret of its success? This new leaven, which changed the spirit of Buddhism so profoundly, was as alien from the native vein of the Indic as it was from that of the Hellenic philosophy.[3] Was it the fruit of the

[1] The Hellenic conception of Man's relation to God is illuminatingly illustrated by some observations of Aristotle's in a passage (1158B–1159A) of his *Ethica Nicomachea*: 'There would appear to be a difference in the meaning of the term equality in its respective applications in the realm of rights and in that of friendship. In the realm of rights moral equality is primary and quantitative equality secondary, whereas in the realm of friendship this order of precedence is inverted. This is clear where there is a wide discrepancy in goodness, badness, wealth or what not; for such a discrepancy rules out not only the possibility of friendship but even the pretension to it. This is most evident in the case of gods, who enjoy a crushing superiority in advantages of all kinds; but it is also clear in the case of kings; for no pretension to friendship with kings, any more than with gods, is made by their extreme inferiors—and likewise none to friendship with the moral and intellectual *élite* by people of no account. It is, no doubt, impossible exactly to define the limit up to which friends can still remain friends in despite of a quantitative inequality between them. Friendship can survive the subtraction of many advantages [from one of the two parties], but it cannot survive where the gulf has become as broad as that which separates a god [from a man]. This raises the puzzling question whether a friend can really desire for his friend superlative advantages; for being a god is an advantage that is assuredly superlative, and yet, when your friend has become a god, you can no longer be a friend for him, and therefore no longer an asset (which is what a friend is). If, therefore, we have been right in supposing that a friend's motive in desiring advantages for his friend is altruistic, then he is bound to want his friend to remain the mere human being that he now is.'

[2] An analysis of the meaning of *bhakti* will be found in Eliot, Sir Ch.: *Hinduism and Buddhism* (London 1921, Arnold, 3 vols.), vol. ii, pp. 180–4.

[3] The contrast between this aspect of the Mahāyāna and the authentic doctrine and êthos of the historical Buddha, Siddhārtha Gautama, is brought out very clearly in Stcherbatsky, Th.: *The Conception of Buddhist Nirvana* (Leningrad 1927, Academy of Sciences of the U.S.S.R.). 'The denial of soul as a separate substance . . . provoked, in the Buddhist community itself, opposition which grew ever stronger and resulted, five hundred years after the demise of the Master, in what may be called a quite new religion, reposing on a quite different philosophic foundation' (p. 4). 'The great change produced by the Mahāyāna consisted in the view that the Absolute was immanent to the World' (p. 34). The rise of the Mahāyāna was part of the same movement as the rise of the worships of Vishnu and Shiva—pantheism and a radical monism being common features of the Mahayanian and the Hindu faith (pp. 50–1). 'Buddhist art of the ancient period represented Buddha by an empty place or a symbol, which later on is replaced by a divine figure of the Apollo type. . . . The only explanation [of the former manner of representation] seems to be that the total disappearance of Buddha in Nirvana was thus given pictorial expression' (ibid., p. 36, footnote 2)—whereas, in the Mahāyāna, 'the sage Gautama became in practice, if not in theory, a god, with his ears open to the prayers of the faithful, and served by a hierarchy of Bodhisattvas and other beings acting as mediators between him and sinful men' (Smith, V. A.: *The Early History of India*, 3rd edition (Oxford 1914, Clarendon Press), p. 266). For the role of Love in the Mahāyāna see further V. C (i) (*d*) 11, vol. vi, p. 164, footnote 3, below. 'The Buddha-statue played its part in that conversion of [the] Buddha from a man into a god which took place in the Mahāyāna' (Tarn, op. cit., pp. 407–8). Both the idea of representing the Buddha in human form and the earliest of the types in which this idea was worked out were of Hellenic origin; and Tarn (op. cit., pp. 395–404) demonstrates, from a piece of numismatic evidence, that the prototype of the Apollinean statue of the Buddha must have been carved, at latest, early in the last century B.C. The Indic artists accepted the Hellenic device of anthropomorphism but discarded the Apollinean type in favour of a more spiritual representation of their saviour (ibid., pp. 405–7).

spiritual experience of an Indic internal proletariat which had previously been ignored by the supercilious philosopher-members of the dominant minority, and which was belatedly entering into its kingdom now that the philosophers' confidence in their own spiritual powers had been shaken by the impact of Hellenism? This conjecture is suggested by the fact that the Mahāyāna was not the only Indic 'higher religion' in which the spirit of *bhakti* made its appearance.[1] Or was this vital fire in the Mahāyāna no Indic fire at all, but a spark caught from the Syriac flame which had already kindled Zoroastrianism and Judaism and was soon to kindle Mithraism and Christianity as well? This latter conjecture is commended by the chronological fact that the epiphany of the Mahāyāna was preceded by the fusion of Indic with Syriac populations under the rule of the Greek kings of Bactria and their Kushan successors. In default of patent evidence, however, we must confess that the provenance of the vital element in the Mahāyāna is still uncertain.[2] We must be content to take note of the fact that, with the arrival of this Buddhaic 'higher religion' upon the scene, the religious history of the Indic Society began to take the same course as that of the Syriac Society which we have already surveyed.

As a 'higher religion' which went forth from the society in whose bosom it had arisen in order to evangelize a dominant Hellenic World, the Mahāyāna is manifestly an Indic counterpart of Christianity and Mithraism; and, with this key in our hands, we can easily identify the respective Indic counterparts of the other rays into which the light of Syriac religion was diffracted by the interposition of a Hellenic prism. If we look for the Indic equivalent of those 'fossils' of the pre-Hellenic state of the Syriac Society that have survived in the shapes of the Jewish and Parsee 'Diasporàs', we shall find what we are looking for in the latter-day Hinayanian Buddhism of Ceylon and Burma and Siam, which is a relic of the pre-Mahayanian philosophy of Siddhārtha Gautama and a 'fossil' of the Indic Society as it was before Demetrius of Bactria crossed the Hindu Kush.[3] Again, if we look for the Indic equivalent of a later-deposited stratum of Syriac 'fossils' which is represented by the Nestorian and Mono-

---

[1] It asserted itself simultaneously in the rise of the post-Buddhaic religion of Hinduism (see p. 138, below).

[2] The hypothesis of a Zoroastrian provenance is combated by Thomas, E. J.: *The History of Buddhist Thought* (London 1933, Kegan Paul), pp. 178–9. On the other hand it is more favourably entertained by Eliot, Sir Ch.: *Hinduism and Buddhism* (London 1921, Arnold, 3 vols.), vol. iii, pp. 218–22. In particular, Sir Charles Eliot points out the singular closeness of the resemblance between Amitābha's paradise and Ahuramazda's. Cf. ibid., vol. cit., pp. 451–4.

[3] For these Hinayanian 'fossils' of an extinct Indic Society see I. B (iii), vol. i, p. 35, and I. C (i) (*b*), vol. i, pp. 90–2, above.

physite 'Diasporàs' and fastnesses to-day, we shall find what we are looking for, here again, in the latter-day Tantric Mahayanian Buddhism of Tibet and Mongolia.[1] We have sought to explain Nestorianism and Monophysitism as a pair of Syriac attempts to combat Hellenism, not by the crudely militant tactics of Maccabaean Judaism and Sasanian Zoroastrianism, but by the subtler method of purging the Hellenic alloy out of the Syro-Hellenic religious syncretism of Christianity.[2] On this analogy we may discern in the Tantric version of the Mahāyāna an attempt to provide a 'de-Hellenized' variety of an Indic religion for those 'Zealots' in the Indic World in whose eyes the Catholic form of the Mahāyāna was vitiated—whether they were aware or not of the true reason for their distaste—by its Hellenic tinge. At any rate, the Tantric version of the Mahāyāna had the same fate as Nestorianism and Monophysitism in missing fire;[3] and, just as the Syriac Society had to wait for the emergence of Islam in order to lay its hand upon a religion which was capable of serving as an effective instrument for casting Hellenism out, so we find that the complete and final expulsion of the intrusive Hellenic spirit from the Indic body social was accomplished, not through a 'de-Hellenized' version of the Mahāyāna, but through the purely Indic and utterly un-Hellenic religious movement of post-Buddhaic Hinduism.

This post-Buddhaic Hinduism, which eventually provided the internal proletariat of the Indic Society with its universal church, is an elusive creature. If we fix our attention upon the fact that—in deliberate reaction against every form of Buddhism, pristine or transfigured, philosophic or religious—Hinduism accepts and consecrates the social ascendancy of the Brahman caste, we may be inclined to see nothing more in Hinduism than an archaistic[4] revival of the primitive paganism of the barbarian Aryas whose Völkerwanderung into India out of the Eurasian Steppe was the prelude to the birth and growth of the Indic

[1] For the conversion of the Mongols and the Calmucks to this Tantric form of the Mahāyāna see Part III. A, Annex II, vol. iii, p. 451, IV. C (iii) (c) 3 (α), vol. iv, p. 497, and the present chapter and volume, p. 116, above.

[2] See II. D (vii), vol. ii, pp. 286–7, and the present chapter and volume, p. 127, above.

[3] The parallelism in the diffraction of the Syriac and the Indic religion has a politico-geographical aspect which has been touched upon already in II. D (vi), Annex, vol. ii, p. 405, footnote 1, above. The Tantric version of the Mahāyāna, like the Nestorian form of Christianity, found an asylum beyond the political pale of Hellenism—Nestorianism in 'Irāq, beyond the eastern frontier of the Roman Empire; the Tantric Mahāyāna in Bengal, beyond the eastern limits of the Bactrian and the Kushan Kingdom. When Nestorianism was supplanted in the plains of 'Irāq by its more effective successor Islam, it found a fastness for itself in the highlands of Kurdistan and a new world to conquer on the Eurasian Steppe. Similarly the Tantric Mahāyāna held out upon the plateau of Tibet and eventually spread from Tibet into Mongolia after the Nestorian 'Diasporà' in Mongolia had died out.

[4] For the phenomenon of Archaism in the field of Religion see V. C (i) (d) 8 (δ), vol. vi, pp. 83–94, below.

Civilization;[1] for this Aryan paganism had continued to hold the field in the Indic World until the breakdown of the Indic Civilization evoked the 'mental strife' that expressed itself in the Jain and Buddhist philosophies, and one of the outstanding features in the development of this primitive religion during the growth-phase of Indic history was a steady increase in the Brahmans' prestige and power. On the other hand, if we contemplate the philosophical side of the post-Buddhaic Hinduism, and observe how, among those Hindus who claim to be the greatest adepts, this aspect of Hinduism tends to push all other aspects into the background, we may be inclined to see in Hinduism, not a revival of Aryan paganism, but a mimesis of Buddhist philosophy.[2] We shall not, however, divine the essential nature of Hinduism until we turn our eyes to that personal relation between the god and his devotee[3] which—in contrast to the primitive pre-Buddhaic Aryan paganism[4]—the Hindu worships of Vishnu and Shiva have in common with the Mahayanian worships of the Bodhisattvas[5] and the Egyptiac worship of Isis and the Hittite worship of Cybele and the Syriac worships of Mithras and Christ;[6] and in the light of this comparison we shall perceive that, under a twofold disguise, this Hinduism is in truth a representative of that now familiar 'higher' species of religions that are brought to birth, out of the agony of disintegrating civilizations, by the poignant spiritual experience of their internal proletariats.

[1] For this Völkerwanderung of the Aryas see I. C (i) (b), vol. i, pp. 104–7, above.

[2] The Mahāyāna did not, of course, cease to be a philosophy in becoming a religion as well. In fact, its metamorphosis into a religion was a consequence of its particular philosophic bent, and it is this Mahayanian bent that is followed by the post-Buddhaic Hindu philosophy of the Vedānta. (For the points in common between the Mahayanian philosophy and the Vedānta, and for the reciprocal influence of these two philosophies upon one another from the first to the seventh century after Christ, see Stcherbatsky, Th.: *The Conception of Buddhist Nirvana* (Leningrad 1927, Academy of Sciences of the U.S.S.R.), pp. 38 and 61; Eliot, Sir Ch.: *Hinduism and Buddhism* (London 1921, Arnold, 3 vols.), vol. i, p. xl; vol. ii, p. 211.)

[3] See Aiyangar, S. K.: *Some Contributions of South India to Indian Culture* (Calcutta 1923, University Press), pp. 209, 212, and 228.

[4] For the differences between the pre-Buddhaic religion of the Vedas and the post-Buddhaic Hinduism see Eliot, Sir Ch.: *Hinduism and Buddhism* (London 1921, Arnold, 3 vols.), vol. ii, pp. 136–9.

[5] See p. 136, footnote 1, above. For the common origin of the Hindu worships of Vishnu and Shiva and the Mahayanian cults of Bodhisattvas see Eliot, Sir Ch.: *Hinduism and Buddhism* (London 1921, Arnold, 3 vols.), vol. ii, p. 12; Thomas, E. J.: *The History of Buddhist Thought* (London 1933, Kegan Paul), pp. 178 and 194. For the affinity and contemporaneity of the Hindu worship of Krishna with the Mahayanian cult of Amitābha see Eliot, *Japanese Buddhism*, pp. 87 and 392–3.

[6] While these Indic and Syriac worships can all be classed in one category in virtue of the personal relation, which is to be found in them all, between the worshipper and his god, Christianity differs from all the rest in demanding a devotion that is not merely personal and emotional but is also exclusive. For this difference between Christianity and the worships of Vishnu and Shiva see further V. C (i) (d) 7, vol. vi, pp. 47–9, below. For the possibly Hellenic and Syriac origin of the anthropomorphism and image-worship which are two of the most conspicuous non-Vedic features of the post-Buddhaic Hinduism, see Eliot, *Hinduism and Buddhism*, vol. ii, pp. 139 and 171–5.

We have seen that the Indic philosophy—and the religion into which it was transformed at a certain stage of its development —was diffracted, like the Syriac religion, into four separate rays of philosophic or religious light, and that two of the four (namely the authentic philosophy of Siddhārtha Gautama and the Tantric version of the Mahāyāna) proved abortive, while the Catholic form of the Mahāyāna radiated out of the Indic into the Hellenic World and the post-Buddhaic religion of Hinduism won the allegiance of the Indic internal proletariat in the last chapter of the story. Up to this point the history of the Catholic Mahāyāna corresponds with the history of Catholic Christianity, which likewise found its field of action in the Hellenic World instead of devoting itself to the conversion of the non-Hellenic society from whose bosom it had sprung; but there is a further chapter in the history of the Catholic Mahāyāna to which the history of the Catholic Christian Church can show no parallel.

In the history of Catholic Christianity the first migration was also the last; for, when the Church had conquered the Hellenic World and had taken upon its own head the responsibility for acting as this moribund civilization's executor and residuary legatee, it stood steadfast at its self-appointed post and offered itself as a shelter from the storm during the terrible tribulation of the post-Hellenic interregnum, until, with the slow passage of Time, two new Christian civilizations, both affiliated to the Hellenic, came to birth and began to grow up under the Church's aegis.[1] This lasting association between the legacy of the Hellenic Society and the work of the Catholic Christian Church is not reproduced in the relation between the Hellenic Society and the Catholic Mahāyāna. The Mahāyāna did, indeed, eventually emulate the Christian Church in linking its own fortunes—'for better for worse, in sickness and in health'—with those of a moribund civilization, but it was not in the Hellenic World that it found this permanent partner. Whereas the Christian Church established its head-quarters, once for all, within the pale of the Roman Empire, the Mahāyāna only tarried for a short breathing-space within the limits of the Kushan 'successor-state' of the Greek Kingdom of Bactria[2]—a semi-barbarian commonwealth which was the counterpart of the Roman Empire in the eastern extremity of the Hellenic World during the first few centuries of the Christian Era. The reception which the Mahāyāna met with in the Kushan Kingdom offered it every

[1] For the affiliation of the Western and the Orthodox Christian Civilization to the Hellenic Civilization through the mediation of the Catholic Christian Church see I. B (iv), vol. i, pp. 39–44; I. C (i) (a), vol. i, pp. 52–63; I. C (i) (b), vol. i, pp. 63–7, above, and Part VII, below.

[2] For the relation of the Kushan Rāj to the Bactrian Greek Rāj see p. 133, footnote 1, above.

inducement to settle down; for the Kushan King Kanishka (*regna-bat circa* A.D. 78–123)[1] was as solicitous a patron of the nascent Buddhaic 'higher religion' as the Roman Emperor Constantine was of Catholic Christianity.[2] But, while the policy of the Kushan Crown was an invitation to the Mahāyāna to cease from its pilgrimage, the social geography of the Kushan Kingdom was an incitement to move on; for, unlike the Roman Empire, the Kushan Kingdom was not a terminus; it was a 'roundabout' on which four roads converged: one from the Indic World, one from the Syriac, one from the Hellenic, and one from the Sinic.[3] When, under a Kushan régime which had 'abolished the Hindu Kush', the Mahāyāna made its passage out of the Indus Valley into the Oxus-Jaxartes Basin, it found that it could not halt here and dig itself in; it had to travel on along one or other of the three alternative roads that now opened up before its face; and the circumstances of the age decided that, at this parting of the ways, the Mahāyāna should take the Sinic turning. Travelling across the extremity of a superficially expanded Hellenic World and of the temporarily buried Syriac World whicl lay beneath it, the Mahāyāna completed its long and devious journey from its Indian birth-place to the Far Eastern scene of its life-work by a route which skirted three sides of the four-square Tibetan bastion.[4] It was the destiny of the Mahāyāna to play in the Far East, among the ruins of the Sinic universal state of Ts'in and Han, the role of universal church which was played by the Catholic Christian Church in the Western and the Orthodox Christian worlds among the ruins of the Hellenic universal state that had been embodied in the Roman Empire.

In order to understand the triumphal progress of the Mahāyāna in a Sinic World which was geographically so remote from the Mahāyāna's Indian homeland, we have to examine the history of the Sinic internal proletariat.

Considering the intensity of the tribulation of the Sinic 'Time of Troubles' when it was reaching its climax during 'the Period of Contending States',[5] we should expect *a priori* to find an internal

---

[1] Smith, V. A.: *The Early History of India*, 3rd edition (Oxford 1914, Clarendon Press), p. 270. According to Tarn, W. W.: *The Greeks in Bactria and India* (Cambridge 1938, University Press), p. 352, Kanishka died twenty years earlier, in A.D. 103.

[2] The stages of Kanishka's cautious and gradual conversion from a rather artificial and frigid religious syncretism to the ardent and single-minded proletarian faith that was sweeping over his dominions can be traced—like the development of the similar religious experience of Constantine—in the images and superscriptions on the princely convert's coins (see Smith, V. A.: *The Early History of India*, 3rd edition (Oxford 1914, Clarendon Press), pp. 265–6; Eliot, *Hinduism and Buddhism*, vol. ii, p. 87).

[3] For this historical function of the Kushan Empire as a cultural corridor see II. D (vii), vol. ii, pp. 372–3, above.

[4] For this extraordinary route see II. D (vii), vol. ii, p. 373; II. D (vi), Annex, vol. ii, p. 405, footnote 1; III. C (i) (*a*), vol. iii, p. 131, above.

[5] See I. C (i) (*b*), vol. i, pp. 88–90, above, and V. C (ii) (*b*), vol. vi, pp. 291–5, below.

proletariat being generated on the grand scale in the Sinic World
of that age, and this expectation is confirmed by the historical
evidence. We can watch the Sinic internal proletariat being
recruited from the three regular sources: uprooted members of the
disintegrating society's native body social; conquered members of
alien civilizations; and conquered barbarians. The first source was
drawn upon by the founder of the Sinic universal state, Ts'in She
Hwang-ti (*imperabat* 221[1]–210 B.C.), when he transplanted some
of the desirable elements in the population of his empire in order
to fill the new capital city which he had laid out,[2] and some of the
undesirable elements in order to colonize the barbarian territories
which he was annexing in the south.[3] The forcible enrolment of
barbarians was carried out over a longer period and on a vaster
scale; and it was by this method that the Sinic World had already
expanded, during its 'Time of Troubles',[4] from the modest domain
in the middle and lower valley of the Yellow River, which had
sufficed for its birth and growth,[5] over an area which extended to
the south-eastern fringes of the Eurasian Steppe in one direction
and towards the southern watershed of the Yangtse Basin in
another. North-westward the process of turning recalcitrant barbarians into domesticated proletarians was already complete by
Ts'in She Hwang-ti's time, when on this front the Sinic Civilization found itself in direct contact, all along the line, with the alien
civilization of the Eurasian Nomads.[6] On the southern front the
process was carried on steadily and systematically under the Ts'in
and Han régimes until, rather more than a hundred years after the
foundation of the universal state, it was completed, in this direction
likewise, *circa* 112–111 B.C.,[7] by the annexation of the southern
sea-board—including the territories that now constitute the French
possessions of Tongking and Annam, as well as the sites of the
present Chinese provinces of Kwangsi and Kwangtung and Fukien

[1] The year 221 B.C. was that in which Chêng Wang of Ts'in took the title of She
Hwang-ti ('First Universal Monarch') after the overthrow of Ts'i, which had been
the last surviving Great Power, apart from Ts'in itself, in the Sinic arena. As local
King of Ts'in, Chêng had been on the throne since 246 B.C.

[2] See Cordier, H.: *Histoire Générale de la Chine* (Paris 1920–1, Geuthner, 3 vols.),
vol. i, p. 202; and compare the Armenian successor of the Seleucidae, Tigranes', resort
to the same method of barbarism in order to populate Tigranocerta (*circa* 77 B.C.).

[3] See Franke, O.: *Geschichte des Chinesischen Reiches*, vol. i (Berlin and Leipzig
1930, de Gruyter), p. 244.

[4] If the hall-mark of the Sinic 'Time of Troubles' is the militarization of the states
into which the Sinic body social had come to be articulated, its beginning is probably
to be dated, as we have seen (in IV. C (ii) (*b*) 1, vol. iv, p. 66, above), from the outbreak
of the first great war for hegemony in 634 B.C. From this time onwards the surrounding
barbarians were drawn into the Sinic vortex on an ever-increasing scale—partly through
being conquered by the original states-members of the Sinic constellation, and partly
through being compelled to sinify themselves (as Urartu babylonicized herself) because
this was their only chance of self-preservation.

[5] For the cradle of the Sinic Civilization see II. C (ii) (*b*) 2, vol. i, pp. 318–21.

[6] See II. D (v), vol. ii, pp. 118–19, above.

[7] Cordier, op. cit., vol. i, p. 212; Franke, op. cit., vol. i, pp. 321–4.

and Chekiang. Before the vast barbarian recruitment of the Sinic internal proletariat was thus brought to a close, the enrolment of members of alien civilizations had already begun, and it was the introduction of this third element into the ranks of the Sinic internal proletariat that inoculated the now moribund Sinic body social with the Mahāyāna.

Sinic statesmanship found the Eurasian Nomads, with whom it was now in direct contact on its north-western front, more difficult neighbours to deal with than the sheerly barbarian highlanders by whom the Sinic World had previously been surrounded—on the one-side in Shansi and Shensi, and on the other side along the watershed between the Yangtse and the southern seaboard—and had thus been completely insulated from all other societies of its own species. Ts'in She Hwang-ti himself sought to solve this new problem of 'contact' in negative terms by consolidating into one continuous Great Wall the local fortifications which had been erected against the Nomads by his predecessors on the throne of Ts'in and by the princes of the neighbouring Sinic states that had likewise come to march with the Eurasian Steppe.[1] This enormous work was put in hand in 215 B.C.; yet, even with one of the material Wonders of the World to back it, a merely defensive strategy was found by the rulers of the Sinic universal state to be inadequate for coping with the power of the Hiongnu;[2] and eventually the Han Emperor Wuti (*imperabat* 140–87 B.C.) passed over to the offensive and launched against the Hiongnu a war of aggression which lasted nearly a hundred years (133–36 B.C.) before it resulted in a temporary pacification, under a *Pax Sinica*, of the Nomads' ranges as far westward as the Zungarian Gap.[3] In respect of achieving its main purpose—which was to solve the problem of dealing with Nomad neighbours—Wuti's policy was hardly more successful than Ts'in She Hwang-ti's, for the offensive against the Hiongnu strained the resources of the Sinic universal state almost to breaking-point[4] without permanently relieving it of its Nomad adver-

[1] See II. D (v), vol. ii, p. 119, above, as well as Cordier, op. cit., vol. i, pp. 206–7, and Franke, op. cit., vol. i, pp. 240–4.

[2] The record of the relations between the Sinic universal state and the Nomad Empire of the Hiongnu from the reign of Ts'in She Hwang-ti to the reign of Han Wuti gives the impression that, with the passage of time, the pressure of the Nomads was bearing harder and harder upon the sedentary Power behind the Great Wall. This may have been the effect of a bout of aridity on the Steppe, if there is any truth in the theory of climatic pulsations (for this theory and its application to the problem of the periodic eruptions of the Nomads see Part III. A, Annex II, in vol. iii, above); or it may have had nothing to do with the Nomadism of the Hiongnu, but have been simply an instance of the working of one of the general laws (see Part VIII, below) that govern the relations between a civilization and its barbarian neighbours when they are in long-continuing contact with one another along a stationary frontier.

[3] For the great war between the Prior Han and the Hiongnu see Franke, op. cit., vol. i, pp. 334–57.

[4] The strain of the great war on the Steppes may have been one of the causes of the

saries. An incidental consequence, however, of this hazardous forward policy against the barbarians on the Eurasian Steppe was the astonishing discovery that on the farther coast of this arid ocean[1] there was another world—or, rather three other worlds: the Indic, the Syriac, and the Hellenic.[2] In the last quarter of the second century B.C. the eastern outposts of these new worlds, in the oases of the Tarim Basin,[3] were annexed to the Sinic universal state;[4] their inhabitants were incorporated into the Sinic internal proletariat; and the descendants of these new alien recruits were the carriers of the Mahāyāna, in which the Sinic internal proletariat ultimately found the spiritual bread that it had never been

momentary breakdown of the Sinic universal state during the interregnum between the Prior and the Posterior Han in the first quarter of the first century of the Christian Era (for this interregnum see V. C (i) (c) 3, p. 271, and V. C (ii) (b), vol. vi, p. 295, below).

[1] For the analogy between the Steppe and the Ocean see Part III. A, vol. iii, pp. 7–8, with Annex I, above.

[2] The discovery was made by a party—half exploring expedition and half diplomatic mission—which was sent out into the Unknown West by the Emperor Wuti in 138 B.C., when he was making up his mind to take the offensive against the Hiongnu, and which duly returned to Ch'ang Ngan in the winter of 126/5 B.C. after having discovered Bactria and Parthia (Franke, op. cit., vol. i, pp. 334 and 337–40; Tarn, W. W.: *The Greeks in Bactria and India* (Cambridge 1938, University Press), pp. 279–84). To Sinic minds in the second century B.C. the news brought back by this party must have been even more astonishing than it was for Western minds to learn of the discovery of the Central American and Andean civilizations on the other side of the Atlantic in the sixteenth century of the Christian Era. For Western minds in that age the surprise was particular and not general, since the Western Society had always been aware that there were other societies of its own species in existence besides itself (e.g. Orthodox Christendom and the Syriac Society with its Iranian and Arabic offspring). On the other hand the members of the Sinic Society had always supposed—until the return of Chang K'ien's party to Ch'ang Ngan in 126/5 B.C.—that the Sinic Civilization was the solitary representative of its species in a universe whose only other human denizens were barbarians and savages; and, to minds brought up in this belief, the discovery of the existence of the Indic, Syriac, and Hellenic civilizations must have been as revolutionary in its intellectual effect as the sixteenth-century Western astronomical discovery that the stellar universe was not geocentric. We may compare the discovery of the Babylonic and Hittite civilizations by the members of the Egyptiac Society, in the fifteenth century B.C., in the course of their counter-offensive, across the desert of Sinai, against the Hyksos Eurasian Nomad cousins of the Hiongnu.

[3] In the Tarim Basin, by the time when it came within the Sinic Society's purview in the last quarter of the second century B.C., the elements of the three non-Sinic civilizations which had previously arrived on the scene were already blended; but the Indic element was here still predominant over the Syriac and the Hellenic. According to the local tradition of the Khotan oasis, which has been preserved in a Tibetan medium, the city was founded by settlers from India in Açoka's time, and Buddhism was introduced from India 170 years later (Sir Charles Eliot: *Hinduism and Buddhism* (London 1921, Arnold, 3 vols.), vol. iii, p. 211; Smith, V. A.: *The Early History of India*, 3rd edition (Oxford 1914, Clarendon Press), p. 193). 'In the Turfan frescoes, the drapery and composition are Indian', while 'the faces are Eastern Asiatic (sometimes, however, they represent a race with red hair and blue eyes)'; and 'the paintings testify to the invasion of Far Eastern art by the ideas and designs of Indian Buddhism rather than to an equal combination of Indian and Chinese influence' (Eliot, op. cit., vol iii, p. 195).

[4] The way was first cleared by the conquest, in 121 B.C., of the intervening barrier of Hiongnu territory in the present Chinese province of Kansu. The actual conquest of the Tarim Basin itself was carried out in 104–101 B.C. (Franke, op. cit., vol. i, pp. 342–9). The moment was favourable, since the Greek Power in Bactria had just been overwhelmed, and the Parthian Power in Khurāsān was still hard beset, by the eruption of the Sakas and the Yuechi across the threshold of the Eurasian Steppe between the Pamirs and the Caspian.

able to extract from the Confucian and Taoist philosophies of the Sinic dominant minority.

The transmission of the Mahāyāna along this channel was actually facilitated by the vicissitudes in the political relations between the Sinic universal state and its western dependencies during the three centuries that elapsed between the first assertion of Sinic authority over the Tarim Basin at the end of the second century B.C. and the final break-up of the Sinic universal state itself at the turn of the second and third centuries of the Christian Era.

After having lasted for rather more than a century, the first period of Sinic rule in the Tarim Basin came to an end in A.D. 16,[1] when the collapse of the Prior Han Dynasty enabled the Hiongnu to shake off the Sinic yoke and the oasis-states to repudiate their allegiance; and it was not till A.D. 73 that the Posterior Han, after having re-established the Han Empire in the home-provinces, felt themselves strong enough to begin the reconquest of the lost western dependencies. Thanks to the abilities of one great military commander and colonial administrator, Pan Ch'ao, the enterprise was successfully accomplished by the end of the first century of the Christian Era;[2] and at the moment when the hero re-entered Loyang in triumph in A.D. 102 the westward extension of the Sinic universal state was as wide as it had been in 101 B.C. Pan Ch'ao, however, found no worthy successor; the reconquered peoples became restive as soon as his masterly hand was withdrawn; and this time there was an alien Power on the horizon which could venture to cross swords with the sovereign of 'All that is under Heaven'.

When the Prior Han Emperor Wuti made the first Sinic conquest of the Tarim Basin, the Greek Power in Bactria had just been overwhelmed by the eruption of the Saka and Yuechi Nomads out of the Eurasian Steppe;[3] but while Pan Ch'ao (*militabat* A.D. 73–102) was campaigning in Central Asia, Kanishka (*regnabat circa* A.D. 78–123) was completing the expansion of one of the five petty Yuechi 'successor-states' of Bactria into a Philhellene barbarian kingdom which was as extensive and as powerful as the Bactrian Greek principality at its apogee.[4] In A.D. 90 Kanishka sent an army into the Tarim Basin to dispute Pan Ch'ao's advance, and drew upon himself an ignominious defeat;[5] but after Pan Ch'ao's disappearance from the scene Kanishka repeated his attempt and this time

[1] Franke, op. cit., vol. i, p. 383.
[2] For details see ibid., pp. 395–400.
[3] See p. 143, footnote 4, above.   [4] See p. 133, with footnote 1, above.
[5] Smith, V. A.: *The Early History of India*, 3rd edition (Oxford 1914, Clarendon Press), pp. 251–2.

he succeeded in wresting the greater part of the Tarim Basin out of Sinic hands and bringing it under his own suzerainty.[1] Thereafter the command over the Tarim Basin appears to have been disputed between the Kushan and the Han until both Powers broke down and disappeared in the early decades of the third century of the Christian Era.[2] The details of the history of this frontier warfare are obscure[3] and unimportant; but the entry of the Mahāyāna into the Sinic World through the avenue of this disputed territory in the course of the second century of the Christian Era is a fact which is as certain as it is momentous.[4] By the time when, at the turn of the second and third centuries, the Sinic universal state broke up and the Sinic Civilization went into dissolution, the Mahāyāna had effectively established its claim

[1] Smith, op. cit., pp. 262–3. This reconstruction of events would be difficult, though not impossible, to reconcile with the chronological scheme (see p. 140, footnote 1, above) which dates Kanishka's death A.D. 103 instead of A.D. 123.

[2] See II. D (vii), vol. ii, p. 373, above.

[3] Dated documents that have been recovered by our modern Western archaeologists from the military frontier of the Han Empire in the neighbourhood of Tun-huang show that the Han were in effective occupation of this point between A.D. 98 and A.D. 153 (Eliot, Sir Charles: *Hinduism and Buddhism* (London 1921, Arnold, 3 vols.), vol. iii, p. 193).

[4] See IV. C (ii) (*b*) 1, vol. iv, p. 65, above. The story of the deliberate introduction of Buddhism into the Han Empire in the seventh decade of the first century of the Christian Era by the Emperor Mingti (*imperabat* A.D. 58–75), in obedience to a dream, is rejected as legendary by Franke (op. cit., vol. i, pp. 407–8), who points out the unlikelihood of such a transaction having taken place before the reconquest of the Tarim Basin by Pan Ch'ao. Our own dating of the introduction of Buddhism into the Sinic World will differ greatly according to whether we are speaking of the new Mahayanian religion, to which the Kushan King Kanishka became a convert in the first or second century of the Christian Era, or of the pre-Mahayanian philosophy which was adopted in the third century B.C. by the Mauryan Emperor Açoka. Whereas the Mahāyāna—which was itself only nascent in Kanishka's generation—can hardly have entered upon its conquest of the Sinic World before Kanishka's conversion to the faith and conquest of the Sinic dependencies in the Tarim Basin, the pre-Mahayanian philosophy of Siddhārtha Gautama may have become known in the Sinic World at any time after the dispatch of Chang K'ien's exploring party into the Western *terra incognita* in 138 B.C. For the Hinayanian Buddhist philosophy and the Mahayanian Buddhist religion travelled from their common original centre of dispersion in Northern India in successive waves (see II. D (vi), Annex, vol. ii, p. 405, footnote 1, above); and the Hinayanian wave, which was set in motion by the Indic Emperor Açoka (*imperabat* 273–232 B.C.), if not by the private enterprise of earlier philosophic missionaries, may well have reached the Oxus-Jaxartes Basin, and even the Tarim Basin, within a hundred years of Açoka's death. Franke (op. cit., vol. i, pp. 408–9) calculates—on the strength of a casual reference, in the Sinic records, to the presence of Buddhist monks and laymen as far afield as the present Chinese province of Kiangsu in A.D. 65—that Buddhism must have begun to penetrate the Sinic World before the beginning of the Christian Era. If this inference is legitimate, the Buddhism in question must, of course, have been of the pre-Mahayanian school; for the conception of the Mahāyāna is not older than the first century of the Christian Era; the doctrine of the Fathers who attended Kanishka's oecumenical council *circa* A.D. 100 was not the full-blown flower of the Mahayanian Faith (see Eliot, *Hinduism and Buddhism*, vol. ii, pp. 78–82); and the differentiation of the Mahāyāna from the Hīnayāna was not yet complete in the second century when the Buddhist impulse was being transmitted from the Kushan Kingdom to the Han Empire via the disputed territory in the Tarim Basin. According to Sir Charles Eliot (*Hinduism and Buddhism* (London 1921, Arnold, 3 vols.), vol. iii, p. 213), the Mahāyāna and the Hīnayāna were still not wholly disentangled from one another in the Tarim Basin in the fifth and sixth centuries of the Christian Era, and the Hīnayāna still survived in Kuchā, on the northern rim of the Tarim Basin, when the Far Eastern Buddhist pilgrim, Hiuen Tsiang (Yuan Chwang), passed that way *circa* A.D. 629 (Eliot, op. cit., vol. iii, pp. 205 and 211). The problem discussed in this footnote has been dealt with, by anticipation, in IV. C (ii) (*b*) 1, vol. iv, p. 65, footnote 4, above.

to act—like Christianity, two centuries later, in the Hellenic World —as the moribund society's executor and residuary legatee.

If imitation is the sincerest flattery, the hold which the Mahā-yāna had already gained, by this time, upon the imagination and emotions of the Sinic internal proletariat may be gauged from the fact that, in the Sinic World in this age, one of the indigenous philosophies of the Sinic dominant minority was transformed into a proletarian religion through a metamorphosis which was perhaps even more extraordinary than that which had conjured the Mahā-yāna itself out of the philosophy of Siddhārtha Gautama.[1]

The Sinic philosophy of the Tao, which had been first pro-pounded, like the Confucian philosophy, during the Sinic 'Time of Troubles', as a response to the challenge of the breakdown of the Sinic Civilization,[2] was distinguished from the Confucian sister school by an attitude towards life which rather resembled the Buddha's. The essence of the Tao was its belief in the supreme virtue and efficacy of inaction—in which, by a paradoxical but penetrating intuition, the Taoist philosopher saw the most intense and creative form of true activity.[3] A doctrine which thus not only condemned violence but went so far as to deprecate exertion of every kind, seemed marked out to be an esoteric discipline which would never be appreciated or practised by more than a few rare spirits; and it is somewhat surprising to find a 'Taoism' in which the genuine 'way' was vulgarized into a mere policy of *laisser faire* laying itself out to meet the needs of practical men in the age of lassitude which followed the refoundation of the Sinic universal state by Liu Pang, the first Emperor of the Han Dynasty. During the first half of the second century B.C. this travesty of Taoism actually anticipated Confucianism both in winning acceptance as the official philosophy of the Sinic universal state[4] and in pur-chasing this worldly success at the price of debasing itself into magic;[5] and when, in the reign of the Emperor Wuti (*imperabat* 140–87 B.C.), Confucianism succeeded in supplanting Taoism once for all at the official centre of the Middle Kingdom, the discomfited practical philosophy did not give up the game, but went under-ground and retreated into the provinces—lying low and biding its time until at length, when the Sinic universal state broke up, the name of Taoism attached itself to a proletarian church[6]—with

---

[1] See Eliot, Sir Ch.: *Hinduism and Buddhism* (London 1921, Arnold, 3 vols.), vol. iii, pp. 227–9.   [2] See I. C (i) (*b*), vol. i, p. 89, above.
[3] For this cardinal doctrine of the Tao see III. C (i) (*c*), vol. iii, pp. 187–9, above, and V. C (i) (*d*) 4, in the present volume, pp. 415–17, below.
[4] See V. C (i) (*d*) 4, pp. 418–19, below.
[5] See Hackmann, H.: *Chinesische Philosophie* (Munich 1927, Reinhardt), p. 225.
[6] See the present chapter and volume, p. 178, footnote 1, and also V. C (i) (*d*) 6 (δ), p. 557, below. In the preceding generation Taoism had been taken up again, at the centre of the Sinic universal state, by the Posterior Han Emperor Huanti (*impera-*

monasteries, temples, and liturgical observances on the Mahayanian pattern[1]—which sprang into existence, and converted the population *en masse*, in those *ci-devant* barbarian territories on the southwestern fringes of the Sinic World whose inhabitants had been forcibly enrolled in the Sinic internal proletariat through the conquests that were made in this direction by Ts'in She Hwang-ti and his Prior Han successors.[2] If this metamorphosis is extraordinary, it is more extraordinary still to see the name of the pacific Tao being taken in vain in order to give a religious sanction of legitimacy and guarantee of success to an armed proletarian insurrection against the Han régime which broke out in the last quarter of the second century of the Christian Era in the wild hill-country on the border between the present provinces of Shensi and Szechwan.[3]

It will be seen that the history of the Sinic Civilization conforms very closely, in its disintegration-phase, to the Hellenic pattern. In the misguided hands of a minority that was dominant without being creative, the disintegrating society ran its course from breakdown to dissolution through a 'Time of Troubles' and a universal state and an interregnum; there was a secession of the proletariat; and the internal proletariat found for itself, in the Mahāyāna, a universal church which played the part of the Catholic Christian Church in the foundering Hellenic World, while the abortive Taoist Church may be compared with the abortive Neoplatonic Church of Iamblichus and Maximinus Daia and Julian the Apostate and Sallustius.[4] If we turn next to the history of the disintegration of the Sumeric Civilization, we shall observe that, up to a point, the phenomena are the same, but that the plot of the play does not work out to the same dénouement.

The Legacy of the Sumeric Internal Proletariat.

In Sumeric, as in Sinic and Hellenic, history we can discern a 'Time of Troubles' and a universal state[5] and an interregnum;

bat A.D. 147–68) (Hackmann, H.: *Chinesische Philosophie* (Munich 1927, Reinhardt), p. 249).

[1] Franke (op. cit., vol. i, p. 420) inclines to the belief that the outward organization of this latter-day 'Taoist' proletarian church was a conscious imitation of the contemporary organization of the Mahāyāna. Compare the relation of the Ryobo Shinto Church to the popular Japanese adaptations of the Mahāyāna in the Japanese 'Time of Troubles'.

[2] See p. 141, above.

[3] For this insurrection and its Taoist colouring see Cordier, H.: *Histoire Générale de la Chine* (Paris 1920–1, Geuthner, 3 vols.), vol. i, pp. 189–90; Hackmann, H.: *Chinesische Philosophie* (Munich 1927, Reinhardt), p. 228; Franke, op. cit., vol. i, pp. 419–21. In the present chapter of this Study this latter-day aberration of Taoism is referred to again on p. 178, footnote 1, below.

[4] For this abortive Neoplatonic Church see further V. C (i) (d) 6 (δ), pp. 565–7; V. C (i) (d) 6 (δ), Annex, pp. 680–3; and V. C (ii) (a), vol. vi, pp. 222–3, below.

[5] For the foundation of this Sumeric universal state—'the Empire of Sumer and Akkad'—by Ur-Engur of Ur *circa* 2298 B.C., and its restoration *circa* 1947 B.C. by Hammurabi, see I. C (i) (b), vol. i, p. 106, above, and V. C (ii) (b), vol. vi, pp. 296–7, below.

and the Sumeric, like the Sinic and the Hellenic, Society was compensated for its own dissolution by becoming 'apparented' to younger societies of its own species. The Babylonic and Hittite societies appear to stand to the Sumeric as the main body of the Far Eastern Society in China and its branch in Korea and Japan stand to the Sinic Society, or as the Western and Orthodox Christian societies stand to the Hellenic Society. These points of likeness are offset, however, by one striking difference. In the relation between the Hellenic and Sinic societies and the younger civilizations that were respectively affiliated to them, the link was provided by a universal church which had been created or adopted by the internal proletariat of the disintegrating 'apparented' society and which eventually served as a chrysalis out of which the nascent 'affiliated' societies emerged.[1] The Mahāyāna provided a link of this kind between the Sinic Society and the two Far Eastern societies, and the Catholic Christian Church mediated in the same way between the Hellenic Society and the two Christendoms. On the other hand, when we come to examine the relation between the Sumeric Society and the Hittite and Babylonic societies, we find no trace of the corresponding phenomenon which we should expect to find on the principle of 'the uniformity of Human Nature'.

The religion of the Babylonic World seems to have been taken over, *tel quel*, from the Sumeric dominant minority;[2] the religion of the Hittite World seems to have been derived from the same souice in part, but in the main to have been of non-Sumeric origin—its presumable source being the Anatolian external proletariat of the Sumeric Society which flooded over the Cappadocian provinces of the Sumeric universal state when, after the death of Hammurabi, the Empire of Sumer and Akkad broke up in the nineteenth century B.C.[3] The interregnum intervening between the dissolution of the Sumeric Society and the emergence of the Babylonic and Hittite societies is not spanned by any bridge which we can identify as a Sumeric proletarian church; and we cannot even point to any wreckage—a fallen key-stone or a weathered pier—which might warrant us in hazarding the conjecture that such a bridge did once exist. We know so little about the religious history of the Sumeric Society that, as we have already had to confess,[4] we cannot confidently ascribe to a proletarian origin even those elements in the Sumeric religion—the Penitential Psalms and the worship of Tammuz and Ishtar—

---

[1] For the function of a universal church as a chrysalis for a new civilization see further Part VII, below.   [2] See I. C (i) (*b*), vol. i, p. 115, above.
[3] See I. C (i) (*b*), vol. i, p. 112, with footnote 2, above.
[4] In I. C (i) (*b*), vol. i, p. 115, footnote 1, above.

which assume a distinctively proletarian complexion if we allow
ourselves to interpret the internal evidence in the light of a comparison with other religions which are proletarian in their origin
beyond question. We can only say that, if the worship of Tammuz
and Ishtar really is a monument of the experience and the creativity of the Sumeric internal proletariat, then this attempted act
of creation was abortive in the history of the Sumeric Society
itself, and only came to fruition in so far as it transmitted a spark
of inspiration to kindle spiritual fires in alien souls.

We have already come across one of these remote workings
of the worship of Tammuz and Ishtar in observing[1] how the
worship of Cybele, who was the Sumeric Ishtar in a Hittite dress,
became one of the 'higher religions' of the internal proletariat
of the Hellenic World in the course of this goddess's long journey
from the interior of Anatolia to the coasts of the Baltic and the
North Sea. In this Hittite version of the worship of the Sumeric
pair of divinities the figure of the goddess has dwarfed and
overshadowed that of the god who plays towards her the diverse
and even contradictory roles of son and lover and protégé and
victim. By the side of Cybele-Ishtar, Attis-Tammuz dwindles
to insignificance; and Nerthus-Ishtar seems to stand in solitary
grandeur without the attendance of any masculine consort.[2] This
north-westward road which scaled the Taurus and found its distant
terminus on an island in the North European seas was not, however, the only road that was trodden triumphantly by the pair
of Sumeric gods who found abroad the honour that was perhaps
never wholeheartedly accorded to them in their own country.
We can watch them travelling south-westwards simultaneously—
down Syria into Egypt—and on this journey there seems to have
been an inverse change in the relations between the two divinities
—Tammuz increasing while Ishtar decreased. At any rate, the
Atargatis whose worship spread from a mother-shrine at Bambyce
to a daughter-shrine at Ascalon[3] would appear, from her name,
to have been an Ishtar whose claim to veneration was based upon
her function of serving as Attis' mate; in Phoenicia an Adonis-
Tammuz was 'the Lord' whose yearly death an Astarte-Ishtar
mourned; and in the Egyptiac World an Osiris-Tammuz—who
was associated, in the story of his Passion, with the Phoenician
city of Byblus[4]—overshadowed his sister-wife Isis as decidedly

[1] See the present chapter, pp. 81–2, above.
[2] In the same way Isis-Ishtar, too, eventually eclipsed Osiris-Tammuz, if she did
not actually dismiss him from her train, in her triumphal progress from her Egyptiac
home to her Hellenic mission-field.
[3] Meyer, E.: *Geschichte des Altertums*, vol. iii (Stuttgart 1901, Cotta) p. 137.
[4] For the probable derivation of Osiris and Isis from Tammuz and Ishtar through
Adonis and Astarte see I. C (ii), vol. i, p. 140, above.

as Isis, in her turn, overshadowed Osiris when she subsequently won a spiritual empire for herself in the hearts of the Hellenic internal proletariat.[1] This version of the Sumeric faith in which the suffering and dying god, and not the mourning and ministering goddess, was the figure on which the worshipper's attention and devotion were concentrated, seems even to have spread to the remote barbarians of a Scandinavian Ultima Thule, where Balder-Tammuz, like Adonis-Tammuz, was called 'the Lord' *par excellence* in the local vernacular tongue, while Balder's colourless consort Nanna still retained the personal name of the Sumeric mother-goddess.[2]

In the worship of Osiris the sorely oppressed proletariat of a disintegrating Egyptiac Society found a satisfying expression for a bitter resentment and an ardent hope.[3] The resentment was directed against the indigenous gods of the Egyptiac World, who had allowed the dominant minority to purchase an exclusive claim on their divine benevolence with gigantic oblations—culminating in the Great Pyramids—that could only be offered at the cost of a ruthless exploitation of all but a privileged fraction of the people. From these mercenary and heartless divinities the Egyptiac internal proletariat turned away to a god who had tasted the bitterness of death and had won from this agony a strength which could make even the Pyramid-Builders tremble;[4] and they addressed themselves to Osiris in the hope that this god of their own choice, in whom they had put their trust by a personal act of faith, would bestow upon them the immortality which their oppressors were seeking to purchase at a monstrous price from Re—the Sun-God whose character the Pharaohs had re-minted in their own image.

The resentment and the hope which were thus both expressed in a single proletarian religion were reflected, in the field of action, in that conflict between the spirit of Violence and the spirit of Gentleness with which we have become familiar in the histories of other internal proletariats. The violence discharged

---

[1] See p. 149, footnote 2, above.

[2] For this remarkable equation see Dawson, Christopher: *The Age of the Gods*: re-issue (London 1933, Sheed & Ward), pp. 282–3. For Scandinavia as a 'living museum' of elements of culture which have been radiated from distant sources, see II. D (vii), vol. ii, p. 342, footnote 3, above.

[3] For the conflict between the religions of the dominant minority and the internal proletariat during the disintegration of the Egyptiac Society see I. C (ii), vol. i, pp. 140–3; for the replacement of a creative by a dominant minority in the Egyptiac World in the Age of the Pyramid-Builders see III. C (i) (*d*), vol. iii, pp. 212–15; for the violent proletarian revolt, during the Egyptiac 'Time of Troubles', against the idolization of the Egyptiac Double Crown see IV. C (iii) (*c*) 2 (*β*), vol. iv, pp. 409–11, above; for the proletarian origin of the Osirian Church see Breasted, J. H.: *The Development of Religion and Thought in Ancient Egypt* (London 1912, Hodder & Stoughton), pp. 37–9.

[4] For the dread which Osiris inspired in the Pyramid Builders see ibid., pp. 74–5.

itself, during the Egyptiac 'Time of Troubles', in the subversive revolutionary outbreaks of which we catch an echo in *The Admonitions of a Prophet*[1] and other works of literature in the same vein which were composed in the following age. In these orgies of savage retaliation the Egyptiac internal proletariat took a revenge upon the Pyramid-Builders which was equal in its enormity to the Egyptiac dominant minority's crying offence.

'He hath put down the mighty from their seat, and hath exalted the humble and meek;
'He hath filled the hungry with good things, and the rich he hath sent empty away.'[2]

But, since in this case the avenger was not a just and compassionate god but a gang of exasperated men who had taken the law into their own hands, the revenge was as barren as it was complete; and the exposure of the futility of the Pyramid-Builders' attempt to attain a selfish immortality for themselves at their subjects' expense, by a ruthless and unscrupulous exploitation of their immense material power, did not in itself reveal any alternative way of attaining the spiritual treasure which the Pharaohs had failed to win but which the proletariat had not ceased to long for. The insurgent Egyptiac internal proletariat did not succeed in quenching its spiritual thirst until it had been disillusioned and at the same time enlightened by the experience of reaping the harvest of Violence and finding that it was Dead Sea fruit. In this chastened mood it recoiled from the way of Violence to the way of Gentleness and reached, by this road, the object of its long and agonizing search. In the age of 'the Middle Empire', which was the Egyptiac universal state, we see the proletarian worshipper of Osiris finding his happiness at last in a personal relation with his god; a god whose blessed immortality was not a divine prerogative which he enjoyed *ex officio deitatis*, but was a special grace which he had won for himself—and could therefore impart gratuitously to his human votaries—in virtue of an experience which was unknown to any other god while it was the common lot of every human being. Osiris could bring salvation to Man because he—alone among the Gods—had passed through the human ordeal of Death.[3]

In the 'Indian Summer' of Egyptiac history this twofold mystery of Osiris' death and resurrection and of the worshipper's union with the God in his divine bliss, as well as in his tribulation,

---

[1] See the extracts from this poem in IV. C (iii) (c) 2 (β), vol. iv, pp. 410–11, above.
[2] Luke i. 52–3.
[3] For Osiris as an epiphany of the Dying God see further V. C (ii) (a), vol. vi, p. 276, below.

was enshrined in a holy sepulchre and rehearsed in a passion play; and when the Egyptiac Society was *in articulo mortis* it looked as though an Osirian Church were destined to assume, for this moribund civilization, that role of executor and residuary legatee which has actually been played by the Christian Church for the Hellenic Civilization and by the Mahāyāna for the Sinic. It was only at the thirteenth hour, when the Egyptiac universal state had duly broken up and when the ensuing interregnum had set in, that the course of history was suddenly and violently diverted into an entirely different channel by the vehemence of the revulsion of the Egyptiac internal proletariat, as well as the Egyptiac dominant minority, against the alien tincture in the culture of the Hyksos barbarian invaders.[1]

The historical consequences of this revulsion have engaged our attention in other contexts already[2] and only concern us here in their particular effect upon the fortunes of the Osirian Church. We have seen how the prospects of this church were blighted, when the flower was on the point of bearing fruit, by the establishment of an unnatural 'union sacrée' between the nascent religion of the internal proletariat and the moribund religion of the dominant minority in the mummified carcass of the Egyptiac body social. This ultimate fate of the Osirian Church was as tragic as it was inconsequent; but we must not allow an abnormal epilogue to trick us into forgetting the normality of the main action of the play. The Osirian Church had to be called into existence before it could be cheated of its manifest destiny; and, in itself, the creation of the Osirian Church is a proletarian achievement which is worthy to be compared with the creation of the Christian Church or with the creation of the Mahāyāna, while the antecedent struggle between the spirits of Violence and Gentleness in the souls of the Egyptiac internal proletariat is not less illuminating for a historian—or less moving for a fellow human being—than the similar struggle, with the similar outcome, between the gentleness of Eleazar the Scribe and Jesus of Nazareth and the violence of Judas Maccabaeus and Judas of Galilee.

The Symptoms in the Western World.

In order to complete our survey of internal proletariats we have still to examine one more case. Do the characteristic phenomena, with which we have now made ourselves familiar, reappear in

---

[1] See I. C (ii), vol. i, p. 139, footnote 1, and p. 144; IV. C (ii) (*b*) 2, vol. iv, p. 85; IV. C (iii) (*c*) 2 (*β*), vol. iv, p. 421; and Part V. A, in the present volume, pp. 2–3, above, and V. C (i) (*c*) 4, pp. 351–2, below.

[2] In I. C (ii), vol. i, pp. 144–6, and in the present Part, Division A, in the present volume, pp. 2–4, as well as in V. C (i) (*b*), pp. 28–9, above.

the history of the West? When we call for the evidence for the existence of a Western internal proletariat, we may find ourselves overwhelmed by an *embarras de richesses*.

We have already noticed that one of the regular sources for the recruitment of an internal proletariat has been drawn upon by our Western Society on a stupendous scale. The 'man power' of no less than ten disintegrating civilizations has been conscripted, wholesale, into the Western body social within the last four hundred years;[1] and on the common level of membership in our Western internal proletariat, to which they have thus been reduced, a process of standardization has been at work which has already blurred—or even quite effaced—the characteristic features by which these heterogeneous masses of human beings were once distinguished from one another before they were devoured and masticated by the great Leviathan of the West. Nor has the monster been content just to prey upon his own kind. Within the same four centuries he has also hunted down and swallowed up almost all the primitive societies that had not become the prey of other predatory civilizations before the beginning of the sixteenth century of the Christian Era; and, while some of the primitive populations that have been rounded up in this way into our Western internal proletariat have simply died of the shock (like the Caribs and the Bushmen and the Tasmanians and the Australian Black-fellows and the great majority of the Red Indian peoples on the North American Continent north-east of the Rio Grande),[2] there are others (like the Negroes of Tropical Africa) who have managed to survive and to set the Niger flowing into the Hudson.

Under the lash of our Western dominant minority (which has chastised these human rivers with more effect than ever followed from Xerxes' scourging of the insensitive waters of the Dardanelles), the Congo, too, has been made to flow into the Mississippi, and the Yangtse into the straits of Malacca; for in our modern Western World since the opening of the sixteenth century of the Christian Era—as in the Hellenic World after the opening of the third century B.C.—the populations of alien or primitive culture which have been swept into an expanding civilization's net have been not merely subjugated but also uprooted. The Negro slaves who have survived 'the Middle Passage' across the Atlantic from Africa to America, and the Tamil and Southern Chinese coolies who have been shipped to the equatorial or antipodean coasts of the Indian Ocean, are the counterparts of the slaves who,

---

[1] See the present chapter, pp. 89–90, above.
[2] For the statistical aspect of the Red Indians' fate see II. D (vii), vol. ii, p. 277, above.

in the last two centuries B.C., were consigned from all the coasts of the Mediterranean to the ranches and plantations of Roman Italy.[1]

There is another contingent of conscripted aliens in our Western internal proletariat who have been uprooted and disoriented spiritually without having been physically evicted from their ancestral homes. In any community that is attempting to solve the problem of adapting its life to the rhythm of an exotic civilization to which it has been either forcibly annexed or freely converted, there is need of a special social class to serve as a human counterpart of the 'transformer' which changes an electric current from one voltage to another; and the class which is called into existence—often quite abruptly and artificially—in response to this demand has come to be known generically, from the special Russian name for it, as the intelligentsia (a word whose meaning is expressed in its very formation, in which a Latin root and a Western idea are acclimatized in Russian by being given a Slavonic termination). The intelligentsia is a class of liaison-officers who have learnt the tricks of an intrusive civilization's trade so far as may be necessary to enable their own community, through their agency, just to hold its own in a social environment in which life is ceasing to be lived in accordance with the local tradition and is coming more and more to be lived in the style that is imposed by the intrusive civilization upon the aliens who fall under its dominion.

The first recruits to this intelligentsia are military and naval officers who learn as much of the domineering society's art of war as may be necessary in order to save the Russia of Peter the Great from being conquered by a Western Sweden, or the Turkey and Japan of a later age from being conquered by a Russia who by this time has herself become sufficiently Westernized in the sphere of military technique to be able to launch out upon a career of aggression on her own account against her still un-Westernized neighbours. Then comes the diplomatist who learns how to conduct with Western governments the negotiations that are forced upon his community by its failure to hold its own in battle against Western armies and navies. We have seen the 'Osmanlis enlisting their *ra'īyeh* for this diplomatic work—and grudgingly allowing them the licence and influence and affluence which are the necessary reward of their services—until a further turn of the Western screw compels the 'Osmanlis at last to master for themselves this despised and distasteful trade.[2] Next come the merchants—the

---

[1] For the transplantation of Chinese coolies see II. D (vi), vol. ii, pp. 217–18, and II. D (vii), vol. ii, p. 315; for the transplantation of Negro slaves see II. D (vi), vol. ii, pp. 218–20, above.

[2] See II. D (vi), vol. ii, pp. 224–8, and Part III. A, vol. iii, pp. 47–50.

Hong Merchants at Canton;[1] the compradores of a later generation at Shanghai; the Levantine,[2] Sephardī,[3] Greek,[4] and Armenian[5] subjects of the Ottoman Pādishāh in the Échelles du Levant—who manage to hold the long spoons with which any self-respecting non-Western society prefers at first to sup when it is shamefacedly doing commercial business with the Western devils. And finally, as the leaven—or virus—of Western Civilization works deeper into the social life of the society which is in process of being penetrated and assimilated, the intelligentsia develops its most characteristic types: the schoolmaster who has learnt the trick of teaching Western subjects; the civil servant who has picked up the practice of conducting the public administration according to Western forms; the lawyer who has acquired the knack of applying a version of the *Code Napoléon* in accordance with a nineteenth-century French judicial procedure.

This spectacle of the creation of an intelligentsia will occupy our attention again at a later stage when we are studying,[6] for its own sake, the phenomenon of the contacts between civilizations. In this place we merely have to observe that, wherever we find an intelligentsia in existence, we may infer, not only that two civilizations have been in contact, but that one of the two is now in process of being absorbed into the other's internal proletariat. We can also observe another fact in the life of an intelligentsia which is written large upon its countenance for all to read: an intelligentsia is born to be unhappy.

This liaison-class suffers from the congenital unhappiness of the bastard and the hybrid, who is an outcast from both the families —or a sport in both the races—that have guiltily combined to beget him. An intelligentsia is hated and despised by its own people because its very existence is a reproach to them. Through its awkward presence in their midst it is a living reminder of the hateful but inescapable alien civilization which cannot be kept at bay and which therefore has to be humoured. The Pharisee is reminded of this each time when he meets the Publican, and the Zealot when he meets the Herodian. The intelligentsia's unpardonable offence in the eyes of its own kith and kin is the very indispensability of the social services which the intelligentsia performs—a hard fact which the Pharisees never overtly acknowledge yet perpetually recognize and resent in their hearts. And, while the intelligentsia thus has no love lost upon it at home, it also has no honour

[1] See II. D (vi), vol. ii, p. 232, above.
[2] See II. D (vi), vol. ii, pp. 230–2, above.
[3] See II. D (vi), vol. ii, pp. 243–7, above.
[4] See II. D (vi), vol. ii, pp. 223–4, above.
[5] See II. D (vi), vol. ii, p. 236, above.   [6] In Part IX, below.

paid to it in the country whose manners and customs and tricks and turns it has so laboriously and ingeniously mastered. In the earlier days of the historic association between India and England a Hindu intelligentsia which the British Rāj had fostered for its own administrative convenience was sometimes ridiculed by English philistines who dishonoured their own nation in insulting their Indian fellow subjects.. The more facile 'the babu's' command of English, the more sardonically 'the sahib' would laugh at the subtle incongruity of those minute errors that still inevitably crept in.[1] The philistine perhaps seldom paused to reflect that his own knowledge of Hindustani was far too imperfect to expose him to the same kind of ridicule vice versa, and he did not ask himself whether his depreciation might not be a left-handed kind of praise and his scorn a mask for an unconfessed envy of a virtuosity which the dominant alien was perhaps affecting to despise because he himself lacked either the skill or the application to attain to it. The philistine simply gave rein to his feelings; and, however captious his criticism might be, the shaft of malice would only too often strike home.

The intelligentsia is at the philistine's mercy because the essence of the intelligentsia's profession is, after all, mimesis; its art consists in a *tour de force*; and in other contexts we have already probed the weak points of mimesis and assessed the penalty that has to be paid for making the audacious attempt to add a cubit to one's stature. The insipid mechanicalness of mimesis,[2] and the pathological distortion and abandoned vulgarity that are apt to result from the division of labour and the practice of mimesis in a society in process of civilization,[3] are vices which find a uniquely congenial soil to grow in on the border-line of contact and fusion between one disintegrating civilization and another; and this means that the intelligentsia is exposed to the danger of being infected with these moral maladies *ex officio*. In these circumstances the taunts with which the intelligentsia is assailed by its critics are likely to hit the mark—even though the missile may recoil, like a boomerang, upon the heads of the critics themselves when they do not hesitate to make use, for their own profit, of those valuable social services through the faithful performance of which the intelligentsia acquires its characteristic faults.

It will be seen that the intelligentsia complies in double measure

---

[1] The present writer can enter personally into the feelings of the Anglophone Hindu through having been brought up to express his own feelings in Greek elegiac verse. He can imagine what game would be made of the verses printed at the beginning of volume i of this Study if an Antipater of Sidon or a Meleager of Gadara were to cast his eye over them in a malicious mood.

[2] See IV. C (iii) (a), vol. iv, pp. 119–33, above.

[3] See IV. C (iii) (b) 14 and 15, vol. iv, pp. 232–45, above.

with our fundamental definition of a proletariat[1] by being 'in' but not 'of' two societies and not merely one;[2] and while it may console itself in the first chapter of its history with the ironical reflection that it is an indispensable organ of both these bodies social, and that this very indispensability is the head and front of its offending, it is robbed of even this consolation as time goes on. For the adjustment of supply to demand is almost beyond the wit of Man when 'man-power' itself is the commodity; and, just because an intelligentsia is an emergency-product which has to be called into existence rather suddenly and artificially *ex nihilo* in the first instance, the measures taken to stimulate production are apt to lead to over-production in the end.

A Peter the Great wants so many Russian chinovniks or an East India Company so many Bengali clerks or a Mehmed 'Alī so many Egyptian mill-hands and shipwrights: incontinently they set to work to perform their conjuring-trick of creating something out of nothing with all the vigour and resourcefulness of the consummate man of action which the successful Westernizer has to be; and then, in the next chapter of the story, they find themselves in the quandary of the hero in the fairy-tale who has learnt the magic formula for making the mill grind salt but has forgotten to acquaint himself with the complementary formula for stopping the machinery when the mill has ground out all the salt that the magician requires. The process of manufacturing an intelligentsia is still more difficult to stop than it is to start; for the contempt in which the liaison-class is apt to be held by those who profit by its services is more than offset by its prestige in the eyes of those who are eligible for enrolment in it; and the competition becomes so keen that the number of the candidates rapidly increases out of all proportion to the number of opportunities for employing them. When this stage is reached, the original nucleus of an intelligentsia which is consoled by being employed becomes swamped by the adventitious mass of an 'intellectual proletariat' which is idle and destitute as well as outcast. The handful of chinovniks is reinforced by a legion of 'Nihilists', the handful of babus who thankfully drive their quills, or resignedly tap their typewriters, by a legion of 'failed B.A.s'. And the bitterness of the intelligentsia is incomparably greater in this latter state than it is in the former.

[1] In I. B (iv), vol. i, p. 41, footnote 3, above.
[2] This painful insulation is particularly in evidence in the history of the Russian intelligentsia during the century ending in the Bolshevik revolution of 1917:
'From the first, the revolution, whether theoretical or political, had no base of support among the masses. . . . The revolutionary circle had a world of its own, and formed a state within the state.'—Masaryk, T. G.: *The Spirit of Russia* (English translation: London 1919, Allen & Unwin, 2 vols.), vol. ii, p. 106. The whole chapter (pp. 105–14) from which this quotation is taken is illuminating.

Indeed, we might almost formulate a social 'law' to the effect that an intelligentsia's congenital unhappiness regularly increases in acuteness in geometrical ratio with the arithmetical progress of time. The Russian intelligentsia, which dates from the close of the seventeenth century, has already discharged its accumulated spite in the shattering Bolshevik Revolution of A.D. 1917. The Bengali intelligentsia, which dates from the latter part of the eighteenth century, is displaying to-day a vein of revolutionary violence which is not yet to be seen in other parts of British India,[1] where the local intelligentsia did not come into existence till fifty or a hundred years later. In Egypt and Java and China and Japan, where the intelligentsia is of about the same age as it is in Gujerat or in the Panjab, it is also in about the same mild state of exasperation to-day; but in Java and Japan, at any rate, the latest symptoms seem to portend the approach of paroxysms of a Russian or Bengali fury.[2]

Nor is the rank growth of this social weed confined to the soil in which it is a native plant. While, in our latter-day Westernized World, the intelligentsia has made its first appearance on non-

[1] For this contrast see the present chapter, p. 106, above.

[2] The symptoms of unrest in the 'intellectual proletariat' of Japan thrust themselves upon the attention of the writer of this Study during a visit to the Far East in the autumn of 1929. The Japanese Government's extreme nervousness about 'dangerous thought' was exhibited to the traveller when, upon landing in Japan, he was required, as part of the regular passport and customs procedure, to make a complete return of any books and pamphlets that might be included in his luggage. Evidently the Japanese authorities believed that some important element in the population was particularly prone to catch the mental infection of foreign subversive ideas; and, equally evidently, they were terrified about the possible consequences of the disease if once it did gain a hold upon the Japanese body social. Some of the grounds for this anxiety on the Japanese dominant minority's part were soon revealed to the writer when, in the university town of Kyoto, he was informed that, out of the last graduation-class of students, only 20 per cent. of the young men and women had succeeded in finding employment. Since a majority of the students were the children of poor parents—mostly workers on the land—and had been given their university education (which incidentally unfitted them for pursuing their ancestral calling) at the cost of heavy sacrifices and privations on their family's part, the failure of their education to bring in any economic return was nothing less than a social disaster. The unemployed ex-student was thrown back, without prospects, to live upon his family in an over-populated and insolvent country-side, and he was embittered by a humiliating sense of failure and frustration, while his relatives were equally embittered by a feeling that all their sacrifices had been in vain. Here indeed was food for 'dangerous thought' to feed on! Finally, on his way home to Europe from the Far East via Siberia, the writer was taught to admire the enterprise and courage of this Japanese 'intellectual proletariat', in its desperate straits, by hearing the personal story of a Japanese girl who was travelling in the same train. Having studied and qualified for being a school-mistress, and having then realized how poor her prospects were in a profession that was already so terribly overcrowded, she was spending her small savings on the venture of taking a year's course in dressmaking at Paris, on the calculation that within the next few years there would be a demand in Japan for *modistes à l'occidentale* owing to the growing tendency for Japanese women to follow the men's example in adopting Western dress. It seemed only too likely that if this admirable Japanese initiative and fortitude in the face of adversity were cheated, by circumstances beyond its control, of its morally due reward, it would find vent sooner or later in a violent explosion. These trivial experiences of the writer in the autumn of 1929 cast a flood of light, for him, upon the Japanese outbreak which duly occurred, two years later, in the autumn of 1931. In the militant policy which the Japanese Empire has been pursuing since then, the driving force has been the revolutionary passion of the young naval and military officers and the rejected cadets; and these are typical members of the Japanese intelligentsia.

Western ground that has been in process of being annexed to the domain of an expanding Western Civilization, it has latterly begun to spread to the homelands of the aggressive society. A lower middle class which has received a secondary and even a university education without being given any corresponding outlet for its trained abilities is the backbone of the post-war Fascist Party in Italy and National-Socialist Party in Germany; and the demoniac 'driving-force' which has carried a Mussolini and a Hitler to the pinnacle of power has been generated out of this 'intellectual proletariat's' exasperation at finding that its painful efforts at self-improvement are not sufficient in themselves to save it from being crushed between the upper millstone of a politically organized Capital and the lower millstone of a politically organized Labour. In Fascist Italy and National-Socialist Germany we can thus identify some of the symptoms that have notoriously accompanied the production of an 'intellectual proletariat' in a half-Westernized Japan or Java or Bengal or Russia. But Italy and Germany are no alien appendages to the Western body social; they are bone of its bone and flesh of its flesh; and it follows that the social revolution which has taken place yesterday in Italy and Germany under our eyes may overtake us in France or England or the Netherlands or Scandinavia to-morrow.

As a matter of fact, we do not have to await our present Post-War Age in order to see a Western internal proletariat being recruited from the native tissues of the Western body social; for in the Western, as in the Hellenic, World it is not only the subjugated primitive and alien populations that have been torn up by the roots. In Western Christendom, as in Hellas, the original nucleus of an ever growing internal proletariat has been formed out of *déracinés* who were born and bred in the bosom of the disintegrating society before they were disinherited and driven into exile by the winnowing fan of civil strife which so perversely scatters the grain and leaves the chaff lying on the threshing-floor.[1] As early as the second chapter of our Western history—in the so-called 'Medieval' Age which runs from the last quarter of the eleventh to the last quarter of the fifteenth century of our era—we can see this scourge afflicting the Italian cosmos of city-states; and the figure of Dante stands at the head of the long line of Western exiles, as Thucydides heads the parallel line

---

[1] For the inverse social selection which is one of the penalties of *stasis* see Seeck, O.: 'Die Ausrottung der Besten' in his *Geschichte des Unterganges der Antiken Welt*, 4th edition (Stuttgart 1921, Metzler, 6 vols., with supplements), vol. i, part (2), chap. 2. (This chapter of Seeck's work has been cited already in IV. C (ii) (*b*) 1, vol. iv, p. 63, footnote 1, above.)

in the history of the decline and fall of Hellas.[1] In our Western history, however, this social malady of exile, as the penalty for being left upon the losing side in civil dissensions, did not become rife throughout the Western World until after the Italianization of the Transalpine and Transmarine countries of Western Christendom at the opening of the 'Modern' Age;[2] and in the West in this age a personal and political hatred of the kind that animated the Florentine and Roman and Athenian faction-feuds has been envenomed with an *odium theologicum*.

The sixteenth-century and seventeenth-century Wars of Religion[3] brought in their train the penalization or eviction of the discomfited Catholic faction in every country where the sovereign power fell into Protestant hands, and of the discomfited Protestant faction in every country where a Catholic Government succeeded in maintaining itself; and the odious rule '*Cuius Regio eius Religio*',[4] which was accepted by Catholics and Protestants alike in their common idolization of the fetish of absolute sovereignty in a parochial state, has left its mark down to this day—on a world which has long since forgotten the Catholic-Protestant quarrel— in the dispersion of the descendants of French Protestant exiles who are scattered over the face of the Earth from Prussia to South Africa and the descendants of Irish Catholic exiles who are scattered, even more widely, from Chile to Austria and from the United States to Australia. Nor has the plague been stayed by the peace of lassitude and cynicism in which our Western Wars of Religion tardily came to their close.[5] For the fanaticism which seemed to have burnt itself out before the opening of the eighteenth century had lighted up again, before that century came to an end, in a new and larger and still more inflammable pile of fuel. In another context we have observed how the Wars of Religion have been followed, after the briefest respite, by the Wars of Nationality;[6] and in our modern Western World the spirit of religious fanaticism and the spirit of national fanaticism are manifestly one and the same evil passion masquerading under a superficial diversity of interest and objective.

Our modern Western nationalism has an ecclesiastical tinge; for, while in one aspect it is a reversion to the idolatrous self-

---

[1] For the effect of exile upon the careers of Thucydides and Dante see III. C (ii) (*b*), vol. iii, pp. 291–2 and 331–2, above.

[2] For this process of Italianization see III. C (ii) (*b*), vol. iii, pp. 299–306 and 357–63, above.

[3] For the part played by the Wars of Religion in Western history see further V. C (i) (*d*) 6 (δ), Annex, pp. 668–72, and V. C (ii) (*b*), vol. vi, pp. 315–19, below.

[4] See IV. C (iii) (*b*) 11, vol. iv, pp. 221–2, above.

[5] See V. C (i) (*d*) 6 (δ), Annex, pp. 668–72, below.

[6] See IV. C (iii) (*b*) 3 and 4, vol. iv, pp. 150–67, above, and also V. C (ii) (*b*), vol. vi, pp. 319–20, below.

worship of the tribe[1] which was the only religion known to Man before the first of the 'higher religions' was discovered by an oppressed internal proletariat,[2] this Western neo-tribalism is a tribalism with a difference. The primitive religion has been deformed into an enormity through being power-driven with a misapplied Christian driving-force. The Golden Calf—or Lion or Bear or Eagle, or whatever the tribal totem may happen to be —is being worshipped in our world to-day with an intensity of feeling and a singleness of mind which ought not to be directed by human souls towards any god but God Himself.[3] And it is not surprising to find that we have been propitiating these blasphemously idolized tribal deities with the human sacrifices which they relish and exact. How should we do otherwise when our Protestant and Catholic forefathers have set us the example by making the same impious oblations to a God whose delight is in mercy and not in Man's cruelty to Man? Thus we see the eviction of the Protestants from France in A.D. 1685 and from Salzburg in A.D. 1731-2 being followed in A.D. 1755 by the eviction of the Acadians from Nova Scotia (a name which tells its own tale of national rivalry) and in A.D. 1783 by the eviction of 'the United Empire Loyalists' from the new-born United States;[4] and these are the vanguard of a fresh host of exiles—the French aristocratic *émigrés* of 1789; the European liberal *émigrés* of 1848; the Russian 'White' *émigrés* of 1917; the Italian and German democratic *émigrés* of 1922 and 1933; the Austrian Catholic and Jewish *émigrés* of 1938—who have been uprooted in the effort to impose a spiritual uniformity by force: an ideal which loses none of its perversity—though assuredly most of its excuse—for being transferred to the national from the ecclesiastical arena.

To these victims of a politico-religious fanaticism we have to add the tale of exiles who have been carried into captivity from the centre to the fringes of an expanding Western World as a punishment for crimes (some serious, some trivial; some real, some imaginary), and, in particular, the convicts who have been transported from the British Isles to North America before, and to Australia since, the establishment of the independence of the United States. These British convict-exiles to the New World overseas are the counterparts of the criminals whom the Sinic Emperor Ts'in She Hwang-ti planted in the newly conquered barbarian territories of the south,[5] and of the *déracinés* whom

[1] See IV. C (iii) (c) 2 (β), vol. iv, p. 351, above, and V. C (i) (c) 3, in the present volume, pp. 230-1, below.
[2] See the present chapter and volume, p. 79, with footnotes 2 and 3, above.
[3] See Part I. A, vol. i, p. 9, footnote 3, and IV. C (iii) (c) 3 (β), vol. iv, pp. 581-2, above.   [4] See IV. C (ii) (b) 4, vol. iv, p. 165, above.
[5] See the present chapter, p. 141, above.

the Achaemenidae marooned on the islands of the Red Sea.[1] There are also counterparts, in our modern Western internal proletariat, of that floating urban population—irretrievably divorced from the country-side yet never properly acclimatized to the life of the city—which we see silting up in Rome and in the smaller towns of Sicily and Italy in the last two centuries B.C. Indeed, in our own world this element in the proletariat has come to occupy so prominent a place, and to weigh so heavily upon the consciences of statesmen as well as philanthropists, that when we pronounce the word 'proletariat' it is this element, to the exclusion of all the rest, that is apt to present itself to our minds.

We have seen how in Sicily and Italy, during the Hellenic 'Time of Troubles', the free population was uprooted from the country-side and driven into the towns by an economic revolution in the conduct of the rural industries of agriculture and stock-breeding. The new rural economy was the offspring of War, which presented the *entrepreneur* with the *tabula rasa* of a devastated area and with the edged tool of the cheap labour-force which the enslavement of the prisoners-of-war had thrown upon the market. By placing these two instruments simultaneously in the *entrepreneur*'s hands, War taught him the secret of drawing an unprecedented and almost fabulous profit from the land by a new-fangled process of mass-production for export.[2] The up-rooting and eviction of the free peasant proprietor who had formerly supported himself by subsistence farming on the site of the new plantations and ranches was an incidental consequence of the rural economic revolution which War and the *entrepreneur* had brought about between them. And, when the disinherited peasant was first reduced to the status of a seasonal wage-labourer on the land and was eventually shouldered off the land altogether and penned up in a slum inside the walls of the city, nobody imagined or pretended that there was anything but unmitigated evil in this degradation of a self-supporting peasant into an unemployed town-dweller whose life was just kept in his body by the grudging distribution of a public dole. The capitalist who was making his fortune out of a slave-tilled country-side displayed as ugly a countenance as his patron-god Mars himself; and, for any disinterested spectator of the joint work of this grim pair of partners, it was not surprising to find wickedness producing results which were morally repugnant and socially disastrous.

[1] See the present chapter, p. 124, footnote 2, above.
[2] For this rural economic revolution in the western parts of the Hellenic World in and after the fifth century B.C. see III. C (i) (b), vol. iii, pp. 168–71, and IV. C (ii) (a), vol. iv, pp. 48–9, above.

In our modern Western history we have seen an almost exact repetition of this Hellenic social disaster in the rural economic revolution which made it irresistibly profitable to substitute cotton plantations worked with Negro slaves for the mixed farming of White freemen in 'the Cotton Belt' of the Southern States of the American Union in the earlier decades of the nineteenth century.[1] The 'White trash' which was thus degraded to the ranks of the Proletariat in this Transatlantic annex of the modern Western World was of the same quality as the dispossessed and pauperized 'free trash' of Roman Italy who were 'called the lords of the World' without having 'a single clod of earth to call their own;'[2] and this rural economic revolution in North America which produced these two cancerous social growths of White pauperdom and Black slave-labour was only a logically ruthless application, in an overseas environment, of a similar rural economic revolution in England which had been taking place more gradually in the course of the preceding three centuries. The English *entrepreneurs* of the early Modern Age had not followed the bad example of the Portuguese in introducing African slave-labour into a European country-side, but they had imitated the Roman and anticipated the American planters and stockbreeders in uprooting a free peasantry for the sake of economic profit, by turning ploughland into pasture and common-land into enclosures. This modern Western rural economic revolution has not, however, either in Europe or overseas, been the principal cause of the flow of population from the country-side into the towns in the Modern Age of our Western history. The motive-force that has been mainly operative in bringing about this movement on a material scale which dwarfs the Hellenic counterpart of it has been not a push but a pull. While the *ci-devant* self-supporting rural population of the Western World has partly been driven into the towns by a rural agricultural revolution which has deprived it of its former livelihood on the land, it has mostly been drawn into the towns by an urban industrial revolution which has inveigled it into tearing up its own roots by dangling before its dazzled eyes the lure of abundant urban employment at lucrative wages.

When this Western Industrial Revolution broke out first on English ground about a hundred and fifty years ago, its economic profitableness appeared to be so immense and so secure that the great change was welcomed and blessed—social consequences and all—by many observers who were not less well-meaning than a

[1] See III. C (ii) (*b*), vol. iii, pp. 171–2, and IV. C (iii) (*b*) 2, vol.i v, pp. 139–40, above.
[2] Tiberius Gracchus, quoted in the present chapter on p. 70, above (see also IV. C (iii) (*c*) 3 (β), vol. iv, p. 508, above, and V. C (ii) (*a*), Annex II, vol. vi, p. 381, with Table VIII, logion (α), p. 414, below).

Spartan Agis or a Roman Tiberius Gracchus. While deploring the long hours of labour to which the first generation of factory workers, including the women and children, were condemned, and the sordid and unhealthy conditions of their new life in both the factory and the home, the panegyrists of the Industrial Revolution were confident that these were transitory evils which could and would be removed, and they denounced, as an improvident folly, any proposal to check the impetus of Man's crowning victory over Physical Nature for the sake of sparing Society the inevitable growing-pains. If only (they urged) the Industrial Revolution were allowed to work itself out unhindered, the total wealth of Society would be so vastly increased that the workers themselves could not fail to obtain a handsome share of this well-earned increment; and, when once the spoils of Man's conquest of Nature had been gathered in and divided out, then the temporary inconveniences with which the first and second generation of urban industrial workers had been required to put up would be compensated a hundred-fold by the solid comfort in which the third and fourth and subsequent generations would live happily ever after.

The ironical sequel has been that this rosy prophecy has largely come true—in defiance of the gloomy forebodings of the nineteenth-century prophets of woe—but that the blessings of this marvellous entry into an earthly paradise 'in real life' are being neutralized to-day by a curse which was hidden from the eyes of the pessimists, as well as the optimists, of a century ago. On the one hand, child labour has been abolished, women's labour has been tempered to women's strength, hours of labour have been shortened, the conditions of life and work in factory and home have been improved out of all recognition, and at the same time the workers' share in the spoils won from Nature by Industry has been substantially increased—as is shown by the steady proportionate increase of the wages bill by comparison with the profits in the employers' balance-sheet. In all these ways the urban industrial workers' position has improved beyond the most sanguine expectations of the enthusiasts for the Industrial Revolution in the generation of its outbreak. But there is another side to the shield; and this aspect daunts even our optimists to-day when a world that is gorged with the wealth ground out by the magic industrial machine is at the same time overshadowed by the spectre of unemployment. *À la fin du compte* the transfer of population from country-side to town has produced the same cancer in the Western as in the Hellenic body social: the cancer of an urban proletariat which has lost its roots in the country, has struck no roots in the town, and is reminded—every time that it draws its dole—that it is 'in' but not 'of' the society which has to serve as the unwilling 'host' of this unhappy social parasite.

Through the ingenuity of Industrialism the modern Western World has evaded the curse of Adam—'in the sweat of thy face shalt thou eat bread'[1]—which has weighed hitherto upon the life of every human society that has started, from the primitive level, to clamber up the face of the precipice of Civilization.[2] We have slily transferred the primal curse from our own muscle and bone to the immeasurably more potent material forces of Inanimate Nature; and now we find ourselves trapped by the very brilliance of the success of our technological manœuvre; for our new-found economic abundance has taken us morally unawares. Morally we have allowed ourselves no time to revise the dispensation under which we and our forefathers have been living during six thousand years of Adamic scarcity—a dispensation which prescribes that we shall work 'with labour and travail night and day that we' may 'not be chargeable to any of' our neighbours, and which commands 'that if any' will 'not work, neither' shall 'he eat'.[3] And now that an unmanageable abundance has made nonsense of the precept that 'with quietness they work, and eat their own bread',[4] we find ourselves morally at a loss in our relations with the millions that 'walk among' us 'working not at all'[5] to-day through no fault of their own. Manifestly these helpless human victims of callously triumphant machines are not the 'disorderly busybodies'[6] which they would have been if they had been work-shy idlers in the aeon of scarcity; for a 'technological' unemployment cannot be exorcised by an honest will to work. Yet still it cannot be incurred without bringing upon its victims those moral pains and penalties—the sense of frustration and the consciousness of losing caste—which were the proper and inevitable retribution for a wilful work-shy idleness but are a cruel aggravation of an unavoidable lock-out.

This revenge of Nature upon her Western conquerors has been hastened and sharpened by the triumph of an industrialized Western Society over the human as well as over the physical environment. Since the outbreak of the Industrial Revolution in the eighteenth century in England, we have not only completed our industrial conquest of Nature in Western Europe. We have also taught the tricks of our West European trade to the new communities of Western culture which have been established by our West European colonists overseas, and to the old communities of alien culture which have been forcibly enrolled in the Western

---

[1] Gen. iii. 19.
[2] For this simile see Part II. B, vol. i, pp. 192–5, above.
[3] 2 Thess. iii. 8 and 10.   [4] 2 Thess. iii. 12.   [5] 2 Thess. iii. 11.
[6] Op. cit., loc. cit.

internal proletariat. The sleight of hand which replaced the poorly remunerated hard labour of human and bovine and equine muscles by the fabulously productive facile labour of iron and coal and steam and oil and electricity has been applied in the cities—and even on the fields—of America and Russia and India and China and Japan, as well as in those of England and Belgium and France and Germany; and, with the physical plethora of plenty, the spiritual curse of plenty—the curse of an unavoidable yet intolerable unemployment—is now spreading from the European metropolis of our latter-day Great Society to its American and Asiatic provinces. We may even live to see the cancer fasten upon the heart of Tropical Africa, where in the post-war years the latest and most primitive of the alien recruits to our Western internal proletariat have been flung into the furnace of Industrialism by the discovery of the copper ores of Northern Rhodesia and Katanga— a discovery which has led the African's latter-day European masters to provide themselves with a Native industrial 'labour-force' by deliberately driving the African out of the kraal into the labour-market through the imposition of poll-taxes and hut-taxes at a rate at which they cannot be paid out of the produce of African subsistence-farming.

In other words,

The ground of a certain rich man brought forth plentifully, and he thought within himself, saying: 'What shall I do, because I have no room where to bestow my fruits?' And he said: 'This will I do: I will pull down my barns and build greater; and there will I bestow all my fruits and my goods. And I will say to my soul: *Soul, thou hast much goods laid up for many years. Take thine ease, eat, drink and be merry.*' But God said unto him: 'Thou fool, this night thy soul shall be required of thee: then whose shall those things be which thou hast provided?' So is he that layeth up treasure for himself and is not rich toward God.[1]

If the souls of a modern Western dominant minority have indeed now been summoned to appear before God's judgement-seat, their intelligences must be inquiring, with an anxious curiosity, into the temper of that vast Western internal proletariat whose membership we have cursorily reviewed from the earliest victims of a political revolution in a medieval Italian city-state to the latest victims of the industrial revolution in the primitive kraals of Central Africa. Do we find the two veins of Violence and Gentleness reappearing in our Western internal proletariat's reaction to the proletarian ordeal? And, if both the two alternative tempers are displayed, which one of the two is in the ascendant?

[1] Luke xii. 16–21.

Manifestations of the militant temper in our Western underworld are not far to seek. We can find them in every secret conspiracy or open insurrection of down-trodden social classes and religious or national minorities during the last four centuries: in the revolt of the High German peasantry against their feudal lords in 1524-5; in the seizure of the Low German city of Münster[1] by a band of Anabaptist 'Zealots' who converted a medieval princebishopric into a communistic New Jerusalem and successfully defied a world in arms for seventeen months in 1534-5;[2] in the French revolutions of 1789 and 1830 and 1848 and 1871; in the Russian revolutions of 1905 and 1917; in the Bavarian and Hungarian 'Red' revolutions which followed the defeat of the Central Powers in the General War of 1914-18; and in the Haitian revolution of 1795-1803, in which a modern Western band of plantation-slaves wrested an enduring success out of that desperate enterprise of exterminating their masters and establishing a freedmen's state which had proved to be beyond the powers of the Zanj slave-insurgents in 'Irāq in the ninth century of the Christian Era[3] and the Syrian slave-insurgents in Sicily in the second century B.C.[4] The wreckage left behind by these explosions of Violence litters the track of our Western Society's recent history; but, when we turn to look for corresponding evidence of a counteracting and constructive spirit of Gentleness, the traces of this hitherto are, unhappily, far to seek.

[1] The revolutionary establishment of an Anabaptist commonwealth at Münster in 1534 was not a unique or unprecedented event. In 1528 a band of Anabaptist Tyrolese peasants had similarly seized and momentarily held the city of Brixen, and, after the collapse of the Anabaptist commune at Münster, there were a number of abortive Anabaptist 'putsches' in the Netherlands.

[2] The original stimuli and aims of the insurgent peasants and the Anabaptists were not the same, though in the course of their revolt the peasants came under revolutionary religious influences. The peasants were moved to rise against their lords by a recent increase in the weight of their feudal burdens (partly owing to the reception of Roman Law in place of local custom), by an abuse of money-lending, and by the growth of a rural landless proletariat in the south-western and central parts of Germany through which the revolt spread. The substance of the peasants' demand was a reduction of their burdens to the customary amounts and, as far as this essentially conservative programme came to be tinged with more radical ideas, these were more akin to the French ideas of 1789 than to the Russian ideas of 1917 (see Schubert, H. von: *Der Kommunismus der Wiedertäufer in Münster und seine Quellen*) (Heidelberg 1919, Winter), p. 9; Schönebaum, H.: *Kommunismus im Reformationszeitalter* (Bonn and Leipzig 1919, Schroeder), p. 27). On the other hand, Anabaptism was an urban movement which was led into communism by considerations that were not economic but religious (see Schubert, op. cit., pp. 7-9 and *passim*; Schönebaum, op. cit., pp. 24 and 41; Carew Hunt, R. N.: 'Some Communist Experiments of the Sixteenth Century' in *The Edinburgh Review*, No. 504, vol. 247, April 1928, p. 285). The revolutionary-minded towns-people sympathized, however, with the rural insurgents and infected them with their ideas. The Swabian peasantry were influenced by Anabaptist secessionists from the Zwinglian Church at Zürich (Schönebaum, op. cit., pp. 30-1), the Franconian and Thuringian peasantry by Thomas Müntzer, one of the 'prophets of Zwickau' who had seceded from the Lutheran Church at Wittenberg (op. cit., p. 25), and who lost his life at the battle of Frankenhausen, at which the tide of war turned, on the 25th May, 1525, against the peasants and in favour of the feudal lords (see Carew Hunt, R. N., in *The Church Quarterly Review* for July 1938 and January 1939).

[3] See the present chapter, p. 129, footnote 2, above.

[4] See the present chapter, pp. 69-70, above.

It is true that we can point to many victims of the cruel process of disinheritance and eviction who have refrained from taking to violent courses. In another context[1] we have passed in review several examples of refugees from religious or political persecution in the European homelands of our Western Civilization whose response to the challenge of having their roots plucked up has been to strike fresh root in virgin soil overseas. Many—perhaps a majority—of the Protestants who were expelled from France and the Catholics whose native Ireland under a Protestant ascendancy became too hot to hold them and the Loyalists who had to leave their homes in the former Thirteen Colonies in 1783 and the Liberals who had to flee from Germany in 1848 have made fortunes and founded families in the overseas countries of their adoption— in South Africa or Chile or Australia or Canada or the United States or whatever the country may be. The same *tour de force* has been achieved by the American and Australian descendants of many English indentured servants and deported convicts. Even the liberated descendants of the Negro slaves in the United States and the Antilles (to leave out of account the victorious rebels in Haiti) have not entirely failed to find a second home in the house of exile. In 'the Black Belt' of the New World to-day there are Negro populations to be found who have settled down as self-supporting peasants on a land in whose features they can recognize the kindly Mother Goddess that nurtured their forebears in Africa before they were torn from her bosom by the slave-raider's sacrilegious hand. But these successful responses to the stimulus of penalization—admirable though they may be in themselves—are none of them examples of the gentle response to the ordeal of serving in the ranks of the Internal Proletariat; for these diverse ways of meeting and conquering adversity all agree in one point: they are all of them ways of refusing to join the Proletariat—or at any rate refusing to remain in it. They are solutions of the proletarian's problem which avoid the necessity of choosing between the violent and the gentle alternative courses by finding ways and means of escaping altogether from the dilemma. In our search for modern Western exponents of the gentle response our only finds will be the German Anabaptist refugee settlers in Moravia and the Dutch Anabaptist Mennonites and the members of the English Society of Friends; and even these three rare specimens of a gentle proletarian êthos will slip through our fingers; for, when we follow up their later history, we shall find that, in the end, the Moravian Anabaptists and the Mennonites and the Quakers have each been re-absorbed, in their turn, into the general Western body social.

[1] In II. D (vi), vol. ii, above.

The failure of the Moravian Anabaptists and the Mennonites to preserve their separate communal life is the more extraordinary considering that a secession from the Western Church Universal was the essence of the Anabaptist movement and the significance of the symbolic act of re-baptism from which the movement acquired its name.[1] The problem of asserting this separateness in face of a hostile and intolerant majority of the society from which they were deliberately and defiantly seceding confronted all Anabaptists in virtue of the cardinal point in their creed; and the pacifist

[1] For a general account of the Anabaptist movement see McGothlin, W. J. M., s.v. 'Anabaptism', in Hastings' *Encyclopaedia of Religion and Ethics.* An interesting sketch, in small compass, will also be found in Piette, M.: *John Wesley in the Evolution of Protestantism* (English translation: London 1937, Sheed and Ward), pp. 18–36. The Anabaptists welcomed the destructive part of Luther's work, but disapproved of his endeavour to construct a new Church Universal on the ruins of the Church of Rome (Müller, L.: *Der Kommunismus der Mährischen Wiedertäufer* (Leipzig 1927, Heinsius), pp. 65–6). They quarrelled with Zwingli likewise for his unwillingness to fall in with their view that the elect ought to be separated off from the rest of Mankind (op. cit., p. 68). The Anabaptist sect may be said to have come into existence when the first re-baptism was performed at Zollikon near Zürich in February 1525 (Müller, op. cit., p. 69; Carew Hunt, op. cit., pp. 277–8; Schönebaum, op. cit., pp. 29–31). In its essence the Anabaptist movement was thus a recrudescence of the movement for the establishment of a separate church of the elect which had declared itself once before in Western Christendom in the twelfth-century vogue of Catharism and other kindred sects (for this affiliation of the Anabaptist movement see Müller, op. cit., p. 65; for Catharism see IV. C (iii) (c) 2 (β), vol. iv, pp. 369–71; IV. C (iii) (c) 3 (β), vol. iv, pp. 559–60; IV. C (iii) (c) 2 (β), Annex III, vol. iv, pp. 624–34; IV. C (iii) (c) 3 (β), Annex, vol. iv, pp. 652–6, above).

The following note has been communicated to the writer of this Study by Mr. R. N. Carew Hunt:

'The essential characteristic of Anabaptism is the demand that the Church should be a *Sonderkirche*: that is, that it should consist of believers only, who, after attesting their faith, should be admitted to membership through "believers' baptism". . . . But "believers' baptism", however important, is subordinated in their thought to the *Sonderkirche* idea and to the necessity for a return to Primitive Christianity. Baptism was the means, the *Sonderkirche* the end.

'The movement started in Germany and Switzerland in 1523–4. In Germany the principal exponent was Thomas Müntzer, who had been influenced, through Niclas Storch at Prague, by Taborite opinions, and himself visited Bohemia in 1522–3 [see Mr. Carew Hunt's articles in *The Church Quarterly Review*, cited on p. 167, footnote 2, above.—A.J.T.]. Müntzer was not a thoroughgoing Anabaptist. . . . But he preached, and no one more vehemently, the Anabaptist doctrine of a Church of the Elect, though he did not regard "believers' baptism" as the divinely appointed means of entering it. In his writings and letters he taught, further, that it was for the Elect to arise and slay the godless, and he thus represents the militant spirit which was to come out in the Münster revolt.

'Meanwhile there had arisen in Switzerland a movement against Zwingli of which Conrad Grebel and Felix Manz were the most important leaders. As early as 1523 they began to pester Zwingli to set up a Church of the Elect into which the faithful should be baptized (see Egli, E.: *Die Züricher Wiedertäufer zur Reformationszeit* (Zürich 1878, Schulthess), pp. 10 seqq.; Kidd, B. J.: *Documents Illustrative of the Continental Reformation* (Oxford 1911, Clarendon Press), pp. 450–8). . . . On the 18th January, 1525, the Council of Zürich ordered infant baptism, and the Opposition set up a church at Zollikon, where, on the 9th February, Grebel baptized Blaurock. From this action Anabaptism, as a sect, technically dates.

'In both German and Swiss Anabaptist circles there was a good deal of talk of communism before 1525; but none of the leaders advanced any clearly defined policy of social reform, and their insistence on communism was no more than a part of their general demand for the establishment of a church modelled on that of the early Christians, whose members had possessed all their goods in common. But the Swiss Anabaptists from the first disallowed the use of force against the ungodly, which Müntzer advocated, and the letter which Grebel, Manz and others addressed to him on the 5th September, 1524, shows the measure of their disagreement.'

communities in the Netherlands and Moravia, as well as the militant messianic commonwealths at Brixen and Münster,[1] were attempts to respond to this formidable challenge. The social pressure to which the Anabaptists were reacting was so heavy that in their violent and in their gentle reaction alike they were driven to extremes.

The violent reaction at Münster (*saeviebat* 9th February, 1534, to 25th June, 1535)[2] was in an apocalyptic vein.[3] An Anabaptist prophet, Melchior Hofmann, whose head-quarters were at Strassburg, had declared himself to be the first of two witnesses to the imminence of the Second Coming, and had proclaimed that the divine event would take place in Strassburg at a precise date and hour in A.D. 1533. After this date had been surmounted without incident, Hofmann's Netherlander khalîfah, Jan Matthys the baker of Haarlem, declared himself to be the second witness and changed the *venue* to Münster, where he duly established his militant Messianic commonwealth in February 1534. After Matthys' death in a sortie against the Prince Bishop's free lances on the Easter Day of that year, the prophet's mantle fell on the shoulders of Matthys' disciple Jan Bockelson the tailor of Leyden. And this epigonus of Hofmann's diadochus styled himself 'King of the New Jerusalem' and 'King of Righteousness with universal dominion', to whom God had given the sceptre of David and the sword that was 'to cleave its way through all the World, for the punishment of the unrighteous and the protection of the godly'.[4] From first to last the Anabaptist régime in Münster was a reign of terror. In the early days of the revolution Matthys preached in a sermon the killing of all Lutherans, Papists, and other unbelievers, in accordance with the Anabaptist doctrine that the ungodly ought to be, not merely boycotted socially, but also physically exterminated. As a compromise with mercy, all who refused to be re-baptized were driven out of the city destitute two days later.[5] The exiles' goods were impounded by the newly established rulers of the revolutionary commonwealth. The city guilds were overthrown, and communal workshops, breweries, and bakeries were set up, as well as communal eating-houses.[6] For the sanctification of his own lusts the Messianic King John compelled his subjects to adopt polygamy.[7]

[1] See the present chapter, p. 167, above.
[2] See Cornelius, C. A.: *Geschichte des Münsterischen Aufruhrs* (Leipzig 1855–60, Weigel, 2 vols.). A collection of documents relating to the affair will be found in Löffler, K.: *Die Wiedertäufer zu Münster, 1534–5* (Jena 1923, Diederichs).
[3] Schubert, op. cit., p. 50; Carew Hunt, op. cit., pp. 281–2.
[4] See Schubert, op. cit., p. 54; Carew Hunt, op. cit., p. 285; eundem: 'John of Leyden' in *The Edinburgh Review*, No. 507, vol. 249, January 1929, p. 89.
[5] Schubert, op. cit., p. 53; Carew Hunt, 1928, p. 282; idem, 1929, p. 84.
[6] Carew Hunt, 1928, pp. 283–4; Schubert, op. cit., p. 10.
[7] Carew Hunt, 1928, p. 284; idem, 1929, pp. 87–8.

At the very time when the short-lived Anabaptist New Jerusalem at Münster in Westphalia was being established and defended by the swords of the Netherlanders Jan Matthys and Jan Bockelson, the Netherlander Menno Simons[1] and the Tyrolese Jacob Hutter were organizing, in Holland and in Moravia respectively, two other Anabaptist communities which were likewise segregatory, communistic, and authoritarian,[2] but which differed from the disastrous experiment at Münster in the capital point of being pacifist instead of militant.[3] Hutter's and Menno's policy for dealing with the ungodly was not to draw the sword against them but to take pains not to give them provocation to draw their own swords against the elect; and since in Moravia, Westphalia, the Netherlands, and indeed everywhere the Anabaptist Chosen People were overwhelmingly outnumbered by the Catholic and Protestant Gentiles, this difference of policy spelled, for Menno's and Hutter's followers and their descendants, the whole difference between extermination and survival. Instead of perishing with the sword like the Melchiorites, the Mennonites and the Hutterites brought upon themselves the more surprising and ironic fate of being slowly stifled by the inevitable rewards of their own distinctive virtues.

Hutter interpreted the Anabaptist institution of communism, not as conferring a licence to spoil the Egyptians, but as imposing upon the Chosen People themselves a religious duty of working unselfishly, conscientiously, and indefatigably for the benefit of the elect community.[4] Starting with a technological superiority over the native Moravian Slavs,[5] the German Anabaptist refugees on Moravian soil soon concentrated their energies upon handicraftsmanship in preference to agriculture[6] and won powerful protectors by making themselves useful to the Moravian landlords as artisans and bailiffs. The very practical success of this policy

---

[1] See Krahn, C.: *Menno Simons, 1496–1561* (Karlsruhe 1936, Schneider).

[2] For the key-points in Hutter's system see Müller, op. cit., p. 77. For the origins of the Moravian branch of the Anabaptist movement see Beck, J. von, and Loserth, J: 'Der Anabaptismus in Tirol,' in *Archiv für Österreichische Geschichte*, vols. 78 (1892), 79 (1893), and 81 (1895); and Loserth, J.: *Balthasar Hubmaier und die Anfänge der Wiedertaufe in Mähren* (Brünn 1893, Winiker). See further Hrubý, F.: 'Die Wiedertäufer in Mähren' in *Archiv für Reformationsgeschichte*, vol. xxx (1933), pp. 1–36 and 170–211, and vol. xxxi (1934), pp. 61–102.

[3] The contrast between Menno and Hutter, on the one side, and the ghāzīs of Münster, on the other, is reminiscent of the contrast between Johanan ben Zakkai and the Jewish Zealots in A.D. 66–70 (see the present chapter, pp. 75–6, above). In the view of Mr. R. N. Carew Hunt, as expressed in a letter to the writer of this Study, 'the Münster revolt was really a caricature of the movement, which was essentially pacific, and it contained all the worst aspects of Müntzer's teaching (e.g. its emphasis on the Old rather than on the New Testament). Certainly it showed what fanaticism will accomplish; and all Western Europe, Catholic and Protestant, was appalled by it. But it was repudiated by all responsible Anabaptist leaders, and its whole policy and direction was opposed to the generally accepted tenets of the sect.'

[4] Müller, op. cit., p. 90.   [5] Ibid., p. 99.

[6] Ibid., p. 91.

of Gentleness seems gradually to have softened the Hutterites'
moral fibre, and this moral decay seems already to have gone
too far to be arrested by the blow which the sect suffered in A.D.
1622, when it was expelled from its settlements in Moravia and
was confined to the daughter colonies in Hungary and Transylvania.[1] In the colony at Velké Leváry, in Hungary, the fundamental Anabaptist institution of the community of goods was
formally abandoned in 1685.[2] In 1733 these degenerate Anabaptists renounced the symbolic rite from which they derived their
name, and allowed their children to be baptized thenceforward
in infancy into the Catholic Church.[3] In 1741 they departed
from the pacifism which was the Hutterites' distinctive mark, and
supplied the Royal Hungarian Government with two recruits to
fight as hussars against Frederick the Great.[4] Finally, in 1760-4,
they submitted to a forcible wholesale conversion to Catholicism.[5]
Thereafter a fraction of the former Hutterite community at
Alvintz in Transylvania found asylum first in Wallachia and
eventually in the Ukraine, where their descendants have survived
down to this day and have even planted North American offshoots
in South Dakota and Alberta.[6] These survivors, however, are
no more than a 'living museum' of the Hutterite Anabaptist
imperium in imperio in Moravia which had its brief *floruit* in the
latter part of the sixteenth century; and the history of the Mennonites has run a parallel course of re-assimilation which has
been the more remarkable inasmuch as it has been accomplished
without any pressure from outside and without any formal abjura-
tion of the community's separatist tenets. With the inevitability
of gradualness 'the epoch of heroic exaltation gives place to the
banality of a petty tradesman's life'.[7] And thus, while the Anabaptists who took the path of Violence duly perished by the
sword within ten years of the foundation of the sect in 1525,
those who chose the alternative way of Gentleness have also
been eliminated in due course by the slower yet ultimately not
less effective process of re-absorption into the main body of the
Western body social.

Within a narrower range of action and on a lower emotional
key the history of the Anabaptists has been repeated in that
of the Quakers.

In the first generation of the life of this English sect a vein of
Violence, which found vent in naked prophesyings and in noisy
disturbances of the decorum of church services, drew down upon

---

[1] Müller, op. cit., pp. 104 and 106.   [2] Ibid., p. 107.
[3] Ibid., p. 108.   [4] Ibid., pag. cit.
[5] Ibid., p. 109.   [6] Ibid., pp. 110-14.
[7] Piette, op. cit., p. 34.

the Quakers a savage chastisement from Episcopalians in England and from Presbyterians in Massachusetts. This Violence, however, was quickly and permanently superseded by a Gentleness which became the Quakers' supreme and characteristic rule of life; and the Society of Friends then for a time seemed destined to play in a modern Western World the classic role of the Primitive Christian Church on whose spirit and practice, as set forth in *The Acts of the Apostles*, they devoutly modelled their own lives, like the Hutterites and the Mennonites before them. But, while the Friends of later generations have never fallen away from the victorious rule of Gentleness, they have long ago travelled right out of the proletarian path which their history for a short time seemed to lay down for them, and, like the Hutterites and the Mennonites again, they have been, in a sense, the victims of their own virtues. It might indeed be said of the Friends that they have achieved material prosperity in their own despite; for much of their success in business can be traced to formidable decisions which Friends have taken at the bidding of conscience, with a trustful faith in God, in the belief that they were acting to the detriment of their own material interests. The first step in their march to material prosperity was taken, all unwittingly, when this originally rural sect migrated from the country-side to the cities, not because they had lost their hereditary agrarian livelihood or because they were tempted by the lure of higher urban profits, but because a voluntary migration seemed the most obvious way of reconciling a conscientious objection to the payment of tithes to the Episcopalian Established Church of England with an equally imperious objection to the alternative course of resisting the tithe-collector by force.[1] Thereafter, when Quaker brewers took to manufacturing cocoa and chocolate because they had come to doubt the lawfulness of supplying their fellow men with an intoxicant, and when Quaker retail shopkeepers took to marking their goods with fixed prices because they scrupled to vary their price in 'the haggling of the market', they were deliberately risking their fortunes for the sake of their faith; and no doubt it seemed to them—as it did to a malevolently quizzical audience of philistine spectators—that in obeying their conscience they were facing blue ruin. The opposite event has illustrated the little-heeded truths that 'honesty is the best policy' and that 'the meek . . . shall inherit the Earth'; but by the same token it has debarred us from retaining any members of the Society of Friends upon the muster-roll of our Western internal proletariat.

In order to find any lasting or recent example of the proletarian

[1] On this point see II. D (vi), vol. ii, p. 220, footnote 2, above.

Gentleness for which we are in search, we must range beyond the limits of the native Western body social and must bring within our purview the societies of alien culture which have been annexed to our Western internal proletariat by some military or economic or cultural act of conquest. If we allow ourselves this licence, then we can place to the Western proletariat's credit the gentleness of a Gandhi eschewing the violence of the Bengali revolutionaries[1] and the gentleness of a Tolstoy condemning the violence of the Russian Nihilists, to reinforce the native Western pacifism of a Lansbury and a Sheppard.

When we have cast our net for Gentleness and taken so small a catch, it almost goes without saying that we shall fare no better when we scan the works of our Western internal proletariat in search of evidence of a creative religious activity; for, in our survey of the histories of other internal proletariats, we have seen already that it is the gentle and not the violent vein which is apt to be fruitful in the religious field.

If we follow the clues that are offered to us by the histories of the 'higher religions' which were adopted or adapted or created by the Hellenic internal proletariat, we shall find two rather faint modern Western analogues of Christianity and Manichaeism and the worships of Mithras and Isis and Cybele in two religious movements of Islamic origin, the Bahā'īyah[2] and the

---

[1] See the present chapter, pp. 106 and 158, above.

[2] The Bahā'īyah Sect is a derivative of the Bābī Sect, whose founder Sayyid 'Alī Muhammad of Shīrāz declared himself to be 'the Bāb' (i.e. 'the Gate' of the Twelfth Imām Mahdī of the Imāmī Shī'ah) in A.D. 1844, and eventually claimed to be the inaugurator of a new dispensation, and a manifestation or incarnation of God. The Bābī movement was promptly denounced by the Imāmī Mujtahids and persecuted by the Persian Government; and the Bāb himself, after being thrown into prison at Mākū, was put to death at Tabrīz in 1850. After the persecution had become intensified as a result of an attempt to assassinate Nāsir-ad-Dīn Shāh which was made by Bābī fanatics in 1852, a band of Bābīs was led into exile by the Bāb's at that time generally acknowledged successor, the Subh-i-Azal Mīrzā Yahyā. Their first asylum was Baghdad, and here the party was joined by Mīrzā Yahyā's elder half-brother, Mīrzā Husayn 'Alī. In 1864 the exiles were transferred from Baghdad to Constantinople, and thence to Adrianople, by the Ottoman authorities. At Adrianople, in 1866–7, Mīrzā Husayn 'Alī, who had long since been the leader of the exiles de facto, declared himself to be 'Him whom God shall make Manifest': the greater prophet of whom the Bāb had professed himself—at least in one phase of his teaching—to be the forerunner. This declaration may be taken as the genesis of the Bahā'ī Sect; since Mīrzā Husayn 'Alī, under the title of Bahā'u'llāh ('the Manifestation of the Beauty of God'), captured from his brother the allegiance of all but an insignificant minority of the Bābīs, in Persia as well as abroad, and was thenceforth regarded by his followers as the founder of their religion, while the figure of the Bāb tended to diminish in stature and to recede into the background (compare the progressive eclipse of Marx by Lenin in the Communist Church of the Soviet Union). In 1868 the Ottoman Government banished Subh-i-Azal to Famagusta in Cyprus and Bahā'u'llāh to 'Akkā on the Syrian coast, where Bahā'u'llāh continued to reside until his death in 1892. The rigorous internment to which the head of the Bahā'ī community was at first subjected at 'Akkā was gradually relaxed, but it was re-imposed upon Bahā'u'llāh's son and successor 'Abd-al-Bahā from 1901 until the Ottoman Revolution of 1908. These physical restrictions, however, did not prevent the propagation of the new religion into Europe and America; and after his liberation in 1908 Abd-al-Bahā went in person on a missionary journey which lasted from 1911 to 1913 and carried him as far afield as the Pacific coast of the United

Ahmadīyah.[1] These two variations upon Islam have arisen in the Iranic World—the Bahā'īyah in Persia and the Ahmadīyah in the Panjab—since the time when the Iranic World first began, about a hundred years ago, to feel our Western pressure, just as the five Oriental religions which we have cited as Hellenic parallels arose in the Hittite and Egyptiac and Syriac worlds after these had been overrun and overlaid by an expanding Hellenism. Again, the Bahā'-īyah and the Ahmadīyah movements are alike distinguished by a spirit and cult and practice of gentleness[2] which stand out in sharp contrast to the militancy of the Islam[3] from which they are both derived; and this contrast recalls the similar antithesis between the gentle êthos of Christianity and Manichaeism and the violent êthos of Maccabaean Judaism and Sasanian Zoroastrianism.[4] A further point of resemblance is that—again like Manichaeism and Christianity—the Bahā'īyah and the Ahmadīyah have been persecuted in their own world and have gone out to seek a kindlier soil for

States. (For the history and doctrines of Babism see Browne, E. G.: 'The Bābīs of Persia' in the *Journal of the Royal Asiatic Society*, vol. xxi [new series] (London 1889), pp. 485–526 and 881–1009; eundem: *A Traveller's Narrative written to illustrate the Episode of the Bāb*, edited and translated (Cambridge 1891, University Press, 2 vols.); eundem: Mīrzā Huseyn's *New History of the Bāb* translated (Cambridge 1893, University Press); eundem: 'Personal Reminiscences of the Bābī Insurrection at Zanjān in 1850, translated from the Persian' in *J.R.A.S.*, vol. xxix [new series], (London 1897); eundem: *Kitāb-i-Nuqtatu'l-Kāf*, being the earliest history of the Bābīs, compiled by Hājjī Mīrzā Jānī of Kāshān = E. J. W. Gibb Memorial Series, vol. xv (London 1910, Luzac); eundem: *Materials for the Study of the Bābī Religion* (Cambridge 1918, University Press); eundem: *A Literary History of Persia*, vol. iv (Cambridge 1928, University Press). For an account of Bahaism from the Bahā'ī standpoint see Esslemont, J. E.: *Bahā'u'llāh and the New Era* (London 1923, Allen and Unwin). For the injustice done to the Bahā'ī community in 'Irāq by the Government of the newly fledged sovereign independent 'Irāqī State, at the instigation of the local Shī'ī community, see Toynbee, A. J., and Boulter, V. M.: *Survey of International Affairs, 1934* (London 1935, Milford), pp. 119–22.)

[1] The Ahmadīyah Sect was founded in 1882 by Ghulām Ahmad of Qādyān (a place in the Ghūrdāspūr district of the Panjab), who claimed to be the Messiah and the Mahdī. After the death of the founder on the 26th May, 1908, the Ahmadīyah split into two branches, with head-quarters at Qādyān and Lahore respectively (the Lahore branch being the more susceptible to Western ideas). Both branches have embarked on missionary activities not only in the Islamic World, but in Great Britain, the United States, and Germany. (See M. Th. Houtsma : 'Le Mouvement Religieux des Ahmadiyya aux Indes Anglaises' (in *Revue du Monde Musulman*, i, 1907, pp. 533–76); H. A. Walter: *The Ahmadiya Movement* (Calcutta 1918, Oxford University Press); Mīrzā Bashīr-ad-Dīn Mahmūd Ahmad [son of the founder, and head of the Qādyān branch]: *Ahmad the Messenger of the Latter Days*, Part I (Qādyān 1924; and Madras 1924, Addison Press); eundem: *Ahmadiyyat or the True Islam* (Qādyān 1924); Mawlānā Muhammad 'Alī [head of the Lahore branch]:''The Ahmadiyya Movement' (in *The Light* of Lahore, 16th October, 1925, translated in *Oriente Moderno*, vi, 2, pp. 108–23).)

[2] Bahā'u'llāh declared for Non-Violence (see Browne in *J.R.A.S.*, vol. xxi [new series], pp. 954–9, and in *A Traveller's Narrative*, vol. ii, p. xl), in contrast to the militancy into which the Primitive Bābīs had lapsed after the imprisonment of the Bāb at Mākū in A.D. 1847.

[3] The Sunnah has been militant from first to last, and, while the Shī'ah has sometimes taken on an appearance of gentleness, this has perhaps usually reflected a lack of the power rather than the will to take to violent courses. The Carmathians in the tenth century of the Christian Era and the Ismā'īlīs in the eleventh and twelfth centuries were more violent than any Sunnīs; and violence has also been the keynote of the militant revival of Imāmī Shī'ism by Ismā'īl Shāh Safawī (see I. C (i) (b), Annex I, in vol. i, above, and V. C (i) (d) 6 (δ), Annex, pp. 661–5, below.).

[4] See the present chapter, pp. 125–6, above, with the references there given.

their seed in the alien world which has imposed itself upon theirs so masterfully. When the Bāb, who was the forerunner of the prophet of Bahaism, was put to death by his Persian countrymen, and when life in Persia was made almost impossible for the martyred prophet's disciples, the Bāb's successor Subh-i-Azal sought asylum at Baghdad; after the eviction of the exiles from 'Irāq, Subh-i-Azal's supplanter Bahā'u'llāh eventually found a secure resting-place at 'Akkā on the Mediterranean coast of Syria; and from this last well-sited base of operations the Bahā'īs have launched their propaganda into the Western World and have gathered Western converts into their fold as far afield as Chicago. The same road has been trodden by the Ahmadīs, who have gained a footing in Europe and America while they have been ignored in their native Panjab and persecuted in their nearest mission-field in Afghanistan.[1] We are reminded of the westward march of Christianity and Manichaeism into the Hellenic World after Jesus had been put to death at Jerusalem and Mani at Ctesiphon, while the relation of Bahaism to Babism calls to mind the relation between Pauline Christianity and the more nebulous pre-Pauline faith that was grasped and shaped and clarified by the Apostle to the Gentiles.

When we turn from the alien 'higher religions' to the alien philosophies that made simultaneous conquests in the Hellenic World, we shall find a counterpart of the Babylonic pseudo-science of Astrology in the Hindu pseudo-science of Theosophy, whose exponents address themselves to a Western public of much the same kind as the Hellenic public which once succumbed to the Chaldaean *mathematici*: a public which has become too conceitedly sophisticated to abide in its own ancestral traditions, but which has not learnt either how to fill for itself the self-inflicted spiritual void in its soul or how to appraise at their proper worth or worthlessness the pretentious alien spiritual wares which are dangled before its uncritical eyes by a swarm of skilful and not always scrupulous salesmen.

We may also now perhaps venture to prophesy that our indigenous modern Western Science will undergo in the course of time a metamorphosis like that which has transformed the philosophy of Siddhārtha Gautama into the Mahāyāna[2] and the philosophy of Plato into the religion of Neoplatonism[3] and the philosophy of the

---

[1] For the persecution of the Ahmadīyah in Afghanistan in A.D. 1924–5 see Toynbee, A. J.: *A Survey of International Affairs, 1925*, vol. i (London 1927, Milford), p. 568.

[2] See the present chapter, pp. 133–6, above, and V. C (i) (d) 6 (δ), p. 552, below.

[3] See IV. C (iii) (c) 2 (α), vol. iv, pp. 271–2, above, and V. C (i) (d) 6 (δ), pp. 545–52, below.

Tao into an explosive mixture of magic and militancy.[1] Already we are beginning to doubt whether our classic nineteenth-century scientific method of weighing and measuring, in which we have put our intellectual trust, is really a talisman which can be counted upon to transmute subjective thought into objective truth; and in the youthful postures of Psycho-analysis, which is the callowest of our Western scientific disciplines, we can see the first tentative essays in a new attitude of mind and cast of feeling and bent of will. Under the mask of a super-intellectualism we detect the resurgent and rebellious spirit of Primitive Man in the act of stealthily slinking back towards its Kingdom of Ancient Night in the hope that, in this reassuring disguise, the truant may be able to elude the vigilance of the secularized angel who wields the flaming sword of scientific scepticism. Is it the humiliating destiny of our Western Science to pander to our *nostalgie de la boue*? Will the twenty-fourth century of the Christian Era bring forth some Rumanian Iamblichus, or the twenty-fifth century some Mexican Proclus, to conjure a rank Neohuxleian theurgy out of a senile experimental technique? The hard-headed chemist or biologist of the present generation whose first impulse will be to scout this vision of our Western mental future as an extravagantly fantastic *jeu d'esprit* will do well to pause and take stock of a not less strange metamorphosis which has actually been taking place under his nose in one great province of the Westernized World of to-day; for in Marxian Communism we have a notorious example in our midst of a modern Western philosophy which has changed, in a lifetime, quite out of recognition by transforming itself into a proletarian religion, taking the path of Violence, and carving out its New Jerusalem with the sword on a Russian scale which utterly dwarfs the sixteenth-century Anabaptist Messianic city-state in Westphalia.

If Karl Marx had been challenged by some Victorian *censor morum* to give his spiritual name and address, no doubt he would have described himself, in all good faith, as a disciple of the great modern Western philosopher Hegel, and would have added that he had made it his own personal philosophic task to apply the Hegelian dialectic to the economic and political phenomena of modern Western social life. In the same Hegelian tradition Lenin, the Russian disciple of Marx, and perhaps—who knows?—even Stalin, the Caucasian disciple of Lenin, would have thought and spoken of himself as a philosopher first and foremost,[2] and would

---

[1] See the present chapter, pp. 146–7, above, and V. C (i) (d) 6 (δ), p. 557, below.

[2] 'Whereas in France, England, Germany, and everywhere throughout the West, Socialism first manifested itself as Christian or religious socialism, Russian socialism was from the outset a philosophic movement, influenced by Western philosophic doctrines.'—Masaryk, T. G.: *The Spirit of Russia* (English translation: London 1919, Allen and Unwin, 2 vols.), vol. ii, pp. 356–7.

have taken an even greater pride in his mastery of the dialectic method than in his power of controlling economic forces and ruling the hearts of men. Yet all the time it is patent to the judicious observer that the picture which paints Communism as a kind of applied philosophy is ludicrously inadequate and misleading; for even in the original Marxian ideology, not to speak of its Leninian and Stalinian application to life, the Hegelian dialectic is only one of the ingredients—and not the dynamic one at that! The elements which have made Marx's version of Hegelianism an even more explosive mixture than Chang Ling's version of Taoism[1] are not derived either from Hegel or from any other modern Western philosopher: they most of them bear on their face their certificate of origin from the ancestral religious faith of Western Christendom —a Christianity which in the nineteenth century, three hundred years after the delivery of the modern Western philosophic challenge by Descartes, was still being drunk in by every Western child with its mother's milk and inhaled by every Western man and woman with the air which the creature breathed. And such of the dynamic elements in Marxism as cannot be traced to Christianity can be traced to Judaism—the 'fossilized' parent of Christianity which had been preserved by a Jewish Diaspora in the Western World and had been volatilized through the opening of the Ghetto and the emancipation of the Western Jewry in the generation of Marx's grandparents.

The distinctively Jewish (or perhaps originally Zoroastrian) element in the traditional religious inspiration of Marxism is the apocalyptic vision of a violent revolution which is inevitable because it is the decree, and irresistible because it is the work, of God himself, and which is to invert the present roles of Proletariat and Dominant Minority in a tremendous *peripeteia*—a reversal of roles which is to carry the Chosen People, at one bound, from the lowest to the highest place in the Kingdom of This World.[2] Marx has taken the Goddess 'Historical Necessity' in place of Yahweh for his omnipotent deity,[3] and the internal proletariat of the

[1] For the (perhaps partly legendary) story of Chang Ling, the Taoist philosopher-alchemist who received a supernatural command from his (perhaps quite legendary) master, Lao-tse himself, to give happiness to Mankind, and who fulfilled this behest by founding, on the borders of the present Chinese provinces of Shensi and Szechwan, a model community which, in the reign of the founder's grandson, played a militant part in the proletarian insurrections against the expiring Han régime in the last quarter of the second century of the Christian Era, see Cordier, H.: *Histoire Générale de la Chine* (Paris 1920–1, Geuthner, 3 vols.), vol. i, pp. 189–90; Hackmann, H.: *Chinesische Philosophie* (Munich 1927, Reinhardt), p. 228; Franke, O.: *Geschichte des Chinesischen Reiches*, vol. i (Berlin and Leipzig 1930, de Gruyter), pp. 419–21. This latter-day aberration of Taoism has been mentioned already in the present chapter, pp. 146–7, above.

[2] For the originally mundane emplacement of the Messianic Kingdom in the futuristic expectations of the Jews see V. C (i) (d) 9 (γ), vol. vi, pp. 120–3, below.

[3] This Marxian Jewish Goddess 'Historical Necessity' has a sister in the Falasha Jewish Goddess Sanbat (see II. D (vi), Annex, in vol. ii, p. 406, above) and in the

modern Western World in place of Jewry;[1] and his Messianic Kingdom is conceived as a Dictatorship of the Proletariat.[2] But the salient features of the traditional Jewish apocalypse protrude through this threadbare disguise, and it is actually the pre-Rabbinical Maccabaean Judaism that our philosopher-impresario is presenting in modern Western costume; for it is of the essence of the Marxian apocalyptic doctrine that the Messianic Kingdom is not only to be a material kingdom in This World but is also to be won by a victorious stroke of violence. If this archaic Futurism is the distinctive Jewish element in the Marxian faith, the distinctively Christian element is an Oecumenicalism which is positively antipathetic, and not merely foreign, to the Jewish tradition. 'Go ye into all the World and preach the Gospel to every creature'[3] is an injunction which Marx feels to be laid upon himself, and which he lays in turn upon his followers, as imperiously as the duty of establishing the kingdom of righteousness by force. It is not merely a revolution but a world revolution that the good Marxian is in duty bound to strive for.[4]

It is a far cry from the Hegelian dialectic to the embattled church militant of a Soviet Union Communist Party[5] which with one hand is defending and organizing, through the Government of the Soviet Union, the ground which the Marxian Faith has now already won by the sword, while with the other hand it is working for the completion of the World Revolution through the agency of the Third International. The Marx who has conjured this matter out of that spirit by blending Syriac religion with Western philosophy is a mighty magician. He has performed as extraordinary a feat of 'materialization'[6] as his Hellenic prototype Blossius of Cumae:[7] the Stoic prophet of revolution[8] who was not

Elephantinian Jewish (or Judaeo-Samaritan) Goddesses 'Anath-Yahū and 'Anath-Bethel (see V. C (i) (d) 7, vol. vi, p. 46, footnote 1, below).
 [1] Compare the substitution of the internal proletariat of the Hellenic World for Jewry by the Christian Church under the influence of the Apostle to the Gentiles.
 [2] In the Marxian eschatology the Dictatorship of the Proletariat is represented as a transient régime which is destined to give place to a stateless form of society as soon as Socialism has become ingrained into the fabric of human life sufficiently to work by itself without any further need of organized force to back it. A similar transitoriness is, of course, one of the traditional features of the Jewish Messiah's millennial reign on Earth. [3] Mark xvi. 15.
 [4] For the socialist element in Marxism and its relation to Christianity see V. C (i) (c) 2, Annex II, below.
 [5] The Bolshevik or Majoritarian wing of the Russian Social-Democratic Party renamed itself 'the Russian Communist Party' (in homage to the Paris Commune of A.D. 1871) in March 1918 and 'the Soviet Union Communist Party' in May 1924 (in consonance with the by then accomplished fact of the reorganization of the former Russian Empire into a Union of Soviet Socialist Republics in which the Russian Soviet Federative Socialist Republic was only one (albeit the largest and strongest) of the half-dozen original states members of the Union).
 [6] Or of 'counter-etherialization' in the language of the terminology which we have coined in this Study (see III. C (i) (c), in vol. iii, above).
 [7] See further V. C (ii) (a), vol. vi, p. 249, below.
 [8] The question whether it was because of, or in spite of, his Stoicism that Blossius

only Zeno's disciple but was also the master of Tiberius Gracchus and Aristonicus.[1]   And, if it had pleased the Goddess fortune to crown Aristonicus's proletarian insurrection with success, then no doubt the names of the Italiot Greek prophet and his Pergamene khalīfah would be resounding down to this day as loudly as the names of Marx and Lenin do ring in the ears of a generation which has witnessed the triumphant establishment, on Russian ground, of a Marxian counterpart of that Blossian 'City of the Sun'[2] which Aristonicus tried and failed to establish in Asia Minor in the second century B.C.

Fortune decided otherwise; and the god Helios, to whom Aristonicus's commonwealth was dedicated, no more availed to save his Asiatic Heliopolis than the goddess Atargatis availed to save the contemporary Sicilian freedmen's state that was placed under her auspices by the Syrian slave-prophet Eunus.[3]   These attempts in a disintegrating Hellenic World to convert a prole-tarian religion and a proletarianized philosophy into political coin by force of arms were both promptly crushed by Roman military intervention, and they simply served to prove in action a truth which was put into words more than a century later by another leader of the Hellenic internal proletariat when he re-fused, in the crisis of his earthly career, to follow in Eunus's and Aristonicus's footsteps: 'for all they that take the sword shall perish with the sword.'[4]   The historical verdict which was pronounced in the Roman military victory over Eunus and Aristonicus was not shaken by the desperate attempts to reverse it which were made in succession by the authors of the Second Sicilian Slave-Revolt and by Spartacus and by Catiline; and some time before the tormented Hellenic World obtained the respite of the *Pax Augusta* it had already become clear that its destiny, whatever it was to be, was at any rate not foreshadowed in the apocalyptic vision of an internal proletariat which had gone, in desperation, upon the war-path.

oecame a revolutionary and went into practical politics on the forlorn hope of attempting to translate his dream into reality is a matter of controversy among modern Western scholars. According to one view, 'pour tirer les opprimés de leur inertie apathique, il fallut un grand élan de mysticisme dont les missionnaires stoïciens se firent les propagateurs' (Bidez, J.: *La Cité du Monde et la Cité du Soleil chez les Stoïciens* (Paris 1932, Belles Lettres), p. 50). According to another view, 'the slavery question shows that Aristonicus's inspiration was not Stoicism, i.e. Blossius (as Bidez thinks). . . . What moved Blossius was doubtless sympathy with the under-dog and perhaps a family tradition of hostility to the Roman Optimates' (Tarn, W. W.: *Alexander the Great and the Unity of Mankind* (London 1933, Milford), p. 34, footnote 54).

[1] For Aristonicus see the present chapter, pp. 69–70, above, with the references there given.

[2] For the worship of the Sun as the divinity who takes up the cause of the Internal Proletariat, see V. C (i) (d) 6 (δ), Annex, p. 692, footnote 2, below.

[3] For Eunus see further V. C (ii) (a), Annex II, vol. vi, *passim*; for the First Sicilian Slave-Revolt, of which Eunus was the leader, see the present chapter, pp. 69–70, above.

[4] Matt. xxvi. 52.

In our Western World in our generation the Leninian attempt
to fulfil the scripture of the Marxian apocalypse has been treated
more kindly by Fortune, at least in the first chapter; for Lenin's
proletarian commonwealth on Russian soil has successfully repulsed the first attempt of the Western dominant minority (or 'the
Capitalist Society' as it is called in the monomaniacally economic
language of the Marxian Sociology) to overthrow the new régime
in its puny infancy. More fortunate than his counterparts in the
second century B.C., who had to face a dominant minority whose
forces were then united under the single command of the omnipotent and ubiquitous power of Rome, Lenin made his *coup* in a
world in which the dominant minority was still profoundly divided
against itself and was engaged at that very moment in an internecine world-war; and the contending 'Capitalist' states all played
their unwilling part in working for the cause of their common
arch-enemy. The German Reich gave Lenin his first opening
by battering the Russian Tsardom to pieces; and the German
authorities actually conveyed the formidable exile himself from
Switzerland to Russia across German territory in order that he
might complete—to their profit, as they fondly imagined—the
task of destruction in which the donkey-work had already been
done by German arms. Then, when Lenin succeeded in his
enterprise too brilliantly for the Germans' liking, the victorious
Allies unintentionally came to Lenin's rescue and saved his work
in Russia from being hacked to pieces by the German sword
when, for their own purposes, they compelled their defeated
German adversaries to evacuate all the occupied Russian territories which Lenin, with his tongue in his cheek, had just ceded
to the Central Powers in the Peace of Brest-Litovsk. And after
that the nascent military strength of the rising Bolshevik state
proved just sufficient for fending off the half-hearted attacks
which the war-weary Allies proceeded to make upon the fringes
of the Bolshevik domain in the futile hope of dispatching with
their own blunted swords the monster whom they had not permitted their German opponents to slay.

In this world of mutually hostile 'Capitalist Powers' which
were more concerned to thwart one another than to crush their
common proletarian enemy, Lenin's infant Communist Commonwealth in Russia survived the ordeal to which Eunus's Sicilian
freedmen's state and Aristonicus's Asiatic Heliopolis both alike
succumbed. In the fourth year after Lenin's seizure of power at
Petrograd in 1917 it was already clear that the Bolshevik régime
was going to maintain itself in all but the outskirts of the derelict
domain of the fallen Russian Empire; and eighteen years later

again, in the year 1938, the Union of Soviet Socialist Republics
was still 'a going concern', instead of having faded into the mere
'curiosity of history' which was all that was left, within a year or
two of Aristonicus's *coup*, of the Blossian militant revolutionary's
pathetic attempt to establish a Hellenic Utopia 'in real life'.
This striking difference, up to date, between the respective
fortunes of our modern Western Hegelian philosophy militant
and of its Zenonian counterpart in Hellenic history raises a
question in our case which hardly arose in the other. We are
driven to ask ourselves whether it may perhaps be the destiny
of our Western Society to be taken captive by this militant movement—as formidable as it is bizarre—which claims intellectual
descent from a modern Western philosophy, has caught its spirit
of violence from an archaic strain in Judaism, has commandeered an
ample base of operations in the vast Russian province of a Westernized World, and has been inspired by an echo of the Christian
tradition to attempt the conversion of the whole of Mankind.

Ever since Lenin's advent to power at Petrograd in A.D. 1917
this question has been exercising the minds of men and women
all over the World and has been arousing their hopes or their fears
in accordance with their diverse outlooks and situations. The
established Communist masters of the Soviet Union have hoped
that they will not taste of death till they have beheld the world-
wide triumph of the Marxian creed and régime which their own
hands have already carried to victory in Russia. The non-Russian
Communist 'Diasporà' *in partibus infidelium*—or in *Dār-al-Harb*,
to use the corresponding Islamic term which seems more appropriate to the militancy of the Marxian êthos—has hoped that
it may live to see for itself the coming of the Dictatorship of the
Proletariat which in Russia is already an accomplished fact; and
this hope has perhaps been shared to some extent by some of
the non-Communist elements in the Western internal proletariat
—for instance, among the avowedly subject or nominally independent peoples of alien culture to whom the propaganda of the
Third International has been assiduously addressed in the hope
of persuading them to join in building up a common 'anti-Capitalist' and 'anti-Imperialist' front. On the other hand the Western
dominant minority beyond the borders of the Soviet Union,
which has been the principal target of the Third International's
attack, has hoped to see the march of Communism towards the
World Revolution arrested at least at the present frontiers of the
U.S.S.R.; and the *ci-devant* dominant minority in Russia, in so far
as it still survives either at liberty in exile or in its homeland under
the Bolshevik yoke, has ventured to hope—unfeignedly or in

secret, according to its place of domicile—that a successful repulse
of the Communist offensive abroad may some day be followed
up by a counter-attack upon the Communist stronghold in
Russia, and that this may eventually result in the repatriation of
the *émigrés* and the liberation of those who, under the Bolshevik
régime to-day, are sitting in darkness and in the shadow of death.

Officially, the opponents of Communism have been expecting
daily—every day since the 8th November, 1917—that the Bolshevik régime will collapse to-morrow, while the Latter-Day Saints
of the Communist Church Militant have been awaiting, with
the same official certitude, a denouement in the opposite sense
on the lines laid down in the militant Jewish apocalyptic tradition.
According to the orthodox Communist apocalypse, the heathen
Capitalist Powers are sooner or later to join forces in a supreme
effort to take the Soviet Socialist Jerusalem by storm and to
overwhelm the Communist Chosen People; and on that day,
when—on the plains of a Manchurian or Ukrainian Armageddon
—the Communist Church Militant is standing at bay against
a world of aggressors and is apparently facing hopeless odds,
her patron goddess Historical Necessity will manifest her power
by putting all the hosts of Midian out of action once for all at
a single miraculous stroke. Such are the official expectations on
either side; but they give little light to any one who is genuinely
seeking to forecast the outcome of the conflict; for it has been
evident for some time that both parties have ceased to believe
in the respective apocalypses to which they are officially committed. For light we have to look, not to dogmas, but to acts;
and, when we examine the recent internal political struggles and
external political relations of the Soviet Union, we may feel
inclined to predict that neither the Communist nor the anti-
Communist apocalypse is likely to come true.

The domestic political life of the U.S.S.R. has been dominated,
since Lenin's death in 1924, by a schism[1] in the ranks of his
companions—not on any point of theoretical Marxian or Leninian
doctrine or 'ideology', in which they all subscribe to an identic
orthodoxy, but on the practical question of how these sacrosanct
principles are to be translated into action here and now. One
faction among the Union Communist Party leaders have taken
the line that their immediate and paramount task is to bring about
the world-wide triumph of the Communist Revolution, and that,

---

[1] For this schism and its effects upon the domestic politics and foreign policy of the
Soviet Union see Florinsky, M.: *World Revolution and the U.S.S.R.* (London 1933,
Macmillan), pp. 125–68; Toynbee, A. J., and Boulter, V. M.: *Survey of International
Affairs, 1927* (London 1929, Milford), pp. 255–6; *Survey, 1934* (London 1935, Mil-
ford), pp. 362–8.

for this purpose, the economic and political and military resources of the U.S.S.R. must be placed unreservedly at the disposal of the Third International. But this Trotskian policy of 'continuous revolution' has been challenged by an opposing Stalinian policy of 'Socialism in a single country'—a policy which does not question the orthodox Communist doctrine that the Communist Revolution ultimately must be, and will be, world-wide, but does contest the Trotskian contention that the furtherance of the World Revolution ought to be a first charge upon the assets of the Soviet Union. The first thing to be done, in Stalin's view, is to make Socialism a going concern and a practical success in the one great country in which a Communist régime is already in power; and Stalin contends that this first objective can be attained within the frontiers of the U.S.S.R. independently of what may be happening—or not happening—at the moment in the rest of the World, while admitting that 'Socialism in one country' is only a means to the end of 'Socialism throughout the World', and that, until this consummation is reached, even the most brilliant and imposing achievements in a single country must still be regarded as provisional and precarious. In the year 1938, when the schism was fourteen years old, it was possible to pronounce with some assurance that the Stalinian policy had won. While Stalin was sitting in the Kremlin, Trotsky was vegetating in exile and Zinoviev was rotting in a grave to which he had been sent by the bullets of a firing-squad; and, while the socialization of the Soviet Union was by then an accomplished fact, the Communist World Revolution seemed to be farther off than it had ever been in a world in which Germany had turned National-Socialist. In fact, 'Socialism in a single country' had driven 'continuous revolution' off the field in the arena of Soviet Union domestic politics; and it was noteworthy that the definitive victory of Stalin over Trotsky in Moscow had been quickly followed by an almost sensational change in the relations between the Soviet Union and the states of 'the Capitalist World'.

Since Japan ran amok in the Far East in 1931, and Herr Hitler came into power in Germany in 1933, the Soviet Government has ceased in practice to act upon its official theory of knowing no distinctions between one Capitalist Power and another, and of expecting to see the world-wide triumph of Communism precipitated by a combined attack of all the Capitalist Powers upon the U.S.S.R. Instead, it has begun to show a lively fear lest a concerted attack upon the Soviet Union on the part of two aggressive Capitalist Powers alone may be sufficient to bring about, not the triumph of Communism throughout the World, but its overthrow in its present Russian citadel; and Soviet statesmanship has sought to parry this threat by making friends among the Mammon of Unrighteousness. As early as 1932 the Soviet Union entered into a political *entente* with France; in 1934 she became a member of the League of Nations; in 1935 she signed treaties of mutual assistance with both France and Czechoslovakia.

These positive acts are proof that Soviet statesmanship no longer expects to see the downfall of Capitalism abroad within any measurable time; for they imply a belief in the reality of the menace to the Soviet Union from the side of Germany and Japan, as well as a belief in the efficacy of an alliance with France and an adherence to the League as expedients for warding the danger off, whereas the peril and the safeguard alike would have to be dismissed in the same breath as sheer illusions by any one who was sincerely convinced that Germany and Japan and France and all the states members of the League were vessels of destruction *ipso facto* because they were products and expressions of an officially doomed Capitalist order of society. Thus the Soviet Government's foreign policy since 1932 presupposes, on the Communist side, a renunciation of the hope of seeing the world-wide triumph of the Communist régime brought to pass within the lifetime of the present generation; and conversely we may infer, on the Capitalist side, a corresponding renunciation of the last lingering hope of living to see the collapse of the Communist régime within the borders of the Soviet Union; for French statesmanship was quite as active as Soviet statesmanship in negotiating the Franco-Soviet *entente* of 1932, and in 1934 most of the existing states members of the League were quite as eager to secure the Soviet Union's adherence as the Soviet Union was to win their consent to its admission; and this attitude implies a belief, in the minds of the statesmen of the Capitalist countries, that the Soviet Union is a valuable associate and not a ramshackle empire that is on the point of falling to pieces. On this showing, it might be said, in the year 1938, that the Soviet Union and a majority, at any rate, of its Capitalist neighbours[1] had reciprocally and simultaneously come to the conclusion that the Communist and the Capitalist régimes were likely to go on existing side by side in the same world for as long a time to come as it was possible for statesmanship to take into account.

[1] Germany, Japan, and Italy are perhaps to be excluded from the list in view of the conclusion of a German-Japanese 'anti-Comintern Pact' on the 25th November, 1936 (see Toynbee, A. J., and Boulter, V. M.: *Survey of International Affairs, 1936* (London 1937, Milford), pp. 925–9), and the adhesion of Italy to this pact, with the status of an original party to it, on the 6th November, 1937 (*Survey, 1937*, vol. i, pp. 43–4). On the other hand, some belief in the stability of the Communist régime in the U.S.S.R. was presumably implied in the diplomatic recognition which was belatedly accorded to the Soviet Union by the Government of the United States in 1933.

We may remind ourselves of the similar conclusion which was arrived at—likewise reciprocally and simultaneously—by the Protestant and the Catholic commonwealths of Western Christendom in the last quarter of the seventeenth century of the Christian Era; and the parallel is illuminating. In that earlier case, as we can now see in the retrospect of the intervening two hundred and fifty years, the mutual decision to live and let live has been followed by a steady convergence, towards a single standard type, between two groups of states whose citizens had previously felt themselves to be divided by so great a gulf that, for the first hundred and fifty years after the outbreak of the Reformation, they had assumed with one accord that Christendom was too small to hold them both. Can we see any symptoms of an analogous approximation to-day between the Communism of the Soviet Union and the Capitalism of the rest of the World? We have only to put the question for it to answer itself decidedly in the affirmative.

We can already discern a pronounced tendency towards convergence in this case likewise, and we can observe that this converging movement is proceeding simultaneously from both sides. The 'Socialism in one country' which is the watchword of the Stalinian régime is manifestly generating a new Soviet Socialist nationalism which is finding its basis not in an old-fashioned uniformity of language but in a new-fangled uniformity of institutions which has its counterparts in the Fascist nationalism of post-war Italy and the National-Socialist nationalism of post-war Germany. Conversely, not only these two dictatorially governed communities but also all the other post-war Capitalist national states in their degree are becoming more and more socialist in their constitution as their nationalism becomes more intense. The convergence between the nationalistic socialism of the Soviet Union and the socialistic nationalism of her neighbours is unmistakable; and we can already make out the lineaments of the new common standard type of community towards which our post-war Capitalist and Communist states are thus all tending. The common goal towards which they are headed is a 'totalitarian' régime in a parochial socialist national state which commands the religious as well as the political allegiance of its subjects and imposes itself upon their souls as their supreme and indeed exclusive object of worship.[1]

If we are right in this forecast, it is the destiny of the would-be world-wide movement of Communism to be frustrated thrice over:

[1] For the idolatrous self-worship of the primitive tribe see IV. C (iii) (c) 2 (β), vol. iv, p. 351, above, and V. C (i) (c) 3, in the present volume, pp. 230–1, below. For the relapse of societies in process of civilization into this primitive form of idolatry see the same section of Part IV, *passim*.

first by being imprisoned within the frontiers of a single parochial state; next by being degraded into a local variety of Nationalism after having started its career as a social panacea for all Mankind; and finally by seeing the particular state that has enslaved it gradually assimilate itself to the other sixty or seventy states of the contemporary world by approximating to a common standard type.

This is just the fate by which we should expect to see Communism overtaken on the analogy of the history of other religious or philosophico-religious movements that have similarly turned militant. For example, the militant anti-Hellenic Judaism and Zoroastrianism of the Syriac World in the post-Alexandrine age became imprisoned respectively in the Maccabaean Kingdom[1] and in the Sasanian Empire;[2] the militant Imāmī Shī'ism of the Iranic World became imprisoned in the Safawī Empire;[3] the militant Muslim-Hindu syncretistic religion of Sikhism became imprisoned in the principality of Ranjit Singh;[4] and all the four imprisoning states showed the same tendency to approximate in type to their neighbours. The Sikh State became one of those ephemeral 'successor-states' of the Mughal Rāj in India— the Oudes and Rohilcunds—which made their appearance for a moment on the troubled surface of Indian political life before the broken *Pax Mogulica* was re-established as a *Pax Britannica*. The Maccabaean Kingdom played a corresponding role—until, under the Herodian usurpers, it became scarcely distinguishable in type from the Cappadocias and the Commagenes—as a 'successor-state' of the Seleucid Empire during the brief interval of anarchy which supervened before all these *peritura regna* were expunged by the *Pax Romana*.[5] The Sasanian Empire both influenced and was influenced by its sole neighbour and rival, the Roman Empire, during the four centuries of their existence in the same world side by side until, on the eve of the Primitive Arab Muslim assault upon them both, it might have needed a practised eye to distinguish the court of Chosroes from the court of Caesar. And South West Asian history repeated itself when a Safawī counterpart of Chosroes prostituted his hereditary head-

[1] For this spiritual imprisonment of Judaism see V. C (i) (d) 6 (δ), Annex, pp. 657–9, below.
[2] For this spiritual imprisonment of Zoroastrianism see V. C (i) (d) 6 (δ), Annex, pp. 659–61, below.
[3] See I. C (i) (b), Annex I, vol. i, pp. 366–93, above, and V. C (i) (d) 6 (δ), Annex, pp. 661–5, below. In this connexion we may recall the fact—already mentioned in the present chapter, p. 175, footnote 2, above—that the latter-day emanation from the Imāmī Shī'ism which is known as Babism has been blighted on its native Persian ground as a penalty for its lapse into militancy. It is not in Iran but in the Ottoman Empire and the Western World, and not in its primitive form but in the new guise of Bahaism, that the seed sown by the Bāb has eventually fallen into good ground and brought forth fruit.   [4] See V. C (i) (d) 6 (δ), Annex, pp. 665–8, below.
[5] On this point see Tacitus: *Histories*, Book V, chap. 8.

ship of a religious order to the mundane political ambition of becoming the *Gegenkaiser* to the Ottoman *Qaysar-i-Rūm*. The same historic penalty for the sin of militancy is apparently being exacted from Communism in our world to-day; and we can now almost foresee the time when Communism and Capitalism will be interchangeable names for a uniform idolatrous worship of the community in a standardized parochial 'totalitarian' state. On this showing, we shall be looking in vain if we look to Communism to provide the internal proletariat of a disintegrating Western Society with the makings of a universal church.

The upshot of our present inquiry seems to be that, while the evidence for the recruitment of an internal proletariat is at least as abundant in the recent history of our Western World as it is in the history of any other civilization, there is singularly little evidence in our Western history so far for the laying of any foundations of a proletarian universal church or even for the emergence of any strong-winged proletarian-born 'higher religions'. Communism seems not to 'fill the bill' any better than Anabaptism or Quakerism or Bahaism or Ahmadism; and these five movements, which make so oddly assorted a company, are a small catch to take in a net which we have thrown so wide.

How is this apparent spiritual barrenness of our Western internal proletariat to be interpreted?

On first thoughts we might perhaps be tempted to draw an encouraging conclusion. We might account for this dearth of creative achievement by the fact, which we have already observed,[1] that some of the finest of the plants that have been uprooted in our Western garden have managed hitherto to strike root again on virgin soil. In other words, some of the most promising of the recruits to our Western internal proletariat have been prevented from making any appreciable contribution to a new proletarian culture by the fact that they have been successfully reabsorbed into an unruptured Western body social; and this is a fact on which we may surely congratulate ourselves; since it may be taken to mean that, in our Western Society, the schism between Proletariat and Dominant Minority has been partially repaired, and that the breakdown of our civilization (if it has broken down) has been to that extent retrieved. The talents of these rehabilitated proletarians may have been lost to the proletariat, but they have certainly not been lost to our society as a whole. So far from that, these *déracinés*' descendants—Nonconformist English, French Protestant South Africans, United Empire Loyalist Canadians, and Irish and German Americans—

---

[1] See the present chapter, pp. 168–73, above.

are reckoned to-day among the most valuable members of the
communities on to which they have been grafted or re-attached.
On this line of reasoning the spiritual barrenness of the Western
proletariat, so far from being a cause for shame or regret, is
actually to be taken as presumptive evidence that the condition
of our Western body social as a whole, though it may be serious,
is not by any means beyond hope. And if, in our own day, our
system shows signs of being able still to conquer and transmute
so strong a virus as Communism, we may surely flatter ourselves
that there is life and health in our Western Society yet.

These may be our first thoughts; but our optimism will be
damped when we look narrowly at the price at which our boasted
conquest of Communism is being purchased; for the all-absorbing
Western institution to which the Marxian Church Militant shows
signs of succumbing turns out, as we have seen, to be the pagan
parochial 'totalitarian' state; and, if we remind ourselves of the
fate of other civilizations that have come to be articulated into
states of this kind, we shall find reason to fear that the future
history of our own civilization may be 'nasty, brutish, and short'.[1]
An unceasing round of internecine warfare of ever increasing
intensity between deified parochial states has been the principal
cause of the breakdown and disintegration of some, and perhaps
most, of the civilizations that have already gone the way of all
flesh. The bones of the Hellenic and Sinic societies—to pick out
two conspicuous skeletons—lie whitening ominously on fratricidal battlefields. If our own Western Society in its turn is now
assuming this fatal posture and falling into this deadly rhythm,
then its prospects, so far from being encouraging, are about as
bad as they can be;[2] for the 'drive' of Democracy and Industrialism, which are the two master-forces in our Western World
in this latest age, has already entered into both our parochialism
and our warfare; and this terrific head of steam seems likely to
carry us at an unprecedented speed to an unparalleled disaster.[3]
On these second thoughts we may be inclined to look for some
alternative solution of our puzzle which will not involve the
assumption that, in spite of appearances to the contrary, our
Western Civilization is really still flourishing like a green bay tree.

If our Western body social is articulating itself to-day into
a congeries of parochial 'totalitarian' states which are irreconcilable
with one another because each of them refuses to recognize any
higher object of worship than itself, then certainly we are approxi-

---

[1] Hobbes, T.: *Leviathan*, Part i, chap. 13.
[2] See V. C (ii) (*b*), vol. vi, pp. 312–21, below.
[3] See IV. C (iii) (*b*) 3 and 4, vol. iv, pp. 141–85, above.

mating to the condition in which the Hellenic Society found itself at the moment of its breakdown in the fifth century B.C.; but at this point we shall be struck by a significant difference between Hellenic and Western history. In Hellenic history this parochial paganism was the first state of the ailing society as well as the last; but it has certainly not been the first state—even if it is the present state—of a Western Society which was once entitled to speak of itself as Western Christendom.[1] Moreover, even if we have now at last succeeded in sloughing off our Christian heritage, the process of apostasy has been slow and laborious, and with the best will in the world we are unlikely to have carried it through with all the thoroughness that we might wish; for, after all, it is not so easy to get rid of a tradition in which we and our forebears have been born and bred since the time, now more than twelve hundred years ago, when our Western Christendom was born—a feeble infant—from the Church's womb. When Descartes and Voltaire and Rousseau and Marx and Machiavelli and Hobbes and Lenin and Mussolini and Hitler have all done their best or worst, in their diverse spheres, to de-christianize the various departments of our Western life, we may still suspect that their scouring and fumigating has been only partially effective. The Christian virus or elixir is in our Western blood—if, indeed, it is not just another name for that indispensable fluid—and it is therefore difficult to suppose that the spiritual constitution of our Western Society can ever be refined to a paganism of a Hellenic purity.

Besides, the Christian element in our system is not only ubiquitous: it is also Protean; and one of its favourite tricks is to escape eradication by insinuating a strong tincture of its own essence into the very disinfectants that are so vigorously applied, with intention to sterilize it, by our latter-day neo-pagan social physicians. We have noticed,[2] for example, the surprising strength and importance of the Christian ingredient in a Communism which purports to be an anti-Christian application of a modern Western philosophy to the practical problems of social life; and, while the violent-handed missionaries of this militant faith betray the extent of their debt to Christianity in the passion with which they deny it, the prophets of Gentleness in a Western or Westernized World—the Tolstoys and the Gandhis—have never sought to conceal their Christian inspiration. The same inspiration is avowed *a fortiori* by those walkers in the way of Gentleness who acknowledge and proclaim themselves Christians like the members

---

[1] See I. B (iii), vol. i, pp. 32–4, above.
[2] See the present chapter, pp. 178–9, above.

of the Society of Friends; and we may now remind ourselves of
one profoundly touching and impressive religious movement in
the bosom of our Western internal proletariat which we have not
considered yet in the present context.

Among the many diverse contingents of disinherited men and
women who have been subjected, within the last four centuries, to
the common ordeal of being enrolled in this Western internal proletariat, the worst sufferers of all have been those Primitive African
Negroes who have been uprooted from their homes and sold into
slavery on the opposite coasts of the Atlantic. In these slave-
emigrants from Tropical Africa to North America we have found
our Western analogue of the slave-immigrants who were swept
into Roman Italy from all the other coasts of the Mediterranean at
the acme of the Hellenic 'Time of Troubles' in the last two centuries B.C.; and we have observed that the Americo-African, like
the Italo-Oriental, plantation-slaves met their tremendous social
challenge with a religious response. In comparing the two responses at an earlier stage in this Study,[1] we dwelt upon their
points of likeness, but there is also a point of difference which
is equally striking and also particularly relevant to our present
inquiry; and that is the difference in the sources from which these
two sets of uprooted plantation-slaves respectively drew their
religious inspiration. The Egyptian and Syrian and Anatolian
slave-immigrants into Roman Italy found their religious consolation in those ancestral religions which were the sole element in
their heritage that they had been able to carry with them into
their land of exile; on the other hand the African Negro slave-
immigrants into post-Columbian America have lost the whole
of their heritage—religion and all[2]—and have turned for their
religious consolation to the hereditary religion of their masters.

How is this difference to be accounted for? In part, no doubt,
by the difference in the nature of the social antecedents of the two
sets of slaves. The plantation-slaves of Roman Italy were largely
drawn from an ancient and deeply cultivated Oriental population
whose children might be expected to cling to their cultural heritage
with all their might, whereas the African Negro slaves who were
imported into America were primitives whose ancestral religion

[1] In II. D (vi), vol. ii, pp. 213–16 and 218–20, above.
[2] This statement requires qualification, for the modern American Negro converts to
Christianity, like the North European barbarian converts of an earlier age, have blended
their acquired 'higher religion' with a primitive religious alloy of their own, and the
American Negro debasement of the Western Christian religious coinage seems to have
been carried to the greatest lengths in those American Negro communities that have
been the most successful in emancipating themselves from the White Man's control.
In the sovereign independent Negro Republic of Haiti we can observe to-day, in the
shape of Voodooism, a recrudescence of the Primitive Tropical African paganism which
has quite thrown off the Christian mask.

was no more fit than any other element in their hereditary culture to hold its own against the overwhelmingly superior civilization of their European White masters. This is a partial explanation of the difference in the sequel; but, in order to explain it completely, the cultural difference between the two sets of masters, as well as that between the two sets of slaves, has to be taken into consideration.

We have already observed[1] that the Oriental slaves in Roman Italy had actually nowhere to look, outside their own native religious heritage, for the religious consolation for which they were athirst, since their Roman masters were living in a spiritual vacuum; and even if the Hellenic dominant minority had not already lost faith in the impersonal Italic *numina* and the barbaric Achaean Pantheon, these crude primitive worships which had been repudiated long since by the Hellenic philosophers would scarcely have been embraced by the Oriental worshippers of Cybele and Isis and Mithras and Christ. In fact, in the Hellenic case the pearl of great price was to be found in the religious heritage of the slaves and not in that of their masters, while in our Western case the spiritual treasure, as well as all the worldly wealth and power, has lain in the hands of the slave-driving dominant minority.

It is one thing, however, to possess a spiritual treasure, and quite another thing to impart it; and, the more we think over it, the more astonishing we shall find it to be that these Christian slave-owners' hands should have been able to transmit to their primitive pagan victims the spiritual bread which they had done their worst to desecrate by the sacrilegious act of enslaving their fellow men. How could a slave-driver evangelist ever touch the heart of the slave whom he had morally alienated by doing him a grievous personal wrong? And why was the religion which he brazenly preached to his slave-victims not utterly discredited, in the slave-catechumen's eyes, by the glaring contrast between the precept and the practice of the master-preacher? This Christian religion which has been repudiated in act and deed by the American slave-owner, as well as by the French philosopher in thought and word, must be animated by an invincible spiritual power if it can still win converts under such conditions. It must still be keeping alive, with a life that is all its own, after the dominant minority in a *ci-devant* Western Christendom has presumed to slough its ancestral Christianity off as though a religious integument were as easily shed as the winter skin of a snake in spring-time. And since Religion has no dwelling-place on Earth except in human souls, it

[1] In II. D (vi), vol. ii, pp. 215–16, above.

follows that there must be Christian men and women still abroad in a neopagan world who have never renounced their Christian birthright of citizenship in the *Civitas Dei* in order to become the subjects of King Mammon or King Moloch. 'Peradventure there be fifty righteous within the city';[1] and a glance at the American slave mission-field will show us some of these persistent Christians at work; for the American Negro convert to Christianity does not, of course, really owe his conversion to the ministrations of a plantation-gang overseer with a Bible in one hand and a whip in the other. The real workers of the miracle have been the John G. Fees[2] and the Peter Clavers.

In this miracle of the slaves' conversion to the ancestral religion of their masters we can see the familiar schism between the Proletariat and Dominant Minority being healed in our Western body social by a Christianity which our dominant minority has been trying to repudiate; and the conversion of the American Negro servile wing of our modern Western internal proletariat is only one among the triumphs of a latter-day Christian missionary activity. The eighteenth-century Methodist preachers who sowed the seed of Christianity in the hearts of the North American slaves were at the same time converting other members of the same internal proletariat who were neither slaves in status nor Negroes in physique: for example, the remote backwoodsmen in the Appalachian mountains and the neglected slum-dwellers in the nascent mining and industrial areas of Wales and Northern England. Nor has the Christian revival in a paganized Western World been confined to the Revivalist Movement in the Protestant Churches. In our post-war generation, in which the lately brilliant prospects of a neopagan dominant minority have been rapidly growing dim, the sap of life is visibly flowing once again through all the branches of our Western Christendom; and this spectacle suggests that perhaps, after all, the next chapter in our Western history may not follow the lines of the final chapter in the history of Hellenism. Instead of seeing some new church spring from the ploughed-up soil of an internal proletariat in order to serve as the executor and residuary legatee of a civilization that has broken down and gone into disintegration, we may yet live to see a civilization which has tried and failed to stand alone, being saved, in spite of itself, from a fatal fall by being caught in the arms of an ancestral church which it has vainly striven to push away and keep at arm's length. In that event a tottering civilization which has shamefully

[1] Genesis xviii. 24.
[2] See Fee, John Gregg: *Autobiography* (Chicago 1891, National Christian Association).

succumbed to the intoxication of a showy victory over Physical Nature, and has applied the spoils to laying up treasure for itself without being rich towards God,[1] may be reprieved from the sentence—which it has passed upon itself—of treading out the tragic path of κόρος-ὕβρις-ἄτη; or, to translate this Hellenic language into a Christian imagery, an apostate Western Christendom may be given grace to be born again as the *Respublica Christiana* which is its own earlier and better ideal of what it should strive to be.

Is such spiritual re-birth possible? If we put Nicodemus's question, we may take his instructor's answer.[2]

3. *External Proletariats*

The Estrangement of the Proselyte.

The External, like the Internal, Proletariat brings itself into existence by an act of secession from the Dominant Minority of a civilization that has broken down and gone into disintegration; and the schism in which the secession results is in this case palpable; for, in contrast to the Internal Proletariat, which continues to live intermingled geographically with the Dominant Minority from which it has come to be divided by a moral gulf, the External Proletariat is not only alienated from the Dominant Minority in feeling but is also actually divided from it by a frontier which can be traced on the map.

The crystallization of such a frontier is indeed the sure sign that the Secession of the External Proletariat has taken place; for, as long as a civilization is still in growth, it has no hard and fast boundaries except on fronts where it happens to have collided with some other member or members of its own species. Such collisions between two or more civilizations give rise to a set of social phenomena which we shall have occasion to examine in a later part of this Study,[3] but at the present stage, for convenience' sake, we will take the licence of leaving out of account these geographical contacts of civilizations with one another, and— for our immediate purpose of studying the disintegrations of civilizations—we will confine our attention for the moment to the situation in which a civilization has for its neighbour, not another society of its own kind, but a society of the primitive species. In these circumstances we shall find that, so long as a civilization is in growth, its frontiers are indeterminate; for, if we first place ourselves at the geographical focus of a civilization that is still in growth—taking our stand at some point where the creative minority of the day can be seen at home and at work—and if we

---

[1] Luke xii. 21, quoted in the present chapter on p. 166, above.
[2] See John iii. 1-8.   [3] In Part IX, below.

then proceed to travel outwards, in any direction that we choose, until we find ourselves sooner or later in another social environment which is not only different but is unmistakably primitive, we shall not be able—at any point on this journey out of the full light of Civilization into the pitch-black darkness of Savagery—to draw a line and set up a mark and inscribe on our boundary-stone: 'Here Civilization ends and we enter the Primitive World.'

This problem of defining limits is one which does not present itself in the relations between the creative minority and the uncreative mass out of whose midst the minority has arisen; for *ex hypothesi*, if a civilization is still in growth, the creative minority of the day, which has found itself through an act of withdrawal, will also have justified itself by making a successful return; and the success will have consisted—*ex hypothesi* again—in the persuasion of the uncreative mass to adopt that response to the challenge of the day which the creative minority has worked out.[1] A returning minority which had failed to cast its spell over the mass would be like a pinch of yeast which had pioved too flat to leaven the lump or like a lamp which had proved too dim to light the room. It would have patently broken down in its ambitious attempt to play the creator's part; and the breakdown of a would-be creative minority brings with it the breakdown of the civilization to which this minority has tried, and failed, to give a lead. Our hypothetical civilization, however, is still—*ex hypothesi*—in growth; and this means that, as a matter of fact, the room has been successfully lit and the lump successfully leavened.

No doubt the creative minority's task of converting its uncreative kith and kin is always difficult to achieve, since it is notorious that 'a prophet hath no honour in his own country';[2] but we have a double proof that the difficulty is not insuperable. We know this empirically from the patent historical fact that civilizations do grow—or, in other words, do respond successfully not merely to a single challenge but to a series of challenges.[3] And we can also tell *a priori* that the task is not impossible because we can see that it is not unlimited in its extent. The room which has to be illuminated may be a cavern of darkness, yet the lamp-light will strike—if only it can radiate so far—upon four walls and a ceiling. The lump which has to be leavened may be a mountain of dough, yet the yeast—if only it can permeate so deep—will eventually have worked its way right through this mountainous lump from top to bottom. In the body social of a

---

[1] For the relation between a creative minority or individual and the uncreative mass in the process of the growths of civilizations see III. C (ii), *passim*, in vol. iii, above.
[2] John iv. 44; cf. Matt. xiii. 57=Mark vi. 4; Luke iv. 24.
[3] For the serial aspect of the growths of civilizations see Part III. B, in vol. iii, above.

growing civilization we may take it that the whole of the uncreative mass has been touched and stirred by the creative minority
in some way or other whenever a challenge receives a successful
response. For those who do not catch the inspiration in their
souls, 'like a light caught from a leaping flame',[1] are induced to
conform externally by the enlistment of their faculty of mimesis.

Thus, when a creative minority successfully performs its role
in the life of a growing civilization, the spark which it has kindled
gives light unto all that are in the house;[2] but when this light
strikes the walls it is not arrested there, for the walls of a growing
civilization are walls of glass in a city that is set on a hill and that
cannot be hid.[3] The light streams out and on to shine before
men;[4] and, when once the rays have passed through the transparent envelope of the crystal chamber out of which they are
radiating, they enter a boundless field in which there is nothing
to limit their range except the inherent limitations of their own
carrying-power. Accordingly, when the light of a growing civilization shines out upon the primitive societies round about, it travels
on until it has faded away to vanishing-point. The luminous
focus shades off into a penumbra and the penumbra into an outer
darkness; but the gradations are infinitesimal, and it is impossible
to demarcate a line at which the last glimmer of twilight flickers out
and leaves the heart of darkness in undivided possession of the field.

To re-translate our simile into human terms, we find that in a
growing civilization the creative minority of the day exercises its
attraction not only upon the uncreative mass in whose midst it has
arisen but also upon the primitive societies round about, and that
it sometimes makes its influence felt at points that are astonishingly
remote from the centre of radiation. The Sumeric Civilization
sends forth its gods to win honour in Scandinavia;[5] the Syriac
Civilization radiates its Alphabet into Manchuria;[6] the Hellenic
Civilization makes its aesthetic influence felt in the coinage of
Britain[7] and in the statuary of India.[8] In fact, the carrying-power
of the radiation of civilizations among primitive societies is so
great that although the younger of the two species of societies is
still very young indeed—perhaps not more than six thousand
years old as against the hundreds of thousands of years of Primitive Man's existence on Earth up to date[9]—it has long ago suc-

---

[1] Plato's Letters, No. 7, 341 B–E, quoted in III. C (ii) (a), vol. iii, p. 245, above.
[2] Matt. v. 15.   [3] Matt. v. 14.   [4] Matt. v. 16.
[5] See V. C (i) (c) 2, pp. 82 and 149–50, above.
[6] See III. C (i) (a), vol. iii, pp. 130–1, above, and V. C (i) (d) 6 (γ), in the present
volume, p. 500, below.   [7] See V. C (i) (d) 6 (β), p. 482, below.
[8] See III. C (i) (a), vol. iii, p. 131; III. C (ii) (a), vol. iii, p. 247, footnote 2; and V. C
(i) (c) 2, in the present volume, pp. 134–5, above.
[9] See I. C (iii) (c), vol. i, p. 173, above.

ceeded (if the word can be used of an activity that has been mostly
unintentional and unconscious) in permeating, at least in some
minute degree, the whole congeries of surviving primitive societies.
The social radiation that has emanated from the twenty-one
civilizations, living and extinct, which we have succeeded in
identifying, is diffused to-day throughout the Primitive World
like the starlight which just relieves the blackness of a moonless
night. And it would probably be impossible for our twentieth-
century Western anthropologists to discover—even behind a
curtain-wall of limestone precipices in the heart of Papua[1]—a
primitive society which had entirely escaped the influence of
some civilization or other. We may confidently affirm that there
is no such thing to be seen in the World to-day as a society in the
pristine state in which all societies were living before the first of
the civilizations emerged.[2] The societies that we now describe as
primitive can only be called so by courtesy; for these latter-day
primitives are no longer the untutored—or unspoiled—savages
that their forefathers were; instead, they have turned into partially—
if only infinitesimally—civilized barbarians; and in a world in
which the goal of Civilization has never yet been reached by any
society in process of civilization, even at its highest flights, the
least civilized of the barbarians are perhaps less far removed from
our semi-civilized selves than they are from their own primitive ancestors of the seventh or hundred-and-seventh millennium B.C.

This all-pervasiveness of the influence of the civilizations in what
remains of the Primitive World is the aspect of the relations between
the two species of Society which strikes us most forcibly when we
view these relations through the primitive societies' eyes and embrace in our survey the whole Time-span of the six thousand years
or so that have now elapsed since the first civilizations appeared on
the scene. On the other hand, if we look at the same process from the
standpoint of the civilizations and narrow down our survey to the
Time-span of a single civilization's age of growth, we shall be
struck no less forcibly by the fact that the strength of the influence
that is radiated out wanes *pari passu* with the extension of its
geographical range. As soon as we have recovered from our
astonishment at detecting the influence of Hellenic art in a coin

---

[1] For the discovery, in A.D. 1935, of a previously quite unknown society in a region
in the interior of Papua which has been insulated physically by the caprice of Nature,
see *The Times*, 14th August, 1935, and Hides, J. G.: *Papuan Wonderland* (London 1936,
Blackie). The feature in the life of these Tari Furora that made the deepest impression
upon the mind of the Western public, when it read the report of the discovery, was the
unexpectedly high level of their culture, at any rate on the material side. From some
civilization or other, at some unknown date, this secluded people had already acquired
the technique of an intensive cultivation of the land and an orderly lay-out of the country-
side.
[2] On this point see Part II. A, vol. i, pp. 185–7, above.

that was struck in Britain in the last century B.C. or on a sarcophagus that was carved in Afghanistan in the first century of the
Christian Era, the edge is taken off our admiration by the hard
fact that Hellenism has only achieved the *tour de force* of travelling
so far as this at the price of shedding most of its virtue in the
course of the journey. Our British coin looks like a caricature of
an original stater of Philip the son of Amyntas, and our Gandharan
sarcophagus is convicted of being a vile product of 'commercial art' as soon as we set it side by side with the Alexander
Sarcophagus. At this remove mimesis passes into travesty. Yet
this only happens at the outer extremity of the radiating civilization's range of action; and even the clumsiest and most perfunctory mimesis has its value—as a means of self-education for
the party by whom the act of mimesis is performed, and as
a tribute of admiration and token of friendship for the party
towards whom the mimesis is directed.

Mimesis is evoked by charm; and we can now see that the
charm which is exercised, during the growth of a civilization, by
a succession of creative minorities preserves the house not only
from being divided against itself but also from being attacked by
its neighbours—in so far, at least, as these neighbours happen to
be societies of the primitive species. Wherever a growing civilization is in contact with primitive societies, the creative minority
of the day attracts their mimesis as well as the mimesis of the
uncreative majority in whose midst it arises; and, thanks to this
attractive power, a growing civilization seldom finds itself in
direct contact with savages whose cultural level is so far below
its own as to preclude a friendly understanding. It usually finds
itself surrounded by a ring of buffer-societies which are continually absorbing its radiation into their own bodies social and
then passing it on, diminuendo, to an outer ring, which receives
and transmits in its turn until the current of energy finally gives
out at the extreme range of the civilization's carrying-power.

If this is the normal relation between a civilization and the
primitive societies round about so long as the civilization is in
growth, a profound change sets in if and when the civilization
breaks down and goes into disintegration. This change can be
described in two different ways, according as we speak in the
language of Life or in terms of Inanimate Nature.

In the language of Life the breakdown consists in the disappearance from the scene of the creative minorities that have
won a voluntary allegiance by the charm which their creative
power exerts, and in their replacement by a Dominant Minority
which attempts to usurp a heritage that it does not deserve to

inherit, and seeks to gain its end by substituting, for the charm which it lacks, the physical force which still remains at its command.[1] This policy, as we have seen, has the moral effect of alienating the victims of it. It goads them into acts of secession; and, while the secession of the masses in whose midst the Dominant Minority stands gives birth to an Internal Proletariat, an External Proletariat is generated by the secession of the primitive societies round about who, so long as the civilization was in growth, were accepting and transmitting its radiation. It would not, however, be an accurate or a complete account of the change in the attitude of these surrounding primitive societies to describe their act of secession as a withdrawal of mimesis from the now disintegrating civilization; for in falling into disintegration a society ceases to be a whole on which other societies can model themselves, or decline to model themselves, consistently and integrally. The cause of breakdown, as we have seen, is a failure of self-determination;[2] this failure declares itself in a loss of proportion and harmony and inward unity; and—if we now transpose our description of the phenomena into terms of Physical Science—we shall find that this disintegration (in the literal sense) of the broken-down society's fabric is reproduced in the texture of the rays of the radiation which it continues to emit so long as it remains in existence.

While the rays of social radiation that are emitted by a growing civilization may be likened to rays of white light, in which all the constituent elements of light are blended into a single clear beam, the rays emitted by a disintegrating civilization may be likened to physical light which has been diffracted into a sheaf or fan of separate strands that follow distinct paths and display their diverse elemental colours. In social radiation this change in the texture of the ray, which we have just described as diffraction by analogy with a physical phenomenon, has an important effect on its range; for the three elements—cultural, political, and economic—of which a 'white-light' ray of social radiation is composed differ greatly in their carrying-power; and this difference makes itself felt as soon as they are disentangled from one another.

So long as they are interwoven in a single composite ray, the three strands of social radiation travel at an even speed and to an equal distance—a mean distance and a mean speed which strike the average between their respective capacities. But when once they are set free to go each its own way, the three strands begin to travel at the different speeds and to the different distances which are respectively natural to each of them; and the result is

---

[1] See IV. C (iii) (a), vol. iv, pp. 123–4 and 131–2, above.
[2] See IV. C (iii), *passim*, in vol. iv, above.

a differentiation of the disintegrating society's radio-activity—an enhancement of this activity on one plane and a reduction of it on another.[1] Since the carrying-power of the economic element is the highest of the three and is therefore above the average, one effect of the breakdown and disintegration of a civilization is an increase in the expansion of its economic influence; there is sometimes also an increase, above the previously maintained average, on the political plane likewise; and this accounts for an apparent 'law'—which has been revealed in another context[2] by an empirical survey—to the effect that the geographical expansion of a civilization is apt to go hand in hand with its social disintegration. We have now, however, to observe that this enhancement of radiation on the economic plane—and sometimes even on the political plane—which a civilization gains by going into disintegration, is offset by a proportionate reduction of its radiation on the cultural plane; for the natural rate of radiation on this plane is below the average; and, while in the 'white-light' ray of a growing civilization the cultural element is speeded up beyond its own natural pace, and is carried beyond its own natural range, by its unison with two other elements of greater carrying-power, it drops to its own intrinsic range and pace as soon as it is disentangled from them, just as they rise to their longer intrinsic ranges and higher speeds as soon as they are disentangled from it. In fact, while a disintegrating society surpasses a growing society in its radiation on one, or even two, of the three social planes, it simultaneously falls behind it on one plane at least; and, if we now substitute qualitative for quantitative standards of measurement, we shall be left in no doubt that the net result is a moral loss and not a moral gain.

The difference in value between the three elements of social life is, indeed, extreme; for what we have called the cultural element in a civilization is its soul and life-blood and marrow and pith and essence and epitome, while the political and, *a fortiori*, the economic element are, by comparison, superficial and non-essential and trivial manifestations of a civilization's nature and vehicles of its activity. It is only in so far as it succeeds in radiating itself out on the cultural plane that a civilization can ever genuinely and completely assimilate an alien body social with which it has come into contact; for the most spectacular triumphs of economic and political radiation are imperfect and therefore precarious.

---

[1] We have already come across this differentiation of a society's radio-activity, on the three different planes of economic, political, and cultural action, in attempting to trace backwards in Time, from the situation as it stands at the present day, the variations in the spatial extension of our Western Civilization (see I. B (iii), vol. i, pp. 26–33, above).

[2] In III. C (i) (*a*), vol. iii, pp. 139–53, above. See also IV C (ii) (*b*) 1, vol. iv, p. 57, above.

Accordingly it is more profitable, both for the society which is emitting the radiation and for the society which is receiving it, that an inch should be gained on the cultural plane than a mile on the political plane or a league on the economic.

On this showing, the expansion of a growing civilization is to be commended for being slow but sure; for in a growing civilization the three elements are either completely blended or at worst only slightly diffracted; and under such conditions all the ground that is won is won on the cultural plane as well as on the other two, while at the same time rather more ground is won by the three elements in combination than could have been won by the cultural element in isolation. By contrast, the expansion of a disintegrating civilization is exposed as being showy but unsound; for, while it forges ahead on the economic plane, and perhaps on the political plane as well, the ground thus superficially gained is never definitively secured by a cultural conquest, since the cultural radiation of a disintegrating civilization is losing momentum in exact proportion to the enhancement of its political and economic radioactivity. In fact—to vary our simile—the economic and political seed which a disintegrating civilization contrives to scatter so far afield is sickly seed sown among thorns.[1]

If we now return to the standpoint of the barbarian society which has been receiving the radiation of a growing civilization and has been reacting to it by directing its own faculty of mimesis towards the alien source of this new light and life, we shall see that, when the barbarian society's reaction changes after the civilization's breakdown, the new sense of alienation from a neighbour who has lost his soul and changed his countenance, and the act of secession in which this estrangement issues, do not necessarily involve a complete cessation of all mimesis on every plane. The

[1] 'The tree that grows and flowers is tied to the patch of soil in which it is rooted ... but its ripe fruits can be sown by every wind no matter how far afield. Strassburg Minster could not have grown to be what it is anywhere but in Strassburg, and the Haghía Sofía not anywhere but in Constantinople; but a "modern building in the Renaissance style" can "be produced" just as well at the South Pole as in the primeval forests of Brazil.'—Frobenius, L.: *Paideuma* (Frankfurt a.M. 1928, Frankfurter Societäts-Druckerei), p. 172. Compare the contrast, noted in the present Study in IV. C (iii) (b) 14, vol. iv, p. 243, above, between the performance of an Attic play at one of the regular festivals in the Theatre of Dionysus at Athens, where the Attic drama had its roots, and the performance of the same play, *post Alexandrum*, by the Διονύσου Τεχνῖται, anywhere in the world, from Parthia to Spain. This objective phenomenon of the diffraction of the rays of a disintegrating civilization has a subjective counterpart in 'the sense of promiscuity' which is examined in V. C (i) (d) 6, pp. 439–568, below. The psychological shock that is an apparently inevitable accompaniment of the external disturbance involved in the experience of social 'deracination' seems to be so severe that its effects may be devastating even when the social milieu from which the subject is uprooted is itself an artificial and abnormal environment. For example, when barbarian war-bands break through a *limes* (see p. 208, below)—in a Völkerwanderung which first uproots them from the no-man's-land in which they have come into being, and then deposits them in the interior of a *ci-devant* universal state—the consequent shock is apt to throw them into a state of demoralization which is examined in Part VIII, below.

estranged and disillusioned barbarian society may abandon its cultural mimesis of a neighbour whose culture has lost its savour, without ceasing to borrow this neighbour's practical institutions or material technique. In fact, by continuing to borrow these it may be providing itself with the most effective means of ensuring that it shall not be compelled to receive the no longer attractive alien culture except in so far as it chooses; for the Dominant Minority with which the barbarians now have to deal will almost certainly act after its kind by seeking to impose its repudiated culture by force; and this force may perhaps be most effectively repelled by adopting and turning against the aggressor one of his own institutions (e.g., his political institution of dictatorship) or some part of his own technique (e.g., his art of war).[1]

'Cette pénétration étroite de la sauvagerie et de la civilisation c'est justement ce qui fait la barbarie redoutable: des organismes humains qui ont une résistance et une détente animales; et à leur disposition pourtant l'acquis des vieilles civilisations. C'est l'histoire éternelle, les Francs n'ont pas été autre chose.'[2]

This disastrous miscarriage in the relations between a civilization and its primitive neighbours has been described in an illuminating passage from the pen of another modern Western scholar:

'There tends to grow up round every centre of the higher civilization a zone of lower culture which is to some extent dependent or parasitic upon its civilized neighbours, while at the same time possessing a higher degree of mobility and a greater aptitude for war. Thus to the settled Semitic civilizations of Mesopotamia and Syria and South Arabia there corresponds the predatory Nomad culture of the Bedouin, and to Egypt the pastoral culture of the Libyans and the other Hamitic peoples of North Africa. So, too, in Eastern Asia we find a similar zone of Nomad Mongolian peoples on the north-western frontiers of China, and in Central Asia the peoples of the Steppes have owed their culture to the settled civilization of Persia and Turkistan; while in prehistoric Europe the same relation existed between the peasant cultures of the Danube and the Dniepr and the warlike peoples to the north and east. . . .

'It is . . . probable that it was the civilized peoples who were the first aggressors, and that it was from them that the barbarians first learnt the possibilities of organized warfare, as well, no doubt, as the

---

[1] A perversely ingenious barbarian instinct of self-defence sometimes even turns to military account a piece, or an instrument, of technique that the civilization from which this impromptu weapon has been borrowed has never thought of employing on its own account for any but peaceful purposes. Thus the camel, which was introduced into North Africa by the Romans as a means of civilian transport for economic objects, was converted into a means of mobility in military operations by the war-bands of the North African Nomad barbarians in the steppe and desert hinterland of the Roman dominions (see Gautier, E. F.: *Les Siècles Obscurs du Maghreb* (Paris 1927, Payot), pp. 162 and 184).   [2] Gautier, op. cit., p. 317.

use of weapons of metal.[1] Certainly the great wave of invasion of the men of Gutium from the north which overwhelmed Mesopotamia in the twenty-sixth century B.C. followed close upon the period of Sargon and Naramsin, who were the first to lead Mesopotamian armies into the uncivilized mountainous regions to the north and east of Tigris;[2] and in the same way in Egypt the later days of the Old Kingdom had been marked by expeditions of conquest against "the Sand Dwellers" of the north and the Nubians of the south, which may have helped to provoke the subsequent movement of invasion.[3] However this may be, the ultimate advantage was all on the side of the barbarians; for every fresh invasion increased their warlike efficiency, whereas the destructive effects of warfare on the higher civilization[4] were cumulative.'[5]

Broadly speaking, we may say that, when a society in process of civilization has been split by the schism which is the penalty of breakdown, the Proletariat is apt to withdraw its mimesis from all the ideals of the Dominant Minority except its worship of violence, and from all its institutions and techniques except those in which this spirit of violence is embodied.

In our foregoing survey of the experiences and reactions of internal proletariats we have observed how the path of Violence allures them; and we have also seen that, when they do yield to their human passions and attempt to repay their oppressor in his own coin, they usually defeat their own ends and bring disaster upon themselves into the bargain. In his own chosen field of force the hangman-commissary of the Dominant Minority is more than a match for any members of the Internal Proletariat who may be rash enough to take up arms against him. The Theudases and Judases inevitably perish with the sword; and it is only when it follows a prophet who leads it along the path of Gentleness that the Internal Proletariat has a chance of taking its conquerors captive—by taking them unawares on an unfamiliar field of action

[1] Plato (*Leges*, 678 E) has put forward the conjecture that metallurgy, and in consequence war (both civil and international), is in abeyance in a primitive state of society—which, in Plato's view (see IV C (i), vol. iv, pp. 24-7, and IV. C (i), Annex, vol. iv, pp. 585-8, above), is a state that is perpetually recurring as an aftermath of periodical cosmic catastrophes.—A.J.T.
[2] For Naramsin's militarism and its nemesis see further I. C (i) (*b*), vol. i, p. 109, above, and the present chapter and volume, p. 262; V. C (ii) (*a*), vol. vi, p. 184; and V. C (ii) (*b*), vol. vi, p. 296, below.—A.J.T.
[3] For this invasion of the Egyptiac World by Asiatic barbarians in the latter days of 'the Old Kingdom', on the eve of the onset of an Egyptiac 'Time of Troubles', see Part III. A, Annex II, vol. iii, p. 404, above, and the present chapter and volume, pp. 266-7, below.—A.J.T.
[4] For the social 'law' that, while the military efficiency of a community is proportionate to the degree of its civilization, its capacity for social recuperation from the devastating effects of war is in inverse ratio both to the degree of its civilization and to the standard of its military efficiency, see the present Study, IV. C (iii) (*c*) 2 (*β*), vol. iv, pp. 393-4, above.—A.J.T.
[5] Dawson, Christopher: *The Age of the Gods*, reissue (London 1933, Sheed & Ward), pp. 241 and 245.

on which the hangmen are inexpert and defenceless. In an ordeal by battle the Dominant Minority's victory over the Internal Proletariat is virtually assured *a priori* because its intrinsic superiority in military strength is reinforced—in dealing with this opponent—by the tactical advantage of fighting the action on a limited field on which the victor can be certain of securing a decision. We have seen, for example, in the Hellenic case, how hopeless it was for the Hellenic internal proletariat in the last two centuries B.C. to cross swords with a dominant minority whose force was not only superior in itself but was also by this time concentrated in the hands of the single ubiquitous Roman Power.[1] How do the External Proletariat's chances compare with those of the Internal Proletariat if it ventures, in its turn, to meet the Dominant Minority in battle?

The intrinsic inferiority of the External Proletariat to the Dominant Minority in military prowess is perhaps as extreme as that of the Internal Proletariat—at any rate on the morrow of the schism which has put the Proletariat and the Dominant Minority into a state of war with one another. We have convincing presumptive evidence of this in the fact—which we have observed in a previous context—that one of the regular sources of the recruitment of an Internal Proletariat lies in the conquest of members of the External Proletariat by the Dominant Minority.[2] In so far as they are simply subjugated instead of being annihilated or evicted, the conquered external proletarians are transferred from the External to the Internal Proletariat by the act of conquest; and this is perhaps the usual fate of those layers of the External Proletariat of a disintegrating civilization that lie nearest to the Dominant Minority's base of operations. At the same time the External Proletariat has one great advantage over the Internal Proletariat in trying conclusions with the Dominant Minority by force of arms. Whereas the whole of the Internal Proletariat lies, *ex hypothesi*, within the Dominant Minority's reach, some part, at any rate, of the External Proletariat is likely to find itself beyond the effective range of the Dominant Minority's military action—and this, again, *ex hypothesi*, since, as we have seen, the radiation of a civilization into the Barbarian World is not, as a rule, brought to a halt by any external obstacle, but runs on unimpeded until it gradually dies away through a progressive diminution of its own energy as it approaches the inherent limits of its carrying-power.

In such circumstances it is evident that, when a growing

[1] See V. C (i) (c) 2, pp. 68–71 and 180, above.
[2] See V. C (i) (c) 2, *passim*, above.

civilization has broken down, and when the charm exerted by a creative minority has been replaced by the Dominant Minority's substitute of violence, this radiation of force—like the radiation of attractiveness which it has superseded, and indeed *a fortiori*—must come sooner or later, as it travels out into Space, to a point that is so distant from its original place of emission that its effectiveness here dwindles to an infinitesimal quantum. In other words, even if the innermost layer of the External Proletariat succumbs to conquest, and the same fate then overtakes the next layer, or even the next after that, it is only a question of distance for an outer layer to be reached which is so remote from the Dominant Minority's base of operations that the aggressor's intrinsic superiority in military strength is here effectively counteracted by the geographical handicap. At this remove the External Proletariat will be able to take up arms against the Dominant Minority with impunity, in the assurance of being able to hold its own.

It is true that, on certain fronts, some physiographical accident may deprive the External Proletariat of this geographical advantage by compelling it to fight—as the Internal Proletariat always has to fight, if it fights at all—with its back to the wall in a confined space where the Dominant Minority can insist upon bringing it to battle and obtaining a decision. In the Hellenic World the barbarians of the Iberian Peninsula had to fight at this disadvantage against the Roman Power—by contrast with those of North-West Africa on the one side and of Transpyrenaean Europe on the other. In both these other war-zones the depth of the *terrain* which was at the barbarians' disposal for manœuvre far exceeded the range of Rome's power to strike. On the Transmediterranean front in North-West Africa the Roman arm which struck down a Jugurtha in Numidia was not long enough to reach the remoter layers of Berbers in the highlands of the Atlas or on the steppes of the Sahara; and on the Transappennine front in Europe a Power which could both reach and hold the line of the Rhine could not hold the line of the Elbe or even reach the line of the Vistula.[1] In the Iberian Peninsula, on the other hand, the barbarians were trapped between the Pyrenees and the sea; and, when Caesar had finally cut them off from all communication with their Transpyrenaean kin and kind by extending the Roman hold upon Gaul from the Mediterranean slope to the coast of the Atlantic, the last of the independent Iberian barbarians, in the strong but narrow natural fastness between the crest of the Asturian and Cantabrian Mountains and the waters of the Bay of

[1] See V. C (i) (c) 3, Annex I, pp. 591–5, below.

Biscay,[1] were followed up into their lairs and reduced to subjection by Augustus—some two centuries after the date at which the first Roman soldier had set foot in the Iberian Peninsula in the course of the Hannibalic War.

In the histories of other civilizations we can think of parallel cases in which a detachment of the External Proletariat has been caught by the Dominant Minority in a geographical trap of this kind and has then been either subjugated or annihilated until, on this particular front, the victorious Dominant Minority has successfully carried its advance up to a frontier with no further layer of barbarians beyond it—a 'natural frontier' that is defined and defended by some unnavigated sea or untraversed desert or unsurmounted mountain range.

In the Indic World, for example, under the Maurya régime, the Dominant Minority subjugated the barbarians of Southern India almost up to the tip of the Indian Peninsula and thereby acquired, on this front, a natural frontier which was washed by the sea. Again, in the Sinic World under the Ts'in and Han régime, the Dominant Minority completed the subjugation of the Southern Barbarians up to the unfrequented coasts of the South China Sea and the unscaled eastern escarpment of the Tibetan Plateau.[2] In Russian Orthodox Christendom the backwoodsmen never gave the barbarian denizens of the north-eastern forests time to throw up a stockade. Within two hundred years of the conversion of Vladímir in A.D. 988/9 the pioneer Russian communities of Novgorod and Vyatka had pushed their way to the White Sea and the Urals; and, when the watershed between Volga and Ob had once been crossed by the Cossacks in A.D.

---

[1] For the part played by the Biscayan fastness, in a later age, in the collision between the Syriac Society, in its re-integrated universal state, and a nascent Western Christendom, see II. D (vii), Annex VIII, in vol. ii, pp. 446–52, above. After more than four hundred years of acquiescence in the *Pax Romana* the Basques and Cantabrians of the Biscayan highlands, like the Isaurians of the Taurus (see IV. C (iii) (c) 2 (β), vol. iv, p. 325, above), had shaken off the authority of the tottering Hellenic universal state and (unlike the Isaurians) had succeeded in maintaining their newly recovered independence. Indeed, they maintained it against successive bands of incoming barbarians—first the Vandals and Sueves and Visigoths and then the Arabs. Nor did they fall under the dominion of the Syriac universal state which the Arabs restored to life in the shape of the Umayyad Caliphate. Farther west, the Asturian highlanders submitted to the Vandals and the Sueves and the Goths, but held out against the Arabs as indomitably as their Cantabrian and Basque neighbours. Compare the tenacity of the resistance opposed by the Three Basque Provinces and Asturias to the Castilian Nationalists and their Italian and German allies in the war that broke out in Spain in July 1936. Compare, further, the survival of a primitive 'Adoptionist' version of Christianity in an Asturian fastness, where there is evidence for its persistence down to the latter part of the eighth century (see IV. C (iii) (c) 2 (β), Annex III, vol. iv, pp. 625, 629, 630, and 633, above). Compare, finally, the survival down to the present day, in the Peninsular provinces of Viscaya, Guipuzcoa, and Navarre, as well as in the adjoining districts of France on the other side of the Pyrenees, of a pre-Indo-European language which has no living counterpart on a continent on which—except in this one corner—all older linguistic strata have been buried and obliterated, centuries ago, under Indo-European and Ural-Altaic deposits.   [2] See V. C (i) (c) 2, pp. 141 and 147, above.

1586, it took them little more than fifty years to push on across
the Siberian Taiga and Tundra to a natural frontier on the coasts
of the Arctic Ocean and the Sea of Okhotsk.[1] In the Arabic World
the penetration of Tropical Africa from the Saharan and Nilotic
fringes of the Sudan and from the African coast of the Indian
Ocean would almost certainly have been rounded off, before the
close of the nineteenth century of the Christian Era, by a subjugation of the whole 'Dark Continent' if the Arab invaders had
not been overtaken and supplanted, at the eleventh hour, by the
more redoubtable Franks. Within the fifty or sixty years ending
in 1938 the Powers of Europe had partitioned the soil, and subjugated the primitive Negro 'Natives', of the whole of Tropical
Africa, from ocean to ocean and from desert to desert; and
between the 12th September, 1935, when these lines were written,
and the 7th August, 1938, when they were revised for the press,
one of these Powers, which had received short measure in the
scramble for Europe's African spoils, had broken its own engagements and had defied the verdict and the sanctions of its peers in
conquering the last surviving independent Native African state:
the Empire of Ethiopia.[2] In earlier chapters of the history of our
Western World in its Modern Age the European colonists overseas kept the Red Indian barbarians on the run in North America
from the moment of their first landing on the Atlantic coast of
the continent until the time—some two hundred and fifty years
later—when they reached their natural frontier on the shores of
the Pacific;[3] and in the South Seas they decimated the Australian
Blackfellows and exterminated the Tasmanian aborigines until
they had made themselves masters of the whole surface of both
the continent and the island. Nearer home other modern militant
pioneers of our Western Civilization have almost as recently
made an equally 'clean job' of the White barbarians in the highlands and isles of Scotland[4] and the bogs and mountains of Ireland;
and our subjugation of these barbarians of 'the Celtic Fringe' has
its analogue in the Far Eastern World in the subjugation—or

---

[1] See II. D (v), vol. ii, p. 157, above.
[2] For the Italian aggression against Abyssinia in and after A.D. 1935 see further pp.
334–7, below. For the previous history of Abyssinia see II. D (vii), vol. ii, pp. 364–7,
above. In A.D. 1935 Abyssinia could accurately be described as the only surviving
independent Native African state, since Liberia, which was also both African and independent, was ruled, not by Native Africans, but by the repatriated descendants of
Africans who had been sold into slavery in North America. On the other hand the
Amharan rulers of the Empire of Ethiopia could fairly claim to be Native Africans, in
spite of the fact that their mother tongue was a Semitic language which had been
brought in by conquerors from the other side of the Red Sea before the beginning of
the Christian Era.
[3] See the present chapter, pp. 328–32, below.
[4] See II. C (ii) (a) 1, vol. i, p. 237; II. C (ii) (a) 1, Annex, vol. i, pp. 465–7; and
II. D (vii), vol. ii, p. 311, above; and the present chapter and volume, pp. 320, 321,
and 322–3, below.

extermination—of the Ainu barbarians in the Japanese Archipelago.[1]

In these and similar cases, where Geography sets bounds to the battlefield, an external proletariat which ventures to cross swords with a dominant minority has to fight at the same disadvantage—and with the same desperate prospects—as an insurgent internal proletariat. Such cases, however, are exceptional; and the normal sequel to the outbreak of war between an external proletariat and a dominant minority is not a running fight that continues until the barbarians have been eliminated by being either exterminated or subjugated up to the line of some natural frontier. While the dominant minority usually draws the first blood and cuts deep into the flesh of the surrounding barbarian body social, its arm is seldom long enough to complete the work of destruction or conquest. At a certain remove from the enemy base of operations the barbarians generally manage to make a stand and hold their own; and therewith the running fight, instead of being brought to an end by the barbarian combatant's annihilation or surrender, simply changes from a war of movement into a war of positions without passing over from war into peace.

When this stage is reached in the warfare between the Dominant Minority and the External Proletariat of a disintegrating civilization, it brings with it the completion of a change—which begins as soon as the civilization breaks down—in the nature of the geographical contact between the civilization and its barbarian neighbours. So long as the civilization is in growth, its home territory, where it prevails in full force, is insulated, as we have seen, from the unreclaimed wilderness of Savagery by a broad threshold or buffer-zone across which Civilization shades off into Savagery in a long series of fine gradations. On the other hand, when a civilization has broken down and fallen into schism, and when the hostilities between the Dominant Minority and the External Proletariat have ceased to be a running fight and have settled down into trench warfare, we find that the buffer-zone has disappeared. The geographical transition from Civilization to Barbarism is now no longer gradual but is abrupt. To use the appropriate Latin words, which bring out both the kinship and the contrast between the two kinds of contact, the *limen* or threshold, which was a zone, has been replaced by a *limes* or military frontier, which is a line that has length without breadth. Across this line a baffled Dominant Minority and an unconquered

---

[1] See II. C (ii) (a) 1, vol. i, pp. 229–30 and 236; II. D (v), vol. ii, p. 159; II. D (vii), vol. ii, p. 311; III. C (i) (a), vol. iii, pp. 144–5; IV. C (ii) (b) 2, vol. iv, p. 94; and V. C (i) (c) 2, in the present volume, pp. 95–6, above.

External Proletariat now face one another under arms; and this military front is a bar to the passage of all social radiation except that of military technique[1]—an article of social commerce which makes for war and not for peace between those who give and take it.

The social phenomena which follow when the warfare between the Dominant Minority and the External Proletariat of a disintegrating society becomes stationary along a *limes* will occupy our attention later;[2] and at this point we will not anticipate our coming study of 'heroic ages' and Völkerwanderungen except so far as to mention the single cardinal fact that this stationary warfare along a sharply drawn line is not a stable or permanent equilibrium, but is a temporary and precarious balance which invariably ends in a barbarian break-through because, in this situation, Time works inexorably on the barbarians' side.[3] The

---

[1] See pp. 202–3, above.   [2] In Part VIII, below.

[3] We have already come across several illustrations of the working of this law in other contexts. We have seen, for example, how the Celtic Völkerwanderung, which broke upon the Hellenic World in a succession of waves between *circa* 425 and *circa* 225 B.C., was provoked by two rash and ill-sustained offensives which were launched by two Hellenic Powers against the Continental European barbarian hinterland of the Hellenic World. The first of these Celtic onslaughts, which descended like an avalanche upon Italy, was a retort to the rashness of the Etruscan maritime colonists of the Maremma in pushing their aggression against the continental barbarians right across the Appennines until the aggressors were brought to a halt along an indefensible *limes* at the foot of the Alps (see II. D (vii), vol. ii, pp. 280–1, above). The second Celtic onslaught, which was directed against Greece and Anatolia, was a similar retort to the inconsequence of Alexander the Great and his successors in diverting the whole military strength of Macedonia, first to the task of conquering the Achaemenian Empire and then to the luxury of fighting over the spoils, after Alexander's father Philip had carried the Continental European frontier of Macedonia deep into the interior of the Balkan Peninsula and had thereby saddled his kingdom with a *limes* which it would have taxed her strength to maintain—even if she had not squandered this strength in other directions (see II. D (vii), vol. ii, p. 281, footnote 1, above). We have also seen (in II. D (vii), vol. ii, pp. 344–5, and IV. C (iii) (c) 3 (α), vol. iv, p. 490, above) how the Scandinavian Völkerwanderung was similarly provoked by Charlemagne's rashness in carrying the *limes* of the Austrasian Empire from the right bank of the Rhine to the left bank of the Eider without having the strength or staying power to bring his offensive against the North European barbarians to a victorious conclusion by pressing on to the natural frontier of the Arctic Circle.

We may here observe in passing that the two civilizations which made these gross strategic blunders in their warfare with the European barbarians both escaped more lightly than they deserved; for, while the Etruscan and Macedonian and Carolingian *limites* were all duly broken through, the Celtic and Scandinavian counter-attacks were abortive. The common reason for their failure was that they were all made at a time when the civilization which they were attacking still had forces in reserve. The Hellenic Civilization and the Western Civilization were still each in their growth-stage at the respective times when the Celtic counter-offensive was opened and when the Scandinavian counter-offensive was delivered; and in the Hellenic World the Roman Power took its stand in the breach through which the Etruscans and the Macedonians had allowed the Celts to pass (see II. D (v), vol. ii, pp. 160–4, above), while in Western Christendom the Scandinavians, with whom the Carolingians had failed to cope, were brought to a halt, within a hundred years of the first Viking raid, by the rising Powers of Wessex and France (see II. D (v), vol. ii, pp. 194–202, and II. D (v), Annex, vol. ii, p. 401, above).

On the other hand the Iranic World paid the full penalty for Timur Lenk's inconsequence in diverting the energies of Transoxania to the conquest of her sedentary neighbours before he had carried to completion his brilliant feat of using Transoxanian arms to harry the Eurasian Steppe and to break the power of the Nomads (for Timur's career

explanation of this 'law' that will be found to govern the history of the *limites*, or anti-barbarian military frontiers, of disintegrating civilizations is not essential to our immediate purpose, which is simply to bring the External Proletariat on to the stage; and this inquiry can therefore conveniently stand over until the time comes for giving the actor his cue to play out his part. Our first task is to muster the External Proletariat in as large an array of examples as we can contrive to collect by making an empirical survey; and in this survey, as before, we will begin by examining the Hellenic instance.

A Hellenic Instance.

The growth-phase of Hellenic history is rich in illustrations of the *limen* or buffer-zone with which the home-territory of a healthily growing civilization tends to surround itself.

Towards Continental Europe the quintessence of Hellas shaded off, north of Thermopylae, into a semi-Hellenic Thessaly, and, west of Delphi, into a semi-Hellenic Aetolia; and Aetolia and Thessaly, in their turn, were insulated by the demi-semi-Hellenism of Epirus and Macedonia from the undiluted barbarism of Illyria and Thrace.[1] None of these gradations was so brusque or precipitous as to be impassable; for even on the Thracian border, where the Macedonian backwoodsmen extended the bounds of Hellenism by annihilating the barbarian Eordaei and evicting the barbarian Pieres and Bottiaei,[2] these methods of barbarism were perhaps less characteristic of the propagation of the Hellenic Civilization than the way of Orpheus, the legendary prophet and minstrel whose music captivated barbarian hearts and whose spiritual conquests were sealed by his martyrdom.[3]

see II. D (v), vol. ii, pp. 144–50, and IV. C (iii) (c) 3 (α), vol. iv, pp. 491–5, above). The retort was the Uzbeg Nomad invasion of Transoxania at the turn of the fifteenth and sixteenth centuries of the Christian Era; and this barbarian counter-attack was never effectively met; for at that critical moment the Iranic Civilization broke down and the forces which it still had in reserve were diverted, in their turn, from the urgent common task of dealing with the barbarian enemy, and were expended instead in the fratricidal warfare between the Sunnah and the militant Shi'ism of Ismā'īl Shāh Safawī (see I. C (i) (b), Annex I, vol. i, pp. 366–400, above).

We have still to observe (see the present chapter and volume, pp. 284–8, below) that the responsibility for provoking the Scandinavian Völkerwanderung was shared with Charlemagne by contemporary Khazar Nomad empire-builders on the Great Western Bay of the Eurasian Steppe, with consequences for Khazaria which were as disastrous as those which Transoxania and Etruria brought upon themselves by committing the same strategico-political error in their dealings with their own respective barbarian hinterlands.

An abortive Egypto-Ottoman expansion in the Sudan in the nineteenth century of the Christian Era, which evoked a Baggara Arab Nomad counterstroke before that century reached its close, is also noticed in the present chapter and volume, pp. 294–5, below.

[1] For this semi-Hellenism and demi-semi-Hellenism of Northern Continental Greece in the growth-phase of Hellenic history see III. C (ii) (b), Annex IV, vol. iii, p. 478, above.   [2] Thucydides, Book II, chap. 99.

[3] For the mythical figure of Orpheus as a type of the creative minority of a civilization in its growth-stage see IV. C (iii) (a), vol. iv, p. 123, above. For the historical higher

Towards Asia Minor, again, the quintessence of Hellas shaded off likewise, in the hinterland of the Aeolian and Ionian and Dorian and Lycian city-states of the Asiatic seaboard, into the semi-Hellenism of Caria and the demi-semi-Hellenism of Lydia, before passing over into the barbarism of the Thracian interlopers—Mysians, Phrygians, and the like—who had squatted among the ruins of the Hittite Civilization on the Anatolian Plateau. On this Asiatic border we see Hellenism taking its barbarian conquerors captive, Orpheus-fashion, for the first time in the full light of history. The spell was so strong that, in the second quarter of the sixth century B.C., the conflict between Philhellenes and Hellenophobes came to the forefront of Lydian politics; and even when a Philhellene aspirant to the Lydian throne—the Ionian queen's son Pantaleon—was worsted by his half-brother the Carian queen's son Croesus,[1] the protagonist of the anti-Hellenic party proved so impotent to swim against the pro-Hellenic tide that he became famous for being as generous a patron of Hellenic shrines as he was a credulous consultant of Hellenic oracles.

Even in the hinterlands of the Greek colonies overseas, where the cultural gulf between Hellenism and barbarism might have been expected to be wider and the political relations between the two worlds proportionately more hostile, peaceful relations and gradual transitions appear to have been the rule. The enserfment of the Anatolian Mariandyni by the Greek founders of Heraclea Pontica seems to have been as exceptional a barbarity in the overseas Hellenic World as the enserfment of the Messenians by the Spartans was in Hellas Proper; and the extermination of the Itali[2] and the Chônes, in the 'toe' of the Italian Peninsula, by the makers of Magna Graecia, is the only overseas analogue of the extermination of the Eordaei by the Macedonians.[3] The barbarians of the hinterland were sometimes brought under the political suzerainty of the colonial Greek city-states. In Sicily,

religion of Orphism see I. C (i) (*b*), vol. i, pp. 95–100, and V. C (i) (*c*) 2, in the present volume, pp. 84–7, above.   [1] See Herodotus, Book I, chap. 92.

[2] It is one of the curiosities of history that this small and obscure people, which was wiped out of existence before it had had time to bequeath anything to Posterity except its name, should eventually have conferred this name upon a territory extending from the 'toe' of Italy, in which the Itali had their home, to the distant summit of the Alps. In the history of the latter-day expansion of our own Western Society we may compare the capricious and ironic preservation of a few vestiges of the names, and fragments of the languages, of the extinct Red Indian 'Natives' of North America in the outlandish nomenclature of the states and the provinces, the cities and the rivers, of the United States and Canada: Massachusetts and Saskatchewan, Chicago and Winnipeg, Ottawa and Mississippi. Apart from these incongruous memorials, 'the names they bore in common are forgotten, their language perishes, and all traces of their origin disappear. Their nation has ceased to exist, except in the recollection of the antiquaries of America and a few of the learned of Europe' (de Tocqueville, A.: *Democracy in America*, English translation, new edition (London 1875, Longmans, Green, 2 vols.), vol. i, p. 345).

[3] For the element of violence in the overseas expansion of the Greeks in this age see I. B (ii), vol. i, p. 24, II. D (ii), vol. ii, pp. 42–3, and III. C (ii), vol. iii, p. 121, above.

for example, Syracuse and Agrigentum each established a minia-ture empire over the neighbouring native Sicilian communities. But there are at least as many examples of *ententes* like that between the Greek colony of Cyrene and the local Libyans, or alliances like that which was eventually established between the Greek colony of Tarentum and the Messapians in the 'heel' of Italy. And, underlying this diversity of political relations, there is a striking uniformity, on the cultural plane, in the peaceful penetration of the interior by Hellenism. In Sicily in the last century B.C., less than five hundred years after the founda-tion of the latest Greek colony on Sicilian soil, it would have been impossible (as will be apparent to any reader of Cicero's *Verrines*) any longer to distinguish the descendants of native Sicels from those of Greek Siceliots in a population which had long ago been unified by its common Hellenic culture, its common Greek speech, and its common sufferings under Roman misrule.[1] In the Continental Italian hinterland of Tarentum Hellenism spread so rapidly, and 'took' so strongly, among the Illyrian-speaking peoples between the tip of the 'heel' and the 'spur' of Monte Gargano that, as early as the fourth century B.C., Apulia advertised her conversion to Hellenism by becoming the busiest (though not the most exquisite) workshop for the production of red-figure vases. Still farther afield the Sicels' continental kinsmen in Latium took so heartily to the exotic Hellenic institution of the city-state that Greek observers accepted the Latins as Hel-lenes by adoption.[2] The earliest mention of Rome in extant literature is a notice, in a surviving fragment of a lost work from the hand of Plato's pupil, Heracleides Ponticus, in which this Latin commonwealth is described as 'a Hellenic city';[3] and we have seen already[4] how Rome earned this compliment by spreading at any rate the political elements of Hellenic culture from the Latin Campagna[5] into the Sabine and Picentine highlands.

Thus, on all the fringes of the Hellenic World in its growth-stage, we seem to see the same gracious figure of Orpheus casting his spell upon the barbarians round about, and even inspiring

[1] For a sketch of the Janus-face of the Philhellene-Hellenophobe Sicel leader Ducetius see V. C (ii) (*a*), vol. vi, pp. 235-6, below.

[2] See IV. C (i), vol. iv, pp. 19-20, and V. C (i) (*c*) 1, in the present volume, p. 55, with footnote 4, above.

[3] 'A faint and blurred report of the bare event of the catastrophe which Rome suffered in being captured [by the Gauls *circa* 390 B.C.] does appear to have penetrated at the time to Hellas; for Heracleides Ponticus, whose own date is not so very much later, mentions, in his treatise on the Soul, the currency of a story from the West to the effect that a host had burst in from the outer darkness of the land of the Hyperboreans and had captured a Hellenic city called Rome (πόλιν Ἑλληνίδα Ῥώμην) which lay at the back of beyond, somewhere in the direction of the Atlantic (ἐκεῖ που κατῳκημένην περὶ τὴν μεγάλην θάλασσαν).'—Plutarch: *Life of Camillus*, chap. 22.

[4] In IV. C (iii) (*c*) 2 (β), vol. iv, pp. 310-13, above.

[5] For the history of the name Campagna see II. D (i), vol. ii, p. 19, footnote 1, above.

them to rehearse his magic music, on their own simpler lyres, to the ruder peoples of the farther hinterland.[1] This idyllic picture vanishes, however, in a trice upon the Hellenic Civilization's breakdown. As the harmony breaks into a discord, the spell-bound listeners seem to awaken with a start; and, relapsing into their natural ferocity, they now hurl themselves—with more excuse than there ever was for their womenfolk's legendary assault upon the authentic Orpheus—against the sinister man-at-arms whom they have caught masquerading under the gentle prophet's cloak.

The first move in a thousand years' war between barbarians and Hellenes was made, in Orpheus' own Thracian mission-field, in the third year of the Hellenic civil war of 431–404 B.C., when Sitalces the Odrysian invaded and harried Macedonia and put all the Hellenes in a tremor from the Strymon to Thermo-pylae.[2] Sitalces' raid was abortive; and, although the voluntary self-Hellenization of Thrace was checked and blighted from that time onwards, Hellas had little further serious trouble with this obstinate Thracian outpost of barbarism at her gates during the four hundred and seventy-four years of cultural stalemate that followed on this front, from 429 B.C. to A.D. 46, before the Odrysian Kingdom was converted into a Roman province, in order to be Hellenized by force, in the reign of the Emperor Claudius (*imperabat* A.D. 41–54). The militant reaction of the external proletariat to the breakdown of the Hellenic Civilization was both more violent and more effective in Magna Graecia, where the Bruttians and Lucanians now began to avenge the Chônes and the Itali by entrenching themselves in their extinct barbarian predecessors' desolate fastnesses and insinuating themselves, like hermit crabs, into one Italiot Greek city after another.

Within less than a hundred years after the outbreak of the

---

[1] On the political plane we can watch the gradual and spontaneous spread of republi-can at the expense of monarchical institutions from the city-states of Hellas Proper, where monarchy is already obsolete at the earliest date to which our surviving records reach back, to the seaboard of Epirus by 430 B.C. (see III. C (ii) (*b*), Annex IV, vol. iii, p. 478, above); to the Paeonian and Thracian peoples of the Lower Strymon Valley by 383 B.C. (see III. C (ii) (*b*), Annex IV, vol. iii, p. 483, above); to the Romans at some date unknown which was perhaps earlier than either of these; and to the peoples of Gaul (with the exception of the Belgae) before the time of Caesar's conquest. By the time when Tacitus was writing his *Germania*, the wave of republicanism had travelled on into the German zone of barbarism; and at this date the primitive form of kingship was definitely on the wane—even beyond the Rhine—among the Frisians and the Cherusci. Among the Suebi, however, it was still holding its own; and among the Goths and, above all, the Swedes, it was still intact (Chadwick, H. M.: *The Origins of the English Nation* (Cambridge 1907, University Press), pp. 298–9). For the subsequent replacement of both the adoptive republicanism and the indigenous monarchical institu-tions of the North European barbarians beyond the Roman pale by a new military despotism, which was one of the products of the barbarians' reaction to the challenge of the Roman *limes*, see V. C (i) (*d*) 7, vol. vi, p. 4, footnote 4; V. C (ii) (*a*), vol. vi, pp. 228–36; and Part VIII, below.   [2] See Thucydides, Book II, chap. 101.

Atheno-Peloponnesian War, which was the 'beginning of great evils for Hellas',[1] the few remaining survivors among the formerly prosperous and powerful communities of Magna Graecia were summoning knight-errants—or condottieri—from the mother-country to save them from being driven into the sea.[2] And these erratic reinforcements were of such little avail for stemming the Oscan tide that the inflowing barbarians had already crossed the Straits of Messina and acquired, in that city itself, a base of opera-tions for the conquest of Sicily before the whole movement was brought to an abrupt end by the intervention of the Oscans' Hellenized Roman kinsmen. The Romans showed themselves to be more discerning, as well as more effective, champions of Hellenism in Italy than their discomfited Epirot adversary Pyr-rhus. The Epirot knight-errant had sought to save the mere political independence of Magna Graecia—at the expense of the Hellenism which it was Magna Graecia's mission to propagate beyond her borders—by making common cause with the barbarian enemies at the Italiot Greek cities' gates against the most Hel-lenic of all the native Powers of Italy; Roman statesmanship saved not merely Magna Graecia but the whole Italian Peninsula for Hellenism by taking the Oscans in the rear, attacking these now inveterate barbarians in overwhelming force, and imposing a common Roman peace upon Italian barbarians and Italiot Greeks.

Thus the South Italian front between Hellenism and barbarism, on which Hellenism had been fighting a losing battle in the fourth century B.C.,[3] was suddenly wiped out in the third century B.C. by the Romans' master-stroke; and thereafter successive feats of Roman arms extended the dominion of the Hellenic dominant minority almost as far afield in Continental Europe and the Iberian Peninsula and North-West Africa as it had already been extended in Asia by the conquests of Alexander of Macedon.[4] But these Macedonian and Roman conquests could not, and did

---

[1] Thucydides, Book II, chap. 12, quoted in IV. C (ii) (b) 1, vol. iv, p. 62, above.

[2] For these knight-errants see IV. C (iii) (c) 2 (β), Annex I, vol. iv, pp. 589–91, above.

[3] The Oscan barbarian counter-attack, which did not begin earlier than the fourth century B.C. in Magna Graecia, had begun before the end of the fifth century B.C. in Campania; but in the Campanian field the breakdown by which the counter-attack was evoked was not the general breakdown of the Hellenic Society—which may be dated from the outbreak of the Atheno-Peloponnesian War in 431 B.C.—but the earlier local breakdown of the Hellenized Etruscan settlers on the west coast of Italy, who had been as rash in pushing their way inland from the Campanian stretch of the Italian coast as they had been, on a larger scale, farther north. The advancement of the Etruscan *limes* in Campania to the south-western foot of the Abruzzi produced as provocative an effect upon the Oscan highlanders as was produced upon the Celts by the contemporary advancement (discussed in II. D (vii), vol. ii, pp. 280–1, and in the present chapter and volume, p. 209, footnote 3, above) of the other Etruscan *limes* in the Po Basin to the foot of the Alps.

[4] See III. C (i) (a), vol. iii, pp. 140 and 150–1; III. C (i) (d), vol. iii, p. 197; IV. C (iii) (c) 2 (α), vol. iv, p. 265, and IV. C (iii) (c) 2 (β), vol. iv, pp. 305–6, above; and V. C (ii) (b), vol. vi, pp. 289–90, below.

not, relieve a disintegrating Hellenic Society from a social malady that was one of the unescapable penalties of its breakdown. The effect of this morbid military expansion of the Hellenic World was not to eliminate its anti-barbarian fronts but rather to add to their length as it pushed them farther afield from the Hellenic dominant minority's bases of operations; and this progressive lengthening of the lines of communication, as well as of the front itself, diminished the dominant minority's striking power while increasing its commitments.

In another context[1] we have already observed how Rome's very success in stepping into the breach and taking over the Etruscans' commitments against the Celts and the Tarentines' commitments against the Oscans and the Macedonians' commitments against the Thracians and Dardanians led her on, inexorably, step by step, into assuming the sole responsibility for the maintenance of an anti-barbarian front that ran across the whole length of the European Continent from the North Sea to the Black Sea coast[2] and thus brought the Hellenic Society into a direct and hostile contact with the formidable Eurasian Nomads in the Hungarian Alföld and the Lower Danube Basin, as well as with the sedentary European barbarians in the Teutoberger Wald and the Hercynian Forest and Transylvania. Moreover this vast extension and aggravation of an anti-barbarian front which the disintegrating Hellenic Civilization had inherited from its own past was only part of the additional burden which an ailing society was wantonly taking upon its shoulders; for simultaneously the Hellenic dominant minority was taking over no less than four other anti-barbarian fronts from a Syriac Society which had been forcibly incorporated into the Hellenic World by the Macedonian and Roman wars of conquest.

From an annihilated Carthage Rome inherited one anti-barbarian front in the Iberian Peninsula and another in Numidia, while from a ham-strung Seleucid Monarchy,[3] which was itself the Hellenic heir of the Achaemenian Empire, Rome also inherited the task of defending South-Western Asia against assaults both from the Eurasian Nomads who were always ready to pour in through the gateway between the Caspian and the Pamirs[4] and from the Afrasian Nomads of the Arabian Peninsula whose grazing-fleets were always cruising expectantly off the desert-coast of Syria with an eye to turning pirates at any favourable

[1] In II. D (v), vol. ii, pp. 161–4, above.
[2] This European frontier of the Roman Empire is discussed in V. C (i) (c) 3, Annex I, pp. 591–5, below.
[3] A board of Roman commissioners did literally ham-string the Seleucid stud of war-elephants at Apamea in 162 B.C. (see V. C (i) (d) 9 (γ), vol. vi, p. 122, footnote 5, below).
[4] For this gateway see Part III. A, Annex II, vol. iii, pp. 400–1, above.

opportunity.[1] It is true that Rome did not have to carry all these additional burdens to the end of her days; for, as we have seen,[2] she succeeded, in Augustus's day, in wiping out the front in the Iberian Peninsula, as she had wiped out the front in Southern Italy before the outbreak of the first of the Romano-Carthaginian wars; and in Asia the flood-waters of Eurasian Nomadism, which had spread from the line of the Jaxartes to the line of the Euphrates in the second century B.C.,[3] evaporated in the third century of the Christian Era when the Nomad Power of the Parthians was ignominiously suppressed by the resurgent Syriac Empire of the Sasanidae.[4] In this latter case, however, the net weight of the burden which Rome had to carry was not diminished, but on the contrary was heavily increased, when the barbarian King Log who had been sitting so inertly on the throne at Ctesiphon was suddenly supplanted by a Syriac King Stork with a mission to wage an anti-Hellenic 'Holy War';[5] and the series of Romano-Sasanian wars of ever-increasing frequency and intensity which occupied the next four hundred years eventually exhausted the belligerents to a degree that left them impotent to prevent the Arab barbarians from breaking out in the seventh century of the Christian Era and overwhelming them both.[6]

This four-hundred-years-long struggle between the Roman and Sasanian Empires, and between the civilizations which they respectively embodied, will call for examination later on in other contexts.[7] In this place we are concerned only with the anti-barbarian fronts of the disintegrating Hellenic Civilization; and we will confine our attention to four which had a continuous existence from the turn of the third and second centuries B.C.— when Rome 'knocked out' all the other Great Powers of the contemporary Hellenic World and thus acquired a monopoly of all the assets and liabilities of the Hellenic dominant minority—down to the interregnum (*circa* A.D. 375–675) which followed the break-up of the Roman Empire at the turn of the fourth and fifth centuries of the Christian Era. The four fronts in question are the front against the sedentary barbarians of Continental Europe from the North Sea coast to Transylvania;[8] the front against the

---

[1] See Part III. A, Annex II, vol. iii, pp. 412 and 445, above.
[2] In the present chapter, pp. 205–6, above.
[3] See pp. 239–40, below.   [4] See p. 240, below.
[5] For the disastrous effect of this Sasanian militancy upon the fortunes of the Zoroastrian Religion see V. C (i) (*d*) 6 (δ), Annex, pp. 659–61, below.
[6] This nemesis of a common Militarism did not, however, fall upon the two warring empires with equal weight; for, while the Sasanian Empire was utterly destroyed, its Roman antagonist escaped with its life at the cost of losing its limbs (see Part III. A, Annex II, vol. iii, p. 450, and V. C (i) (*c*) 2, in the present volume, p. 128, above).
[7] For example, in Parts IX and XI, below.
[8] This Continental European front had an insular extension in the British Isles which

Eurasian Nomads (and the Nomadicized sedentary intruders upon the Nomads' ranges)[1] in the Lower Danubian bay and the Middle Danubian enclave of the Great Eurasian Steppe; the front against the barbarians in the interior of North West Africa (Nomads on the Sahara and highlanders in the Atlas); and the front against the Arabs beyond the desert-coast of Syria who constituted the Asiatic wing of the Afrasian Nomad forces.

When we compare the military annals of these four fronts during the span of some nine hundred years (circa 225 B.C.— A.D. 675) over which their history extends from first to last we find that there is a close chronological correspondence between the respective alternating bouts of military activity and relatively

we will pass over in our present survey since we have already dealt with it in our study of the abortive Far Western Christian Civilization (see II. D (vii), vol. ii, pp. 322–40, and II. D (vii), Annexes II, III, and IV, in vol. ii, pp. 420–33, above).

[1] For the alternation between the Nomads' eruptions and the sedentary societies' encroachments in the exposed salients and detached enclaves of the Steppe see Part III. A, Annex II, vol. iii, pp. 425–8, above. The ex-sedentary North European barbarian intruders upon the western fringes of the Eurasian Steppe who played a historic role in the history of the disintegration of the Hellenic Civilization were the Goths, who made themselves at home on the Steppe in the third century of the Christian Era during an interval of quiescence between the subsidence of the Sarmatian Nomad eruption and the outbreak of the Hun Nomad eruption. During the century and a half of their residence on Nomad territory the Goths were nomadicized profoundly—and this in their êthos as well as in such external things as their art of war (for the adoption, by these sedentary interlopers, of the Sarmatian Nomad cataphracts' equipment and tactics see IV. C (iii) (c) 3 (α), vol. iv, pp. 439–44, above). The extent of their conversion from a sedentary form of barbarism to the Nomadic culture can be measured by the difference between their subsequent history and that of their kinsmen the Franks: a sedentary North European barbarian people who had not ventured out of their native forest on to the Steppe and who had therefore not acquired any tincture of the Eurasian Nomad Civilization. When the collapse of the Roman Power gave the signal for both Franks and Goths to break through the Roman limes and begin their Völkerwanderung, the Goths responded with an initial brilliance which threw the Franks quite into the shade. Within less than half a century after their passage of the Lower Danube on sufferance, as suppliant refugees who were fleeing before the face of the uns and were throwing themselves on the Roman Government's mercy (see IV. C (iii) 3 (α), vol. iv, p. 440, footnote 4, above), the Visigoths had entered the Imperial City itself as conquerors and had then swept on to carve out an appanage for themselves at the farthest extremity of the Empire, on the Gallic shores of the Bay of Biscay. By the close of the fifth century the Visigoths had made themselves masters of the whole of Gaul south of the Loire and west of the Rhône, together with the whole of the Iberian Peninsula except the north-west corner and the highland hinterland of the Biscay coast (see p. 206, footnote 1, above), while the Ostrogoths, following at their heels, had secured the still choicer prize of Italy, together with the Western Illyricum. In the year A.D. 500 it looked as if the Goths had won for themselves the lion's share of the Roman heritage; but at this point in a hitherto brilliant career they began to show that fatal lack of staying-power, and that incurable inability to strike root, which are characteristic, as we have seen (in Part III. A, vol. iii, pp. 22–5, above), of the Nomad conqueror in partibus agricolarum. When the Visigoths, who had fought their way from the Baltic to the Black Sea and from the Black Sea to the Mediterranean and the Atlantic, collided at Vouillé, in A.D. 507, with the Franks, who had taken as long a time to advance from the right bank of the Rhine to the right bank of the Loire, it was the Franks and not the Goths that won the day (see II. D (v), vol. ii, p. 166; II. D (vii), vol. ii, p. 380; and II. D (vii), Annex IV, vol. ii, p. 428, above); and the ruin of the Goths was completed when the Ostrogoths were exterminated in the Great Romano-Gothic War of A.D. 535–52, and when the half of the Visigothic Kingdom which the Franks had spared in A.D. 507 was overwhelmed in A.D. 711 by the Arabs. This ultimate political failure of the Goths has, however, brought with it a literary reward which has been withheld from the Franks by their ultimate political success. It is the unsuccessful Goths, and not the successful Franks, that have provided a fruitful theme for 'heroic' poetry (see V. C (i) (c) 3, Annex III, pp. 610 and 613, below).

V   H

peaceful stagnation on each of them;[1] and in this uniform rhythm we can discern three periods of storm and stress in which the barbarians attempted to break through—on the first two occasions in vain, but the third time with success.

At the height of the Hellenic 'Time of Troubles' during the last two centuries B.C.[2] we find the Sarmatian barbarians advancing from the east bank of the Don to new ranges in the Lower and the Middle Danube Basin, where they hovered menacingly on the north-eastern flank of the Hellenic World from that time onwards. Contemporaneously, at the turn of the second and the last century B.C., the Arabs[3] drifted into the derelict domain of a moribund Seleucid Monarchy in Mesopotamia and Syria. On the North-West African front the Numidians took advantage of the overthrow of Carthage in the Hannibalic War and her annihilation in 146 B.C. in order to encroach upon the derelict Carthaginian province on the African mainland. And last of all, on the North European front, the first extension of the Roman rule into Transalpine Europe—into Gaul on one side and into Noricum on the other—towards the close of the second century B.C. was answered by the formidable counter-attack of the Cimbri and the Teutones, who bore down on Italy itself along war-paths that were now no longer blocked by the semi-barbarian buffer Powers which had just been crippled or shattered by Roman arms. On three fronts out of the four the Romans found themselves compelled to intervene in order to bring the barbarian offensives to a standstill; and on the North European front they had to fight for their lives—even in this first of the three historic paroxysms of barbarian aggression. In Europe and in Africa the situation was saved by Marius, who snatched victory out of defeat in the war against the Numidian aggressor Jugurtha (*gerebatur* 112–106 B.C.) and in the war against the Cimbri (*gerebatur* 105–101 B.C.).[4]   In Asia the last remnant of the Seleucid heritage was salvaged from the depredations of the Arab war-bands by Pompey when he organized

[1] In order to make the comparison in equivalent terms for all fronts, we have to allow for the possible intervention of a climatic factor—an alternating rhythm of humidity and aridity on the Steppes—on those fronts on which the transfrontier barbarians were Nomads. The question whether a climatic factor of this nature is one of the causes of the occasional eruptions of the Nomads out of their own domain on the Steppes into the adjoining domain of the sedentary societies round about them has been discussed in Part III. A, Annex II, vol. iii, above.

[2] It should be noticed that this critical period in the disintegration of the Hellenic Civilization partly coincided in date—if we are to accept the theory of climatic pulsations —with a bout of aridity on the Steppes which lasted from *circa* 225 B.C. to *circa* A.D. 75. In view of this coincidence we may find ourselves at a loss to determine, in the case of the Nomads, whether their movements of aggression against the Hellenic World between these dates were produced by a social pull or by a climatic push.

[3] See p. 215, above.

[4] For the stimulus which was given to the organization and technique of the Roman Army by these Marian wars against the barbarians of Africa and Europe see III. C (i) (b), vol. iii, p. 166, and IV. C (iii) (c) 2 (γ), vol. iv, p. 439, above.

the Roman province of Syria in 63–62 B.C. Thereafter, when a band of Suevi—undeterred by their Cimbrian cousins' and predecessors' recent fate—set their feet upon the same European war-path, Caesar jumped at the opportunity of improving the Transalpine frontier of the Roman dominions by carrying it (*bellum gerebat* 58–51 B.C.) up to the line of the Rhine, on which it continued to stand, with a few brief fluctuations, for the next four centuries.

The second abortive attempt, on the barbarian side, at a break-through on all four fronts was made in the middle of the third century of the Christian Era, when the Roman Empire suddenly tottered—and then almost as suddenly recovered itself[1]—like a man who has been smitten by a first paralytic stroke in a late but still vigorous middle age. This time it was the Eurasian, and not the North European, front that was subjected to the heaviest pressure. On this front in this crisis the Goths not only thrust their way overland across the Lower Danube into the heart of the Balkan Peninsula, but also took to the water and harried the coasts of the Black Sea and the Aegean. On the Arabian front the tribesmen likewise returned to the attack—this time under the leadership of the oasis-dwellers of Palmyra[2]—and, thus led and organized, they momentarily overran not only Syria but Egypt and Anatolia as well. In North-West Africa the Berbers once more went on the war-path for the first time since Jugurtha's day. On the North European front the Franks and Alemanni now crossed the Rhine and treated themselves to a taste of the flesh-pots of Gaul. In this second paroxysm of simultaneous concentric barbarian attacks the Roman Power succeeded in saving the situation once again. The death of the Emperor Decius (*imperabat* A.D. 249–51) at the hands of the Goths was avenged by the Emperor Claudius Gothicus (*imperabat* A.D. 268–70). The blow which Zenobia had dealt to Roman prestige was effaced when the audacious Palmyrene princess was led in triumph through the streets of Rome behind the chariot of Aurelian. The Berbers were cleared out of the African provinces, and the Germans out of Gaul. In fact, all the broken fronts were for the second time restored; but this time the victory had been preceded by heavier reverses and deeper humiliations; it had been purchased at a higher price; and it had only superficially restored the *status quo ante*; for, while the old frontiers had been re-established (except in Swabia and in Transylvania), the relative strength of the Roman and barbarian forces had been permanently changed in the barbarians' favour.

---

[1] For this temporary collapse of the Empire see IV. C (i), vol. iv, p. 8, above, and V. C (i) (*d*) 6 (δ), Annex, in the present volume, p. 649, and V. C (ii)'(*b*), vol. vi, p. 284, below. For the Illyrian soldiers who set the Empire on its feet again see V. C (ii) (*a*), vol. vi, p. 207, below.   [2] For the history of Palmyra see II. D (i), vol. ii, pp. 9–12, above.

We are thus prepared for the decisive success of the third barbarian offensive, which began in the last quarter of the fourth century of the Christian Era and was kept up, on this front or on that, for some three hundred years (*circa* A.D. 375–675).[1]

This time, again, the action opened on the Eurasian front, where the eruption of the Hun Nomads blew the nomadicized Goths right off the Steppe into the far interior of the Roman body politic—as rocks and trees are uprooted and hurled through the air by an exploding shell.[2] From the end of the fourth century to the end of the sixth the pressure continued to be heavier on this front than on any other, as the ebb of the Hun wave was followed by the onrush of the Avar wave, and the vacuum left by the violent propulsion of the Goths was filled by the gentle infiltration of the Slavs.[3] It was only in the seventh century, when the onslaughts of pagan Huns and Avars were outmatched by the demoniac outbreak of the Muslim Arabs, that the main pressure shifted from the Eurasian front to the Arabian.

The organized and purposeful military campaigns of the Muslim Arabs were very different from the half automatic and barely conscious pressure of their ancestors against the yielding desert-frontier of a decaying Seleucid Empire in the second and the last century B.C. They are more comparable to the momentary Arab occupation of the Syrian, Egyptian, and Anatolian territories of the Roman Empire under Palmyrene leadership in the third century of the Christian Era.[4] But they utterly surpassed both these anticipatory reconnaissances in the potency of their driving-force.[5] While the Arab encroachments in the last two centuries B.C. had got no farther than the line of the Lebanon and the Orontes,[6] and the momentary Palmyrene conquests in the third century of the Christian Era had come to a halt at the banks of the Nile and of the Black Sea Straits, the Muslim Arab conquerors penetrated as

---

[1] In attempting to account for the movements of the Nomads between these dates, it has to be borne in mind that the interregnum which followed the dissolution of the Hellenic Civilization coincided in time—and this even more closely than the Hellenic 'Time of Troubles' (see p. 218, footnote 2, above)—with a bout of aridity on the Steppes (if the theory of climatic pulsations is to be accepted). For this hypothetical bout of aridity *circa* A.D. 375–675 see Part III. A, Annex II, vol. iii, p. 414, above.

[2] See Part III. A, Annex II, vol. iii, p. 426, above.

[3] See II. D (vii), vol. ii, pp. 317–19, and IV. C (iii) (c) 2 (β), vol. iv, pp. 327–8 and 397–8, above, and V. C (ii) (a), vol. vi, pp. 224–5, below.

[4] This comparison has been made already in I. C (i) (b), vol. i, p. 74, footnote 4, and in Part III. A, Annex II, vol. iii, pp. 397–8, above.

[5] This immense superiority, in potency, of the third of the three Arab offensives against the Hellenic World was almost certainly due to the most conspicuous of its distinctive features: that is to say, to the fact of its having been launched under the auspices of Islam. For the effect of alien religious influences—such as the Jewish and Christian influences that went to the making of Islam—in precipitating eruptions of Nomads see Part III. A, Annex II, vol. iii, pp. 450–1, above.

[6] See Jones, A. H. M.: *The Cities of the Eastern Roman Provinces* (Oxford 1937, Clarendon Press), pp. 255–6.

far as their Palmyrene predecessors towards the north-west, while on the south-west they left them far behind. In Asia Minor the Constantinopolitan Government succeeded—at the price of abandoning its commitments and cutting its losses on all other fronts—in pushing the Muslim Arabs back from the line of the Straits to the line of the Taurus and holding them there at the cost of grievously overstraining and fatally deforming the nascent body social of Orthodox Christendom.[1] In Africa, however, the wave of Muslim Arab conquest swept on from the Nile to the Atlantic—meeting and overpowering and carrying along with it the lesser wave of Berber aggression which was at that time breaking, likewise for the third time, upon the remnant of the African domain which Rome had inherited from Carthage.

At the Straits of Gibraltar the united Arab and Berber wings of the Afrasian Nomad forces collided with the epigoni of the Visigoths, who had settled down in the Iberian Peninsula at the end of a Völkerwanderung which had carried them across the whole breadth of the Roman Empire from a starting-point on the Great Western Bay of the Eurasian Steppe.[2] When these Gothic pupils of the Eurasian Nomads now encountered the Afrasian Nomad invaders of the Roman Empire at a point on the Empire's extreme western verge which was almost equally remote from the original mustering-grounds of both the rival war-bands, it was the Afrasian Nomadism that was victorious;[3] for the united Arab-Berber forces were not flung back from the Straits of Gibraltar by Roderick in A.D. 711 as the Arabs were flung back from the Bosphorus by Constantine IV in A.D. 677 and again in A.D. 718 by Leo Syrus. Scattering the Goths like chaff, the Arabs and Berbers pressed on across the Pyrenees and reached the banks of the Rhône and the Loire before they collided with the Franks and fared as ill at their hands in A.D. 732 on the road to Tours[4] as the ancestors of the Arabs' discomfited Gothic adversaries had fared at the same Frankish hands at Vouillé in A.D. 507.[5] It was characteristic of the heavy-footed gait[6] of the sedentary North European barbarians that, at dates which were two hundred and twenty-five years apart, they should win their successive victories over their mobile rivals from the Ukraine and the

---

[1] See II. D (vii), vol. ii, pp. 367–9; IV. C (iii) (c) 2 (β), vol. iv, pp. 321–2, above.
[2] For the Völkerwanderung of the Goths see p. 217, footnote 1, above.
[3] The victory of the Afrasian Nomads over the Visigothic representatives of the Eurasian Nomadism at Xeres, on the Iberian threshold of Europe, in A.D. 711, has the same piquancy as the victory of the Indian over the African elephants at Raphia, on the Egyptian threshold of Africa, in 217 B.C.
[4] See II. D (v), vol. ii, pp. 203–4; II. D (vii), vol. ii, pp. 361–2 and 378–81; II. D (vii), Annex IV, vol. ii, pp. 427–33; and IV. C (iii) (c) 2 (β), vol. iv, p. 341, above.
[5] For the Battle of Vouillé between the Frankish war-lord Clovis and the Visigothic war-lord Alaric II see II. D (v), vol. ii, p. 166; II. D (vii), vol. ii, p. 380; II. D (vii), Annex IV, vol. ii, p. 428; and the present chapter and volume, p. 217, footnote 1, above.
[6] See p. 217, footnote 1, above.

Hijāz on battlefields that were something less than twenty miles distant from one another as the crow flies.[1] Charles Martel allowed the Arabs to come that much nearer to the home territory of the Frankish Power in the basins of the Seine and the Rhine[2] than Clovis had allowed the Visigoths to advance in the same direction before marching out to defeat them; but the event was the same. At Tours in A.D. 732, as at Vouillé in A.D. 507, the immovable Franks remained masters of the field.

These Frankish victories over Goths and Arabs were a double triumph for the tortoise who had been content to crawl from the Rhine to the Loire during the time that it had taken one hare to sprint from the Ukraine, and another to sprint from the Hijāz, to the tortoise's doorstep in Aquitaine. In this contest between the barbarians for the division of the Hellenic dominant minority's territorial spoils the race was certainly not to the swift, though the battle may have been to the strong.[3] But this revelation of the relative strengths of the rival barbarian war-bands is not the main interest of the two battles in which they tried conclusions with one another. The outstanding historical event to which the battles of Vouillé and Tours bear witness is not the discomfiture of the Goths and the Arabs by the Franks, but the collapse of the resistance of the Roman Power which had been the common arch-adversary of all the three combatants. By the time when, in the heart of the *Orbis Romanus*, the war-bands from beyond one of the four anti-barbarian frontiers encountered and defeated—on derelict Roman ground—the war-bands from beyond each of the other three frontiers, it was manifest that the third of the three attempts of the external proletariat to take the Hellenic universal state by storm had been completely and definitively successful.

After this cursory review of the Hellenic external proletariat's successive relations with the Hellenic dominant minority, from the beginning of the schism down to the dominant minority's collapse, we may be inclined to raise two general questions which are suggested by analogy with our foregoing study of internal proletariats.[4] In the External Proletariat's reaction to the Dominant Minority's pressure, can we see any symptoms of a gentle as well as a violent response? And can we credit the External Proletariat with any creative activities?

[1] The battle between the Austrasians and the Arabs which is traditionally known by the name of Tours seems actually to have been fought in the neighbourhood of Old Poictiers, in the angle between the rivers Elain and Vienne.
[2] Charles Martel's sluggishness in marching to the help of the Aquitanians in A.D. 732 may be compared with the sluggishness of the Spartans in-coming to the Athenians' aid in 490 B.C. and again in 479 B.C.
[3] Ecclesiastes ix. 11.   [4] In V. C (i) (c) 2, above.

At first sight it might seem that, in the Hellenic case, the answer to both questions was in the negative. We can observe our anti-Hellenic barbarian in diverse postures and positions. As Ariovistus, he is driven off the field by Caesar; as Arminius, he holds his own against Augustus; as Odovacer, he takes his revenge upon Romulus Augustulus. But in all warfare there are these three alternatives of defeat and equal honours and victory; and, in each alike of the three situations, violence monotonously rules and creativity is uniformly at a discount. We may be encouraged, however, to look beyond this first view of the External Proletariat's êthos and achievement when we recollect that the Internal Proletariat is apt to display an equal violence and an equal barrenness in its earlier reactions, while the gentleness which eventually expresses itself in such mighty works of creation as a 'higher religion' and a universal church usually requires both time and travail in order to gain the ascendancy. With this clue in our hands we can perhaps detect some faint and rudimentary parallels in the history of the Hellenic external proletariat to the Internal Proletariat's generic saving graces.

In the matter of gentleness, for example, we can at any rate perceive a certain difference of degree in the violence of the various barbarian war-bands.[1] We can see that, on the whole, the Goths compare favourably with the Huns and Vandals and Lombards and Franks, while the Franks, in their turn, compare favourably with the English, the Lombards with the Avars, and the Arabs with the Berbers, Franks, and Goths. If we were given the chance of transferring our lives to the post-Hellenic interregnum, instead of having to live them out in the present age of our own Western history, we should probably find that we had definite preferences, as between the tyranny of one barbarian war-band and another, when it came to choosing the exact time and place for our exchange of fortunes.

To begin with, we would assuredly rather live through the Visigothic sack of Rome in A.D. 410 than through the Vandal and Berber sack in A.D. 455; for, although the first violation of an imperial city which had seen no enemy within her gates for eight hundred years may have given the greater shock to a Roman who heard the news at a distance (as Jerome heard of the Gothic blow at Bethlehem),[2] we may conjecture that for the victim on the spot

---

[1] This point has been touched upon already in V. C (i) (b), pp. 26–7, above.

[2] 'While this [theological war] was being waged in Jerusalem, terrible news arrived from the West. We learnt how Rome had been besieged, how her citizens had purchased immunity by paying a ransom, and how then, after they had been thus despoiled, they had been beleaguered again, to forfeit their lives after having already forfeited their property. At the news my speech failed me, and sobs choked the words that I was dictating (*haeret vox, et singultus intercipiunt verba dictantis*). She had been captured—

the tempered barbarism of an Alaric must have been distinctly less hard to bear than the unmitigated barbarism of a Genseric. Indeed, the impression made upon contemporaries, when they heard the whole story, by Alaric's grant of asylum in the churches of Rome to the inhabitants of the captured city is commemorated in one of the most celebrated passages of Latin literature.

'All the devastation, massacre, depredation, arson and assault of every kind that has been perpetrated in the catastrophe by which Rome has just been overtaken has been done according to the custom of war; but in this catastrophe there has also been a new departure, an unprecedented spectacle. The dreaded atrocity of the barbarians has shown itself so mild in the event that churches providing ample room for asylum were designated by the conqueror, and orders were given that in these sanctuaries nobody should be smitten with the sword and nobody carried away captive. Indeed, many prisoners were brought to these churches by soft-hearted enemies to receive their liberty, while none were dragged out of them by merciless enemies in order to be enslaved.'[1]

In another passage of his *magnum opus* tne same Roman man-of-letters and Christian exponent of the philosophy of history upbraids his pagan Roman contemporaries for their ingratitude towards a God who had shown mercy to them beyond their deserts in allowing a divinely ordained capture of Rome by barbarian hands to be executed in A.D. 410 by the comparatively gentle hands of an Alaric rather than in A.D. 406 by the cruel hands of a Radagaisus.

'There is a merciful and miraculous act of God—an act performed within living memory and, indeed, quite recently—which our pagan contemporaries not only refuse to commemorate by returning thanks for it, but actually endeavour, so far as lies with them, to bury, if possible, in a universal oblivion. We should be showing ourselves as ungrateful as they are if we were to pass this mercy over in silence for our part. [The fact to which I refer is that] when Radagaisus, king of the Goths, at the head of a huge and savage war-band, had occupied a position close to the city, where his axe-edge was within striking distance of Roman necks, the barbarian invader was defeated in one day's fighting with such speed and at so slight a cost that, without one single

the City by whom the whole World had once been taken captive (*capitur Urbs quae totum cepit Orbem*). Worse than that, famine had anticipated the work of the sword, so that scarcely a remnant had survived to fall into captivity.'—Saint Jerome, Ep. cxxvii, cap. 12, written *circa* A.D. 412 (in Migne's *Patrologia Latina*, vol. xxii, col. 1094).

[1] Saint Augustine: *De Civitate Dei*, Book I, chap. 7: 'Quod in eversione Urbis quae aspere gesta sunt de consuetudine acciderint belli; quae vero clementer, de potentia provenerint nominis Christi.' In order to follow Augustine's own argument—which is to demonstrate, not the clemency of the Visigoths, but the power of Christ's name and the blessings of the Christian Era—the passage quoted in the text should be read in its context from the beginning of the Preface to the end of the chapter from which the present quotation has been taken.

Roman casualty—not to speak of the loss of a single Roman life—more than a hundred thousand of the enemy's host were laid low, while the leader himself was promptly captured and put to the death that he so richly deserved. If this fanatically heathen war-lord, with his vast and likewise fanatically heathen forces, had entered Rome, whom would he have spared? What martyrs' shrines would he have respected? In whose person would he have shown a fear of God? Whose blood would he have cared to save from being shed, whose chastity from being violated? . . . And yet our wretched pagans refuse to give thanks to the immense mercifulness of a God who, when He had determined to chastise with a barbarian irruption a generation that had earned a still heavier chastisement by its vices, still tempered His indignation with an immense compassion—of which He gave proof first in causing Radagaisus miraculously to be defeated . . . and then in allowing the capture of Rome to be executed by a different band of barbarians who, contrary to the whole custom of war as it has been waged in the past, gave quarter, out of veneration for the Christian Religion, to all who took sanctuary in our holy places.'[1]

Yet, without contesting Augustine's thesis that Rome had been let off comparatively lightly in being delivered into Alaric's hands rather than into Radagaisus's, the inhabitant of Rome who had saved himself alive in A.D. 410 by taking the asylum which Alaric had given must still have breathed a sigh of relief when Alaric died and his gentler brother-in-law Atawulf took command of the Visigothic host. And an equal relief must have been felt in A.D. 489–93 by the grandson of our survivor of the catastrophe of A.D. 410 when the barbarian war-lordship in Italy was wrested out of the hands of the Scirian Odovacer by the Ostrogoth Theodoric. Conversely, we know for a fact that on the battlefield of Vouillé, in A.D. 507,

---

[1] Saint Augustine: *De Civitate Dei*, Book V, chap. 23: 'De bello in quo Radagaisus, rex Gothorum, daemonum cultor, uno die cum ingentibus copiis suis victus est.' The title of the chapter shows that Augustine's own argument here is to demonstrate, not the difference of degree between the more savage barbarism of a Radagaisus and the less savage barbarism of an Alaric, but, once again, the blessings of the Christian Era and the power of the Christians' God. In the second of the passages omitted from the above quotation Saint Augustine suggests that God's paramount purpose in bringing upon Radagaisus his miraculous defeat was 'to save the minds of the weak from being confounded by the glory that would then have been given to the demons of whom Radagaisus was a notorious worshipper'. And the contingency here referred to is explained in the earlier of the two omitted passages. 'What fine things our pagans would have had to say for their gods, and with what exultant insolence they would have boasted that the secret of Radagaisus's victory (if he had won the day), and of his potency (if a victory had proved it), was that he was placating and soliciting the Gods by daily sacrifices when the Romans were inhibited by the Christian Religion from doing likewise. Why, when Radagaisus was on his march to the place where he was crushed by the effortless exertion of the will of God's Majesty (*nutu summae maiestatis*), and when he was "in the news" all over the World, we were hearing at Carthage that the pagans [at Rome] were believing and propaganding and boasting that, in virtue of the protection and assistance that Radagaisus was receiving from gods who were his friends because he offered sacrifice to them every day (so it was said), the barbarian invader was quite invincible in face of Roman opponents who would not perform, and would not allow any one else to perform either, any corresponding acts of worship to the Gods of Rome.'

the grandson of an Arvernian nobleman who had striven to save his native canton from falling under the Visigothic yoke showed himself worthy of his grandfather by fighting and dying under the Visigothic banner to save Aquitaine from being snatched out of the grasp of her first barbarian conquerors by the yet more barbarous Franks.[1] In Aquitaine, as in Italy, at the turn of the fifth and sixth centuries of the Christian Era, a Roman *vir senatorius* can have felt no hesitation in preferring a Gothic to a Frankish or a Scirian master; and two hundred years later an Andalusian peasant perhaps found as little difficulty in determining his preference when the Arabs replaced the Visigoths as the barbarian warlords of the Iberian Peninsula; for the Muslim conquerors treated their new Christian subjects in the west no differently from their older Christian subjects in the east, and we have explicit testimony to the lightness of the Umayyad yoke towards the close of the seventh century in the former Oriental provinces of the Roman Empire. In a chronicle which reflects the views of the conquered provincials it is recorded of the Umayyad Caliph Yazīd I (*imperabat* A.D. 680–3) that

'he was a delightful character and enjoyed an extreme personal popularity among all the subject peoples of his dominions, because he never thirsted for any of the pomp which is universally regarded by princes as the prerogative of their high estate, but made himself accessible to everybody and lived like a simple commoner.'[2]

Between a Yazīd, who receives this mead of praise from his subjects, and an Attila who is remembered by his victims as 'the Scourge of God', there is a diversity of barbarian temper which cannot be ignored; and the spiritual history of one of the barbarian war-lords of the post-Hellenic interregnum, who has already been honourably mentioned above, is illuminated by a deposition from Roman lips which shows him in the act of conversion from Violence to Gentleness.

'I myself also [writes Augustine's disciple Orosius, at the close of his chronicle of the tribulations of the Hellenic Society] once was present at a conversation, in the town of Bethlehem in Palestine, between the most blessed Jerome the priest and a gentleman from Narbonne who had had a distinguished military career under the Emperor Theodosius and was also a man of deep piety, mature judge-

---

[1] See II. D (v), vol. ii, p. 166, above.
[2] 'Iucundissimus et cunctis nationibus regni eius subditis vir gratissime habitus, qui nullam unquam, ut omnibus moris est, sibi regalis fastigii causa gloriam appetivit, sed communis cum omnibus civiliter vixit.'—*Continuatio Isidori Byzantia Arabica*, § 27, in Mommsen, Th.: *Chronica Minora*, vol. ii (Berlin 1894, Weidmann), p. 345. In the same paragraph Yazīd's son and successor Mu'āwīyah II is praised for being like his father; and in § 38 (Mommsen, p. 357) 'Umar II is described as being 'tantae ... benignitatis et patientiae ... ut hactenus tantus ei honor lausque referatur a cunctis, etiam ab externis, quantus ulli unquam viventi regni gubernacula praeroganti adlatus est'.

ment and sterling character in his private life. This gentleman told us that at Narbonne he had become extremely intimate with Atawulf, and that he had often been told by him—and this with all the earnestness of a witness giving evidence —the story of his own life which was often on the lips of this barbarian of abounding spirit, vitality and genius. According to Atawulf's own story, he had started life with an eager craving to wipe out all memory of the name of Rome, with the idea of turning the whole Roman domain into an empire that should be—and be known as—the Empire of the Goths. His dream was to see "Gothia" substituted for "Romania" (if I may be pardoned for introducing these convenient "slang" terms) and Atawulf seated on the throne of Caesar Augustus. In time, however, experience had convinced him that on the one hand the Goths were utterly disqualified by their uncontrolled barbarity for a life under the rule of Law, while on the other hand it would be a crime to banish the rule of Law from the life of the State, since the State ceases to be itself when Law ceases to reign in it. When Atawulf had divined this truth, he had made up his mind that he would at any rate make a bid for the glory, that was within his reach, of using the vitality of the Goths for the restoration of the Roman name to all—and perhaps more than all—its ancient greatness; for in that event the barbarian war-lord who had found it beyond his powers to wipe Rome out might still be remembered by Posterity as the architect of her restoration.'[1]

This passage is perhaps the *locus classicus* for evidence of a change from Violence towards Gentleness in the êthos of the external proletariat of a disintegrating Hellenic Society; and in the light of this ascertained fact we can identify certain accompanying symptoms of spiritual creativity—or, at any rate, originality—in partially reclaimed barbarian souls.

Atawulf, for example, was an adherent of the same religion as his brother-in-law Alaric; and Alaric's religion was not the paganism of his forebears—as Augustine points out in drawing his contrast between the Christian Goth Alaric and the pagan Goth Radagaisus.[2] At the same time, Alaric's Christianity was not the Catholic Christianity of Augustine himself and of Augustine's and Alaric's contemporaries in the derelict Empire on whose territory the barbarian war-lord and his followers were trespassing. On the European front the barbarian invaders of the Roman Empire during the post-Hellenic interregnum, in so far as they were not still pagans, were Arians; and, although their original conversion to Arianism instead of Catholicism had been a matter of chance, their subsequent fidelity to Arianism was deliberate.

[1] Orosius, P.: *Adversum Paganos*, Book VII, chap. 43. The vividness of this report of Atawulf's own account of his political conversion may call to mind another famous passage of Hellenic literature in which Plato puts into Socrates' mouth an account of the speaker's intellectual conversion from an interest in the Macrocosm to an interest in the Microcosm (Plato: *Phaedo*, 96–7, quoted in III. C (i) (c), vol. iii, pp. 186–7, above).

[2] See the passage quoted on pp. 224–5, above.

The North European barbarians who broke into the Roman Empire as Arians at the turn of the fourth and fifth centuries of the Christian Era were the children of fathers who had been converted by Arian missionaries while they were encamped in the no-man's-land beyond a then still standing Roman *limes*;[1] and the Arians of the Empire had been able to carry out this missionary enterprise in the wilderness because, at the time, they were enjoying, at home, the favour of the Imperial Government of the day. In the middle decades of the fourth century Arianism had been the personal religion of the Emperors Constantius II (*imperabat* A.D. 337–61) and Valens (*imperabat* A.D. 364–78) and therefore at the same time the state religion of those portions of the Empire over which the direct authority of these two emperors extended; and the temporary ascendancy to which Arianism attained within the Imperial frontiers, thanks to the active support of these two powerful patrons, was neither seriously impaired by the lukewarm Catholicism of their brothers who ruled in the western provinces nor effectively interrupted by the militant Neoplatonism which momentarily took the place of Arianism as the officially favoured religion during the brief reign of Julian (*imperabat* A.D. 361–3).[2] In these circumstances the barbarians beyond the Roman pale who became converts to Arianism in the fourth century no doubt accepted, together with the Arian creed, the Arian missionaries' claim to be preaching the form of Christianity which had come into the ascendant—and come to stay—on the Roman side of the line;[3] and thus the converts, so far as they were aware, were taking a new departure which would bring them nearer, spiritually and culturally, to their Roman neighbours instead of widening the existing ·social gulf between those who found themselves on opposite sides of the geographical barrier of the *limes*.

This was, however, an illusion which could not, and did not, persist after the barbarians had broken through the Roman frontier defences in their third offensive, which began before the fourth century closed. In A.D. 378, on the battle-field of Adrianople,

---

[1] See I. C (i) (*b*), vol. i, p. 96, footnote 4, above.

[2] The Catholic restoration under Jovian, between the death of Julian in the summer of A.D. 363 and the accession of Valentinian and Valens in the winter of 363–4, was too brief to count.

[3] This impression that Arianism was the prevalent form of Christianity in the Roman Empire would be strengthened by the fact that the barbarians to whom the Arian missionaries first addressed themselves were encamped opposite the Lower Danube sector of the Roman frontier, and were therefore within close range of Constantinople, which was the seat of government of both the Arian Emperor Constantius II and the Arian Emperor Valens. From the nomadicized Goths in the Great Western Bay of the Eurasian Steppe Arianism spread to the Goths' poor relations the Gepids in the borderland between the Eurasian Steppe and the North European forests, and thence to some of the forest-dwelling barbarians of Central Europe, such as the Vandals, Burgundians, and Lombards.

the Arian Goths with their own hands deprived the last of the Arian Emperors of his diadem and his life; and in the next generation, as they flooded in through the breach which had been only momentarily repaired by Valens's militantly Catholic successor Theodosius the Great, the Arian barbarians found themselves masters of the military and political situation in the defenceless territories of a decrepit empire whose Government was now as orthodoxly Catholic as was an overwhelming majority of the provincial population. Under these altered conditions the Arianism to which the triumphant barbarians continued to adhere could no longer be explained away as a half-unconscious tribute to the cultural prestige of the civilization whose body social they were physically assailing. Whatever it may have been before, this Arianism was now a badge[1]—deliberately worn and sometimes insolently displayed—of the conquerors' social distinction from a conquered population with which they were now determined not to identify themselves (for the victorious barbarians were eager to exploit the political fruits of their military victory by stepping into the *ci-devant* Imperial Government's shoes and establishing themselves as a privileged ruling caste). This interpretation of the Arian barbarians' attitude towards their sectarian faith after they had carved their 'successor-states' out of the Roman body politic is supported by the fact that, the more truculent an Arian war-band was in its treatment of its provincial victims, the more fanatical it was apt to be in its hostility to Catholicism. While the subject Catholic populations in the Iberian Peninsula and Aquitaine and Italy were treated with tolerance by their Gothic masters, the more atrocious Vandal masters of a subject Catholic population in North-West Africa capped economic exploitation and political oppression with religious persecution.

While an Arianism which its barbarian converts had taken as they found it thus eventually became the distinctive badge of these particular bands of barbarian conquerors *in partibus subditorum*, there were other barbarians on other frontiers of the Empire who showed in their religious life a certain originality, or even creativeness, which was inspired by something more positive than a pride of caste. On the frontier in the British Isles, for example, the barbarians of 'the Celtic fringe', who were converted by Christian missionaries from the Roman Empire almost a hundred years later than the barbarians beyond the

---

[1] Barbarian or *ci-devant* barbarian conquerors sometimes advertise their distinctiveness by wearing badges that are visible and tangible. For example, Hammurabi continued to dress his hair in the traditional style of his Amorite Badu forefathers (cropped head, shaven upper lip, long beard) when he was the Emperor of the Sumeric universal state (see Meyer, E.: *Geschichte des Altertums*, vol. i, part (2), third edition (Stuttgart and Berlin 1913, Cotta), p. 632).

Lower Danube, and were therefore converted to a Catholic instead of to an Arian Christianity, were not content to adopt the alien religion *tel quel*, but moulded it, as we have seen, to fit their own barbarian heritage.[1] On the frontier facing the Arabian section of the Afrasian Steppe the transfrontier barbarians showed an independence which was greater still in their reaction to the same religious influences from the Roman side of the Syrian *limes*. In the creative soul of Muhammad[2] the radiation of Judaism and Christianity[3] was transmuted[4] into a spiritual force which discharged itself—whether this was the Prophet's original intention or not—as a new 'higher religion' with its own distinctive message and independent organization.[5] Nor were the Arabs and the Celts the only members of the Hellenic external proletariat who showed a greater originality in the religious field than the Teutonic converts to Arianism. The ancestors of these Eastern Teutons had already tasted the experience of a religious revolution at least once before the Arian missionaries came to preach to them in the Transdanubian wilderness; for the paganism from which these missionaries redeemed their converts was not the primeval paganism which the remoter ancestors of the Transdanubian barbarians must originally have shared with the rest of Primitive Mankind.

The religion of Primitive Mankind is a worship of the community in any or all of the diverse aspects in which the community is revealed by the vital activities on which it depends for its perpetuation.[6] In the life of a primitive community that is either quite untouched or only faintly titillated from a long way off by the social radiation of the civilizations, the two key-activities are the procreation of the human stock and the acquisition of the food-supply (an economic activity which presents itself, almost as a matter of course, in the form of procreation on the human

---

[1] See II. D (vii), vol. ii, pp. 322–8, above.

[2] And also in the soul of the Hijāzī Arab prophet's Najdī Arab contemporary and counterpart Maslamah (see III. C (ii) (a), vol. iii, p. 238, above). According to Nöldeke, Th., and Schwally, F.: *Geschichte des Qorāns*, 2nd edition (Leipzig 1909–38, Dieterich, 3 parts in 6 instalments), part i, pp. 56–7, Maslamah was a prophet of a genuine originality, and the similarities between his teaching and Muhammad's are traceable to the two Arabian prophets' common debt to Christianity.

[3] According to Nöldeke and Schwally, op. cit., part i, pp. 6–7, the Jewish influence that can be discerned in the Qur'ān is more considerable than the Christian influence—though one of the channels along which the Jewish influence percolated into Arabia may have been an Oriental Christianity.

[4] 'Islam is the form in which Christianity made its way into Arabia at large (*in Gesamt-Arabien Eingang gefunden hat*).'—Nöldeke and Schwally, op. cit., part i, p. 8.

[5] See III. C (ii) (b), vol. iii, pp. 276–7, and Part III. A, Annex II, vol. iii, pp. 450–1, and V. C (i) (c) 2, in the present volume, pp. 127–8, above, and V. C (i) (d) 6 (δ), Annex, in the present volume, pp. 673–8, below.

[6] For the primitive 'totalitarianism' in which the religious and political and economic aspects of social life are inseparable and indeed indistinguishable, see IV. C (iii) (c) 2 (β), vol. iv, p. 351, and V. C (i) (c) 2, in the present volume, pp. 160–1, above.

pattern when the food-supply is obtained by agriculture[1] and stock-breeding, and by no means necessarily in the form of strife and slaughter even when hunting is the principal economic resource).[2] A primitive community in this pristine state is apt to be worshipped mainly in the guise of a god or goddess of fertility, and only secondarily, if at all, in the guise of a destructive power. But, since the religion of Primitive Man is always a faithful reflection of his social conditions—whatever these conditions may be—a revolution in his religion is almost bound to take place when his social life is violently deranged by being brought into a contact with an alien human body social that is both close and hostile; and this is what happens when a primitive community which has hitherto been gradually and peacefully absorbing the beneficent influences of a growing civilization tragically loses sight of the gracious figure of Orpheus with his enchanting lyre,[3] and finds itself brusquely confronted, instead, by the ugly and menacing countenance of the Dominant Minority in a civilization that has broken down and gone into disintegration. In this event the primitive community is transformed into a fragment of an External Proletariat; and this social revolution goes to extremes in that inmost layer of the External Proletariat which is in immediate contact with the body social of the disintegrating civilization across a regular military frontier.

In this situation there is a revolutionary inversion[4] of the relative importance of the procreative and the destructive activities in the barbarian community's life. Procreation still counts for something—at least, in the human sphere—since without a supply of warriors it is impossible to make war at all; but, apart from the necessity of satisfying this demand for military 'man-power', it is now the destructive activity which is all-important. With the Dominant Minority's sword at its throat the External

---

[1] For the spiritual light which Mankind has gained by allowing its feelings and thoughts to play upon the parallelism between the life of plants and the life of men, see III. C (ii) (b), vol. iii, pp. 256–63, above.

[2] A hunting community is apt to look upon its game not as a hostile and hateful enemy but as a beneficent and amiable friend. The act of slaughtering the game does not seem to loom very large in the hunter's feelings and thoughts about his relation with the animals through whose death he lives; and at moments, and in situations, in which he cannot avoid recognizing the ugly truth that, for his own selfish ends, he is depriving the animal of a life which the animal does not wish to lose, the hunter usually shows embarrassment and ruefulness. He prefers to think of the animal—or the god incarnate in the animal—as a benefactor who is voluntarily sacrificing his life for Man's sake. In fact, the primitive hunter's attitude towards his game is not at all like his more sophisticated successor the warrior's attitude towards his human adversary. It is actually more like the Christian's attitude towards Christ.

[3] See IV. C (iii) (a), vol. iv, p. 123, and the present chapter and volume, p. 210, above.

[4] It will be seen that this particular vein of revolutionary change illustrates the thesis, put forward in IV. C (iii) (b) 1, vol. iv, pp. 135–6, above, that all revolutions are retarded acts of mimesis, in which the individual or community or society that is undergoing the revolution is responding to a 'challenge' from some other party.

Proletariat has to fight for its life; and its impulses towards strife and slaughter are thus diverted from the relatively innocent task of hunting animals to the sinister business of waging war against other human beings. War now becomes the community's all-absorbing occupation—in the first place because the urgency of self-defence drives all other social needs into the background, and secondly because the militarized barbarian gradually discovers —as the balance along the stationary *limes* inclines more and more in his favour[1]—that a profession which has been thrust upon him as a necessity for his self-preservation can be turned to economic account as well on a frontier where the barbarian raider has gained the upper hand. When War thus becomes more lucrative, as well as more exciting, than the dull and laborious pursuit of agriculture, how can Demeter, or even Aphrodite, hope to hold her own any longer against Ares as the supreme expression of a deified community that is now no longer mainly intent upon either Aphrodite's or Demeter's work? In the last stage of this process of hammering out the External Proletariat on the anvil of War the once pacific and industrious primitive community resolves itself into a war-band; and when these Martians call upon their god, their cry is

'Blessed be the Lord my strength, which teacheth my hands to war and my fingers to fight.'[2]

The god whom a completely militarized External Proletariat has refashioned in its own image is a divine war-lord who employs his superhuman strength on the sub-human business of committing robbery and rape at the head of a divine war-band. We have come across divinities of this barbaric strain in the Olympian Pantheon which was worshipped by the Achaean external proletariat of the Minoan 'thalassocracy';[3] and we have seen that these deified brigands in their eyrie on Olympus have their counterparts in the denizens of Asgard who were worshipped by the Scandinavian external proletariat of the Carolingian Empire, as well as in the gods of the Aryas who broke out of the Eurasian Steppe into the derelict domains of the Indus Culture and the Sumeric Civilization and the Egyptiac Civilization in the second millennium B.C.[4] Another pantheon of the same kind was worshipped by the Teutonic barbarians beyond the European frontiers of the Roman Empire before the Eastern Teutons were

---

[1] For this 'law' of the *limes* see Part VIII, below.   [2] Psalm cxliv. 1.
[3] See I. C (i) (b), vol. i, pp. 96–7, above.
[4] For the family likeness between the Achaean, Scandinavian, and Aryan pantheons see II. D (vii), Annex V, vol. ii, pp. 434–7, above. For the Völkerwanderung of the Aryas and their Hyksos *apodasmos* see I. C (i) (b), vol. i, pp. 104–7, and II. D (vii), vol. ii, pp. 388–91, above.

converted to Arianism in the fourth century of the Christian Era
and the Franks and the English to Catholic Christianity towards
the close of the fifth and the close of the sixth century respectively.
And, since Woden and his band were quite as far removed as the
garrisons of Asgard and Olympus were from the worthier objects
of the worship of an unspoiled Primitive Mankind, the evocation
of these predatory divinitiès in their militarized worshippers' own
image must be reckoned as a creative work that has to be placed
to the credit of the Teutonic external proletariat of the Hellenic
World.

Having gleaned these wisps of creative activity in the field of
Religion, can we add to our slender harvest by drawing upon
analogy once again? The 'higher religions' which are the glorious
discoveries of the Internal Proletariat are notoriously associated
with a sheaf of creative activities in the field of art. Every 'higher
religion' that has come to flower has expressed itself in architecture
and pageantry and music and singing and poetry, as well as in
prayer and sacrifice. Have the 'lower religions' of the External
Proletariat any corresponding works of art to show? Have they
made any atonement in the aesthetic sphere for their moral
ugliness?

These questions answer themselves in the affirmative; for, as
soon as we try to visualize the Olympian Gods, we see them with
our mind's eye as they are portrayed in the Homeric Epic; this
poetry is associated with that religion as inseparably as Gregorian
plain song and 'Romanesque' and 'Gothic' architecture are
associated with medieval Western Catholic Christianity; and the
brilliant poetic achievement of the barbarian makers of the Olympian Pantheon is by no means unique. In another context[1] we have
observed that the Greek epic poetry of Ionia has its counterparts in the Teutonic epic poetry of England and in the Scandinavian Saga of Iceland. All three of these schools of literary
art are expressions of a creative response to the stimulus of new
ground on the part of barbarian war-bands who have made their
Völkerwanderung by sea; and the three corresponding pantheons
are manifestly another fruit of the same creative activity. The
Scandinavian Saga is bound up with Asgard, and the English
Epic—of which *Beowulf* is the principal surviving masterpiece—
with Woden and his divine *comitatus*, as the Homeric Epic is
bound up with Olympus. And when we inquire whether perchance the lesser stimulus of migration overland, which has been
potent enough to evoke the Vedic Pantheon in the imaginations
of the Aryas, has also moved them to any works of literary creation,

[1] In II. D (iii), vol. ii, pp. 94–6, above.

the answer is in the affirmative again; for the epic poetry which was precipitated by the Völkerwanderung of the Aryas, when they poured out of a Eurasian no-man's-land into the domain of the Indus Culture before the birth of the Indic Civilization, is to be found embedded—like a pearl in an oyster or like a fly in amber —in the *Mahābhārata* and the *Rāmāyana*.[1]

Moreover, if we turn our attention from the North European to the Arabian *limes* of the Roman Empire, we shall see that epic poetry is not the only form of literary self-expression to which the transfrontier barbarians may be stimulated by the rising tension of their relations with the Dominant Minority on the opposite side of the military front. If the Arabic poetry which is traditionally ascribed to the pre-Islamic period is to be accepted as genuine, it affords us an example of a barbarian literature of 'the Heroic Age' which is lyrical in its vein and personal in its interest; and, even if the alleged examples of this pre-Islamic school of Arab literary art are to be rejected as spurious, we can still infer, from the unquestionably authentic rhymed prose of the Qur'ān, that there were poets before the Prophet Muhammad's day in the ranks of the Arabian wing of the external proletariat of the Hellenic World.

Our examination of the genesis, history, and achievements of this Hellenic sample of the External Proletariat is now complete; and we can sum up our findings as follows.

The secession of an external proletariat from the dominant minority of a disintegrating Hellenic Civilization produced a state of war between these two fractions of a formerly undivided and harmonious body social. The resulting hostilities began as a running fight and then turned into a stationary warfare along each of several different fronts. In this stationary warfare there were alternating bouts of activity and sluggishness; and these alternations were synchronous on all fronts. The bouts of activity took the form of successive attempts on the barbarians' part to break through into the dominant minority's domain. The first of these bouts coincided in date with the culmination of the disintegrating civilization's 'Time of Troubles'; the second coincided with a momentary collapse, in mid-career, of the disintegrating civilization's universal state; the third coincided with the social interregnum which followed the final break-up of the universal state and the simultaneous dissolution of the civilization itself. The first two barbarian attempts to break through were abortive, but the third was a success; and this successful break-through re-

---

[1] The relation of the Sanskrit Epic, in the form in which we have it, with the Völkerwanderung of the Aryas is discussed in V. C (i) (c) 3, Annex II, pp. 596–606, below.

sulted in a Völkerwanderung in which the triumphant barbarian war-bands swept over the derelict provinces of the decrepit universal state and carved out for themselves 'successor-states' in which they tried to settle down in order to exploit their victory and to live upon the conquered population as a privileged caste.

In all these vicissitudes of their struggle with the disintegrating civilization's dominant minority the barbarians walked undeviatingly in the path of Violence; but in the hour of their victory the several war-bands went to different lengths in the degree of the atrocity with which they treated their victims. Among some of them there was at least a tendency to incline from Violence towards Gentleness; and there was at any rate one victorious war-lord who was convinced by his personal experience that the fame for which he thirsted could only be won by his making it his mission to fulfil and not to destroy the work of the age-long adversary whose dominance had been broken at last. Nor was even the violence of the barbarians altogether uncreative. On one front they made for themselves, in the likeness of the war-lord and his band, a new pantheon which bore no closer a resemblance to the pristine objects of the worship of Primitive Mankind than it bore to the vision of God which was beheld by the prophets of the 'higher religions' that were arising, in the same age, in the bosom of the Hellenic internal proletariat. On other fronts they took some one of these 'higher religions' and either refashioned it into something new, or modified it to fit their own barbarian heritage, or at least adopted it in a sectarian form which became their own distinctive barbarian badge. These were rudimentary acts of creation, and this barbarian vein of creativity revealed itself not only in the field of religion but also in works of literary art. The North European barbarians who invented Woden and his band of deified freebooters were also the makers of *Beowulf* and the Continental Teutonic epic poetry. The Arabian barbarians who created Islam out of broken lights of Judaism and Christianity which flickered over their steppes were also the makers of a lyric poetry with a personal note which the Prophet Muhammad turned to religious account in the rhymed prose of the Qur'ān.

The Minoan External Proletariat.

If we have truly succeeded in making out the main features in the portrait of the external proletariat of the Hellenic Society, this scrutiny may provide us with a clue for carrying out the rest of our present survey. Let us now proceed to pass in review the external proletariats of the other civilizations that have broken down and gone into disintegration, and mark whether any of the same features appear in their portraits too.

If we begin with the Minoan Civilization, to which the Hellenic Civilization is 'affiliated', we shall at once be able to locate the position of one Minoan *limes* which is commemorated down to this day by the still standing walls of Tiryns and Mycenae.[1] Those walls were built to keep at bay the barbarians of Continental Europe; and, while our archaeological evidence does not tell us whether any barbarian raiders from the no-man's-land beyond this frontier had a hand in the first destruction of the palaces at Cnossos and Phaestus at the end of 'Middle Minoan II'—a catastrophe in which we seem to see the culmination of a Minoan 'Time of Troubles'[2]—Archaeology and Literature corroborate one another in their record of the Völkerwanderung in which these Continental European barbarians, after capturing the continental outposts of the Minoan Power and taking to the sea,[3] eventually swept over the Minoan World—and hurled

---

[1] For the contrast between these Minoan frontier fortresses on the European mainland of Greece and the unwalled metropolises of the Minoan universal state on the island of Crete see II. D (v), vol. ii, pp. 159–60, above.

[2] See I. C (i) (b), vol. i, p. 92, footnote 3, and IV. C (ii) (b) 1, vol. iv, pp. 64–5, above, and V. C (ii) (b), vol. vi, p. 312, below.

[3] For the Vandal-like audacity which was shown by the Continental European external proletariat of the Minoan Society in accepting the challenge of the Sea and bearding the Minoans on their own element see I. C (i) (b), vol. i, p. 93, and II. C (ii) (b) 2, vol. i, p. 333, above. The Achaeans can hardly have performed this feat without already having made themselves masters of the former Minoan fortresses on the mainland; but the archaeological evidence does not enable us to determine the date at which Mycenae and Ti ns changed hands; and it therefore remains uncertain whether the mainlanders who sacked Cnossos *circa* 1400 B.C. were the Achaean assailants or the Mycenaean wardens of the Continental European marches of the Minoan World. It is possible that the Mycenaeans turned upon the Minoans *circa* 1400 B.C. (as, in Japan, the pioneer barons in the Kwanto turned upon the Imperial Court in Yamato in the twelfth century of the Christian Era), before the Achaean barbarians took advantage of this dissension among their adversaries in order to overwhelm Mycenaeans and Minoans alike. For this possibility see II. D (v), vol. ii, p. 160, above. In the opinion of Glotz, G.: *La Civilisation Égéenne* (Paris 1923, Renaissance du Livre) p. 61 (cf. p. 245), our archaeological evidence proves that the Minoan Power in Crete was overwhelmed by the concerted action of the Mycenaean Power and 'the New Empire' of Egypt, which entered into direct relations with the Mycenaeans in the reigns of the Egyptiac Emperors Amenhotep II (*imperabat circa* 1450–1415 B.C.) and Amenhotep III (*imperabat circa* 1405–1370 B.C.). 'Ces cadeaux sont de véritables documents d'histoire diplomatique. Ils annoncent un évènement considérable: le soulèvement du monde mycénéen contre la Crète qui l'avait converti et transformé, un choc en retour qui allait détruire la puissance de Cnosse.' According to the same scholar the archaeological evidence proves further that the preceding radiation of Minoan culture from Crete into the Mycenaean domain on the mainland of European Greece had been ominously selective. When, towards the close of the seventeenth century B.C., the Minoan Civilization 'took' on the mainland (see the passage quoted from Glotz, op. cit., in I. C (i) (b), vol. i, p. 94, footnote 1, above), the continental ladies adopted all the Cretan fashions (for the style of these see the passage quoted from Glotz, op. cit., in I. C (iii) (c), vol. i, p. 174, footnote 1, above), but the continental men were refractory and, in particular, were unwilling to follow the Cretan men's fashion of shaving clean (Glotz, op. cit., pp. 78–9, 87, 91). If these external manners and customs (to which alone it is possible for archaeological evidence to bear direct witness) may be taken as outward visible signs of inward spiritual states, perhaps we are warranted in inferring, from the evidence in question, that the male half of the Mycenaean body social was never captivated, as the womenfolk

themselves against the ramparts of the Egyptiac World beyond it—[1] during the post-Minoan interregnum (*circa* 1425-1125 B.C.).

This story is written—for living eyes still to read—in the abiding marks of the fire that seared the faces of the gigantic earthenware jars in the Imperial store-houses at Cnossos on the day when the barbarians broke through the wooden walls of the 'thalassocracy'—which had been the Minoan universal state—round about the year 1400 B.C.;[2] and if, as we stand among the ruins of Cnossos, we fix our eyes on those sinister smirches that have been brought to light in our day, and then call to mind Saint Augustine's and Saint Jerome's descriptions[3] of what their own feelings were when they heard the news of Alaric's sack of Rome in A.D. 410, we can perhaps enter into the feelings of unknown devotees of a falling Minoan Civilization who may have suffered as sharp an agony[4] without having left any written memorial for a modern Western scholar to decipher. For our literary evidence of the final catastrophe of the Minoan Civilization we must turn to documents which are not the work of the Minoan dominant minority. The archives of the Egyptiac universal state have yielded up the official narrative in which the Government of 'the New Empire' has recorded its own success—through a victory bought at the price of social prostration[5]—in bringing the last and most violent onset of this post-Minoan Völkerwanderung to a tardy halt on the threshold of Egypt itself.[6] And in the tale of the siege of Troy the barbarians' own epigoni have perhaps preserved the memory of a preliminary assault upon an outpost of the Hittite World on the eve of the great migration of 1200/ 1190 B.C.[7] If the siege of Troy is an authentic historical event,

were, by the exotic Minoan culture, but always remained at least semi-barbarian at heart—in a state of repressed spiritual revolt which eventually broke out into an act of flagrant savagery at the turn of the fifteenth and fourteenth centuries.

[1] See I. C (i) (*b*), vol. i, p. 93, above, and the present chapter and volume, p. 269, and V. C (i) (*c*) 4, p. 352, and V. C (ii) (*a*), vol. vi, p. 207, below.

[2] See I. C (i) (*b*), vol. i, p. 93, and IV. C (ii) (*b*) 1, vol. iv, p. 64, above.

[3] See the present chapter and volume, pp. 223-5, above.

[4] See I. C (i) (*b*), vol. i, p. 93, footnote 1, above.

[5] See IV. C (iii) (*c*) 2 (*β*), vol. iv, p. 422, above.

[6] See I. C (i) (*b*), vol. i, pp. 93 and 100-2, above.

[7] For the westward expansion of the Khatti Power in Anatolia, up to the threshold of a Minoan World which was then in its last throes, after the peace-settlement of 1278 B.C. between Khatti and 'the New Empire' of Egypt, see I. C (i) (*b*), vol. i, p. 114, above. Within the last few years the royal archives of the Khatti capital at Khattusas (the present Boghazkiöi) have yielded up documents which appear to give us glimpses of some of the movements in the post-Minoan Völkerwanderung between the sack of Cnossos *circa* 1400 B.C., which is recorded in the present condition of the ruins of the palace, and the grand finale of 1200/1190 B.C., which is recorded in the inscriptions of the Egyptiac Emperor Ramses III. These Hittite documents, like the Homeric Epic, show us the sea-roving descendants of the Continental European external proletariat of the Minoan World bearing down upon the seaboard of the Khatti Empire in Anatolia; but the maritime province which has to bear the brunt of the attack in this chapter of the story is Pamphylia and not the Troad. As early as the time of King Mursil II of Khatti (*regnabat circa* 1345-1320 B.C.) we find the name Akhkhiyawa (? Achaia) applied to a

it must, of course, have been a minor affair by comparison with the successful raid on Cnossos and the abortive assault upon Egypt; and of these two great exploits there is no echo in the *Iliad* and the *Odyssey*. But, if the Homeric Epic is true to type in ignoring the greatest events of the age by which it has been inspired, and in exaggerating the importance of the affair which it has chosen to take for its theme,[1] it is incomparable in the art with which it has created 'a possession for ever' out of the fruitless deeds and ephemeral experience of one particular set of barbarian war-bands. In this Greek 'heroic' poetry the creative potentialities of an external proletariat have come to their finest flower. The magnificence of the Ionian Epos as a work of art is matched only by the inadequacy of the Olympian Pantheon as an object of worship.

The Syriac External Proletariat.

If we turn next to the Syriac Civilization, we shall find that several of the anti-barbarian fronts which formed themselves on its borders in the course of its disintegration have come to our attention already in considering the fortunes of the Hellenic dominant minority which took these fronts over as a result of Alexander's conquests in Asia and the Roman conquests in North-West Africa and the Iberian Peninsula.

These Syriac fronts set hard in the sixth century B.C., when both the main body of the Syriac Society in Syria and Iran and its offshoot in the western settlements of the Phoenicians overseas passed out of a Syriac 'Time of Troubles' into a universal state. The universal state of the main body was the Achaemenian Empire, which also embraced within its political frontiers the whole of the Babylonic World and that more mature half of the Egyptiac World that lay to the north of the First Cataract.[2] The universal state of the Syriac transmarine world was the Carthaginian Empire. Both these Syriac empires were in contact with the Hellenic World—indeed, it was a Hellenic pressure that

maritime district of Southern Anatolia which seems to correspond to the country which in the Hellenic Age, after the post-Minoan interregnum, was known as Pamphylia, and which was inhabited, in this later age, by a Greek-speaking population. The king of Akhkhiyawa who was Mursil's contemporary appears to have borne the name Tawagalawas (? 'Ετεοκλέϝης or Eteoclês), while about a century later the same country was under the rule of an Attarissiyas (? Atreus). These fragments of the archives of Khatti point to the possibility that the Achaean ancestors of the later Greek-speaking Pamphylians may have already gained a firm enough footing in Pamphylia to impose the Achaean name upon the province within less than a hundred years of the sack of Cnossos *circa* 1400 B.C. (see Meyer, E.: *Geschichte des Altertums*, vol. ii, part (1) second edition (Stuttgart and Berlin 1928, Cotta), pp. 546–50; Schachermeyr, F.: *Hethiter und Achäer* (Leipzig 1935, Mitteilungen der Altorientalischen Gesellschaft, vol. ix, Heft 1/2, Harrassowitz), *passim*).

[1] The relation in which 'heroic' poetry stands to history is discussed in V. C (i) (c) 3, Annex III, pp. 607–14, below.

[2] For the political partition of the Egyptiac World at the First Cataract from the fifth decade of the seventh century B.C. onwards see II. D (v), vol. ii, pp. 116–17, above.

had prevailed upon the Phoenician colonies in the west to unite
their forces under Carthaginian leadership—but either empire
also had its anti-barbarian frontiers. The Carthaginian Empire
marched with the Afrasian Nomads in the Sahara and with the
sedentary barbarians of North-West Africa and Spain. The
Achaemenian Empire marched with the Afrasian Nomads in
Arabia; with the Eurasian Nomads on the threshold of the
Eurasian Steppe between the Pamir Plateau and the Caspian
Sea; and with the sedentary barbarians of Europe in Thrace.[1]

The history of the warfare between the Syriac dominant minority
and the transfrontier barbarians on these five different fronts is
rather intricate on several different accounts. In the first place
there was no inner connexion—and therefore no significant correspondence in dates—between the respective courses of events on
the Achaemenian and on the Carthaginian sectors.[2] In the second
place the history of the Syriac Civilization was interrupted, in this
field of action as in others, by the violent intrusion of the Hellenic
Society through the force of Macedonian and Roman arms.

For the first two hundred years after the overthrow of the
Achaemenian Empire by Alexander all the anti-barbarian fronts
of the Syriac World in Asia were occupied and held against the
barbarians by Hellenic Powers; and, when, in the sixth decade of
the second century B.C., Carthage was supplanted by Rome in
Africa as well as in Spain, there was a moment when every single
front of all the five—in Europe, Africa and Asia alike—was in
Hellenic hands. This situation did not last; for, before the third
quarter of the second century B.C. had run out, the Eurasian
Nomads on the front between the Pamirs and the Caspian had
broken the Bactrian Greek Power,[3] and the defence of this front
had devolved upon the Parthians.[4] These Parthians, however, were

---

[1] These sedentary barbarians in Thrace screened both the Achaemenian dominions
in Asia Minor and the Hellenic World in Peninsular Greece from a direct contact with
the Eurasian Nomads on the Great Western Bay of the Eurasian Steppe; but the screen
was thin. The Odrysae themselves, who in this age were the dominant Thracian community in the Basin of the Maritsa, were perhaps of Nomad origin, if their name testifies
to a kinship with the Agathyrsi of the Hungarian Alföld (see Part III. A, Annex II,
vol. iii, p. 425, footnote 2, above), and there is no doubt about the Nomadism of the
Getae, who ranged the Lower Basin of the Danube between the Balkans and the
Transylvanian Carpathians. When, at some date before the close of the sixth century
B.C., Darius the Great carried the Achaemenian frontier out of Asia into Europe across
the Black Sea Straits, he broke right through the screen of sedentary barbarians and
made an unsuccessful attempt to subdue the Scythian Nomads in the hinterland of the
Milesian Greek colonies on the north coast of the Black Sea.
[2] There was, of course, a certain inner connexion between the respective relations
of the Achaemenian and the Carthaginian Empire with the Hellenic World. This
connexion is examined in Part IX, below.
[3] See Tarn, W. W.: *The Greeks in Bactria and India* (Cambridge 1938, University
Press), chap. 7: 'The Nomad Conquest of Bactria'.
[4] See II. D (v), vol. ii, p. 141, footnote 2, and p. 144, and Part III. A, Annex II, vol.
iii, pp. 412 and 449, above, and the present chapter and volume, pp. 275 and 310, and V.
C (i) (c) 3, Annex II, in the present volume, p. 601, footnote 4, and p. 602, footnote 5, below.

themselves the epigoni of Nomads who had drifted out of Trans-caspia into Khurāsān little more than a hundred years before;[1] and, in summing up the history of South-Western Asia between the irruption of the Sakas[2] and the Yuechi[3] *circa* 130–129 B.C.[4] and the Battle of Carrhae in 53 B.C., it would be as true to say that the Parthians had carried the banners of Eurasian Nomadism into the heart of the Syriac World from the Caspian Gates to the banks of the Euphrates[5] as it would be to say that they had shielded the heart of the Syriac World by stemming the tide of Nomad invasion at the Khurasanian escarpment of the Iranian Plateau.[6] To the peasantry and townsfolk of Western Iran and 'Irāq their Parthian 'saviours' were perhaps hardly distinguishable from the Saka destroyers whom the Parthian arms were keeping at bay; and, in so far as the Parthians acquired a tincture of sedentary culture in the course of their south-westward advance, it was Hellenism rather than the Syriac Civilization that attracted them. Indeed, from first to last, they were better Philhellenes[7] than they were Zoroastrians. It was not until the Arsacidae had been overthrown and supplanted by the Sasanidae *circa* A.D. 226/232[8] —some five hundred and fifty years after the overthrow of the Achaemenidae by Alexander —that the Khurasanian frontier over against the Eurasian Nomads for the first time passed back into the keeping of a purely Syriac Power; and, even when the Sasanids' other mission of completing the ejection of Hellenism from the Syriac World had been executed—after four hundred years of unsuccessful Sasanian efforts—by the Sasanids' conquerors the Primitive Muslim Arabs, another hundred years had still to pass before the Umayyad Power brought to an end, in A.D. 737–41, a Nomad domination over the Oxus-Jaxartes Basin which by then had lasted for eight centuries and three-quarters.[9]

This Arab conquest of the Oxus-Jaxartes Basin restored, over

---

[1] See II. D (vii), vol. ii, p. 371, above.

[2] The Saka invaders of Parthia in 129 B.C. appear to have consisted mainly of Massa-getae and Sacaraucae (Tarn, op. cit., p. 294).

[3] The Yuechi appear to have been a horde of Tochari led by an aristocracy of Asii (Tarn, op. cit., pp. 284–7).

[4] The *termini post quem* and *prae quem* are respectively 141 B.C. and 128 B.C. The conventionally accepted approximate date *circa* 135 B.C. has been corrected to *circa* 130 B.C. for the Nomad invasion of Bactria, and 129 B.C. for the Nomad invasion of Parthia, by Tarn in op. cit., cap. cit., p. 294. According to the same authority, pp. 278–9, Farghānā had already been conquered from the Greek princes of Bactria by Sakas of the Sai-Wang horde *circa* 159 B.C.   [5] See p. 216, above.

[6] For the consequent diversion of these flood-waters from the Syriac World to India see V. C (i) (c) 3, Annex II, pp. 601–4, below.

[7] This Parthian Philhellenism did not, however, amount to much (see V. C (i) (c) 4, p. 355, footnote 2, below).   [8] See p. 216, above.

[9] For the history of the Oxus-Jaxartes Basin from the irruption of the Sakas and Yuechi *circa* 130 B.C. down to the Umayyad conquest in A.D. 737–41 see II. D (v), vol. ii pp. 140–1, and II. D (vii), vol. ii, pp. 370–84, above. Since the publication of the first three volumes of the present work a masterly study of the subject has appeared in W. W. Tarn's *The Greeks in Bactria and India* (Cambridge 1938, University Press).

against the Eurasian Nomads between the Pamirs and the Caspian, that frontier of the Syriac World which had been originally established in the sixth century B.C. by the Achaemenidae[1] and which had survived the overthrow of the Achaemenian Empire for two hundred years. During the brief span of the fifth decade of the eighth century of the Christian Era, the Umayyad Caliphate united, in a single reintegrated Syriac universal state, not only the whole of the former domain of the Achaemenian Empire (save for its north-western provinces in Anatolia and Thrace),[2] but also all, and more than all, the former domain of the Carthaginian Empire in North-West Africa and the Iberian Peninsula.[3] This momentary political unity was lost when the 'Abbasids overthrew and supplanted the Umayyads in Asia in A.D. 750; for a fugitive Umayyad succeeded in saving Andalusia for his House; and even in Africa the authority of the 'Abbasids was never very effectively or securely established west of Egypt. But, if the political re-union of the Syriac World under Umayyad rule was thus ephemeral, the accompanying social unification survived the division of the Caliphate and endured as long as the Syriac Civilization itself. From the eighth century of the Christian Era down to the close of the post-Syriac interregnum (*durabat circa* A.D. 975–1275) there was a unison in the movement of life through all the members of the Syriac body social from Andalusia to Transoxania. In the interior of the Syriac World this unison in this age declared itself in an active and rapid circulation of ideas and emotions and persons and commodities from end to end of this vast domain.[4] On the anti-barbarian frontiers in the same age the same unison declared itself in a similarity and simultaneity in the vicissitudes of the military struggle on all fronts. In this respect the history of the relations between the Syriac dominant minority and its external proletariat under the 'Abbasid Caliphate and the Andalusian Umayyad Caliphate resembles the history of the Hellenic dominant minority and its external proletariat under the Roman Empire.

On the other hand the external proletariat of the Syriac

---

[1] See II. D (v), vol. ii, pp. 138–9, above.

[2] In the eighth century of the Christian Era the Thracian and Anatolian territories that had once belonged to the Achaemenian Empire were welded into an East Roman Empire by the genius of Leo Syrus and his son the Emperor Constantine V (see the references in IV. C (iii) (c) 2 (β), vol. iv, p. 322, footnote 2, as well as IV. C (iii) (c) 2 (β), vol. iv, pp. 340–5, above).

[3] See II. D (v), vol. ii, pp. 203, above.

[4] The intellectual monument of this social solidarity of the Syriac World in the Age of the 'Abbasids is the Arabic literature of the eighth to the thirteenth century of the Christian Era, which is the product of a Republic of Letters in which Cordovans and Samarqandīs worked hand in hand. A signal example of the activity of the circulation on the economic plane is the spread through the Syriac World of the art of manufacturing, and the habit of using, paper (see Carter, T. F.: *The Invention of Printing in China and its Spread Westward*, revised edition (New York 1931, Columbia University Press), pp. 97–100).

Civilization has distinguished itself from other representatives of its class by performing on two occasions on three different fronts—and each time with momentous historical results—the *tour de force* of enlisting in its own ranks, and carrying away with it in its own marauding adventures, the children of an alien civilization.

The barbarians who broke through the Thracian front of the Achaemenian Empire and overthrew its Government and over-ran its territories in the third quarter of the fourth century B.C. were not the wild highlanders of the Istranja Dagh or Rhodope, and they were not even the Odrysae of the Maritsa Basin with their possible Nomadic antecedents and their undoubted talent for holding together a barbarian principality. The barbarian destroyers of the Achaemenian Empire were the Macedonian backwoodsmen of the Hellenic World; and they made their impetuous entry onto the Syriac stage in a dual role—as apostles of Hellenism and not merely as plunderers and exploiters of the society that was the victim of their prowess in arms. Similarly, in a later age, the Armenian barbarian soldier of fortune who bat-tered down the defences of the Melitenian march of the 'Abbasid Caliphate[1] was fighting in the service of an East Roman Empire which was the premier state of a politically precocious Orthodox Christian Civilization,[2] while the Basque and Cantabrian and Asturian barbarians who broke through the European front of the Andalusian Umayyad Caliphate during the post-Syriac interreg-num (*circa* A.D. 975–1275) were reinforced by their Western Chris-tian co-religionists and European neighbours the Franks—wayward children of an infant Western Christian Civilization who readily relapsed into barbarism when their primitive passions were re-awakened by the scent of blood and the prospect of plunder.

The true date of the beginning of the Crusades[3] is not A.D. 1095, when Pope Urban II made his historic call to arms, with a Levantine objective, in the market-place at Clermont, but A.D. 1018, when the first war-band of warriors from the northern side of the Pyrenees came over the mountains to join the Christian barbarians of the Iberian Peninsula in their assault upon the tottering defences of the Andalusian Umayyad Caliphate;[4] for,

[1] See the present chapter, pp. 253–4, below.
[2] For the political precocity of the Orthodox Christian Civilization and its untoward results see IV. C (i) (c) 2 (β), vol. iv, pp. 320–408, above.
[3] See I. B (iv), vol. i, p. 38, and II. D (vii), vol. ii, pp. 362–3, above, and V. C (i) (c) 4, in the present volume, p. 354, below.
[4] In a different context we have studied the collision between the Syriac and the Western Christian Society in the Iberian Peninsula from the Western Christian point of view, and have watched how the Arab thrust from the Straits of Gibraltar towards the line of the Loire in A.D. 711–32 was answered by a Western Christian counter-thrust which was carried across the Pyrenees by Charlemagne in A.D. 778 and eventually across the Atlantic by Christopher Columbus in A.D. 1492 (see I. B (iv), vol. i, p. 38; II. D (v), vol. ii, pp. 202–6; and IV. C (iii) (c) 2 (β), vol. iv, p. 341, above). But, when

when once the young commonwealth of Western Christendom
had joined in this Transpyrenaean hue and cry, the flame of barbarian aggression spread like wildfire along the whole length of
the Mediterranean, from west to east,[1] and found fuel in Orthodox

we look at the same collision of social forces from the Syriac standpoint, the Arab conquest of the Iberian Peninsula in A.D. 711–13 takes on the appearance of a long-deferred
but none the less legitimate recovery for the Syriac World of a colonial domain which
had been captured for Hellenism by sheer force of Roman arms in the Hannibalic War
after it had been fairly won for the Syriac Civilization from Barbarism by a long line
of Phoenician empire-builders—beginning with the maritime explorers who gained the
first Phoenician foothold on the Iberian coast of the Atlantic at some date in or before
the eighth century B.C., and culminating in the person of Hannibal's own father Hamilcar
Barca, who carried the Carthaginian Peace into the interior of the Peninsula. It was the
dominion exercised in the Peninsula by Hamilcar and Hannibal between the end of
the First and the outbreak of the Second Punic War that was re-established, more than
nine hundred years later, by Mūsā for the benefit of an Umayyad Caliph at Damascus
(see II. D (v), vol. ii, p. 203, and II. D (vii), Annex IV, vol. ii, p. 432, above); and
although, as we have observed (on p. 241, above), the political union of the whole
Syriac World, from the Eurasian frontier of Transoxania to the Atlantic coasts of
Morocco and the Iberian Peninsula, was thus achieved by the Umayyads only to be
undone, within less than a decade, through a partition of the Arab Caliphate, in two
extremely unequal portions, between the Umayyads and the 'Abbasids, the surviving
Andalusian Umayyad Caliphate, in which a scion of Umayyah's House contrived still
to reign over a remnant of his vast ancestral heritage, continued to play in the Peninsula
the role of a reintegrated Syriac universal state which had been usurped by the rival and
triumphant 'Abbasid Caliphate in the Asiatic and African provinces of the Syriac
World. The two Caliphates not only lived on side by side to perform an identical social
function in their respective domains : they also both dissolved simultaneously in the
general post-Syriac interregnum of A.D. 975–1275; and in this world-wide débâcle the
Basque and Asturian barbarians from beyond the European frontier of the Andalusian
Umayyad Caliphate competed with the Murābit and Muwahhid Berbers from beyond
its African frontier for the possession of the Umayyads' now derelict Peninsular domain
(see II. D (v), vol. ii, p. 204, above).

It was in these circumstances that the children of Western Christendom on the farther
side of the Pyrenees enlisted in the ranks of the European external proletariat of the
Syriac World by joining in their Basque and Asturian co-religionists' barbarian invasion
of Andalusia. The first of these Transpyrenaean marauding expeditions from France
was made in A.D. 1018 (ten years before the Andalusian Umayyad Caliphate finally broke
up into a bevy of indigenous 'successor-states') by a Norman war-band under the leadership of Roger de Toeni. These Norman pioneers were followed in A.D. 1033 by a
Burgundian war-band which was recruited by Odilo, the Abbot of Cluny, and which
presented to the Abbey the booty won from the Muslims. Guy-Geoffrey, Duke of
Aquitaine, followed in 1063; Thibaut de Semur, Count of Chalon, in 1065. Eble,
Count of Rouci and Rheims, who was the son-in-law of Robert Guiscard and brother-
in-law of Sancho King of Aragon and Navarre, took the same road in 1073 under the
patronage of Pope Gregory VII. Duke Hugh of Burgundy came to fight for King Sancho
in 1078; and from that time onwards, until the stream was diverted from Andalusia to
Syria in 1095, there was a steady flow of Crusaders across the Pyrenees from Burgundy
—'not that the Burgundians were more adventurous than many others, but because the
great Abbey of Cluny recruited them and launched them against the Unbeliever' (Petit,
E.: Histoire des Ducs de Bourgogne, vol. i, p. 223, quoted in Bédier, J.: Les Légendes
Épiques, 2nd edition, vol. iii (Paris 1921, Champion), p. 371).

'La France, comme on voit, n'a point attendu le concile de Clermont pour concevoir
l'idée de la croisade et pour la réaliser. Normands, Champenois, Gascons, Provençaux,
Bourguignons surtout, les aventuriers de toutes nos provinces y ont collaboré. Les
Clunisiens — eux qui devaient plus tard inspirer la Chronique de Turpin et soutenir le
mouvement du pèlerinage de Compostelle — ont commencé par organiser des expéditions armées en Espagne. Avant de guider sur les routes de paisibles cortèges de pèlerins,
ils y ont convoyé des bandes d'hommes équipés en guerre.' (Bédier, op. cit., loc. cit.)

These Transpyrenaean Crusaders who came over the mountains in the eleventh
century of the Christian Era to reinforce the Christian barbarians of the Iberian Peninsula in their warfare against the Andalusian Umayyads and these Umayyads' indigenous
successors may remind us of the Transalpine Gaesatae who came to the help of the
Celtic barbarians of Italy in their struggle against the Romans in 225 B.C. (see II. D
(vii), vol. ii, p. 345, footnote 2, above).

[1] See II. D (vii), vol. ii, p. 362, footnote 5, above.

Christendom as well as in Dār-al-Islām. The Pisans and Genoese chased the African Muslims out of Corsica[1] and Sardinia; the Normans chased them out of Sicily and pursued them as far as their own African coasts from a base of operations in Apulia and Calabria which the first generation of Norman adventurers in Southern Italy had captured from the East Roman Empire.[2] In the next stage of their aggressive advance the European barbarians—who needed no scratching to make them betray their primitive natures beneath their Western Christian veneer—could hardly be restrained from laying their covetous hands upon the metropolitan provinces of the East Roman Empire as they trekked across Romania on their way to carve out the Frankish 'successor-states' of the 'Abbasid Caliphate in Syria; and their great day came in A.D. 1204 when they sacked Constantinople itself and divided up the remnants of the East Roman Empire in Greece and the Archipelago. The longing to commit this crime, which was carried into effect in the Fourth Crusade, had by then been smouldering, unavowed, in the hearts of four generations of cross-marked adventurers ever since the Franks who went on the war-path in the First Crusade had noted the riches of the Imperial City of Orthodox Christendom when they were received within her gates as her citizens' co-religionists and allies. The sack of Constantinople by the Crusaders is a barbarian exploit that deserves to be commemorated on the same roll of dishonour as the sack of Rome by the Vandals and the sack of Cnossos by the Achaeans.

Without attempting to trace the history of the relations between the Syriac dominant minority and its external proletariat through all these complications on each of its five fronts, we can perhaps gain some idea of its likeness to, or difference from, the corresponding passages of Hellenic history by first tracing the alternation of paroxysms and lulls on the principal Syriac anti-barbarian front—that is, the front over against the Eurasian Nomads between the Pamirs and the Caspian—and then surveying synoptically the simultaneous barbarian offensives which broke through the *limes* of a then divided Caliphate[3] on all five fronts in the last act, during the post-Syriac interregnum of A.D. 975–1275.

On the Eurasian front we meet with the first great barbarian inroad in the age in which we should expect to find it on our Hellenic analogy. The Cimmerian and Scythian Nomad invasion of South-Western Asia in the eighth and seventh centuries B.C. coincided in date with the culmination of the Syriac 'Time

---

[1] See further V. C (i) (d) 6 (γ), Annex I, p. 622, footnote 3, below.
[2] See II. D (v), vol. ii, p. 201; III. C (i) (a), Annex, vol. iii, pp. 458–9; and IV. C (iii) (c) 2 (β), vol. iv, p. 392, footnotes 1 and 2, and pp. 401–2, above, and the present chapter and volume, pp. 291–2, below.   [3] See p. 242, footnote 4, above.

of Troubles';[1] and on this occasion the Nomad trespassers from
the Desert on to the Sown penetrated almost as far as their predecessors the Aryas in the second millennium B.C.;[2] for the
Scythians, too, made their way from Transoxania to Cisjordania—
though, unlike the Hyksos, they were brought to a standstill at
Gaza and never watered their horses in the Nile. The tide of
barbarian invasion which thus momentarily submerged the whole
of South-Western Asia towards the end of the seventh century B.C.
was swept back in the sixth century to the north-eastern side of
'the Caspian Gates' by the Medes, and to the other side of the
Jaxartes by the Achaemenidae;[3] and the Achaemenian watch on
the Steppe was so well kept that the Nomads did not move when
the Achaemenian Empire stumbled and recovered itself in the
middle of the fourth century B.C.[4] Indeed, they did not even take
advantage of the sudden and unexpected overthrow of the Achaemenidae, a few years after this recovery, by a Macedonian invader who broke into the domain of the Syriac universal state from
the opposite quarter, out of the Thracian no-man's-land on the
European side of the Black Sea Straits; and, even when they were
given an opening at last by the break-up of the Achaemenian
Empire's Seleucid Macedonian 'successor-state', they did not
succeed in emulating the exploits of the Scythians or the Hyksos;
for the Parthians, as we have seen, got no farther into the Syriac
World than the line of the Euphrates, and the Sakas no farther
than the Khurasanian escarpment of the Iranian Plateau; and
eventually—when the Arsacids had been supplanted by the
Sasanids, and the Sasanids in their turn by the Umayyads—these
Umayyad sovereigns of a reintegrated Syriac universal state re-
established the Central Asian frontier that had originally been
won by Cyrus, and handed this restored frontier on to their own
supplanters the 'Abbasids. It was only when the break-up of the
'Abbasid Caliphate brought with it the dissolution of the Syriac
Society that the Eurasian Nomads broke into South-Western
Asia once again and, on this occasion, repeated the Hyksos'
feat when, in A.D. 1250, the 'successor-state' of the 'Abbasid

---

[1] It also coincided with an apparent period of aridity—and therefore of explosivenes
—on the Steppes (see Part III. A, Annex II, vol. iii, p. 410, above).
[2] See the references on p. 232, in footnote 4, above.
[3] See II. D (v), vol. ii, pp. 138–9, above.
[4] The Central Government of the Achaemenian Empire had to fight for its life *circa*
366–359 B.C., when a number of satraps in the Asiatic provinces west of the Euphrates
made a concerted revolt with the support of Egypt, which had been independent *de facto*,
under an Egyptiac nationalist Government, since 404 B.C. The crisis, however, was
successfully met. In or about the year 360 B.C. the revolt of the satraps collapsed; and,
when the Emperor Artaxerxes Ochus achieved the reconquest of Egypt in 343–2 B.C.,
it looked as though the Achaemenian Power had acquired a new lease of life (see further
V. C (i) (c) 2, p. 94, above, and V. C (ii) (a), vol. vi, p. 207; V. C (ii) (b), vol. vi, p. 302;
and V. C (ii) (a), Annex II, vol. vi, p. 442, below).

Caliphate in Syria and Egypt was usurped from the Kurdish Ayyubids by their Turkish mamlūks.

During this post-Syriac interregnum (*durabat circa* A.D. 975–1275)[1] the successive waves of the barbarian offensive on the Eurasian front all had their counterparts on each of the other four fronts.

In the latter part of the tenth century of the Christian Era, when the Eurasian Nomad Ilek Khans were breaking upon the Transoxania, and the Saljūqs upon Transcaspia, at the head of their respective Turkish war-bands, Arabian Nomads (Banu 'Uqayl and Banu Asad and Banu Kilāb) were breaking upon 'Irāq and the Jazīrah and Syria—partly at the instigation of the militant Shī'ī Carmathians, and partly under the leadership of a host of petty Arab war-lords (the Banu Asad under the Mazyadids and the Banu Kilāb under the Mirdāsids)[2] whose thirst for plunder did not disguise itself as religious enthusiasm.[3] At the foot of the Taurus and the Amanus these tenth-century Arab barbarian invaders of the Syriac World from its Arabian hinterland collided with 'borderers' (ἀκρῖται) of the East Roman Empire who were bearing down upon the Mesopotamian and Cilician and Syrian lowlands from the Anatolian plateau;[4] and the two competing gangs of scavengers divided the local spoils of the 'Abbasid Caliphate mainly by ordeal of battle but partly also by pacific agreement.[5]   At the same moment the Katāma Berber high-

[1] This post-Syriac interregnum coincided exactly in date with an apparent bout of aridity on the Steppes, just as the second paroxysm (*circa* 825–525 B.C.: see V. C (ii) (*b*), vol. vi, p. 303, below) of the Syriac 'Time of Troubles' had been contemporaneous with an earlier apparent bout of aridity which may have lasted from about 825 to 525 B.C.

[2] See Part III. A, Annex II, vol. iii, p. 416, above. These minor Arab trespassers upon the fringes of a derelict 'Abbasid Caliphate at the turn of the tenth and eleventh centuries of the Christian Era may be compared with the Arab trespassers on the fringes of the Seleucid Empire in the same districts at the turn of the second and the last century B.C. (see pp. 215–6 and 218, above).

[3] Shi'ism had, however, been professed by the Hamdānid leaders of the Banu Taghlib, who had made themselves masters of the Jazīrah and Northern Syria in an earlier generation (they had gained possession of Mawsil (Mosul) between A.D. 873 and A.D. 904, and of Aleppo in A.D. 944).

[4] See IV. C (iii) (*c*) 2 (β), vol. iv, pp. 399–401, above, and the present chapter and volume, p. 242, above, and pp. 253–4, below.

[5] The Nomad Arab war-band of the Banu Habīb, who had taken up their quarters in the Syrian provinces of the 'Abbasid Caliphate, went over, bag and baggage, to the East Roman camp in A.D. 928 (Grégoire, H.: 'L'Épopée Byzantine et ses Rapports avec l'Épopée Turque et l'Épopée Romane' in Académie Royale de Belgique: *Bulletin de la Classe des Lettres et des Sciences Morales et Politiques*, 5ᵉ série, tome xvi (Brussels 1930, Lamertin), p. 466; idem: 'Autour de Digénis Akritas' in *Byzantion*, vol. vii (Brussels 1932, Secrétariat de la Revue), p. 288; for the capitulation, in the same year, of the Margrave of the Melitenian march of the 'Abbasid Empire see the present chapter, p. 254, below). The East Roman 'borderers'' aggression was vigorously contested by the first of the Hamdānid Arab war-lords of Aleppo, Sayf-ad-Dawlah (*dominabatur* A.D. 944–67); but his successor Sa'd-ad-Dawlah (*dominabatur* A.D. 967–91) gave up the struggle and submitted to an East Roman protectorate in A.D. 969. (For the treaty establishing this relation see Vasiliev, A. A.: *Histoire de l'Empire Byzantin* (Paris 1932, Picard, 2 vols.) vol. i, p. 409; there is a Latin translation of the Arabic text in the Bonn edition of the East Roman historian Leo Diaconus (Bonn 1828, Weber), pp. 392–4.

landers from Eastern Kabylia, under their 'Fātimid' leaders, were bearing down upon Egypt after having already submerged the Aghlabī 'successor-state' of the 'Abbasid Caliphate in Ifrīqīyah.[1] And at the same moment, likewise, the Iberian highlanders of Asturias and Navarre were making their first conquests at the expense of Dār-al-Islām in Andalusia. In the middle of the eleventh century of the Christian Era, when the Saljūq Turks were following the Parthian trail from Transcaspia to the Euphrates, the Banu Hilāl and the Banu Sulaym were breaking out of Arabia across Egypt into Ifrīqīyah,[2] while the Lamtuna Sanhāja Nomad Berbers from the Sahara, under their Murābit leaders,[3] were pouring across the Straits of Gibraltar to contend for the possession of Andalusia with the North Iberian Christian barbarians and their French co-religionists and allies from beyond the Pyrenees.[4] In the third quarter of the eleventh century the Saljūq Turks collided with the East Roman 'borderers' in a race between these two barbarian competitors for the possession of the 'Abbasid Caliphate's Armenian Monophysite Christian 'successor-states';[5] and before the close of the eleventh century the Saljūq Turks and the Katāma Berbers and the French Franks, in the course of their simultaneous invasions of the Syriac World from opposite quarters, had all come into collision, in a 'three-cornered duel', in Syria itself. In the middle of the twelfth century, when the Eurasian Nomad Ghuzz were treading on the Eurasian Nomad Saljūqs' heels in Transcaspia and Khurāsān, the Muwahhid Masmuda Berber highlanders from the Atlas were pursuing the Murābit Lamtuna Berber Nomads across the Straits.[6] It was not until the twelfth century had passed over into the thirteenth that the Eurasian Nomads gave a decisive demonstration of their superiority in staying-power over all their barbarian competitors in the contest for the division of a moribund Syriac Society's heritage.

In the thirteenth century, when the East Roman 'borderers' were fighting their last rear-guard action on the Anatolian side of the Black Sea Straits, when the Arabian and North-West African reservoirs of aggressive barbarian 'man-power' had both temporarily run dry, and when the Frankish barbarian invaders of Syria were barely managing still to cling to their last footholds on the Syrian coast, the Eurasian Steppe delivered itself of the most violent and destructive eruption of Nomads that has ever been recorded in the annals of any of the sedentary civilizations.

[1] See Gautier, E. F.: *Les Siècles Obscurs du Maghreb* (Paris 1927, Payot), pp. 311–29.
[2] See Part III. A, Annex II, vol. iii, pp. 445–6, and Part III. C (ii) (*b*), Annex III, vol. iii, pp. 473–4, above.
[3] See Gautier, op. cit., p. 333.   [4] See II. D (v), vol. ii, p. 204, above.
[5] See IV. C. (iii) (*c*) 2 (β), vol. iv, pp. 400 and 401, above.
[6] See II. D (v), vol. ii, p. 204, above.

In this century the Mongols—not content with invading the Far Eastern World in one direction and the Russian Orthodox Christendom in another—simultaneously flung themselves upon the Syriac World through the gap between the Pamirs and the Caspian, and devastated it with a ferocity which quite eclipsed the performances of the Ghuzz and the Saljūqs. The Mongol conquerors of Transoxania and Iran and 'Irāq pushed on across the Euphrates into Syria; and they would certainly have reached the Nile, and perhaps even the Atlantic, if they had not been repulsed on Syrian battlefields by their Turkish cousins the Egyptian Mamlūks, a pack of Eurasian Nomad wolves who had been trained by their Ayyubid masters to serve as Syriac watchdogs.[1]

This rather perfunctory survey has perhaps brought to light a sufficient resemblance between the respective histories of the Syriac and Hellenic external proletariats to raise the question whether similar experiences have produced similar spiritual effects. We have seen that the Hellenic external proletariat was stimulated by its struggle with the Hellenic dominant minority into displaying a certain creativity in the two fields of religion and literature. In the same two fields do we find that the Syriac external proletariat has any creative works to its credit?

In the field of religion we shall search the record of the Syriac external proletariat in vain for any parallel either to the North European barbarians' creation of a pantheon in the image of the war-lord and his war-band or again to the Prophet Muhammad's achievement of conjuring a new 'higher religion' out of the religious influences that were radiating from the Hellenic World into the Arabia of his age. On the other hand we shall find several parallels in the history of the intercourse between the external proletariat and the dominant minority of the Syriac World to the Goths' adoption of an Arian instead of a Catholic Christianity and to their deliberate persistence in an originally undesigned sectarianism as a distinctive badge to mark them off from a Catholic subject population after their successful breach of the Roman *limes* had made their fortunes by suddenly promoting them to the status of a privileged ruling caste from their former status as outcasts wandering in the wilderness beyond the pale.

An inclination to resist conversion to the established religion

---

[1] For the successive Mongol invasions of Syria which were repulsed by the Egyptian Mamlūks see I. C (i) (*b*), Annex I, vol. i, p. 350, and IV. C (iii) (*c*) 2 (γ), vol. iv, p. 447, above. This successful stand against the Mongol Nomads which was made in Syria by the ex-Nomad Mamlūks may be compared with the successful stand against the Saka Nomads which was made in Khurāsān by the ex-Nomad Parthians (see II. D (v), vol. ii, p. 141, footnote 2, and the present chapter and volume, pp. 239–40, above, and V. C (i) (*c*) 3, Annex II, in the present volume, p. 601, footnote 4, and 602, footnote 5, below).

of the Syriac World of the day, without closing their ears to the preaching of the same faith in an unorthodox sectarian form, can be detected among the Syriac external proletariat both in the Sasanian Age, when the established religion was Zoroastrianism, and in the Age of the Arab Caliphate, when the established religion was Islam.

Between the Zoroastrian Church and the Eurasian Nomads there was a secular antipathy, which can be traced back to Zarathustra's own lifetime.[1] While the Iranian prophet addressed himself to the Nomads[2] as well as to the members of the sedentary society to which he himself belonged, he seems to have found the Nomads impervious to his teaching—as was indeed to be expected, considering that the substance of Zarathustra's message, on the social side, was a call to abandon the Nomadic for the sedentary way of life. Zarathustra's own personal hostility to Nomadism was conscious and avowed; and it seems to have evoked, among Nomads who persisted in the error of their ways, an answering hostility which was perhaps less articulate but which was not on that account less genuine. The Parthians, for example, were never more than lukewarm half-hearted Zoroastrians down to the day when they were overthrown by the zealous Sasanid Defenders of the Zoroastrian Faith—though by that time more than four and a half centuries had elapsed since the moment in the third century B.C. when an Arsacid war-lord had led his followers out of the desert of Transcaspia into the sownland of Khurāsān. Nor did the official patronage of the Arsacids' Sasanian successors avail to enable a Zoroastrianism which was now the established religion of Iran[3] to propagate itself even among the *ci-devant* Nomad masters of the Oxus-Jaxartes Basin—not to speak of the unreclaimed Nomads on the open Steppe beyond.

In the Oxus-Jaxartes Basin—which had been thrown open to a constant radiation of Indic cultural influence ever since the crossing of the Hindu Kush by the first Bactrian Greek conqueror in the second century B.C.[4]—the Zoroastrian established church of the Sasanian Empire found the Mahāyāna already in possession of the field[5] in the first half of the third century of the Christian Era; and four hundred years later, on the eve of the Sasanian

---

[1] See V. C (i) (c) 2, p. 121, footnote 1, above.
[2] See Pettazzone, R.: *La Religione di Zarathustra* (Bologna 1920, Zanichelli), p. 91.
[3] The official establishment of the Zoroastrian Church by the Sasanian Dynasty, so far from being a boon to Zoroastrianism, cast a blight upon it (see V. C (i) (d) 6 (δ), Annex, pp. 659–61, below).
[4] See II. D (v), vol. ii, p. 141, footnote 2, and II. D (vii), vol. ii, pp. 369–85, and V. C (i) (c) 2, in the present volume, pp. 132–3, above.
[5] See V. C (i) (c) 2, p. 136, above.

Empire's fall, when the Chinese Buddhist pilgrim Hiuen Tsiang
(Yuan Chwang) travelled across the Oxus-Jaxartes Basin *circa*
A.D. 629, on his way to India, it is evident from his narrative that
the Mahāyāna had not yet disappeared from Central Asia, even
if its hold there had been weakened.[1] This survival of the
Mahāyāna at the Sasanian Empire's gates is evidence of the ill
success of the Zoroastrian Church's missionary propaganda;
and corroborative evidence, which is more cogent still, is to be
found in the fact that, while the ebb of the Mahāyāna in Central
Asia in the Sasanian Age was undoubtedly due to a return of
the tide of native Syriac cultural influences, the native Syriac
religions which won ground in Central Asia in this age at the
Mahāyāna's expense were Manichaeism,[2] which was proscribed
and persecuted in the Sasanian Empire, and Nestorianism, which
was grudgingly and precariously tolerated[3] by the Sasanian
Government for the negative reason that this sectarian form of
Christianity was proscribed and persecuted in the contemporary
Roman World. While the Zoroastrian missionary propaganda
failed to make any headway beyond the north-east frontier of the
Sasanian Empire, the Nestorian missionaries had succeeded, by
A.D. 636, in carrying their faith right across the Eurasian Steppe
to the capital of the T'ang Empire in the Far East;[4] and in A.D.
762 the Manichaean missionaries succeeded in converting the
Uighur Nomad masters of the Turfan Basin.[5] The hold which
Nestorianism obtained upon the Nomads, as well as upon the
oasis-dwellers, in Eurasia was so strong that it even survived the
overthrow of the Nestorian Nomad Karāyits and Naimans by
the pagan Nomad Mongols at the beginning of the thirteenth century of the Christian Era. The Mongol victors took the conquered
Nestorians into their service; and there were occasions, during
the last and greatest eruption of the Eurasian Nomad Völkerwanderung into the Syriac Society's domain, on which it pleased
the pagan Mongol conquerors of South-Western Asia to show
their disdain for a Muslim subject population by ostentatiously
bestowing their favours upon the religion of their Nestorian
Christian secretaries and accountants.[6]

While the establishment of Zoroastrianism as the official religion of the Sasanian Empire had this unintended effect of commending a sectarian Manichaeism and Nestorianism to the Eurasian

---

[1] For Hiuen Tsiang's evidence see II. D (vii), vol. ii, p. 375, above.
[2] See V. C (ii) (c) 2, Annex I, pp. 575–80, below.
[3] This toleration alternated with short but sharp outbursts of persecution.
[4] See II. D (vi), vol. ii, pp. 263–8, above. The date is vouched for by the evidence
of the Nestorian inscription of Si Ngan (see II. D (vii), vol. ii, p. 375, footnote 2, above).
[5] See Part III. A, Annex II, vol. iii, p. 415, above.
[6] See II. D (vi), vol. ii, pp. 237–8, above.

Nomad wing of the Syriac external proletariat, the next chapter of Syriac history—in which the Sunnah took the place of Zoroastrianism as the established religion of the Sasanian Empire's 'successor-state' the Arab Caliphate—shows us the Shī'ah, which was proscribed and persecuted throughout the Sunnī Caliph's dominions, making converts among the transfrontier barbarians in no less than three different directions: among the pagan Berbers in Africa; among the Zoroastrian Iranian highlanders in the Caspian Provinces;[1] and among the nominally Sunnī Arab Nomads in Hasā. And the sweeping success of this Shī'ī missionary enterprise in these three barbarian hinterlands of the Sunnī Caliphate procured for the Shī'īs the same revenge upon their orthodox Muslim opponents and persecutors that the discomfited Arians obtained for themselves against the victorious Catholic majority in the Roman Empire through the conversion to Arianism of the Goths and the Vandals.[2]

In the tenth century of the Christian Era, when the frontier-defences of the reintegrated Syriac universal state collapsed, the East Arabian barbarian harriers of 'Irāq and Syria and the Daylamī barbarian conquerors of Western Iran and Baghdad and the Katāma Berber conquerors of Ifriqīyah and Egypt all alike broke through as Shī'ī invaders of a Sunnī World; and the 'successor-states' of the 'Abbasid Caliphate which were founded by these victorious barbarians' Carmathian and Buwayhid and Fātimid leaders did not merely impose the military yoke of a victorious external proletariat upon the necks of a no longer dominant minority; they also established a Shī'ī minority's dominion over a Sunnī majority.[3] This momentary Shī'ī ascendancy in Dār-al-Islām was brought to an end when the first wave of barbarian invaders from the threshold of the Syriac World was swamped by a second wave from an outer zone of barbarism which had never been reached by the Shī'ī missionaries; for these remoter barbarians had been converted, before they broke out of the wilderness, to the Sunnah—and this in an ultra-orthodox form.[4] In Iran and 'Irāq the Shī'ī régime of the Daylamī Buwayhids

---

[1] For the parallelism, vis-à-vis the Arab Caliphate, between the position of these Zoroastrian barbarian highlanders in the Caspian provinces of Iran and the position of the Christian barbarian highlanders in the Biscayan provinces of the Iberian Peninsula see II. D (vii), Annex VIII, vol. ii, pp. 446–52, above.

[2] See pp. 227–9, above.

[3] For this temporary ascendancy of the Shī'ah over the Sunnah in the 'successor-states' of the 'Abbasid Caliphate in the tenth and eleventh centuries of the Christian Era see I. C (i) (b), Annex I, vol. i, pp. 354–6, above.

[4] See I. C (i) (b), Annex I, vol. i, p. 357, above. It may perhaps be conjectured that these belated Sunnī missions to an outer circle of pagan barbarians beyond the pale were stimulated, like the preceding Shī'ī missions, by the spur of adversity at home. At any rate, the Sunnī missionaries who converted the Sanhāja and the Saljūqs must have been operating from their respective bases of operations in Ifriqīyah and in Iran

was overthrown by the Sunnī Saljūqs, while the Fātimid Shī'ī Caliphate which had been established by the strong arm of the Kabylian Katāma was overwhelmed in Ifrīqīyah by the Katāma's western neighbours the fanatically Sunnī Murābit Sanhāja,[1] and was extinguished in Egypt by a studiously orthodox Saladin.[2] Yet down to the end of the post-Syriac interregnum the Shī'ah continued to exercise its power of attraction upon the barbarian rulers of Sunnī subjects; for at the turn of the thirteenth and fourteenth centuries of the Christian Era, when the Mongol Il-Khans were experimenting in alternative substitutes for their ancestral paganism, they toyed with the Shī'ah,[3] as well as with Nestorian Christianity, before they capitulated to the Sunnī orthodoxy which was the faith of the majority of the population of their dominions.

Thus the Syriac external proletariat resembles the Hellenic external proletariat in showing at least a certain originality—though perhaps not a positive creativity—in the field of religion. When we turn from religion to literature, do we find any poetic achievement of the Syriac external proletariat that can be regarded as an analogue of the Teutonic Epic? The answer is in the affirmative; for, while the African contingents of the Syriac external proletariat have not charged the air with any winged words to commemorate their historic experiences, their Asiatic and European comrades-in-arms have not remained dumb. The Macedonian *conquistadores* who broke through the Thracian front of the Achaemenian Empire in the fourth century B.C. have left a literary echo of their barbarian feat of arms in the Alexander Romance.[4] The East Roman 'borderers' who broke through the Euphratean front of the 'Abbasid Caliphate in the tenth century of the Christian Era[5] have left behind them an echo of their corresponding feat of arms in the epic of which the hero is Basil Digénis Akrítas. And the French Crusaders who broke through the Pyrenaean front of the Andalusian Umayyad Caliphate in the eleventh century of the Christian Era have created a work

at a time when these regions were under the Shī'ī rule of the Fātimids and the Buwayhids. We may remind ourselves that the Arian Lombards were at the gates of Rome at the moment when Pope Gregory the Great sent out his missionaries to convert the pagan English barbarians in Ultima Thule to Catholicism (see III. C (ii) (b), vol. iii, p. 269, above).

[1] Gautier, E. F.: *Les Siècles Obscurs du Maghreb* (Paris 1927, Payot), pp. 333–9.

[2] This overthrow of the Katāma and Daylamite barbarian converts to Shī'ism by the Sanhāja and Saljūq barbarian converts to the Sunnah may be compared with the overthrow of the Arian Visigoths by the Frankish converts to Catholicism.

[3] See I. C (i) (b), Annex I, vol. i, p. 363, above.

[4] For the divergence, which began within Alexander's own lifetime, between the literary tradition that grew into the Alexander Romance and the historical record of Alexander's authentic acts see Annex III to the present chapter, p. 608, and V. C (ii) (a), Annex II, vol. vi, pp. 441–4, below.

[5] See V. C (iii) (c) 2 (β), vol. iv, pp. 399–400, above.

of art which is the parent of all the poetry that has ever been written in any of the vernacular languages of the Western World. The *Chanson de Roland*, at any rate, has outstripped *Beowulf* in its historical importance just as signally as it surpasses the *chef d'œuvre* of the Teutonic Epic in its intrinsic literary merit.

The geographical and social environment in which the Byzantine Greek Epic of Basil Digénis Akrítas came to birth is proclaimed in the hero's standing epithet; for 'Akrítas' means 'Borderer',[1] and the scene of action of every incident in the poem is located within the East Anatolian highland no-man's-land[2] where the East Roman Empire marched with the Arab Caliphate.[3] The historical nucleus of the literary character that is the central figure of the poem seems to be an East Roman officer of the Anatolic army-corps[4] named Diogenes, whose death in battle against the Arabs is recorded by the chronicler Theophanes (*sub Anno Mundi* 6281 = A.D. 788).

'Ces choses se passaient . . . dix ans apres que fut tombé dans la *clisura* de Roncevaux le Digénis Akritas des Francs, le paladin Roland, aussi obscur, aussi fameux que le héros d'Anatolie, mais mieux chanté que lui.'[5]

The original home of the epic which crystallized round this eighth-century East Roman officer's memory seems to have lain in the Taurus defiles and on the Cilician plain;[6] but in the course of its growth the epic seems to have laid under contribution the personality and exploits of a later historical personage, the Armenian soldier of fortune Mleh (*Graecè* Melias),[7] who conquered from a by then tottering 'Abbasid Caliphate the March of Lykandos on the East Roman Government's behalf in the

---

[1] See p. 246, above.

[2] For this no-man's-land, which gave birth not only to the East Roman Epic but also to both the 'Isaurian' and the 'Macedonian' dynasty of East Roman Emperors, see III. C (ii) (*b*), vol. iii, p. 274, footnote 2; IV. C (iii) (*c*) 2 (β), vol. iv, p. 365, footnote 4; and IV. C (iii) (*c*) 2 (β), Annex III, vol. iv, p. 630, above.

[3] The lay of the Akrítas Basil Digénis is not the only piece of Byzantine Greek epic poetry to which this Romano-Arab borderland has given birth. It has also generated the heroic ballad of Armourópoulos, which seems to have been precipitated by historical events which occurred in the ninth century (see Grégoire, H.: 'Autour de Digénis Akritas' in *Byzantion*, vol. vii (Brussels 1932, Secrétariat de la Revue), pp. 292–3, and the present chapter, p. 255, footnote 3, below), and likewise the cycle of Andronicus and Constantine Ducas, who are historical personages of the tenth century (see Grégoire, H.: 'L'Âge Héroïque de Byzance' in *Mélanges Offerts à M. Nicolas Jorga* (Paris 1933, Gamber), p. 391; eundem: 'Études sur l'Épopée Byzantine' in *Revue des Études Grecques*, vol. xlvi (Paris 1933, Leroux), pp. 48–61).

[4] For the origin and character of this East Roman army-corps and military district, see II. D (iii), vol. ii, p. 81, with footnote 1, and II. D (v), vol. ii, p. 153, with footnote 1, and IV. C (ii) (*b*) 1, vol. iv, p. 73, above.

[5] Grégoire, H.: 'Le Tombeau et la Date de Digénis Akritas (Samosate, vers 940 après J.-C.)' in *Byzantion*, vol. vi (Brussels 1931, Secrétariat de la Revue), p. 499. Cf. eundem: 'L'Épopée Byzantine et ses Rapports avec l'Épopée Turque et l'Épopée Romane' in Académie Royale de Belgique: *Bulletin de la Classe des Lettres et des Sciences Morales et Politiques*, 5ᵉ Série (Brussels 1930, Lamertin), p. 464.

[6] Grégoire, 'L'Épopée', p. 464.   [7] See p. 242, above.

reign of the Emperor Leo VI (*imperabat* A.D. 886–911) and afterwards cooperated with the East Roman general John Curcuas
in the more ambitious conquest of the larger and more important
Arab March of Malaṭīyah, on the right bank of the Upper Euphrates, in A.D. 928.[1] The scene of the Byzantine Greek epic hero's
imaginary life was transferred from the Taurus to this conquered
territory farther north-east, and the domain in the ancient district of Commagene which is assigned by the poet to the Cappadocian Akrítas corresponds exactly with the domain which is
known to have been assigned by the East Roman Government to
their Armenian servant, Mleh 'in real life'.[2]

It will be seen that, from the Arab point of view, the East
Roman 'borderers' whose features have been combined to compose the imaginary portrait of the hero of a Byzantine Greek
epic poem were members of an external proletariat who had
broken through the north-western *limes* of the 'Abbasid Caliphate
when the Syrian universal state, which the Arabs had re-established,[3] was *in extremis*; and the celebration of such barbarian
feats of arms in epic poetry is something that we have now learnt
to expect on the strength of the instances that have already come
to our notice in the histories of other alien invaders of other
collapsing universal states. The content of the Byzantine Greek
Epic has, however, been enriched—and its history, by the same
token, complicated—by reason of two facts which are both of
them peculiar to this particular example of the phenomenon that
we are now studying.

In the first place the East Roman Empire was something more
than the barbarian no-man's-land which it looked like in the
eyes of Arab wardens of the 'Abbasid marches whose acquaintance
with the enemy's country was confined to the wilder regions
adjoining the border. The East Roman Empire was, as we have
seen in another context,[4] a deliberate reconstruction of a Roman
Empire which had been the Hellenic universal state, and in
Byzantine Greek eyes it was the East Roman 'borderers' who
were the wardens of the marches of Civilization and their Arab
neighbours who were the transfrontier barbarians. The Arabs

---

[1] For the East Roman wars of aggression against the 'Abbasid Caliphate and its
'successor-states' which began with the campaigns of Curcuas see IV. C (iii) (c) 2 (β),
vol. iv, pp. 399–400, above. The submission of Malaṭīyah in A.D. 928 seems to have
been followed by a military occupation in 934.
[2] Grégoire, 'L'Épopée', p. 464; idem: 'Études sur l'Épopée Byzantine' in *Revue
des Études Grecques*, vol. xlvi (Paris 1933, Leroux), pp. 64–8; idem: 'Autour de Digénis
Akritas', p. 288. Compare Goossens, R.: 'Autour de Digénis Akritas' in *Byzantion*,
vol. vii (Brussels 1932, Secrétariat de la Revue), p. 316: 'Les chants épiques ont suivi,
de la Cappadoce à l'Euphrate et à la Syrie, les frontières changeantes des deux empires
dont ils retracent les luttes.'   [3] See I. C (ii) (b), vol. i, pp. 76–7, above.
[4] In IV. C (iii) (c) 2 (β), vol. iv, pp. 322–3 and 340–5, above.

had, indeed, actually played the part assigned to them in the Byzantine mental picture of Arabo-Byzantine relations. Before ever the East Roman 'borderers' found their opportunity to take the offensive at the 'Abbasid Caliphate's expense, the Arabs had conducted, twice in every year, regular seasonal raids into East Roman territory from a *place d'armes* on the Cilician Plain at Tarsus;[1] and the other Arab raiders who had been operating less systematically, and on a smaller scale, from a secondary base at Malatīyah had anticipated the East Roman 'borderers' in running true to the type of barbarians on the war-path. These Melitenian marchmen of the 'Abbasid Caliphate had celebrated their exploits on East Roman ground in a local epic of their own, which, like the contemporary Byzantine Greek Epic, was precipitated by the deeds of two historical personages. The first of these (corresponding to the East Roman officer Diogenes) was the Sayyid Battāl,[2] who died fighting against the East Romans in A.D. 739, at the Battle of Akroinon. The second (corresponding to the East Roman Government's Armenian henchman Mleh) was a margrave of Malatīyah named 'Umar, who played a part in the capture of the East Roman fortress of Amorium in A.D. 838[3] and was finally overtaken, defeated, and killed in A.D. 863, in the course of a raid on Amisus, by the East Roman General Petronas.[4] This Muslim Melitenian Epic seems also to have derived some of its inspiration from the ninth-century exploits of the Paulicians in the adjoining district of Tephrice,[5] who, though not co-religionists of the Melitenian Arabs, had in common with them a perpetual feud with their other neighbours the East Romans. In the earliest of the foreign versions in which the Melitenian Arab Epic has come down to us at second hand the historical Paulician leaders Chrysocheir and Carbeas are made into the Amīr 'Umar's father and

---

[1] See II. D (vii), vol. ii, p. 368, with footnote 1, and IV. C (iii) (c) 2 (β), vol. iv, p. 400, footnote 2, above.

[2] See Grégoire, 'L'Épopée', pp. 468–70 and 480; eundem: 'Comment Sayyid Battāl, martyr musulman du viiie siècle, est-il devenu, dans la légende, le contemporain d'Amer (†863)?' in *Byzantion*, vol. xi (Brussels 1936), pp. 570–5.

[3] Amorium was not only the principal fortress in the Anatolic army-corps district; it was also the strategic key-point of all the Asiatic territories of the East Roman Empire, since it commanded the several routes leading from the south-eastern frontier to the Asiatic shores of the Bosphorus. The fall of Amorium in A.D. 838 made an impression on East Roman hearts and minds of which the depth and strength are attested by the existence of a Byzantine Greek heroic ballad of which the hero (Armourópoulos = the son of one of the East Roman defenders of Amorium whom the victorious Arabs had carried away captive) avenges and effaces the disaster by the feat of crossing the Euphrates and defeating the Arabs in their own territory (Grégoire, H.: 'L'Âge Héroïque de Byzance' in *Mélanges Offerts à M. Nicolas Jorga* (Paris 1933, Gamber), pp. 388–9; idem, 'Études', pp. 32–47; idem, 'Le Règne de Michel III' in *Byzantion*, vol. v (Paris 1930, Champion), p. 329).

[4] For 'Umar's death see Grégoire, 'L'Épopée', p. 469; eundem: 'Le Règne de Michel III dans l'Épopée Byzantine' in *Byzantion*, vol. v (Paris 1930, Champion), p. 332.

[5] For the death-struggle between the Paulician Republic of Tephrice and the East Roman Empire in the ninth century of the Christian Era see IV. C (iii) (c) 2 (β), vol. iv, pp. 364–6, above.

uncle respectively, and the capture of Amorium in A.D. 838 is attributed to them.[1]

This Melitenian Arab Epic with a Paulician tincture in it must have already taken shape by the year A.D. 928, when the 'Abbasid March of Malatīyah was incorporated into the East Roman Empire. If the annexation of this Muslim territory had been carried out in the same grim spirit and brutal manner as that of the Paulician Republic of Tephrice some fifty-three years before, in or about A.D. 875, the East Romans might never have deigned to acquaint themselves with the work of the Melitenian minstrels' art and would certainly never have allowed it to have any influence on their own epic literature. What has complicated the history of the Byzantine Greek Epic is the fact that the incorporation of Arab Malatīyah into the East Roman Empire was achieved in the end by a voluntary capitulation which satisfied the *amour propre* of both parties and which was followed by a fraternization between these ancient enemies. The Melitenian Arab margrave Abu Hafs who tendered his submission to the East Roman general John Curcuas in A.D. 928[2] thenceforward fought, side by side with his conqueror, in the East Roman campaigns against Abu Hafs' own co-religionists in the interior of the 'Abbasid Empire.[3] The East Romans responded by taking their new companions-in-arms to their bosom; and they gave a gracious literary expression to this union of hearts by incorporating into their own epic of the Akrítas the Melitenian Epic in which the leading figure was Abu Hafs' grandfather the Amīr 'Umar.[4] The association of the Melitenian

---

[1] Grégoire, 'Études', p. 64; idem, 'Le Règne de Michel III', p. 329. These attributions are made in the Byzantine Greek version of the Melitenian Arab Epic which now figures as Part One of the final form of the epic poem of Basil Digénis Akrítas.

[2] Grégoire, 'L'Épopée', p. 466.

[3] Grégoire, 'Le Tombeau et la Date de Digénis Akritas', p. 497.

[4] The tenth-century Byzantine Greek version of the Melitenian Epic which constitutes Part One of the poem of Digénis in its final form is not the only trace of the Melitenian Epic that has come down to us. It can also be traced in one of the stories in the Arabian Nights (see Goossens, R.: 'Autour de Digénis Akritas: la "Geste d'Omar" dans les Mille et une Nuits' in *Byzantion*, vol. vii (Brussels 1932), pp. 305–12) and in an Arabic romance of the Romano-'Abbasid wars called *Dhāt al-Himmah wa 'l-Battāl* (see Goossens, op. cit., p. 317, and Canard, M.: 'Delhemma: Sayyid Battāl et 'Omar al-No'mān' in *Byzantion*, vol. xii (Brussels 1937), pp. 183–8). Moreover the Melitenian Epic seems to have enriched a non-Arabic literature twice over. After having, in the tenth century of the Christian Era, provided the materials for the present Part One of the Byzantine Greek epic poem of Digénis Akrítas, it similarly provided, in the twelfth century, the materials for a Turkish Epic of which the hero is the Sayyid Battāl (though the Akrítas figures in this Turkish poem, too, as a secondary character under the name of Akrates). The *terminus post quem* for the composition of this Turkish version of the Melitenian Epic is the conquest of the March of Malatīyah by the Muslim Turkish barbarian invader Gumushtigīn son of Dānishmand at the end of the eleventh century of the Christian Era in the wake of the Saljūqs (see I. C (i) (b), vol. i, p. 106, footnote 1; I. C (i) (b), Annex, vol. i, p. 349, footnote 1; IV. C (ii) (b) 1, vol. iv, p. 71; and IV. C (iii) (c) 2 (β), vol. iv, p. 398, above). The *terminus prae quem* cannot be very much later, since the last historical event mentioned in this Turkish Epic is the First Crusade (*gerebatur* A.D. 1096–9), while the last 'Abbasid Caliph mentioned is Mu'tasim (*imperabat* A.D. 833–42), who was the contemporary of the Amīr 'Umar of Malatīyah,

margrave 'Umar with the Cappadocian akrítas Diogenes was neatly effected by a slight manipulation of the name of a Byzantine Greek literary hero whose historical nucleus had long since faded out of mind.

'L'Émir, que chantait sans doute plus d'une cantilène de Malatia, devint le père du héros grec, et Akritas lui-même, étant Digénis[1] ou fils de deux races, put être le héros commun des Grecs et des Syriens, des Cappadociens et des Euphratésiens. Le poème grec, avec ses deux parties, est la traduction poétique de l'annexion de Malatia.'[2]

In the poem of Digénis as we have it, Part One is devoted to the glorification of Digénis' suppositious father 'the Amīr', and the poem breathes throughout a spirit of reconciliation between Greek and Arab. The Amīr is represented as abandoning Islam for Christianity out of love for the Greek princess who is to be Digénis' mother.[3] The Amīr's raids into East Roman territory are celebrated as heroic feats of arms, while Digénis is never made to fight Arabs, but only East Roman outlaws.[4] There is no touch, in the poem, of religious animosity.[5]

The weaving of the tenth-century Byzantine Greek epic poet's[6] rope out of the diverse strands[7] which offered themselves to his hand on either side of the Romano-'Abbasid military frontier[8] has been deftly epitomized by the Belgian scholar who has taken the lead in unravelling this complex piece of literary history.

the hero of Part One of the poem of Digénis (see Grégoire, 'L'Épopée', pp. 471-3 and 480; Canard, 'Delhemma', pp. 186-7).

[1] Sic, for 'Diogenes'.—A.J.T.
[2] Grégoire, 'L'Épopée', p. 478.
[3] Grégoire, 'L'Épopée', p. 465.
[4] Grégoire, 'L'Épopée', p. 465.
[5] Grégoire, 'L'Épopée', pp. 466-8.

[6] The tenth-century rhapsode who composed the poem of Digénis as we have it was perhaps the pupil of Paphlagonian ballad-singers who are casually mentioned by Arethas of Caesarea (vivebat A.D. 850-932) (see Grégoire, 'Autour de Digénis Akritas', p. 291)

[7] See Grégoire, 'Le Tombeau et la Date de Digénis Akritas', p. 491; eundem, 'Autour de Digénis Akritas', p. 289.

[8] The only sources of the poem of Digénis that concern us for our present purpose are the Byzantine Greek heroic poetry from the East Roman side of the border and the Arab heroic poetry from the March of Malatīyah; but at least two other sources which have also been laid under contribution have been detected by the critics. One of these is the contemporary sophisticated Byzantine literature written in Attic Greek: e.g. the work of the historian Genesius (Bonn edition, pp. 121-6) appears to have been drawn upon by the rhapsode who made the present Part One of the poem of Digénis out of the Arab Epic of Malatīyah (Grégoire, 'Le Règne de Michel III', pp. 329-31; idem, 'Le Tombeau et la Date de Digénis Akritas', pp. 493-4). Another source was archaeological. Certain conspicuous ancient monuments of Hellenic origin in Commagene (the southern fringe of the Arab March of Malatīyah, between the Taurus and the Euphrates) were associated with Digénis Akrítas in the rhapsode's imagination when the scene of the Byzantine epic hero's life and exploits was translated to this district after the incorporation of the March of Malatīyah into the East Roman Empire in A.D. 928 (Grégoire, 'Le Tombeau et la Date de Digénis Akritas', pp. 500-6). Similarly the name of one of Digénis' legendary adversaries, the Amazon Maximó, seems to have been taken from an ancient Greek inscription of circa A.D. 200 at Sebastopolis Pontica in honour of a certain 'Maxima alias Amazonis' (Grégoire, H., in Byzantion, vol. xi (Brussels 1936), pp. 607-10).

'De Digénis, héros du viiie siècle (?), un versificateur du temps du
Porphyrogénète [*imperabat* A.D. 911—59][1] fit à la fois, en l'honneur du
fondateur de la dynastie macédonienne, un Basile, et, en l'honneur
des vaillants soldats du dernier thème-frontière, un éponyme de ce
thème de Lykandos ou des Akrites. Réunissant sur sa tête la gloire
impériale de Basile le Macédonien, les exploits récents et historiques
de l'Arménien Mleh; évoquant par son second nom des prouesses
fabuleuses comme la lutte contre le dieu de la mort; enfin, grâce à
l'habile "calembour" d'un rhapsode, recueillant, lui, soldat chrétien,
toute la célébrité d'une ascendance musulmane et paulicienne où
figuraient les plus redoutables ennemis de Byzance au ixe siècle: Amer,
Chrysochir, Carbeas, ainsi que toute la renommée d'une antique souche
cappadocienne, les Kinnamos, et des deux familles historiques quasi-
impériales, les Moselès et les Dukas — Basile Digénis Akritas, le plus
composite des héros, nous apparaît comme la somme de la gloire
militaire arabo-byzantine au milieu du xe siècle.'[2]

It will be seen that on the Euphratean front of the 'Abbasid
Caliphate the creative effect, on the literary plane, of the border
warfare between Arabs and East Romans was not one-sided but
was reciprocal. Before the barbarian experience of breaking
through the *limes* of a tottering Syriac universal state had inspired Byzantine Greek bards to compose the epic poem of which
the hero is Basil Digénis Akrítas, the Melitenian Arab marchmen
of the 'Abbasid Empire in its heyday had tasted, for their part,
the selfsame barbarian experience in their own raids into the
East Roman Empire, and had been inspired by their exultation
over these exploits to express themselves in a work of the self-
same epic genre of literature. The literary reciprocity between
the two contending parties on this particular military border is
commemorated in the mixed birth attributed to the hero of the
Byzantine Greek Epic and in the duplication of the poem, which
celebrates in Part One the exploits of the East Roman 'borderer's'
Melitenian Arab adversaries before dealing in Part Two with
the exploits of the Akrítas himself.[3] This peculiar feature of the

---

[1] The date of the composition of the poem as we now have it can be located within
narrower chronological limits than those of Constantine Porphyrogenitus's forty-eight
years-long reign. Part One must have been incorporated, from its Melitenian Arab
source, after the capitulation of Abu Hafs to John Curcuas in A.D. 928 (see above). On
the other hand the political geography of the Romano-'Abbasid frontier, as this is presented in the poem, shows that the poet must have finished his work before A.D. 969,
when the situation described or taken for granted in the poem was radically changed
as a result of the conquests made by the East Roman Emperor Nicephorus Phocas.
More than that, we can infer that the poem was completed before A.D. 944, since it
refers to the sacred relic of Edessa, which was transferred to Constantinople in that
year, as being at Edessa, without any allusion to its translation (on this question of date
see Grégoire, 'L'Épopée', pp. 463–4; eundem, 'Le Tombeau et la Date de Digénis
Akritas', pp. 486–7).—A.J.T.   [2] Grégoire, 'Études', p. 69.

[3] The way in which this literary reciprocity worked has been analysed as follows by
Grégoire, H.: 'Échanges Épiques Arabo-Grecs' in *Byzantion*, vol. vii (Brussels 1932),
p. 378:
'Il y a eu, d'un camp à l'autre, des échanges et des emprunts constants de motifs

Byzantine Greek epic poem of Digenis, which was precipitated by the East Roman 'borderers" barbarian feat of breaking through the *limes* of the 'Abbasid Caliphate in the tenth century of the Christian Era, is not to be found in the French *Chanson de Roland*, which appears to have been precipitated in the eleventh century by a corresponding barbarian feat of the French 'borderers' at the expense of the Andalusian Umayyad Caliphate and its indigenous 'successor-states' in the Iberian Peninsula. The problem presented by the *Chanson de Roland* is of a different order.

The original assonanced version of the *Chanson de Roland* is known to have been composed some time between A.D. 1080 and 1130;[1] and all the seventy or eighty *chansons de geste* of which the *Roland* heads the list are works of the twelfth and thirteenth centuries.[2] So much is common ground. But, because the heroes of this twelfth-century and thirteenth-century French heroic poetry are mental projections of mortal men who lived in the flesh in the generation of Charlemagne, while the date of the historical Battle of Roncesvalles is known to have been A.D. 778, it has been assumed by one school of modern Western scholars that a twelfth-century poem which has Roncesvalles for its theme and Roland for its protagonist must be the late flower of a work of art which had grown like a plant and had sprung from a seed that had been sown—as the seed of the corresponding Byzantine Greek Epic may have been sown[3]—more than three hundred years earlier. On this view we should have to believe that at least the elements of the *Chanson de Roland* took shape on the morrow of those eighth-century events that are celebrated in the poem as we have it. It has been left for a perhaps more judicious scholar of our own generation to maintain by weighty arguments that the earliest extant version of the *Chanson de Roland* is not the ultimate outcome of a long plant-like growth, but is the original creation of a single poet; and the gist of the demonstration consists in a circumstantial proof that the historical events that have kindled this twelfth-century poet's imagination are not those eighth-century campaigns of Charlemagne that have provided Turoldus with his theme, but are eleventh-century expeditions of crusading French war-bands[4] which were the liveliest living

---

"épiques". Mais toujours, et c'est naturel, le poète ou le conteur, soit byzantin, soit musulman, a introduit dans le thème plus ou moins banal une pointe à l'adresse des ennemis, ou des personnages d'origine étrangère. Ce sont ainsi de perpétuels renversements de rôles. Le problème se complique du fait même que les emprunts ne viennent pas toujours du même côté du *limes*. Une partie de la geste de Mélitène a été empruntée par les Grecs. Mais les Arabes ont riposté, en reprenant à leurs adversaires des histoires byzantines dont ils ont pour la plupart *retourné* la tendance.'

[1] Bédier, J.: *Les Légendes Épiques*, 2nd edition, vol. iii (Paris 1921, Champion), p. 191.
[2] Bédier, op. cit., vol. iii, p. 3.
[3] See p. 253, above.   [4] See pp. 242–3, above.

social experiences of the poet's countrymen in the poet's own age.

'La *Chanson de Roland* n'étant rien qu'un épisode d'une guerre sainte en Espagne, à quelle époque naît l'idée de guerre sainte? Est-ce au temps de Charlemagne? Non; ce n'est ni de son temps, ni au ixe siècle, ni au xe;[1] mais bien au xie, dans la période qui précède immédiatement l'apparition de la *Chanson de Roland*.

'Cette période, des expéditions de chevaliers français en Espagne l'ont remplie. . . . Pour rendre compte de la *Chanson de Roland*, "il serait . . . naturel de rappeler ce qui s'était passé ou se passait au moment où le trouvère composait ses laisses, c'est-à-dire la guerre permanente que les seigneurs français faisaient aux Sarrasins d'Espagne depuis le début du xie siècle; tel est le fait d'histoire qui a déterminé l'auteur et inspiré son travail entier."[2]

'Ces chevaliers en effet qui au xie siècle s'acheminaient vers les antiques champs de bataille de Guillaume et de Roland, prenons garde qu'ils ont ressemblé au Guillaume des chansons de geste plus encore que le Guillaume de l'Histoire lui-même, au Roland des chansons de geste plus encore que le Roland de l'Histoire. Le Roland de l'Histoire meurt dans les Pyrénées en combattant les Basques, des Chrétiens; mais les chevaliers du xie siècle traversaient les Pyrénées pour s'offrir aux coups de vrais Sarrasins. Pour eux, bien plus que pour le Roland historique, la guerre sainte fut une réalité.

'Ce sont eux, croyons-nous, qui, les premiers, ont réveillé sur les routes le souvenir des expéditions de Charlemagne. . . . Comme Charlemagne ils s'arrêtaient à ces étapes nécessaires: Bordeaux, Sorde, Dax, Saint-Jean-Pied-de-Port. Ils campaient à Blaye, bivouaquaient à Roncevaux. A Blaye les clercs de Saint-Romain leur montraient la tombe de Roland; à Roncevaux ils vénéraient le lieu de son martyre.'[3]

If we accept the theory of the origin and inspiration of the *Chanson de Roland* which is set forth in these terms by Monsieur Bédier, we are entitled to describe the French Epic as a creation of the European wing of the external proletariat of the Syriac

[1] Compare the absence of any trace of the crusading spirit in the tenth-century version of the Byzantine Greek epic poem of Basil Digénis Akrítas (see p. 257, above). —A.J.T.

[2] Luchaire, A., in *Histoire de France depuis les Origines jusqu'à la Révolution*, publiée sous la direction d'Ernest Lavisse, vol. ii, part (2) (Paris 1911, Hachette), p. 392.

[3] Bédier, op. cit., vol. iii, pp. 368–9 and 372–3. The tomb at Blaye, which was exhibited as the tomb of Roland to the eleventh-century French war-bands on the Pyrenaean war-path, as well as to the pilgrims of later generations who followed the Crusaders' trail to the shrine of Saint James at Compostella, will recall to the mind of a classical scholar the grave-mounds that stand out on the sky-line above the shore of the Troad as the ship on which he is travelling from the Peiraeus to Constantinople approaches the mouth of the Dardanelles; for in the Classical Age of Hellenic history these mounds were known to fame as the graves of Achilles and Patroclus. Since he first made this note, the writer has learned from Monsieur H. Grégoire ('Le Tombeau et la Date de Digénis Akritas', pp. 500–2) that the tomb attributed to Roland's Byzantine counterpart was in fact a grave-mound of precisely this type and location—standing out, as it did, on the sky-line within conspicuous view of one of the main overland thoroughfares in Commagene.

World, corresponding to the Byzantine Greek Epic[1] of Basil Digénis Akrítas which was created by the Asiatic wing of the same external proletariat under the stimulus of the same experience of breaking through the *limes* of a tottering Syriac universal state. In both the French and the Byzantine Greek Epic we can also see a true analogue of the Teutonic Epic which was created by the North European wing of the external proletariat of the Hellenic World, and with equal justification we may compare them both with the Homeric Epic which was created by the Continental European external proletariat of the Minoan 'thalassocracy'. The emergence of this set of correspondences is possibly an indication that we are on the right track, and is certainly an encouragement to persevere in our present line of exploration.

The Sumeric External Proletariat.

Now that we have finished our examination of the Syriac Civilization's external proletariat, the Babylonic Civilization thrusts itself next upon our attention; but, just because the histories of the Syriac and Babylonic worlds are so closely intertwined in their disintegration-phases, we shall not win much more grist for our mill by threshing a harvest from the Babylonic field. When we scan the last two centuries of the Babylonic 'Time of Troubles' (*durabat circa* 1000–600 B.C.),[2] we behold the selfsame barbarian war-bands that have already become familiar to us in our study of the almost contemporaneous Syriac 'Time of Troubles' (*durabat circa* 925–525 B.C.). We see the Cimmerians and Scythians bearing down upon South-Western Asia out of the Eurasian Steppe, and the Arabs simultaneously encroaching upon the desert borders of Babylonia and Syria.[3] But we have observed and noted these particular barbarian offensives already; and we may therefore take leave to pass on at once to the history of the Sumeric Civilization which looms up in the Babylonic Society's historical background.

The Sumeric 'Time of Troubles' was opened, as we have seen,[4] by the destructive career of Lugalzaggisi, the militarist master of Erech (Uruk) and Umma (*dominabatur circa* 2677–2653 B.C.), and it was brought to a close (*circa* 2298 B.C.) when

---

[1] Save for the apparent absence, in the French Epic, of any trace of that reciprocal literary influence between the contending parties on the two sides of the border which is an outstanding feature of the Byzantine Greek Epic (see pp. 254–9, above).

[2] The annihilation of the Assyrian state, army, and people in the war of 914–910 B.C. (see IV. C (iii) (c) 3 (α), vol. iv, pp. 468–70 and 482–4, above) may be taken as the culmination and close (see V. C (ii) (b), vol. vi, p. 308, below) of a 'Time of Troubles' which was followed by the establishment of a short-lived indigenous Babylonic universal state in the shape of the Neo-Babylonian Empire (see I. C (i) (b), vol. i, pp. 79 and 119, above).

[3] See Part III. A, Annex II, vol. iii, p. 410, above.

[4] In I. C (i) (b), vol. i, p. 109, and IV. C (ii) (b) 1, vol. iv, p. 64, above. See also V. C (ii) (b), vol. vi, p. 296, below.

Ur-Engur of Ur established 'the Empire of Sumer and Akkad' which became the Sumeric universal state.[1] This age of Sumeric history witnessed the formation of three anti-barbarian frontiers: one towards the Anatolian Plateau, another towards the Iranian Plateau, and a third towards the North Arabian Steppe.

On the Anatolian front the peaceful penetration of Cappadocia by Assyrian traders and prospectors, which had been going on while the Sumeric Society was in growth, was transformed, after the breakdown, into a military occupation in the twenty-seventh century B.C., when the Akkadian conqueror Sargon of Agade (*dominabatur circa* 2652–2597 B.C.) led his troops across the Taurus.[2] By the twenty-sixth century the relations between the dominant minority of the Sumeric Society and its external proletariat had similarly passed over from peace into war on the Iranian front too; for one of the finest of the monuments of Sumeric sculpture that have been recovered by our modern Western archaeologists is a stele of Naramsin (*dominabatur circa* 2572–2517 B.C.) which displays the militarist Sargon's like-spirited descendant in the act of attacking and slaughtering the highlanders of the Zagros in their mountain-fastnesses. Thereafter, in the twenty-fifth century B.C., when some two hundred and fifty years of unbridled militarism had exhausted the Sumeric body social to a degree at which it became impotent even in warfare, the great-grandchildren of Naramsin's barbarian victims in the Zagros avenged the wrongs of their ancestors by launching a counter-offensive which resulted in a barbarian triumph. For more than a hundred years (*circa* 2429–2306 B.C.) the homeland of the Sumeric Society in 'Irāq had to bear the yoke of the victorious barbarian Gutaeans;[3] and this first experience of the bitterness of servitude to a barbarian master lasted until the eve of the foundation of the Sumeric universal state at the turn of the twenty-fourth century B.C. and the twenty-third.

In the meantime, while these Gutaean 'invaders from beyond the Zagros frontier were battening like vultures upon the heart of the Sumeric World, the Amorite Nomads from Arabia must have been engaged already on their slower but surer penetration of the western borderlands; for the Sumeric Emperor Hammurabi (*imperabat circa* 1947–1905 B.C.), who emulated Ur-Engur's achievement by reviving the Sumeric universal state which Ur-Engur had founded, was an Amorite in sentiment and tradition as well as in descent; the principality of Babylon, which was Ham-

[1] See I. C (i) (*b*), vol. i, p. 107, above, and V. C (ii) (*b*), vol. vi, p. 296, below.
[2] See I. C (i) (*b*), vol. i, p. 110, above, and V. C (ii) (*a*), vol. vi, p. 184, below.
[3] See I. C (i) (*b*), vol. i, p. 109, and the present chapter and volume, p. 203, above, and V. C (ii) (*a*), vol. vi, pp. 184 and 234, and V. C (ii) (*b*), vol. vi, pp. 296–7, below.

murabi's ancestral patrimony, was not only, as its name records, a mythical 'Gate of the Gods', but was also the historical gateway through which the Amorite barbarian interlopers found their way into the Land of Akkad out of the North Arabian Steppe; and, since we know that the First Dynasty of Babylon, in which Hammurabi is the greatest figure, had been founded—about a hundred years before his accession—*circa* 2049 B.C., we may perhaps infer that the Amorite barbarian invaders of the Sumeric World were already on the war-path[1] before the foundation, at the beginning of the twenty-third century B.C., of the Sumeric universal state which was to be revived and administered, in the fullness of time, by a Babylonian Amorite saviour of the Sumeric Society.

It will be seen that, on at least two fronts out of the three, the culmination of the Sumeric 'Time of Troubles' was marked by encroachments or attacks on the part of the external proletariat, and that one of these attacks was unusually successful. If we set ourselves to translate these Sumeric transactions into terms of more familiar events in Hellenic history, we shall find our parallel to the Amorite infiltration into Syria and Akkad in the Arab infiltration into the same regions during the death agonies of the Seleucid Empire,[2] while we shall be inclined to compare the Gutaean invasion of the valley of the Tigris and Euphrates with the invasion of the valley of the Po by the Teutones and Cimbri.[3] But, in order to make this second comparison work out, we shall have to reverse the historical outcome of the decisive battle on the Raudian Plains outside the walls of Vercellae, and to imagine the barbarians of Northern Europe enjoying in the last century B.C., before the establishment of the *Pax Augusta*, a foretaste of the triumph which in fact they never achieved until the fifth century of the Christian Era, after the Hellenic universal state had both come and gone. Our comparison shows that the synchronization of a bout of exceptionally severe barbarian pressure with the climax of a 'Time of Troubles' is still more emphatically marked in Sumeric history than it is in Hellenic; and, when we reach the last act of the play and watch the curtain rise over the scene of the post-Sumeric interregnum, we find, here again, another bout of barbarian aggression at a stage in the action at which our Hellenic analogy would lead us to look for it.

In the post-Sumeric interregnum the first of the victorious barbarian onslaughts appears to have been delivered on the Zagros front by a horde of Nomads from a distant Eurasian

---

[1] For the indications of an Amorite Völkerwanderung about the middle of the third millennium B.C. see Part III. A, Annex II, vol. iii, p. 404, above.
[2] See pp. 215–16 and 218, above.   [3] See p. 218, above.

hinterland. The Aryas whose advance-guard burst into Egypt
out of the Syrian extremity of the Sumeric World about the year
1680 B.C. must have broken out of the Eurasian Steppe between
the Pamirs and the Caspian, and swept on south-westward across
the plateau of Iran and the plains of 'Irāq, within the two hundred
years that intervened between the moment when these invaders
eventually arrived at the north-east frontier of the Egyptiac
universal state and the earlier date at which the revived Sumeric
universal state had broken up irretrievably after the death of
Hammurabi *circa* 1905 B.C.[1] In contrast to the profound effect of
their impact upon Egyptiac history, these Nomads left so little
trace of their passage across 'Irāq that even the date of it is a matter
of inference; but we may conjecture that it was the Aryan invaders'
audacious trespass upon the home territories of the Sumeric Society
that revealed, in a flash, the decrepitude of the Sumeric universal state under the rule of Hammurabi's Babylonian Amorite
successors; and that it was this revelation that moved to action
certain other barbarian invaders who made a deeper mark.
At any rate we know that Sargon's aggression against the barbarians beyond the Taurus was paid back in the post-Sumeric
interregnum—more tardily but not less effectually than Naramsin's
aggression in the Zagros had been paid back by the Gutaeans
during the Sumeric 'Time of Troubles'—when King Mursil I
of Khatti, the principal barbarian 'successor-state' of the Empire
of Sumer and Akkad in Anatolia, not only raided the Land of
Shinar but actually captured and sacked the city of Babylon,[2]
which was the latter-day capital of the Sumeric universal state.
The Cappadocian raiders were content to evacuate Babylon, as
Alaric evacuated Rome in A.D. 410, with their hands full of booty
and their souls satisfied by the achievement of a revenge which by
this time was perhaps as much as nine hundred years overdue;
but, while this barbarian wave from beyond the Taurus ebbed as
rapidly as the Nomad wave from beyond the Zagros had rolled on,
the Land of Shinar did not have peace; for the withdrawal of the
Hittites back to the Taurus was followed immediately by the
descent of the Kassite highlanders down from the Zagros; and
the Kassites, like their predecessors the Gutaeans, came to stay.
They sat ponderously upon the neck of a prostrate Babylonia
from 1749 to 1173 B.C.[3]

[1] For the circumstances and date of the Aryan invasion of South-Western Asia and
the lower valley of the Nile and the upper valley of the Indus see I. C (i) (*b*), vol. i,
pp. 104–7 and p. 111, footnote 1; and II. D (vii), vol. ii, pp. 388–91, above.
[2] See I. C (i) (*b*), vol. i, pp. 110–11, and IV. C (ii) (*b*) 1, vol. iv, p. 64, with footnote
1, above. As has been noted already in the latter of these two places, this event is dated
as early as *circa* 1806 B.C. by Delaporte and as late as *circa* 1750 B.C. by Meyer.
[3] See I. C (i) (*b*), vol. i, p. 111, and IV. C (ii) (*b*) 1, vol. iv, p. 64, above.

In this post-Sumeric interregnum, again, we catch glimpses of an originality, and even a creativity, in the barbarian camp along the lines with which we have become familiar in our Hellenic prototype.

We may conjecture, for example, that the Aryas were profiting from the stimulus of their experience in breasting, and eventually breaking through, the north-east frontier of the Sumeric universal state when they created a characteristically barbarian religion and poetry which have been embedded—not in the Land of Shinar, but on the adjacent soil of the Indus Culture—in the Vedic Pantheon[1] and the Sanskrit Epic[2] of an Indic Civilization that sprang from this soil after the dust of the Aryan Völkerwanderung had settled down. There is no corresponding trace of these Aryan works of religious and poetic creation on Egyptiac soil during the brief episode of the Hyksos' occupation of the Delta of the Nile; yet this extreme right wing of the Aryan horde displayed at least a negative originality in refusing to capitulate to the established religion of the Egyptiac World which these migrant Nomads had overrun. During the hundred years of their dominion over the derelict domain of 'the Middle Empire' which had been the Egyptiac universal state, the Hyksos were not converted either to the worship of Re and the other gods of the Egyptiac dominant minority or to the worship of Osiris which was the 'higher religion' of the Egyptiac internal proletariat. They gave their allegiance to Set, who was the villain of the piece in the Osiris myth. And we may conjecture that it was the odiousness of the part which this God of Evil played in the Egyptiac Mythology that commended him to the Hyksos invaders and induced them to substitute Set for—or to identify Set with—their own Indra or whatever other Aryan name may have been borne by the barbarian war-god whom they had brought with them into Egypt as the divine leader of their raid.[3]

As for the Hittites and the Kassites, their religious history has less in common with that of the Hyksos than with that of the

---

[1] For the Vedic Pantheon see II. D (vii), Annex V, in vol. ii, and the present chapter, p. 232, above.

[2] In V. C (i) (c) 3, Annex II, below, an attempt is made to reconstruct the fifteen-hundred-years-long process of literary development through which the Sanskrit Epic, as we have it, grew out of the heroic poetry of the Aryan invaders of the Indus Valley in the second millennium B.C.

[3] For this worship of Set by the Hyksos and for its effect upon the course of Egyptiac religious history see I. C (ii), vol. i, p. 144; V. A, in the present volume, p. 3, footnote 4; and V. C (i) (c) 2, in the present volume, p. 152, above, and V. C (i) (c) 4, in the present volume, p. 351, below. The remnants of the Hyksos horde which survived in Syria after their expulsion from Egypt in the sixteenth century B.C. must have carried their Set-worship with them; for the name turns up, in a later age, in the Syriac Mythology. An Egyptiac priest would have found it hard to recognize his God of Evil in the human Seth of Genesis iv. 25–6, who is 'the good boy' in the family of Adam and Eve, and who is rewarded for his virtue by being made the progenitor of Noah.

Aryan invaders of the Indus Valley. Both the Hittite masters of Cappadocia and the Kassite masters of the Land of Shinar appear to have amalgamated a barbarian pantheon of their own creation with the pantheon of the Sumeric dominant minority; but the two resultant syncretistic religions evidently differed markedly in the respective proportions in which the several ingredients entered into the mixture. The sluggish Kassites, who had exposed themselves to the full blast of the Sumeric Civilization's influence by settling upon the metropolitan territory of the Sumeric World, were content to adopt the native worships of Marduk-Bel and Shamash under the names of their own imported gods Kharbe and Buriash;[1] and even these names would have passed into oblivion if they had not happened to enter into the compound titles of Kassite kings who sat on the Throne of Babylon. On the other hand the lively Hittites substituted their own barbarian pantheon for all but a remnant of those Sumeric worships that had managed to obtain a foothold in the outlying Cappadocian province of the Sumeric Society's domain.[2]

The Egyptiac External Proletariat.

In the Egyptiac World we find three anti-barbarian fronts: first the north-eastern front—facing towards South-Western Asia across the Desert of Sinai—through which the Hyksos broke in about the year 1680 B.C.; second a southern front, up the Nile, over against the barbarians of Tropical Africa; and, third, a north-western front which faced towards North-West Africa across the Libyan Desert.

On the Asiatic front the Egyptiac 'Time of Troubles', as well as the post-Egyptiac interregnum, was signalized by an accentuation of barbarian pressure; for the Hyksos who broke through this front at the beginning of the interregnum, in the earlier part of the seventeenth century B.C., had been anticipated by an earlier horde of Asiatic barbarian invaders who had delivered their attack in the middle of the third millennium B.C. and who are perhaps to be identified with the Amorite Afrasian Nomads who, at that very time, were drifting out of the North Arabian Steppe into the western fringes of the Sumeric World.[3] Unlike the Hyksos, these earlier Asiatic invaders suffered a repulse; but the Egyptiac Society only saved itself from a barbarian conquest on this occasion at the cost of a supreme military effort[4] which

---

[1] See I. C (i) (b), vol. i, p. 116, above, and V. C (i) (d) 6 (δ), in the present volume, p. 529, below.   [2] See I. C (i) (b), vol. i, p. 112, above.
[3] See Part III. A, Annex II, vol. iii, p. 404, and the present chapter in the present volume, pp. 203 and 262–3, above.
[4] Meyer, E.: Geschichte des Altertums, third edition, vol. i, part (2) (Stuttgart and Berlin 1913, Cotta), pp. 232–3.

brought on, with a run, the disintegration of the Egyptiac Civilization. The Asiatic barbarians were repelled by King Pepi I (*regnabat circa* 2400–2380 B.C.), and the crash[1] came in the reign of the victor's successor King Pepi II (*regnabat circa* 2376–2282 B.C.).[2]

The Asiatic barbarian offensive in the time of Pepi I appears to have been a retort to a previous Egyptiac movement of aggressive expansion which had begun, with the beginning of the Egyptiac 'Time of Troubles', under the Fifth Dynasty;[3] and the Sixth Dynasty, of which Pepi I was the third representative on the Pharaonic Throne, seems not only to have kept up this offensive on the Asiatic front until the eve of the Asiatic barbarian counter-stroke, but also to have taken the offensive on the Upper Nile front as well.[4]

In another context[5] we have already made some study of the effect of this southern anti-barbarian frontier of the Egyptiac World upon the internal life of the Egyptiac Society; and we have observed that the foundation of the Egyptiac universal state *circa* 2070/2060 B.C., as well as the foundation of the United Kingdom *circa* 3200 B.C., was the work of empire-builders who arose in the Southern March and whose military prowess had presumably been acquired in frontier-warfare against the adjoining barbarians. After the Theban princes of the Eleventh and Twelfth Dynasties had accomplished their oecumenical task of giving internal unity and peace to an Egyptiac World that had been distracted by a 'Time of Troubles', they turned back as Emperors of an Egyptiac universal state, with all the resources of the Egyptiac World now at their command, to fulfil their own special mission of serving as wardens of the Southern March.

[1] Meyer, op. cit., vol. i, part (2), pp. 234–5, and the present Study, IV. C (ii) (*b*) 2, vol. iv, p. 84, above.

[2] These dates are reckoned on the basis of Eduard Meyer's chronology for the period of Egyptiac history before the foundation of 'the New Empire' by the first Emperor of the Eighteenth Dynasty, Amosis, *circa* 1580 B.C. While there is a consensus among modern Western scholars in regard to the chronology of the periods of Egyptiac history *post* 1580 B.C., there is still a wide divergence of opinion in regard to the earlier—and historically far more important and interesting—ages. Meyer's reconstruction, which is one of the shortest in span, appears to the writer of this Study to be the most convincing; and the approximate dates here assigned to the reigns of the two Pepis are arrived at by a comparison of two passages in Meyer's *Geschichte des Altertums*: vol. i, part (2), third edition (Stuttgart and Berlin 1913, Cotta), p. 236, and 'Die ältere Chronologie Babyloniens, Assyriens und Ägyptens' (Stuttgart and Berlin 1925, Cotta), p. 68. The dating cannot be more than approximate owing to the defectiveness of our information. The combined duration of the Sixth and Eighth Dynasties is known to have been 181 years, which Meyer equates with the years 2423–2243 B.C.; and we also know that Pepi I and Pepi II were respectively the third and the fifth king in this series; that Pepi I reigned for 20 years and Pepi II for 94(!); and that there was an intervening reign of four years' duration. Unfortunately the lengths of the reigns of the first two kings of the series, as well as the seventh to the tenth inclusive, are unknown to us.

[3] Meyer, op. cit., vol. i, part (2), p. 209.

[4] See Meyer, op. cit., vol. i, part (2), pp. 211, 230–1, and 261.

[5] In II. D (v), vol. ii, pp. 112–18, above.

The military conquest of the Nile Valley from the head of the First Cataract to a point above the head of the Second was accomplished by a series of warlike emperors beginning with Amenemhat I (*imperabat circa* 2000–1971 B.C.) and ending with Senwosret III (*imperabat circa* 1887–1850 B.C.). And this forward movement on this front was merely retarded, without being reversed, by the decline of 'the Middle Empire' and by its disastrous end in the successful breach of the Asiatic front by the Hyksos. For, when the Hyksos were expelled and the Egyptiac universal state was restored by another dynasty of Theban princes, the emperors of this Eighteenth Dynasty followed the example of their predecessors of the Twelfth Dynasty in resuming the work of southward expansion as soon as they had fulfilled their prior task in the interior of the Egyptiac World. Under 'the New Empire' the southern military frontier against the Tropical African barbarians was carried forward, as early as the reign of Thothmes I (*imperabat circa* 1557–1505 B.C.), as far as the foot of the Fourth Cataract; and in this chapter of the history of the Southern March the military conquest was followed up by a cultural assimilation of the conquered barbarians which was carried out so thoroughly that the subsequent decay of 'the New Empire' did not bring with it any weakening of the hold of the Egyptiac culture upon the population of 'the New Empire's' Nubian dominions.

Upon the break-up of the 'New Empire' at the turn of the twelfth and eleventh centuries B.C. the frontier-fortress of Napata, which had been planted at the foot of the Fourth Cataract by Thothmes I, now became the capital of one of 'the New Empire's' local 'successor-states'; during the hundred years ending about the year 655 B.C. this Napatan principality came near to success in emulating the thrice-repeated Theban achievement of uniting the entire Egyptiac World into a single state; and, even after it had been forced to renounce this oecumenical ambition, the Napatan Power remained in being for another nine hundred years—during which it maintained its own political independence against the successive Achaemenian and Macedonian and Roman conquerors of the Lower Nile Valley below the First Cataract, and at the same time preserved and even extended the domain of the Egyptiac culture in the Upper Nile Valley. By 300 B.C. the social centre of gravity of this Ethiopian half of the Egyptiac World had moved so far to the south that Napata, which had been first the frontier-fortress of 'the New Empire' and then the capital of its Ethiopian 'successor-state', was forced to surrender this latter honour to Meroe, at the foot of the Sixth Cataract. It was not until the third century of the Christian Era that these successive encroachments of the Sixth[1] and Twelfth and Eighteenth Dynasties and their successors the Napatan and Meroitic princes of Ethiopia upon the domain of Tropical African barbarism at last evoked an effective barbarian counterstroke. In this century, when the Roman Empire only just succeeded in beating off the barbarian attacks that were launched against it simultaneously on all its four anti-barbarian fronts,[2] the principality of Ethiopia was overwhelmed and extinguished by a host of Nubian barbarian conquerors.

As for the third of the Egyptiac anti-barbarian frontiers, which faced across the Libyan desert towards North-West Africa, we find no certain trace of barbarian pressure here before the thirteenth century B.C.; and it is possible that the Libyan invasions of the Egyptiac World in this century and the next were not the direct results of hostile intercourse between the Egyptiac Society and the North-West African barbarians, but were rather a product of the post-Minoan Völkerwanderung. At any rate, these Libyan barbarian assaults upon Egypt overland coincided in date with those overseas attacks on the part of the sea-peoples of the Aegean that were undoubtedly a backwash from the troubling of the waters at the foundering of the Minoan 'thalassocracy'.[3] In some instances it is evident that the Libyan and Aegean offensives were not merely simultaneous, but were deliberately concerted. And it is likely to have been the Minoan rather than the Egyptiac Civilization whose radiation into North Africa stirred the local primitive peoples up and set them on the move; for North Africa was much more easily accessible to the Minoan pioneers across the waters of the Mediterranean than it was to any Egyptiac pioneers who may have had the hardihood to venture out among the Libyan sand-dunes.

In the supreme crisis of the barbarian offensive against the Egyptiac World on the Libyan and Aegean fronts at the turn of the thirteenth and twelfth centuries B.C. the Libyan as well as the Aegean invaders were repulsed;[4] but, unlike their Aegean comrades-in-arms, the vanquished Libyan war-bands did not take 'No' for an answer. While the discomfited Philistines and Teucrians settled down once for all in the Shephelah,[5] the Libyans who had been hurled back when they presented themselves as invaders soon returned to offer themselves as mercenaries, and within a few generations the children had captured by 'peaceful penetration' the promised land which the fathers had failed to

---

[1] See p. 267, above.   [2] See the present chapter, pp. 219–20, above.
[3] See I. C (i) (b), vol. i, p. 93, and the present chapter and volume, pp. 236–8, above, and V. C (i) (c) 4, p. 352, below.
[4] See I. C (i) (b), vol. i, pp. 93 and 101, IV. C (ii) (b) 2, vol. iv, p. 85, and IV. C (iii) (c) 2 (β), vol. iv, p. 422, above, and V. C (i) (c) 4, in the present volume, p. 352, and V. C (ii) (a), vol. vi, p. 207, below.   [5] See I. C (i) (b), vol. i, pp. 101–2, above.

take by storm. From the eleventh century B.C. onwards the domain
of the Egyptiac Society from the Delta as far southward as the
First Cataract was partitioned between the intrusive Libyan war-
lords in their garrison-towns and the tenacious Egyptiac priesthood in its temple-states.[1]

The Sinic External Proletariat.

In the Sinic World, as in the Babylonic and Syriac worlds, the
crucial anti-barbarian front was the frontier against the Eurasian
Nomads;[2] and in this case, as in those, a civilization which was
expanding in the course of its disintegration wantonly placed
itself in contact with these formidable neighbours through its own
act in breaking through a screen of highlander barbarians which
had formerly insulated the Desert from the Sown. Just as the
Assyrian conquest of the Medes in the eighth century B.C. opened
the door for an invasion of South-Western Asia by the Cimmerians
and the Scyths,[3] so the conquest of the barbarians in the Shensi
and Shansi highlands by the Sinic principalities of Ts'in and Chao
and Yen in the fourth century B.C. brought the Sinic World into
contact with the Hiongnu;[4] and, though in the Sinic arena 'the
Contending States' did not bring down upon themselves the
catastrophe of a Nomad avalanche, they dammed it back at
the cost of a Herculean effort.

During the last hundred years of the Sinic 'Time of Troubles'
the states on the Eurasian border managed to divert part of their
energies from their own fratricidal struggle for existence to the
still more urgent task of building dykes to stem the Nomad flood;
and, after the delivery of 'the knock-out blow' in the Sinic internal
struggle by King Chêng of Ts'in in 221 B.C.,[5] the victor justified
his assumption of the title of 'the first universal monarch'—*She
Hwang-ti*—by consolidating these haphazard local defences into
the Great Wall.[6] Yet even the construction of this classic artificial
limes did not solve the problem of the relations between the Sinic
Society and its Eurasian Nomad neighbours; for the unification of
the Sinic World into a universal state was answered by a counter-
unification of all the Nomads in the hinterland of the Great Wall,

[1] See IV. C (iii) (c) 2 (β), vol. iv, p. 422, above, and V. C (i) (c) 4, in the present
volume, pp. 352-3, below.
[2] The Sinic dominant minority were also confronted by an external proletariat in the
south, towards the southern watershed of the Yangtse Basin; but in this quarter they
succeeded in preventing the formation of an anti-barbarian frontier; for they kept the
southern barbarians on the run until, in this direction, they had extended the borders
of the Sinic World up to 'natural frontiers' which were furnished by the water's edge
of the South China Sea and by the eastern escarpment of the Tibetan Plateau (see V. C
(i) (c) 2, pp. 141-2 and 147, and the present chapter, p. 206, above).
[3] See II. D (v), vol. ii, p. 136, and the present chapter and volume, pp. 244-5, above.
[4] See II. D (v), vol. ii, pp. 118-19, and III. C (i) (b), vol. iii, p. 167, footnote 1, above.
[5] See I. C (i) (b), vol. i, p. 89, above.   [6] See II. D (v), vol. ii, p. 119, above.

from the Upper Sungari to the Upper Irtish, into a barbarian
anti-state under the leadership of the Hiongnu; and, within less
than a hundred years after Ts'in She Hwang-ti had done his work,
his successor Han Wuti (*imperabat* 140–87 B.C.) found the policy
of standing on the defensive behind a fortified line so unsatisfactory that he deliberately embarked on the hazardous enterprise
of conquering and subjecting the Hiongnu as an alternative to
holding them at bay. The progress and eventual success of Sinic
arms in this hundred years' war (*circa* 133–36 B.C.) have been mentioned in the foregoing chapter in their bearing upon the entry of
the Mahāyāna into the Sinic World.[1] In this place we need only
add that even the radical solution which Han Wuti put in train,
and which was carried to its completion by Han Yuanti's general
Ch'ên T'ang, was not, after all, definitive, because these conquests
beyond the Great Wall, extensive though they were, did not bring
the northern border of the Sinic universal state up to any 'natural
frontier' which could insulate the Sinic World from contact with
the barbarians in this quarter. When the frontier stood at the
relatively remote line of Lake Baikal and the Altai, there was still
an apparently boundless barbarian hinterland on the farther
side—just as there had been when the frontier had stood at the
relatively close-drawn line of the Great Wall. And an ineffectually
militant Sinic Society did not even succeed in permanently
subjugating, not to speak of assimilating, the barbarian population of the newly annexed territories. When the Prior Han
régime collapsed[2]—perhaps partly under the strain of this titanic
war of conquest—the momentarily prostrated Nomads shook
themselves free again in the second decade of the first century of
the Christian Era; and it was not until the eighth decade of the
same century that Pan Ch'ao (*militabat* A.D. 73–102) could begin
to reconquer for the Posterior Han that dominion over the Steppes
which had been established for the Prior Han by Ch'ên T'ang
more than a hundred years earlier.

Moreover, this second annexation of Eurasia to the Sinic
universal state was as ephemeral as the first; for Pan Ch'ao's
work began to crumble and dissolve as soon as the hero himself
disappeared from the scene of action.[3] On the Eurasian front the
power of the Posterior Han was on the wane throughout the second
century of the Christian Era; and the balance of power went on
shifting more and more in the barbarians' favour when the post-

---

[1] See V. C (i) (c) 2, pp. 144–5, above.
[2] For the temporary relapse of the Sinic World into anarchy at the turn of the last
century B.C. and the first century of the Christian Era, between the fall of the Prior Han
and the rise of the Posterior Han, see V. C (i) (c) 2, p. 142, footnote 4, above, and V.
C (ii) (b), vol. vi, p. 295, below.   [3] See V. C (i) (c) 2, pp. 144–5, above.

Sinic interregnum set in, as it did before the century closed. To outward appearance the irretrievable collapse of the Sinic Society was staved off for another hundred years, during which the Empire of the Posterior Han first lingered on through a final phase of impotence (A.D. 172–221), then temporarily broke up into a trio of indigenous 'successor-states'[1] ('the Three Kingdoms' *gerebantur* A.D. 221–280), and was afterwards momentarily restored under the rule of the Western or United Tsin (*imperabant* A.D. 280–317).[2] But these successive political façades masked a social *dégringolade* which went to its greatest extremes in the relations between the dissolving Sinic Society and the inflowing Eurasian barbarians.

Even in the age when Pan Ch'ao was repeating the exploits of Wuti, the reassertion of Sinic authority on the Steppe was successfully disputed by a new Nomad Power which now loomed up above the Sinic horizon in the no-man's-land beyond the frontier between Korea and the Khingan Range. In A.D. 93 the Northern Hiongnu were conquered by the Sien Pi;[3] and in A.D. 132 the name which had dominated the Eurasian hinterland of the Sinic World for the past five hundred years faded out of history when the Northern Hiongnu went into limbo in order to escape from an intolerable servitude to their fellow Nomad Sien Pi masters, while the Southern Hiongnu found shelter from the blizzard on the Steppes by drifting into the domain of the Sinic universal state[4] and settling down on the lee side of a Great Wall which was no longer effectually manned for obstructing the passage of Nomad trespassers.[5] These formidable movements of barbarian warbands on the Eurasian threshold of the Sinic World produced their inevitable consequences. At the turn of the third and fourth centuries of the Christian Era, at a moment when the political

---

[1] Although 'the Three Kingdoms' were of indigenous and not of barbarian origin, there was a strain of barbarism in their êthos which found literary expression in a romantic chronicle of their fratricidal wars that may be compared with the Alexander Romance. In the haze of this romantic tradition a military adventurer of the age, Kuang Yü, who lived and died as a man of flesh and blood, was gradually increased in stature and enhanced in potency until, in A.D. 1590, he was officially deified as the war-god of the Far Eastern World (Cordier, H.: *Histoire Générale de la Chine* (Paris 1920–1, Geuthner, 3 vols.), vol. i, p. 299).

[2] See IV. C (ii) (*b*) 1, vol. iv, p. 65, footnote 3, above.

[3] See Cordier, op. cit., vol. i, pp. 275 and 278–9.

[4] See Cordier, op. cit., vol. i, p. 292.

[5] This passage of the Great Wall of China by the Southern Hiongnu in the second century of the Christian Era may remind us of the passage of the Lower Danube frontier of the Roman Empire, some two hundred years later, by the Visigoths, when these former denizens of the Great Western Bay of the Eurasian Steppe were fleeing before the face of a Hunnish horde of Nomads in whom some scholars have thought to recognize the descendants of those Northern Hiongnu who had made their escape out of Mongolia in a westerly direction, through the Zungarian Gap, in A.D. 132. For the circumstances of and sequel to the lodgement of the Visigoths on Roman territory in the last quarter of the fourth century of the Christian Era see Part III. A, Annex II, vol. iii, p. 426; IV. C (iii) (*c*) 2 (*γ*), vol. iv, p. 440, footnote 4; and the present chapter and volume, p. 217, footnote 1, and p. 220, above.

unity of the Sinic World was nominally intact once more under the Western Tsin régime, we are confronted by the apparently sudden emergence, in the Eurasian marches, of three new 'successor-states' with archaistic names;[1] but a closer inspection reveals that both the character of the names and the suddenness of their assumption were deliberate ruses in a desperate and transparent attempt to keep up Sinic appearances. These respectable titles had been assumed with intent to veil the vulgar reality of a barbarian dominion on Sinic soil, and there was actually nothing new about this distressing state of affairs except the open acknowledgement of an accomplished fact which was the cumulative result of some two hundred years of silent and gradual social change. The 'Pe Yen' ('Northern Yen') principality in the Liao-tung Peninsula was the Sinic dominion of the Sien Pi; the 'Pe Han' ('Northern Han') Empire in Eastern Shansi was the Sinic dominion of the Southern Hiongnu; the 'Wei' principality in Western Shansi was the Sinic dominion of the To Pa.

The epigoni of these last-named To Pa barbarian conquerors of Sinic ground turned right-about-face and embarked upon a new war of conquest against their own 'poor relations' on the Steppe in A.D. 370;[2] and in A.D. 386 they celebrated this successful repetition of the Eurasian achievements of the authentic Han by assuming the imperial title in rivalry with their own 'Pe Han' barbarian contemporaries;[3] but this enlistment of barbarian arms in a Sinic war of revenge upon the barbarian world was a brief interlude in the course of the post-Sinic barbarian Völkerwande-rung;[4] for the Eurasian conquests of the 'Wei' Empire were quickly undone[5] when, at the turn of the fourth and fifth centuries, the vanished Nomad Empire of the Hiongnu was reconstituted by the Juan Juan;[6] and yet another wave of barbarian attack upon the ruins of the Sinic World was still to follow. In the sixth decade of the sixth century of the Christian Era the Juan Juan were overthrown and replaced by their former subjects the Turks between Altai and Khingan;[7] and in the same decade, between

---

[1] See IV. C (ii) (b) 1, vol. iv, p. 65, above.

[2] For the cultural *volte-face* of which this military *volte-face* was a corollary, see V. C (i) (d) 6 (α), pp. 477-8, below.

[3] See Cordier, op. cit., vol. i, p. 318.

[4] The post-Sinic interregnum lasted from about A.D. 175 to about A.D. 475, and thus partly overlapped in time with an apparent period of relative aridity (and therefore of Nomad effervescence) on the Steppes which may have prevailed from about A.D. 375 to about A.D. 675 (see Part III. A, Annex II, vol. iii, p. 414, above). The conquest of the Steppe by 'Wei' was carried out on the eve of the onset of this apparent bout of aridity and effervescence; and the date is perhaps sufficient in itself to explain why the conquest was ephemeral.

[5] On the other hand the 'Wei' Empire succeeded in handing on its pacific cultural achievements to a chain of 'successor-states' which led on to the *imperium redivivum* of the Sui and the T'ang (see V. C (i) (c) 4, p. 356, footnote 6, below).

[6] Cordier, op. cit., vol. i, p. 346. [7] Cordier, op. cit., vol. i, p. 351.

Khingan and Korea, the Khitan came treading on the heels of the Sien Pi.[1]

The Indic External Proletariat.

If we turn from the Sinic to the Indic World, we shall find that in Indic history too the successful barbarian invaders were Eurasian Nomads, but we shall also find that the Indic body social—unlike either the Sinic or the Sumeric or the Babylonic or the Syriac—was never in direct contact with the Nomads across a military front. The Nomads who broke into the Indic World had to traverse both the Oxus-Jaxartes Basin and the north-eastern corner of the Iranian Plateau on their way from the Eurasian Steppe to the Indus-Ganges Plain; and during the life-span of the Indic Civilization—which extended from the close of the post-Sumeric interregnum about the middle of the second millennium B.C. to the beginning of the post-Indic interregnum in the fifth century of the Christian Era—these intervening territories were held, or at any rate overshadowed and dominated, by the Babylonic and Syriac and Hellenic civilizations in succession, and finally by the Syriac Civilization once again, when, in the third century of the Christian Era, the Syriac culture decisively re-asserted itself over Hellenism in Iran and 'Irāq.[2]

Whether the Indic Society was already the victim of Eurasian Nomad assaults across this intervening alien ground during the Indic 'Time of Troubles' (saeviebat circa 725–325 B.C.)[3] is a question that has to be left unanswered for lack of evidence.[4] The first Eurasian Nomad invasion of the Indic World that is adequately attested (after the Aryan Völkerwanderung which was

---

[1] Cordier, op. cit., vol. i, p. 359.
[2] For the expulsion of Hellenism from the Transeuphratean tracts of the Syriac World by the Sasanidae see p. 216, above.
[3] See I. C (i) (b), vol. i, pp. 86–7, above.
[4] It is tempting to conjecture that some of the warlike communities that were encountered by Alexander the Great in the Indus Valley in 327–324 B.C. were the descendants of Eurasian Nomads who had been deposited there by a more recent Völker-wanderung than that of the Aryas. The most recent period of aridity and effervescence on the Steppes may have run from about 825 to about 525 B.C. (see Part III. A, Annex II, vol. iii, p. 410, above), and this period partly coincides in date with both the Babylonic 'Time of Troubles' (saeviebat circa 1000–600 B.C.) and the Syriac 'Time of Troubles' (saeviebat circa 925–525 B.C.). In that age South-Western Asia had been overrun by the Eurasian Nomad Cimmerians and Scyths. Did one wing of this invading horde turn south-eastward after breaking out of the Steppe between the Pamirs and the Caspian, as the Aryan conquerors of the Indus Valley had turned south-eastward in their day when their Hyksos comrades had swept on across 'Irāq and Syria into Egypt? Perhaps the Pactyes on the Indo-Iranian border (Herodotus III, 102; IV, 44; VII, 67 and 85) were an apodasmos of the same horde as the Pactyes in Cappadocia (Herodotus III, 93), and are to be identified with the Cimmerians. Is this hypothetical Indo-Iranian settlement, post 825 B.C. and prae 525 B.C., of Eurasian Nomads bearing the Pactyan name, and presumably belonging to the Iranian-speaking wing of the Nomad natives of the Eurasian Steppe, commemorated in the name Pashtu, by which the living Iranian vernacular language of the north-eastern corner of the Iranian Plateau is known at the present day?

the prelude to the rise of the Indic Civilization) is one which was consequent—in the causal as well as in the temporal sense—upon the intrusion of the Hellenic Society on the Indic Society's domain; and this intrusion did not take place until after the Indic 'Time of Troubles' had been followed by the rise and fall of the Maurya Empire which was the first attempt at an Indic universal state.

We have seen[1] how in the second century B.C. North-Western India was united politically with both North-Eastern Iran and the Oxus-Jaxartes Basin under the rule of the Greek princes of Bactria; and we have also seen[2] how, before the century ran out, this Bactrian Greek Empire was swept away by an avalanche of Eurasian Nomads—the Sakas in the van, with the Yuechi at their heels—who broke out of the Steppe, across the former Achaemenian frontier between the Pamirs and the Caspian, about the years 130–129 B.C. In this eruption the Nomads were prevented from sweeping straight on south-westwards by the stubborn resistance of the Arsacid power in Khurāsān; and while the Yuechi were content to vegetate, for the next hundred and fifty years,[3] in the *ci-devant* Bactrian Greek provinces, north-west of the Hindu Kush, which they had overrun at their first onset, the Sakas—who were caught between a Yuechi devil at their rear and

---

[1] In I. C (i) (*b*), vol. i, p. 80; II. D (v), vol. ii, p. 143; and V. C (i) (*c*) 2, in the present volume, p. 133, with footnote 1, above.

[2] In II. D (v), vol. ii, p. 141, footnote 2, and p. 144, and in the present chapter and volume, pp. 239–40, above. See also p. 310, below.

[3] By the time, in or shortly before 130 B.C., when the Yuechi ousted the Far Eastern Greeks from their possessions in the Upper Oxus-Jaxartes Basin, north-west of the Hindu Kush, these Nomad intruders had been constantly 'on the run', with more powerful Nomad enemies at their heels, since at the latest 174 B.C., and, after these forty years of wandering in the wilderness, they told the Han Power's envoy Chang-K'ien (see V. C (i) (*c*) 2, p. 143, footnote 2, above), when he overtook them at last, in 128 B.C., in Sogdiana (they had not, by then, yet troubled to cross the Oxus as well as the Jaxartes), 'that they were weary of trekking and fighting and only wanted to live in peace' (Tarn, W. W.: *The Greeks in Bactria and India* (Cambridge 1938, University Press), pp. 276–7) and that they were therefore unwilling to entertain the proposal, which the envoy had brought with him from the Court of Ch'ang Ngan, for a concerted convergent assault by the Yuechi and the Sinic Power upon their common enemies the Hiongnu. The first of the five Yuechi war-bands to recover from this lassitude were the Kushans. By about 50 B.C. we find the Kushans not only across the Oxus, but also across the Hindu Kush, on the northern edge of the basin of the Kābul River, somewhere between the Panjshir district and Chitral (Tarn, op. cit., pp. 342 and 506); and the energy which had carried them thus far afield in less than 80 years since the date of Chang-K'ien's visit moved them to respond to the call of a later envoy of the Sinic Power, who was successful in mobilizing the Kushan chief Miaos to fight for the local Greek prince Hermaeus against the Parsians of Côphênê (see V. C (i) (*c*) 2, p. 133, footnote 1, above). Miaos' descendant and eventual successor Kadphises I (*regnabat post* A.D. 25 to A.D. 50) united all five Yuechi war-bands under Kushan leadership and conquered the country of the Paropamisadae (see loc. cit.). The conquest of Taxila, the capital of the Western Panjab, followed *circa* A.D. 60–4 (Tarn, op. cit., p. 353, footnote 1) in the reign of Kadphises II (*regnabat circa* A.D. 50–68); and the second Kadphises' famous successor Kanishka (*regnabat circa* A.D. 78–123) reigned, from Jaxartes to Ganges, over an empire as extensive as the Bactrian Greek prince Demetrius's in 183–175 B.C. (see loc. cit.). By the time, however, when the Kushans were making their conquests in India, they were no longer barbarians but were authentic and self-conscious heirs of the by then almost extinct Far Eastern Greeks.

the Parthian deep sea straight ahead—evaded annihilation by swerving south-eastward and throwing themselves upon the Indian provinces of a Greek Power in the Far East which had been weakened by becoming divided against itself before being smitten by the impact of the Yuechi upon its Transoxanian frontier facing the Eurasian Steppe.[1] After winning and losing an ephemeral dominion (*circa* 110 B.C.–A.D. 19) in the Indus Valley, these Saka Nomad barbarian intruders on Indic ground succeeded in taking permanent possession of the plateaux of Mālwā (*circa* A.D. 78) and Mahārāshtra (about, or shortly before, the middle of the second century of the Christian Era).[2] The overthrow of the last of the Saka 'satraps' in Western India at some date between A.D. 388 and A.D. 401 was the decisive act in the restoration of the Indic universal state by the Guptas.[3]

The Saka Nomad incursion into Indic history during the interlude between the Maurya and the Gupta régimes was not, however, the last Indic social catastrophe of the kind; for, while we have no sure evidence of Nomad assaults upon the Indic World during the Indic 'Time of Troubles' which preceded the foundation of the Maurya Empire by Chandragupta (*imperabat* 322–298 B.C.), a succession of Nomad invasions is a prominent feature of the post-Indic interregnum which set in after the death of the Gupta Emperor Skandagupta (*imperabat* A.D. 455–*circa* A.D. 480).[4] On this occasion the history of the preceding Nomad assault upon India repeated itself, with the Huns playing the Sakas' part.[5]

The last quarter of the fourth century of the Christian Era saw the advent of a bout of apparent aridity[6] and manifest effervescence on the Steppes which, on the sector of the steppe-coast between the Khingan Range and the Tien Shan, was signalled by the menacing emergence of the Juan Juan horde above the northern horizon of the Sinic World.[7] At the opposite extremity of Eurasia the same troubling of the waters of Nomadism declared itself with greater violence in a simultaneous outbreak of the Huns between

[1] For a discussion of the route, and the stages, by which the Sakas reached their Indian destination, see V. C (i) (*c*) 3, Annex II, pp. 602–3, below.
[2] For these conquests of the epigoni of the original Saka invaders of India see V. C (i) (*c*) 3, Annex II, pp. 603–4, below.
[3] See Smith, V. A.: *The Early History of India*, 3rd edition (Oxford 1914, Clarendon Press), pp. 290–2. For the part which the Sakas may have played in the evolution of both the Sanskrit and the Iranian Epic, see V. C (i) (*c*) 3, Annex II, below.
[4] It will be noticed that the post-Indic interregnum (*circa* A.D. 475–775) partly coincided in time with an apparent bout of aridity (and therefore of effervescence) on the Steppes which may have prevailed from about A.D. 375 to A.D. 675 (see Part III. A, Annex II, vol. iii, p. 414, above).
[5] This historical parallel has been noticed already in Part III. A, Annex II, vol. iii, p. 449, above.
[6] For this bout, which may have prevailed from *circa* A.D. 375 to *circa* A.D. 675, see Part III. A, Annex II, vol. iii, p. 414, above.
[7] See the present chapter, p. 273, above.

the Pamirs and the Caspian and between the Caspian and the Urals.[1] Perhaps the most convincing explanation of the origin of these several Nomad offensives which were so widely dispersed in Space yet so closely synchronous in Time is to see in them the uniform effects of a single physical cause which was in operation on—and all over—the Steppe itself; but in attempting to account for the diversity of the subsequent fortunes of the several erupting hordes, after they had left their native Steppes behind and had invaded the domains of their sedentary neighbours, we have to look for an explanation in human instead of in physical terms, and we shall find it in the diverse conditions, at the time, of the different sedentary societies with which the Nomad invaders collided.

The Juan Juan, for example, were prevented from penetrating beyond the fringes of the Sinic World by the resistance of those 'successor-states' of the United Tsin Empire that had been founded in the marches by the Juan Juan's own forerunners the Sien Pi and Hiongnu and To Pa; for these *ci-devant* Nomad principalities served as effective buffers against the next wave of Nomad invasion. On the other hand the principality which the Gothic sedentary barbarians from Northern Europe had established in the Ukraine,[2] between the main body of the Eurasian Steppe and the Lower Danube frontier of the Roman Empire, during the foregoing bout of apparent humidity and manifest quiescence,[3] not only failed to break the shock of the impact of the Huns upon the Hellenic World but actually caused this shock to be more profoundly felt and the blow to strike deeper; for the Hun explosion blew the Gothic principality to pieces, and the flying fragments made breaches in the Roman *limes* through which the Nomad horsemen were able to ride unhindered.[4] Under the leadership of Attila (*dominabatur circa* A.D. 433–453) the right wing of the Hunnish horde, which had taken the road between the Caspian and the Urals, was able to penetrate, in the track of the exploded Goths, into the heart of the Roman Empire before the united efforts of Goths and Romans succeeded in flinging the Nomads back into the Steppes from which they had issued. Meanwhile the White Huns or Ephthalites, who formed the left wing of the erupting Hunnish horde, had parted company with their comrades-in-arms in order to take the alternative road between the Caspian and the Pamirs; and on this road they met with

[1] For the synchronism between the eruption of the Huns and the emergence of the Juan Juan see Part III. A, Annex II, vol. iii, p. 423, above.
[2] See Part III. A, Annex II, vol. iii, p. 426, above.
[3] For this bout see Part III. A, Annex II, vol. iii, p. 413, above.
[4] See p. 220, above.

experiences which were different, again, from those of Attila's Huns in Europe as well as from those of the Juan Juan in the Far East.

The sedentary societies which the Juan Juan and the Black Huns found in their path happened, at the time, to be in an advanced stage of dissolution. At the turn of the fourth and fifth centuries of the Christian Era the Hellenic Society was approaching, in Europe,[1] the end of its universal state, while the Far East was floundering in the trough of a post-Sinic interregnum. On the other hand, in contemporary South-Western Asia the Syriac Civilization was at this time in process of recovery from the stunning blow of a Hellenic assault. It was at last regaining the upper hand, and was preparing to complete its half-fulfilled task of evicting the intrusive Hellenic Civilization from the Syriac domain. The political instrument of this cultural rally was the Sasanian Empire;[2] and this young and militant Power was a much more formidable antagonist for the Huns than an old and weary Roman Empire. When they broke out of the Desert into the Sown on the Pamir-Caspian front, the White Huns overthrew the 'successor-states' of the Kushan Empire in the Oxus-Jaxartes Basin as easily as, in the same region some five hundred years before, the Bactrian Greek Empire had been overthrown by the Sakas and the Yuechi; but beyond the Oxus and the Murghab, at the foot of the Khurasanian escarpment of the Iranian Plateau, the new invaders found the Sasanian Power waiting to receive their attack as the Arsacid Power had once stood on the same line to withstand the Sakas. In this second battle, on the same field, between Iran and Turan, the representative of the sedentary civilization was once again victorious; and, as before, his Nomad assailant swerved aside into India[3] when he found his line of advance into South-Western Asia blocked by a resistance which he was unable to overcome.

The first Hun attack, across the Hindu Kush, upon the Gupta Empire appears to have been delivered at the moment of Skandagupta's accession in A.D. 455; and this attack was repulsed. But in the last decade (*circa* A.D. 470–480) of Skandagupta's reign, when the restored Indic universal state was verging towards its fall, the Nomad assault was renewed in greater force and with greater persistence; and, when the Gupta Empire broke up after Skandagupta's death, the Hun invaders maintained for half-a-

---

[1] For the differentiation, in the course of the fifth century of the Christian Era, between the simultaneous responses of an identic Roman Empire to identic challenges in its western provinces and in its central and eastern provinces respectively see IV. C (iii) (c) 2 (β), vol. iv, pp. 323–6, above.

[2] See p. 216, above.

[3] For the history of this Hun invasion of India during the post-Indic 'Time of Troubles' see Smith, V. A., op. cit., pp. 309–23.

century (*circa* A.D. 480–528) a reign of terror in India[1] in which the war-lord Mihiragula (*militabat circa* A.D. 510–540) played Attila's part. Like his Black Hun cousin, this White Hun 'Scourge of God' made himself so intolerable that he drove the rival successors of the Empire on whose domain he was trespassing to make common cause against him; and the reverse which Mihiragula suffered *circa* A.D. 528 at the hands of Bālāditya and Yasodharman[2] was more severe than that which had been inflicted upon Attila by Aetius and Theodoric. But it was neither the defeat nor the death of the Ephthalite invader that gave a devastated Indic World security against a repetition of the calamity. The ravaging of India by the White Huns was only brought to an end when this first wave of the Nomad flood in the ebullition of A.D. 375–675 was followed by a second. Between A.D. 563 and A.D. 567 the Turks burst out of the Steppe into the Oxus-Jaxartes Basin and succeeded—in alliance with the Sasanid Power, which thus revenged the disaster of A.D. 484—in annihilating the Ephthalites in their home territory, without pushing their own conquests farther in the direction of India than the Kābul Valley.[3]

Evidence from the New World.

In passing from the Old World to the New, we shall find ourselves handicapped again—as we have been handicapped in attempting to review the Indic 'Time of Troubles'—by a dearth of evidence.

In the history of the disintegration of the Andean Civilization, for example, we can catch no more than a glimpse or two of the relations between a dominant minority and an external proletariat before we reach the date of the establishment of the Andean universal state. We have already observed[4] that the Incas trained themselves for the task of empire-building by serving as the wardens of the marches of the Andean World against the savages in the forests of Amazonia, and we may now observe that the Chancas—who came nearer than any of the

---

[1] The Ephthalites won a free hand to concentrate their marauding energies upon India when, in A.D. 484, they defeated and killed the Sasanian Pādishāh Pīrūz, who had rashly attacked them on their own ground in the Oxus-Jaxartes Basin, instead of being content with his predecessors' achievement of holding the frontier of Khurāsān.

[2] See Smith, V. A., op. cit., p. 318.

[3] That is, if the Gurjara Nomads—whose descendants we find established in North-Western India in a later age (see II. D (v), vol. ii, p. 130, footnote 3, above)—were not a spill-over from the crest of this Turkish wave when it broke against the Hindu Kush. In the Hindu records the Gurjaras are mentioned in association with the Huns (see Smith, V. A., op. cit., pp. 321–2), and the most natural inference would be that they were an allied horde which descended upon India in the same avalanche as the Huns themselves; but the association may signify no closer relationship between Huns and Gurjaras than is involved in the facts that both were Nomads and that both entered India in the course of the post-Indic interregnum (*circa* A.D. 475–775).

[4] In II. D (v), vol. ii, pp. 206–8, above.

Incas' other Andean adversaries to cutting the Incas' career of conquest short[1]—are believed to have been the descendants of barbarian intruders of Amazonian origin. In the last days of the Inca Empire, on the eve of the Spanish conquest, we find that, in addition to the Amazonian front, the Andean universal state had two other anti-barbarian frontiers to defend: one at the south-eastern escarpment of the plateau (on the edge of the highlands that are now included in the south-eastern extremity of Bolivia and in the north-western extremity of Argentina) and the other on the Pacific sea-board at the line of the River Maule (in what is now Chile). Both the Araucanian barbarians beyond the Maule and the Guarani barbarians in the Chaco were as warlike as the Amazonian savages;[2] and on the Chaco front the Inca Power had to cope, in A.D. 1526, with a Guarani invasion[3] which penetrated farther than the Guaranis' Paraguayan descendants ever succeeded in advancing in their war with Bolivia some four hundred years later.

As for the Mexic World, the Aztec Power, which was on the point of establishing a Mexic universal state at the moment when the Spanish conquerors arrived on the scene,[4] had arisen, like the Inca Power in the Andean World, in an anti-barbarian march.[5] While Cuzco was a frontier-fortress against the savages of the Amazonian forest, Tenochtitlan was a frontier-fortress against the barbarians of the North American desert; and the Aztec masters of Tenochtitlan were themselves the descendants of barbarian interlopers from beyond the pale.[6]

We may add that, in the Spanish Viceroyalty of New Spain, as in the Spanish Viceroyalty of Peru, the alien usurpers found themselves compelled to assume responsibility for a conquered commonwealth's anti-barbarian fronts as the price for their seizure of the spoils of victory.[7] While in South America the *conquistadores* had to carry on the Incas' warfare with the Amazonians

---

[1] See II. D (iv), vol. ii, pp. 102–3, above.

[2] See Baudin, L.: *L'Empire Socialiste des Inka* (Paris 1928, Institut d'Ethnologie), p. 211.

[3] See Baudin, op. cit., pp. 44 and 168; Nordenskiöld, E.: 'The Guarani Invasion of the Inca Empire in the Sixteenth Century' in *The Geographical Review*, August 1917.

[4] See IV. C (ii) (*b*) 2, vol. iv, p. 105, above.

[5] See II. D (v), vol. ii, pp. 206–8, above.

[6] It will be seen that the Aztecs were the Mexic counterparts of the Chancas and not of the Incas; and, if the decisive battle of Sacsahuana (see II. D (iv), vol. ii, p. 103, above) had ended in a Chanca victory, the course of Andean history from A.D. 1347 onwards might have been characterized by that brutality which was conspicuous by its presence in the Aztecs and by its absence in the Incas. See further V. C (i) (*c*) 4, p. 357, below.

[7] Just as the Romans had to take over the Etruscan frontier in Northern Italy and the Carthaginian frontiers in the Iberian Peninsula and North-West Africa and the Macedonian frontier in the Balkan Peninsula and the Seleucid frontiers against the Arabs and the Parthians (see II. D (v), vol. ii, pp. 161–4, and the present chapter and volume, pp. 215–16, above).

and Guaranis and Araucanians, in North America they had to carry on the Aztecs' warfare with the even more ferocious Apaches and Comanches.[1]

Evidence from the Eurasian Steppe.

Before we extend our survey from extinct to extant civilizations, we may notice several examples of the phenomena with which we are now concerned—namely, the secession of external proletariats and the delivery of barbarian counter-offensives—in the histories of certain Nomad Powers which have extended their rule over sedentary populations on the fringe of the Steppe and have thereby liberated themselves from the Nomadic Society's peculiar destiny of being a civilization without a history,[2] but have won this liberty at the price of exposing themselves to those perils of breakdown and disintegration that beset the path of growth.

In another context[3] we have detected the plot of a drama in three acts—quiescence, prosperity, and demoralization—which has been performed on at least three distinct occasions when a Nomad horde has erupted out of the heart of the Eurasian Steppe into its Great Western Bay and has there established a political ascendancy over the sedentary primitive societies in the Northern Forest, while itself falling under the cultural ascendancy of one or more of the sedentary civilizations of the South. In a different context, again,[4] we have observed that Nomad empires *in partibus agricolarum* carry within themselves the seeds of their own rapid decay, and that the evil day is merely postponed, without being averted, for those Nomad empires on the Great Western Bay of the Eurasian Steppe whose rulers have embarked on the dangerous experiment of substituting human for horned and hoofed cattle without committing the further folly of transferring their own habitation from the Desert to the Sown.[5] In the end the Royal Scythians and the Khazars and the Golden Horde, who dominated their sedentary subjects from a base of operations on the Steppe, each travelled the same road to destruction as their respective cousins and contemporaries the vagrant Scythians, who terrorized South-Western Asia for less than a hundred years in the seventh and sixth centuries B.C., the Pseudo-Avars, who terrorized Central and Eastern Europe for perhaps less than fifty years in the sixth and seventh centuries of the Christian Era, and the Il-Khans, who in the thirteenth and fourteenth centuries

[1] The extraordinary conservatism of Spanish military technique on this North American anti-barbarian front has been noticed in III. C (i) (a), vol. iii, p. 136, above.
[2] For this aspect of Nomadism see Part III. A, vol. iii, pp. 7–22, with Annex II, above. [3] In Part III. A, Annex II, vol. iii, pp. 428–30, above.
[4] In Part III. A, vol. iii, pp. 22–5, above.
[5] See Part III. A, vol. iii, p. 25, footnote 8, above.

reigned for less than eighty years over Iran and 'Irāq. And in the decline and fall of each of the three marginal steppe-empires we can observe the phenomena that have become familiar to us in our survey of sedentary societies. In these steppe-empires, too, an external proletariat duly secedes from a Nomad dominant minority and eventually passes over from the defensive to the offensive in the resulting warfare between the two fractions of a house divided against itself.

The Golden Horde had a special name—Qāzāq[1]—for the contumacious barbarian who hovered or lurked, just out of range of the Horde's long whip-lash,[2] on the fringes of the vast appanage of Chingis Khan's eldest son Jūjī: a steppe-empire which extended, at its widest, from the Altai Mountains to the Iron Gates and from the Sea of Aral to the Gulf of Finland, and which exercised a suzerainty over the Iranic sedentary community of Khwārizm (Khiva) on one flank and over the Orthodox Christian sedentary society in Russia on the other.[3] This technical term for the external proletariat of the long since vanished Golden Horde has survived down to the present day as the national name of two separate communities which differ from one another

[1] The word is a regular substantival formation from the Turkish verb *qāzmaq* meaning 'to dig'. Its technical significance in the political vocabulary of the Khans of the Golden Horde is an almost exact equivalent of 'External Proletariat' in the sense in which that term is used in this Study. (For this sense of the term 'Qāzāq' see Czaplicka, M. A.: *The Turks of Central Asia in History and at the Present Day* (Oxford 1918, Clarendon Press), p. 38.) This usage of the nickname 'Diggers' to describe the external proletariat of the Golden Horde suggests that the section of this external proletariat to which the term was first applied must have been some agricultural population—e.g. the Cossacks of the Dniepr (compare the Scythae Arotêres or 'Ploughboy Scythians', and the Scythae Geôrgoi or 'Agriculturist Scythians', who were to be found in the fifth century B.C. up the River Dniepr on the fringe of the Nomad Scythians' pastures, according to Herodotus, Book II, chaps. 17 and 18)—and that the technical sense of the term must eventually have eclipsed its etymological meaning so completely that it could come to be applied to *all* sections of the external proletariat alike—whether they happened to be sedentary communities like the Dniepr Cossacks (see II. D (v), vol. ii, pp. 155-7, above) or Ishmaelites like the Kirghiz Qāzāqs who, so far from being diggers in the literal sense, were more capriciously vagrant than the more or less disciplined Nomads who took their orders from the Khans of the House of Jūjī.

[2] See Herodotus, Book IV, chaps. 1-4, for the story of how the Scythians eventually broke the *moral* of their rebellious serfs—who had fortified themselves in a Crimean fastness masked by a dyke and flanked by the mountains and the sea—by laying aside their spears and bows and taking to their horsewhips. 'So long', observed the Scythian psychologist who recommended this gesture, 'as they have seen us bearing arms against them, they have felt on an equality with us, but when they see us armed with whips instead of weapons they will remember that they are our slaves, and when they realize this they will no longer be able to face us in the field.' According to the tale, the baffled Scythians took the psychologist's advice, with the precise result which he had predicted.

[3] For the extent of Jūjī's appanage see I. C (i) (*b*), Annex I, vol. i, p. 373, and ii. D (v), vol. ii, pp. 145 and 146-7, above. This steppe-empire was founded between A.D. 1219, when the Mongols erupted westwards through the Zungarian Gap, and A.D. 1241, when they raided, but withdrew from, Hungary. It may be said to have come to an end when Shaybānī Khān Uzbeg, the leader of the last intact troop of the Golden Horde, abandoned the Steppe and plunged into Transoxania in A.D. 1500, and when the head-quarters of the Golden Horde at the Saray on the Volga were captured in A.D. 1502 by the Mongols' former tributaries the Muscovites (see I. C (i) (*b*), Annex I, vol. i, pp. 372-4, above).

profoundly in origin and in culture but which nevertheless have in common an identic historical experience which their common name commemorates. Either of these still living peoples is derived from a wing of the long since extinct Golden Horde's external proletariat, and between them they have now occupied almost the whole of the Qipchāq Steppe which was once the Golden Horde's preserve. The Turkish-speaking 'Kirghiz Qāzāq' Nomads,[1] who range to-day from the left bank of the Irtish to the left bank of the Lower Volga, and who have given their name to a Qāzāq Soviet Socialist Republic which was one of eleven direct constituent states members of the Soviet Union according to the Constitution of the 5th December, 1936,[2] are descended from Nomad outlaws who once hovered on the Baraba Steppe, on the farther side of the Irtish, where the writ of the Khan at Saray-on-Volga did not run. The Russian-speaking Orthodox Christian Cossack husbandmen and watermen, whose canton-ments were strung along the banks of the Eurasian rivers, from the Don to the Ussuri, until the Russian Communist revolution broke them up, are descended from sedentary outlaws who once lurked, under the nose of the Khan at Saray, in their water-girt 'Sich' on an island in the Dniepr.[3] The convergent Qāzāq counter-offensive from both flanks, to which the Golden Horde eventually succumbed, seems to have been opened in the latter part of the fourteenth century of the Christian Era and to have triumphed before the end of the sixteenth.

If we now examine the history of the Royal Scythians and the Khazars in the light of this barbarian counter-offensive which signalized and expedited the decline and fall of the Golden Horde, we shall find counterparts, in either case, of both the Cossacks and the Kirghiz Qāzāqs. The respective Nomad outlaws who eventually broke into the Scythians' and the Khazars' preserves out of the hinterland on the Steppe were the Sarmatians and the Pechenegs;[4] the respective sedentary outlaws who broke in out of the hinterland covered by the Northern Forest were the Bastarnae and the Varangians.[5] And, just as, after the dissolution of the Golden Horde at the beginning of the sixteenth century of

[1] 'The Kirghiz Qāzāqs' are so named by the Russians in order to distinguish them from the Russian Cossacks on the one hand and from the Qāra Kirghiz on the other hand; but the so-called Kirghiz Qāzāqs speak of themselves as 'the Qāzāqs', *par excellence*, with no distinctive additional epithet.
[2] See the English text of the Constitution (Fundamental Law) of the Union of Soviet Socialist Republics adopted [on the 5th December, 1936] at the Extraordinary Eighth Congress of Soviets of the U.S.S.R. (Moscow 1937, Co-operative Publishing Society of Foreign Workers in the U.S.S.R.), chap. 2, arts. 13 and 28.
[3] For the Cossacks see II. D (v), vol. ii, pp. 155-7, above.
[4] See Part III. A, Annex II, vol. iii, pp. 426-30 and 441-3, above.
[5] See II. D (vii), vol. ii, p. 349, with Annex VI, and Part III. A, Annex II, vol. iii, p. 426, above.

the Christian Era, the Cossacks met and fought the Kirghiz Qāzāqs for the possession of the derelict steppe, so the Bastarnae contended with the Sarmatians after the fall of the Royal Scythians, and the Varangians with the Pechenegs (and with the Ghuzz and the Cumans[1] who followed at the Pechenegs' heels) after the fall of the Khazars.

Of the three Nomad empires on the Great Western Bay of the Eurasian Steppe that are here under consideration, the Empire of the Khazars is the most interesting—and this not only in itself but also in virtue of the reaction which it evoked from the transfrontier barbarians in the Northern Forest and on the farther side of it.

The Khazars were deposited at the mouth of the Great Western Bay, between the Lower Volga and the Lower Don, about the middle of the sixth century of the Christian Era, by the same explosion that blew the [Pseudo-]Avars into the Hungarian Alföld and the Magyars into the Black Sea Steppe between Don and Dniestr and the Turks into the Oxus-Jaxartes Basin; and at the moment of their simultaneous emergence above the horizon of the neighbouring sedentary societies the Khazars gave no sign that they had any greater capacity for civilization than these other Nomads in front of them or than the Pechenegs and Ghuzz and Cumans in their rear. In the seventh century of the Christian Era the Khazars still wore a savage mien for the Azerbaijani peasants whose fields they ravaged as mercenaries in Heraclius's expeditionary force, or for the citizens of Constantinopie whose dethroned tyrant-emperor Justinian II consoled himself for his banishment to the Crimea by marrying a Khazar princess. The Khazars were, indeed, one of the scourges of an age which was a time of tribulation for the civilizations of the South. In the eighth century, however, both the nascent Orthodox Christian Society and the senescent Syriac Society began to see better days. Orthodox Christendom coped with its problems by conjuring up a ghost of the Roman Empire; and, although the East Roman Empire eventually became a disastrous incubus,[2] the first effect of its establishment was to give an impetus to the development of the Orthodox Christian Civilization. Simultaneously in the Syriac World the Umayyad Caliphs emulated and surpassed both the work of Leo Syrus and the work of the Achaemenidae by incorporating the whole of the Syriac Society's domain into a

---

[1] *Alias* Qipchāq, after whom, as the horde whom they dispossessed (or, it might be more accurate to say, subdued and incorporated), the Mongol Golden Horde named the vast expanse of steppe, between the western foot of the Altai and the eastern foot of the Carpathians, which became Jūjī Khan's appanage.
[2] See IV. C (iii) (*c*) 2 (*β*), vol. iv, pp. 320–408, above.

single universal state extending from Andalusia in one direction
to Transoxania in the other.[1] After the completion of the Arab
conquest of the Oxus-Jaxartes Basin in A.D. 741 Khazaria was
subjected to a concentric fire of Orthodox Christian cultural
radiation from the south-west, across the Black Sea and the
Caucasus,[2] and Syriac cultural radiation from the south-east,
across the Steppe; and, under this bombardment, the Khazars
underwent a social transformation which was profound as well as
rapid. About the middle of the century they abandoned their
primitive paganism for the Jewish Faith,[3] and changed themselves
from warlike Nomads who sold their military services in the South
into peaceful men of business who hired Southern mercenaries to
police their cities and trade-routes.

This self-metamorphosis of the Khazars in the middle of the
eighth century of the Christian Era was a remarkable achievement
for a Nomad horde; but it was also a hazardous adventure; for at
the moment when they were abandoning their ancestral military
tradition the Khazars were acquiring an empire, beyond the borders
of their native Steppe, which was bound sooner or later to become
a serious military commitment. The cause of the change in the
Khazars' way of life had been a taste for the profits of commerce,
and the motive had been a desire to reap these profits to the full.
The strength of the Khazars' trading position lay in their geographical situation midway between the luxury-markets of
Constantinople and Baghdad and the Southern furriers' source
of supply in the Northern Forest; and from the middle of the
eighth century onwards[4] the Khazar *coureurs des bois* pushed their
way up the Dniepr and over the portage to the northern waters
that descended into the Baltic—imposing on the Slav inhabitants
of the woods a tribute of furs and wax, and setting up trading-
posts which soon turned into embryonic city-states with a measure

[1] See pp. 240–1, above.
[2] For this early cultural expansion of Orthodox Christendom north-eastward, which
was one of the first symptoms of the emergence of a new Orthodox Christian Civilization, see I. C (i) (b), vol. i, p. 64, above.
[3] See II. D (vi), Annex, vol. ii, p. 410, and Part III. A, Annex II, vol. iii, p. 429,
above. The Khazars' choice of Judaism, in preference to either Orthodox Christianity
or Sunni Islam, is probably to be interpreted as a deliberate and ingenious attempt to
have the best of both worlds. They wanted to civilize themselves, and recognized that
the necessary means to this end was the adoption of some 'higher religion'. At the same
time they wanted to preserve their own distinct social identity, and therefore refrained
from adopting either of the two 'higher religions' that were officially established in the
two great sedentary empires next door to the Khazar Steppe. If this reading of the
Khazars' conversion to Judaism is correct, we may contrast their deliberate acquisition
of a distinctive 'higher religion' in the eighth century of the Christian Era with the
Eastern Teutons' accidental achievement of the same result through their conversion
to Arianism in the fourth century (see pp. 227–9, above).
[4] The date is established by finds of Arab coins in the Dniepr Basin—if we may assume
that these coins were brought by the Khazar pioneers (see Kliutschewskij, W. [Kluchev-
ski, V.]: *Geschichte Russlands*, vol. i (Berlin 1925, Obelisk-Verlag), pp. 122–3).

of political command over their respective commercial hinter-lands.[1]

This Khazar penetration of the Russian sector of the Northern Forest is recorded to have been eminently peaceful; and the finds of Arab coins[2] in the region which the Khazars thus opened up suggests that even the 'tribute' may have been of the nature of a voluntary commercial transaction rather than a toll exacted by an assertion of superior physical force. In this respect the Khazars' activities in their new dominion compare favourably with Charle-magne's contemporary work in the westernmost sector of the Forest, where the Austrasian empire-builder was setting himself to subjugate the Saxons to Frankdom, and to convert them to the Christian Faith, by sheer violence, and was thereby evoking a desperate resistance from his victims.[3] In one respect, however, the Khazars' advance from the northern fringe of the Steppe to the northern slope of the watershed between the Black Sea and the Baltic resembled both Charlemagne's simultaneous advance from the Rhine to the Eider and the Etruscans' advance, in another age, from the west coast of Italy to the southern foot of the Alps.[4] Like these other two unfortunate adventures, the Khazar enter-prise was an intrusion upon a boundless barbarian world in which the rash intruder had not the staying-power or the strength to find safety by pushing on to a 'natural frontier', so that he was condemning himself to evoke a barbarian counter-movement which he lacked the power to meet and stem.[5] The Khazars' experience was to demonstrate that the nemesis of a hasty advance 'into the blue' was much the same, whether the forward move-ment itself had been pacific or militant.

While the Slavs appear to have been as pacific in the eighth and ninth centuries of the Christian Era as the Khazars were in that age and as the Slavs' own ancestors had shown themselves in A.D. 591,[6] the Khazars' progress through the forests, from the landward fringe of the Black Sea Steppe towards the Continental coast of the Baltic, had brought their northernmost outposts within range of the warlike barbarians of Scandinavia, who at

---

[1] Kluchevski, op. cit., German translation, vol. i, pp. 120–1 and 131. The opening-up of the Russian forests by the Khazar fur-traders in the eighth and ninth centuries of the Christian Era may be compared with the opening-up of the North American forests by the French-Canadian fur-traders in the eighteenth and nineteenth centuries. The geographical location of Kiev-on-Dniepr, which became the *entrepôt* of the Russian fur-trade, corresponds to that of Montreal *mutatis mutandis*—that is to say, with the geographical role of the Gulf of St. Lawrence being played by the Great Western Bay of the Eurasian Steppe.   [2] See the preceding page, footnote 4, above.
[3] See II. D (vii), vol. ii, pp. 344–5, and IV. C (iii) (c) 3 (α), vol. iv, pp. 488–90, above.
[4] See II. D (vii), vol. ii, pp. 276, 280, and 345, above.
[5] A number of illustrations of the historical 'law' that can be seen here in operation have been given on p. 209, footnote 3, above.
[6] See the incident cited in II. D (vii), vol. ii, p. 318, above.

this very moment were being awakened from their 'heavy winter dream'[1] by Charlemagne's provocative hammering upon their southern gate. The Arab coins that, under Khazar auspices, had made their way, salmon-wise, up the Dniepr cataracts travelled on over the portage and down the northern waters and across the Baltic until they came into Scandinavian hands in Rothrsland— the seaboard of Sweden in the neighbourhood of Stockholm.[2] And, while the main body of the Vikings launched their ships on the waters of the North Sea and sought their fortunes on the coasts of France and the British Isles and Iceland, there were other Scandinavian ships'-companies that set sail upon the Baltic to trace the alluring dirhems and dinars to their Khazar source.

According to the legend,[3] these Rothrslanders—or Rhôs, as their name was contracted by their victims—came in as peacefully as the Khazars had come before them when they made their first lodgement on the Russian ground that has inherited their Swedish name. It is as difficult to identify the moment, in the early part of the ninth century, at which these Swedish 'warings' or 'varangians' superseded the Turkish Khazars in the effective control of a Slav Novgorod and a Slav Kiev as it is to say exactly when the Achaeans superseded the Mycenaeans at Mycenae and Tiryns during the decline of the Minoan 'thalassocracy'.[4] It is certain, however, that from the beginning—whatever the exact date may have been—the Varangian régime in the forest country differentiated itself from the preceding Khazar régime by taking to violence instead of emulating the Khazars' gentleness.

Violence had, indeed, already gained the upper hand in the heart of the Khazar dominions before the first Varangian fighting trader—or trading pirate[5]—broke out of the forest on to the Steppe in his descent of the Dniepr. The fortress of Sarkel which was built by East Roman military engineers for an already hard-pressed Khazar Khāqān about the year 835[6] had not availed to hold at bay the other Qāzāqs on the Khazars' opposite anti-barbarian frontier; and we have seen[7] how, some fifty years later, the Khāqān's ingenious attempt to catch the Transvolgan Pechenegs between two fires and thus annihilate them merely resulted in precipitating the Pecheneg 'break-through' which the Khazar statesman had dreaded. Although the last strongholds of the

---

[1] See II. D (vii), vol. ii, pp. 343 and 345, above.
[2] See Kluchevski, op. cit., German translation, vol. i, p. 165.
[3] See II. D (iii), vol. ii, p. 99, above.
[4] See the present chapter, p, 236, footnote 3, above.
[5] The delicate distinction is discussed in Kluchevski, op. cit., German translation, vol. i, p. 129.   [6] Kluchevski, op. cit., German translation, vol. i, p. 125.
[7] In Part III. A, Annex II, vol. iii, pp. 441–3, above.

Khazars at the mouths of the Volga and the Don did not fall into the hands of Russian raiding-parties till as late as about A.D. 966,[1] the widespread Khazar Empire which had been established in the eighth century had ceased to exist by the time when, in the last decade of the ninth century, a Pecheneg horde which had driven all its Nomad competitors off the Steppe between the right bank of the Don and the left bank of the Lower Danube collided, along a line that ran a day's journey south-east of Kiev,[2] with a Scandinavian principality, seated in that city, which had already established its hegemony over the kindred Scandinavian principalities in its rear as far to the north as the shores of Lake Ladoga.[3]

The Scandinavian war-bands[4] which thus usurped the Khazars' heritage[5] in the Northern Forest in the course of the ninth century of the Christian Era display, beyond mistake, the now familiar features of an external proletariat in its hour of triumph. While they were keen traders as well as fine fighters,[6] they had lost their roots in the soil, and they left the task of cultivation, and also even the more lucrative craft of hunting and trapping, to their forest-born Slav subjects, who were sundered socially from their more sophisticated but also more ferocious Russian masters by a sharp cleavage.[7] Moreover these barbarian invaders of the Khazar World have left an echo of their deeds and experiences in a 'heroic' poetry which sets its scene in the landscape of the Ukrainian Steppe, with the city of Kiev for its cynosure[8]—though the only places in which the oral tradition of chanting this poetry is known for certain to survive down to the present day are the Olonetz district, between Lakes Ladoga and Onega, at an extremity of the Varangian war-bands' former field of operations which is as remote as could be from Kiev, and the valley of the river Kolyma in North-Eastern Siberia, where the descendants of the most adventurous of all the post-Varangian Russian pioneers rub shoulders now on the Arctic Circle with the Palaearctic rear-guard of Primitive Mankind.[9]

[1] See Part III. A, Annex II, vol. iii, p. 427, above.
[2] Kluchevski, op. cit., German translation, vol. i, p. 159.
[3] For the establishment of the supremacy of Kiev over the other Scandinavian 'successor-states' of the Khazar Empire see Kluchevski, op. cit., German translation, vol. i, pp. 144–8.
[4] For an account of these Varangian war-bands, which came to be known as *druzhinas* in the Slavonic tongue of the subject population which they had captured, like cattle, from the Khazars, see Kluchevski, op. cit., German translation, vol. i, pp. 197–9.
[5] The fact that these Scandinavian war-lords regarded themselves as successors of the Khazars is demonstrated by their adoption of the Khazar title Khāqān (see Kluchevski, op. cit., German translation, vol. i, p. 161).
[6] Kluchevski, op. cit., German translation, vol. i, p. 163.
[7] Kluchevski, op. cit., German translation, vol. i, p. 166.
[8] Chadwick, N. K.: *Russian Heroic Poetry* (Cambridge 1932, University Press), p. 25; Chadwick, H. M. and N. K.: *The Growth of Literature*, vol. ii (Cambridge 1936, University Press), pp. 23–5, 81, and 93–4.
[9] See Chadwick, *Russian Heroic Poetry*, pp. 2–5; Chadwick, *The Growth of Literature*,

This Russian 'heroic' poetry is a living monument—remote though it be, to-day, in place as well as in time—of the Varangian war-bands' Völkerwanderung into the domain of the Khazar Empire in the ninth century of the Christian Era. Have other barbarian invaders of other steppe-empires been moved by the same experience to give proof of a similar creativity? The question may remind us that the only 'heroic' poetry of any consequence that is known to have existed in any Turkish language is that which can still be heard to-day on the lips of 'Kirghiz Qāzāq' minstrels[1] whose audience are descendants of the Nomad constituents of the external proletariat of the Golden Horde.[2]

The External Proletariat of the Main Body of Orthodox Christendom.

When we turn to the history of the Orthodox Christian Civilization, we find that the first of the barbarian offensives which the main body of Orthodox Christendom had to meet was that of the Varangians, whose flotilla of war-canoes bore down upon the Bosphorus out of the Black Sea in A.D. 860 as swiftly and unexpectedly as a swarm of wasps.[3] These Russian barbarian invaders of the Orthodox Christian World cannot, however, be regarded as members of an external proletariat which had been generated by Orthodox Christendom itself; for, as we have seen, the stimulus that drove the Rothrslanders on to the war-path was proximately the Khazar penetration of the Northern Forest, and ultimately Charlemagne's aggressive war of extermination in Saxony, and was not any move that had been made by any Orthodox Christian dominant minority. The Varangian assaults on the East Roman and Bulgarian Empires in the ninth and tenth centuries of the Christian Era were incidental effects of the Scandinavian Völkerwanderung into the domain of the adjoining

vol. ii, pp. 10 and 11. The majority of the Russian heroic poems that were recaptured and reduced to writing in the middle of the nineteenth century—when the oral tradition was on the point of becoming extinct—through the labours of modern scholars, were heard in the Olonetz district.

[1] See Vambéry, Arminius: *Das Türkenvolk in seinen Ethnologischen und Ethnographischen Beziehungen* (Leipzig 1885, Brockhaus), pp. 292–8. For the vestiges of a 'heroic' poetry, centring round the figure of Köroghlu, among the Western Turks see Chodsko: *Specimens of the Popular Poetry of Persia as found in the Adventures and Improvisation of Kurroglu, the Bandit Minstrel of Northern Persia, and in the Songs of the People inhabiting the Shores of the Caspian Sea* (London 1842, Allen, for the Oriental Translation Fund).

[2] See pp. 282–3, above.

[3] In the element of suddenness and surprise this Russian naval attack on Constantinople in A.D. 860 is reminiscent of the Gothic naval attack on the Black Sea coasts of the Roman Empire *post* A.D. 250 and of the Cossack naval attack on the Black Sea coasts of the Ottoman Empire *post* A.D. 1637 (for the intermittent occupation of the Great Western Bay of the Eurasian Steppe by bands of non-Nomadic barbarians from the Northern Forest see Part III. A, Annex II, vol. iii, pp. 426–8, above). According to Kluchevski (op. cit., German translation, vol. i, p. 127), there is evidence for Russian raids on the Black Sea coasts of the East Roman Empire at a date which must be earlier than A.D. 842.

Khazar Empire—just as the assaults of other sea-rovers upon 'the New Empire' of Egypt in the thirteenth and twelfth centuries B.C. were incidental effects of a Central European barbarian Völkerwanderung into the domain of the Minoan 'thalassocracy'.[1]

In Egyptiac history this backwash from the foundering of a neighbour civilization inflicted serious damage, because the Egyptiac Society itself happened, at the time, to be in a far-advanced stage of decline and exhaustion in which it no longer possessed the necessary reserves of strength for meeting with impunity an unexpected call upon its energies.[2] On the other hand the Orthodox Christian Civilization was still in growth throughout the period which began with the East Roman Empire's repulse of the surprise attack of Askold's war-canoes in the Bosphorus in A.D. 860, and which culminated in the expulsion of Svyatoslav's warbands from the Balkan Peninsula in A.D. 972 by the Emperor John Tzimisces;[3] and the struggle did not end in either the overwhelming or the crippling of the East Roman Empire and the Orthodox Christian Civilization—as the Khatti Empire and the Hittite Civilization were overwhelmed, and 'the New Empire' and the Egyptiac Civilization were crippled, by the impact of the post-Minoan Völkerwanderung. Like 'the New Empire' of Egypt, and unlike the Empire of Hatti, the East Roman Empire proved to the rampant barbarians, on the battle-field, that it was stronger in arms than they were; but the defeated Varangians, unlike the defeated Philistines and Teucrians, were then quickly captivated by the civilization of the victors. The discomfiture of Svyatoslav in A.D. 972 was followed in A.D. 988/9 by the conversion of Vladímir;[4] and, therewith, the Scandinavian 'successor-state' of the Khazar Empire in the Northern Forest was transmuted into a state-member of Orthodox Christendom, and the trading-post of Kiev into a Russian equivalent of Constantinople. This establishment of a new branch of Orthodox Christendom on Russian soil, which was achieved in the hour of the breakdown of the parent stem, was the last, but also perhaps the greatest, creative act of the Orthodox Christian Civilization.[5]

[1] See I. C (i) (b), vol. i, pp. 93 and 100–1, and the present chapter and volume, pp. 236–7 and 269, above.

[2] See p. 269, with the references in footnote 4 on that page, above.

[3] For Svyatoslav's overland invasion of the Bulgarian Empire in A.D. 969–72 see IV. C (iii) (c) 2 (β), vol. iv, pp. 389–90, above. According to Kluchevski, op. cit., German translation, vol. i, p. 153, the complete list of Russian attacks on the East Roman Empire is as follows: Askold's in A.D. 860; Oleg's in A.D. 907, Igor's in A.D. 941 and 944; Svyatoslav's in A.D. 971; Yaroslav's in A.D. 1043. It will be noticed that all of them except the last were anterior to the breakdown of the Orthodox Christian Civilization in A.D. 977.

[4] See II. D (vii), vol. ii, pp. 352–3, above.

[5] For the genesis of the Russian offshoot of the Orthodox Christian Civilization see I. C (ii), vol. i, pp. 132–4; II. D (iii), vol. ii, p. 80, footnote 2, and II. D (v), vol. ii, p. 154, above.

In forcing themselves upon the East Roman Empire in their alternating roles of pirates and traders, the Varangians were partly moved by the commercial motive of bringing to the market of Constantinople, by the water-route of the Dniepr and the Black Sea, the commodities which they collected in their annual tribute-taking tours of their subject territories in the Northern Forest.[1] But there was also perhaps a political motive which moved the war-lords without their being able to avow it to their war-bands. The most famous of the Varangian princes of Kiev, Vladímir the Great (*dominabatur* A.D. 980–1015), who was responsible, as we have seen, for the conversion of his henchmen and subjects to the Orthodox Christian religion and culture, seems to have been anxious to find an outlet for the formidable energies of the Scandinavian mercenaries who flocked into his camp on the Dniestr in embarrassing numbers; and his solution of the problem was to 'pass on' his superfluous warriors to the East Roman Empire without much caring whether they went as marauders or as mercenaries.[2] In the course of the eleventh century the same trick was played upon the East Roman Empire on a larger scale, and with more serious results for the victim, by two other neighbours: the rising Western Society on the north-west and the declining Syriac Society on the south-east. The French no doubt breathed a sigh of relief when the great-grand-children of the Viking companions of Rollo, whom Charles the Simple had perforce accepted as settlers on French soil in A.D. 911,[3] rode off across the Pyrenees in A.D. 1018 to fight for the Christian barbarians of the Iberian Peninsula against the Andalusian Umayyad Caliphate,[4] and across the Alps in A.D. 1016 to fight for the Catholic Lombard rebels against the authority of the Orthodox East Roman Empire in Apulia.[5] And in the next generation the Sunnī Muslims of Iran and 'Irāq were assuredly no less pleased when their Saljūq converts and conquerors began to look for pastures new in the Anatolian dominions of the infidel East Roman Empire in A.D. 1037,[6] and in the Syrian dominions of the schismatic Fātimid Caliphate in A.D. 1071.[7]

This same year 1071—which saw the East Roman Emperor Romanus Diogenes taken prisoner by the Saljūqs on the field of Manzikert and the East Roman metropolis in Apulia, Bari, fall

---

[1] See Kluchevski, op. cit., German translation, vol. i, pp. 150–2.
[2] Ibid., p. 134.
[3] See II. D (vii), vol. ii, p. 347, above.
[4] See the present chapter, pp. 242–4 and 259–61, above.
[5] For the Norman mercenaries whom Melo of Bari employed in his abortive incursion into East Roman territory in A.D. 1017–18 see IV. C (iii) (c) 2 (β), vol. iv, p. 392, foot-notes 1 and 2, and p. 401, above.
[6] See IV. C (iii) (c) 2 (β), vol. iv, p. 401, and the present chapter and volume p. 247, above.
[7] See p. 247, above.

into the hands of the Normans[1]—was a disastrous year in the history of the relations between the main body of Orthodox Christendom and the barbarians. These Norman and Saljūq barbarian invaders now carved out of a broken-down East Roman Empire the 'successor-states' which their Varangian forerunners had failed to carve out of an Orthodox Christian body social that was still in growth at the time when they were assailing it.[2] In one point, however, the Varangians and the Normans and the Saljūqs were all of a piece from the Orthodox Christian standpoint. They were all of them alien barbarians who had been 'passed on' into the Orthodox Christian World by the societies which had bred them. It was not until the Orthodox Christian 'Time of Troubles' (*saeviebat circa* A.D. 975–1375) had entered upon its last and worst phase, after the Frankish sack of Constantinople in A.D. 1204, that Orthodox Christendom's homegrown barbarians began to play their part in the barbarian assaults upon a tortured and prostrated Orthodox Christian body social.

At the moment of the breakdown of Orthodox Christendom in A.D. 977 there were three directions in which the Orthodox Christian culture was being radiated out among barbarians, and in which it was therefore to be expected, on analogy, that anti-barbarian fronts would crystallize as the broken-down civilization went into disintegration. One of these barbarian thresholds of the Orthodox Christian World was in the Abruzzi, where Lombard Western Christian barbarians were absorbing the cultural influence, while they were kicking against the political suzerainty, of the East Roman Viceroyalty of Apulia. Another was in Armenia, where Gregorian Monophysite Christian barbarians—a Mleh[3] and a John Tzimisces[4]—had been finding careers for themselves among the 'borderers' in the East Roman military service. There was also a third barbarian threshold in Jugoslavia and Albania, where the last survivors of the Continental European barbarians—Arnauts and Serbs and Bosniaks—were in relations with the Bulgarian Empire that resembled the relations of the Armenians and the South Lombards with the East Roman Empire. On two thresholds out of these three the front did not have time to form, since the Normans and the Saljūqs, breaking in from the back of beyond, respectively overwhelmed the Lombards and the Armenians and usurped their roles. It was only on the Continental European

---

[1] See IV. C (iii) (c) 2 (β), vol. iv, p. 392, footnote 2, above.

[2] Between the Varangian prince Svyatoslav's abortive invasion of the Balkan Peninsula in A.D. 969–72 and his Norman kinsmen's successful conquest of the Byzantine dominions in Italy in and after A.D. 1040 the main body of Orthodox Christendom had inflicted on itself the disaster of the Great Romano-Bulgarian War of A.D. 977–1019 (see IV. C (iii) (c) 2 (β), vol. iv, pp. 390–1, above).

[3] See pp. 242 and 253–4, above.   [4] See IV. C (iii) (c) 2 (β), vol. iv, p. 400, above.

front of the Bulgarian Empire that the home-grown external proletariat of the main body of Orthodox Christendom succeeded in the end in playing its normal part.

The Serb barbarians were the *tertii gaudentes* in the life-and-death struggle between the two principal Powers of the Orthodox Christian World. They were drawn, as humble allies of the East Roman Empire, into the Romano-Bulgarian War of A.D. 913–27;[1] and, although, after the East Roman victory in the Great Romano-Bulgarian War of A.D. 977–1019, 'the Serbs received for their reward what the Bulgars received for their punishment',[2] and were temporarily incorporated into the East Roman body politic, they fared better than the Bulgars in the next chapter of the story; for they recovered their political freedom more than a hundred years earlier[3] and made greater play with it during the time that was at their disposal before Serbs and Bulgars and Greeks were all compelled to lie down with one another under a *Pax Ottomanica*.[4] In the middle of the fourteenth century of the Christian Era, when the remnant of the revived Bulgarian Empire was in almost as miserable a state as the Nicene Greek principality which had reoccupied the East Roman Imperial Throne at Constantinople,[5] the Serbian war-bands were marching down the valley of the Vardar and making themselves masters of that Macedonian hinterland of Salonica which had been the battle-field of Greeks and Bulgars for the past five hundred years. And, while the Serbs pushed on into Thessaly and beyond, as far as Thermopylae, the Albanians—now heard of for the first time in Orthodox Christian history[6]—were staking out

---

[1] See IV. C (iii) (c) 2 (β), vol. iv, pp. 385–6, above.

[2] To parody the famous epigram which was originally uttered apropos of the uniform repression to which the Croat loyalists and the Magyar rebels were subjected by the Hapsburg Government after the political convulsions of 1848–9 in the Danubian Monarchy.

[3] The Serbs shook off the East Roman yoke *de facto* in, or soon after, A.D. 1081; the Bulgars not until A.D. 1186. The nominal suzerainty of the East Roman Government over the Serbs did, however, last until the death of the East Roman Emperor Manuel I Comnenus in A.D. 1180; and during the last thirty years of his reign (that is, since A.D. 1149) Manuel appears to have asserted his authority over the Serbs more effectively than any of his predecessors had asserted theirs since the loosening of the Empire's hold upon the western part of the Balkan Peninsula in consequence of the Norman invasion launched in A.D. 1081 by Robert Guiscard.

[4] See IV. C (ii) (b) 2, vol. iv, p. 82, footnote 3, above.

[5] For the role of these Nicene Greeks as forerunners of the 'Osmanlis see Part III. A, vol. iii, p. 27, above.

[6] It is impossible to say that this was the first time that the Albanians had intervened in the history of any civilization, since we may guess that their ancestors had played a part in Hellenic history. We do not know, however, whether it is from the Illyrians or from the Thracians that the Albanians are physically descended. On *prima facie* geographical grounds we might be inclined to trace the Albanians' ancestry back to the Illyrians, whose national home in the Hellenic Age included the Albanians' present habitat. On the other hand the linguistic evidence points rather to a Thracian pedigree for the Albanians, since the Albanian, like the Thracian, language is unquestionably a member of the Satem-group of the Indo-European Family, whereas the Illyrian language appears to have belonged to the Centum-group, to judge by the extant monuments of the Venetic and Messapic dialects of the Illyrian settlers in Italy.

corresponding claims on the East Roman heritage in Central Greece and the Peloponnese. The whole domain of Ortho-dox Christendom in the Balkan Peninsula might have been parcelled out, before the close of the fourteenth century, into Serb and Albanian barbarian principalities if the barbarians' progress had not been cut short abruptly by the arrival on the scene of the Ottoman founders of an Orthodox Christian universal state, who conquered Macedonia in A.D. 1371–2 and completed their work in this quarter by annexing the Peloponnese in A.D. 1460.

This tardily arrested incursion of the home-grown external proletariat of the Orthodox Christian World into the heart of Orthodox Christendom on the eve of the establishment of the Orthodox Christian universal state has its pendant, as we should expect, in a second offensive movement of the same barbarian forces at the moment when the universal state broke up. In a different context[1] we have detected the rudiments of a barbarian invasion of the Ottoman Empire, on the same Continental European front, at the turn of the eighteenth and nineteenth centuries of the Christian Era, with the same barbarians playing the same parts. In A.D. 1769–79 a band of Albanian mercenaries in the Ottoman service emulated the past exploits of their fellow tribesmen, four hundred years back, by making themselves momentarily masters of the Peloponnese; and in A.D. 1804 the Serbs rose against the Ottoman régime, as they had risen against the East Roman régime *circa* A.D. 1081.

We may also remind ourselves that, in the abortive post-Ottoman interregnum which began in the last quarter of the eighteenth century, the Albanian and Serb upheavals on the Continental European front of the Ottoman Empire were synchronous with other barbarian upheavals on other anti-barbarian fronts for which the 'Osmanlī empire-builders of the sixteenth century had made themselves responsible by their conquests at the expense of the Iranic and the Arabic World.[2] The 'Osmanlis had thereby acquired a highland frontier in Kurdistan and also two desert frontiers—one on the Syrian and 'Irāqī fringes of the Afrasian Steppe in North Arabia, and another on the Egyptian fringe in Nubia—and, when the Ottoman Empire broke down, these African and Asiatic fronts both likewise lit up. The Kurdish highlanders and the Arabian Nomads began to assert themselves before the close of the eighteenth century, at the same moment

---

[1] In IV. C (ii) (*b*) 1, vol. iv, pp. 68 and 69, and IV. C (ii) (*b*) 2, vol. iv, p. 76, above.

[2] For the tardy and reluctant expansion of the Ottoman Empire in these two directions see I. C (i) (*b*), Annex I, vol. i, pp. 384–90, above.

as the Albanians and the Serbs, while the Sudanese Nomads
followed suit in A.D. 1883.[1]

We have seen that[2] on all these four anti-barbarian fronts of the
Ottoman Empire 'the triumph of Barbarism' was cut short by
the far more potent social movement of Westernization. Yet, brief
though their career was, these barbarian heroes of an abortive post-
Ottoman interregnum did not succumb to their alternative fates of
being killed off by modern Western lethal weapons or taking to top-
hats, as the price of being given quarter, without leaving behind them
some of the characteristic monuments of a barbarian creativity.

In the sphere of religion there was a marked tendency among
the barbarians in the hinterland of several of these fronts to adopt
the 'higher religion' of the dominant minority of the day in a
form that was sufficiently schismatic to be distinctive. In the
Orthodox Christian 'Time of Troubles', for instance, the Bosniak
section of the Jugoslav external proletariat of Orthodox Christendom did not follow the example of their kinsmen and neighbours
the Serbs in accepting the Orthodox Christian Faith. Instead, they
took to Bogomilism, a Bulgarian Slav adaptation of a Paulician
Adoptionist Christianity which had lingered on among the transfrontier barbarians beyond the Armenian front of the East
Roman Empire, and which had been subsequently carried into
the European provinces of the Empire by Paulician deportees.[3]
Again, under the Ottoman Empire which performed the function
of an Orthodox Christian universal state, the 'higher religion'
which won its way among the Albanians was not the orthodox
Sunnī Islam that was the official religion of the Ottoman dominant
minority. The Islam to which the Albanians yielded themselves
was the esoterically heterodox school of the Bektāshī Order of
Dervishes.[4] Finally, during the post-Ottoman interregnum, the
Najdī Arabs rose up against the Ottoman régime in Asia, and the
Kordofānī Arabs against the Egypto-Ottoman régime in Africa,
under the impetus of a Wahhābī and an Idrīsī puritanism[5] in the

[1] This counterstroke of the Baggara Arab Nomads of Kordofan against the Egyptian
Viceroyalty of the Ottoman Empire was both retarded and provoked by a policy of
reckless expansion into the heart of Tropical Africa which had been initiated by Mehmed
'Alī when he conquered Sannār and founded Khartum in A.D. 1821, and which had
been persisted in by Mehmed 'Alī's successors in the Pashalyq of Egypt until, at the
moment of the explosion in A.D. 1883, the Egyptian flag was flying at the sources of
the White Nile in the short-lived province of Equatoria. This Egypto-Ottoman advance
into the boundless barbarian world of Tropical Africa is comparable to the Khazar
advance into the Northern Forest and to the Etruscan advance into the Po Basin. The
same rashness drew down upon itself the same nemesis in this case as in those.
[2] In IV. C (ii) (b) 2, vol. iv, pp. 76–8, above.
[3] See IV. C (iii) (c) 2 (β), vol. iv, pp. 367–9, and IV. C (iii) (c) 2 (β), Annex III,
vol. iv, pp. 624–34, above, and the present chapter and volume, p. 327, below.
[4] See IV. C (ii) (b) 1, vol. iv, pp. 68–9, and V. C (i) (c) 2, in the present volume, p. 111,
above.
[5] The Idrīsī Sayyids who ruled at Sabyā, on the Asīrī section of the Arabian Tihāmah,
from the date of their successful defiance of Ottoman authority in A.D. 1910 until the

sight of which the official Sunnī orthodoxy of the contemporary Ottoman 'Westernizers' was no better than outright Infidelity.

In the sphere of literature the Continental European external proletariat of the Orthodox Christian World has transmuted into 'heroic' poetry the experience of its conflict with the Ottoman makers and masters of the Orthodox Christian universal state. The Serb ballads, which have found their principal theme in the Battle of Kosovo, are true to type in concentrating upon a tragic story as a more promising field than any record of worldly success for the exercise of the epic minstrel's art.[1] At the same time the Kosovo Cycle is peculiar, and perhaps unique, among the works of barbarian poetic genius in being inspired by the experience of a frustrated offensive at the climax of a 'Time of Troubles', instead of reflecting the exhilaration of a 'break-through' at the beginning of an interregnum. For the Battle of Kosovo (*commissum* A.D. 1389) was the disaster that shattered the Serbian barbarians' dream of entering into the heritage of a broken-down Orthodox Christian Society which had not yet passed through its universal state.[2]

It is true that the Serb *guslari* (minstrels) have not left unsung the later chapters in the history of their warriors' struggle against the 'Osmanlis.

'The heroic songs of the historical cycle deal further with the period of subjugation to the Turks, their oppression and individual reprisals carried out by the *hajduci* and *uskoci*, the memory of whom is preserved in the two cycles thus named, both of which contain many beautiful songs. (The *hajduci* were a kind of guerilla warriors who fought the Turks while they kept Serbia subdued; while the *uskoci* were the Jugoslavs who had fled to Dalmatia and the Croatian littoral after the fall of Herzegovina in 1482, where, as mercenaries of the [Hapsburg] Emperors, they defended the borders from the Turks, often raiding and pouncing upon them.)

absorption of their principality into the dominions of the Wahhābī empire-builder 'Abd-al-'Azīz b. Saʿūd between the years 1926 and 1934, were puritans of the same sect as the Sudanese Mahdī Muhammad Ahmad who led the barbarian counter-attack against the Egypto-Ottoman régime in the Upper Nile Basin in A.D. 1883.

[1] For this (no doubt, unconsciously practised) trick of the epic minstrel's trade see further V. C (i) (c) 3, Annex III, p. 610, below.

[2] The 'Time of Troubles' in the history of the Orthodox Christian Civilization may be said to have run from the last quarter of the tenth century of the Christian Era to the last quarter of the fourteenth; the universal state (i.e. the Ottoman Empire) from the last quarter of the fourteenth century to the last quarter of the eighteenth. The historical events of which some memory is embedded in the Serb 'heroic' poetry of the Classical School—which includes the several cycles of Kosovo, Marko Kraljević, George Branković, Vuk 'the Dragon-Despot', and the Jakšića (see Chadwick, *The Growth of Literature*, vol. ii, pp. 310–25)—fall within the years 1371–1485 (see ibid., pp. 447–8 and 454). There is, however, also a hazy recollection of the great Czar Stjepan Dušan, who reigned in Macedonia from 1331 to 1356, just before the overthrow of the Serbs by the 'Osmanlis (ibid., pp. 310 and 454). Compare the recollection, in the Teutonic Epic, of the great Ostrogothic war-lord Hermanoric (*Anglicè* Eormenric), who reigned in the Ukraine in the third quarter of the fourth century of the Christian Era, just before the overthrow of the Ostrogoths by the Huns (Chadwick, *The Heroic Age*, pp. 23 and 37).

'The liberation of Montenegro and Serbia at the beginning of the eighteenth and nineteenth centuries respectively has been described in the two cycles thus named . . . . The *guslari* [chanted] for the leaders of the First Rising of the Serbs, during the first two decades of the last century. Filip Višnjić, for instance, spent four years in the district of Mačva, and almost all his songs, which he recited for Vuk Karadžić a few years later, describe the fighting between the Serbs and the Turks which took place in that district while he was there, and glorify the deeds of the contemporary Serbian leaders. There are several instances which prove that many Serbian leaders of that period had their own *guslari*, and these very often composed songs in which the heroic deeds of their masters were glorified. This, perhaps, explains the fact that heroic songs which deal with the liberation of the Serbs, and those which chant the achievements of the *hajduci* and *uskoci*, are far more numerous than those dealing with the events and personalities of mediaeval Serbian history.'[1]

The quality, however, of this Serbian 'heroic' poetry of a later age is in inverse ratio to its quantity; for the Hajduk and Uskok cycles

'both—and the former especially—relate true historical events with very little poetry. They differ greatly in this respect from the earlier heroic songs. These are, perhaps, the least interesting and the least beautiful'.[2]

Such as they are, the Hajduk and Uskok cycles of Serb 'heroic' poetry have an Albanian analogue of approximately the same date,[3] and also a Greek analogue in songs which celebrate the prowess of *klephts* and *armatolí* who were the Greek contemporaries and counterparts of the Serb *hajduci* and *uskoci* in the interior of the Ottoman Empire.[4] The Greek Armatole and Klephtic cycles

---

[1] Subotić, D.: *Yugoslav Popular Ballads: Their Origin and Development* (Cambridge 1932, University Press), pp. 17 and 23–4. [2] Ibid., p. 17.
[3] See Chadwick, *The Growth of Literature*, vol. ii, pp. 455–6. In its style this Albanian 'heroic' poetry 'seems to resemble Greek "heroic" poetry of the same period, rather than Jugoslav'. In addition to the school of Albanian 'heroic' poetry corresponding in date and in inspiration to the Hajduk and Uskok cycles of Serb 'heroic' poetry, there seems also to be an earlier school, celebrating the exploits of the fifteenth-century Albanian hero Scanderbeg, which would correspond to the Serb Classical School in being a monument of a barbarian experience·of the last phase of the Orthodox Christian 'Time of Troubles'.
[4] Whereas the *hajduci* and *uskoci* were transfrontier barbarians of the Ottoman Empire in the literal and exact meaning of the term, the *klephts* were insurgents whose bases of operations lay within the Ottoman frontiers. It will be seen that, in terms of the history of the Roman Empire, the Serb *hajduci* who crossed the Save and broke into the Serb-inhabited districts of the Empire in A.D. 1804 correspond to the German war-bands which crossed the Rhine and broke into the Roman provinces of Upper and Lower Germany on the last day of A.D. 406, while the contemporary upheaval of the Basque and Isaurian highlanders in the interior of the Roman Empire has its analogue in the upheaval of the Rumiliot and Moreot Greek *klephts*. As for the Rumiliot *armatolí*, these were a local Greek Orthodox Christian hereditary militia which had been tolerated, and indeed encouraged, by the Ottoman Power as an instrument for keeping the *klephts* in check on the principle of setting a thief to catch a thief (κλέπτης is the Greek for thief, while ἁρματωλός is a Greek version of the Italian word *armatore*, meaning an outfitter of piratical craft: see Vlakhogiánnis, G.: Κλέφτες τοῦ Μοριᾶ (Athens 1935, no imprint of publisher's name), pp. 14 and 17).

of 'heroic' poetry[1] belong to the same school as the Serb Hajduk and Uskok cycles,[2] and like these, again, they wilted away in the

[1] These Greek cycles confront the student of history with some intricate and obscure preliminary problems of literary analysis and criticism from which the contemporary and corresponding Serb cycles would appear to be free; and those literary difficulties are in their turn due, at any rate in part, to three historical facts. The first of these facts is that the principal seed-bed of this Modern Greek 'heroic' poetry lay, not in the Morea, but in Continental Greece north of the Isthmus of Corinth (a region which, under the Ottoman régime, formed part of the Empire's European metropolitan province of Rumili). The second fact is that before, during, and after the Greek national uprising of 1821 the Rumiliot klephts and armatolí alike were successfully and permanently crushed by the 'Osmanlis (in 1783 'Ali Pasha of Yannina was appointed by the Porte to be general Derbend Aghasy of Rumili, with the mission of destroying both the klephts and the armatolí of his province; 'Ali carried out this mission efficiently till his fall in 1820; and the ruin of the martial elements in the Greek population of Rumili was consummated through the ultimate failure in Rumili of the Greek national uprising of 1821 which was ultimately successful in the Morea: see Vlakhogiánnis, op. cit., pp. 181–2). The third fact is that the life and poetry of the Rumiliot Greek warriors whose history ended in this 'heroic' failure won an immense prestige among their comparatively feeble and inglorious Moreot 'opposite numbers' who scored, contemporaneously, the solid worldly success of liberating their peninsula from Ottoman rule and making of it the nucleus of a 'successor-state' of the Ottoman Empire in the shape of a Greek national state on the contemporary Western pattern (see p. 299, below). If the institution of armatolí had ever existed in the Morea, it had been destroyed in the turmoil of the Venetian intrusion (durabat A.D. 1684–1715: see IV. C (iii) (c) 2 (α), vol. iv, pp. 279–80, above, and V. C (i) (d) 6 (γ), Annex I, in the present volume, pp. 637–8, below); upon the Ottoman reconquest the duties performed by the Greek armatolí in Rumili were assigned in the Morea by the reinstated Ottoman authorities to an alien Albanian militia (Vlakhogiánnis, op. cit., pp. 13–25) which continued to perform these duties here throughout the restoration period (durabat A.D. 1715–1821); the only ra'íyeh ín the Morea who were authorized to bear arms during this period were the tame apparitors (called Κάποι) of the local Orthodox Christian civilian notables (the khŏja-bāshis); and the Moreot klephts (see ibid., pp. 34–74 and 110–35), who ventured to raise their heads only between 1770 and 1806, and who were never more than 150 strong all told (ibid., pp. 88, 159, 176), were more of a plague to their own co-religionists than they were to the local representatives of the Ottoman 'Ascendancy' (ibid., pp. 37, 155, 160–2, 180–1), and were eventually hunted down or forced to fly the country by a general hue and cry in which law-abiding Christian and Muslim Moreots joined with equal alacrity, and which attained its objective within a few weeks (ibid.; pp. 136–82). These inglorious antecedents stung those survivors of the Moreot klephts and kapi who distinguished themselves in the War of 1821–9 into attempting to ennoble themselves by claiming a fictitious 'Moreot armatole' ancestry; and to this end they seem to have gone to prodigious lengths in forging for themselves a 'heroic' history and literature on Rumiliot models (ibid., pp. 11 and 257). These two kinds of Moreot fake are exemplified respectively in the Kolokotronaic family cycle of spurious 'heroic' ballads (see p. 299, footnote 3, below) and in the memoirs of the most illustrious member of this house, Theodore Kolokotrónis, which he dictated in his old age under the title of Διήγησις Συμβάντων τῆς Ἑλληνικῆς Φυλῆς, 1770–1836 (Athens 1889, Estía, 2 vols.). In this work, on p. 40 of that edition, there is a romantic sketch of the life of the (in truth sordid) Moreot klephts and the (in truth non-existent) Moreot armatolí which has been devastatingly exposed, for the fancy picture that it is, by Vlakhogiánnis in op. cit., pp. 42–3. The critic shows that Kolokotrónis has purloined his fictitious Moreot colours and outlines from the true portrait of the Rumiliot armatolí whose acquaintance he first made as their fellow refugee in Zante in and after 1806. Some of the details of Kolokotrónis' sketch appear to have been taken (Vlakhogiánnis, op. cit., pp. 42–3) from a still unpublished account by an eye-witness of the life of the Rumiliot armatolí in the Aspropótamo district during the years 1821–4. It will be seen that the authentic life and literature of the full-blooded Rumiliot armatolí and klephts are exceedingly difficult to reconstruct.

[2] The literary affinity here is indeed so close that a Western scholar is said to have discovered the existence of the Modern Greek 'heroic' poetry by inference from his knowledge of the existence of the Serb 'heroic' poetry, as an astronomer sometimes suspects the existence of a hitherto undetected star by inference from his observations of the movements of other heavenly bodies. According to an anonymous article in the Athenâ of the 8th November, 1858 (quoted in Vlakhogiánnis, op. cit., pp. 198–9), a German scholar from the Rhineland, who was brought to Vienna in 1814 by business relating to the international peace congress that was being held in that city in that year,

hour in which the historic deeds that were the minstrels' theme were crowned with success. How are we to explain this apparently premature drying up of the springs of a barbarian poetic inspiration? Was it the very success of the 'heroes' in real life that debarred their fictitious doubles, who were being conjured into a poetic existence in the minstrels' imagination, from entering upon a career in that 'other world' of literary life in which the Siegfrieds and the Guthheres have grown to so vastly taller a stature than was ever attained by the petty war-lords whose historic names are borne by these famous creatures of imagination?[1] No doubt the Karageorgević or the Obrenović who had laid aside his weapons and stepped out of his forest fastness in order to receive an Imperial patent from a discomfited Pādishāh and then take his seat, as a duly recognized princeling, upon a tawdry little throne, had thereby made himself as poor a subject for 'heroic' poetry as Theodoric when he stepped into Odovacer's shoes in the guise of the Emperor Anastasius's viceroy in Italy, or as Clovis when he accepted the insignia of the consulship from the same Emperor's envoys after his victory over the Visigoths at Vouillé.[2] On this analogy[3] we may surmise that the 'heroic' poetry of the Serb and Greek external proletariat of the Ottoman Empire would in any event have had a short life after the successful establishment of a Serb 'successor-state' of the Empire in the Morava Basin and a Greek 'successor-state' in the Peloponnese. We have noticed, however,[4] that these barbarian 'successor-states'

suggested to the Director of the Imperial Library in Vienna, Kopitar, who had published a collection of Serb folk-songs, that an inquiry might reveal the existence of a corresponding school of poetry among the Greeks. Kopitar passed on this suggestion to a member of the Greek colony in Vienna, and eventually the Greek colonies in Vienna and Paris, between them, duly collected a number of Greek folk-songs (most of which appear to have been supplied by a Viennese Greek's grandmother, who was living in her grandson's household) and placed their collection in the hands of a French scholar who had made his mark in this field by publishing a collection of French folk-songs. This was the origin of C. Fauriel's *Chants Populaires de la Grèce Moderne* (Paris 1824–5, Firmin-Didot, 2 vols.).

[1] On this point see further V. C (i) (c) 3, Annex III, pp. 612–13, below.
[2] On this point see further V. C (i) (c) 3, Annex III, pp. 613–14, below.
[3] A worldly success which might put its winner out of the running for becoming the popular hero of a genuine 'heroic' poetry might, of course, at the same time place it within the barbarian *arriviste*'s power to make good the lack of genuine poetry in his honour by procuring the fabrication of fakes. According to Vlakhogiánnis, op. cit., pp. 215–25, the Greek ballads of which the Kolokotronaîoi, individually or collectively, are the heroes, are none of them genuine, but are the offspring of a series of literary forgeries perpetrated by, or on behalf of, the family in the course of the half-century beginning in 1821. According to the same scholar again (op. cit., *passim*), this faking of the Kolokotronaic cycle of Modern Greek 'heroic' ballads is merely the classical example of a contemporary orgy of fabrication for which the motives were the glorification of particular individuals, families, and districts. Any student of history who wishes to arrive at an independent opinion of his own on the subject of Monsieur Vlakhogiánnis' iconoclastic thesis will find a collection of the Kolokotronaic ballads at the end of the second volume of Theodore Kolokotrónis' memoirs in the edition cited above on p. 298, footnote 1. Three are printed in Polítis, N. G.: *'Εκλογαὶ ἀπὸ τὰ Τραγούδια τοῦ Ἑλληνικοῦ Λαοῦ* (Athens 1914, Estía), Nos. 53, 60, 64.
[4] In IV. C (ii) (b) 2, vol. iv, pp. 76–8, above.

of the Ottoman Empire had hardly begun to take shape before
they underwent a transformation into the totally different species
of states members of the Western comity. And it seems probable
that their 'Westernization' was a still more potent factor than
their material success in killing the Serb and Greek 'heroic'
tradition.

The revolutionary change of social environment which was
brought about, within the span of a single lifetime, by the inrush
of Western technique and ideas and institutions that accompanied
the Greek insurrection against the 'Osmanlis is vividly depicted
in the words of a *ci-devant* Peloponnesian *klepht* who had made
his name and fortune as a warrior-patriot in the Greek national
'uprising' (*epanastasis*) of A.D. 1821–9. The passage occurs in
the memoirs of Theodore Kolokotrónis which were dictated to an
amanuensis by this illiterate leader of a barbarian war-band in
his old age, when, after having fought and quarrelled and pillaged
his way through the Greek War of Independence, he was living,
like a shark out of water, under the sovereignty of a king who had
been imported from Bavaria in order to guide the feet of the
victorious *klephts* into the way of Western Civilization.[1]

'In the days when I was young and might have learnt something,
schools and academies didn't exist. There were only just a few schools
in which they learnt to read and write. The old-time *khōja-bāshīs*,
who were the leading men of a place, hardly knew how to write their
own names. The majority of the archpriests knew nothing but what
they had picked up of the ecclesiastical routine; not one of them
had had a real education. The Psalter, the Eightfold Chant, the Book
of Monthly Offices and other prophetical works were the books
that I read. It was not till I went to Zante[2] that I found the History

---

[1] King Otto's task was no sinecure. The exotic throne on to which he had mounted
with youthful optimism in A.D. 1833 was shaken by a revolution in 1843 and was finally
pulled away from under him in 1863. And the Danish dynasty which has since tried
its hand in Greece has fared almost as ill as its Bavarian predecessor. In 1938 it was
not yet possible to guess what was to be the ultimate sequel to the arbitrary restoration
of a monarchical régime in Greece by a military *coup d'état* which had been announced
on the day—the 11th October, 1935—on which these lines were being written in the
first draft of the present Part of this Study.

[2] The Ionian Islands, of which Zante was one, had been incorporated into the Western
World since their seizure from the East Roman Empire by a Norman admiral and a
Genoese pirate towards the close of the twelfth century of the Christian Era. They had
eventually all been acquired by Venice, and they remained in Venetian hands until
Napoleon took them as part of the French share of the spoils when he partitioned the
Venetian dominions with the Danubian Hapsburg Monarchy in A.D. 1797. The Islands
were then taken from the French by a Russian expeditionary force, which was in occupation
in 1806 when Kolokotrónis sought refuge in Zante after having been hunted out of his
native Morea as one among some 150 Moreot *klephts* who were suppressed, as a public
nuisance, in the first quarter of 1806, by the law-abiding majority of their local compatriots and co-religionists under Ottoman leadership (Vlakhogiánnis, op. cit., pp. 142–
65). In 1807 the Russians retroceded the islands to the French; but all of them except
Corfù were promptly wrested out of French hands by the British. Kolokotrónis enlisted
in a Greek force which the British Government raised in the islands, and he remained
in the British service until two years after the close of the Napoleonic Wars: that is,

of Greece in plain Greek. The books that I read often were the History of Greece, the History of Aristomenes and Gorgo, and the History of Scanderbeg. In my opinion it was the French Revolution and Napoleon that opened the eyes of the World. Before that, the nations were not heard of; the kings were treated like gods on Earth; and whatever those kings did was praised as a matter of course. On this account, by the way, it is more difficult to govern people nowadays. In my time, trade was very small; money was scarce; the dollar fetched three gurush; and anybody who had a thousand gurush was "a big noise": with that amount one could do business which one couldn't do now with a thousand of Venetian currency. There was little intercourse; it was only our Revolution that brought all the Greeks together. You could find people who didn't know the next village an hour's walk from their own. Zante seemed as far away then as the ends of the Earth seem now. What America is to us now—that is pretty well what Zante was to them. When they went to Zante, they called it "going to the Western World" (ἔλεγαν εἰς τὴν Φραγκιά)."[1]

The headlong onset of 'Westernization' that is sketched in this passage will convincingly account for the galloping consumption which overtook both the Greek and the Serb school of 'heroic' poetry in the nineteenth century in a doubly deleterious atmosphere of sophistication and commercialization. In Greece 'the ballads of 1821 were not given time to attain their final form, because the prosaic political and social life which descended upon them brought their [natural] evolution to a halt'.[2] In Bosnia, Herzegovina, and Montenegro the life, and with it the minstrelsy, of 'the Heroic Age' survived until the Austro-Hungarian occupation of the two former provinces in and after A.D. 1878;[3] and even in the sooner westernized Kingdom of Serbia new 'heroic' poems are credibly reported to have been composed to celebrate incidents in the wars of 1912–18.[4] Yet there is also a record of a man being approached, in Montenegro, as far back as 1876 with the 'business proposition' that 'he could have his name brought into

till about four years before the outbreak of the Greek War of Independence in 1821 gave him his opportunity to return, in the *beau rôle* of a patriot, to a native land from which he had been evicted as a malefactor fifteen years earlier.—A.J.T.

[1] Kolokotrónis, op. cit., vol. i, pp. 48–9. The foregoing first-hand account of how the *ra'iyeh* lived 'in real life' in the last days of the Ottoman Empire is oddly reminiscent of the archaistic Utopia which is sketched as an ideal in the *Tao-te King* (see the passage quoted in V. C (i) (d) 8 (α), vol. vi, p. 59, below). The Moreots' feeling in the years before 1821, to which Kolokotrónis here testifies, that Zante was an *alter orbis* must have been borne in upon the writer by an incident which he himself records at an earlier point (p. 18). In 1805, when the Moreot *klephts* had made their own country too hot to hold them, Kolokotrónis went on a personal reconnaissance to Zante and then came back home with the intention of recruiting some of his Moreot fellow malefactors for mercenary service in the neighbouring island. Though they all knew that on their native heath their days were numbered, Kolokotrónis' comrades rejected his proposal, replying to him with one accord: 'We will not go to Phrangiá; we want to die in our native land.'

[2] Vlakhogiánnis, op. cit., p. 266.
[3] Chadwick, *The Growth of Literature*, vol. ii, pp. 337 and 434
[4] Ibid., p. 337.

a poem—presumably as a hero—on payment of two plete, i.e. forty kreuzer or about eightpence'.[1] After the turn of the century

'oral tradition among the Orthodox Christians had largely been displaced by printed books of poems, owing to the enterprise of a printer in Nikšić. In the Montenegrin army there was a regular organization of minstrels under a *kapetan od guslara* or "chief of the minstrels". These men composed their poems collectively and sent them to the printer, who in his turn, apparently after some revision, supplied them with printed copies.'[2]

By the year 1936 the two English students of the subject who have just been quoted found on inquiry

'that nearly every one [in the Serb-speaking parts of Jugoslavia] now can read, and that printed collections of poems are purchasable everywhere, not to mention gramophone records and wireless performances. Moreover, even the most remote districts are no longer inaccessible to external influence'.[3]

This explanation of the decay of the Serb and Greek schools of 'heroic' poetry is borne out by the fact that the Russian school, which took no harm from the 'Byzantinization' of Kiev in and after the reign of Vladímir (*regnabat* A.D. 980–1015), has proved unable to survive the Westernization of Muscovy in and after the reign of Peter the Great (*imperabat* A.D. 1682–1725).

'The intellectual outlook of the Russian minstrels has hardly kept pace with the growing dignity of their subjects. This increasing disparity becomes most obvious when we come to the last large body of narrative heroic poetry which Great Russia has produced—that on the Napoleonic Wars. In the Tsar Alexander, as in his enemy Napoleon, the poets had subjects which might well have inspired a new school of heroic poetry. Tolstoy's *War and Peace* reflects the consciousness which was felt by all Russians, whether in the officers' quarters or in the Moscow and Petrograd drawing rooms, that they were living in an age of heroes. Yet when we read the *byliny* [heroic poems] on the capture of Smolensk, and observe the part assigned to the Cossack General Platov and to the Tsar himself, we are conscious of a paradox. The function of heroic poets is to glorify human action and exalt human beings; but in the pictures of Platov at the French court, of the Tsar Alexander cutting his beard or receiving the intimation of Napoleon's approach, the poet has unconsciously reduced his heroes far below their actual human dignity. The epic manner and formulae are still preserved, but the exaltation has vanished, the epic figures have become puny. Above all, the presentation of the facts is distorted and unworthy of the great events and changes which were taking place. The breach between the minstrels and their old patrons, which shows itself in the poverty of the treatment of exalted subjects, has become

---

[1] Chadwick, op. cit., vol. ii, p. 439, following M. Murko.
[2] Ibid.   [3] Ibid., p. 434.

final—a breach which was perhaps first foreshadowed when the travels of Peter the Great in search of enlightenment[1] were described by an indulgent but uncomprehending minstrel as "amusing himself abroad".'[2]

When the rulers of Muscovy 'went Western', they were betaking themselves beyond the range of the Russian minstrel's capacity for imaginative comprehension; and in these circumstances it was so much the worse for the Russian tradition of 'heroic' poetry that these changelings thenceforth monopolized the field of action that was fit to become a 'heroic' theme. Unable to treat of high matters that passed his understanding, the minstrel was reduced to harping upon prosaic trivialities. Deprived of the grain that was its due, the Russian epic genius quickly died of inanition on a starvation-diet of chaff.

The Hindu External Proletariat.

When we pass from the main body of Orthodox Christendom— with its alien Varangian and Norman and Saljūq barbarian incursions at the beginning of its Romano-Bulgarian 'Time of Troubles' and with the abortive 'heroic age' of its home-bred Albanian and Serb and Greek barbarians at the dissolution of its Ottoman universal state—we shall find some of the same features reappearing in the history of the relations between the external proletariat and the dominant minority of the Hindu World.

In Hindu history the earliest of the barbarian offensives that accompanied the Hindu 'Time of Troubles' (*saeviebat circa* A.D. 1175-1575)[3] was likewise delivered by invaders from the back of beyond who had been 'passed on' by a neighbour civilization. The Turkish war-bands whom Sebuktegīn of Ghaznah and his son and successor Mahmūd led down from Zābulistān upon the Panjab at the turn of the tenth and eleventh centuries of the Christian Era[4] were the kinsmen as well as the contemporaries of the Saljūqs who trespassed out of Transcaspia into Iran in A.D. 1026 and who were 'passed on' into the Anatolian territories of Orthodox Christendom in A.D. 1037.[5] But, just as, in the Orthodox

---

[1] For an estimate of the true significance of Peter's Western tour in A.D. 1697-8 see III. C (ii) (b), vol. iii, pp. 281-3, above.—A.J.T.
[2] Chadwick, N. K.: *Russian Heroic Poetry* (Cambridge 1932, University Press), p. 23. Compare Chadwick, H. M. and N. K.: *The Growth of Literature*, vol. ii (Cambridge 1936, University Press), pp. 91-2. [3] See IV. C (iii) (b) 2, vol. iv, p. 99, above.
[4] See IV. C (ii) (b) 2, vol. iv, pp. 98 and 100, above.
[5] This cleavage in the host of Nomad invaders of South-Western Asia, at the turn of the tenth and eleventh centuries of the Christian Era, into a right wing which swept on into Anatolia and Syria and Egypt and a left wing which swerved away over the Hindu Kush into India has its analogue in the cleavage between the Hyksos conquerors of Egypt and the Aryan conquerors of India in the second millennium B.C. This analogy has been pointed out in another connexion in I. C (i) (b), vol. i, pp. 104-7, above.

Christian 'Time of Troubles', the barbarians from the back of beyond—Varangians and Saljūqs and Normans—were followed, in their invasion, by the home-grown Serbs and Albanians, so in the Hindu 'Time of Troubles' the Turkish Nomad invaders from the Eurasian Steppe were followed by other barbarians whose native haunts were nearer at hand, on the south-eastern rim of the Iranian Plateau.[1] The great 'break-through', which carried the barbarian invaders, at one swoop, from the line of the Sutlej to the coast of Bengal, was achieved by the Ghūrīs—an Iranian mountain-people from the highlands between Ghaznah and Herāt and Qandahār[2] who had previously supplanted the Ghaznawīs both in Zābulistān and in the Panjab. And, although the Eurasian Nomads came to the front again in the war-bands of the 'Slave-Kings' and the Taghlāqīs who ruled over Hindustan in the thirteenth and fourteenth centuries,[3] their successors the Lōdī Afghans, whose reign coincided in time with the last and worst phase of the Hindu 'Time of Troubles',[4] were highland barbarians of the same breed as the Ghūrīs, from the threshold of the Hindu World beyond the North-West Frontier.

This Hindu 'Time of Troubles', in which the Turkish Nomads and the East-Iranian highlanders had thus taken turn and turn about in serving as 'the scourge of God', was brought to an end by the establishment of a Mughal Rāj which gave the Hindu Society its universal state;[5] and in the subsequent chapters of Hindu history the home-grown East Iranian external proletariat of the Hindu World has had the field to itself; for since the reign of Akbar (*imperabat* A.D. 1556–1602), who was the true author of the *Pax Mogulica*,[6] the Eurasian Nomads have not again appeared above the Hindu horizon. When the *Pax Mogulica* prematurely dissolved in the eighteenth century, the barbarians who rushed in—to contend for the possession of the carcase with the Marāthā protagonists of a militant Hindu reaction against an alien universal state—were the East Iranian Rohillas and Afghans; and, when Akbar's work was reperformed by other alien hands, and the Hindu universal state was re-established in the shape of a British in place of a Mughal Rāj, the defence of the North-West Frontier, over against the wild highlanders of North-Eastern Iran, proved to be by far the heaviest of all the frontier-commitments that the

---

[1] We may also bring into the comparison the descent of the Hittites and the Kassites upon the Land of Shinar, after the passage of the Hyksos, during the post-Sumeric interregnum; and the descent of the Medes upon Assyria, after the passage of the Cimmerians and the Scyths, during the Babylonic 'Time of Troubles'.
[2] See IV. C (ii) (*b*) 2, vol. iv, p. 99, footnote 1, above.
[3] See Part III. A, vol. iii, pp. 30 and 31, footnote 1, above, and V. C (ii) (*b*), vol. vi, p. 301, below.   [4] See V. C (ii) (*b*), vol. vi, p. 301, below.
[5] See IV. C (ii) (*b*) 2, vol. iv, pp. 97–8, above, and V. C (ii) (*b*), vol. vi, p. 301, below.
[6] See V. C (ii) (*a*), vol. vi, p. 191, below.

British empire-builders in India had to take over from the vanquished rival candidates for the succession to the Mughal heritage.[1]

By the year 1938 the gravity of this British commitment could be estimated in the light of a mature experience; for by then more than a hundred years had passed since the British masters of India had first addressed themselves to the task of finding a solution for the North-West Frontier problem; and, so far, none of the alternative possibilities had proved, on trial, to be altogether satisfactory.

The first alternative which the British empire-builders tried was to conquer and annex outright the whole of the East Iranian barbarian threshold of the Hindu World right up to the line along which the Mughal Rāj, at its apogee, had marched with its own Uzbeg 'successor-states' in the Oxus-Jaxartes Basin and with the Safawī Empire in Western Iran. The adventurous reconnaissances which were carried out, from A.D. 1831 onwards, by Alexander Burnes,[2] were followed up by the still more hazardous step of dispatching a British-Indian military force to Afghanistan in 1838; but this ambitious attempt at a 'totalitarian' solution of the North-West Frontier problem had a disastrous ending. For, in the first flush of their triumphantly successful conquest of all India, south-east of the Indus Basin, between 1799 and 1818,[3] the British empire-builders had over-estimated their own strength and under-estimated the vigour and effectiveness of the resistance that their aggression would provoke among the untamed barbarians whom they were proposing now to subdue.

At a time when the Panjab was still in the hands of the fully sovereign and formidably martial Power of the Sikhs, while the amīrs of Sind were bitterly hostile to British designs which they could not resist by force, Afghanistan was really beyond the effective reach of a British Rāj whose military operations in the East Iranian highlands had to be conducted from such distant bases as Calcutta and Bombay; and, if the military omnipotence of the British at this time in the Indian territories east of the Indus and south of the Sutlej thus gave no measure of British military strength

[1] Compare the heaviness of the frontier-commitment on the Continental European border of the Hellenic World which the Romans had to take over from the Etruscans and Tarentines and Macedonians (see II. D (v), vol. ii, pp. 161–4, and the present chapter and volume, pp. 215–16, above, and V. C (i) (c) 3, Annex I, pp. 591–5, below).

[2] Burnes, A.: *Travels into Bokhara; being the account of a journey from India to Cabool, Tartary and Persia; also, narrative of a voyage on the Indus, from the Sea to Lahore, with presents from the King of Great Britain; performed under the orders of the Supreme Government of India, in the years 1831, 1832 and 1833* (London 1834, John Murray, 3 vols.); idem: *Cabool: A personal narrative of a journey to, and residence in, that city, in the years 1836, 1837 and 1838*, 2nd edition (London 1843, John Murray).

[3] Before 1799 the British Rāj was in effect confined to Bengal. Bombay, Madras, and the Circars were mere enclaves in non-British territory, and had no communications with Bengal except by sea.

at Ghaznah or Kābul, conversely the perpetual political dissensions and civil wars in which the barbarians of Afghanistan were consuming their energies gave no measure of their ability to make common cause against an alien invader who threatened to deprive them all alike of their unanimously cherished privilege of living in a state of anarchy. Times had changed in the East Iranian highlands since the seventeenth century of the Christian Era, when the Mughal and Safawī and Uzbeg Powers had contended with one another for command of the frontier-fortresses of Qandahār and Herāt and Balkh while the highlanders remained sullenly submissive or passively aloof. In the eighteenth century, when the Mughal and Safawī Empires had broken up, while the Uzbeg Khanates were sinking into an ever deeper decay, the highlanders had been having their fling. They had usurped the throne of Shāh 'Abbās from 1722 to 1730,[1] and had raided the plains of Hindustan from 1745 to 1761;[2] and, although their licence had been curbed before the eighteenth century had run out, and they had ebbed back into the mountains from which they had descended, the memory of their eighteenth-century marauding adventures still inspired them, in the nineteenth century, with a self-conceit and self-confidence that made them rise in vehement revolt against a British effort to reduce them to submission in their native fastnesses. For these various reasons the British attempt to solve the Indian North-West Frontier problem by conquering the entire barbarian hinterland ended, in 1841–2, in a disaster of greater magnitude than the Italian disaster in the Abyssinian highlands in 1896.

After this first resounding failure the second chapter in the history of the British attempt to cope with the North-West Frontier opened in 1849, when the annexation to the British Rāj of Sind in 1843, and of the Sikh principality in the Panjab in consequence of the Anglo-Sikh wars of 1845–9, had carried the north-western boundary of British India forward, along the whole front, to the south-eastern foot of the escarpment of the Iranian Plateau.[3] Since 1849 the British Rāj has always possessed the geographico-strategical facilities, which it so conspicuously

[1] See Browne, E. G.: *A Literary History of Persia*, vol. iv (Cambridge 1928, University Press), pp. 122–33.

[2] By 1745 the power of the Rohilla Afghan military adventurers in the country on the left bank of the Upper Ganges, on which they have stamped the name Rohilkund, had been already established by their first leader 'Alī Muhammad Khān. The invasions of Hindustan by the Abdālī or Durrānī Afghan military adventurer Ahmad Shāh began in 1747 and culminated in his victory over the Marāthās at Panipat in January 1761.

[3] The earliest British attempt to organize and pacify the piedmont frontier of the Panjab is graphically described at first hand in Edwardes, H. B.: *A Year on the Punjab frontier in 1848–49* (London 1851, Bentley, 2 vols.). The author was serving in the name of a Panjābī Sikh Rāj which had already been taken under tutelage by the British Rāj but had not yet been formally superseded by it.

lacked in 1838, for applying the original policy of conquest to the untamed barbarians in the East Iranian highlands; but, though there have been two more Anglo-Afghan wars since then—one in 1879–81 and another in 1919—the British ambition to make a permanent conquest of the highlands has not ever, in fact, been more than tentatively revived, and the variations in British frontier policy since 1849 have been tactical rather than strategic, since they have all alike been subject to the unvarying fundamental postulate that—whatever the line along which the frontier was to run, and whatever the military and political expedients by which it was to be maintained—there was now to be no question of eliminating by force of arms the untamed barbarian war-bands beyond the pale.

Within the limits allowed by this postulate there have, of course, been considerable variations in method—some local and some temporary.[1] In the south-western section of the frontier the effective military and political front has been established on the summit of the plateau, on the farther side of the wall of mountains by which the plateau is surrounded. In the north-eastern section the front has been kept below the foot of the mountains, part way between the water-shed of the Indus Basin and the channel of the river Indus itself; and on this sector there have been alternations between a tendency to move the limit of effective occupation forward, towards the juridical frontier between India and Afghanistan,[2] and a tendency to leave unadministered as broad a zone as possible of the barbarian territory that is juridically subject to the Government of India's sovereign authority. In the counsels of the British Indian military and political authorities the 'forward' and the 'close border' frontier policies have alternately prevailed, and then each time each in turn lost credit, as the particular drawbacks and inconveniences of each have once again been exposed under the test of a practical trial. And this history of British Indian frontier policy bears out a social 'law'—which we have mentioned, by anticipation, at the beginning of this chapter, and which we shall seek to demonstrate in a later part[3]—to the effect that, on a stationary frontier between Civilization and Barbarism, Time does not tell in Civilization's favour. The cogency of this 'law' was being brought home by

[1] See de Watteville, H.: *Waziristan, 1919–1920* (London 1925, Constable), pp. 6–14 and 28–45.

[2] This juridical frontier—the so-called 'Durand Line'—was laid down in 1893, by agreement between the British Indian and Afghan Governments, from a point abutting on the Persian frontier in Seistan to a point at the head of the Kurram Valley. Towards its north-eastern extremity this line traversed barbarian territory which, except at a few points, had not yet, by the year 1938, been brought under the effective authority of either of the two contracting parties (see Toynbee, A. J.: *Survey of International Affairs, 1925*, vol. i (London 1927, Milford), p. 549). [3] In Part VIII, below.

current events at the time of writing of the first draft of this chapter in the autumn of the year 1935, when the Government of India was finding itself once again constrained to undertake elaborate military operations against one of the barbarian war-bands[1] in the non-administered zone of the North-West Frontier Province.

The External Proletariat of the Main Body of the Far Eastern Society.

When we pass from the Hindu World to the main body of the Far Eastern Society, the spectacle that meets our eyes there is the same *mutatis mutandis*. The Far Eastern 'Time of Troubles' (*saeviebat circa* A.D. 875–1275), which set in with the decline and fall of the T'ang Dynasty, was punctuated by a series of barbarian encroachments upon the Far Eastern Civilization's domain in which the Eurasian Nomads opened the first breach and were afterwards followed up by home-grown highlander barbarians from the threshold of the invaded society's territory.[2] The Khitan Nomads, who *circa* A.D. 550[3] had appeared on the horizon of a nascent Far Eastern World at the extremity of the Eurasian Steppe between Korea and the Khingan Mountains, gained a footing south of the easternmost section of the Great Wall *circa* A.D. 927–37.[4] Some two hundred years later these Nomadic Khitan were supplanted, and their encroachments at the Far Eastern Society's expense were extended, by the Kin barbarians[5] from the forest-clad highlands between the Manchurian Steppe and Korea (as, in the Hindu World, the Ghūrīs supplanted and out-ranged the Ghaznawī Turks,[6] and, in the Syriac World, the Muwah-hid highlanders from the Atlas followed at the heels of the Murābit Nomads from the Sahara[7]). In the thirteenth century of the Christian Era the Kin, in their turn, were supplanted by the Khitan's fellow Nomads the Mongols, who completed the barbarian conquest of the main body of the Far Eastern World and thereby provided it with a universal state (as the Mughals performed a corresponding service for the Hindu World and the

---

[1] The Upper Mohmands.
[2] A brilliant and penetrating study of the continental anti-barbarian frontiers of the main body of the Far Eastern World will be found in Lattimore, O.: *Manchuria Cradle of Conflict* (New York 1932, Macmillan). The author has made his observations at first hand; and, both on this account and because of his powers of analysis and generalization, his work throws a flood of light not only on the particular field with which he is concerned but also on the whole subject of anti-barbarian frontiers. The technical term 'reservoir', which Mr. Lattimore has coined for his own use in his book, refers to the same geographico-social phenomenon as the term 'threshold' or *limen*, in the sense in which that is used in this Study (see the present chapter, pp. 208–10, above).
[3] See the present chapter, p. 274, above.
[4] See II. D (v), vol. ii, p. 121, and IV. C (ii) (*b*) 2, vol. iv, p. 86, above, and V. C (ii) (*b*), vol. vi, p. 307, below.
[5] See the references in the preceding footnote.
[6] See p. 304, above.
[7] See p. 247, above.

'Osmanlis for the main body of Orthodox Christendom). There-after, when the Mongols had been driven out again to their own side of the Great Wall by the Chinese militant nationalist reaction that was led by the Ming,[1] the Nomadic Mongols' work of establishing a Far Eastern universal state was eventually reperformed by the Kin's fellow highlanders the Manchus.[2]

Upon all these barbarian invaders of the Far Eastern World, whether Nomads or highlanders, the influence of the culture of the conquered society has worked so swiftly and penetrated so deep that they have had little need, or opportunity, to exercise any creative faculties of their own. The Manchus, in particular, have shown themselves whole-hearted converts to a Far Eastern Civilization which they had been imbibing from the long-established Chinese settlers in South Manchuria before ever they committed their own trespass across the Liaotung Pale and on beyond, through Shanhaikwan. Of all the four successive hosts of in-truders—Khitan and Kin, Mongols and Manchus—the Mongols alone have offered a conscious and obstinate resistance to the process of Sinification. The Mongols' native Nomadism, which was the first barrier that divided them from the peasants and litterati of the Far Eastern World, was reinforced, before their intrusion upon Far Eastern ground, by the tincture of Syriac culture which the Nestorian missionaries on the Eurasian Steppe had imparted to the Karāyits and the Naimans.[3] And the Mongols thus brought with them into China a distinctive culture of their own. Thereafter their determination to retain their separate social identity was displayed in their attitude towards the Mahā-yāna, with which their conquest of China brought them into contact. In spite of the attraction which this 'higher religion' exercised upon these primitive pagans, the Mongols did not embrace the Catholic Mahāyāna which had become the universal church of the Far Eastern World.[4] They turned, in preference, to the Tantric form of Mahayanian Buddhism which had been begotten in Bengal and had found a second home in Tibet.[5] Qubilay Khan (*imperabat* A.D. 1259–94) himself showed favour to, and interest in, the Tibetan Lamas; and three hundred years after his time, and two

[1] See II. D (v), vol. ii, pp. 121–2; IV. C (ii) (*b*) 2, vol. iv, p. 87; Part V. A, in the present volume, p. 3; and V. C (i) (*c*) 1, p. 54, above; and V. C (i) (*c*) 4, p. 351; V. C (ii) (*a*), vol. vi, p. 193; and V. C (ii) (*b*), vol. vi, p. 305, below.
[2] For the origin of the Manchus see II. D (v), vol. ii, p. 122, footnote 2, above.
[3] See II. D (vi), vol. ii, pp. 237–8; Part III. A, Annex II, vol. iii, p. 451; and V. C (i) (*c*) 1, in the present volume, p. 54, above, and V. C (i) (*c*) 4, p. 348, below.
[4] For the conquest of the Far East by the Catholic Mahāyāna during the post-Sinic interregnum see V. C (i) (*c*) 2, pp. 139–46, above.
[5] For this Tantric or Lamaistic form of the Mahāyāna see I. B (iii), vol. i, p. 35; I. C (i) (*b*), vol. i, pp. 90–2; II. D (vi), Annex, vol. ii, p. 405, footnote 1; and V. C (i) (*c*) 2, in the present volume, p. 137, above.

hundred years after the expulsion of his successors from China to the Nomads' own side of the Great Wall, the Mongols at length adopted this Tantric Buddhism *en masse* in A.D. 1576–7.[1] The adoption of a distinctive religion is, as we have observed,[2] one of two characteristic manifestations of originality in the souls of barbarians who feel moved to retain and express their own barbarian êthos instead of succumbing to the faded charms of the moribund civilization at whose expense they are running amok. The second characteristic form of barbarian self-expression is the creation of a 'heroic' poetry;[3] and inquiry reveals that the re-calcitrant Mongol barbarian 'borderers' on the Eurasian frontier of the main body of the Far Eastern World have expressed themselves in this way as well. Among the Mongol Nomads whose ranges lay within the boundaries of Manchuria, there could be heard sung, in 1935,[4] ballads celebrating the exploits of Mongol bandits in the *ci-devant* Imperial Pastures of the Manchu Crown which had been turned, in 1902, into an ordinary administrative district (*hsien*) of the Chinese Republic, where the Mongols' Nomadism would be challenged thenceforth by the advance of the Chinese peasant-colonist's plough.

The Iranic External Proletariat.

In the history of the Iranic World the breakdown of the Iranic Civilization—which we have equated with the schism in the Iranic body social in the generation of Shāh Ismā'īl[5]—was accom-panied by the Uzbeg barbarian Nomads' occupation of the Oxus-Jaxartes Basin.[6] This Nomad encroachment, which corresponds to the Khitan's intrusion upon the Far Eastern World after the fall of the T'ang, was never carried farther; for, at the Khurasanian escarpment of the Iranian Plateau, the Uzbegs were brought to a halt by the Safawis, as the White Huns had been arrested at the same line by the Sasanids and the Sakas by the Arsacids.[7] Yet, for nearly four hundred years after the Uzbeg occupation of the Oxus-Jaxartes Basin, the Persians had to put up with the perpetual raids of the Uzbegs' Türkmen protégés in Transcaspia;[8] and in

[1] See IV. C (iii) (*c*) 3 (α), vol. iv, p. 497, and V. C (i) (*c*) 2, in the present volume, p. 137, above.   [2] On pp. 227–33, above.   [3] See pp. 233–4, above.
[4] See Lattimore, O.: *The Mongols of Manchuria* (London 1935, Allen & Unwin), pp. 223–4.   [5] See I. C (i) (*b*), Annex I, in vol. i, above.
[6] See I. C (i) (*b*), Annex I, in vol. i, pp. 371–81; and IV. C (iii) (*c*) 3 (α), vol. iv, pp. 498–9, above.
[7] See II. D (v), vol. ii, p. 141, footnote 2; Part III. A, Annex II, vol. iii, p. 449; and the present chapter and volume, pp. 239–40, above, and V. C (i) (*c*) 3, Annex II, pp. 601–2, below. It may be noticed that the Uzbegs, when they were prevented from advancing into South-Western Asia, contented themselves with their conquests in the Oxus-Jaxartes Basin like their sixth-century Turkish predecessors, and did not seek an alternative field for further expansion in India, like the White Huns and the Sakas.
[8] For the eventual subjugation of these Türkmens by the Russians in A.D. 1873–86 see the present chapter, p. 323, footnote 3, below.

the first quarter of the eighteenth century of the Christian Era,
when the Iranic 'Time of Troubles' was overtaken by its next
paroxysm, the Afghan highlander barbarians from North-Eastern
Iran also momentarily overran the derelict territories of a decrepit
Safawī Empire (as we have noticed incidentally in our foregoing
survey of the external proletariat of the Hindu World).[1]

The Russian External Proletariat.

In the offshoot of Orthodox Christendom in Russia the 'Time of
Troubles'[2] set in, after an exotic bloom that had lasted for less than
a hundred years from the date of Vladímir's conversion, upon the
decay of the authority of the principality of Kiev towards the end
of the eleventh century of the Christian Era.[3] And, in Russian
history too, this first stage in the disintegration of a civilization was
signalized by the scourge of Nomad barbarian assaults. The
Russians, however, were more successful than the Hindus or the
Chinese or their own co-religionists in the East Roman Empire in
coping with their Nomad adversaries. The Ghuzz and the
Cumans, who broke in rapid succession out of the heart of the
Eurasian Steppe into the Great Western Bay in the sixth decade of
the eleventh century,[4] when Byzantine Kiev was verging towards
her decline, were held at the borderline between Steppe and
Forest, and were prevented from trespassing on Russian ground,
as effectively as, some hundred and sixty years earlier, the Pechenegs had been checked at the same line by a Varangian Kiev[5]
which, in the ninth century, had been in the first vigour of a barbarian adolescence.[6] And though, less than two hundred years
after the Cumans had been brought to a halt, the Russian forest

---

[1] See the present chapter, p. 306, above.

[2] The chapter of Russian history which is officially known as the 'Time of Troubles'
is, of course, not this, but an interlude at the beginning of the seventeenth century when
there was a momentary collapse of a Muscovite Empire which was the Russian universal
state (see I. C (i) (a), vol. i, p. 53, footnote 2; II. D (v), vol. ii, pp. 157 and 176; and
IV. C (ii) (b) 2, vol. iv, pp. 90 and 91–2, above; and V. C (ii) (a), vol. vi, p. 195, footnote 2,
and V. C (ii) (b), vol. vi, p. 311, below).

[3] See IV. C (ii) (b) 2, vol. iv, p. 96, footnote 1, above.

[4] See Part III. A, Annex II, vol. iii, p. 416, above.

[5] The Varangian principality of Kiev had held, for the benefit of all the other
Varangian 'successor-states' of the Khazar Empire, the front along which the Varangian
Viking heirs of the forest-clad dependencies of the Khazar Empire in the north-west
had come to march with the rival Pecheneg Nomad heirs of the Khazar Empire's home
territory in the Great Western Bay of the Eurasian Steppe (see p. 288, above). No doubt
it was in virtue of their service as wardens of the marches of the Scandinavian World
that the Varangian princes of Kiev acquired a hegemony over all the other Scandinavian
'successor-states' of the Khazar Empire, from the banks of the Middle Dniepr to the
shores of Lake Ladoga (see p. 288, footnote 3, above, together with II. D (v), *passim*,
in vol. ii).

[6] Even, however, in this time of her youth and strength Kiev had found her powers
taxed to the utmost by the task of barely keeping the Nomads at bay, and this historical
fact is faithfully reflected in the mirror of the Russian 'heroic' poetry (see pp. 288–9,
above). 'The warfare of the Kiev Cycle is almost wholly defensive' (Chadwick, H. M.
and N. K.: *The Growth of Literature*, vol. ii (Cambridge 1936, University Press), p. 95).

bowed to the earth under the unprecedentedly furious impact of
the Mongol tornado—a blast which had been gathering momentum all the way as it swept across Eurasia from the Kerulen to
the Dniepr—these Russian tree-trunks even then bent without
breaking.

During the two and a half centuries that elapsed between Bātū
Khan's sack of Kiev in A.D. 1240 and the Muscovites' capture of
Saray-on-Volga in A.D. 1502, the states of Russian Orthodox
Christendom—including distant Novgorod on the Baltic slope, as
well as the Russian communities in the basins of the Dniepr and
the Volga—were all of them for most of the time under the Tatar
yoke, except in so far as they succumbed, instead, to the alternative barbarian domination of the forest-dwelling Lithuanians.[1]
Successive Russian attempts to throw off the Tatar suzerainty
were severely punished. Even as late as A.D. 1382, when the principality of Muscovy had already succeeded in uniting a large part of
the Russian World under its own lordship, a Muscovite repudiation of allegiance to the Khan of the Golden Horde was conclusively proved to be premature by Toqatmysh's retaliatory sack
of Moscow.[2] And it was only the union of Muscovy with Novgorod in A.D. 1478—exactly a hundred years after the first Muscovite act of defiance—that created at last a Russian Power which
was of a calibre to defy with impunity a Tatar Power which was now
in articulo mortis. These facts show how long and how heavily the
Russians were weighed down by the Tatar incubus; yet they never
allowed it to crush them. Their servitude did not go beyond the
payment of tribute to Tatar overlords who continued to dwell on
their native steppes; and there was no installation of a Tatar
ruling caste in the Russian cities, after the fashion of the Manchu
'bannermen' in China or the Turkish war-bands of the 'Slave-
Kings' and their successors in Hindustan.

This successful Russian passive resistance to Nomad aggression
during the Russian 'Time of Troubles'[3] prepared the ground for
Russian Orthodox Christendom to pass over to the offensive in
the age of the universal state that was brought into existence by

---

[1] For the south-eastward expansion of these pagan Lithuanian barbarians, at the
White Russians' and the Red Russians' expense, until in A.D. 1363 they reached the
shores of the Black Sea between the mouths of the Dniepr and the Dniestr, see II. D
(v), vol. ii, p. 172, and Part III. A, Annex II, vol. iii, pp. 424 and 428, above. The
Red Russians are, of course, identical with the Ruthenians, and these with the Ukrainians.
For the relative prosperity of the Red Russian principality of Galicia, by comparison
with other parts of Russia, during the first century of the Mongol domination which
was the sequel to Batu's raid, see V. C (ii) (b), vol. vi, p. 310, footnote 2, below. In
the course of the fourteenth century of the Christian Era Galicia was annexed to the
Western World through being united politically with the Kingdom of Poland and
ecclesiastically with the Western Christian Church.
[2] See I. C (i) (b), Annex I, vol. i, p. 374, footnote 1, and II. D (v), vol. ii, p. 147, above.
[3] In the sense in which the term is used in this Study (see p. 311, footnote 2, above).

the union of Novgorod with Muscovy. And this Russian counter-offensive against the Eurasian Nomadism has been a unique operation in the annals of the warfare between the Eurasian Nomads and the sedentary societies round about; for the Russians have gained a victory over the Nomads which, to all appearance, is complete and definitive.

In this last chapter of the history of Russian Orthodox Christendom's anti-Nomad front the master-stroke of the Empire of All the Russias has been to enlist in its service, as disciplined hunting-dogs, the Cossacks who had made their first entry into the Eurasian amphitheatre as wild wolves snapping at the flanks of the Golden Horde.[1] This remarkable metamorphosis of the Cossacks from barbarians into barbarian-fighters was not accomplished without a struggle;[2] and the parent Cossack war-band in the 'Sich' in the Dniepr eventually proved intractable. These Dniepr Cossacks could never forget their original freedom from any master; and, even when, in the sixteenth century, they had found it necessary to compromise their liberty by entering into political relations with one of the neighbouring sedentary Powers, their first choice for their suzerain had been Poland-Lithuania. They had only subsequently come under the suzerainty of Muscovy—and this by a voluntary transfer of allegiance which was transacted, in A.D. 1654, through the negotiation of a formal treaty between the Cossack Hetman and the Muscovite Tsar. With this history behind them it is not surprising that the Dniepr Cossacks were unable to accommodate themselves to the requirements of a Muscovite autocracy which, from Peter the Great's time onwards, was inspired by the modern Western as well as by the medieval Byzantine tradition of absolutism. After the last great Cossack revolt against Muscovite authority in A.D. 1773 the Dniepr 'Sich' was dissolved, and the Cossack 'Die-Hards' fled to the Ottoman dominions, where new homes in the neighbourhood of the Danube Delta were granted to them by the Pādishāh. The majority of the Dniepr Cossacks, however, submitted, in this extremity, to the Tsar, and suffered themselves to be deported from their island fastness in the Dniepr, where they had been ensconced for some four hundred years, to more fertile fields along the right bank of the Kuban, where they were now set to guard the western half of the Russian Empire's anti-barbarian front over against the highlanders of the Caucasus, between the coast of the Sea of Azov and the right flank of the Cossacks of the Terek. In the meantime the Russian Imperial Government had met with less recalcitrance from the daughter

---

[1] See II. D (v), vol. ii, pp. 155–6, and the present chapter, pp. 283–4, above.
[2] See V. C (i) (c) 2, p. 104, above, and V. C (i) (a), vol. vi, pp. 227–8, below.

Cossack war-bands on the Terek[1] and the Don and the Yaik; and, when once these had been gradually and peacefully incorporated into the Imperial administrative system, it was an easier step still for the Imperial Government to garrison hitherto unguarded river-lines with new Cossack settlements whose fighting-men were ready to eat out of the hand of an Imperial master to whom their *stanitzas* owed their very existence.[2]

Under the Imperial Russian Government's authority and direction the two new 'hosts' of Orenburg Cossacks and Siberian Cossacks were planted, in the course of the eighteenth century, beyond the left wing of the Yaik Cossacks, across the wide gap in the Russian frontier-defences on the northern threshold of the Eurasian Steppe between the Ural Mountains and the Altai. Thereafter, in 1867, the Siberian dominions of the Empire, north of the Steppe, were linked up with the new dominions, south of the Steppe, in the Oxus-Jaxartes Basin, which the Imperial Government was then in process of conquering,[3] by the establishment of a Semiriech Cossack 'host' between the left flank of the Siberian Cossacks, on the right bank of the Upper Irtish, and the newly acquired province of Farghānā in the valley of the Upper Jaxartes.[4] This settlement of the Semiriech Cossacks was proof positive of the Eurasian Nomads' utter discomfiture, for the new Cossack line cut the Eurasian Steppe in two by closing the Zungarian Gap between the Altai and the Tien Shan.

Nevertheless the occupation of this vital line across 'the Seven Rivers' by the Semiriech Cossack 'host' in A.D. 1867[5] is not to be

[1] The Cossack community on the Terek seems to have been founded in A.D. 1579 and to have formally acknowledged the sovereignty of the Muscovite Empire in A.D. 1712 (Allen, W. E. D.: *A History of the Georgian People* (London 1932, Kegan Paul), p. 164; idem, in *The Baltic and Caucasian States* (London 1923, Hodder & Stoughton), p. 194).

[2] A map of Eurasia, showing the area covered by the Steppe and the territories occupied by Cossack 'hosts', within the framework of the Russian Empire, on the eve of the Bolshevik Revolution of 1917, will be found in *The Round Table*, issue of June 1918, facing page 562. It will be seen from this map that, in addition to the several Cossack 'hosts' that were established in order to hold the anti-barbarian frontiers of the Russian Empire against the Eurasian Nomads and the Caucasian highlanders, three further 'hosts'—the Transbaikal, Amur, and Ussuri Cossacks—were established in the Far East in order to confirm the Russian hold upon the new territories which the Tsardom had acquired from the Manchu Empire in the sixth decade of the nineteenth century.

[3] The Uzbeg Khanates in the Oxus-Jaxartes Basin were all conquered by the Russian Empire between A.D. 1863 and A.D. 1873.

[4] This first essay in forging a direct link between the West Siberian and the Transoxanian territories of the Russian Empire was followed up sixty-three years later, in A.D. 1930, by the opening of the 'Turk-Sib' railway along a route which was approximately coincident with the line of the Semiriech Cossack cantonments. The Bolshevik régime had swept the Cossacks away, yet it continued to pursue, by other means, the policy of expansion and consolidation in Eurasia for which the Cossacks, in their day, had shown themselves effective instruments in the hands of the Tsardom (for the progress of this expansion under the Soviet régime see Hubbard, G. E., in Toynbee, A. J., and Boulter, V. M.: *Survey of International Affairs, 1934* (London 1935, Milford), pp. 685–9).

[5] The foundation of the Semiriech Cossack 'host' in that year was the latest instance of the effective establishment of a new Cossack community; but an abortive attempt to carry out the traditional policy on a new front was made, on the eve of the fall of the

compared, for audacity, with the occupation of the line of the Yaik in the sixteenth century by the Cossack 'host' which took its name from that single stream; for the Semiriech Cossacks were established, with the whole strength of the Russian Empire behind them, at a date when the effective resistance of the Nomads had long since been broken, whereas the Yaik Cossacks performed their feat of cutting off the Great Western Bay from the heart of the Eurasian Steppe on their own unsupported initiative—and this in an age when a fresh Nomad eruption was still to come. In A.D. 1616 the newly formed Cossack line along the Yaik was broken through by the impact of the Torgut Calmucks;[1] but it was broken without being swept away; and, when the Don Cossack line brought the tide of Calmuck invasion to a standstill, the Yaik Cossack line closed in again at the Nomad invaders' rear and cut them off from their kin and kind. This successful absorption of the Calmuck shock by the elasticity of the Cossack buffer in the first quarter of the seventeenth century was the beginning of the end of the long struggle between the Russian Orthodox Christendom and its Nomad adversaries; and the eventual Russian counterstroke—which was delivered when the epigoni of the Calmuck intruders ebbed back into the heart of the Steppe in A.D. 1771[2]—was already a foregone conclusion in 'the sixteen-twenties'.

This apparently conclusive settlement of the problem of the Russian Orthodox Christendom's Eurasian Nomad frontier between A.D. 1616 and A.D. 1771 was facilitated by the *floruit*, in that age, of a restored Far Eastern universal state under the rule of Manchu empire-builders who, like the Cossacks, were sedentary barbarians from the borderland of the Steppe; for the Manchus, likewise, were as masterful towards the Eurasian Nomadism as they were familiar with it;[3] and, when, in the latter part of the

Tsardom, during the General War of 1914–18. During this war 'the Russian military authorities on the Armenian front began to create a new Cossack line in the occupied Ottoman territory. Russian colonists were placed on the lands of the Armenians whom the Turkish atrocities had removed, and the infamous project was only put an end to by the Revolution' (*The Round Table*, issue of June 1918, p. 542).

[1] See Part III. A, Annex II, vol. iii, pp. 418 and 428, above.

[2] See Part III. A, vol. iii, p. 19, footnote 3, and IV. C (iii) (c) 3 (α), vol. iv, pp. 497–8, above.

[3] For the non-Nomadic origin of the Manchus and for their attitude to the Eurasian Nomadism and to the Far Eastern Civilization respectively see II. D (v), vol. ii, p. 122, footnote 2, and Part III. A, vol. iii, pp. 16 and 19, with Annex II, p. 423, footnote 1, above. In the Manchu Imperial Government's policy towards the Nomads it is perhaps possible to detect a certain duality. While the Manchu Government showed the same determination and persistence as the contemporary Russian Government in imposing its authority upon recalcitrant and aggressive Nomads like the Zungar Calmucks, it adopted a patronizingly conciliatory policy towards quiescent Nomads, such as the Mongols were at this date, and especially towards the Imperial Manchus' own Nomad Manchu poor relations on the Transkhingan enclave of the Eurasian Steppe. The Imperial Manchus, who were reducing the Zungars to subjection with China's resources and for China's benefit, were at the same time seeking to enlist the Nomad Manchus and the Mongols as reinforcements for the barbarian garrison with which the Imperial

seventeenth century of the Christian Era, the Manchu and Muscovite Empires came into contact with one another in Trans-
baikalia, the Eurasian Steppe was encircled—for the first time in
history, so far as is known—by an unbroken ring of anti-Nomad
Powers. Thereafter the Russian blow at the Torgut Calmucks
which was delivered in A.D. 1771 was anticipated by the greater
feat of the Manchu Emperor Ch'ien Lung (*imperabat* A.D. 1735–96)
in breaking the power of the Torguts' more formidable kinsmen
the Zungars.[1]

Through the simultaneous coercive action of the Manchu and
Muscovite Powers—a converging movement which was not the
less éffective for not having been concerted—it looked as though a
greater and more momentous historical result had been achieved
than the mere victory of this or that sedentary society over the
Eurasian Nomads of a particular time and place. It looked as
though, in the Eurasian arena, the Nomadic Civilization itself had
at last been defeated decisively in its vaster struggle with a long
array of civilizations of the sedentary class. And, though the blows
delivered in 1755 and in 1771 broke the Nomads' military and
political power without thereby putting a stop to the Nomadic way
of life, it seemed merely a question of time for the Nomad herds-
man himself to vanish from the face of the Earth before the relentless and irresistible advance of the cultivator and the industrialist.[2]
The Great Society of a Westernized World seemed to have
licence to commit the most outrageous crimes and follies against
itself without jeopardizing its apparently automatic progress at the
Eurasian Nomadism's expense. The Chinese Revolution of A.D.
1911 might throw a China that was in process of Westernization
into interminable social disorders, and yet the colonization of the
Nomads' ancestral ranges in Inner Mongolia and Manchuria by
Chinese peasant settlers might be actually stimulated by the
pressure of brigandage, war, pestilence, and famine which the
Revolution had brought to bear upon the settlers' ancestral homes
in Honan or Shantung. The Russians might be driven to the

Manchus were also holding China down. For the provenance and organization of the
Manchu Power's garrisons in China see Lattimore, O.: *The Mongols of Manchuria*
(London 1935, Allen & Unwin), pp. 146–8. The unit was the 'banner', which always
included a Manchu battalion, and usually a Chinese and a Mongol sister battalion as
well. These composite 'banners' were stationed, in groups of varying strength, in the
principal cities of Manchuria-within-the-Pale and Intramural China. 'Mongol "banners",
forming battalions of the Manchu "banner" regiments, had no tribal function; they consisted of Mongols recruited from the tribes and thereby detached from their native tribal
organizations to form hereditary professional troops.' At the same time (see Lattimore,
op. cit., pp. 145–6 and 148–51), as the Manchus progressively imposed their rule upon
Mongolia as well as upon China, they put the existing Mongol tribal units on a regular
permanent footing by organizing them as 'banners' in a second meaning of the term
which is not to be confused with its usage to denote a cadre of the Manchu standing army.
[1] See IV. C (iii) (c) 3 (α), vol. iv, pp. 497–8, above.
[2] For the Nomad's apparent doom see Part III. A, vol. iii, pp. 16–22, above.

slaughter by the million in the European War of 1914–18 and
might finally fall out of this frying-pan into the fire of revolution,
and yet Russian hands could find time between August 1914 and
October 1917 to cause the death of thousands of Qāra Kirghiz[1]
Nomads who had been stampeded into a panic by rumours that
they were to be wrenched out of the only way of life that they could
conceive, in order to be conscripted for non-combatant service
behind the Russian military front.[2] Thus it seemed until the other
day as though the Nomads could only be implicated in the
sedentary civilization's self-inflicted fate and could not look for a
reprieve from it.

This continued to be the outlook until the autumn of 1931; but
by 1938 the Japanese military outbreak on the Asiatic Continent,
and the policy of aggressive expansion which the powers behind
the throne at Tokyo had been pursuing for seven years by then,
had put a different complexion upon the Nomads' prospects; for
the Nomads' two latter-day oppressors, the Chinese and the
Russians, were the Japanese imperialists' principal victims, and
therefore their principal adversaries, in their continental adventure; and it was a short step from this for the Japanese to single
out the rear-guard of the Nomads to be their own protégés and
allies. In making up their puppet-state of 'Manchukuo' out of the
four conquered Chinese Eastern Provinces, the Japanese empire-
builders ostentatiously granted the local Mongol 'banners' their
autonomy and put a stop to the process of Chinese peasant colonization at the Mongols' expense.[3] And next door, in the Inner
Mongolian territories west of the Mongolian province of Jehol
which had been incorporated into 'Manchukuo', the Mongols
were consequently able to make a bargain for themselves, on
equivalent terms, with the Government of the Chinese Republic—
under tacit threat of opening the way for a further westward
enroachment of Japanese imperialism at China's expense, unless
the Chinese were willing to make it worth the Mongols' while
to remain faithful to their allegiance to Nanking.[4] As for Outer

[1] *Sic*, and not 'Kirghiz Qāzāqs', as erroneously stated in Toynbee, A. J.: *The Western
Question in Greece and Turkey*, in the passage quoted in this Study, Part III. A, vol. iii,
p. 18, above.
[2] See Czaplicka, M. A.: *The Turks of Central Asia in History and at the Present Day*
(Oxford 1918, Clarendon Press), p. 17, cited in Part III. A, vol. iii, p. 19, above. A
damning confirmation of this Polish scholar's indictment, out of the ulprit's own mouth,
will be found in the extracts translated from the official provincial gazette *Semiriechen-
skiya Oblastniya Viedomosti*, Nos. 200–15, in the British Admiralty publication *Manual
on the Turanians and Pan-Turanianism* (London, no date, H.M. Stationery Office),
pp. 229–34.
[3] See Toynbee, A. J., and Boulter, V. M.: *Survey of International Affairs, 1932*
(London 1933, Milford), pp. 443–5 and 459.
[4] See Hubbard, G. E., in Toynbee, A. J., and Boulter, V. M.: *Survey of International
Affairs, 1933*, pp. 464–6; *1934*, pp. 683–5.

Mongolia, which had accepted a Russian in place of a Chinese suzerainty after the Chinese Revolution of 1911, and had become a Soviet Socialist Republic in 1924,[1] it remained to be seen whether its 'bannermen' would be affected in their turn by the revival of hope and ambition with which the Mongols of Inner Mongolia and 'Manchukuo' had already been inspired since the advent of the Japanese. By the year 1938, however, the Japanese imperialists had put their country's continental fortunes to the touch in a supreme military hazard; and, in the act, they had drawn into their arena the broad territories in the heart of Eurasia which the Mongols had managed still to retain at the end of four centuries of Russian and Chinese encroachment. Across the pasture-lands of their Mongol protégés—or pawns—the Japanese were then attempting to drive a wedge that was to prise asunder their common Chinese and Russian enemies.

Now that Gobi or Shamo had suffered the grievous misfortune of becoming an East Asian Armageddon, what was likely to be the fate of its last surviving Mongol Nomad denizens? Would they be able to extort a new lease of their old Nomadic life as the price of their military support? Or would they be exterminated to the last horde and herd? Or would they be saved alive—to lead a life-in-death—by being converted *en masse* into standardized replicas of the sedentary *Homo Mechanicus* who had been their bane? For Nomads of the Mongols' indomitably recalcitrant spirit, mechanization—if this third alternative was their destiny—might be more excruciating than annihilation.

[1] See Toynbee, A. J.: *Survey of International Affairs, 1920–3* (London 1925, Milford), pp. 428–31; and Hubbard, G. E., in *Survey of International Affairs, 1934* (London 1935, Milford), pp. 685–6. This Soviet Socialist Republic of Outer Mongolia was not taken into membership of the U.S.S.R.; and in the treaty of the 31st May, 1924, between the Soviet Government at Moscow and the Chinese Government at Peking, which had been signed a few months before the 'People's Republic of Outer Mongolia' was proclaimed, the U.S.S.R. had recognized Outer Mongolia as being an integral part of China under Chinese sovereignty (Art. 5). By the terms of the same article, however, the question of the Moscow Government's military occupation of Outer Mongolia had been left for future settlement (*Survey of International Affairs, 1925*, vol. ii, pp. 334–5); and the Russian troops not only remained in command of Outer Mongolia: they also organized, trained, and equipped a Red Mongolian Army. It will be seen that the effect upon the Mongols of the impact of Russian and Japanese influences in the twentieth century of the Christian Era was running exactly counter to the effect of the impact of Tibetan influence in the sixteenth century. The conversion of the Mongols to the Tantric form of the Mahāyāna had counteracted their traditional militarism; their conversion to the Russian form of Western Communism or to the Japanese form of Western Capitalism seemed likely to bring back to Mongol ears the sound of 'ancestral voices prophesying war'. On the 12th March, 1936, the Soviet Governments of the U.S.S.R. and of Outer Mongolia signed a Protocol of Mutual Assistance, in which they undertook to come to one another's aid with their respective armed forces in the event of either of them becoming a victim of aggression at the hands of a third state. After this transaction had been made public, the Government at Moscow assured the Chinese Government that nothing had been donè to change the *status quo ante* in the relations between the Soviet Union, Outer Mongolia, and China (Hubbard, G. E., in *Survey of International Affairs, 1936* (London 1937, Milford), pp. 934–5).

Vestiges and Rudiments in the Western World.

When we come, in conclusion, to the history of the relations between our own Western Civilization and the primitive societies which it has encountered, we can discern an early stage in which, like Hellenism in its growth-phase, this Western Christendom won converts through the sheer attraction of its charm. The most signal of these early converts were the members of the abortive Scandinavian Civilization, who eventually succumbed—and this in their native lairs in the Far North and in their distant settlements in Iceland, as well as in their encampments on Christian ground in the Danelaw and in Normandy—to the spiritual prowess of the civilization which these barbarians had been assailing by force of arms.[1] The contemporary conversion of the Nomad Magyars and the forest-dwelling Poles was equally spontaneous and is almost equally impressive. Yet, if these feats of peaceful penetration are worthy to rank with a growing Hellenic Civilization's cultural conquests in Italy and Asia Minor,[2] this early age of Western expansion into a barbarian world is also marred by crimes which surpass the criminality of the Hellenic pioneers' subjugation of the Mariandyni and eviction of the Piéres and extermination of the Eordaei and the Chônes.[3]

Through the misguided zeal of Charlemagne the Saxons were dragged into the fold of Western Christendom by the scruff of the neck;[4] and, when, two centuries later, their own turn came to extend the bounds of Western Christendom at the expense of the rest of the North European barbarism, the converted descendants of Charlemagne's pagan Saxon victims went beyond the bad example that had been set them in the eighth century by their Austrasian conqueror. Between the latter part of the tenth century and the latter part of the twelfth the Saxons evicted the Slavs between the Elbe and the Oder;[5] and beyond the Vistula, in the thirteenth and fourteenth centuries, the Teutonic Knights went so far as to exterminate the Prussians. On this sector of medieval Western Christendom's barbarian threshold it is evident that the relations between the growing civilization and the barbarians within its range went from bad to worse during the passage of

---

[1] See II. D (vii), vol. ii, pp. 347–60, above.

[2] See the present chapter, pp. 210–13, above.

[3] For these crimes of the Hellenic Society in its growth-phase see the present chapter, pp. 210–11, above.

[4] See II. D (v), vol. ii, p. 167; II. D (vii), vol. ii, pp. 345–6; IV. C (iii) (c) 2 (β), vol. iv, p. 322; IV. C (iii) (c) 3 (α), vol. iv, pp. 488–90; IV. C (iii) (c) 3 (β), vol. iv, p. 523; and the present chapter and volume, pp. 286–7 and 289–90, above.

[5] See II. D (v), vol. ii, pp. 168–9, above. The only Slavs in this region who survived were the Abotrites, who saved themselves at the eleventh hour, after a protracted resistance, by volunteering to receive baptism. These Abotrite Slavs are the direct ancestors, after the flesh, of our latter-day Mecklenburger Germans.

the four and a half centuries that elapsed between the opening of
Charlemagne's campaign against the Saxons in A.D. 772 and the
beginning of the extermination of the Prussians by the Teutonic
Knights after their evacuation of the Mediterranean and their
migration to the Baltic in A.D. 1228; and the same melancholy
picture of moral deterioration meets our eyes when we turn away
from the Continent to watch the contemporary progress of Roman
Christianity in the British Isles. In this insular story the first
chapter is the conversion of the English heathen by a tiny band of
Roman missionaries without any force to back them; and these
spiritual conquerors of Ultima Thule had been dispatched from
Rome on their distant and perilous enterprise by a Pope who had the
greatness of heart to take thought for a remote tribe of pagan barbarians at a moment when the schismatic barbarian Lombards were
beleaguering him in his own see.[1] It is a sad fall from this height
to the level of the next chapter, which records the coercion of the
Far Western Christians of 'the Celtic Fringe' by a series of turns of
the screw which began with the decision at the Synod of Whitby
in A.D. 664 and culminated in the armed invasion of Ireland by
King Henry II of England, with Papal approval, in A.D. 1171.[2]

It will be seen that, in the record of our Western Christendom's
relations, in this early phase, with the primitive societies round
about, there are more entries on the debit and fewer on the credit
side than in the corresponding chapter of the Hellenic Society's
account. Nor was this chapter in our own Western account
entirely closed by the almost complete elimination of the North
European barbarians before the end of the fourteenth century of
the Christian Era through the combined operation of the diverse
processes of conversion, subjugation, eviction, and extermination.
It is true that by A.D. 1400 Western Christendom had expanded
up to the 'natural frontiers' of the Atlantic Ocean on the west and
the Arctic Circle on the north, while on the east it now marched with
Orthodox Christendom from a point on the coast of the Adriatic
to another point on the coast of the Arctic Ocean;[3] and it is also
true that, after the Lithuanians had insured themselves—through
an alliance with the Poles and a simultaneous act of conversion to
Western Christianity[4]—against being overtaken by their Prussian
kinsmen's cruel fate, the only surviving patches of Continental
European barbarism were a few scattered enclaves in such natural
fastnesses as Bosnia and the Scottish Highlands and Western
Ireland. But the tradition of 'frightfulness' to which the Western

---

[1] See III. C (ii) (b), vol. iii, p. 269, above.
[2] See II. D (vii), vol. ii, pp. 333–40, with Annexes II and III, above.
[3] See II. D (v), vol. ii, pp. 168–9, above.
[4] See II. D (v), vol. ii, pp. 172–4, above.

Christians had enslaved themselves in their medieval warfare with primitive peoples on the Baltic and the Celtic fronts was unhappily to show a greater vitality than the European barbarians themselves who had been its first victims. Habits acquired by generations of English and Scottish borderers along the Irish Pale and the Highland Line have continued to assert themselves in the behaviour of these medieval Western barbarian-fighters' descendants towards the previously unknown barbarians of a new world which has been brought within our range by the maritime discoveries at the beginning of the Modern Age. And the North American Indian and the Tropical African Negro have been, in their turn, the victims of a ruthlessness which was first evoked on this side of the water in long since forgotten struggles with 'Wild Highlanders' and 'Wild Irishmen'.[1]

In the expansion of our Western Civilization over the whole face of the planet in the course of the Modern Age of Western history the impetus of the expanding body social has been so strong, and the disparity in strength so extreme between the aggressive West Europeans and their primitive victims, that the movement of expansion has been apt to sweep on unchecked, from the line at which the West Eourpean pioneers have made their first impact on the 'Natives',[2] until this running fight between two unequally matched forces has reached its term at a 'natural frontier'. We have seen how the English settlers in North America have swept the Red Indians almost out of existence from the Atlantic to the Pacific coast, and how the later opening-up of Tropical Africa by the competitive enterprize of half a dozen West European Powers has resulted in the subjugation of the African Negroes from the Atlantic to the Indian Ocean and from the Sahara to the Kalahari Desert.[3] In this world-wide modern Western offensive against the rear-guard of the primitive societies extermination or eviction or subjugation has been the rule and conversion the exception. Indeed, we can count on the fingers of one hand the number of the primitive societies that our modern Western Society has taken into partnership with itself.

There are the Scottish Highlanders,[4] who were one of those

---

[1] For this load of *karma* see II. C (ii) (*a*) 1, Annex, in vol. i, pp. 465–7, above.

[2] For the connotation of this word in the vocabulary of Modern Western Imperialism see I. B (iii), vol. i, p. 33, and I. C (iii) (*b*), vol. i, pp. 151–3, above.

[3] See the present chapter, p. 207, above. One of the incidents in this opening-up of Africa by West European Powers in the last quarter of the nineteenth century of the Christian Era was the extinction of the militant barbarian Power which had been established in the Eastern Sudan by the Baggara Arabs, under the leadership of the Mahdī Muhammad Ahmad, on the ruins of the abortive Egypto-Ottoman empire in the upper basin of the Nile (see the present chapter, pp. 295–6, above, and 324, below).

[4] See II. C (ii) (*a*) 1, vol. i, p. 237; II. C (ii) (*a*) 1, Annex, vol. i, pp. 465–7; II. D (vii), vol. ii, p. 311, and the present chapter and volume, p. 207, above.

rare enclaves of untamed European barbarians that were bequeathed[1] to the modern Western World by a medieval Western Christendom. There are the Maoris, who were encountered by the Scottish and English settlers in New Zealand in the nineteenth century. And there are the Araucanians in the barbarian hinterland of the Chilean province of the Andean universal state,[2] with whom the Spanish settlers in Chile have had to deal since the Spanish conquest of the Inca Empire in the sixteenth century. In these three instances the process of cultural conversion has finally prevailed over the alternatives; but even here this solution has only been accepted by the aggressor after the methods of coercion have been tried and found not worth the price of the desperate resistance which they were evoking.[3]

The test case is the history of the incorporation of the Scottish Highlanders into our modern Western body social after the failure of these White Barbarians' last kick against the pricks in A.D. 1745; for the social gulf between a Dr. Johnson or a Horace Walpole and the war-bands that carried Prince Charlie to Derby was probably not much less difficult to bridge than the gulf between the Western Society of the nineteenth century and the contemporary Maoris and Araucanians. At the present day the great-great-grandchildren of Prince Charlie's shaggy warriors are undoubtedly of one standardized social substance with the descendants of those bewigged-and-powdered Lowlanders and Englishmen who were the victors in the last round of a struggle that reached its end nearly two hundred years before the present volume was published. To-day the epigoni of both parties to that ancient warfare are partners in business and politics and recreation and literature and art, without its being possible for the sharpest-sighted observer to detect even a trace of the historic social cleavage. Yet this happy result cannot be claimed as a clear and unalloyed triumph of the way of Gentleness in contrast to the way of Violence; for, on an impartial examination of the methods by which this act of social assimilation has been accomplished

---

[1] See the present chapter, pp. 320–1, above.
[2] For these Araucanian barbarians beyond the frontier of the Inca Empire along the River Maule see the present chapter, p. 280, above.
[3] 'For over two hundred years the frontier-line [between Araucanian natives and Spanish colonists in Chile] shifted back and forth of the River Biobio, with a story of struggle exactly similar to that between the Saxons and the Wendish Slavs at the River Elbe from the ninth to the twelfth centuries in Europe. The Araucanians were never conquered, and held all their territory. In 1870 they accepted peacefully the sovereignty of Chile, and traders with disease and alcohol, and farmers with their ploughs, entered their country; but no compulsory training in civilized ways was imposed upon them. Steadily their aboriginal population declined, and continues to decline' (Macleod, W. C.: *The American Indian Frontier* (London 1928, Kegan Paul), pp. 117–18). With slight changes, this passage could be adapted to give an accurate description of the history of the relations between the Maoris and the British settlers in New Zealand.

since the middle of the eighteenth century, it might be difficult
for an honest jury to declare that the implacable repression of the
Highlanders' ancestral costume and customs has been a less potent
factor in the process than the generous admission of the discomfited barbarians to share in the privileges and opportunities of
modern Western social life as lived in the United Kingdom.

There are, of course, other barbarians who have managed, in
the midst of an elsewhere Westernized World, to hold their own—
both unconverted and uncoerced—until to-day, or at any rate until
yesterday. But, like the successfully converted Araucanians, these
still obstinately persisting barbarian enclaves have been legacies
from non-Western civilizations that have not yet been completely absorbed into our Western body social.

We have seen, for example,[1] that the modern Western empire-
builders in the Hindu World have been obliged to take over from
their Sikh and Mughal predecessors the responsibility for holding
the North-West Frontier of India against the highlander barbarians of Eastern Iran; and we have also observed that the
British Rāj has had this Indian North-West Frontier problem on
its hands for no less than a hundred years without having yet
succeeded in solving it. We can now call to mind several other
anti-barbarian frontiers of the same kind that have been inherited
from other non-Western civilizations by other Western or Westernized Powers. In the eighteenth century a Westernized Russian
Empire inherited from a Byzantine Muscovy one anti-barbarian
frontier over against the Eurasian Nomads and another over
against the highlander barbarians in the Caucasus, while a nineteenth-century France has inherited from a broken-down Arabic
Society in the Maghrib one anti-barbarian frontier over against
the Afrasian Nomads in the Sahara and another over against the
highlander barbarians in the Atlas. When we compare the French
and Russian handling of the barbarians on these four fronts
with the British handling of the barbarians on the North-West
Frontier of India, we shall notice that both the Russians and the
French have carried out that 'totalitarian' policy of conquering
the barbarians outright which the British first tried and then
abandoned in Afghanistan.[2] The Russians subjugated the Eurasian
Nomads in the eighteenth century[3] and the Caucasian highlanders

---

[1] In the present chapter, pp. 304–5, above.
[2] See the present chapter, pp. 305–8, above.
[3] See the present chapter, pp. 313–16, above. The only horde of Eurasian Nomads
who were still beyond the reach of the Russian arm at the end of the eighteenth century
were the Türkmens in Transcaspia, who lived by raiding Persia from their oasis-
fastnesses—carrying away not only goods and cattle but also Shī'ī slaves for the Sunnī
slave-markets in the Uzbeg Khanates. The Russians left these Transcaspian Türkmens
alone until after the completion of their conquest of the Caucasus, and then attacked

in the nineteenth, while the French had mastered the Sahara before the nineteenth century closed, and have now completed in Morocco the military task upon which they entered in A.D. 1911[1] by reducing to submission, in the year 1934, the last of the 'dissident' Atlas Berbers.[2] In another part of the African field, in the Eastern Sudan, we have already recorded[3] the abortive attempt of an imperfectly Westernized Egypto-Ottoman Power to push its anti-barbarian frontier southward from the First Cataract to the Equatorial sources of the White Nile. This Egypto-Ottoman commitment in the Nile Basin was subsequently taken over by the British; and in the last decade of the nineteenth century British arms eliminated the recalcitrant enclave of barbarism in this quarter by conclusive military operations[4] in the manner of the Russians in the Caucasus and Transcaspia—in contrast to the less drastic British handling of the barbarians beyond the North-West Frontier of India.

If at this point we pause to ask ourselves our usual question—whether the External Proletariat has been stimulated, by its struggle for life, to any acts of creativity in the fields of religion and poetry—we shall find it hard to bring together in a single view the straggling army of barbarians with which our Western Civilization has had to deal in the course of a history which has ranged so widely both in Time and in Space. It would be superfluous to re-examine over again the brilliant creative works of those barbarian rear-guards in 'the Celtic Fringe' and in Scandinavia whose attempts to give birth to civilizations of their own were rendered abortive by their unsuccessful encounters with the nascent civilization of Western Christendom.[5] We may pass on at once to the Modern Age of

them from a Transcaucasian base, from which they were able, thanks to their naval command of the Caspian, to make a lodgement on the opposite coast of that sea. Yet although the Türkmens were thus assailed from an unexpected quarter by adversaries who now had at their disposal the modern Western material technique—including both the steamboat and the railway—their resistance was so stubborn that it took the Russians thirteen years—from 1873 to 1886—to overcome it, whereas it had taken them no more than ten years—from 1863 to 1873—to conquer all the Uzbeg Khanates in the Oxus-Jaxartes Basin (see p. 314, footnote 3, above).

[1] The French had reached the north-western foot of the Atlas *massif* when they had occupied Wajda (Oujda) in 1907, but it was not until they had completed their subsequent occupation of the Atlantic lowlands of Morocco by their entry into Fez (Fās) in the spring of 1911 and into Marrākish in the autumn of 1912 that they took over from the Sharifial *Makhzan* the task of holding the Moroccan 'highland line' and asserting the Sharif's title to sovereignty on the highland side of it.

[2] For the competition between the Western Civilization, as represented by the French, and the Arabic Civilization, as represented by the Arabized Sunnī Muslim population of the Atlantic lowlands of Morocco, for the cultural allegiance of the nominally Muslim, but practically still almost primitive barbarian, Berber highlanders in the Atlas see Toynbee, A. J.: *Survey of International Affairs, 1925*, vol. i (London 1927, Milford), pp. 126–7, and Toynbee, A. J., and Boulter, V. M.: *Survey of International Affairs, 1937*, vol. i, pp. 524–7.

[3] In the present chapter, pp. 209, footnote 3, 294–6, and 321, footnote 3, above.

[4] See p. 321, footnote 3, above, and V. C (ii) (*a*), vol. vi, p. 227, below.

[5] See II. D (vii), vol. ii, pp. 322–60, above.

Western history; and here we may content ourselves with a single example of barbarian creativity in each of the two spheres in which we have learnt to be on the look-out for it.

In the poetic field we may take note of the 'heroic' poetry which was cultivated in the sixteenth and seventeenth centuries of the Christian Era by the Bosniak barbarians[1] beyond the south-eastern frontier of the Danubian Hapsburg Monarchy. And this example is interesting, because it is an apparent exception which in reality proves the prevailing rule that the External Proletariat of a disintegrating civilization is not apt to be stimulated to the creation of 'heroic' poetry until the civilization with which the barbarians are at war has passed through its universal state and fallen into an interregnum which gives opportunity for a barbarian Völkerwanderung. In our survey up to the present point the only prominent exception to this rule which has come to our notice is the genesis of the 'heroic' poetry of the Serb external proletariat of Orthodox Christendom, which apparently goes back to the last phase of the Orthodox Christian 'Time of Troubles' on the eve of the establishment of an Orthodox Christian universal state in the shape of the Ottoman Empire.[2] On this showing, we should not expect to find any examples of 'heroic' poetry among the external proletariat of our Western World, since it is certain that our Western Civilization has not yet entered into a universal state, and uncertain whether it has even broken down.[3] There is, however, one frontier of the Western World on which the local equivalent of a universal state was called into existence more than four hundred years ago by the formidable pressure of an alien civilization; and it is in the hinterland of this front that our Bosniak example of 'heroic' poetry presents itself.

We have seen[4] that the Danubian Hapsburg Monarchy sprang from the defensive union, in A.D. 1526, of the states—or remnants of states—in the south-eastern marches of Western Christendom which were at that moment within striking distance of the Ottoman aggressor; and we have also seen that this hastily concluded union

---

[1] Accounts of this Bosniak school of 'heroic' poetry will be found in Chadwick, H. M.: *The Heroic Age* (Cambridge 1912, University Press), pp. 101–3; Subotić, D.: *Yugoslav Popular Ballads: Their Origin and Development* (Cambridge 1932, University Press), pp. 18–21; Chadwick, H. M. and N. K.: *The Growth of Literature*, vol. ii (Cambridge 1936, University Press), pp. 325–30, 356–8, 365.

[2] See the present chapter, p. 296, above. The historical events that have contributed themes to the repertory of the Classical School of Serb 'heroic' poetry fall within the years 1371–1485. The establishment of the Ottoman Empire may be taken as dating from the Ottoman conquest of Macedonia in A.D. 1371–2 (see Part III. A, vol. iii, p. 26, above); but the key-stone of the Ottoman arch was not fitted into its place until the conquest of Constantinople in A.D. 1453 by Sultan Mehmed II (*imperabat* A.D. 1451–81) (see V. C (ii) (*a*), vol. vi, p. 191, with footnote 1, below).

[3] See I. B (iv), vol. i, pp. 36–7, above, and V. C (ii) (*b*), vol. vi, pp. 313–15, below.

[4] In II. D (v), vol. ii, pp. 177–90, above.

was preserved—by the continuance of the same external pressure that had produced it in the first instance—until our own lifetime, when, in A.D. 1918, the Danubian Hapsburg Monarchy fell to pieces in the political convulsion that gave the *coup de grâce* to the Monarchy's efficient cause, the Ottoman Empire. In terms of a simile which we have used in another place,[1] the Danubian Hapsburg Monarchy was a carapace which the Western Christian body social grew for itself, out of its own living substance, as a special means of protection against a particular and peculiar external danger; and this simile may be instructive for our present purpose, since it draws attention to the diversity in the appearance of the Monarchy as viewed from outside and viewed from within.

Looked at from a standpoint in the heart of Western Christendom, by an observer standing on the banks of the Rhine or the Po or the Scheldt, the Danubian Hapsburg Monarchy could never, even in its heyday, be mistaken for anything but a hollow shell which was as thin and as brittle as it was hard. Though the Hapsburg potentate at Vienna might pile the Imperial Crown of the Holy Roman Empire[2] upon the insignia of so many Danubian kingdoms and lands, no citizen of any state to the west of the Emperor's direct and hereditary dominions could possibly regard as a universal monarch a prince whose writ did not even run in the other principalities of the ramshackle empire of which he was the titular head—not to speak of the admittedly independent kingdoms of France and Spain and Portugal and England and Scotland and Denmark and Sweden and Poland-Lithuania. So far from having entered into a universal state, the Western World in the sixteenth century was farther away from political unity than it had been at any time since the days before Charlemagne's conquest of Lombardy. But though this was the truth about sixteenth-century Western Christendom, it was not the picture that presented itself either to the subjects of the Hapsburg Emperor or to his adversaries beyond the south-eastern frontier of his dominions. To these two contending parties in the drama in which the Emperor was a protagonist, he wore an aspect which he could never wear to any Western European spectator. On his own Danubian ground the Hapsburg filled the political horizon of friends and foes alike as the authentic *Caesarea Majestas*: the supreme head of a Western Christian World which had entered into an *union sacrée* under his leadership in order to stand at bay, in an oecumenical solidarity, against an Ottoman threat to its

---

[1] In I. C (iii) (*b*), vol. i, p. 156, footnote 1, above.
[2] The actual Imperial Crown of Charlemagne was still one of the historic treasures of Vienna down to the annexation of Austria by Germany in A.D. 1938.

existence. Thus, to all intents and purposes, the Danubian Hapsburg Monarchy did perform the part of a Western universal state from 1526 to 1918 in the eyes of all Europeans whose homes lay anywhere south-east of the Inn and the Isonzo. And it is perhaps not simply chance that a barbarian South-East European community living only just beyond the Hapsburg Monarchy's south-eastern pale should have produced in the sixteenth and seventeenth centuries of the Christian Era, when the Viennese Caesar was most conspicuously fulfilling his oecumenical mission, the only school of 'heroic' poetry that has yet arisen in any section of the external proletariat of the modern Western World.

The Bosniaks, who were the authors of this particular 'heroic' tradition, were a rear-guard of the Continental European barbarians who had previously had to endure the unusual—and unusually painful—experience of being taken between the two fires of an aggressive Western and an aggressive Orthodox Christendom. The radiation of the Orthodox Christian Civilization, which had been the first of the two to reach the Bosniaks, had been rejected by them, as we have seen,[1] when it came in its orthodox form; and it had only been able to insinuate itself in the schismatic guise of Bogomilism. This adherence to a Christian heresy had drawn upon the Bosniaks the hostile attentions of their Western Christian as well as their Orthodox Christian neighbours; and in these straits they had welcomed the advent of the 'Osmanlis and had made sure of the good-will of these all-powerful patrons by abandoning their Bogomilism and turning Muslim *en masse*.[2] Thereafter, under Ottoman protection, these Jugoslav converts to Islam took to playing, on the Ottoman side of the Ottoman-Hapsburg frontier, the same part as was played on the Hapsburg side by the Jugoslav Christian refugees from the territories which had fallen under the Ottoman domination.[3] The two opposing sets of Jugoslav barbarian war-bands found an identical occupation in raiding on the one side the Ottoman Empire, which was now performing the function of a universal state for Orthodox Christendom, and on the other side the Hapsburg Monarchy, which was providing the façade of a universal state for the Western World;[4]

---

[1] In the present chapter, p. 295, above.
[2] See IV. C (iii) (c) 2 (β), vol. iv, p. 368, footnote 3, above.
[3] For the refugee Serb *uskoci* (*Italicè* Morlacchi) and *hajduci*, see the present chapter, p. 296, above.
[4] Compare the two likewise opposing sets of Arab war-bands that conducted their raids and counter-raids across the North Arabian borderland between the Roman and Sasanian Empires in the age immediately preceding the Primitive Muslim Arab conquest of South-Western Asia. The Sasanian Empire was raided by the Ghassānī Arab wardens of the Roman marches east of Jordan and Orontes; the Roman Empire by the Lakhmī Arab wardens of the Sasanian marches west of Euphrates. The Banu Ghassān were Monophysite Christians, while the subjects of the Lakhmī princes of Hīrah were divided between Monophysitism, Nestorianism, and paganism (see Browne, L. E.: *The*

and on the same fertile soil of border warfare two independent schools of barbarian 'heroic' poetry, both using the medium of the Serbo-Croat language, grew up and flourished side by side[1]— to all appearance, without exercising any influence upon one another.[2]

If we now wish to find among the external proletariat of our modern Western body social an example of creativity in the religious field, we must wing our flight from the Old World to the New and must take leave of the seventeenth-century frontier of the Danubian Hapsburg Monarchy in Jugoslavia over against the Bosniaks in order to reconnoitre the nineteenth-century frontier of the United States of North America over against the Red Indians.

It is remarkable that the North American Indians should have been capable of making any creative religious response at all to the challenge of European aggression, considering that they were almost continuously 'on the run' from the moment of the arrival of the first English settlers on the Virginian shore of the Atlantic coast of North America in the first decade of the seventeenth century down to the crushing of the last Indian attempt at armed resistance to the power of the United States in the Sioux War of 1890. It is still more remarkable that this Indian religious response, when it came, should have been, not violent, but gentle.

A priori a gentle reaction would not readily have been predicted of a primitive people whose martial qualities—a pride, an endurance, and a demonic energy on the war-path—have made so deep and so lasting an impression upon their White assailants and destroyers that to-day a legendary portrait of a Red Indian warrior

Eclipse of Christianity in Asia (Cambridge 1933, University Press), p. 13). For the conversion of the Serbs and Bosniaks from marauders into mercenaries see V. C (i) (*d*) 6 (α), pp. 462–3, below.

[1] Like the Orthodox Christian Serbo-Croat 'heroic' poetry of Bosnia, Herzegovina, and Montenegro, the Muslim Serbo-Croat 'heroic' poetry of Bosnia and Herzegovina survived the turn of the nineteenth and twentieth centuries of the Christian Era. 'One *beg* took a minstrel with him when he went to visit the spa of Rohitsch-Sauerbrunn in Styria in 1913' (Chadwick, *The Growth of Literature*, vol. ii, p. 438).

[2] Notwithstanding this apparent absence of reciprocal influence, the Serb and the Bosniak school displayed one prominent common feature which was doubtless acquired by both of them from the uniform impress of a common social environment. Like the epic poetry of the French external proletariat of the Andalusian Umayyad Caliphate, but unlike the general run of barbarian literature, the two Jugoslav schools of 'heroic' poetry were largely inspired by the 'politico-religious' *motif* of the Holy War (Chadwick, *The Growth of Literature*, vol. ii, p. 365). In this respect the literary history of the Ottoman-Hapsburg frontier in the sixteenth and seventeeth centuries of the Christian Era offers a sharp contrast to that of the 'Abbasid–East Roman frontier in the ninth and tenth centuries. On this latter frontier the contending 'borderers' were divided from one another not only by their differences of religious and political allegiance, but by a difference of language as well, and yet here, as we have seen (in the present chapter, pp. 256–7, above), the two schools of 'heroic' poetry which were generated on opposite sides of the line by the border warfare were both of them innocent of 'politico-religious' animus and each of them eager to seek inspiration from the other.

who is now physically extinct in consequence of the White Man's
ruthlessness has become the conventional type of 'the Noble
Savage' throughout the Western World.[1] It might rather have
been expected that, if the Red Indians reacted by adopting the
religion of their adversaries with some distinctive difference, they
would seize upon, and exaggerate, the fanatical militancy of the
New Englander's Puritan Calvinist Protestantism,[2] as in the Old
World the Wahhābī and Idrīsī and Sanūsī religious movements
among the Afrasian Nomads have in fact seized upon the corresponding elements in Sunnī Islam in order to nerve their devotees
for the ordeal of fighting, with their backs to the wall, against a
Westernizing Ottoman Power and its British and French and
Italian supplanters.[3] Alternatively, if the Red Indians reacted by
creating a new religion of their own out of their native religious
experience, then this new Red Indian religion might have been
expected to conform to the general type of the worship of a divine
war-lord and his war-band with which we have now become
familiar from Scandinavian and Gothic and Achaean and Hittite
and Aryan examples which have come under review at earlier
points in this chapter. So far from that, the new religion which the
Red Indians did create—under stress of their rapid and tragic
retreat towards an inexorable annihilation before the White Man's
remorseless advance—displays the distinctive characteristics of the
'higher religions' that have been discovered by those prophets of
the Internal Proletariat who have taken the path of Gentleness.

These distinctive characteristics present themselves with an
impressive uniformity and persistence in the teaching and practice
of a series of Red Indian prophets[4] who arose from time to time
between 'the seventeen-sixties' and 'the eighteen-eighties'. The
series begins with two anonymous figures: the prophet of the
Delawares (*profatus* A.D. 1762) and the prophet of the Munsee
branch of the same tribe (*profatus circa* A.D. 1766–75); it continues
in the Shawnee Tenkswatawa, 'the Open Door' (*profatus* A.D.
1795), and the Kickapoo prophet Kanakuk (*profatus* A.D. 1819–
post 1831); and it culminates in the Far Western trio Smohalla
(*profatus post* A.D. 1850) and the two Paiute prophets: Tavibo the

---

[1] 'Woe unto you! For ye build the sepulchres of the prophets and your fathers killed
them' (Luke xi. 47) is a damning stroke of irony which could be applied to the European
colonists and the Red Indian 'Natives' of North America almost as justly as it is applied
in the Gospel to the doctors of the Jewish Law and the prophets of Yahweh.

[2] For this element in Protestantism, and for its share in the creation of our modern
Western Race-feeling, see II. C (ii) (a) 1, vol. i, pp. 211–27, above.

[3] For this militant religious reaction of the Afrasian wing of the external proletariat
of the Ottoman Empire see the present chapter, pp. 295–6, above.

[4] For an illuminating account of these prophets, with indications of their spiritual
affinity with other religious leaders in other times and places, see Macleod, W. C.:
The American Indian Frontier (London 1928, Kegan Paul), pp. 505–32.

Forerunner (*profatus prae* A.D. 1870) and Wovoka the Messiah (*profatus circa* A.D. 1886). The Delaware and Shawnee prophets arose in what has since become the State of Ohio;[1] Kanakuk in what has since become the State of Minnesota; Smohalla in the Rocky Mountains, near the border between the United States and Canada; Tavibo and Wovoka in the more southerly western highland region of Nevada. It will be seen that the locus of the birthplace of the prophet of the day moved westward with the movement of the frontier itself. In each generation the would-be saviours of the primitive Red Indian society in North America made their epiphany in the neighbourhood of the line along which the White Man's pressure was being exerted at the time. They addressed themselves successively to the communities which at successive moments were in imminent danger of being subjugated or evicted or exterminated; and among these exposed and threatened communities the influence of each of the prophets in turn spread far and wide, partly as the result of long missionary journeys undertaken by the prophets themselves, and partly through the flocking of pilgrims to the prophets' own headquarters.

It is the more remarkable to find that the principal message of almost all these prophets was one of peace. And while they preached the establishment of this peace in the first instance between the Indian peoples themselves, as a necessary preliminary to to an *union sacrée* against the White intruders, they did not make their call upon their Indian hearers to cease fighting one another in order to direct their followers' arms against a common alien enemy. While they proclaimed that the Indians were a chosen people who were destined to a life of bliss in an earthly paradise in which the living would be rejoined by the souls of their ancestors, this Red Indian Messianic Kingdom was not to be conquered with tomahawks, and still less with bullets. It was to come through an act of God; and God would perform His act when His chosen people had done what was pleasing in His sight. The Indians' part was the spiritual task of watching and praying and the ritual duty of discarding all the innovations that they had accepted from the White Man. The prophets taught that it was the adoption of these alien tools and techniques that had drawn down God's displeasure upon His people, and that an abandonment of these unclean things was the sovereign means of recapturing God's

[1] The territory now occupied by this state member of the North American Union was not the ancestral domain of the Delaware and Shawnee tribes into which these three prophets were born. It was merely the temporary camping-ground of broken fragments of tribes which had long since been evicted from their original homes. Before it gave birth to a prophet, each of these tribes had been 'on the run' before the face of the White aggressor for at least a hundred years.

blessing.[1] The first of the tools that they instructed their followers
to lay aside were fire-arms (an injunction which sufficiently proves
the good faith of their exhortation to render unto the White Caesar
the things that were his, by submitting themselves to the authority
of the White Man's Government). The prohibition further extended to peaceful utilities like the flint and steel which had been
replacing the Indian's primitive fire-sticks; and it was even applied
to agriculture by Smohalla, in whose remote homeland the art of
cultivation had been unknown until the White Man's advent.[2]

The Indian prophets' general advocacy of Non-Violence in face
of implacable aggression and intolerable provocation was justified
by the event in the rare cases in which either the prophets or their
followers lost their difficult faith in the virtue of forbearance.
In the first generation of the series the Delaware prophet's
religious movement was fatally compromised by the unhappy
results of an experiment in militancy on the part of the Delaware's
Ottowa disciple Pontiac, who had doubly perverted his master's
doctrine by preaching that the object of establishing peace between warring tribes of Indians was to turn their united forces
against the British, and that these alien intruders could not be
fought effectively without resort to the two exotic weapons of the
musket and a French alliance.[3] In the next generation Tenkswatawa 'the Open Door' brought his own movement to destruction
when in A.D. 1809 he abruptly abandoned the doctrine of Non-
Violence which he had been preaching for fourteen years, and took,
instead, to a militancy which was the practice of his brother
Tecumseh 'the Meteor'.[4] Finally, the Ghost Dance Religion—the

[1] This notion that, in coping with a more potent culture than one's own, the disastrous
error—or deadly sin—is to attempt to fight the aggressive culture with its own weapons,
is the fundamental idea of the 'Zealot' reaction (for the alternative 'Zealot' and 'Herodian' reactions to the impact of an alien culture see Part IX, below). The classic exponents of the idea have been the Jewish Zealots from the days of Judas Maccabaeus to
the days of Bar Kōkabā (see V. C (i) (c) 2, pp. 68 and 126, above, and V. C (i) (d) 6 (δ),
Annex, pp. 657–9, and V. C (i) (d) 9 (γ), vol. vi, pp. 120–3, below, with the references
in the footnotes); but the Jewish Zealots of that age, like the Wahhābīs at the present
day, combined their puritanism with militancy, whereas the Red Indian prophets, like
Johanan ben Zakkai and his rabbinical successors, have combined a similar puritanism
with a doctrine of non-resistance.

[2] Agriculture and the worship of agrarian fertility gods were, of course, indigenous
in the New World; and the art had spread from the Mexican Plateau to the region of
the Great Lakes before the arrival of the first Europeans on the American side of the
Atlantic (see II. C (ii) (a) 2, vol. i, p. 265, with footnote 1, above). The first English
settlers in New England found the local Indians cultivating maize; and the three
Delaware and Shawnee prophets all arose in communities in which the indigenous
agriculture of the New World was in use. These Indian prophets in the east of the
Continent thus had no reason to repudiate agriculture, since it would never have
occurred to them to class it with fire-arms as a European invention.

[3] For Pontiac's 'Beaver War' (gerebatur A.D. 1763–5) see Macleod, op. cit., pp. 407–23.
For the untoward effect of Pontiac's unsuccessful excursion into militancy upon the
fortunes of the Delaware prophet's religion see ibid., p. 515.

[4] For the Battle of Tippecanoe (commissum A.D. 1811) and its disastrous effects upon
the fortunes of Tenkswatawa's religion see Macleod, op. cit., pp. 519–21. In A.D. 1814
a comparable disaster overtook the Creek converts to Tenkswatawa's religion when the

fine flower of the Red Indian Messianic Movement, which Tavibo
the Forerunner created and handed on to Wovoka the Messiah—
sustained a mortal blow when Wovoka's Sioux converts made their
desperate and disastrous military outbreak in 1890, and this in
spite of the fact that the Sioux insurrection against the United
States Government had not been directly inspired by Wovoka's
teaching.[1] The Ghost Dance Religion of Tabivo and Wovoka
could not give victory to the Sioux warriors in their forlorn hope;
but the Dreamer Religion of the older western prophet Smohalla
did inspire Chief Joseph and his Nez Percés in 1877 to endure the
horrors of a thirteen-hundred-and-twenty-miles-long retreat under
the pursuit of a relentless enemy.[2] As a sheer feat of heroic endurance the Nez Percés' trek in 1877 is worthy to rank with the
Torgut Calmucks' trek in 1771;[3] and these two long-drawn-out
agonies of revolt and flight may be remembered in history as Abel's
last protest against Cain in the Old World and in the New World
respectively.

At the time of writing it looked as though, for the few antique
barbarian communities that still remained on the map of a by this
time almost completely Westernized world, the only chance of
survival would lie in adopting the tactics of the Abotrites and the
Lithuanians, who, in the medieval chapter of the history of the
expansion of Western Christendom, had had the foresight to anticipate a forcible by a voluntary conversion to the culture of an
aggressive civilization which was too strong for them to resist.[4]
In our latter-day remnant of an antique barbarian world there
were still standing out, in 1938, two closely beleaguered fastnesses
of Barbarism in each of which an enterprising barbarian war-lord
had latterly been making a determined effort to save a perhaps not
yet quite hopeless military and political situation by launching a
vigorous cultural offensive defensive.

In North-Eastern Iran it seemed possible in 1938 that the
North-West Frontier problem of the British Indian Empire might
find its solution, not in any drastic military action against the untamed barbarians on the Indian side of the Indo-Afghan frontier,
but rather in the Westernization of Afghanistan herself; for one of
the crucial issues in this at that time still callow social movement in
Afghanistan was the question whether the Central Government at
Kābul could succeed in establishing its effective authority over the

---

local exponents of the Shawnee prophet's faith followed their master's inauspicious
example by plunging, in their turn, into militancy (ibid., p. 520, footnote 2).
[1] See Macleod, op. cit., p. 528, with footnote 2.   [2] Ibid., pp. 499–501.
[3] See Part III. A, vol. iii, p. 19, IV. C (iii) (c) 3 (α), vol. iv, p. 498, and the present
chapter and volume, p. 315, above.
[4] See II. D (v), vol. ii, pp. 172–4, and the present chapter and volume, p. 319, footnote 5, and p. 320, above.

untamed barbarians on the Afghan side of the same line; and, if this Afghan endeavour were to achieve success, one of the effects would be to place the war-bands on the Indian side between two fires and thereby make their position ultimately untenable. The Westernizing movement in Afghanistan, with which the Indian frontier problem was bound up, had been launched by King Amā-nallāh (*regnabat* A.D. 1919–29) with a radical excess of zeal[1] which was a caricature of the contemporary statesmanship of a Mustafā Kemāl Atatürk and a Rizā Shāh Pehlevī; and this intemperance had cost the royal revolutionary his throne. Yet King Amānal-lāh's personal fiasco was perhaps less significant than the fact that the check had not proved fatal to a movement which had had this unfortunate start. By 1929 the process of Westernization had already gone too far, and a desire for it—or, at least, an acquies-cence in it—had become too widespread, for the people of Afghan-istan to put up with the unmitigated barbarian reaction of the brigand-rebel Bacha-i-Sakkā ('the Water-Carrier's Son'); and under the régime of King Nādir and his successor the process had been unobtrusively resumed and carried on with a tact which seemed to promise more substantial results in the long run than the ex-King Amānallāh's provocatively sensational gestures.[2]

The outstanding Westernizer of a beleaguered barbarian fastness in A.D. 1938 was 'Abd-al-'Azīz b. 'Abd-ar-Rahmān Āl Sa'ūd, the King of the Najd and the Hijāz: a soldier and a statesman who, since A.D. 1901, had raised himself out of the political exile into which he had been born until he had made himself master of all Arabia west of the Rub'-al-Khālī and north of the Yamanī Kingdom of San'ā.[3] During the thirty-eight years of his public career up to date Ibn Sa'ūd had been as resolute in asserting his authority against rivals and rebels as he has been moderate in the terms which he had accorded to his defeated adversaries. As a barbarian war-lord he could bear comparison with the Umayyad Yazīd I for affability[4] and with the Amalung Atawulf for enlightenment.[5] As a Westernizer he had apprehended the potency of the modern Western scientific technique and had shown a discerning eye for those applications of it—artesian wells and motor-cars and aero-planes—that were particularly effective on the Central Arabian Steppe. But, above all, he had seen that the indispensable founda-

[1] See V. C (i) (d) 9 (β), vol. vi, p. 103, and V. C (ii) (a), vol. vi, p. 234, below.
[2] For the history of, and sequel to, Amānallāh's 'raging tearing campaign' of Westerni-zation in Afghanistan see Toynbee, A. J.: *Survey of International Affairs, 1925*, vol. i, pp. 564–9; *1928*, pp. 188–234; *1930*, pp. 182–8.
[3] For King 'Abd-al-'Azīz's career and policy see Toynbee, A. J.: *Survey of International Affairs, 1925*, vol. i, pp. 271–346; *1928*, pp. 284–307; *1930*, pp. 177–82; *1934*, pp. 306–8 and 310–21.   [4] See the present chapter, p. 226, above.
[5] See the present chapter, pp. 226–7, above.

tion for a Western way of life was law and order. 'Abd-al-'Azīz Āl
Sa'ūd stood head and shoulders above the most eminent of his
Afghan contemporaries in moral and intellectual stature; and, since
this was assuredly a case in which personality counted for more
than any material conditions, Sa'ūdī Arabia appeared in 1938 to
have a better prospect than Afghanistan of transferring herself from
the ranks of the doomed barbarian war-bands to those of the states
members of a Westernized Great Society—notwithstanding the fact
that the steppes were more vulnerable than the highlands to military
attack by the mechanical devices of twentieth-century warfare.

When the last obstinate enclave of antique barbarian life has
been eliminated, in one or other of the alternative ways, from the
cultural map of a Westernized World, shall we be able to congratulate ourselves on having seen the last of Barbarism itself?
A complete elimination of the Barbarism of the External Proletariat would warrant no more than a mild elation, since we have
convinced ourselves[1] (if there is any virtue in this Study) that the
destruction which has overtaken a number of civilizations in the
past has never been the work of any external agency, either human
or inanimate, but has always been in the nature of an act of suicide.

'We are betrayed by what is false within.'[2] And this line of
poetry, read in the light of our Western history since the autumn
of the year 1935, may give an unintended turn to a passage in this
Study on the subject of Abyssinia which was written in the
autumn of 1931.

' "The common Christianity" of Abyssinia and the West, in a world
which the radiation of our Western Christian Civilization has now
unified upon a Western Christian basis, is a theme for satire to which
only a Voltaire or a Gibbon could do justice.'[3]

The theme had not gone stale through seven years' keeping, but
the intervening events[4] had raised the question which of the two
parties was to be the satirist's target. In plain words: Who were
the barbarians? Which party had cast itself for the part? The
Abyssinians, who in the interval had made a vain effort to defend
themselves against an unprovoked attack? Or the Italians, who
within the same span of time had broken their own deliberately
given pledges under the Covenant of the League of Nations and
the Briand-Kellogg Pact and the Italo-Abyssinian treaty of 1928
in order to break the Law of Nations, as well as the Law of God,
by setting out to conquer a country which was not theirs and by
levying war upon a miserably armed people with all the deadly

---

[1] In Part IV, *passim*, above.
[2] Meredith, G.: *Love's Grave*, quoted in IV. C (iii) (*a*), vol. iv, p. 120, above.
[3] II. D (vii), vol. ii, pp. 364-5, above.   [4] See p. 207, above.

weapons—including poison gas—that have been added to our modern Western armoury by our modern Western science? If we are to pass beyond the baldly technical sense of the word 'barbarian', and to use it in its deeper moral connotation, then we are bound to declare that, when the Italians attacked and defeated and conquered their Abyssinian victims in East Africa in A.D. 1935–6, the reign of Barbarism in our Great Society was not curtailed but was, on the contrary, most formidably extended.

Who, let us ask ourselves again, are the true barbarians to-day, and where are they to be found? The familiar barbarians of the antique type may have been effectively wiped out of existence through the elimination of the last remaining no-man's-land beyond anti-barbarian frontiers which have now been carried up to the limits set by Physical Nature on every front in the World. But this unprecedented triumph will have profited us nothing if the barbarians, in the hour of their extinction beyond the frontiers, have stolen a march on us by re-emerging in our midst. And is it not here that we find our barbarians embattled to-day? 'Ancient civilizations were destroyed by imported barbarians; we breed our own.'[1] Are we not seeing a host of neobarbarian war-bands being recruited nowadays under our eyes in one country after another— and these in the heart, and not on the outskirts, of what has hitherto been a Christendom? What else but barbarians in spirit are the fighting-men in these *Fascii di Combattimento* and these *Sturmabteilungen*? Have they not been taught that they are the stepchildren of the Society out of whose bosom they have come, and that, as an aggrieved party with a score to pay off, they are morally entitled to conquer 'a place in the sun' for themselves by a ruthless use of force? And is not this precisely the doctrine that the warlords of the External Proletariat—the Generics and the Attilas— have always proclaimed to their warriors as they have led them 'over the top' to plunder some world that has lost the power to defend itself? Black shirts, and not black skins, were assuredly the badges of barbarism in the war that was waged in Africa in 1935–6. So much we can confidently declare; and with no less confidence we can add that the shirted barbarian is a more formidable menace to Society and a more appalling portent for the sociologist than the berserker of whom he has made a prey. The blackshirt is a portent because he is deliberately sinning against inherited lights, and he is a menace because, for the commission of this sin, he has at his disposal an inherited technique[2] which he is free to

---

[1] Inge, W. R.: *The Idea of Progress* (Oxford 1920, Clarendon Press), p. 13.
[2] 'It is the possession of funded civilization which makes the illiterate and morally wild American hunter of the prairies more powerful in fight than the Red Man—the savage of Civilization more terrible than the savage of Barbarism. It is the funded

divert from God's to the Devil's service.¹ But in arriving at this conclusion we have not yet dug down to the root of the matter, for we have not yet asked ourselves what the source may be from which this Italian neobarbarism has been derived.

Towards whom was a Mussolini on the war-path directing his faculty of mimesis? Assuredly not towards his Abyssinian victims, whom he affected altogether to despise.² Our Italian war-lord fancied himself as the builder and not as the destroyer of an empire. In his own estimation he was not a Mihiragula but a Clive. He had stated, in terms, that he thought 'for Italy as the great Englishmen who have made the British Empire have thought for England, as the great French colonizers have thought for France'.³ His intended role was that of an eighteenth-century English or a nineteenth-century French empire-builder; and his West European critics should pause to reflect before angrily or contemptuously dismissing this latter-day Italian caricature of the deeds of their own forebears. A good caricature may be an illuminating portrait; and the Italians, after all, are noted for being past masters of the caricaturist's art. In the repulsive Italian countenance of a neobarbarian apostate from the path of Civilization we may be compelled, with shame and grief, to confess to a recognition of our English ancestors' authentic features. And a twentieth-century Italian dictator's naïve assumption of this old-fashioned West European mien is a formidable indictment of the character of his nineteenth-century and eighteenth-century French and English models. The indictment is formidable just because it is tendered, in complete good faith, as a tribute of admiration. For an imitation which is the sincerest flattery may also be the most'crushing condemnation. 'In the last analysis' the inspiration of Signor Mussolini's neobarbarian imperialism would appear to be a Romagnol's Anglomania; and as soon as we admit this

civilization that they possess that alone makes *les classes dangereuses* really dangerous.'—
Meadows, T. T.: *The Chinese and their Rebellions . . . to which is added an Essay on Civilization* (London 1856, Smith Elder), p. 518.
¹ The perversity which thus misuses the cultural heritage of Civilization is of the essence of Barbarism; and it is likewise practised, as we have already observed (on pp. 202-3, above), by those antique barbarians that are recruited direct from the ranks of Primitive Mankind. Its effectiveness, and, by the same token, its deadliness, is, however, far greater when the practitioners are neobarbarians who have been recruited, not from the extremities, but from the heart, of a body social that has broken down and gone into disintegration as a consequence of failure in an attempt at Civilization.
² While Signor Mussolini and his kind would have sincerely and indignantly repudiated the charge that they were leading their followers back to Barbarism, they bore unintended witness against themselves in their own unconscious attitudes and gestures. See L. S. Woolf:¡*Quack! Quack!* (London 1935, Hogarth Press) for synoptic photographs showing snapshots of Signor Mussolini and Herr Hitler addressing their followers set side by side with the 'still life' of graven images of barbarian war-gods. The unmistakable resemblance is as instructive as it is amusing.
³ Signor Mussolini in an interview given to the French publicist Monsieur de Kerillis, quoted in *The Times*, 1st August, 1935.

unpalatable truth we find ourselves compelled to trace back the origin of the neobarbarism in our midst to earlier events than the formation of the first *fascii di combattimento* in a post-war Italy. Are not these latter-day Italian Fascist war-bands the spiritual descendants of the ships'-crews of certain Elizabethan patron saints of the British Empire—a beard-singeing Drake and a slave-trading Hawkins?[1] To a Castilian historian the affiliation must be plain; and a Hindu philosopher who had the discernment to recognize, and the generosity to declare, that a conscience-smitten generation of post-war Englishmen and Englishwomen was sincerely and earnestly striving to shake off a disreputable English past might ask us gently—in a voice half compassionate and half ironic—whether we were really still so ignorant of the workings of the Universe as to flatter ourselves that a single good resolution would suffice to release us from a load of *karma* which had been accumulated for us by twelve successive generations of impenitently imperialist ancestors.

But must we not pursue our importunate question still farther? Ought we not to remind ourselves, at the close of this chapter, of our observation that, in the warfare between external proletariats and dominant minorities, it is usually the dominant minorities that denounce themselves as the aggressors by being the first to declare war and to take the offensive?[2] We have always to remember that the annals of this warfare between 'Civilization' and 'Barbarism', like those of the warfare between the sedentary societies and the Nomads,[3] have been written almost exclusively by members of one only of the two parties to the dispute. The classic picture of the external proletarian, which portrays him in the act of carrying his barbarous fire and slaughter into the fair domain of some defenceless civilization, is therefore likely, *a priori*, to be not so much an objective presentation of the truth as an expression of the 'civilized' party's resentment at being made the target of a counter-attack which his own previous aggression has in due course brought down upon his head. The complaint against the barbarian, as drafted by his mortal enemy's pen, perhaps amounts to little more than an elaborate variation upon a simple theme which has been 'shown up' once for all by a nineteenth-century French wit:

> Cet animal est très méchant:
> Quand on l'attaque, il se défend![4]

---

1 This point has been touched upon, by anticipation, in I. B (i), vol. i, p. 18, above.
2 See the present chapter, pp. 201–3, above.
3 See Part III. A, vol. iii, p. 18, footnote 1, above.
4 'Théodore P. K.': *La Ménagerie* (1868).

4. *Alien and Indigenous Inspirations*

The first criterion that we have applied in order to determine whether a particular civilization, in a particular stage of its history, is in process of disintegration has been the appearance of schism in the body social;[1] and in the course of a long empirical survey we have made ourselves familiar with the lines along which a disintegrating civilization is apt to split, and also with the composition and nature and characteristic works of each of the resulting fractions of the broken-down society. The tripartite division of a disintegrating civilization into three such fractions—a Dominant Minority and an Internal and an External Proletariat—was originally accepted at an early point in this Study[2] as a provisional working hypothesis on the strength of the single case of the breakdown and disintegration of the Hellenic Civilization. Our present muster of other examples will perhaps have confirmed us in the belief that these are, in fact, the three camps into which any disintegrating civilization tends to divide against itself; and in the light of our survey we shall perhaps also have come to the conclusion that the characteristic works of dominant minorities are schools of philosophy and universal states, and that internal proletariats display their creative power in the creation of 'higher religions' and of universal churches, while external proletariats express themselves in barbarian or dissenting religions and in 'heroic' poetry. Now that we have completed our study of schism in the body social, the next step that suggests itself is to attempt a complementary study of schism in the Soul. But, before we turn the page, we may pause to ask ourselves whether the foregoing investigation suggests any general considerations that may be worth dwelling upon for a moment.

One question of the kind, which almost thrusts itself upon our attention at this point, is that of the source from which the inspirations of these creative works of a disintegrating civilization are derived.

Our earliest definition of societies of the species 'civilizations' was that they were 'intelligible fields of study';[3] and this empirical account of them, from the subjective standpoint of an historical observer, turned out to carry with it certain implications about the objective nature of the field of observation. It meant that, on the whole, the course of the lives of civilizations was self-determined, so that, for the most part, this course could be studied and understood in and by itself, without requiring constant allowance for

[1] See V. C (i) (*b*), pp. 23–35, above.
[2] In I. B (iv), vol. i, pp. 40–2, and I. C (i) (*a*), vol. i, pp. 52–63, above.
[3] See Part I. B, vol. i, above.

the play of alien social forces. In this objective as well as subjective independence we found an important point of difference
between civilizations, seen steadily and whole, and those fragments
of civilizations called national states which our modern Western
egotism has tried to erect into universes in themselves,[1] while our
modern Western paganism has bowed down and worshipped them
as idols.[2] In contrast to these fragmentary national units the bodies
social of societies in process of civilization appear to have a genuine
life of their own. This appearance has been borne out by our study
of civilizations in their geneses[3] and in their growths;[4] and so far
it has not been dispelled by our subsequent study of them in
their breakdowns[5] and disintegrations.[6] For, although a disintegrating society may split into fragments, each one of these
fragments turns out to be a chip of the old block. We have seen,
for example, that even the External Proletariat is recruited (notwithstanding the name with which we have labelled it) from
elements that are already within the disintegrating society's
field of radiation—even though they may be only on its fringe.[7]
At the same time our survey of the several fractions of societies
in disintegration—and this is true, not only of external proletariats, but of internal proletariats and dominant minorities as
well—has frequently required us to take alien as well as indigenous
actors into account in our efforts to follow the plot of the play.
And this frequent call to extend our mental horizon beyond the
limits of the particular society momentarily under view—even
after allowing these limits their widest construction—in order
to understand what is going on, is a definitely new and distinctive element that has entered into our Study at this stage
of it.

The empirical survey which we have now just completed has,
in fact, made it clear that, while the definition of a civilization
as being 'an intelligible field of study' can be accepted virtually
without qualification so long as the particular civilization that we
are studying is still in growth, this definition can only be maintained with reservations when we come to the disintegration stage.
True though it be that the breakdowns of civilizations are due to
an inward loss of self-determination and not to any external
blows,[8] it is not true that the process of disintegration, through

[1] See Part I. A, vol. i, pp. 9–13, above.
[2] See IV. C (iii) (c) 2 (β), passim, in vol. iv, above.
[3] See Part II, passim, in vols. i and ii, above.
[4] See Part III, passim, in vol. iii, above.
[5] See Part IV, passim, in vol. iv, above.
[6] See Part V. A, B, and C (i) (c), 1–3, in the present volume, pp. 1–337, above.
[7] See V. C (i) (c) 3, pp. 194–203, above.
[8] See IV. C (iii) (a), vol. iv, pp. 119–33, above.

which a broken-down civilization has to pass on its way to dissolution, is equally intelligible without reference to external agencies and activities. In the study of the life of a civilization in the disintegration-stage the 'intelligible field' has proved to be distinctly wider than the ambit of the single society that is the immediate object of observation. And this means that, in the process of disintegrating, the substance of a body social does not merely tend to break up into its component elements but also tends at the same time—in consequence of this dislocation—to resume its liberty to enter into new combinations with extraneous elements derived from foreign bodies—just as the physical disintegration of a bar of iron is accompanied by an amalgamation of certain molecules of the metal, which the process of disintegration releases, with molecules of oxygen that are yielded up by the air. The formation of this oxide or rust, through a dislocation of the molecules of the disintegrating material and through the entry of an alien element into the chemical process, is, of course, the outward visible sign that the iron bar is weathering away; and in the disintegration of a body social the intrusion of alien social elements has a corresponding significance. It will be seen that, now that we have come to the study of the disintegrations of civilizations, we are finding that the ground on which we took our stand at the beginning of this Study is slipping away from under our feet. At the beginning we chose civilizations for the objects of our Study just because they presented the appearance of being 'intelligible fields' which lent themselves singly to being studied in isolation. We now find ourselves already on the move from this standpoint towards a different standpoint which we shall have to take up when we examine, in later Parts,[1] the contacts between one civilization and another—in the Space-dimension first and in the Time-dimension later. Meanwhile, in anticipation of this later systematic study of 'contacts' for their own sake, we may find it convenient at this point to distinguish and compare the respective effects of the alien and the indigenous inspirations that can be discerned in the activities of the several fractions of the body social of a civilization that is in process of disintegration.

Our survey has shown us that in the activities of all three fractions—the Dominant Minority as well as the two sections of the Proletariat—alien inspirations are apt to enter in. But if we now cast our minds back over the results of our survey, with our present purpose in view, we shall notice that the effects of these alien inspirations differ—and indeed are diametrically opposite to one another—in different cases, and that the difference

---

[1] In Parts IX and X, below.

of circumstance which produces the difference of effect is a difference in the identity of the party which is the recipient and exponent of the alien cultural influence. In the works of the Dominant-Minority and the External Proletariat an alien inspiration is apt to result in discord and destruction, whereas in the works of the Internal Proletariat it is apt to produce the exactly opposite effects of harmony and creation.

To begin with the Dominant Minority, we may recall the fact—which has been brought out in our survey[1]—that the majority of the universal states that are provided for disintegrating civilizations by their dominant minorities are the work of empire-builders who are indigenous to the society for which they are performing this social service. These indigenous empire-builders may be frontiersmen[2] from the outer edge of the world upon which they confer the blessing of peace through the imposition of political unity; but this origin does not, in itself, convict them of having any alien tinge in their culture.[3] At the same time our survey has also brought to our notice certain cases in which the moral débâcle of a Dominant Minority has been so rapid and has gone to such lengths that, by the time when the disintegrating society has arrived at the natural term of its 'Time of Troubles', and is ripe for entering into a universal state, there is no longer any remnant of the original indigenous dominant minority that is still possessed of the empire-building virtues. In these rather rare cases the task of providing a disintegrating civilization with a universal state is not usually allowed to remain unperformed on account of the indigenous dominant minority's default. The usual denouement is for some alien empire-builder to step into the breach and to perform for the ailing society the service that ought to have been performed by native hands.[4]

We have now to observe that this involuntary acceptance of a universal state from an alien source is a practical confession of social bankruptcy, and that such a confession is seldom or never made with impunity. The alien empire-builder's little finger is apt to be thicker than the native empire-builder's loins.[5] The outsider who intervenes in order to save a situation with which

---

[1] See V. C (i) (c) 1, pp. 52–5, above.
[2] See V. C (i) (c) 1, pp. 54–5, above. The stimulus of pressures to which the frontiersmen of a society are exposed, and from which, if they respond successfully to this challenge, they thereby shield—or starve—their neighbours of the same culture in the interior of the same world, has been examined in II. D (v), vol. ii, pp. 112–208, above. The misdirection—in the malady of Militarism—of the energies that are evoked by a successful response to the stimulus of pressures on a cultural frontier has been examined in IV. C (iii) (c) 3 (α), vol. iv, pp. 501–4, above.
[3] See V. C (i) (c) 1, pp. 55–6, above.
[4] See V. C (i) (c) 1, pp. 53–4, and V. C (i) (c) 2, pp. 88–95 and 105–17, above.
[5] 1 Kings, xii. 10.

the indigenous dominant minority has shown itself incompetent to cope is naturally unwilling to undertake this arduous and ungrateful task 'for love'. He recoups himself for his pains in taking command of a desperate situation by charging an exorbitant fee; and since, *ex hypothesi*, he is in power, he can assess this charge at as high a figure as he likes and can exact the payment as harshly as he chooses. The beneficiary—or victim—of the alien empire-builder's high-handed service has precluded himself, in advance, from the possibility of insisting upon fair terms or reasonable accommodation. He has no choice, at the moment, but to pay whatever price may be extorted from him. But, of course, the less he is able to resist, the more bitterly he resents the necessity of submitting. Impotence is transmuted into vindictiveness; and the retaliation which is beyond the subject's power here and now is saved up for a future settlement of scores against a hated master, at compound interest.

This means that the universal peace which an alien empire-builder provides is never perfect—even in a prosaic worldly sense—because it is never able to grow out of being an external repression that depends for its efficacy upon a perpetual exertion of the physical force by which it was imposed in the first instance. This same crude physical force is, no doubt, the usual means by which any empire-builder—alien or indigenous—establishes his authority at the moment when he is actually founding his universal state; for the 'Time of Troubles', upon which the universal state supervenes, is in its essence an age of violence, and the final paroxysm of this frenzy is usually the worst.[1] Even the best-intentioned and highest-minded empire-builder can hardly be expected to do his business without behaving in the fashion of his age to some extent; and indeed this hardly avoidable initial recourse to violent means seldom provokes any deep resentment; for 'beggars cannot be choosers', and a society which has travelled so far along the path of disintegration as to have reached the culmination of its 'Time of Troubles' must, *ex hypothesi*, have been so cruelly buffeted and battered by the lawless play of force already that by this time, most likely, it will be prepared to acquiesce in one more bout of violence if, at this price, there is some hope of its being able at last to purchase admission into the haven of a genuine and enduring peace. On this account all universal states—whether their founders are natives or strangers—are apt to be accepted with resignation, if not with enthusiasm, at the outset; and it is only in the later chapters of the story that divergences begin to appear in the development of the relations between the rulers and

[1] For evidence of this see V. C (ii) (*b*), *passim*, in vol. vi, below.

their subjects. When these divergences do appear, however, they tend to be sharply marked.

In general we find that in a universal state which has been established by native hands—as the Hellenic universal state was established by the hands of the Roman frontiersmen of the Hellenic World[1]—Time heals the wounds that the work of empire-building has inflicted, and transforms a submission extorted by force into an allegiance accorded by consent or even tendered with enthusiasm.

In the history of the Hellenic Society the Age of the Antonines—though this was but a brief 'Indian Summer' which might delay, but could not avert, the onset of the winter storms[2]—did at least achieve one notable permanent moral result in the conversion of the Greek Republic of Letters from a passive hostility and resentment[3] to an active affection and gratitude towards the Roman Empire. The successors of Greek philosophers and rhetoricians who had still remained unreconciled to Roman rule in the time of the Emperor Domitian (*imperabat* A.D. 81–96), which was already more than a hundred years removed from the date of the original establishment of the *Pax Augusta* in 31 B.C. over the dead body of the last of the Greek Great Powers, were moved by the time of Marcus (*imperabat* A.D. 161–180) to return to the 'real life' of their day—from the asylum of an archaistic wonderland into which they had made their pedantic way through a literary looking-glass[4]—in order to add their cultivated Greek voices to a swelling chorus of praise with which Dea Roma was now being honoured, in all sincerity, by the loyal descendants of her formerly disaffected subjects. Let us listen for a moment to the voice of the Emperor Marcus's academic contemporary Publius Aelius Aristeides, who knew how to express, in Greek that was both elegant and eloquent, the sentiments of millions of his British and Arabian and Pontic and Mauretanian fellow-subjects:

'You have made one single household of the entire Inhabited World.... Before the establishment of your empire the World was in confusion, upside down, adrift and out of control; but as soon as you Romans intervened the turmoils and factions ceased, and life and politics were illumined by the dawn of an era of universal order . . . so that to-day the Earth and all they that dwell therein are endowed with a clear and comprehensive security. . . .

'The entire Inhabited World now speaks with one voice in closer

---

[1] See II. D (v), vol. ii, pp. 161–4, above.
[2] See IV. C (ii) (b) 1, vol. iv, pp. 58–61, above.
[3] See V. C (i) (c) 1, pp. 55–6, above.
[4] See V. C (i) (d) 8 (γ), vol. vi, pp. 78–80, below.

unison than a chorus; and the common prayer which this oecumenical chorus utters is for the eternal duration of a Roman Empire which is kept in such masterly order by its emperor-conductor..... You Romans are the only rulers known to History who have reigned over freemen. .... You have endowed the entire Inhabited World with the constitutional liberties of a world-wide city-state.... The lustre of your rule is unsullied by any breath of ungenerous hostility; and that is because you yourselves set the example of generosity by sharing all your power and privileges with your subjects ... with the result that in your day a combination has been achieved which previously appeared quite impossible—the combination of consummate power with consummate benevolence.... No one is debarred from being a citizen of Rome either by an estranging sea or by an intervening continent. In this matter no distinction has been drawn between Europe and Asia. Every privilege of Roman citizenship lies within everyone's reach, and no one is treated as an alien who is worthy of responsibility and trust. In fact, the Roman Empire is a world-wide democracy under the governance of one supreme magistrate who is singled out for his pre-eminence in virtue; and Mankind comes together in a common forum where each can be sure of receiving fair measure. As an ordinary city-state stands to its own parochial territory, so stands this city of Rome to the entire Inhabited World. Rome is a town which has the World for its countryside. Rome is a citadel which has all the peoples of the Earth for its villagers. And Rome has never failed those who have looked to her. As the surface of the Earth bears all Mankind, so Rome receives all the peoples of the Earth into her bosom, as the rivers are received by the Sea. And this likeness of Rome to the Sea extends to a further point. The sea is not increased in volume by the inflow of the rivers. There seems to be some law of Nature which adjusts the Sea's capacity to the rivers' discharge. And it is the same with Rome: she does not run to any unseemly enormity, but ... ever keeps and displays her own proper proportions.'[1]

This Greek panegyric of Rome from the second century of the Christian Era may be capped with the Latin testimony of two poets who were writing about a quarter of a millennium later than Aristeides, the one just before, and the other just after, the débâcle of A.D. 406–10,[2] and who came from the opposite extremities of the *Orbis Romanus*—the one from Egypt and the other from Gaul.

This is how Rome is addressed by Claudian of Alexandria in a Latin which was a *tour de force* in the mouth of a Greek citizen of the Roman Commonwealth:

> Haec est, in gremium victos quae sola recepit,
> humanumque genus communi nomine fovit

---

[1] Aristeides, P. Aelius: *In Romam*, pp. 396, 360, 362, 376, 373–4.
[2] Claudian's Third Book *De Consulatu Stilichonis* appears to have been written in A.D. 400, Rutilius's *De Reditu Suo* in A.D. 416.

matris, non dominae, ritu, civesque vocavit
quos domuit, nexuque pio longinqua revinxit.[1]

And this is how she is addressed by the Gaul Rutilius in a Latin
which was likewise an alien tongue in the mouth of a descendant of
Celtic-speaking barbarians:

Fecisti patriam diversis gentibus unam:
    profuit invitis, te dominante, capi;
dumque offers victis proprii consortia iuris,
    Urbem fecisti quod prius Orbis erat.
auctores generis Venerem Martemque faetmur,
    Aeneadum matrem Romulidumque patrem:
mitigat armatas victrix clementia vires;
    convenit in mores numen utrumque tuos.
hinc tibi certandi bona parcendique voluptas:
    quos timuit, superat; quos superavit, amat. . . .
te, dea, te celebrat Romanus ubique recessus,
    pacificoque gerit libera colla iugo.
omnia perpetuo quae servant sidera motu
    nullum viderunt pulchrius imperium.[2]

The Gallic poet who, in A.D. 416,[3] made this famous declaration
of admiration and love for a Rome that, six years earlier, had been
smitten and humiliated by the hand of Alaric,[4] had inherited the
right to utter these ardent words; for he was descended from
ancestors who had been brought under Roman rule by force of
arms—and this, at the earliest, not very much more than five
hundred years before the poet's own day.[5] Rutilius was moved

[1] Claudian: *De Consulatu Stilichonis*, Book III, ll. 150–3.
[2] Rutilius Namatianus, C.: *De Reditu Suo*, Book I, ll. 63–72 and 79–82.
[3] A.U.C. 1169 (Book I, ll. 135–6) = A.D. 416.
[4] The memory of the *Clades Gothica* was still fresh in Rutilius's mind (ll. 39–42 and 115–44). For the impression which the news of the capture of Rome by Alaric had made, at the time, upon the minds of Saint Jerome and Saint Augustine, see V. C (i) (c) 3, pp. 223–5, above. Between Saint Jerome's letter on the subject, which has been quoted in V. C (i) (c) 3, p. 223, footnote 2, above, and the first four lines of the passage just quoted, in the present context, from Rutilius's poem, there is a twofold verbal correspondence. Saint Jerome's *capitur Urbs quae totum cepit Orbem* has recognizable echoes in Rutilius's *capi* and in his *Urbem-Orbis*. The chronological facts would allow us to account for these echoes by supposing that Rutilius had read and remembered Jerome's words; for Jerome's letter seems to have been written *circa* A.D. 412, while Rutilius tells us (see the preceding footnote) that the date of his poem is A.D. 416. But this chronological possibility is a psychological impossibility and an historical improbability; for Rutilius, as he also tells us in his poem, had a violent hatred for Christian anchorites and all their works; he would never have been willing to be consciously beholden to Saint Jerome for a phrase or an idea; and it is most unlikely that a letter addressed by Jerome, from Bethlehem, to a Christian correspondent should have come into Rutilius's hands during the Gallic poet's sojourn in Rome as *Praefectus Urbi* in A.D. 414, even if Jerome's correspondent Principia was still resident in Rome in A.D. 412. We must therefore assume that the figures of speech that are common to these two approximately contemporary pieces of Latin literature were commonplaces which were 'in the air' in the second decade of the fifth century of the Christian Era. We can, indeed, already discern them in embryo in the passage, already ancient in Jerome's and Rutilius's day, which we have quoted above from Aelius Aristeides.
[5] That is to say, if the poet's home (which he does not deign to mention precisely) lay in Gallia Narbonensis. If it lay beyond the Rhône and the Cevennes, somewhere

to write by the emotions that welled up within him as he travelled
back to his Gallic home after a sojourn in the Imperial City.
The feeling that chiefly inspired him was home-sickness; but the
home that held his affection was the spiritual home that he was
now leaving, and not the distant countryside that was his birth-
place and habitual domicile.

> At mea dilectis fortuna revellitur oris,
>   indigenamque suum Gallica rura vocant.[1]

And his year's sojourn in the metropolis of his world has been
all too short for his taste.

> Velocem potius reditum mirabere, lector,
>   tam cito Romuleis posse carere bonis.
> quid longum toto Romam venerantibus aevo?
> nil unquam longumst quod sine fine placet.[2]

Nor is this surprising in Rutilius's case; for the business which
had brought him on this long journey to the city that had forcibly
imposed her yoke upon his forebears' necks was not the payment
of a tribute or the performance of a *corvée* but was a call to investiture with one of the most distinguished offices of state—and
this not some oecumenical magistracy which was concerned
with the Empire as a whole, but the distinctively metropolitan
Praefectura Urbis, which might well have been reserved—if any
Roman public honour had been thus reserved in this age—for
Roman citizens who had been born and bred within the precincts
of the city. These happy beings were objects of the departing
poet-prefect's wistful and respectful envy.

> O quater et quotiens non est numerare beatos
>   nasci felici quo meruere solo![3]

And his gratitude overflowed at the thought that he had been
generously summoned from his own provincial birthplace in
order to be co-opted into this goodly company.[4] No wonder that,
as he left the city of his dreams after having lingered there for
more than twelve months beyond the end of his golden year
of office, Rutilius had to shame himself into a faint blush of human

---

in that larger part of Gaul which had first been brought under Roman rule by Caesar,
then Rutilius was a Roman *ressortissant* of less than five hundred years' hereditary
standing.   [1] Book I, ll. 19–20.   [2] Book I, ll. 1–4.   [3] Book I, ll. 5–6.

[4] The list of those doubly-distinguished Prefects of the City who, unlike Rutilius,
were of metropolitan origin, was not to close before it had included the future Pope
Gregory the Great, who appears to have held the *Praefectura Urbis* in or about the
year A.D. 573 (see III. C (ii) (b), vol. iii, p. 267, above), some 160 years after Rutilius,
who appears to have held the office in A.D. 414. In Rutilius's own words (Book I, ll. 7–8)
Gregory was one of those

> Qui Romanorum procerum generosa propago
> ingenitum cumulant Urbis honore decus.

feeling for his dull Gallic native land by reminding himself that her war-scarred countenance had a claim upon his pity.

Sed quam grata minus, tam miseranda magis.[1]

In the lines[2] immediately following the first of the passages that have been quoted above, the poet goes on to throw into relief the greatness and goodness of the Roman Empire against a foil which he finds in the work of other empire-builders; and it is interesting to observe the uniformly alien origin of the examples that he picks out: the Assyrians who afflicted a Syriac World with a Babylonic reign of terror; the Medes who imposed a Syriac rule upon their Assyrian oppressors; the Macedonian *conquistadores* who won for Hellenism a dominion over the domain of a Syriac universal state that embraced the Egyptiac and the Babylonic World as well as the Syriac; the Eurasian Nomad Parthians who usurped the heritage of the Achaemenids' Seleucid successors.

It was assuredly true that the Gallic poet's crowning eulogy of Rome—'Quod regnas minus est quam quod regnare mereris'[3]— would never have been uttered by any of these alien empire-builders' subjects—not even in the evening of their reign, when Time had done all that he could to temper the odiousness of their rule with the opiate of familiarity. The Babylonian priests who welcomed Alexander as a deliverer in 331 B.C. were more bitterly hostile to the Achaemenian régime than their predecessors had been two hundred and eight years back, when, in 539 B.C., they had seen the first Achaemenian conqueror, Cyrus, ride in.[4] And their pent-up feelings burst out with all the greater violence because, for the past century and a half, they had been too heavily crushed to repeat the periodical armed revolts with which they had enlivened the first half-century of their subjection to an alien Syriac yoke. Alexander's reception by the Babylonians may remind an English scholar of the Hindus' acquiescence in the British Rāj in the early days when there was still a popular memory of the more obnoxious alién régime of the Mughals;[5] and on this analogy we may conjecture that, if the Babylonic Civilization had not solved all its problems by the *ultima ratio* of becoming extinct in the last century B.C.,[6] Hellenism

---

[1] Book I, l. 22.   [2] Book I, ll. 83–6.   [3] Book I, l. 91.
[4] See IV. C (ii) (*b*) 2, vol. iv, p. 100, footnote 4, and V. C (i) (*c*) 2, in the present volume, pp. 94 and 123, with footnote 2, above, and V. C (ii) (*a*), vol. vi, pp. 187–8, and V. C (ii) (*a*), Annex II, vol. vi, p. 442, below.
[5] The Babylonians' attitude towards the Hellenic culture appears to have resembled the Hindus' attitude towards the Western culture. They readily adopted the externals, but were careful to keep the heart of their own culture intact (see Tarn, W. W.: *The Greeks in Bactria and India* (Cambridge 1938, University Press), pp. 56–60).
[6] The latest document in the Akkadian language and cuneiform script that has yet been recovered by our modern Western archaeologists dates from 7 B.C. (Tarn, op. cit., p. 57).

might eventually have come to stink in Babylonian nostrils as odiously as the Western Civilization which is embodied in the British régime has actually come to stink in the nostrils of our latter-day Bengali revolutionaries. Certainly the alien *Pax Otto-manica* which had been welcomed in the first quarter of the fourteenth century of the Christian Era by the Greek adherents of the founder of the Ottoman Commonwealth on the Asiatic shores of the Marmara had become an object of loathing to the Greeks who rose in the Morea and in Rumili against the Government of Sultan Mahmūd II in A.D. 1821. In this case the passage of five centuries had produced in Greece a change of sentiment which was the exact inverse of the change in Gaul from the Romano-phobia of a Vercingetorix to the Romano-philia of a Rutilius Namatianus or a Sidonius Apollinàris.

Another prominent example of the hatred that is aroused by empire-builders with an alien culture is the animosity of the Chinese towards the Mongol conquerors who provided a distracted Far Eastern World with a sorely needed universal state.[1]

The vehemence of this Chinese feeling will impress us when we remind ouselves that the tincture of alien civilization which the Mongols had acquired[2] before they took it upon themselves to provide the Far East with a *Pax Mongolica* was far too slight to discolour more than infinitesimally the straightforward and inoffensive barbarism which was their native hue. Yet, faint though it was, this taint of discoloration never escaped the sharp sight of the Mongols' Chinese subjects and also never won pardon from their resentful hearts. To a distant observer's eyes the difference of tint between the fly-blown barbarism of the Mongols and the uncontaminated barbarism of the Manchus, who eventually re-established the Far Eastern universal state which the Mongols had originally founded, is so fine that it is barely perceptible, even under a scholar's lens. Yet this fine shade made a world of difference between the respective outcomes of the Mongol and the Manchu attempts at an identical enterprise.

The Mongols were expelled from China, neck and crop,[3] only ninety-two years after Qubilay's capture of Hangchow;[4] the Manchus were suffered to reign over China for the 267 years that elapsed between their entry into Peking in A.D. 1644 and the

---

[1] This has been touched upon by anticipation in Part V. A, pp. 3-4, and in V. C (i) (c) 1, p. 54, above.
[2] See II. D (vi), vol. ii, pp. 237-8; Part III. A, Annex II, vol. iii, p. 451; and V. C (i) (c) 3, in the present volume, p. 309, above.
[3] See II. D (v), vol. ii, p. 121, above.
[4] Hangchow capitulated to Qubilay's general Bayan in A.D. 1276; Qubilay's successor Tughān Tīmūr was driven out beyond the Great Wall in A.D. 1368.

Chinese Revolution which extinguished their effective authority in the same city in A.D. 1911. And, even then, the treatment which the discomfited Manchus received at Chinese hands was entirely different from that which had been meted out to their Mongol forerunners. The Mongols, with their indelible brand of uncleanness in Chinese eyes, had been physically expelled to the farther side of the Great Wall and had then and there resumed with ease—and possibly with relief—their great-grandfathers' nomadic life on their great-grandfathers' pasture-lands. The Sinified epigoni of the Manchu conquerors who were put down from their seat in 1911 had by then long since lost all personal touch with their ancestral homes far away in the forests above the headwaters of the Sungari. And, if they had been returned, on disapproval, to this wilderness beyond the pale which was their historical place of origin, they would have been no more capable of resuming the pristine Manchu way of life than a butterfly is capable of resuming the life of a caterpillar. Marooned in the Manchurian forests, these latter-day Manchu princes and 'bannermen' would have perished as helplessly there as a Chinese litteratus or a Mongol new-born baby; and their former Chinese subjects, who had opposed them without animus and deposed them without vindictiveness, did not now expose them to this fate. They showed a nicer tact —and perhaps also a keener malice—in simply leaving them where they were, to sink unromantically, like lumps of lead, from the top to the bottom of the social scale of a Far Eastern Civilization that these *ci-devant* barbarians had embraced 'to have and to hold . . . for better for worse, for richer for poorer, in sickness and in health'.

This Chinese tolerance—at first respectful and finally contemptuous—towards the Manchus in the mandarins' midst presents a striking contrast to the violence of the antagonism which the Mongols, with their alien henchmen, excited in Chinese breasts from the beginning to the end of the Mongols' ill-starred attempt to play the part of the Imperial people in a Far Eastern universal state. That Chinese feeling is made manifest in two incidents which have been recorded by a Western Christian man of affairs who worked in China in the service of the Mongol Khāqān Qubilay. In the one case the targets of Chinese xenophobia were Orthodox Christian soldiers; in the other case they were Muslim administrators; but the temper of both Chinese outbreaks was the same.

The story of the encounter between Qubilay's Orthodox Christian soldiers and the Chinese civilian population of a Far Eastern World on which the Mongols were unable to impose their peace without making a desert of it first[1] is recounted by Marco Polo as follows:

'At the time of the conquest of the great province of Manzi [the Empire of the Sung], when Bayan was in command, he sent a company of his troops, consisting of a people called Alans, who are Christians,[2] to take this city [of Changchow]. They took it accordingly; and, when they had made their way in, they lighted upon some good wine. Of this they drank until they were all drunk, and then they lay down and slept like so many swine. So, when night fell, the townspeople, seeing that they were all dead-drunk, fell upon them and slew them all; not a man escaped. And, when Bayan heard that the townspeople had thus treacherously slain his men, he sent another admiral of his with a great force, and stormed the city, and put the whole of the inhabitants to the sword.'[3]

The story of the anti-Muslim conspiracy is still more illuminating, since the feeling which it reveals is not the hot-blooded homicidal mania that breaks out where there is a state of war, but is a colder animosity which smoulders on in peace-time.

'A certain Saracen named Ahmad [from Banākath or Fanākant in Transoxania], a shrewd and able man, . . . had more power and influence with the Great Khan [Qubilay] than any of the others; and the Khan held him in such regard that he could do what he pleased. . . . In such authority did this man continue for two-and-twenty years. At last the people of the country, to wit the Cathayans [i.e., the Chinese], utterly wearied with the endless outrages and abominable iniquities which he perpetrated against them, . . . conspired to slay him and revolt against the Government. . . . [The principal conspirators, who were two Chinese military officers in Qubilay's service with commands at Peking,] sent word to their friends in many other cities that they had determined on such a day, at the signal given by a beacon, to massacre all the men with beards, and that the other cities should stand ready to do the like on seeing the signal fires. The reason why they spoke of massacring the bearded men was that the Cathayans naturally have no beard, whilst beards are worn by the Tatars, Saracens and Christians. And you should know that all the Cathayans detested the Great Khan's rule because he set over them governors who were Tatars, or still more frequently Saracens, and these they could not endure, for they were treated by them just like slaves. You see, the Great Khan had not

---

[1] 'Ubi solitudinem faciunt, pacem appellant.'—Tacitus: *Agricola*, chap. 30, *ad fin.*

[2] The Alans were a rear-guard of the Sarmatian Nomads who had lingered on in the borderland between the Great Western Bay of the Eurasian Steppe and the northern foot-hills of the Caucasus. Their conversion to Christianity in the eighth century of the Christian Era had been one of the earliest cultural conquests of a nascent Orthodox Christian Civilization; and the descendants of these converts had survived to be overtaken by the tidal wave of Mongol invasion in the thirteenth century, and to find their deaths, in the circumstances here described, at the opposite end of their new masters' immense dominions. (For the conversion of the Alans see I. C (i) (b), vol. i, p. 64, above.)—A.J.T.

[3] Polo, Marco: *The Book of Ser Marco Polo*, translated and edited by Colonel Sir Henry Yule, 3rd edition (London 1903, John Murray, 2 vols.), vol. ii, pp. 178–9 = Book II, chap. 74.

succeeded to the dominion of Cathay by hereditary right, but held it by conquest; and thus, having no confidence in the natives, he put all authority into the hands of Tatars, Saracens or Christians who were attached to his household and devoted to his service, and were foreigners in Cathay.'[1]

The measure of the hostility which is evoked by alien authors of universal states—a hostility which is evidently only exacerbated, instead of being mitigated, by the passage of Time—is given by the uniformly fanatical êthos of the thoroughbred indigenous régimes which sometimes succeed in bringing such alien universal states to a premature end. This touch of fanaticism is shared by the Ming, who expelled the Mongols from China between A.D. 1351 and A.D. 1368,[2] with the Marāthās who were the executors of the Hindu Society's revenge upon the Mughals in the eighteenth century; and we can detect the same temper, not only in the anti-British revolutionary movement in twentieth-century Bengal, but also in the successive Babylonian revolts against Darius the Great and Xerxes, and in the Moreot Greek revolt against Ottoman rule in A.D. 1821.

A no less fanatical temper is apt to be evoked by barbarians with a tinge of alien culture when they present themselves in their normal role of predatory members of the External Proletariat without having gone out of their way to take upon themselves a Dominant Minority's neglected task of establishing a universal state. For example, the Hyksos, who broke into the domain of the Egyptiac Society after the break-up of the indigenous Egyptiac universal state that is known as 'the Middle Empire', were hated with as burning a hatred, and were expelled at the first opportunity, neck and crop, in as vehement a *Befreiungskrieg*,[3] as the Mongol trespassers upon the sacred soil of China; and this similarity of the emotional reaction in two encounters which were so widely separated in Time as well as in Space is satisfactorily explained by the identity of the colour of the rag which in each case infuriated the bull. It was the alien Sumeric tinge in the culture of the Hyksos that made the Egyptians 'see red', as it was the alien Far Eastern Christian tinge in the culture of the Mongols that maddened the Chinese. And in the Egyptiac case, as in the Far Eastern, our explanation is borne out by the contrast between this morbid fury and the common-sense stolidity with which the momentary maniac afterwards put up with a visitation from a second uninvited guest who was equally unwelcome in himself

---

[1] Ibid., vol. i, pp. 416–18 = Book II, chap. 23.
[2] See II. D (v), vol. ii, pp. 121–2, and Part III. A, Annex II, vol. iii, p. 417, above.
[3] See I. C (ii), vol. i, p. 139, footnote 1, and p. 144; IV. C (ii) (b) 2, vol. iv, p. 85; IV. C (iii) (c) 2 (β), vol. iv, p. 412; Part V. A, in the present volume, pp. 2–3; and V. C (i) (c) 2, p. 152, above.

but who happened to be innocent of the one offence that was unforgivable.

We have seen that the Far Eastern universal state which had originally been founded, with such explosive consequences, by the Mongols, was eventually re-established with impunity by Manchus whose sole, but decisive, point of diversity from their Mongol predecessors lay in the fact that their barbarism was free from any alien cultural taint. There is a parallel in Egyptiac history to this repetition-with-a-difference; [1]for, when the Egyptiac universal state had been re-established in the shape of 'the New Empire' by the Theban expeller of the Hyksos, Amosis, and when 'the new Empire', in its turn, was overtaken by the decadence into which 'the Middle Empire' had fallen in its day, two new barbarian clouds appeared, as we have seen, above the Egyptiac dominant minority's horizon. In the thirteenth and twelfth centuries B.C. a decaying Egyptian Empire was assaulted simultaneously by sea-peoples from the Aegean (the mingled destroyers and survivors of a broken-down Minoan 'thalassocracy') and by Libyan Nomads from the African side of the Afrasian Steppe;[2] and in resisting the assailants of Minoan complexion the military emperors of the Nineteenth Dynasty and their immediate successor the second emperor of the Twentieth Dynasty, Ramses III, displayed the same energy as the formidable militarists of the Eighteenth Dynasty—Amosis himself or the first and the third Thothmes—in contrast to the unwarlike intervening reigns of the third and the fourth Amenhotep.[3] In so far as the Libyans made common cause with the invaders from the Aegean in this age, both assailants were repelled with equal animosity, and also with equal success, by the pugnacious holders of the beleaguered Egyptiac fort.[4] But an extraordinary change of temper came over Egyptiac souls after Ramses III, *circa* 1200/1190 B.C., had expended the last ounce of energy that remained in the Egyptiac body social on the task of stemming the last and greatest tidal wave of the post-Minoan Völkerwanderung. Thereafter, when the sea-peoples' offensive had been brought to a halt, once for all, at the Asiatic gates of Egypt between Pelusium and Gaza, the Libyan barbarians from beyond the North-West African frontier of the Egyptiac World found themselves knocking at an open

---

[1] This parallel has been mentioned, by anticipation, in IV. C (iii) (c) 2 (β), vol. iv, pp. 421–3, above.

[2] See I. C (i) (b), vol. i, p. 93, and V. C (i) (c) 3, in the present volume, pp. 236–7 and 269–70, above.

[3] Amenhotep IV is, of course, identical with the Imperial heretic Ikhnaton.

[4] See I. C (i) (b), vol. i, pp. 93 and 101; IV. C (ii) (b) 2, vol. iv, p. 85; IV. C (iii) (c) 2 (β), vol. iv, p. 422; and V. C (i) (c) 3, in the present volume, pp. 237 and 269, above; and V. C (ii) (a), vol. vi, p. 207, below.

door as soon as they sought admission by, as well as for, themselves, without any obnoxious confederates from the Aegean to cast doubt upon the Libyans' own clean bill of social health as untainted barbarians.

During the period of social prostration which followed the death of Ramses III (*imperabat circa* 1200–1168 B.C.),[1] the *rois fainéants* who make up the rest of the tale of the Twentieth Egyptiac Dynasty allowed the descendants of the Libyan aggressors, who had repeatedly been hurled back by these shadow-emperors' predecessors, to encroach upon the sacred soil of the Egyptiac World step by step—with no single step ever effectively opposed—in the role of brigands and mercenaries. And by the tenth century B.C. we find these impudent Libyan intruders in command of all the provinces that had not been reserved by the Egyptiac priesthood for the benefit of their own new-fangled temple-states.[2] These sacerdotal legatees of the Egyptiac dominant minority and internal proletariat were evidently at this date in virtual collusion with the external proletariat's Libyan representatives; and at first sight it seems extraordinary that this Libyan barbarism should have been tolerated, at these close quarters, by a fanatically-minded hierarchy which had shown itself uniformly intransigent towards the Philistines as well as towards the Hyksos. On second thoughts, however, we may conjecture that the Libyan interlopers' unmitigated barbarism was the quality which commended them to the complacent proprietors of the domain on which they were now unobtrusively trespassing. To the professional eye of trustees of the Egyptiac tradition who were capable of taking a long view, these shapeless plastic lumps of Libyan clay were less disconcerting than those rudimentary Philistine and Hyksos figurines which had begun to set hard in an alien mould before ever they were thrown upon an Egyptiac potter's wheel.

A similar preference for the raw over the 'semi-manufactured' barbarian made itself manifest in the Syriac World during the interregnum (*durabat circa* A.D. 975–1275) which was the final

---

[1] See I. C (i) (*b*), vol. i, p. 101, above.

[2] See IV. C (iii) (*c*) 2 (β), vol. iv, p. 422, footnote 3, and V. C (i) (*c*) 3, in the present volume, pp. 269–70, above. The process is described as follows by Meyer, E.: *Geschichte des Altertums*, vol. ii, part (1), second edition (Stuttgart and Berlin 1928, Cotta), p. 589:

'[After their defeat at the hands of Ramses III] the Libyan tribes did not ever attempt any further invasions [of the Egyptiac World], so far as we know; but their peaceful dissemination over Egypt (a process which was promoted by Ramses' settlements [of Libyan prisoners of war on Egyptian soil]) went forward all the more vigorously for that. At the same time the [Egyptian] army drew on the Libyans more and more heavily for recruits. . . . As, at the same time, the enlistment of mercenaries from overseas [i.e. from the Minoan World] entirely came to an end after Ramses III's day, and the military vigour of the [native] Egyptians died away to vanishing point, these Libyan troops gradually became the only militarily effective portion of the Egyptian army. The consequence was that, two hundred years later, under Shoshenq I, these Libyans who had been Egypt's serfs converted themselves into Egypt's masters.'

chapter in its long history. Of all the barbarians who, in this age, fell upon the Syriac Society's moribund carcass, the Franks were perhaps the least barbarous. They were, indeed, the children of an adolescent Western Christian Civilization which had already begun to develop a distinctive culture of its own; and—perhaps just on this account—they were invariably rejected by the *Plebs Syriaca* in favour of alternative barbarian masters, wherever and whenever there was a choice. In the derelict domain of the Andalusian Umayyad Caliphate in the Iberian Peninsula the victimized provincials put their necks under the successive yokes of the Murābit Sanhāja Berber Nomads,[1] who were as barbarous in fact as in name, and of the Muwaḥḥid Masmuda Berber highlanders,[2] who out-berbered the Murābits, rather than submit to the dominion of the Basque and Asturian Christian barbarians with their reinforcements from the French side of the Pyrenees.[3] In the derelict domain of the ʿAbbasid Caliphate in Syria the provincials who had been conquered by the Frankish founders of the Crusader principalities[4] made a corresponding choice when they welcomed as deliverers the Turkish and Kurdish barbarian war-bands[5] of Zengı and Nūr-ad-Dīn and Shīrkūh and Saladin.

We can perhaps even venture to formulate something like a general social 'law' to the effect that the barbarian invaders who present themselves free from any cultural taint are apt to make their fortunes—and this even if they persist in their barbarian paganism instead of abandoning it in favour of the orthodox religion of their newly conquered subjects—while those who, before their Völkerwanderung, have acquired either an alien or a heretical tinge must go out of their way to purge themselves of the unclean thing, through some positive act of conversion which their subjects will accept as satisfactory, if they are to escape an otherwise inevitable doom of being either ejected or exterminated.[6]

To take the undiluted barbarians first, we may remind ourselves

---

[1] See II. D (v), vol. ii, p. 204, and V. C (i) (c) 3, in the present volume, p. 247, above.
[2] See II. D (v), vol. ii, p. 204, and V. C (i) (c) 3, in the present volume, p. 247, above.
[3] See II. D (v) ,vol. ii, pp. 204–6, and V. C (i) (c) 3, in the present volume, pp. 242–4, above.
[4] For the Crusades see I. B (iv), vol. i, p. 38; II. D (vii), vol. ii, pp. 362–3; and V. C (i) (c) 3, in the present volume, pp. 242–4 and 247, above.
[5] The Kurdish, unlike the Turkish, warriors who supplied the man-power for this counter-offensive were not in the strict sense members of the external proletariat of the Syriac World. They were an imperfectly tamed highland community in the heart of the Syriac World who—like the Ghūrī highlanders of North-Eastern Iran (see IV. C (i) (b) 2, vol. iv, p. 99, footnote 1, and V. C (i) (c) 3, in the present volume, p. 304, above)—had reasserted their barbarian independence upon the downfall of the ʿAbbasid Caliphate, as the Isaurians and the Basques had reasserted theirs upon the downfall of the Roman Empire (see V. C (i) (c) 3, p. 206, footnote 1, above).
[6] This 'law' that can be seen at work in the diversity of the fortunes of barbarian conquerors is a particular application of a still wider 'law' which Ibn Khaldūn has brought to light in the field of the arts and sciences (*Muqaddamāt*, de Slane's translation (Paris 1863–8, Imprimerie Impériale, 3 vols.), vol. ii, pp. 366–7: chapter headed: 'He

that the Aryas and the Hittites and the Achaeans, who each invented a barbarian pantheon of their own during their sojourn on
the threshold of a civilization,[1] and who persisted in this authentic
barbarian worship after they had broken through and made their
conquests, each also succeeded, notwithstanding this 'invincible
ignorance', in becoming the fathers of new civilizations: the
Indic, the Hittite, and the Hellenic. As for the Kassites and the
Parthians, who made a half-hearted and ineffective compromise
between the religion which they had brought in with them and
the religion which they found in the conquered land, even they
were rewarded for their innocence of any alien cultural taint[2] by
being suffered to enjoy a parasitic dominion which was as protracted as it was inglorious, before the society upon which they
had billeted themselves lost patience at last and spued out of her
mouth these lukewarm Laodiceans.[3] When we pass on to the
undiluted barbarians who have been converted whole-heartedly
from their own barbarian religion to the orthodox faith of their
subjects—whatever that faith may have been in any given case[4]—
we find that these robuster converts have won the signal reward
of being co-opted into the fellowship of a civilization which has not
owed its origin to their endeavours, and which might, if it had
chosen, have gone on its own way without accepting their services.

For example, the Frankish and English and Scandinavian and
Polish and Magyar converts from a native paganism to the
Western Catholic Christianity secured the opportunity to play a
full, and even a leading, part in the building up of Western Christendom. The conversion of the Sakas and the White Huns and
the Gurjaras to Hinduism enabled the Sakas to contribute to
the foundation of a Hindu universal church in the course of the

who possesses the capacity for practising some particular art very rarely manages to
acquire another art perfectly'):
'A tailor, for instance, who possesses a capacity for sewing, who uses it with the
greatest skill, who is really master of his art, and who has made it part and parcel of
himself, will be unable afterwards to acquire, to perfection, the art of being a cabinet-
maker or a mason. If he did achieve this, that would mean that he did not yet possess,
to perfection, the former capacity; it would mean that the dye of that capacity in him
had not yet taken fast. Here is the explanation: it is that the capacities—being attributes
of the Soul or colours which the Soul is apt to take—cannot overlay one another on
the Soul and can only settle on the Soul one at a time. In order to acquire a capacity
easily, and to be in a favourable condition for the reception of it, the Soul must be in the
primitive state of its nature. Afterwards, when it takes the colour of this or that capacity,
it departs from its primitive state; and, since the tincture which has now just been
imparted to it is bound to have weakened in the Soul its aptitude for receiving another
tincture, the Soul no longer has as much strength as before for acquiring a second faculty.'
  [1] See I. C (i) (b), vol. i, pp. 96–7; II. D (vii), Annex V, vol. ii, pp. 434–7: and V. C
(i) (c) 3, in the present volume, pp. 230–3, above.
  [2] The Philhellenism of the Parthians was so superficial that it can hardly have counted
among the offences for which the Parthians were eventually condemned and executed
by the Syriac 'Zealots' of the Zoroastrian persuasion (see V. C (i) (c) 3, pp. 216 and 240,
above).   [3] Rev. iii. 16.
  [4] For the general principle of policy that may be summed up in the maxim 'Religio
Regionis Religio Regis' see V. C (i) (d) 6 (δ), Annex, pp. 704–12, below.

first four centuries of the Christian Era,[1] and the Huns and Gurjaras
to play, in the first chapter of the history of the resulting Hindu
Civilization, the part which was played in the first chapter of our
Western history by the Franks.[2] Similarly, the conversion to
Buddhism of the Kushans when they crossed the Hindu Kush,[3]
and of the To Pa when they established themselves in Shansi,[4]
conferred upon the Kushans the privilege of serving to speed a
nascent Mahāyāna on its way across the Oxus from India to the
Far East,[5] while the subsequent acceptance of the full-blown
Catholic Mahāyāna by the To Pa singled out these hitherto
obscure Eurasian Nomads to enjoy the honour of laying the foundations for the Far Eastern United Kingdom of the Sui and the
T'ang.[6] In the post-Syriac interregnum the conversion of the
Saljūqs on the one side and the Murābits and Muwaḥḥids on the
other to the Sunnah[7] cast these Turks and Berbers for the roles
that were played in the post-Hellenic interregnum by the Franks
and the English and in the post-Indic interregnum by the Huns
and the Gurjaras.[8] In the disintegration of the main body of
Orthodox Christendom we can see that the Serb barbarians, who
were converted to Orthodox Christianity,[9] found a wider field—

---

[1] See V. C (i) (c) 3, Annex II, pp. 605–6, below.
[2] The evidence for the Hun and Gurjara origin of the Rājputs, who were the ruling
element in the Hindu World from the emergence of the Hindu Civilization in the eighth
century of the Christian Era until its breakdown in the twelfth, is set out in Smith, V. A.:
The Early History of India, 3rd edition (Oxford 1914, Clarendon Press), pp. 407–15.
The crucial act in the metamorphosis of the Eurasian Nomad raider into the Rājput
paladin seems to have been his conversion to Hinduism.
[3] See V. C (i) (c) 2, p. 133, with footnote 1, and V. C (i) (c) 3, p. 275, with footnote
3, above.
[4] See IV. C (ii) (b) 1, vol. iv, p. 65, and V. C (i) (c) 3, in the present volume, pp. 272–
3, above.
[5] See IV. C (ii) (b) 1, vol. iv, p. 65, and V. C (i) (c) 2, in the present volume, pp.
139–40 and 143–6, above.
[6] The To Pa barbarian 'successor-state' of the Han Empire in Shansi blossomed out,
after its conversion to the Catholic Mahāyāna, into the Kingdom of the United Wei
(*florebat circa* A.D. 420–534), which absorbed into itself two sister barbarian 'successor-
states', Pe Han and Pe Yen (see V. C (i) (d) 6 (α), p. 477, below), besides momentarily
subduing the unreclaimed Nomads in its own rear on the Steppe (for this latter feat see
V. C (i) (c) 3, p. 273, above; for the Sinification of the To Pa themselves by one of the
princes of the United Wei, Hiao-wên ti (*regnabat* A.D. 490–9), see V. C (i) (d) 6 (α),
pp. 477–8, below). After half a century of renewed division—this time into two fractions (the Eastern Wei with their successors the Pe Ts'i (*durabant* A.D. 534–77) and the
Western Wei with their successors the Pe Chóu (*durabant* A.D. 535–77), the former
dominions of the United Wei were reunited through the Pe Chóu conquering the Pe
Ts'i (A.D. 577). The Pe Chóu only enjoyed the fruits of this victory for four years before
being supplanted (in A.D. 581) by the new dynasty of the Sui; but this dynastic change
not only left the work of consolidation unimpaired but also quickly resulted in its
completion; for in A.D. 589 the Sui reunited the South of the Far Eastern World with
the North under a single sovereignty, and this put an end to a separation between South
and North which had lasted, in all, for 272 years since the fall of the United Tsin in
A.D. 317. After this it only remained for the T'ang to enter into the labours of the Sui,
as once, in the history of the apparented Sinic Civilization, the Han had entered into
the labours of Ts'in She Hwang-ti.
[7] See I. C (i) (b), Annex I, vol. i, p. 357, and V. C (i) (c) 3, in the present volume,
pp. 251–2, above.   [8] See p. 355, above.
[9] See V. C (i) (c) 3, pp. 293–4, above.

and this for more effective action—than their kinsmen and neighbours the Bosniaks, who were converted to the heresy of Bogomilism.[1] Finally, we may observe that the Aztecs—who were on the
point of imposing their own grim peace upon a distracted Mexic
World when the Spaniards suddenly burst in and wrested out of
the Aztecs' hands the role of serving as the empire-builders of a
Central American universal state—were undilutedly barbarian interlopers[2] who had embraced, apparently without reserve, the religion
which the Mexic Society had inherited from its Mayan predecessor.[3]

If we now survey the barbarians who have yielded, like the
Bosniaks, to the attractions of an alien or a heretical faith, we
shall observe that the Bosniaks themselves are in a category of
barbarian heretics that have elected to save themselves alive by
capitulating to the prevailing orthodoxy before it has been too
late. The Bosniaks prudently exchanged their invidious Bogomilism for the Sunnī Islam which was the religion of the alien
Ottoman founders of an Orthodox Christian universal state.[4]
The Burgundians and Visigoths and Lombards exchanged their
Arianism for the Catholicism of their subjects. And the Mongol
Il-Khans of Iran and Irāq, after toying with both Nestorianism[5]
and the Shī'ah,[6] had the wisdom in the end to opt for a Sunnah[7]
which in their days was the faith of the vast majority of the
population in the territories over which the Il-Khans' rule extended.

The statesmanship of these barbarian apostates is commended
by the spectacle of the untoward fate of their comrades who
hardened their hearts; for if 'Paris is worth a mass', it is presumably to be allowed, *a fortiori*, that any apostasy is justified, on
Machiavellian standards, when the alternative to it is eviction
or extermination; and one or other of these unpleasant experiences
seems to have overtaken every one of the heretical barbarian war-
bands that have insisted upon making themselves unnecessarily
odious to their subjects by perversely persisting in the error of
their religious ways. The Hyksos worshippers of Set were evicted
from the Egyptiac World by Amosis.[8] The Ostrogoth Arians were

---

[1] See IV. C (iii) (c) 2 (β), vol. iv, pp. 368–9, and V. C (i) (c) 3, in the present volume,
p. 295, above.
[2] See II. D (v), vol. ii, p. 207, and V. C (i) (c) 3, in the present volume, p. 280, above.
[3] See I. C (i) (b), vol. i, p. 127, above, and V. C (i) (d) 5, in the present volume, p. 437,
ootnote 3, below.
[4] See IV. C (iii) (c) 2 (β), vol. iv, p. 368, footnote 3, and V. C (i) (c) 3, in the present
volume, p. 327, above.
[5] See II. D (vii), Annex VIII, vol. ii, pp. 449–52, above.
[6] See I. C (i) (b), Annex I, vol. i, p. 363, above.
[7] See I. C (i) (b), vol. i, Annex I, pp. 364 and 401, and Part III. A, Annex II, vol. iii,
pp. 439 and 450, above.
[8] See p. 351, with the references in footnote 3, above.

evicted from Italy, and the Vandal Arians exterminated in Africa, by Justinian. The Mongols, with their Nestorian Christian taint and their Tantric Mahayanian Buddhist proclivities, were evicted from China by the Ming.[1] The Katāma and Daylamī and East-Arabian Shiʻites, whose Fātimid and Buwayhid and Carmathian leaders seemed destined for a moment to divide between them the heritage of the Sunnī ʻAbbasid Caliphate, were all brought to naught at the moment when the prize seemed to be within their grasp. The Buwayhids were supplanted by the Saljūqs; the Fātimids were deposed by Shīrkūh; the Carmathians were hurled back from the borders of ʻIrāq and Syria and were left to die of inanition in the deserts in which they had made their lair.[2] Finally we may notice that the Far Western Christians of 'the Celtic Fringe', who obstinately clung to their own peculiar usages, were absorbed into the body social of Roman Christendom by a process of subjugation, instead of being taken into partnership on equal terms like the Scandinavians. The Scandinavians were no more successful than the Far Western Christians were in their attempt to erect a promising barbarism into an independent civilization in face of the Roman Christendom with which they had collided; but, in the terms of their capitulation to a victorious Roman Christendom, they profited conspicuously, by contrast with the Celts, from the facts that they passed straight out of a native barbarian religion into the Roman form of Christianity and that they made this change through a voluntary act of conversion.[3]

The outstanding exception to this particular clause of our 'law' is presented by the history of the Primitive Muslim Arab external proletariat of the Roman Empire, who succeeded in making their fortunes—and this with an unparalleled brilliance—notwithstanding their obstinacy in clinging to their barbarian version (or travesty) of Syriac religion[4] instead of abandoning Islam for the Monophysite Christianity of their new subjects in the conquered Roman provinces of Syria and Egypt. This is, however, one of those exceptions which do not discredit a rule but rather confirm it; for we have noticed, in other contexts,[5] that

[1] See II. D (v), vol. ii, p. 121, and the present chapter and volume, p. 348, above.
[2] For this passage in the history of the Shīʻah see I. C (i) (b), Annex I, vol. i, pp. 355–7, above.
[3] For this contrast between the fortunes of the Far Western Christians and the fortunes of the Scandinavians see II. D (vii), vol. ii, pp. 322–60, with Annexes II, III, and IV, above.
[4] For this description of Primitive Islam, as conceived and expounded by the prophet who was its author, see I. C (i) (b), vol. i, p. 83, III. C (ii) (b), vol. iii, pp. 276–8, with Annex II, and V. C (i) (c) 2, in the present volume, p. 128, above.
[5] In I. C (i) (b), vol. i, pp. 72–7; II. D (vi), vol. ii, p. 235; II. D (vii), vol. ii, pp. 285–8; and V. C (i) (c) 2, in the present volume, pp. 128–9, above. See further V. C (i) (d) 6 (δ), Annex, pp. 672–7, below.

the Muslim Arab barbarian conquerors of these Roman provinces had a subsequent career which was utterly different from
that of their Berber and North European and Eurasian Nomad
companions-in-arms who broke through the frontiers of the same
empire on other fronts. Through the Arabs' incidental conquest
of the entire Sasanian Empire, in the course of their victorious
assault upon the Oriental provinces of the Roman Empire, the
barbarian 'successor-state' of the Roman Empire which the Arabs
had founded on Syrian soil transformed itself into a restoration
of the Syriac universal state which had been prematurely destroyed, a thousand years before, when the Achaemenidae had
been overthrown by Alexander; and the vast new political mission
with which the Muslim Arab conquerors were thus, almost accidentally, invested, opened up a new horizon for Islam itself. Alone
among barbarian heresies, the Arab prophet Muhammad's
amalgam of Christianity and Judaism escaped the scrap-heap
which is the usual destination of such crude barbarian black-
smith's work. Under the normal operation of our rule the Arab
war-bands that settled upon Syria and Egypt in the seventh
century of the Christian Era ought either to have abandoned
their Muhammadan heresy or to have been cast out again into
their native Arabian steppes before the close of the eighth century.
In the actual event the year 800 saw the Arabs politically firm
in the saddle through the length and breadth of the Syriac World
from Andalusia to Farghānā; and by the same date Islam, so far
from being extinct, had already turned into a 'higher religion'
with a 'manifest destiny' to provide the Syriac internal proletariat with its long-sought universal church.[1]

It will be seen that this history of Islam is a special case which
does not invalidate the general results of our inquiry.[2] In general
we are evidently justified in concluding from an empirical survey
that, for external proletariats and for dominant minorities alike,
an alien inspiration is a curse, because it is a fruitful source of
friction and frustration for either of them in their dealings with
members of the other two fractions of the three into which a
disintegrating society splits up. If we turn now to examine the
influence of alien inspirations upon the lives and fortunes of
internal proletariats, a survey of the field in this case will lead to
a conclusion which is exactly the opposite. For internal proletariats
we shall find that an alien inspiration, so far from being a curse,
is a blessing which confers upon those who receive it an apparently

---

[1] See II. D (vii), vol. ii, p. 288, above, and V. C (i) (d) 6 (δ), Annex, pp. 677–8, below.
[2] The history of Islam is also a special case in respect of another social 'law' to the
effect that religions bring ruin on themselves by going into politics (see V. C (i) (d) 6 (δ),
Annex, pp. 672–8, below).

superhuman power of taking their conquerors captive[1] and of attaining the end to which they have been born.[2] And if we hesitate on first thoughts to accept this conclusion, because we can see no reason why an identic cause should have these diametrically opposite effects when it is acting upon different fractions of the same body social,[3] we must be content in the first instance to verify the fact in the hope that it may begin to explain itself as we study it at closer range and in greater detail. Our thesis can best be tested by an examination of those 'higher religions' and universal churches which are the Internal Proletariat's characteristic works; and our survey of these has shown that their potency depends upon the presence, and varies in proportion to the strength, of an alien spark of vitality in their spirit.[4]

This alien spark is visible in most of the 'higher religions' which we have identified in an earlier chapter;[5] for a 'higher religion' usually turns out to have originated in some section of the Internal Proletariat that has at any rate been profoundly influenced by some alien culture, even if it has not actually been recruited from a population which has been forcibly detached and transferred from some alien body social by an act of conquest on the Dominant Minority's part.

For example the worship of Osiris, which was the 'higher religion' of the Egyptiac proletariat, can be traced back tentatively (as we have seen)[6] to an alien origin in the Sumeric worship of Tammuz; and the manifold and competing 'higher religions' of the Hellenic internal proletariat can all be traced back to various alien origins with certainty. In the worship of Isis the alien spark

---

[1] Horace, *Epp.*, Book II, Ep. i, l. 156.   [2] John xviii. 37.

[3] The question why, for the Internal Proletariat, an alien inspiration is a social 'asset', instead of being the social 'liability' that it is for the External Proletariat and for the Dominant Minority, must, of course, be kept distinct from the different question why, for the Proletariat of both kinds, an alien inspiration is attractive. The answer to this second question is obvious. The Proletariat is drawn towards alien elements of culture for the negative reason that these have no associations with a Dominant Minority against whose domination the Proletariat is in revolt. In the case of the External Proletariat we have come across this motive already in observing the External Proletariat's proneness, even when it accepts a 'higher religion' from the Dominant Minority's side of the *limes*, to take this 'higher religion' in some heretical form (see V. C (i) (c) 3, pp. 227–30 (Arianism, Celtic Christianity, Islam), pp. 250–2 (Manichaeism, Nestorianism, the Shi'ah), pp. 295–6 (Bogomilism, Bektashism, Wahhabism, Idrisism), pp. 309–10 (Tantric Mahayanian Buddhism), pp. 328–32 (the North American Indian prophetic religions)). Some of the corresponding considerations in the mind of the Internal Proletariat are brought out in the following note by Professor Gilbert Murray:

'The Proletariat (1) craves an imaginary world, or world of faith, to compensate the real world in which all God's chillen obviously have not got wings—or shoes; and (2) feels sure that, whatever the truth is, it cannot be what their masters know or believe (as the English labourer knows that it cannot be the Squire's "Church of England", or the factory hand that it cannot be the Employer's "Liberalism"). Therefore anything from a foreign source is welcome.'

[4] See I. B (iv), vol. i, pp. 40–1; I. C (i) (a), vol. i, p. 57; II. D (vi), vol. ii, pp. 213–16; and V. C (i) (c) 2, in the present volume, *passim*, above.

[5] In V. C (i) (c) 2, *passim*, above.   [6] In V. C (i) (c) 2, pp. 147–50, above.

is Egyptiac; in the worship of Cybele it is Hittite; in Christianity and Mithraism it is Syriac; in the Mahāyāna it is Indic; and in each of these cases we are acquainted with the historical circumstances in which the vital fire was introduced into the Hellenic tinder. The first four of the 'higher religions' in this Hellenic list were created by Egyptiac and Hittite and Syriac populations which had been conscripted into the Hellenic internal proletariat through Alexander's conquest of the Achaemenian Empire in and after the year 334 B.C., while the fifth—namely the Mahāyāna—was created by an Indic population which had been likewise conscripted into the Hellenic internal proletariat, in and after the second decade of the second century B.C. through the Euthydemid Bactrian Greek princes' conquests in the Indic World.[1]

Profoundly though they may differ from one another in their inward spiritual essence, all these five 'higher religions' have at least this superficial feature in common. They are all of them attempts to translate some non-Hellenic religious inspiration into Hellenic terms—devotional or philosophic or aesthetic.[2] In the first four of them this feature is notorious; but it is also unmistakably recognizable in the Mahāyāna. One of the decisive steps towards the creation of a 'higher religion' out of the philosophy of Siddhārtha Gautama was taken when Buddhist sculptors made use of the plastic medium of representation, which the intrusive Hellenic culture had placed in their hands, in order to portray the Buddha in concrete anthropomorphic form.[3]

This visualization of the Buddha as a being of the Apollinean Hellenic type was attained by a utilization of Hellenic technique on Indic soil, before the nascent 'higher religion' had begun to spread beyond the bounds of the society that had given it birth. But the Buddha who had been clothed in this Hellenic body—a body of cold marble and not of flesh and blood—had only been invested with the bare externals of divine personality. The would-be worshipper had still to discover the living god within the lifeless statue; and this act of intuition was not achieved until, in the next chapter of the story, the statue itself had been spiritualized by an Indic chisel,[4] and, in the next chapter after that, the

---

[1] See I. C (i) (b), vol. i, p. 86; II. D (v), vol. ii, p. 143; V. C (i) (c) 2, in the present volume, p. 133, with footnote 1, and p. 139; and V. C (i) (c) 3, pp. 275–6, above.
[2] On this point see further pp. 366–7, below.
[3] See III. C (ii) (a), vol. iii, p. 247, footnote 2, and V. C (i) (c) 2, in the present volume, p. 134, above.
[4] The Apollinean type of Buddha statue, which seems to have been the creation of Greek artists working in Gandhāra near the beginning of the last century B.C. at the latest, was discarded, in favour of a more spiritual type, by an Indic school of artists working at Mathurā after the beginning of the second century of the Christian Era, at the earliest (see Tarn, W. W.: The Greeks in Bactria and India (Cambridge 1938, University Press), pp. 396–408).

ci-devant Indic philosophy, with its mantle of thus Indicized Hellenic art, had been propagated from the Indic into the Syriac provinces of the Bactrian Greek Empire's Kushan 'successor-state'.[1] In the Oxus-Jaxartes Basin under the Kushan régime Buddhism underwent a further translation—this time on the devotional plane—into terms of the other alien culture which it encountered here. On this Syriac ground the Indic philosopher portrayed as an Indicized Olympian god was transfigured, to all appearance, into a Zoroastrian saviour;[2] and it was this second mutation that completed the metamorphosis of Gautama's philosophy into the religion of the Mahāyāna. Thus the Mahāyāna was miraculously born from an Olympian's head and was then still more miraculously brought to life like Pygmalion's statue. And, if, in the next chapter after that, the new religion had travelled westwards in order to compete with its four sisters for spiritual supremacy in the Hellenic World, the Mahāyāna would have presented itself to its Hellenic converts as a Hellenized proletarian-born 'higher religion' with a twofold alien inspiration—part Indic and part Syriac.

In this Indo-Syriac duality the Mahāyāna would not have been an altogether peculiar portent in the spiritual landscape of the Roman Empire, for it would have had a counterpart in Mithraism, which—with its strong infusion of the Babylonic astral philosophy[3]—might be regarded as a dual Syro-Babylonic rather than as a simple Syriac graft upon a Hellenic stem. As it happened, however, the direction in which the Mahāyāna travelled from its temporary camping-ground on the banks of the Oxus was not westward but eastward.[4] Under the Kushan régime, as we have observed, it spread from the Oxus-Jaxartes Basin to the Tarim Basin in the age when the two were politically united in the Kushan Empire; and from the Tarim Basin—which was a province of the Sinic universal state again after, as it had already been before, the interlude of the Kushan occupation—the Mahāyāna travelled on to conquer a vast new spiritual empire in the Sinic World.[5]

---

[1] See V. C (i) (c) 2, pp. 139–40, above.

[2] See V. C (i) (c) 2, p. 136, above. This transfiguration did not, of course, take the form of a direct deification of the historical human figure of Siddhārtha Gautama the Sakya aristocrat from Kapilavastu. When the man Gautama had come to be regarded as an epiphany of Buddhahood, it was a natural, and perhaps inevitable, step for a religion of Indic origin to assume that this epiphany was a term in a series. The new step was to expand the series by an exercise of the devotional imagination. And it was the mythical epiphanies—an Avalokita and a Maitreya and an Amitābha (Amida)—that became the saviour-gods of the Mahāyāna. (For the cult of Amitābha see V. C (i) (d) 11, vol. vi, p. 164, footnote 3, below. For the Japanese adaptation of this cult see V. C (i) (c) 2, in the present volume, pp. 96–103, above.)

[3] See V. C (i) (c) 1, pp. 56–7, above.

[4] See II. D (vi), Annex, vol. ii, p. 405, footnote 1; IV. C (ii) (b) 1, vol. iv, p. 65; V. C (i) (c) 2, in the present volume, pp. 139–40 and 144–6; and the present chapter, p. 356, above. [5] See V. C (i) (c) 2, pp. 143–5, above.

The victory of the Mahāyāna in the Far East is a triumph which is comparable in magnitude to the victory of Christianity in the Near East and the West; and the irresistible inference is that an alien inspiration cannot be a source of friction and frustration when the party that is fired by it is an internal proletariat and not either an external proletariat or a dominant minority. The Christian religion of the Hellenic internal proletariat was not debarred by its Syriac 'taint' from conquering the Hellenic World; and the Mahāyāna conquered the Sinic World in spite of being saturated with an alien 'taint' that was neither single nor even dual but actually triple—for in Sinic eyes the Indic and the Hellenic and the Syriac elements in the Mahāyāna were all equally exotic; and the Hellenic style of the Mahayanian Buddhist art, which would have served the Mahāyāna as a passport for admission if it had been knocking at the gates of Antioch or Rome, only emphasized its outlandishness in the sight of citizens of Ch'ang Ngan and Loyang. Nevertheless the Mahāyāna triumphantly made its conquest of the outgoing Sinic Civilization and successfully impressed upon the incoming Far Eastern Civilization an imprint of Hellenic art and Syriac devotion and Indic philosophy, though these traits were all decidedly alien from the êthos of the apparented Sinic Society to which this nascent Far Eastern Society was affiliated. These indisputable historical facts would appear to suggest that for an internal proletariat an alien 'taint' is no handicap, but is rather a positive advantage. For, while it might perhaps be arguable (though the argument would be a *tour de force*) that Christianity conquered Hellenism in spite, and not because, of the conquering religion's non-Hellenic spark of Syriac inspiration, it would be almost beyond belief that, if alienness were really a hindrance and not a help to the spread of a 'higher religion', the Mahāyāna could ever have conquered the conservative-minded latter-day Sinic World under the crippling handicap of being alien three times over.

Our conclusion will not be shaken by a consideration of certain cases in which an attempt to conquer a society has been made by an alien 'higher religion' without success. There is the abortive attempt of the Shī'ah to become the universal church of the main body of Orthodox Christendom under the Ottoman régime;[1] and

[1] See I. C (i) (*b*), Annex I, vol. i, pp. 382–3, and V. C (i) (*c*) 2, in the present volume, p. 111, above. The process through which the Shī'ah introduced itself into the internal proletariat of the main body of Orthodox Christendom resembles the process by which the Mahāyāna introduced itself into the internal proletariat of the Sinic Society. In this case, as in that, the intrusive religion was able to make its entry owing to the vicissitudes in the history of a border province in which it had gained a foothold. In the case of the Mahāyāna this border province was, as we have seen, the Tarim Basin: an outlying annex of the Indic World which was conquered for the Sinic World by the Prior Han; reconquered for the Indic World (and for the Syriac and Hellenic worlds as well)

the abortive attempt of Catholic Christianity to become the universal church of the Far Eastern Society—in China during the last century of the Ming and the first century of the Manchu régime, and in Japan at the moment of transition from the Japanese 'Time of Troubles' to the Tokugawa Shogunate. Again, the role which has been played by Catholicism in the Far East and by the Shī'ah in the main body of Orthodox Christendom has been played in the Russian Orthodox Christendom, *post Petrum*, by the Protestant variety of Western Christianity. In each of these cases the intrusive 'higher religion' has failed to make its conquest, in spite of the alienness of its origin; but in each case the failure has a convincing explanation which has nothing to do with the question whether the inspiration of the successful religion has been alien or indigenous.

In Russia, for example, Protestantism has been driven off the field in our day by the competition of a rival movement of the same alien origin: the Marxian philosophy. At the time of going to press in A.D. 1938 the triumph of Marxism in Russia was still so recent that it would have been rash to assert that it was definitive or to rule out the possibility that Protestantism—which had shown more fight, under the Marxian persecution, than the native Russian Orthodoxy—might some day return to the attack. But whether it is Marxism or Protestantism that is eventually to be victorious in Russia is a question that does not affect the present argument, considering that both these competing faiths alike have come in from abroad. The defeat—whether temporary or permanent—of Protestantism by Marxism in the Soviet Union is simply an incident in the struggle between competing alien religions, like the defeat which was inflicted upon Mithraism by Christianity in the corresponding struggle for the spiritual conquest of the Roman Empire.

As for the Shī'ah in the Ottoman Empire and Catholicism in Japan, they were both cheated of their prospective spiritual

by the Kushans; and finally conquered back by the Posterior Han for a Sinic World which quickly caught fire from a Mahayanian spark that had been conveyed into the Tarim Basin from the west during the Kushan occupation. In the process by which the Shī'ah introduced itself into the main body of Orthodox Christendom, the geographical role of the Tarim Basin was played by Central and Eastern Anatolia: an integral part of the homeland of Orthodox Christendom which was detached, and annexed to the Syriac World, as a result of the Saljūq conquest (see II. D (v), vol. ii, pp. 153–4; IV. C (ii) (*b*) 1, vol. iv, pp. 72–5; and IV. C (iii) (*c*) 2 (β), vol. iv, pp. 395–9, above). When the Syriac World went into dissolution, this alien territory which it had conquered *in extremis* was included in the domain which the defunct civilization bequeathed to the 'affiliated' Iranic Society; but in the fifteenth century of the Christian Era this lost Anatolian territory was reannexed to the Orthodox Christian World by the Ottoman founders of the Orthodox Christian universal state. The Shī'ism which then tried and failed to become the universal church of the Ottoman Empire had entered Anatolia from the east during the four centuries (*circa* A.D. 1065–1465) which elapsed between the Saljūq conquest of the Anatolic army-corps district of the East Roman Empire and the Ottoman conquest of the principality of Qaramān.

conquests by being exploited—or at any rate suspected of being exploited—for illegitimate political ends. In either case the Government of the empire which the missionary religion was seeking to convert suddenly abandoned a policy of complacency for the policy of repression because it became convinced that the alien religion whose progress it had been tolerating in its dominions was being insidiously used by a foreign and hostile Power as an instrument for undermining the loyalty, and capturing the allegiance, of an unoffending neighbour's subjects. The Shī'ī insurrection of A.D. 1511 in Ottoman Anatolia under the leadership of Shāh Ismā'īl's agent Shāh Qūlī convinced the sluggish Sultan Bāyezīd's vehement son Sultan Selīm that he was faced with a choice between losing his Asiatic dominions to the Safawis or purging them of Shi'ism; and accordingly he made an end of Shi'ism in Anatolia in the massacre of A.D. 1514:[1] an atrocity which blighted for ever the prospects of the Shī'ah in the Orthodox Christian World. It was on similar grounds in Japan that Catholicism, after being allowed to win a foothold and make some headway during the second half of the sixteenth century of the Christian Era, was afterwards frowned upon by Hideyoshi (*dominabatur* A.D. 1582–98) and was finally extirpated remorselessly by the Tokugawa between A.D. 1612 and A.D. 1638. The Japanese Government's objection to Catholicism was of the same political order as the Ottoman Government's objection to Shi'ism. It was believed that both the European Catholic residents in Japan and the Japanese converts were being turned to an illegitimate use by the Spanish Crown as agents in underhand preparations for a Spanish attack on Japanese independence; and it was in order to anticipate this supposed danger that the Japanese Government proceeded to stamp Catholicism out.

The failure of Catholicism in China was not, like its failure in Japan, the incidental effect of an extraneous political cause. In China this alien religion was eventually rejected on religious—or perhaps rather on philosophical—grounds. Yet, even here, it was not its sheer alienness that was fatal to it. In China, too, the prospects of Catholicism were blighted by the action of a foreign Power, though in this case the Power that intervened with disastrous results was of an ecclesiastical and not of a political order. The fatal act was a refusal, on the part of the Vatican and its representatives, to allow the Jesuit missionaries in China to carry on their work of translating an alien Catholic religious idiom into the traditional language of Far Eastern philosophy and ritual.[2] And this veto

---

[1] For these events see I. C (i) (*b*), Annex I, vol. i, pp. 382–4, above.
[2] See Jenkins, R. C.: *The Jesuits in China* (London 1894, Nutt).

dealt a death-blow to the Catholic propaganda in China; for the process of cultural translation is one of the indispensable conditions for the propagation of any alien 'higher religion' in any mission-field.

Our empirical survey has led us to the conclusion that an alien origin is a help and not a hindrance to a 'higher religion' in winning converts; and the reason for this is not far to seek. The light from an alien spark is, *ex hypothesi*, a new revelation; and it is the newness that makes it attractive; but, before it can become attractive, a truth has to be made intelligible; and until this necessary work of exposition has been performed, the new truth will be inhibited from making its potential appeal. On this account the translation of the alien religion into terms of the prospective converts' native culture is a task of vital importance in any missionary enterprise. The progress of the Mahāyāna and Christianity and Mithraism, and of the worships of Isis and Cybele, in the Hellenic World went *pari passu* with the process of their translation into terms of Hellenic art and literature and philosophy, and even into terms of Hellenic ritual and piety[1] (though in these latter points the act of translation touched the very quick of the incoming alien faiths). We may also observe that this process of Hellenization was carried to greatest lengths, and was at the same time carried out with the greatest insight and discrimination, in the metamorphosis of the religion which was the eventual victor among these competitors for the captivation of Hellenic souls.[2] The Christian victory in the Roman Empire could hardly have been won if the Fathers of the Christian Church had not exerted themselves perseveringly, during the first four or five centuries of the Christian Era, to translate the Christian doctrine into terms of Hellenic philosophy; to build up the Christian ecclesiastical hierarchy on the pattern of the Roman civil service; to portray the Christ in the lineaments of an Orpheus; to descry the Cross athwart the disk of Sol Invictus;[3] to mould the Christian ritual on the model of the Mysteries; and even to convert pagan into Christian festivals,[4] and replace pagan cults of heroes by Christian cults of saints.

Whether the Jesuit Catholic missionaries in China were consciously following the precedent of the Early Christian Church in the Roman Empire, or whether they were acting on an inde-

---

[1] See pp. 361-3, above.

[2] See I. C (i) (*b*), vol. i, pp. 83 and 91; I. C (iii) (*b*), vol. i, p. 155; and II. D (vii), vol. ii, p. 374, above.

[3] For Professor N. H. Baynes' interpretation of the vision of Constantine the Great see V. C (i) (*d*) 6 (δ), Annex, pp. 693-4, below.

[4] For the conversion of the birthday of Sol Invictus into Christmas Day see V. C (i) (*d*) 6 (δ), Annex, p. 693, footnote 2, below.

pendent intuition of their own in seeking the same solution for the same problem, they were unquestionably doing what had been done, not only by the Early Christian Fathers, but by the missionaries of every alien religion that had ever made a spiritual conquest. Matteo Ricci (*in Oriente Extrema Fidem Catholicam propagabat* A.D. 1582–1610) did for Christianity at Macao the service that a Clement (*vivebat circa* A.D. 150—*prae* 215) and an Origen (*vivebat* A.D. 185–254) had done for the same faith at Alexandria some fourteen hundred years earlier.[1] Clement and Origen commended Christianity to the respectful and even sympathetic attention of cultivated Hellenes by deliberately winning recognition for themselves as accomplished Hellenic philosophers. Ricci—the supreme *virtuoso* in the Christian missionary's art—performed the still greater *tour de force* of obtaining for himself a tablet in a Far Eastern hall of fame as an accomplished Confucian litteratus. And if he and his successors had been allowed to persevere in their work for three centuries, instead of being pulled up short after they had been little more than one century in the field, who can say whether, in the year 1938, the former domain of the Far Eastern universal state might not have been as thoroughly permeated with Christianity as the former domain of the Hellenic universal state actually was in A.D. 538, after the unhindered completion of the Early Fathers' long and far-reaching expository work?[2]

[1] See further V. C (i) (*d*) 6 (δ), p. 539, below.
[2] The Jesuit missionaries in China had to contend with two adverse forces: the jealousy of their Franciscan and Dominican rivals in the China mission-field and the ignorance of the Vatican and its representatives. It was the combined operation of these two forces that eventually brought the Jesuits' work in China to naught. And this may perhaps explain why it was that the Jesuits failed in an enterprise in which the Early Fathers succeeded; for, although the rivalry between Jesuits and Friars in China has numerous parallels in the internal struggles within the bosom of the Early Christian Church in the Roman Empire, there is no parallel in this other chapter of Christian history to the obstacle which was placed in the Jesuits' path in China by the Vatican's ignorance of Far Eastern conditions. In order to translate this obstacle into Early Christian terms we should have to draw an imaginary picture of Origen and Clement doing their work at Alexandria under the authority of a supreme ecclesiastical Power whose seat was geographically remote from the Hellenic World, in some Syriac fastness into which the radiation of Hellenism had never penetrated. Supposing that our Alexandrian Christian philosophers had been bound to render an account of their stewardship to a Holy Father whose see lay in the Yaman or in Hyrcania, we may conjecture that they would have been peremptorily called to order. Even as it was, Origen did not altogether escape the stigma of heresy, though the ecclesiastical judges before whose bar his theology had to appear had all been born and brought up in Origen's own Hellenic environment and were therefore able to appreciate, in the light of their personal experience, the full strength of the case for a Christian policy of Hellenization. On this showing, it is not to be wondered at that the Jesuits' policy of Confucianization should have shocked the Vatican, which had no understanding of, or taste for, the Confucian culture to which Ricci and his successors had been making their concessions. Some of these concessions could not fail to be startling to Latin minds which had not been compelled—by the challenge of a missionary's life and work—to grapple with the problem of distinguishing between the sacrosanct essence of Christianity and its local and temporary Syriac and Hellenic and Western accidents. The Vatican's ignorance and lack of imagination were, in fact, pardonable and perhaps even inevitable; but these venial faults of head and heart were none the less disastrous for the prospects of Catholi-

Thus the failure of certain alien religions, in certain circumstances, to achieve a spiritual conquest to which they had aspired is no disproof of our thesis that alienness is, in itself, a help and not a hindrance to the spread of a 'higher religion'. We may now go on to suggest that in the histories of the 'higher religions' an inspiration that is alien and not indigenous has not only been a potent aid to success whenever it has been present, but has also been one of the regular distinguishing features of this particular species of the genus 'religions', while, conversely, a successful 'higher religion' whose inspiration is indigenous to the society in which the religion wins its way is an exceptional and abnormal phenomenon.

Our muster of 'higher religions' which appear, at first sight, to have had indigenous inspirations will include Judaism and Zoroastrianism and Islam—three religions which have found their field in the Syriac World and have also undoubtedly drawn their inspiration from the same quarter—as well as Hinduism: a religion which has found its field in the Indic World and has at the same time manifestly had an Indic inspiration. If we are to take account of imperfect representatives of the class, we may further cite Nestorianism and Monophysitism: two revised versions of Christianity which found their field in the Syriac World and which did their best to purge themselves of the Hellenic element in the Syro-Hellenic syncretism of which Christianity consists.[1] These two Syriac religious reactions against Hellenism have their Indic counterpart in the Tantric Mahāyāna: a branch of the Mahayanian Church which retreated into the interior of the Indic World, and entrenched itself in Bengal,[2] in the age when the Catholic Mahāyāna was breaking the bounds of its Indic birth-place and was boldly venturing out into Central Asia and thence into the Far East. Like the Nestorian and Monophysite Christianities, the Tantric

cism in China, since they had the effect of deeply offending Chinese susceptibilities which the Jesuit missionaries had been scrupulously careful to spare. As a matter of fact the irreparable damage was not done by the Papal Legate de Tournon—a young and inexperienced Savoyard who was sent out to the Far East without any expert knowledge. The mortal offence was given by the Papal Vicar-General in Fukien, Bishop Maigrot, who ought to have known better, since, as a resident in the Far East, he had as good an opportunity as the Jesuit missionaries of grasping the local situation and seeing how it appeared in Confucian eyes. The crisis was precipitated by Bishop Maigrot's edict of A.D. 1693, and it was brought to a head by his audience with the Emperor on the 12th December, 1706, when the local representative of the head of the Western Catholic Church was publicly convicted, by the head of the Far Eastern universal state, of an utter ignorance of the Confucian philosophy. This was an exposure which the Jesuit propaganda in China could not retrieve and did not survive. (See further V. C (i) (d) 6 (δ), p. 539, and V. C (i) (d) 7, vol. vi, pp. 23–4, below.)

[1] See I. C (i) (b), vol. i, pp. 83 and 91; I. C (iii) (b), vol. i, p. 155; II. D (v), vol. ii, p. 203; II. D (vi), vol. ii, p. 235; II. D (vii), vol. ii, pp. 286–7 and 374; and V. C (i) (c) 2, in the present volume, p. 127, above.
[2] See II. D (vi), Annex, vol. ii, p. 405, footnote 1, and V. C (i) (c) 2, in the present volume, pp. 136–7, above.

Mahāyāna sought to adapt itself to a native mission-field by purging itself of all but the native element in its amalgam. Nestorianism and Monophysitism tried to separate their Syriac gold from the single alloy of Hellenism; the Tantric Mahāyāna tried to separate its Indic gold from the twofold alloy of the Syriac conception and the Hellenic portrayal of Buddhahood. It will be seen that our assembly of religions with an indigenous inspiration remains singularly small, even when we have brought in the stragglers from the highways and hedges. If we now inspect our recruits, we shall find that two of them really belong to the 'alien' class after all, and that those which are genuinely 'indigenous' or 'semi-indigenous' are the exceptional products of peculiar circumstances.

In the first place, if we remind ourselves of the origins of Judaism and Zoroastrianism, we shall remember that, while they are indeed, both of them, religions with a Syriac inspiration which have made their first appearance in a Syriac milieu, the Syriac populations among which they came to birth between the eighth and the sixth century B.C. were broken peoples which had been forcibly conscripted into the internal proletariat of the Babylonic Society by the Assyrian men-at-arms of the Babylonic dominant minority. It was this challenge of Babylonic aggression and domination that evoked the Jewish and Zoroastrian religious responses from the Syriac souls that were subjected to the ordeal.[1] And on this showing it is evident that we ought to classify Judaism and Zoroastrianism, not as Syriac religions with an indigenous Syriac inspiration, but rather as religions which were introduced by Syriac conscripts into the internal proletariat of a Babylonic Society upon whose native religious tradition and consciousness the Syriac inspiration of Judaism and Zoroastrianism impinged as an alien spiritual force.

Thus, in the rise and spread of Judaism and Zoroastrianism in the Babylonic World after the Assyrian annexation of the Syriac populations of Syria and Iran to the Babylonic internal proletariat we have an exact parallel to the rise and spread of Christianity and Mithraism in the Hellenic World after the Macedonian annexation of the Syriac populations of South-Western Asia to the Hellenic internal proletariat.[2] And, if the disintegration of the Babylonic Civilization had been as long drawn out as that of the Hellenic Civilization, and had passed through all the same successive stages, then the birth and growth of Judaism and Zoroastrianism would present themselves, in historical perspective, as events in Babylonic history—as the birth and growth of Christianity and Mithraism do, in fact, present themselves as events

[1] See V. C (i) (c) 2, pp. 119–21, above.   [2] See V. C (i) (c) 2, pp. 80–2, above.

in Hellenic history. Our perspective has been thrown out by the accident that Babylonic history—unlike Hellenic history—came to a premature end owing to the abnormal deadliness of the Babylonic malady of Assyrian militarism.[1] Though the Babylonic World did just manage to struggle out of its 'Time of Troubles' into a universal state, the effort which had been required in order to extinguish the Assyrian conflagration had been so exhausting that the Chaldaean founders of the Neo-Babylonian Empire were left without the strength to accomplish the tremendous task of reconstruction which they had taken upon their shoulders. This Chaldaean attempt at a Babylonic universal state collapsed; and the Syriac conscripts in the Babylonic internal proletariat were able not only to throw off their chains but also to turn the tables on their Babylonic conquerors by taking them captive in body as well as in spirit.[2] The Iranians became converts to the Syriac and not to the Babylonic culture; the Achaemenian Empire which was founded by Cyrus the Persian played the part of a Syriac universal state instead of taking over the mission of the abortive Babylonic universal state which it had supplanted;[3] and within little more than five hundred years of Cyrus's entry into Babylon in 539 B.C. the last remnants of a prematurely disintegrated Babylonic Society had been absorbed into the tissues of the Syriac body social. It is in this perspective that Judaism and Zoroastrianism take on their present appearance of being Syriac religions with an indigenous inspiration. We can now see that in their origin they were religions of a Babylonic internal proletariat to which their Syriac inspiration was alien.

As for the partially de-Hellenized Syriac and Indic religions of Nestorianism and Monophysitism and the Tantric Mahāyāna, and the thoroughly de-Hellenized Syriac and Indic religions of Islam[4] and Hinduism,[5] we have already observed in other contexts[6] that these were all of them expressions, in Syriac and Indic re-

---

[1] See IV. C (iii) (c) 3 (α), vol. iv, pp. 468–84, above.

[2] See I. C (i) (b), vol. i, pp. 79–81 and 119; II. D (v), vol. ii, p. 138; IV. C (iii) (c) 3 (α), vol. iv, p. 471; and V. C (i) (c) 2, in the present volume, pp. 94 and 122–3, above.

[3] The entente between Cyrus and the Syriac victims of his vanquished Babylonic adversaries was signified in his gracious act of granting the Jews permission to return home from the land of exile; and the Iranian conqueror's Syriac proclivities were appreciated and extolled by these Jewish beneficiaries. This Iranian saviour of Jewry from a Babylonian captivity was the first temporal ruler to be hailed by a Jewish poet with the title of Messiah.
'Thus saith the Lord to his anointed, to Cyrus (Septuagint: τῷ Χριστῷ μου Κύρῳ), whose right hand I have holden, to subdue nations before him. . . . For Jacob my servant's sake, and Israel mine elect, I have even called thee by thy name; I have surnamed thee, though thou hast not known me' (Isaiah xlv. 1 and 4).

[4] See I. C (i) (b), vol. i, p. 83; II. D (vii), vol. ii, p. 288; III. C (ii) (b), vol. iii, pp. 276–8, with Annex II, V. C (i) (c) 2, in the present volume, pp. 127–8, and the present chapter, pp. 358–9, above, and V. C (i) (d) 6 (δ), Annex, pp. 672–8, below.

[5] See V. C (i) (c) 2, pp. 137–8, above, and V. C (i) (d) 7, vol. vi, pp. 47–9, below.

[6] See the references on p. 368, footnotes 1 and 2, above.

ligious terms, of a revolt in the Syriac and Indic worlds against the intrusive social force of Hellenism. This means that these religions are genuine representatives of the class of 'higher religions' whose inspiration is indigenous; and, while Nestorianism, Monophysitism, and the Tantric Mahāyāna may be imperfect specimens, this cannot be said of either Hinduism or Islam. At the same time we may notice that this Syriac and Indic revolt against Hellenism is only the last chapter in the history of the encounter between these three civilizations. This chapter of revolt and estrangement had been preceded by a chapter of forbearance and intercourse; and this earlier and happier relation[1] had likewise found expression in religious terms of its own. Its monuments are the syncretistic religions of Catholic Christianity and the Catholic Mahāyāna; and both of these religions were discovered by the Hellenic internal proletariat in the light of an alien inspiration—Syriac in the one case and Indic in the other. This chapter which saw the birth of a Catholic Christianity and a Catholic Mahāyāna was assuredly a more fruitful and important and significant phase in the encounter between Hellenism and its two neighbours than the later chapter which gave birth to Nestorianism and Monophysitism and the Tantric Mahāyāna, and afterwards to Islam and Hinduism.

In this last sentence we have implicitly made a judgement of value as between one 'higher religion' and another. We have judged that Catholic Christianity is a more valuable representative of its species than Nestorianism or Monophysitism or Islam, and that the Catholic Mahāyāna is more valuable than the Tantric Mahāyāna or Hinduism. Are we warranted in taking a liberty with religions that we have scrupled to take with civilizations? At an early point in this Study[2] we debated whether we should take account of possible differences of value in comparing one civilization with another, and in this case we decided not to presume to act as judges or dividers.[3] When we pass from the study of civilizations to the study of religions, are we going to abandon this discreet attitude of neutrality and to take the perilous plunge into passing judgements and meting measures?[4] Our reply to this question may perhaps be postponed until we come to deal, in a later Part,[5] with those universal churches in

---

[1] We have, however, also seen that there was an earlier chapter still which—like the third, and unlike the second—was a chapter of war and not of peace, though in this first chapter it was the intrusive Hellenic Civilization, and not its Syriac or Indic victim, that took the offensive. In this first chapter, too, the Syriac reaction expressed itself in religious forms: in the militant 'Zealot' outbreaks of a Eunus of Enna and a Judas Maccabaeus (see V. C (i) (c) 2, pp. 68–9, above).

[2] In I. C (iii) (d), vol. i, pp. 175–7, above.   [3] Luke xii. 14.

[4] Matt. vii. 2.   [5] In Part VII, below.

which the victorious 'higher religions' have embodied themselves. In the present chapter we must turn to the consideration of a point which presents itself as a corollary to our conclusion that the 'higher religions' which have alien, and not indigenous, inspirations are the normal representatives of their species.

If a religion has an alien inspiration, then manifestly the origin and the nature of that religion cannot be understood without taking account of a contact between at least two civilizations: on the one hand the civilization in whose internal proletariat the new religion arises, and on the other hand the different civilization (or civilizations) from which the alien inspiration (or inspirations) of the rising religion is derived. This point about the study of 'higher religions' is simple and self-evident; but—all the more imperatively on that account—it compels us to make a radical new departure; for it requires us to relinquish the basis on which this Study has so far been built up.

So far we have been dealing in terms of civilizations; and we have assumed that any single civilization will afford a practicable field of study because, at the outset of our inquiry,[1] we satisfied ourselves that any given civilization constituted a social 'whole' which was intelligible in isolation from whatever social phenomena might present themselves outside the spatial and temporal limits of this particular society. Indeed, we originally defined a civilization as 'an intelligible field of study'; and our approach to the identification of our twenty-one representatives of this species of societies was subjective as well as empirical. We started our inquiry from the observation that the national community—which has been the actual standard unit employed in most of the historical study that has been carried out in our Western World in its Modern Age—proves to be a fragmentary, and therefore unintelligible, slice of some field of greater magnitude; and we then mapped out the bounds of this wider field in our own social landscape by exploring outwards beyond the ragged edges of one particular parochial community—and also backwards behind the brief span of one particular generation—and observing, as we went on enlarging our spatial and our temporal horizon, that the intelligibility of the social landscape at first rose steadily in degree, but then reached a maximum at a certain remove, and afterwards fell off until—long before we had embraced in our field of vision the whole living generation and past ancestry of Mankind on the surface of the planet—the degree of intelligibility of our field of vision had sunk once more to the level at which it had stood to begin with, when we were confining our view within the 'short

[1] In Part I. B, vol. i, above.

and narrow-vergèd shade' of 'some single herb or tree' in the tribal forest. It was by this empirical manoeuvre from a subjective starting-point that we approximately ascertained the extension, in Space and in Time, of our own Western Society; and it was only after this that we went on to identify twenty other representatives of the same species of society by analogy with our first-found specimen.

This resumé of the overture to our inquiry[1] may serve to remind us that a civilization, in the sense in which we have defined and employed the term, is 'in the last analysis' a field of study which appears to be intelligible within its own limits; and up to this point we have found ourselves able to work on the assumption that the intelligible field is always and everywhere of the order and the dimensions that are exhibited in our own Western body social and in its twenty sisters. By enlarging our field of operations from the nation to the civilization of which the nation is a fragment, we have found it possible to make a study of History in terms of civilizations and their careers—from genesis to growth and from breakdown to disintegration. But 'the relativity of historical thought'[2] has now caught us out in our turn, as we have seen it catch out the historians who have allowed their horizon to be determined by the narrower frontiers of some single national community or city-state; for the particular 'intelligible field' that has sufficiently well served our purpose so far is manifestly relative, in magnitude to the length, and in locus to the position, of the particular base-line from which we first set out to survey the extent of this field and to plot out its limits. Our original base-line, as we have reminded ourselves, was the modern Western national community which the national historian accepts as his social universe; and it is perhaps really surprising that a survey conducted from this base of operations should have carried us so far as it has; for the national community is far indeed from being adequate to the historian's purpose, even when it is taken as a base-line and not as a boundary.

The first step in our inquiry made it clear to us that the national community, as we know it in our modern Western World, is both eccentric in its position in the historical landscape and petty in its scale; and the combination of these two untoward features makes it a peculiarly unfavourable starting-point for a study of History. For us, in our time and place, it was not within our power to start from anywhere else; for the national community is the social prison-house in which our modern Western souls are incarcerated.

---

[1] See Part I, *passim*, especially I. B (v) and I. C (ii), in vol. i, above.
[2] See Part I. A, in vol. i, above.

The best that we could do was to peer over the battlements and extend our field of vision, beyond the imprisoning walls, as far as the eye could reach. But we have come now to a parting of the ways in this mental voyage of exploration. If we cannot or will not now break out of these prison walls, then we must be content to abandon our inquiry at the present point; for we have now surveyed the whole of the landscape that is visible from within the *enceinte* of this outlandish and close-cribbed *donjon*. We have, in fact, now surveyed the whole of the intelligible field that falls within the horizon of an observer who is tied down to a national standpoint; and from this observation-post we can see no farther, however intently we may crane our necks and strain our eyes. From our parochial standing-ground the single civilization is the widest field of vision that can be attained; and, since our reconnaissance has now reached this limit in all four quarters of the compass, one of the alternatives before us is to recite, for the second time, the famous words[1] in which Pindar renounces the pursuit of his quest into the Ocean beyond the Pillars of Hercules.

Probably this would have been the alternative to which a Hellenic inquirer would have resigned himself if he had found himself in our present situation; for his Theban or Athenian horizon was bounded for him by the limits of his Hellas as rigidly as the English or French horizon is bounded for us by the limits of our wider, yet still finite, Western World. We children of Western Christendom, however, have not the same excuse as Pindar and his Hellenic contemporaries for giving up the game at this point; for an alternative course lies open to us; and the way has been pointed by one of the Fathers of our Western Christian Civilization. In the fifth century of our era, when the post-Hellenic interregnum had set in and the Gothic sack of Rome had proclaimed the break-up of the Hellenic universal state, one child of the age—a Hellene who was also a Christian, and a genius who was also a saint—had the spiritual insight to see that the venerable social edifice which was falling about his ears was after all a prison-house, and that the Hellene's catastrophe might spell the Christian's liberation. The falling walls of Jericho which were giving entry to the Israelite invader would also set the Canaanite captive free. And so Augustine's reply to the challenge of Alaric's stroke was to spring out of the shattered prison-house of the City of Man into the infinite liberty of an inviolate and inviolable City of God.[2]

---

[1] Pindar's Third Olympian Ode, *ad fin.*, quoted in II. C (i), vol. i, p. 205, above.
[2] Saint Augustine's theme in the *De Civitate Dei* has been touched upon in V. C (i) (c) 3, p. 224, footnote 1, and p. 225, footnote 1, above. The spirit of Saint Augustine, as it is revealed in the *De Civitate Dei*, may be both compared and contrasted with the spirit

Can we escape from our own present *impasse* by following the lead of this Christian mentor and master? The mental—or rather spiritual—feat that is required of us is to burst the cramping bounds of our English or French or German or American social prison-house—whichever of the nationalisms it may be that has been holding us hide-bound—and to re-occupy the place that belongs to us in a greater kingdom which was Augustine's by right of spiritual conquest and is still ours to-day by privilege of cultural inheritance. If once we can escape from the parochial standpoint of an American or German or French or English member of a Western brood of nations, and can take our stand, instead, upon our birthright in Christendom, which was the spiritual habitation of our forebears,[1] then our social horizon will assuredly expand to farther distances which we have not yet begun to explore. For the 'intelligible field of study' which unfolds itself to an observer whose feet are planted on the mountain-heights of one of the 'higher religions' quite outranges the limits of the single civilization which is the widest field that can be surveyed from the squat battlements of a national prison-fortress. We have just observed[2] that the single civilization, which, when regarded from the standpoint of one of its national fragments, has worn the appearance of a fully 'intelligible field of study', shrivels up, in its turn, into an unintelligible fragment of some far larger whole when we place ourselves at the standpoint, no longer of a national community, but of one of those churches in which the 'higher religions' embody themselves. Within the ambit of a single civilization the origin and nature of a 'higher religion' are unintelligible *ex hypothesi*, since we have seen that the birth of a 'higher religion' presupposes a foregoing contact and intercourse between two civilizations at the least. In a mental voyage of discovery which takes its departure from a church and not from some parochial political community, it is evident that the 'intelligible field of study' will be of an altogether

that is attributed to Epicurus in a magnificent passage of Lucretius's *De Rerum Natura* which has been quoted at an earlier point in this Study (in II. C (ii) (*b*) 1, vol. i, p. 299, above). Like the Hellenic philosopher, the Christian father boldly defied a power which was apparently irresistible, and won by his audacity a passage from a prison-house to freedom; but this superficial likeness covers a fundamental difference; for Epicurus broke his way out of the Hell of Superstition into the Material Universe of Science through a defiance of God, whereas Augustine took the Kingdom of Heaven by storm through a defiance of human forces that were destroying the Kingdom of This World. (For Saint Augustine's vision of the Kingdom of God see further V. C (i) (*d*) 11, vol. vi, pp. 152–4 and 166–7, and V. C (i) (*d*) 11, Annex II, vol. vi, pp. 365–9, below.)

[1] For the loss of the consciousness of common citizenship in the Western *Respublica Christiana*, simultaneously with the emergence of the consciousness of parochial nationality, at the beginning of the Modern Age of our Western history see I. B (iii), vol. i, pp. 33–4, above. In the Russian Orthodox Christendom the corresponding consciousness of common Christianity lasted longer. In Russia the ordinary word for 'peasant' was *Khrestianin* down to the Revolution of A.D. 1917.　　[2] On p. 372, above.

higher order of magnitude than that of the single civilization which has sufficed us hitherto. Possibly we shall find that our new field also extends into a different spiritual dimension—but this is a possibility which we can now examine at our leisure;[1] for, almost without noticing what we have been doing, we have chosen and taken our course. The Pillars of Hercules are behind us, and the sea on which we are sailing is no longer the familiar land-bound *Mare Nostrum*.

(d) SCHISM IN THE SOUL

1. *Alternative Ways of Behaviour, Feeling, and Life*

The schism in the Human Body Social, which we have been examining in the foregoing chapter as one of our criteria of the disintegration of a civilization, is an experience which is collective and therefore superficial. Its significance lies in its being the outward visible sign of an inward spiritual rift; and this spiritual rift is riven in human souls; for, among all the almost infinitely various manifestations of Human Nature, the Soul alone is capable of being the subject of spiritual experiences and the author of spiritual acts.[2] A schism in the souls of human beings will be found at the heart of any schism that reveals itself on the surface of the society which is the common ground of these human actors' respective fields of activity;[3] and the several forms which this inward schism may take must engage our attention now, if we wish to pursue our search for a criterion on a deeper level of reality.

Schism in the souls of the human 'members' of a disintegrating civilization displays itself in a variety of shapes because it arises in every one of the various ways of behaviour, feeling, and life which we have found to be characteristic of civilizations—or, rather, of the action of the human beings who play their part in civilizations —in those phases of social history which we have labelled 'genesis' and 'growth'. In the disintegration-phase each of these single lines of action is apt to split into a pair of mutually antithetical and antipathetic variations or substitutes, in which the response to a challenge is 'polarized' into two alternatives—one passive and the other active, but neither of them creative. A choice between the active and the passive option is the only freedom that is left to a soul which has lost the opportunity (though not, of course, the capacity) for creative action through being cast for a part in the

---

[1] See V. C (i) (d) 11, vol. vi, pp. 149–68, below.

[2] This elementary truth—which has not ceased to be true through being unpalatable to many modern Western minds—has been acknowledged already in this Study in III. C (ii) (a), vol. iii, pp. 230–1, above.

[3] For this definition of the nature and structure of a society see III. C (ii) (a), in vol. iii, above.

tragedy of social disintegration as either one of the villains or one of the victims of the piece. As the process of disintegration works itself out, the alternative choices tend to become more rigid in their limitations, more extreme in their divergence, and more momentous in their consequences. That is to say, the spiritual experience of schism in the Soul is a dynamic movement, not a static situation.

We may now pass these alternative substitutes for creative activity in review, and take a bird's-eye glance at their interactions with one another, before we attempt an empirical survey of the historical manifestations of each of them.

To begin with, there are two ways of personal behaviour which are alternative substitutes for the exercise of the general faculty of creativeness.[1] Both of them are attempts at self-expression. The passive attempt consists in an *abandon* (ἀκράτεια) in which the Soul 'lets itself go', in the belief that by giving free rein to its own spontaneous appetites and aversions it will be 'living according to Nature'[2] and will automatically be receiving back, from the cornucopia of this mysterious and therefore possibly puissant goddess,[3] the precious gift of creativity which the sick Soul has been conscious of losing. The active alternative to this passive *abandon* is an effort at self-control (ἐγκράτεια) in which the Soul 'takes itself in hand' and seeks to discipline its 'natural passions'—through a régime of spiritual exercises which is conceived on the analogy of the physical training (ἄσκησις) of an athlete—in the opposite belief that Nature is the bane of creativity and not its source, and that to 'gain the mastery over Nature' is the only way of recovering the lost creative faculty.

Then there are two ways of social behaviour which are alternative substitutes for that mimesis of creative personalities which we have found to be a necessary, though perilous, short cut on the road of social growth.[4] Both of these substitutes for mimesis are attempts to step out of the ranks of a phalanx whose 'social drill' has failed to work—with the result that the uncreative mass, which formerly followed its leaders through intricate evolutions in orderly formation, now stands immobilized, irresolute, and apprehensive: a helpless target for hostile attack. The passive attempt

---

[1] An attempt to apprehend—'through a glass darkly'—the nature of creativeness in itself has been made in II. C (ii) (*b*) 1, in vol. i, above.

[2] 'The Return to Nature' is interpreted as a symptom of social disintegration by Oswald Spengler in *Der Untergang des Abendlandes*, vol. i (Munich 1920, Beck), p. 286. Besides being a gesture of *abandon*, it is also an expression of archaistic-mindedness (see V. C (i) (*d*) 8 (α), vol. vi, pp. 58–9, below).

[3] The deification of Nature is a classic example of the human weakness which takes *omne ignotum pro magnifico* (Tacitus: *Agricola*, chap. 30).

[4] See III. C (ii) (*b*), vol. iii, pp. 245–8, and IV. C (iii) (*a*), vol. iv, pp. 122–33, above.

to break this formidable social deadlock takes the form of committing the misdemeanour of truancy. The soldier realizes with dismay that the regiment has now lost the discipline which has hitherto fortified his *moral* and secured his safety and given strength to his right arm; and, in this unforeseen and unbargained-for situation, the truant-minded soldier allows himself to believe that he is absolved from his military duty. In that unedifying frame of mind the truant steps out of the ranks backwards—in the contemptible and futile hope of saving his own skin by leaving his comrades in the lurch. There is, however, another alternative way of facing the same ordeal which is illustrated by the famous story[1] of the two Spartiate soldiers Aristodâmus 'the Truant'[2] and Eurytus.

The story relates that the two men were on leave together in hospital behind the front—both of them incapacitated for active service by an acute attack of ophthalmia—when the news was brought to them that the rest of the devoted band of three hundred Spartiates were being outflanked at Thermopylae by a turning movement and were therefore now doomed to certain death in consequence of King Leonidas' decision not to retreat. In these circumstances Eurytus and Aristodâmus were 'both presented with the possibility of returning safely home to Sparta together unless they preferred the alternative of losing their lives with their comrades', and, 'when this choice was presented to them, they could not make up their minds to agree, but took different views of their duty'. While Aristodâmus slunk off home to Sparta, Eurytus made his batman lead him to the battlefield; and when, upon reaching the front, the Helot servant turned and fled, his Spartiate master flung himself—blind-eyed—into the mêlée in order to meet death still more swiftly, and against still more fearful odds, than his two hundred and ninety eight comrades whom he had rejoined—unbidden—by this heroic *tour de force*. It is evident that Eurytus's way of distinguishing himself from the rank and file was the antithesis of Aristodâmus's. Instead of stepping backwards, he stepped forwards. Instead of lapsing into truancy, he rushed into martyrdom.

A martyr is primarily a soldier who takes it upon himself to bear witness to the supreme value and the absolute obligation of the military virtues in a situation in which his only means of giving his testimony is to sacrifice his own life on a forlorn hope. His self-sacrifice may have the incidental aim of carrying his comrades to victory by breaking a breach in the enemy line—as when

---

[1] See Herodotus, Book VII, chaps. 229–31, and Book IX, chap. 71.
[2] ὁ τρέσας Ἀριστόδημος.

Arnold von Winkelried threw himself upon the Hapsburg pikes; or when Alessandro Pizzoli drew the fire of the Neapolitan cannon by dropping down into the lane which the piece commanded, and then charging the cannon's mouth at point-blank range;[1] or when the Decii dedicated themselves to Tellus and to the Di Manes as sacrificial victims who were to get themselves slain on the battle-field by the enemy's hand.[2] But the fundamental motive of martyrdom is not to secure material success here and now for the cause to which the martyr has dedicated himself. The Spartan soldier Eurytus chose to bear witness to the virtues of the Lycurgean *agôgê* by sacrificing his life in an action in which an utter physical defeat was a foregone conclusion; and the same *esprit de corps* has inspired the innumerable heroes of innumerable stricken fields who have died rather than surrender to an already victorious adversary. In essence the martyr is a soldier who steps out of the ranks on his own initiative[3] in a forward direction in order to

[1] Trevelyan, G. M.: *Garibaldi and the Making of Italy, June–November, 1860* (new impression, London 1928, Longmans, Green), p. 84.

[2] For this Roman practice of *devotio*, which was a literal self-sacrifice on the part of the general commanding, see Livy, Book VIII, chaps. 9–10, and Book X, chaps. 28–9.

The practice outraged the Romans' Greek antagonist Pyrrhus both as a rationalist and as a 'clean fighter', and, upon receiving intelligence, on the eve of the Battle of Ausculum, that the commander of the opposing Roman army, Publius Decius Mus the Third, intended to dedicate himself in this fashion on this occasion, Pyrrhus is said to have made an allocution on the subject to his troops, with the twofold object of removing from their minds any superstitious fears which the report of Decius's intention might have aroused, and at the same time instructing them to make the Roman commander's gesture fall flat by insisting upon taking him alive. On the first point Pyrrhus is reported to have observed that 'a single man cannot defeat a multitude by dying, nor can a piece of spell-binding and black art ($\epsilon\pi\omega\delta\grave{\eta}\nu$ καὶ μαγγανείαν τινά) prove more than a match for armaments and valour (κρείττω τῶν ὅπλων καὶ τῶν ἀνδρῶν γενέσθαι)'. On the second point he was not content with giving orders to his own troops to refuse Decius all opportunity of finding the death which he was proposing to seek: he also sent a message to Decius himself to warn him that his purpose would not meet with success, and further to threaten him that he would be put to death in an unpleasant way after being taken alive (ζωγρηθέντα κακῶς ἀπολεῖσθαι). The story relates that, on receiving this message, Decius gave up the idea (Dio Cassius: fragments of Book X = Zonaras, Book VIII, chap. 5, §§ 1–3. The passage will be found in U. P. Boissevain's edition of Dio, vol. i (Berlin 1895, Weidmann), p. 133).

According to Beloch, K. J.: *Römische Geschichte bis zum Beginn der Punischen Kriege* (Berlin and Leipzig 1926, de Gruyter), pp. 440–2, the alleged *devotiones* of the first Publius Decius Mus at Veseris in 340 B.C. and of his son and namesake at Sentinum in 295 B.C. are both apocryphal and are both to be accounted for as alternative transfers of a genuine *devotio* of the third Publius Decius Mus in 279 B.C. at Ausculum. In Beloch's view P.D.M. III really did commit *devotio*; and the story that Pyrrhus successfully frustrated his intention was afterwards invented in deference to the awkward fact that at Ausculum the Romans actually suffered a heavy defeat, whereas a successfully committed *devotio* ought to have been an infallible means of procuring a victory. This is perhaps an excessive indulgence in 'the higher criticism'!

[3] A critic may here object that a martyr is often inspired by the heroic example of a predecessor whom he loves and admires. When Publius Decius Mus devoted himself at Sentinum in 295 B.C., we must suppose (if, *pace* Beloch, we accept the three successive *devotiones* in the tradition as being all alike authentic) that he was consciously imitating his father and namesake who had devoted himself in 340 B.C. at Veseris; and unquestionably every Christian martyr is consciously imitating the Crucifixion of Christ. Martyrdom, the critic may conclude, is not a substitute for mimesis: on the contrary, it is an illustration of it. We may reply that an act of martyrdom, like any other act, may become an object of mimesis, but that the crucial case is the conduct of the protomartyr in any given series, and that, when we examine this original act of martyrdom, we invariably

go beyond the demands of duty. While in normal circumstances duty demands no more of the soldier than that he should risk his life to the minimum extent that may be necessary for the effective execution of his superior officer's orders, the martyr courts death for the vindication of an ideal, without necessarily having any expectation at all that his self-sacrifice will secure a material victory for his tribe or country. And, if this is true of the military prototypes of martyrhood, it is true *a fortiori*, as we shall see, of the nobler army of martyrs who lay down their lives in contests which make as exacting a demand as any military action can make upon the courage and generosity and faith of the combatant, without offering him those adventitious aids to his *moral* that are provided by the physical excitement and the mass-suggestion of the literal battle-field.

When we pass from the plane of behaviour to that of feeling, we may first take note of two ways of personal feeling which are alternative reactions to a reversal of that movement of Promethean *élan* in which the nature of growth appears to reveal itself.[1] Both these feelings reflect a painful consciousness of being 'on the run' from forces of evil which have not only taken the offensive but have also established their ascendancy so potently that they now march from victory to victory and go from strength to strength.[2] The passive expression of this consciousness of continual and progressive moral defeat is a sense of being adrift in a Universe in which Evil is triumphant in the Macrocosm. The routed Soul is prostrated by a perception of its objective failure to master and control its environment; and it is tempted to resign itself to the belief that the Universe, including the Soul itself, is at the mercy of a power which is as irrational as it is invincible: the ungodly goddess with the double face who is propitiated under the name of Chance (*Τύχη*) or is endured under the name of Necessity (*Ἀνάγκη*). Alternatively, the moral defeat which desolates the routed Soul may be felt as a failure to master and control the Soul's own self; and in that case the expression of the Soul's consciousness of defeat will be active. The Soul will then be possessed by a sense of sin; and, turning its gaze inwards from the Macrocosm to the Microcosm, it will gird itself for the arduous spiritual enterprise of attacking and overcoming *Karma*: the cumulative burden of the excess of evil over good in the Soul's own action in the past.

We have also to notice two ways of social feeling which are alter-

---

find that it is a voluntary action which goes beyond the call of duty and which is evoked by a social situation in which the normal 'social drill' of mimesis has broken down. The very object of the protomartyr is to give a new example.

[1] The nature of growth has been discussed in Part III. B, in vol. iii, above.
[2] Psalm lxxxiv. 7.

native substitutes for the sense of style—a sense that is the subjective counterpart of the objective process of the differentiation
of civilizations through their growth.[1] Both these feelings betray
a loss of this same sensitiveness for form; but their respective ways
of responding to an identic challenge are poles apart. The passive
response is an acquiescence in the total loss of all sense of form
as a consequence of the loss of the particular style of the particular
civilization that has now passed over from growth into disintegration. The Soul surrenders itself to the melting-pot; and a negative
sense of promiscuity then comes to pervade every sphere of social
activity. In the sphere of social intercourse it results in a blending
of incongruous traditions and in a compounding of incompatible
values (παμμιξία); in the media of language and literature and
visual art it declares itself in the currency of a *lingua franca* (κοινή)
and of a similarly standardized composite style of literature and
painting and sculpture and architecture; in the realm of philosophical ideas and of religious beliefs and practices it produces
ritual and theological syncretisms. This passive response is not
always sharply distinguished by students of the phenomena of
social disintegration from the active response which is really its
extreme antithesis. This active response takes the loss of a style
of living which has been local and ephemeral as an opportunity,
and a call, to adopt another style which partakes of what is universal and eternal: *quod ubique, quod semper, quod ab omnibus*.[2]
When it rises to this active response, the Soul finds that the efface-
ment of the characteristic form of the disintegrating civilization
has brought it face to face, not with a Chaos void of any form at
all, but with a Cosmos whose circumambient form and divine
architecture are now at last coming into view through the rents in
the screen of lath-and-plaster work with which Man has sought
to shut out an overwhelming vision of Eternity and Infinity.[3]

[1] For this differentiation through growth see III. C (iii), in vol. iii, above.
[2] Saint Vincent of Lérins: *Commonitorium Primum*, chap. 2 (Migne, J.-P.: *Patrologia
Latina*, vol. i, col. 640).
[3] An almost naïvely self-complacent boast of juvenile proficiency in this art of self-
protective spiritual jerry-building is made in the following passages from Mr. H. G. Wells'
Experiment in Autobiography, vol. i (London 1934, Gollancz), pp. 78–9, 96, and 144:
  'I was glad to think that between the continental land masses of the World, which
would have afforded an unbroken land passage for wolves from Russia and tigers from
India, and this safe island on which I took my daily walks, stretched the impassable
moat of the English Channel. I read, too, in another book, about the distances of the
stars, and that seemed to push the All Seeing Eye very agreeably away from me. . . .
  'I felt it must be rather empty and cheerless beyond the stars, but I did not let my
mind dwell on that. My God, who by this time had become entirely disembodied, had
been diffused through this space since the beginning of things. He was already quite
abstracted from the furious old hell-and-heaven Thunder God of my childish years.
His personality had faded. . . .
  'It must be hard for intelligent people nowadays to realize all that a shabby boy of
fifteen could feel as the last rack of a peevish son-crucifying Deity dissolved away into
blue sky, and as the implacable social barriers, as they had seemed, set to keep him in

This active response is an awakening to a sense of unity which broadens and deepens as the vision expands from the unity of Mankind, through the unity of the Cosmos,[1] to embrace the unity of God.

If we pass on, in the third place, to the plane of life, we shall encounter, here again, two pairs of alternative reactions to match the two pairs that have already presented themselves on each of the two preceding planes of feeling and behaviour. On this third plane, however, the picture departs from the previous pattern in three respects. For one thing the alternatives which here replace the single movement that is characteristic of the stage of growth are variations on that movement rather than substitutes for it. Secondly both pairs of alternatives are variations upon the same single movement—a movement which we have described[2] as a transference of the field of action from the Macrocosm to the Microcosm. Thirdly the two pairs of alternative ways of life that make their appearance in the life of a disintegrating civilization, as variations upon the process of transference, are differentiated from one another by a difference which is sufficiently profound to account for the duplication. In one pair the temper of the reactions is violent; in the other it is gentle.

This parting of the ways into violent and gentle courses in the history of a disintegrating society first caught our attention when we were examining the response of the internal proletariat of the Hellenic Society to the challenge from the dominant minority. We stumbled upon the contrast in the famous antithesis between the violent spirit of Theudas and Judas of Galilee and their partisans and the gentle spirit of Jesus and his disciples.[3] In that context

---

that path unto which it had pleased God to call him, weakened down to temporary fences he could see over and presently perhaps hope to climb over or 'push aside.'

The unconscious irony of these passages is heightened by the very expressiveness of the author's literary genius. Mr. Wells here reveals himself building up defensive screens and fancying all the time that he is pulling down constricting barriers; contracting the spiritual bounds of his microcosm and imagining that he is enlarging the span of the Universe because he is pushing the physical frontiers of his macrocosm out to a mathematical infinity. To all appearance he is unaware of the truth that, as God dissolves into blue sky, the shades of the prison-house are closing around the growing boy.

[1] A human 'political animal' who has apprehended the unity of the Cosmos can most aptly describe his spiritual discovery in the political metaphor of citizenship in a cosmic society; and the Greek name for this cosmic society is Κοσμόπολις; but in the current usage of the English language the adjective 'cosmopolitan', which has been coined from the Greek substantive, has been divorced from its proper meaning in order to describe the παμμιξία which the melting-pot produces. This arbitrarily incorrect usage has no doubt played its part in the blurring of the sharp and vital distinction between the true Cosmopolis and its exact antithesis the Melting-Pot. The English adjective which comes nearest to expressing the connotation of the Greek word Κοσμόπολις is 'catholic' in the non-ecclesiastical meaning of the term.

[2] In III. C (i) (d), in vol. iii, above.

[3] See V. C (i) (c) 2, pp. 72–3, above. A distinction between several different positive realities underlying the negative phenomenon of Gentleness or Non-Violence is drawn in V. C (i) (c) 2, Annex III, pp. 588–90, below.

we went on to notice that the same contrast could be discerned —unmistakably, though perhaps not quite so clearly—in the responses of the Hellenic dominant minority and external proletariat. In the history of the dominant minority we detected this contrast in the antithesis between the destructive temper of the Roman militarists from the time of the Hannibalic War to the time of Augustus and the constructive êthos of the Roman civil servants from the time of Augustus to the time of Alexander Severus.[1] In the history of the external proletariat we detected a corresponding contrast, in the last chapter of the story, between the temper of a Genseric and the temper of a Theodoric.[2] In the rest of our long review of internal and external proletariats we have come across this distinction between violent and gentle courses time and again; and, now that we have passed on from the superficial study of schism in the Body Social to the deeper study of schism in the Soul, we shall find that the prominence of this parting of the ways between Violence and Gentleness in the landscape of social disintegration is no mere fortuitous optical effect of an empirical survey, but is an essential feature in the plot of the spiritual drama which the social process half expresses and half obscures.

With this preface our violent and our gentle pair of variations on the movement of transference from the Macrocosm to the Microcosm may now be brought on to the stage. In the violent pair the passive reaction may be described as Archaism and the active as Futurism. In the gentle pair the passive reaction may be described as Detachment and the active as Transfiguration.

Archaism and Futurism are two alternative attempts to substitute a mere transfer in the Time-dimension for that transfer of the field of action from one spiritual plane to another which is the characteristic movement of growth. In both Archaism and Futurism the effort to live in the Microcosm instead of the Macrocosm is abandoned for the pursuit of a Utopia[3] which would be reached —supposing that it could actually be found 'in real life'—without any challenge to face the arduous change of spiritual clime. This external Utopia is intended to do duty, in place of the inward spiritual cosmos, as an 'Other World'; but it is an 'Other World' only in the shallow and unsatisfying sense of being a negation of the Macrocosm in the momentary present state of the Macrocosm's existence here and now. The Soul that has been daunted by finding that it has been called on to play its part in life in the

[1] See V. C (i) (c) 1, pp. 38–9, and V. C (i) (c) 2, pp. 78–9, above.
[2] See V. C (i) (c) 3, pp. 223–7, above.
[3] For Utopias as attempts to 'peg' falling civilizations see Part III. A, vol. iii, pp. 88–106, above.

tragedy of social disintegration still cannot repudiate all movement or aim or purpose, since that would mean committing outright spiritual suicide; so it seeks to 'get by' through taking the easiest spiritual option that is open to it. Instead of continuing to attempt to make the formidable passage from the Macrocosm to the Microcosm, it now seeks to fulfil the bare letter of the Law of Life by making a perfunctory transfer which does not involve any departure from the level of the Macrocosm to a different spiritual height or depth. It proposes to perform what is required of it by making its move from the Macrocosm as it is to-day to a goal which is simply another state of the self-same Macrocosm as it may once have been in the Past or as it may some time come to be in the Future. Archaism places in the City of Cecrops[1] the treasure that it withdraws from the City of Pericles, while Futurism withdraws its treasure from the same City of Pericles in order to place it in the City of the Sun.[2]

In terms that we have coined for ourselves in earlier passages of this Study, Archaism may be defined as a reversion from the mimesis of contemporary creative personalities to a mimesis of the ancestors of the tribe: that is to say, as a lapse from the dynamic movement of Civilization to the static condition of Primitive Mankind in its latest state.[3] It may be defined, again, as one of those attempts at a forcible stoppage of change which result, in so far as they succeed, in the production of social enormities.[4] In the third place, Archaism may be taken as an example of that attempt to 'peg' a broken-down and disintegrating society which, in another context,[5] we have found to be the common aim of human Utopias and of those insect societies to which the arrested human societies approximate. In corresponding terms we may define Futurism as a repudiation of any mimesis of anybody—present or past, creative or conservative—and also as one of those attempts at a forcible accomplishment of change which result, in so far as they succeed, in the production of social revolutions that defeat their own purpose by tumbling over into reaction.[6] In fine, Futurism only avoids the static immobility of Archaism at the price of moving like a convict on a treadmill or like a captive

---

[1] For the City of Cecrops (the patron divinity of archaic Athens) as a title for the Archaistic Utopia see Marcus Aurelius Antoninus: *Meditations*, Book IV, chap. 23.
[2] For the City of the Sun (the patron divinity of the Oecumenical Proletariat that is scattered through all the lands on which the god Helios shines, without possessing a single clod of earth to call its own) see V. C (i) (c) 2, pp. 69–70, 111, footnote 2, and 179–80, above, and V. C (i) (d) 6 (δ), Annex, p. 692, footnote 2, and V. C (i) (d) 11, Annex I, vol. vi, p. 351, below.
[3] See Part II. B, vol. i, pp. 191–2, above.
[4] See IV. C (iii) (b), *passim*, in vol. iv, above.
[5] In Part III. A, in vol. iii, pp. 88–106, above.
[6] See IV. C (iii) (b), *passim*, in vol. iv, above.

mouse in a revolving cage; and the futility of this revolutionary motion is summed up in the devastating aphorism *Plus ça change, plus c'est la même chose.*[1]

For those who put their trust in either of these would-be substitutes for the transfer of the field of action from the Macrocosm to the Microcosm, there lies in wait an ironical common fate. In seeking their alternative easy options these 'defeatists' are actually condemning themselves—whether blindly or with open eyes—to a violent denouement which is bound to overtake them, when once they have set their feet on either the archaistic or the futuristic path, because in both cases they are attempting something which is contrary to the order of Nature. The quest of the inner life, which seems—and is—so formidable an undertaking, is at any rate no impossibility for a Soul that is playing its temporary part on the stage of the External World; for, since the Microcosm and the Macrocosm are different planes of spiritual experience and activity, the transference of the Soul's treasure from the outward to the inward life is equally difficult, or equally easy, whatever the momentary state of the Macrocosm may be. On the other hand it is intrinsically impossible for the Soul, in so far as it is living in the outward life, to extricate itself from its present place in the current of the 'ever-rolling stream' by taking either a flying leap backward upstream into the Past or a flying leap forward downstream into the Future. The archaistic and the futuristic Utopia alike are Utopias in the literal sense of being localities which have no real existence. These two alluring *alibis* are thus both of them unattainable *ex hypothesi*; and the sole and certain effect of striking out towards either of them is to produce a troubling of the waters with a violence that brings no healing.

The crescendo movement of violence that is set in motion by Futurism has been described, with an inimitable combination of exactitude and vividness, by a famous nineteenth-century Western socialist.

'Lorsqu'arrive le temps des époques critiques ou de destruction,[2] c'est que des faits nouveaux se sont produits; c'est que la société éprouve des besoins nouveaux, que ne comporte pas et que ne peut comprendre le cadre trop étroit, et devenu inflexible, de la croyance établie et de l'institution politique qui la réalise. Cependant, ces faits nouveaux, ces exigences d'avenir, cherchent à se faire jour, à prendre place; d'abord ils viennent se briser contre l'ordre ancien; mais, par

---

[1] Alphonse Karr: *Les Guêpes,* Janvier 1849 (ed. Michel Lévy, vol. vi, p. 304), according to Harbottle, T. B., and Dalbiac, P. H.: *Dictionary of Quotations (French and Italian)* (London 1901, Swan Sonnenschein).

[2] For the sense in which this term is used in the Saint-Simonian philosophy see the present Study, Part II. B, vol. i, pp. 199–200, above.—A.J.T.

leur choc répété, ils finissent par l'ébranler et par le renverser lui-même. La société alors ne présente plus que l'image d'une guerre acharnée, d'une anarchie profonde, au sein de laquelle les sentiments haineux semblent les seuls qui puissent se développer. Bientôt les esprits, effrayés de la confusion qui les frappe, ne pouvant encore apercevoir l'ordre qui doit s'établir, n'éprouvant que de répugnance pour l'ordre qui vient de périr, et dans lequel ils ne voient qu'une longue et oppressive déception, ne tardent point à arriver à cette idée que le monde est livré au désordre. . . .

'Les époques critiques se divisent en deux périodes distinctes: l'une formant le début de ces époques,[1] pendant laquelle la société, ralliée par une foi vive aux doctrines de destruction, agit de concert pour renverser l'ancienne institution religieuse et sociale; l'autre, comprenant l'intervalle qui sépare la destruction de la réédification, pendant laquelle les hommes, dégoûtés du passé et incertains de l'avenir, ne sont plus unis par aucune foi, par aucune entreprise commune. Ce que nous avons dit de l'absence de moralité aux époques critiques ne doit s'entendre que de la seconde des deux périodes qu'elles comprennent, mais non point de la première, non point des hommes qui y figurent et qui, par une sorte d'inconséquence, prêchent la haine par amour, appellent à la destruction en croyant édifier, provoquent le désordre parce qu'ils désirent l'ordre, établissent l'esclavage sur l'autel qu'ils élèvent à la liberté. Ceux-là . . . sachons les admirer, plaignons-les seulement d'avoir été soumis à la mission terrible qu'ils ont remplie avec dévouement, avec amour pour l'humanité; plaignons-les, car ils étaient nés pour aimer, et toute leur vie a été consacrée à la haine.'[2]

In its tragic climax Futurism expresses itself as Satanism.

'The essence of the belief is that the World Order is evil and a lie; goodness and truth are persecuted rebels. . . . The belief has been held by many Christian saints and martyrs, and notably by the author of the Apocalypse. But we should notice that it is diametrically opposed to the teaching of almost all the great moral philosophers. Plato, Aristotle and the Stoics, St. Augustine and St. Thomas Aquinas, Kant and J. S. Mill, and Comte and T. H. Green, all argue or assume that there exists in some sense a Cosmos or Divine Order; that what is good is in harmony with this order, and what is bad is in discord against it. I notice that one of the Gnostic schools[3] in Hippolytus the Church Father actually defines Satan as "The Spirit who works against the Cosmic Powers":[4] the rebel or protestant who counteracts the will of the whole, and tries to thwart the community of which he is a member.'[5]

This inevitable ultimate outcome of the spirit of revolution is

---

[1] Compare the work here being quoted, vol. xli, pp. 87–8.—A.J.T.
[2] Bazard: 'Exposition de la Doctrine Saint-Simonienne' in Œuvres Complètes de Saint-Simon et d'Enfantin, vol. xlii (Paris 1877, Leroux), pp. 18 and 20–1.
[3] The school of Saturnilus of Antioch, a contemporary of Basileides.—A.J.T.
[4] Ἄγγελον ἀντιπράττοντα τοῖς κοσμικοῖς (Hippolytus: Refutatio Omnium Haeresium, edited by Duncker, L., and Schneidewin, F. G. (Göttingen 1859, Dieterich), Book VII, chap. 28).
[5] Murray, Gilbert: 'Satanism and the World Order' in Essays and Addresses (London 1921, Allen & Unwin), p. 203.

an accepted commonplace among all men and women who are not themselves revolutionaries;[1] and it is not difficult to lay our finger on historic illustrations of the working of this spiritual law.

For example, in the Syriac Society—both in its Iranian and in its Syrian wing—the Messianic form of Futurism made its first appearance as a positive attempt to follow the way of Gentleness. Instead of persisting in a disastrous attempt to maintain his political independence here and now against the assaults of Assyrian militarism, the Israelite, like the Mede, bowed his neck to a present political yoke and reconciled himself to this painful act of resignation by transferring all his political treasure to the hope of a saviour-king who was to arise and restore the fallen national kingdom at some hidden future date. When we trace out the history of this Messianic Hope in the Jewish community,[2] we find that it worked in favour of Gentleness for more than four hundred years—from 586 B.C., when the Jews were carried away into a Babylonish captivity by Nebuchadnezzar, until 168 B.C., when they were subjected to a Hellenizing persecution by Antiochus Epiphanes.[3] The first Jewish martyrs who gave their lives for Judaism in its three-hundred-years-long struggle with Hellenism all suffered and died without offering any physical resistance. Yet the discord between a confidently expected mundane future and an excruciatingly experienced mundane present resolved itself in Violence in the end. The martyrdom of Eleazar and the Seven Brethren was followed, within two years, by the armed insurrection of Judas Maccabaeus; and the Maccabees inaugurated that long line of ever more fanatically militant Jewish Zealots—the innumerable Theudases and Judases of Galilee—whose violence reached its appalling climax in the Satanic Jewish *émeutes* of A.D. 66–70 and 115–17 and 132–5.[4]

[1] It is not surprising to find this commonplace expressed with a classic French precision—'La révolution est satanique dans son essence'—by so militant a counter-revolutionary as Joseph de Maistre. Sombart has taken the same theme as his text for a definition of 'Revolutionismus':

'I am using this term to describe a settled spiritual attitude which seeks to confer upon Luciferism a recognition in principle and an application in practice. In entering into this idea the Revolution ceases to be what it originally was—simply a means to an end —and becomes an end in itself. . . . The revolutionary *must* not concern himself with the question of shaping the Future, because that would cripple his revolutionary energy. He may not think about construction; he must devote himself exclusively to the task of sabotage.'

The writer of this Study owes both these quotations to Curtius, E. R.: *Deutscher Geist in Gefahr* (second edition: Stuttgart and Berlin 1933, Deutsche Verlags-Anstalt), p. 38.

It will be seen that, when Futurism rankles into Satanism, it defeats its own original purpose.

[2] For this history see further V. C (i) (d) 9 (γ), vol. vi, pp. 120–32, below.

[3] See further V. C (i) (d) 9 (β), vol. vi, pp. 103–5, below.

[4] See V. C (i) (c) 2, pp. 68 and 73, above. For the militancy into which Zoroastrianism likewise eventually fell in the Age of the Sasanidae, see II. D (v), vol. ii, p. 203; II. D (vii), vol. ii, pp. 285–7 and 374; and V. C (i) (c) 3, in the present volume, p. 216, above; and V. C (i) (c) 2, Annex I, pp. 578–9, and V. C (i) (d) 6 (δ), Annex, pp. 659–61, below.

The nemesis of Futurism, which is illustrated by this classic Jewish case, is not unfamiliar; but it is perhaps more surprising to find Archaism being overtaken by the same nemesis at the end of its own apparently opposite path; for, so far from being a commonplace, it may seem something of a paradox to suggest that a pandemonium of Violence is the inevitable outcome of this retrograde movement likewise. Nevertheless the facts of history show that our paradox is as true as our commonplace; and, in anticipation of a survey of the facts, we may point the truth by citing, here again, a single classic case.

In the history of the political disintegration of the Hellenic Society the first statesmen to take the archaistic road were the Eurypontid King Agis IV in the Lacedaemonian commonwealth and in the Roman commonwealth the Tribune of the Plebs Tiberius Gracchus;[1] and there was a singular resemblance in character, as well as in policy, between the Roman and the Spartiate reformer. They were both of them men of unusual sensitiveness and unusual gentleness; and, born (as they both were) into an age of distress and discord, they both set themselves the political task of righting a social wrong, and thereby averting a social catastrophe, through a return to what they believed to have been the ancestral constitution of the commonwealth in the already half legendary 'Golden Age' before the breakdown. Their aim was the restoration of concord and the preservation of peace; yet, because their archaistic policy was an attempt to reverse the current of social life, it inevitably led them into a course of Violence which was contrary both to their policy and to their êthos; and the gentleness of their spirit, which moved them to sacrifice their lives rather than go to extremes in combating the fiercer Counter-Violence which their own reluctant Violence had swiftly provoked, did not avail to arrest the avalanche of Violence which they had unintentionally set in motion. Their self-sacrifice merely inspired a successor to take up their work and seek to carry it to success by a ruthless use of the Violence in which the martyr had shown himself half-hearted. The gentle Eurypontid King Agis IV was followed by the violent Agiad King Cleomenes III; the gentle Roman Tribune Tiberius Gracchus by his violent brother Gaius. And this tragic sequence was not the end of the story; for the ruthlessness of Gaius and Cleomenes was only temporarily and superficially successful in

---

[1] These two historical representatives of the Hellenic dominant minority both had posthumous literary careers as heroes of 'folk-tales' which took shape in the underworld of the Hellenic internal proletariat (see V. C (ii) (a), Annex II, passim, in vol. vi, below). For their political careers 'in real life' see Part III. A, vol. iii, pp. 76–7; IV. C (iii) (b) 9, vol. iv, p. 205; IV. C (iii) (c) 3 (β), vol. iv, p. 508; and V. C (i) (c) 2, in the present volume, p. 78, above; and V. C (i) (d) 8 (α), vol. vi, pp. 52–3, and V. C (ii) (a), vol. vi, pp. 219–20, below.

achieving Tiberius's and Agis' frustrated purpose. In either case the successor's career merely illustrated the truth that 'all they that take the sword shall perish with the sword'[1] whether they draw it right out and lay about them, or hold it back, half-drawn, in the scabbard. The ultimate result of the violent successor's ruthless work was simply to give fresh momentum to the wave of Violence which his gentle predecessor had undesignedly set in motion. Between them, the two archaizing Heracleidae and the two archaizing Gracchi let loose a spate of Violence which did not subside[2] until it had swept away the whole fabric of the commonwealth which the would-be reformers had sought to save.[3]

Our Hellenic illustration of the fruits of Archaism and our Syriac illustration of the fruits of Futurism perhaps demonstrate, between them, our thesis that both these two variations upon the movement of transference of the field of action end invariably and inevitably in disastrous Violence; for this is their outcome even when they are set in motion by leaders who, by temperament as well as out of policy, are sincere believers in Gentleness. If we now pursue our Hellenic and our Syriac story into the next chapter, we shall find that the pandemonium of Violence which had been let loose by the cult of Archaism in the one case and of Futurism in the other was eventually allayed by an astonishing resurrection of that very spirit of Gentleness which the surging tide of Violence had overborne and submerged and silenced. In the Hellenic dominant minority the gang of conquerors and wastrels and hang-

---

[1] Matt. xxvi. 52. See V. C (i) (c) 2, p. 78, above; and V. C (i) (d) 8 (α), vol. vi, pp. 52–3; V. C (ii) (a), vol. vi, p. 178; and V. C (ii) (a), Annex II, vol. vi, pp. 391–2 and 527–8, below.

[2] For Cleomenes' ultra-violent successor Nabis and Gaius's ultra-violent successor Sulla see V. C (ii) (a), vol. vi, p. 220, below.

[3] It is strange that the moral of Cleomenes' and Gaius's failure was not observed and taken to heart by Machiavelli, who searched the scriptures of Hellenic history with such diligence and such acumen for illustrations of his empirically established social 'laws'. In this case the Florentine philosopher's insight failed him; for there is a passage in *The Prince* in which he expounds the precise argument for the efficacy of Violence which was drawn by Cleomenes from the history of Agis, and by Gaius from the history of Tiberius, with such fatal consequences for the policies of both of the two 'armed prophets' of the Hellenic dominant minority who acted on this line of reasoning:

'All the armed prophets have been victorious, while the unarmed prophets have come to grief, because . . . the nature of the peoples is inconstant, and it is easy to persuade them of a thing, but difficult to hold them to that persuasion. Accordingly it is expedient to be so equipped that, when their belief gives out, one will have it in one's power to make them believe by force. Moses, Cyrus, Theseus, and Romulus would not have been able to secure the observance of their constitutions very long if they had been unarmed—as may be inferred from what happened in our own times to Brother Girolamo Savonarola, who came to grief over his new dispensation because, when the multitude began to lose belief in it, Brother Girolamo himself lacked the means of either retaining his hold upon those who had once believed or compelling belief on the part of the unbelievers. No doubt the armed prophets encounter great difficulties, and they are assailed *en route* by all the dangers of their undertaking—dangers which it is their business to overcome by their efficiency—but, when once they have overcome them, and have begun to evoke veneration, thanks to having wiped out all their inveterate detractors, they then remain puissant, secure, honoured and happy ever after.'—Machiavelli, Niccolò: *Il Principe*, chap. 6.

men who worked their will upon a distracted world during the last two centuries B.C. begot, as we have observed,[1] a breed of public servants with the conscience and the ability to organize and maintain a universal state; and at the same time the epigoni of the violent-handed archaizing reformers turned into a school of aristocratic philosophers[2]—Arria, Caecina Paetus, Thrasea Paetus, Seneca, Helvidius Priscus, Arulenus Rusticus, Herennius Senecio —who took no satisfaction in the exercise of their hereditary dominance even in the public interest, and who carried this abdication to the point of obediently committing suicide when the word of command was uttered by a Claudius or a Nero or a Vespasian or a Domitian. Similarly, in the Syriac wing of the Hellenic internal proletariat, the fiasco of the Hasmonaean attempt to establish by force of arms a Messianic Kingdom in This World—in the trough between the ebbing wave of the Hellenic Power of the Seleucidae and the oncoming wave of the Hellenic Power of Rome[3]—was followed by the triumph of a King of the Jews whose servants were forbidden to fight because his Kingdom was not of This World,[4] while in the next generation, on a narrower range of spiritual vision, the savagely heroic forlorn hope of the militant Zealots John of Gischala and Simon of Gerasa was retrieved, in the hour of annihilation, by the sublimely heroic non-resistance of the Rabbi Johanan ben Zakkai.[5] How was it that, in both these cases, a tide of Violence which seemed to have swept away every barrier in its path was thus, after all, brought to a standstill and reversed? In either case the miraculous reversion from Violence to Gentleness can be traced to a change in ways of life. In the souls of the Roman fraction of the Hellenic dominant minority the ideal of Archaism had been supplanted by that of Detachment; in the souls of the Jewish fraction of the Hellenic internal proletariat the ideal of Futurism had been replaced by that of Transfiguration.

What is the nature of these two ideals, which—in the two instances in which we have just been watching them make their unexpected appearance and produce their amazing effect—are historically later arrivals upon the terrestrial scene than the ideals of Archaism and Futurism? Their posteriority in point of time would seem to bear witness to their superiority in spiritual worth; for,

[1] See V. C (i) (c) 1, pp. 38–9, above. For the corresponding breed in other dominant minorities see the same chapter, pp. 47–52, above.

[2] See V. C (i) (d) 3, p. 405, and V. C (ii) (a), vol. vi, p. 250, below.

[3] The hard fact that the Hasmonaeans owed their ephemeral military and political success to a passing accident in the political history of the Hellenic World, and not to the strength of their own right arm, was perceived and pointed out by Tacitus (*Histories*, Book V, chap. 8): 'Iudaei Macedonibus invalidis, Parthis nondum adultis (et Romani procul erant), sibi ipsi reges imposuere.' The explanation was as deeply humiliating for the Jewish futurists as the fact itself was momentarily fortunate for them.

[4] John xviii. 36.   [5] See V. C (i) (c) 2, pp. 75–6, above.

whereas we have seen Gentleness degenerating into Violence under the baneful auspices of Archaism and Futurism, we see Violence giving place again to Gentleness when the spirits of Detachment and Transfiguration begin to move upon the face of the angry waters. Perhaps we can apprehend the distinctive qualities of these two gentle ways of life in the same view as their historical geneses if we approach each of them first through the personality and the life-history of a notable convert: for example, Cato Minor the Roman archaist who became a Stoic philosopher,[1] and Simon Bar Jonas the Jewish futurist who became Peter the disciple of Jesus.[2] In both of these great men there was a streak of spiritual blindness which obscured their greatness by misdirecting their energies so long as they were pursuing the respective Utopias to the service of which they had first sought to dedicate themselves. And in each of them the long baffled and bewildered soul was enabled, through its conversion to a new way of life, to realize at last its highest potentialities.

As the Quixotic champion of a romantically conceived Roman πάτριος πολιτεία which had never existed in any past age 'in real life',[3] Cato was almost a figure of fun. In the politics of a generation which he obstinately refused to take as he found it, he was perpetually chasing the shadow and missing the substance; and, when at last he stumbled into playing a leading part in a civil war for the outbreak of which he himself bore no small share of unadmitted responsibility, his political make-believe was doomed to suffer a shattering disillusionment whatever the event might be, since the régime which would have been the consequence of a Republican victory would have been at least as repugnant to Cato's archaistic ideal as the eventually victorious Caesarean dictatorship. In this dilemma, which seemed to offer Cato merely a choice between alternative roads to frustration and failure, the Quixotic politician was redeemed from ineptitude by the heroic philosopher. The man who had lived as an archaist in vain now met his death as a Stoic to such good purpose that, after all, he gave Caesar—and Caesar's successors for more than a century after him—more trouble than all the rest of the Republicans together. The story of Cato's last hours—sublimely magnificent and at the same time profoundly moving—made an impression upon his contemporaries which can be recaptured down to this day by any reader of Plutarch's narrative. With the instinct of genius

[1] For Cato Minor see further V. C (i) (d) 3, p. 405, and V. C (ii) (a) ,vol. vi, p. 250, below.
[2] Peter's conversion from the way of Violence to the way of Gentleness has been touched upon by anticipation in V. C (i) (c) 2, p. 74, above.
[3] For this expression of institutional Archaism see further V. C (i) (d) 8 (α), vol. vi, pp. 52–6, below.

Caesar apprehended the gravity of the blow which had been dealt
to his cause by the Stoic death of an antagonist whom he had never
found it necessary to take very seriously as a live politician; and,
in the midst of the titanic labour of reconstructing a world while
he was stamping out the embers of a civil war, the militarily triumphant dictator found time to reply to Cato's sword with Caesar's
pen—the only weapon, as this versatile genius knew well, which
might avail to ward off an attack that had been transferred from
the military to the philosophic plane by Cato's disconcerting gesture of turning his sword against his own breast. Yet Caesar, for
all his versatility, was unable to cope with the Cato who had struck
this tremendous parting stroke; and Cato's death irresistibly produced the result which Caesar had feared. It gave birth to a school
of philosophic opponents of Caesarism who were inspired by their
founder's example to put the new tyranny out of countenance by
removing themselves, with their own hand, from a situation which
they would not accept and which they could not mend.[1]

As for Peter, his Futurism seemed at first as incorrigible as
Cato's Archaism. The first of the disciples to hail Jesus as the
Messiah,[2] he was also the foremost in protesting against his
acknowledged Master's consequent revelation that his Messianic
Kingdom was not to be a Jewish version of the Iranian world-
empire of Cyrus;[3] and so, having earned a special blessing as the
reward for his impulsive faith, he immediately drew down upon
himself a crushing rebuke for his obtuse and aggressive insistence
that the Master's vision of his own kingdom must conform to the
disciple's *idée fixe*.

'Get thee behind me, Satan; thou art an offence unto me. For thou
savourest not the things that be of God, but those that be of men.'[4]

Satanism, in Hippolytus's meaning of the term,[5] was indeed the
essence of Peter's own untutored Messianic Hope. For, even when
his error had been held up before his eyes by his Master's terrible
reproof, the lesson made so little effect upon the stiff-necked
disciple that he failed again under the next test. When he was
chosen out to be one of the three witnesses of the Transfiguration,
he immediately took the vision of Moses and Elias standing at his
Master's side as the signal for the beginning of a *Befreiungskrieg*,
and betrayed his prosaic misconception of what the vision meant
by proposing to build on the spot the nucleus of a camp[6] of the
kind that the Theudases and Judases of Galilee were wont to

---

[1] See p. 390, above, and V. C (ii) (*a*), vol. vi, p. 250, below.
[2] Matt. xvi. 16 = Mark viii. 29 = Luke ix. 20.
[3] Matt. xvi. 22 (= Mark viii. 32), quoted in V. C (i) (*c*) 2, on p. 74, above.
[4] Matt. xvi. 23 = Mark viii. 33.   [5] See p. 386, above.
[6] Matt. xvii. 4 = Mark ix. 5 = Luke ix. 33.

establish in the wilderness during the brief interval of grace before the Roman authorities received intelligence of their activities and sent out a flying column of troops to disperse them. At the sound of this jarring note the vision vanished in an echo of admonition to accept the Messiah's own revelation of the Messiah's path.[1] Yet this second lesson was still not enough to open Peter's eyes. Even at the climax of his Master's earthly career—when all that the Master himself had foretold was patently coming true—the incorrigible futurist drew his sword to fight in the garden of Gethsemane;[2] and he was so utterly confounded by the decisive veto with which his Master quashed his instinctive recourse to Violence once again[3] that he rebounded from a forlorn hope into a dastardly betrayal.[4] Indeed, even after this crowning experience of his life, when the Crucifixion and the Resurrection and the Ascension had taught him at last that Christ's Kingdom was not of This World, Peter was still fain to believe that even in this transfigured kingdom the franchise must be restricted to the Jews, just as it would have been in the futurist's Messianic Utopia—as though a society that embraced God in Heaven as its King could be bounded on God's Earth by a frontier excluding from it all but one of the tribes of God's human creatures and children. In one of the last scenes in which Peter is displayed to us in the Acts of the Apostles, we see him characteristically protesting against the clear command which accompanied the vision of the sheet let down from Heaven.[5] Yet Peter does not give place to Paul as the protagonist in the story until the narrative has recorded his comprehension, at last, of a truth which Paul the Pharisee had apprehended in a trice through a single overwhelming spiritual experience. The long work of Peter's enlightenment was completed when the vision on the roof was followed by the arrival of Cornelius's messengers at the gate.[6] And in his confession of faith in Cornelius's house at Caesarea[7] and his defence of his action there before the bar of the Jewish-Christian community upon his return to Jerusalem[8] Peter preached the Kingdom of Heaven in words that would have drawn no reproof from the Christ.

What are these two ways of life which produced these vast spiritual effects when they were respectively adopted in place of Archaism by Cato and in place of Futurism by Peter? In peering into spiritual depths which may prove unfathomable, let us begin by taking note of the common differences between Detachment

[1] Matt. xvii. 5 = Mark ix. 7 = Luke ix. 35.
[2] Matt. xxvi. 51 = Mark xiv. 47 = Luke xxii. 49–50 = John xvii. 10.
[3] Matt. xxvi. 52–4 = Mark xiv. 48 = Luke xxii. 51 = John xviii. 11.
[4] Matt. xxvi. 69–75 = Mark xiv. 66–72 = Luke xxii. 54–62 = John xviii. 15–18 and 25–7.   [5] Acts x. 9–16.   [6] Acts x. 17–33.
[7] Acts x. 34–48.   [8] Acts xi. 1–18.

and Transfiguration on the one hand and Archaism and Futurism on the other, and then go on to examine how Detachment and Transfiguration differ from each other.

Transfiguration and Detachment alike differ from both Futurism and Archaism in substituting a genuine change in spiritual clime, and not a mere transfer in the Time-dimension, for the particular form of transference of the field of action from the Macrocosm to the Microcosm which we have found to be the criterion of the growth of a civilization. The kingdoms that are their respective goals are both of them 'otherworldly' in the sense that neither of them is an imaginary past or future state of mundane existence. This common 'otherworldliness', however, is their only point of resemblance; and in every other respect they present a contrast to one another.

The way of life which we have called 'Detachment' has been given a variety of names by various schools of adepts. From a disintegrating Hellenic World the Stoics withdrew into an 'Invulnerability' ('Aπάθεια)[1] and the Epicureans into an 'Imperturbability' ('Aταραξία). From a disintegrating Indic World the Buddhists withdrew into an 'Immutability' (Asamskṛta) or an 'Unruffledness' (Nirvāna)—a state in which the wind is hushed and the fire extinct. The positive content of the concept of Nirvāna is even harder to apprehend than that of its Hellenic counterparts; for the authoritative descriptions of it define it as being neither one nor other of successive pairs of opposites—for example, neither Permanence nor Annihilation—and in the Buddhist philosophy the question 'whether after death a tathāgata (a released person) exists or not, whether he exists and does not exist, whether he is neither existent nor non-existent', is one of those questions that are dogmatically declared to be undetermined.[2] A positive apprehension of the meaning of 'Detachment' is perhaps, however, not only impossible but also unnecessary; for the four names—two Greek and two Sanskrit—for this way of life which we have just cited are all of them abstract substantives with a negative prefix; and it is the negativeness of the way that is the point of it.

It is a way that leads out of This World; its goal is an asylum; and the fact that that asylum excludes This World is the feature

[1] The connotation of the Greek word ἀπάθεια, in its Stoic usage, is perhaps more expressively conveyed in English by the word 'invulnerability' than by the word 'apathy'; for, though 'apathy' is the etymological counterpart of ἀπάθεια, the Greek word has changed colour in the process of being Anglicized. 'Apathy' has come to mean an insensibility that is neither an effort nor a virtue, whereas ἀπάθεια means a spiritual 'invulnerability' which can be neither achieved nor maintained without the exercise of a self-discipline of an almost heroic severity.

[2] Thomas, E. J.: The History of Buddhist Thought (London 1933, Kegan Paul), p. 124. The whole of chapter 10, 'Release and Nirvana', is illuminating in the light which it throws upon the field of our present inquiry.

that makes it attractive—as the goal has to be if the philosophic traveller is to make the renunciations and subject himself to the disciplines which are the indispensable conditions for pursuing his arduous and depressing spiritual journey. The impulse that carries him along is a push of aversion and not a pull of desire. He is shaking from off his feet the dust of the City of Destruction —'The worldling says: "O beloved City of Cecrops"; and shalt *thou* not say: "O beloved City of Zeus"?'[1]—but Marcus's 'City of Zeus' is not the same as Augustine's *Civitas Dei* which is 'the city of the Living God',[2] and the journey is a 'withdrawal according to plan' rather than a pilgrimage inspired by faith. For the philosopher a successful escape from This World is the true and ultimate end of Man; and for this reason the philosopher, if he faces the whole of the truth, must confess that at bottom it does not really matter what he does with himself, or whether he does anything at all, or whether such a thing as his self any longer exists, when once he has crossed the threshold of his city of refuge. The Hellenic philosophers pictured the state of the liberated sage as one of blissful contemplation (θεωρία)[3]—the intellectual bliss of admiring the form of some perfect geometrical figure or 'watching the stars go round',[4] or the emotional bliss of an ecstatic union with the divine element in the Universe—and the earliest and greatest of them, who was born in the first generation after the breakdown, when the iron had not yet had time to enter right into their souls,[5] made a brave show of finding a supreme positive value in this 'otherworldly' condition or activity. Yet Plato himself, in the simile of the Cave, betrays a temptation to cherish the sunlit Other World for its negative value of being an *alibi* from this one;[6] Plotinus repudiates Plato's reluctant injunction to return from that world to this;[7] and Siddhārtha Gautama the Buddha frankly declares that, so long as all possibility of returning has been ruled out

[1] Marcus Aurelius Antoninus: *Meditations*, Book IV, chap. 23 (quoted above on p. 384 and again in V. C (i) (d) 7, Annex, vol. vi, p. 335, below).

[2] Hebrews xii. 22.

[3] See III. C (ii) (b), vol. iii, p. 253, above.

[4] Bevan, Edwyn: *Stoics and Sceptics* (Oxford 1913, Clarendon Press), p. 111, citing Seneca, L. Annaeus: *Ad Marciam de Consolatione*, chap. 25.

[5] Plato was born *circa* 430 B.C. (i.e. on the morrow of the outbreak of the Peloponnesian War), but he lived on till *circa* 347 B.C. (i.e. to the eve of the birth of the fourth generation to be born since the catastrophe); and, though, even in his old age, he may still have remained unseared at heart, he never recovered from the shock which he had suffered in his early manhood when the disastrous ending of a twenty-seven-years-long fratricidal war had been followed by the judicial murder of Plato's master Socrates. One effect of this shock can be observed in the archaistic antedating of the imaginary dates of Plato's dialogues to the extent of about half a lifetime (see V. C (i) (d) 8 (γ), vol. vi, p. 79, below).

[6] See the passages quoted from *The Republic* in III. C (ii) (b), vol. iii, pp. 249–52, above.

[7] See the passage quoted from Monsieur Henri Bergson in III. C (ii) (b), vol. ii, p. 254, above.

once for all, the nature of the alternative state in which the *tathā-gata* has come to rest is a matter of no consequence.

This unknowable and neutral *Nirvāna* or 'City of Zeus', which is the goal of the philosophic movement of Detachment, is the very antithesis of the Kingdom of Heaven or *Civitas Dei*, which is entered by way of the religious experience of Transfiguration. While the philosophic 'Other World' is in essence a world that is exclusive of ours on Earth, the divine 'Other World' transcends the earthly life of Man without ceasing to embrace it.

'And when he was demanded of the Pharisees, when the Kingdom of God should come, he answered them and said: "The Kingdom of God cometh not with observation; neither shall they say *Lo here!* or *Lo there!* for, behold, the Kingdom of God is within[1] you." '[2]

The meaning of this passage in the Gospel according to Saint Luke may be expressed in a simile from the ever-changing landscape of the Physical Cosmos as this happens to be depicted at the moment by our Western men-of-science. We may say that the Kingdom of This World is possessed and informed by the *Civitas Dei* as Matter is said to be penetrated and shot through by Radiation. The realms are not external to one another in the dimensions of Space and Time, since only the lower of the two is confined to these dimensions, whereas the higher simultaneously occupies and transcends them—and, in virtue of this all-pervasiveness, coexists with the Kingdom of This World all the time and everywhere. Accordingly the soul that aspires to rise to the higher realm from the lower will find its way, not by seeking to reduce to zero the dimensions of its former spiritual existence, but rather by seeking to expand them to infinity. Just as, by the scientist's sleight of hand, the human ear that is wont to hear sounds conveyed through the medium of Matter can be attuned to catch the sounds that are conveyed by Radiation, so, by God's grace, the Soul can be made aware of the eternal omnipresence of God—a presence which per-

---

[1] The original Greek words ἐντὸς ὑμῶν may mean either 'within you' or 'among you', but this ambiguity does not affect the significance of the passage for our present purpose. On either interpretation the Kingdom of God is represented as existing in This World as well as outside it. The words would also appear to imply that the immanence of the Kingdom of God in This World, in the hearts of human beings who are its citizens, is a state of things which is present—and, indeed, perpetual. This reading of the passage is contested, however, by A. von Gall in Βασιλεία τοῦ Θεοῦ (Heidelberg 1926, Winter), pp. 474-5. Von Gall—taking ἐντὸς ὑμῶν to mean 'among you'—reads a future meaning into the present tense of the concluding sentence ('before you know where you are, you will find the Kingdom already there'), and he maintains that Jesus (as presented in this passage) agrees with the Pharisees in regarding the advent of the Kingdom as a future event (and not a present reality). According to von Gall, Jesus differs from the Pharisees merely in declaring that this future advent of the Kingdom will take the form of a sudden *fait accompli*, which will take the living generation by surprise, instead of being advertised in advance by signs and portents.—A.J.T.

[2] Luke xvii. 20-21.

vades This World just in virtue of transcending it—through being rapt into a supra-mundane mode of spiritual being.[1]

It will be seen that the *Civitas Dei* is as positive in its nature as the 'City of Zeus' is negative, and that, whereas the way of Detachment, which leads to the 'City of Zeus', is a sheer movement of withdrawal, the way of Transfiguration, which leads to the *Civitas Dei*, is a movement of withdrawal-and-return[2]—though this on a different spiritual plane from any of those on which we have seen this movement taking place in the growths of civilizations.

This completes our preliminary review of the alternative ways of behaviour, feeling, and life which are opened up by that Schism in the Soul which is always to be found at the heart of the disintegration of any body social. If we are to be faithful to our well-established method, our next task will be to make an empirical survey of each of these spiritual phenomena as they have manifested themselves in the disintegrations of as many civilizations as have left a sufficiently intimate record of their 'members'' experience. But before we launch out on to this ocean we may pause for a moment to take our bearings by observing the links between the history of the Soul and the history of Society.

Granting, *ex hypothesi*, that every spiritual experience must be that of some individual human being, shall we find that certain experiences, among those which we have been reviewing, are peculiar to members of certain fractions of a disintegrating society? We shall find, if we cast a glance back at our muster of experiences with this question in our minds, that all the four personal ways of behaviour and feeling—a passive *abandon* and an active self-control, a passive sense of drift and an active sense of sin—can be detected in members of the Dominant Minority and members of the Proletariat alike. On the other hand, when we come to the social ways of behaviour and feeling, we shall have to distinguish, for our present purpose, between the passive and the active pair. The two passive social phenomena—the lapse into truancy and the surrender to a sense of promiscuity—are apt to appear first in the ranks of the Proletariat and to spread from there to the ranks of the Dominant Minority, which usually succumbs to the sickness of 'proletarianization' in so far as it has not already perished through self-inflicted violence. Conversely, the two active social phenomena—the quest of martyrdom and the awakening to a sense of unity—are apt to appear first in the ranks of the Dominant

---

[1] For this and other similes which may perhaps imperfectly convey at least some of the aspects of the relation between This World and the *Civitas Dei*, see V. C (i) (*d*) 11, vol. vi, pp. 157–61, below.

[2] For this likeness and difference between the two movements see also III. C (ii) (*b*), vol. iii, pp. 248–63, above, and V. C (i) (*e*), vol. vi, pp. 170–1, below.

Minority and to spread from there to the ranks of the Proletariat, where Agis' gentle martyrdom is emulated by a proletarian Eleazar, and Cleomenes' violent martyrdom by a proletarian Judas Maccabaeus, while the proletarian who hungers after a cosmic society finds his equivalent for a philosophic *Cosmopolis* in a religious catholicism. Finally, when we consider our four alternative ways of life, we shall find that here, conversely, the passive pair are apt to be associated in the first instance with the Dominant Minority and the active pair with the Proletariat. Archaism and Detachment make their epiphany in the ranks of the Dominant Minority; and, while Archaism finds adherents among the External Proletariat as well, it is never adopted by the Internal Proletariat, and Detachment never by either section of the Proletariat, Internal or External. On the other hand, Futurism and Transfiguration make their epiphany in the ranks of the Proletariat and propagate themselves from this starting-point—Futurism gaining converts from the Dominant Minority among the baffled and disillusioned devotees of an Archaism that has failed to bring salvation, while Transfiguration works its miracle in any human soul that awakens to the presence, and aspires to the citizenship, of the *Civitas Dei*.

From these historical associations between the several ways of behaviour, feeling, and life and the several fractions of a society in disintegration we may gain some knowledge of the relations in which the spiritual experiences and activities stand to one another. In general we can see that the passive reactions are apt to be the more barren and the active the more fruitful. For example, at one end of the scale *abandon* leads nowhere, whereas self-control is a constant element in all the virtues which the disintegrations of civilizations bring to flower; and similarly, at the other end of the scale, the life of Detachment, in which Passivity achieves its spiritual *chef d'œuvre*, is put out of countenance by the supremely active life of Transfiguration. Again, when we analyse the components of Detachment, with an eye to distinguishing the points in which it can bear comparison with Transfiguration from the points in which it reveals its inadequacy, we find that Detachment rises to the heights of Transfiguration in its readiness for martyrdom and in its conviction of sin, but is depressed to a lower spiritual level through a failure to rid itself of a clinging taint of truancy and Fatalism when it succumbs to an almost pardonable shrinking from the duty of returning to the night-bound Cave, and to an almost admirable acceptance of the inexorable laws of an impersonal Universe. Here we see two passive ways of behaviour and feeling acting as drags upon their two active counterparts; and there is a corresponding contrast between the effects of the passive surrender to a sense of promiscuity and the active awakening to a sense of unity. A horror of the melting-pot inspires the two forlorn hopes of an Archaism and a Futurism in quest of Utopia; a yearning after a harmony that is not of This World inspires both the sublime failure of Detachment and the miraculous triumph of Transfiguration.

2. 'Abandon' and Self-Control

The particular manifestations of *abandon* and self-control which are characteristic of societies in disintegration are perhaps rather difficult to identify, just because these two ways of personal be-haviour are apt to be exhibited by human beings in every variety of social circumstances. In the life of the primitive societies, for instance, in the static condition in which alone we have knowledge of it,[1] it is already possible to distinguish an orgiastic and an ascetic vein; and in this primitive life, with its cyclic rhythm, the two antithetical moods may be seen predominating in alternation with one another, according to the season, in the tribe's ceremonial corporate expression of its members' emotions. The same two moods can likewise be seen working in harmony—though this on a more intricate pattern and in a more highly sophisticated spirit—in the life of civilizations in the growth stage; and it is in this stage that their interaction is creative. It is only when we come to examine civilizations in their disintegration that we find the same two ways of personal behaviour still indeed both at work, but now at odds in an unreconciled opposition instead of playing in with one another in a creatively harmonious rotation.

In the histories of declining civilizations the phenomenon of *abandon* in our precise meaning of a way of personal behaviour is not, of course, to be confused or equated with the whole of that welter of demoralization of conduct and inversion of ranks and roles and values which is the most prominent of the outward visible signs of any process of breakdown and disintegration.[2] *Abandon*, as we have defined it,[3] implies something more than a mere external rack and ruin. It means a state of mind in which antinomianism is accepted—consciously or unconsciously, in theory or in prac-tice—as a substitute for creativeness.

Examples of *abandon* in this inward spiritual sense can perhaps be identified with least uncertainty if we try to take them in a

---

[1] See I. C (iii) (e), vol. i, pp. 179–80, and Part II. B, vol. i, pp. 190–5, above.

[2] See, for example, the picture of the Egyptiac 'Time of Troubles' that is given in a passage, quoted above in IV. C (iii) (c) 2 (β), vol. iv, pp. 410–11, from *The Admonitions of a Prophet*; and the corresponding pictures of the Hellenic 'Time of Troubles' (in two successive phases) that are given in a passage of Thucydides quoted above in V. C (i) (c) 2, pp. 59–60, and in a passage of Polybius quoted above in IV. C (iii) (c) 3 (β), vol. iv, pp. 505–6.   [3] In V. C (i) (d) 1, p. 377, above.

single synoptic view side by side with examples of that self-control which is the alternative substitute for creativeness in the same ages of social decline.

In the Hellenic 'Time of Troubles', for instance, in the first generation after the breakdown, a pair of contrasted incarnations of *abandon* and self-control are presented to us in Plato's portraits of Alcibiades and Socrates in *The Symposium* and of Thrasymachus and Socrates in *The Republic*—Alcibiades, the slave of his own passion, standing for *abandon* in practice, and Thrasymachus, the advocate of *Faustrecht*, for the same mood in theory. It is in the next chapter of the Hellenic story that we find the exponents of each of the two attempts at 'self-expression' in lieu of creation seeking an authoritative sanction for their respective ways of behaviour by claiming that these are ways of 'living according to Nature'.

This merit was claimed for the mood of *abandon* by those vulgar hedonists who took in vain, and brought into disrepute, the name of Epicurus, and who for this offence were chidden by the censure of an Epicurean poet who had inherited the genuine austerity of his Master.

> Hoc etiam faciunt ubi discubuere tenentque
> pocula saepe homines et inumbrant ora coronis,
> ex animo ut dicant: 'Brevis hic est fructu homullis;
> iam fuerit neque post unquam revocare licebit.'[1]

On the other side we see the sanction of 'naturalness' being claimed for the ascetic life of self-control in the crudely literal practice of the Cynics and, with a greater refinement, by the Stoic practitioners of a kindred philosophy. In all things that were 'indifferent'—and for a Stoic nothing was either good or evil in itself except the rightness or wrongness of his own will—it was the whole duty of the sage to mortify those human desires which were accepted by the hedonist as the promptings of Nature; and to carry this mortification to a degree at which the sage became able to accept, as natural, not the impulses of the hedonist's 'natural man', but the trials, whatever they might be, that were put upon him by the chances and changes of this mortal life. The course of Nature, thus conceived, must be borne by the Stoic sage with cheerfulness if he was capable of rising to this counsel of perfection, and at all events with calmness and tranquillity if he was to be accounted worthy of being numbered at all among the disciples of Zeno.

The melancholy vein of Stoic self-control is reflected in the *Meditations* of the philosopher-emperor Marcus Aurelius, whose philosophy never could quite brace him to bear on his lonely shoulders the Atlantean load of a collapsing world.

[1] Lucretius: *De Rerum Natura*, Book III, ll. 912–15.

'The power that rules within, when it is in tune with Nature, has an attitude towards events which enables it to adapt itself easily to any-thing—within the limits of possibility—that is presented to it. . . .'[1]

'Be like the headland against which the waves continually break; but the headland stands firm while the tormented waters sink to rest around it. . . .'[2]

'This infinitesimally short span of time is something to be passed through in tune with Nature and passed out of with a good grace—like an olive that falls when it is ripe with a blessing for Nature who has brought it forth and a gratitude to the tree which has borne it.'[3]

The temper to which the careworn Stoic emperor wistfully aspires in the last of the three sentences above quoted had been duly attained by the lame Stoic slave who had been the most conspicuous wearer of Zeno's mantle in the preceding generation.

'What else should we be doing, in public and in private, but singing the praises of the Godhead and speaking good of His name and attempting to express our thanks to Him? Digging or ploughing or eating, should we not ever be singing our hymn to God? . . . And, since most of you have gone blind, was it not meet that there should be somebody occupy-ing this place and singing the hymn to God on behalf of us all? And what else can I, a lame old man, do but sing the praises of God? Were I a nightingale, I would sing like a nightingale; or, were I a swan, I would sing like a swan. But I happen to be a being endowed with reason, and so I must sing the praises of God. This is my work, so I am doing it, and I will never desert this post so long as it continues to be assigned to me. And I call upon the rest of you to sing the same song. . . .'[4]

'And, when Death overtakes me, I hope to be found by him prac-tising what I preach, in order that I may be able to say to God: "Did I ever transgress Thy commandments? Did I ever use, for any other purposes than Thine, the talents or the senses or the innate ideas (ταῖς προλήψεσιν) that Thou gavest me? Did I ever reproach Thee? Did I ever blame Thy governance? I was sick, when that was Thy will (my fellows were sick likewise, but when *I* was sick, I did not rebel). By Thy will I knew poverty, but I rejoiced in it. I never bore rule, because it was never Thy will that I should; but I never desired it. Didst Thou ever see me turn sullen on that account? Was there ever an occasion on which I presented myself before Thee with other than a cheerful countenance, or without being ready for any command or signal that Thou mightest choose to give? And now it is Thy will that I should leave the festival, so I am taking my leave—with my heart full of gratitude to Thee, because Thou hast deigned to allow me to cele-brate the festival with Thee and to behold Thy works and to watch the course of Thy governance. When Death overtakes me, may these

---

[1] Marcus Aurelius Antoninus: *Meditations*, Book IV, chap. 1.
[2] Ibid., chap. 49.   [3] Ibid., chap. 48.
[4] Epictetus: *Dissertations*, Book I, chap. 16, §§ 15–16 and 19–21.

thoughts be in my mind and these words on my pen or on the page that my eyes are reading.'[1]

Such was the ascetic mastery over Nature that was attained, in the course of the disintegration of the Hellenic Society, by the noblest adepts of the Stoic school of philosophy. And in the final chapter of Hellenic history we can see the ascetic tradition of an expiring dominant minority blending with the less negative asceticism of the proletariat when the Hellenic philosophy, in its Neoplatonic close and climax, rises to a pitch of mystical feeling at which its dying song of praise to God comes almost into unison with the younger and stronger voice of Christianity.[2]

If we pass from the Hellenic to the Syriac World in its 'Time of Troubles', we shall find the same unreconciled opposition between *abandon* and self-control reappearing in the contrast between the sedately sceptical theory of the Book of Ecclesiastes and the piously ascetic practice of the monastic community of the Essenes. And in another field again, in the philosophic strife of the Sinic 'Time of Troubles', we shall see Yang Chu suffering Epicurus's fate of being exploited by hedonists[3] and at the same time castigated by moral disciplinarians who in the Sinic case were of the Confucian and Mencian school. Similarly, in a latter-day 'Time of Troubles' in Japan which preceded the enforcement of the peace of the Tokugawa Shogunate, the same antithesis reveals itself again in the clash between the abandoned immorality of the Japanese high politics of the age[4] and the almost inhumanly perfect self-dedication of the contemporary samurai to his feudal lord.

There is another group of civilizations—the Indic, the Babylonic, the Hittite, and the Mayan—which seem, as they disintegrate, to be reverting to the êthos of Primitive Man in their apparent insensibility to the yawning breadth of the gulf between the abandoned sexualism of their religion and the exaggerated asceticism

---

[1] Epictetus, op. cit., Book III, chap. 5, §§ 7–11. The second of the two passages here quoted reappears in Book IV, chap. 10, §§ 14–17, in the following variant:

'If, after this, Death overtakes me, it is sufficient for me if I am able to lift up my hands to God and say: "I have not neglected the talents that I received from Thee in order that I might perceive Thy governance and follow it. I have not disgraced Thee as far as it lay within me. Behold how I have used my senses and my innate ideas (ταῖς προλήψεσιν). Did I ever blame Thee? Did I ever take badly anything that happened, or wish that it had happened in some other way? Did I ever transgress the laws of my nature (μή τι τὰς σχέσεις παρέβην;)? Because Thou hast begotten me, I am grateful for what Thou hast given me. So long as I have been using that which is Thine, it has sufficed for me. Now take back that which is Thine own and assign it to whatever place Thou wilt. For everything was Thine; it was Thou that gavest me all that I had. Should one not be content to depart in this frame of mind? Or is there any better or fairer life, or happier death, than a life and death like these?'

[2] For this momentary *rapprochement* between Hellenic philosophy and Christianity see further V. C (i) (d) 6 (δ), pp. 550–3, below.

[3] For these Sinic hedonists see Waley, A.: *The Way and its Power: A Study of the Tao Tê Ching and its Place in Chinese Thought* (London 1934, Allen & Unwin), pp. 39–43.

[4] See V. C (i) (c) 2, pp. 95–103, above, and V. C (ii) (b), vol. vi, pp. 303–5, below.

of their philosophy. In the Indic (which is the classic) case there is a contradiction which at first sight looks insoluble between lingam-worship and yoga; and we are similarly shocked by the corresponding contrasts between the temple-prostitution and the astral philosophy of a disintegrating Babylonic Society, between the human sacrifices and the penitential self-mortifications[1] of the Mayas, and between the orgiastic and the ascetic aspects of the Hittite worship of Cybele and Attis. Perhaps it was the common vein of sadistic extravagance which entered into their practice of *abandon* and their practice of self-control alike that maintained, in the souls of the members of all these four civilizations in their decadence, an emotional harmony between practices which seem to defy reconciliation when they are observed with the coldly analytic eye of an alien spectator.

If we turn, in conclusion, to the history of our own Western Society, our attention will be caught first by the clash of *abandon* with asceticism in the disintegration of the medieval Italian city-state cosmos. In fifteenth-century Florence the Thrasymachean political theory of Machiavelli and the Epicurean social practice of the Medicean circle were confronted by the puritanical religious fervour of Savonarola;[2] and in sixteenth-century Lombardy Rodolfo Gonzaga supplied the foil—a murky halo—for his brother Aluigi within the bosom of a single family.[3]

Are the two conflicting ways of behaviour now re-performing their play upon the broader stage of our Western Society in the modern chapter of its history? There is no lack of evidence for the resurgence of *abandon*; for in the domain of theory it has found its prophet in Jean-Jacques Rousseau with his alluring invitation to 'return to Nature',[4] while, for the practice of *abandon* by the living generation of Western and Westernized men and women, in Europe and overseas, *si monumentum requiris circumspice*. On the other hand we may still search in vain for traces of a counter-resurgence of asceticism, and may perhaps tentatively draw from this negative evidence the cynical conclusion (which may comfort us or leave us unconsoled, according to the nature of the faith by which we live) that, if our Western Civilization has indeed already broken down in its Modern Age, its disintegration cannot yet be very far advanced.

[1] For these see Gann, T., and Thompson, J. E.: *The History of the Maya* (London 1931, Scribner), p. 143.
[2] Machiavelli's own consciousness of this antithesis is attested by the passage from *The Prince* which has been quoted in V. C (i) (*d*) 1, on p. 389, footnote 3, above.
[3] See V. C (i) (*c*) 1, pp. 40 and 48, above.
[4] Rousseau's outlook is taken as a psychological symptom of social disintegration by Oswald Spengler in *Der Untergang des Abendlandes*, vol. i (Munich 1920, Beck), p. 487. Besides being a gesture of *abandon*, it is also an expression of archaistic-mindedness (see V. C (i) (*d*) 8 (α), vol. vi, pp. 58-9, below).

3. *Truancy and Martyrdom*

If, in our survey of truancy and martyrdom, we follow the same comparative method that we have just been employing in our survey of *abandon* and self-control, we shall find, if we again address ourselves to Hellenic history first, that the contrast between these two ways of social behaviour which are alternative substitutes for the expedient of mimesis comes out repeatedly in successive stages of the Hellenic Society's decline and fall.

In the first generation after the breakdown the truancy of the Attic slaves who ran away from their masters to find asylum within the enemy lines at Decelea in the second act of the Atheno-Peloponnesian War provides a foil for the martyrdom of the Athenian citizen Socrates, who refused to elude a death-sentence by condescending either to abscond from the prison where he was awaiting trial or to prevaricate at the trial when this duly took place[1]—though, in the judgement of most of Socrates' own friends and admirers, either of these ways of playing truant would have seemed far less blameworthy than the 'get-away' of the miner-slaves from the *ergastula* at Laurium. In the contemporary Lacedaemonian camp the moral truancy of Gylippus, which ended in his ignominious exile,[2] was as truly an outcome of the 'beginning of great evils for Hellas' in 431 B.C. as was the vindication of the Spartiate military tradition by Brasidas through the giving of a heroic example which ended in the hero's glorious death.

Some two centuries later, when the fate of the Hellenic World was once more 'on the razor's edge' between the first rally after the original breakdown and the first relapse,[3] both Athens and Sparta played truant, at the critical moment, from the common cause of federalism, though the championship of this cause offered the only hope of saving the independence of the historic states at the heart of the Hellenic World now that these had been dwarfed and overshadowed by a ring of giant states on the periphery which the expansion of a disintegrating Hellenism had latterly called into existence.[4] The Spartan statesman who was perhaps more responsible than any other man of his day for this second blighting of the prospects of the city-states of Greece was King Cleomenes III; and this self-same Cleomenes was one of the two members of the pair of Spartan martyr-kings who gave Sparta her last sunset

---

[1] For Socrates' repeated and persistent refusals to accept the various loopholes for escaping death which were almost officiously opened for his benefit, see Plato's *Crito*, *Apology*, and *Phaedo, passim*, and also the present study, V. C (ii) (*a*), Annex II, vol. vi, pp. 490–2, below.   [2] See Part III. A, vol. iii, p. 70, above.

[3] See V. C (ii) (*b*), vol. vi, pp. 287–9, below.

[4] See III. C (ii) (*b*), vol. iii, p. 341, footnote 1, and IV. C (iii) (*c*) 2 (α), vol. iv, pp. 265 and 268, above.

glow of glory[1] and at the same time transmitted to the internal proletariat of the Hellenic Society as a whole an inspiration which can perhaps be detected, in the fullness of time, in one aspect of the spirit of Christianity.[2]

In the course of the subsequent relapse[3] the antithetic roles of truant and martyr were replayed both on the Roman and on the Syrian section of a Hellenic arena which had now been enlarged to the dimensions of a colosseum. The Gylippan demoralization of the majority of the young men of the Roman governing class in the generation that came to manhood after 'the crowning mercy' of Pydna—when the overthrow of the last surviving rival Great Power within range of Rome had suddenly relaxed a tension under which every Roman of that class had been living, with scarcely a respite, ever since the beginning of the Hannibalic War a full half-century back—was an example of mass-truancy which threw into all the sharper relief the unrotted virtue of a Scipio Aemilianus[4] and the clear-eyed self-sacrifice of the Gracchi: a pair of Roman martyrs who retrod, step for step, the *via dolorosa* which had been trodden before them, a hundred years earlier,[5] by the Spartan pair of Heracleidae.[6] As for the submerged Syriac wing of the Hellenic internal proletariat, it was the years immediately following the definitive establishment, at Pydna, of Rome's supremacy in the Hellenic World that witnessed in Judaea the parting of the ways between the truancy of the Hellenizing Jewish High Priest Jason[7] and the martyrdom of Eleazer and the Seven Brethren in response to the challenge of Antiochus Epiphanes' policy of forcible Hellenization.[8]

In the last bout of the Roman civil wars, which marks the transition from the first relapse of a disintegrating Hellenic Society to its second rally, the martyrdom of Cato Minor finds its antithesis in the truancy of Mark Antony; and, if the inspiration of Cato's example can be discerned in the deaths of a series of Roman aristocrats who likewise gave their lives for the republican ideal in the course of the next century,[9] the spirit of Antony's craven and futile flight from a nightmare which was inescapable, because it was a true reflexion of his own defeated soul, has been expressed

---

[1] See the references in V. C (i) (d) 1, p. 388, footnote 1, above.

[2] See IV. C (iii) (c) 2 (α), vol. iv, p. 269, above, and V. C (ii) (a), Annex II, *passim*, in vol. vi, below.

[3] See V. C (ii) (b), vol. vi, pp. 290–1, below.

[4] See IV. C (iii) (c) 3 (β), vol. iv, pp. 505–6, above.

[5] For the time-lag in Roman social evolution in this chapter of Hellenic history see IV. C (iii) (b) 9, vol. iv, p. 205, above, and V. C (ii) (b), vol. vi, p. 288, below.

[6] See the references in V. C. (i) (d) 1, p. 388, footnote 1, above.

[7] See V. C (i) (d) 9 (β), vol. vi, pp. 103–5, below.

[8] See V. C (i) (c) 2, pp. 68 and 72, above.

[9] For this effect of Cato's example see V. C (i) (d) 1, pp. 390 and 392, above, and V. C (ii) (a), vol. vi, p. 250, below.

with an insidiously imaginative sympathy by the freedman-poet
Horace in the sixteenth poem of his Book of Epodes.

> Altera iam teritur bellis civilibus aetas,
>   suis et ipsa Roma viribus ruit:
> quam neque finitimi valuerunt perdere Marsi
>   minacis aut Etrusca Porsennae manus
> aemula nec virtus Capuae, nec Spartacus acer
>   novisque rebus infidelis Allobrox,
> nec fera caerulea domuit Germania pube
>   parentibusque abominatus Hannibal—
> impia perdemus devoti sanguinis aetas
>   ferisque rursus occupabitur solum.
>   . . . .
>
> Forte quid expediat communiter aut melior pars
>   malis carere quaeritis laboribus;
> nulla sit hac potior sententia: Phocaeorum
>   velut profugit exsecrata civitas
> agros atque Lares patrios, habitandaque fana
>   apris reliquit et rapacibus lupis,
> ire pedes quocumque ferent, quocumque per undas
>   Notus vocabit aut protervus Africus.
>   . . . .
>
> Nos manet Oceanus circumvagus: arva, beata
>   petamus arva divites et insulas,
> reddit ubi Cererem tellus inarata quotannis
>   et imputata floret usque vinea.
>   . . . .
>
> Juppiter illa piae secrevit litora genti,
>   ut inquinavit aere tempus aureum—
> aere, dehinc ferro duravit saecula, quorum
>   piis secunda vate me datur fuga.[1]

In the 'escapism' of this Horatian conceit of a 'get-away' from
an irreparably ruined real world to the Utopia of some Lotus
Eaters' Land or Calypso's Isle[2] the truancy of the Hellenic dominant minority comes to its dramatic climax at the same moment as
the Hellenic 'Time of Troubles'; but the denouement is staved off
by the successful establishment of a Hellenic universal state; and
we have to sit expectantly until the passage of two centuries has
brought us within sight of the bankruptcy of the Roman Peace
before we again see the antithetic roles of truant and martyr being
played on the Hellenic stage by eminent pairs of mutually antipathetic performers. On the Imperial Throne in the gathering
gloom of the outgoing decades of the second century of the
Christian Era we behold in the person of Marcus a prince whose

---

[1] Horace: *Epodon Liber*, carmen xvi, ll. 1–10, 15–22, 41–4, 63–6.
[2] For the temptations of Odysseus see II D (i), vol. ii, pp. 22–4, above.

title to the martyr's crown is not invalidated, but is on the contrary confirmed, by Death's refusal to cut this martyr's ordeal short by any *coup de grâce*; while in Marcus's son and successor Commodus we are presented with the spectacle of an Imperial truant who makes scarcely an effort to shoulder the burden of his heritage before he turns tail and is off, in headlong moral flight, along the sordid cinder-track of 'proletarianization'.[1] In the next generation after Commodus's we see the contrast between Marcus and his unworthy son being displayed once again, on the same Imperial Throne, by a pair of cousins who both wear the now hallowed Antonine name as a transparent cloak over their notorious Syrian provenance. While Elagabalus dies by violence in retribution for his truancy in neglecting the strenuous duties of a Roman Emperor in a time of crisis in order to indulge—under the aegis of a Roman Peace that can now no longer be taken for granted—in the lascivious relaxations of a High Priest of the Baal of Emesa,[2] Alexander Severus dies the same death as a martyr to his intrepid attempt to carry out—with the self-sacrificing public spirit of his predecessor and ensample Marcus—the alien, uncongenial, and unpromising task of restoring the antique discipline of the Roman Army.

This ill-assorted pair of Syrian recruits is the last conspicuous entry on our roll of truants and martyrs from the Hellenic dominant minority; for the social class in which the Hellenic culture had hitherto been preserved and handed down, in defiance of the spirit of an age of disintegration, as a continuous and a vital tradition, was almost annihilated in the terrible relapse into the downward path into which the Hellenic World was precipitated by the assassination of Alexander Severus.[3] On the other hand the two generations—one of unbridled anarchy and another of ruthless reconstruction—which elapsed between the death of Alexander in A.D. 235 and the death of Galerius in A.D. 311 were signalized by a classic exhibition of both martyrdom and truancy in the ranks of a Christian Church which had been expanding from its original standing ground in the Syriac section of the Hellenic internal proletariat until it had won converts, and put forth branches, in every province of the Hellenic universal state.[4]

[1] For this phenomenon of 'proletarianization' see further V. C (i) (d) 6 (α), pp. 439–80, below.

[2] For Elagabalus's religion and religious policy see V. C (i) (c) 2, p. 82, footnote 4, above, and V. C (i) (d) 6 (δ), Annex, pp. 649 and 685–8, below.

[3] For this relapse see IV. C (i), vol. iv, p. 8, and V. C (i) (c) 3, in the present volume, p. 219, above, and V. C (i) (d) 6 (δ), Annex, in the present volume, p. 649, and V. C (ii) (b), vol. vi, pp. 284 and 291, below.

[4] The Church's unanimity-in-ubiquity had already been proclaimed in the second century of the Christian Era, before the end of the Antonine 'Indian Summer' of Hellenic history, by the Christian Father Saint Irenaeus of Lyon:

'Having received this gospel and this faith, as we have already related, the Church, in spite of her dispersal throughout the World, preserves these treasures as meticulously

The Christian Church was the principal target for the parting strokes of a Hellenic dominant minority which turned savage in its death-agony;[1] for this dying pagan ruling class refused to face the heart-rending truth that it was itself the author of its own downfall and destruction; even *in articulo mortis* it tried to salvage a last shred of self-respect by persuading itself that it was perishing as the victim of a dastardly assault on the part of the proletariat;[2] and, since the external proletariat was now marshalled in formidable barbarian war-bands which were able for the most part to defy or elude the Imperial Government's attempts at retaliation for their galling raids, the brunt fell upon the Christian Church, which was the master-institution of the internal proletariat and at the same time was not, as the barbarians were, beyond the physical reach of the dominant minority's now distractedly vindictive arm.[3] Under the test of this ordeal the sheep in the Christian fold were divided unequivocally from the goats by the challenge of being called upon to make the tremendous choice between renouncing their faith and sacrificing their lives. The renegades were legion—indeed, their numbers were so great that the problem of how to deal with them became the burning question of ecclesiastical politics as soon as the persecutions came to an end—but the tiny band of martyrs was spiritually potent out of all proportion to its

as though she were living under one single roof. She believes in these truths as unanimously as though she had only one soul and a single heart, and she preaches them and expounds them and hands them down as concordantly as though she had only one mouth. While the languages current in the World are diverse, the force of the [Church's] tradition is one and the same everywhere. There is no variety in the faith or in the tradition of the churches that have established themselves in the Germanies or in the Spains or among the Celts or in the East or in Egypt or in North-West Africa, or, again, of the churches that have established themselves at the World's centre. Just as God's creature the Sun is one and the same throughout the World, so likewise the Gospel of the Truth shows its light everywhere.'—Irenaeus: *Contra Haereses*, Book II, chap. 10, § 2 (Migne, J.-P.: *Patrologia Graeca*, vol. vii, cols. 552–3). Cf. Book V, chap. 20, § 1 (col. 1177).

[1] For the Roman Government's persecution of the Christian Church see also IV. C (i), vol. iv, p. 8, and V. C (i) (c) 2, in the present volume, pp. 76 and 80, above, and V. C (i) (d) 6 (α), pp. 456–7, and V. C (ii) (a), vol. vi, pp. 201–2, below.

[2] Compare the Hitlerian legend that, in the General War of 1914–18, Germany was defeated, not by the Allied and Associated Powers on the battle-field, but by Liberal, Marxian, and Jewish traitors at the rear. The question whether the break-up of the Roman Empire and the dissolution of the Hellenic Society can properly be described, in Gibbon's phrase, as 'the triumph of Barbarism and Religion', has been discussed in IV. C (ii) (b) 1, vol. iv, pp. 58–63, above.

[3] In this respect the recurrent bouts of systematic persecution to which the Christian Church in the Roman Empire was subjected between A.D. 235 and A.D. 311 will remind a reader of this Study of the systematic persecution of the Jews in a National-Socialist German Reich. In this post-war Germany the Jews were made the scapegoats for the sufferings and humiliations which had befallen the German people in and after their military defeat in the General War of A.D. 1914–18; and the reason why the Jews were singled out for victimization—on account of a German military defeat with which in truth they had had nothing to do—was because the Germans were unwilling to confess that they had mainly themselves to blame for their own misfortunes, and at the same time were unable (at least in the earlier years of the Nazi régime) to wreak their vengeance upon their Gentile ex-enemies at whose hands they had met with their overthrow in A.D. 1918.

numerical strength. Thanks to the prowess of these heroes who, at the critical moment, stepped forward from the Christian ranks in order to bear their witness at the cost of life itself, the Church emerged victorious from her contest with the melancholy sternness of a Decius and with the boorish brutality of a Daia; and that small but noble army of Eurytus-minded Christian men and women[1] have received no more than their due meed of fame in being remembered by History as 'the martyrs' *par excellence*, in antithesis to 'the traitors' (*traditores*).[2]

This survey of the recurrent conflict between the two contrary impulses towards truancy and towards martyrdom during the long-drawn-out disintegration of the Hellenic Society may close with a glimpse of two contrasted figures which appear for an instant on a tottering Hellenic stage in the last wild scene of all. On the eve of the dissolution of Hellenism in the break-up of the Roman Empire we see a noble Christian embodiment of the pagan political martyr in the Emperor Majorian (*imperabat* A.D. 457–61), who courted the death that overtook him[3] when he refused to play the puppet's part for which he had been designed by the barbarian king-maker Ricimer, and insisted, instead, upon fulfilling the now desperate duty of his Imperial office by attempting to inflict upon barbarian war-bands that were by this time firmly seated in the Roman saddle the chastisement that had been meted out to less formidable predecessors of the fifth-century Franks and Vandals by a Marius or a Claudius Gothicus. As a foil to Majorian's martyrdom we may set the truancy of a renegade Greek man-of-business who in A.D. 448, nine years before Majorian's elevation to the purple, had crossed the path of the Greek historian and Roman diplomatist Priscus of Panium when Priscus was representing the Constantinopolitan Government on a mission to Attila, the Khāqān of the Black Huns, at the Nomad war-lord's camp on the Hungarian Alföld.[4] The essence of the truant's state of mind is revealed in the ambassador's account of his conversation with this nomadized *ci-devant* citizen of the Roman Empire and member of the Hellenic Society.[5] According to the narrator of the story the renegade's first confident exposition of the signal advantages

---

[1] For the story of Eurytus the Spartiate see V. C (i) (d) 1, p. 378, above.

[2] These original recipients of the opprobrious title 'traitor' (*traditor*) were Christians who delivered up the holy scriptures or the sacred vessels of the Church at the demand of the pagan Imperial authorities.

[3] Officially Majorian died of dysentery five days after Ricimer had compelled him to abdicate as a punishment for having reigned too much in earnest. Actually there can be little doubt that his death was brought about by foul play on Ricimer's part.

[4] See the fragment of Priscus's *History of His Own Times* in *Historici Graeci Minores*, edited by Dindorf, L.: vol. i (Leipzig 1870, Teubner), pp. 305–9.

[5] Priscus's renegade is cited again—this time as an example of 'proletarianization'—in V. C (i) (d) 6 (α), pp. 473–4, below.

of 'going native' over staying Hellene broke down lamentably under Priscus's counter-attack on behalf of Hellenic culture and Roman law.

'My interlocutor', the historian records, 'was reduced to tears, and he confessed that the laws were excellent and that the Roman Constitution was admirable, if only the rulers had not so hopelessly lost the spirit of their predecessors that they were ruining Society.'

This Hellenic renegade might well weep when he was confronted by a loyal Hellene and Roman who commanded the ability to state the loyalist's case; for the renegade had not merely repudiated the spiritual and political allegiance to which he had been brought up: he had actually thrown himself into the service of hard-bitten barbarians who were the mortal enemies of both Hellenism and the Empire. This Hellenic act of truancy at the moment of the Hellenic Society's final dissolution has an analogue in the Manchurian marches of the Far Eastern World in the seventeenth century of the Christian Era on the eve of the conquest of Intramural China by the Extramural Manchu barbarians:

'The Chinese in Southern Manchuria . . . while characteristically Chinese in culture and social organization . . . had taken on [before the date of the Manchu conquest of Intramural China] a strong "frontier" colour. . . . Thus they were, for their part, willing to accept the authority, and identify themselves with the drive, of the rising and aggressive Manchu group, which promised them a share of the power and wealth to be garnered in China—the rich land, the land of civilization and luxury; a land whose promise altogether overshadowed any promise of growth and expansion toward the barbarian wilderness. . . . During the rise of the Manchu Power any Chinese who shaved his forehead and grew a queue (thus making it difficult for him to desert at short notice to an anti-Manchu political faction) could be recruited into a Chinese "banner"[1] [of the Manchu Army].'[2]

In the Syriac World in its 'Time of Troubles', when it was being battered by an Assyrian flail, we see the Prophets of Israel and Judah offering themselves as martyrs in protest against the truancy of a paganizing faction who were seeking an escape from intolerable miseries in a deliberate repudiation of the Chosen People's priceless peculiar heritage, with the base intention of purchasing some relief from pressure at the cost of re-merging the potter's

[1] See V. C (i) (c) 3, p. 315, footnote 3, above, and V. C (i) (d) 6 (α), p. 447, below.—A.J.T.
[2] Lattimore, O.: *Manchuria Cradle of Conflict* (New York 1932, Macmillan), pp. 45 and 61. These passages bring out the distinction between 'playing truant' and 'going native'; for these Manchurian Chinese recruits to Manchu barbarian war-bands committed the same heinous crime of truancy as Priscus's renegade without also being guilty, as he was, of the additional crime of 'proletarianization'. For a Chinese example of the converse process of 'going native' without at the same time playing truant see V. C (i) (d) 6 (α), p. 474, footnote 2, below.

half-shaped vessel into the still shapeless common clay of the unregenerate Gentiles.

In our own modern World of the West can we discern any traces of the two antithetical ways of social behaviour which we have now observed in the disintegration of three different civilizations? Assuredly we can put our finger on a portentous modern Western act of truancy in 'la trahison des clercs';[1] and the roots of this treason spring from a depth to which the gifted Frenchman who has coined the phrase might perhaps hesitate to trace them—though he has virtually confessed how deep-rooted the mischief is by choosing the medieval ecclesiastical name to denote and indict our modern Western 'intellectuals'. Their treason did not begin with the pair of treasonable acts—a cynical loss of faith in the recently established principles, and a nerveless surrender of the recently won gains, of Liberalism—that have been perpetrated by our 'intellectuals' within living memory. The truancy that has given this latest exhibition of itself was set on foot, centuries earlier, when the 'clerks' repudiated their clerical origin—and in the same act cut our Western culture off from the possibility of drawing nourishment any longer from the sap of the Tree of Spiritual Life—by trying to shift the rising edifice of our Western Christian Civilization from a religious to a secular basis.[2] This was the original act of *hybris* which is being requited in our day by an *âtê* that has been accumulating for centuries at compound interest.[3]

If we cast our eyes some four hundred years back and then focus them upon the patch of Western Christendom which is known as England, we shall there see in Thomas Wolsey—the precociously modern-minded clerk who pleaded guilty, in the bitter hour of his political disgrace, of having served his God less well than he had served his King—a truant whose truancy was shown up in all its blackness, less than five years after his ignominious end,[4] by the martyrdom of his contemporaries Saint John Fisher and Saint Thomas More. The modern Western clerkly proto-truant Wolsey has never lacked successors. It remains to be seen whether the blood of the modern Western protomartyrs will be proved, by fresh testimony in our day, to have been the seed of the Church[5]—as was the blood of their forerunners in the Hellenic World in the generations of Decius and Galerius.

[1] See the book with this title by Benda, Julien (Paris 1927, Grasset).
[2] On this matter see further Part VII, below.
[3] For *hybris* and *âtê* see IV. C (iii) (c), *passim*, in vol. iv, above.
[4] After his downfall in the autumn of 1529 Wolsey lingered on rather more than a year before dying a natural death on the 4th November, 1530; Saint John Fisher and Saint Thomas More were put to death by King Henry VIII on the 22nd June and on the 6th July, 1535, respectively.
[5] See the phrase from Tertullian's *Apologeticus* that is quoted in V. C (ii) (a), vol. vi, p. 202, footnote 3, below.

4. *The Sense of Drift*

The sense of drift, which is the passive way of feeling the loss of the *élan* of growth, is one of the most painful of the tribulations that afflict the souls of men and women who are called upon to live their lives in an age of social disintegration; and this pain is perhaps a punishment for a commission of the sin of idolatry through a worship of the creature instead of the Creator;[1] for in this sin we have found one of the causes of those breakdowns from which the disintegrations of civilizations follow. In terms of the Christian Theology:

'The consequence of the Fall, as a declension of the Soul from allegiance to the Creator to concern with the creature, was, in a word, idolatry. To the early converts this idolatry appeared primarily as the worship of images and of the innumerable gods who were themselves creatures fallen from grace, if not mere phantoms of human conceit; but the most stubborn foe of the Christian, as it had been of the Platonic, Faith was that homage to the idols of the Reason which wears the mask of Philosophy. Call it Stoicism or call it Epicureanism, call it Science or Deism or Realism or mere indifference or what you will, the most insidious and obstinate enemy of Religion was, and is, the subservience of the mind content to see in the World only a huge fatalistic mechanism or a heterogeneous product of Chance or, as the modern Darwinians would have it, a monstrous combination of both. Whatever form the error may take, it is a denial of the Logos as the creative wisdom and purpose of God, a magnification of the creature, a refined, but not the less devastating, species of idolatry.'[2]

Chance and Necessity[3] are the alternative shapes in which this idol is saluted by its votaries;[4] and, though at first sight the two notions may appear to contradict one another to the point of being mutually exclusive, they prove, when probed, to be merely different facets of one identical illusion.

The notion of Chance is expressed in the literature of the Egyptiac 'Time of Troubles' through the simile of the giddy spinning of a potter's wheel,[5] and in the literature of the Hellenic 'Time of Troubles' through the simile of a ship that has been abandoned,

---

[1] For this definition of idolatry, which is the sense in which the term is used in this Study, see Part I. A, vol. i, p. 9, footnote 3, and IV. C (iii) (c) 2 (α), in vol. iv, pp. 261–2, above.

[2] More, P. E.: *Christ the Word = The Greek Tradition from the Death of Socrates to the Council of Chalcedon: 399 B.C.–A.D. 451*, vol. iv (Princeton 1927, University Press) p. 305.

[3] For a discussion and rejection of the view that Necessity is the cause of the breakdowns of civilizations see IV. C (i), vol. iv pp. 7–39, above.

[4] 'Mihi haec et talia audienti in incerto iudicium est fatone res mortalium et necessitate immutabili an forte volvantur.'—Tacitus: *Annals*, Book VI, chap. 22, *init*. The rest of the chapter is devoted to an exposition of the alternative hypotheses.

[5] See the passage from *The Admonitions of a Prophet* which is quoted in IV. C (iii) (c) 2 (β), vol. iv, pp. 410–11, above.

without a steersman, to the mercy of the winds and waves.[1] In a disintegrating Hellenic Society the sense of drift—'imus, imus praecipites'[2]—sought expression and relief in a worship of Chance which came near to becoming the prevailing religion of the Hellenic World as the Hellenic 'Time of Troubles' worked up towards its climax;[3] and the deeply ingrained anthropomorphic habit of the Hellenic imagination conferred upon this new goddess, who was being raised to power by the defeat of a human attempt at self-determination, a 'local habitation and a name'.[4] Timoleon dedicated to Fortune ('Ιερῷ Δαίμονι) a house which had been given him by the Syracusans in acknowledgement of their gratitude to the liberator of their city; and in this house he built a chapel in which he offered sacrifices to 'Our Lady Automatism' (Αὐτοματία).[5] In later generations the same goddess won worship farther afield as Τύχη Ἀντιοχέων or Fortuna Praenestina sive Antias.[6]

> O diva gratum quae regis Antium,
>   praesens vel imo tollere de gradu
>   mortale corpus vel superbos
>   vertere funeribus triumphos:
>
> te pauper ambit sollicita prece
>   ruris colonus; te, dominam aequoris,
>   quicumque Bithyna lacessit
>   Carpathium pelagus carina.
>
> te Dacus asper, te profugi Scythae
>   urbesque gentesque et Latium ferox
>   regumque matres barbarorum et
>   purpurei metuunt tyranni,

[1] See the passage from Plato's *Politicus* which is quoted in IV. C (i), vol. iv, pp. 26-7, above. This simile, which Plato applied to the Universe, was transferred by Seneca to the field of human psychology: 'Pauci sunt qui consilio se suaque disponant; ceteri, eorum more quae fluminibus innatant, non eunt sed feruntur.'—Seneca, L. Annaeus: *Epistulae Morales ad Lucilium*, Book III, ep. ii [xxiii], chap. 8.
[2] Persius Flaccus, A.: *Satires*, No. III, ll. 41-2.
[3] 'In the outlook of the general public, [as well as in that of the philosophers,] the [personal] rule of the Gods retires farther and farther into the background, and its place in the determination of human destinies is taken by Tyche or by Automatism—that is to say, by Luck and by Chance.'—Seeck, O.: *Geschichte des Untergangs der Antiken Welt*, vol. iii, 2nd edition (Stuttgart 1921, Metzler), p. 84.
[4] *A Midsummer Night's Dream*, Act V, Scene i. See I. C (iii) (e), Annex, vol. i, p. 443, above. This Hellenic personification of Chance was an expression of the same incorrigible anthropomorphic-mindedness as the impertinence of the unknown Greek sculptor in Gandhāra who carved the first statue of the Buddha in human form (see V. C (i) (c) 2, p. 135, footnote 3, above). [5] Plutarch: *Life of Timoleon*, chap. 36.
[6] Even Constantinople was furnished by its Christian founder with a temple dedicated to the Roman Tychê (Parker, H. M. D.: *A History of the Roman World from A.D. 138 to 337* (London 1935, Methuen), p. 301). The worship of this goddess on this spot survived both the definitive triumph of Christianity at the close of the fourth century of the Christian Era (see IV. C (iii) (b) 12, vol. iv, pp. 226-7, above) and the breakdown of the *Pax Romana* in the Greek heart of the Hellenic World in the latter part of the sixth century (see IV. C (iii) (c) 2 (β), vol. iv, pp. 326-8, above). For this survival of the worship of the Roman Tychê of Constantinople into the Byzantine Age see Cumont, Fr.: 'L'Éternité des Empereurs Romains' in *Revue d'Histoire et de Littérature Religieuses*, vol. i (Paris 1896, Macon et Protat), p. 452.

iniurioso ne pede proruas
stantem columnam, neu populus frequens
ad arma cessantes, ad arma,
concitet, imperiumque frangat.[1]

Has this frank and concrete Hellenic worship of Tychê any analogue in the histories of other civilizations? We shall find a more subtle version of it prevalent in the Sinic World on the morrow of the foundation of the Sinic universal state, and a less straightforward version in our Western World at the present day.

When we look into our hearts, we find the Hellenic goddess now enthroned there—notwithstanding our boast of being hard-headed scientists who deal in facts and not in fictions[2]—as potently as she was in the hearts of the Hellenes themselves in their decadence. The following profession of faith in the omnipotence of Tychê may be quoted from the preface of a notable book from the pen of one of the most highly distinguished among our living Western historians:

'One intellectual excitement has . . . been denied me. Men wiser and more learned than I have discerned in History a plot, a rhythm, a predetermined pattern. These harmonies are concealed from me. I can see only one emergency following upon another as wave follows upon wave; only one great fact with respect to which, since it is unique, there can be no generalizations; only one safe rule for the historian: that he should recognise in the development of human destinies the play of the contingent and the unforeseen.'[3]

This brilliantly phrased passage cannot be dismissed as a scholar's conceit; for the writer is a Liberal who is formulating a creed which Liberalism has translated from theory into action, and his irony is a sword with a rapier-point which flickers out into the world beyond the walls of the intellectual fencer's study. This modern Western belief in the omnipotence of Chance gave birth in the nineteenth century of the Christian Era, when things still seemed to be going well with Western Man, to the policy of *laisser faire*: a philosophy of practical life which was founded on a faith in the miraculous enlightenment of self-interest. In the light of a transitorily gratifying experience our nineteenth-century grandfathers claimed to 'know that all things work together for good for them that love'[4] the goddess Tychê. And even in the twentieth century, when the goddess had begun to show her teeth, she was still the oracle of British foreign policy. The view that was prevalent

---

[1] Horace: *Carmina*, Book I, Ode xxxv, ll. 1–16.
[2] For the vanity of this boast on the lips of our modern *Homo Occidentalis* see I. C (iii) (*e*), Annex, vol. i, pp. 442–5, above.
[3] Fisher, H. A. L.: *A History of Europe* (London 1935, Eyre & Spottiswoode, 3 vols.), vol. i, p. vii.   [4] Romans viii. 28.

among the people, as well as in the Cabinet, of the United Kingdom during the fateful period of Western history which opened
in the autumn of A.D. 1931 was accurately expressed in the following sentence from the files of a great English Liberal newspaper:

'A few years of peace are always a few years gained, and a war that is
due in a few years' time may never come off at all.'[1]

The doctrine of *laisser faire* which had brought the Western
World to the pass in which it found itself in the autumn of 1938
cannot be claimed as an original Western contribution to the
common stock of human wisdom. It was current coin in the Sinic
World some two thousand years before it captivated modern
Western minds; and, while the Sinic Society's pretensions to have
anticipated us in our recently acquired technical command over
Physical Nature are perhaps not to be taken *au pied de la lettre*,[2]
there is no doubt that the spiritual 'defeatism' which has accompanied our own material triumphs of the last hundred and fifty
years can also be detected in Sinic souls in the second century B.C.
This Sinic worship of Chance differs, however, from ours in de-
riving from a less sordid origin. The eighteenth-century French
bourgeois came to believe in *laisser faire laisser passer* because
he had noticed and envied and analysed the prosperity of his
English 'opposite number', and had come to the conclusion that
the bourgeoisie might prosper in France as well as in England if
only King Louis could be induced or compelled to follow the
example of King George in allowing the bourgeois to manufacture
what he chose, without restrictions, and to send his goods to any
market, free from tolls. In fact, the catchword of our modern Western
philosophy of drift has the prosaic original meaning of 'No state
interference with business'. On the other hand the line of least
resistance along which a weary Sinic World allowed itself to
drift during the earlier decades of the second century B.C.[3] was

---

[1] This quotation is taken from a leading article published in *The Manchester Guardian*
of the 13th July, 1936.
[2] See, for example, the anecdote in III. C (i) (c), vol. iii, pp. 188–90, above.
[3] It will be seen that in Sinic history the psychological self-surrender of a disintegrating society to the drift of the Universe was contemporaneous with the closure of the
international anarchy of 'the Contending States' (see V. C (ii) (b), vol. vi, pp. 291–5,
below) by the establishment of a universal state in the political arena. The captivation
of Sinic souls by the dark power of Chance was of older date than this. It can be traced
back into the second, at least, of the two bouts of the Sinic 'Time of Troubles'. In this
earlier age, however, the Sinic response to the challenge of Chance had taken an active
and not a passive form. The princes of 'the Contending States' did not resign themselves
to the mercy of the winds and waves: they sought rather to take advantage of the movements of these elemental forces—tempestuous and menacing though these might be
—for the furtherance of their own designs. According to Granet, M.: *La Pensée
Chinoise* (Paris 1934, Renaissance du Livre), p. 428, the ideas that were in the ascendant
in that age are summed up in two words which are almost impossible to translate:
'*chou* [anglicè *shu*], recettes, méthodes, artifices, et *che* [*she*], conditions, situations,
circonstances, forces, influences. Notre mot "chance" est, peut-être, celui qui rend le

conceived of, not as a pack-horse's beaten track from a humming mill to a lucrative market, but as a way which was the truth and the life:[1] the *tao* which 'meant "the way the Universe works"—and ultimately something very like God, in the more abstract and philosophical sense of that term'.[2]

The Sinic form of the worship of Chance was in fact a subtly decadent perversion of an original and authentic Taoist philosophy which—illuminated by knowledge born of suffering[3]—had apprehended the truth of 'etherialization',[4] had resolved to live by it, and had acted on its resolve by taking one of the highest and most arduous flights ever essayed by the Sinic spirit.

In the theistic language of the Syriac religious genius[5] the Taoist intuition of an absolute energy which is indistinguishable from an absolute tranquillity[6] has been expressed in the poetic image of God's self-revelation to Elijah through the still small voice which made itself heard when the wind and the earthquake and the fire had come and gone;[7] and this Hebrew poetry has been transposed into Christian theology in a single sentence of Saint Augustine which is as terse as it is sublime: *Novit quiescens agere et agens quiescere*.[8] In the language of the Sinic philosophy the same truth is presented in such passages as the following from the *Tao Te King*:[9]

Great Tao is like a boat that drifts;
It can go this way; it can go that.
The ten thousand creatures owe their existence to it, and it does not
    disown them;
Yet, having produced them, it does not take possession of them.
Tao, though it covers the ten thousand things like a garment,
Makes no claim to be master over them,
And asks for nothing from them.
Therefore it may be called the Lowly.

moins mal le mot "che". Les situations et conditions diverses de temps et de lieu recèlent des occasions dont il faut se mettre en état de capter l'influence et la force pour risquer le sort avec le maximum de chances.' [1] John xiv. 6.

[2] Waley, A.: *The Way and its Power* (London 1934, Allen & Unwin), p. 30.

[3] Πάθει μάθος—Aeschylus: *Agamemnon*, l. 177, quoted in I. C (iii) (*b*), vol. i, p. 169, footnote 1; II. C (ii) (*b*) 1, vol. i, p. 298; IV. C (iii) (*b*) 11, vol. iv, p. 218; IV. C (iii) (*c*) 3 (β), vol. iv, p. 584, footnote 1; and V. C (i) (*c*) 2, in the present volume, p. 78, above, and V. C (ii) (*a*), vol. vi, p. 275, below.

[4] For the principle of 'etherialization' see III. C (i) (*c*), vol. iii, pp. 174–92, above.

[5] For the differentiation between a sense of unity which apprehends the unifying principle in a ubiquitous and irresistible law and a sense of unity which apprehends the same principle in a unique and omnipotent deity, see V. C (i) (*d*) 7, vol. vi, pp. 15–18, below.

[6] For this Taoist conception of Wu Wei see III. C (i) (*c*), vol. iii, p. 187, above.

[7] 1 Kings xix. 11–12.

[8] Aurelius Augustinus: *De Civitate Dei*, Book XII, chap. 18. Cf. the *Tao Te King*, chap. 81: 'Heaven's way is to sharpen without cutting.'

[9] The English translation here given is Mr. Arthur Waley's, in op. cit. The selection of the passages is inevitably rather arbitrary, since the paradox of the *Tao* is the subject of the whole treatise—or, rather, poem—and almost every chapter is a variation on the anonymous author's inexhaustible theme.

The ten thousand creatures obey it,
Though they know not that they have a master;
Therefore it is called the Great.[1]

This 'Way of the Universe' can only be apprehended by human
souls through an act of cognition which is at the same time an
act of will; and the Taoist sage attains his knowledge of 'the Way'
by walking in it himself:

So, too, the sage, just because he never at any time makes a show of
    greatness, in fact achieves greatness.
Without leaving his door
He knows everything under Heaven.
Without looking out of his window
He knows all the ways of Heaven.
For the further one travels
The less one knows.
Therefore the sage arrives without going,
Sees all without looking,
Does nothing yet achieves everything.[2]

If only the lesson of the sage's life were taken to heart by the
rulers of This World!

Tao never does;
Yet through it all things are done.
If the barons and kings would but possess themselves of it,
The ten thousand creatures would at once be transformed.
And if, having been transformed, they should desire to act,
We must restrain them by the blankness of the Unnamed.
The blankness of the Unnamed
Brings dispassion;
To be dispassionate is to be still.
And so, of itself, the whole Empire will be at rest.[3]

The philosophy that is hinted at in these passages is as noble as
it is profound; and yet, for a human being who sets himself to

---

[1] *Tao Te King*, chap. 34, Waley's translation (cf. chap. 40).

[2] Ibid., chaps. 34 and 47, Waley's translation (cf. chaps. 45, 48, 81).

[3] Ibid., chap. 37, Waley's translation. Compare a passage from chap. 67 of the *Tao Te King* which is translated as follows by Forke, A.: *Die Gedankenwelt des Chinesischen Kulturkreises* (Munich and Berlin 1927, Oldenbourg), p. 195:

'Whoso seeks to rule the state through knowledge is a scourge to the state; whoso rules it not through knowledge, a blessing.'

This Sinic dictum has a remarkably exact Arabic parallel in the following passage of Ibn Khaldūn's *Muqaddamāt* (Book I, chap. 24):

'Benevolent government is rarely associated with a ruler whose mind is over-alert and intelligence over-developed. Benevolence is most commonly found in rulers who are easy-going or who behave as if they were. The worst defect in the alert-minded ruler is that he lays burdens upon his subjects which are greater than they can bear; and he does this because his mental vision outranges theirs and because his insight penetrates to the ends of things at the beginnings—with disastrous consequences for them. . . . The ideal is the Golden Mean . . . and for this reason a man who is over-intellectual has Satanic attributes attributed to him.'

walk in the way of the *Tao*, the path is not without pitfalls; for the superhuman effortlessness of the divine activity may be confounded in human eyes with the human vice of sloth. A warning against this error is uttered by Saint Augustine in the chapter above quoted: *Non in eius vacatione cogitetur ignavia, desidia, inertia, sicut nec in eius opere labor, conatus, industria.* Nevertheless, when the flesh is weak, the Taoist sage's posture may sink into being little more than a pose that saves a sluggard's face. And Taoism was in fact perverted to this base use by the desperation of a Sinic Society which had found itself cheated, through the swift collapse of Ts'in She Hwang-ti's universal state,[1] of the repose for which it was panting after the hard labour of a 'Time of Troubles'.

'The First Empire lasted only fifteen years (221–206 B.C.). After seven years of terrific wars the country was again united under the Han Empire; but civil wars did not end till 195 B.C. The long years of revolution and war had devastated the country, and the new empire found everything in ruins. . . . What was needed was not positive and meddlesome reforms, but peace and order to allow the people to live and recuperate. So the early statesmen of Han practised the policy of peace and *laissez faire*, and scholars and thinkers tended to exalt the philosophy of Taoism, which taught non-action and non-interference with Nature.'[2]

The modern Chinese scholar, Dr. Hu Shih, who is the writer of these lines, goes on to quote[3] a description of this misapplied Taoism of the early second century B.C. from the brush of a contemporary observer, Sse-ma T'an:[4]

'The Taoists say "Do nothing"; but they also say "Nothing is undone". It sounds subtle, but is in reality easy to work out. Its method lies in postulating nothingness or non-being as the basis of all things, and in following natural evolution as the principle of activity. They recognise no ready-made situation nor constant form; they are therefore able to understand the reality of things. They do not wish to anticipate things too prematurely, nor do they wish to lag behind the times; therefore they are masters of all things.'

'This attitude,' Dr. Hu Shih remarks,[5] 'suited the temper of the age admirably well; and for nearly three-quarters of a century the people enjoyed peace and throve in prosperity'—until the Emperor Wuti (*imperabat* 140–87 B.C.) abandoned this travesty of Taoism in order to establish, as the official philosophy of the Sinic uni-

---

[1] See V. C (ii) (a), vol. vi, p. 187, below.

[2] Hu Shih: 'The Establishment of Confucianism as a State Religion during the Han Dynasty' in *The Journal of the North China Branch of the Royal Asiatic Society*, vol. lx (1929), p. 22.   [3] Ibid., p. 23.

[4] Dr. Hu Shih mentions that this philosopher Sse-ma T'an was the father of the historian Sse-ma Ts'ien.

[5] Hu Shih, op. cit., p. 22; cf. Franke, O.: *Geschichte des Chinesischen Reiches*, vol. i (Berlin 1930, de Gruyter), pp. 286–8.

versal state, a form of Confucianism which was perhaps almost as remote from the teaching of Confucius himself as the contemporary Taoism was from the teaching of the *Tao Te King*.[1]

This misapplied Taoism of the second century B.C. might be described equally well as a *modus vivendi* with Chance or as a surrender to Fate;[2] for the goddess of *laisser faire* has another face, under which she is worshipped, not as Chance, but as Fate or Necessity.[3]

The two notions of Necessity and Chance are correlative by reason of their very antithesis; for this antithesis does not lie between two alternative and incompatible conceptions of the nature of things, but merely between the human being who feels that he is adrift and the mighty waters that seem to him to be tossing him about as callously as though he were an inanimate piece of flotsam. In a self-regarding mood the castaway views the force that is defeating him in a negative light, as a sheer chaotic disorder, and it is in this mood that he gives the name of Chance to his irresistible adversary and mistress. But the notion of disorder, as Bergson has pointed out,[4] is essentially relative, like the notion of order itself.[5] Neither order nor disorder can be conceived except

---

[1] For the contamination of both Confucianism and Taoism with popular superstition in the Han Age see V. C (i) (*d*) 6 (δ), pp. 555–7, below. For the official adoption of Confucianism by the Emperor Wuti see V. C (i) (*d*) 6 (δ), Annex, pp. 654 and 707–8, below.

[2] That Fate works mechanically had been a tenet of the Taoist philosopher Lieh-tse (*vivebat circa* 440–370 B.C.); that Heaven is a blind mechanical force had been a tenet of Hsün-tse (*vivebat circa* 310–230 B.C.) (see Forke, A.: *Die Gedankenwelt des Chinesischen Kulturkreises* (Munich and Berlin 1927, Oldenbourg), pp. 67 and 55).

[3] For the 'rationalization' of this surrender to Fate in the Babylonic philosophy of Astrology see V. C (i) (*c*) 1, pp. 56–7, above.

[4] See Bergson, Henri: *L'Évolution Créatrice*, 24th edition (Paris 1921, Alcan), pp. 239–58.

[5] The following extracts from the passage just cited may be quoted as examples of the great French philosopher's masterly lucidity in the exposition of his thought:

'If, at a venture, I select a volume in my library, I may replace it on the shelves, after taking a glance at it, with the remark "This isn't verse". But is this really what I perceived when I was turning the pages? Clearly not. I did not see, and I never shall see, an absence of verse. What I did see was prose. But, as it is poetry that I am wanting, I express what I find in terms of what I am looking for; and instead of saying "Here is some prose" I say "This isn't verse". Inversely, if it takes my fancy to read some prose and I stumble on a volume of verse, I shall exclaim "This isn't prose"; and in using these words I shall be translating the data of my perception, which shows me verse, into the language of my expectation and my interest, which are set upon the idea of prose and therefore will not hear of anything else. . . .

'Now let us suppose that there are two species of order and that these two orders are two contrary species embraced in a single genus. Let us further suppose that the idea of disorder arises in our minds every time when we look for one of the two species of order and find the other. The idea of disorder would then have a definite meaning in practical life: it would objectify, for expression in words, the disappointment of a mind which finds itself in the presence of an order that is different from the one which it wants—in the presence of an order for which, at the moment, it has no use, and which in this sense is non-existent for it. . . .

'An order is contingent, and appears so to us, in relation to the inverse order, in the way in which verse is contingent in relation to prose and prose in relation to verse. Just as all speech which is not prose is verse and is necessarily conceived of as verse, and just as all speech which is not verse is prose and is necessarily conceived of as prose, so every manner of being which is not one of the two orders is the other and is necessarily conceived of as the other. But it is possible for us to place a fog of affective states between

in contrast to its opposite. Every time that we make the observation that, in such and such a case, we are confronted with a disorder, our judgement is subjective. What we mean is that we are here being disappointed of some particular form of order which it has been our pleasure, here and now, to impose, in thought or in act, upon the face of the Universe. And the intractable state of the facts upon which we are taking a verbal revenge by giving it the bad name of disorder may—and indeed must—at the same time be an exemplification of the principle of order when the situation is viewed from one or other of the infinitely numerous possible alternative standpoints to that single arbitrary one which happens to be ours at the moment. For instance, the dizzy motion of the Egyptiac potter's wheel, which stands for the acme of disorder in the eyes of an Egyptiac poet[1] whose imagination animates the clay that is helplessly spinning on this wheel's whirling surface, is at the same time an example, on the mathematical plane of existence, of an orderly cyclic motion, while on the teleological plane it is an obedient instrument for impressing upon the clay the spiritual order that is represented by the potter's will.

> Said one among them: 'Surely not in vain
> My substance from the common earth was ta'en
>   And to this figure moulded, to be broke
> Or trampled back to shapeless earth again?'[2]

In a similar way the disorderly motion of a rudderless ship, which stands in Plato's eyes for the chaos of a Universe abandoned by God,[3]

ourselves and our representation of what we are conceiving of, and between ourselves and our perception of the idea that is really present to our minds. . . .

'If we analyse the idea of chance, which is a near relation to the idea of disorder, we shall find the same elements. When the purely mechanical operation of the causes which bring the roulette to a halt on a particular number makes me win and so behaves as a good genius would have behaved if he had been looking after my interests, and when the purely mechanical force of the wind snatches a tile from the roof and flings it down on my head—thus acting as an evil genius would have acted if he had been plotting against my life—in both cases I find a mechanism in a place where I would have looked for—and ought, it would seem, to have encountered—an intention; and that is what I am expressing when I speak of "chance". And in describing an anarchic world, where the phenomena follow one another at the pleasure of their caprice, I shall say, again, that this is the reign of chance, and I shall mean by this that I find myself confronted by acts of will, or rather by "decrees", when what I was looking for was mechanism. . . . The idea of chance simply objectifies the state of mind of someone whose expectation has been directed towards one of two species of order and who then encounters the other.

'Chance and disorder are, then, necessarily conceived of as relative.'

A glimmer of Bergson's clear vision of the meaning of the ideas of 'Chance' and 'Disorder' has been caught by Oswald Spengler in *Der Untergang des Abendlandes*, vol. i (Munich 1920, Beck), pp. 210–11:

'Strange as this may sound, Chance in the everyday sense of the term has an intimate affinity with the principle of Causality. The link between them is the inorganic element and the absence of anything in the nature of "direction".'

For the idea of 'direction' see Part III. B, vol. iii, pp. 124–7, and IV. C (i), vol. iv, pp. 34–8, above.

[1] See IV. C (iii) (c) 2 (β), vol. iv, pp. 410–11, and the present chapter and volume, p. 412, above.

[2] Edward Fitzgerald's translation of the *Rubā'iyāt* of 'Umar Khayyām, Quatrain lxxxiv.

[3] See IV. C (i), vol. iv, p. 26, and the present chapter and volume, pp. 412–13, above.

can be recognized, by a mind endowed with the necessary knowledge of dynamics and physics, as a perfect illustration of the orderly behaviour of waves and currents in the media of wind and water.[1] When the Human Soul adrift thus apprehends that the force which is baffling it is not simply a negation of the Soul's own will or caprice but is a thing in itself—albeit something that the Soul is failing to grasp or control—then the countenance of the unknown invincible goddess changes from a subjective aspect under which she is known as Chance to an objective aspect under which she is known as Necessity—but this without any corresponding change in the essence of this inhuman power's nature.

In approaching a divinity of so cold and implacable a mien as Necessity wears when she is recognized for what she is, her votaries are tempted to make some pretence of retaining a shadow of freedom which might save them, if it were genuine, from being driven to confess that they are utterly at the goddess's mercy.

At the dwarfed and daunted political heart of the Hellenic World in the second century B.C.,

'Philopoemen admitted that unquestionably a time would come sooner or later when the Greeks would find themselves constrained to obey, without option, any orders which the Romans might choose to give. "But we have still", he said, "some latitude in regard to dates. Do we want to bring this consummation to pass as quickly as possible, or on the contrary to put off the evil day to the latest possible date? Surely the latter?" And so, as he explained it, the difference between his policy and Aristaenetus's policy was this: Aristaenetus was eager to accelerate the march of Destiny (τὸ χρεών) and to do everything in his power to co-operate with it, while his own (Philopoemen's) policy was to resist and show fight to the limit of his strength.'[2]

The Achaean politician who was Philopoemen's opponent was acting, whether consciously or not, in the exact spirit of the famous prayer which the Stoic philosopher Cleanthes (*vivebat circa* 300–220 B.C.) had addressed to Necessity under the synonyms of Fate and Zeus:

ἄγου δέ μ', ὦ Ζεῦ, καὶ σύγ', ἡ Πεπρωμένη,
ὅποι ποθ' ὑμῖν εἰμὶ διατεταγμένος,
ὡς ἔψομαί γ' ἄοκνος· ἢν δέ γε μὴ θέλω,
κακὸς γενόμενος, οὐδὲν ἧττον ἔψομαι.[3]

---

[1] It may be added that, in the *Politicus*, the simile of the ship adrift is only one of two elements that make up, between them, the picture which Plato is painting in the colours of myth. The state in which the Universe drifts at the mercy of Chance alternates, in an endlessly recurrent cycle, with a contrary state in which it is steered by the hand of God according to Plan.

[2] Polybius, Book XXIV, chap. 13 (ed. Büttner-Wobst, vol. iv, Berlin and Leipzig 1904, Teubner), *ad annum* 181–180 B.C.

[3] Cleanthes in von Arnim's *Stoicorum Veterum Fragmenta*, vol. i (Berlin and Leipzig 1905, Teubner), p. 118. The lines have been quoted, apropos of the decline and fall of the 'Osmanlis, in Part III. A, vol. iii, p. 47, footnote 1, above.

This sense of uncontrollable drift on the sweep of Necessity's tide was felt, in the Hellenic World of the second century B.C., in the sheltered garden of scientific research as well as on the blasted heath of international politics.

'The most remarkable feature in [the] history [of Hellenistic science] was its failure to lead on from its first successes to a continuous growth like that which the modern pioneers of science inaugurated. This general falling off from an earlier promise can hardly be attributed to ignorance of scientific method. The best specimens of Hellenistic research reveal precisely that blend of observation and reasoning which usually yields the most solid results in scientific discovery. A more valid if partial explanation is that Hellenistic science lacked instruments of precision, such as the telescope and microscope, and this at a stage when observation by the unaided eye could not carry them much further. This deficiency would help to explain the eventual stagnation of astronomy, botany and medicine. But the chief reason is, no doubt, to be found in that general loss of the spirit of hope and adventure which befell the Greek nation in the second century [B.C.][1] It is significant that in the second century the Greek World became addicted to the practices of Astrology[2] and Magic. In pursuing these delusive short cuts to success, it proved that it had lost the faculty of patient research which distinguished the earlier Hellenistic pioneers.'[3]

The story of the progressive surrender of the Hellenic spirit to a sense of drift expressed in an ever more servile worship of Necessity has been recapitulated in the following terms by a modern Western historian of Hellenic thought:

'To ascribe knowledge and certainty to Physical Science and to deny Man's inner freedom by imprisoning the spirit in a huge mechanism of fixed and calculable Natural Law is to invert the whole order of the

---

[1] On this dictum a caveat is entered by Tarn, W. W.: *The Greeks in Bactria and India* (Cambridge 1938, University Press), pp. 34–9. 'There is small sign of "decadence" down to about the middle of the 2nd century B.C.' In the Middle East the Greek of the last century B.C. 'did not essentially differ from the Greek of the third'. And as late as the first century of the Christian Era, as far afield as Babylonia, the city-state of Seleucia-on-Tigris still preserved intact both its Greek race and its Hellenic culture and êthos according to the testimony of two Roman men-of-letters of that age ('Neque in barbarum corrupta, sed conditoris Seleuci retinens' (Tacitus: *Annals*, Book VI, chap. 42); 'Libera hodie ac sui iuris Macedonumque moris' (Pliny: *Natural History*, Book VI, chap. 122)).—A.J.T.

[2] See V. C (i) (c) 1, p. 57, with footnote 3, above. For the Fatalism which was instilled by Astrology into Hellenic souls, and for the attempts to find a religious way of escape from the astral Wheel of Existence along the alternative avenues offered by the worship of Isis, the rite of 'the Mithras Liturgy', Judaism, and Christianity, see Wendland, P.: *Die Hellenistisch-Römische Kultur* (Tübingen 1912, Mohr), pp. 156–7, 172, with footnote 1, and 399–400; and Dey, J.: Παλιγγενεσία (Münster i. W. 1937, Aschendorff), pp. 95–6 and 109. 'Whatever way men took it [Astrology], behind it loomed the gigantic and terrible figure of the Babylonian Fate, immutable and inexorable, neither loving nor hating, which ruled the Universe and before which gods and men were alike puppets playing their pre-determined parts, a figure which outraged the Greek sense of freedom till the history of Hellenistic religion might almost be summed up as a series of attempts to find a way of escape' (Tarn, op. cit., p. 60).—A.J.T.

[3] Cary, M.: *A History of the Greek World from 323 to 146 B.C.* (London 1932, Methuen), pp. 352–3.

Platonic philosophy. The result of such an inversion is shown strikingly
in the different connotations of the word "Necessity" in Plato and
Marcus Aurelius. To the former, Necessity meant the resistance of the
meaningless and incomprehensible flux of things, whether in Nature
or [in] the Human Soul, to the government of order and happiness; it
was the exact contrary of the spirit, which is shrined in liberty. To the
Imperial Stoic, Necessity was the binding force of the whole World,
leaving to the spirit this poor relic of freedom alone, that it might form
its own opinion as to the moral character of the universal flux of which
it was itself also a part, and so might persist in praising that as good
which it felt to be evil.'[1]

A classical exposition of this latter-day 'totalitarian' Determinism of the Hellenic spirit has been placed on record by an Antio-
chene adept in Astrology who is believed to have been the Emperor
Marcus's contemporary:[2]

'Life is a plaything and a wandering in the wilderness and a passing
show. . . . This is the work of Fate ($Eἱμαρμένης$) and Chance ($Τύχης$),
who ever so softly escort us human beings in order to make the
lives of some of us happy and the lives of others unhappy with
out rhyme or reason. So life travels its wandering and brutal course,
and, as it goes, it brings some things to such increase and glory and
prosperity and prominence that many fall in love with these prizes,
while other things are wounded by Life and corroded and blighted
and landed in oblivion and in peril and in odium. . . . For Fate
has enacted, to operate in the life of each one of us, an unalter-
able series of irrevocably accomplished facts. . . . In these circumstances those who are either innocently or wilfully ignorant of the
art of prognostication are harried and fleeced by the goddesses Hope
and Chance. . . . On the other hand, those who have studied the art and
have attained to the truth which it reveals are able to call their souls
their own in a freedom that has no taint of slavishness about it. These
freemen contemn Chance, do not cling to Hope, do not fear Death, and
live unperturbed ($ἀταράχως$), because they have given their souls an
anticipatory training in fortitude. They no longer either rejoice at good
fortune or are cast down by bad fortune, but are satisfied with what
comes to them. They are not in love with the impossible, and so they
bear with self-control ($ἐγκρατῶς$) the enactments [of Fate], and, weaning
themselves from all pleasure and servility, they enlist as Fate's soldiers.
It is impossible for a man by prayers or sacrifices to overcome the
destiny that has been laid down for him from the beginning and to
establish a different one for himself according to his desires. What has
been given will come to be, even without our prayers; and what has not
been fated will not come to pass, even if we pray for it. So, just as the
actors on the stage change their make-up to fit the book of the words
and play, with a professional propriety, sometimes kings, sometimes

[1] More, P. E.: *Platonism*, second edition (Princeton 1926, University Press), pp. 238–9.
[2] This is the most probable date of Vettius Valens according to W. Kroll in his
editio princeps of Vettius's *Anthologiae* (Berlin 1908, Weidmann), p. vi.

brigands, and sometimes yokels or cockneys or gods, in the same way we too ought to play the parts with which we are invested by Fate, and to conform to them without morally capitulating (οὐ συγγιγνώσκοντες) to the chances and changes of Life. If any man rebels, "he will have disgraced himself without modifying his destiny by one jot".[1]

The Antonine astrologer's cherished freedom seems to be limited to the single privilege of voting in the affirmative when Queen Fate takes a vote of confidence in her dictatorial régime; and there is equally little substance in the show of freedom that is left to the human will in the classic form that has been given to the Islamic theory of Predestination by the masterful theologian Abu'l-Hasan al-Ash'arī (vivebat circa A.D. 873–935). Al-Ash'arī attempts to resolve the apparent contradiction between God's Predestination and Man's Free Will by propounding the doctrine of Iktisāb, according to which the human will accepts for itself the destiny which God has already assigned to it. On this showing, 'Man is still an automaton, although part of his machinery is that he believes himself free'.[2]

---

[1] Vettius Valens: *Anthologiae*, edited by Kroll, W. (Berlin 1908, Weidmann), p. 246 (Book VI, chap. 1); p. 240 (Book VI, Introduction); pp. 219 and 220–1 (Book V, chap. 9). The quotation at the end of the last of these passages—κακὸς γενόμενος αὐτὸ τοῦτο πείσεται—is a garbled version of the Stoic philosopher Cleanthes' verse κακὸς γενόμενος οὐδὲν ἧττον ἔψομαι which has been quoted in this Study in Part III. A, vol. iii, p. 47, footnote 1, and in the present chapter and volume, p. 421, above.

One of the strangest passages in a strange work is an outburst of resentment at the exhaustion of an atmosphere of freedom of thought without which even Vettius's pseudo-science of Astrology could not live:

'In writing what I have written above I have been filled with pride for my own part in the heavenly science (θεωρία) in which I have been clad by the Deity—though nowadays this science is dishonoured and spurned, in spite of its venerable antiquity and its sovereign control over everything in life. Without it, nothing either is or can be, and yet sometimes even to have a name for being an adept in it brings one into odium—in sad contrast to the position of our predecessors, who used to boast of possessing the gift and to congratulate themselves upon it. This fills me with resentment and with envy of those ancient kings and despots who were enthusiasts for the science. Why did I not have the good fortune to live in those spacious days and to breathe the fresh air of their spiritual freedom for research? . . . At the present day the effective investigation of facts is obscured and blighted by Fear. The intellect, driven into negation and no longer fortified by ratiocination, has lost its stability. It has become inconsequently volatile to a degree at which it threatens to reassume its primaeval unconsciousness (λήθην).'—Vettius Valens, op. cit., ed. cit., pp. 241 and 242 (Book VI, Introduction).

Evidently it had never crossed our author's mind that his own beloved pseudo-science of Astrology itself was both a symptom and a cause of the death, which he is here lamenting, of the Hellenic intellect.

[2] *The Encyclopaedia of Islam*, vol. ii (London 1927, Luzac), s.v. Ḳadar. Al-Ash'arī's doctrine clearly approaches much nearer towards Predestination than towards Free Will, yet it was intended to establish a middle position between two extreme views which had previously been at war with each other on the arena of Islamic Theology. One of these two earlier opposing views was a thorough-going Fatalism; for, while the Qur'ān contradicts itself on the issue of Predestination *versus* Free Will, its author had gradually inclined towards Fatalism, and—no doubt largely in consequence of this tendency in the Prophet Muhammad's own mental evolution—the earliest conscious Muslim attitude towards the problem had been uncompromisingly fatalist. A revolt against this position had, however, broken out—apparently under Christian influences—before A.D. 700; and from that time until the generation of al-Ash'arī the Primitive Muslim Fatalism had been vigorously attacked by the Qadarīyah movement, whose supporters maintained that Man has *Qadar* (i.e. command) over his own actions.

After this preliminary observation of the hesitant fatalist's tendency to capitulate in the end to the full rigour of the creed which he has espoused, we may briefly pass in review the graven images of diverse substance in which the same goddess Necessity is worshipped by her whole-hearted devotees. There is, no doubt, an unspeculative form of Fatalism which is content to record Necessity's mighty works without making any inquiry into her nature. This attitude is exemplified in a formula—'Evil had to befall so-and-so, and therefore such-and-such things happened'—which repeats itself, like a refrain, in the history of Herodotus.[1] But more commonly Necessity is envisaged, in less abstract terms, as a force that operates in some particular medium—physical or economic or psychic or theistic.

The dogma of the omnipotence of Necessity on the physical plane of existence seems to have been introduced into Hellenic thought by Democritus—a philosopher whose long life-span (*vivebat circa* 460–360 B.C.) gave him time to grow to mature manhood before becoming a witness of the breakdown of the Hellenic Civilization, and thereafter to watch the process of social disintegration for at least another three score years and ten. 'By Necessity', Democritus pronounced, 'are foreordained all things that were and are and are to come'; and in this proposition 'a full and unhesitating Determinism' was indeed 'asserted as a base-principle of the Universe,' in contrast to the half-hearted Determinism of Democritus's predecessor Leucippus.[2] Yet Democritus appears to have ignored the problems involved in an extension of the empire of Determinism from the physical to the moral sphere;[3] and Epicurus, who was content in general to follow Democritus's lead in sketching out his own perhaps rather perfunctory chart of the Physical Universe, took the drastic step of introducing an infinitesimal dose of rebellious caprice—the famous παρέγκλισις or *clinamen*—into the physical department of Necessity's realm, because Epicurus—believing, as he did, that the Soul had a physical basis—was at the same time unwilling to admit the absolute sovereignty of Necessity in the sphere of morals.

'It were better', Epicurus declared, 'to follow the myths about the Gods than to become a slave to the "Destiny" of the natural philosophers

---

[1] See, for example, Herodotus: Book I, chap. 8; Book IV, chap. 79; Book V, chap. 33; Book V, chap. 92, δ; Book VI, chap. 64; Book VI, chap. 135; Book VII, chap. 11; Book VII, chaps. 17–18; Book VIII, chap. 53; Book IX, chap. 109. Translations of these ten passages will be found in Toynbee, A. J.: *Greek Historical Thought* (London 1924, Dent), pp. 160–1.

[2] Bailey, C.: *The Greek Atomists and Epicurus* (Oxford 1928, Clarendon Press), pp. 120–2.

[3] Ibid., pp. 186–8. It is curious to find this devotee of Physical Necessity castigating, in the field of human action, the weakness of the character that bows down and worships Chance.

(τῇ τῶν φυσικῶν εἱμαρμένῃ δουλεύειν); for the former suggests a hope of placating the Gods by worship, whereas the latter involves a necessity which knows no placation.'[1]

The dogmatic belief in an unmitigated Physical Determinism which was thus proposed by Democritus and declined by Epicurus in the course of the development of Hellenic thought was the foundation of the astral philosophy of the dominant minority in a disintegrating Babylonic World, as we have already had occasion to observe;[2] and we have also observed that the astrologers did not shrink from carrying to their logical conclusion the scientific principles of the uniformity of Nature and the mutual sympathy of all her creatures by extending the empire of Determinism from the motions of the heavenly bodies to the lives and fortunes of human beings. According to the thesis of at least one distinguished modern Western authority[3] Nabonidus's Babylonia contributed more than Democritus's Abdera to inspire Zeno of Citium with the 'totalitarian' Fatalism that distinguishes his philosophy from that of his Athenian contemporary Epicurus. If we now turn from Hellas and Babylon to our own Western World, we shall observe that our modern Western physical scientists have adopted the creed of Physical Determinism with the wholeheartedness of a Democritus, while, in the sphere of the humanities, our moral philosophers have been more ready to follow suit to the physicists, as Zeno did, than to protest in company with Epicurus.

However that may be, the modern Western World seems to have broken virgin soil in extending the empire of Necessity into the economic field—which is, indeed, a sphere of social life that has been overlooked or ignored by almost all the minds that have directed the thoughts of other societies. The classic exposition of Economic Determinism is, of course, that philosophy—or religion[4] —whose founder is Karl Marx; but in the Western or Westernized World of to-day the number of the souls who testify by their acts to a conscious or unconscious conviction that Economic Necessity is Queen of All is vastly greater than the number of professing Marxians, and would be found in fact to include a phalanx of archcapitalists who would repudiate with horror and indignation any suggestion that they were fundamentally at one, in the faith by which they lived, with the execrable prophet of Communism.

[1] Epicurus, *Letters*, No. 3, § 134. This translation of the passage, together with the original Greek, will be found in Bailey, op. cit., on p. 318.
[2] In V. C (i) (c) 1, pp. 56–7, above.
[3] See Bidez, J.: *La Cité du Monde et la Cité du Soleil chez les Stoïciens* (Paris 1932, Les Belles Lettres), *passim*, and especially p. 52.
[4] For the transformation of the original Marxian philosophy into a new-fangled proletarian religion see V. C (i) (c) 2, pp. 176–7, above.

The sovereignty of Necessity in the psychical sphere has also been proclaimed by one faction, at least, in our fledgling school of modern Western psychologists, who have been tempted to deny the existence of the Soul—in the sense of a personality or self-determining spiritual whole—in the excitement of an apparent initial success in an endeavour to analyse the Soul's processes of psychic behaviour. And, young though the science of Psycho-analysis is, the worship of Necessity in the medium of soul-stuff can already claim as its convert the most sensationally successful politician of the age.

'I go my way with the assurance of a somnambulist, the way which Providence has sent me.'

These words are quoted from a speech which was delivered by Adolf Hitler at Munich on the 14th March, 1936; and they sent a cold shudder through the frames of millions of European men and women beyond the frontiers of the Third Reich (and perhaps inside them too) whose nerves had not yet had time to recover from the preceding shock of the German military reoccupation of the Rhineland seven days before.

There is another version of the creed of Psychical Determinism which breaks the bounds of the narrow Time-span of a single human life on Earth and carries the chain of spiritual cause and effect both backwards and forwards in Time without a break—backwards to the first appearance of Man on this terrestrial stage, and forwards to his final exit from it. This more formidable appli-cation of the dogma of Determinism to spiritual affairs was already a burning question many centuries before either National Social-ism or Psycho-analysis were first heard of; and this older and deeper doctrine is found in two variants which, to all appearance, have arisen quite independently of one another. One variant is the Christian conception of 'Original Sin'; the other is the Indic conception of *Karma*, which has entered into both the philosophy of Buddhism and the religion of Hinduism.

These two renderings of one doctrine agree with one another in the essential point of making the chain of spiritual cause and effect—and the corresponding debit-and-credit account in the Book of Judgement—run on continuously from one earthly life to another. In both the Christian and the Indic view the character and conduct of a human being whom we behold alive on Earth to-day are held to have been causally conditioned by the nature of certain actions that have been performed in other lives[1]—or in one other life[2]—lived in the past, while the life that is now being

---

[1] The Indic variant.   [2] The Christian variant.

lived is believed not only to have had a spiritual heritage entailed upon it, but also to be destined to bequeath a spiritual heritage to lives that are to be lived in the future.[1] To this extent the Christian and the Indic conception coincide, but beyond this point they diverge from one another.

The Christian doctrine of 'Original Sin' affirms that a particular personal sin of the progenitor of the Human Race has entailed upon all his offspring an untoward spiritual heritage which they would all have been spared if Adam had not fallen from grace; that every descendant of Adam, *ex officio stirpis*, is foredoomed to inherit this Adamic blemish; that he does in fact find himself saddled with it automatically; and that this hereditary spiritual infection is transmitted by physical descent without the moral plague being stayed by the psychic insulation of soul from soul (although this psychic insulation or 'individuality' of each and every soul is both absolute and all-important, according to the Christian belief). It will be seen that this Christian affirmation of the fact, and conception of the nature, of spiritual heredity in Mankind[2] anticipates the doctrine of a school of modern Western biologists who hold that the physical heritage of living creatures is handed down from one generation to another, across the ever-recurring gulf which divides the successive individual representatives of a species, without any modification of the original specific type through the subsequent transmission of characteristics that may have been personally acquired by individual descendants of the first member of the series. In the spiritual, as in the physical, version of the doctrine of 'Original Sin' the power of transmitting

---

[1] This conception of 'Original Sin' or *Karma* is accepted by Christianity and by Buddhism alike; and in this measure both Christianity and Buddhism explicitly recognize the sovereignty of the goddess Necessity; but of course it would be a travesty of the truth to classify either of these two faiths as a form of Necessity-worship or Fatalism; for, while they both of them take as their premiss the proposition that Man, in his unredeemed state, is in bondage *de facto* to 'Original Sin' or to *Karma*, the purpose of both faiths is to find for Man some method of release from Necessity's yoke, and their claim to Man's attention and allegiance rests on their conviction that they are able to offer him a method of release that is capable of being effective. 'The difference for Greeks between the teaching of Babylon and the teaching of Buddha' is underlined by Tarn in op. cit., p. 60. This difference—which likewise distinguishes the teaching of Babylon from the teaching of Christ—is momentous, not merely for Hellenes, but for all men in all cultural climes and in all ages.

[2] The topic of 'Original Sin' has, of course, become one of the main arenas of theological controversy between contending Christian sects; yet the differences between their conflicting views on this subject—wide though these differences may be and bitterly though the points of conflict may be contested between them—seem to presuppose a certain common foundation of belief which is identical in all the contending schools of Christian Theology. The propositions which appear to be accepted by all Christian theologians universally and without contention are (i) that Adam, through a personal sin, has transmitted to all his physical descendants a spiritual heritage which is (a) untoward, (b) automatically inherited; (ii) that this faculty of physically transmitting an acquired spiritual characteristic (which in Adam's case happens to have been a state of lapse from grace) is a property, peculiar to the progenitor of the Human Race, which has never been possessed, and never will be possessed, by any of Adam's descendants, either for good or for evil.

an acquired characteristic from one individual to another is ascribed to Adam but is denied to every one of Adam's descendants.

The apparently arbitrary inner contradictions which are thus latent in the Christian conception of 'Original Sin' are not likewise implicit in the Indic conception of *Karma*. According to this Indic doctrine the spiritual characteristics that an individual acquires through his own acts are all transmitted from first to last, and for good or for evil, without exception; and the bearer of this cumulative spiritual heritage is not a genealogical tree representing a procession of successive separate personalities, but is a spiritual continuum (either a single permanently subsisting self or else a selfless continuum of psychological states)[1] which appears and reappears in the World of Sense through a series of reincarnations in a succession of phenomenal existences whose semblance of separateness from one another and of respective individuality is merely an hallucination in the minds of spectators.[2] These are the presuppositions of the Indic conception of *Karma*: a Sanskrit word which literally means just 'Action', but which has been restricted, in the technical terminology of philosophy and religion, to bear the special meaning of moral action, flowing from deliberate acts of will, which produces an abiding effect upon the character of the agent and which thus mounts up cumulatively, in an ever-open debit-and-credit account, from one re-incarnation to another.[3]

Finally we have to take notice of the theistic form of Determinism—a form which is perhaps the most bizarre and perverse of all, since in this Theistic Determinism an idol is worshipped in the likeness of the True God. The addicts to this covert idolatry still theoretically ascribe to the object of their worship all the attributes of a divine personality, while at the same time they insist upon the single attribute of transcendence with an emphasis so disproportionate that their God becomes transformed into a being as unapproachable, unknowable, unaccountable, implacable, and impersonal as Saeva Necessitas herself.

The 'higher religions' that have emanated from the internal

[1] The analysis of the human personality into a (not indissoluble) continuum of psychological states is a cardinal point of Buddhist doctrine which can be traced back, almost with certainty, to Siddhārtha Gautama himself; and this psychological scheme involves, at any rate implicitly, a denial of the existence of any such thing as a permanently abiding self (see Thomas, E. J.: *The History of Buddhist Thought* (London 1933, Kegan Paul), chap. 8).

[2] The spectators who suffer from this hallucination include not only outsiders but also the subject himself in his incarnation of the moment, if and when he is not in a state of enlightenment. It is only through attaining to enlightenment that the subject of *Karma* can make his memory leap the gulf between his present incarnation and his former lives, and thus become aware of the whole of the spiritual continuum of which his momentary embodiment is a temporary vehicle.

[3] For the effect of a belief in the operation of this law upon the Indic conception of the nature of the Universe see V. C (i) (d) 7, vol. vi, pp. 19–20, below.

proletariat of the Syriac Society are the spiritual fields in which this idolatrous perversion of a transcendental Theism seems most apt to break out. The two classic examples of it are the notion of *Qismet*—a popular version, current in the modern Islamic World, of al-Ash'arī's classical doctrine of *Iktisab*[1]—and the doctrine of Predestination as this has been formulated by Calvin on the alleged authority of Saint Augustine and has been presented in this guise by the modern Western Protestant revolutionary as a return to the original and fundamental teaching of the Christian Church.

Qismet is an Arabic word which means literally just 'distribution', but which has acquired the special meaning of the lot assigned to a human being for his life in This World.

'It is this meaning of the Turkish that is best known. In Turkish, however, *Kismet* is not so much an expression of theological doctrines concerning Predestination as of a practical Fatalism which accepts with resignation the blows and vicissitudes of Fate. The same sentiment is often expressed among Persian and Turkish poets by the words *falak* and *čarkh* to express the irrational and inevitable influence exercised by the spheres.'[2]

The following description of the practical working of this notion of *Qismet* in ordinary life comes from the pen of an acute English observer who was resident in Turkey over a long span of years in the latter part of the seventeenth century of the Christian Era: that is to say, in an age when the Iranic culture of the 'Osmanlis was already in full decadence without having yet begun to be contaminated by the intrusion of the alien culture of the modern West.

'The doctrine of the Turks in this point [of the nature of Predestination] seems to run exactly according to the assertion of the severest Calvinists. . . .

'They are of opinion that every man's destiny is wrote in his forehead, which they call *Narsip* [*Nasīb*] or *Tactir* [*Taqdīr*], which is the Book wrote in Heaven of every man's fortune, and is by no contrary endeavours, councels or wisdom to be avoided; which tenent is so firmly radicated in the minds of the vulgar that it causes the souldiery brutishly to throw away their lives in the most desperate attempts, and to esteem no more of their bodies then as dirt or rubbish to fill up the trenches of the enemy. And, to speak the truth, this received assertion hath turned the Turks as much to account as any other of their best and subtilest maximes.

'According to this doctrine, none ought to avoid or fear the infection of the Plague—Mahomet's precepts being not to abandon the city-house where infection rages, because God hath numbered their dayes and predestinated their fate—and upon this belief they as familiarly attend the beds and frequent the company of pestilential persons as we

---

do those that are affected with the gout, stone or ague. And, though they evidently see that Christians—who fly into better airs, and from infected habitations—survive the fury of the years of pestilence when whole cities of them perish and are depopulated with the disease, yet so far is this opinion rooted amongst them that they scruple not to strip the contagious shirt from the dead body and to put it on their own. Nor can they remove their aboad from the chambers of the sick—it being the custom in the families of great men to lodge many servants on different palets in the same room, where the diseased and healthful lie promiscuously together; from whence it hath happened often that three parts of a Pashaw's family, which perhaps hath consisted of two hundred men, most youthful and lusty, hath perished in the heat of July and August's pestilence. And in the same manner many whole families every summer have perished, and not one survivor left to claim the inheritance of the house—for want of which, the Grand Signior hath become the proprietor.

'Though the Mahometan Law obliges them not to abandon the city nor their houses, nor avoid the conversation of men infected with the pestilence where their business or calling employs them, yet they are counselled not to frequent a contagious habitation where they have no lawful affair to invite them. But yet I have observed, in the time of an extraordinary plague, that the Turks have not confided so much to the precept of their Prophet as to have courage enough to withstand the dread and terrour of that slaughter the sickness hath made, but have under other excuses fled to retired and private villages—especially the *Cadees* [*Qādis*] and men of the Law, who, being commonly of more refined wits and judgments then the generality, both by reason and experience have found that a wholsome air is a preserver of life, and that they have lived to return again to their own house in health and strength, when perhaps their next neighbours have through their brutish ignorance been laid in their graves.'[1]

In this picture of the prevailing Turkish êthos in the decadence of the Iranic Civilization the sense of drift is the feature that dominates the psychological landscape.

---

[1] Rycaut, Sir Paul: *The Present State of the Ottoman Empire* (London 1668, Starkey & Brome), pp. 115–16. This seventeenth-century English observer's picture of the Turkish state of mind in his own day may be supplemented by the following testimony to the hold of Fatalism over eighteenth-century Turkish souls which is given by two twentieth-century Western scholars:

'As for the prevalence of Fatalism, no European observer of the Ottoman Empire in the eighteenth century fails to dwell on it; for it produced striking results: whole quarters of Istanbul were perpetually being burnt down; every few years the population would be decimated by plague. Yet nothing would make the Muslims build their houses of anything but wood or take the slightest precautions, for themselves or their families, against infection. They were, it is true, quite inconsistent: for instance, they would call in a physician to treat a patient and would do their best to extinguish these conflagrations: what constituted flying in the face of Fate was settled rather by convention than otherwise. The one unpardonable blasphemy was to complain of misfortune; for this was to imply either that an event might occur otherwise than by the will of God, or else that the will of God was unjust. The correct response was an immovable calm and a reference to *Qismet* or *Taqdīr*' (Gibb, H. A. R., and Bowen, H.: *Islamic Society and the West*, vol. i (Oxford 1939, University Press), chap. 13).

5. *The Sense of Sin*

While the sense of drift is a passive feeling[1]—even when it finds expression in the seemingly dynamic activities of a militant predestinarianism[2]—it has an active counterpart and antithesis in the sense of sin which is an alternative reaction to an identical consciousness of moral defeat.

In essence and in spirit the sense of sin and the sense of drift present the sharpest contrast to one another; for, while the sense of drift has the effect of an opiate in instilling into the soul an insidious acquiescence in an evil that is assumed to reside in external circumstances beyond the victim's control, the sense of sin has the effect of a stimulus because it tells the sinner that the evil is not external after all, but is within him[3] and is therefore subject to his will— if only he wills to carry out God's purpose and so to render himself accessible to God's grace. There is here the whole difference between the Slough of Despond and the Faith that moves mountains; yet at the same time we can see that there may be a margin of common ground between the mountains and the slough in practical life—an intermediate zone of feeling and conduct across which a soul in travail with the spiritual pangs of an age of social disintegration may make an arduous passage from the passive to the active mood.

The existence of this no-man's-land in which the two moods overlap is implicitly assumed in the Indic conception of *Karma*;[4] for, although on the one hand *Karma*, like 'Original Sin', is conceived of as a spiritual heritage with which the Soul or the continuum of psychological states is saddled without the option of repudiating it, the accumulation of *Karma*, as it stands at a given moment, is also the net result of a number of acts which—good and evil acts alike—have all been deliberate acts of will; and at any moment it is possible, through other such acts of will, either to increase the weight of the inherited burden or to diminish it. Thus, while *Karma* can be regarded in one aspect as a burden forcibly imposed by the inexorable working of the law of causation, there is an alternative light in which it can be viewed as a burden that is deliberately increased or diminished, assumed or thrown off, by acts which are all within the scope of the agent's own volition.[5]

---

[1] See V. C (i) (*d*) 1, p. 380, and V. C (i) (*d*) 4, pp. 412–31, above.
[2] See V. C (i) (*d*) 4, Annex, pp. 615–18, below.
[3] See IV. C (iii) (*a*), vol. iv, pp. 120–2, above.
[4] See V. C (i) (*d*) 4, pp. 427–9, above.
[5] These two at first sight irreconcilable aspects of *Karma* can perhaps be brought into harmony by the consideration that, while the chain of acts that generates *Karma* is a chain of cause and effect, the acts themselves are all of them deliberate acts of volition.

When viewed under this aspect, *Karma* presents itself as the work of the soul (or bundle of psychoses) that is its subject, and no longer as the work of a Destiny that is external to the subject and unamenable to his (or its) control; and under this aspect *Karma* resolves itself into Sin instead of Fate. It turns out, that is, to be an evil of which the subject is himself the author, but which, by the same token, he has the power to diminish and perhaps even in the end to extinguish.

The same passage to a conquerable Sin from an unconquerable Fate can be made along a Christian road; for the Christian soul is offered a possibility of purifying itself from the taint of 'Original Sin', which is its heritage from Adam, by seeking and finding God's grace; and this divine grace does not operate as a sheerly transcendent spiritual force that scours off from the Soul an impurity which is likewise external to it. Grace comes as a divine response to a human effort; and, in order to merit this aid, the effort has to be directed towards overcoming—not, of course, the infectious primal sin which was committed by Adam and which must therefore *ex hypothesi* be impervious to the human action of any human being except Adam himself—but the personal sin of the particular soul that is now striving to win release. This personal sin may be traceable, *sub specie theologiae*, to an innate predisposition towards concupiscence which is Adam's untoward legacy to every one of his descendants; but a predisposition is not tantamount to a predetermination nor a temptation to a fall. And a sinner cannot find excuse for his sin by pleading that, in committing it, he has been yielding to a congenital frailty. For Adam's offspring, as for their progenitor, the responsibility for the sinner's own personal sin rests on the sinner himself. But, on that hypothesis, this personal sin is an evil which the Soul is capable of resisting and overcoming with the help of God's grace.

An awakening to the sense of sin can be detected in the development of the Egyptiac conception of the Life after Death in the course of the Egyptiac 'Time of Troubles';[1] but the classical case is the spiritual experience of the Prophets of Israel and Judah in the Syriac 'Time of Troubles'. When these prophets were

---

[1] In the time of 'the Old Kingdom' the attainment of bliss in the After Life was held to depend upon the fulfilment, in This World, of ritual requirements involving a material outlay. By the time of the establishment of 'the Middle Empire' the attainment of bliss in the After Life had come to be held to depend upon the living, in This World, of a righteous life. The aspirant to happiness after death no longer expected to be able to extort the prize from the Gods by the exercise of magic: he expected to stand a trial in which the Gods would be the judges, the Soul's moral conduct on Earth would be the subject of the divine scrutiny, and the alternatives of happiness and torment would be respectively the reward and the punishment that awaited the Dead alternatively according to whether the verdict were favourable or adverse (see I. C (ii), vol. i, p. 143, above, and also Meyer, E.: *Geschichte des Altertums*, vol. i, part (2), third edition (Stuttgart and Berlin 1913. Cotta), p. 242).

discovering their truths and delivering their message, the society out of whose bosom they had arisen, and to whose members they were addressing themselves, was lying in helpless agony in the grip of the Assyrian tiger, with the monster's claws lacerating the prostrate victim's flesh and its teeth splintering his bones like matchwood.[1] For souls whose body social was in this fearful plight, it was a heroic spiritual feat to reject the obvious and specious explanation of their misery as the work of an irresistible external force of a material kind, and to divine that, in spite of all outward appearances, it was their own sin that was the true cause of their tribulations[2] and that it therefore lay in their own hands to win their true release.

This saving truth which had been discovered by the Syriac Society in the ordeal of its own breakdown and disintegration was inherited from the Prophets of Israel, and was then propagated in a Christian guise, by the Syriac wing of the internal proletariat of the Hellenic World. Without this instruction from an alien source in a principle which had already been apprehended by Syriac souls with an altogether un-Hellenic outlook, the Hellenic Society might never—even in its own 'Time of Troubles'—have succeeded in learning a lesson which was so much at variance with the dominant mood in the Hellenic êthos. At the same time the Hellenes might have found it still more difficult than they did find it to take this Syriac spiritual discovery to heart if they had not, of their own motion, been moving in the same direction themselves.

This native awakening to a sense of sin can be traced in the spiritual history of Hellenism many centuries before a Hellenic trickle mingled with a Syriac stream in the river of Christianity.[3]

If we have been right in our interpretation of the origin, nature, and intention of Orphism,[4] there is evidence that, even before the Hellenic Civilization broke down, at least a few Hellenic souls had become so painfully conscious of a spiritual void in their native cultural heritage that they had resorted to the *tour de force* of artificially inventing the 'higher religion' with which the apparented Minoan Civilization had failed to endow them. It is at any rate certain that, in the very first generation after the breakdown of 431 B.C., the apparatus of Orphism was being used—and abused— for the purpose of providing satisfaction for souls that were already convicted of sin and were groping, however blindly, for release from it. For this we have the testimony of a passage of Plato which might almost have flowed from the pen of Luther.

---

[1] See V. C (i) (c) 2, pp. 117–19, above.
[2] Reasons for pronouncing a verdict of suicide, and not one of murder, upon the death of the Syriac Society have been suggested in IV. C (ii) (b) 1, vol. iv, pp. 67–8, above.　　　　[3] See V. C (ii) (a), Annex II, vol. vi, p. 537, below.
[4] See V. C (i) (c) 2, pp. 84–7, above.

'There are the quacks and diviners who peddle their wares to the rich and make them believe that these cheapjacks possess powers, procured from the Gods by sacrifices and incantations, for healing with diversions and festivities any sin that has been committed either by oneself or by one's forebears. Conversely—supposing that one wants to plague an enemy—they pretend to the command of corresponding powers for inflicting injury (upon the just and the unjust indifferently) by charms and spells at a modest price. This they claim to do by inducing the Gods to minister to their purposes; and as their authorities for all this rigmarole they cite the poets ... and produce a host of books purporting to have been written by Musaeus and Orpheus, whom they palm off as the offspring of the Moon and the Muses. They follow these books in their hocus-pocus; and they persuade even Governments, as well as private people, that a release and purification from sin can be obtained by means of sacrifices and agreeable child's-play! They further maintain that these "rites" (as they call them in this connexion) are as efficacious for the dead as they are for the living. "Rites" liberate us from the torments of the world beyond the grave, while a dreadful fate awaits us if we neglect here and now to make sacrifices.'[1]

This first glimpse that is given to us of a native sense of sin in the souls of the Hellenic dominant minority in its 'Time of Troubles' looks as unpromising as it is repulsive. Yet two and three and four centuries later, in the tender consciences of an Agis and a Cleomenes and a Tiberius and a Gaius Gracchus[2] and in the tardy yet sincere repentance of Augustus,[3] we see a native Hellenic sense of sin which has been purified, out of all recognition, in the fires of suffering; and there is almost a Christian note in the voice of the Hellenic dominant minority in the Augustan Age as this makes itself heard in the poetry of Virgil:

> Ergo inter sese paribus concurrere telis
> Romanas acies iterum videre Philippi;
> nec fuit indignum superis bis sanguine nostro
> Emathiam et latos Haemi pinguescere campos. . . .
> Di Patrii, Indigetes, et Romule Vestaque mater,
> quae Tuscum Tiberim et Romana Palatia servas,
> hunc saltem everso iuvenem succurrere saeclo
> ne prohibete. satis iam pridem sanguine nostro
> Laomedonteae luimus periuria Troiae. . . .
> quippe ubi fas versum atque nefas; tot bella per orbem;
> tam multae scelerum facies; non ullus aratro
> dignus honos: squalent abductis arva colonis
> et curvae rigidum falces conflantur in ensem.

[1] Plato: *Respublica*, 364B–365A.
[2] For these four archaistic-minded social reformers see the references in V. C (i) (d) 1, p. 388, footnote 1, above.
[3] See V. C (i) (c) 2, p. 78, above, and V. C (i) (d) 6 (δ), Annex, p. 648, and V. C (ii) (a), vol. vi, p. 187, below.

hinc movet Euphrates, illinc Germania bellum;
vicinae ruptis inter se legibus urbes
arma ferunt; saevit toto Mars impius orbe;
ut cum carceribus sese effudere quadrigae,
addunt in spatio, et frustra retinacula tendens
fertur equis auriga neque audit currus habenas.[1]

This is a prayer for delivery from a torturing sense of drift
which is conveyed in the last three lines by one of the most vivid
strokes of Virgil's art. The prayer takes the form of a confession
of sin; and, though the sin from which the poet implores Heaven
for release is nominally an 'original sin' inherited from Laomedon
—a minor character in the Greek Epic Cycle of Troy who by
Virgil's time had come to be adopted as a legendary Trojan progenitor for an authentic Roman dominant minority—the tremendous *ergo* which is the first word of the first line and the key word
of the whole passage tells the reader that the sin which the Romans
were expiating in Virgil's day was really the sin which they themselves had been committing during the two-centuries-long rake's
progress upon which they had entered when they plunged into the
Hannibalic War[2]—a sin that, in its fearful climax, had driven the
Sun himself to veil his countenance,

cum caput obscura nitidum ferrugine texit,
impiaque aeternam timuerunt saecula noctem.[3]

Within a century of the year in which Virgil's poem was written,
the spirit that breathes through these passages had become predominant in a stratum of the Hellenic Society which had hardly yet come
within range of the radiation of Christianity.

'From whatever quarter, a new spiritual vision had opened, strange
to the Ancient World. It is not merely that the conception of God has
become more pure and lofty: the whole attitude of the higher minds
to the eternal had altered. A great spiritual revolution had concurred
with a great political revolution. The vision of the Divine World which
satisfied men in the Age of Pericles or in the Punic Wars, when Religion,
Politics, and Morality were linked in unbroken harmony[4]—when, if
spiritual vision was bounded, spiritual needs were less clamorous, and
the moral life less troubled and self-conscious—could no longer appease

---

[1] Virgil: *Georg.* I, ll. 489–92, 498–502, 505–14. Some of these lines have been quoted
already in IV. C (iii) (c) 3 (β), vol. iv, p. 509, above.

[2] See IV. C (iii) (c) 3 (β), vol. iv, pp. 505–8, above.

[3] Virgil: *Georg.* I, ll. 467–8. The crime which, according to Virgil, had been signalized by this portent of diurnal darkness was, of course, the assassination of Caesar and
not the crucifixion of Christ. This traditional association of an eclipse of the Sun with
the death of a hero who is being cut off in his prime by a heinous piece of foul play
can be traced back to the legend of Hêraklês (see V. C (ii) (a), Annex II, vol. vi, p. 473,
below).

[4] For the diffraction, during the process of social disintegration, of the rays of social
radiation which are blended into a single clear beam during the process of social growth,
see I. B (iii), vol. i, pp. 26–33, and V. C (i) (c) 3, in the present volume, pp. 199–203
above.—A.J.T.

the yearnings of the higher minds. Both Morality and Religion had become less formal and external, more penetrating and exigent. Prayer was no longer a formal litany for worldly blessings or sinful indulgence, but a colloquy with God in a moment of spiritual exaltation. The true sacrifice was no longer "the blood of bulls" but a quiet spirit. Along with a sense of frailty and bewilderment men felt the need of purification and spiritual support. The old mysteries and the new cults from the East had fostered a longing for sacramental peace and assurance of an Other Life, in which the crooked should be made straight and the perverted be restored.'[1]

This picture of the spiritual state of the Hellenic dominant minority about a hundred years later than the generation of Augustus has been painted by a modern Western scholar with authentic colours that have been preserved in the literature of the age; and it is a different picture indeed from the sketch drawn by Plato some five hundred years earlier. In retrospect it is plain that the generations of Seneca and Plutarch and Epictetus and Marcus were unwittingly preparing their hearts for an approaching enlightenment from a proletarian source out of which these sophisticated Hellenic 'intellectuals' would never have augured the coming of any good thing.[2]

The Hellenic and Syriac societies are assuredly not the only civilizations in which there has been an awakening to the sense of sin through the shock of seeing an ancient social structure collapse in ruin. We may tentatively interpret the penitential self-mortifications of the Mayas[3] in their age of social decadence as an outward visible sign of an inward spiritual state; and we may draw the same inference in the same tentative fashion from certain relics of the Sumeric religion: the Penitential Psalms and the worship of Tammuz and Ishtar.[4] In the Sumeric and in the Mayan field the historian is working almost entirely in the dark, with only a rare glimmer of uncertain light to guide him. It is strange to find ourselves equally at a loss to answer the question whether a native sense of sin can be detected in the present state

[1] Dill, S.: *Roman Society from Nero to Marcus Aurelius* (London 1905, Macmillan), pp. 420–1. Compare the passages quoted in V. C (i).(*d*) 6 (δ), pp. 550–1, below.
[2] John i.46. On this point see further V. C (i) (*d*) 6 (δ), pp. 550–68, below.
[3] See V. C (i) (*d*) 2, p. 403, above. This vein in the religion of the Mayas in the time of the Mayan universal state duly reappears in the Mayan religious heritage of the Mexic Society (for this heritage see I. C (i) (*b*), vol. i, p. 127, and V. C (i) (*c*) 4, in the present volume, p. 357, above). Dirges on the themes of mutability and death are a prominent feature in the literature of the interloping barbarian Aztec empire-builders who embraced the religion of the Mexic World (see V. C (i) (*c*) 4, p. 357, above) and came within an ace of anticipating the Spaniards in establishing a Central American universal state (see Spinden, H. J.: *Ancient Civilizations of Mexico and Central America* (New York 1922, American Museum of Natural History, Handbook No. 3), pp. 212–13).
[4] For the difficulty of replacing these relics of the Sumeric religion in their historical setting so long as we are handicapped by our present dearth of historical evidence see, I. C (i) (*b*), vol. i, p. 115, footnote 1, and V. C (i) (*c*) 2, in the present volume, pp. 148–9, above.

of mind of the society in which we ourselves actually live and move and have our being.

The sense of sin is, no doubt, a feeling with which our modern Western homunculus is quite familiar. A familiarity with it is, indeed, almost forced upon him; for the sense of sin is a cardinal feature of the 'higher religion' which we have inherited from the dead civilization to which ours is affiliated. In this case, however, familiarity seems latterly to have been breeding—not so much contempt as the more violent reactions of aversion and hostility. And the contrast between this temper of the modern Western World and the contrary temper of the Hellenic World in the sixth century B.C. shows up the vein of perversity in human nature. Though our historical evidence for the early age of Hellenic history is too scanty to be conclusive, it indicates, as we have seen,[1] that the Hellenic Society, starting life with the jejune and unsatisfying religious heritage of a barbarian pantheon, became conscious of its spiritual poverty and exerted itself to fill the void by inventing, in Orphism, a 'higher religion' of the kind that some other, perhaps more fortunate, civilizations have inherited from their predecessors; and the character of the Orphic ritual and doctrine makes it clear that the sense of sin was the pent-up religious feeling for which the Hellenes of the sixth century B.C. were eager, above all, to find a normal outlet. In contrast to the Hellenic Society our Western Society is one of those more generously endowed civilizations that have grown up under the aegis of a 'higher religion' and within the chrysalis of a universal church; and it is perhaps just because Western Man has always been able to take his Christian birth-right for granted that he has persistently depreciated and finally repudiated it.

The history of this graceless *Homo Occidentalis* who has turned against the Christianity that found him a barbarian and has promoted him to the lordship of creation is a tale of ὕβρις which has been told in the parable of Jeshurun.

'He found him in a desert land and in the waste howling wilderness; He led him about, He instructed him, He kept him as the apple of His eye. . . .

'He made him ride on the high places of the Earth that he might eat the increase of the fields, and He made him to suck honey out of the rock and oil out of the flinty rock. . . .

'But Jeshurun waxed fat and kicked . . . then he forsook God which made him, and lightly esteemed the rock of his salvation.'[2]

Of all the gifts of Christianity against which our modern Western Jeshurun has been kicking in these latter days, the sense of sin

---

[1] In V. C (i) (c) 2, pp. 84–7, above.   [2] Deut. xxxii. 10, 13, and 15.

is perhaps the one which has moved him to the direst fury of rebellion. You have only to mention the sense of sin in order to be sure of making the modern-minded Westerner 'see red'. The degree to which he flatters himself that he has succeeded in plucking this sense out and casting it from him is for him almost the measure of his success in his struggle to emancipate himself from the bondage of that Christian tradition in which he has been bred. And the cult of Hellenism, which has been so potent, and in many ways so fruitful, an ingredient in our secular Western culture during the last four centuries, has been partly fostered and kept alive by a conventional conception of Hellenism as a way of life which gloriously combines with all our own modern Western virtues and attainments an innate and effortless freedom from that hateful sense of sin which Western Man is now industriously purging out of his *ci-devant* Christian spiritual heritage.[1]

Will modern Western Man repent of, and recoil from, his ὕβρις before it finds its nemesis in ἄτη? If this is the riddle of the destiny of our Western Civilization, the answer cannot yet be forecast in a generation which has been born into the critical act of the tragic drama. But we may anxiously scan the landscape of our contemporary spiritual life for any symptoms that may give us ground for hope that we are regaining the use of a spiritual faculty which we have been doing our worst to sear and sterilize. Dare we allow ourselves to see at any rate a favourable omen in the emphasis that is laid upon a conviction of sin in the 'revivalist' version of Protestantism which has been rife on the English-speaking fringe of the Western World during the last two hundred years and which—winning its first foothold in a nascent industrial proletariat, and spreading thence to a rising lower-middle class—has lately been carried into the citadel of a paganized dominant minority by the shock-tactics of the so-called 'Oxford Groups'?

6. *The Sense of Promiscuity*

(α) *Pammixia and Proletarianization.*
The Receptivity of Empire-Builders.

A sense of promiscuity is the passive substitute for that sense of style which develops *pari passu* with the growth of a civilization.[2] This state of mind takes practical effect in an act of self-surrender to the melting-pot; and in the process of social disintegration an identical mood manifests itself in equivalent action in every province of social life:[3] in Religion and Literature and Language and

---

[1] For the element of truth in this picture of Hellenism as an historic example of the blessedness of being spiritually 'once-born' see II. D (vii), vol. ii, pp. 355–7, above.
[2] See III. C (iii), vol. iii, pp. 377–90, above.
[3] See V. C (i) (*d*) 1, p. 381, above.

Art, as well as in a wider and vaguer field that may be labelled 'Manners and Customs'. In attempting an empirical survey of the manifestations of this sense of promiscuity in the declines and falls of those civilizations that have broken down up to date within the brief span of some five or six thousand years during which this species of societies has been in existence so far, it will be convenient to sift out the phenomena for separate consideration under these different heads. It will also be convenient to begin operations in the field of 'Manners', since this is the field which has the widest range, while the spiritual crop that it bears is not to be despised if there is any truth in the adage that 'Manners makyth Man'.

In looking out for the earliest and strongest evidence for the emergence of a sense of promiscuity in the body social of a disintegrating society we shall perhaps be inclined to turn our eyes with the greatest expectancy towards the Internal Proletariat. In bringing the representatives of the Internal Proletariat on to our stage in an earlier chapter[1] we have observed that their common and characteristic affliction is the torture of being torn up by the roots; and this terrible experience of social 'deracination' might be expected, above all other experiences, to produce a sense of promiscuity in souls that had been compelled to undergo it. This *a priori* expectation is not, however, borne out by the historical facts; for, more often than not, the ordeal to which an internal proletariat is subjected seems to strike that optimum degree of severity at which the challenge acts as a stimulating spur and not as a crushing sledge-hammer;[2] and we see the uprooted and ex-patriated and enslaved men and women of whom an internal proletariat is composed not only keeping a firm hold upon any shreds of their torn and trampled native social heritage that they have been able to carry with them into exile or captivity, but actually going on to impart these fragmentary remnants of their ancestral culture to a dominant minority who, *a priori*, might have been expected—so far from receiving any cultural impress from that quarter—to impose their own 'culture-pattern' upon the mob of waifs and strays whom they have caught in their net and forced under their yoke.

[1] See V. C (i) (c) 2, *passim*, above.
[2] For the notion of Challenge-and-Response see Part II. D, vol. ii, *passim*, above. 'The Golden Mean' in the working of Challenge-and-Response is discussed in II. D (vii). The application of these principles to the life of the Internal Proletariat has been touched upon, in this context, in II. D (vi), which deals with the stimulus of penalizations. The ordeal of 'deracination', which is thus apt to evoke a victorious response from members of the Internal Proletariat, is on the contrary apt to have a demoralizing effect upon members of the External Proletariat when these are uprooted and transplanted in consequence, not of exile or enslavement, but of a Völkerwanderung in which their war-bands break through a *limes* and migrate from a no-man's-land into an Eldorado as military conquerors (see V. C (i) (c) 3, p. 201, footnote 1, above, and Part VIII, below).

It is still more surprising to see—as, again, we do see—the
Dominant Minority showing itself similarly receptive to the cultural influence of the External Proletariat, considering that these
truculent war-bands are insulated from the Dominant Minority
by a military frontier and that their barbarian social heritage
might have been expected to be lacking in both the charm and the
prestige that manifestly still cling even to the tatters of those
mellow civilizations to which the Internal Proletariat is heir in
the persons of some, at least, of its involuntary recruits.

Nevertheless we do find, as a matter of fact, that, of the three
factions into which a disintegrating society is apt to split, it is the
Dominant Minority that succumbs to the sense of promiscuity the
most readily, and this in its military intercourse with the External
Proletariat beyond the *limes* as well as in its economic intercourse
with the Internal Proletariat in the *ergastulum*. The ultimate
result of these two parallel processes of 'proletarianization' to
which the Dominant Minority yields itself is a disappearance of
that schism in the body social which is the index and the penalty
of a social breakdown. The Dominant Minority atones, in the
end, for its sins by closing a breach that has been its own handiwork; and it closes it by merging itself in the Proletariat in so far
as it does not forestall the completion of this process of 'proletarianization' by an act of suicide.

Before we attempt to follow the course of 'proletarianization'
along its two parallel lines, it may be illuminating to glance at
the evidence for the receptivity of empire-builders, since this
pre-disposition may partly explain the sequel.

The universal states of which these empire-builders are the
architects are, for the most part, the products of military conquest,
and we may therefore look for our finest examples of receptivity
in the sphere of military technique. We may begin by citing
testimony to the military receptivity of the Romans which has
been given by a Greek witness who was himself a member of the
Hellenic dominant minority of the age in which he was writing.

'At the present day', Polybius records, 'the equipment of the Roman
cavalryman is practically identical with that of his Greek companion-
in-arms. Originally, however, it was otherwise. . . . [Here follows a
detailed technical description of the Roman cavalryman's original
equipment.] . . . When experience proved their own equipment unsatisfactory, the Romans speedily replaced it by the Greek, which possesses the following advantages. . . . [Technical specifications follow.]
. . . The Romans were not slow to make these advantages their own
when once they had apprehended them—the fact being that the Romans
are without rivals among the nations of the World in their adaptability

and their enthusiasm for progress (ἀγαθοὶ γάρ, εἰ καί τινες ἕτεροι, μετα-
λαβεῖν ἔθη καὶ ζηλῶσαι τὸ βέλτιον καὶ 'Ρωμαῖοι).'[1]

A similar receptivity in the sphere of military technique was
shown by the Theban founders of 'the New Empire' of Egypt in
borrowing the horse-and-chariot, as a weapon of war, from their
defeated *ci-devant* Nomad antagonists the Hyksos; by the marchmen
of the Sinic World over against the Eurasian Steppe in following
their Nomad neighbours in the substitution of cavalry for chariotry
as a more effective way of employing the horse in warfare;[2] by
the Parnian[3] and Saka Eurasian Nomad supplanters of Greek
empire-builders in Parthia and in India in respectively employing
against their Greek antagonists the two Greek weapons of catapults
for besieging cities[4] and naval flotillas for commanding navigable
rivers;[5] by the 'Osmanlis in borrowing the Western invention of
fire-arms; by the Mughals in adopting this same Western innovation at second hand from the 'Osmanlis;[6] and by the military
Powers of the modern Western World in borrowing, in their turn,
from their 'Osmanli debtors the immensely potent weapon of a
disciplined professional infantry armed with muskets and uniformly
dressed and drilled.[7]

The vein of receptivity in the empire-builders which is revealed
in this readiness to exchange old lamps for new on points of military technique is not, however, by any means confined to the
soldier's business in which these empire-builders have made their
fortunes. They show themselves almost equally receptive to
'gadgets' and to habits that have little or nothing to do with the
art of war. For example, the Parnian Nomad founders and

---

[1] Polybius, Book VI, chap. 25, §§ 3–11. A translation of the passage, including the
technicalities that have been omitted here, will be found in Toynbee, A. J.: *Greek
Civilisation and Character* (London 1924, Dent), pp. 92–3. This receptivity in the
sphere of military technique was still being displayed by the Romans in an age, some
three hundred years later than Polybius's day, when conservatism had become the note
of Roman life in almost every other line of activity.
'The tactics of the Romans in the second century A.D. represent the evolution of a
system of warfare based on the experience of centuries of fighting. If the cohort formation and the military camp were essentially Roman products, the phalanx was the
contribution of Macedon, and the *gladius* and *lancea* the discoveries of Spain and Gaul.
In this effective combination of inventions and inheritances Rome worked out her
military organization and strategy, and the secret of her success lay in her willingness
to learn from her enemies, and to assimilate the gifts which they had to offer' (Parker,
H. M. D.: *The Roman Legions* (Oxford 1928, Clarendon Press)).
[2] See III. C (i) (*b*), vol. iii, p. 167, footnote 1, and IV. C (iii) (*c*) 2 (γ), vol. iv, p. 439,
footnote 4, above. The Sinic war-lord to whom this innovation is attributed was, it is
true, a prince of Chao and not a prince of Ts'in, which was the border principality that
gave birth to the Sinic universal state.
[3] See II. D (vii), Annex V, vol. ii, p. 435, footnote 1, above.
[4] Tarn, W. W.: *The Greeks in Bactria and India* (Cambridge 1938, University Press),
p. 21, footnote 1.
[5] Tarn, op. cit., pp. 91, 320, 322, 329, 349.
[6] For Bābur's acknowledgements of his indebtedness to the 'Ghazis of Rum' for the
chefs d'œuvre of his military technique see I. C (i) (*b*), Annex I, in vol. i, p. 352, above.
[7] For this military debt of the modern Western World to the 'Osmanlis see Part III A,
vol. iii, p, 38, footnote 2, and IV. C (iii) (*c*) 2 (γ), vol. iv, p. 450, above.

masters of the Parthian 'successor-state' of the Seleucid Greek 'successor-state' of the Achaemenian Empire appear to have borrowed a number of administrative devices both from their Seleucid Greek predecessors and from their Euthydemid Greek neighbours.[1] Again, the Saka Nomad founders and masters of 'successor-states' of a Bactrian Greek empire on Indian ground borrowed administrative devices from their Greek predecessors and a religion, a language, and perhaps also a literature from their Indian subjects.[2] This wider range of receptivity is also strikingly illustrated by the following description, from a Greek observer's pen, of the Persian builders of the Achaemenian Empire—a description which is noteworthy for the abruptness of the contrast between the Persians' receptivity in practice and their exclusiveness in theory:

'Next to themselves, the Persians rate highest the peoples that live nearest to them, next highest the next nearest—and so on in a graduated scale in which appreciation varies in inverse ratio to distance, with the remotest nations at the bottom of the honours list. For they consider their own selves to be by far the finest specimens of Mankind in all points, and they grade the rest on the scale aforementioned, which condemns the remotest nations to rank as the worst. . . . There is no nation like the Persians for adopting foreign manners and customs (ξεινικὰ δὲ νόμαια Πέρσαι προσίενται ἀνδρῶν μάλιστα). For instance, the civilian dress of the Medes seemed to them handsomer than their own, so [in peace time] they wear that, while on active service they wear Egyptian breast-plates. They are also addicted to all kinds of outlandish self-indulgences which they have picked up—among others, unnatural vice, which they have learnt from the Hellenes.'[3]

A better taste in promiscuity appears to have been shown by the Inca empire-builders of the Andean universal state.

'Ce n'est pas un des moindres mérites des Inka que de s'être mis toujours à l'école des vaincus. Ils ont beaucoup emprunté au point de

---

[1] According to Tarn, in op. cit., the 'Parthians' borrowed from their Euthydemid Greek neighbours in Bactria the constitutional expedient of appointing sub-kings (p. 90) and the administrative device of raising ci-devant Seleucid eparchies to the status of satrapies (p. 240), while from the Seleucidae they borrowed the devices of an official era (p. 65), a division of the empire into a senior western and a junior eastern kingdom (pp. 203–4), and the appointment of a queen regent (p. 317).

[2] According to Tarn, in op. cit., the Sakas borrowed from their Bactrian Greek predecessors their administrative organization (pp. 241–3), their mints (p. 323), and their calendar (p. 359). Their subsequent borrowings from their Indian subjects were more momentous. They became converts to Hinduism and patrons of the archaistic revival of the classical Sanskrit language (see V. C (i) (d) 8 (γ), vol. vi, pp. 75–7, below). Their patronage may also have played a part in the precipitation of the Indic Epic in its present form (see V. C (i) (c) 3, Annex II, in the present volume, p. 606, footnote 3, below).

[3] Herodotus, Book I, chaps. 134–5. This receptivity of the Persian builders of the Achaemenian Empire is compared with that of the Arab builders of the Caliphate by Meyer, E.: Geschichte des Altertums, vol. iii (Stuttgart 1901, Cotta), p. 38.

vue matériel au Royaume de Quito; ils ont peut-être aussi emprunté au point de vue spirituel au Royaume des C[h]imu.'[1]

A precocity in promiscuity is ascribed to the Athenians by one of themselves who has left us a vivid thumb-nail sketch of the cosmopolitan manners that his countrymen acquired as the makers and masters of a premature and abortive Hellenic universal state[2] which subsisted, from first to last, for barely three-quarters of a century; and, while 'the Old Oligarch's' testimony against a democratic Athens in which he and his kind were at a discount has in general to be received with caution, what he writes in the following passage is corroborated by all the other evidence that has come down to us.

'If we may be excused for mentioning trivialities, we may add to our catalogue of the consequences of the Athenians' command of the sea first and foremost the eclectic fashion of high living which they have elaborated out of what they have picked up here, there and everywhere in their intercourse with foreigners. Their command of the sea has enabled them to assemble on one table tit-bits from Sicily, Italy, Cyprus, Egypt, Lydia, the Pontus, the Peloponnese or anywhere that you will.'[3]

These exotic ingredients in the diet of Cleonian Athens cannot fail to conjure up, in the mind of any modern Western reader who has tasted 'the Old Oligarch's' Attic salt, a considerably longer catalogue of trivialities that have become woven by now into the very texture of the everyday life of our modern Western World, and which yet are, all of them, 'souvenirs' of the empire-building activities of a *Homo Occidentalis* who during the past four centuries has been ranging over the face of the planet 'as a roaring lion . . . seeking whom he may devour'.[4] Our tobacco-smoking commemorates our extermination of the red-skinned aborigines of North America to make room for the repeopling of 'the New World' (as it has been for us) by a population of European origin and Western culture.[5] Our coffee-drinking and tea-drinking and polo-playing and pyjama-wearing and taking of Turkish baths commemorate the enthronement of the Frankish man-of-business in the seat of the Ottoman Qaysar-i-Rūm and of the Mughal Qaysar-i-Hind. And our jazzing, which is the most recent addition to this repertory of a Western bourgeois household's common round and daily task, commemorates the enslavement of the African

---

[1] Baudin, L.: *L'Empire Socialiste des Inka* (Paris 1928, Institut d'Ethnologie), p. 61, footnote 3.
[2] For this aspect of 'the First Athenian Empire' see Part III. B, vol. iii, p. 122, footnote 3; III. C (ii) (*b*), vol. iii, p. 340; and IV. C (iii) (*b*) 10, vol. iv, pp. 208, 211, and 213, above, and V. C (ii) (*b*), vol. vi, p. 287, below.
[3] Auctor Atheniensis Anonymus: *Institutions of Athens* (edited by Kalinka, E.: Leipzig and Berlin 1913, Teubner), chap. 2, § 7.   [4] 1 Peter v. 8.
[5] See II. C (ii) (*a*) 1, Annex, in vol. i; II. D (vii), vol. ii, p. 277, footnote 2; and V. C (i) (*c*) 1, in the present volume, p. 46, above.

Negro and his transportation across the Atlantic to labour on American soil in plantations which had taken the place of the hunting grounds of the vanished Red Indian.[1]

After this prefatory recital of some of the more notorious evidence for the receptivity of the Dominant Minority in a disintegrating society, we may now proceed to our survey, first of the vulgarization of the Dominant Minority through its pacific intercourse with an Internal Proletariat which lies physically at its mercy, and then of its barbarization through its warlike intercourse with an External Proletariat which eludes its yoke.

The Vulgarization of the Dominant Minority.

While the intercourse of the Dominant Minority with the Internal Proletariat is pacific in the sense that the proletarians of this class have already become physically subject to the Dominant Minority *ex hypothesi*, nevertheless it often happens that the first social contact between subjects and rulers—and even between slaves and masters, where the gulf is of that width—takes the form of an introduction of proletarian recruits into the empire-builders' permanent garrisons or standing armies which have been originally established as instruments of domination and have therefore, at the outset, been recruited, with a jealous exclusiveness, from members of the Dominant Minority only.

The classic example of this dilution of military labour is the recruitment of the Slave-Household of the Ottoman Pādishāh from renegades, prisoners-of-war, and child-conscripts supplied by the Pādishāh's own Orthodox Christian *raʿīyeh*;[2] for this dilution of the Ottoman standing army and administrative service set in at an early stage of the ʿOsmanlis' history as empire-builders; it was the principal cause of their marvellous military and political triumphs; and it was carried to such extremes that in the heyday of the Ottoman Empire the Imperial slave's career was the sole avenue to power, and yet at the same time every free-born Muslim subject of the Pādishāh was debarred from following this career by the stigma of a birth which in almost every other society would have given him a paramount or exclusive title to bear rule. In a rather cruder form this apparent contradiction-in-terms—a proletarian dominant minority—re-appears in the Mamlūk régime in Egypt,[3] and we have found traces of it in the substructure of the

[1] See IV. C (iii) (b) 2, vol. iv, pp. 137–41, above. For the less trivial influence which the uprooted African Negro recruit to the overseas section of the proletariat of the modern Western World may be destined to have upon our religion, see II. D (vi), vol. ii, pp. 218–20, and V. C (i) (c) 2, in the present volume, pp. 191–3, above.

[2] An account of the recruitment, training, organization, and employment of the Ottoman *qullar* has been given, in a different context, in Part III. A, vol. iii, pp. 22–44, above.   [3] See Part III. A, vol. iii, pp. 30–1, above.

Mughal Rāj in Hindustan and in the superstructure of the régime under which Hindustan was ruled by the Mughals' forerunners in the fourteenth century of the Christian Era.[1]

This *tour de force* of attaching disabilities instead of privileges to noble birth is the peculiarity of empires built *in partibus agricolarum* by *ci-devant* Nomads whose line of least resistance, in seeking to adapt themselves to their new circumstances, lies in applying to an internal proletariat of human stock the technique that their own ancestors have worked out, on their native steppes, for the domestication of animals.[2] But at the same time this is only an extreme example of a tendency which is more widely prevalent; for the same process of dilution can be seen at work likewise in the standing armies of dominant minorities of non-Nomadic antecedents.

The history of the standing army of the Roman Empire, for example, is the story of a progressive dilution which began almost on the morrow of the Roman army's transformation from an *ad hoc* and amateur conscript force to a permanent and professional volunteer force by the act of Augustus. From the beginning the Augustan Imperial army included units of *auxilia*, recruited from subjects or semi-subjects of the Empire who were not Roman citizens,[3] besides the legions which still at first continued to be composed of citizens exclusively; the *auxilia* perhaps at no time accounted for less than half the total strength of the regular establishment;[4] and the differentiation between the 'auxiliary' and the 'legionary' branch of the service steadily diminished in significance as the privilege of Roman citizenship came to be extended to an ever widening circle, until the old distinction vanished altogether when Caracalla (*imperabat* A.D. 211–17) completed the process of enfranchisement by conferring Roman citizenship *ex officio* upon every free adult male inhabitant of the Empire who was either a citizen or a subject of any one of the hundreds of local city-

---

[1] See Part III. A, vol. iii, p. 31, footnote 1, above.

[2] This point has been made in Part III. A, vol. iii, p. 28, above.

[3] These *auxilia* were, indeed, already a well-established arm of the Roman Army by the date of the Augustan reorganization; for they were the successors of, and substitutes for, an older non-citizen force in the shape of the cohorts furnished by the Italian communities that had formerly been *socii* and not citizens of the Roman state. When these Italian *socii* of Rome had at last extorted, by the *ultima ratio* of armed insurrection, an enfranchisement that had long been overdue, the Roman Government had found itself constrained to look elsewhere for non-citizen troops to brigade with the legions. 'By the enfranchising laws of 90–89 B.C. the recruiting area for legionary troops was extended to all Italy south of the Po. The *socii* disappeared, and the Roman Army was now composed of legions of citizen-soldiers and *auxilia* or detachments of foreign troops serving either as volunteers or as mercenaries' (Parker, H. M. D.: *The Roman Legions* (Oxford 1928, Clarendon Press), p. 46).

[4] See *The Cambridge Ancient History*, vol. x, pp. 228–9, for the numerical ratio between *auxilia* and legions in the Roman Army as reorganized by Augustus. For the recruitment, character, and history of the *auxilia* see Cheesman, G. L.: *The Auxilia of the Roman Imperial Army* (Oxford 1914, Clarendon Press).

states that were the cells of the Imperial body politic.[1] Thereafter (until the radical reorganization of the Imperial army by
Diocletian and Constantine) the legions, which had long since
struck local roots in their respective cantonments in the provinces,
were each recruited almost entirely from the surrounding population within their local radius, and the only surviving units in
which the troops were Roman soldiers without being Roman
citizens were now those raised (it is true, in growing numbers)
from barbarian sources of man-power outside the Imperial
frontiers.[2]

The history of the Roman standing army in a Roman Empire
which was the Hellenic Society's universal state is reproduced in
the history of the standing army in the Far Eastern universal state
as this was reconstructed in the seventeenth century of the
Christian Era by Manchu empire-builders;[3] and the same tendencies are illustrated by the history of the Arab standing army
in the dominions of the Umayyad and the 'Abbasid Caliphate.
In its inclusion of Chinese as well as Manchu 'banners'[4] the Manchu military establishment is an exact counterpart of the Roman
with its units of *auxilia* brigaded with the legions.[5] And the Man-
chu-Chinese comradeship-in-arms which grew up in the South
Manchurian march of the Far Eastern World has a parallel in the
Arab-Iranian comradeship-in-arms which grew up in the Syriac
World's border-province (as it was in that age) of Khurāsān.[6] We
may also take note of the far-going dilution of the Mongol standing
army, within less than a hundred years of the beginning of
Chingis Khan's military career, which is illustrated by the episode
of the annihilation of the Alan unit in a force which was being
employed by Chingis' grandson Qubilay for the conquest of

---

[1] For this view of the scope of the Caracallan enfranchisement see Jones, A. H. M.:
'Another Interpretation of the *Constitutio Antoniniana*' in *The Journal of Roman
Studies*, vol. xxvi, part 2 (1936).

[2] Unlike the *auxilia* of the first and second centuries of the Christian Era, these
fourth-century and fifth-century *foederati* served in their own native equipment and
formations and even under their own native commanders; and this difference was
inimical to assimilation

[3] See IV. C (ii) (b) 2, vol. iv, p. 87, and V. C (i) (c) 1, in the present volume,
pp. 53–4, above.

[4] For the Manchu Imperial military organization see V. C (i) (c) 3, p. 315, footnote
3, and V. C (i) (d) 3, p. 410, above.

[5] The analogy goes still farther; for, if the Chinese 'banners' of the Manchu establishment are strictly comparable with the units of *auxilia* which were recruited from the
non-citizen subjects of the Roman Empire, the Mongol 'banners' correspond, with the same
exactness, to those units of *foederati* that were recruited from the transfrontier barbarians.

[6] Khurāsān was the border-province of the Syriac World over against the Eurasian
Nomads during the period of little less than nine hundred years (from the latter part of
the second century B.C. to the earlier part of the eighth century of the Christian Era)
during which the Oxus-Jaxartes Basin was under Nomad occupation. For this episode
of Syriac frontier-history and for the historical connexion between the fraternization
of Arabs and Iranians in Khurāsān and the replacement of the Umayyad by the
'Abbasid dynasty in the Caliphate see II. D (v), vol. ii, p. 141, above.

Southern China.[1] The dilution of the standing army of the Achaemenian Empire must have been at least as thorough and at least as rapid, if we may draw any general inference from a glimpse of the organization and *personnel* of a single unit—the garrison of Elephantinê, on the Nubian frontier of Egypt—which has been given to us by our modern Western archaeologists through their discovery of some local records written on papyrus[2] in the Aramaic *lingua franca* to which the Achaemenidae had given an official currency in all their western provinces.[3] A modern Western scholar need not, however, look so far afield as the Nile Valley in the fifth century B.C. in order to observe, in the life, how a military machine may serve as an instrument of vulgarization. He can watch the process at work under his eyes in his own world in his own day. For, though the Western Society has not yet entered into a universal state, the parochial states into which it is still articulated have been driven, by the twofold driving-force of Democracy and Industrialism, into following, one after another, the sinister lead given by France when she raised her *levée en masse* in A.D. 1793.[4] Since that date we have witnessed, in a Western World that has in the meantime been expanding to a literally world-wide range, a transformation of the eighteenth-century professional standing armies—numerically insignificant forces which were segregated from the civilian population and were stamped, by a Draconian discipline, with the Dominant Minority's mark—into national short-service armies through which the entire able-bodied male population is passed, generation by generation, and in which the conscripts drawn from the Dominant Minority are outnumbered to an extent at which they are, not merely diluted, but swamped by the masses of the Internal Proletariat.

If we now try to estimate the importance of the part which has been played by comradeship-in-arms in the breaking down of the barrier between the Dominant Minority and the Internal Proletariat, we shall find, as we might expect *a priori*, that this factor has been of the greatest account in those cases in which the Dominant Minority has been represented by empire-builders who have been not merely frontiersmen but also men from the wrong side of the frontier—empire-builders, that is, of barbarian origin.[5] For

---

[1] See V. C (i) (c) 4, p. 350, above.
[2] See Meyer, E.: *Der Papyrusfund von Elephantine*, 2nd edition (Leipzig 1912, Hinrichs); Hoonacker, A. van: *Une Communauté Judéo-Araméenne à Éléphantine, en Égypte, aux vie et ve Siècles av. J.-C.* (London 1915, Milford).
[3] For this currency of Aramaic as a *lingua franca* in he Achaemenian Empire see V. C (i) (d) 6 (γ), pp. 487–91 and 499–501, below.
[4] For this impact of Democracy and Industrialism upon War in the modern Western World see IV. C (iii) (b) 3, vol. iv, pp. 141–55, above.
[5] For the several alternative provenances of empire-builders of universal states see V. C (i) (c) 1, pp. 52–6, above.

the barbarian conqueror is likely to be still more receptive than the marchman to amenities of life which he finds in use among the epigoni of peoples whom he has reduced by his own prowess to the status of a subject population.

Such, at any rate, was the sequel to the comradeship-in-arms between the Manchus and their Chinese neighbours in the debatable territory in South Manchuria outside the Great Wall, but inside the Willow Palisade:

'The Manchus were, from the beginning, without either the strong tribal consciousness or the strong historical traditions of the Mongols.[1] . . . This very immaturity facilitated their extraordinarily rapid and thorough assumption of Chinese characteristics. Indeed, nothing could be more evident . . . than that the Manchus, from a very early period, not only looked on China as a country to conquer, but on Chinese civilization as something to aspire to. . . . The Manchus . . . had taken on a thoroughly Chinese colour. Their two emperors who ruled from Mukden before the entry into China were emperors in the Chinese manner. . . . It cannot be doubted that the *racial* character of certain laws of privilege passed by the Manchus has been greatly overemphasized. There was a residuum of racial feeling in some of these laws; but all of them, in operation, had an almost purely social function; and in any case their nominal racial character is vitiated by the fact that, from the beginning, Chinese 'bannermen' were counted as Manchus. The 'banners' themselves were purely a military, never a racial, formation. . . . There was no restriction on marriage between Manchus and Chinese 'bannermen', and . . . at an early period Manchus began to marry non-'banner' Chinese girls, although not giving their own daughters in marriage to non-'banner' Chinese men.'[2]

The same tendency to abandon a *de jure* segregation in favour of a *de facto* symbiosis can be traced, as we have already noted, in the history of another body of barbarian empire-builders: the Primitive Muslim Arab conquerors of South-Western Asia, who were unintentionally and unconsciously restoring a Syriac universal state which had first taken shape in the prematurely shattered empire of the Achaemenidae.[3]

In Syria, under the régime of the Caliph Muʿāwīyah (*in Syria*

---

[1] The Mongols in the Far Eastern World, like the Hyksos in the Egyptiac World, paid the penalty of eviction for their unreadiness to soak themselves through and through in the culture of the sophisticated people whom they had conquered. The happier fortune which was common to the Mongols' Manchu successors and the Hyksos' Libyan successors is an indication that, for a barbarian empire-builder, a cultural self-surrender is an indispensable act of atonement and that, if he cannot bring himself to this, he can never hope to win forgiveness for his political presumptuousness. (On this point see V. C (i) (c) 4, pp. 348–53, above.)—A.J.T.

[2] Lattimore, O.: *Manchuria, Cradle of Conflict* (New York 1932, Macmillan), pp. 44–7.

[3] For this view of the Primitive Muslim Arab empire-builders' work see I. C (i) (b), vol. i, pp. 75–7, above. For the comparison drawn by Eduard Meyer between the receptivity of the Arab builders of the Caliphate and that of the Persian builders of the Achaemenian Empire see the present chapter, p. 443, footnote 3, above.

procurabat circa A.D. 640–61; *per Orbem Terrarum imperabat* A.D. 661–80),

'The distinction between masters and subjects appears not to have been so sharp as it was, to begin with, in 'Irāq. In Syria the Muslims did not live segregated in cantonments specially laid out for them: they lived at close quarters with the natives of the country in the old cities— Damascus, Emesa, Qinnasrīn, etc.—and sometimes they actually went shares with the natives in the use of a place of public worship, which then became half church and half mosque.'[1]

In Khurāsān, under the last of Mu'āwīyah's Umayyad successors, on the eve of the transference of the Caliphate in A.D. 750 from the Umayyads to the 'Abbasids,

'Arabs and Iranians were not separated from each other by any segregation of domiciles. In the Arab garrison towns—Naysābūr (Bivard, Sarakhs, Nasā), Marv, Marvrūd and Herāt—the indigenous population lived on, though the citadels were naturally occupied by the conquerors. Moreover the Arabs did not keep together in compact settlements at just a few points, and did not confine themselves to the towns which they had selected as sites for military colonies. They had properties, with serfs, in the country-side, and they spent part of their time there as well—especially in the oasis of Marv, where the town constituted the centre for a host of villages in a unitary system of irrigation. They kept Iranian retainers and married Iranian women; and this influence was bound to make itself strongly felt already in the second generation. . . . The Arabs acclimatized themselves; they felt themselves at one with the natives of the country as inhabitants of the province which was their common home. They, too, were now Khurāsānīs; and they wore trousers like the Iranians, drank wine, and celebrated the festivals of Nawrūz and Mihrigān. The Arab notable adopted the style of the M rzbāns. The daily round and common task brought in their train the need for an understanding with the Iranians; and even in Kūfah and Basrah Persian was at least as much in use as Arabic as the language of business.'[2]

When we turn to the histories of dominant minorities which have arisen—as dominant minorities normally do arise—from within and not from beyond the disintegrating society's pale, we shall not be able to leave the military factor out of account; for the proletarianization of the Manchu barbarian empire-builders of a Far Eastern, and of the Arab barbarian empire-builders of a Syriac, universal state through a comradeship-in-arms with recruits from the Internal Proletariat is a social phenomenon which is reproduced, as we have already seen, in the histories of the

---

[1] Wellhausen, J.: *Das Arabische Reich und sein Sturz* (Berlin 1902, Reimer), p. 84.
[2] Ibid., p. 307.

Roman army in the Imperial Age and of the conscript armies of the national states of the modern Western World.[1] At the same time we shall find that, in a disintegrating society in which the Dominant Minority is indigenous, a comradeship-in-arms is apt to be replaced by a partnership-in-business as the form of intercourse that is the most effectively instrumental in breaking down the social barrier and achieving the passage from segregation to symbiosis.

This comes out clearly in an account—by a contemporary observer whom we have quoted already—of a change in the social relations between masters and slaves at Athens that resulted from the Athenians' premature and abortive attempt to establish a Hellenic universal state in the fifth century B.C.

'Slaves . . . and permanently domiciled aliens enjoy an extreme degree of licence at Athens, where it is illegal to assault them and where the slave will not make way for you [in the street]. The reason why this is the local custom shall be explained. If it were legal for the slave—or the alien or the freedman—to be struck by the free citizen, your Athenian citizen himself would always have been getting hit through being mistaken for a slave. The free proletariat at Athens are no better dressed than the slaves and aliens, and no more respectable in appearance. If any reader is surprised at the further fact that at Athens they allow the slaves to live in luxury and in some instances to keep up an imposing establishment, it would not be difficult to demonstrate the good sense of their policy in this point as well. The fact is that, in any country that maintains a naval establishment, it is essential for slaves to bring in money by their services, in order that I [the master] may receive at least the royalties on the profits of my slave's labour;[2] and this involves [eventual] manumission.[3] In a country, however, in which wealthy slaves exist, it is no longer desirable that my slave should be afraid of you—as he is, for example, in Lacedaemon. If your slave is afraid of me, that fact will keep him under a perpetual threat of having to stand and deliver his own money [to me as blackmail]. This is the reason why we have put our slaves on a social equality (ἰσηγορίαν) with our freemen; and we have placed our permanently domiciled aliens on the same footing vis-à-vis our citizens because our country needs these aliens' services on account of the multiplicity of our industries, as well

---

[1] See pp. 446–7 and 448, above.

[2] The logical connexion between sea-power and making slavery pay is not here explicitly stated by the writer because, in his time and place, it was so notorious that he could count upon his readers' taking it for granted. The connexion is, of course, that, in a Hellenic city-state that maintained a navy, this expensive public luxury had to be paid for by the well-to-do slave-owning class in a burden of taxation which was so heavy as to make it impossible for slave-owners to keep their slaves employed on such occupations as domestic service, in which the capital sunk in the purchase-price of the slave would be, from the financial point of view, an unproductive investment.—A.J.T.

[3] In the Hellenic World it was a psychological and economic commonplace that the only way of inducing a slave to work 'on his own' in a competitive trade with the zest of a freeman was by allowing him to put by a proportion of his earnings in order to save up for his eventual purchase of his own freedom.—A.J.T.

as on account of the navy. These are our reasons—and they are good ones—for giving social equality to the aliens as well.'[1]

When we find that the *Gleichschaltung* of citizens with aliens and of freemen with slaves in the Hellenic Society had been carried as far as this at Athens in the first generation after the breakdown of 431 B.C., it is not surprising to find further that four hundred years later, when the Hellenic 'Time of Troubles' had burnt itself out and when the Hellenic universal state, which the Athenians had tried and failed to establish, had come into being at last in the shape of the Roman Empire, the elements in the proletarian underworld which were the fittest to survive in the vicious social environment of a disillusioned and demoralized age had not only maintained the favourable social position which they had reached at Athens before the end of the Atheno-Peloponnesian War, but had gone on steadily climbing from one rung of the social ladder to the next till they had attained to dizzy heights of wealth and influence.[2] In the latter days of the Roman Republic the management of the Roman aristocrats' households, with their huge *personnel* and their elaborate organization, had already become a perquisite of the ablest of the freedmen of the nominal master; and, when Caesar's household, outgrowing and overtopping all its rivals, actually went into partnership with the Senate and People in the management of a Roman commonwealth which had become responsible for the government of the entire Hellenic World, then Caesar's freedmen became the cabinet ministers of a Hellenic universal state. Nor was theirs a hidden hand, like the authority that is exercised with such a discreet self-effacement by the permanent civil servants in the parochial states of our latter-day Western World. So far from that, the three principal portfolios held by freedmen in the Imperial Cabinet— the ministries *ab epistulis, a libellis,* and *a rationibus*—came to be part of the recognized insignia of the Imperial office—so much so, that, *imperante Nerone,* in A.D. 64, a member of the Roman aristocracy

---

[1] Auctor Atheniensis Anonymus: *Institutions of Athens* (edited by Kalinka, E.: Berlin and Leipzig 1913, Teubner), chap. 1, §§ 10–12, quoted in IV. C (iii) (*b*) 4, vol. iv, p. 156, footnote 3, above.

[2] Such careers as these were not, of course, typical of the contemporary experience of the whole class to which these self-made men belonged; for one of the effects of the four-centuries-long ordeal which the Hellenic 'Time of Troubles' imposed upon the Hellenic internal proletariat was to produce an extreme differentiation of fortunes between different elements in the proletarian mass. While some proletarians, who had the ability and the desire to adapt themselves to the spirit of the age, were able to rise to dizzy, though precarious, pinnacles of worldly success, the majority were ground down to a degree of misery that evoked from them a powerful spiritual reaction—either the violent reaction of Satanism or the gentle reaction which eventually found its expression in Johanan ben Zakkai's Judaism and in Christianity. (For this process of differentiation in the Hellenic internal proletariat see II. D (vi), vol. ii, pp. 213–16, as well as V. C (i) (*c*) 2, in the present volume, pp. 72–8, and V. C (i) (*d*) 1, *passim,* above, and V. C (i) (*c*) 2, Annex III, pp. 588–90, and V. C (ii) (*a*), Annex II, vol. vi, pp. 376–8 and 504–8, below.)

was hounded to death on a charge of treasonable designs against
the reigning emperor because, in a fit of childish ostentation, he
had rashly taken in vain the titles of the three secretaryships of
state by conferring them on three freedmen of his own who,
in the management of his private estate, were charged with the
corresponding duties.[1]

It will be seen that the Imperial freedmen in the early years of
the Roman Empire enjoyed a plenitude of power which was comparable to that of those members of the Ottoman Sultan's Slave-
Household who attained to the equally powerful—and equally
precarious—office of Grand Vizier.[2] And we shall be reminded
again of the rise of the Hellenic internal proletariat to the top of
the social tree in the household of Caesar if we turn to the history
of the Arab Caliphate and watch clients and patrons slowly but
surely changing places with one another in the vast households
which the Primitive Arab Muslim conquerors of the first few
generations gathered round themselves by throwing the mantle
of their protection over men of parts who were members of the
non-Muslim subject communities.

In all cases of symbiosis between the Dominant Minority and the
Internal Proletariat in which the relation attains to a certain degree
of intimacy, both parties are affected by it, and the effect on each
of them is to set them in motion on a course which leads towards
an assimilation to the other class. On the superficial plane of
'manners' the Internal Proletariat moves towards enfranchisement,
and the Dominant Minority towards vulgarization. The two
movements are complementary, and both are taking place all
the time; but, while it is the enfranchisement of the Proletariat
that is the more conspicuous of the two in the first chapter of the
story, in the last chapter it is the vulgarization of the Dominant
Minority that forces itself upon our attention.

The classic example is the vulgarization, in 'the Silver Age', of
the Roman governing class: a sordid tragedy which has been
inimitably recorded—or caricatured—in a Latin literature which
still preserved its old genius, or at least its old vigour, in the
satirical vein long after it had lost its last breath of inspiration in
every other *genre*.

This Roman rake's progress can be followed in a series of
Hogarthian pictures in each of which the central figure is not
merely an aristocrat but an emperor.

'Caligula . . . gave an immense impetus to the rage for singing,

---

[1] The victim's name was D. Iunius Torquatus Silanus. He was accused *inter libertos
habere quos ab epistulis et libellis et rationibus appellet—nomina summae curae et
meditamenta*. He anticipated a death-sentence by committing suicide (Tacitus: *Annals*,
Book XV, chap. 35).   [2] For instances see Part III. A p. 40, footnote 1, above.

dancing, and acting, for chariot-driving and fighting in the arena, not unknown before, which Juvenal and Tacitus brand as the most flagrant sign of degenerate morals. There was indeed a great conflict of sentiment under the early Empire as to some of these arts. Julius Caesar had encouraged or permitted Roman senators and knights to fight in the gladiatorial combats, and a Laberius to act in his own play. But a decree of the Senate, not long afterwards, had placed a ban on these exhibitions by men of noble rank. Tiberius, who was, beyond anything, a haughty aristocrat, at a later date intervened to save the dignity of the order. But the rage of the rabble for these spectacles had undoubtedly caught many in the ranks of the upper class. And Caligula and Nero found, only too easily, youths of birth and breeding, but ruined fortune, who were ready to exhibit themselves for a welcome *douceur*, or to gain the favour of the prince, or even to bring down the applause of the crowded benches of the amphitheatre or the circus. . . .

'Amid all this elaborate luxury and splendour of indulgence there was a strange return to the naturalism of vice and mere blackguardism. A Messalina or a Nero or a Petronius developed a curious taste for the low life that reeks and festers in the taverns and in the stews. Bohemianism for a time became the fashion. . . . The distinguished dinner party, with the Emperor at their head, sallied forth to see how the people were living in the slums. . . . In the fierce faction fights of the theatre, where stones and benches were flying, the Emperor had once the distinction of breaking a praetor's head.'[1]

While Nero was content to emulate the proletarian music hall *artiste* ('Qualis artifex pereo!'[2]), Commodus, a century later, could not satisfy his craving for proletarianization by any milder feat of exhibitionism than a public appearance in the gladiatorial arena.

'The influence of a polite age and the labour of an attentive education had never been able to infuse into his rude and brutish mind the least tincture of learning; and he was the first of the Roman emperors totally devoid of taste for the pleasures of the understanding. Nero himself excelled, or affected to excel, in the elegant arts of music and poetry. . . . But Commodus, from his earliest infancy, discovered an aversion to whatever was rational or liberal, and a fond attachment to the amusements of the populace—the sports of the circus and amphitheatre, the combats of gladiators, and the hunting of wild beasts. . . . The servile crowd, whose fortune depended on their master's vices, applauded these ignoble pursuits . . . [and], elated with these praises, which gradually extinguished the innate sense of shame, Commodus resolved to exhibit, before the eyes of the Roman people, those exercises which till then he had decently confined within the walls of his palace and to the presence of a few favourites. On the appointed day the various motives of flattery, fear and curiosity attracted to the amphitheatre an innumerable multitude of spectators; and some degree of applause was de-

---

[1] Dill, S.: *Roman Society from Nero to Marcus Aurelius* (London 1905, Macmillan), pp. 73-6.   [2] Suetonius: *Nero*, chap. 49.

servedly bestowed on the uncommon skill of the Imperial performer. Whether he aimed at the head or heart of the animal, the wound was alike certain and mortal. . . . But the meanest of the populace were affected with shame and indignation when they beheld their sovereign enter the lists as a gladiator and glory in a profession which the laws and manners of the Romans had branded with the justest note of infamy. . . . He now disdained the appellation of Hercules. The name of Paulus, a celebrated *secutor*, was the only one which delighted his ear. It was inscribed on his colossal statues, and repeated in the redoubled acclamations of the mournful and applauding Senate.'[1]

The last stage in the process of vulgarization is displayed in the portrait of an emperor of the next generation.

'The demeanour of Caracalla was haughty and full of pride; but with the troops he forgot even the proper dignity of his rank, encouraged their insolent familiarity, and, neglecting the essential duties of a general, affected to imitate the dress[2] and manners of a common soldier.'[3]

Caracalla's way of 'going proletarian' was neither so sensational nor so pathological as Commodus's way or Nero's, but, just on that account, it is perhaps of greater significance as a sociological symptom. A Hellenic dominant minority which had reached the last stage in the repudiation of its social heritage was fitly represented by the figure of an emperor who took refuge in the proletarian freedom of the barrack-room from a freedom of the Academy and the Stoa which he found intolerable just because he knew that it was his birth-right. Indeed, by this date, on the eve of the next relapse of the Hellenic Society into its downward course after the respite of the Augustan rally,[4] the relative volumes and momenta and speeds of the two mutually contrary streams of influence that flowed respectively from the Dominant Minority and from the Internal Proletariat had changed, in the proletarian stream's favour, to a degree at which the latter-day observer may find himself wondering whether, after all, he has not been

---

[1] Gibbon, E.: *The History of the Decline and Fall of the Roman Empire*, chap. iv.

[2] 'Dressing the part' is one of the ways in which the social turncoat advertises his intention to declass himself; and the proneness of the Roman governing class, in its decadence, to this crude form of exhibitionism is commemorated in the nicknames 'Caracalla' and 'Caligula', under which two *apaches* who were raised by Fortune to the Roman Imperial Throne have succeeded in making themselves remembered by Posterity. The sovereign who wears his own livery may of course be moved by motives of petty policy as well as by a taste for low life; for this is one of the easiest and cheapest ways at his command for currying favour with his lackeys. Suleymān the Magnificent sought to propitiate the Janissaries, who were already beginning to get out of hand before the end of his reign, by enrolling himself in one of their units and drawing a private's pay. Is this trick of Ottoman statecraft the origin of the custom, which is now *de rigueur* for the heads of our Western states, of wearing their own uniforms and holding honorary rank in their own service? (See Part III. A, vol. iii, p. 38, footnote 2, § 3, above.) —A.J.T.   [3] Gibbon, op. cit., chap. vi.

[4] For this relapse see IV. C (i), vol. iv, p. 8, and V. C (i) (c) 3, in the present volume, p. 219, above, and V. C (i) (d) 6, Annex, p. 649, V. C (ii) (a), vol. vi, p. 207, and V. C (ii) (b), vol. vi, p. 284, below.

watching the movement of a single current which now, at a certain moment, has simply reversed its direction. Though this is an illusion, it is true that in the earlier stages of disintegration our attention is more apt to be caught by the downward percolation of emotions and ideas from the Dominant Minority to the Internal Proletariat,[1] while in the later stages we become more and more clearly aware that the Dominant Minority is taking its colour from the Internal Proletariat instead of continuing to exercise that function of leadership which is the Dominant Minority's sole *raison d'être* (and that a doubtful one!).

This increasing moral subservience of a sinking Dominant Minority to a rising Internal Proletariat is illustrated in the history of the Hellenic dominant minority's orientation towards Christianity;[2] for, in each successive phase, the dominant minority can be convicted of having adopted towards Christianity, tardily and reluctantly, the attitude, whatever it might be, that had shown itself to be prevalent among the internal proletariat of the day. In an age in which a majority of the internal proletariat was still both non-Christian and anti-Christian, the Roman authorities bowed to popular feeling in the last resort by stooping from time to time to a half-hearted official persecution of the unpopular faith. On the other hand, when the Christian Church eventually succeeded —whether in spite of persecution or because of it—in overcoming the proletarian opposition and establishing its own ascendancy over the internal proletariat's life, the dominant minority signified its unenthusiastic acceptance of the proletariat's revised verdict by a wry-faced announcement of its own conversion to a religion which had now decisively proved its title by its sensational victory in the proletarian arena. Nor is this the whole of the story; for, in so far as the dominant minority played its successive proletarian parts of persecutor and convert with a certain scepticism and cold-bloodedness, it was still betraying, under its proletarian shirt, the sophisticated temper of a Gallio. We shall not have taken the full measure of the dominant minority's repudiation of its own traditional êthos until we have watched it exchanging this traditional Gallionic indifference for a savagery which, in Gàllio's day, would have branded any one who exhibited it as the classmate of a Theudas and Judas of Galilee and a John of Gischala.

'In accordance with the law that governs the religious development of the Imperial Age throughout, the religious zeal which inspired the

[1] This percolation from above downwards is discussed, *à propos* of a concrete case, in V. C (ii) (*a*), Annex II, in vol. vi, below. See, in particular, the passage quoted on pp. 456–7 from Seeck, O.: *Geschichte des Untergangs der Antiken Welt*, vol. iii, 2nd edition (Stuttgart 1921, Metzler), pp. 203–4.

[2] On this see also V. C (i) (*c*) 2, pp. 76 and 80, and V. C (i) (*d*) 3, pp. 408–9, above, and V. C (ii) (*a*), vol. vi, pp. 201–2, below.

populace to its deeds [of violence] mounted slowly from below upwards. As the new faith gradually penetrated the ruling strata of Society, the hatred with which Christianity was regarded by its adversaries made its way among the rulers *pari passu*. We see here two currents beating against one another which are both of the same nature.'[1]

In concrete terms, we see the pagan levity of a Gallienus giving place to the pagan grimness of a Galerius; the lukewarm Christianity of a Philip changing into the fervent Christianity of a Constantine; and the Hadrianic tolerance, which Constantine never sacrificed to the fervour of his own less philosophic age, being thrown to the winds by the pagan fanaticism of a Julian and by the Christian fanaticism of a Theodosius with an equal recklessness.[2]

If we now turn our eyes from the Hellenic to the Far Eastern World, we shall see the first chapter in our story of the proletarianization of the Roman governing class in the act of reproducing itself in the history of the Manchus at the present moment. And here we are in a position to observe the process at first hand by doing sociological field-work of the kind that is exemplified in the following record from the pen of a living Western scholar, who shows us the struggle for enfranchisement giving way to the drift towards proletarianization within the compass of the single generation that separates a Manchuized Chinese father from his own proletarianized son:

'It was . . . possible, in Manchuria, for a Chinese from China Proper to become, in his own lifetime, an out-and-out "Manchu". An instance of this phenomenon came within my own experience when I formed an acquaintance with a Chinese military officer and his old father. The father, born in Honan, had gone to Manchuria as a young man, had travelled over the most remote parts of the three provinces, and had finally settled at Tsitsihar. One day I said to the young man: "Why is it that you, who were born in Tsitsihar, speak just like the generality of Manchurian Chinese, while your father, who was born in Honan, has not only the speech, but exactly the manner and even gestures, of the old-fashioned Manchus of Manchuria" [which differ somewhat from those of Peking Manchus]? He laughed, and said: "When my father was a young man, it was difficult for a *min-jen* [non-'banner' Chinese, 'a civilian', 'one of the people'] to get on in the world up in the northern regions. The Manchus dominated everything, and they harassed the *min* Chinese. In Tsitsihar, where he settled down, they had a custom of 'chasing out the *min*' twice a year. All the Chinese who had filtered in were liable to be driven out, and often beaten and robbed. Of course many of them came back; but the only way to

---

[1] Seeck, op. cit., vol. cit., 2nd edition, p. 301.
[2] For the eventual victory of fanaticism over tolerance in the Hellenic World in the course of the fourth century of the Christian Era see IV. C (iii) (*b*) 12, vol. iv, pp. 226–7, above.

become secure was to 'follow' [as the phrase went] the Manchus and become so like them as to be undetectable. So my father, when he had learnt their ways, 'entered the banners' and married a Manchu [which, of course, was against the strict law] and has always remained like them. But when I was growing up it was no longer any use to be a 'bannerman', and therefore I became like all the other young men of my generation." This is a story which illustrates the processes of the present as well as of the past; for the young Manchus of Manchuria are becoming rapidly indistinguishable from Manchuria-born Chinese.'[1]

In this record of the social history of a Chinese father and son we see the stream of vulgarization in the life of a Manchu dominant minority encountering and overwhelming the stream of snobbery in the life of a Chinese internal proletariat. While in the father's generation the proletarian who meant to rise was still compelled to resort to a servile mimicry of his masters, in the son's generation the children of a *ci-devant* proletariat and a *ci-devant* dominant minority were already meeting and mingling on the common level of a proletarian vulgarity.

An Englishman who was moved at this time to do some work of his own in this field of sociological research on living subjects had no need to put himself to the expense of booking a berth on the Trans-Siberian express; for the social changes that were witnessed by our twentieth-century American observer on the banks of the Nonni River could be seen and studied quite as well on the banks of the Thames by his stay-at-home English contemporaries. The proletarianization of a dominant minority could be watched in the London metropolitan area in the year 1938 by any one who entered the doors of either a cinema or a club; for in the cinema he would see people of all classes taking an equal pleasure in films that had been artfully designed to cater for the taste of the proletarian majority of the audience, while in the club he would find that the black ball did not exclude the yellow press. Indeed, if our latter-day British Juvenal was a family man, he could stay indoors and still find his copy. He had merely to open his ears (which was perhaps easier than to close them) to the jazz-music which his children were conjuring out of the wireless set. And then, when, at the end of the holidays, he saw his boys off to school, let him not forget to ask them to point out to him 'the bloods' among their schoolfellows assembling on the platform of the London railway terminus. As, at this passing show, our quizzical paterfamilias discreetly took smart young Commodus's measure, he would notice the rakish proletarian angle at which 'the public schoolboy's' trilby hat was cocked, and would observe

<hr>

[1] Lattimore, O.: *Manchuria Cradle of Conflict* (New York 1932, Macmillan), pp. 62-3.

that the *apache* scarf, with its convincing air of negligence, had really been carefully arranged so as not to reveal the obligatory white collar. Here was proof ocular and positive that in twentieth-century London, as in second-century Rome, the proletarian style was *à la mode*. And, since a straw really does show which way the wind is blowing, the satirist's trivialities may be grist for the more ponderous mill of the historian.

The Barbarization of the Dominant Minority.

When we pass from the vulgarization of the Dominant Minority through their pacific intercourse with the Internal Proletariat to examine the parallel process of their barbarization—a social change which arises out of their warlike intercourse with the External Proletariat beyond the pale—we find that the plot of both plays is the same in its general structure. In this case, as in that, either party exercises an assimilative influence on the other; and in both cases alike it is the influence of the Dominant Minority upon its proletarian servitor or antagonist that claims our attention in the first act. This time once again, however, there is a second act in which the two actors exchange their roles; and the curtain does not fall until the Dominant Minority has been barbarized in this encounter as decisively and irretrievably as we have already seen it vulgarized in the companion play.

In our present play the *mise-en-scène* is an artificial military frontier—the *limes* of a universal state—across which the Dominant Minority and the External Proletariat are seen confronting each other, when the curtain rises, in a posture which, on both sides alike, is one of aloofness and hostility. As the play proceeds, the aloofness turns into an intimacy which does not, however, bring peace; and, as the warfare goes on, Time tells progressively in the barbarian's favour, until at last he succeeds in breaking through the *limes* and overrunning the vast domain—a whole world in itself—of the universal state which the Dominant Minority's garrison has hitherto successfully protected. The causes and consequences of this denouement of the play on its military side are discussed in a later part of this Study;[1] and in the present place we shall concern ourselves exclusively with the social side: that is to say, with the social assimilation of the two adversaries to one another—an assimilation which is partly the effect, but also partly the cause, of their growing intimacy, and which ends in their fusion into a social amalgam in which the dominant element is the barbarian one.

In the first act the barbarian appears in the successive roles of

---

[1] See Part VIII, *passim*, below.

hostage and mercenary, and in both these roles he comes on to the Dominant Minority's ground in a figurative as well as in a literal sense; for, in both, he comes over as a more or less docile apprentice. In the second act he still crosses the line, but now only in a sense which is literal with a vengeance; for he now comes neither by command nor by invitation but unbidden and unwanted as a raider who eventually settles down to stay as a colonist or a conqueror. Thus, between the first act and the second, the military ascendancy passes out of the Dominant Minority's hands into the barbarian's; and, although the change is not always easily perceptible while it is in the act of taking place—since the barbarian conqueror may be a time-expired mercenary, and his seizure of the land may be legalized *ex post facto*, by a Dominant Minority eager to save its face, as a payment in kind for military services rendered—all the same, in the end, the reversal of fortune is sensational; for, while at the opening of the play the barbarian is well content if he can hold his own and prevent the frontier of Civilization from being pushed still farther forward at his expense, the close of the play sees the *ci-devant* Dominant Minority resigning itself to the permanent establishment of a barbarian invader on the wrong side of the old front line as the new lord and master, *de facto*, of a ravished world. This sensational transfer of the kingdom, the power, and the glory from the Dominant Minority's to the barbarian's banners has a profound effect upon the Dominant Minority's outlook; and, long before the military and political process is complete, the revolutionary inversion of prestige is proclaimed by the discomfited party itself in deeds that are more eloquent than words. It is now the Dominant Minority that comes on to the barbarian's ground—not, indeed, in the literal sense, for the time has now long since gone by when the garrison of the *limes* could show its mettle by making punitive expeditions into no-man's-land. In the literal sense the Dominant Minority is now yielding ground to the barbarian in an unbroken retreat that is threatening to turn into a rout. But, just for the reason that the barbarian is now manifestly gaining the upper hand, the Dominant Minority seeks to retrieve its rapidly deteriorating military and political position by taking one leaf after another out of the barbarian's book; and imitation is assuredly the sincerest form of flattery.

Having now sketched out the plot of the play, we may pause to survey the scene more closely as it displays itself in the several acts. We may watch the barbarian make his first appearance on the stage as the Dominant Minority's apprentice; see the Dominant Minority begin to 'go native'; catch a glimpse of the two

adversaries at a fleeting moment at which, in their rival mas-
querades in one another's borrowed plumage, they assume the
grotesque generic resemblance of the griffin to the chimaera; and
finally watch the *ci-devant* Dominant Minority lose the last traces
of its original form by sinking to meet the triumphant barbarian
at a common level of barbarism that is quite unmitigated.

Our list of barbarian war-lords who have made their *début* as
hostages in the hands of a 'civilized Power' includes some famous
names. Theodoric served his apprenticeship as a hostage at the
Roman Court of Constantinople,[1] and Scanderbeg[2] his at the
Ottoman Court of Adrianople, where he received the education
of an *ich-oghlan*.[3] We may perhaps hesitate to number among the
barbarians the hostage-son of Amyntas who learnt at Thebes from
Epaminondas and Pelopidas the arts of war and peace which he
afterwards practised to such brilliant effect when he had mounted
his father's throne as King Philip II of Macedon. But we may
mention a living example of the type in the person of Muhammad
'Abd-al-Karīm al-Khattābī: a chief of the tribe of the Banu
Wuryāghal in the Moroccan Rīf who annihilated a Spanish expeditionary force at Anwāl in 1921 and in 1925 performed the
greater feat of momentarily shaking the French power in Morocco
to its foundations. For 'Abd-al-Karīm's apprenticeship was served
in an eleven-months-long sojourn in a Spanish prison at Melilla.[4]

The treatment that the Rīfī war-lord received at his Frankish
gaolers' hands turned him immediately and inevitably into their
implacable enemy; but 'Abd-al-Karīm's experience was the exception and not the rule; for common sense usually moves a
dominant minority which is anxious to hold its barbarian frontier
with the minimum of trouble and expense to bind its barbarian
hostages in chains that are so pleasantly gilded that the captive
will be tempted to hug them. Through such tactful handling the
young barbarian who comes as a hostage may be induced to stay
on as a mercenary; and Theodoric and Scanderbeg both completed their apprenticeship in this fashion by serving for a time,
on a more or less voluntary footing, in the army of the empire
which they afterwards made it their life-work to combat.[5]

---

[1] For Theodoric see further pp. 472–3, below.

[2] For Scanderbeg see Pisko, J.: *Skanderbeg* (Vienna 1894, Frick).

[3] For the system of education which was the making of the Ottoman Pādishāh's
Slave-Household in 'the Golden Age' of Ottoman history see Part III. A, vol. iii, pp. 28–44,
above.

[4] See Toynbee, A. J.: *Survey of International Affairs, 1925*, vol. i (London 1927,
Milford), p. 111.

[5] If it is so manifestly politic for the Dominant Minority to slur over the distinction
between mercenary and hostage, it is not surprising that the historian should sometimes
find himself at a loss to know whether this or that barbarian warrior ought to be assigned
to this or that category. For example, was it as a hostage in Roman hands or as a
mercenary in the Roman service that the Cheruscan war-lord Hermann-Arminius

The list of barbarians who have 'come' and 'seen' as mercenaries, before imposing themselves as conquerors, is a long one. The Teutonic and Arab barbarian conquerors of Roman provinces in the fifth and in the seventh century of the Christian Era were respectively the descendants of many generations of Teutons and Arabs who had done their military service in the Roman forces;[1] and the careers of a Theodoric and a Mu'āwīyah are foreshadowed by those of a Maximinus Thrax and a Philippus Arabs —a pair of third-century barbarians who rose in the Roman service from the ranks to the purple. Again, the Turkish bodyguard of the 'Abbasid Caliphs in the ninth century of the Christian Era prepared the way for the Turkish buccaneers who carved the Caliphate up into its eleventh-century 'successor-states'. And the present Kingdom of Jugoslavia, which is a barbarian 'successor-state' of the Ottoman Empire on the one hand and of the Danubian Hapsburg Monarchy on the other, perhaps ultimately owes its existence to past generations of Serbs who served an Ottoman military apprenticeship as hirelings of the Pādishāh,[2] and later on as *qullar* in the Slave-Household, and a Western military ap-

---

earned his title to be described by a contemporary Roman man-of-letters as *adsiduus militiae nostrae prioris comes, iure etiam civitatis Romanae decus equestris consecutus gradus* (Velleius Paterculus, C.: *Historia Romana*, Book II, chap. 118)? It is perhaps significant that Hermann is remembered by Posterity under the Latinized form of his native barbarian name, and Scanderbeg [i.e. Iskender Bey] under his Ottoman *nom de guerre* and not under his Christian name George Castriota. Again, the hero and champion (*el Campeador*) of the Western Christian barbarians beyond the pale of the Andalusian Umayyad Caliphate has been made famous—and this by his own people— under his Arabic title of the Cid and not under his Christian name of Rodrigo Diez de Bivar. We may also notice that a Latin name was borne by one, and a Greek name by another, of the seven kinglets of the Teutonic barbarian Alemanni whose war-bands were caught on the wrong side of the Rhine and roughly handled by the Caesar Julian in A.D. 357; and the Latin historian—who was himself 'miles quondam et Graecus'— has considerately gratified our curiosity by telling us how the Alemannian prince who bore the Greek name had come to be called by it:

'Latus vero dextrum Serapio agebat: etiam tum adultae lanuginis iuvenis, efficacia praecurrens aetatem, Mederichi fratris Chnodomarii filius, hominis quoad vixerat perfidissimi, ideo sic appellatus quod pater eius diu obsidatus pignore tentus in Galliis, doctusque Graeca quaedam arcana, hunc filium suum, Agenarichum genitali vocabulo dictitatum, ad Serapionis transtulit nomen' (Ammianus Marcellinus: *Res Gestae a Principatu Caesaris Nervae*, Book XVI, chap. 12, § 25).

These tell-tale names bear witness that, while the barbarian who has once been domesticated may break loose again and turn all the more savage for having at one time worn chains, the most truculent defiance in after-life can still never quite efface the marks that have been made upon him by an education to which he has been subjected at the impressionable age of youth or early manhood. Even when he is ranging at large again in no-man's-land as the notorious captain of a barbarian war-band, his transmogrified name commemorates his earlier experience of domestication as surely as the 'little bald spot' which Mowgli's finger was able to feel under the fur of Bagheera's throat betrayed the fact that the panther who was now enjoying the freedom of the Jungle had at one time languished in a cage (Kipling, Rudyard: *The Jungle Book*, 'Mowgli's Brothers').

[1] For the mercenary service, in the Roman forces, of the Teutonic-speaking barbarians on the European Continent and in Scandinavia, and also of the Celtic-speaking barbarians in the British Isles, see Chadwick, H: M.: *The Heroic Age* (Cambridge 1912, University Press), pp. 445-7.

[2] This is the true history of Marko Kraljević, who has been transfigured into a hero by the genius of Serbian minstrelsy (see V. C (i) (c) 3, Annex III, p. 609, below).

prenticeship as *granichari* in the border regiments [1] with which the
Hapsburg Government garrisoned the frontiers of the territories
that it wrested out of the 'Osmanlis' grasp at the turn of the
seventeenth and eighteenth centuries.[2] As for the Libyan interlopers who eventually usurped the derelict heritage of 'the New
Empire' of Egypt, they reversed the usual order of proceedings;
for, after a series of premature attempts (which all ended disastrously for the presumptuous barbarian aggressors) to exchange
the mercenary's role for the conqueror's at the turn of the thirteenth and twelfth centuries B.C., the Libyans put their pride in
their pocket and reverted to their mercenary calling; and they
were rewarded for their humility by being permitted to win after
all, through a process of peaceful penetration, the prize that had
been brusquely denied to them when they had tried to snatch it
by main force.[3] Finally, if we may venture to treat the Greeks as
the barbarians that they appeared to be in Egyptiac and Syriac
eyes, we may find the precursors of Alexander's world-conquering
army in those 'Brazen Men' of Carian and Ionian provenance who
had risen so obligingly from the sea to take mercenary service with
the first Psammetichus and with the Pharaohs who followed after
him during the next three centuries;[4] or, more pertinently still,
in those fourth-century mercenaries drawn from almost every city-
state of a distracted Hellas who fought with the same professional
loyalty and political insouciance at Cunaxa for Cyrus the Younger
against his Achaemenid brother Artaxerxes and at Gaugamela for
the last Darius against Alexander himself.

Our list might be longer still if the historical records of the last
agonies of civilizations were not so fragmentary as they are apt to
be. But we may at least conjecture that the sea-roving barbarians
who hovered round the fringes of the Minoan thalassocracy and
sacked Cnossos itself *circa* 1400 B.C. had served their apprenticeship as the hirelings of Minos before they aspired to supplant him;
for the contemporary Egyptiac records tell us that 'the Peoples of
the Sea' competed with the Libyans in the lucrative business of
soldiering for 'the New Empire' of Egypt, and went into partnership

[1] In addition to these regiments of Jugoslav regulars whose task was to guard the
frontiers that marched with the Ottoman Empire, the Hapsburg Government, under the
stress of its struggle with Frederick the Great, also enlisted Jugoslav irregulars who
made themselves a scourge under the name of Pandours. These Pandours are presumably homonyms of the Pindaris who so obstinately resisted the establishment of the
Pax Britannica in Central India.
[2] For the previous stages in the history of the Serbs and Bosniaks see IV. C (ii) (*b*) 1,
vol. iv, pp. 68 and 69; IV. C. (ii) (*b*) 2, vol. iv, p. 76; and V. C (i) (*c*) 3, in the present
volume, pp. 292–7, 301–2, and 327–8, above.
:See IV. C (iii) (*c*) 2 (β), vol. iv, p. 422; V. C (i) (*c*) 3, in the present volume,
pp. 269–70, and V. C (i) (*c*) 4, pp. 352–3, above.
[4] The most distinguished name on the roll of Greek mercenaries in the Egyptiac
service is that of King Agesilaus of Sparta (*regnabat* 400–361 B.C.).

with the Libyans in the confederated barbarians' unsuccessful
attempt to deal with Egypt as they had dealt with Crete. Can we
likewise infer from the semi-legendary figure of Ogier the Dane,
who makes his appearance among Charlemagne's paladins in the
French Epic, that the Vikings who were already raiding the coasts
of the Carolingian Empire before Charlemagne was in his grave
were preceded by Scandinavian mercenaries in the Austrasian
service?[1] And did the Han dynasty enlist the Eurasian Nomads
from beyond the Great Wall—whose descendants were ultimately
to reign on Sinic soil as the Han's eventual successors—for patrol-
ling the frontiers of the Sinic universal state?

'The policy for the Middle Kingdom is to employ the barbarians for knocking the barbarians on the head' is a maxim which
is to be found in an essay from the brush of Kia Yi, a Sinic political
philosopher of the second century B.C.;[2] but in practice we hear
less of Nomad soldiers in the Sinic Imperial service than of Nomad
settlers planted, on the Imperial Government's initiative, on Intramural territory; and these settlers evidently correspond not so
much to the units of barbarian *foederati* in the Roman Imperial
army as to the barbarian agricultural colonists known as *laeti*[3] who
were recruited from time-expired mercenaries or from prisoners-
of-war or even from raiders whom the Government was too lazy
to drive out, and who were planted for the purpose of recultivating
and repeopling the provinces which these settlers' own kinsmen,
or perhaps even the settlers themselves, had previously devastated
and depopulated.[4] It was perhaps in this more peaceful fashion,
rather than with weapon in hand, that the Northern Barbarians
gained their footing on Sinic soil; and this surmise would appear
to be borne out by the notorious fact that the Sinic universal state
was not supplanted immediately by 'successor-states' of barbarian
origin even in the northern marches. 'The Three Kingdoms',

---

[1] This conjecture is favoured by the fact—which is known for certain—that the
Vikings who embarked on the waters of the Baltic and not on those of the North Sea,
and who made their fortunes at the expense of the Khazar Empire in the Russian forests
(see V. C (i) (c) 3, pp. 286–8, above), instead of making them at the expense of the
Carolingian Empire in North-Western Europe, gained entrance as mercenaries before
they rose to be masters. 'In the commercial centres, into which the warlike foreign
elements were particularly active in pushing their way, their status changed without
difficulty. From trading partners or salaried wardens of the trade-routes they easily
turned into rulers.'—Kliutschewskij, W. [= Kluchevski, V.]: *Geschichte Russlands*,
vol. i (Berlin 1925, Obelisk Verlag), pp. 133–7.

[2] The general tenor of this essay is reproduced by Franke, O.: *Geschichte des Chinesischen Reiches*, vol. i (Berlin 1930, de Gruyter), pp. 332–3.

[3] For a list of instances of the settlement of barbarian colonists on the land, in districts
inside the Roman Imperial frontiers, by the Roman authorities from the reign of Augustus
(*imperabat* 31 B.C.–A.D. 14) to the reign of Valens (*imperabat* A.D. 364–78) inclusive,
see Dill, S.: *Roman Society in the Last Century of the Western Empire*, 2nd edition
(London 1905, Macmillan), pp. 292–5. See also Seeck, O.: *Geschichte des Untergangs
der Antiken Welt*, vol. i, 4th edition (Stuttgart 1921, Metzler), Book II, chap. 6.

[4] The comparison is drawn by Franke in op. cit., vol. ii (Berlin 1936, de Gruyter),
pp. 30–6.

which were the direct heirs of the Posterior Han, were all indigenous; and, between them, they covered the whole domain of
the universal state which they replaced. It was not till about
a hundred years after the break-up of the Han Power (which
occurred *de facto* in the last quarter of the second century of the
Christian Era, though officially the dynasty lingered on till A.D.
221) that the descendants of the Nomad settlers in the northern
marches openly took the sceptre into their own hands.[1]

We can also espy several instances in which the barbarian mercenary has missed his 'manifest destiny'. For example, the East
Roman Empire might have fallen a prey to the Varangian Guard
if it had not been ravished by the Normans and the Saljūqs, carved
up by the French and the Venetians, and finally swallowed whole
by the 'Osmanlis. And the Ottoman Empire, in its turn, would
assuredly have been partitioned among the Bosniak and Albanian
mercenaries who were fast asserting their mastery over the provincial pashas and even over the Sublime Porte itself at the turn
of the eighteenth and nineteenth centuries of the Christian Era
if the Frankish man-of-business had not come treading on the
heels of the Albanian man-at-arms to give the last chapter of
Ottoman history an unexpected turn by flooding the Levant with
Western political ideas as well as with Manchester goods.[2] The
Oscan mercenaries, again, who found a market for their services
in the Greek city-states of Campania and Magna Graecia and
Sicily made a practice of ejecting or exterminating their Greek
employers whenever they gained the opportunity, and there is little
doubt that they would have carried on this game—in which the
Greeks themselves never ceased to play into their hands—until
there would not have been one single Greek community left on
the western side of the Straits of Otranto, if the Romans had not
taken the Oscan homelands in the rear at the critical moment.[3]
Finally, we may venture to prophesy that, if these Roman tamers
of the Oscans had succumbed in their turn to Hannibal, the profits
of that great Punic soldier's success would not have long remained
in the pockets of the petty-minded Carthaginian oligarchy whom
he was attempting (as it turned out, vainly) to save in spite of
themselves. For some three hundred years before Hannibal's
time Carthage had been fighting her battles with the arms of
barbarian mercenaries whom she recruited from all the hinterlands
of the Western Mediterranean; and, after she had escaped destruction at Roman hands in the First Punic War, she had courted it

[1] See IV. C (ii) (*b*) 1, vol. iv, p. 65; V. C (i) (*c*) 3, in the present volume, pp. 272–3.
and V. C (i) (*c*) 4, p. 356, above, and the present chapter, pp. 477–8, below.
[2] See IV. C (ii) (*b*) 2, vol. iv, pp. 76–8, above.
[3] For this Roman intervention see V. C (i) (*c*) 3, pp. 213–4, above.

at the hands of her own hirelings, whom she exasperated into mutiny by her close-fistedness in the settlement of their pecuniary claims upon her. The four years of this war at her own gates with the mercenaries (240–237 B.C.) were perhaps as terrible for Carthage as the twenty-four years of the antecedent war with Rome, which had been fought entirely on or over the sea (except for the African expedition of Regulus, which had ended disastrously for the Roman invader). If, in the second trial of strength between Carthage and Rome, the genius of Hannibal had availed to give Carthage the immediate victory, the ultimate victors would as-suredly have been Hannibal's native troops: his Libyan and Spanish infantry and his Numidian horse.

This Carthaginian case may remind us of a living instance in which we cannot yet read the riddle of Destiny. At the time of writing the military strength of the French Republic resided—not indeed to a Carthaginian degree, but nevertheless in a formidable measure—in White African man-power drawn from the Carthaginian recruiting-grounds in the Maghrib and Black African man-power drawn from trans-Saharan sources which Carthage never tapped (though her maritime explorers may have rounded Cape Verde). Was it France's destiny, under the increasing strain of an effort to maintain her weakening position in Europe, to serve as the military vehicle through which the valley of the Rhine was to fall under the dominion of barbarians from the Senegal? To an Englishman in his armchair this suggestion might appear to be nothing more serious than a rhetorical question that had been drafted in a German National-Socialist Ministry of Propaganda. On the other hand, to any native of the Rhineland who had not been living abroad between the autumn of 1918 and the 30th June, 1930, the picture of a Europe cowed by African bayonets would suggest, not a piece of fantastic *Zukunftsmusik*, but a grim reality with which he was already acquainted through his personal experience.

In the same sober spirit an Indian of the same generation might speculate on the future role, in India's destinies, of those barbarians—entrenched in a warlike independence in their fastnesses beyond the limits of the Government of India's administration or control—from among whom no less than one-seventh of the Indian Regular Army was recruited in A.D. 1930.[1] Were the Gurkha mercenaries and the Pathan raiders of that day marked out to be remembered in history as the fathers or grandfathers of barbarian conquerors who were to carve out on the plains of Hindustan the 'successor-states' of the British Rāj?[2]

[1] For these figures see II. D (v), vol. ii, p. 128, footnote 1, above.
[2] For the British Indian Government's local practice and experience in employing

Whether Englishmen and Afridis or Frenchmen and Kabyles were likely, in course of time, to exchange their respective roles was a question which still lay on the knees of the Gods at the time when this volume was published. In cases such as these, in which we find ourselves in the middle of the story, we can only say that such a denouement appears not impossible in the light of the clear evidence that the like has actually occurred in other cases in which the whole of the drama has already been played out. One such case, in which we are acquainted in some detail with the second act of the play as well as with the first, is the story of the relations between the Hellenic Society in its universal state and the European barbarians beyond the northern *limes* of the Roman Empire. On this historic stage we can watch from beginning to end the parallel processes by which the Dominant Minority sinks into barbarism while the barbarians are making their fortune at the Dominant Minority's expense.

In this performance the play opens in a liberal atmosphere of free contract and enlightened self-interest.

'The Empire was not an object of hatred to the barbarians. Indeed, they were often eager to be taken into its service; and many of their chiefs, like Alaric or Ataulphus, had no higher ambition than to be appointed to high military command. On the other hand there was a corresponding readiness on the Roman side to employ barbarian forces in war. From the earliest days of the Empire these auxiliaries appear on the army lists. Germans are found in the bodyguard of Augustus. They fought under Vitellius in the foremost ranks at the battle of Cremona. Vespasian had special confidence in the loyalty of the Sueves, and had two of their chiefs in his service. Marcus Aurelius formed some corps of Germans for his war with their countrymen on the Danube. In the third century the tendency becomes even more marked. Valerian, in a despatch to Aurelian, describes an army which included troops from Ituraea, Arabia and Mesopotamia, and officers bearing such unmistakable German names as Hariomundus, Hildomundus and Haldagates. Claudius II, after the great defeat which he inflicted on the Goths, enrolled a large number of them under his standards. Probus recruited the frontier garrisons with 16,000 from the wreck of the great host which had devastated Gaul. The army of Constantine, in the battle of the Milvian Bridge, was chiefly composed of Germans and Celts and Britons. Of similar composition was the army with which Theodosius defeated Eugenius on the Frigidus.'[1]

The scholar from whose work this passage is quoted goes on in the same context[2] to trace the individual careers of a number of

a Wazīrī militia to guard the North-West Frontier of India in the Waziristan sector see de Watteville, H.: *Waziristan, 1919–1920* (London 1925, Constable), especially pp. 8–9 and 13–14.
[1] Dill, S.: *Roman Society in the Last Century of the Western Empire*, 2nd edition (London 1905, Macmillan), pp. 291–2.   [2] Ibid., pp. 295–6.

barbarian military officers who made their mark in the Roman service in the fourth and fifth centuries of the Christian Era: the *laetus* Magnentius; the Franks Arbogastes and Merobaudes and Richomer and Bauto; the Goths Munderich and Gainas and Fravitta; and the Vandal Stilicho. The 'Scythian' Modares, likewise, is proclaimed a barbarian by his name, while his generic epithet tells us that he was a child of the Eurasian Steppe; and 'how many more may have disguised their nationality under Roman names no one can tell'.[1] It appears, however, that, about the middle of the fourth century, the Germans in the Roman service started a new practice of retaining their native names;[2] and this change of etiquette, which seems to have been abrupt, points to a sudden access of self-consciousness and self-assurance in the souls of a barbarian *personnel* which had previously been content to 'go Roman' without any reservations in favour of its own 'native' past.

It is all the more significant that this new insistence on the barbarians' side upon a cultural individuality of their own, which they were now asking their Roman employers to accept as something distinctive and inalienable, did not evoke on the Romans' part any counter-demonstration of an anti-barbarian exclusiveness. So far from that, the barbarians in the Roman service began, at this very time, to obtain admission into an inner sanctum of Roman public life which had never been thrown open to them in earlier centuries when their own attitude had been less aggressively self-assertive.

'German chiefs [now] not only obtained the great military commands; they also rose to the consulship, the highest civil honour which the Emperor had to bestow. Dagelaephus and Merobaudes were colleagues of Gratian in this great office. In the reign of Theodosius, Merobaudes, Richomer and Bauto were consuls in successive years, and at least five more German names appear in the reigns of the last emperors of the West. When an office which the Emperor himself was proud to hold was given so freely to men of barbarian origin, it is plain that the old exclusiveness had disappeared and that the Germans had stolen their way into the very citadel of the Empire long before its distant outworks were stormed.'[3]

This social triumph of the fifth-century barbarian *novi homines* attained its culmination when the Emperor Theodosius's son and successor Arcadius (*imperabat* A.D. 395–408) deigned to take in marriage the barbarian Bauto's daughter Eudoxia—without scrup-

[1] Dill, op. cit., loc. cit.
[2] Lot, F.: *Les Invasions Germaniques* (Paris 1935, Payot), p. 230.
[3] Dill, S.: *Roman Society in the Last Century of the Western Empire*, 2nd edition London 1905, Macmillan), pp. 296–7.

ling to raise the child of a Frankish soldier-of-fortune to the rank
of Augusta, the highest honour open to a woman in the Imperial
society of the age.

While the barbarians were thus setting their feet upon the top-
most rungs of the Roman social ladder, the Romans themselves
were beginning to move in just the opposite direction; for, in the
generation before that in which the Teutonic mercenary Bauto
achieved the double feat of winning the consular *laticlavium* for himself and the Imperial purple for his daughter, the Roman Emperor
Gratian (*imperabat* A.D. 375–83) had succumbed to a new-fangled
form of inverted snobbery, a mania, not for vulgarity, but for
barbarism.

'The most skilful masters of every science and of every art had
laboured to form the mind and body of the young prince. . . . But the
influence of this elaborate instruction did not penetrate beyond the
surface; and, . . . as soon as time and accident had removed those faithful
counsellors from the throne, the emperor of the West insensibly
descended to the level of his natural genius; abandoned the reins of
government to the ambitious hands which were stretched forwards to
grasp them; and amused his leisure with the most frivolous gratifica-
tions. . . . Among the various arts which had exercised the youth of
Gratian, he had applied himself with singular inclination and success
to manage the horse, to draw the bow, and to dart the javelin; and these
qualifications, which might be useful to a soldier, were prostituted to
the viler purposes of hunting. Large parks were enclosed for the
Imperial pleasures, and plentifully stocked with every species of wild
beasts; and Gratian neglected the duties, and even the dignity, of his
rank to consume whole days in the vain display of his dexterity and
boldness in the chase. The pride and wish of the Roman emperor to
excel in an art in which he might be surpassed by the meanest of his
slaves reminded the numerous spectators of the examples of Nero and
Commodus; but the chaste and temperate Gratian was a stranger to
their monstrous vices; and his hands were stained only with the blood
of animals.

'The behaviour of Gratian, which degraded his character in the eyes
of Mankind, could not have disturbed the security of his reign if the
Army had not been provoked to resent their peculiar injuries. As long
as the young emperor was guided by the instructions of his masters,
he professed himself the friend and pupil of the soldiers; many of his
hours were spent in the familiar conversation of the camp;[1] and the
health, the comforts, the rewards, the honours of his faithful troops
appeared to be the object of his attentive concern. But, after Gratian

[1] It will be noticed that the respectable Gratian begins his rake's progress at the
point which had been the ruffianly Caracalla's limit (see p. 455, above). The inverse
contrasts between the two careers and the two characters give the measure of the distance
along the road towards proletarianization that had been travelled by the Hellenic
dominant minority in the Roman Empire between the first quarter of the third century
and the last quarter of the fourth.—A.J.T.

more freely indulged his prevailing taste for hunting and shooting, he naturally connected himself with the most dexterous ministers of his favourite amusement. A body of the Alani was received into the military and domestic service of the palace; and the admirable skill which they were accustomed to display in the unbounded plains of Scythia was exercised, on a more narrow theatre, in the parks and enclosures of Gaul. Gratian admired the talents and customs of these favourite guards, to whom alone he entrusted the defence of his person; and, as if he meant to insult the public opinion, he frequently showed himself to the soldiers and people with the dress and arms, the long bow, the sounding quiver, and the fur garments of a Scythian warrior. The unworthy spectacle of a Roman prince who had renounced the dress and manners of his country filled the minds of the legions with grief and indignation.[1] Even the Germans, so strong and formidable in the armies of the Empire, affected to disdain the strange and horrid appearance of the savages of the North, who, in the space of a few years, had wandered from the banks of the Volga to those of the Seine.'[2]

This craze for barbarian dress and manners eventually cost Gratian his life; but the poor young prince's grisly end did not choke off the rising generation of his class from following the fashion which Gratian had inaugurated.

'There are signs that even in smaller things, such as toilet and dress, Germans, at the beginning of the fifth century, were setting the fashion. Three edicts of Honorius, between 397 and 416, forbid the wearing of trousers,[3] long hair and fur coats of the barbarian style within the precincts of the city. The tone of the law of 416 leaves no doubt that the

---

[1] Yet poor Gratian was only doing what was done with impunity in the eighteenth century by the enlightened monarchs of a modern Western World when they dressed up their troopers (and on occasions their own selves) in the outlandish 'Scythian' kit of a Hungarian 'hussar' or a Polish 'uhlan' (*Turcicè* 'oghlan', i.e. one of 'the boys' in the American sense).—A.J.T.

[2] Gibbon, E.: *The History of the Decline and Fall of the Roman Empire*, chap. xxvii.

[3] The hesitating steps by which the Hellenic dominant minority gradually took to trousers are significant marks of the successive stages in its descent down the slippery slope of barbarization, because trousers were the common badge of the barbarians beyond two frontiers: on the one hand, of the Germans and Dacians beyond Rhine and Danube, and, on the other hand, of the Parthians beyond Euphrates. (The trousers of Iran and those of Northern Europe were, of course, alike derived from the Eurasian Steppe, whence they had been introduced by Nomad invaders: the common descent of the Parthians and the Dacians from the same Eurasian Nomad horde has been mentioned already in II. D (vii), Annex V, vol. ii, p. 435, footnote 1, above.) On this account, trousers were originally regarded as the very insignia of barbarism by the polite society of the Roman Empire, which was at bay on two frontiers against a threat of invasion by war-bands clad in these 'inexpressibles'. When Virgil has to refer to trousers, he resorts to the decent periphrasis 'barbara tegmina crurum' (*Aeneid*, Book XI, l. 777); and in the revolutionary year A.D. 69 the commander of the force that marched on Rome from the Rhine in order to secure the Imperial throne for Vitellius did perceptible damage to his cause by imprudently continuing to wear, on the Italian side of the Alps, a garment to which he had become addicted in the harsher climate of a Rhenish garrison-town. 'Caecina, velut relicta post Alpis saevitia ac licentia, modesto agmine per Italiam incessit. ornatum ipsius municipia et coloniae in superbiam trahebant, quod versicolori sagulo, bracas [*breeches*] indutus, togatos adloqueretur' (Tacitus: *Histories*, Book II, chap. 20). As late as A.D. 274 it was the trousers on the legs of the captive Gallic pretender Tetricus that caught the eye of the crowd which watched the Emperor Aurelian's triumphal procession (see V. C (i) (c) 3, p. 219, above) traversing

rage for German fashions was wide-spread and that the previous edicts had been disregarded.'[1]

The fifth century was the age in which the Romans who were 'going barbarian' and the barbarians who were 'going Roman' met one another, in their respective courses, mid-way, and lingered for a moment abreast—until the Romans drifted on again along their downward road towards barbarization and now carried the half-Romanized barbarians backwards with them This brief phase of social parity in an unstable compromise between Barbarism and Civilization may be illustrated by bringing together the portraits of two men both of whom may claim to rank among the outstanding figures of that world in that penultimate phase of its history. Aetius, who was the older man of the two, was officially a Roman, while Theodoric the Ostrogoth, who was a child of the succeeding generation, was officially a barbarian. Both alike, however, were born frontiersmen; and the birth-place of both was the same sector of the *limes*. It was that Lower Danubian sector where the pressure was always particularly high because at this point the north-eastern corner of the Roman Empire touched the head of the Great Western Bay of the Eurasian Steppe (a funnel up which the flood of Nomadism was apt to surge with the speed and force of the tide in an estuary).[2] While their identity of birth-place thus constituted an initial bond between these two distinguished sons of Moesia Secunda, their respective upbringing happened in either case to be such as to bring them still nearer together by counteracting their diversity of social heritage; for, while Aetius

the streets of Rome. 'The use of braccae, breeches or trowsers was still considered in Italy as a Gallic and Barbarian fashion', is Gibbon's observation (*The History of the Decline and Fall of the Roman Empire*, chap. xi, footnote 86). 'The Romans, however,' Gibbon adds, 'had made great advances towards it.' And Gibbon himself was destined soon to see the polite society of his own world do likewise. There is extant a letter dated the 21st June–7th July, 1778, which was written to the Countess of Carlisle by her husband the Fifth Earl when that nobleman was on a diplomatic mission in America (as one of the Royal Commissioners who had been appointed on the 12th April, 1778, in the forlorn hope of persuading the now indomitable insurgent colonists to accept, at the thirteenth hour, some accommodation which would avert a complete severance of the revolted colonies' political connexion with the British Crown); and in this letter the following passage occurs:

'The gnats in this part of the River [Delaware] are as large as sparrows; I have armed myself against them by wearing trousers, which is the constant dress of this country.' (Historical Manuscripts Commission: Fifteenth Report, Appendix, Part VI: The Manuscripts of the Earl of Carlisle, preserved at Castle Howard (London 1897, Eyre & Spottiswoode), p. 345.)

It was only a few years after this, again, that the French disciples of the American revolutionaries earned the nickname of *sans-culottes* for appearing in public, not in nothing but their shirts, but shockingly clad in liberal trousers instead of conservative knee-breeches. A superstitious antiquary might be tempted to infer that the act of going into trousers was an infallible outward visible sign of the demoralization of a *ci-devant* dominant minority.—A.J.T.

[1] Dill, S.: *Roman Society in the Last Century of the Western Empire*, 2nd edition (London 1905, Macmillan), p. 297.

[2] See Part III. A, Annex II, vol. iii, pp. 401 and 426–8, above.

was brought up as a hostage among the Goths and Huns, Theodoric was brought up as a hostage at the Roman Imperial Court
of Constantinople. The two sketches that here follow both come
from the deft pen of the same modern Western scholar:

'Aetius . . . était Romain. Il était né . . . à Durostorum (aujourd'hui
Silistrie).[1] Son père . . . avait fait une carrière brillante. . . . C'est
évidemment parce qu'il appartenait à une famille militaire distinguée
qu'Aetius, jeune garçon, fut donné comme otage à Alaric. Le chef des
Visigoths distingua l'enfant romain, l'instruisit dans le métier des armes.
Puis Aetius passa, toujours comme otage, chez les Huns, sur lesquels
régnait le roi Rougila. . . . Il connut à sa cour le neveu du Khan, Attila,
et se lia avec lui. Ainsi les deux fameux adversaires de la célèbre
bataille du Campus Mauriacus, où devaient s'affronter d'un côté la
Romania et les fédérés germains, de l'autre la Barbarie tatare avec ses
sujets germains, alains, etc., se sont connus dès leur prime jeunesse.[2]

'Ce séjour chez les Huns eut des conséquences importantes. Aetius
conserva des intelligences chez ce peuple. C'est chez lui qu'il aimait à
puiser les mercenaires dont il composera les armées dites "romaines"
pendant une quinzaine d'années. En 424, alors qu'il favorisait l'usurpation de Johannès contre Valentinien III, Aetius avait été chercher une
armée hunnique. En 432, lorsqu'il dut prendre la fuite, vaincu sous
Rimini par son rival Boniface, Aetius se réfugia chez les Huns et revint,
l'année suivante, avec une armée que lui fournit le roi Rougila. Par la
terreur, il se fait alors octroyer le titre de généralissime (*magister
utriusque militiae*) et la dignité de "patrice": c'est-à-dire, de père adoptif
de l'empereur. Le romain Aetius n'agit pas autrement que le visigoth
Alaric ou, plus tard en Orient, l'alain Aspar, l'ostrogoth Théodoric.
Il est plus barbare d'éducation et de tempérament que le vandale
Stilichon.

'Aetius nous est connu surtout par les panégyriques de Mérobaude
et un fragment de la chronique de Renatus Profuturus Frigeridus. Ces
deux écrivains latins du ve siècle sont, comme l'indiquent leurs noms,
d'origine germanique: signe des temps.

'Il faut reconnaître que, si l'Empire a pu tenir trente ans encore en
Occident, de 424 à 454, c'est [dû] à la connaissance approfondie que
le patrice Aetius avait des hommes et des choses du monde barbare,
tant tatare que germanique, non moins que du monde romain.'[3]

It is instructive to examine this portrait of Aetius in the same
synoptic view as the following portrait of Theodoric from the
hand of the same artist:

'Nul barbare ne fut plus comblé de faveur que Théodoric. L'empereur Zénon le nomma patrice, l'adopta même comme fils d'armes

---

[1] Durostorum was one of the fortresses that guarded the Roman military frontier
along the south bank of the Lower Danube.—A.J.T.
[2] It is for this reason that another modern Western scholar (quoted in I. C (i) (a),
vol. i, p. 60, footnote 1, above) describes the conflict between Aetius and Attila as
presenting 'the image of a civil war'.—A.J.T.
[3] Lot, F.: *Les Invasions Germaniques* (Paris 1935, Payot), pp. 89–90.

(476). Plus tard il sera fait *magister militum*, désigné pour le consulat. Théodoric n'était pas étranger au monde gréco-latin. Donné comme otage par son père en 465, il avait passé à Constantinople dix années, de 8 à 18 ans, les années décisives de l'homme, celles de sa formation. S'il avait été seul, il aurait fait sa fortune au service de l'Empire d'Orient, comme tant d'autres chefs barbares, comme son rival et homonyme Théodoric le Louche. Mais Théodoric appartenait à la race illustre des "Amales". Le peuple ostrogothique, qui le reconnaissait pour son chef, avait mis en lui toute sa confiance. Ce sont les revendications incessantes de ses compatriotes qui expliquent son attitude ambiguë vis-à-vis de l'Empire, tantôt déférente et soumise, tantôt subitement agressive. En 488 enfin, Zénon trouva l'occasion de se débarrasser de ce sujet indocile. Il lui concéda le pays d' "Hespérie" (L'Italie), à charge de s'en rendre maître aux dépens d'Odoacre.'[1]

If, having examined and compared this pair of fifth-century portraits, we were now to break off our survey and shut our eyes, we might flatter ourselves that we had already witnessed the closing scene in the play, and that the spectacle on which the curtain was falling was a stable amalgam of Roman and barbarian manners on a level which must be at any rate as high as Theodoric's, though it might also be as low as Aetius's. There is, however, still another scene to come; and this further scene—which is really and truly the final one—has met our eyes already in our portrait-gallery of truants.[2] We have there taken notice of a picture of a *ci-devant* Roman citizen which was drawn from the life in A.D. 448 by a Greek man-of-letters who paid a visit in that year to Attila's camp in the Hungarian Alföld on a diplomatic mission from the Roman Imperial Court at Constantinople. This contemporary of Aetius who is portrayed for us by Priscus had the same taste as Aetius himself—and Aetius's forerunner Gratian —for a barbarian way of life; but the canny Greek (for such he was by birth, like the historian who has immortalized him) had managed to indulge in Gratian's craze without incurring Gratian's fate; for Fortune had enabled him to carry his barbarization to a length from which even Gratian would probably have recoiled. The story is best told in the words of Priscus the Roman envoy and Greek historian.

'While I was waiting' [Priscus tells us, for an audience with Attila's minister Onegesius,] 'and was pacing up and down in front of the enclosure surrounding the establishment, I was approached by an individual whom I presumed, from his Nomad dress, to be a native, but who addressed me in Greek with the words "Good morning" ($\chi a\hat{\imath}\rho\epsilon$)! —a greeting which intrigued me, for here was good Greek issuing from the lips of a Nomad. The Nomads, being the sweepings of the

---

¹ Lot, F., op. cit., p. 135.　　² See V. C (i) (d) 3, pp. 409–10, above.

V　　　　　　　　Q

Earth, supplement their diverse vernaculars by some study of either Hunnish or Gothic or Latin (in so far as they have intercourse with the Romans),[1] while none of them readily speak Greek except the prisoners carried off from Thrace or from the Adriatic sea-board. These unfortunates, however, were recognizable at sight. Their tattered clothing and unkempt heads marked them out as people who had come down in the world, whereas my friend had all the appearance of a prosperous Nomad, with his clothes so smart and his hair so neatly bobbed.

'After returning his greeting, I inquired who he was and where he had lived before he had crossed into No-Man's-Land and adopted the Nomadic Life. He retorted by asking the motive of my eagerness to learn these details. I told him that the cause of my curiosity was his knowledge of Greek. Thereupon he laughed and told me that he was a Greek ($\Gamma\rho\alpha\iota\kappa\delta s$) by race who had come on business to the Moesian town of Viminacium on the Danube. He had stayed there a long time, married a local heiress, and enjoyed a spell of prosperity; but he had been stripped of all this when the town fell into the hands of the barbarians—on which occasion his former wealth had caused him to be reserved for Onegesius himself in the division of the spoils. The well-to-do captives, he mentioned, were the special perquisite (after Attila had taken his choice) of the *élite* in the Nomadic World, because they fetched the highest price when disposed of. However, he continued, he had distinguished himself in the subsequent actions against the Romans and against the [?Khazar] horde; had made over his winnings on active service to his native master, according to the Nomad etiquette; and had thus obtained his freedom. He had married a native wife; he was the father of children;[2] he was an honoured guest at Onegesius's table; and he considered his present life preferable to his past.'[3]

[1] Latin was at this time the language of all the Danubian provinces of the Roman Empire from the Black Forest to the Black Sea, while Greek was hardly spoken any longer anywhere to the north of the Balkan Range (see IV. C (iii) (c) 2 (β), vol. iv, p. 326, footnote 2, above).—A.J.T.

[2] In due course Priscus's renegade might have become the progenitor of a new Nomad tribe or horde, if the dominion of the Huns on Roman ground had not collapsed at Attila's death but had lasted on for nine or ten generations, like the dominion of the Manchus in the Far East. In the territory of the Jasakto Khan 'Banner' of Mongols, in the southern division of the Hsingan Province of 'Manchukuo', there was in 1935 an enclave which was at that date still occupied by a tiny autonomous community of prosperous Nomadic stock-breeders who were known as the Manchu-Mongols. The story of this little horde is told as follows by a modern Western scholar who has obtained his knowledge at first hand (Lattimore, O.: *The Mongols of Manchuria* (London 1935, Allen & Unwin), pp. 228–32):

'In the reign of Ch'ien Lung (*imperabat* A.D. 1736–96) a Manchu Imperial princess was given in marriage to the ruling prince this of [the Jasakto Khan] "banner". In her following were seven "slaves" who were later given Mongol wives. On the death of the princess the then prince established them in their present territory. At the same time he gave them a kind of charter, exempting them from taxes and service, except for the expenses of the annual sacrifices at the tomb of the princess. . . . They have increased to over a hundred families, numbering about a thousand people. . . . The fact that this group is called "Manchu-Mongol" is, in my opinion, misleading. The original seven men were undoubtedly Chinese, and were called Manchu simply because they came as the servants of a Manchu princess. There is a tradition that they were artisans—a carpenter, a mason, and so on—and artisans coming from Peking in the eighteenth century were not likely to be Manchus. The Peking Manchus of that time,

For footnote [3] see opposite page, at bottom.

This *ci-devant* Greek renegade who was encountered by the historian Priscus in Attila's *ordu* in A.D. 448 was a portent of things to come; for he stands at the head of a line of truants from an expiring Hellenic dominant minority who managed to make themselves at home in a barbarian environment and who took to this adoptive barbarism so whole-heartedly that they began to lend a hand in fighting the battles of Hun or Teuton war-lords whose ancestors had been employed by their own ancestors as mercenaries. In a different context[1] we have already noted how at Vouillé in A.D. 507, when the Visigoths and the Franks were fighting out by the ordeal of battle the question which of two barbarian war-bands was to become the permanent possessor of the derelict Roman Imperial heritage in Gaul, there fought and died at the side of the Visigoth war-lord Alaric a grandson of the Latin man-of-letters Sidonius Apollinaris. The grandfather had been a mild and cultivated Gallo-Roman country-gentleman who could have comfortably worn the shoes of Jane Austen's Mr. Woodhouse, but who would have rubbed his eyes at the spectacle of his little grandson breaking Sarmatian lances instead of turning Latin verses as a gentleman should. Yet young Sidonius was acting no differently from other Gallo-Romans of his generation. At Vouillé there were Gallo-Roman forces engaged on the Frankish as well as on the Gothic side; it was the man-power of the Gallo-Roman population of the Seine Basin, whose allegiance Clovis had previously captured from their native leader Syagrius, that furnished the Frankish adventurer with the means of overthrowing all the rival barbarian war-lords within his reach;[2] the survivors among young Sidonius's Arvernian contemporaries who lived to fight another day had in their turn to exchange an Amalung for a Merowing *heretoga*; and in the sixth century it was the habit of the Frankish kings of Gaul to fight their wars, both civil and foreign, with an unwieldy *levée en masse* in which their Latin and Teutonic subjects were

being at the height of their prestige, were a leisured class who did not have to work as artisans. Furthermore the surnames Wang and Li, given for three of the families, were not Chinese names that were commonly taken by Manchus during the period when they were at pains to distinguish themselves socially from the Chinese. This group offers, therefore, a well established and clearly dated example of Chinese "turning Mongol". The numbers are not important; the amount of Chinese blood in a hundred families descended from seven men of the eighteenth century must be very small indeed. It is the process that is important. It undoubtedly was common in the past; for something of the same sort can still be seen in regions where the Chinese penetrate among the Mongols in small numbers.'

This testimony of Lattimore's from the opposite extremity of Eurasia affords an interesting corroboration of Priscus's story.—A.J.T.

[1] In II. D (v), vol. ii, p. 166, above.

[2] See Taylor, H. O.: *The Medieval Mind* (London 1911, Macmillan, 2 vols.), vol. i, p. 120.

[3] Priscus of Panium: *History of His Own Times*, in *Historici Graeci Minores*, edited by Dindorf, L., vol i (Berlin and Leipzig 1870, Teubner), pp. 305-9.

conscripted promiscuously.[1] There is no evidence that in this age the descendants of the Roman provincials showed any less alacrity in following a *Führer* on the war-path than was shown by the contemporary descendants of barbarians to whom, for centuries past, the war-game had been the breath of life.

'Ces populations gallo-romaines désarmées par la méfiance de l'Empire romain reprirent le goût de la guerre avec une rapidité incroyable. On les voit, dès le viᵉ siècle, se battre avec rage contre elles-mêmes pour soutenir les querelles insensées d'un Chilpéric, d'un Sigebert, d'un Gontran. L'armement, l'instruction militaire, la tactique furent copiés sur ceux des Francs. Même en temps de paix, le Gallo-Romain prit l'habitude de porter l'épée au côté et de se vêtir d'habillements serrés au corps, à la façon des Barbares. À sa mort, il voulut être enseveli avec ses armes, comme le guerrier franc. De là, l'aspect tout barbare des nécropoles de ce temps. Les prétendus "cimetières francs" sont en réalité, pour la plupart, des cimetières gallo-romains.'[2]

In the rare intervals when there was no dynastic bickering among their Frankish war-lords to give these sixth-century Gallo-Romans an excuse for indulging in their new-found barbarian sport the Gallo-Roman cities—reviving the pugnacious tradition of international relations between the city-states of the Hellenic World before the establishment of the Roman Peace—now indulged, in flat defiance of the peace of a barbarian 'successor-state', in private wars against one another.[3] And the local history of the progress of this cult of Barbarism among the epigoni of a Roman governing class can also be traced, and this perhaps most clearly of all, in a change of fashion in names. We have noticed above[4] that, about half-way through the fourth century, the barbarians in the Roman Imperial service had dropped the practice —handed down by previous generations of barbarian hostages and mercenaries—of Latinizing their barbarian names or even giving them up in order to take good Latin names in place of them. The following century saw, in Gaul, the earliest examples of an inverse move, on the part of true-born Romans, to assume German names instead of imposing them;[5] in the last third of the sixth century this late-fifth-century fashion abruptly gained the upper hand; and before the end of the eighth century it had become universal.[6]

[1] For instances see Dill, S.: *Roman Society in Gaul in the Merovingian Age* (London 1926, Macmillan), pp. 119–20 and 274.
[2] Lot, F.: *Les Invasions Germaniques* (Paris 1935, Payot), p. 210.
[3] Dill, S., op. cit., p. 265.   [4] On p. 468.
[5] The process of fusion must have been expedited by the legalization, in A.D. 497, of marriages between Romans and Franks in the Frankish dominions (see Taylor, op. cit., vol. i, p. 120). The Franks do not seem to have thought of treating their Roman fellow subjects as members of a separate and inferior race (Taylor, op. cit., vol. i, p. 123).
[6] These socially significant changes of nomenclature are recorded by Lot in op. cit., pp. 229–34. In the Visigothic 'successor-state' of the Roman Empire in the Iberian

By Charlemagne's time every inhabitant of Gaul was sporting a German name, regardless of whether his or her ancestry was actually Frankish or provincial.

This trivial point of manners tells us how unsubstantial was the ghost of the Roman Empire that was officially evoked in Western Christendom in Charlemagne's reign and person;[1] and this Gallic testimony is confirmed by the history of a parallel cult of barbarism in the decline and fall of the Sinic World; for this Sinic story has a singularly different ending from that of our tale of Gaul.

If we make a chronological equation between the break-up of the Roman Empire in the West at the turn of the fourth and fifth centuries and the break-up of the Sinic Empire of the Han at the turn of the second and third centuries of the Christian Era, and if we concentrate our attention, in both cases, upon those ex-Imperial territories that were carved up into barbarian 'successor-states', then the century in the post-Sinic interregnum in Northern China that will correspond to the eighth century of the Christian Era in the post-Hellenic interregnum in Western Europe will be the sixth century or thereabouts. When we examine, however, what was happening by that time in those northern marches of the defunct Empire of the Han which had been carved up, at the close of the third century, into barbarian 'successor-states' under the dominion of *ci-devant* Eurasian Nomads,[2] we behold a revolution of manners which is the exact inverse of the revolution which was consummated in the eighth century in Gaul.

The respective Sien Pi and Hiongnu and To Pa founders of the three earliest barbarian 'successor-states' of the Sinic universal state had already taken care to drape the nakedness of their barbarism under a veil of decency by archaistically bestowing upon their new political creations the polite Sinic names of 'Pe Yen' and 'Pe Han' and 'Wei';[3] and some two hundred years later, after the To Pa principality of 'Wei' had annexed both of its two neighbours and rivals,[4] the cue of 'de-barbarization' was taken up and followed out to its logical consequences by one of the princes of 'Wei', Hiao-wên ti (*regnabat* A.D. 490[5]–499).[6] In A.D. 494 this Sinomane

---

Peninsula the fusion between Romans and Goths seems to have been completed by the middle of the seventh century of the Christian Era (Taylor, op. cit., vol. i, p. 118).

[1] The hollowness of 'the Holy Roman Empire' has already struck us by contrast with the solidity of the rival structure which was erected in the same century in Orthodox Christendom. For this contrast between 'the Holy Roman Empire' of Charlemagne and the East Roman Empire of Leo Syrus see IV. C (iii) (c) 2 (β), vol. iv, pp. 322–3, above.

[2] See IV. C (ii) (b) 1, vol. iv, p. 65; V. C (i) (c) 3, in the present volume, pp. 272–3; V. C (i) (c) 4, p. 356; and the present chapter, p. 465, above.

[3] See V. C (i) (c) 3, p. 273, above.   [4] See V. C (i) (c) 4, p. 356, footnote 6, above.

[5] This was the date of Hiao-wên ti's effective accession. He had been on the throne as a minor, under a regency, since his father's abdication in A.D. 471.

[6] For Hiao-wên ti's reign and policy see Franke, O.: *Geschichte des Chinesischen Reiches*, vol. ii (Berlin 1936, de Gruyter), pp. 208–15.

prince of To Pa barbarian origin transferred the seat of his government from his forefathers' camping-ground at P'ing-ch'êng, in the barbarized marches, to the derelict site of the ancient Imperial capital of Loyang; in the same year he prohibited the wearing of barbarian dress by any of his subjects; in 495 he banned the use of the barbarian vernaculars at Court and compelled the barbarian-descended families in the population to exchange their barbarian names for Sinic substitutes; and finally, in 496, he changed the name of his own dynasty from the tell-tale barbarism of 'To Pa' to the respectable Sinism of 'Yuan'. If the Sinic tradition could cast so strong a spell as this over the native prince of a barbarian 'successor-state' some three hundred years after the break-up of the Sinic universal state, it is not surprising to find the universal state itself being resuscitated, after the passage of another hundred years, by the Sui and the T'ang[1] with an effectiveness that is likewise characteristic of the corresponding work of an Anatolian Leo Syrus, but which is conspicuously lacking in the work of an Austrasian Charlemagne.[2]

Before closing our inquiry into the barbarization of dominant minorities, we may pause to ask ourselves whether any of the symptoms of this social phenomenon are discernible in our own world of the modern West. On first thoughts we shall perhaps be inclined to think that our question has received a conclusive answer in the recent conquest of one of the strongest of the surviving fastnesses of Barbarism by one of the weakest of the Western Great Powers of our day. Even if there be a dominant minority in our twentieth-century Western World which may find itself constrained to plead guilty to a charge of vulgarization, can this other danger of barbarization be taken very seriously in a world where the last of the transfrontier barbarians are being subjugated or exterminated under our eyes? The spectacle of Ethiopia may impel us to dismiss our question with a curt answer in the negative; yet, before we finally condemn it as inane, we may do well to look farther afield and remind ourselves of the rather disconcerting fact that, in the present heart of our Western Society's 'New World' of North America, there is to-day a large and widespread population of European blood and Western Christian social heritage which has been unmistakably and profoundly barbarized by being marooned in the Appalachian backwoods after serving a preliminary term of exile on 'the Celtic Fringe'.[3]

[1] See V. C (i) (c) 4, p. 356, footnote 6, above, for the historical development, through a number of intervening stages, of the *imperium redivivum* of the Sui and the T'ang out of the Han Empire's To Pa barbarian 'successor-state' in Shansi.

[2] This likeness of the Sinic *imperium redivivum* of the Sui and the T'ang to the East Roman Empire, in a common contrast to 'the Holy Roman Empire', is examined further in Part X, below.   [3] See II. D (vii), vol. ii, 311–12, above.

The barbarizing effect of the American frontier has been described with equal eloquence and insight by an American historian who is a master of the subject.

'In the settlement of America we have to observe how European life entered the continent and how America modified and developed that life and reacted on Europe. Our early history is the study of European germs developing in an American environment. . . . The frontier is the line of most rapid and effective Americanization. The wilderness masters the colonist. It finds him a European in dress, industries, tools, modes of travel and thought. It takes him from the railroad car and puts him in the birch canoe. It strips off the garments of civilization and arrays him in the hunting shirt and the moccasin. It puts him in the log cabin of the Cherokee and Iroquois and runs an Indian palisade around him. Before long he has gone to planting Indian corn and plowing with a sharp stick; he shouts the war-cry and takes the scalp in orthodox Indian fashion. In short, at the frontier the environment is at first too strong for the man. He must accept the conditions which it furnishes, or perish; and so he fits himself into the Indian clearings and follows the Indian trails. Little by little he transforms the wilderness; but the outcome is not the old Europe. . . . The fact is that here is a new product that is American.'[1]

The thesis is that, although the Indian frontier of the United States has ceased to exist as a physical fact with a precise geographical locus, it has succeeded nevertheless in immortalizing itself by setting a permanent spiritual impress upon the national life of a new nation of European origin which, as the frontier travelled westward across the Continent,[2] was steadily growing in stature on American ground. If this thesis is correct, then we are bound to declare that, in North America at any rate, a social pull of prodigious force has been exerted upon one section of the dominant minority of our modern Western World by one section of the external proletariat. For, on this showing, the influence of the now physically obsolete Indian frontier is visible not only in the 'living museum' of barbarized frontiersmen who have been left stranded in an Appalachian fastness by the westward-rolling tide of American 'nation-building': the frontier has also carved for itself a vaster monument in a more lasting medium by introducing a vein which is certainly distinctive, and possibly predominant, into the new-made American national character. When we remind ourselves of the initial disparity—and this in spiritual culture as well as in corporate physical strength—between the incomers from Europe who have built this new nation up and the American aborigines whom they have swept out of their path, and when

[1] Turner, F. J.: *The Frontier in American History* (New York 1921, Holt), pp. 3–4. Part of this passage has been quoted already in II. D (vii), vol. ii, p. 312, footnote 1, above.   [2] See V. C (i) (c) 3, pp. 207 and 328–32, above.

we further recall that the Indian frontier of the European colonies
in North America was in physical existence for barely two centuries and a half, reckoning from the landing of the first settlers
on the Atlantic coast down to the time when their descendants
reached and occupied their natural frontier on the Pacific sea-board
of the North American Continent, we shall be more astonished
than ever at the strength of the influence exerted by a barbarism
which was continually 'on the run' upon an invading civilization
which hardly paused in its march across the American Continent
and which was animated by the 'driving-power', and backed by
the weight, of the whole body social of Western Christendom in
its European homeland. In the light of this American portent it
would be rash to assume that the spiritual malady of barbarization
is a peril which our modern Western dominant minority can afford
to disregard. On our American precedent an Ethiopian barbarism
that has been crushed by methods more barbarous than its own
may perhaps be expected to revenge itself by transferring its habitation from Abyssinian to Italian souls and perpetuating itself, no
longer innocuously in a primitive Africa, but lethally in a decadent
Europe.

(β) *Vulgarity and Barbarism in Art.*

If we pass next from the general field of 'Manners and Customs'
to the special field of Art, we shall find the sense of promiscuity
betraying itself, here again, in the two alternative forms of vulgarity and barbarism with which we have now made ourselves
familiar. In one or other of these forms the Art of a disintegrating
civilization is apt to pay for an abnormally wide and rapid geographical diffusion by forfeiting that distinctiveness of style which
is the sign manual of well-being in Art perhaps even more conspicuously than it is in any of the other activities of a civilization
that is still in its growth.

Two classic examples of vulgarity in Art are the fashions in
which a disintegrating Minoan and a disintegrating Syriac Society
successively radiated their aesthetic influence round the shores of
the Mediterranean. The interregnum (*circa* 1425–1125 B.C.) which
followed the overthrow of the Minoan 'thalassocracy' is marked—
in the 'artifacts', disinterred by our modern Western archaeologists,
which are our sole evidence for the course of Minoan history—by
the vulgar fashion, labelled 'Late Minoan III', which outranges
in its diffusion all the earlier and finer Minoan styles;[1] and similarly

---

[1] For its range see Glotz, G.: *La Civilisation Égéenne* (Paris 1923, Renaissance du
Livre), pp. 64 and 248–50. In this age when it was *in articulo mortis*, the Minoan culture
spread from the Aegean to Macedonia in one direction and to Cyprus in another, and
Syrian princesses took to dressing *à la crétoise*.

the 'Time of Troubles' (*circa* 925–525 B.C.) which followed the breakdown of the Syriac Civilization is marked by the equally vulgar and equally widespread mechanical combination of *motifs* drawn promiscuously from Egyptiac and from Babylonic sources which was diffused from Tyrian and Sidonian workshops into the sister Hellenic World in the Aegean, as well as into the barbarian hinterlands of Carthage and of Gades.

In the history of Hellenic art a corresponding vulgarity found expression in the excessively rich decoration which came into vogue with the Corinthian order of architecture—an extravagance which is the very antithesis of the distinctive note of the Hellenic genius; and, when we look for outstanding examples of this fashion, which reached its climax in the Imperial Age of Hellenic history (*circa* 25 B.C.–A.D. 375), we shall not find them at the geographical heart of the Hellenic World. As illustrations of this florid display of aesthetic decadence, the surviving columns of the Olympieum at Athens are not so characteristic as the remains of the temple of a non-Hellenic divinity at Ba'lbak, or as the sarcophagi that were manufactured by Hellenic 'monumental masons' to harbour the mortal remains of Philhellene barbarian war-lords on the far eastern rim of the Iranian Plateau.[1]

If we turn from the archaeological to the literary record of the disintegration of the Hellenic Civilization, we find that the 'highbrows' of the first few generations after the breakdown of 431 B.C. bewailed the vulgarization of Hellenic music and the deplorable effect upon the Hellenic êthos of a change for the worse in an art to which Hellenic souls were particularly sensitive. And we have already noticed in another context[2] the vulgarization of the Attic drama at the hands of Διονύσου Τεχνῖται ('United Artists, Ltd.') who tore it up from its roots in the theatre of Dionysus at Athens in order to hawk it up and down the world from Parthia to Spain.

In the modern Western World we may observe that it is the floridly decadent and not the severely classical style of Hellenic architecture that has inspired our Western Hellenizing fashions of Baroque and Rococo. And in the so-called 'chocolate-box style' of our Victorian and Edwardian 'commercial art'[3] we can discern an analogue of 'Late Minoan III' that bids fair to conquer, not merely the Mediterranean Basin, but the whole face of the planet in the service of a peculiarly Western commercial technique of visually advertising the tradesman's wares.

---

[1] See III. C (i) (*a*), vol. iii, p. 131; III. C (ii) (*a*), vol. iii, p. 247, footnote 2; V. C (i) (*c*) 2, in the present volume, pp. 134–5; and V. C (i) (*c*) 3, p. 196, above.
[2] In IV. C (iii) (*b*) 14, vol. iv, p. 243, above.
[3] For the corresponding modern Western monstrosity of 'commercial architecture' see the passage quoted from Frobenius in V. C (i) (*c*) 3, p. 201, footnote 1, above.

The fatuousness of 'the chocolate-box style' is so desolating that it has provoked even a generation as aesthetically obtuse as ours[1] into attempting desperate remedies. Our archaistic flight from vulgarity into a pre-'Pre-Raphaelite' Byzantinism is discussed in a later chapter;[2] but in this place we have to take note of the contemporary and alternative flight from vulgarity into Barbarism. Self-respecting Western sculptors of the present day who have not found a congenial asylum in Byzantium have turned their eyes towards Benin; and it is not only in the glyptic branch of art that a Western World whose own sources of creativeness have apparently run dry has been seeking fresh aesthetic inspiration from the barbarians of West Africa. West African music and dancing, as well as West African sculpture, have been imported into the heart of the Western World on the lips and in the limbs of African conscript-immigrants; Congolese slaves have carried them into America, and Senegalese mercenaries into Europe; and the effect upon the êthos of our Western dominant minority has been so swiftly and so deeply demoralizing that, if Plato could have witnessed it, he would assuredly have lifted up his hands and given thanks to Apollo for Timotheus.

This triumph of a Negro art in the northern states of America and in the western countries of Europe represents a much more signal victory for Barbarism than the progressive barbarization of the Hellenic image and superscription on the staters of King Philip's mintage in the course of the long and slow journey of this Hellenic coin-type from the banks of the Strymon to the banks of the Thames in Ultima Thule.[3]

To a layman's eye the flight to Benin and the flight to Byzantium seem equally unlikely to lead the latter-day Western artist to the recovery of his lost soul.

> Hoc se quisque modo fugitat, quem scilicet, ut fit,
> effugere haud potis est.[4]

And yet, even if he cannot save himself, it is still not impossible that he may be a means of salvation for others. 'A mediocre teacher, giving mechanical instruction in a science that has been created by men of genius, may awake in some one of his pupils the vocation which he has never felt in himself';[5] and, if the 'commercial art' of a disintegrating Hellenic World performed the astonishing feat of evoking the supremely creative art of Mahayanian

---

[1] On the aesthetic obtuseness of modern Western Man see the acute observations of Dean Inge that have been quoted in III. C (iii), vol. iii, p. 387, above.
[2] See V. C (i) (d) 8 (β), vol. vi, p. 60, below.
[3] See V. C (i) (c) 3, p. 198, above.
[4] Lucretius: De Rerum Natura, Book III, ll. 1068–9, quoted already in I. C (i) (a), vol. i, p. 55, above.
[5] Bergson, quoted already in III. C (ii) (a), vol. iii, p. 247, above.

Buddhism through its encounter with the religious experience of another disintegrating world on Indic ground,[1] we cannot venture to pronounce *a priori* that the modern Western 'chocolate-box style' is incapable of working similar miracles as it is flaunted round the globe on the advertiser's hoardings and sky-signs.

(γ) *Lingue Franche*.

In the field of Language the sense of promiscuity in a disintegrating society reveals itself in the change from a local distinctiveness to a general confusion of tongues.

Though the institution of Language exists for the purpose of serving as a means of communication between one human being and another, the social effect of Language in the history of Mankind up to date, as far as we have knowledge of it, has actually been on the whole to divide the Human Race and not to unite it; for hitherto this institution (which in itself is one of the clearest of the criteria that distinguish men from brutes) has been current in so great a number of such extremely diverse forms that even the languages which have won the widest currency and enjoyed the longest vogue have never yet become common to more than a fraction of Mankind. Even within the narrower subjective world of the individual human being's experience in his brief personal span of Time and Space it has hitherto been rare for him to find himself speaking a language that has been common to all other human beings who have come within his ken either by intercourse or by report. An element which has seldom been absent from Man's mental picture of the world in which he lives is a consciousness of the existence of 'foreigners' whose principal hall-mark is their unintelligible speech; and thus it has come about that an institution which is common to all Mankind and which distinguishes Man from all other embodiments of Life on this planet has hitherto served in practice to distinguish and divide one human community from another as well as to identify and unite with one another the respective members of each one of these innumerable separate linguistic communities into which the Human Family has hitherto been parcelled out. This is the penalty which Mankind has had to pay for the narrowness of the limits of mutual intelligibility. For in fact, so far as our modern Western knowledge goes, there has never really yet been a time when 'the whole Earth was of one language and of one speech'.[2] A mutual intelligibility that knows no exceptions and no limits is a potential achievement of the power of speech which may be its ultimate purpose and its

[1] See III. C (i) (*a*), vol. iii, p. 131; III. C (ii) (*a*), vol. iii, p. 247, footnote 2; V. C (i) (*c*) 2, in the present volume, pp. 134–5; and V. C (i) (*c*) 3, p. 196, above.
[2] Gen. xi. 1.

eventual goal; but, if so, we can only say that the purpose has never yet been attained and that the goal still lies hidden in the Future. Hitherto, any widespread uniformity—even within limits far short of a world-wide range—has been exceptional, while an extreme variety of tongues has been the rule. We find this rule of linguistic diversity prevailing, not only in primitive societies like those which still survive in the Sudan,[1] but also in civilizations in their growth stage. The Hellenic World, for example, included non-Greek-speaking Carians and Lycians, as well as Greek-speaking peoples, within the ambit of its city-state culture since the earliest date to which our records of Hellenic history go back;[2] and among the Greek-speaking majority there was a diversity of dialect and script between one district and another, and even between one city-state and another within the same district, which was jealously preserved as the distinctive shibboleth and hall-mark of a diversity of local character and was only ironed out into complete uniformity by the last tribulations of the Hellenic 'Time of Troubles'.[3] Again, in our modern Western World in our own day—whether we are living already in a 'Time of Troubles' or still in an age of growth[4] —a local diversity of language within an oecumenical uniformity of culture is an even more conspicuous feature than it was in the Hellenic World in the early and the middle chapters of Hellenic history.

It is in disintegrating civilizations at an advanced stage of their decline that we are apt to see languages—following the fortunes of the communities that speak them as their mother-tongues— waging internecine wars with one another and conquering, when victorious, wide dominions at their discomfited rivals' expense; and, if there is any grain of historical fact in the legend[5] of a confusion of tongues in the land of Shinar at the foot of an unfinished ziggurat in a recently built city of Babel, the story perhaps takes us to Babylon in an age in which the Sumeric universal state was breaking up, and the Sumeric Civilization dissolving, after the death of Hammurabi (*imperabat circa* 1947–1905 B.C.).[6] Babylon had been the capital of the Sumeric universal state in those latter days when 'the Empire of Sumer and Akkad' was being kept alive

---

[1] See Part III. A, Annex I, vol. iii, p. 393, above.
[2] On the other hand it was not until after the breakdown of the Hellenic Civilization that the Greek-speaking barbarians north and north-west of the Thermopylae–Naupactus line were brought into the Hellenic fold (see III. C (ii) (*b*), Annex IV, vol. iii, p. 478, above).
[3] See Buck, C. D.: *Introduction to the Study of the Greek Dialects* (Boston 1910, Ginn), pp. 154–5 and 157.
[4] This not yet soluble problem of historical diagnosis has been noticed in I. B (iv), vol. i, pp. 36–7, above, and is considered further in V. C (ii) (*b*), vol. vi, pp. 313–14, below.   [5] Gen. xi. 1–9.
[6] See I. C (i) (*b*), vol. i, pp. 106 and 110, and IV. C (ii) (*b*) 1, vol. iv, pp. 63–4, above, and V. C (ii) (*b*), vol. vi, pp. 297–8, below.

by a Babylonian dynasty of Amorite princes of whom Hammurabi himself was the most eminent representative;[1] and it might well be remembered in a 'folk-memory'[2] that 'the Lord did there confound the language of all the Earth, and from thence did the Lord scatter them abroad upon the face of all the Earth'; for in this catastrophic last chapter of Sumeric history the Sumerian language became a dead language after having played an historic role as the original linguistic vehicle of the Sumerian culture, while even the Akkadian language, which had attained to an upstart parity with Sumerian in the course of the Sumeric decline and fall, had now to contend with a host of external proletarian vernaculars—Hyksos and Hittite and Kassite—which had been brought into the derelict domain of the Sumeric universal state by barbarian war-bands that were ranging over it and settling down upon it during the post-Sumeric Völkerwanderung.[3]

We may thus perhaps venture to interpret this famous legend as the persistent echo of a bitter lament for the passing of a language which had formerly been current for a season, not indeed over the whole Earth, but at least over the whole domain of a single disintegrating civilization; and we may then go on to surmise that a uniform medium of linguistic communication which was looked back to with such poignant regret after it had passed out of currency may have been looked forward to with a proportionately keen longing in an earlier age when the very idea of an oecumenical language was still only a hope or a dream. This conjecture is fully in accord with the picture of the characteristic social circumstances of a 'Time of Troubles' which has already unfolded itself in this Study in other contexts. In a 'Time of Troubles', when a society is violently plucked up by the roots, those traditional articulations of the social structure which have grown up gradually and naturally through the ages are suddenly confounded. The once distinct and separate local communities now collide and intermingle with one another; the Orontes flows into the Tiber;[4] and the agony which these tribulations are bound in any case to inflict on the human beings who are called upon to endure them is aggravated by the special pains of loneliness and helplessness so long as the victims of the social convulsion, when they are thrown together in their strange new relations of hostility or comradeship, continue

---

[1] See I. C (i) (b), vol. i, pp. 103 and 106, above, and V. C (ii) (b), vol. vi, pp. 297-8, below.

[2] For the nature and operation of 'folk-memory' see V. C (ii) (a), Annex II, vol. vi, pp. 438-64, below.

[3] For this Völkerwanderung see I. C (i) (b), vol. i, pp. 104-11, and V. C (i) (c) 3, in the present volume, pp. 263-6, above.

[4] The famous passage of Juvenal has been quoted already in V. C (i) (c) 2, p. 67, above.

to be divided by the barriers of linguistic diversity that are a legacy of their former state. The legend of the confusion of tongues is true to life in fastening upon this state of mutual unintelligibility as being a sovereign impediment to concerted social action in face of a new and unprecedented social crisis; and this association of linguistic diversity with social paralysis can be illustrated by examples that stand out conspicuously in the full light of history.

In our Western World in our own generation this was one of the fatal weaknesses of that Danubian Hapsburg Monarchy which perished in the General War of 1914–18; and even in the inhumanly efficient Slave-Household of the Ottoman Pādishāh in its age of maturity, in A.D. 1651, we see the curse of Babel descending upon the *Ich-oghlans* within the precincts of the Seraglio and reducing them to impotence at the critical moment of a palace revolution. In their excitement the boys forgot their artificially acquired 'Osmanli idiom; and the astonished ears of the spectators were smitten by the sound of 'a tumult . . . with different voices and languages—for some cried in Georgian, others Albanian, Bosnian, Mingrelian, Turkish and Italian'.[1] In this historical instance of 'speaking with tongues' the multitude were not miraculously hearing from the lips of others, but were automatically rearticulating on their own lips, their 'own tongue wherein' they had been 'born',[2] while they were momentarily forgetting the new common language in which they had been sedulously instructed for the very purpose of enabling them to act effectively by acting in concert. We may allow ourselves to surmise that the memory of this paralysing experience inspired this batch of *Ich-oghlans* in after-life to master their 'Osmanli language of official intercourse with as thorough a command as they possessed over their now disconcerting mother-tongues. But all the circumstances of this trivial incident of Ottoman history are inverted in the momentous episode in which a 'speaking with tongues' is reported for the first time in the Acts of the Apostles.[3] In that scene depicted in the saga of the infancy of the Christian Church the tongues which are spoken are foreign to the lips of the speakers; these speakers are unlettered Galilaeans, who have hitherto never spoken, and seldom heard, any other language than their native Aramaic; their sudden outbreak into other tongues is represented as being a miraculous gift from God, which they exercise 'as the Spirit' gives 'them utterance'; and this gift is the first in which their new inspiration is manifested; for, according to the tale, the miracle of the Apostles

---

[1] Rycaut, P.: *The Present State of the Ottoman Empire* (London 1668, Starkey & Brome), p. 18.   [2] Acts ii. 8.   [3] Acts ii. 1–13.

speaking 'with other tongues' breaks out immediately after the descent of the Holy Ghost upon them.

While this tale may be diversely interpreted as history or as legend, there will be no dispute about the point in it which here concerns us. It is clear that, in the view of the writer of the Acts, the gift of tongues was the first enhancement of their natural faculties that was needed by Apostles who had been charged with the tremendous task of converting Mankind to a newly revealed 'higher religion'. Indeed, the world-wide range of their mission and the enhancement of their natural faculties through an in-pouring of the spirit of God are two things which the writer expressly brings into direct relation with one another in an earlier passage:

'Ye shall receive power after that the Holy Ghost is come upon you; and ye shall be witnesses unto me both in Jerusalem and in all Judaea and in Samaria and unto the uttermost part of the Earth.'[1]

Since the Acts of the Apostles is a mirror of the minds of the Christian missionaries of the first generation, these passages are evidence that the boon of an oecumenical medium of communication was as ardently desired by the pioneer propagators of a new-born Christianity as the loss of an historic *lingua franca* must have been keenly regretted by those survivors of the shipwreck of the Sumeric Society to whose grievous experience we may tentatively trace back the legend of the confusion of tongues in the Book of Genesis. In the view of the authorities behind the author of the Acts the pentecostal gift of tongues is in fact a miraculous substitute for a natural facility—the currency of a *lingua franca*—for lack of which the early Christian missionaries might otherwise have found themselves almost prohibitively handicapped.

If this is a true reading of the passage, the eagerness and grati-tude of these early Christian missionaries for the gift of speech in a multitude of local vernacular languages may still, however, at first sight seem surprising when we consider that the Apostles' world in the first century of the Christian Era was far less ill sup-plied with *lingue franche* than our world is to-day. The mother-tongue of the Galilaeans of that age was an Aramaic which would carry any Palestinian speaker of it northwards as far as the Amanus and eastwards as far as the Zagros and westwards as far as the Nile, while the Greek in which the Acts themselves are written would carry the writer in Saint Paul's company overseas through 'the Isles of the Gentiles'[2] as far as Rome—and on beyond Rome to the Rhône and the Pyrenees and the Atlas, if the swords of Paul's

---

[1] Acts i. 8.   [2] Gen. x. 5.

Roman gaolers would drop their points to give further passage to the intrepid Greek-speaking preacher of an Aramaic-speaking Christ. Any child of that age who commanded both these two oecumenical languages had it in his power to address himself—through the written word, at any rate—to a public which extended, east and west, from the countrymen of the learned Magi to the subjects of the cultivated King Juba—as is testified by a celebrated contemporary of the anonymous author of the Acts. The Jewish historian Josephus[1] tells us in the preface to one of his works[2] how he first wrote the book in Aramaic for the information of half his world and then, for the instruction of the other half, published a translation of it in Greek.

In Josephus's opinion the previously published works on the Romano-Jewish War of A.D. 66–70 which had been written in Greek by non-Jewish authors were without exception highly unsatisfactory.

'Such works consist of alternate invective and encomium, without a vestige of historical accuracy; and this has induced me to offer to the public of the Roman Empire, in a Greek translation, a work of my own, originally composed in my native language [i.e. in Aramaic] and published in the non-Hellenic Orient (ἃ τοῖς ἄνω βαρβάροις τῇ πατρίῳ συντάξας ἀνέπεμψα πρότερον).... I felt it a paradox that the truth concerning events of such importance should be allowed to remain in doubt, and that the Parthians, the Babylonians, the most remote peoples of Arabia, my own compatriots beyond the Euphrates and the inhabitants of Adiabene should be accurately informed, through my labours, of the origin, vicissitudes and issue of the war, while the Greeks and all Romans who did not serve in the campaign should have nothing better at their disposal than flattering or fictitious accounts which conceal the truth.'

It will be seen that the world for which Josephus was writing was uncommonly well equipped in the matter of *lingue franche* if a command of no more than two languages would suffice to enable an author to bring his book within reach of all potential readers of it. Perhaps the reason for this trivial yet striking exception to the general disharmony and frustration which were the outstanding features of the social life of Josephus's time and place was that Josephus's world was composed of the overlapping domains of no less than three civilizations—the Babylonic, the Syriac, and the Hellenic—which had successively broken down and had so given play for the spread of *lingue franche* in the course of their own disintegration. In the world-wide Great Society of the present age it would be difficult for any writer to reach so large a propor-

---

[1] For Josephus's career as an example of Withdrawal-and-Return see III. C (ii) (*b*), vol. iii, pp. 294–6, above.
[2] Josephus: *The Romano-Jewish War*: Preface = Book I, chaps. 1–16.

tion of his potential public as Josephus was able to reach without having to do more than simply write his book in his own mother-tongue and then translate it into a single other language. In our world neither a Russian book with a French translation nor an Arabic book with an English translation would command so wide a range of readers as was accessible to a book written in Aramaic and translated into Greek by a Palestinian Jew in the first century of the Christian Era.

We may next observe that the peoples mentioned in the cata-logue[1] of those in whose local mother-tongues the Apostles miraculously began to speak on the Day of Pentecost are almost all of them included either in the Aramaic-reading or in the Greek-reading portion of Josephus's public. The Parthians and Arabians are mentioned by name in the Acts as well as in Josephus's cata-logue of Aramaic-readers; Josephus's Aramaic-reading Babylon-ians and Adiabenians are next-door-neighbours of the 'Medes and Elamites and the dwellers in Mesopotamia' whom the writer of the Acts has included in his list; and we may presume that the Aramaic language was also current among these three peoples likewise. Why was it, then, that the Apostles' own native Galilaean Aramaic did not serve them, without any special gift of tongues, for speaking to such of their audience as belonged at any rate to those five out of the fifteen nationalities mentioned, as well as to the Aramaic-speaking dwellers in Judaea? And, as for the other nine—the dwellers in 'Cappadocia, in Pontus and Asia, Phrygia and Pamphylia, in Egypt and in the parts of Libya about Cyrene, and strangers of Rome (Jews and proselytes)', together with the 'Cretes'—could not the Apostles have anticipated Josephus by reaching them, one and all, in a single non-Aramaic language, namely Greek? Was not the gift of a dozen other tongues, in addition to their native Aramaic, a superfluous prodigality? Would it not have sufficed for these hereditarily Aramaic-speaking preachers of the Word to be miraculously endowed with an addi-tional power of speech in Greek, and in Greek only?

This apparent inconsequence may find its explanation in the fact that the people whom the Apostles were addressing were drawn from the same range of countries as Josephus's public without being drawn from the same class. Whereas Josephus was undoubtedly writing for an intellectual *élite*, it seems likely that the 'Jews, devout men, out of every nation under heaven', who, dwelling in Jerusalem, there suddenly (as the story goes) heard issuing from the Apostles' lips the local vernaculars of their re-spective countries of origin, will for the most part have been

[1] Acts ii. 9–11.

people of a humbler and less highly sophisticated sort.[1] And one of the points of difference between these two different social strata was probably just this, that the people on the lowlier level were masters of their mother-tongue only, while those of the superior rank were masters of one or more *lingue franche* in addition to their mother-tongue, unless they happened (as was the happy fortune of an Aramaic-speaking Galilaean or Judaean or a Greek-speaking Pamphylian or 'Crete') to have inherited as their mother-tongue one of the languages of wider currency.[2] One reason why Josephus was able to reach his far-flung public through the medium of no more than two languages was because this public belonged exclusively to a cultured, and therefore bilingual or trilingual, minority. If, instead of setting out to write a 'serious work' for 'high-brows', Josephus had been called, like the Apostles, to preach salvation to the unlettered multitude, neither his own native Aramaic nor his laboriously acquired Greek would have carried him anything like so far. His Aramaic preaching would have been understanded of the people from Judaea and Mesopotamia and Babylonia and Adiabene, while his Greek preaching might have been partially intelligible to those from Crete and Cyrene and Pamphylia, as well as to some of those from Asia and from Rome; but, when he came to the pilgrims from the back parts of Arabia and Iran and Anatolia, he would soon have found himself praying for the miraculous gift of tongues as his only hope of being able to enter into communication with these outlandish potential converts whose exotic native vernaculars were the only media through which the Word could be conveyed to them.

This contrast between the respective linguistic problems with which the Apostles and Josephus had to cope brings out more clearly what the difference is between the linguistic situation in a disintegrating society and the situation in other social circumstances. In a disintegrating society, as in other places and times, the masses are masters of their mother-tongue only, and of no other language besides; but at the same time the process of social disintegration is accompanied by two linguistic processes which are specially characteristic of it: in the first place, the original

---

[1] Such, at any rate, is to-day the general character of the corresponding element in the Jewish community at Jerusalem—in contrast, for example, to the Zionists.

[2] To pursue our analysis of the respective social ingredients in the Palestinian Jewry of the first and of the twentieth century of the Christian Era, we should perhaps likewise find to-day that, among the 'devout men' belonging to the *Agudath Israel*, only a minority would be masters of a second language in addition to their mother-tongue (whether they were East-European Yiddish-speaking Jews or Central-Asian Tajik-speaking Jews or Yamani Arabic-speaking Jews). On the other hand we should find that all the Zionists possessed at least a-smattering of Neo-Hebrew, and that many of them were also masters of one of the world-languages of the day—e.g. English or French—even when they were Jews who had been born and brought up in some European country in which neither English nor French was the local vernacular.

mother-tongue of some communities or countries is ousted by an intrusive language (as, in the case in point, Hebrew had been ousted by Aramaic in Judaea and Assyro-Babylonian by Aramaic in Babylonia and in Adiabene);[1] and in the second place certain of these aggressive languages also become *lingue franche* on the lips of an intellectual *élite* over a far wider geographical range than the regions in which they have succeeded in supplanting the original mother-tongue of the masses (as, in the case in point, Aramaic had gained currency as a *lingua franca* in Parthia and Media and Elam and Arabia without having at the same time supplanted the local Iranian and Arabic vernaculars).[2]

In the social circumstances in which the need for such a *lingua franca*, or supplementary language of more than local currency, has begun to make itself felt, there are several alternative means through which the growing demand may be supplied in different degrees of efficacy.

The simplest media of mental communication across the boundaries of parochial language-areas are not languages nor even scripts, but are mere systems of numerical notation. The classic example is the famous Incaic system of *quipus*—sets of cords which were variously coloured and knotted to convey a wide range of meanings with the aid of an elaborate scheme of mnemonics—and these unwritten records which spoke the same wordless language to men of different tongues were one of the essential instruments in the administration of an Incaic Empire which grew to the stature of an Andean universal state. A cruder form of the same material device, in the shape of 'tallies', was employed in one of the most efficiently administered kingdoms in the Transalpine part of medieval Western Christendom; and a more elegant form is in daily use in our own world to-day in the shape of the Arabic numerals—which have now won their way to an almost ubiquitous currency, though the numbers for which they stand are known in different languages by a vast variety of names conveyed in a considerable variety of scripts.

When we pass from numerals to 'characters',[3] we see the Latin

---

[1] See I. C (i) (*b*), vol. i, p. 79; IV. C (iii) (*c*) 3 (α), vol. iv, p. 484; and V. C (i) (*c*) 2, in the present volume, pp. 117–19, above, and the present chapter, p. 499, footnote 5, below.

[2] See V. C (i) (*c*) 2, p. 123, footnote 2, above, and the present chapter, pp. 499, below.

[3] On the border-line between numerical notations and scripts that convey, not numerals, but the sounds of articulate human speech, we may conjecturally place the still undeciphered scripts (representing several distinct systems) which have been recovered from the debris of the Minoan World by the enterprise of our modern Western archaeologists (see V. C (i) (*c*) 2, p. 84, above). In the present context we may take note of the fact that, in the history of the Minoan system of writing or notation, as far as it is as yet possible for us to reconstruct it, an original variety seems to have given way to a subsequent uniformity at about the time of the foundation of a Minoan

Alphabet steadily winning its way towards as wide a currency as that of the Arabic numerals, thanks to the convenient fact that the same letters can be employed in different languages with an almost endless variety of phonetic values—while the only rival of the Latin Alphabet which is stubbornly refusing to be driven off the field is the ideographical Sinic script, in which every 'character' stands for a more or less precise and constant meaning, though there may be no recognizable affinity between the respective sounds in which, in different dialects, the same 'character', with the same meaning, is translated out of brushwork into the living speech that can be uttered by human mouths and heard by human ears.[1] If the Arabic numerals are an example of an international notation and the Latin Alphabet an example of an international script, the Sinic ideograms show how a script that has already gained an international currency may go half-way along the further road of evolution into an international language as well; for this ideographical script has achieved the feat of giving a more than parochial currency to mental meanings as well as to visual 'characters'. Yet, regarded strictly as an international language, the Sinic system of ideograms is evidently imperfect, since its success in standardizing the painted sign and the associated meaning has not been crowned by a standardization of the sounds in which this meaning is conveyed in living speech; and, for the social purposes of a *lingua franca*, aural intelligibility is even more important than visual. In order to be complete, a *lingua franca* must be equipped with uniform 'phonemes' or articulate sounds which convey constant meanings to the ear, as well as with the uniform 'characters' by which constant meanings are conveyed to the eye.

Such a *lingua franca*, complete in all its parts, may be deliberately invented—as, for instance, Esperanto has been invented in our own world and age. Indeed, it might have been expected *a priori* that this would turn out to be the usual origin of *lingue franche*; for, in a language which *ex hypothesi* has to be learnt by an effort of will in a utilitarian spirit, instead of being acquired unconsciously as a mother-tongue, it is manifest that the two supreme desiderata will be simplicity and regularity, and these

universal state—if that event is to be equated with the beginning of the period which the archaeologists have labelled 'Middle Minoan III' (for this equation see I. C (i) (a), vol. i, pp. 92–3; IV. C (ii) (b) 1, vol. iv, p. 64; and V. C (i) (c) 3, in the present volume, p. 236, above; and V. C (ii) (b), vol. vi, p. 312, below). In 'Middle Minoan II', which presumably coincided in date with the final paroxysm of a Minoan 'Time of Troubles', two separate hieroglyphic scripts, known as 'A' and 'B', simultaneously made their appearance. At the beginning of 'Middle Minoan III' a new linear script, composed eclectically out of all the earlier systems, suddenly came on the scene and superseded the two hieroglyphic scripts completely (Glotz, G.: *La Civilisation Égéenne* (Paris 1923, Renaissance du Livre), p. 429).

[1] See III. C (i) (c), vol. iii, p. 175, above.

two qualities are imparted to works of art more easily than they are found in unkempt Nature. As a matter of experience, however, it is notorious that there is no known instance of a synthetic *lingua franca* becoming a really effective instrument of social intercourse; for the utmost intellectual ingenuity that may have been expended on an artificial language by a cunning verbal artificer will not compensate for the absence of the emotional associations that accompany, and invigorate, any natural language—even one which has had half its roots cut away in the process of being converted from a mother-tongue into a linguistic second string for use when wanted over a wider range of intercommunication. An empirical survey will show us that every *lingua franca* that has played a historic role up to date has been a natural language which has first appeared on the scene as the mother-tongue of some local community and has subsequently extended its currency from an original range that may have been very narrow.[1]

In examining the causes and the consequences of such transformations of local mother-tongues into oecumenical *lingue franche* we shall find, on the one hand, that a language which wins this kind of victory over its rivals usually owes its success to the social advantage of having served, in an age of social disintegration, as the tool of some community which has been potent in war or else in commerce. On the other hand, we shall find that languages, just like the human beings who speak them, are unable to win victories without paying a price. And the price which a language pays for gaining the currency of a *lingua franca* is the sacrifice of its native subtleties and niceties; for it is only on lips that have learnt it in infancy that any language is ever spoken with that effortless perfection which is the dower of Nature and the despair of Art. In fact, a language—even a natural language—cannot gain an artificial currency without a risk of becoming vulgarized. A flagrant example of this process in the modern Western World is the vulgarization of the Low Dutch mother-tongue of the Netherlanders into Afrikaans on the lips of ex-French-speaking Huguenot refugees in South African territories that were once dominions of the Dutch Republic. These strangers have clumsily broken the sharp edges, and crudely confounded the lights and shades, of an alien language which they have adopted without enthusiasm in the house of exile as one of the incidental hardships of a cruel destiny. The aesthetic and intellectual impoverishment which forces itself

[1] There is a suggestive parallel between the failure of artificial languages like Esperanto to win their way into current use as *lingue franche* and the failure of abstract philosophical or scientific conceptions of deity to win their way into current acceptance as representations of the One True God (see V. C (i) (d) 7, vol. vi, pp. 18–28, below). There is a corresponding parallel between the triumph of the natural languages and the triumph of Yahweh (see V. C (i) (d) 7, vol. vi, pp. 38–49, below).

painfully upon the attention of any unprejudiced outsider who sets himself to compare Afrikaans with its European parent is a change for the worse which is characteristic of the evolution of all the *lingue franche*; and we may observe at this point that so grievous a loss of a cherished spiritual heritage is unlikely to be accepted with indifference—and, *a fortiori*, with complacency— in any highly sensitive social milieu. *Lingue franche* are rare in primitive societies and also rare in civilizations while these are still in growth. *Lingue franche* only flourish on a spiritual soil that has been coarsened by that loss of sensitiveness and that appetite for promiscuity which are symptoms of the process of social disintegration.

This vulgarization of a *lingua franca* in the course of its spread, and its indebtedness for its vulgar success to the adventitious aid of war or commerce or both, are characteristic features, to judge by the frequency of their recurrence in the careers of *lingue franche* that have made their mark on History. This judgement can be verified by a survey of the historical evidence.

In the history of the disintegration of the Hellenic Society we see two languages one after the other—first Attic Greek and subsequently Latin—starting as the respective mother-tongues of the two tiny districts of Attica and Latium and then spreading out from these small beginnings until, on the eve of the Christian Era, we find Attic being employed in the chancery of a Greek principality on the east bank of the Jhelum and Latin in the camps of Roman legions on the west bank of the Rhine. In the career of Attic Greek the first step in the expansion which eventually went to these vast lengths can be observed in the time of the Athenian 'thalassocracy' in the fifth century B.C., when the city-state of Athens made herself the naval mistress of the Aegean and took advantage of her political ascendancy in order to divert to the Peiraeus the trade of Aegina and Miletus. Thereafter the fortunes of Attic Greek were made, once for all, when this foreign dialect was adopted as the official language of the Macedonian Court by King Philip the son of Amyntas (*regnabat* 359–336 B.C.).[1] As for Latin, its fortunes followed the flag of the Latin-speaking city-state of Rome which succeeded in the fullness of time in establishing that Hellenic universal state which the abortive Athenian 'thalassocracy' had prematurely and hazily foreshadowed.[2] Even, however, when we have taken due account of these adventitious advantages, we shall be lost in admiration at the stupendous triumph of a pair of

---

[1] Attic belonged to the Ionic branch of the Greek linguistic family, whereas the native Macedonian Greek dialect appears to have been a variety of Aeolic (see Hoffmann, O.: *Die Makedonen* (Göttingen 1906, Vandenhoeck & Ruprecht), especially pp. 111–15). [2] See IV. C (iii) (*b*) 10, vol. iv, p. 208, above.

local dialects which won their way, each in its turn, to an oecumenical currency—and then, if we exchange the economist's and the publicist's spectacles for those of the philologist and the man-of-letters, we shall be struck no less forcibly by the spiritual impoverishment which the material victory brought with it.

In the history of Attic Greek the ravages of vulgarization were already conspicuous before the Athenian 'thalassocracy' had come to grief. The contemporary Athenian observer whom we have quoted more than once already in other contexts tells us that his countrymen

'have their ears constantly bombarded by all the languages of the World, and have responded by picking up one expression from one language and another from another—with the result that, while the Hellenes in general tend to cultivate a particularism in their speech, as well as in the rest of their manners and customs, the Athenians have made themselves conspicuous by talking a jargon compounded of ingredients for which the whole World—barbarian as well as Hellenic—has been laid under contribution'.[1]

In this picture, which was drawn before the close of the fifth century B.C., we can perceive already at work the tendencies which were eventually to transform the exquisite parochial Attic mother-tongue of Aeschylus and Sophocles into the vulgar Attic κοινή of the Septuagint and Polybius and the New Testament.[2] A similar price for a comparable extension of its currency in the Time-dimension as well as in the Space-dimension has been paid by Latin in its vulgarization from the classical language of the Augustan Age to the 'Dog Latin' that was handed down through the slums and the *ergastula* of the western provinces of the Roman Empire to an affiliated Western Christian Society which continued to use this inelegant yet accommodating *lingua franca* for all serious forms of international intercourse until a modern *Homo Occidentalis* who had made up his mind to emancipate himself at all costs at last abandoned 'Dog Latin' for French no longer ago than the seventeenth century.[3]

[1] Auctor Atheniensis Anonymus: *Institutions of Athens* (edited by Kalinka, E.: Berlin and Leipzig 1913, Teubner), chap. 2, § 8.
[2] A concise professional account of the evolution of the Attic κοινή will be found in Buck, op. cit., pp. 156-9. A curious stage in the process by which a vulgarized Attic gradually supplanted all the non-Attic dialects of Ancient Greek is represented by the Doric and the North-West Greek κοιναί: intermediate forms in which these non-Attic dialects were fused together, and at the same time vulgarized in an Attic direction, as a first step towards that complete Atticization which was their eventual fate. It may also be noted that the history of the Attic Greek language has been reproduced, *mutatis mutandis*, in that of the Attic Greek Alphabet. This Alphabet has succeeded in making itself the vehicle for a number of languages—Coptic and Armenian and Georgian, as well as Bulgarian and Ukrainian and Russian and Serbo-Croat, in addition to Modern Greek—but it has made its foreign conquests at the price of being distorted—in some cases, almost out of recognition.
[3] In the realm of learning we may date the change at the generation of the Hano-

In the long-drawn-out disintegration of the Egyptiac Civilization we see the New Egyptian language breaking through the
long-since-dead crust of Classical Egyptian in the fourteenth
century B.C. in order to establish itself for a short season as the
lingua franca of a tottering 'New Empire', and for a much longer
season as the literary language of an Egyptiac World which had
been shorn of all its foreign annexes. The beginning of the end
of 'the New Empire' of Egypt was contemporaneous with the
beginning of the use of the New Egyptian language as a medium
of official and literary intercourse. Both movements date from the
reign of the Emperor Ikhnaton (*imperabat circa* 1370–1352 B.C.);[1]
and within less than two hundred years of Ikhnaton's accession
the loss of the senile empire's non-Egyptiac provinces was complete; yet this short currency as a *lingua franca* with an ever-
dwindling geographical range set a stamp upon the New Egyptian
language which was never effaced. In the later age when New
Egyptian, in its turn, had become a dead language like the Classical
Egyptian which it had supplanted, 'particular attention' had to be
paid by those who studied it to 'the many foreign words and
barbarous names in which' it 'abounded'.[2]

In the disintegration of the Sumeric Civilization the victory
went to the Akkadian language, which in all probability[3] had made
its first appearance above the Sumeric horizon as the barbarian
mother-tongue of a swarm of Semitic-speaking squatters who had

verian philosopher Leibnitz (*vivebat* A.D. 1646–1716), who wrote in Latin and in French
indifferently (perhaps in both senses of the word). In the realm of public affairs we
may remind ourselves that the English poet Milton (*vivebat* A.D. 1608–74) was employed by Cromwell as his Latin Secretary. In the old-fashioned eastern fringes of
Western Christendom 'Dog Latin' remained in use as a *lingua franca* for some two
hundred years longer—and this not only on paper but *viva voce*. The Hungarian
parliament, for example, transacted its business in Latin down to A.D. 1840 (and in
A.D. 1938 it could be seen, in retrospect, that the abandonment of the use of this neutral
language was one of the detonators of an internecine struggle of intermingled nationalities
which had burst out in 1848 and had thenceforward never ceased until it had broken
the Crown of St. Stephen into fragments in 1918). In Poland, too, 'Dog Latin' lingered
on; and the writer of this Study can remember once meeting a countryman of his own
who—travelling as a young man in the Polish provinces of the Russian Empire during
the insurrection of A.D. 1863–4—had successfully turned his knowledge of Latin to
account for communicating with the insurgent Polish gentry. If the Polish gentry had
still gone on speaking Latin in the generation of Marshal Pilsudski, Europe might have
been spared the post-war feud between Poland and Lithuania!

[1] 'In the great revolution at the end of the Eighteenth Dynasty, which we associate
with the name of Amenophis IV [Amenhotep IV = Ikhnaton], . . . men began to write
poetry in the actual language of the day, and in it is composed the beautiful hymn to
the Sun, the manifesto of the reformed religion. But, whereas the other innovations of
the heretical régime disappeared after the collapse, this particular one survived—doubtless because the conditions hitherto existing had become impossible. Under the Nineteenth and Twentieth Dynasties there burst forth into flower a vigorous literature
written in the new language.'—Erman, A.: *The Literature of the Ancient Egyptians*,
English translation (London 1927, Methuen), p. xxvi. Cf. Meyer, E.: *Geschichte des
Altertums*, vol. ii, part (1), second edition (Stuttgart and Berlin 1928, Cotta), p. 508.
[2] Erman, op. cit., p. 187.
[3] In attempting to reconstruct the early chapter of Sumeric history to which we must
assign the first settlement of the Akkadians in the Land of Shinar, we are thrown back
upon inference in the absence of positive historical evidence.

been attracted out of the Arabian Steppe into the fringes of a
rising and growing Sumeric World in an early chapter of Sumeric
history. The fortune of the Akkadian language was made by the
fact of its being the mother-tongue of all but the first of the four
outstanding militarists of the Sumeric 'Time of Troubles';[1] and,
when a Sumerian-speaking saviour of the disintegrating society
arose at last in the person of Ur-Engur of Ur, who brought the
Sumeric 'Time of Troubles' to an end through the establishment
of a universal state,[2] the Akkadian language was placed on an
official parity with the Sumerian, and this elevation of its status
was proclaimed in the very title of 'the Empire of Sumer and
Akkad'. The position thus accorded to the Akkadian language *de
jure* almost certainly, however, did less than justice to the currency
which had already been gained by Akkadian *de facto*; for, while in
the following age, when the Sumeric universal state was being
laboriously held together by an Amorite dynasty from Babylon,
Sumerian gave way to Akkadian, even in Sumer itself, as the
language of everyday intercourse, and only lived on in the precarious life-in-death of ceremonial usage and learned reminiscence,
the Akkadian language still went from strength to strength. In the
heyday of the Sumeric universal state, when Elam was one of the
provinces of 'the Empire of the Four Quarters', Akkadian temporarily supplanted Elamite, not indeed as the spoken vernacular
language of the country, but as the notarial language for private
business transactions as well as the language of state.[3] And, after
Elam had regained its independence and the Empire of Sumer and
Akkad had broken up and the Sumeric Society itself had gone into
dissolution, the Akkadian language not only held its own among
the ruins, but actually rose to the zenith of its career as a *lingua
franca*; for during the post-Sumeric interregnum, when the derelict provinces of the Sumeric universal state were parcelled out
into barbarian 'successor-states'—Hittite and Hyksos and Kassite
and Mitannian—which were all alike under the dominion of non-
Semitic-speaking intruders, the ancient Semitic language of Akkad
continued to serve as the common language of diplomatic and
commercial intercourse for the whole of South-Western Asia for
at least six centuries after the death of Hammurabi; and it was in
this age that this Akkadian tongue won what was perhaps the

[1] The Sumerian militarist was Lugalzaggisi; his Akkadian successors were Sargon
of Agade, Sharrukin, and Naramsin (see I. C (i) (b), vol. i, p. 109, above, and V. C (ii) (a),
vol. vi, p. 184, and V. C (ii) (b), vol. vi, p. 296, below).
[2] See I. C (i) (b), vol. i, p. 106, above; and V. C (i) (d) 6 (δ), Annex, in the present
volume, pp. 650-1; V. C (ii) (a), vol. vi, p. 190; and V. C (ii) (b), vol. vi, pp. 296-7, below.
[3] See I. C (i) (b), vol. i, p. 117, footnote 4, above. At the same time the Sumerian
form of the cuneiform script, which had been adapted to convey the Akkadian language
likewise, temporarily ousted in Elam the Elamite variant of cuneiform which had been
struck out for the purpose of conveying the Elamite language in an earlier age.

greatest triumph in its history. For, when 'the New Empire' of
Egypt established its footing on the wreck of the Hyksos power
and eventually extended its rule over the former possessions of the
Hyksos Empire in Syria, an Egyptiac Society which had always
been inclined towards exclusiveness, and which had recently been
exacerbated to an unprecedented pitch of xenophobia by its experience of the Hyksos domination,[1] condescended to borrow
from the barbarian upstarts whom it had just overthrown one of
the most conspicuous elements in their detested veneer of Sumeric
culture. The Government of the reconstituted Egyptiac universal
state deigned to correspond even with its own client princes in
Syria, as well as with the independent Powers beyond Euphrates
and Amanus, in the prevailing South-West Asian *lingua franca*;
and, while this use of Akkadian was no doubt virtually forced upon
Pharaoh's chancery by the practical necessity of entering into
diplomatic relations with the denizens of the strange new world
into which 'the New Empire' had allowed itself to be carried by
the impetus of a *revanche*, nevertheless the trove of diplomatic
documents in the cuneiform script and the Akkadian language
which has turned up in Ikhnaton's archives at Tell-el-Amarna is
an astonishing testimony to the Akkadian language's power of
penetration as a medium of international intercourse.

In the disintegration of the Indic Civilization we may see so
many rival competitors for the role of *lingua franca* in the several
vernaculars (prākrits) that were respectively employed by Açoka
in his inscriptions in different provinces of the Indic universal
state; and yet another competitor is to be seen in the closely
related Pālī dialect of the voluminous Hinayanian Buddhist scriptures. Pālī was the linguistic medium in which an Indic culture
which was all the time expanding as it disintegrated made its conquest of Ceylon; and on the opposite fringe of the Indic World,
in the Tarim Basin, we find the sense of promiscuity acquiescing
in the evolution of local *lingue franche* that were blends of the
mother-tongue of the native population with intrusive elements of
Indic speech. The language that has been labelled 'Nordarisch'
by the modern Western archaeologists who have unearthed it has
an Iranian base, but it contains an infusion of prākrit, and the
resulting amalgam is conveyed in the Brāhmī Indic script.[2]
Another local hybrid language, which was current as a medium
of administration in the third century of the Christian Era, has a
prākrit base but a large foreign element in its vocabulary, and this

---

[1] For the psychological effect of the Hyksos domination upon the Egyptiac êthos
see I. C (ii), vol. i, p. 144, and V. C (i) (c) 4, in the present volume, pp. 351–2, above.
[2] See Eliot, Sir Ch.: *Hinduism and Buddhism* (London 1921, Arnold 3 vols.), vol. iii,
p. 190,

inversely compounded amalgam is likewise conveyed in an Indic script, which in this case is the Kharosthī.[1]

In the disintegration of the Babylonic and Syriac civilizations the ruins of the two simultaneously collapsing societies became ever more indistinguishably intermingled, the thicker they came to be strewn over their common *Trümmerfeld*; and across the broken surface of this promiscuous debris the Aramaic language spread itself with the luxuriance of a weed which flourishes where no crop can grow and which stretches its creeping tendrils, with an undiscriminating alacrity, over every shattered column or splintered pinnacle that can offer them a hold. The expansion of this Aramaic *lingua franca* of the declining Babylonic and Syriac worlds was fostered first by the Assyrian and later by the Achaemenian political power; but the impulsion which it thus received from the operation of political forces was not, in either case, a deliberate act like King Philip's when he chose Attic for his Macedonian Kingdom's language of state, or like the Emperor Açoka's when he made his selection of prākrits for employment in his inscriptions. The Assyrians propagated the Aramaic language and Alphabet involuntarily as an incidental consequence of their ruthless conquests and deportations;[2] and the Achaemenidae made a determined attempt to give, through their official patronage, an oecumenical currency to three languages—none of which was Aramaic or was even conveyed in the Aramaic script[3]—before they bowed to a *fait accompli* and accepted Aramaic, with its own Alphabet to convey it, as the regional language of official business for all the western provinces of their empire—including Egypt and Anatolia, where Aramaic had never established itself as the vernacular language of ordinary life.[4] This was the origin of the Aramaic *lingua franca* in which, in the first century of the Christian Era, Josephus wrote his *magnum opus* before translating it into the Attic κοινή.[5]

[1] See Burrow, T.: *The Language of the Kharosthi Documents from Chinese Turkestan* (Cambridge 1937, University Press).

[2] See I. C (i) (*b*), vol. i, p. 79; IV. C (iii) (*c*) 3 (α), vol. iv, p. 484; and V.C (i) (*c*) 2, in the present volume, pp. 117-19, above.

[3] The three favoured languages were Elamite, Medo-Persian, and Assyro-Babylonian (the last phase of Akkadian); and these three were selected, perhaps rather academically, as the languages current at the time in the three Imperial capitals: Susa, Ecbatana, and Babylon. All three were conveyed in variants of the cuneiform script, and the drastically simplified cuneiform syllabary which was used for the Medo-Persian language would appear to have been specially invented for the purpose (see V. C (i) (*c*) 2, p. 123, footnote 2, above).

[4] See V. C (i) (*c*) 2, p. 123, footnote 2, above.

[5] See pp. 488-91, above. The area within which the Aramaic language supplanted the previous local vernaculars was, of course, narrower than the range over which it established itself merely as a *lingua franca*; yet even as a vernacular it conquered the whole of 'the fertile crescent' that skirts the northern fringes of the Arabian Steppe. Radiating from its homelands in Eastern Syria and in Western Mesopotamia, Aramaic supplanted the previous local Semitic vernaculars first in the Judaeo-Samaritan military colony at

The currency of the Aramaic language, however, seems short-lived and narrow-verged by comparison with that of the Aramaic Alphabet.[1] The standard Aramaic Alphabet that had been current under the Achaemenian régime broke up—upon the break-up of the Achaemenids' Seleucid 'successor-state' in the second century B.C.—into a number of variants,[2] several of which have had the privilege of becoming in their turn the vehicles for great governments or great literatures or great religions. The list of offshoots of the Aramaic Alphabet within the former Achaemenian frontiers includes 'Square Hebrew', Nabataean (a humble script which has left its mark on human history as the parent of the Arabic), Palmyrene, Syriac (which has gradually differentiated itself into separate Nestorian and Jacobite styles), and Pehlevi (the parent of Avestan) —besides the obscurer variants that have been worked out in the bosom of the Mandaean and the Manichaean churches for the conveyance of their scriptures.[3] In the extreme eastern march of the Achaemenian Empire the Aramaic Alphabet gave birth to the Kharosthī script which was used by the Emperor Açoka to convey his prākrit texts in two out of the fourteen inscriptions of his that are known to us;[4] and in the extreme north-eastern march, again, at a later date, it gave birth to yet another variant—the so-called 'Sogdian'[5]—which gradually made its way eastwards from the banks of the Jaxartes to the banks of the Amur within less than two thousand years after the destruction of the Achaemenian Empire by Alexander the Great.[6]

It will be seen that the spread of the Aramaic script and language

Elephantinê on the southern frontier of Upper Egypt, then in Palestine (where Hebrew was already falling into disuse in the third quarter of the fifth century B.C.: see Nehemiah xiii. 24, and the present Study, V. C (i) (d) 8 (γ), vol. vi, p. 70, footnote 3, below), next in Assyria and Babylonia, and last of all in Phoenicia (Meyer, E.: *Geschichte des Altertums*, vol. iii (Stuttgart 1901, Cotta), p. 137; idem: *Der Papyrusfund von Elephantine*, 2nd ed. (Leipzig 1912, Hinrichs), pp. 17–19; Hoonacker, A. van: *Une Communauté Judéo-Araméenne à Éléphantine, en Égypte, aux vi⁰ et v⁰ siècles av. J.-C.* (London 1915, Milford), pp. 31–2).

[1] See Jensen, H.: *Geschichte der Schrift* (Hanover 1925, Lafaire), pp. 122–33.

[2] Ibid., p. 122.

[3] Mani's innovation consisted in abandoning the clumsy Pehlevi Alphabet, with its use of Aramaic words as ideograms (see I. C (i) (b), vol. i, p. 80, with footnote 3, above, and the present chapter and volume, p. 501, footnote 4, below) and with its rudimentary vowel pointing, and in adopting, in its place, an adaptation of the Syriac Alphabet for writing in the Middle Persian language as well as in the Syriac language (Christensen, A., *L'Iran sous les Sassanides* (Copenhagen 1936, Levin & Munksgaard), pp. 185–6 and 194).

[4] A prākrit written in Kharosthī was also current as an official language in the Tarim Basin in the third century of the Christian Era (see Burrow, T.: *The Language of the Kharosthi Documents from Chinese Turkestan* (Cambridge 1937, University Press)).

[5] The Sogdian Alphabet was derived, not from the Pehlevi Alphabet that was officially current in the Parthian and in the Sasanian Empire, but from the Manichaean version of the Syriac Alphabet (Christensen, op. cit., loc. cit.).

[6] See III. C (i) (a), vol. iii, pp. 130–1, and V. C (i) (c) 3, in the present volume, p. 196, above. Alexander completed the subjugation of the Achaemenian provinces in the Oxus-Jaxartes Basin in 328 B.C.; and in A.D. 1599 the Manchu Alphabet was borrowed from the Modern Mongol which had been derived from the fourteenth-century Galik which had been based on the Uigur which had arisen out of the Sogdian

both within and far beyond the bounds of the Syriac World was not interrupted by the unceremonious intrusion of Hellenism; and when, after the passage of nearly a thousand years, the work of Alexander's Macedonians was at last undone by the Primitive Muslim Arabs, and the Syriac universal state which had found its first embodiment in the Achaemenian Empire was re-embodied in the Umayyad and 'Abbasid Caliphates,[1] the career of the Aramaic language was emulated by the sister Semite Arabic language, and the career of the Aramaic Alphabet by the derivative Alphabet in which the Arabic language was conveyed.

While Aramaic owed less of its fortune than was owed by Attic Greek to political influences, Arabic has been indebted to the Arab Caliphate as deeply as Latin to the Roman Empire. Unofficially the conquerors' language radiated from their military cantonments and tribal settlements in the conquered territories.[2] Officially Arabic was substituted for Greek in the ex-Roman provinces of the Caliphate, and for Pehlevi in the ex-Sasanian provinces, in the reign of the Caliph 'Abd-al-Malik (*imperabat* A.D. 685–705).[3] And, though the Arabic Alphabet has not succeeded in pushing its way eastwards so far into the heart of Asia as the Aramaic Alphabet, it has at least made a deeper impression as far as it has gone; for, in adopting the Arabic Alphabet in place of the Aramaic to convey their non-Semitic mother-tongues, the Persians and the Turks have allowed the new script to bring in its train an invading host of alien Arabic words into their native vocabularies.[4]

variant of the Aramaic Alphabet (see Jensen, op. cit., pp. 213–16). It is possible that the Sogdian Alphabet may also be the ancestor of the script used in the Turkish inscriptions of the eighth century of the Christian Era in the basins of the Orkhon and Yenisei rivers; but the origin of this script, like that of the Baltic Runes, is uncertain, and it is possible that it, too, may be derived, not from the Aramaic Alphabet, but from the Greek (Jensen, op. cit., pp. 208–10).

[1] See I. C (i) (*b*), vol. i, pp. 76–7, above.

[2] The spread of Arabic through this channel was powerfully promoted by the Arab conquerors' practice of recruiting 'clients' from among the members of the subject communities (see V. C (i) (*d*) 6 (α), pp. 449–50, above).

[3] Wellhausen, J.: *Das Arabische Reich und sein Sturz* (Berlin 1902, Reimer), pp. 136–7. In Egypt this official replacement of Greek by Arabic is known to have taken place in the Islamic year A.H. 87.

[4] In thus adopting an Arabic vocabulary as well as an Arabic script, New Persian has gone a step farther than Pehlevi ever went in laying itself open to a Semitic influence. This difference is not apparent to the eye; for in a Pehlevi text, just as in a New Persian text, Semitic words (in this case Aramaic) will be found interspersed among Iranian words written in the same Semitic script. Whereas, however, the Arabic words in New Persian are pronounced as they are spelt (like the French and Latin and Greek words in Modern English), it is believed that the Aramaic words in Pehlevi were employed as ideograms and were pronounced, not according to their spelling, but as though they were their Iranian equivalents (see I. C (i) (*b*), vol. i, p. 80, with footnote 3, above). If this is the fact, then in Pehlevi (unlike New Persian) the Semitic element was confined entirely to the script, and did not extend to the vocabulary, even where an Iranian word was represented by an ideogram which would make a Semitic word if it were pronounced phonetically; and in the spoken, as opposed to the written, form of the Pehlevi language there will then have been hardly a trace of Semitic influence. On the other hand, in the spoken as well as in the written form of both New Persian and Turkish, the Arabic inlay in the vocabulary is conspicuous. It is true that, in both

If we turn next to the abortive cosmos of city-states with its main focus in Northern Italy which arose within the ambit of Western Christendom during the so-called 'medieval' period of Western history,[1] we shall see the Tuscan dialect of Italian eclipsing its rivals, as Attic eclipsed the rival dialects of Ancient Greek, and at the same time being propagated round all the shores of the Mediterranean by Venetian and Genoese seamen and traders and empire-builders, as well as by Pisans and Florentines who spoke Tuscan as their mother-tongue; and this Pan-Mediterranean currency of the Italian language in its Tuscan shape outlived the prosperity, and even the independence, of the medieval Italian city-states. In the sixteenth century of the Christian Era Italian was the service language of an Ottoman Navy that was then fast driving its Venetian and Genoese opponents out of Levantine waters; and in the nineteenth century, again, the same Italian was the service language of a Hapsburg Navy whose Imperial-Royal masters were successful from 1814 to 1859 in reducing Italy herself to the mere 'geographical expression' that Metternich had pronounced her to be. In fact, the 'Osmanlis and the Hapsburgs each in turn found themselves constrained to employ an Italian medium of communication as an indispensable element in the construction of a war-machine which they were creating for the purpose of holding the Italian people in check; and thus the Italian language succeeded twice over in forcing itself down the throats of strangers who were so far from speaking it by nature that they were actually the mortal enemies of the people who had inherited it as their mother-tongue. This Tuscan Italian, however, was no more able than the Attic Greek had been to make such extraordinary foreign conquests with impunity; and we are confronted with an Italian analogue of the Greek κοινή in the historical Lingua Franca, which may be accurately described, in the very words which our anonymous Athenian author has used of his own fast-changing Attic tongue, as 'a jargon compounded of ingredients . . . for which the whole World has been laid under contribution'.[2] This Lingua Franca of the Levant, with its Italian base almost buried under the load of its miscellaneous foreign accretions, is such an admirable example of the genus which it represents that its historic name has come to bear a generic meaning.

Latterly, however, this historic Lingua Franca has been replaced

languages, there has eventually been a reaction against this process of Arabicization. In New Persian the weeding out of Arabicisms was begun a thousand years ago by Firdawsī; and in our own day President Mustafā Kemāl Atatürk set himself to liberate the Ottoman Turkish language from its Arabic vocabulary as well as from its Arabic script.

[1] For this city-state cosmos within the medieval Western World see III. C (ii) (b), vol. iii, pp. 341–50, above.   [2] See the passage quoted on p. 495, above.

by a substitute, even in its congenial Levantine haunts; and this successor that has supplanted it is not a purified Italian but a vulgarized French.

In the history of the decline and fall of the medieval Western city-state cosmos, French came treading on the heels of Italian as, in the decline and fall of Hellenism, Latin followed Attic Greek, or as Arabic followed Aramaic in the longer-drawn-out disintegration of the Syriac Civilization. The fortune of the French language has been made by the fact that during the 'Time of Troubles' of the broken-down cosmos of Italian and German and Flemish city-states—a phase in the history of this sub-society's disintegration which set in towards the close of the fourteenth century of the Christian Era and which lasted until the close of the eighteenth[1]— France carried off the victory in the contest among the Great Powers round the periphery of this still expanding world for the mastery over its now decaying centre.[2] From the age of Louis XIV (*regnabat* A.D. 1643–1715) onwards, France forged ahead of the ungainly Hapsburg Power which had been her principal competitor; French culture began to exert an attraction which kept pace with the progress of French arms;[3] and, when Napoleon at length achieved his Bourbon forerunner's ambition of piecing together a mosaic with a French design out of all the broken fragments of medieval city-states which strewed the face of Europe at the French nation's doors from the Italian shores of the Gulf of Genoa and the Adriatic to the German shores of the North Sea and the Baltic, the Napoleonic Empire proved itself to be a cultural force as well as a military system.

It was, indeed, its cultural mission that was the Napoleonic Empire's undoing; for the ideas of which it was the 'carrier' (in the clinical sense of the word) were the expression of a modern Western culture which had sprung to maturity among the ruins of the medieval city-state cosmos and had transmuted the legacy of a medieval Italian culture into a new spiritual force. In the

---

[1] The various local catastrophes in the last quarter of the fourteenth century which may be taken as signs of the breakdown of the medieval Western cosmos of city-states have been touched upon in III. C (ii) (*b*), vol. iii, pp. 347–50, above.

[2] For this contest, and for the light which it throws upon the general principles of the working of the Balance of Power, see III. C (ii) (*b*), vol. iii, pp. 300–5, above, as well as V. C (i) (*d*) 6 (*γ*), Annex I, in the present volume, pp. 624–33, below.

[3] In Germany the triumph of a French culture conveyed in the French language was already assured before the birth of Germany's French military conqueror Napoleon as all but a Genoese subject in Corsica; for the French-writing movement which Leibniz had begun was carried to its climax by Frederick the Great. In the most critical period of the Seven Years' War Frederick spent the short daily ration of leisure and relaxation which he allowed himself on the literary exercise of writing French Alexandrine couplets! This was surely as great a triumph for the French language as was scored by Italian when it was adopted as the service language of the Ottoman and the Hapsburg Navy. (For Frederick's literary recreations, see *Frederick the Great: The Memoirs of his Reader Henri de Catt (1758–1760)*, translated by Flint, F. S. (London 1916 Constable, 2 vols.).)

Revolutionary and Napoleonic Age that force was still in the flood tide of its youthful energy; and 'the Ideas of the French Revolution', imbued as they were with this dynamically restless spirit, were not calculated to act as a sedative which might reconcile the Italians and Flemings and Rhinelanders and Hanseatics to the yoke of the French empire-builders by whom these ideas were being introduced. So far from that, the revolutionary impact of Napoleonic France gave these stagnating peoples a stimulating shock which roused them from their torpor and inspired them to rise up and overthrow the French Empire as a first step towards taking their places as new-born nations in a modern Western World side by side with France herself.[1] Thus the Napoleonic Empire carried within itself the seeds of its own inevitable failure in the Epimethean role of serving as the universal state of a decadent world which, once, in its long-past noonday, had created the splendours of Florence and Venice and Bruges and Ghent and Nürnberg and Lübeck.[2]

The actual task which the Napoleonic Empire did involuntarily perform was to tow the stranded galleons of a derelict medieval armada back into the racing current of Western life, and at the same time to stimulate their listless crews into making their vessels sea-worthy for sailing on a broader ocean than the landlocked seas on which they had hazarded their lives in times past; and this actual French performance was a short and thankless business in the nature of the case. The French Empire has been—as it was bound to be—abortive; the genius of Napoleon I could not avail to sustain this political *tour de force* for even a full score of years after the first passage of the Rhine and the Alps by the armies of Revolutionary France; and all the king's horses and men could not reinstate Humpty Dumpty when once he had suffered the great fall of 1812–14. 'The Hundred Days' were a *fiasco* and the Second Empire ended in a débâcle. Since 1871 the French Empire has been dead and buried not only as a European reality but even as a French dream.[3] Yet in the Great Society of to-day there is

---

[1] This repayment of the modern Western World's debt to the medieval Italian culture through the requickening of Italian life from a new Transalpine source of spiritual energy has been touched upon in IV. C (i), vol, iv, p. 19, and in IV. C (iii) (c) 2 (α), vol. iv, pp. 283–4, above. The Italian experience was not, of course, unique; for the German and Flemish epigoni of the medieval cosmos of city-states were inoculated from the same source and in the same generation with the same new fund of spiritual energy. Heine's *Reisebilder* give a vivid picture of the reanimation of the Rhenish city of Düsseldorf as the result of a dose of French conquest and Napoleonic rule. For a systematic account of the effect of this spiritual medicine upon the German province of the *ci-devant* city-state cosmos see Fisher, H. A. L.: *Studies in Napoleonic Statesmanship in Germany* (Oxford 1903, Clarendon Press).

[2] For this aspect of the Napoleonic Empire see V. C (i) (d) 6 (γ), Annex I, below.

[3] For the transfer of the field of French imperial aspirations and activities from Europe to the Maghrib see Toynbee, A. J., and Boulter, V. M.: *Survey of International Affairs, 1937*, vol. i (London 1938, Milford), pp. 489–92.

one substantial legacy of the two-hundred-years-long role, with its brief Napoleonic culmination, which was sustained by France in the last phase of the decline and fall of the medieval city-state cosmos. The French language has succeeded in establishing itself as the *lingua franca* of that central portion of our Western World, and it has even extended its dominion to the far extremities of the former domains of the Spanish and Ottoman Empires, which, from the fifteenth century to the seventeenth, were two of the competitors of France for the hegemony over the colonies and the metropolitan territories of the Italian commonwealths. In Germany and Italy a 'totalitarian' nationalism has latterly been doing its best to efface the marks of French influence; but a knowledge of French will still carry the traveller through Belgium and Switzerland and the Iberian Peninsula and Latin America and Rumania and Greece and Syria and Turkey and Egypt;[1] and the Latin Alphabet, riding on the shoulders of the French language, has superseded a Slavonic Alphabet as the vehicle of Rumanian, and an Arabic Alphabet as the vehicle of Turkish.[2]

In its haste to reap the fruits of commercial and military and political labours that have all been so much labour lost, the French language—like the other languages that have followed the same questionable career—has stooped to the indignity of vulgarization. And any member of the cultivated nation that enjoys, as not the least valuable part of its birth-right, the privilege of speaking perfect French without ever having consciously to acquire this accomplishment, must feel a horrid tingling in his sensitive ears if ever he is compelled to hear his delicate mother-tongue being butchered to make an Argentinian intelligible to a Pole, or a Brazilian to a Greek—unless, perchance, he may be saved from this excruciation by a blissful unawareness of the fact that South

[1] The vogue of the French language in Egypt has triumphantly survived a British military occupation which lasted for 54 years before it was at length brought to an end as the result of the signature of an Anglo-Egyptian treaty of friendship and alliance on the 26th August, 1936. French never ceased to be the official medium of communication between the representatives of the Egyptian Government and their British advisers; and, when the British High Commissioner in Egypt, Lord Allenby, on the 23rd November, 1924, read to the Egyptian Prime Minister, Zaghlūl Pasha, *in English*, two communications conveying an ultimatum which had been provoked by the assassination of the Sirdar, Sir Lee Stack, the unusual choice of language was doubtless intended to be taken as a mark of displeasure or even discourtesy. Even then, the British High Commissioner deposited written copies of his communications *in French* in order to make sure that their purport should be understood by their Egyptian recipient (see Toynbee, A. J.: *Survey of International Affairs, 1925*, vol. i (London 1927, Milford), p. 216).

[2] For the substitution of the Latin for the Arabic Alphabet in Turkey in A.D. 1928 on the initiative of President Mustafā Kemāl Atatürk see Toynbee, A. J., and Boulter, V. M., *Survey, 1928* (London 1929, Milford), III A. (viii). It is perhaps even more significant that the Latin, and not the Russian, Alphabet was adopted—and this with the approval, and even encouragement, of the ruling authorities in the U.S.S.R.— as the new vehicle for conveying the twenty-seven Turkish dialects that were spoken in various parts of the territory of the U.S.S.R. at this time (see op. cit., pp. 223–7).

America and Eastern Europe are boasting themselves to be talking
Racine's tongue when they are holding intercourse with each other
in their voluble *lingua franca*.[1]

If this French *lingua franca* is a monument, in the modern
Western World, of the decline and fall of a medieval sub-society
within the Western body social, we may see in the English *lingua
franca*—which, since the War of 1914–18, has been raised to even
an official parity with French as an alternative medium of diplomatic international intercourse—a product of that gigantic process
of *pammixia* (whatever it may portend) which has expanded—and,
in the process, diluted—our modern Western World into a 'Great
Society' of literally world-wide range. In this world-wide arena
the English language has now gained the ascendancy over French,
as well as over Dutch and Spanish and Portuguese; and its definitive victory,[2] in a struggle which lasted for some two hundred
years, was won in the Seven Years' War.[3]

[1] We may assume with some confidence that no Frenchman—not even so rare an
anglomane as Monsieur Clemenceau himself—would have recognized his own mother-
tongue in the 'French' to which Mr. Lloyd George is reported to have laid claim when he
deftly eluded the effort of a malicious interlocutor who had sought to put him out of
countenance by asking him in public how on earth, without knowing French, he had
managed to get on at the Peace Conference of Paris. 'But I do understand French', Mr.
Lloyd George is reported to have answered very placidly; and, having thus tripped his
adversary up, he finished his sentence by adding demurely—'when it is spoken by
Lord Grey.' This story is corroborated, if it is not inspired, by Lord Grey's own
testimony, apropos of a conference in Paris in 1916 between the French Cabinet and
a deputation from the British Cabinet consisting of Mr. Lloyd George, Lord Grey, and
Lord Oxford.

'Such part as was taken by us was left to, or, it would be more correct to say, thrust
upon myself. Asquith would not, Lloyd George could not, and I *had* to speak French.
. . . When the council was over, and we three British Ministers were safely outside,
Lloyd George said to me: "You know, your French was the only French that I could
understand." If this suggests to a mocking spirit a doubt whether the French Ministers
understood it, I can reply that on other occasions when I have had to speak French,
I have had proof that it was intelligible even to French ears' (Grey of Falloden, Viscount:
Twenty-Five Years (London 1925, Hodder & Stoughton, 2 vols.), vol. ii, p. 245).

[2] This victory of the English language has mainly taken the form, not of supplanting
the discomfited competitor languages in regions where they had already established
themselves as vernaculars or even merely as *lingue franche*, but of encircling them and
circumscribing their possibilities of further expansion. For example, Dutch has been
supplanted by English as the vernacular of the European colonists of the Hudson
Valley, but it is still the *lingua franca* of Indonesia; and a Dutch public servant once
recounted to the present writer—half proudly and half whimsically—how a party of
Javanese 'regents' who had been making the grand tour exclaimed, when they reached
Holland in due course, what a relief it was at last to find themselves once more in a
place where every one spoke the world-language! As for the French colonists in the
St. Lawrence Valley, they have stubbornly retained their French mother-tongue for
their vernacular, while succumbing to a passable familiarity with an English that has
now become the *lingua franca* of all North America. The Spanish and Portuguese
languages have been still more successful in maintaining their currency in the vast
domains which they had staked out for themselves before the English language entered
the lists against them. The Philippine Archipelago is perhaps the only place where
Spanish has given way to English; and in the Philippines Spanish (thanks to the liberal
policy of the Spanish Crown in this matter) was never forced upon the natives in substitution for their own mother-tongues; so that in the Philippines it has merely been a
question of a change of *lingua franca* (see Wyndham, H.: *Native Education* (London
1933, Milford), pp. 103–4).

[3] The view that the Seven Years' War marked a turning-point in the struggle between
the French and English languages is supported by the testimony of the life and letters

This triumph of the English language was a corollary of the triumph of Great Britain herself in a military and political and commercial struggle for the mastery of a new world overseas which was being annexed to the domain of a once parochially West European civilization through the competitive growth and expansion of the rival nations into which a medieval Western *Populus Christianus* had latterly broken up in the Western Society's West European homeland; and therefore it is not surprising to find the English language established to-day as the principal vernacular of the North American continent and as the dominant *lingua franca* of the Indian sub-continent, since these two regions were the scenes of Great Britain's eighteenth-century victory over France in these two European Powers' twofold competition in Asiatic empire-building and in American colonization. The prowess of the English language, as distinct from that of the English people and its daughter nations overseas, is perhaps more impressively attested by the present currency of English as a *lingua franca* in the Far East; for here the direct material impact of the English-speaking peoples did not begin to make itself felt until some two hundred years later than the date when it was first felt in India and North America; and, during the hundred and fifty years or so during which the Far East has been subject to the present second bout of Western social pressure,[1] this Western impact has largely taken the peaceful forms of missionary and commercial enterprise, while, by comparison at any rate with the older history of Western penetration into the Indies and the Americas, the corresponding expansion of the Western Powers in the Far East has been accompanied by few aggressive wars, still fewer permanent conquests, and scarcely any colonization. Thus in the Far East the adven-

---

of Edward Gibbon (*vivebat* A.D. 1737–1794). Gibbon's first work, an *Essai sur l'Étude de la Littérature*, was written in French in 1759, and published in the same language in 1761, while the Seven Years' War was in progress and its issue still in doubt. Thereafter Gibbon continued to use French as his medium in his study *Sur la Monarchie des Mèdes*, which appears to have been still unfinished at the opening of the year 1763 (see Low, D. M.: *Edward Gibbon, 1737–1794* (London 1937, Chatto & Windus), p. 206), as well as in his abortive *Introduction à l'Histoire Générale de la République des Suisses*, which was finished in 1768. On the other hand, *The History of the Decline and Fall of the Roman Empire*, which was conceived on the 15th October, 1764, on the morrow of the peace settlement of 1763, was composed in English between October 1772 and the 27th June, 1787 (see IV. C (iii) (*b*) 3, vol. iv, p. 148, footnote 3, above). For the considerations which determined Gibbon's choice of English in preference to French as the vehicle for his *magnum opus* see further V. C (i) (*d*) 6 (γ), Annex II, below.

[1] In this second bout, which began towards the close of the eighteenth century of the Christian Era, the principal agents of Western penetration have been Protestant missionaries and British, French, and American sailors and men-of-business. In the first bout, which began towards the middle of the sixteenth century and came to an end soon after the beginning of the eighteenth, the missionaries were Catholic and the sailors and traders were Spanish and Portuguese. The policy and fortunes of the Catholic missionaries in China, from Ricci's generation to de Tournon's inclusive, are touched upon in V. C (i) (*c*) 4, pp. 365–7, above, and in V. C (i) (*d*) 6 (δ), p. 539, and in V. C (i) (*d*) 7, vol. vi, pp. 23–4, below.

titious aid that the English language has received has been distinctly less forceful than elsewhere; and therefore, so far as the language has succeeded in making its way here also, this success can more confidently be ascribed to the language's own intrinsic powers. Accordingly the present currency of English in the Far East may be taken as the measure of its achievements and its prospects in the World at large; and we may venture to rate these high when we find English being employed as a *lingua franca* in Far Eastern cities which have never been under the rule of either the British Empire or the United States, and on the lips of speakers who have been speaking English in the act of carrying on a propaganda campaign against 'British interests'.

English was, in fact, the medium of communication between the people of Southern and Central China and Mr. Michael Borodin, the political adviser who was lent in the summer of 1923 to the Kuomintang Government at Canton by the Soviet Government at Moscow[1] for the purpose of instructing the Kuomintang in the art of launching an anti-foreign mass-movement which was to be pointedly anti-capitalist and still more pointedly anti-British. Mr. Borodin knew no Chinese; and his strenuous political activities during the four years for which his mission in China lasted left him no leisure for mastering a difficult foreign language with the facility that would have been required for making popular appeals to mass-meetings. At the same time the Kuomintang were unable to find on the southern sea-board of China, or even in the Yangtse Valley, Chinese linguists who were sufficiently well acquainted with Russian to be able to serve Mr. Borodin as interpreters from Russian into Chinese. On the other hand there was no difficulty in finding Southern Chinese with an adequate knowledge of English; and, since this was a *lingua franca* which Mr. Borodin, too, could understand and speak, the English language became a vital link in this Russian emissary's anti-British propaganda campaign in a Chinese mission-field. The Chinese invasion of the British Concession at Hankow on the 3rd–5th January, 1927, was the sequel to a series of inflammatory speeches which had been delivered in Hankow by Mr. Borodin in December;[2] and, in addressing the Chinese mobs whom he was inciting to attack the British, the Russian agitator had to employ the cumbrous method of speaking in English to a Chinese interpreter who then translated the orator's ardently anti-British words out of their original English dress into the local Chinese vernacular.

This English means of communication between a Chinese audi-

---

[1] See Toynbee, A. J.: *Survey of International Affairs, 1925*, vol. ii (London 1928, Milford), pp. 311 and 322, and *Survey, 1926* (London 1928, Milford), pp. 283–4.
[2] Ibid., pp. 347–51.

ence and a Russian orator on the banks of the Yangtse[1] is not, however, the most striking of the illustrations of the currency of English as a *lingua franca* in the Far East that have come to the notice of the present writer; for, on board an American ship *en voyage* from Shanghai to Kobe in 1929, he witnessed at first hand the employment of English by Chinese as a means of communication, not with foreigners, but with one another.

In this American ship's saloon I was given my place at a table where all the other seats were occupied by Americans or English people, while at the next table to ours the party was entirely Chinese. In a lull in the conversation at our own table we noticed that we were not alone in talking English; for at the Chinese table an English conversation was in full swing—and this in an English which was not less fluent than ours. Why, we speculated, were our Chinese neighbours speaking English among themselves? There was no suspicion that they might be 'showing off' their mastery of the world-language, for they were manifestly quite un-self-conscious; and, even if we had not been able to read this on their countenances at a glance, we could have been sure *a priori* that it would never have occurred to Chinese men and women of good breeding (such as these were) to take any pride in performing the tricks of foreign trades. Their use of English in talking among themselves must therefore serve some strictly practical purpose; and, as we fell into exchanging surmises as to what the point of it might be, I contributed the guess that our Chinese party might be made up of passengers from different provinces, including some of those on the southern and south-eastern seaboard where each province speaks its own local dialect and not the elsewhere current 'mandarin',[2] so that English might be the only language in which they were all of them sufficiently well versed to be mutually intelligible to one another. By this time our English and American curiosity had become so eager that we ventured to interrupt the neighbouring conversation in order to learn the answer to our riddle—whereupon our Chinese fellow passengers told us, with much good humour, that my explanation was the right one.

The admirable English that was being talked by Chinese passengers on board an American ship in A.D. 1929 is not, however, the only form in which the language may be heard nowadays on lips to which it has not come as a birthright. Indeed, we have not

---

[1] This was not the last occasion on which the English language was to serve as a means of Russo-Chinese communication. The Russo-Chinese Pact of Friendship and Non-Aggression which was concluded on the 21st August, 1937, was drawn up in an English text (Art. 4).

[2] For this latter-day Chinese *lingua franca* see pp. 512-14, below.

far to seek in order to discover that 'ingredients . . . for which the whole World has been laid under contribution' now also infest the English that is spoken as a mother-tongue in North America and in the South Seas and even in England itself—for the Germanisms[1] in North American English are decidedly less exotic than the Indianisms[2] of a metropolitan Kiplingese. If 'the Old Oligarch' whose lot was cast in Periclean Athens had been able to turn his attention to this latter-day metropolitan English of ours, he would assuredly have castigated it in terms even more sardonic than those which he was provoked into using in order to express what he felt about the vulgarization, in his own day, of his own metropolitan Attic Greek. We can picture the extremity of disgust to which this Periclean Athenian aristocrat would have been moved if he could have lived to hear a post-Alexandrine Attic κοινή being spoken by Susan priests or Gerrhaean sailors or Bactrian villagers. Yet, so far as we know, the Attic κοινή—even in its remotest outposts and even in its most degenerate days—never fell into the plight to which English has been reduced as the *lingua franca* of Chinese coolies.

In this 'Pijin English' we have the spectacle of a colloquial Chinese masquerading in an English costume. The tendency—already strong in the native English remnant of our modern English vocabulary—to reduce every word to a monosyllable has been carried, in 'Pijin English', to a Chinese degree. In 'Pijin English' monosyllables are the rule; and, having taken the Chinese cue in this *reductio ad absurdum* of the admirable principle of linguistic simplicity, 'Pijin English' has followed suit to colloquial Chinese in adopting a Chinese cure for a Chinese malady. Colloquial Chinese has worked out an ingenious device for parrying the ambiguity which is apt to beset a monosyllabic language owing to the diversity of meanings which each monosyllable has to bear. It has sought to make its meaning clear by expressing every idea in a pair of monosyllables which happen to be more or less synonymous, and it has thus begun to revert from monosyllabism to dissyllabism in its word-structure. In 'Pijin English' we can observe a reflection of this latest tendency in the indigenous language which has here been moulding the English *lingua franca* of the Far East into accord with the Chinese genius. For instance,

---

[1] e.g. 'nix' (*nichts*) meaning 'of no account' and 'dumb' (*dumm*) in the sense of lacking, not in the faculty of speech, but in mother wit (to be dumb in this American sense is quite compatible with being voluble!).

[2] e.g. 'pyjamas' (meaning in Persian 'leg-wear') and 'gymkhana' (meaning in Hindustani 'a ball house'). Both these two compound words are packed with linguistic history; for, while three out of the four components are Persian, the English language has acquired them, not from Persian direct, but through the two intermediate stages of Hindustani and Urdu (for these two *lingue franche* of a disintegrating Hindu Society see further pp. 517-18, below).

in monotonously employing the couplet 'look-see' to describe every visual act, 'Pijin English' has sacrificed the proper English discrimination between the passive connotation of 'see' and the active connotation of 'look', for the sake of ensuring that the one nondescript 'hyphenated' word shall at least convey unmistakably the general category of meaning that is common to both its constituents.

The English that has undergone this conversion into a cheap *chinoiserie* may prove puzzling to ears which have been accustomed to hear nothing but English from their infancy; and this un-Englishness of 'Pijin English' is illustrated by a story to which the present writer, as a child, was never tired of listening as it was told by an old great-uncle of his[1] who had served in the English merchant marine and had risen to the command of an East-Indiaman. The incident related in this story purports to be an historical event dating from one of those middle decades of the nineteenth century of the Christian Era when the narrator was navigating his ship in Chinese waters and when the trade which made such a distant voyage worth while for European merchant-men was being forced upon China at the cannon's mouth by European men-of-war. The story tells that, in a lull between the successive naval wars of aggression in which the Western Powers were at that time forcing open the Far Eastern hermit empire's hitherto almost hermetically sealed doors, one Power which had recently been at war with China made an offer to the Chinese Government, through the diplomatic channel, for building a hospital at the foreign Government's own expense at a point on Chinese territory which these unexpectedly benevolent foreigners took the trouble to designate. The offer was made in proper form and in courteous language; but the site which the foreign Government had selected for its benefaction was one of such conspicuous strategic importance that the Imperial Government's suspicions were aroused. To invert the terms of Clausewitz's epigram,[2] the policy of the European Power that was making the offer was shrewdly suspected by the mandarins of being 'a continuation of war by other means'. However, they had now been taught by painful experience to take every possible precaution against giving these bellicose 'South Sea Barbarians' any shadow of excuse for resorting to arms on the ground that they had been insulted by the Imperial Government's behaviour; so, with an uneasy mind, the mandarins accepted the offer in phrases still more courteous than those in which it had been laid before them. Their uneasiness did

---

[1] Captain Henry Toynbee (*vivebat* A.D. 1819–1909).
[2] Quoted in III. C (ii) (*b*), vol. iii, p. 298, footnote 2, above.

not diminish as the work progressed; for the building which now swiftly began to rise on the crown of an island commanding the estuary of one of China's finest navigable rivers seemed singularly inappropriate for the philanthropic service to which it was officially dedicated. The windows—mere slits—were as narrow as the walls —veritable ramparts—were massive. And when the roof was on and the donors began to land the medical stores with which the new hospital was to be equipped for performing its works of mercy, the cases were reported by the coolies, hired to carry them up from the beach, to weigh as heavy as lead. At this stage the Imperial Government, feeling that the time for action had arrived, passed the word to a trustworthy gang of its public-spirited coolie-subjects to drop one of the cases, *en route*, with a clumsiness sufficient to break it. The accident was duly contrived; and, sure enough, the bursting medicine-chest disgorged, not Epsom salts or cupping-glasses, but stands of muskets with powder and shot to match. At this shattering exposure one of the coolies who had staged it exclaimed to his European taskmasters, with a consummately innocent air of surprise: 'Hi-yah! Me no savey sick man yam gun.' It would perhaps have been difficult to go farther in denaturing the English medium of an *impromptu* diplomatic retort of which the ironic Chinese point could hardly have been presented more sharply in the most carefully conned note from the officials of the Imperial Ya-men.

After this glance at the vicissitudes with which the English language has met in its career as the *lingua franca* of a Westernized World, we may pass on to consider the fortunes of other living *lingue franche* which have been overtaken by English—and overridden by it, in different degrees—in the course of their own less ambitious careers of expansion over the narrower domains of non-Western societies that have latterly been enmeshed in a world-enveloping Western net.

In the main body of the Far Eastern World, for example, the political unity which has been maintained, off and on, ever since the close of the sixth century of the Christian Era[1] has had its linguistic counterpart in the spread of the so-called 'mandarin' dialect. This Imperial *lingua franca* has now become current through the greater part of the vast area that is occupied at the present day by a Chinese-speaking population; and the mutual intelligibility which it has established as it has spread is such that

---

[1] This political unity has worn the appearance of a ghost of the universal state of the Sinic Civilization to which the Far Eastern Civilization is affiliated. This aspect of the empire of the Sui and T'ang and Sung and Yuan and Ming and Ch'ing as a resuscitation of the empire of the Ts'in and Han is touched upon in V. C (i) (c) 4, p. 356, footnote 6, and in V. C (i) (d) 6 (α), pp. 477–8, above, and is discussed in Part X below.

to-day an inhabitant of the south-western province of Yunnan, on the far side of the Upper Yangtse, can travel all the way to the extreme north-eastern province of Kirin, which is washed by the Amur, without finding himself, at any stage of his journey, unable to understand the local speech or to make his own speech understood by the local inhabitants. On the other hand there is a chain of five provinces along the southern and south-eastern seaboard—including the province of Kiangsu, which bestrides the estuary of the Yangtse and contains both Nanking and Shanghai—where the local dialects are not only different from 'mandarin' but are so far removed from it, and at the same time so highly differentiated from one another,[1] that in this region the areas of mutual intelligibility rarely exceed the limits of a single province, in sharp contrast to the vastness of the area (some twenty provinces, all told, including those in Inner Mongolia and Manchuria) over which the 'mandarin' dialect uniformly prevails.[2]

We have already overheard the members of a party of Chinese travellers which included a contingent from some of the non-'mandarin'-speaking provinces communicating with one another in English in the saloon of an American steamer;[3] and it is conceivable that the Pan-Chinese oral and auditory *lingua franca*[4] which is one of China's present crying needs will in fact be provided in the form of an utterly alien Indo-European language, imported from the far side of the Old World, which, in linking the several vernacular language-areas of China with one another, will at the same time be linking up the whole of China with all the rest of the World in virtue of having become the oecumenical language

[1] In spite of this diversity from one another, all the southern and south-eastern Chinese dialects apparently display one common difference from 'mandarin' in the shape of a certain old-fashionedness. These outlying dialects are in some respects living specimens of Chinese speech in a 'pre-mandarin' stage (see III. C (i) (a), vol. iii, p. 138, above).

[2] During the seven years ending in the autumn of 1938 a number of the Chinese provinces here mentioned had been at least temporarily overlaid by new administrative structures that were the products and at the same time the instruments of Japanese aggression against the main body of the Far Eastern Society. Yet, notwithstanding the immense destruction of life which was inflicted on these ravished Chinese provinces by the Japanese aggressors, it was beyond the power of Japanese militarism to curtail the domain of either the Chinese population or the 'mandarin' *lingua franca* in continental Eastern Asia—as was shown by the fact that 'mandarin' was adopted, as a matter of course, as the official language of every one of the 'puppet states', beginning with 'Manchukuo', which were successively established by the Japanese interlopers on the territory of the Chinese Republic. [3] See p. 509, above.

[4] China has, of course, from time immemorial been in possession of a *lingua franca* that can be painted with the brush and read with the eye, in the shape of the classical characters, which convey constant and uniform meanings in spite of the extreme variety of their pronunciation in different times and places (see p. 492, above). This ideographical *lingua franca* is common to-day not only to all parts of China but to Korea and Japan and Tongking and Annam besides. It appears to have taken shape during the second bout of the Sinic 'Time of Troubles' (*circa* 403–221 B.C.: see V. C (ii) (b), vol. vi, p. 294, footnote 3, below), and to have been standardized by the Emperor Ts'in She Hwang-ti, who was the first founder of the Sinic universal state (see Granet, M.: *La Pensée Chinoise* (Paris 1934, Renaissance du Livre), p. 457).

of 'All that is Under Heaven' in the literal as well as in the Sinic sense of that term. It is also possible, however, that, while English will indeed become (as would seem, indeed, to be its manifest destiny) the medium of both visual and vocal communication between China and the outer world, it will not, after all, snatch away from the 'mandarin' dialect of Chinese the different function of serving as a universal means of internal communication by mouth and ear within the boundaries of the immense region in which the vernacular languages are all of them dialects of Chinese. For within the last few years the leading spirits in the non-'mandarin'-speaking provinces have been setting themselves to make 'mandarin' as familiar there as it is in the rest of China.[1]

At Shanghai in 1929 the writer of this Study was told by the Chinese scholar and philosopher Dr. Hu Shih—who has dedicated his life to the foundation of a popular literature in a simplified form of 'mandarin'—that he had recently hesitated to accept an invitation to go on a lecture tour in the South because the experiment had not proved a success when he had tried it on a former occasion not so very long before. On this previous tour Dr. Hu Shih had not found adequate audiences in the South that could follow him in 'mandarin', while he himself was, of course, unable to address the intelligentsia of each southern province in its own parochial patois. He put these difficulties which he had then encountered to the Southerners who were now inviting him to visit them for the second time; and he received in reply an emphatic assurance that—thanks to the progress which had been made in the South in the intervening years in spreading a familiarity with 'mandarin' there—he need no longer fear any repetition of his previous aggravating experience.

In the Iranic World, before it began to succumb to the process of Westernization, the New Persian language, which had been fashioned into literary form in mighty works of art during the post-Syriac and pre-Iranic interregnum (*circa* A.D. 975–1275),[2] at the same time gained a currency as a *lingua franca*; and at its widest, about the turn of the sixteenth and seventeenth centuries of the Christian Era, its range in this role extended, without a break, across the face of South-Eastern Europe and South-Western Asia from the Ottoman pashalyq of Buda, which had been erected out of the wreckage of the Western Christian Kingdom of Hungary after the Ottoman victory at Mohacz in A.D. 1526, to

---

[1] This new linguistic policy in the provinces of the southern and south-eastern seaboard of China is a sign that, in linguistic and educational matters, the old provincial particularism has now given way to a nationalism on a Pan-Chinese scale; and a change which has thus already taken place on the cultural plane may be expected to follow on the political plane sooner or later.

[2] See I. C (i) (*b*), Annex I, vol. i, p. 363, footnote 3, above, and Part VI, below.

the Muslim 'successor-states' which had been carved, after the
victory of the Deccanese Muslim princes at Talikota in A.D. 1565,
out of the carcase of the slaughtered Hindu Empire of Vijayanagar.[1] For this vast cultural empire the New Persian language was
indebted to the arms of Turkish-speaking empire-builders—reared
in the Iranic tradition and therefore captivated by the spell of
the New Persian literature—whose military and political destiny
it had been to provide one universal state for Orthodox Christendom[2] in the shape of the Ottoman Empire[3] and another for the
Hindu World in the shape of the Timurid Mughal Rāj.[4] These
two universal states of Iranic construction on Orthodox Christian
and on Hindu ground were duly annexed, in accordance with
their builders' own cultural affinities, to the original domain of
the New Persian language in the homelands of the Iranic Civilization on the Iranian Plateau and in the Basin of the Oxus and the
Jaxartes; and in the heyday of the Mughal, Safawī, and Ottoman
régimes New Persian was being patronized as the language of
litterae humaniores by the ruling element over the whole of this
huge realm, while it was also being employed as the official language of administration in those two-thirds of its realm that lay
within the Safawī and the Mughal frontiers.

The new Persian language and literature were staples in the
intellectual education of the *Ich-oghlans* who were the *corps d'élite*
among the neophytes in the Ottoman Pādishāh's Slave-Household,[5] and the influence of this Persian mental background naturally persisted among the adult lights and leaders in the Ottoman
court and camp. The redoubtable Ottoman militarist Sultan Selīm
the Grim amused his leisure by writing Persian verse[6] with better
success than ever attended the Hohenzollern militarist King Frederick the Great's poetic efforts in French;[7] and the lavish patronage
of the Muslim courts in India has piled up, through a long series
of command performances, a corpus of poetry in the Persian
tongue which is as preponderant in mass as it is inferior in merit
to the classical Persian poetry that has sprung spontaneously from
a less heavily manured Iranian soil that is this fine flower's native

[1] This Empire of Vijayanagar had been founded in A.D. 1336 as a last asylum in
which a remnant of the Hindu Society might continue to lead its own life in a state of
independence after the Turkish and Iranian Muslim invaders of the Hindu World had
conquered the greater part of the Deccan (in sequence to their previous conquest of
Hindustan) at the turn of the thirteenth and fourteenth centuries of the Christian Era.

[2] Not, of course, including the domain of the Russian offshoot of the Orthodox
Christian Society, which was shaking off the Turkish domination of the Golden Horde
at the very time when the main body of Orthodox Christendom was succumbing to the
Turkish domination of the 'Osmanlis.

[3] See Part III. A, vol. iii, pp. 26–7, and IV. C (ii) (b) 1, vol. iv, p. 68, above, and
V. C (ii) (b), vol. vi, pp. 298–300, below.

[4] See IV. C (ii) (b) 2, vol. iv, p. 97, above.

[5] See Part III. A, vol. iii, p. 39, footnote 4, above.

[6] See I. C (i) (b), Annex I, vol. i, p. 353, above.   [7] See p. 503, footnote 3, above.

earth. As for the career of the Persian language on Indian ground
as an official vehicle of administration, it was not till A.D. 1829 that
Persian began to be discarded for this purpose, in favour of
English, in the territories which the British East India Company
had taken over from the Mughal Rāj and its 'successor-states'.[1]

It is not surprising to find that the New Persian language has
had to pay for this ephemeral vogue as a *lingua franca*[2] by submitting in its day to as radical a vulgarization as has since been the
lot of that European language to which Persian has eventually
been forced to give way in Hindustan. To begin with, Turkish
and not Persian was the mother-tongue of the war-lords and war-
bands who were the empire-builders of the Safawī and the Mughal
as well as the Ottoman Empire; and all three dominant minorities
—including the two which went the length of employing Persian
for their public administration as well as for their private literary
recreation—retained the use of their native Turkish for the hum-
drum domestic business of everyday life. In these linguistic circumstances all three of them sought to reconcile nature with culture
by doctoring their raw Turkish mother-tongues with a potent
infusion of Persian elements.[3] The Turkī, Azerbaijānī, and Ottoman Turkish languages, as we know them to-day—or knew them
yesterday before a generation of purists or pedants arose to reverse
the process—are virtually composite languages with a Persian
superstructure that counts for more than the Turkish basis.[4]

[1] In 1829 Lord William Bentinck substituted English for Persian as the linguistic
medium of the Sirkar's diplomatic correspondence with Indian princes. On the 7th
March, 1835, Lord William Bentinck announced his decision to make English, and
not Persian or any other Oriental language, the medium of higher education in British
India. Finally, Persian was deposed, in British India, from its previous function
of serving as the instrument of public business, and was replaced by the local vernaculars in the conduct of both judicial and fiscal proceedings.

[2] At the present day the one country where Persian is the official language without
at the same time being the people's mother-tongue is Afghanistan; for, although the
vernaculars of a majority of the tribes within the Afghan frontiers likewise belong to
the Iranian family of languages, they all differ very widely from the classical Farsī.
There are also, of course, certain districts, not only in Afghanistan but in Persia, in
which the local vernaculars are not Iranian at all, but Turkish. A Turkish dialect is
spoken in the provinces of Afghanistan between the Hindu Kush and the Oxus, and
again in the Persian province of Azerbaijan; and in Fars itself there are tribes of
Turkish origin which still continue to speak their ancestral mother-tongue in this
citadel of the New Persian language and literature.

[3] In Ottoman Turkish the handful of borrowed Persian particles has been a more
precious acquisition than the host of borrowed Persian nouns (see III. C (i) (c), vol. iii,
p. 178, above).

[4] It is mainly through this Persian channel—and not, for the most part, direct—that
the Turkish languages of the Iranic culture-circle have imbibed their infusion of
Arabic. It was likewise the Persian version of the Arabic Alphabet, and not the Arabic
original, that these Turkish languages employed for their script until they discarded
it, in favour of the Latin Alphabet, only the other day. The iconoclasts who have now
substituted the Latin for the Perso-Arabic Alphabet as the vehicle of this westerly group
of Turkish languages point out that, after all, the Perso-Arabic Alphabet is not the
first in which a Turkish language has ever been reduced to literary form. Long before
the Turkish-speaking peoples of the Iranic culture-circle had been carried into their
present domiciles, and been there exposed to New Persian cultural influences, as a
result of their Völkerwanderung, *circa* A.D. 975–1275, into the derelict domain of the

These Turco-Persian linguistic alloys do not, however, represent the final degree of the New Persian language's debasement; for in the Indian dominions of the Mughal Empire and in the European dominions of the Ottoman Empire the Persian *lingua franca* of the Timurid and 'Osmanlī empire-builders came into contact, not only with these dominant minorities' Turkish mother-tongues, but also eventually with the indigenous languages of the Hindu and Orthodox Christian worlds when the cultures of the subject populations began to captivate their Iranicized Turkish conquerors.

'The character of Akbar, so far as it depended upon heredity, was . . . based on three distinct non-Indian strains of blood existing in his proximate ancestors: namely, the Turk or Turkī, the Mongol or Mogul, and the Persian or Iranian strains. The manners and customs of his court exhibited features which were derived from all the three sources: Turkī, Mongol, and Iranian. During the early years of his reign Indian influences counted for little—the officers and courtiers surrounding him being divided into two parties: the Turks (Mongol or Chaghatāy and Uzbeg) on the one side and the Persians on the other. But after Akbar had attained maturity the pressure exercised by his Indian environment rapidly increased, so that in sentiment he became less and less of a foreigner until, in the later years of his life, he had become more than half an Hindu. His personal conduct was then guided by Hindu *dharma* or rules of duty, modified considerably by the precepts of Iranian Zoroastrianism. The Turkī and Mongol elements in his nature were kept so much in the background that he was reputed by Hindus to be a reincarnation of a Brahman sage.'[1]

This Indianization of Akbar's soul found its linguistic reflexion in the formation of a new alloy of the Persian language with a vein of base metal that was Indian instead of being Turkish.

'Both Turkī and Persian were spoken at his court, but the former tongue in the course of time dropped out of use, while the latter became the recognized official and literary language. The highly Persianized form of [Western] Hindī known by the name of Urdū, or the camp language,[2] which developed gradually as a convenient instrument

'Abbasid Caliphate, the Uighur Turkish language had been reduced to writing in an Alphabet of Aramaic origin, and the Altaian Turkish language in the Alphabet of the inscriptions in the basins of the rivers Orkhon and Yenisei—a script which, whatever its origin may be, is certainly not derived from the Arabic Alphabet (see p. 500, footnote 6, above). It may be added that the starkly consonantal Arabic Alphabet is peculiarly ill equipped for conveying any member of a family of languages which has a genius—as the Turkish family has—for both the differentiation and the harmonization of vowel sounds.
[1] Smith, V. A.: *Akbar the Great Mogul*, 2nd ed. (Oxford 1919, Clarendon Press), pp. 10-11. The religious aspect of Akbar's eclecticism is examined in V. C (i) (d) 6 (δ), Annex, pp. 699-704, below.
[2] 'Urdū' = 'ordū' = 'horde'. In Turkey at the present day this Mongol word 'ordū' is used with the technical meaning of 'army-corps'. In the Mughal Empire 'Urdū-i-Mu'allā' was the name of the Imperial military bazaar outside the palace at Delhi (*The Imperial Gazetteer of India*, new edition, vol. i (Oxford 1907, Clarendon Press), p. 365).—A.J.T.

of communication between natives and foreigners,[1] was often almost identical in vocabulary with Persian as spoken in India, while retaining the grammatical structure of an Indian tongue.'[2]

The Persian influence on Western Hindī has been so strong that the Hindustānī language has accommodated itself—even in its less impure form, in which the influx of the Persian vocabulary has been kept within more modest limits—to employing the Perso-Arabic Alphabet as an alternative vehicle to the indigenous Brāhmī script—though the latter still serves to convey the greatest of all Hindī works of poetic art: the Eastern Hindī *Rām-Charit Mānas* of Akbar's Hindu contemporary and subject, Tulsī Dās.[3]

This penetration of a Hindī element into the everyday speech of Akbar's court and camp has a rudimentary analogue in the prevalence, in the same age, of Jugoslav as the domestic language of the Ottoman Pādishāh's Slave-Household; and, if the master institution of the Ottoman Empire had not, after the death of Suleymān the Magnificent, been reduced to a premature decadence by a breach of the fundamental rule that the recruits must be infidel-born,[4] a Perso-Jugoslav alloy might be playing in the Near East to-day a role corresponding to that of the Perso-Hindī alloy which is still current under the name of Urdu as a *lingua franca* in India. This possibility was blighted by the socially disastrous

---

[1] The basis of Urdu is Hindustānī: i.e. 'that dialect of Western Hindī whose home is the Upper Gangetic Doāb, in the country round Meerut. The city of Delhi lies close to the southern border of this tract. Here the dialect was in general use, and from here it was carried everywhere in India by the lieutenants of the Mughal Empire' (*The Imperial Gazetteer of India*, new edition, vol. i, p. 365).—A.J.T.

[2] Smith, op. cit., p. 11. 'When this infusion of borrowed words is carried to an extreme . . . the language is intelligible only to educated Musulmāns and to those Hindus who have been educated on Musulmān lines. . . . The extreme Persianization of Urdū is due to Hindu rather than to Musulmān influence. Although Urdū literature is Musulmān in origin, the Persian element was first introduced in excess by the pliant Hindu kāyasths and khattīs employed in the Mughal administration and acquainted with Persian, rather than by Persians and Persianized Mughals, who for many centuries used only their own language for literary purposes. . . . During the first centuries of its existence Urdū literature was entirely poetical. Prose Urdū owes its origin to the English occupation of India and to the need of text books for the College of Fort William. The Hindī form of Hindustānī was invented at the same time by the teachers at that college. It was intended to be a Hindustānī for the use of Hindus, and was derived from Urdu by ejecting all words of Arabic and Persian birth, and substituting in their place words borrowed or derived from the indigenous Sanskrit. Owing to the popularity of the first book written in it, and to its supplying the need for a *lingua franca* which could be used by the strictest Hindus without their religious prejudices being offended, it became widely adopted and is now the recognized vehicle for writing prose by those inhabitants of Upper India who do not employ Urdū. . . . Urdū, as becomes its origin, is usually written in a modified form of the Persian character, while Hindī is generally written, like Sanskrit, in the Deva-nāgarī character' (*The Imperial Gazetteer of India*, new edition, vol. i, pp. 365-6). For this archaistic form of Hindī see further the present Study, V. C (i) (*d*) 8 (γ), vol. vi, p. 77, footnote 2, below.

[3] Tulsī Dās *vivebat circa* A.D. 1530-1623; Akbar *vivebat* A.D. 1542-1605. Though Akbar delighted in giving his patronage to eminent Hindus, the genius—and, indeed, even the existence—of Tulsī Dās seems never to have been brought to the Emperor's notice (Smith, op. cit., pp. 417-18).

[4] For the value of this rule and the fatal consequences of its violation see Part III. A, vol. iii, pp. 34-5 and 44-7, above.

political success of the Pādishāh's free Muslim subjects in taking the Pādishāh's Slave-Household by storm; for most of the free Muslim recruits who forced their way into the Household in and after the later decades of the sixteenth century of the Christian Era were drawn from the Turkish-speaking Muslim population of the metropolitan provinces of the Empire in the Anatolian and Balkan peninsulas. This usurpation of the Ottoman seat of power by a ring of predominantly Turkish-speaking Muslim freemen in the place of a ring of predominantly Jugoslav-speaking Christian slaves has been reflected in the respective fortunes of the rival languages. The Jugoslav language has missed its destiny of becoming, under a Persian veneer, a *lingua franca* for the whole of the Near East, and has been reduced to the modest role of serving as the parochial vernacular of a single one among the Ottoman Empire's numerous 'successor-states'. On the other hand the Turkish language of the original 'Osmanlī empire-builders has escaped the fate—which has overtaken the sister Turkī tongue of the Timurid empire-builders in India—of ceasing to be spoken by the empire-builders' own descendants in the conquered territories. There is, indeed, a striking contrast between the extinction of Turkī in India and the survival of Turkish in Anatolia, where the Ottoman Turkish language has not been content merely to hold its own against the Greek and Armenian which it found in occupation, but has steadily won converts at their expense until in the end it has driven both these predecessors right off this Anatolian field.[1]

The most remarkable trophy of the Turkish language's victory here has been its capture of ex-Greek-speaking and ex-Armenian-speaking minorities[2] who have 'turned Turk', not as an incidental consequence of becoming converts to the Islamic faith of their Turkish conquerors, but in spite of an unbroken loyalty to the Orthodox and to the Gregorian Monophysite Christianity which are their respective religious heritages from a pre-Turkish-speaking past. This now Turkish-speaking remnant of the ancient Christian communities of Anatolia has so utterly lost the command of its pre-Turkish speech that it has come to use a Turkish version of the Orthodox and Gregorian Christian liturgies and to inscribe Turkish texts (in Greek or Armenian letters) upon the tombstones that commemorate its dead. A passing stranger who happened, before the mass-evictions of A.D. 1915–22, to find himself in some Christian village among the secluded mountain fastnesses

---

[1] See IV. C (ii) (b) 1, vol. iv, p. 75, and IV. C (iii) (c) 2 (β), vol. iv, p. 398, above, with the authorities cited on p. 398, footnote 3.

[2] For the commercial prowess of the ex-Greek-speaking Orthodox Christian Qāramānlīs see II. D (vi), vol. ii, p. 223, above.

on the watershed between the Halys and the rivers of Cilicia could not have told by the ear that these villagers were of a different religion from their Muslim neighbours. He must use his eyes to observe that the local house of worship was not a mosque but a church; and he must then look still closer—at the tombstones in the graveyard and at the books behind the screen—in order to determine whether the Christianity of these Turcophone Christians was of the Greek-lettered Orthodox or of the Armenian-lettered Gregorian kind.

It is true that this conversion to the Turkish language without a conversion to Islam has not carried with it that sense of political affinity which in the Near East has invariably accompanied a change of faith—even when this has not been followed by a corresponding change of speech. This truth has been recognized on both sides; and the recognition has been acted upon in an interchange of populations—partly by way of forcible eviction, but also partly by way of a more or less voluntary migration—through which the formerly intermingled *millets* of the old Ottoman Empire have sorted themselves out, in the course of about a hundred years ending in 'the nineteen-twenties', into a number of separate and severally homogeneous *blocs* on the pattern of the distribution of nationalities in Western Europe.[1] If we examine the demographic map of the Near East as it stands to-day, when this agonizing process of geographical segregation is practically complete, we shall find that the Turkish-speaking Orthodox Christians who learnt their Turkish, without giving up their Christianity, in their native Anatolia have now been transplanted to Greece, because they are felt, and feel themselves, to be Greeks in virtue of their religion— while conversely the Greek-speaking and Bulgar-speaking and Jugoslav-speaking Muslims who respectively became converts to Islam, without any change of speech, in their native Crete and Rhodope and Bosnia, have now been transplanted to Turkey because, on the same religious criterion, they are felt, and feel themselves, to be Turks.

On this showing, it might perhaps be imagined that the difference in religion between, for example, a Turkish-speaking Gregorian Christian Armenian and a Turkish-speaking Muslim Ottoman Turk would count for everything, and their identity of language for nothing at all, in determining their attitude towards each other. Did not the religious antagonism between these two Turkish-speaking communities harden the Turkish-speaking Muslims' hearts to the point of attempting to exterminate the Turkish-

[1] See IV. C (ii) (*b*) 2, vol. iv, pp. 76–8, and IV. C (iii) (*b*) 5, vol. iv, pp. 185–90, above, and Part IX, below.

speaking Christians in A.D. 1915-16, without any scruple about acting in this inhuman way towards victims who shared their butchers' mother-tongue?[1] And could the moral gulf between the perpetrators and the survivors of those hideous deportations and massacres ever be bridged? The writer of this Study (whose melancholy task it once was to edit a collection of documents relating to this grim episode in Near Eastern history)[2] was convinced— until he was presented one day with decisive evidence to the contrary—that the gulf was quite unbridgeable; and, even if it had been foretold to him that a happier relation between at least one Turk and one Armenian would soon be re-established neverthe-less, he still would not have guessed that the community of Turkish speech between the Armenian Christian and his Turkish Muslim enemy would be the social substance out of which this miraculous moral bridge would be built. Yet so it was in the experience of a Turkish friend of the writer's, from whose lips he heard the story.

The narrator was Yūsuf Kemāl Bey, an eminent Turkish lawyer who had rallied to Mustafā Kemāl Pasha in his Cave of Adullam at Angora and had distinguished himself as an amateur diplo-matist in the service of what seemed a hopeless cause when the Ottoman Turkish people was fighting for its life in the Anatolian war-after-the-war of 1919-22. After the conclusion of peace with honour at Lausanne, Yūsuf Kemāl Bey was appointed Turkish Ambassador at the Court of St. James's; and, as the Turkish Embassy in London had by then been closed for some ten years— ever since the suspension of diplomatic relations between Turkey and the United Kingdom upon the outbreak of war between them in 1914—the new Ambassador found that his official residence was not immediately habitable as it stood when he arrived to re-open it. During the uncomfortable days which had to be passed while the necessary redecorations were being carried out, the Ambassador, with his family and his suite, took his dinner night by night in a neighbouring restaurant; and, in their temporarily forlorn and homeless state, the Turkish diplomatic party were cheered and touched by the markedly cordial solicitude on their behalf which was invariably shown by one, in particular, of the

---

[1] As a matter of fact, such scruples were both felt and shown by the Turkish-speaking Muslim neighbours of the Turkish-speaking Armenian deportees from Cilicia; and in this district, at any rate, it seems improbable that the traditional relations of good-neighbourliness between the two Turkish-speaking communities would ever have been disturbed if they had been left to themselves. The deportations were engineered and carried out on the initiative of the Committee of Union and Progress: a recently founded Turkish Muslim organization, with its head-quarters far away at Salonica, which was inspired by a fanatical determination to apply throughout the Ottoman Empire the exotic and inappropriate Nationalism of the modern Western World.

[2] See the British parliamentary paper on *The Treatment of the Armenians in the Otto-man Empire, 1915-16 = Cd.* 8325 (1916) = Misc. No. 31 (1916).

waiters who here served them at table. On their last visit to the restaurant before the Embassy kitchen was in working order once again, the Ambassador singled this waiter out for a parting expression of his thanks; and then at last the waiter's tongue was loosed. 'O Your Excellency,' he burst out in Turkish, 'you really need not thank me at all, for it is I myself, entirely, that have been the gainer through the stroke of good luck that put me in the way of waiting on you and yours. You see, I am an Armenian from' such and such a place (it was an out-of-the-way spot in Anatolia); 'and now, for years on end, I have had to spend my life earning my living here in London, with the whole breadth of Europe between me and home and without ever hearing a word of my native tongue. And so, Your Excellency, when you and your party came in here for the first time the other night and started to talk Turkish, I felt almost as though I were at home again, and my heart leapt up. Night by night, since then, I have just feasted my ears. Simply by talking to each other, you and your friends were doing me a world of good without ever suspecting it. So you see, Your Excellency, it is really I that am in debt to you!' Here was at least one native of the Near East who was more deeply moved by the sound of his mother-tongue than by the bitter memories of a communal vendetta! As the Ambassador told the story, his countenance beamed with his pleasure at this unlooked-for welcome in London from an Armenian Turkish-speaking mouth; and the Turkish narrator's English listener took the tale as a happy augury for the opening of a new chapter of Near Eastern history.

If we pass now from the Iranic World, with its Indian and Near Eastern annexes, to the sister Arabic World, and then cast our eyes over the borderland between the domain of this Arabic Civilization and its Tropical African hinterland, we can trace the progress of the Arabic language as it has pushed its way westward from the west coast of the Indian Ocean towards the Lakes, and southward from the south coast of the Sahara into the Sudan, in the train of successive bands of Arab or semi-Arabicized stock-breeders and slave-raiders and traders. And the linguistic side of this movement can still be studied to-day in the life; for, while the physical impact of Arab intruders upon the domain of the native Negro peoples in this African 'living museum'[1] of Primitive Humanity has been brought to a standstill by European intervention within the last fifty or sixty years, the linguistic impact of the Arabic language upon the native vernaculars has actually received fresh impetus from an 'opening-up of Africa' which has latterly been taken out of Arab hands and been carried to completion as a

[1] See II. C (ii) (b) 2, vol. i, p. 313, above.

European enterprise. Under the European flags that signify the imposition of a Western régime the Arabic language is proceeding with its advance into the heart of Tropical Africa with better facilities than it ever commanded before the present railways and motorroads and postal and telegraph and telephone services were placed at its disposal by the energy and ability of European pioneers; and these material services do not exhaust the tale of benefits which have been conferred upon the Arabic language and culture in Tropical Africa by European colonial Powers. Perhaps the greatest benefit of all has been the official encouragement that they have given—for the sake of supplying an administrative need of their own—to the mixed languages that have arisen on the different cultural coasts on which the flowing tide of an Arabic *lingua franca* has been seeping in through native African mangrove swamps. It is French imperialism on the Upper Niger and British imperialism on the Lower Niger and British and German imperialism side by side in the East African hinterland of Zanzibar that have respectively made the fortunes of Fulani and Hausa and 'Swahili'; and all these three languages are linguistic alloys—with an African base and an Arabic infusion—that have been reduced to writing in the Arabic Alphabet. Sawāhīlī, the East African 'language of the coasts', is an Arabo-Bantu counterpart of the Perso-Hindī alloy which is the Indian 'language of the camp' or Urdū; and the body that has been given to 'Swahili' by an East African dialect of Bantu has been given to Fulani and Hausa by two of the local non-Arabic vernaculars of the semi-nomadic peoples on the Saharo-Sudanese borderland between the Desert and the Sown.[1]

When we pass from the Old World to the Americas, we find the Inca empire-builders of the Andean universal state displaying in their linguistic policy, as in everything else, a characteristic authoritarianism which has not yet been emulated by European administrators in Africa. Having come to the conclusion that their subjects could not function as fully efficient human instruments of a 'totalitarian' régime unless they were equipped with some common *lingua franca*, the Incas selected the Quichua language for this purpose and then not merely encouraged but actually compelled all the inhabitants of their empire to make themselves familiar with it.[2] This linguistic regimentation of the Andean

[1] For Fulani and Hausa see the references given in Part III. A, Annex I, vol. iii, p. 393, above.
[2] Joyce, T. A.: *South American Archaeology* (London 1912, Lee Warner), p. 213; Markham, Sir Clements: *The Incas of Peru* (London 1910, Smith Elder), p. 137. The Incas evidently looked upon Quichua as a vulgar tongue; for they had another esoteric classical language of their own, which they kept to themselves. The ordinance prescribing a compulsory universal proficiency in Quichua is ascribed to the Emperor Pachacutec (*imperabat circa* A.D. 1400–48) by Baudin, L.: *L'Empire Socialiste des Inka* (Paris 1928, Institut d'Ethnologie), pp. 116–17.

peoples at their Inca masters' hands has had lasting consequences, notwithstanding the premature and violent interruption of the Incas' work by the Spanish *conquistadores* who hurled them from the seat of power and enthroned themselves in their stead.[1] For the missionaries of the Catholic Christian Church espied a new world ripe for spiritual conquest in the wreckage of an Incaic earthly paradise which had been ravished and devastated by the material weapons of Pizarro and his ruffianly companions;[2] and they perceived that a *lingua franca* which was already a 'going concern' throughout the vast domain of the shattered Andean universal state might be as useful an instrument for the propagation of the Christian Faith as it had been for the operation of the Incaic system of government. Accordingly the dissemination of the Quichua language, which the Inca administrators had begun, was carried further by the Catholic Christian hierarchy which partitioned the Incaic heritage with the Spanish Crown; and it is perhaps mainly thanks to this ecclesiastical policy that, on the Andean Plateau to-day, Quichua is still spoken by a numerous population.[3] No doubt this consecutive Incaic enforcement and Catholic furtherance of a knowledge of Quichua in the Andean World for three or four centuries on end did much to prepare the ground for the subsequent spread of Spanish over the same area.

This Spanish, unlike the Quichuan, *lingua franca* of a post-Incaic Andean Society serves not merely as a medium of internal intercourse but also as a means of communication with other regions of that Westernized World of literally world-wide extent into which the Andean Society's formerly secluded domain has been incorporated as one of the consequences of the Spanish conquest. Within that 'Great Society' of the present age a common command of Spanish links the Andean World with Spain itself and with those South American territories—now occupied by the republics of Chile and Argentina and Uruguay —in which a sparse and backward aboriginal population has been

---

[1] This interruption of the Incas' work by the Spaniards has a parallel in the interruption of the work of the Achaemenidae by the Macedonians.

[2] When the Spanish Crown at length succeeded in Peru in asserting its authority over the demonic licenciousness and destructiveness of the *conquistadores* and their diadochi, the viceroys sought to make the best of a bad business by deliberately restoring as much as possible of the Incaic régime; but the damage had been done and the restoration was a caricature (Baudin, op. cit., p. 241). The Catholic Church showed at any rate a greater ability than the Spanish Crown, if not a greater goodwill, to save something from the wreck.

[3] The policy was carried out in the grand style. To begin with, the Catholic missionaries gave the Quichua language the benefit of the art of writing, which they had brought with them to the Andes from the Old World, by reducing Quichua to literary form in the Latin Alphabet. In A.D. 1576 a chair of Quichua was founded at the University of Lima, where it was maintained until 1770; and in 1680 a knowledge of Quichua was made in Peru an obligatory qualification for any candidate for ordination to the Catholic Christian priesthood (ibid., p. 117).

evicted and replaced by a Spanish-speaking population of European origin. At the same time this common Spanish *lingua franca* is a bond between the Andean World and the domain of a neighbouring society in Central America with which the Andeans appear to have had little direct intercourse before the fates of these two indigenous civilizations of the New World were brought into a tragic conjunction by the common calamity of a Spanish conquest which overwhelmed both of them alike in the early decades of the sixteenth century of the Christian Era. In Central America, south-west of the Rio Grande, the Spanish language to-day enjoys as wide a currency as anywhere south of the Isthmus of Panamá—and this in spite of the fact that in Central America no indigenous *lingua franca* has prepared the ground for Spanish as Quichua has prepared it in the Andes. The Spanish conquest which followed the establishment of an Andean universal state by the Incas anticipated the establishment of a Central American universal state by the Aztecs;[1] and, owing to this historical accident, the Western culture—of which the Spanish language has been the vehicle in the Central American as well as in the Andean portion of the vast tract that has now become Latin America—has been compelled in Central America to make its way for itself, instead of finding, as it has found in the Andes, the valleys filled and the rough ways made smooth[2] by the antecedent cultural labours of indigenous empire-builders.

It may seem strange that any *lingua franca* which has originally been imposed as a result of a military conquest should ever afterwards be able to shake itself free from this odious historical association in the minds of the conquered peoples who have had it forced down their throats. Yet Spanish and Quichua are by no means unique in having been started on their careers in this fashion; this has been the history of more than half the *lingue franche* in our catalogue; and a final example may be cited to illustrate how hard it is for bitter memories to hold their own against convenient habits.

At the Peace Conference of Paris the writer's wife was acting as assistant to the special correspondent of *The Manchester Guardian*; and in the course of her work it fell to her lot one day to accompany her principal when he was waiting on the Georgian delegation in their hotel in order to obtain an interview from them. The leading Georgian delegates who were then in Paris were men whose names had become widely known in a previous chapter of history as those of prominent Menshevik Social-

---

[1] See I. C (i) (*b*), vol. i, p. 124; IV. C (ii) (*b*) 2, vol. iv, pp. 105–6; and V. C (i) (*c*) 4, in the present volume, p. 357, above.   [2] Luke iii. 5.

Democratic deputies in the Imperial Russian Duma at Petrograd; but in Paris in 1919 they were presenting themselves in another role—not as members of one of the great political parties of the *ci-devant* Russian Empire, but as representatives of a non-Russian nationality which was now 'rightly struggling to be free' from a forcibly imposed Russian yoke. In accordance with their professed political metamorphosis the delegates opened the conversation— which was conducted through an interpreter belonging to their staff—by dwelling upon the distinctiveness of the Georgian from the Russian culture; and they sought to drive their point home by reminding their visitors that the Georgian language was not even remotely akin to Russian—as English, for example, was—but actually belonged to an utterly different language-group which had no affinity whatever with the Indo-European family. This picturesque insistence upon the outlandishness of the speakers' mother-tongue caught the assistant-correspondent's fancy; and, whenever the Georgian delegates were priming their interpreter with the representations that he was to pass on to her principal and herself in French, she took advantage of these pauses in her own work of taking notes in order to gratify her curiosity by listening to the cadences of a language whose chief title to consideration seemed to lie in being *sans pareil*.

As the interview proceeded in this fashion—with the touch of tedium that is inevitable in a conversation that has to be interpreted—the listener's mind gradually began to wander; and presently she found herself stumbling on the thought that apparently one has only to open one's ears for a certain length of time to a wholly unknown language in order to begin to catch some glimmerings of an understanding of it. The absurdity of this idea recalled the dreamer, with a start, to wakeful consciousness. How fatuous the mind can be when one allows it to go wool-gathering! And then, as she went on listening with her attention now at full stretch, it was suddenly borne in upon her that perhaps, after all, she had not been so silly as she had supposed; for surely the language which the delegates were talking with the interpreter was Russian—a language of which she did, as it happened, possess a certain knowledge. With her curiosity now sharply whetted, she took the first opportunity to put in a word to the interpreter on her own account. 'I wonder', she said, 'if you would allow me to ask you what language you and the delegates were talking together just now?' And at this the interpreter, looking slightly embarrassed, held a whispered conversation with his chiefs. 'The delegates desire me to tell you,' he finally answered her, 'that, as a matter of fact, they were talking Russian just then; but they were only talking it for a moment, and you must not attach any importance to that. They have, of course, been talking Georgian all the rest of the time.'

Good manners forbade any cross-examination; but the interpreter's explanation of an unfortunate *lapsus linguae* was hardly convincing; and a different tale was told with greater eloquence by the disconcerted countenances of the delegates themselves. The questioner drew the conclusion (which, no doubt, was correct) that even a Georgian patriot's mind fell into thinking in Russian, the moment it was off its guard, if the subject of its thoughts was political. The Great Russian *lingua franca* of the Muscovite Empire was, after all, the vehicle which had first conveyed to Transcaucasia the exotic political ideas of a Western World that was sundered from Georgia by the redoubtable breadth of all the Russias; and, if your Georgian was being constrained to think in terms of 'natural rights' and 'constitutions' and 'plebiscites' and 'minorities', it stood to reason that it would be exceedingly difficult for him to utter or even frame such thoughts in any other medium than the parliamentary language of a Russian Duma in which he had served his apprenticeship and made his name as a politician. On the conscious plane of his mental life this Georgian politician *à la Russe* might have made up his mind to repudiate his Russian political past and to throw himself into the novel part of a Georgian nationalist; on the subconscious plane, however, he was evidently apt, at unguarded moments, to relapse in a trice into his indelibly Russian political self. It will be seen that the Georgian politician's Russian *lingua franca* was something more than a convenient social tool which could be employed or laid aside at its master's good pleasure; it was a vehicle of thought without which a Georgian could not live the life of a political animal any more than a fish could swim on dry land or a bird fly in a vacuum. In fact, a Georgian political programme of secession from the Russian body politic was in 1919 a political contradiction in terms.

(δ) *Syncretism in Religion.*

In the field of Religion, as in the fields of Language and Art and Manners, syncretism is an outward manifestation of that inward sense of promiscuity which arises from the schism in the Soul in an age of social disintegration.

The phenomenon of religious syncretism may be taken, with some assurance, as a symptom of disintegration in the social milieu in which the phenomenon presents itself, because the apparent examples of religious syncretism in the histories of civilizations in their growth-stage turn out, on inspection, to be illusory. For instance, when we see the parochial mythologies of innumerable city-states being co-ordinated and harmonized into a single Pan-Hellenic system by the labours of Hesiod and the 'catalogue poets' and the 'logographers' in the early stages of the growth of the Hellenic Civilization, we are watching a mere juggling with names which is not accompanied by any corresponding fusion of different rites or blending of diverse religious emotions. Similarly, when we see Latin *numina* being identified with Olympian divinities—a Juppiter with a Zeus or a Juno with a Hera—what we are watching, in effect, is the mere replacement of a primitive Latin animism by the anthropomorphic pantheon of the Hellenic World in the course of the peaceable conversion of a primitive Latin society to Hellenism.[1] These equations between Latin and Greek names of gods do not bear witness to any dilution of Greek with Latin religious ceremonies or ideas; there has been no give-and-take; for the giving has been all on the Greek and the taking all on the Latin side when Zeus has been installed on the Capitol under the name of Juppiter, no less than when Polydeuces has been installed as 'Pollux', and his brother Castor under his own undistorted Greek name, on a site in the Forum Romanum within a stone's-throw of Zeus-Juppiter's Capitoline seat. It makes no difference whether a Castor and an Apollo are translated from Greece to Latium under their exact original names; or whether, in the process of translation, a Polydeuces is distorted into a 'Pollux' and a Heracles into a 'Hercules' and a Persephone into a 'Proserpine'; or whether a Hestia and a Zeus are transposed into their philological equivalents Vesta and Jovis; or whether a Hephaestus is dubbed 'Vulcanus' and a Demeter 'Ceres' in spite of the absence of any kinship here between the Latin name and the Greek. This arbitrary variety of usage in the matter of nomenclature covers a uniform cultural process which is not a case of syncretism at all, but consists in the introduction of a Greek divinity, *de toutes pièces*, into a Latin vacuum.[2]

---

[1] For this conversion of the Latins to Hellenism during the growth stage of the Hellenic Civilization see IV. C (i), vol. iv, pp. 19–20; V. C (i) (c) 1, in the present volume, p. 55, footnote 4; and V. C (i) (c) 3, p. 212, above.

[2] 'Les Latins attribuaient à Neptune les aventures de Ποσειδῶν.'—*Œuvres de Turgot* (Paris 1844, Guillaumin, 2 vols.), vol ii, p. 621 ('Géographie Politique'). There is an almost exact parallel to this process in the history of the Japanese offshoot of the Far Eastern Society, where, after the introduction of the Mahāyāna into Japan, the indigenous Japanese *numina* (*Japonicè 'kami'*) were systematically identified with famous Mahayanian Bodhisattvas (Holtom, D. C.: *The National Faith of Japan: A Study in Modern Shintō* (London 1938, Kegan Paul, Trench, Trubner), pp. 35–8; Kato, Genchi: *A Study of Shinto, the Religion of the Japanese Nation* (Tokyo 1926, Meiji Japan Society), pp. 134–6). In this system of 'Ryobu' or 'Dual' Shinto the Bodhisattvas were given the place of honour, as archetypes or ideas (in the Platonic sense) of which the Shinto *kami* were reflexions in the phenomenal world. This relation was reversed by Urabe Kanetomo (*vivebat* A.D. 1435–1511) in a counter-system entitled 'Yui-itsu' or

There is a different class of identifications between names of gods in which these verbal equations do occur in an age of social disintegration and also do bear witness to the prevalence of a sense of promiscuity, but which nevertheless will be found on examination to be no genuine religious phenomena, but merely politics under a religious mask. Such are the identifications that are made between the names of different local gods in an age when a disintegrating society is being forcibly unified on the political plane as the mechanical consequence of a series of inter-necine wars between parochial states into which the society has articulated itself previously in its growth-stage.[1]

For example, when, in the concluding chapters of Sumeric history, Enlil the Lord (Bel) of Nippur was merged into Marduk of Babylon, and when Marduk-Bel of Babylon in his turn went incognito for a time under the name of Kharbe,[2] the *pammixia* commemorated in this deliberate confounding of distinctions between the names of different gods was of a political and not of a religious order. The political significance of this juggling with divine names is indeed prodigious. When the god who was the lord of Nippur was given his lordly title—Bel—in the Akkadian language, we can infer that this Semitic dialect must by that time have been supplanting Sumerian in a city-state which had hitherto been the hub of the Sumeric universe. When Marduk of Babylon was identified with the Bel of Nippur, this was a record of the rehabilitation of a Sumeric universal state through the prowess of a Babylonian dynasty. And, when we find Bel-Marduk of Babylon going under the Kassite name of Kharbe, we can tell that the Sumeric universal state which had been momentarily rehabilitated by Hammurabi has now been superseded, even in its metropolitan territory, by a barbarian 'successor-state' under the rule of Kassite war-lords. Again, in the affiliated Babylonic Society, when we find the same pantheon enthroned in both Babylonia and Assyria, name for name, except that in Assyria the pre-eminent position of the Babylonian Marduk-Bel is occu-pied by a god called Asshur,[3] the true inference is not that there was any substantial difference between Assyrian and Babylonian religious practices and beliefs, but merely that, in the political life of the Babylonic Society, the Assyrians had developed a

'Only One' Shinto, in which the *kami* are promoted to the rank of archetypes and the Bodhisattvas degraded to that of shadows (Holtom, op. cit., pp. 38–41; Kato, op. cit., pp. 136–7).

[1] This internecine warfare which ends in an amalgamation of the local gods begins as a competition between them in which they experience the same changes of fortune as the local communities by which they are respectively worshipped. The vicissitudes in the fortunes of some of the local gods of the Sumeric city-states during the Sumeric 'Time of Troubles' are noticed by Sir Leonard Woolley: *Abraham* (London 1936, Faber), pp. 224–5.   [2] See I. C (i) (b), vol. i, p. 116, above.   [3] See loc. cit.

strongly pronounced national consciousness which they expressed in religious terms by calling the high god of the Assyro-Babylonian Pantheon by the name of their own eponymous Assyrian national divinity in preference to using the name of Marduk-Bel with its distinctively Babylonian political associations.

In a similar way in the Egyptiac World, when the obscure local god Amon of Thebes—who seems originally to have been a double of the neighbouring local god Min of Coptos--was identified with Re the Sun-God, who was not only a Pan-Egyptiac divinity but was actually the high god of the Egyptiac Pantheon,[1] this was a mere reflexion, in religious terms, of the political facts that the Egyptiac universal state had not only been founded in the first instance by one Theban prince but had afterwards been reinstituted by another empire-builder from the same southern march of the Egyptiac World after the interlude of a Hyksos barbarian domination.[2] The god Amon's fortune was made by the prowess of the human rulers who happened to have inherited him as their parochial object of worship; and it is significant that Amen-emhat ('Amon was in the Beginning') was the name of the first Theban Emperor of the Twelfth Dynasty, whose reign inaugurated the 'Indian Summer' of the Egyptiac universal state.[3] Thereafter, when, after the Hyksos interlude, Amon had returned to power in the train of another Imperial dynasty—the Eighteenth—from the god's native canton of Thebes, the Emperor Thothmes III organized an ecclesiastical counterpart of the restored Egyptiac universal state in the shape of a Pan-Egyptiac hierarchical corporation under the presidency of the Chief Priest of Amon-Re's Theban sanctuary.[4]

[1] In the Egyptiac World the Sun-God had been raised to this eminence in the course of the 'Time of Troubles' between the breakdown of 'the Old Kingdom' and the establishment of 'the Middle Empire' by Theban hands. This epoch saw 'the completion of a far-reaching progressive transformation of the Egyptiac religion. The ideas, evolved at Heliopolis, regarding the unity of the divine power which reveals itself in the creative energy of the Sun—ideas which had first found their liturgical expression in the Sun-worship of the Fifth Dynasty—now obtained general currency. [The doctrine was that] in truth there is only one single godhead, namely the Sun who is sprung from Nunu, the primeval waste of waters, and this whether the god who dwells in the Sun is called Atum, Re, Khepre "the Creator", or what you will. . . . This is the Solar Monotheism of the Egyptiac Theology. All other gods that are worshipped locally here and there in the Egyptiac World sink to being either mere names for "the One" or, alternatively, to being his assistants and servitors. This doctrine, which had been worked out at Heliopolis, . . . was now propagated all over the Egyptiac World as a piece of esoteric wisdom belonging to the priesthood, and the higher orders, the "Knowing", were initiated into it.'—Meyer, E.: *Geschichte des Altertums*, vol. i, part (2), third edition (Stuttgart and Berlin 1913, Cotta), pp. 243–4.
[2] See I. C (ii), vol. i, p. 144; II. D (v), vol. ii, pp. 112–13; V. C (i) (c) 3, in the present volume, p. 268, and V. C (i) (c) 4, p. 352, above.
[3] See V. C (ii) (a), vol. vi, p. 192, below. For the foregoing foundation of the Egyptiac universal state by Amenemhat I's predecessor Mentuhotep IV see I. C (ii), vol. i, p. 137; II. D (v), vol. ii, p. 117, footnote 1; IV. C (ii) (b) 2, vol. iv, p. 85; and V. C (i) (c) 3, in the present volume, p. 267, above; and V. C (ii) (a), vol. vi, p. 190, below.
[4] See I. C (ii), vol. i, p. 145, footnote 5, and IV. C (iii) (c) 2 (β), vol. iv, pp. 413 and 421, above, and V. C (i) (d) 6, Annex, in the present volume, pp. 653–4 and 695, below.

Through the glory reflected upon him by this political advancement of both his local human prince and his personal human servitor, Amon rose to a pinnacle of greatness to which the Theban god would scarcely have dreamed of aspiring in the days of his obscurity during the growth-phase of Egyptiac history; but, for this immense aggrandisement, Amon had to pay the price of ceasing to be himself. 'His old local characteristics, whatever they may have been,[1] have been supplanted by those of the Sun-God, and the ancient local Amon has been completely solarized. In this way it has been possible to raise him to the supreme place in the Pantheon.'[2] 'As Amon-Re, he receives a new, and less indecent, shape.'[3] 'On the whole, Amon-Re is actually nothing more than the old powerful Sun-God Re,[4] Harakhti, Atum, Khepre and whatever else he was called. Like him he sails over the celestial ocean, and like him he wars with the cloud-dragon Apophis; and all that Re possesses in the way of sanctuaries, ships, names and crowns becomes his property.'[5]

'The Ennead was joined in thy limbs, . . . every god was united with thy body. Thou didst emerge first that thou mightest begin the commencement, O Amon, whose name is hidden from the Gods, great aged one, older than these, Tenen who did shape himself as Ptah. . . .

'Of mysterious form and gleaming shape, the wondrous god with many forms. All gods make their boast in him in order to magnify themselves with his beauty, for he is so divine.

'Re himself is united with his body, and he is the great one who is in Heliopolis.'[6]

This Egyptiac conception of a single universal godhead manifesting itself under a host of local names was not only extended from Re of Heliopolis to Amon-Re of Thebes. In an age when the Egyptiac Civilization itself was on the eve of extinction we find an Egyptiac Isis who by this time had conquered a spiritual empire for herself in an alien Hellenic World laying claim to the same Protean universality in her epiphany to the hero of Apuleius's pornographico-devotional romance.

[1] Amon seems originally to have been, like Min, a local ithyphallic fertility god—an aspect of godhead which is at the very farthest remove from the etherial and oecumenical figure of the Sun-God with whom Amon now came to be identified.—A.J.T.
[2] Breasted, J. H.: *The Development of Religion and Thought in Ancient Egypt* (London 1912, Hodder & Stoughton), p. 318.
[3] Erman, A.: *Die Religion der Ägypter* (Berlin 1934, de Gruyter), p. 104.
[4] Long before the course of Egyptiac political events had led to the identification of Amon with Re, Re himself had been 'politicized' by becoming 'a kind of celestial reflection of the earthly sovereign' (Breasted, J. H.: *Development of Religion and Thought in Ancient Egypt* (London 1912, Hodder & Stoughton), p. 17, cited already in I. C (ii), vol. i, p. 141, above).—A.J.T.
[5] Erman, A.: *The Literature of the Ancient Egyptians*, English translation (London 1927, Methuen), p. 283.
[6] Chapters 90 and 200 of *The Thousand Songs* in honour of Thebes and A-mon-Re (quoted in Erman, *Literature*, English translation, pp. 298–9).

'En adsum tuis commota, Luci, precibus, rerum naturae parens, elementorum omnium domina, saeculorum progenies initialis, summa numinum, regina manium, prima caelitum, deorum dearumque facies uniformis, quae caeli luminosa culmina, maris salubria flamina, inferum deplorata silentia nutibus meis dispenso: cuius numen unicum multiformi specie, ritu vario, nomine multiiugo totus veneratur orbis. inde primigenii Phryges Pessinuntiam deum matrem, hinc autochthones Attici Cecropeiam Minervam, illinc fluctuantes Cyprii Paphiam Venerem, Cretes sagittiferi Dictynnam Dianam, Siculi trilingues Stygiam Proserpinam, Eleusinii vetustam deam Cererem, Iunonem alii, Bellonam alii, Hecatam isti, Rhamnusiam illi, et qui nascentis dei Solis inchoantibus inlustrantur radiis Aethiopes Ariique priscaque doctrina pollentes Aegyptii caerimoniis me propriis percolentes appellant vero nomine reginam Isidem.'[1]

The same deliberate policy of establishing identifications between divinities that were originally local and unrelated comes into evidence in the Andean World in the time of the universal state that was constructed by the Incas;[2] and the Inca Pachacutec (*imperabat circa* A.D. 1400–48), in whose reign this political unification of the Andean World was substantially completed,[3] performed a feat of ecclesiastical organization which was exactly analogous to the Egyptiac performance of the Pharaoh Thothmes III. Pachacutec convened a congress of priests from all parts of his dominions at Corichanca—the great temple in Cuzco which was the seat of the Incas' own ancestral Sun-worship—and arranged that all the gods of the Incaic Empire should be marshalled into a pantheon with the Corichancan Sun-God in the role which was assigned by Thothmes III to his own Theban Amon-Re.[4] Like Thothmes again, Pachacutec provided his heavenly pantheon with an earthly hierarchy in which the Chief Priest of the temple of the Sun at Corichanca occupied the position of the Chief Priest of Amon-Re at Thebes; and in the Andean, as in the Egyptiac, World the central shrine of the high god of the pantheon was reproduced in a host of local Sun-temples at the seats of provincial administration, while the whole ecclesiastical establishment was endowed with the produce of lands which were set aside for this purpose in all parts of the empire.[5]

[1] Apuleius: *Metamorphoses*, Book XI, chap. 5.
[2] See Joyce, T. A.: *South American Archaeology* (London 1912, Lee Warner), p. 152.
[3] See II. D (iv), vol. ii, p. 103, footnote 2, above.
[4] Pachacutec carried out his policy in a way that was more literal and more drastic than anything that Thothmes ventured to do; for in the Andean case the idols of the local divinities were physically removed from their local shrines in order to be assembled at Corichanca (see Baudin, L.: *L'Empire Socialiste des Inka* (Paris 1928, Institut d'Ethnologie), p. 62).
[5] See Means, P. A.: *Ancient Civilisations of the Andes* (New York and London 1931, Scribner), pp. 427–8; Joyce, op. cit., pp. 156–9; Baudin, op. cit., p. 62; Markham, Sir C.: *The Incas of Peru* (London 1910, Smith Elder), pp. 105–6; and the present Study, V. C (i) (d) 6 (δ), Annex, in the present volume, pp. 653 and 694, below.

In this Protean capacity for metamorphosis, which is common to Enlil-Bel-Marduk-Kharbe-Asshur and to Min-Amon-Re-Ptah and to the gods who were regimented by the Incas into their Andean Pantheon, we are witnessing not so much a religious phenomenon as politics working through an ecclesiastical medium; and in our own Western World a classical example of this process of political syncretism in an ecclesiastical mould is to be seen in the ecclesiastical history of the English and Scottish Crowns during the last two and a half centuries. Since the time of the Anglo-Scottish political and ecclesiastical settlement which was inaugurated by the accession of King William III to the two thrones, and which was completed by the constitutional union of the two kingdoms themselves in A.D. 1707, the common sovereign with whom the churches that are respectively established in England and in Scotland have each, in virtue of their establishment, continued to be in official relations[1] (though this on quite different terms in the two cases) has so far always been deemed, and has deemed himself, to be a member of both churches.[2] At the same time, in the same settlement, the churches themselves not only freely went their respective ways and, in doing so, parted company once for all in rite and constitution, if not in doctrine: their respective freedom was also reciprocally guaranteed in a political Act of Union which was formally passed in the common sovereign's name—though in fact, of course, it was a transaction between the two parliaments, or indeed between the two nations, since the monarchy had become constitutionally limited after the deposition of King James II.[3] In this Western case we are witnessing, not indeed a theological union of different godheads, but a personal union of different forms of worship of one and the same god through

The ecclesiastical empire of the Sun-temple at Cuzco was divided into nine or ten 'dioceses' with a 'bishop' in charge of each of them under the Cuzcan 'Pope's' supervision (see Cunow, H.: *Geschichte und Kultur des Inkareiches* (Amsterdam 1937, Elsevier), pp. 198–201). In the contemporary Mexic World a process of religious amalgamation seems likewise to have accompanied the process of political unification which, in this world, was heading towards the establishment of a Mexic universal state by force of Aztec arms when the work of the Aztec empire-builders was cut short, on the verge of its completion, by the advent of the Spaniards (see Thompson, J. E.: *The Civilisation of the Mayas* (Chicago 1927, Field Museum of Natural History), p. 36).

[1] The situation in which an English and a Scottish established church are severally in official relations with a single sovereign has, of course, existed since 1603, when the two crowns were first united on the head of King James I/VI.

[2] King William III's predecessor King James II, as a Roman Catholic, had been a member neither of the English nor of the Scottish Established Church. It may be noted that both King William III himself and Kings George I and II were actually members, not merely of two churches, but of three, since King William was also a member of the Calvinist Church of the United Netherlands, while the first two Georges were also members of the Lutheran Church of Hanover. The Calvinist Church of the Netherlands had the same doctrine as that of Scotland, but the Lutheran Church of Hanover had a doctrine and an ecclesiastical constitution which differed from both the Anglican and the Scottish.

[3] For the happy political consequences of this ecclesiastical *Ausgleich* between the English and Scottish constituent state of the United Kingdom see V. C (i) (*d*) 6 (δ), Annex, pp. 711-12, below.

the common participation of a single crowned head in the membership of different churches.

The foregoing survey has brought out the fact that the parochial gods who come to be identified with one another in a disintegrating society, as a consequence and an acknowledgement of the unification of the parochial states, are apt to have a certain antecedent affinity with one another in virtue of their being in most cases the ancestral gods of different sections of one and the same dominant minority. For this reason the amalgamation of godheads that is demanded, at this stage of a society's history, by *raison d'état* does not, as a rule, go seriously against the grain of religious habit and sentiment. In order to find examples of a religious syncretism that cuts deeper than *raison d'état* and touches the quick of religious practice and belief, we must turn our attention from the religion which the Dominant Minority inherits from a happier past to the philosophy which it strikes out for itself in response to the challenges of a 'Time of Troubles'; and we must watch rival schools of philosophy colliding and blending not only with one another but also with the new 'higher religions' that are imported into the life of a disintegrating society by the alien recruits to the Internal Proletariat. Since these 'higher religions', too, collide with one another besides colliding with the philosophies, it will be convenient first to glance at the relations between 'higher religions' *inter se* and philosophies *inter se* in their originally separate social spheres, before we go on to consider the more dynamic spiritual results that follow when the philosophies on the one side come into relation with the 'higher religions' on the other.

In the disintegration of the Hellenic Society the generation of Poseidonius (*vivebat circa* 135–51 B.C.) seems to mark the beginning of an epoch in which the several schools, which had hitherto delighted in lively, acrimonious, and interminable controversies, now tended with one accord (with the solitary exception of the Ishmaelitish Epicureans) to notice and emphasize the points that united them rather than those that divided them,[1] until a time came, in the first and second centuries of the Roman Empire, when every non-Epicurean philosopher in the Hellenic World of the age subscribed to much the same eclectic set of tenets, whether he chose to call himself a Stoic or a Peripatetic or an Academic. A similar tendency towards promiscuity in philosophy displays itself in the history of the disintegration of the Sinic Society at a

---

[1] This new tendency towards consensus was facilitated by a likewise new tendency towards dogmatism (see Meyer, E.: *Ursprung und Anfänge des Christentums*, vol. iii. (Stuttgart and Berlin 1923, Cotta), pp. 329 and 536) which set in simultaneously; and this dogmatism tended to take a more and more religious and emotional, and a less and less scientific and intellectual, colour (see pp. 550–68, below).

corresponding stage. In the second century B.C., which was the first century of the Empire of the Han, eclecticism was equally the note of the Taoism[1] which was at first in favour at the Imperial Court and of the Confucianism which eventually supplanted it.

'Taoism is a term invented about this time to designate that great eclecticism which was taking place during the second century B.C. and which attempted to embrace all the essential doctrines of the various schools of thought that had flourished during the preceding age of philosophical speculation. . . . "Its method" [says Sse-ma Tan][2] "consists of observing the seasonal regularities of the natural forces as taught by the astrologers, and in selecting the best elements in the teachings of the Confucianists and Mo-ists and incorporating into itself the essentials of the schools of the Logicians and the Jurists".'[3]

This so-called 'Taoism', which was the prevalent philosophy of the Sinic dominant minority during the first two generations of the Han régime, was officially superseded in the reign of the Emperor Han Wuti (*imperabat* 140–87 B.C.) by a 'Confucianism' which

'was not at all what Confucius taught or Mencius philosophized about, but was something so different from the original teachings of the school that we must call it "the Han Confucianism" in order to distinguish it from the moral and social teachings of Confucius and Mencius on the one hand and the Neo-Confucianist philosophy of the Sung Dynasty on the other'.[4]

This syncretism between rival philosophies which we observe in the disintegration of the Sinic Society as well as in that of the Hellenic has its parallel in the relations between rival 'higher religions' nurtured in the bosom of the Internal Proletariat.

For example, in the Syriac World from the generation of Solomon onwards we find a strong tendency towards a *rapprochement* between the Israelitish worship of Yahweh and the worships of the local Baalim of other Syriac communities which were Israel's neighbours;[5] and the date is significant, because we have seen reason[6] to believe that the death of Solomon heralded the break-

---

[1] For this travesty of Taoism see V. C (i) (*d*) 4, pp. 418–19, above.
[2] For this Sinic philosopher of the second century B.C. see loc. cit.—A.J.T.
[3] Hu Shih: 'The Establishment of Confucianism as a State Religion during the Han Dynasty' in *The Journal of the North China Branch of the Royal Asiatic Society*, vol. lx, 1929, pp. 22–3. For the distinctive tenets of the diverse Sinic schools of philosophy which had grown up during the foregoing 'Time of Troubles', see Waley, A.: *The Way and its Power* (London 1934, Allen & Unwin), Introduction.
[4] Hu Shih, op. cit., p. 28.
[5] We may assume that the *rapprochement* which followed the collision between the worship of the god of Israel and the worships of the gods of Moab and Ammon and Phoenicia and Philistia was a matter of give-and-take, even though our records tell us only of the religious influences to which the worship of Yahweh was exposed, while they are silent about any influences that the worship of Yahweh may have imparted to other local cults. The *argumentum ex silentio* would be more than usually hazardous in this case, considering that the evidence at our disposal comes exclusively from the Israelitish side. (On this point, see II. D (ii), vol. ii, p. 50, above.)
[6] In IV. C (ii) (*b*) 1, vol. iv, p. 68, above.

down of the Syriac Civilization and the beginning of a Syriac 'Time of Troubles'. No doubt the remarkable and momentous feature in the religious history of Israel during that age is the exceptional success of the Prophets in combatting the sense of promiscuity and diverting the stream of Israelitish religious development out of the facile channel of syncretism into a new and arduous channel which was peculiar to Israel itself. Yet, when we look at the credit instead of the debit side of the Syriac account of reciprocal religious influences, we shall recall that the Syriac 'Time of Troubles' may have seen the worship of Yahweh make an impact upon the religious consciousness of the peoples of Western Iran in whose midst a 'Diasporà' of Israelitish deportees had been planted by the Assyrian militarists;[1] and it is at any rate certain that there was a powerful counter-impact of the Iranian upon the Jewish religious consciousness in the time of the Achaemenian Empire, which was the Syriac universal state, and in the succeeding age when the Seleucid successors of the Achaemenidae were reigning over the defunct empire's former provinces in Asia. By the second century B.C. the mutual interpenetration of Judaism and Zoroastrianism had gone to such lengths that our modern Western scholars find the utmost difficulty in determining and disentangling the respective contributions that these two sources of Syriac religious experience have severally made to the stream which was fed by their united waters.[2]

Similarly, in the development of the 'higher religions' of the internal proletariat of the Indic World we see a fusion—which goes much deeper than a mere equation of names—between the worship of Krishna and the worship of Vishnu.[3]

At this point we may also take note of a type of religious syncretism which is peculiar to the abnormal situation that arises when a disintegrating civilization is provided with its universal state by alien empire-builders, owing to a failure on the part of the indigenous dominant minority to perform even this service for its society.[4] In this situation there is sometimes, as we have

[1] See I. C (i) (b), vol. i, p. 81, with footnote 1, and V. C (i) (c) 2, in the present volume, p. 121, above.

[2] There is a wide discrepancy between the estimates of the influence of Zoroastrianism upon Judaism that have been made by different modern Western scholars. For a conservative estimate see Meyer, E.: *Ursprung und Anfänge des Christentums* (Stuttgart and Berlin 1921–3, Cotta, 3 vols.), vol. ii. For a less cautious estimate see von Gall, A.: Βασιλεία τοῦ Θεοῦ (Heidelberg 1926, Winter). All scholars, however, seem to be agreed that in this age Zoroastrianism and Judaism did influence one another in some degree. (On this point see V. C (i) (c) 2, p. 121, above, and V. C (i) (d) 7, vol. vi, pp. 43–4; V. C (i) (d) 9 (γ), vol. vi, p. 126, footnote 5, and p. 129, footnote 2; and V. C (i) (d) 11, vol. vi, p. 163, footnote 1, below.)

[3] For the failure of Hinduism to transcend the residual separateness of Vishnu-Krishna from Shiva see V. C (i) (d) 7, vol. vi, pp. 47–9, below.

[4] These universal states of alien origin have been discussed in V. C (i) (c) 1, pp. 53–4; V. C (i) (c) 2, pp. 105–17; and V. C (i) (c) 4, pp. 347–51, above.

observed in another context,[1] a fusion between the hereditary religion of the alien empire-builders who have earned the status of a dominant minority in the society which they have provided with a universal state, and the hereditary religion of the indigenous dominant minority which has forfeited its birth-right and has in consequence been degraded to the ranks of the internal proletariat. For example, on the morrow of the endowment of the main body of Orthodox Christendom with an alien universal state in the shape of the Ottoman Empire a syncretism between the Islam of the 'Osmanlis and the Christianity of their subjects was propagated by Sheykh Bedr-ed-Dīn of Simāv.[2] On the eve of the establishment of an alien universal state in the Hindu World by the Timurid Mughals a syncretism between the Islam of the pre-Mughal Iranic empire-builders in Hindustan and the Hinduism of the indigenous populations, whom these alien intruders were conquering, was conceived in the soul of Kabīr and realized in the Sikh Church Militant.[3] And, when the short-lived alien universal state that had been built for the Hindu Society by Timurid hands was reconstructed, after its premature collapse, by a second fatigue-party of alien empire-builders who were recruited, this time, from the West, a syncretism between Hinduism and the Protestant Christianity of the Timurids' English successors was compounded by Ram Mohan Roy.[4] Finally, in the main body of the Far Eastern World, on the eve of its incorporation into a Great Society with an oecumenical range and a Western framework, the T'aip'ing movement was generated by a blend between the indigenous Far Eastern religious and philosophical tradition and the Protestant Christianity of English intruders who were the apostles of Westernization in the Far East as well as in India.[5]

Such breaches in the barriers between religion and religion or philosophy and philosophy in times of disintegration will

[1] In V. C (i) (c) 2, pp. 106–7 and 111, above.
[2] See IV. C (ii) (b) 1, vol. iv, p. 68, and V. C (i) (c) 2, in the present volume, p. 111, above.
[3] See IV. C (iii) (b) 13, vol. iv, p. 231, and V. C (i) (c) 2, in the present volume, p. 106, above, for the Hindu-Islamic syncretism which was precipitated in the fifteenth century of the Christian Era by the genius of Kabīr. At the present day there are believed to be about one million non-Sikh Kabīr-panthīs in India, some of whom regard themselves as Hindus and others as Muslims (Eliot, Sir C.: *Hinduism and Buddhism* (London 1921, Arnold, 3 vols.), vol. ii, p. 266). But the most important of the spiritual heirs of Kabīr are not these followers of Kabīr himself but those of his younger contemporary Nanak (*vivebat* A.D. 1469–1538), who founded the Fraternity of the Sikhs—largely under the inspiration of Kabīr's ideas. The metamorphosis of a fraternity which was originally a purely religious association into a militant political community —a sinister transformation which was carried out, by stages, between the last quarter of the sixteenth and the last quarter of the seventeenth century of the Christian Era— is discussed in V. C (i) (d) 6 (δ), Annex, pp. 665–8, below.
[4] See IV. C (iii) (b) 13, vol. iv, p. 231, and V. C (i) (c) 2, in the present volume, p. 106, above.
[5] See V. C (i) (c) 2, in the present volume, p. 107, above.

evidently open the way for *rapprochements* between philosophies and religions; and in these philosophico-religious syncretisms, in which the sense of promiscuity achieves its spiritual *chefs d'œuvre*, we shall find again that the attraction is mutual and that the move is made from both sides. Just as, astride the military frontiers of a universal state, we have watched the soldiers in the imperial garrisons and the warriors in the barbarian war-bands gradually approximating towards one another in their ways of life until at length the two social types cease to be distinguishable,[1] so, in the interior of a universal state, we can watch a corresponding movement of convergence between the adherents of the philosophic schools and the devotees of the popular religions. And the parallel runs true; for in this case, as in that, we find that, while the representatives of the Proletariat do come a certain distance to meet the representatives of the Dominant Minority, the latter go so much farther along their own path of proletarianization that the eventual fusion takes place almost entirely on proletarian ground. In studying the *rapprochement* from both sides it will therefore be convenient to survey the shorter spiritual journey of the proletarian party first before attempting to follow the longer spiritual journey of the Dominant Minority.

When 'higher religions' that have been nurtured in the bosom of the Internal Proletariat find themselves face to face with the Dominant Minority, their advance along the path of adaptation may sometimes stop short at the preliminary step of commending themselves to the Dominant Minority's notice by assuming the outward fashions of the Dominant Minority's style of art. Thus, in a disintegrating Hellenic World, the Mahāyāna and the worships of Mithras and Cybele and Isis all sought to promote the success of their respective missionary enterprises on Hellenic ground by recasting the visual representations of their divinities into forms that might be expected to prove agreeable to Hellenic eyes. Up to this point these eventually unsuccessful rivals of Christianity for the conquest of Hellenic souls were taking the same course as Christianity itself; but none of them made any appreciable move towards taking the further step of Hellenizing itself inwardly as well as outwardly. It was Christianity, alone among them all, that went the length of expressing its creed in the language of Hellenic philosophy.[2]

In the history of Christianity the intellectual Hellenization of a religion whose creative essence was of Syriac origin was foreshadowed in the employment of the Attic, instead of the Aramaic,

---

[1] See V. C (i) (d) 6 (α), pp. 459–80, above.
[2] On this point see V. C (i) (c) 4, p. 366, above.

κοινή[1] as the linguistic vehicle for the New Testament; for the very vocabulary of this vulgarized yet sophisticated form of Greek carried with it a host of unsuspected philosophic implications.

'In the Synoptic Gospels Jesus is regarded as the Son of God, and this belief is carried on and deepened in the body of the Fourth Gospel. But also in the prologue to the Fourth Gospel the idea is thrown out that the Saviour of the World is the Creative Logos of God. Implicitly, then, though the statement is not made explicitly, the Son of God and the Logos of God are one and the same: the Son as the Logos is identified with the creative wisdom and purpose of deity, the Logos as the Son is hypostatized into a person beside the person of the Father. At one bound the philosophy of the Logos has become a religion'[2]—

or, to describe the same spiritual mutation in the inverse terms, the religion of the Dying God Incarnate has found a new expression for itself in the hitherto abstract and frigid philosophy of the Logos.

Nor has this first occasion been the only one on which the missionaries of the Christian Faith have translated their good tidings into the language of the philosophers. The legitimate intellectual arts by which the scholarly Alexandrian Fathers Clement and Origen commended Christianity to a Stoic-minded Hellenic dominant minority were reapplied some fourteen hundred years later when Matteo Ricci and his fellow members of the Society of Jesus addressed themselves—with an ability and a discernment which barely failed to win the triumph that they deserved—to the comparable task of converting the souls of a Confucian-minded dominant minority of Far Eastern litterati.[3]

This device of preaching Religion in the language of Philosophy —an intellectual manœuvre to which Christianity has already resorted twice, with an overwhelming success at the first essay which was all but repeated at the second—was one of the heirlooms which Christianity had inherited from Judaism. It was Philo the Jewish philosopher of Alexandria (*vivebat circa* 30 B.C.–A.D. 45) who sowed the seed from which Philo's Christian fellow citizens and fellow philosophers Clement and Origen were to reap so rich a harvest within two centuries of Philo's day; and it was perhaps from the same quarter that the author of the Fourth Gospel gained his vision of the Divine Logos with which he identifies his Incarnate God.[4] No doubt this Alexandrian Jewish forerunner of Alexandrian

[1] For these two *lingue franche* see V. C (i) (*d*) 6 (γ), pp. 487–91, 494–5, and 499, above.
[2] More, P. E.: *Christ the Word = The Greek Tradition from the Death of Socrates to the Council of Chalcedon: 399 B.C.–A.D. 451*, vol. iv (Princeton 1927, University Press), p. 298.   [3] See V. C (i) (*c*) 4, pp. 366–7, above.
[4] On the other hand, in the opinion of Eduard Meyer (*Ursprung und Anfänge des Christentums* (Stuttgart and Berlin 1921–3, Cotta, 3 vols.), vol. ii, p. 318, the Johannine

Christian Fathers was led into the path of Hellenic philosophy through the gate of the Greek language, like the Christian philosophers themselves; for it was assuredly no accident that Philo lived and philosophized in a city in which the Attic κοινή had become the vernacular language of a local Jewish community that had so utterly lost command of Hebrew, and even of Aramaic, that it had been driven by dire necessity to desecrate its Holy Scriptures by translating them into the impious language of the Isles of the Gentiles. Yet in the history of Judaism itself this Jewish father of a Christian philosophy is an isolated figure. He was not the spiritual progenitor of either the Zealot John of Gischala or the Rabbi Johanan ben Zakkai;[1] and his ingenious effort to derive the Platonic philosophy from the Mosaic Law remained, for Judaism, a barren aetiological conceit which was 'Alexandrian' in the depreciatory meaning of the epithet.

When we pass from Christianity to Mithraism, which was the Syrian 'higher religion's' Iranian counterpart and rival[2] in a competition for the spiritual conquest of the Hellenic World, we shall observe that, on its voyage westwards from its Iranian homeland, Mithra's barque took on board a heavy cargo of the Babylonic astral philosophy[3] from the now half-submerged continent of the *ci-devant* Babylonic World. Indeed,

'the Chaldaean conception of the Powers of Destiny that manifest themselves in the planets and the stars—the belief that everything has its proper "hour", which is fixed and calculable—becomes a common mental possession of all peoples.'[4]

In similar fashion the Indic 'higher religion' of Hinduism barefacedly despoiled a senile Buddhist philosophy of its intellectual panoply[5] in order to acquire for itself the last and most potent of the weapons that it needed in order to drive its philosophical rival right out of their common homeland in the Indic World. And it is the opinion of at least one eminent modern Western Egyptologist that the proletarian worship of Osiris only won its

'Logos' was not derived, either through Philo or through any other channel, from the Hellenic philosophical tradition, but was a translation of the Aramaic 'Memra': the Word of God which, in the Judaism of this age, had come to be endowed with something that might almost be called a personality of its own which was felt to be distinct from the personality of its utterer Yahweh. Eduard Meyer also points out, in the same context (op. cit., vol. ii, p. 317), that the Johannine concept of the Logos has an exact analogue in the Islamic concept of the Uncreated Qur'ān.
[1] See V. C (i) (c) 2, pp. 75–6, above.
[2] Both the Syrian religion of Christianity and the Iranian religion of Mithraism were, of course, 'Syriac' in the cultural sense in which that term is used in this Study.
[3] For this implacably determinist philosophy see V. C (i) (c) 1, pp. 56–7, above.
[4] Meyer, E.: *Geschichte des Altertums*, vol. iii (Stuttgart 1901, Cotta), p. 172. See also the present Study, V. C (i) (c) 1, in the present volume, p. 57, above.
[5] See V. C (i) (c) 1, p. 58, above.

way into the citadel of the Egyptiac dominant minority's hereditary
pantheon by usurping from Re the ethical role—originally quite
foreign to the Osirian Faith—of a divinity that reveals and vindi-
cates Righteousness. According to Breasted, this role had already
been assumed by Re before the fall of 'the Old Kingdom'—at a
time, that is to say, when the Egyptiac Civilization had been still
in its growth-stage—and had then been etherialized, always still
in Re's person, through the wisdom born of the suffering of an
Egyptiac 'Time of Troubles',[1] whereas Osiris was little better
than a hypocrite who gained his entry into the exclusive upper
circle of an Egyptiac celestial society under the false pretence of
patronizing an ideal of goodness that had not originally been his.[2]
And it was in the strength of this borrowed ideal that the proletarian worshippers of Osiris made their eventual conquest of the
Egyptiac World in the time of a 'Middle Empire' which was the
Egyptiac universal state. In fact,

'the Lord gave the people favour in the sight of the Egyptians, so that
they lent unto them such things as they required. And they spoiled the
Egyptians'[3]—

and this is not only the story of the religion of Osiris in its appro-
priation of an ethic that had been cultivated by an Egyptiac
dominant minority in a 'Time of Troubles': it is likewise (as we
have seen) the story of Hinduism in its dealings with Buddhism and
of Mithraism in its dealings with Astrology and of Christianity
in its dealings with Stoicism and Neoplatonism.

This 'spoiling of the Egyptians', however, may sometimes cost
a 'higher religion' dear—as is illustrated by the Egyptiac case in
point. In the Egyptiac case an aspiring Osirian Church, which
sought to help itself on its way by commandeering an ethic that
was the creation of a dominant minority, had to pay for these
unceremoniously borrowed plumes by putting itself into the hands
of the party that was being constrained to lend them. The master-
stroke of the old Egyptiac priesthood was to place itself at the
disposal—and, in so doing, also place itself at the head—of a rising
proletarian religious movement which it had found itself unable
to suppress or even hold at bay, and which might eventually have
swept the old established hierarchy away if, at the critical moment,
these priests of a pre-Osirian Egyptiac Pantheon had not deftly
checkmated their opponents by ostensibly going over to their

---

[1] 'It is Re who is dominant in the thinking of [the] social philosophers of the Feudal
Age. . . . The moral obligations emerging in the Solar theology . . . wrought the earliest
social regeneration and won the earliest battle for social justice of which we know anything in history' (Breasted, op. cit., p. 250).
[2] For this (no doubt, controversial) theory see Breasted, op. cit., pp. 170–8.
[3] Exodus xii. 36.

side.[1] By their astuteness in thus taking the Osirian religion under their wing the Egyptiac priesthood raised their order to a pinnacle of power which it had never attained in the days before Osiris had appeared, as a formidable newcomer, above the Egyptiac dominant minority's horizon.[2]

Astute as it was, this feat of the Egyptiac hierarchy is not unique. The capture of the Osirian religion by the priests of the old Egyptiac Pantheon has its parallels in the capture of the post-Buddhaic Hinduism by the Brahmans[3] and in the capture of Zoroastrianism by the Magi.[4] But there is another, and still more insidious, way in which a 'higher religion' that has made its epiphany out of the bosom of an internal proletariat is apt to fall into the hands of a dominant minority which this rising religion is successfully despoiling of its accumulated spiritual treasures; for the priesthood which gains control over a proletarian church and then abuses this control in order to govern that church in the Dominant Minority's spirit and interest—in impudent defiance of the church's own origin and mission—need not be an ancient priesthood belonging to the Dominant Minority by descent; it may actually be recruited from among the leading lights of the proletarian church itself.

In an early chapter of the political history of the Roman Republic the *stasis* between Plebeians and Patricians was notoriously brought to an end by a 'deal' in which the Patricians took the leaders of the Plebeians into partnership on the tacit understanding that, in consideration of their own admission into the sanctum of the politically and socially privileged class, the appointed champions of the unprivileged lower order would cynically betray their trust by leaving the Plebeian rank-and-file in the lurch.[5] In a similar fashion on the religious plane, in the history of the internal proletariat of a disintegrating Hellenic World, the rank-and-file of Jewry had been betrayed and deserted, by the time of Christ, by their own former leaders the Scribes and Pharisees. These

---

[1] See I. C (ii), vol. i, pp. 143–4, and V. C (i) (c) 2, in the present volume, p. 152, above. In these other contexts we have observed that, in its achievement of this *tour de force*, the Egyptiac priesthood was assisted by the fanatical reaction in the Egyptiac body social against the Hyksos barbarian domination—a reaction of which the priesthood took advantage in order to draw the Osiris-worshippers in the internal proletariat into an 'union sacrée' with the Re-worshippers in the dominant minority.

[2] See I. C (ii), vol. i, p. 145, footnote 5; II. D (v), vol. ii, p. 116, footnote 1; IV. C (iii) (c) 2 (β), vol. iv, p. 421; and IV. C (iii) (c) 3 (β), vol. iv, pp. 515–17, above.

[3] See IV. C (iii) (c) 2 (β), vol. iv, p. 421, footnote 3, and V. C (i) (c) 2, in the present volume, p. 137, above.

[4] See V. C (i) (d) 6 (δ), Annex, p. 705, footnote 1, below.

[5] The traitorous Plebeian leaders were assisted in 'putting over' this 'deal' at the expense of their own followers by the temporary relief from economic pressure which the rank-and-file of the Roman Plebs obtained through land-settlement on lands which came into the possession of the Roman Government as one of the fruits of the Roman conquest of Italy (see IV. C (iii) (b) 9, vol. iv, p. 205, above).

Jewish 'separatists' lived to deserve their self-imposed name in a sense which was the opposite of their meaning at the time when they originally assumed it. The original Pharisees were Jewish puritans who separated themselves from the Hellenizing Jews when these renegades were joining the camp of an alien dominant minority.[1] On the other hand the distinguishing mark of the Pharisees of the time of Christ was their separation of themselves from the rank-and-file of the loyal and devout members of the Jewish community to whom they still hypocritically professed to be setting a good example.

'The learned in the Scriptures, as well as the worldlings, belong to the upper strata of Society; and their attitude is one of condescension mingled with contempt as they look down upon the masses of the working population whom it is their intention to instruct and lead. In [the souls of] these masses, however, the religious life pulsates with a far fiercer intensity. With a fervent credulity they have taken the Law into their bosoms complete. It fills their whole life. . . . At every moment of their existence they feel themselves to be in direct communication with the Godhead, and they discern His operation anywhere and everywhere. The course of events in this chapter of Jewish religious history is the same as it is in all other similar cases—we will confine ourselves here to recalling the various phases of [Christian] monasticism, the Pietists and Methodists, Sufism, and, in the field of Buddhism, the transcendental doctrine of "the Great Vehicle" (the Mahāyāna). In Judaism, likewise, the refinement and etherialisation (*Fortbildung und Verinnerlichung*) of Religion proceeds, not from the learned, but from those strata of the common people that have taken Religion to heart. It is the silent folk of the land (*die Stillen im Lande*)[2] who live and labour (*leben und weben*) in these ideas. They call themselves "the Pious" *sans phrase*: *chasīdīm*, meaning literally "the Partakers in Grace", to whom God, in His grace, has granted the proper conduct, godfearingness and piety. Already in the Psalms the word is used—side by side with the much more common *Saddīqīm*, "the Righteous"—as a party name for those who feel themselves to be the true Church of God, the poor and oppressed who put their trust in God alone, in contrast to "the Wicked" (*Resha'īm*), the selfseeking and ungodly worldlings who ostensibly are masters of the situation in This World but who all the time are living under threat of punishment in the Judgement which will bring all their pomp to a fearful end when God's longsuffering is exhausted.'[3]

This is the historical background of the scathing denunciation of the Pharisees which echoes through the pages of the Gospels.

[1] See V. C (i) (c) 2, p. 73, with footnote 3, above, and V. C (i) (d) 9 (β), vol. vi, pp. 103–5, below.
[2] The same phrase is used by Jung in the passage quoted on p. 567, below.—A.J.T.
[3] Meyer, E.: *Ursprung und Anfänge des Christentums*, vol. ii (Stuttgart and Berlin 1921, Cotta), pp. 41–2.

'The Scribes and the Pharisees sit in Moses' seat: all, therefore, whatsoever they bid you observe, that observe and do; but do not ye after their works; for they say and do not. For they bind heavy burdens and grievous to be borne, and lay them on men's shoulders; but they themselves will not move them with one of their fingers. . . . They . . . love the uppermost rooms at feasts and the chief seats in the synagogues and greetings in the markets, and to be called of men "Rabbi, Rabbi". But be not ye called "Rabbi"; for one is your master, even Christ; and all ye are brethren. . . . Neither be ye called "masters" . . . but he that is greatest among you shall be your servant. And whosoever shall exalt himself shall be abased; and he that shall humble himself shall be exalted.'[1]

Here, through the eyes of the rank-and-file of the Jewish contingent in a Hellenic internal proletariat, we see the Pharisees as Jewish ecclesiastical counterparts of Jewry's Roman political masters; and in the exordium to the parable of the Pharisee and the Publican, in which the parable is described as being addressed 'unto certain which trusted in themselves that they were righteous, and despised others',[2] we are given a complementary definition of a Pharisee which would as aptly describe a Stoic philosopher. Nor was this assimilation of the *ci-devant* spiritual leaders of Jewry to both the two main types of their former Hellenic adversaries just a curiosity of history without practical consequences. In the tragedy of the Passion of Christ we see the Scribes and Pharisees not merely inclining in the privacy of their hearts to the spirit and behaviour of a dominant minority, but also actively ranging themselves at the side of the Roman authorities in the public light of the forum in order to compass the death of a prophet of their own race who had been putting them to shame by doing the very works of which these 'whited sepulchres'[3] made no more than a hollow pretence.

'When he saw the multitudes, he was moved with compassion on them, because they fainted and were scattered abroad, as sheep having no shepherd.'[4]

This clear and reproachful apprehension of the treachery that the Pharisees had perpetrated in heartlessly deserting their flock was Jesus's unforgivable offence in the Pharisees' resentful eyes.

Are there other instances of this spiritual treason which the Pharisees exemplify? When we observe the Pharisaic tendencies of the Manichaean and Paulician *electi*,[5] we may speculate whether

---

[1] Matt. xxiii. 2–12; with these verses and the rest of the chapter compare Mark xii. 38–40; Luke xi. 39–52; and Luke xx. 46–7.   [2] Luke xviii. 9.
[3] Matt. xxiii. 27.   [4] Matt. ix. 36, with a reminiscence of Zech. **x**. 2.
[5] For the Paulician *electi* see IV. C (iii) (c) 2 (β), Annex III, vol. iv, p. 628, above; for the Manichaean *electi* see Burkitt, F. C.: *The Religion of the Manichees* (Cambridge 1925, University Press), p. 46.

these 'separatist' leaders of two later Syriac religious movements might not have relieved the Pharisees of the invidious distinction of serving as the classical examples of the type, supposing that Manichaeism had succeeded in conquering the Hellenic World in the fourth century of the Christian Era, or Paulicianism Western Christendom in the thirteenth.

If we pass now to our examination of the complementary movement in which the philosophies thought out by the Dominant Minority make their approach towards the religions discovered by the Internal Proletariat, we shall find that on this side the process begins earlier, besides going farther. It begins in the first generation after the breakdown; and it passes from curiosity through devoutness into superstition.

The earliness of the first infusion of a religious tinge into the Dominant Minority's philosophical speculations is attested, in the classical Hellenic case, in the *mise en scène* of Plato's *Republic*. The scene is laid in the Peiraeus—the oldest crucible of social *pammixia* in the Hellenic World—at some moment before the end of the Peloponnesian War;[1] the master of the house in which the dialogue is supposed to take place is a resident alien and not an Athenian either by origin or by naturalization; and the alleged narrator, Socrates, begins by telling us that he has walked down to the port from the city of Athens, where his own house is situate, 'in order to pay' his 'respects to the Thracian goddess Bendis, and at the same time out of curiosity to observe how they are going to keep the festival that is being celebrated in her honour at the Peiraeus for the first time on this occasion'. Socrates is delighted with the procession of the townspeople, but he is also delighted as much, or even more, with that of the Thracian strangers in whose train the Thracian goddess has come to Greece; and when, as he starts back for home, he is induced to turn aside and spend the rest of the day at Cephalus's house, he finds his host engaged in the concluding rites of a domestic act of worship. Thus, in the atmosphere of this *chef d'œuvre* of Hellenic philosophical literature, Religion is in the air; and the religious celebrations that catch the eye are alien and even exotic. Here, surely, is an introduction which prepares us for the sequel that is described by a modern Western scholar in the following words:

'The extraordinary thing . . . is that, despite the alien source of the new myth, the theology and philosophy of the Greek Fathers should have turned out in essential matters so thoroughly Platonic, or, more

[1] The date at which the dialogue is to be imagined as taking place is nowhere expressly indicated by the author, and the internal evidence, which our modern Western scholars have industriously searched for a clue, has been diversely interpreted. Boeckh places the imaginary date in the year 411 B.C., Adam in the year 410.

accurately expressed, could have been adopted from Plato with so few modifications. Such a coalescence may lead us to conjecture that the mythology which Plato sought to substitute for the old tales of the Gods was not so much antagonistic to the faith of Christianity as imperfectly Christian. . . . From hints here and there it could even be surmised that Plato himself was dimly aware of a theophany to come, of which his allegories were a prophecy. Socrates in the *Apology* had warned the Athenians of other witnesses to the Soul who should appear after him and avenge his death; and elsewhere he had admitted that, for all the reasoning and high imaginings of Philosophy, the full Truth could not be known until revealed to Man by the grace of God (*theia moira*).'[1]

The religious curiosity which brought Socrates from Athens to the Peiraeus to witness the festival of Thracian Bendis at some date that was previous to the close of the fifth century B.C. was still alive at Athens, not much less than five hundred years later, among 'certain philosophers of the Epicureans and of the Stoics' who 'took . . . and brought . . . unto the Areopagus' a 'babbler' from abroad, 'saying, "May we know what this new doctrine, whereof thou speakest, is?" '—because he seemed 'to be a setter forth of strange gods'.[2] In the first century of the Christian Era it remained as true as it had been in the fifth century B.C. that 'all the Athenians and strangers which were there spent their time in nothing else but either to tell or to hear some new thing'.[3] And while, as we have noticed in another context,[4] it was the tragedy of Athens that the promise of *The Republic* was not fulfilled in *The Acts*, still the Hellenic philosophy which had first come to flower on Attic soil did fulfil its destiny of transposing itself into religious terms, and into religious feelings and practices as well, in other provinces of the empire of Hellenism—a cultural empire which was continually expanding as the Hellenic Civilization itself continued to decline.[5]

Our historical record of this metamorphosis of Philosophy into Religion is ample enough in the Hellenic case to enable us here to follow the process clearly through its successive stages.

The cool intellectual curiosity which is the Platonic Socrates' attitude in *The Republic* towards the Thracian religion of Bendis is also the mood of the historical Socrates' contemporary Herodotus in his incidental disquisitions on the comparative study of Religion. The interest, here, is essentially scientific in character; and, to Herodotus's mind, it was evidently of hardly any genuinely

---

[1] More, P. E.: *Christ the Word* = *The Greek Tradition from the Death of Socrates to the Council of Chalcedon: 399 B.C. to A.D. 451*, vol. iv (Princeton 1927, University Press), pp. 6–7.   [2] Acts xvii. 18–19.
[3] Acts xvii. 21.   [4] In IV. C (iii) (c) 2 (α), vol. iv, pp. 269–71, above.
[5] For the correlation between physical expansion and social and spiritual disintegration see III. C (i) (a), vol. iii, pp. 139–54, and V. C (i) (c) 3, in the present volume, pp. 199–201, above.

religious consequence at all whether this or that Syriac or Egyptiac or Babylonic divinity was, or was not, in truth identical with this or that member of the Hellenic Pantheon.[1] Such theological problems of identity or difference came to be matters of somewhat greater practical concern to members of the Hellenic dominant minority after the overthrow of the Achaemenian Empire by Alexander the Great, when the Hellenic or Hellenizing princes of the 'successor-states' had to make some ritual provision for the religious needs of mixed populations in which the non-Hellenic and Hellenic elements were coming to be ever more intricately intermingled.[2] At the same time the founders and propagators of the Stoic and Epicurean schools of philosophy were making it their concern to provide a ration of spiritual comfort for individual souls which found themselves forlornly astray in a spiritual wilderness, as a result of their sudden liberation from the social bondage —or expulsion from the earthly paradise—of the close-knit corporate life of the pre-Alexandrine Sovereign City-State. If, however, we take as our gauge of the prevalent tendency of Hellenic philosophy in this age the tone and temper of the school which had been the first in the field and which looked back to the prince of the philosophers as its founder, we shall observe that, in opposition to the Stoa, the Academy, during the first two centuries *post Alexandrum*, was pushing ever farther along the path of scepticism. A course that had been set by Arcesilaus was continued by Carneades (*vivebat circa* 213–129 B.C.), who made it his life-work to unpick the threads of a Stoic web that had been woven by Chrysippus (*vivebat* 280–207 B.C.). It was not till after Carneades' death that the litigiously contending schools were moved to look for points of contact and agreement instead of keeping their eyes open for subjects of dispute.[3] But, when at last they did set them-

---

[1] See, for example, Herodotus's chronological proof, in Book II, chaps. 43–5, that the Egyptiac divinity whom the Hellenes of his day called Hêraklês might be the same as the Tyrian divinity to whom they applied the same name, but that it was impossible to regard either of these alien divinities as being identical with the native Hellenic Hêraklês whose father was Amphitryon.

[2] See, for instance, the post-Alexandrine examples of the description of a divinity by a long string of titles, some of them Hellenic and some of them non-Hellenic, which are cited in Wendland, P.: *Die Hellenistisch-Römische Kultur in ihren Beziehungen zu Judentum und Christentum*, 2nd and 3rd editions (Tübingen 1912, Mohr), p. 131. The most interesting of the composite titles there quoted is that from the inscription of King Antiochus I of Commagene (*regnabat circa* 70–29 B.C.) on the Nimrud Dagh (for the identities of the four divinities named in this inscription see Christensen, A.: *L'Iran sous les Sassanides* (Copenhagen 1936, Levin & Munksgaard), p. 152). Alexander's political expedient of arranging literal marriages between Macedonian officers and Iranian ladies (see V. C (i) (d) 7, vol. vi, pp. 6–7, below) has its politico-religious reflexion in a symbolic marriage—celebrated in an Aramaic inscription of the second century B.C. which has been found at Arabsun in Cappadocia—between the *genius loci*, under the name of Bel, and the Zoroastrian Religion, under the name of Dēn Mazdayasn. This metaphorical marriage appears to signify the 'reception' (in the juristic sense) of Zoroastrianism in the *ci-devant* domain of the Hittite Civilization (see Christensen, op. cit., pp. 152–3). [3] See p. 534, above.

selves to walk in step with one another, they found their single
track in a path leading away from an intellectual nihilism towards
an emotional faith.¹

After Carneades' death the Academics and the Sceptics suffered
an eclipse;² and the Syrian Greek Stoic philosopher Poseidonius
of Apamea (*vivebat circa* 135–51 B.C.), who was the leading intellectual light of his age, avenged Chrysippus upon Carneades by
opening the gates of the Stoa for the reception of popular religious
beliefs and practices to an extent that might have startled, not only
Chrysippus himself, but even Poseidonius's own immediate predecessor the Rhodian aristocrat Panaetius.³ Poseidonius lived to
see the Academy itself capitulate to the *Zeitgeist* of which the
Stoic philosopher was the spokesman. About 80 B.C., at a time
when Athens was lying stunned on the morrow of the harrowing
experiences which she had brought upon herself through her
intervention in the conflict between Rome and Mithradates of
Pontus,⁴ another Syrian philosopher, Antiochus of Ascalon, who
was at that time president of an Academy that had obstinately
remained à citadel of scepticism down to the reign of his immediate
predecessor Philo of Larisa, declared that 'Philosophy must go
into reverse'.⁵

¹ This emotional faith, like the intellectual nihilism against which it was a reaction,
was a pathological exaggeration (see IV. C (iii) (c) 2 (γ), Annex, in vol. iv, above) of
one among the several constituents of the harmoniously balanced philosophy with
which the founder of the Academy had been inspired by his own master Socrates.
In the soul of Socrates three impulses—'an intellectual scepticism, a spiritual affirmation, and a tenacious belief in the identity of virtue and knowledge'—are distinguished
by More, P. E.: *Platonism*, 2nd edition (Princeton 1926, University Press), p. 2. According to the same scholar (*Hellenistic Philosophies = The Greek Tradition from the
Death of Socrates to the Council of Chalcedon: 399 B.C. to A.D. 451*, vol. ii (Princeton
1923, University Press), p. 375, the post-Socratic schools of Hellenic philosophy con-
cocted the diverse fare which they offered, in competition with one another, to a hungry
Hellenic public, out of crumbs which had all fallen from their common master's table.
Epicureanism was a combination of Socrates' rationalism with his hedonism; Stoicism
was a combination of his rationalism with his optimistic endurance (καρτερία); Neoplatonism was a combination of his rationalism with his spiritual affirmation; Pyr-
rhonism was a combination of his scepticism with his hedonism and his endurance. In
making these diverse excerpts from the philosophy of Socrates all the schools alike were
aiming at the same goal: namely, a reconciliation of liberty with security under the
watchword of αὐτάρκεια.
² More, P. E.: *Hellenistic Philosophies = The Greek Tradition from the Death of
Socrates to the Council of Chalcedon: 399 B.C. to A.D. 451*, vol. ii (Princeton 1923, University Press), p. 317. In the strength of the rally which the Hellenic Society succeeded
in making when it passed out of its 'Time of Troubles' into its universal state in the
generation of Augustus, an archaistic revival of the Hellenic philosophy of Scepticism
was set on foot, at the beginning of the Christian Era, by Aenêsidêmus. The author
of the chief extant Greek treatise on this Neo-Scepticism, Sextus Empiricus, lived in
the last generation of the *Pax Augusta*, circa A.D. 150–230. In Sinic history there was
a comparable revival of sceptical thought—in this case, likewise, with an archaistic
savour—in a rally that was also reflected in the restoration of the Sinic universal state
by the Posterior Han Dynasty after an interlude of anarchy. The moving spirit in this
Sinic Neo-Scepticism was Wang Ch'ung (*vivebat circa* A.D. 27–100) (Granet, M.: *La
Pensée Chinoise* (Paris 1934, Renaissance du Livre), p. 580).
³ See Meyer, E.: *Ursprung und Anfänge des Christentums*, vol. iii (Stuttgart and
Berlin 1923, Cotta), p. 536, and Seeck, O.: *Geschichte des Untergangs der Antiken Welt*,
vol. iii, 2nd ed. (Stuttgart 1921, Metzler), pp. 142–3.
⁴ See IV. C (iii) (c) 2 (α), vol. iv, p. 266, above. ⁵ Seeck, op. cit., loc. cit.

This conversion, which began to take effect in the sensitive souls of philosophers as early as the turn of the second and the last century B.C., took some time to communicate itself to the Hellenic dominant minority as a whole. At a date some three hundred years later than Antiochus of Ascalon's day, in the pale light of an Antonine 'Indian Summer', a vestige of the prosaic *raison d'état* of Antiochus of Commagene is still visible, through the rising mist of piety, in the syncretism that was cultivated, in his private religious life, by the Emperor Alexander Severus (*imperabat* A.D. 222–35).

'The philosophic devotion of that emperor was marked by a singular but injudicious regard for the Christian religion. In his domestic chapel he placed the statues of Abraham, of Orpheus, of Apollonius and of Christ, as an honour justly due to those respectable sages who had instructed Mankind in the various modes of addressing their homage to the supreme and universal deity.'[1]

The state of mind here displayed in private life by one of the rulers of the Hellenic universal state on the eve of its first collapse can also be detected unmistakably in the following account of the public religious policy of the second founder[2] of the Sinic universal state, Liu Pang, the first emperor of the Han Dynasty:

'When the unification of the empire was completed, the city of Ch'ang Ngan was made the capital of the new empire, and all the tribal and local religions and cults were fully represented in the capital, where each sect had its own shrines, priesthoods, and ceremony. There were the Liang Priestesses, representing the sects of the western peoples of modern Szechuan; the Tsin Priestesses representing the tribal worships of modern Shensi;[3] the Ts'in Priestesses representing the peoples of modern Shensi and further west; the Chin Priestesses, representing the races of the valleys of the Han and the Yangtse. . . . And, when the Emperor Wuti conquered the tribes of modern Kwangtung (111 B.C.),[4] the Yueh Priestesses were added to the numerous tribal and local priesthoods at the capital city and were allowed to worship their own gods and spirits and practise their peculiar method of divination by means of chicken-bones.'[5]

In fact, in the Sinic, as in the Hellenic, World the original attitude of cultivated minds in the Dominant Minority to the religious practices and beliefs of the Internal Proletariat was that depicted

[1] Gibbon, Edward: *The History of the Decline and Fall of the Roman Empire*, chap. xvi. Gibbon's account is based on the following passage of 'the Life of Alexander Severus' (chap. 29) in the so-called *Historia Augusta*: 'Usus vivendi eidem hic fuit: Primum [ut], si facultas esset—id est, si non cum uxore cubuisset—matutinis horis in larario suo, in quo et divos principes, sed optimos electos, et animas sanctiores, in quis et Apollonium et (quantum scriptor suorum temporum dicit) Christum, Abraham et Orpheum et huiuscemodi ceteros habebat et maiorum effigies, rem divinam faciebat.'
[2] For the historical relation between Liu Pang and Ts'in She Hwang-ti see V. C (ii) (a), vol. vi, pp. 187 and 190, below.   [3] Shansi ?.—A.J.T.
[4] See V. C (i) (c) 2, p. 141, above.—A.J.T.   [5] Hu Shih, op. cit., pp. 30–1.

in a famous description, in the Acts of the Apostles, of how the Roman Governor of the province of Achaia behaved when the Jewish community at Corinth hailed Paul, the Apostle of Christ, before his judgement-seat,

'saying· "This fellow persuadeth men to worship God contrary to the Law". And, when Paul was now about to open his mouth, Gallio said unto the Jews: "If it were a matter of wrong or wicked lewdness, O ye Jews, reason would that I should bear with you; but, if it be a question of words and names and of your law, look ye to it; for I will be no judge of such matters". And he drave them from the judgment-seat. Then all the Greeks took Sosthenes, the chief ruler of the synagogue, and beat him before the judgment-seat. And Gallio cared for none of those things.'[1]

Yet this Marcus Annaeus Gallio, who has so strangely acquired a reflected fame from a wandering Jew who happened to cross the Roman administrator's path when Gallio was Proconsul of Achaia, had a brother named Lucius Annaeus Seneca who is justly famous in his own right as a philosopher; and

'Seneca is the earliest and most powerful apostle of a great moral revival. . . . He adheres formally to the lines of the old Stoic system in his moments of calm logical consistency. But, when the enthusiasm of humanity, the passion to win souls to goodness and moral truth, is upon him, all the old philosophical differences fade; the new wine bursts the old bottles. The Platonic dualism, the eternal conflict of flesh and spirit, the Platonic vision of God, nay, a higher vision of the Creator, the pitiful and loving Guardian, the Giver of all good, the Power which draws us to Himself, who receives us at death, and in whom is our eternal beatitude—these ideas, so alien to the older Stoicism, transfigure its hardness, and its cold repellent moral idealism becomes a religion. . . .'[2]

'Hardly less striking is the warmth of devout feeling which suffuses the moral teaching of Epictetus and Marcus Aurelius. They have not, indeed, abandoned the old Stoic principle that Man's final good depends on the rectitude of the will. But the Stoic sage is no longer a solitary athlete, conquering by his proud unaided strength and in his victory rising almost superior to Zeus.[3] Growing moral experience had taught humility and inspired the sense of dependence on a higher Power in sympathy with Man. No true Stoic, of course, could ever forget the divine element within each human soul which linked it with the Cosmic Soul, and through which Man might bring himself into harmony with the great polity of gods and men.[4] But somehow the Divine Power immanent in the World, from a dim cold impalpable Law or Fate or

---

[1] Acts xviii. 13–17.
[2] Dill, S.: *Roman Society from Nero to Marcus Aurelius* (London 1905, Macmillan), pp. 304–5.
[3] Cf. Luke xviii. 9, quoted on p. 544, above.—A.J.T.
[4] For the Hellenic conception of the *Cosmopolis* see V. C (i) (d) 7, Annex, vol. vi, pp. 332–8, below.—A.J.T.

impersonal force, slowly rounds itself off into a Being, if not apart from Man, at any rate his superior, his Creator and Guardian, nay, in the end, his Father, from whom he comes, to whom he returns at death. . . .[1]

'We are now on the threshold of another world from which many voices were coming to the age of Plutarch.[2] After Philosophy has done its utmost to mould the life of sixty or seventy years into a moral harmony, with its music in itself, the effort ends in a melancholy doubt. The precept of Seneca and Plutarch, that you should live under the tutelary eye of some patron sage of the past, revealed a need of exterior help for the virtuous will. The passion for continued existence was sobered by the sense of continued moral responsibility and the shadow of a judgement to come. Vistas of a supernatural world opened above the struggling human life on Earth and in far mysterious distances beyond. When Philosophy had done its utmost to heal the diseases of Humanity, it was confronted with another task: to give Man a true knowledge of God and assurance of His help in This World and the Next. . . .[3]

'Some may think this a decline from the lofty plane of the older school. The answer is that the earlier effort to find salvation through pure reason in obedience to the law of the Whole,[4] although it may have been magnificent, was not a working religion for Man as he is constituted. The eternal involution of Spirit and Matter in the old Stoic creed, the cold impersonal unknowable Power which under whatever name—Law, Reason, Fate, Necessity—permeates the Universe, necessarily exclude the idea of design, of providence, of moral care for Humanity. The unknown Power which claims an absolute obedience has no aid or recognition for his worshipper. The monism of the old Stoics breaks down. The human spirit, in striving to realize its unity with the Universal Spirit, realizes with more and more intensity the perpetual opposition of Matter and Spirit, while it receives no aid in the conflict from the Power which ordains it; it "finds itself alone in an alien world". The true Stoic has no real object of worship.'[5]

In the spiritual experience of Hellenic souls the yearning after God which suffused this latter-day Stoicism with a warm religious glow had already found expression, six hundred years earlier—before the age of growth had ended in a breakdown—in the deliberately manufactured religion of Orphism;[6] and within the

---

[1] Dill, op. cit., pp. 390–1.
[2] For Plutarch's contribution to the pious work of suffusing Hellenic philosophy with religion—and with superstition and demonology in the same breath—see Seeck, O.: *Geschichte des Untergangs der Antiken Welt*, vol. iii, 2nd ed. (Stuttgart 1921, Metzler), pp. 150–2. 'Among the pagan men of learning who deserve the name, he [Plutarch] is the first to renounce completely the ideal of researching, without prejudice, into the Truth, and to turn Philosophy, unconditionally, into a missionary of Faith.'—A.J.T.
[3] Dill, op. cit., pp. 416–17.
[4] A modern Western presentation of the philosophy of 'Holism' will be found in General J. C. Smuts' *Holism and Evolution*, 2nd ed. (London 1927, Macmillan).—A.J.T.
[5] Dill, op. cit., p. 391. Compare the passage quoted from the same author and work in V. C (i) (d) 5, pp. 436–7, above.
[6] See V. C (i) (c) 2, pp. 84–7, above.

next two hundred years, at the hour of sunset, the glow was to flare out for one fleeting moment into the gorgeous colours of Neoplatonism.

In another context[1] we have already seen a corresponding metamorphosis overtaking the Indic philosophy of Buddhism and changing it into the 'higher religion' of the Mahāyāna.

'The Buddhas and Bodhisattvas are conceived as mighty beneficent beings rivalling the gods of the surrounding Hinduism. They may not have been conceived as gods in the sense of the ultimate reality of things; but popular thought was not concerned with such problems. It sought objects of worship, and it found them in the Buddhas and Bodhisattvas. . . . The element of devotion (*bhakti*)[2] was thus introduced into Buddhism. . . . In the popular mode of expression the *Tathāgata* does manifest himself. He does so "when men have become unbelieving, unwise, ignorant, careless, fond of sensual pleasures". In the same way the god Krishna in the *Bhagavadgītā*[3] says: "Whenever there is a decay of righteousness and a rising of unrighteousness, then I emanate myself. In order to save the good and to destroy evil-doers, to establish righteousness I am born from age to age." The actual historical relations between Buddhism and Krishnaism or Vaishnavism are not known, but here we have popular Mahāyāna Buddhism conforming exactly to the beliefs of contemporary Hinduism. . . . The Buddha has become an eternal being and an object of worship not differing in powers or qualities from the gods of the rival religions.'[4]

It was in this hardly recognizable form of a 'higher religion' appealing to the Proletariat that the Mahāyāna made its subsequent conquest of the Sinic World,[5] and at the same time stimulated the Sinic philosophy of Taoism to enter into competition with it after accomplishing a similar metamorphosis.[6]

In this phase of suffusion with religious feeling the philosophies of the Dominant Minority show themselves capable of rising, in their highest flights, within range of those heights of spiritual sublimity that are attained by the religions which spring from the bosom of the Internal Proletariat. There are passages in Seneca's philosophical works that are so arrestingly reminiscent of passages in the Epistles of Saint Paul that some of the less critical-minded Christian theologians of a later age have duplicated Philo's conceit of Plato's debt to Moses, and have allowed themselves to imagine that the Roman philosopher was in correspondence with the Christian missionary. Such conjectures are as superfluous as they are improbable; for, after all, there is nothing to surprise us in

---

[1] In V. C (i) (c) 2, pp. 133–6, above.   [2] See V. C (ii) (c) 2, p. 135, above.—A.J.T.
[3] *Bhagavadgītā*, iv, 7, 8.
[4] Thomas, E. J.: *The History of Buddhist Thought* (London 1933, Kegan Paul), pp. 178 and 184–5.
[5] See V. C (i) (c) 2, pp. 139–46, above.   [6] See V. C (i) (c) 2, pp. 146–7, above.

these harmonies of tone between two pieces of spiritual music
which were the fruits of the same social experience and the products of the same age—albeit in different souls. On this common
ground between the Dominant Minority and the Internal Proletariat, at a certain moment, Seneca stands on a level with Paul,
as, at another moment and on different ground which is common
to the Dominant Minority and the External Proletariat, Aetius
matches Theodoric;[1] and this is only what we should expect. On
the other hand it is not only extremely surprising, but also deeply
disconcerting, to find that the parallel which we have just drawn
continues to run true in the sequel. We have seen[2] that the military guardian of the physical frontiers of a universal state does not
succeed in making a stable combination of the barbarian's virtues
with his own. When once he has let himself begin to 'go barbarian',
he cannot check his course at some optimum point of his own
choosing midway, but runs on willy-nilly till he reaches a full stop
in a barbarism that is unmitigated. Worse still, he drags down
again, with him, his barbarian 'opposite number' who had been
making notable headway in the direction of civilization under the
frontiersman's earlier influence. This melancholy history of the
limitaneus whose duty lies in holding the physical frontiers of
the Dominant Minority's domain against an outer darkness has
a parallel, which is still more tragic, in the history of the philosopher whose mission is to hold frontiers that are spiritual against
a darkness arising from within. The philosophies of the Dominant
Minority blossom into Religion at one moment only to rankle into
Superstition at the next.

'Up to this point [in Hellenic history] all progress in religious thought
had proceeded from the highest circles of Society and of the life of the
Spirit; the Oriental worships, on the other hand, pushed their way up
from the dregs of the populace. In Rome the first initiates of Isis had
been roués and whores; the gospels of the Great Mother and of
Mithras had found their apostles in slaves, pirates and common
soldiers. "The extermination of the élite"[3] made itself felt in the religious sphere too; and here its consequence was that the leadership in
matters of Religion was no longer retained by those who had a claim
to it in virtue of their greater maturity in culture, and that the lower
classes and the spiritual paupers forced their superstition upon the
higher social strata. It would be nearer the truth to say that these latter
themselves sank lower and lower, and, in thus sinking, gradually reverted to the lower religious level of their underlings. Even Philosophy,
which once upon a time had tolerated the popular religion, *de haut en
bas*, solely as a crutch for cripples, now saturated itself with this popular

---

[1] See V. C (i) (*d*) 6 (α), pp. 471-3, above.   [2] In loc. cit.
[3] This terrible phrase of Seeck's—'die Ausrottung der Besten'—has been quoted
already in IV. C (ii) (*b*) 1, vol. iv, pp. 62-3, above.—A.J.T.

religion and soon found its mission in either defending or explaining the very thing which, once upon a time, Philosophy itself had undermined.'[1]

A tendency which thus displays itself throughout the whole field of the religious life of a Hellenic Society in disintegration can also be seen uniformly at work at different geographical points and at different social levels. It can be observed, for example, on Syrian ground under a Hellenic political régime, in the evolution of an Oriental religion which has surpassed all its sisters and rivals in historical interest and importance through its having given birth to Christianity.

'The double-edged ambiguity of the new development [in Judaism] declares itself at once in the fact that here, as in Zoroastrianism, it flings the doors wide open for the entry of Demonology, Superstition and Magic. It fills the World with spirits, whose nature and operation, as well as their names, it strives to apprehend more and more exactly; it sees everywhere the operation of supernatural powers, rejects the rational comprehension of the understanding, and puts in its place the mystical intuition of a spiritually unbalanced sensibility and phantasy, which then—and this is the most disastrous step of all—is paradoxically reduced to an absurd system by the application of the most hard-headed logic. Hereby the "Wisdom" of the learned is perverted into its own opposite, and the road is blocked against the acquisition of any genuinely scientific knowledge. This is the course of development through which all advanced religions (*fortgeschrittene Religionen*) have passed— the Egyptiac religion in ever increasing measure since the fiasco of Ikhnaton's monotheistic reformation, and not only the Egyptiac religion but likewise the Babylonic (under the tyranny of Astrology),[2] the Persian religion of the Magi, the Indian religions, and in Hellas the mystery religions (this development is already under way in Hesiod) and Orphism, and thereafter, since the beginning of the reaction against the Enlightenment, Neopythagoreanism and Philosophical Eclecticism. Everywhere we find an increase in the moral depth of Religion going hand in hand with a relapse into the most primitive forms of Religion, forms that have long since been completely transcended.'[3]

Thus, in Hellenic history, the philosophies of the Dominant Minority and the religions of the Internal Proletariat gradually approach one another until at length they contrive to meet on the common ground of Superstition.

In tracing the nemesis of the self-idolization of Athens we have already been witnesses of the portentous spectacle of latter-day Athenian professors of philosophy stooping to practise out of school the primitive arts of the rain-making magician;[4] and, if we

---

[1] Seeck, O.: *Geschichte des Untergangs der Antiken Welt*, vol. iii, 2nd ed. (Stuttgart 1921, Metzler), p. 138.   [2] See V. C (i) (*c*) 1, pp. 56-7, above.—A.J.T.
[3] Meyer, E.: *Ursprung und Anfänge des Christentums*, vol. ii (Stuttgart and Berlin 1921, Cotta), pp. 118-19. Cf. pp. 357-8.
[4] See IV. C (iii) (*c*) 2 (α), vol. iv, pp. 271-2, above.

now examine the activities of these Hellenic philosophers' Sinic counterparts at a corresponding stage in the disintegration of the Sinic Civilization we shall receive a second shock in seeing these Confucian sages of the last two centuries B.C. making precisely the same exhibition of themselves as the Attic Neoplatonists of the fifth century of the Christian Era.

'It was in . . . an atmosphere of occultism and superstition that Confucianism was elevated to be the orthodox system of teaching in the [Han] Empire. It was impossible for Confucianism and for the Confucian scholars to escape from the contagious influence of this tremendously powerful atmosphere of the popular superstitions. Indeed, a number of the great Confucianists never attempted to escape from it. Mencius once remarked that Confucius was a timely sage. Confucianism, too, was always a timely system of teaching; it always caught up the fashions of the age. Shu-sen Tung, who was the real founder of [the] Confucianism of the Han Empire, was described by his own disciples as a sage that knew what the time needed. The same may be said of a number of the leading Confucianists of the age. Tung Chungshu, the greatest representative of Confucian thought of the [Han] Dynasty, was well known in history for his method of praying for rain—which consisted in closing all southern gates of the city and forbidding all use of fire while our Confucian philosopher stood on the northern gate spraying the passers-by with drops of water.[1] Another great scholar of the Confucian School, Liu Hsiang, was an alchemist believing in the possibility of converting base metals into gold through the magic intervention of spirits; and he was once sentenced to death on the charge that he had deceived the Emperor Hsuanti (*imperabat* 73–49 B.C.) with his alchemical forgeries.

'It is to be expected that the New Confucianism established under the patronage of a ruler of such multifarious and insatiable credulity and under the leadership of such equally credulous scholars—this New Confucianism should be a great synthetic religion into which were fused all the elements of popular superstition and state worship, rationalized somewhat in order to eliminate a few of the most untenable elements, and thinly covered up under the guise of Confucian and pre-Confucian classics in order to make them appear respectable and authoritative. In this sense the New Confucianism of the Han Empire was truly the national religion of China. It was a great conglomeration of popular beliefs and practices of the time through a thin and feeble process of rationalization. . . . One may easily see that the New Confucianism of the Han Empire was quite different from the agnostic humanism of Confucius or the democratic political philosophy of Mencius. . . .

'The whole religious and intellectual atmosphere, even in the highest quarters of nobility and royalty, was primitive and crudely supersti-

---

[1] Another activity of Tung Chung-shu's was the interpretation of the prodigies recorded in the annals of history as evidence for the sympathy between the workings of Physical Nature and the vicissitudes of human affairs (see Granet, M.: *La Pensée Chinoise* (Paris 1934, Renaissance du Livre), pp. 579–80).—A.J.T.

tious. It was but natural that the New Confucianism which was patronized and nurtured in this environment should take on much that was primitive and crudely superstitious. It frankly discarded the naturalistic philosophy of a previous age which had been accepted by such prominent Confucian thinkers as Hsün-tse. It frankly rejected the agnosticism of Confucius himself and openly took a theistic position similar to that of the school of Mo Ti, whom the earlier Confuci[an] philosophers had condemned. These New Confucianists of Han believed that they knew the will of God and were capable of interpreting [the] hidden meaning of all its manifestations in Heaven and on Earth. They believed in magic and practised alchemy. They borrowed their methodology from the astrologers and spent their lives in trying to interpret the significance of physical catastrophes and anomalies by means of historical and scriptural analogies. Yet, for all that, we must forgive them. These Confucian scholars were children of an environment which alone was responsible for their primitiveness and crudity.'[1]

These rank weeds of Superstition which sprang up and choked a senile Confucianism as well as a senile Neoplatonism have also been the death of the Mahāyāna;[2] and in the Westernized Great Society of the present day no open-eyed observer will fail to detect symptoms of similar things to come. Already our Natural Science can be seen sprouting into 'Christian Science' and our psychical research into 'Spiritualism' and our comparative study of religions into 'Theosophy'. And, if the Marxian version of Hegelianism succeeds in holding its ground—either in its present posture of an oecumenical faith or even in the more modest role of a distinctive way of life for the peoples of the Soviet Union—we may foresee that the 'red line' which has already run from Hegel through Marx to Lenin will be continued (like the Platonic 'Golden Chain' that once upon a time ran through the sceptics Arcesilaus and Carneades to the medicine-man Proclus) in successors who, in entire good faith, will interpret their Marxian dogma and develop their Marxian practice into shapes which the Fathers of the Communist Church would perhaps hardly be able to recognize as any legacy of theirs if they were one day to revisit the Earth for an inspection of the results of their labours.[3]

Such is the miserable end of the philosophies of the Dominant

---

[1] Hu Shih, op. cit., pp. 34–5, 39, and 40.

[2] The classic Mahayanian sutra that bears the title of *The Lotus of the True Doctrine* includes a chapter on spells as well as a statement of the abstruse metaphysical doctrine of the Void (see Thomas, op. cit., pp. 184 and 186). In the sequel it has been the matter of chapter 21 of *The Lotus*, and not that of chapter 15, that has pervaded the consciousness and attracted the interest of most of the latter-day adherents of a Mahayanian universal church. This sutra was taken as the holy scripture of one of those popular forms of the Mahāyāna that were put into currency among a Japanese internal proletariat after the breakdown of the Far Eastern Civilization in Japan and the onset of a Japanese 'Time of Troubles' (see V. C (i) (c) 2, p. 101, above).

[3] For the inspiration and evolution of Communism see also V. C (i) (c) 2, pp. 177–87, above.

Minority, and this even when they have striven with all their might
to win their way on to that kindlier proletarian spiritual soil that is
the seed-bed of the 'higher religions'. It profits these philosophies
nothing that they, too, have at last broken into flower when this
tardy and reluctant flowering revenges itself upon them by degenerating almost at once into an unhealthy and enervating luxuriance.
In the last act of the dissolution of a civilization the philosophies
finally dry up and wither away, while the 'higher religions' keep
alive and in consequence become the defunct philosophies' residuary legatees, with an undisputed claim upon the Future. In a
dissolving Hellenic World Christianity survived and succeeded to
Neoplatonism (which found no elixir of life in discarding the
rationality of Stoicism). In a dissolving Indic World Hinduism
similarly survived and succeeded to the Mahāyāna (which could
not keep Buddhism alive on its native Indian ground by throwing
to the winds the sobriety of the Hīnayāna).[1] And in a dissolving
Sinic World a Mahāyāna which had succeeded in completing its
metamorphosis from an esoteric philosophy into a popular religion
in the course of a long and roundabout journey from the Ganges
to the Yellow River through a Helleno-Syriac corridor,[2] encountered at its Sinic goal a Taoism that knew how to emulate the
Mahāyāna's peculiar *tour de force* of transmuting itself from a
philosophy into a religion[3] without requiring the Mahāyāna's
special stimulus of being driven to wander in an alien wilderness
beyond the pale of its native social environment. The result was
that on Sinic ground these two new popular religions with philosophic antecedents which they had both of them succeeded in
living down now triumphantly divided between them the heritage
of a Confucianism that had failed, after all, to season itself by the
sordid device of steeping its Master's sovereign common sense in
a mud-bath of vulgar Superstition.

This empirical survey, brief though it be, will perhaps have
sufficed to bring out the apparent truth that, when philosophies
and religions meet, the religions must increase while the philosophies must decrease;[4] and we cannot turn away from our study
of the encounter between these respective spiritual discoveries of
the Internal Proletariat and the Dominant Minority without
pausing to look into the question why it is that this defeat of the
philosophies is—as history testifies—a foregone conclusion.

What, then, are the weaknesses that doom Philosophy to dis-

[1] For this victory of Hinduism over Buddhism—even as travestied in the most
extreme of the divers Hinduistic metamorphoses of the Indic philosophy—see V. C
(i) (c) 2, pp. 136–9, above.
[2] See II. D (vi), Annex, vol. ii, p. 405, footnote 1, and V. C (i) (c) 2, in the present
volume, pp. 133–46, above.   [3] See V. C (i) (c) 2, pp. 146–7, above.   [4] John iii. 30.

comfiture when it enters the lists as a rival to Religion? The fatal and fundamental weakness, from which all the rest derive, is a lack of spiritual vitality.

'The geometry of the Ancients[1] was able to provide particular problems with solutions which look like anticipatory applications of our [modern Western] general methods. But it was not able to extract these methods themselves, because it had not the *élan* that could make the jump from statics to dynamics. The Ancients had simply pushed to the extreme limit a simulation of dynamics in static terms. We receive an impression of the same kind when we compare the doctrine of the Stoics . . . with Christian morality. The Stoics proclaimed themselves citizens of the World, and they added that all men are brothers because they are all children of the same God. These were almost the same words [as those of the Christian Gospel]; but they did not find the same echo, because they were not spoken with the same accent. The Stoics set some magnificent examples. If they did not succeed in drawing Mankind after them, that was because Stoicism is essentially a philosophy. The philosopher who is taken with a doctrine of such loftiness, and who puts himself into it, does, no doubt, lend life to it by practising it— as Pygmalion's love breathed life into the marble that had already been carved into a statue. But it is a far cry from Pygmalion's love to the enthusiasm which propagates itself from soul to soul without limit, like a conflagration.'[2]

This lack of *élan* lames Philosophy in two ways. On the one hand it diminishes its attractiveness for the mass of Mankind, and on the other hand it discourages the minority to whom it does appeal from throwing themselves into the task of converting their fellows.

One manifest secondary weakness is the proneness of Philosophy to provide for the Intellect out of all proportion to its provision for the other faculties of the Soul.

'The warning voice had sounded out clear to the World and was heard through all the places where men disputed and reasoned; the four hundred volumes of Hasdrubal-Cleitomachus, the compact effective arguments of Aenêsidêmus, the penetrating irony of Lucian, all these things were there, palpable and audible, during the centuries when the determination of the people of the Graeco-Roman World slowly matured to put themselves under the authority of a new dogma. Men did not answer the Sceptical arguments: they simply went past them, turned their backs upon them. Why was this? Why was the logic of the Sceptics impotent to arrest this movement of the Human Spirit? I think that, as we look at the history more closely, we see why. . . . There was one respect in which the Sceptical Philosophy hopelessly broke down; it broke down just where all Agnosticism must break down, before the exigencies of Life—before the fact that Man is not

[1] i.e. the Hellenes.—A.J.T.
[2] Bergson, H.: *Les Deux Sources de la Morale et de la Religion* (Paris 1932, Alcan), p. 58.

only a spectator of Reality but a maker of it. If we were minds suspended in Space merely watching what went on, we might well, so far as I can see, take the advice of the Sceptic to hold back from all belief; we might simply wait and see what happened. But we have to act, to-day and to-morrow and all the days to come. It was, when all was said and done, because men wanted guidance for action that they turned, in spite of all [that] the Sceptics could urge, to dogmatic systems—to Stoicism, to Epicureanism, and later on to Neoplatonism and the Church. There was an imperious need which the dogmatic systems set out to supply, and which Scepticism could neither supply nor set aside.'[1]

Another secondary weakness of Philosophy as a rival to Religion is the proneness of Philosophy to address itself to an intellectual *élite* within the Dominant Minority and to deliver its message in the elaborate and sophisticated terms which will commend it to these cultivated minds, but which, by the same token, will hardly be understanded of the people at large, outside this narrow circle.[2] Alexander's vision of the unity of Mankind[3] effaced the ancient division between Hellenes and Barbarians without exorcizing the spirit of exclusiveness itself from the souls of the Hellenic dominant minority; and a spirit which had been quelled in one quarter promptly found vent in another direction.

[1] Bevan, E.: *Stoics and Sceptics* (Oxford 1913, Clarendon Press), pp. 140–2. In the light of this Hellenic example an analogous course of spiritual development in the modern Western World has been predicted by Spengler, O.: *Der Untergang des Abendlandes*, vol. i (Munich 1920, Beck), pp. 608–9:

'I declare it in advance: this current century, which has been the epoch of scientific-critical Alexandrianism, will not have passed without having seen [the Western Soul] outlive its will to win victories for Science. European Science is on the road towards a self-annihilation through a refinement of the intellect. First (in the 18th century) we tested the resources of Science, and then (in the 19th century) its power; at the end of the story, to-day, we are seeing through its historical role. From Scepticism there is a path that leads to "the Second [Bout of] Religiosity"—the religiosity of the dying mammoth-cities (*Weltstädte*), of that morbid inner life that comes, not before a culture, but after a culture, bringing a touch of warmth to wizzened souls, as was done by the Oriental religions in latter-day Rome.'

While it remains to be seen whether Spengler's proleptic analogy between the respective spiritual histories of the Hellenic and the Western World is to be justified by the event, the rebound from scepticism into credulity which Mr. Bevan has observed in the course of Hellenic history has a Sinic parallel which is likewise already an accomplished fact. The occultism and the superstition to which the Confucian philosophy abandoned itself in the Imperial Age of the Han Dynasty (see pp. 555–6, above) followed hard upon the heels of the esotericism and the scepticism that had been the distinguishing marks of the Confucianism of the philosopher Hsün-tse (see Hackmann, H.: *Chinesische Philosophie* (Munich 1937, Reinhardt), p. 202; and Granet, M.: *La Pensée Chinoise* (Paris 1934, Rennaissance du Livre), p. 579).

[2] The spirit of intellectual exclusiveness which inspired the Hellenic philosophy from the outset is pithily expressed in the notice which is said to have been inscribed over the gate of the Academy: Μηδεὶς ἀγεωμέτρητος εἰσίτω (Tsetzes: *Chiliades*, Book VIII, l. 973). With this Platonic warning we may contrast the Christian boast: ἔξεστι γὰρ τῷ καθ᾿ ἡμᾶς πολιτευομένῳ καὶ ἄνευ γραμμάτων φιλοσοφεῖν· . . . κοινὴ γὰρ ἁπάντων τῶν ἀνθρώπων τῶν γε ἑλομένων ἡ σωφροσύνη (Clement of Alexandria: *Stromata*, Book IV, chap. 8, § 58, quoted by Meyer, E.: *Ursprung und Anfänge des Christentums*, vol. iii (Stuttgart and Berlin 1923, Cotta), p. 539, footnote 1). These are the words of an Alexandrian Greek Father of the Church who had made it his life-work to express Christianity in terms of Hellenic philosophy.

[3] See V. C (i) (*d*) 7, vol. vi, pp. 6–10, below.

'The distinction between Hellenes and Barbarians is translated into one between the cultivated and the uncultivated; and the cultivated alone—to the exclusion of the residual masses—are qualified for attaining to the correct apprehension of the truth, and this only if they have genuinely achieved, to perfection, the inward education of the spirit.'[1]

This intellectual exclusiveness was not purged out of the Hellenic philosophy by its latter-day suffusion with Religion.

'The gospel of philosophy expounded by Seneca was rather an esoteric or aristocratic creed. With all his liberal sentiment, his cosmopolitanism, his clear conception of human equality and brotherhood, Seneca always remains the director of souls like his own, enervated by wealth, tortured with the ennui of jaded sensibility, haunted by the terror of the Caesars. Indeed, Stoicism was always rather a creed for the cultivated upper class than for the crowd. In its prime its apparatus of logical formulae, its elaborate physics and metaphysics, its essentially intellectual solution of the problems both of the Universe and [of] human life, necessarily disabled it from ever developing into a popular system. . . . In the first century [of the Christian Era] Stoicism came to be much more a religion than a philosophy or even a theology. Its main business, as conceived by men like Seneca, is to save souls from the universal shipwreck of character caused by the capricious excesses of luxury, the idolatry of the world and the flesh, which sprang from a riotous pride in the material advantages of imperial power, without a sobering sense of duty or a moral ideal. But, in the nature of things, this wreck of character was most glaringly seen among the men who were in close contact with the half insane masters of the World in the first century, and who possessed the resources to exhaust the possibilities of pleasure or the capacities of the senses to enjoy. It is to people of this class who still retained some lingering instincts of goodness—weary with indulgence, bewildered and tortured by the conflict of the lower nature with the weak but still disturbing protests of the higher—that Seneca addresses his counsels.'[2]

It will be seen that, in the Hellenic case, the approach of Philosophy towards Religion which began to declare itself openly in Seneca's day was not accompanied in the narrow circle of the elect by any serious practical attempt to bring the philosopher's esoteric creed within the mental range of a wider public which was likewise hungering for spiritual bread; and this ominous failure of the latter-day Hellenic philosopher's new faith in a supramundane Power to express itself in new works of charity towards the semi-convert's fellow human beings is perhaps, after all, not surprising; for by this time the tradition of intellectual, and even

---

[1] Meyer, E.: *Ursprung und Anfänge des Christentums*, vol. iii (Stuttgart and Berlin, 1923, Cotta), p. 325.
[2] Dill, S.: *Roman Society from Nero to Marcus Aurelius* (London 1905, Macmillan), pp. 334-5.

social, exclusiveness had become deeply ingrained in the practice of all the Hellenic schools of philosophy, with the honourable exception of the Cynics.[1] In the pre-Senecan generation of Augustus the cultivated poet Horace could write without any prick of compunction or fear of bringing odium on himself:

> Odi profanum vulgus et arceo;
> favete linguis: carmina non prius
> audita Musarum sacerdos
> virginibus puerisque canto.[2]

And a contemporary man of science has expressed the same sentiment in even more brutal language.

'A rabble of women and promiscuous vulgarians cannot be induced to answer to the call of Philosophic Reason if you are wanting to lead them into piety and holiness and faith. In dealing with people of that sort, you cannot do without Superstition; and Superstition, in its turn, has to be fed with fairy-tales and hocus-pocus.'[3]

This inhuman prescription of the Hellenic Enlightenment for giving the Proletariat a stone in lieu of bread[4] stands in diametrical opposition to the lord's injunction to the servant in a parable[5] which was soon to be disseminated through the Hellenic World in the scriptures of the Christian Church:

'Go out into the highways and hedges and compel them to come in, that my house may be filled.'[6]

The contrast is presented in the following terms by a modern Western master of the subject:[7]

'The difference of individualities is recognized by Christianity too: "Many be called, but few chosen."[8] Here, however, the differentiating

---

[1] For this exception see Seeck, O.: *Geschichte des Untergangs der Antiken Welt*, vol. iii, 2nd ed. (Stuttgart 1921, Metzler), pp. 68–9.

[2] Horace: *Carmina*, Book III, carm. i, ll. 1–4.

[3] Strabo: *Geographica*, Book I, ch. 8, p. 19: οὐ γὰρ ὄχλον γε γυναικῶν καὶ παντὸς χυδαίου πλήθους ἐπαγαγεῖν λόγῳ δυνατὸν φιλοσόφῳ καὶ προσκαλέσασθαι πρὸς εὐσέβειαν καὶ ὁσιότητα καὶ πίστιν, ἀλλὰ δεῖ καὶ δεισιδαιμονίας· τοῦτο δ' οὐκ ἄνευ μυθοποιίας κα ἰτερατείας. Compare the passage of Polybius quoted in V. C (i) (d) 6 (δ), Annex, pp. 646–7, below. This tendency towards intellectual exclusiveness on the part of the cultivated *élite* of the Hellenic World also comes to light in a philological observation made in the second century of the Christian Era by the Latin scholar Aulus Gellius, who points out (*Noctes Atticae*, Book XIII, chap. 16) that the Latin word 'humanitas' is used in the meaning, not of the Greek word φιλανθρωπία, but of the Greek word παιδεία: 'Qui verba Latina fecerunt . . . "humanitatem" non id esse voluerunt quod vulgus existimat quodque a graecis φιλανθρωπία dicitur . . . sed "humanitatem" appellaverunt id propemodum quod Graeci παιδείαν vocant, nos eruditionem institutionemque in bonas artes dicimus.' That is to say, a word which, in virtue of its origin and its literal meaning, ought to stand for something which unites a cultivated man with the mass of his fellow men, has come to stand for something which distinguishes and divides him from them.

[4] Matt. vii. 9 = Luke xi. 11.

[5] Luke xiv. 15–24; cf. Matt. xxii. 1–14. This parable has been cited already, as an illustration of the phenomenon of περιπέτεια, in IV. C (iii) (c) 1, vol. iv, p. 247, above.

[6] Luke xiv. 23.

[7] Meyer, E.: *Ursprung und Anfänge des Christentums*, vol. iii (Stuttgart and Berlin 1923, Cotta), pp. 325–6.

[8] Matt. xx. 16, and xxii. 14.

factor is not the intellect and not the individual's own ability, but is the divine grace; and for precisely this reason the preaching of the word is addressed in principle to the whole of Mankind, and in the first place to the middle and lower, and not to the upper, strata of Civilized Society—to those uncultivated and simple souls which are neither born nor bred to pass a logical judgement or to acquire a philosophical apprehension of the truth, but which follow the obscure drift of their sensibilities and are for that reason accessible to the πνεῦμα. To these circles Christianity offers something which neither the philosopher nor the Cynic preacher of "moral uplift" can offer to them, and that is a firm foundation for Life and Thought. This foundation is won through Faith: that is, through an acceptance, without reservation, of the revelation that is preached to them, however strange —and, to cultivated minds, nonsensical—its contents may appear to be. A further condition is their willing submission to the divine authority which is showing compassion on them. This is nothing less than a denial of everything that is of the essence of philosophical thought and of its spiritual freedom. The ideal of Philosophy is the sage who relies on himself; the ideal of Christianity is the believer who sinks himself in God.'[1]

The first penalty that an enlightened Hellenic dominant minority had to pay for its spiritual frigidity was the loss of its moral and material power.

'The leadership slips out of the hands of the cultivated class because they have lost the power to fulfil the tasks with which they are confronted. They have nothing more to offer to the world: intellectual life founders in the trifling business of rhetoric, government is abandoned to the professional civil servants, while, as for the sword, they have let it pass out of their hands and have shuffled off the duty of military service—which in their eyes is unworthy of a cultivated world which attends to its affairs in peace—on to the shoulders of the culturally lowest strata of the population and eventually on to those of mercenaries recruited from beyond the frontiers. The rise of the religious movement and the victory of Christianity is merely the reverse side of the unlimited extension of the military régime since the days of Severus and Caracalla, and after them the Illyrians, in the third century. The state moulded by Augustus had been based on the conception that the upper classes had a vocation to bear rule; as and when these upper classes fail, the decision falls into the hands of the gross, loutish masses; and

---

[1] 'Here we touch the really decisive point of difference. Philosophy is a movement that comes from above and that is the offspring of the Enlightenment, of the emancipation of the Spirit from the traditional ideas of Religion and of the social heritage (*des Herkommens*); and for this reason Philosophy is in principle unbelieving; it begins with doubt, and this doubt then leads, through scrutiny, either to a complete rational system of knowledge of the World and of Man, or else to scepticism. Christianity, on the other hand, like all the other phenomena of the same order, is a movement that comes from below and that is the offspring of Religion and of the ideas—to which the masses cling so obstinately—of mythical thought and of the supernatural powers, the good and the bad, with their magical properties and their arbitrary operations. For this reason these phenomena are in principle irrational and authoritarian.'

the ascendancy of the masses carries with it an ascendancy of the views and feelings by which these masses are governed (whether consciously or unconsciously) and of an intellectual and religious life that is shaped to fit the masses' needs.'[1]

At this point the *ci-devant* governing class began to hunger after the spiritual bread which they had so long and so contemptuously rejected; but their tardy repentance only served to bring down upon their heads the nemesis which the Gospel announces:

'I say unto you that none of those men which were bidden[2] shall taste of my supper.'[3]

The breath of Religion which momentarily animated the cold and clear-cut marble of the Hellenic intellect in the generations of Seneca and Epictetus rapidly staled, after the generation of Marcus, into a stuffy religiosity; and the heirs of the Hellenic philosophical tradition fell lamentably between two stools. They threw away their precious heritage of Reason without finding their way, through this supreme sacrifice, to the hearts of the masses; and in ceasing to be sages they dropped into crankiness instead of rising to sainthood.[4]

In the moribund Hellenic Society of the fourth century of the Christian Era,

'The motive that impelled Athanasius to idealize Antony was not unlike that which led Julian, the philosopher in the World, to turn from Socrates to Diogenes for his model of Philosophy out of the World. And Diogenes alone—or, let us say, the legendary Diogenes—could stand with the martyrs of the Church, as he stood with the terrible ascetics. . . .

'It might seem as if Socrates would have served such a purpose better than Diogenes, for he had in fact faced Death for his convictions and conquered its fears; but . . . the death of Socrates, as had been his life, was too calm and reasoned to satisfy the religious craving of that age. Julian might make a brave pretence of appealing to the verdict of intelligence, but at heart he was a child of his own generation, and for centuries the World had been receding farther and farther from the old hope of finding salvation in the clear conception of Truth and of what we know and do not know. The change shows itself in the eclectic merging of the various, even contradictory, sects of Philosophy, with a vein of Neopythagorean obscurantism predominating over all.[5] It is

---

[1] Meyer, op. cit., vol. cit., p. 335.

[2] This refers, of course, not to the guests who were now to be brought in from the highways and hedges, but to other guests who had accepted invitations in advance and then, at the last moment, had sent messages praying the master of the house to have them excused.—A.J.T.   [3] Luke xiv. 24.

[4] Monsieur Henri Bergson has pointed out in *Les Deux Sources de la Morale et de la Religion* (Paris 1932, Alcan), p. 249, that the saint is not afflicted with the philosopher's morbid aversion from the work of evangelizing the masses.

[5] For this merger see the present chapter, p. 534, above.—A.J.T.

notable in the waves of emotional superstition that were supplanting the humanized mythology of Olympus.[1] Most conspicuously it is seen in the victory of the Christian Faith, foretold by Saint Paul in the declaration that God hath "made foolish the wisdom of This World"[2] and verified in the exultant cry of Tertullian: [*Credibile est*] *quia ineptum est! [Certum est] quia impossibile!*[3] Over and over again we find the Fathers, even those most favourably disposed to Plato and most ready to admit that God had not left himself without a witness among the Gentiles—again and again we find them reproaching Philosophy with its inability to convert the stubborn hearts of men and to save the masses. And the Fathers were right. In whatever terms we may choose to state the fact, it is true, as Ambrose said, that "it hath not pleased God to give his people salvation in dialectic".[4] It is simply true that, in setting the emphasis so strongly upon knowledge and intelligence, and in leaving so little room for the will and the instinctive emotions, Classical Philosophy, even the Philosophy of Plato, had left the great heart of Mankind untouched.'[5]

Indeed, in this tragi-comic last act, the epigoni of Plato and

---

[1] The Olympian Faith was dead before its rival heirs broke into the Hellenic arena to fight over the corpse (see I. C (i) (a), vol. i, p. 57, and II. D (vi), vol. ii, pp. 215–16, above). 'The decay of religious feeling reveals itself most plainly of all in the fact that the oracles, which once had attained to so great a power, almost all of them gradually became extinct during the last centuries before Christ, because nobody any longer felt it worth while to consult them' (Seeck, O.: *Geschichte des Untergangs der Antiken Welt*, vol. iii, 2nd ed. (Stuttgart 1921, Metzler), p. 84).—A.J.T.

[2] 1 Cor. i. 20. See also the passages from the same chapter of the same epistle that are quoted in IV. C (iii) (c) 1, vol. iv, p. 249, above, and in V. C (i) (d) 11, vol. vi, p. 150, below.—A.J.T.

[3] Tertullian: *De Carne Christi*, 5 (Migne, J.-P.: *Patrologia Latina*, vol. ii, col. 761). The maxim of Tertullian has been popularized, but scarcely travestied, in the words: *Credo quia absurdum.*—A.J.T.

[4] Ambrose: *De Fide*, Book I, chap. 5, § 42: 'Non in dialectica complacuit Deo salvum facere populum suum.' The Milanese master's aphorism was to become his Hipponian disciple's commonplace. 'Sed forsitan dicet aliquis: "Etsi ipse humiliter natus est, in discipulorum nobilitate iactare se voluit"? Non elegit reges aut senatores aut philosophos aut oratores: immo vero elegit plebeios, pauperes, indoctos, piscatores. Petrus piscator, Cyprianus orator. Nisi fideliter praecederet piscator, non humiliter sequeretur orator'.— Augustine, *Sermo* cxcvii, fragm. 2. Cf. eundem, *Sermo* xliii, chap. 5 (apropos of 1 Cor. i. 26–8): Peter was a fisherman, not an orator, senator, or emperor; *Sermo* lxxxvii, chap. 10 (apropos of the same passage of Scripture): 'Dominus noluit prius eligere senatores, sed piscatores'; *Sermo* ccclxxxi (apropos of Psalm cxii. 7–8): 'Nisi prius eligeretur vilitas infirmorum, non sanaretur inflatio superborum'; *Enarratio in Psalmum xxxvi*, *Sermo* ii, chap. 14 (apropos of 1. Cor. i. 27): 'Et non de oratore piscatorem, sed de piscatore lucratus est oratorem, de piscatore lucratus est senatorem, de piscatore lucratus est imperatorem'; *De Civitate Dei*, Book XXII, chap. 5: 'Ineruditos liberalibus disciplinis et omnino, quantum ad istorum doctrinas attinet, impolitos, non peritos grammatica, non armatos dialectica, non rhetorica inflatos, piscatores Christus cum retibus fidei ad mare huius saeculi paucissimos misit atque ita et ex omni genere tam multos pisces et tanto mirabiliores, quanto rariores, etiam ipsos philosophos cepit.' In this matter the two fourth-century Latin fathers Saint Ambrose and Saint Augustine are supported by the nineteenth-century French prophet of the modern Western heresy of Racialism. 'Ce n'est pas l'érudition qui sauve un peuple arrivé à la décrépitude '(de Gobineau, le Comte J. A.: *Essai sur l'Inégalité des Races Humaines* (Paris 1853–5, Firmin Didot, 4 vols.), vol. i, p. 278).—A.J.T.

[5] More, P. E.: *Hellenistic Philosophies = The Greek Tradition from the Death of Socrates to the Council of Chalcedon: 399 B.C. to A.D. 451*, vol. ii (Princeton 1923, University Press), pp. 297–9. In the present Study this operation of the principle of περιπέτεια in the intellectual field is touched upon in IV. C (iii) (c) 1, vol. iv, p. 248–9, above, and in V. C (i) (d) 11, vol. vi, pp. 149–54, below.

Zeno confessed the inadequacy of their own great masters and ensamples by abandoning themselves to an imitation of the Internal Proletariat which was in very truth the sincerest flattery of this *profanum vulgus*. Nor was their imitation directed solely towards the inward êthos of the rising religions that had made their first epiphany in a proletarian environment: it was also extended, with an undiscriminating zeal, to the details and even the trivialities of these religions' external rites and organization.

'In Iamblichus—as contrasted with Plotinus and also still with Porphyry—the individual religious experience, with the whole of its inspiration, is eliminated. Its place is taken by a mystical church with sacraments, a scrupulous exactness in carrying out the forms of worship, a ritual that is closely akin to magic, and a clergy. To give all this its finishing touch Iamblichus introduces a fanaticism which in the Ancient World is something quite new. Porphyry, for example, is vehemently attacked—without regard to any merit that he may have acquired as an opponent of Christianity—because he does not seem to stand on entirely positive ground. This attitude in itself proclaims the advent of a new age. Julian's attempt to found a pagan state church has hitherto been written off as a completely isolated enterprise of the Ancient Civilization in its last phase; but this view, thus expressed, is not correct. In this field, likewise, the Roman emperor has merely executed the Syrian philosopher's design. To adapt a well-known phrase from Modern History, Julian is an Iamblichus on horseback.

'Julian's ideas about the elevation of the priesthood reproduce . . . exactly the standpoint of Iamblichus, whose zeal for the priests, for the details of the forms of worship, and for a systematic orthodox doctrine had prepared the ground for the construction of a pagan church. Julian's role is simply to develop this conception further. The project of establishing a church of this kind is thus one piece of that organic development in which the rising fervour of pagan piety expressed itself.'[1]

The accident of Julian's birth and office made it possible for the emperor-archaist momentarily to shore up the shaky structure of this would-be Neoplatonic universal church by buttressing it with the massive masonry of a not yet fallen Hellenic universal state. Yet Julian's impetuous dedication of these vast political means to that bizarre religious purpose merely served to make it plain that

> All the King's horses and all the King's men
> Could not set up Humpty-Dumpty again.[2]

[1] Geffken, J.: *Der Ausgang des griechisch-römischen Heidentums* (Heidelberg 1920, Winter), pp. 113 and 131. See also the present Study, V. C (i) (c) 2, p. 147, above; and V. C (i) (c) 2, Annex II, p. 584; V. C (i) (d) 6 (δ), Annex, pp. 680–3; and V. C (ii) (a), vol. vi, pp. 222–3, below.

[2] For a more general examination of the relations between churches and governments see V. C (i) (d) 6 (δ), Annex, below.

Julian's state-supported pagan ecclesiastical establishment collapsed in a trice at the news of the death of its Imperial architect and patron; and thereafter nothing remained of Iamblichus's grandiose dream save a pathetically futile coterie of cranks.

'The sketches of the anti-Christian Eunapius give a picture, which is as remarkable as it is vivid, of the inner life of Hellenes—both men and women—in the fourth century. The picture reveals a society of passionately religious philosophers rapt in contemplation and ecstatically absorbed in the Divine. The spirit of the age breaks out in them, almost morbidly, when they are still in their tender years. This amazing state of things seems hardly capable of being keyed up to any higher pitch; and yet it is not till the fifth century that it attains the acme of its eccentricity. No doubt the contemporary Christian Church likewise displays similar features and produces a fair number of very queer saints; but among the Christians we never find, on quite this scale, any community of people who are completely extravagant, and almost entirely engrossed in unprofitable thoughts and actions, such as we find among these late pagan philosophers who drift like sleep-walkers through a Utopian world of their own.

'The special characteristic of these representatives of Paganism is a mutual resemblance which is so close that their common psychic condition absolutely hits the observer in the eye. . . . What is the goal at which these latter-day Hellenes are aiming? It is holiness, purity, the mortification of the flesh, a union with the World of the Gods. This holiness becomes a fixed programme which is followed out with complete singleness of mind. The means employed to this end are an asceticism, an observance of special fast days, and an anchorite's existence which is filled with a constant intentness upon heavenly things. . . .

'As a genuine regard for science diminishes . . . theurgy—and the magic that is directly bound up with it—gain proportionately in prestige. . . . As the lord of Physical Nature, the philosopher makes rain like a primitive warlock, and knows how to ban an earthquake. He drives out devils through the sheer force of his personality . . . though it is true that there is a painful consciousness that this holy lore is beginning to be lost—a consciousness which inspires enthusiasm for such isolated depositories of the ancient theurgy as still survive.

'So their life is lived in a world of miracles and legends—and also of inept and undesignedly ludicrous old-wives'-tales. . . . A mystical catalepsy and a religious transport strip away all that is natural in the life of body and soul. . . . And the disappearance of all simple and natural feeling finds compensation in an accentuation of supernatural powers. . . .

'Pythagoreanism has bequeathed a legacy to this age in the participation—which becomes more and more vigorous—of female adepts in the philosophers' spiritual life. Sosipatra is followed by Hypatia, Asclepigenea, Aedesia. The mystical eccentricity of the men communicates itself to the women as a matter of course; and then the women in their turn win the men's unstinted admiration if they prove themselves receptive pupils of the theurgi and perhaps go on to practise rain-making under the cloak of "Nephelomancy", like Anthusa of Cilicia.

'The studies of these sages are naturally confined, in essentials, to Religion—apart from the acquisition of the formal sophistic accomplishments. They plunge deep into the hieratic lore of the Egyptians and tread in the footsteps of innumerable predecessors in their interpretations of the animal-worship of the Holy People; and all other known religions are laid under contribution with equal enthusiasm. Proclus, for instance, as his biographer boasts of him, was acquainted with the whole corpus of Theology, Greek and Barbarian. He addressed his prayers to Marnas of Gaza, to Aesculapius Leontuchus of Ascalon, to Theandrites the god of the Arabs, and to Isis of Philae. Hê kept the religious festivals of all nations. In his eyes the philosopher was the whole World's hierophant.'[1]

A fitting epitaph for Proclus—and not for this last of the Neoplatonists alone, but also for his Buddhist and Taoist and Confucian counterparts—is offered us in the following passage from the pen of an eminent living Western psychologist who is manifestly thinking, as he writes, of a world that is neither Julian's nor Skandagupta's[2] nor Hsuanti's,[3] but is the writer's very own:

'Great innovations never come from above; they come invariably from below, just as trees never grow from the sky downward, but upward from the earth, however true it is that their seeds have fallen from above. The upheaval of our world and the upheaval in consciousness is one and the same. Everything becomes relative and therefore doubtful; and, while Man, hesitant and questioning, contemplates a world that is distracted with treaties of peace and pacts of friendship, Democracy and Dictatorship, Capitalism and Bolshevism, his spirit yearns for an answer that will allay the turmoil of doubt and uncertainty. And it is just people of the lower social levels who follow the unconscious forces of the Psyche; it is the much-derided, silent folk of the land[4]—those who are less infected with academic prejudices than

[1] Geffken, J.: *Der Ausgang des griechisch-römischen Heidentums* (Heidelberg 1920, Winter), pp. 190–200. This picture of the last phase of Hellenism is curiously reminiscent of a description of the last phase of the abortive Scandinavian Civilization in Iceland which has been quoted in II. D (vii), vol. ii, p. 358, above.

[2] In the generation of Skandagupta (*imperabat circa* A.D. 455–80), on the eve of the break-up of an Indic universal state that had been re-established by the Gupta Dynasty after the intrusion of Hellenism upon the Indic World (see I. C (i) (b), vol. i, pp. 85–6, above), Hinduism was gaining ground, under Imperial patronage, at the expense of a Buddhism that was at the same time rapidly ceasing to be distinguishable from the rising religion that was supplanting it (see Smith, V. A.: *The Early History of India*, 3rd ed. (Oxford 1914, Clarendon Press), p. 303).

[3] For the credulity of the Han Emperor Hsuanti (*imperabat* 73–49 B.C.) see the passage quoted on p. 555, above, from a paper by Dr. Hu Shih.

[4] The same phrase is used by Meyer in the passage quoted on p. 543, above.—A.J.T.

great celebrities are wont to be. All these people, looked at from above, present mostly a dreary or laughable comedy; and yet they are as impressively simple as those Galilaeans who were once called blessed.'[1]

[1] Jung, C. G.: *Modern Man in Search of a Soul*, English translation (London 1933, Kegan Paul), pp. 243–4. Compare the quotation from Eduard Meyer in V. C (i) (d) 9 (β), vol. vi, pp. 114–15, below.

ROMAN POLICY TOWARDS PRIMITIVE PEOPLES

THE exception which proves the rule of habitual humanity in the record of the Romans' treatment of primitive peoples is their behaviour towards the Gallic natives of the lowlands between the Appennines and the Po, and the Ligurian natives of the North-West Appennine valleys, during the quarter of a century running from 197 to 173 B.C. This black chapter in the history of the Roman conquest of the European barbarians was distinguished by those acts of eviction, deportation, and extermination which we have cited above[1] as examples of the ruthlessness of the Hellenic dominant minority on the war-path. This Roman application of the policy of 'frightfulness' was, however, strictly local and temporary, and it can be accounted for as the exceptional result of a combination of special causes.[2]

In the first place the quarter of a century in question was the post-war period after the Hannibalic War, when the war-generation of the Populus Romanus was still distraught by the eighteen-years-long agony which it had just had to endure. In the second place the Romans bore a special grudge against these Gallic and Ligurian tribesmen because they had taken Hannibal's side as soon as he had appeared over the crest of the Alps, and had enlisted in his army. The tribesmen had thereby done their worst to bring about the defeat of Rome in her life-and-death struggle with an implacable adversary, and they had undoubtedly helped Hannibal materially to prolong the struggle and so to inflict that deadly wound upon the Roman body social in Italy which was his permanent legacy of revenge upon a Power that was the bane of Carthage. In the third place the Roman Government was desperately in need of lands for the resettlement of ex-servicemen who had been uprooted in formidable numbers from their homes in the Cisappennine war-zone, and who could not be replanted easily in the devastated areas. The lands which were now confiscated from Hannibal's Gallic and Ligurian confederates after the Cartha-

---

[1] In V. C (i) (c) 1, on pp. 37–8, above.

[2] The only precedent for the eviction of the Boii in 191 B.C. was the previous eviction of this tribe's kinsmen and neighbours, the Senones, in 283 B.C. This previous act of inhumanity, which was committed two generations before the outbreak of the Hannibalic War and not on the morrow of it, had no excuse. It can only be said that the Roman Government had at first made a moderate use of its victory over the Senones by founding on their territory the single *colonia Latina* of Sena Gallica as a frontier-fortress (Polybius, Book II, chap. 19). The subsequent alienation (in 232 B.C.) of all the rest of the lands of the Senones in allotments to Roman citizens was a demagogic measure which was carried through by Gaius Flaminius in the face of sharp criticism and strong opposition (Polybius, Book II, chap. 21).

ginian invader's defeat were turned to account, between 189 and 175 B.C., in order to add ten new constituent city-states[1] to the Roman Commonwealth;[2] and the residue that remained in the hands of the Roman State, after the ex-servicemen who were enrolled as citizens of these new communities had been provided with allotments on a generous scale, was divided up, in 173 B.C., into freehold homesteads for individual settlers.[3] These were the circumstances in which the four acts of inhumanity above mentioned were committed by the Roman authorities; and in this connexion there are two further points to be noted. In the first place each of the acts in question had either some excuse or some mitigation; in the second place the policy which prevailed from 197 to 173 B.C. was deliberately and effectively changed for the better in 173–172 B.C. by the active intervention of the Senate, which in this age exercised the supreme authority in the Roman body politic.

As regards the first of these two points, the confiscation of the lands of the Boii was mitigated by the restriction of this harsh measure to one half (though this, no doubt, the better half) of the tribal territory.[4] The deportation of the Apuani was mitigated by the facts that they were granted permission to take their movable property with them; that the move was financed at the cost of the Roman Treasury; that land-allotments were provided for the deportees in their new homes; and that a further Treasury grant was made to them for building and furnishing their new houses.[5] Again, the eviction of the Gallic settlers from Venetia was partly mitigated by the restoration to them of their movable property and was partly excused by the fact that they had only just arrived—and this without asking permission—from beyond the Alps;[6] while the extermination of the Ligurian 'Die-Hards' on Mounts Letus and Balista was provoked by the indefensible behaviour of the victims. (After having tendered their submission, they had revolted as soon as the Roman troops had been withdrawn; they

[1] The *coloniae Latinae* Placentia, Cremona, Bononia, Aquileia, and Luca; the *coloniae civium Romanorum* Parma, Mutina, and Luna; and the *oppida civium Romanorum* Florentia and Pistoria. Of these, Placentia and Cremona were not new foundations but restorations. They had been in process of foundation in 218 B.C., when Hannibal arrived on the scene; and the natives had seized the opportunity to wipe them out.

[2] For the system of 'dual citizenship' on which the Roman Commonwealth was constructed, and for the Roman practice of enlarging the material scale of the structure by founding new city-states on politically virgin soil. see IV. C (iii) (c) 2 (β), vol. iv, pp. 311–13, above.

[3] Livy, Book XLII, chap. 4. The individual settlers appear to have been organized into *oppida civium Romanorum* (*vici, fora, conciliabula*). Among the townships which owed their origin to the *senatusconsultum* of 173 B.C. we may probably identify Caesena, Forum Livii, Faventia, Forum Cornelii, Claterna, Tannetum, Fidentia, Florentia (a second foundation of the name, between Parma and Placentia), Forum Novum (between Parma and Luna), and Forum Druentinorum.   [4] Livy, Book XXXVI, chap. 39.

[5] Livy, Book XL, chap. 38.   [6] Livy, Book XXXIX, chaps. 22, 45, and 54.

had then attacked, plundered, and momentarily occupied the newly founded Roman colony of Mutina (Modena); and, upon the approach of a punitive force, they had carried their prisoners off with them to their mountain fastnesses and had massacred them there.)[1]

The second point—that is, the new turn given to Roman policy by the Senate in 173-172 B.C.—is an historical event of considerable interest and importance.[2]

In 173 B.C. Marcus Popillius Laenas, who was one of the two Consuls of the year, invaded, without provocation, the territory of a Ligurian tribe, the Statelli, who had never been at war with Rome; forced the tribesmen to give battle by making open preparations to attack their capital town; inflicted on them a sanguinary defeat; and then, when they surrendered unconditionally, proceeded to disarm the surviving fighting men, raze the town to the ground, and sell the whole population into slavery, besides selling up their property. When the Senate received the Consul's dispatches boasting of what he had done, they passed a strong resolution censuring him, directing him to make restitution, and recalling him from his province; and, when he showed himself contumacious and opened a second campaign against the Statelli after returning to the province as Proconsul in the following spring, the Senate brought him to heel. By refusing to transact any public business until this public scandal had been removed, they prevailed upon two Tribunes of the Plebs to propose a plebiscite—which was carried by a large majority—empowering the Senate to appoint a commissioner with authority to hold an inquiry and take disciplinary action. The Senate thereupon appointed one of the Praetors of the year; and the insubordinate Proconsul duly appeared before the Praetor's tribunal. Characteristically he was let off with this lesson and was spared—through a deliberate protraction of the judicial proceedings beyond the end of the official year—the humiliation of having sentence passed upon him (a humiliation which might have affected the prestige of the whole governing class). On the other hand effective measures were taken to make what restitution could be made to Popillius's Ligurian victims. The Senate passed a resolution instructing the magistrates of the year (172 B.C.) to liberate all enslaved Ligurians who had not borne arms against Rome since the end of the year 179 B.C.,[3] and to settle them on lands beyond

---

[1] Livy, Book XLI, chaps. 14 and 18.
[2] The story will be found in Livy, Book XLII, chaps. 7–9 and 21–2.
[3] Evidently this date was chosen in order to withhold the amnesty from the enslaved survivors of the Briniates, who had treacherously taken up arms again in 177 B.C., after having made their submission in 179 B.C. (see above).

the River Po. 'Through this resolution of the Senate many thousands of souls were restored to liberty and were transplanted to the farther side of the Po, where lands were duly allotted to them.'

This intervention of the Senate against the Consul Marcus Popillius Laenas achieved more than the redress of a single flagrant act of injustice: it gave a new turn to the policy of Rome towards primitive peoples. From that time onwards the Roman state did in truth act for the most part—at any rate in its dealings with peoples on the primitive level of culture—upon the maxim *parcere subiectis et debellare superbos*[1] which was formulated by Virgil retrospectively in words which gave an immortal expression to what had been the normal practice from 172 B.C. down to the poet's own day.

The fact that this great reform of policy was not only introduced but was also subsequently maintained is impressive when we consider that the problem of finding land for uprooted Roman citizens had by no means been solved by the land distributions at the Gauls' and Ligurians' expense between the years 197 and 173 B.C. The Hannibalic War did not merely produce a temporary economic and social disturbance which could be surmounted by emergency measures for tiding over a transitional period: the shock which it administered to the Roman body social and economic in Peninsular Italy was so profound[2] that it set in motion movements of a secular wave-length as well. There were two of these not only new but also persistent factors—namely the perpetual drafting off of Roman peasant proprietors to serve on long-drawn-out campaigns in distant war-zones overseas[3] and an irreversible revolution in economic technique which was making it profitable to buy up small peasant properties and consolidate them into vineyards, olive-yards, and cattle-ranches[4]—that were now combining to uproot the Roman peasantry from their ancestral free-holds in Peninsular Italy as ruthlessly as they had been uprooted by Hannibal's *Landsknechts*; and consequently the pressure upon the authorities to find ever new supplies of free land continued without relief. With these facts in mind we may conjecture that Popillius's undoubtedly unprovoked and apparently wanton attack upon the Statelli in 173 B.C. was a purposeful and not an aimless atrocity: in fact, that the Consul was doing what he conceived to be his public duty by manufacturing a pretext for acquiring a new,

---

[1] Virgil: *Aeneid*, Book VI, l. 853.
[2] See IV. C (ii) (a), vol. iv, pp. 48–9, with the references on p. 49, footnote 2, above.   [3] See V. C (i) (c) 2, pp. 62–3, above.
[4] For the untoward social consequences of this economic advance see III. C (i) (b), vol. iii, pp. 168–71, and V. C (i) (c) 2, in the present volume, pp. 65–7, above.

and urgently needed, reserve of public land for colonization.[1] If this conjecture is right, and if we may assume that this aspect of the issue was in the minds of the Senate and the Tribunes of the Plebs and the Plebs itself, as well as in the mind of the Consul, then we must conclude that the *senatusconsulta* and *plebiscitum* of 173–172 B.C. were extremely creditable to the Roman Government and People. The Romans were now perhaps deliberately refusing to seek, in cold blood, a solution for their own internal economic and social problem at their external proletariat's expense.

What were the historical consequences of this affair? In one sense the Romans had their reward for their virtue; for a change of policy which placed before the barbarians' eyes a hope of security in return for submission, instead of the previous fear of eviction from their ancestral lands or outright extermination, was a change which made the threat of Roman conquest a tolerable prospect, and which thus paved the way for an extension of Roman rule, in the course of the next two centuries, over hundreds of recalcitrant but not desperate or irreconcilable barbarian tribes from the Appennines and the Po to the Rhine and Atlantic and Sahara.[2] In another sense, however, the Romans paid—and paid heavily —for their deliberate and persistent refusal to confiscate the lands of the primitive peoples who came under Roman rule by conquest; for, while the Roman People's native subjects in the provinces, like the wild animals in Italy, still had some hole or lair which they could call their own, the Roman citizens who were the provincials' masters and Italy's defenders were now sinking to the condition of proletarians without a stake in the country—houseless

[1] At the moment when the first draft of this sentence was being written in July 1935, Popillius's behaviour towards the Statelli was on the point of being emulated in Signor Mussolini's policy towards the Abyssinians. It may be noted, as one of the minor curiosities of history, that the Romagnol dictator of Italy in A.D. 1935 was a native of the territory from which the Boii were evicted in 191 B.C.

[2] This statesmanlike consideration was probably in the minds of the Senate in 172 B.C., since the allotment to Roman citizens, in 232 B.C., of the residue of the land that had been confiscated in 283 B.C. from the Senones had immediately provoked the surviving Gallic tribes in the Po Basin to rise in arms against Rome and to recruit reinforcements from the Gallic backwoodsmen beyond the Alps, under the impression 'that the Romans' war-aims were no longer mere political supremacy or even domination, but had come to be nothing short of the complete eviction and extermination of their victims' (Polybius, Book II, chap. 21). In 225 B.C. the Romans had had to meet, on their own ground south of the Appennines, a torrent of invasion in which the whole of Barbarian Europe seemed to be coming down upon Italy in spate. It was no doubt the vivid memory of this disconcerting sequel to Flaminius's ruthless act that led the Senate, in 183 B.C., to send envoys to the Transalpine barbarians in order to explain the Roman Government's reasons for sending the unauthorized Gallic settlers back to their own side of the mountains (Livy, Book XXXIX, chap. 55). In the Western Society of our own age the practice and spirit which were characteristic of the Roman Government's treatment of barbarians from 172 B.C. onwards have been recaptured by the French Republic's great proconsul, Marshal Lyautey, in his dealings with the primitive Berber highlanders in the Atlas (see V. C (i) (c) 3, p. 324, footnote 2, above). At the time of writing it looked as though, in the French Zone of Morocco, the genius of a single great man had succeeded in setting upon the policy of France that lasting stamp that was set upon the policy of Rome by the action of the Senate in 173–172 B.C.

and homeless wanderers over the face of the Earth whose share in
the good things enjoyed by their fellow members of Society was
limited, now, to the air that they breathed and the sunlight that
shone impartially on the evil and on the good.[1]

This increasing host of disinherited and unemployed Roman
citizens had sooner or later to be provided for somehow; and, if
the provision was not to be made unjustly, at the expense of
primitive peoples who had thrown themselves on the mercy of
their Roman conquerors, then justice must be done by adopting
the only alternative and carving homesteads for the landless citizen
proletariat out of the state domain in Italy itself which the Roman
Government had acquired as a consequence of the Hannibalic
War. By rejecting Marcus Popillius Laenas' cynical solution of
the land-question in 172 B.C. the Senate had logically committed
itself to an eventual acceptance of the naïve solution which was
proposed by Tiberius Sempronius Gracchus forty years later.
The Gracchan solution was naïve because, during the seventy
years which had elapsed by then since Hannibal's evacuation of
Italy, a formidable vested interest in the usufruct of this state
domain had been acquired by the prosperous heirs of speculative
planters and stockmen to whom this usufruct had originally been
granted. Yet it was no policy at all to reject both, in succession,
of the only two solutions that were feasible; and accordingly the
rejection of the Gracchan alternative precipitated a revolution
which continued for a century and was only brought to an end by
the establishment of a Caesarean dictatorship.

[1] For a comparison between the λόγιον ascribed to Tiberius Gracchus in Plutarch's
Lives of the Gracchi, chap. 9, and the λόγιον ascribed to Jesus in Matt. viii. 19–20, and
Luke ix. 57–8, see IV. C (iii) (c) 3 (β), vol. iv, pp. 508 and 510, and V. C (i) (c) 2, vol. v,
pp. 70–1, above, and V. C (ii) (a), Annex II, vol. vi, p. 381, with Table VIII, logion (α),
on p. 414, below.

THE ROLE OF MANICHAEISM IN THE ENCOUNTER BETWEEN THE SYRIAC INTERNAL PROLETARIAT AND HELLENISM

IN the chapter to which this Annex attaches, we have descried in the Nestorian and Monophysite 'Diasporàs' the monuments of a second abortive attempt on the Syriac Society's part to cast Hellenism out by fighting it with its own intellectual weapons.[1] We may go on to ask ourselves whether Nestorianism and Monophysitism were the only two movements in which this attempt was made, or whether we can catch another echo of the same passage of Syriac history in the voice of Manichaeism: a Syriac religion, founded in the third century of the Christian Era, which has not survived even as a 'fossil'. This question, which we have touched upon already,[2] may occupy our attention once again for a moment in the present context.

Was it the mission of Manichaeism, too, to reclaim a Syriac spiritual treasure for the Syriac World by purging a Syro-Hellenic religious syncretism of its Hellenic alloy? We might be tempted to answer this question in the affirmative if we ventured to interpret the Manichaean Mythology[3] as a 'higher critic' reads the Book of Daniel or as a psycho-analyst explains his patient's dreams.

For example, the invasion of the realm of Light by the ruler of Darkness might be taken to signify the invasion of the Syriac World by Hellenism. The Primal Man who is brought into being by the King of Light in order to fight the Darkness might typify the Achaemenid,[4] and the Bright Elements which are his weapons might be Judaism and Zoroastrianism.[5] The stunning of Primal Man and the swallowing of the Bright Elements by the Dark Powers might describe the conquest of the Achaemenian Empire by Alexander.[6] The descent of Primal Man into the Abyss, where

---

[1] See V. C (i) (c) 2, p. 127, with footnote 3, and also I. C (i) (b), vol. i, pp. 83 and 91; I. C (iii) (b), vol. i, p. 155; II. D (v), vol. ii, p. 203; II. D (vi), vol. ii, p. 235; II. D (vii), vol. ii, pp. 286–7 and 374; and IV. C (iii) (c) 2 (β), vol. iv, pp. 325–6, above.

[2] In II. D (vii), vol. ii, p. 374, footnote 3, above.

[3] The presentation of the Manichaean Mythology which is adopted in the present Annex is that which is given in Burkitt, F. C.: The Religion of the Manichees (Cambridge 1925, University Press). See also Christensen, A.: L'Iran sous les Sassanides (Copenhagen 1936, Levin & Munksgaard), pp. 178–84.

[4] The establishment of a Syriac universal state in the shape of an Achaemenian Empire just forestalled the establishment of a Hellenic ascendancy over the Egyptiac, Syriac, and Babylonic worlds in the sixth century B.C.

[5] For the role of these two 'higher religions' of the Babylonic internal proletariat as alternative potential nuclei for a Syriac universal church see V. C (i) (c) 2, pp. 120–2, above. The number of the bright elements in the Manichaean Mythology was, however, not two but five (Christensen, op. cit., p. 179).

[6] By conquering the Achaemenian Empire in the fourth century B.C. Alexander won

he cuts the roots of the Dark Elements and thereby ensures that these shall never increase, might represent the counter-captivation of the heart of the Hellenic World by a Syriac Underworld which brings its own 'folklore',[1] own religion,[2] and own êthos with it and, by propagating these *in partibus infidelium*, overcomes the Hellenic culture in its own citadel. In the defeat and capture of the Dark Archons we might see an image of the military disasters that were inflicted on the Seleucid brothers Demetrius Nîcâtôr and Antiochus Sîdêtês[3] and on their Roman successor Crassus[4] by the Parthians. In the two problems which Light now has to solve—the walling off of the realm of Darkness and the extraction, from the captive Archons, of the particles of Light which they have swallowed—we might recognize the political problems of containing the Roman Empire within the line of the Euphrates and dismembering the Hellenic 'successor-states' of the Achaemenian Empire east of the Euphrates in order to use the recaptured territories as a building-site for the Parthian, and later for the Sasanian, Empire. In the lust which is excited in the appetites of the captive Dark Powers by the Light which is successfully extracted, we might find an allegory of the passion which Hellenic souls came to conceive for certain elements of Syriac religion when these had been 'peptonized', to suit Hellenic palates, by having been passed through a Hellenic cultural medium.[5] And the Sin which is thus incidentally produced by the process of salvaging the Light might be identified with the creation of such Syro-Hellenic religious syncretisms as Christianity and Mithraism (the latter being symbolized in the sin-dragon which falls into the sea and is slain). In the Adam who is generated by the Dark Powers as a receptacle to retain the rest of the stolen Light which the Light Powers are seeking to recapture, we might discern a portrait of the Hellenized Oriental; and when Jesus rouses Adam from his sleep and throws him into a mental agony by revealing to him the duality of his nature, we might fancy ourselves watching that Syriac reaction to Hellenism which we have detected in the Nestorian and Monophysite movements and which may perhaps be the motive of the Manichaean movement as well—a desperate reaction of the Hellenized Oriental against the dark Hellenic envelope in which his soul-spark of Syriac light has been imprisoned.

for Hellenism the Oriental dominions which it would have won for itself some two hundred years earlier if in the sixth century this prize had not been snatched, at the eleventh hour, out of the grasp of Ionian and Carian pi·ates, mercenaries, and merchants by the prowess of Cyrus, Cambyses, and Darius the Great.

[1] See V. C (ii) (*a*), Annex II, vol. vi, pp. 438–64, below.
[2] See II. D (vi), vol. ii, pp. 215–16, and V. C (i) (*c*) 2, in the present volume, pp. 81–2, above. [3] See I. C (i) (*b*), vol. i, p. 75, above.
[4] See III. C (i) (*b*), vol. iii, p. 164, and IV. C (iii) (*c*) 2 (γ), vol. iv, p. 440, above.
[5] See V. C (i) (*d*) 6 (δ), pp. 538–40, above.

Such interpretations of the Manichaean Mythology are perhaps not unprofitable exercises of the fancy; but we should be rash to take them so seriously as to conclude, on the strength of them, that Manichaeism is to be placed in the same category of Syriac religious phenomena as Monophysitism and Nestorianism.

If this tentative classification is to be confirmed, it must be shown that Manichaeism stands to Mithraism in the relation in which Nestorianism and Monophysitism both alike stand to Catholic Christianity: i.e., in the relation of a child to a parent against whom the child is in reaction. Manichaeism, however, is not the child of Mithraism; at the closest it is only its first cousin, and it may prove to be only its first cousin once removed. For the closest kinship that can be traced between Manichaeism and Mithraism is through a common Zoroastrian, or perhaps pre-Zoroastrian, element in their respective origins,[1] since Manichaeism derives from Zoroastrianism (in so far as that is its source), not through Mithraism, but direct. While Mithraism is Zoroastrianism—or, alternatively, is a pre-Zoroastrian Iranian paganism—in a Hellenic dress, Manichaeism is Zoroastrianism in a Christian dress.[2] Further, though it is true that the Christianity which Mani has incorporated into his system is the Christianity of Marcion and the Christianity of Bardesanes, and not Catholicism, it is also a fact that any form of Christianization involves some measure of Hellenization as well. The Hellenic elements in Manichaeism may be slight, but they are unmistakable.[3] There can be no mistake, for instance, about the Greek origin of the term $\beta\hat{\omega}\lambda o s$; and we may conjecture that the source of the term was likewise the source of the bizarre doctrine which the term embodies.[4] Again, the Manichaean account of the origin and nature of Adam is strongly reminiscent of the anthropological teaching of the abortive Hellenic 'higher religion' of Orphism.[5] On this showing, the tendency of

[1] The bifurcation of the respective lineages of Manichaeism and Mithraism has to be dated back to the Pre-Zoroastrian Age of Iranian religious history if Mithraism is to be regarded, not as a derivative of Zoroastrianism (in the sense in which Manichaeism is a derivative of Zoroastrianism and Christianity of Judaism), but as a separate and independent development out of a pre-Zoroastrian Iranian paganism (according to the view put forward in Pettazzone, R.: *La Religione di Zarathustra* (Bologna 1920, Zanichelli), p. 167). On this question see further the always suggestive and often brilliant but sometimes fanciful work of Autran, C.: *Mithra, Zoroastre, et la Préhistoire Aryenne du Christianisme* (Paris 1935, Payot).

[2] See Christensen, op. cit., pp. 186–7. Mani seems to have proclaimed himself to be the Paraclete (Christensen, op. cit., p. 178).

[3] See Burkitt, op. cit., pp. 65–6 and 93 seqq.

[4] Compare the Greek name ($B\hat{\eta}\mu a$) of the Manichaean festival commemorating Mani's martyrdom. At this festival the Prophet's unseen presence was signified in the erection of an empty tribune (*Graecè* $\beta\hat{\eta}\mu a$) (Christensen, op. cit., p. 193). Compare the empty tent that was erected by Eumenes, as a symbol of the unseen presence of Alexander the Great, in the camp of the Argyraspides (Plutarch: *Life of Eumenes*, chaps. 11–13).

[5] This resemblance may, of course, be the consequence, not of any direct borrowing from 'Orpheus' on the part of Mani, but rather of a common Zoroastrian inspiration in

Manichaeism, so far from being in reaction against, or opposite to, that of its cousin Mithraism, would actually be in harmony with it, while, so far from being the same as the tendency of Nestorianism and Monophysitism, it would turn out to be the exact antithesis of that. While these two versions of Christianity can properly be described as attempts to purge the parent religion of its Hellenism, we should have to regard Manichaeism as being, like Mithraism, an attempt to blend an Iranian religion with a Hellenic alloy.[1]

But what could have moved a Syriac prophet to adulterate with Hellenism a pure Syriac religion, such as Zoroastrianism had contrived to remain, in an age when the tide of Syriac feeling was already setting strongly in an anti-Hellenic direction?[2] Perhaps we may find an explanation in the brilliant conjecture of an Italian scholar,[3] who points out that Mani preached his new religion in a generation which saw the foundation of the Sasanian state and the official adoption of Zoroastrianism as the new state's established church. In becoming the established church of an empire which was dedicated to the task of fighting Hellenism with political weapons,[4] Zoroastrianism was patently repudiating its former mission of providing a universal church for the Syriac internal proletariat.[5] Signor Pettazzone suggests that Mani was a religious genius who had the insight to understand, and the sensibility to regret, that Zoroastrianism was taking this disastrous turn;[6] and he interprets Manichaeism as a deliberate attempt to meet this religious emergency by calling into existence a new religion which was to redress the overturned balance between Religion and Politics by assuming the spiritual role which Zoroastrianism had abandoned and by filling the void which this act of betrayal had left in the Syriac religious universe. Pettazzone's theory would explain why it was that Mani's activities were in the end[7] so actively combated and so ruthlessly repressed by the Sasanian Govern-

both Orphism and Manichaeism (for Zoroastrian elements in Orphism see V. C (i) (c) 2, p. 85, above).

[1] See II. D (vii), vol. ii, p. 374, footnote 3, above.

[2] See I. C (i) (b), vol. i, pp. 75–6, above.

[3] Pettazzone, R.: La Religione di Zarathustra (Bologna 1920, Zanichelli), p. 193.

[4] See II. D (v), vol. ii, p. 203; II. D (vii), vol. ii, pp. 285–7 and 374; and V. C (i) (c) 3, in the present volume, p. 216, above, and V. C (i) (d) 6 (δ), Annex, pp. 659–61, below.

[5] 'It was solely due to outward circumstances that both [Zoroastrianism and Buddhism] were given a national stamp, and that the teaching of Zarathustra actually became the national religion of Iran. Wherever the possibility was open, Zoroastrianism, just like Buddhism and (later) Christianity and Islam, carried on an energetic propaganda beyond the frontiers of the Iranian nationality' (Meyer, E.: Geschichte des Altertums, vol. i, part (1), 4th ed. (Stuttgart and Berlin 1921, Cotta), p. 155).

[6] For the disastrousness of it see also II. D (vii), vol. ii, p. 375, above, and V. C (i) (d) 6 (δ), Annex, in the present volume, pp. 659–61, below.

[7] Mani was put to death in A.D. 276 by Vahrām I (imperabat A.D. 273–6) after having been well treated by Shapur I (imperabat A.D. 241–72) (Christensen, op. cit., pp. 189–93).

ment. The Sasanian policy of welding State and Church together into a single 'totalitarian' body politic and ecclesiastic would have been condemned to frustration if this exploitation of Syriac religion for Sasanian political ends had resulted in a wholesale conversion of the votaries of the old 'higher religion', which had now allowed itself to be perverted into an instrument of secular policy, to a new 'higher religion' which promised to furnish hungry souls with the spiritual bread that Zoroastrianism could now no longer offer them.

If this explanation of Mani's Ministry and Passion is the right one, then our tentative comparison of Manichaeism with Nestorianism and Monophysitism falls to the ground. On this showing, the true parallel lies between Manichaeism and Primitive Christianity —Manichaeism standing to a Sasanian Zoroastrianism as Primitive Christianity stands to a Maccabaean Judaism.[1] In this case, as in that, when the older religion went into politics and immured itself in the prison-house of a particular parochial state, the younger religion took up its predecessor's abandoned vocation of saving the souls of Mankind and preaching a gospel to the ends of the Earth.[2] More than that, it was the Hellenic World that was the principal mission-field of the Manichaean as well as the Christian—and the Mithraic—missionary. This fact is apt to be overlooked because Manichaeism spread from its original 'Irāqī centre of dispersion[3] in two directions—north-eastwards towards Central Asia as well as westwards towards the Mediterranean—and, while in the western field Manichaeism, like the worship of Mithras, rapidly succumbed to Catholic Christianity, in the Central Asian field it survived, like Nestorianism, in 'Diasporà' till the thirteenth century of the Christian Era.[4] This now extinct Central Asian 'Diasporà' is the source of our fragmentary first-hand evidence in regard to Manichaean doctrine and practice.[5] But we must be on our guard against the fallacy of gauging the relative importance of the two Manichaean mission-fields by the relative value of the raw materials which they have respectively yielded to our modern Western captains of historical industry.[6] The true measure is given by the

[1] For the perversion of Judaism into a political instrument in the hands of the Maccabees see V. C (i) (d) 6 (δ), Annex, pp. 657–9, below.

[2] 'I am come from the land of Babylon to make a cry heard throughout the World.'— Mani, Fragment M 4 a, quoted in Christensen, op. cit., p. 178.

[3] Mani's home-country was Mesene, which was approximately coincident with the present province of Basrah (see IV. C (iii) (c) 2 (β), Annex III, vol. iv, p. 629, footnote 1, above). This 'Irāqī prophet seems, however, to have been of Iranian extraction. His father is said to have come to Mesene from Hamadan, and his mother is said to have been of Arsacid birth (Christensen, op. cit., p. 177).

[4] The greatest single triumph of Manichaeism in its Central Asian mission-field was the conversion of the Uighurs in A.D. 762 (see Part III. A, Annex II, vol. iii, pp. 415, 425, footnote 1, and 451, above).

[5] See Christensen, op. cit., p. 196.

[6] This fallacy has been exposed already, in the classic example of Ptolemaic Egypt and Seleucid Asia, in Part I. A, vol. i, pp. 5–7, above.

distribution of the efforts and the orientation of the hopes of the Manichaean missionaries themselves; and on this criterion the rapidly defeated Manichaean mission in the Hellenic World takes precedence over the temporarily successful mission in Central Asia. If Manichaeism had succeeded in supplanting Catholic Christianity in the Mediterranean Basin, instead of merely succeeding in surviving for a time, side by side with Nestorianism, in Central Asia, then Mani would have to be numbered among the prophets who have given a decisive turn to the fortunes of Mankind. The western mission of Manichaeism was, as we have observed, abortive; yet the strength of its appeal to Hellenic souls, in competition with Christianity, is illustrated by the fact that in the fourth century of the Christian Era in North-West Africa it made a temporary convert of Augustine of Madaura.

MARXISM, SOCIALISM, AND CHRISTIANITY

THE advocates of Marxism will perhaps protest that in a rather summary account of the Marxian Philosophy or Faith[1] we have made a show of analysing this into a Hegelian and a Jewish and a Christian constituent element without having said a word about the most characteristic and most celebrated part of Marx's message to his fellow men. In the mind of 'the man in the street', the Marxian apologist will point out, Marxism means Socialism; and he will add that 'the man in the street' is substantially right in making this popular equation. Socialism, the Marxian will tell us, is the essence of the Marxian way of life; it is an original element in the Marxian system which cannot be traced to a Hegelian or a Christian or a Jewish or any other pre-Marxian source; and it is a supremely philanthropic ideal—so much so that, when we place it in its proper position at the heart of the Marxian dispensation, the whole of this dispensation will appear in an utterly different light from the lurid colour in which it is maliciously painted by its enemies. As soon as we view it thus in its true proportion and perspective, we shall perceive (we shall be told) that Marxism is eminently humane and constructive in its ulterior aims and in its ultimate effects, and that the destructive violence upon which its enemies have seized as a pretext for discrediting it is no more than an incidental and transitory means to an end which is purely beneficent. Our champion of Marxism will probably follow up this vigorous defence by passing over to the offensive. He will accuse the opponents of his Faith of giving a false pretext for their hostility because they are ashamed of confessing the true reasons. What they really hate and fear in Marxism (he will suggest) is not its revolutionary violence but the fact that its programme of Socialism is a threat to existing anti-social vested interests and an exposure of the inadequacy of pre-Marxian philosophies and religions. The sages and prophets who have left it to Karl Marx to proclaim what is Man's elementary social duty to his neighbour must have been either hypocrites or imbeciles.

In attempting to reply to a Marxian protest on such lines as these we shall readily admit the humaneness and the constructiveness of the ideal for which Socialism stands, as well as the importance of the part which this ideal plays in the Marxian 'ideology'; but we shall find ourselves unable to accept the Marxian contention

---

[1] This account will be found in V. C (i) (c) 2, pp. 177–87, above.

that Socialism is Marx's own original discovery. We shall have to point out, on our part, that there is a Christian Socialism which was practised as well as preached before the Marxian Socialism was ever heard of; and, when our turn comes for taking the offensive, we shall venture to make two assertions. We shall maintain that the Marxian Socialism is derived from the Christian tradition as unmistakably as is the Marxian concern to convert the World. We shall also maintain that the Marxian version of the Christian ideal of philanthropy is an excerpt which has omitted the one thing needful—and indeed indispensable—for making any form of Socialism work.

The social arrangements of the primitive Christian community are only referred to incidentally in the books of the New Testament, because the authors' minds are pre-occupied with other aspects of the life of the Founder and his companions; but these incidental allusions give us glimpses of a picture of a common way of life which is undoubtedly Socialism and indeed Communism in the economic sense[1] of a community of goods and services.

In the story of the Passion as told in the Gospel according to Saint John, Jesus and his companions are represented as having a common purse which is in Judas Iscariot's keeping.[2] And in the preface to the story of Ananias and Sapphira, as told in the Acts of the Apostles, the economic régime of the infant Church on the morrow of the Ascension is depicted as being that of a miniature and rudimentary yet authentic Communist commonwealth.

'The multitude of them that believed were of one heart and of one soul; neither said any of them that ought of the things which he possessed was his own; but they had all things common. And with great power gave the Apostles witness of the resurrection of the Lord Jesus; and great grace was upon them all. Neither was there any among them that lacked; for as many as were possessors of lands or houses sold them and brought the prices of the things that were sold and laid them down at the Apostles' feet; and distribution was made unto every man according as he had need.'[3]

The complete community of goods that is described in this passage did not, of course, become one of the permanent institu-

---

[1] For the political meaning of Communism as a revival of the Paris Commune of A.D. 1871 see V. C (i) (c) 2, p. 179, footnote 5, above. It was this sense of the word that Lenin had in mind when he re-named the Russian Social-Democratic Party 'the Russian Communist Party' in A.D. 1918. The Paris Commune of A.D. 1871 was itself called after the communes of medieval Western Christendom; and these were self-governing commonwealths in which the thing that was shared in common was not property but sovereignty. This medieval usage of the Latin word *commune* in the sense of a self-governing body politic is a perfectly correct piece of Latinity for which classical authority can be found in the works of Cicero and in the C.I.L.

[2] John xii. 6, and xiii. 29.   [3] Acts iv. 32-5.

tions of the Christian Church (as, for that matter, it is not being
insisted upon to-day in the Soviet Union either); nor can the testimony of the Acts be taken as conclusive evidence that the picture
here presented was ever strictly true to the life of the Church
even in the Apostolic Age[1] (any more than the first written constitution of the Union of Soviet Socialist Republics can be taken as
conclusive evidence for the social condition of Russia even in the
lifetime of Lenin). What the passage does attest is the social ideal
of the early Christian milieu in which the Acts was conceived
and written. And, even if this contemporary testimony were lacking, the Christian social ideal of the Apostolic Age could still be
reconstructed by inference from the testimony of succeeding centuries, in which the Church was famous for a sensitiveness—that
declared itself in material as well as in spiritual good works—to
the emotional attitudes and moral responsibilities implied in being
one's brother's keeper. This ingrained philanthropic vein in the
post-Apostolic Christian tradition comes out in the legend of how
St. Lawrence replied to the Roman Government's summons to

[1] As evidence for social facts (though not, of course, as evidence for social ideals)
the passage just quoted from the Acts of the Apostles is suspect on account of certain
coincidences of content, and even of words, which seem too numerous and too close
to be dismissed as fortuitous, with other works of literature, both Syriac and Hellenic.
For instance, the first sentence in Acts iv. 34 sounds like an echo of the first sentence
in Deuteronomy xv. 4; and the whole passage here quoted corresponds in so many
points, both of content and of language, with a description of the life of the primitive
Pythagorean community at Croton in Iamblichus's *Life of Pythagoras*, §§ 167–9, that
it is hardly possible to account for these correspondences on any hypothesis except
that of there being some literary relationship between the two passages. (Their literary
affinity positively leaps to the eye when they are set out in parallel columns, as they
are in Schubert, H. von: *Der Kommunismus der Wiedertäufer in Münster und seine
Quellen* (Heidelberg 1919, Winter), p. 36.) *A priori* there are two alternative possible
relationships. Since Iamblichus lived and wrote no earlier than round about the turn
of the third and fourth centuries of the Christian Era, it is chronologically possible that
his picture of an early Pythagorean Communism may be a copy of the picture of an
early Christian Communism in the Acts; or, alternatively, it is possible that the points
of likeness in the two passages may have been inherited independently from some
common literary ancestry. Of these two alternative possibilities the former may be
ruled out; for, while it is true that by Iamblichus's time the Christian Scriptures were
not only accessible but also notorious in pagan circles, it is at the same time almost
inconceivable that the spiritual father of a Neoplatonic Antichurch (see V. C (i) (d)
6 (δ), p. 565, above) should have brought himself to borrow any of the properties
of a Christian Church which he so passionately hated and despised. We are left with
the possibility of a common literary ancestry; and von Schubert (op. cit., p. 37, footnote 1) traces both passages back to a passage of Plato, namely *Respublica*, Book V,
462 c. Presumably there are missing intermediate links in both chains of literary ascent.
According to Bertermann, W.: *De Iamblichi Vitae Pythagorae Fontibus* (Königsberg
1913, [dissertation], p. 74, as cited by von Schubert in op. cit., p. 36, Iamblichus's
immediate source was the work of the Siceliot Greek historian Timaeus of Tauro-
menium (*vivebat circa* 352–256 B.C.). As for the immediate inspiration of the author
of the Acts, von Schubert conjectures (op. cit., p. 38) that he may have been emulating
Josephus's description (in *The Romano-Jewish War*, Book II, chap. 8) of the social life
of the contemporary Jewish ascetic confraternity of the Essenes, who practised Communism, were regarded, by Hellenic and Hellenized Jewish observers, as Jewish
counterparts of the Pythagoreans, and may in truth have borrowed some of their beliefs
and institutions from a Pythagorean source. The general question of correspondences
between passages of the New Testament and passages of pagan Hellenic literature is
discussed in V. C (i) (d) 11, Annex I, *passim*, in vol. vi, and in V. C (ii) (a), Annex II,
passim, in vol. vi, below.

deliver up the Church's treasures by collecting a crowd of the poor and needy from the slums of Rome and presenting himself, at their head, to the public authorities. But we need not appeal to an unverifiable Christian legend when we can cite the unimpeachable testimony of Julian the Apostate. The virtual monopoly of social-welfare work by the Christian Church in the Hellenic World of the fourth century of the Christian Era is sorrowfully confessed by Julian in a pastoral letter[1] to one of the pagan prelates of his Neoplatonic Antichurch:[2]

'If Hellenism [i.e. Neoplatonism] is not yet making the progress which we have a right to expect, it is we, its devotees, who are to blame. . . . Are we refusing to face the fact that Atheism [i.e. Christianity][3] owes its success above all to its philanthropy towards strangers and to its provision for funerals and to its parade of a high puritanical morality? These are all, surely, virtues which we ourselves ought to put into practice *bona fide*. . . . You must establish in every city [in your see] an ample number of hospices, in order that strangers may have the benefit of a philanthropy which will be recognized as ours; and this service must not be confined to strangers of our own persuasion; it must be at the disposal of anybody whatsoever who is in need. I have already provided for the allocation to you of the necessary funds. . . . A fifth of this grant should be spent on the poor who are in the clientèle of the [pagan] clergy; the balance should be distributed to strangers and beggars. It is a disgrace to us that our own people should be notoriously going short of assistance from us when in the Jewish community there is not a single beggar, while the impious Galilaeans are supporting not only their own poor but ours as well. You should instruct the votaries of Hellenism to make voluntary contributions towards these charitable services, and the Hellenic [i.e. pagan] parishes [in your see] to dedicate their first fruits [for this purpose]. You must get our Hellenic community into the habit of doing good works of this kind by instructing them that this is one of our most ancient traditional activities—as is testified by Homer. . . . Do not let us allow hostile competitors to outdo us in our own strong points while we give way to a slackness and indifference which are not merely a disgrace to our religion but a downright betrayal of it.'

These passages from the correspondence of the Emperor Julian and from the Acts of the Apostles and from the Gospel according to Saint John will perhaps suffice to demonstrate our three propositions. In the first place they make it clear that Socialism—and

[1] Letter from the Emperor Julian to Arsaces, the Chief Priest of Galatia (= Letter No. 84 in Bidez, J.: *L'Empéreur Julien: Œuvres Complètes*: Tome i, 2ᵉ Partie: 'Lettres et Fragments' (Paris 1924, Les Belles Lettres)).
[2] For this abortive Neoplatonic Antichurch see II. D (vii), vol. ii, p. 378; V. C (i) (c) 2, in the present volume, p. 147; and V. C (i) (d) 6 (δ), pp. 565–7, above; and V. C (i) (d) 6 (δ), Annex, pp. 680–3, and V. C (ii) (a), vol. vi, pp. 222–3, below.
[3] For this Hellenic name for Christianity see IV. C (iii) (c) 2 (β), vol. iv, p. 348, above, and V. C (i) (d) 7, vol. vi, p. 40, footnote 2, and V. C (ii) (a), Annex II, vol. vi, p. 536, below.—A.J.T.

this in the strict formal sense of a community of goods—is one of the principles of the primitive Christian *Weltanschauung*. In the second place they establish a very strong presumption that the Socialism, as well as the Oecumenicalism, of the Marxian scheme is derived from the Christian tradition.[1] In the third place they reveal the element in the Christian Socialism which the Marxian Socialism has left—or cut—out.

The passage in the Acts represents the philanthropy of the primitive Christian Society as flowing from a God-given grace which was the fruit of a belief in the divinity of Jesus. In other words, the charity which is here depicted as moving the primitive Christians to go—in their mutual concern for one another's welfare —to the extreme length of sharing all their worldly goods is not a mere love of Man for Man (which is the limited literal meaning of the word 'philanthropy'), but is a spiritual relation to which God is a party as well as His human creatures. In fact, this Christian Socialism is a practical application, on the economic surface of life, of the fundamental religious truth that the brotherhood of Man is a consequence of the fatherhood of God—a truth which is driven home with special force by a religion which teaches that God is not only the father and creator of Man, but also his saviour who has been incarnate in human shape and has suffered, and triumphed over, Death.[2] Christians believe—and a study of History assuredly proves them right—that (beyond the narrow circle of the tribe, in which a parochial 'honour among thieves' is maintained at the prohibitive moral price of an Ishmaelitish warfare against a world of foreign enemies) the brotherhood of Man is impossible for Man to achieve in any other way than by enrolling himself as a citizen of a *Civitas Dei* which transcends the human world and has God himself for its king.[3] And any one who holds this belief will feel certain, *a priori*, that the Marxian excerpt from a Christian Socialism is an experiment which is doomed to failure because it has denied itself the aid of the spiritual power which

[1] And perhaps, through this Christian tradition, from a Hellenic tributary of the river of Christian faith and works (see p. 583, footnote 1, above). 'A tenuous thread of historical continuity on the plane of ideas (*eine feine ideengeschichtliche Linie*) runs from the man of action John of Leyden to the theorist Plato across an interval of 2,000 years. . . . In motives and in mental scope the Marxian Communism of the present day is something rather different from the Communism of the sixteenth century. Yet now, as then, the idea fills its devotees with an enthusiasm of a religious fervour, and now, as then, again the intolerable tension between the shining ideal and the commonplace realities of life sets in motion the same socio-psychological forces and produces the same chaotic mixture of the most exalted love with the most savage hatred in the heart of Man towards his fellow men—just as at the time of the outbreak at Münster' (Schubert, op. cit., pp. 56–7). For the vein of Communism in the Anabaptist movement see V. C (i) (c) 2, pp. 169–72, above.

[2] For the distinctiveness of this feature in Christianity see further V. C (ii) (a), vol. vi, pp. 275–8, below.

[3] On this point see Bergson, H.: *Les Deux Sources de la Morale et de la Religion* (Paris 1932, Alcan), *passim*.

alone is capable of making Socialism a success. The Christian critic will have no quarrel with the Marxian Socialism for going as far as it does: he will criticize it for not going far enough. Its fatal flaw in his eyes will be a sin of omission and not a sin of commission.

Thus, from the Christian standpoint, the Marxian experiment in Socialism is a tragedy; but this cannot be the Christian observer's last word; for the responsibility for this tragedy is manifestly shared by the Christian Church itself.

How, in face of such evidence as we have cited, are we to explain the Marxian attitude towards Christianity? The Marxians not only maintain that there is no trace of Socialism in the Christian tradition and that their own prophet has been the first to awaken Man's social conscience: they actually declare that Christianity is one of the most formidable obstacles in the way of their own effort to apply Socialism in practice. 'Christianity', they say, 'is the opiate of the People'; and, in the Soviet Union at any rate, this supposed antithesis and incompatibility between Socialism and Christianity has been so sincerely believed in, and so strongly felt, that the votaries of Christianity or of any other theistic religion have been debarred, *ex officio religionis*, from admission to membership of the All-Union Communist Party. In fact, Communism has been definitely and militantly anti-Christian. And, when we ask how this has come to be when Socialism and philanthropy loom as large as they do in the Christian tradition, the answer is, of course, that the Christianity against which the Communists have declared war is neither the first-century Christianity of Jerusalem nor the fourth-century Christianity of the Roman Empire but the nineteenth-century and twentieth-century Christianity of the Western World and Russia. It is our modern Western and modern Russian practice of Christianity that has given this occasion for an enemy to blaspheme; and a practice that has aroused a hatred and contempt which are plainly as sincere as they are vehement must have fallen far indeed below the Christian practice of the first four centuries.

Thus the campaign against Christianity which is to-day an integral part of the propaganda of Marxian Socialism is a challenge to the living generation of Christians to examine their consciences and to throw themselves, once more, into an essential Christian activity which they have neglected, or even abandoned, in modern times; and we may aptly begin by addressing the Apostate's searching questions to ourselves:

'Are we refusing to face the fact that Atheism owes its success above all to its philanthropy? . . . These are virtues which we ourselves ought to put into practice *bona fide*. . . . Do not let us allow hostile competitors to outdo us in our own strong points while we give way to a slackness and indifference which are not merely a disgrace to our religion but a downright betrayal of it.'

Fas est et ab hoste doceri;[1] and, if we do take to heart the self-reproachful words of a noble adversary, we latter-day Christians may still turn a Marxian attack upon Christianity to good account as, seven centuries ago, a Paulician attack was turned to account, in comparable circumstances, under the inspired leadership of Saint Francis and Saint Dominic.[2] In that event the verdict of History may turn out to be that a re-awakening of the Christian social conscience has been the one great positive practical achievement of Karl Marx; and, in bringing Marx's endeavours to this unexpected issue, the irony of History would not be so cruel as might at first appear; for, if we are right in our thesis that the Marxian Socialism is doomed, *a priori*, to be a Socialism *Manqué*, then we must believe that Marx's sole chance of realizing his ideal of a socialized world lies in awaking from its inopportune slumber, and speeding upon its abandoned path, that primitive Christian charity which does know the secret of making Socialism work as one of the terrestrial institutions of a supra-mundane *Civitas Dei*.

---

[1] Ovid: *Metamorphoses*, Book IV, l. 428.
[2] See IV. C (iii) (c) 2 (β), vol. iv, pp. 370–1, and IV. C (iii) (c) 3 (β), Annex, vol. iv, pp. 652–6, above.

THE AMBIGUITY OF GENTLENESS

'GENTLENESS', in the sense in which we have used the word in the chapter to which this Annex attaches, might equally well be called 'Non-Violence'. This alternative description makes it clear that what we are thus labelling is something negative. If we go on to look below this superficial negative label we may expect to find that it covers more than one positive reality; and a first glance will bring to light at least four distinct positive meanings of our term, every one of which can be illustrated by conspicuous cases in point.

At its lowest the practice of Non-Violence may express nothing more noble or more constructive than a cynical disillusionment with the fruitlessness of a Violence which has been previously practised *ad nauseam* without having produced the intended results. A notorious example of a Non-Violence of this unedifying kind is the religious toleration which has been in vogue in the Western World from about the last quarter of the seventeenth century of the Christian Era down to our own day.[1] Alternatively, Non-Violence may express a conviction that Man's divinely allotted role in the economy of the Universe is to adopt a patiently passive attitude towards a mundane scene on which it is God's exclusive prerogative to execute His divine will through His own action—which would be hampered, and not assisted, if Man were to presume to intervene in what is wholly God's business. Such is, for example, the conviction that underlies the Non-Violence of the *Agudath Israel*.[2] This second philosophy of Non-Violence is as pious and as scrupulous as our first is unprincipled and cynical; but at the same time it resembles the Non-Violence of Disillusionment in being unconstructive. Non-Violence may, however, also be practised as a means to some constructive end; and such an end, again, may be either mundane or 'Otherworldly'. A classic example of the practice of Non-Violence for a mundane end is presented in Mahatma Gandhi's political tactics of Non-Violent Non-Co-operation.[3] The aim of Mr. Gandhi and his followers is to obtain for the People of India the political boon of complete self-government; and the pursuit of this aim by these tactics is

---

[1] See IV. C (iii) (b) 3, vol. iv, pp. 142–3 and 150; IV. C (iii) (b) 4, vol. iv, p. 184–5; and IV. C (iii) (b) 12, vol. iv, pp. 227–8, above; and V. C (i) (d) 6 (δ), Annex, in the present volume, pp. 669–71, and V. C (ii) (b), vol. vi, pp. 316–18, below.

[2] See V. C (i) (c) 2, p. 76, above, and V. C (i) (d) 9 (γ), vol. vi, p. 128, below.

[3] The most authoritative account of the origin and aim of Mr. Gandhi's movement is to be found in a book by Mr. Gandhi himself: *Satyagraha in South Africa* (Madras 1928, Ganesan).

evidence of a high degree of intellectual and moral originality; for the aim in view has been valued at its present enormously high current price in a Western Vanity Fair; and our Western nationalists have seldom or never abstained from resorting to Violence— of heart, if not of hand[1]—in their endeavours to gain possession of this coveted pearl. Mr. Gandhi's tactical recourse to Non-Violence is therefore a noteworthy new departure in the political technique of a Westernized 'Great Society'; but it is not, of course, so great a departure as a practice of Non-Violence for reasons which are not just tactical but are strategic. While Mr. Gandhi practises Non-Violence because he considers this to be the most efficacious means of pursuing an aim that is mundane, the Non-Violence of Jesus and Johanan ben Zakkai is a reflexion, on the mundane plane, of a transference of the field of action[2] from that mundane plane to another.

In the New Testament this profound shift of interest and change of objective is a *fait accompli*. Considering that the movement, of which the New Testament is a monument, came out of the bosom of the same Hellenic internal proletariat that threw up the Maccabees and the Zealots and Eunus and Salvius and Spartacus, it is not surprising to find in it, here and there, some trace of a violent vein (for examples of this see V. C (ii) (a), Annex II, vol. vi, pp. 378 and 388, below): what is remarkable is to observe how faint this trace is.

The denunciation of the rich in James v. 1–6, leads on to an exhortation to the poor to—not revolt, but—exercise patience. In general, wealth is represented, not as a material boon to be envied and, if possible, expropriated, but as a spiritual impediment to be deprecated (this is the moral of the simile of the Camel and the Needle's Eye;[3] of the antecedent incident of the Young Man with Great Possessions;[4] and of the pastoral exhortations in 1 Tim. vi. 6–11, and James i. 9–11). Conversely, the poverty which in the sight of a Tiberius Gracchus is damning evidence of the Internal Proletariat's intolerable social grievance is accepted in the New Testament as the distinctive badge of office of the servants of God.[5]

---

[1] In op. cit., chap. xiii, 'Meaning of Satyagraha', Mr. Gandhi draws a sharp distinction between his own instrument of 'soul force' and the English political expedient of 'passive resistence'. He regards 'passive resistence' as a form of militancy: 'the weapon of the weak', to which they resort as a *pis aller* when they do not command a majority of votes or a superiority in arms. On the other hand, Satyagraha and militancy are, in Mr. Gandhi's view, mutually exclusive in principle. As examples of non-Indian Satyagrahis, Mr. Gandhi cites Christ, the early Christian martyrs, and the Dukhobors. 'In Satyagraha there is not the remotest idea of injuring the opponent, Satyagraha postulates the conquest of the adversary by suffering in one's own person.'
[2] See III. C (i) (d), vol. iii, pp. 192–217, above.
[3] Matt. xix. 23–4 = Mark x. 23–5 = Luke xviii. 24–5.
[4] Matt. xix. 16–22 = Mark x. 17–22 = Luke xviii. 18–23.
[5] Contrast Plutarch: *Lives of the Gracchi*, chap. 9, with Matt. viii. 19–20 = Luke ix. 57–8; Luke vi. 20; 1 Cor. iv. 9–14; James ii. 5.

It is in the Other World, not in This World, that Lazarus is comforted and Dives tormented.[1] And even for the rich the hope of gaining entry into the Kingdom of Heaven is not completely ruled out.[2] Finally we may observe that the non-revolutionary attitude of the New Testament towards the current social conflict between Rich and Poor is also its attitude towards the analogous conflicts between Masters and Slaves and between Rulers and Subjects. Examples of this attitude towards Slavery are Ephesians vi. 5–9; Colossians iii. 22–5; 1 Tim. vi. 1–5; Titus ii. 9–10; 1 Peter ii. 18–25; and, above all, the Epistle to Philemon. As for the political conflict, the characteristic attitude of the Primitive Christian Church towards the mundane political authority of the Roman State is expressed in Matt. xxii. 15–22 = Mark xii. 13–17 = Luke xx. 19–26. and in Romans, xiii. 1–7, and not in the Book of Revelation.

The ambiguity of our term 'Gentleness' will now be clear; and at later points in this Part[3] we shall have occasion to distinguish sharply between different meanings of the term which are not merely distinct but are positively antithetical to one another. It would have been premature to introduce these distinctions in the chapter to which this Annex attaches, since the purpose of this chapter has been to bring the historic internal proletariats on to our stage as the necessary first step towards a study of their diverse faiths and works.

[1] Luke xvi. 19–31.
[2] Matt. xix. 25–6 = Mark x. 26–7 = Luke xviii. 26–7.
[3] e.g. in V. C (i) (d) 9 (γ), 10 and 11, vol. vi, pp. 118–68, below.

THE RHINE-DANUBE FRONTIER OF THE ROMAN EMPIRE

THE Rhine-Danube frontier of the Roman Empire is sometimes cited as a classical example of a frontier that is 'natural' or 'scientific'; and this belief, which has been inculcated by our modern Western classical scholars, in the intrinsic rightness or excellence of the long-since obliterated Continental European boundary of the Hellenic universal state has had a perceptible effect upon the political history of our own Western World, since it is one of the grounds of the modern French claim—or ambition—to have the Rhine for the frontier of France from the Alps to the North Sea (an aspiration which was first formulated in the seventeenth century; was translated into fact for a brief span when the Napoleonic Empire was at its height; and was revived, in the dreams of a few Frenchmen, during the Paris Peace Conference of 1918–20).

Whatever may be thought of a Rhine frontier for France, a Rhine-Danube frontier for the Roman Empire undoubtedly does look 'natural' on a small-scale map of Europe on which the two great rivers are apt to show up among the most prominent of the physical features that are picked out for display by the cartographer. Indeed, a river-line is not only conspicuous on the map but is also more precise in actuality than any other physical feature —except a sea-coast—which might serve as a 'natural' basis for a political boundary. Nevertheless a river is apt to be less effective, even as a strategic frontier, than a mountain-range or a desert;[1] and, while mountains and deserts tend to act as social insulators on the economic and the cultural as well as on the military and the political plane, rivers tend, like narrow seas, to bring together rather than to keep apart the populations that face one another across the water. This has certainly been the normal social effect of both the Rhine and the Danube upon the riparian populations ever since the Rhine-Danube frontier of the Roman Empire vanished with the Empire itself—as is witnessed by the present political map of Europe, on which those sections of the courses of the two rivers on which the waterways now serve as political boundaries are very much shorter in the aggregate than those other sections in which either river now runs through the heart of a country and serves as one of its principal internal arteries (the

[1] 'The frontiers of states are either large rivers or chains of mountains or deserts. Of all these obstacles to the march of an army the most difficult to overcome is the desert; mountains come next; and large rivers occupy the third place.'—*The Officer's Manual: Maxims of Napoleon*, translated from the French by Colonel Sir G. C. d'Aguilar (Dublin 1831, Milliken), Maxim 1, p. 5.

role of the Rhine in Holland and Prussia and Hessen, and of the Danube in Württemberg and Bavaria and Austria and Hungary). On the strength of this contemporary evidence we may hazard the conjecture that the Rhine and the Danube may have performed the same function of bringing together, instead of keeping apart, the populations on their opposite banks in that primitive Trans-alpine Europe which was artificially and forcibly partitioned into a Roman and a non-Roman half when the Roman frontier was drawn along the river-line.

In any case, even if it were to be conceded, for the sake of the argument, that a river-frontier is a 'natural' one in principle, it would still remain to be proved that the particular river-frontier to which the Roman Empire resigned itself in Europe was 'scientific'; and to prove this would be difficult indeed.

A 'scientific' military frontier presumably means one that has been chosen out of a number of alternative possible lines because it is the easiest of all of them to hold; and, *ceteris paribus*, the most defensible line is the shortest. A glance at the map will make it evident, however, that, of all the river-frontiers in the interior of Europe that could have been selected for an empire which was based on the Mediterranean Sea and which embraced the whole of the Mediterranean Basin, the Rhine-Danube frontier, so far from being the shortest, was in fact the longest.[1] An Elbe-Danube frontier would have been shorter, an Oder-Danube frontier shorter still, and a Vistula-Dniestr frontier the shortest (and on this count therefore the best) of all.[2] In and after the reign of Vespasian (*imperabat* A.D. 69–79) the Roman Government did manage to shorten the Rhine-Danube frontier slightly—and at the same time to embrace an additional patch of barbarian territory in the Roman pale—by cutting out the Swabian salient between the upper courses of the two rivers and running a line of artificial fortifications overland from the right bank of the Rhine below Coblenz to the left bank of the Danube above Ratisbon. But the saving of length through this substitution of an overland line for the river-line in the Swabian sector was more than offset by Trajan's pro-digality in trespassing beyond the river-line in the Lower Danube sector and annexing to the Empire a Transdanubian bridge-head— the new province of Dacia—which included at least the whole of what are now Little Wallachia and Transylvania. Nor was any

---

[1] This point has been noticed, by anticipation, in II. D (v), vol. ii, p. 162, above.

[2] After the interregnum that followed the break-up of the Roman Empire, the frontier of the new society of Western Christendom was, of course, pushed forward from the Rhine to the Elbe, the Oder, the Vistula, and still farther afield to the Niemen, the Dvina, and finally the Narev in the course of the six centuries following the launching of Charlemagne's attack upon the Saxons in A.D. 772 (see II. D (v), vol. ii, pp. 167–9, above).

great net economy of length achieved when, after the paroxysm in the third century of the Christian Era, Aurelian reversed Trajan's policy and withdrew the frontier to the river-line again in this Lower Danube sector; for in the same emergency the Roman Government was compelled also to abandon the transfluvial land-frontier on the Swabian sector likewise, and the withdrawal to the river-line here meant lengthening the frontier instead of shortening it. While the abandonment of Transylvania to the Goths relieved the empire of its own former salient into Barbaria, the abandonment of Swabia to the Alemanni[1] let a new barbarian salient into Romania; and this new salient pointed menacingly towards the Empire's Italian heart.

Thus, through all its successive local fluctuations, the Rhine-Danube frontier was never anything but the longest 'natural', or mainly 'natural', frontier on the European Continent that the Roman authorities could have chosen. But to imply that they did deliberately choose this line is to beg the question of their skill and insight as frontier-makers when we know as a matter of fact that the Roman Government did not ever choose this line, but simply acquiesced in it as a *pis aller*. The fateful decision was made by Augustus in A.D. 9, after he had reluctantly come to the conclusion that the establishment of an Elbe-Danube frontier, at which he had previously been aiming, could only be achieved at the cost of a greater military and financial effort than he could venture to call for from a Hellenic World which was then in urgent need of rest and relaxation after the protracted and cumulative strain of its four-hundred-years-long 'Time of Troubles'. The attempt to reach the Elbe-Danube line, which Augustus thus confessed to be beyond his strength, was not repeated by any of his successors; but Trajan did, as we have seen, succeed in temporarily substituting the mountain-frontier of the Eastern Carpathians for the river-frontier of the Lower Danube when he annexed Transylvania; and Marcus Aurelius would perhaps have succeeded (if his life had not been cut short when he was on the verge of success) in pushing the frontier forward from the river-line to the mountain-line on the Middle Danube sector as well, where he made a determined effort to annex the territories of the Marcomanni and the Quadi in what was yesterday Czechoslovakia.

The truth is that the Roman authorities were always dissatisfied with the Rhine-Danube frontier and showed their dissatisfaction in the strenuous attempts which they made on almost every sector,

---

[1] Swabia derives its present name from the presumably predominant Suebian element in the σύμμικτος ὄχλος of which the Alemannian war-band was composed. (For the social and psychological effects of a *limes* upon the transfrontier barbarians see V. C (i) (d) 7, vol. vi, p. 4, footnote 4, as well as Part VIII, below.)

at one time or another, to push their way forward to a better line
—Augustus aiming at a shorter river-line and the Flavians at an
elimination of the salient between the Upper Rhine and the Upper
Danube, while Trajan and Marcus Aurelius each sought, on a
particular sector, to get rid of the river-line altogether and to
secure a mountain-frontier instead. It was only in the last phase
of the Empire's existence, during the lull between the second
barbarian offensive and the third,[1] that the Roman frontier in
Europe coincided exactly with the courses of the Rhine and the
Danube throughout their length from the North Sea to the Black
Sea; and in this period the frontier was held at a greater cost and
at the same time with less efficiency than during the century and a
half that had intervened between the establishment of the Swabian
limes during the reign of Vespasian and the temporary collapse of
the whole frontier in the fifth decade of the third century of the
Christian Era.[2]

On this showing, we must decline to pay the Rhine-Danube
frontier of the Roman Empire the compliment of allowing it to be
called either 'natural' or 'scientific'. So far from being a monument of Roman strategical ability, it cannot even be regarded as
the outcome of a deliberate choice on the Roman Government's
part. Meandering, as it did, along the longest axis of Continental
Europe, this unduly praised frontier really registered nothing but
the undesigned and accidental locus of the geographical line along
which two conflicting social forces had come into a transitory
equilibrium. At this distance from the Mediterranean the barbarians of Continental Europe found themselves able to check the
farther advance, at their expense, of a Hellenic dominant minority
which conversely found itself now compelled to leave its European
external proletariat half-unconquered because it had previously
wasted the strength of the Hellenic Society in a series of internecine struggles that had begun with the Peloponnesian invasion
of Attica in 431 B.C. and had ended in 31 B.C. with Augustus's
victory at Actium over Antony and Cleopatra. In fact, the Rhine-
Danube frontier of the Roman Empire, though it held, with certain
temporary lapses, for nearly four hundred years from first to last,
was almost as unnatural and unscientific as the line along which, for

---

[1] For these two offensives see V. C (i) (c) 3, pp. 219–22, above. The lull lasted about
a hundred years, *circa* A.D. 275–375.

[2] In a critique of the policy of Constantine the Great the French philosopher-
administrator Turgot has expressed the opinion 'que l'Empire [Romain] ne fut jamais
assez grand [et] qu'il fallait joindre au projet de transporter la capitale de l'Empire [à
Constantinople] celui de conquérir le Nord de l'Europe et de ne laisser à l'Empire aucun
ennemi à craindre'. In order to conserve the Empire's military energies for this urgently
necessary conquest of Northern Europe the Imperial Government, Turgot argues, ought
to have refrained from aggression against Iran. (Turgot, A. R. J.: *Œuvres* (Paris 1844,
Guillaumin, 2 vols.), vol. ii, pp. 620–1.)

less than four years, an open warfare settled down into a trench warfare on the Western Front after the Battle of the Marne in the General War of A.D. 1914–18. A definitive and therefore satisfactory 'natural' frontier for a civilization on the Continent of Europe was not to be found anywhere short of the limit of human habitation in the latitude of the Arctic Circle. This line—which was never reached by a Hellenic Society that addressed itself to the problem only after it had already gone into decline—was eventually reached by the two affiliated societies of Western and Orthodox Christendom in the fourteenth century of the Christian Era[1] as a result of efforts which had had to be maintained over a span of not less than six hundred years.

[1] See II. D (v), vol. ii, pp. 168–9, above.

THE VÖLKERWANDERUNG OF THE ARYAS AND THE SANSKRIT EPIC

THE Sanskrit Epic, as it has come down to us, clearly cannot be regarded as the work of the Aryan invaders of the Indus Basin, or even as the work of these invaders' epigoni, in the sense in which the Scandinavian Saga and the Greek and English epics are respectively the work of the Norse settlers in Iceland and the Ionian settlers in Asia Minor and the English settlers in Britain.

On this question the dates are decisive. The incursion of the Aryas into the domain of the Indus Culture certainly took place before the end, and probably before the middle, of the second millennium B.C.—considering that the Hyksos, who were evidently an *apodasmos* of the same Eurasian Nomad horde, are known to have pushed their way as far afield as the Asiatic borders of Egypt before 1680 B.C. On the other hand the making of the Sanskrit Epic in its present form is estimated, on internal evidence, not to have been begun before 400–200 B.C. and not to have been completed before A.D. 200–400.[1] Thus in the Time-dimension there is a great gulf fixed between the composition of the Sanskrit Epic and the experience of the post-Sumeric Völkerwanderung, which must be presumed, on analogy, to have been the mental stimulus that inspired the Aryan invaders or their epigoni to make whatever their contribution may have been to the Sanskrit Epic as we have it.

The breadth of this gulf may be measured by the heterogeneity of the contents of the Epic in its final form; for while our scholars can make out at least a plausible case for unity of authorship in their *critiques* of certain famous works of 'heroic' poetry—for instance, the *Odyssey* or the *Chanson de Roland*—not even the boldest 'unitarian' would have the hardihood to call in question

---

[1] Sidhanta, N. K.: *The Heroic Age of India: A Comparative Study* (London 1929, Kegan Paul), pp. 48–9. Cf. Eliot, Sir Ch.: *Hinduism and Buddhism* (London 1921, Arnold, 3 vols.), vol. ii, p. 169. Some independent evidence from the Hellenic side has been brilliantly detected and presented by W. W. Tarn in *The Greeks in Bactria and India* (Cambridge 1938, University Press). The 'heroic' core of the *Mahābhārata* must have been known to the authority followed by the Alexandrian geographer Ptolemy (*vivebat Aevi Christiani saeculo secundo*) when he attributes to the Pandavas of the *Mahābhārata* a territory which had never been occupied by a people of that name at any time since the Indic World had first come within the Hellenic World's horizon (Tarn, op. cit., pp. 511–12). Ptolemy's authority may have been Trogus's Far Eastern Greek source, who seems to have been writing between 87 B.C. and 80 B.C. (Tarn, op. cit., pp. 50). Again, two passages of the *Mahābhārata* (in the form in which we now have it) which apparently belong, not to the original Aryan 'heroic' core but to the much later Hindu religious accretions, are echoed in an inscription on a column at Besnagar which was set up by a certain Heliodorus son of Dio who was in the service of the Far Eastern Seleucid Greek king Antialcidas (*regnabat circa* 130–100 B.C.) (Tarn, op. cit., pp. 313–14 and 380–1).

the compositeness of the authorship of the *Mahābhārata*. It would be fantastic to suggest that the *Bhagavadgītā*—which has been preserved as an episode in the *Bhārata*—is the work of a barbarian minstrel who has been nurtured in the bosom of a war-band and has found his *métier* in celebrating the prowess of his companions-in-arms. The *Bhagavadgītā* is not a piece of 'heroic' literature, but a sophisticated work of religious or philosophico-religious art. And this late and discordant religious element in the Sanskrit Epic does not only make its appearance in separate lays which, like the *Gītā*, can be isolated and detached and lifted bodily out of the main body of the epos. The whole fabric of the epos has been permeated by this religious leaven; and it is evident that, after having passed through the normal earlier stages in the development of a 'heroic' poetry, the literary legacy of the Aryan war-bands fell into the hands of the Brahmans[1] and was eventually incorporated into the scriptures of Hinduism:[2] the 'higher religion' which was discovered, after the breakdown of the Indic Civilization, by the Indic internal proletariat.[3]

This capture and exploitation of an ancient barbarian work of art by the apostles of a latter-day 'higher religion' or philosophy is not altogether without parallel. In the latter days of Hellenic history the Homeric Epic was taken up and taken over, in somewhat the same fashion, by the Fathers of the Neoplatonic Church; and Neoplatonism is an amalgam of the philosophy of the Hellenic dominant minority with the religion of the Hellenic internal proletariat which shows an unmistakable resemblance to Hinduism.[4] The Neoplatonist Fathers, however, never went to the lengths to which the Hindu Fathers permitted themselves to go in taking liberties with their 'heroic' captive. The Neoplatonists contented themselves with re-interpreting 'Homer' allegorically; and, even if they ventured to tamper with the *textus receptus* here and there, they never dreamed of interpolating whole books of 'Orphic' or 'Sibylline' religious verse between the historic cantos of the *Iliad* and the *Odyssey*. The complete smothering of an original 'heroic' nucleus under a pile of later religious accretions is a process that is peculiar to the history of the Sanskrit Epic; and it is one of the most striking illustrations of that tendency towards a predominantly religious *habitus* which is, as we have seen,[5] the special bent of the Indic Civilization.

At the same time we shall observe that the Hindu religious

---

[1] Sidhanta, op. cit., pp. 66–7.   [2] Ibid., p. 110.
[3] See V. C (i) (c) 2, pp. 137–8, above.
[4] For Neoplatonism see II. D (vii), vol. ii, p. 378; V. C (i) (c) 2, in the present volume, p. 147; V. C (i) (d) 6 (δ), pp. 565–7; and V. C (i) (c) 2, Annex II, p. 584, above; and V. C (i) (d) 6 (δ), Annex, pp. 680–3, and V. C (ii) (a), vol. vi, pp. 222–3, below.
[5] In III. C (iii), vol. iii, pp. 384–5 and 387–8, above.

manipulators of the Aryan 'heroic' epos have not succeeded in turning it into an entirely religious work of art which is unitary in the sense of being all of one uniform Hindu êthos and texture; for they have not eliminated—or perhaps even sought to eliminate— the original 'heroic' element altogether. In the Sanskrit Epic as we have it, the residual 'heroic' element is still manifest and even conspicuous; and there are even glaring contradictions between the original Aryan and the interpolated Hindu ideas and ideals which the Hindu manipulators of the *Mahābhārata* have not been able to remove.

The êthos and institutions of a barbarian war-band are unmistakably reflected in the thirst for fame and in the Fatalism which the *Bhārata* attributes to its heroes;[1] in the 'atmosphere of savage heroism' which pervades the *Bhārata* (though it is absent from the *Rāmāyana*);[2] in the importance of the parts that are played by the institutions of kingship and the *comitatus*;[3] in the purely personal basis of international relations;[4] and in the representation of the heroes as being meat-eaters—in contrast to the practice of an Indic Society in which the principle of *Ahimsa* had come to prevail at least as early as the sixth century B.C.[5] The gods of the Vedic Pantheon also behave in the *Bhārata* according to their kind. Indra has a mansion for warriors slain in battle which corresponds to Odin's Valhalla;[6] and he comes down to Earth—like Ares and Apollo and Athena in the *Iliad*—to take part in the warfare between rival human war-bands on an equality with the human combatants. This reduction of Indra to the stature of a mortal man does not trouble the later Hindu editor, for whom Indra is only a literary reminiscence and not a living god; but the latter-day poet falls into serious embarrassment when he allows himself to be decoyed—by his respect for the externals of the Aryan 'heroic' tradition—into bringing on to the battlefield his own Hindu god Shiva, who is the genuine object of a fervently pious worship. How can the omnipotent Shiva be allowed to be worsted, or even challenged, by human arms? And, on the other hand, how can the 'heroic' tradition be maintained if the divine combatant, *ex officio deitatis*, is to carry all before him?[7] In the purely Hindu didactic additions to the *Bhārata* this dilemma does not arise

---

[1] Sidhanta, op. cit., pp. 82–4. [2] Ibid., p. 89.
[3] Ibid., pp. 177 and 172–4.
[4] Ibid., p. 187. For this characteristic feature of 'heroic ages' see further V. C (i) (d) 7, vol. vi, p. 4, footnote 4, below.
[5] Sidhanta, op. cit., p. 169. We may compare the similar contrast between the diet of the Homeric heroes, who feast on beef and have a horror of fish, and the diet of the latter-day urban communities of the Hellenic World, in which fish was the staple flesh-food, while beef and mutton were rarely eaten.
[6] Ibid., pp. 210–12.
[7] For this dilemma see ibid., p. 94.

because the theme is here changed from barbarian warfare to sophisticated speculation; and in these interpolations the Vedic gods are quite eclipsed by Brāhmā, Shiva, and Vishnu.[1]

The frequent *actes de présence* that are made in the Sanskrit Epic by Indra and other members of the Vedic Pantheon are sufficient proof that some part, at least, of the 'heroic' element in the *Mahābhārata* is a genuine legacy from the Völkerwanderung of the Aryas in the second millennium B.C.; and we have corroborative evidence to the same effect in strata of Indic literature which are unquestionably of an early date. For instance, Nārashamsī songs (κλέα ἀνδρῶν) are mentioned in the *Vedas*, and there are allusions to heroic minstrelsy in the *Shatapatha Brāhmana*.[2] These facts would appear to establish, beyond doubt, both the existence of an original Aryan epos which was inspired by the Aryan Völkerwanderung, and also the survival of at least some reminiscence of this ancient epic tradition in the Sanskrit Epic as we have it. Yet there is something extraordinary about this apparent persistence of a 'heroic' literary tradition in an inchoate and fluid form over a period of at least five hundred years between the latest date that can be assigned to the historical events by which this poetry was inspired[3] and the earliest date that can be assigned to the crystallization of the Sanskrit Epic in its present shape. This curious chapter of literary history would become more comprehensible if we had warrant for surmising that, about the time when the Sanskrit Epic did, at last, take its classic shape, the interest in the ancient 'heroic' literary tradition of the Aryas was revived in the Indic World of the day by a contemporary recurrence of the social experiences by which the Aryan 'heroic' tradition had originally been precipitated. Between 400–200 B.C. and A.D. 200–400—which are, as we have seen,[4] the probable *termini post et ante quos* for the composition of the Sanskrit Epic— was there anything in the nature of a new Völkerwanderung and a new 'Heroic Age' in Indic history?

We may perhaps find our answer to this question if we approach it by way of an analogy that is to be found in the history of a comparable 'heroic' tradition which had its home in the Iranian province of the Syriac World.

The Iranian Epic, which has been given its classic and final

[1] Ibid., p. 200.
[2] Ibid., pp. 55–6.
[3] A comparison of the internal evidence of the *Mahābhārata* with evidence afforded by other works of Sanskrit literature which unquestionably date from the early age of Indic history appears to show that the historical characters and events of which there are reminiscences in the *Bhārata* fall within the quarter of a millennium *circa* 1100–*circa* 850 B.C. (Chadwick, H. M. and N. K.: *The Growth of Literature*, vol. ii (Cambridge 1936, University Press), pp. 512–20).
[4] On p. 596, above.

form by the genius of a single great poet,[1] has as long a history as
the Sanskrit Epic; for, while Firdawsī lived from about A.D. 930
to A.D. 1020, and the Pehlevī prose work which is supposed to
have been his source (through the medium of a New Persian translation) is not ascribed to an earlier date than the reign of the last
Sasanian Pādishāh Yazdagird (*imperabat* A.D. 632–51), the mythology which is presented in the *Shāhnāmah* proves to be identical,
even in minor details, with the mythological scheme that is presupposed in the *Avesta*,[2] and some, at least, of these mythical
characters and events appear to be creations of the Iranian imagination in the eighth and seventh centuries B.C., when the Iranian
peoples were living as members of the external proletariat of a
disintegrating Babylonic Society beyond the eastern frontiers of
the Assyrian Empire. There are other elements, however, in the
Shāhnāmah which date from later ages than this, while they are
still considerably older than the age which saw the composition
of Yazdagird's *Khudhāynāmah*. For example, a group of Arsacid
Parthian royal names have found their way into the Iranian 'heroic'
tradition in connexion with one particular episode;[3] and even so
recent an historical event as the death of the Sasanian Pādishāh
Pīrūz at the hands of the Ephthalites in A.D. 484[4] has passed over
into the realm of legend[5] and has there become of one substance
with the mythical exploits of Jāmshīd and Firīdūn.

Another distinct chronological stratum of 'heroic' matter is
perhaps to be found in the tales that are associated with the names
of Zal and Rustam; for, while the figures of these two heroes and
their adversaries loom large in the Iranian Epic in its final form,[6]

---

[1] In strict accuracy we ought perhaps to say 'the genius of two poets'; but—whether
or not Daqīqī would have grown to Firdawsī's stature if Death had not cut his work
short—the older poet's contribution to the *Shāhnāmah* as we have it is completely
dominated by the work of the successor who not only continued the poem but made it
what it now is.

[2] Nöldeke, Th.: *Das Iranische Nationalepos*, 2nd ed. (Berlin and Leipzig 1920, de
Gruyter), p. 1.

[3] Ibid., pp. 7–8. Several of these historical names are associated with one another in
the realm of historical fact as well as in the realm of poetic fiction. An historical King
Gotarzes, who is the namesake of Firdawsī's Gōdharz, had to fight for his throne in
A.D. 49–50 against an historical pretender, Meherdates (a Latin rendering of the Pehlevī
version of the name Mithradates), who is the namesake of Firdawsī's Mīlādh.
Meherdates was supported by the Kāren family, who likewise figure in this episode
of the *Shāhnāmah*.

[4] For the repercussion of this event upon Indic history see V. C (i) (c) 3, p. 279,
footnote 1, above.

[5] Nöldeke, op. cit., p. 9.

[6] The contents of the *Khudhāynāmah* have to be reconstructed by inference, since
neither the original Pehlevī text nor Ibn Muqaffaʿ's Arabic translation (made in the
middle of the eighth century of the Christian Era) is extant (Nöldeke, op. cit., p. 15).
Our inference that the *Khudhāynāmah* did include the Rustam cycle is drawn from the
fact that as early as the first half of the seventh century of the Christian Era, before the
Arab conquest, the name Rustam is borne by private persons in Western Iran and in
ʿIrāq (Nöldeke, op. cit., p. 11)—e.g., by the unfortunate commander of the Sasanian
army which was routed by the Arabs in the Battle of Qādisīyah, *circa* A.D. 637.

there is no trace of them in the *Avesta*.[1] An indication not only of the date but of the source of the Rustam cycle is perhaps to be found in its geographical locus. The legends in this cycle are all definitely associated with the two East Iranian provinces of Seistan and Zābulistān in the basin of the River Hilmand;[2] and the name Seistan, or Sakastene, commemorates the fact that the lower basin of the Hilmand, which had previously been known as Drangiana,[3] was submerged in the second and third quarters of the second century B.C. by a flood of Saka Nomads from the Eurasian Steppe.[4] These Saka invaders were part of the external proletariat of a disintegrating Syriac Society who had assembled in a no-man's-land beyond the Transoxanian frontier of the Achaemenian Empire[5] and had then broken through the former Achaemenian front when the Yuechi Nomads, from the depths of the Steppe, had given an impetus to the Sakas from the rear, and when the forces of the Achaemenian Empire's Macedonian 'successor-state' in Asia had been divided and redivided against themselves by a gradual secession of a Greek principality in Bactria from the Seleucid Monarchy during the latter part of the third century B.C.[6] and by a half-successful Seleucid attempt, in the fourth decade of

[1] Nöldeke, op. cit., p. 9.
[2] Ibid., p. 10. When the Arab conquerors pushed their way into Seistan, they found there a place called 'The Stall of Rustam's Horse [Raksh]' (Nöldeke, op. cit., p. 11).
[3] This older name of the province survived in the name of its capital city, which continued to be known as Zaranj down to the last days of Syriac history in the Age of the 'Abbasids.
[4] See II. D (v), vol. ii, p. 141, footnote 2, and p. 144, and V. C (i) (c) 3, in the present volume, pp. 215–16, 239–40, 275–6, and 310, above. The vanguard of the Saka host which occupied Drangiana in the second century B.C. seems to have planted itself there as early as *circa* 155 B.C., when a body of Saka mercenaries in the service of the Parthian King Mithradates I appears to have made itself at home in this province, without asking its employer's leave, as its self-conferred reward for previous military services which had enabled the Parthian war-lord to conquer Drangiana, Arachosia, and Gedrosia from the Bactrian Greeks in 159 B.C. (see Tarn, W. W.: *The Greeks in Bactria and India* (Cambridge 1938, University Press), pp. 222–3 and 500). The main body of the Sakas erupted out of the Eurasian Steppe into the Parthian Empire in 129 B.C. under pressure from the Yuechi, who had erupted into the Bactrian principality in 130 B.C. or shortly before (see V. C (i) (c) 3, p. 240, footnote 4, above). The momentarily overrun north-eastern provinces of the Parthian Empire, including Drangiana, were recovered for the Arsacid by his vassal the Suren between 124 and 115 B.C. (Tarn, op. cit., pp. 224, 320, and 501), and in the process the bulk of the Saka invaders were driven still farther south-eastwards, out of Drangiana into Sind (see pp. 602–4, below); but a sufficient number of them remained in Drangiana permanently, under the Suren's Parthian rule, to impose upon the province their name (Sakastene) and, with it, perhaps, their social impress. The same Parthian reconquest of Seistan that drove some, though not all, of the Saka invaders south-eastwards into Sind seems to have driven one of the trespassing Nomad war-bands—namely the Pasiani or Parsii—north-eastwards into the highland country, round the headwaters of the Hilmand and Kābul rivers, which subsequently came to be known as Zābulistān. In nationality these Parsian Nomads seem, to judge by their name, to have belonged not to the Saka-speaking but to the Persian-speaking branch of the Iranian family (Tarn, op. cit., pp. 292–5 and 469–73).
[5] For the history of this Eurasian frontier of the Syriac World see II. D (v), vol. ii, pp. 137–44; Part III. A, Annex II, vol. iii, pp. 444–5 and 448–9; and V. C (i) (c) 3, in the present volume, pp. 239–41, 244–6, and 247–8, above.
[6] See Tarn, op. cit., pp. 72–4.

the second century, to recover this lost dominion by force of arms.[1]
It has been conjectured by some of our modern Western scholars
that the Rustam cycle—which is so distinct, both in its local
colour and in its fabulous atmosphere,[2] from the rest of the matter
of the Iranian Epic—may be a literary reflexion of the social
experience of the Sakas in their Völkerwanderung in the second
century B.C.

This attractive conjecture has been rejected by the great scholar
upon whose work we have just been drawing in this Annex.[3] But,
if, in defiance of Nöldeke's formidable authority, we may venture
to entertain the hypothesis unless and until it is decisively refuted,
we may find in it a clue to the solution of the Indic problem which
has led us to take this Iranian question up.

While Seistan was permanently occupied by the Sakas—as is
testified by the permanent change in the province's name—it was
not the final resting-place of the whole Saka horde.[4] The Sakas
took the road to Seistan in and after 129 B.C. simply because this
was their line of least resistance;[5] but Seistan, as well as Herat and

---

[1] See Tarn, op. cit., pp. 183–224.

[2] For this atmosphere see Nöldeke, op. cit., p. 10.

[3] See ibid., p. 11. But the only reason which Nöldeke gives in support of his
adverse judgement is the fact that the personages in the Rustam cycle all bear Iranian
names; and this argument seems scarcely cogent, since it is almost certain that the
Saka Nomad invaders of Drangiana, as well as the sedentary population which they
found in occupation, were an Iranian-speaking people, while the allied war-band of
Parsian Nomad invaders, who were pushed, by the Parthian counter-attack of 124–115
B.C., out of Seistan up the Hilmand Valley into Zābulistān, probably spoke a language
that was not merely Iranian but was actually a member of the Persian branch of that
linguistic family (see p. 601, footnote 4, above).

[4] See p. 601, footnote 4, above.

[5] With their fellow Nomads the Yuechi at their heels the Sakas could not pitch their
tents in the Upper Oxus-Jaxartes Basin (Sogdiana and Bactria), which the Yuechi had
just taken for themselves. One war-band of the Saka Rawaka (Sacaraucae) which was
pushed back to the north-eastern side of the Oxus in the Parthian counter-offensive of
124–115 B.C. 'perished' in consequence (Tarn, op. cit., pp. 306–7). Again, they could
not push, south of the Hindu Kush, up the valley of the Murghab and down the valley
of the Kābul River into the Panjab, partly because of the difficulty of the *terrain* and
partly because the Seleucid Greek principality which had been carved out of the
Euthydemid Greek Empire of Bactria in the fourth decade of the second century B.C.
(see p. 601, above) had not only survived the Yuechi conquest of its provinces in
the Oxus-Jaxartes Basin but had remained strongly entrenched in a natural fastness
between the Hindu Kush Range and the Jhelum River (Tarn, op. cit., p. 312). When
the Parthian counter-offensive of 124–115 B.C. subsequently drove the Parsii out of
Seistan up the Hilmand Valley, they did succeed in pushing across the watershed
into the head of the Kābul Valley (Côphênê) at some date before 87 B.C. (ibid.,
pp. 295, 314, and 332); but (although it was the descendants of these Parsian invaders
of the Kābul Valley that eventually gave the Greek Power in India its *coup de grâce*
both in the Kābul Valley and in the Eastern Panjab: see ibid., pp. 349–50) the
Greeks of the Paropamisadae and Gandhāra proved strong enough to check the
Parsians' progress down the Kābul Valley for some 60 years; and before the end they
even managed, with Kushan military and Han diplomatic assistance, to drive the
Parsians back between *circa* 50 and *circa* 30 B.C. (ibid., pp. 337–43). Thus in the
eighth decade of the second century B.C. the Sakas could not push their way into either
the Upper Oxus-Jaxartes Basin or the Kābul Valley; and at the same time they could
not advance south-westward, into Western Iran and beyond it, owing to the indomitable
defence of the Khurasanian escarpment of the Iranian Plateau by the Arsacid prince
Mithradates the Great (see II. D (v), vol. ii, p. 141, footnote 2; Part III. A, Annex II,
vol. iii, p. 449; and V. C (i) (c) 3, in the present volume, p. 239, above). The only 'get-

Merv, was reconquered by Parthian arms, between 124 and 115
B.C., under the leadership of the Arsacid's vassal the Suren;[1] and,
although a Saka rear-guard settled down, nevertheless, under
Parthian rule, on the banks of the Hilmand, the greater part of
the horde then trekked on still farther south-eastward to find new
homes in the Indic World. After making their way out of the
Hilmand Basin into the Indus Basin over the Bolan Pass, these
Sakas struck the River Indus itself in Northern Sind, took to
the water,[2] and went on to conquer Patalêne (the Indus Delta)
and Surāshtra (Kathiāwār and Gujerāt).[3] By about 80 B.C. they
had established themselves in these provinces so firmly that they
were able to turn northwards and attack the Seleucid Greek
principality which still survived between the Jhelum and the
Hindu Kush. This time, again, the Sakas came by water; and it
was a naval victory on the Indus over their Greek antagonists
that opened for them the way to the conquest of Taxila before
77 B.C., of Gandhāra before 70 B.C., and of Kapisa, in the Paropamisadae, before 60 B.C.[4] While he was thus conquering the
greater part of the Seleucid Greek principality in India with one
hand, the Saka war-lord Maues was at the same time extending
his rule in Central India by conquering Ujjain about 62 B.C.[5] and
Mathurā about 60 B.C.[6] The Euthydemid Greek principality in the
Eastern Panjab, however, still held out between the Jhelum and
the Ravi,[7] and both Greek principalities reasserted themselves when,
in 58 B.C., Maues was defeated by the Mālavas, lost Ujjain, and
met his death.[8] The Euthydemid Greeks won a naval victory over
the Sakas on the Jhelum;[9] the Seleucid Greeks reasserted themselves
in the Paropamisadae;[10] and this collapse of the Saka Power in
India seemed to be confirmed when the Sakas' domain in the
Panjab, as well as both the two Greek principalities on its flanks,
was conquered by the Parsian principality about 30 B.C.,[11] and when
this ephemeral Parsian Empire was conquered in its turn, together
with the remnant of the Saka Empire in Sind and Kathiāwār and
Gujerāt, by the Parthian Suren Gondophares in A.D. 19.[12] The
Sakas, however, were strong both in numbers and in adaptability,[13]

---

away' that was left to the Sakas was to steal up the valley of the Heri Rud, between
Mithradates' right wing and the Kābul Valley Greeks' left wing; and this route led
them straight to Drangiana.
[1] See p. 601, footnote 4, above.
[2] These Saka Nomads who took to the water are the inverse of the Cossack watermen who took to the steppe (see II. D (v), vol. ii, p. 156, above).
[3] Tarn, op. cit., pp. 320–1 and 501.
[4] Ibid., pp. 321–3, 332, and 501.   [5] Ibid., p. 335.
[6] Ibid., p. 325.   [7] Ibid., p. 323.
[8] Ibid., p. 335.
[9] For the numismatic evidence for this see ibid., pp. 326–9.
[10] Ibid., p. 337.   [11] Ibid., pp. 346 and 349–50.
[12] Ibid., pp. 347 and 501.   [13] Ibid., pp. 299–300.

and, though the *ci-devant* Saka Empire of Maues in the Indus
Valley never came to life again, this defunct empire's two great
outlying satrapies—one at Mathurā and the other in Surāshtra
(i.e. Kathiāwār and Gujerāt)— both managed to survive, and the
southern satrapy subsequently extended the Saka Rāj into Central
India far deeper than Maues had ever penetrated in the last century B.C. These epigoni of the Saka conquerors of the Indus
Valley reconquered Ujjain about A.D. 78[1] and made themselves
masters of Mahārāshtra about the same time; and, although the
Saka satrapy in Mahārāshtra was momentarily overthrown by the
Andhra Power, from the Deccan, *circa* A.D. 126, the satrapy in
Mālwā recovered Mahārāshtra for the Saka Rāj between A.D. 126
and A.D. 150. From that time until its extinction at the hands of
the Guptas *circa* A.D. 390,[2] this Saka satrapy bore rule, from its
capital at Ujjain, 'not only over the peninsula of Surāshtra [Kathiā-
wār], but also over Mālwā, Cutch, Sind, the Konkan and other
districts—in short, over Western India'.[3] It will be seen that the
wave of the Saka Völkerwanderung was washing over from the
north-eastern fringe of the Syriac World into the north-western
fringe of the Indic World in the very age in which the Sanskrit
Epic is believed, on quite independent grounds, to have been
crystallizing into its present shape; and it is tempting to conjecture
that the otherwise extraordinary phenomenon of a revival, in the
Indic World in this age, of an interest in a 'heroic' tradition
descending from the Aryan invaders of the Indus Valley in the
second millennium B.C. may partly be accounted for by the arrival
in force, in the course of the last two centuries B.C. and the first
two centuries of the Christian Era, of a Saka swarm of barbarian
invaders who had lately acquired the same literary tastes, as a
result of the same social experience, as their Aryan predecessors
who had trodden the road from Eurasia to India more than a
thousand years earlier.

It is not necessary to suppose that any of the 'heroic' matter of
the Sanskrit Epic, as we have it, is actually of Saka origin—whatever we may think of the theory of a Saka origin of the Rustam
cycle in the Iranian Epic. In the Indic case, at any rate, we need
not go farther than to suggest that the Saka barbarian invaders
who pushed their way into the heart of Western India some time
between the end of the second century B.C. and the beginning of
the second century of the Christian Era were inspired by their own
recent social experience with a taste for that 'heroic' poetry which

---

[1] Tarn, op. cit., pp. 335 and 501.   [2] See I. C (i) (b), vol. i, p. 86, above.
[3] Smith, V. A.: *The Early History of India*, 3rd ed. (Oxford 1914, Clarendon
Press), p. 291.

seems to be the normal form of literary self-expression for barbarians who have been through a Völkerwanderung.

When a demand for 'heroic' poetry arises among barbarian
conquerors who have settled down to live off their conquests as
a ruling caste, this demand can be satisfied in either one of two
alternative ways. Either the barbarians can produce minstrels of
their own to celebrate their own deeds in their own language; or
else they can call upon the subject population to supply them with
the spiritual commodity of 'heroic' poetry as well as with the
material commodities which they are accustomed to take as tribute.[1]
From what we know of the êthos of the Sakas, we should expect
a priori that, if and when they did have an appetite for 'heroic'
poetry, they would prefer to borrow what they wanted rather than
to make it for themselves; for in other fields the Sakas undoubtedly displayed in a high degree the receptivity that seems to be
characteristic of empire-builders.[2] In their administration, coinage,
and calendar they took over the institutions of the Greeks whom
they supplanted,[3] and in the next chapter of their history they
were captivated by the Indic religion of Hinduism and by the
associated archaistic revival of the Sanskrit language.[4] On the
strength of these analogies we may perhaps venture to guess that,
when the Sakas felt a need for 'heroic' poetry, they addressed
themselves to their Indic subjects; and it is evident that, when
this demand is made upon a subject population, its poets will be
prone, like the householder in the parable,[5] to bring forth out of
their 'treasure things new and old'. They will search out and furbish
up, for the delectation of their new barbarian masters, any 'heroic'
matter which their own literary tradition may have preserved from
a more or less remote barbarian past, but at the same time they
will find ways and means of satisfying their own taste, and giving
expression to their own interests, by embroidering this ancient
stuff with incongruous modern trappings. If we imagine a Hindu
poet whose heart—like that of 'every scribe which is instructed
unto the Kingdom of Heaven'[5]—is set upon a new 'higher religion',
being called upon by an importunate barbarian Saka war-lord to
provide him with 'heroic' minstrelsy, is not the Sanskrit Epic, as
we have it, exactly the kind of farrago which we should expect to
see produced by the *tour de force* of an attempt to provide simul-

---

[1] We have already come across a case in point in studying the transformation of
the Norse settlers in the Lower Seine Valley into the Normans. The *ci-devant* barbarians were so completely captivated by the culture of the society which they had
compelled, at the sword's point, to receive them as its adopted sons that they abandoned
their Norse mother-tongue for French and thereafter satisfied their taste for 'heroic'
poetry by lending their ears to the French Epic (see II. D (v), vol. ii, p. 201, above).

[2] See V. C (i) (d) 6 (α), pp. 442–3, above.

[3] See Tarn, op. cit., pp. 241–13, 300, 323, and 358–9.

[4] See p. 606, footnote 3, below.   [5] Matt. xiii. 52.

taneous satisfaction for two tastes that were so diverse and for two
interests that were so far apart?

If we may be allowed to follow up our suggestion *jusqu'au bout*,
we will even venture tentatively to designate a precise place and
time in which the Sanskrit Epic may have taken its final shape.
We will put our finger upon 'Ujjain, one of the most ancient cities
of India, . . . famous as a seat of learning and civilization';[1] and
we will focus our attention upon the age in which Ujjain was the
capital of a Saka satrapy which bore rule over the greater part of
Western India.[2] Is it too rash a guess to conjecture that the
Sanskrit Epic took its final shape at the Saka Court in Ujjain some
time between about A.D. 150 and A.D. 390?[3]

[1] Smith, V. A.: *The Early History of India*, 3rd ed. (Oxford 1914, Clarendon Press),
p. 291.

[2] See the passage quoted from op. cit. on p. 604, above.

[3] This conjecture may be supported by philological as well as social and religious
considerations; for the crystallization of the Sanskrit Epic between 400–200 B.C. and
A.D. 200–400 occurred in close association, not only with the rise of the Hindu religion,
but also with an archaistic revival of the Sanskrit language; and the use of Neo-Sanskrit
for official purposes is believed, on the evidence of coins and inscriptions, to have been
introduced from the North-West into the Deccan, at some date between A.D. 120 and
A.D. 200, by the Saka satraps of Ujjain, who are our hypothetical barbarian patrons
of the Sanskrit Epic. 'The later Saka satraps of Surāshtra seem to have inclined personally much more to the Brahmanical than to the Buddhist cult, and they certainly
bestowed their patronage upon the Sanskrit of the Brahmans rather than upon the
vernacular literature. . . . The restoration of the Brahmanical religion to popular favour,
and the associated revival of the Sanskrit language, became noticeable in the second
century and were fostered by the satraps of Gujerāt and Surāshtra during the third'
(Smith, op. cit., pp. 302–3). The Neo-Sanskrit which was in use in Mahārāstra in the
second century of the Christian Era under the Saka régime was still full of solecisms;
but this very imperfection of the Saka satraps' Neo-Sanskrit style points the fact that
they were the pioneers of the Sanskrit revival in a Pāli-speaking world. In the second
century of the Christian Era Pāli continued to be used for inscriptions not only in the
Andhra Empire, to the south-east of the Saka satrapy of Ujjain, but also in the Indus
Valley (see Franke, R. O.: *Pāli und Sanskrit in ihrem Historischen und Geographischen
Verhältnis auf Grund der Inschriften und Münzen* (Strassburg 1902, Trübner), pp.
78–82). If the Saka satraps patronized the revival of the Sanskrit language, they may
well have extended their patronage to the ancient 'heroic' poetry which, among all the
literary monuments of the favoured language, was the matter which the Sakas themselves would most readily appreciate. (For the archaistic resuscitation of the Sanskrit
language as one of the symptoms of a decadence of the Indic Civilization see also
V. C (i) (d) 8 (γ), vol. vi, pp. 75–7, below.)

HISTORICAL FACT AND 'HEROIC' TRADITION

IN a notable work of both literary and historical scholarship[1] Professor H. M. Chadwick has collated the references to historical events in the Teutonic Epic with the accounts of the same events that have come down to us in the works of Greek and Latin historians; and from this comparison he has brilliantly brought out the fact that, even where the alleged historical event in the epic story turns out to be authentic, there is apt to be no correspondence whatever between the importance that is ascribed to this event in the 'heroic' tradition and its actual importance as our historical records enable us to estimate this quite independently of the 'heroic' version.[2]

For example, the Burgundian war-lord Guthhere or Gunther, whose figure looms so large in the *Nibelungenlied*, proves to have played in fact a very minor part in the barbarian infiltration into Gaul in the fifth century of the Christian Era; and, as for the still more famous literary figure of Siegfried, he 'has been identified with a number of famous princes from Arminius to Sigebert', but 'it cannot be said that any one of these identifications is of a nature to carry conviction; in no case, indeed, have they gained wide acceptance'.[3] Professor Chadwick suggests that

'It was scarcely through the greatness of their power, much less through the effects of their achievements on after generations, that the characters of "the Heroic Age" acquired celebrity; it was far more through the impression made upon their neighbours and contemporaries by their magnificence and generosity, by their personality, and perhaps above all by the adventures and vicissitudes of fortune which fell to their lot.'[4]

In other words, it is not the military or political effectiveness, but the literary 'availability',[5] of a barbarian war-lord that makes his literary fortune; and from this it follows that the literary history of a hero of 'heroic' poetry begins to diverge from his authentic history from the moment—which may fall within the hero's own lifetime—when his actions and his character are taken up as

---

[1] Chadwick, H. M.: *The Heroic Age* (Cambridge 1912, University Press).
[2] Compare Meyer, E.: *Geschichte des Altertums*, vol. i, part (1), 4th ed. (Stuttgart and Berlin 1921, Cotta), p. 222; eundem: *Geschichte des Altertums*, vol. ii, part (2), 2nd ed. (Stuttgart and Berlin 1928, Cotta), p. 295.
[3] Chadwick, op. cit., p. 167.
[4] Ibid. Cf. Meyer, E.: *Geschichte des Altertums*, vol. i, part (1), 4th ed. (Stuttgart and Berlin 1921, Cotta), pp. 220-1.
[5] In the sense in which this word is used of a candidate for the Presidency of the United States.

a literary theme by a poet. That moment sees the creation of a 'character' and a plot which have a separate existence from the personality and the transaction 'in real life' by which these creatures of imagination have been evoked in the poet's soul; and thenceforth these 'fictions' live and grow in accordance with aesthetic laws of their own which have little or no relation to the canons of historical veracity.[1]

'It is possible for an occurrence to be recounted in a way that departs completely from the real course of events, and this immediately after it has taken place, and in the mouths of the spectators and participants themselves. And, the farther the story spreads and the longer it lives, the more radical becomes the transformation, until at last there remains scarcely a vestige of the original facts.'[2]

A classic example of such duality in the literature relating to an historical person is the notorious distinction between the perfectly authentic historical records about Alexander the Great and the essentially imaginative 'Alexander Romance'. In this instance the romance and the records not only both began to take shape simultaneously within the hero's lifetime, but also both originated in the same social milieu, which was none other than Alexander's own personal entourage.[3]

As Professor Chadwick points out,

'Two tendencies are constantly observable: (i) to connect stories or incidents which originally were quite distinct;[4] (ii) within the

---

[1] This point has been touched upon by anticipation in V. C (i) (c) 3, p. 299, above.

[2] Meyer, E.: *Geschichte des Altertums*, vol. i, part (1), 4th ed., p. 221.

[3] See V. C (i) (c) 3, p. 252, above, and V. C (ii) (a), Annex II, vol. vi, pp. 441-4, below. The Alexander Romance may formally be included in our catalogue of 'heroic' literature, since Alexander's conquest of the Achaemenian Empire was, in its Macedonian aspect, a barbarian Völkerwanderung from the Thracian hinterland into the South-West Asian heart of the Syriac World. There is, however, another aspect of Alexander's work that is more prominent and at the same time more important. Besides being a barbarian war-lord, Alexander was a missionary of the Hellenic Civilization; and it was Hellenism, not Barbarism, whose domain was ultimately extended, as the result of Alexander's labours, at the expense of the Syriac Civilization and also of the Egyptiac, Babylonic, and Indic civilizations, whose domains had likewise been embraced within the conquered Achaemenian Empire's frontiers. In fact, the immediate effect of Alexander's conquests was to produce a sudden vast increase in the numbers of the internal proletariat of a disintegrating Hellenic Society (see III. C (i) (a), vol. iii, pp. 140 and 149-51; III. C (i) (d), vol. iii, pp. 197-9; and V. C (i) (c) 2, in the present volume, pp. 64-5, above); and it was in the slums of this Oriental Underworld, and not in the camps of the Macedonian war-bands who were Alexander's comrades-in-arms, that the Alexander Romance took shape eventually (see V. C (ii) (a), Annex II, vol. vi, p. 444, below). This example illustrates the fact that the 'heroic' literature of the External Proletariat has its counterpart in a 'folk' literature of the Internal Proletariat. And the divergence of 'fiction' from fact, which in this Annex we are studying in a 'heroic' proletarian milieu, is characteristic of the 'folk' proletarian literature as well (as will appear from the cases examined in V. C (i) (d) 11, Annex I, vol. vi, and in V. C (ii) (a), Annex II, vol. vi, below).

[4] Cf. Meyer, E.: *Geschichte des Altertums*, vol. i, part (1), 4th ed., p. 221. This tendency is strikingly illustrated by the growth of the legend of one of the heroes of the Classical School of Serb 'heroic' poetry, Marko Kraljević (see Chadwick, H. M. and N. K.: *The Growth of Literature*, vol. ii (Cambridge 1936, University Press), p. 388), and by the attraction, into the *Nibelungenlied*, of elements from different cycles

individual story to lose sight of all except the outstanding characters and incidents.'[1]

In fact, the finer the work of art that is the ultimate product of poetic genius and rhapsodic tradition, the farther the characters and the plot of the epos are likely to travel away from the historical persons and events by which they were originally inspired. The *chef d'œuvre* of creative perversion of the historical truth has perhaps been achieved in the 'heroic' poetry of the Serbian external proletariat of Orthodox Christendom, in which an historical hero, Vuk Branković, has been transfigured into a 'fictitious' traitor, and an historical traitor, Marko Kraljević, into a 'fictitious' hero.[2]

and of characters from distant ages (see Meyer, E.: *Geschichte des Altertums*, vol. ii, part (1), 2nd ed. (Stuttgart and Berlin 1928, Cotta), p. 296). In the Russian 'heroic' tradition the figure of the historical Cossack pioneer Yermak, who led the vanguard in the expansion of the Russian Orthodox Christendom across Siberia in the ninth decade of the sixteenth century of the Christian Era (see II. D (v), vol. ii, p. 157, and IV. C (iii) (c) 3 (α), vol. iv, p. 497, above), has similarly been attracted into the saga of Ilya of Murom in the Kiev Cycle of Russian 'heroic' poetry, which is an echo of historical events that had occurred four hundred years, at the latest, before Yermak's day (see Chadwick, op. cit., vol. ii, p. 50). One of the simplest and most easily intelligible illustrations of this tendency is the coalescence of two historical personages who happen to be one another's namesakes into a single character of 'heroic' saga. For example, the 'Prince Vladímir of Kiev' who is the equivalent of King Arthur in the Kiev Cycle of Russian 'heroic' poetry is a 'fictitious' compound of the two historical war-lords Vladímir I (*militabat* A.D. 980–1015) and Vladímir II (*militabat* A.D. 1113–25) (Chadwick, op. cit., vol. ii, pp. 24 and 34).—A.J.T.   [1] Chadwick, *The Heroic Age*, p. 138.

[2] Subotić, D.: *Yugoslav Popular Ballads, Their Origin and Development* (Cambridge 1932, University Press), pp. 84–7. Compare Chadwick, op. cit., p. 318. For the stages in the evolution of the historical Vuk Branković into a 'fictitious' traitor see Chadwick, H. M. and N. K.: *The Growth of Literature*, vol. ii (Cambridge 1936, University Press), p. 382. For the converse process of the embellishment of the figure of Marko Kraljević see op. cit., pp. 385–8. The good fortune of Marko Kraljević may prove to have been shared by a still more famous hero of 'heroic' saga. A gloss on a passage in the work of the Britanno-Roman historian Nennius (*Historia Brittonum*, chap. 56) gives an odious picture of Arthur. The following note on this point has been most kindly communicated to the writer of this Study by Professor H. M. Chadwick:

'The text of most of the MSS. is as follows (I am quoting from F. Lot's edition): "Tunc Arthur pugnabat contra illos in illis diebus cum regibus Brittonum, sed ipse dux erat bellorum." C and L add the following sentences: "Et in omnibus victor extitit. Mab Uter Britannice, 'filius horribilis' Latine, quoniam a puericia sua crudelis fuit. Artur Latine translatum sonat 'ursum horribilem' vel 'malleum ferreum' quo confringuntur molae leonum." Lot says: "add. de plusieurs mains de C copiée par L." I don't know the MSS., but I am under the impression that the additional passage is a gloss—or rather a series of glosses—in C, and that it is incorporated into the text in L. (C is Corp. Chr. Coll. Cambr. No. 139; L is Cambr. Univ. Libr. Ff. I.27.) In the "Lives" of saints Arthur sometimes behaves in a tyrannical way to a saint. Then the saint performs a miracle, and Arthur becomes penitent and generous. But there is one passage in the Prologue to the Life of St. Cadoc which represents Arthur in a rather more unsympathetic light, and which may perhaps interest you, if you have not seen it. Gwynllyw (Woollo), father of Cadoc, has eloped with Gwladys, daughter of Brychan, and is fleeing to his own country, hotly pursued by Brychan and his army. Arthur is playing dice with Cai and Bedwir on the top of a hill, as they pass. He is enraptured by the girl's beauty, and proposes to appropriate her for himself. But Cai and Bedwir say that this would be disgraceful, and that they ought to protect the distressed. So they come to the rescue of the lovers. Woollo and Gwladys eventually became saints, and Woollo's abode is now the cathedral of Newport. But I should doubt if the above incident is an early story. I have taken it from Rees' *Lives of the Cambro-British Saints*, p. 311 f. The Life of St. Cadoc is believed to date from *circa* A.D. 1075.'

Are we here catching a glimpse of an historical Arthur whose authentic lineaments have been embellished out of all recognition in the 'heroic' tradition from which all our other pictures of Arthur are derived? For the historical Marko Kraljević see also V. C (i) (d) 6 (α), p. 462, footnote 2, above.

Besides taking these enormous liberties with the historical persons and events which it does choose to mention, 'heroic' poetry is apt to pass over in silence the persons and events which are actually of the most outstanding historical importance in the age with which the poems are concerned.

'It is . . . a curious fact that Clovis and his great achievements seem to be entirely unnoticed in poetry; [and] it appears . . . that, though most of the principal Teutonic nations are represented in our stories, the relative prominence assigned to them does not at all correspond to what we should expect. Most remarkable is the fact that in stories relating to the Continent nearly all the chief characters (Eormenric, Theodric, Guthhere, Attila, etc.) belong to nations which had passed out of existence before the end of the sixth century.'[1]

For the historian it is a paradox that 'the Frankish nation, which ultimately became dominant, is but poorly represented'[2] in the Teutonic Epic; but this is by no means the greatest of the paradoxes with which the Teutonic Epic confronts him. The greatest of all is the at first sight astonishing fact that the Teutonic Epic almost entirely ignores the existence of the Roman Empire and *a fortiori* the history of the Hellenic Civilization of which the Roman Empire was the universal state.[3] How is this silence to be explained, when the age with which these Teutonic 'heroic' poems are concerned is precisely the post-Hellenic interregnum which was occupied by the Völkerwanderung of the North European and other transfrontier barbarians into the territories of the Roman Empire?

'The period . . . coincides with what is generally known as the Age of National Migrations (*Völkerwanderungszeit*). It was during this period that many of the Teutonic nations broke through the frontiers of the Roman Empire and carved out for themselves extensive kingdoms within its territories. Among these were the realms of Guthhere and Theodric, and in part also that of Attila. There is no doubt that in all these cases the conquest of the Roman provinces brought with it a great accession of wealth and profoundly affected the life of the invaders.'[4]

More than that, it is this very experience of breaking through the Roman frontiers and becoming masters of a derelict empire, after having been wanderers in a wilderness, that appears to have evoked the Epic in the barbarians' imaginations; and the victorious

---

[1] Chadwick, *The Heroic Age*, pp. 31–2; compare p. 39.
[2] Ibid., p. 39.
[3] 'It is by no means especially the important, nor indeed even the most momentous, events of the age that are immortalized in the [Teutonic] Epic Tradition. So far from that, the tradition knows nothing of the conflicts with Rome, of the invasion of the Roman provinces, or even of the bare existence of the Roman Empire, or, again, of the battle on the Catalaunian Plains.'—Meyer, E.: *Geschichte des Altertums*, vol. ii, part (1), 2nd ed. (Stuttgart and Berlin 1928, Cotta), p. 295.
[4] Chadwick, *The Heroic Age*, p. 28.

feat of arms, with this accompanying outburst of 'heroic' poetry, was the last act in a long drama of frontier warfare between the external proletariat and the dominant minority of the Hellenic Society. It was in response to the challenge of this frontier warfare that the barbarian war-lords and their war-bands and their poetry and their pantheon all arose.[1] What has moved the authors of the Teutonic Epic to leave unsung the Roman *causa causans* of their own barbarian art and barbarian world?

The first point to notice is that this remarkable silence is not unique. While we should never have suspected the existence of the Roman Empire and the Hellenic Society—of which we are so amply informed by contemporary Greek and Latin books, documents, and inscriptions—if the Teutonic Epic had been our only source of information, it is a fact that, until some of the public records of 'the New Empire' of Egypt were discovered and deciphered by our modern Western archaeologists, we actually never did guess from the 'heroic' tradition of Israel, as it has come down to us in the Pentateuch, that Palestine in the second millennium B.C. was under an Egyptiac dominion which had been long established there over the domain of a foregoing abortive Syriac Civilization.[2] In the narrative in the Book of Joshua there is no hint that the Canaanites whom the Israelites were assailing were subjects of 'the New Empire' of Egypt, and that many of the cities of Canaan were held at this time by Egyptian garrisons.[3] Thus the 'heroic' literature of Israel boycotts an Egyptian Empire as rigidly as the Roman Empire is boycotted by the Teutonic Epic. What is the explanation of this consistently strange behaviour of barbarian poets who ignore the empires which their heroes are engaged in destroying? If the barbarian war-lord's strongest desire is for fame, and if the barbarian minstrel's first business is to give this desire satisfaction,[4]

[1] The nature and genesis of this 'heroic' society is examined further in Part VIII, below.

[2] For this abortive Syriac Civilization—which has, of course, to be distinguished from the historic Syriac Civilization which afterwards came to birth in the same region—see II. D (vii), vol. ii, pp. 388–91, above.

[3] On this silence of the Books of Joshua, Judges, and Samuel in regard to an Egyptian rule in Palestine which lasted on into the twelfth century B.C. see Chadwick, *The Growth of Literature*, vol. ii, pp. 634 and 686, and Meyer, E.: *Geschichte des Altertums*, vol. ii, part (1), 2nd ed., p. 487, footnote 1: 'The Israelitish tradition has lost all recollection of these events [the punitive expedition of the Pharaoh Merneptah against the Israelitish settlements in the hill country of Ephraim at some date before the close of the thirteenth century B.C.] as completely as, for example, the Teutonic Saga has lost all recollection of the [North European barbarians'] conflicts with the Romans.' The Pentateuch does, however, contain a hint (though a very inadequate one) of the part which was played in the genesis of the historic live-born Syriac Civilization by refugees from the Minoan World (see I. C (i) (b), vol. i, p. 102, footnote 2, above).

[4] For the 'Heaven' in which the children of the Hellenic internal proletariat are bidden in the Gospel (Matt. vi. 20) to lay up treasure for themselves, the External Proletariat, in its 'Heroic Age', substitutes the glory that is conferred by canonization as a hero of poetry (Teggart, F. J.: *The Theory of History* (New Haven 1925, Yale University Press), pp. 13–14).

why suppress all mention of a feat of arms which is the greatest that any barbarian war-lord can achieve? Why leave unsung the conquest of long-coveted Gaul and of distant sea-girt Africa, and the sack of Rome herself, in order to make poetry out of rival war-lords' petty conflicts with one another μήλων ἕνεκ' Οἰδιπόδαο ?[1]

For the sophisticated historian it is hard to believe that the barbarian poets are not guilty of a conspiracy of silence to which they have been prompted by some inexplicable prejudice or else by sheer caprice. But it is the historian himself who has conjured up this insoluble problem by making the flagrantly unhistorical mistake of ascribing his own interests and outlook to authors who are poets and not historians and whose social milieu is a barbarian war-band and not a civilization.

'The supposition that it is an interest in History that keeps alive [the memory of] historical events [when these are the subject of "heroic" poetry] is merely an illusion in the mind of Posterity. In reality these tales survive thanks to just those elements in them that are unhistorical —elements which may be of a predominantly mythical or religious, or of an exclusively poetical, order. The true course of events is a matter of complete indifference [to the poet and his audience].'[2]

There is, in fact, no warrant for assuming that the authors of 'heroic' poetry are interested in historical truth at all, and *a fortiori* no likelihood that they compose their compositions for the purpose of giving Posterity an accurate and justly proportioned historical record of the age in which their heroes have been living. When once we rid our minds of these rather fantastic *a priori* postulates, we can perceive the patent fact that the silence of the Teutonic Epic in regard to Clovis and to Rome is neither capricious nor deliberate.

It is not capricious; for what the 'heroic' poet wants is a suitable theme for his art; and, from his point of view, both Rome and Clovis would be 'bad subjects'. Clovis is the shrewd calculating politician who has been born into the barbarian war-lord's harness and who successfully overthrows his rivals because he possesses qualities, 'making for success', that are rarely developed in men in his position; but these very qualities that have made Clovis a flaming political success, and therefore an outstanding historical figure, are obviously the marks of a rather prosaic and sordid character which is stony ground for a poet's imagination to cultivate.[3] As a human subject for poetry, how can a mere 'maker of

[1] Hesiod: *Works and Days*, l. 163.
[2] Meyer, E.: *Geschichte des Altertums*, vol. i, part (1), 4th ed., p. 222.
[3] This point has been touched upon, by anticipation, in V. C (i) (c) 3, pp. 296 and 297–9, above, in connexion with the history and the poetry of the Serb external proletariat of the main body of Orthodox Christendom. In this context we have

history' like Clovis compare in poetic interest with an ideal tragic
hero like the historically unimportant Guthheres and Siegfrieds?[1]
And, even in corporate political terms, how can a Frankish tortoise
creeping steadily towards hegemony compare in poetic pathos
with a Gothic hare bounding headlong to destruction?[2] As for
the Romans, it may be true that they have been unintentionally
the prime movers of the *Sturm und Drang* of the barbarian 'Heroic
Age', besides now being the principal victims of it. But how can
an unsophisticated poet make convincing characters for his tale
out of a strange people? How can he attempt to portray, from
within, a soul that, for him, is a sealed book? The contemporary
citizen of the Roman Empire is spiritually quite beyond the ken
of the barbarian minstrel and his barbarian audience in every one
of this Roman stranger's diverse tastes and activities—whether he
is watching a show in the amphitheatre or gossiping in the baths
or discussing the nature of the Trinity or commenting on the
Timàeus or writing a history of his own times. And if the minstrel
knows his business he will not attempt to handle subjects that are
intractable to his imagination.[3]

On this showing, we can see that the Teutonic Epic's silence
regarding the Romans and Clovis, and the Old Testament's silence
regarding the Egyptian officials—and all but silence regarding the
Minoan refugees—in the Promised Land, is so far from being
capricious that it is not even deliberate. Assuredly the poet does
not ever consciously take a decision to avoid mentioning such
people; he passes them over quite unconsciously in his practice

observed that the Hajduk and Uskok cycles of Serb 'heroic' poetry, which have for
their theme the earlier stages of an ultimately successful Serb breach of an Ottoman
limes, are artistically inferior to the works of the Classical School of Serb 'heroic'
poetry, which has for its theme the crushing defeat of the Serb war-bands by the
founders of the *Pax Ottomanica* at the close of the Orthodox Christian 'Time of
Troubles'. In the same context, again, we have seen that the nineteenth-century Serb
counterparts of Clovis have proved to be as refractory as Clovis himself to conversion
into subjects of 'heroic' poetry.

[1] In its disdain for mere material success the Barbarian Society of 'the Heroic Age'
agrees with the Gospel in its negative precept 'Lay not up for yourselves treasures upon
Earth' (Matt. vi. 19).

[2] This contrast between the respective careers of the Goths and the Franks has been
noticed in V. C (i) (c) 3, footnote 1, above.

[3] The soundness of a rule of the barbarian poet's art which has perhaps never been
consciously formulated, yet has certainly seldom been transgressed in practice, is demonstrated by the signal failure of the bards of a Russian school of 'heroic' poetry to find
fruitful subjects for their art in the sophisticated social life of the Westernized Russian
Orthodox Christendom of the Post-Petrine Age (see V. C (i) (c) 3, pp. 302–3, above).
The exceptional aberration, in this Russian case, of the proletarian artist's usually
sagacious sense of tact is perhaps to be explained by the fact that the Westernization of
Russian life was set in train, without any dynastic or even personal break, by a Muscovite
Tsar whose predecessors had provided themes for 'heroic' poetry that were quite after
the poet's heart. If the Western Civilization had been imposed upon Russia, not by
the native hands of a Peter Romanov, but by the alien hands of a Polish King Sigismund
III or a Swedish King Charles XII, we may guess with some confidence that the
contemporary Russian bards would then have passed over in silence the works and
days of such alien performers of a Russian Peter's historic handiwork.

of an art in which he is following the guidance of his artistic intuition without reflecting upon or defining what he is doing and
without ever formulating his practice in rules. It has not occurred
to him to differentiate between fact and fiction.[1] He simply has
an eye for a promising subject and a gift for presenting his theme
in a telling way; and in innocently following these lights he has
stumbled upon a method which Aristotle has ascribed to him—
correctly enough, as regards what our 'heroic' poet actually does,
but with a fantastic perversion of the truth in so far as the sophisticated philosopher takes it for granted that the barbarian artist is
as coldly and consciously purposive when he is composing a poem
as Aristotle himself is when he is constructing a syllogism.

'Homer is the great master of the art of telling falsehoods right. . . .
From him one learns to prefer what is impossible but plausible to what
is possible but incredible.'[2]

For the barbarian artist and his audience Beowulf's adventures
in Grendel's lair in the depths of the lake are more credible than
the life which a Theodoric begins to lead when, as the guerdon
for his victory in the Rabenschlacht, he exchanges the Gothic
camp for the Roman palace in order to rule the Roman People in
Italy as the Viceroy of the Emperor at Constantinople. The poet
does not seek to follow his lost leader through the folds of the
palace-curtains; and as an artist he is right—however culpable his
lack of curiosity might have been in the historian that this poet
has never set out to be.

On this showing, there is nothing either unusual or surprising in
the silence with which the historic sack of Cnossos *circa* 1400 B.C.
and the historic sea-fight off the coast of Egypt *circa* 1200/1190 B.C.
are passed over in the *Iliad* and the *Odyssey*, or in the comparable
silence of the Teutonic Epic in regard to the momentous battle of
A.D. 451 on the Catalaunian Plains and to a sack of Rome in A.D. 410
which reduced Saint Jerome to tears and moved Saint Augustine
to write *De Civitate Dei*.[3]

[1] On this point see I. C (iii) (e), Annex I, vol. i, p. 442, above, and V. C (ii) (a),
Annex II, vol. vi, pp. 438–64, below.
[2] Aristotle: *Poetics*, 1460 A, quoted in I. C (iii) (e), Annex, vol. i, p. 450, footnote 1,
above.
[3] See V. C (i) (c) 3, pp. 223–5, above.

FATALISM AS A SPIRITUAL TONIC

IF we have been right in suggesting that a deterministic creed is an expression of that sense of drift which is one of the psychological symptoms of social disintegration, we have still a problem to solve before we can claim that our proposition has been demonstrated; for it is an undeniable fact that many people—both individuals and communities—who have been avowed determinists have actually been distinguished by an uncommon energy, activity, and purposefulness, as well as by an uncommon assurance.

'The central paradox of religious ethics—that only those are nerved with the courage to turn the World upside down who are convinced that already, in a higher sense, it is disposed for the best by a power of which they are the humble instruments—finds in [Calvinism] a special exemplification.'[1]

Calvinism, however, is only one of several notorious examples of a fatalistic creed which is apparently in contradiction with the conduct of its votaries. The temper displayed by the Calvinists (Genevan, Huguenot,[2] Dutch, and Scottish) has likewise been displayed by other theistic predestinarians: for example, by the Jewish Zealots, by the Primitive Muslim Arabs, and by other Muslims of other ages and races (for instance, by the Janissaries who were observed by Rycaut[3] and by the Mahdists who were overthrown by Kitchener).[4] And in the nineteenth-century Western Liberal votaries of Progress and the twentieth-century Russian Communist Marxians we see two predestinarian sects of an atheistic turn of mind whose êthos is manifestly akin to that of their theistic fellow votaries of the idol of Necessity. The parallel between Communists and Calvinists has been drawn by the brilliant pen of the English historian whom we have quoted above.

'It is not wholly fanciful to say that, on a narrower stage but with not less formidable weapons, Calvin did for the *bourgeoisie* of the sixteenth century what Marx did for the proletariat of the nineteenth, or that the doctrine of Predestination satisfied the same hunger for an assurance that the forces of the Universe are on the side of the Elect as was to be assuaged in a different age by the theory of Historical Materialism. He

---

[1] Tawney, R. H.: *Religion and the Rise of Capitalism* (London 1926, John Murray), p. 109.
[2] For the prowess of the Huguenots there is an alternative explanation. It is possible that it may be due, not to their creed, but to their experience as a penalized minority (see II. D (vi), vol. ii, p. 250, above).
[3] See the quotation from Rycaut in V. C (i) (d) 4, on p. 430, above.
[4] See V. C (i) (c) 3, pp. 295-6, above, and V. C (ii) (a), vol. vi, p. 227, below.

set their virtues at their best in sharp antithesis with the vices of the established order at its worst, taught them to feel that they were a Chosen People, made them conscious of their great destiny in the Providential plan and resolute to realize it. . . . Their triumphs in the past, their strength in the present, their confidence in the future, their faith in themselves and their difference from their feebler neighbours—a difference as of an iron wedge in a lump of clay—made them, to use a modern phrase, class-conscious. Like the modern proletarian, who feels that, whatever his personal misery and his present disappointments, the Cause is rolled forward to victory by the irresistible force of an inevitable evolution, the Puritan *bourgeoisie* knew that against the Chosen People the gates of Hell could not prevail. The Lord prospered their doings.'[1]

The historical link between sixteenth-century Calvinism and twentieth-century Communism is nineteenth-century Liberalism.

'Determinism was much in vogue by this time; but why should Determinism be a depressing creed? The law which we cannot escape is the blessed Law of Progress—"that kind of improvement that can be measured by statistics". We had only to thank our stars for placing us in such an environment, and to carry out energetically the course of development which Nature has prescribed for us, and to resist which would be at once impious and futile. Thus the Superstition of Progress was firmly established. To become a popular religion, it is only necessary for a superstition to enslave a philosophy. The Superstition of Progress had the singular good fortune to enslave at least three philosophies—those of Hegel, of Comte, and of Darwin. The strange thing is that none of these philosophies is really favourable to the belief which it was supposed to support.'[2]

This at first sight contradictory combination of conduct and creed is evidently of too frequent an occurrence to be fortuitous. Are we to infer that a belief in Predestination is actually a spur to action? And, if this conclusion forces itself upon us, can a predestinarian creed still properly be regarded as an expression of the sense of drift?

These pertinent questions may perhaps be met with the following answer. The belief in Predestination does manifestly act on occasions as a spur to action[3]—a spur whose prick is exceedingly stimulating—but (if we may vary the simile in order to discover how far it can be pressed) a predestinarian creed may perhaps also be likened to a tonic which—like the drams drunk at half-time by

---

[1] Tawney, op. cit., pp. 112 and 210.
[2] Inge, W. R.: *The Idea of Progress* (Oxford 1920, Clarendon Press), pp. 8–9.
[3] The same stimulus has even been derived, by at least one famous man of action, from the usually enervating belief in the omnipotence of Chance. 'Imperatorem esse Fortunae est' was a favourite saying of Constantine the Great, but the moral that Constantine drew was 'agendum ut sint imperio digni quos regendi in necessitatem vis fatalis adduxerit'.—*Historia Augusta*, 'Antoninus Heliogabalus', chap. 34.

improvident players in the football-match described in *Tom
Brown's Schooldays*[1]—is transitory in its effect and is also apt to
leave the drinker's last state worse than his first. Taking a hint
from one of the passages quoted above from Professor Tawney,
we may also surmise that Predestinarianism is a belief to which
people do not readily take unless they are consciously in need of
a pick-me-up. 'The hunger for an assurance that the forces of the
Universe are on the side of the Elect' may have to be felt before
Fatalism can become attractive; and such hunger is surely evidence that the person who feels it has been losing faith in his own
power to control events, or, in other words, has been succumbing
to the sense of drift.

On this showing, the adoption of a predestinarian creed may be
interpreted as an attempt to fortify a weakening human will by
making the bold assumption that this human will is coincident
with the Will of God or with the Law of Nature or with the decrees
of Necessity, and is therefore bound, *a priori*, to prevail. If such
a belief is embraced by the convert with even a modicum of sincerity, it is easy to understand how it may give power to his elbow
for a season. But by the same token it is evident that the stimulus
is artificial; and we may also reflect that, if the predestinarian really
believed in Predestination in his heart of hearts, he would turn
quietist—which he does not—instead of turning rampant as he
does.[2] The demoniac effort which the predestinarian is prone to
make for the purpose of ratifying the decrees of Fate by his own
exertions is an idle and indeed an impious activity if the predestinarian's professed convictions are to be taken seriously; and we
may venture to draw the conclusion that his belief in the coincidence of his own will with the inevitable course of Destiny is
hollow in the exact measure of the believer's display of 'dynamism'. It is at any rate indisputable that Predestinarianism does
resemble dram-drinking in this, that the practice revenges itself

[1] 'The leaders are past oranges and apples, but some of them visit their coats and
apply innocent-looking ginger-beer bottles to their mouths. It is no ginger-beer,
though, I fear, and will do you no good. One short mad rush, and then a stitch in the
side and no more honest play: that's what comes of those bottles.'—Hughes, T.: *Tom
Brown's Schooldays*, chap. 3.

[2] It is worth recalling in this context that, in Jewry to-day, Quietism is the attitude
of the *Agudath Israel* towards that hope of a return to the Promised Land which is
cherished by Jews of all persuasions, while the Zionists are activists both on principle
and in practice. The *Agudath Israel* are a strictly orthodox sect who believe implicitly
that an ultimate restoration of Jewry is God's will, and that He is certain to accomplish
this purpose of His in His own way and in His own time. On the other hand the Zionists
partake of the secularist rationalism of the modern Western Goyyim from whom
Zionism has taken the tone of its nationalism (see V. C (i) (c) 2, p. 76, above). In an
earlier chapter of Jewish history the attitude of the Rabbi Johanan ben Zakkai presents
a similar contrast to the behaviour of the Zealots (see loc. cit., pp. 75–6). For the
positive difference between the negatively identical Quietism or Non-Violence of the
Agudath Israel on the one hand and Rabbi Johanan ben Zakkai on the other see V. C
(i) (c) 2, Annex III, pp. 588–9, above.

upon the addict as soon as things begin to go badly with him. For it becomes impossible for him to equate Destiny with his own will as soon as this will of his fails to impose itself triumphantly upon his environment; and, when this failure (which is inevitable sooner or later) eventually overtakes him, then he is driven to equate Destiny, no longer with a will of his own that is now being frustrated, but, on the contrary, with those intractable external circumstances to which this devastating frustration has to be ascribed. When this happens, the predestinarian's artificially stimulated confidence and energy give place abruptly to a proportionately exaggerated discouragement and lassitude. The 'dynamism' of yesterday has to be paid for with the 'defeatism' of the morrow.

THE NAPOLEONIC EMPIRE AS A UNIVERSAL STATE

THE Napoleonic Empire is usually regarded as an episode in the history of France or—on a rather wider view—in the history of the Balance of Power between the Great Powers of the Western World in the modern chapter of Western history; and from this angle of vision the Napoleonic episode wears the appearance of a sensational interlude which is oddly out of relation with both its antecedents and its sequel. In these customary terms the best account of the Napoleonic Empire that we shall find ourselves able to give is that the titanic personal genius of Napoleon, harnessing to its own aims the no less titanic social driving-force which had been generated by the French Revolution, came within an ace of overthrowing a Balance of Power between the principal states of the Western World which had been steadily maintained over a period of some three hundred years before Napoleon entered the arena; but we shall have to add that Napoleon's career was a brief one[1] and that the eventual miscarriage of his all but successful attempt to make France mistress of the Western World by delivering 'knock-out blows' to all the other Great Powers was so decisive that, since the morrow of the Battle of Waterloo, the history of the Western World might appear to have resumed its pre-Napoleonic course as though the Napoleonic episode had been nothing but a pointless aberration.[2] Such an account of the Napoleonic episode is so manifestly unsatisfactory and unconvincing that any student of history will be impelled to question the validity of an outlook from which the object of study assumes so queer a shape.

Can we, then, espy anything radically wrong with that conventional way of looking at the Napoleonic Empire which we have just been essaying? Perhaps the mistake may lie in allowing ourselves to see this so-called 'French Empire' through French eyes;

---

[1] From the Italian campaign of A.D. 1797 to the Hundred Days in A.D. 1815 inclusive, Napoleon's career extended over no more than nineteen campaigning seasons, and the widest extension of the Napoleonic Empire, which did not outlast the year 1812, had not been attained until the close of the year 1809.

[2] The psychological effect of the Restoration of 1814–15 in one of the Rhenish districts of the non-French portion of the Napoleonic Empire has been vividly conveyed, from a deeply felt personal experience, by Heine in the last of the three pieces that constitute the *Reisebilder*. In 'Das Buch Le Grand' the German-Jewish man-of-letters shows us the *Ancien Régime* clicking back into place with an instantaneous precision which made the Napoleonic interlude seem, in retrospect, as though it must have been a mere political mirage.

'Wo man sonst Französisch sprach, ward jetzt Preussisch gesprochen; sogar ein kleines preussisches Höfchen hatte sich unterdessen dort angesiedelt; und die Leute trugen Hoftitel; die ehemalige Friseurin meiner Mutter war Hoffriseurin geworden, und es gab jetzt dort Hofschneider, Hofschuster, Hofwanzenvertilgerinnen, Hofschnapsläden; die anze Stadt schien ein Hoflazareth für Hofgeisteskranke.'

for though, at first sight, it may seem sheer common sense to take a French view of an empire that was built up by French arms round a French nucleus, we find in general that as a matter of fact an empire is apt to play a less important part in the lives of the empire-builders who have exerted themselves to erect it as a monument to their own egotism than it plays in the lives of their involuntary subjects who have been annexed by force of arms and who have been chafing under a yoke which they feel to be both cramping and humiliating.[1] If we are to apply this general law of empire-building to our Napoleonic case, we must begin by concentrating our attention upon the non-French portion of the Napoleonic Empire in order to observe how this composite body politic looks from a standpoint which is just the opposite of that which its historians have usually taken.

Our first step will be to remind ourselves of the territories which this non-French portion of the French Empire embraced at its greatest extension in the years 1810–11; and to define this area we must exclude France proper, up to her pre-imperial limits as these stood in 1792, besides excluding all countries which cannot be reckoned to have been effectively under the government or the control of the Emperor Napoleon, even at the summit of his power. On this criterion we must unquestionably exclude the Ottoman Empire and Great Britain and the Overseas World (none of which ever fell into Napoleon's hands save for an ephemeral occupation of the soil of Egypt and possession of the title-deeds to Louisiana); and we should scarcely be justified in including either Prussia or Austria or Russia—in spite of the fact that, at certain times between 1805 and 1813, all three of these East European Powers were dominated by Napoleon in different degrees. *A fortiori* we cannot include Spain and Portugal, which were partially occupied by Napoleon's armies without ever being completely subdued. We are left with two sets of territories which hang together *de facto* in spite of an arbitrary juridical distinction which was drawn by the French empire-builders on the principle of *divide et impera*. On the one hand we have the non-French

[1] This paradoxical 'law' of empire-building is tested empirically in Part VI, below. In the Hellenic case there is evidence to show that the conception of the Roman Empire as a Hellenic universal state was first conceived in the minds of the Romans' Greek subjects (see the passage quoted in V. C (i) (c) 4, pp. 343–4, above, from Aelius Aristeides' *In Romam*) and that the lesson was only learnt at second hand and against the grain by the Romans themselves, who were slow to acquiesce in the idea that an empire built in the sweat of Roman brows was not, after all, an exclusively Roman affair (see Vogt, J.: *Orbis Romanus* (Tübingen 1929, Mohr), pp. 9–10). In Oswald Spengler's picturesque language, 'Imperialism is so necessary a result of every civilization that it takes a people by the scruff of the neck and hurls them into the role of rulers if they refuse to play. The Roman Empire was not a product of conquest. The *Orbis Terrarum* forced itself into this mould and compelled the Romans to give it their name' (Spengler, O.: *Der Untergang des Abendlandes*, vol. ii (Munich 1922, Beck), p. 529).

territories which were annexed to the French Empire outright:
the new French departments which were constituted out of the
Netherlands; out of the German districts on the left bank of the
Middle Rhine and on the lower reaches of the Ems, Weser, and
Elbe; out of the Italian districts in the Upper Basin of the Po and
along the Mediterranean coast from Nice to Terracina (including
the whole of the basins of the Arno, Ombrone, and Tiber); and
out of the ex-Venetian and ex-Hapsburg territories on the eastern
sea-board of the Adriatic and in its hinterland from the Bocche di
Cattaro to the eastern bank of the Isonzo and to the headwaters
of the Drave. On the other hand we have those dependencies of
the French Empire which were formally not less independent than
Prussia, Austria, Russia, or Spain, but were practically not less
subject to French control than the neighbouring non-French territories which had been reduced officially to the status of integral
parts of the French Imperial body politic; and this second group
includes not only the Napoleonic Kingdom of Italy (which was an
integral part of the French Empire in all but name), but also the
Kingdom of Naples, the states members of the Confederation of
the Rhine, the Duchy of Warsaw, and Switzerland, together with
such small fry as the principalities of Lucca, Piombino, Benevento,
Pontecorvo, and Neufchâtel, and the republics of San Marino and
Danzig.

When these two groups of territories have been amalgamated in
our mind's eye, we shall find that, if we leave out of account the
two outlying dependencies of Warsaw and Naples, the residue
almost exactly coincides in area with the domain of a medieval
city-state cosmos which we have plotted out in another context.[1]
And, if we now set ourselves to think of the Napoleonic Empire
as a belated episode in the history of this medieval galaxy of
Northern Italian and Western German and Flemish city-states,
we shall find historical explanations for the extent and the date and
the duration of Napoleon's conquests, and for the provenance of
Napoleon himself, instead of having to resign ourselves to being
baffled by a series of historical problems that are insoluble so
long as we insist upon thinking of the Napoleonic Empire as a
momentary aggrandizement of modern France in the course of her
latter-day competition with the other Great Powers of the modern
Western World.

In the first place we shall observe that the extent of the Napoleonic Empire, as we have defined it above, is just what we should
expect if its *raison d'être* was to provide the medieval Western
city-state cosmos with a universal state (in the sense in which that

---

[1] In III. C (ii) (*b*), vol. iii ,pp. 344–7, above.

term is used in this Study).[1] For, in embracing the whole of the
cosmos for which it was performing this service, and at the same
time including under the same political aegis a broad circuit of
extraneous territories, the Napoleonic Empire, looked at in relation to that medieval Western cosmos, displays the same political
structure as the Roman Empire looked at as the universal state of
the Hellenic World. In this aspect the Roman Empire can be
dissected into three distinct geographical parts: first, the Greek
core of the Hellenic World which the Roman empire-builders had
succeeded in uniting under their own rule; second, the Italian
marches of the Hellenic World, which had nurtured these Roman
empire-builders and had provided them with the necessary base
of operations; and, third, a fringe of alien territories (Syriac and
Egyptiac in their culture) which had been incorporated into the
Hellenic World in the course of its disintegration and were consequently at the disposal of the Roman empire-builders as materials
for adding an architecturally superfluous Oriental wing to their
Hellenic political edifice. If we regard the Napoleonic Empire as
the universal state of the medieval Western city-state cosmos, we
shall find that it resolves itself into three corresponding component
parts. In the first place it embraced the Tuscan and Lombard
and Swabian and Rhenish and Flemish and Hanseatic core of
the cosmos to which we are relating it; in the second place it
embraced, in France, a march which played the same active part
in the construction of the Napoleonic Empire as was played in the
construction of the Roman Empire by Italy; and in the third place
the Napoleonic Empire embraced, in the Duchy of Warsaw and in
the Kingdom of Naples, certain originally alien territories which
had been penetrated by the cultural influence of the medieval city-
state cosmos during the modern centuries of its decline.

The Kingdom of Naples was a remnant of the colonial domain
which the maritime Italian city-states, in partnership with Norman
and other Transalpine adventurers, had acquired in the Mediterranean at the height of their medieval prosperity;[2] and in this
connexion we may also observe that the Mediterranean island
which was the birthplace of the Emperor Napoleon was one of the
earliest acquisitions of the medieval Italian maritime Powers at
the expense of the Syriac and Orthodox Christian worlds.[3] When

---

[1] An explanation of the Napoleonic Empire in this sense has been foreshadowed in
II. D (iv), vol. ii, p. 104, above.

[2] For the medieval Mediterranean empires of Venice and Genoa and Florence see III.
C (ii) (b), vol. iii, p. 347, footnote 1, above. For the genesis of the Kingdom of the Two
Sicilies as a Norman Western 'successor-state' of the Orthodox Christian East Roman
Empire see IV. C (iii) (c) 2 (β), vol. iv, p. 353, footnote 2, and p. 406, footnote 3, above.

[3] See V. C (i) (c) 3, p. 244, above. The Italian maritime Powers expelled the Arabs
from Corsica in A.D. 1091 (Pirenne, H.: Les Villes du Moyen Âge (Brussels 1927, Lamer-

we remind ourselves that the Buonaparti were not even native Corsicans but were colonists of Florentine origin,[1] we shall perceive that Napoleon's provenance—so far from being one of the curiosities of history, as it is bound to appear if we think of him primarily as a ruler of France[2]—is eminently appropriate to the emperor of a universal state that had been called into existence in order to serve the needs of a cosmos of city-states in which Florence was a focal point and in which even Corsica lay within hail of two such brilliant maritime stars in the galaxy as Genoa and Pisa. When we see this Florentino-Corsican military adventurer in the French service winning his spurs in a campaign resulting in the expulsion of the Austrian 'barbarians' from Italian soil, and then immediately following up this success by cajoling his French employers into entrusting him with the command of a French expeditionary force for the purpose of gaining possession of the lost medieval Italian overseas empire in the Levant, it seems hardly fanciful to suggest that, in these illuminating early chapters of his career, Napoleon was—albeit unconsciously—being drawn into the wake of his medieval Italian forebears.[3]

Again, if we observe the date at which the sudden emergence of

tin), p. 82). Before the close of the eleventh century the Pisans had ousted their Genoese fellow conquerors from both Corsica and Sardinia (Schaube, A.: *Handelsgeschichte der Romanischen Völker des Mittelmeergebiets bis zum Ende der Kreuzzüge* (Munich and Berlin 1906, Oldenbourg), p. 54). But during the next two hundred years the Genoese gradually regained ground in Corsica at the Pisans' expense. In 1138 Pope Innocent II divided the ecclesiastical jurisdiction over the island between the Pisan and Genoese sees. In 1195 the Genoese established themselves at Bonifacio. In 1347 they were requested by a Corsican national assembly to assume sovereignty over Corsica. And, after a century and a half (1298–1447) of struggle for possession between Genoa and Aragon, Corsica did eventually come under a Genoese rule which was exercised first indirectly through the Bank of St. George and then, from 1559 onwards, by the Genoese Government itself.

[1] See II. C (ii) (a) 1, vol. i, p. 242, footnote 3, above.

[2] The date of Napoleon's birth was just late enough to allow him to be born a French subject instead of a Genoese (see V. C (i) (d) 6 (γ), p. 503, footnote 3, above). He was born on the 15th August, 1769, and a Franco-Genoese treaty executing the sale of the sovereignty over Corsica by Genoa to France had been signed on the 15th May, 1768. *De facto* the Genoese Government's exercise of authority in Corsica had been ineffective since 1729; and French troops had landed on the island with Genoese acquiescence in 1764. The resistance of the islanders to their French conquerors had collapsed only two months before Napoleon's birth, when, on the 16th June, 1769, their leaders had sailed from Corsica for Leghorn as refugees on board a British ship.

[3] Consciously, perhaps, Napoleon owed the inspiration of his Egyptian Expedition to the unearthing of a plan which had been submitted to the French King Louis XIV by the Hanoverian philosopher Leibniz and had been preserved ever since, unutilized, in the French Government's archives (see Ghorbal, S.: *The Beginnings of the Egyptian Question and the Rise of Mehemet Ali* (London 1928, Routledge), p. 3); and certainly in French minds Napoleon in Egypt has commonly presented himself in the guise of a successor of Saint Louis (for the *peripeteia* in the relative military efficiency of the French invaders of Egypt and the Egyptian Mamlūks between Saint Louis' day and Napoleon's see IV. C (iii) (c) 2 (γ), vol. iv, p. 450, above). In the modern history of France, however, Napoleon's Egyptian Expedition remains, nevertheless, as oddly detached an episode as the Napoleonic Empire itself, whereas, if we regard Buonaparte in the light of a would-be founder of an Italo-Flemish universal state, his attempt to follow in the Levantine wake of his medieval Venetian predecessors will become just as intelligible as Mark Antony's attempt to follow in the footsteps of Alexander the Great.

the Napoleonic Empire interrupted the regular course of modern
Western history, we shall find that this is just the time when we
should expect to witness the foundation of a universal state in the
history of the medieval Western city-state cosmos; for we have
seen reasons for suggesting that this medieval Western sub-civili-
zation may have broken down in the last quarter of the fourteenth
century of the Christian Era;[1] and, since the average duration of
those 'Times of Troubles' which intervene between the breakdown of a civilization and the rally that is signalized by the foundation of its universal state[2] would appear, on the statistical evidence
at our command, to run to about four hundred years,[3] the end of
the eighteenth century, which is the moment when the Napoleonic
Empire arose, is the very time when we should be expecting the
appearance of some empire of this kind and scale in those parts of
Western Christendom into which the medieval city-state cosmos
had ramified in its heyday.

Finally we shall find that, by relating the Napoleonic Empire,
as we are now doing, to the medieval city-state cosmos, we can
explain the brevity of its life and the completeness of its failure to
make any notable mark upon the course of Western history beyond
assuring the French language of a currency as a *lingua franca*.[4]

If we glance again at the map of the Napoleonic Empire at its
apogee from the morrow of the Danubian campaign of 1809 until
the eve of the retreat from Moscow in 1812, and concentrate our
attention, this time, upon the setting of this empire in the map of
the world of the day, we shall observe that its standing during this
brief spell of three campaigning seasons—A.D. 1810–12—is almost
exactly analogous to that of the Roman Empire during the spell of
twenty-two years which began in 168 B.C. on the morrow of the
Battle of Pydna and ended in 146 B.C. with the annexation of
Africa and Macedonia and the annihilation of Carthage and
Corinth.[5] For the purposes of our comparative study of the standing of the French and Roman Empires in their respective worlds
during these two spells of time, we may equate Austria with
Macedon; Prussia with Carthage; Spain with the Empire of the
Ptolemies; Russia with the Empire of the Seleucidae; Sweden with

---

[1] For the symptoms of breakdown in several portions of this cosmos in the course of
that quarter of a century see III. C (ii) (b), vol. iii, pp. 347–50, above.

[2] For the rhythm of Rout-and-Rally-and-Relapse in the disintegration of a civilization see V. C (ii) (b), vol. vi, pp. 278–87, below.

[3] The statistical evidence for this Time-span is examined in Part XI, below.

[4] For this linguistic legacy of the Napoleonic Empire—a legacy which is the *point
d'attache* of the present Annex to the main thread of this Study of History—see V. C (i)
(d) 6 (γ), pp. 502–6, above.

[5] This comparison has already been foreshadowed in II. D (iv), vol. ii, pp. 103–6.
See also III. C (ii) (b), vol. iii, pp. 310–14 and 339–41, and IV. C (iii) (c) 2 (α), vol. iv,
pp. 265–6 and 268–9, above, and V. C (ii) (b), vol. vi, pp. 290–1, below.

the Pergamene shadow of the abortive Empire of Lysimachus; the Confederation of the Rhine with Rhodes and Numidia and the rest of those small states of the Hellenic World which had found their advantage in siding with Rome against the other Great Powers who were Rome's defeated rivals and these small states' no longer formidable neighbours; the Napoleonic Kingdom of Italy with Continental European Greece to the south of Olympus; the Italian departments of the French Empire with the Roman province of Sicily; and the Rhenish and Netherlandish and Hanseatic departments of the French Empire with Magna Graecia. This elaboration of our analogy will not be labour lost if it serves to bring out the essential points of likeness between the two international situations that we have brought into a synoptic view.

In both tableaux we see the same political landscape with its cluster of venerable and cultivated but minute and broken-down *Kleinstaaten* in the centre and with its ring of large and lusty but upstart and brutal Great Powers round the edges; in both, in the act immediately preceding the respective moments (168 B.C. and A.D. 1810) at which we are raising the curtain on the play, the impotent centre has been serving as an arena in which the boisterous giants from the outskirts have been contending for the maintenance or overthrow of a Balance of Power among themselves; and in both, at the moment of observation, the Balance has in fact been overthrown through a notable triumph of one of the competing Great Powers over its rivals. The victor—Rome in the one case and France in the other—has already set up the conventional trophy of victory in the shape of an exclusive hegemony over the whole cluster of small states in the centre of the ring; and the other Great Powers—though they have not yet been wiped off the map —have been excluded from all influence over the central area, shorn of large slices of their own metropolitan territories, and weakened to a degree at which—if they were ever to venture again to try conclusions with the victor and were to take the obvious precaution of banding themselves into a coalition for the joint conduct of this formidable enterprise—they would scarcely find themselves able, even with united forces, to face their common adversary single-handed.

The political significance of this international map is unmistakable: the old division between the small states at the centre and the Great Powers round the fringes, and the old temperate and therefore recurrent contests[1] between the Great Powers themselves, are both now on the point of being brought to an end through the forcible unification of the whole of this hitherto fragmentary world by the arms of a single Great Power which is at last on the verge of expanding into a universal state. One more round of warfare, and the process can hardly fail to be completed! And in the Hellenic case this expectation was in fact duly realized; for the sixth decade of the second century B.C. saw the extinction of the remnants of Carthage and Macedon and the reduction of the remnants of the Seleucid and Ptolemaic Empires to an impotence at which they found themselves as completely at Rome's mercy as if they had been a Pergamum or a Rhodes. In the Western case, however, the play has a denouement which runs quite counter to the plot; for the inevitable next round of warfare, which was fought out in this case in the years 1812–15 of the Christian Era, did not leave the French Empire in sole and thenceforth unchallengeable possession of a completely prostrate world. On the contrary, it resulted in the utter overthrow of a Power which at the end of the preceding act had seemed to be on the verge of becoming a universal state; and this reversal of the fortunes of France was followed by a complete rehabilitation of those rival Powers which, at the end of the preceding act, had seemed to be on the verge of annihilation. Manifestly it is the Napoleonic and not the Scipionic denouement that demands an explanation. Let us see whether we can discover one.

If we return to our comparison between a Hellenic World of the third and second centuries B.C. over which Rome succeeded in establishing a domination that was exclusive and ubiquitous and lasting, and a Western World of the eighteenth and nineteenth centuries of the Christian Era in which Napoleon tried and failed to emulate this Roman achievement, we shall be able to put our finger upon one point of difference between the two situations which is vital. The Hellenic World of which Rome made herself mistress consisted of the three parts—and these three only—which we have analysed above: first a central cluster of venerable city-states which had been the original Hellas; second an outer ring of parvenu Great Powers of a supra-city-state calibre, including the Roman Commonwealth and its four unsuccessful rivals; and in the third place an appendage of alien territories which had fallen under Hellenic rule in the course of the Hellenic Society's disintegration. We have identified three corresponding components of the world in which Napoleon failed in the nineteenth century of the Christian Era to obtain the conclusive success which the Romans had obtained in their world in the second century B.C.; but we have now to observe that, although this geographical

survey of Napoleon's world does cover the whole of the area of the
medieval Western city-state cosmos up to the farthest limits of its
latest expansion, it is still far from accounting for the whole of the
modern Western World of Napoleon's day—whereas the area over
which the Romans extended their dominion in the second century
B.C. does account for the whole of the Hellenic World of that time.

In another context we have noticed that the medieval Western
city-state cosmos had never succeeded in swallowing up the whole
of Western Christendom at any time—not even in the heyday of
the city-states in the thirteenth and fourteenth centuries.[1] The
pre-existent Western feudal dispensation survived both the rise
and the fall of the medieval Western city-state régime—and this
not only in the Transalpine parts of Western Europe, but also in
a Cisalpine Piedmont at the very gates of Milan and Genoa.[2]
Moreover this recalcitrant major portion of Western Christendom
which had held aloof from the city-state experiment contrived to
be the principal beneficiary from a social and cultural venture on
which it had obstinately declined to stake its own future; for, when
the city-state cosmos broke down at the turn of the fourteenth
and fifteenth centuries, the hitherto impenitently feudal part of
Western Christendom became the residuary legatee of Tuscany
and Lombardy and Flanders, and successfully rejuvenated itself
by grafting the delicate shoots of a Flemish and Italian culture
on to hardier French and Spanish and English stems.[3] This feudal
second-hand version of a medieval city-state culture was propagated, in the course of the Modern Age of Western history, not only
throughout the whole feudal residue of Western Christendom
within its medieval limits, but on beyond into newly discovered
worlds. It made its way overseas into the Indies and Americas and
overland into the Russias. These were the dimensions of the
Great Society into which Napoleon was born and in which he had
to work; and the two new worlds that had been brought within
the ambit of the Western World during the three centuries ending
in Napoleon's generation were the factors that upset Napoleon's
calculations, wore down his strength, and eventually redressed the
balance of the old city-state cosmos, which Napoleon had triumphantly overthrown, by bringing the whole Napoleonic edifice
to the ground in irreparable ruin.

The extent and resources of these new worlds with which
Napoleon failed to reckon can be measured by recurring to our
comparison between the Roman political system in the years

[1] See III. C (ii) (*b*), vol. iii, pp. 346–7, above.
[2] For the imperviousness of Piedmont to the influence of the North-Italian city-state
culture see IV. C (iii) (*c*) 2 (*α*), vol. iv, pp. 285–6, above.
[3] See III. C (ii) (*b*), vol. iii, pp. 351–63, above.

168–146 B.C. and the Napoleonic political system in A.D. 1810–12.
When we have accounted for everything in the Napoleonic system
to which the Roman can supply a counterpart, we shall recollect
that we have not found any anti-Roman counterpart of Great
Britain—a Power which in A.D. 1810–12 was still holding its own
against Napoleon on equal terms—and also that, in taking notice
of Napoleon's incursion into the Iberian Peninsula, we have so far
overlooked the immunity from French invasion which was enjoyed, from beginning to end of the Napoleonic episode, by the
immense Spanish and Portuguese empires overseas under the
aegis of a British Navy which held the command of the sea and
made use of it in order to insulate all the Transmarine appendages
of Western Europe from their normal contact with a continent
that had now fallen under Napoleon's military domination. In the
third place we shall observe that our equation of Russia with the
Seleucid Monarchy—valid though it may be on the points of
social structure and cultural role—breaks down on the point of
political and military strength, which is the crucial point for our
present purpose.

While the reverses which Napoleon inflicted upon Russian
armies on Austrian and Prussian ground in A.D. 1805 and A.D.
1807[1] may be comparable to the Roman victories over the Seleucid
King Antiochus III at Thermopylae and Magnesia in the War of
192–188 B.C., there is no parallel at all, but on the contrary an
extreme antithesis, between the crushing diplomatic humiliation
that was inflicted upon Antiochus IV in 168 B.C. by the Roman
envoy Popillius Laenas[2] and the Russian Tsar Alexander's decisive

---

[1] See II. D (iv), vol. ii, p. 106, above.

[2] Popillius presented himself, without any armed force at his back, at Antiochus's
camp before the walls of Pelusium, at a moment when the Seleucid monarch had in his
grasp the metropolitan territory of the Ptolemaic Empire which was the historic rival
of the Seleucid House. In these circumstances Popillius handed Antiochus an ultimatum from the Roman Government in which the aggressor was called upon to surrender
and renounce all his actual and prospective gains at the Ptolemaic Empire's expense.
When Antiochus, after reading the text of the ultimatum, asked the bearer for time to
consult his ministers on the momentous questions that it raised, Popillius drew a circle
round the King with his stick and insisted upon having his answer before Antiochus
stepped out of the ring. After a brief hesitation Antiochus gave Popillius to understand
that he accepted the Roman Government's terms without reservation. Evidently the
paramount consideration in Antiochus's mind, when he submitted to a public humiliation against which his fiery temperament must have vehemently rebelled, was the knowledge that, if he accepted the Roman challenge, he would assuredly bring upon himself
and his empire a repetition of the disaster into which his father Antiochus III had blun-
dered in the Romano-Seleucid War of 192–188 B.C. At the same time, according to one
modern Western master of the subject (Tarn, W. W.: *The Greeks in Bactria and India*
(Cambridge 1938, University Press), p. 192), Antiochus IV, when he turned the other
cheek to the imperious Roman envoy in 168 B.C., was moved not only by prudence but
also by ambition. According to this interpretation of Antiochus IV's policy and acts, the
conquest of Egypt was for him a secondary aim which he was determined not to allow
to divert his energies and resources from his primary aim of reincorporating into the
Seleucid Empire the whole of the Far East of the post-Alexandrine Hellenic World,
including the vast new dominions which the Bactrian Greek prince Demetrius the son
of Euthydemus had recently acquired on Indian ground south-east of the Hindu Kush.

victory over Napoleon in the military campaign of A.D. 1812. For a Roman parallel to Napoleon's retreat from Moscow we must look, not to any Seleucid feat of arms, but to the annihilating defeat which Crassus suffered in 53 B.C. at the hands of the Parthians; and even Crassus's catastrophe at Carrhae, appalling though it was in itself, did not bring the Roman Empire to the ground, as the Napoleonic Empire was brought down by the retreat from Moscow. It is evident that—in contrast to the utter inability of the Seleucidae to stand up, even in Asia, to a Roman assault—the Russians on their own ground were more than a match for Napoleon.

This military and political strength that was displayed by Russia in response to Napoleon's challenge undoubtedly took Napoleon himself by surprise; and it does indeed demand some explanation, considering that Russia was a semi-barbarous off-shoot of Orthodox Christendom which had not begun to seek initiation into the 'polite society' of the modern Western World until the reign of Peter the Great; for, between the year 1689, which was the date of Peter's effective accession to power, and the year 1812, in which Russia was called upon to undergo the tremendous ordeal of meeting an attack by a military genius who commanded all the resources of Western and Central Continental Europe, Peter's bold experiment of transposing Russian life from a Byzantine to a modern Western key had been given no longer than 123 years to work itself out. How, then, are we to explain the remarkable outcome of the campaign of 1812? The credit for the triumphant reaction of Russia to her searching Napoleonic test cannot all be assigned to the genius of Peter and to the perseverance of his Westernizing successors in the government of the Petrine Russian state; the surprising solidity which the Petrine structure now showed itself to possess must partly be attributed to the excellence of the sources from which Peter and his successors had derived the Western technique and institutions and ideas with which they had been industriously leavening their Byzantine heritage. These Muscovite apostles of Westernization had turned in the first instance to Holland, and thereafter to the Protestant parts of Germany; and from these quarters they had obtained a modern Western version of the medieval Western culture of Flanders and Northern Italy which possibly had more life in it than the Hellenism which the Seleucid Empire imported in the third and second centuries B.C. from an Athens who by then had passed the prime in which she had been 'the education of Hellas'[1] without

---

[1] For the decadence of Athens see IV. C (iii) (*c*) 2 (α), vol. iv, pp. 263–74, above. In the third and second centuries B.C., however, Athens was only one of the sources

having handed on her torch to any younger or more lively disciples.

While this invigoratingly Westernized Russia taxed Napoleon's military strength on the Continent to a point at which it gave way under the strain, the naval and economic discomfiture of the would-be maker of a Western universal state was the work of Great Britain; and here is a second opponent of Napoleon's ambitions who—more clearly still than Petrine Russia—is without a counterpart in the ranks of the adversaries with whom Rome had to settle accounts in the third and second centuries B.C.

England was not, as Russia was, a recent and outlandish recruit to the company of the Great Powers of the Western World. She had been reckoned among their number since the beginning of the modern chapter of Western political history and, in the cultural life of Western Christendom, she had never ceased to play a part which was as intimate as it was active. She had, however, adopted at the turn of the Medieval and the Modern Age,[1] and had persistently pursued ever since, a foreign policy in which she was singular among modern Western or Westernized Powers. For some three centuries, ending in Napoleon's day, all the other combatants in the modern Western gladiatorial arena had been contending on Flemish and Rhenish and Lombard battle-fields, with a zest which seemed to be proof against disillusionment, for the prize of hegemony over the derelict domain of the broken-down medieval city-state cosmos. Great Britain, alone among her peers, had shown herself unwilling to play for this stake. Indeed, the British had avoided being drawn into the Continental European arena at all except to the trifling extent to which they might find it expedient to take a hand in Continental 'side-shows' for

in the heart of Hellas from which the Seleucid Empire drew its draughts of Hellenic culture and its drafts of Greek settlers. In another context (IV. C (i), vol. iv, pp. 20–3, above) we have already observed that the Ionian Greek city-states along the western seaboard of Asia Minor, which had been under an eclipse at the noontide of Athens' brilliance in the fifth century B.C., re-emerged in full splendour *post Alexandrum*, when Athens was in full decline. In the judgement of Tarn (op. cit., p. 34, cited already in V. C (i) (d) 4, p. 422, footnote 1, above) apropos, not of Athens alone, but of Hellas as a whole, 'there is small sign of' decadence 'down to about the middle of the second century B.C.', and 'to talk much about Greek decadence prior at any rate to the Christian Era would . . . give a very false impression'. In the Transeuphratean dominions of the Seleucid Monarchy the retransference of political power from Greek to Iranian hands, which was the political consequence of the collapse of the Seleucid régime in those regions, 'had the somewhat unexpected result of instilling fresh vigour into' the Greeks 'and leading to a stronger assertion of their Greekhood, if we may judge by what happened in the sphere of literature and learning'.

[1] The substitution of abstention for intervention in Continental European affairs as the rule of English foreign policy took place between A.D. 1429 and A.D. 1558. The history of England's foreign relations during that transitional period makes it evident that the abstentionist policy which the United Kingdom was afterwards to pursue with might and main, as one of its most precious privileges, had originally been adopted by England against the grain, under *force majeure* (see III. C (ii) (b), vol. iii, p. 366 above).

the sake of furthering the acquisitive enterprises overseas upon
which all British energies and interests and ambitions were now
being steadily concentrated. The underlying aim of British statesmanship in this age was to take advantage of the other Powers'
infatuation with Continental enterprises which in British estimation were not worth their fabulous market price, in order to sweep
into the British net as many as possible of the overseas annexes
of the modern Western World, which could be won at less cost
and retained with less effort because the statesmen who dictated
the policy of Great Britain's Continental rivals were prone to
estimate the present value of these outlying and undeveloped
estates at a very much lower figure than that at which this value
was assessed by the business acumen of 'a nation of shopkeepers'
who were accustomed to dealing in 'futures'.

This eccentric British policy of eschewing Continental adventures and concentrating upon expansion overseas had become
firmly established long before Napoleon's appearance on the
scene; and, when the Corsican adventurer made his supreme and
all but successful effort to win for his adopted country France—
or perhaps, rather, for the Corsican himself from a convenient
French base of operations—that elusive Continental hegemony
which had been the dream of every Continental Great Power for
the past three hundred years, his brilliant failure in playing this
old-fashioned Continental game produced one definite and permanent result which was certainly the last thing that the Emperor
of the French had either foreseen or desired when he embarked on
his extraordinary career. In failing to achieve his own imperialistic
ambitions, Napoleon incidentally gave his British arch-enemies an
incomparable opportunity for achieving theirs.

The Napoleonic gambit came as a veritable godsend to a generation of British imperialists who, at the turn of the eighteenth and
nineteenth centuries, had hardly yet begun to recover from their
disheartening experience of seeing the first British attempt at
building an overseas empire checkmated in the American Revolutionary War of 1775–83. British statesmanship accordingly exerted
itself to extract the utmost possible advantage out of a situation
in which Napoleon had become master of the Continent while
Great Britain remained mistress of the seas. Beyond the coasts
of his European *terra firma* the Emperor of the French was so
impotent in the face of British sea-power that he could neither
recover the lost French foothold in India[1] nor make any better

---

[1] The only effect of Napoleon's abortive attempts to re-establish relations of diplomatic and military co-operation between France and the rulers of some of the indigenous
'successor-states' of the Mughal Rāj in India was to move the British to sweep off the

use of the title-deeds to Louisiana, when he reacquired them
from Spain,[1] than to sell them cheap to the United States, who
was the only bidder in a position to take delivery.[2] And, when the
Corsican war-lord eventually overran the metropolitan territories
of the Spanish Crown in the Iberian Peninsula, the only permanent
effect of this inconclusive and ephemeral Continental European
exploit of Napoleonic arms was to open to British commerce the
vast Spanish overseas empire in South and Central America—
where the Spanish colonists eagerly seized upon the chance of
throwing off the incubus of the mother-country's hitherto jealously
guarded monopoly of the colonial trade. Again, Napoleon's domination and eventual annexation of Holland gave Great Britain an
excuse—of which she fully availed herself—for taking possession
of the Dutch colonies in Africa and the Indies. Indeed, by the
time when Napoleon was riding for his Russian fall, Great Britain
had succeeded in drawing to herself the markets and sources of
supply of the whole of the Overseas World, and in planting her
flag over a considerable part of it into the bargain; and there
was a double relation of cause-and-effect between these lucrative
British economic and political acquisitions overseas and Napoleon's
fatal march on Moscow. For one thing, Napoleon found one
of his pretexts for making war on Russia in the Tsar's revolt
against the economic sacrifices that his unwilling collaboration in
Napoleon's anti-British 'Continental System' had been exacting
from him; but—more important, by far, than this—it was Great
Britain's access, in defiance of the master of Continental Europe,
to the economic resources of the entire Overseas World that had
supplied her with the financial means of keeping up single-handed
the struggle against Napoleon at the height of Napoleon's power;
and it was the stimulus of this British example, and the expectation of obtaining British financial aid if they had courage to take
the British political cue, that emboldened the poverty-stricken
but populous Powers of Eastern Europe—with Russia in the van

Indian chess-board a number of the pawns that had been lying there at their mercy
ever since they had got this Indian game into their own hands by eliminating the French
player through their victory in the Seven Years' War. The struggle against Napoleon
was carried on by the British Government with so great an economy of British land-
forces on the European Continent that Great Britain found herself able to make extensive and decisive additions to her territorial holdings in India at a time when she was
waging war against Napoleon with all her might at sea and in the economic field.

[1] King Louis' Government had ceded Louisiana to its ally Spain in the peace
settlement of 1763. Napoleon extorted the title-deeds from the Spanish Government
in 1800 and sold them to the United States Government in 1803 (see II. D (ii), vol. ii,
p. 67, above).

[2] The United States was in a position to take delivery of Louisiana, even if Great
Britain had objected to the transaction, because she was the only Power except the
Spanish Empire that marched with Louisiana along a land-frontier, and because (unlike
Spain) the United States was militarily stronger than Great Britain was on the North
American Continent.

and with Prussia and Austria successively swinging back into line with her—to resume, in and after 1812, the struggle on land against a Corsican war-lord who in 1809 had to all appearance established once for all his own military ascendancy on the Continent.

It is manifest, then, that Napoleon's attempt to attain in his own world in the nineteenth century of the Christian Era that complete supremacy which the Romans did attain in their world in the second century B.C. was frustrated by the resistance of two adversaries of a kind and a calibre that the Scipios never had to reckon with. If we mentally eliminate both Great Britain with her overseas hinterland and Russia with her Asiatic hinterland from the list of the factors with which Napoleon still had to settle accounts after his fourth victory over Austria in 1809, and thus leave him (in our imagination) no adversaries to deal with from that time onwards save an already enfeebled Austria and Prussia and a long since decrepit Spain, we can hardly doubt that under these imaginary conditions Napoleon—even if we still condemned him to die as prematurely on an unoverturned throne as he actually died in captivity at Saint Helena—would have succeeded before his early death in 1821 in imposing his own dominion upon the whole of our imaginarily shrunken Western World as decisively as Rome did succeed in imposing hers upon the whole of the Hellenic World by the year 146 B.C. Even, however, if we agree that this conclusion would follow from our hypothesis, there is a further question which we shall have to ask ourselves. Assuming that, in a Western World that we have imaginarily restricted to the confines of Continental Europe west of the Niemen and north-west of the Ottoman frontiers, Napoleon had indeed been successful in establishing a complete universal state in the course of the years that he had at his disposal between 1809 and 1821, would this Napoleonic erection have been likely to be still standing at the present day? In normal circumstances our answer to this question would be confidently affirmative, considering that the normal expectation of life of a universal state is a span of about 400 years.[1] In the case in point, however, there is a particular consideration which suggests that, even if Napoleon had not been prevented from establishing his universal state by the operation of those British and Russian factors which we have now hypothetically eliminated, the Corsican empire-builder's work would have proved ephemeral because it would anyhow have carried in itself the seeds of its own destruction.

These dragon's teeth had been sown, long before Napoleon's

[1] The statistical evidence for this Time-span is examined in Part XI, below.

day, in the French field which was his indispensable base of military and political operations; for there was one vital point in which Napoleon's France departed from the standard type of empire-building communities that serve as instruments for the establishment of universal states.

In our inquiries into the character and the provenance of empire-building communities[1] we have found that, although it is exceptional for them to be wholly alien in culture from the society in whose service they are working, it is usual for them to be out-lying communities which have been trained in the stern school of border warfare against barbarians and have there acquired a military prowess and a political common sense which they even-tually turn to account in forcibly uniting under their own rule the hitherto warring members of the disintegrating body social to which they themselves belong. In this situation, which we may take to be the normal one, the service rendered to a distracted society by the community which provides it with its universal state is apt to be exclusively political and military; and, although the social boon of a universal peace imposed by main force is of inestimable value to a society that has arrived at the extremity of a 'Time of Troubles', the policeman's timely virtues do not exhaust all the surviving values of life, even in a society which has been spiritually as well as materially impoverished by a long course of self-laceration. The moral rally which is perhaps one of the necessary conditions for the successful establishment of a universal state could hardly be achieved if the bruised reed of the afflicted society's cultural heritage had been utterly broken; and the cultural, in contrast to the political and military, materials for the construction of a universal state are apt to be provided, not by the empire-building wardens of the marches, but by the militarily and politically decadent communities in the heart of a disintegrating world whom the empire-builders have forcibly united by subjecting them, willy-nilly, to their own high-handed domination. In fact, there is apt to be a certain exchange of social services between the empire-builders and their subjects on the lines of Horace's famous verses:

> Graecia capta ferum victorem cepit et artes
> Intulit agresti Latio;[2]

and it is this element of reciprocity that paves the way for a mutual understanding between two parties who have been brought into partnership originally by the sheer force of the dominant party's arms.

If we are right in believing that such an exchange of cultural

---

[1] See V. C (i) (*c*) 1, pp. 52–5, and V. C (i) (*c*) 4, p. 341, above.
[2] Horace: *Epistles*, Book II, ep. 1, ll. 156–7.

and politico-military services is a normal process in the life of a
universal state, and that this kind of social commerce between the
divers members of the body politic is no less necessary for the
preservation of health than is the circulation of blood in the human
body, then we cannot feel sure that the Napoleonic universal state,
if it had ever been definitively established, would even then have
been capable of keeping alive; for in the Napoleonic Empire there
was no reciprocity at all between the French empire-builders and
their Italian and Belgian and German subjects; the cultural ideas
were a French contribution, as well as the administrative institutions and the military force;[1] and the political content of these

[1] This exceptionally one-sided economy of the Napoleonic Empire will appear the
more remarkable when we remind ourselves that the conquered epigoni of the medieval
Western city-state cosmos had cultural gifts to give, and that these gifts were of a
kind that has usually been acceptable to the empire-builders of a universal state. The
classical German literature, which was at its zenith at the time when the Napoleonic
Empire was established, was penetrated through and through with both the sense of
promiscuity and the sense of unity (see Bruford, W. H.: *Germany in the Eighteenth
Century* (Cambridge 1935, University Press), pp. 304–8); and the great Franconian
exponent of this school of thought and feeling once met the Corsican empire-builder
face to face. Yet this encounter between Goethe and Napoleon was merely picturesque
and not historic; for Goethe did not captivate Napoleon, whereas Napoleon, for his
part, did captivate Heine. This might, no doubt, be discounted as an easy conquest,
since Heine was a Rhenish man-of-letters who was also a Jew; and for the Jews of the
Rhineland the French conquest spelt social emancipation. A more impressive triumph
of French cultural ideas was their captivation of the Teutonic souls which were the
authors of the *Befreiungskrieg* and the Italian souls which were the authors of the
Risorgimento.
    Why was it, then, that the French (to their own undoing) succeeded in imposing their
ideas, as well as their *imperium*, upon the epigoni of the medieval city-state cosmos
when the Germans, at any rate, had ideas of their own to contribute to the social outfit
of a nascent universal state? Perhaps the explanation is that the *soi-disant* French
'Ideas of 1789' triumphed in the domain of the disintegrating city-state cosmos in
virtue of their original provenance from the very quarters which they were now invading
from abroad.
    In other contexts (for example, in III. C (ii) (b), vol. iii, pp. 350–63 and 369–71;
IV. C (i), vol. iv, p. 19; IV. C (iii) (c) 2 (α), vol. iv, pp. 283–4, above) we have
already observed that the one-sided economy of the Napoleonic Empire was a piece of
poetic justice; for, while there may have been a lack of reciprocity between the living
generation of the French empire-builders and the living generation of their non-French
subjects inasmuch as the cultural as well as the political and military contributions
were now all coming from the French side, the Frenchmen of Napoleon's generation
who were conferring these cultural benefits on their Italian contemporaries and subjects
were thereby repaying a cultural debt which had been contracted by these Frenchmen's
ancestors to Italians of an earlier age. The French culture with which Napoleon inoculated Italy was a Transalpine version of a North Italian culture which had radiated out
into the Transalpine and Transmarine parts of Western Christendom at the time of
transition from the Medieval to the Modern Age of Western history. In the Transalpine
form in which this originally North Italian culture was reintroduced into Italy by the
French empire-builders of the Napoleonic Age, the wine was almost as strange as it
was stimulating to the epigoni of those medieval Northern Italians who had produced
the first vintage of it. At the same time the ultimately North Italian origin of this
·modern Italianistic culture from the farther side of the Alps did not count for nothing—
as can be seen by comparing the avidity with which this French gift was welcomed in
Lombardy and Tuscany and the Romagna with the repugnance that it excited in the
continental half of the Kingdom of the Two Sicilies—a piece of Italian territory which
had been merely a colonial annex (see p. 622, above) to the Italian part of the medieval
Western city-state cosmos. (For the recalcitrance against the Napoleonic régime in
the Kingdom of Sicily beyond the Faro see Johnston, R. M.: *The Napoleonic Empire in
Southern Italy* (London 1904, Macmillan, 2 vols.).).
    Finally, we may observe that, in the precipitation and dissemination of 'the Ideas
of 1789', Flanders as well as Northern Italy played its part. While the arch-disseminator

idées napoléoniennes was a leaven of disruption which was as swift as it was potent in its working.[1]

This internal ferment perhaps did as much to break the Napoleonic Empire up as the external shock of Napoleon's military and economic collisions with Russia and Great Britain; and this was not all; for the fermentation of French ideas in Italian and Belgian and German minds did more than merely wreck the momentary political structure which had served as a carrier for these revolutionary mental germs. This spiritual upheaval also dispelled beyond recall[2] a three-hundred-years-old constellation of political forces in Europe which had made the momentary establishment of a Napoleonic Empire possible. It effectively put an end to a situation in which a central cluster of small weak states had been affording a battle-ground to be fought over and a prize to be competed for by the rival members of a surrounding circle of Great Powers. In fact, the universal state with which the medieval Western city-state cosmos was duly endowed, at the close of its 'Time of Troubles', by the Corsican empire-builder's demonic exertions, had a psychological effect upon its beneficiaries which was just the opposite of that which a universal state usually produces. Instead of serving—as the Roman and the Achaemenian and the Ottoman Empire did each serve—as a sovereign rest-cure, it acted as a dynamic stimulus which spiritually transfigured the North Italians and Swabians and Rhinelanders and Belgians of Napoleon's generation by turning the weary epigoni of an expiring civilization into eager participants in one that was still throbbing with life.[3] In fact, the advent of the Napoleonic régime, at the

Napoleon Buonaparte himself was a Corsican of Florentine ancestry who found himself a citizen of revolutionary France owing to the acquisition of his native island by the French Crown in the reign of Louis XV (see p. 623, footnotes 1 and 2, above), the arch-precipitator Robespierre was a native of Arras who found himself a citizen of revolutionary France owing to the acquisition of his native city-state by the French Crown in the reign of Louis XIV.

[1] Read Heine's brilliant phantasy in 'Das Buch Le Grand':

'Parbleu! wie viel verdanke ich nicht dem französischen Tambour, der so lange bei uns in Quartier lag, und wie ein Teufel aussah, und doch von Herzen so engelgut war, und so ganz vorzüglich trommelte. . . . Monsieur Le Grand wusste nur wenig gebrochenes Deutsch, nur die Hauptausdrücke — Brot, Kuss, Ehre — doch konnte er sich auf der Trommel sehr gut verständlich machen; z. B. wenn ich nicht wusste, was das Wort "liberté" bedeute, so trommelte er den Marseiller Marsch — und ich verstand ihn. Wusste ich nicht die Bedeutung des Wortes "égalité", so trommelte er den Marsch "ça ira, ça ira . . . les aristocrats à la lanterne!" — und ich verstand ihn. Wusste ich nicht, was "bêtise" sei, so trommelte er den Dessauer Marsch, den wir Deutschen, wie auch Goethe berichtet, in der Champagne getrommelt — und ich verstand ihn. Er wollte mir mal das Wort "l'Allemagne" erklären, und er trommelte jene allzu einfache Urmelodie, die man oft an Markttagen bei tanzenden Hunden hört, nämlich Dum-Dum-Dum — ich ärgerte mich, aber ich verstand ihn doch.'

The first people to feel the effects of the German reaction to this French lesson were the French imperialists themselves.

[2] The deadliness of the blow which Napoleon dealt to the *ancien régime* as far as his own empire extended can be gauged from the completeness of the failure of the restoration that was attempted after Napoleon's overthrow.

[3] The classic description of this extraordinary effect of the Napoleonic régime in

turn of the eighteenth and nineteenth centuries, in these derelict areas in the heart of Western Christendom, which had fallen out of the race of Western progress since the close of the Middle Ages, served to draw these stranded Western communities back into the ever-rolling stream of Western life—just as, in the course of the hundred years immediately preceding the Napoleonic Age, certain Orthodox Christian communities under Ottoman rule—the Moreot Greeks and the Morava-Valley Serbs—who had never previously moved in a modern Western orbit, were drawn into the current of modern Western Civilization for the first time[1] by the advent of a Venetian régime in the one case and of a Hapsburg régime in the other.

If we pursue on the political plane our comparison between these three examples of cultural stimulation, we shall observe a remarkable uniformity in the sequence of events. In all three cases the cultural stimulus was brought in by an alien, or virtually alien, political régime; in all three cases this régime had only a short life before it was overthrown—with a violence that it had provoked by the antecedent violence of its own original intrusion —in order to make way for a restoration of the *ancien régime*; in

recalling to life the dead-alive epigoni of the medieval Western city-state cosmos is to be found in Heine's account, in his *Reisebilder*, 'Das Buch Le Grand', of the Napoleonic transformation of Düsseldorf. A brilliant picture of the working of the same miracle over the whole field of the German departments and dependencies of the Napoleonic Empire will be found in Fisher, H. A. L.: *Studies in Napoleonic Statesmanship in Germany* (Oxford 1903, Clarendon Press)—a book which is the fruit of a study of the original documents by an historian of a later age. The recalcitrance of the *ci-devant* Byzantine population of the Kingdom of Sicily-extra-Pharum towards a stimulus to which the Northern Italians, as well as the Western Germans, reacted so eagerly, may be studied in Johnston, op. cit.

The vivifying effect of the Napoleonic régime in Lombardy and the Rhineland is notorious; but we must extend our survey to the Illyrian departments of the French Empire—a strip of ex-Venetian and ex-Hapsburg possessions at the remote south-eastern extremity of the Western World—in order to obtain the most impressive testimony of all to the genius of the Napoleonic system for working miracles within the span of a few years (1806 to 1812 in the case of Istria and Dalmatia; 1810 to 1812 in the case of Krain and Croatia. In these backward marches,

'Under the enlightened, if despotic, rule of Marshal Marmont, the long stagnation of the Middle Ages was replaced by feverish activity in every branch of life. Administration and justice were reorganized, the Code Napoléon superseding the effete medieval codes; schools, primary and secondary, commercial and agricultural, sprang up in every direction; the first Croat and Slovene newspapers appeared; the old guild system was reformed and commercial restrictions removed; peasant proprietary was introduced; reafforestation was begun; and the splendid roads were constructed which are still the admiration of every tourist. . . . A well known story relates how the Emperor Francis, during his visit to Dalmatia in 1818, plied his suite with questions as to the origin of the various public works which struck his eye, and met with the invariable answer: "The French, Your Majesty."—"Wirklich Schad' dass s' nit länger blieben sein" ("It's a real pity they didn't stop longer") exclaimed the astonished Emperor in his favourite Viennese dialect; and there the matter rested for eighty years' (Seton-Watson, R. W.: *The Southern Slav Question* (London 1911, Constable), p. 26).

[1] In an earlier age of Western and Orthodox Christian history the Morea had been subjected to the painful experience of being conquered and dominated by the Frankish adventurers who had gone on 'the Fourth Crusade'. From this Frankish yoke the Moreots had almost completed their own liberation by their own efforts before the arrival of the 'Osmanli empire-builders of an Orthodox Christian universal state.

all three cases, however, this restoration was almost as short-lived as the intrusive régime which it had superseded; and then in all three cases, when the ephemeral restoration had been dismantled in its turn, the subject communities, which had first been stimulated and had then been repressed, at length won their way to political freedom and at once made use of this freedom in order to organize themselves politically into national states of the pattern which had become common form in the Western World[1] by the time of the transition from the Modern Age to that 'post-modern' epoch in which we find ourselves living to-day.[2]

This remarkably uniform sequence of events brings out the at first sight paradoxical yet at the same time unquestionable fact that in all three cases the culture which was introduced by the intrusive empire was directly inimical in the first place to the survival of the empire itself and in the second place to the national interests of the empire-building community. The explanation of this apparent paradox is to be found in a piece of antecedent history that has already come to our notice.[3] We have seen that the modern Western version of the medieval Western city-state culture was, in one of its aspects, an adaptation of this culture to the social conditions of the persistently feudal parts of Western Christendom, and that the necessary adjustment was made by transposing the standard unit of political articulation from the city-state to the kingdom-state scale. This pouring of the new wine of Italian efficiency into the old bottles of Transalpine feudal kingdoms had eventually generated a fresh political force with a new institutional expression.[4] It had brought to birth that modern Western nationalism which can nowhere rest until it has expressed itself in the concrete form of a sovereign independent national state. The France which Napoleon used as the instru-

---

[1] See Part I. A, vol. i, p. 1, above.
[2] The historical analogy which we have followed out above can perhaps be presented more graphically in the form of a table:

Derelict Area.	Intrusive Empire.	Period of Intrusion.	Period of Restoration of the Ancien Régime.	Period of Liberation and Organization into National States.
Northern Italy, Belgium, Swabia, Rhineland, and Hansa	The Napoleonic Empire	1797–1814	1815–1848	1848–1871
The Morea	The Venetian Empire	1690–1715	1715–1821	1821–1829
Serbia	The Danubian Hapsburg Monarchy	1718–1739	1739–1804	1804–1828

N.B. Belgium, in contrast to both Italy and Germany, succeeded in overthrowing the restoration régime as early as 1830 and in establishing her sovereign independence as a national state as early as 1831.
[3] In III. C (ii) (*b*), vol. iii, pp. 350–63, above.
[4] See IV. C (iii) (*b*) 8, vol. iv, p. 198, above.

ment for his empire-building work had already learnt to think of herself as *la Grande Nation*; and it was manifestly inevitable that the Italians and Belgians and Germans who had become the political pupils of the French, in the act of becoming their subjects, should revolt against a French Imperial régime which, for the sake of the aggrandizement of a nationally adult and emancipated France, was illogically and inequitably depriving these other nations in embryo of the 'natural right' to national self-determination which the French had insistently claimed and successfully secured for themselves. It was in this sense that the Napoleonic French Empire carried with it the seeds of its own destruction in the non-French portions of its domain. And we shall be stating the same historical truth in other terms if we say that the principal benefit which Napoleon conferred upon the epigoni of the medieval Italians and Flemings and Swabians and Rhinelanders and Hanseatics by dragooning them all into his universal state lay in the impulse which he thereby communicated to them—in diametrical opposition to his own life-work—to rise up at the first opportunity and insist upon dissecting the non-French territories of this short-lived French Empire into a number of new-fangled national 'successor-states'.

These Belgian and Italian and German 'successor-states' of the Napoleonic French Empire did not supersede their involuntary parent directly; for, as we have observed, the non-French national movements which the French Empire evoked were successfully exploited for a season by the surviving heirs of the *ancien régime*, who made a passing show of complacency towards the anti-French nationalism which had been kindled among their subjects by the experience of Napoleonic rule, until the explosion of the *Befreiungskrieg* had done its negative work in bringing the Napoleonic Empire to the ground—whereupon the legitimists abruptly changed their tactics and stretched out their hands to monopolize for themselves once again a sovereignty which they could never have wrested back from the grip of the Corsican usurper if the German and Italian converts to 'the Ideas of 1789' had not so naïvely laboured for the profit of their hypocritical allies. 'The kings crept out, the peoples stayed at home'; and it took the new-born nations thirty-three years—one third of a century—to win back the national rights which, in 1812–15, they had earned by pouring out their blood and had lost through being made the victims of a political swindle. Thus the non-French national states of a 'post-modern' Western World which ultimately owe their existence to a Napoleonic French stimulus have been founded on the ruins of the post-Napoleonic restoration and not on those of the Napoleonic

Empire itself; and so they cannot be regarded as the immediate
authors of the Napoleonic Empire's overthrow. On the other hand
their establishment has unquestionably had the effect of expung-
ing once for all from the Western political horizon that prospect
of a French hegemony over the Western World which was one
of the constant concerns of Western statesmen not only during
the brief episode of the Revolutionary and Napoleonic wars but
throughout the two centuries ending in 1870; for the preponder-
ance of *la Grande Nation* over rival Powers was due in large
measure to the existence of a political no-man's-land on the
farther side of France's northern and eastern frontiers; and, since the
time when this long-persisting vacuum was turned into a plenum
by the successive crystallizations of a Belgian and an Italian and
a German national state, France has lost her two-hundred-years-
long pre-eminence[1] and has fallen to a level set by the relative
strength of French 'man-power' and French industrial power in a
Western World which has now been politically rearticulated from
one end to the other into an unbroken array of national states
which all conform to a standard French pattern, though one of

[1] By the time, in October 1938, when these lines were being revised for the press,
it had come to look as if the pre-eminence which France had lost in 1870 had passed,
after all, to Germany, notwithstanding the sensational set-back which Germany had
suffered through her eventual defeat in the General War of 1914–18. On the eve of
the twentieth anniversary of the Armistice of the 11th November, 1918, it seemed that
the outcome of that war, so far from blighting Germany's political prospects, might
prove to have ensured the eventual predominance of Germany in Europe. In once for
all establishing the principle of National Self-Determination as the moral basis for the
articulation of Europe into parochial states, the peace settlement of 1919–20 (see IV.
C (iii) (*c*) 2 (α), vol. iv, p. 299, footnote 1, above) had made it certain that, sooner or
later, the 80 million Germans on the Continent would achieve their national unity in a
single Reich which would have almost twice as large a population as the next largest
European national state. At the same time the same peace settlement had also made it
certain that, when this Pan-German Reich did arise, the intrinsic advantage over the
other European Great Powers with which it would be endowed by its superiority in
'man-power' would be reinforced by the adventitious advantage of finding, on the
farther side of its eastern and south-eastern frontiers, a political no-man's-land like
that which France had found beyond her eastern and northern frontiers from the reign
of Louis XIV to the reign of Napoleon III inclusive. When the political vacuum in
Central Europe, from which France had profited for two hundred years, was filled at
last in the nineteenth century by the crystallization of the Belgian, Italian, and German
national states, it was already in process of being replaced by a new vacuum in Eastern
Europe. The break-up of the medieval Central European city-state cosmos in the fourteenth and fifteenth centuries under the impact of the modernized kingdom-states of
feudal Europe has had its historical counterpart in the nineteenth and twentieth centuries in the break-up of the modern East European dynastic states into national 'successor-states' generated by the principle of Self-Determination. This process, which
began in the early decades of the nineteenth century with the secession of the nuclei of
a Serb and a Greek national state from the Ottoman Empire, was completed in the
peace settlement of 1919–20 by the partition of the Ottoman and the Hapsburg Empire
and the mutilation of the Hohenzollern and the Romanov Empire. The result was the
creation, between the eastern frontier of the Weimar Republic and the western frontier
of the Soviet Union, of an East European no-man's-land precariously tenanted by a
dozen *Kleinstaaten*, from Greece to Finland. In this situation it was perhaps inevitable
that the truncated post-war Prussia-Germany should eventually be replaced by a
Greater Germany including the German population which had been left stranded by
the wreck of the Hapsburg Monarchy, and that this 'Third Reich' should then seek to
dominate the non-German *Kleinstaaten* on its eastern and south-eastern flanks.

them has now crystallized, in the shape of a Greater Germany, on a physical scale which dwarfs 'the Third Reich's' French prototype.[1]

Our analysis of the Napoleonic Empire has now perhaps been carried as far as is necessary for the purpose of this Study; and we can sum up our results in the conclusion that Napoleon did not merely fail to achieve his aim but actually produced, through his unsuccessful endeavours, a number of results which he never intended or foresaw and which in combination entailed the paradoxical consequence of making it for ever impossible for any French successor of this fallen titan to emulate his career with a happier fortune. On the one hand Napoleon failed to weld the derelict domain of the medieval city-state cosmos in Italy and Germany and Belgium on to the living body of France in the bonds of a French Empire which was to perform the service of a Western universal state. On the other hand Napoleon unintentionally made the fortune of Great Britain in seeking to ride rough-shod over the obstacle which she obstinately presented to the attainment of the Corsican megalomaniac's superlative ambitions; and he likewise unintentionally compromised the national prospects of France herself by rousing his non-French subjects from their long political slumber and launching them on a new course of political activity which ended in the establishment of a Belgian and an Italian and a German national state on the continental threshold of France within less than three-quarters of a century from the year in which Buonaparte had entered on his meteoric career by descending upon Italy at the head of a revolutionary French army.[2]

---

[1] If we are right in seeing, in the contemporary spectacle of a France now cowering under the menacing shadows of a 'totalitarian' Germany and Italy, the nemesis of the Napoleonic French domination over the Germans and Italians of a hundred years ago, we can put our finger upon corresponding reversals of fortune in the two other cases which we have brought into our comparison. In the same historical perspective the disruption of the Danubian Hapsburg Monarchy through the prise of a Serbian lever in the General War of 1914–18 is to be regarded as the nemesis of the Hapsburg domination over the Serbs in 1718–39; and even the Venetian domination over the Morea in 1690–1715 has subsequently taken its toll from a United Italy by raising an obstacle, in the shape of a liberated and nationally awakened and consolidated Greece, to modern Italian endeavours to re-establish the medieval Italian Empire in the Levant.

[2] It did, however, take the better part of these three-quarters of a century for the immense prestige of the Napoleonic Empire to evaporate.

'France, which had given the impulse to personal freedom, was able to usher in greater freedom of trade through the Napoleonic treaty-system of 1860–70. England might be treated as an exception by other nations. France was always an inspiration; and, although Free Trade had been an accomplished fact in England in the 'forties, and though the European movement was based originally on English economic writers, yet it needed the French advertisement and Napoleon III to make it European. It is difficult for us to realize the glamour which this France, rejuvenated after the wars of 1815, was able to exercise on its contemporaries in the first three-quarters of the nineteenth century' (Knowles, L. C. A.: *Economic Development in the Nineteenth Century: France, Germany, Russia and the United States* (London 1932, Routledge), p. 21).

For the rôle of France in the modern chapter of Western history as interpreter and disseminator of Italian and English ideas see III. C (ii) (b), vol. iii, pp. 369–71, above. For the Free Trade Movement in the Western World in the middle of the nineteenth century see IV. C (iii) (b) 4, vol. iv, pp. 172–4, above.

Thus the note of the Napoleonic episode in our Western history is a striking discord between irony and consolation. The irony appears in the spectacle of the Corsican empire-builder's consummate self-frustration; the consolation makes itself heard in the sound of a revolutionary French trump that proved to possess the miraculous power of raising the dead to new life.[1] The beneficiary of this miracle was the rotting corpse of a medieval Western city-state cosmos which had committed suicide[2] four hundred years before the bustling epiphany of the little man who blew the magic blast. It is amazing that he should have blown it without ever having foreseen what the effect of his rousing music was bound to be.

[1] The *risorgimenti* of communities that have previously passed through a phase of social decadence are discussed in more general terms in IV. C (i), vol. iv, pp. 16–23, above.

[2] See III. C (ii) (b), vol. iii, pp. 348–50, above.

EDWARD GIBBON'S CHOICE OF LINGUISTIC VEHICLE

IN the chapter to which this Annex attaches it has been suggested that, in the competition between the English language and the French for the prize of becoming the *lingua franca* of an oecumenical 'Great Society', English won its definitive victory in the course of the Seven Years' War, and that this view is supported by the testimony of the life and letters of Edward Gibbon, who wrote his *juvenilia* in French while the war was still in progress, and his *magnum opus* in English after the war had ended in the discomfiture of France ánd in the triumph of Great Britain.[1] In this connexion it may be apposite to quote certain passages from Gibbon's own works, and one passage from a letter addressed to Gibbon by Hume, which, when read together, throw some light on the considerations that led Gibbon to adopt French as his vehicle in the first instance and afterwards to abandon French in favour of English.

Gibbon's motives for having recourse to French in his earliest literary venture have been recalled in retrospect by the author himself:

'At Lausanne I composed the first chapters of my Essay[2] in French, the familiar language of my conversation and studies, in which it was easier for me to write than in my mother-tongue. After my return to England I continued the same practice, without any affectation, or design of repudiating (as Dr. Bentley would say) my vernacular idiom. . . . In modern times the language of France has been diffused by the merit of her writers, the social manners of the natives, the influence of the Monarchy, and the exile of the Protestants: several foreigners have seized the opportunity of speaking to Europe in this common dialect, and Germany may plead the authority of Leibniz and Frederic, of the first of her philosophers and the greatest of her kings. The just pride and laudable prejudice of Englând has restrained the communication of idioms; and, of all the nations on this side of the Alps, my countrymen are the least practised and least perfect in the exercise of the French tongue. . . . The vanity of being the first English author in the French language might perhaps be excused; but, in sober truth, I wrote, as I thought, in the most familiar idiom.'[3]

Gibbon's persistence in the use of French in his unfinished and unpublished history of the rise of the Swiss Confederation drew

---

[1] See V. C (i) (d) 6 (γ), p. 506, with footnote 3, above.
[2] *Essai sur l'Étude de la Littérature*, written in 1759 and published in 1761.—A.J.T.
[3] Gibbon, Edward: *The Autobiographies of Edward Gibbon* (London 1896, Murray), pp. 175, 176, and 300.

a friendly criticism from an already famous English man-of-letters who was Gibbon's older contemporary. In a letter addressed to Gibbon on the 24th October, 1767,[1] David Hume took the younger writer to task in the following terms:

'Why do you compose in French, and carry faggots into the wood, as Horace says with regard to Romans who wrote in Greek? I grant that you have a like motive to those Romans, and adopt a language much more generally diffused than your native tongue: but have you not remarked the fate of those two ancient languages in following ages? The Latin, though then less celebrated, and confined to more narrow limits, has in some measure outlived the Greek, and is now more generally understood by men-of-letters. Let the French, therefore, triumph in the present diffusion of their tongue. Our solid and increasing establishments in America, where we need less dread the inundation of Barbarians, promise a superior stability and duration to the English language.'

The impression made upon Gibbon's mind by the last of Hume's points in the letter quoted above is attested by the manifest reminiscence in the following passage in *The History of the Decline and Fall of the Roman Empire*—a passage which appears to have been written at least five years, and possibly as long as thirteen years,[2] after Hume's letter had reached Gibbon's hands:

'If a savage conqueror should issue from the deserts of Tartary, he must repeatedly vanquish the robust peasants of Russia, the numerous armies of Germany, the gallant nobles of France, and the intrepid freemen of Britain; who, perhaps, might confederate for their common defence. Should the victorious Barbarians carry slavery and desolation as far as the Atlantic Ocean, ten thousand vessels would transport beyond their pursuit the remains of Civilized Society; and Europe would revive and flourish in the American World, which is already filled with her colonies and institutions. America now contains about six millions of European blood and descent; and their numbers, at least in the North, are continually increasing. Whatever may be the changes of their political situation, they must preserve the manners of Europe; and we may reflect with some pleasure that the English language will probably be diffused over an immense and populous continent.'[3]

By the time when these words were published, Gibbon had already staked his hopes of lasting fame upon the fulfilment of

---

[1] The full text of this letter will be found in op. cit., p. 277.
[2] For the date of the writing of the 'General Observations on the Fall of the Roman Empire in the West', in which this passage occurs, see IV. C (iii) (b) 3, vol. iv, p. 148, footnote 3, above, in correction of III. C (ii) (b), vol. iii, p. 311, footnote 1.
[3] Gibbon, Edward: *The History of the Decline and Fall of the Roman Empire*, chap. xxxvii: 'General Observations on the Fall of the Roman Empire in the West'. The last of the sentences here quoted is a footnote and not part of the main text, and it is possible that this footnote was added as late as the year 1781, even if the 'Observations' themselves were drafted before the 10th May, 1774 (for this *terminus ante quem* see IV. C (iii) (b) 3, vol. iv, p. 148, footnote 3, above).

Hume's forecast by producing three volumes of *The Decline and Fall* in English; and his eventual choice of language was dramatically justified when an odd volume of *The Decline and Fall*—finding its way into a tract in the heart of North America which had been transformed, since Gibbon's day, from virgin wilderness into the infant State of Illinois—fell into the hands of a certain young backwoodsman, unversed in any tongue but his native English, who was eagerly educating himself with the aid of the few books that he had managed to acquire.[1] It would be a pretty exercise for the fancy to compose, in Gibbon's name and style, some reflections on the American statesman's intellectual debt to the English historian,[2] could the latter have lived to learn of it. We should be on surer ground in guessing that, if Lincoln's as well as Gibbon's life could have been prolonged into the fourth decade of the twentieth century, these two masters of the English language would have been decidedly of one mind—in spite of their vast diversity in genius—in their judgement on the culture of which their mother-tongue had latterly become the vehicle in the Middle Western core of that 'immense and populous continent' over which the English language has now duly been diffused in an ironically barren fulfilment of Hume's far-sighted prophecy.[3] In placing themselves beyond the reach of another barbarian eruption from the Eurasian Steppe the European settlers in North America appear to have escaped from an imaginary danger of being barbarized from outside at the price of undergoing, at any rate for a season, a genuine barbarization of another kind which is far more difficult to withstand because it does not break in from abroad but wells up from the secret places of the heart.

This latest (though assuredly not last) chapter in the cultural history of the Middle West bears out a thesis which has been put forward in this Study already in earlier passages.[4]

[1] See Ludwig, Emil: *Lincoln*: English translation (London and New York 1930, Putnam), p. 36.

[2] This volume of *The Decline and Fall* came into Lincoln's hands at New Salem at a critical moment in his career, in the interval between his momentous voyage down river to New Orleans and back and his first entry into politics. The future statesman was not more than twenty-three years old at the time; his mind at that age must have been at least as impressionable as it showed itself to be in its maturity; and it seems reasonable to assume that the impression made by any particular book would be in inverse ratio to the number of the books that the young man had had an opportunity of reading up to date.

[3] For the deterioration of culture in the Middle West of the United States since the close of the nineteenth century see Lynd, R. S. and H. M.: *Middletown: A Study in American Culture* (London 1929, Constable).

[4] See IV. C (iii) (a), vol. iv, pp. 119–33, and V. C (i) (c) 3, in the present volume, pp. 334–7, above.

CUJUS REGIO, EJUS RELIGIO?

IN the chapter to which this Annex refers we have found reason
for believing that, when the philosophies thought out by the
Dominant Minority and the religions discovered by the Internal
Proletariat encounter one another in a competition for the conversion of souls, the outcome of the contest between them is apt
to bear out the dictum of a modern Western psychologist that
'great innovations never come from above; they come invariably
from below'.[1] On this spiritual plane it is, indeed, the Internal
Proletariat, and not the Dominant Minority, that proves to be the
victor as a rule, on the showing of an empirical survey of a number
of cases in point. But we are still left with the question whether
the Dominant Minority has it in its power to make up for its
spiritual weakness by bringing its physical strength into play and
forcing a philosophy or a religion upon its subjects, from above
downwards, by means of a political pressure which might be none
the less effective for being illegitimate.

If we now examine the historical evidence on this head, we shall
find that in general the Dominant Minority's efforts to impose a
philosophy or a religion upon the Internal Proletariat by political
means are apt to be as unsuccessful—at any rate in the long run—
as its analogous efforts to hold the External Proletariat at bay by
military force along an artificial stationary frontier.[2]

This finding contradicts outright one of the sociological theories
of the Enlightenment during the Hellenic 'Time of Troubles'; for,
according to this theory, the deliberate imposition of religious
practices and beliefs from above downwards, so far from being
impossible or even unusual, has actually been the normal origin
of religious institutions in societies in process of civilization. This
theory has been applied to the religious life of Rome in the following celebrated passage in the work of the historian Polybius (vivebat circa 206–128 B.C.):

'The point in which the Roman constitution excels others most conspicuously is to be found, in my opinion, in its handling of Religion. In
my opinion the Romans have managed to forge the main bond of their
social order out of something which the rest of the world execrates: I
mean, out of Superstition. In dramatizing their Superstition theatri-
cally and introducing it into private as well as into public life, the

---

[1] C. G. Jung, quoted in V. C (i) (d) 6 (δ), on pp. 567–8, above.
[2] For the usual outcome of such relations between the Dominant Minority and the
Barbarians see Part VIII, below.

Romans have gone to the most extreme lengths conceivable; and to many observers this will appear extraordinary. In my opinion, however, the Romans have done it with an eye to the masses.[1] If it were possible to have an electorate that was composed exclusively of sages, this chicanery might perhaps be unnecessary; but, as a matter of fact, the masses are always unstable and always full of lawless passions, irrational temper and violent rage; and so there is nothing for it but to control them by "the fear of the unknown" and play-acting of that sort. I fancy that this was the reason why our forefathers introduced among the masses those theological beliefs and those notions about Hell that have now become traditional; and I also fancy that, in doing this, our ancestors were not working at random but knew just what they were about. It might be more pertinent to charge our contemporaries with lack of sense and lapse from responsibility for trying to eradicate Religion, as we actually see them doing.'[2]

This late Hellenic utilitarian theory of the origins of Religion in societies in process of civilization is about as remote from the truth as the modern Western social-contract theory of the origins of states. If we now proceed to examine the evidence, we shall find that, while political power is perhaps not completely impotent to produce effects upon spiritual life, its ability to act in this field is dependent on the presence of certain special combinations of circumstances; and we shall also find that, even then, its range of action is very narrowly circumscribed. In fact, in the history of the occasional endeavours of political potentates to make their wills prevail in the religious sphere by bringing into play the political means at their command, successes are exceptional and failures are the rule.

To take the exceptions first, we may observe that political potentates do sometimes succeed in establishing a cult when this cult is an expression, not of any genuine religious feeling, but merely of some political sentiment that is masquerading in a religious disguise; and in such a case the feat is perhaps not even very difficult to achieve if the political sentiment which the ruler selects for embodiment in a pseudo-religious ritual is one that is already strongly flowing as a spontaneous popular current—such as, for example, the thirst for political unity in a society that has drunk to the dregs the bitter cup of a 'Time of Troubles'. In these particular circumstances a ruler who has already won a hold over his subjects' hearts as their human saviour[3] may sometimes even

---

[1] In this sentence and what follows, Polybius credits the dominant minority in the Roman Commonwealth with having deliberately and successfully put into practice a precept that is cold-bloodedly commended by Strabo in a passage that has been quoted in V. C (i) (*d*) 6 (δ), p. 561, above.—A.J.T.

[2] Polybius: *Historiae*, Book VI, chap. 56.

[3] For the figure of 'the saviour with the sword' see V. C (ii) (*a*), vol. vi, pp. 178–213, below.

succeed in establishing a cult in which his own office and person and dynasty are the objects of worship.[1]

The classic example of this *tour de force* is the deification of human rulers in a disintegrating Hellenic World. The practice began, in the first generation after the breakdown, with the payment of divine honours in Samos to Lysander—the Lacedaemonian commander who had delivered the 'knock-out blow' in the Atheno-Peloponnesian War[2]—and it continued in the deification of Alexander the Great and his successors, until it reached its climax in the deification of Julius Caesar and Caesar Augustus and the subsequent Roman Emperors for the next two and a half centuries. For that length of time this worship of the Roman Emperors was a success, because it provided an appropriate means of expressing a sense of devout gratitude towards the Principate which was deeply and widely felt. Throughout that age a majority of the inhabitants of the Hellenic universal state which the Caesars had established were devoutly and sincerely grateful for the priceless gift of unity and peace which the Principate had conferred upon the Hellenic World at the end of four centuries of storm and stress; and, as they also appreciated the supreme difficulty of the achievement, as well as its supreme value for themselves, they were ready to acquiesce without much heart-searching (until the advent of Christianity) in the idea that the authors of such acts as this must be beings of a superhuman order.[3]

> Hic vir, hic est, tibi quem promitti saepius audis,
> Augustus Caesar, divi genus, aurea condet
> saecula qui rursus Latio regnata per arva
> Saturno quondam, super et Garamantas et Indos
> proferet imperium.[4]

And this Virgilian acclamation of Augustus as a living god has an equally famous Horatian parallel:

> Caelo tonantem credidimus Iovem
> regnare; praesens divus habebitur
> Augustus adiectis Britannis
> imperio gravibusque Persis.[5]

To evoke such strong feelings as these for a worldly saviour and for a political institution is an impressive achievement. Yet the

---

[1] See IV. C (iii) (c) 2 (β), vol. iv, p. 408, footnote 3, above.
[2] Plutarch: *Life of Lysander*, chap. 18 (citing Duris).
[3] For the sense of the unity of Mankind that is awakened during, and in consequence of the disintegration of a civilization, see V. C (i) (d) 7, vol. vi, pp. 1–49, below. For the gratitude that is evoked by the founders and upholders of universal states, see also V. C (ii) (a), vol vi, p. 181, below. For the penitence of Augustus see V. C (i) (c) 2, p. 78, and V. C (i) (d) 5, p. 435, above, and V. C (ii) (a), vol. vi, p. 187, below.
[4] Virgil: *Aeneid*, Book VI, ll. 791–5. The same semi-religious note of veneration for Augustus is also struck by the same poet in *Aeneid*, Book VIII, ll. 678–81; in *Georgics*, No. I, ll. 500–1; and in *Eclogues*, No. I, *passim*.   [5] Horace: *Carmina*, Book III, Ode v, ll. 1–4.

spontaneous emotional attitude on which the Imperial Cult in the Hellenic universal state depended for its vitality[1] did not survive the first collapse of the Roman Empire at the turn of the second and third centuries of the Christian Era. As soon as the storm rose again and the stress once more made itself felt, the Emperors themselves became conscious that their now fast wilting official divinity was incapable of standing the strain unaided; and those of them who were blessed with foresight and initiative began to cast about for some supernatural sanction behind and beyond their own tarnished and discredited Imperial Genius.[2] While there may have been nothing but the whim of a spoilt and childish pervert behind the religious revolution which was attempted by Elagabalus (*imperabat* A.D. 218–22) when this changeling-Caesar presented himself in Rome as the servant of the local Sun-God of the Syrian city of Emesa whose hereditary high priest he happened to be,[3] we may confidently attribute a higher motive and a more serious purpose to Aurelian (*imperabat* A.D. 270–5)[4] and to Constantius

[1] For the gratitude of the subjects—even more than the citizens—of the Roman Empire to Augustus and his successors in the Principate for the next two centuries see in particular two Greek inscriptions in honour of Augustus that are quoted in Gall, A. von: Βασιλεία τοῦ Θεοῦ (Heidelberg 1926, Winter), p. 453, and in general Charlesworth, M. P.: 'Providentia and Aeternitas' in *The Harvard Theological Review*, vol. xxix, No. 2, April 1936; and the same scholar's Raleigh Lecture on *The Virtues of a Roman Emperor* (London 1937, Milford). For the corresponding transfiguration of Augustus, in his grateful subjects' minds, from an unscrupulous and ruthless dictator into a superhuman Saviour of Society see Wendland, P.: *Die Hellenistisch-Römische Kultur*, 2nd and 3rd ed. (Tübingen 1912, Mohr), pp. 143–4. Augustus was not, of course, the first Roman saviour to evoke this sense of gratitude in the hearts of the Greek and Oriental subjects of Rome and to have divine honours paid to him in consequence. In the preceding generation the same subjects had shown the same feelings in the same way towards Augustus's adoptive father Divus Julius and towards Julius's rival Pompey. It was Pompey who took the first steps on the Roman Government's behalf to restore order in regions which the Senate had been content to leave derelict during the hundred years (167–67 B.C.) that had elapsed since the end of the Third Romano-Macedonian War; and the impression that his work made on the beneficiaries was deep and lasting. Cicero testified that 'omnes nunc in iis locis Gnaeum Pompeium sicut aliquem non ex hac urbe missum sed de caelo delapsum intuentur' (*De Imperio Gnaei Pompeii*, chap. 41). And, nearly two centuries later, the Emperor Hadrian declared that, as he travelled over the World, he found it full of temples dedicated to Pompey (Gall, A. von, op. cit., p. 452).

[2] Even at the zenith of the *Pax Augusta* Divus Caesar had perhaps, after all, been an idol with feet of clay. Though he was acclaimed as a saviour,
'This salvation was merely on the material plane and was limited to life on Earth; and, though it may have brought relief and prosperity to the well-to-do and to the cultivated, it offered little or nothing to the masses, who still, as before, felt the heavy pressure of daily life, and who were incapable of improving their position by their own efforts. Caesar-worship gave just as little satisfaction to those who felt in their hearts the longing for something higher than earthly goods, and to whom the uncertain enjoyment of life on this Earth seemed as hollow and as nugatory as the wisdom of Philosophy and of the Enlightenment with their interminable discussions which left the imagination and the spirit cold.'—Meyer, E.: *Ursprung und Anfänge des Christentums*, vol. iii (Stuttgart and Berlin 1923, Cotta), p. 381.

[3] For Elagabalus's abortive attempt to establish his own divine namesake as the high god of the Roman Pantheon see the present Annex, pp. 685–8, below.

[4] 'Aurelian . . . used to say that the soldiers deceived themselves in supposing that the destinies of the Emperors lay in their hands. For he used to aver that it was God who had bestowed the purple and . . . had decided the period of his reign.'—*Auctor Anonymus post Dionem*, Dindorf's edition, p. 229, quoted by Cumont, F.: 'L'Éternité

Chlorus (*imperabat* A.D. 292–306) when these Illyrian Emperors enlisted under the standard of an abstract and oecumenical Sol Invictus;[1] and we shall also notice that Constantine the Great (*imperabat* A.D. 306–37) took service in his turn, for a season, with his father's Solar tutelary god[2] before he transferred his allegiance, once for all, to one of the gods of the internal proletariat who, by Constantine's day, had proved Himself more potent than either Sol or Caesar. The pitched battle between Caesar-worship and Christianity which had opened with Decius's challenge in A.D. 249 and had closed with Galerius's capitulation in A.D. 311 had been deliberately provoked by a school of blind-eyed and high-handed occupants of the Imperial Throne who rejected the far-sighted policy of fortifying the Imperial Cult with the patronage of some higher divinity in favour of the foolhardy policy of attempting to impose upon all comers, human and divine, by sheer pressure of physical force, a political rite which could now manifestly no longer depend on its old inward spiritual sanction in the hearts of the worshippers.[3] The failure of a Decius and a Galerius to maintain the Imperial Cult by persecution had the same significance as the failure of an Aurelian and a Constantius Chlorus to fortify it by subordinating it to a worship of the Unconquered Sun. Between them, the two failures proved conclusively that Caesar-worship, impressive though it might be, was nevertheless no more than a fair-weather cult which was incapable of riding a storm.

If we turn from the Hellenic to the Sumeric World, we shall observe that there is an analogue of Caesar-worship here in the cult of his own human person which was instituted—not by the founder of the Sumeric universal state, Ur-Engur (*imperabat circa* 2298–2281 B.C.),[4] but by Ur-Engur's successor Dungi (*imperabat circa* 2280–2223 B.C.).[5] We shall also infer—from the fact that

des Empereurs Romains' in *Revue d'Histoire et de Littérature Religieuses*, vol. i (Paris 1896, Macon Protat), p. 447. Compare Timoleon's saying that 'he gave thanks to God for having inscribed Timoleon's name upon His divine decision to save Sicily'.—Plutarch: *Life of Timoleon*, chap. 36.

[1] See V. C (i) (c) 2, p. 82, footnote 4, above, for these two forms of Sun-worship and for the contrast that they present to one another. For the work of the Illyrian Emperors see V. C (ii) (a), vol. vi, p. 207, below.

[2] See Baynes, N. H.: *Constantine the Great and the Christian Church* (London 1929, Milford), pp. 8 and 95–103, as well as the present Annex, pp. 693–4, below.

[3] For the victory of the Christian Martyrs over the Roman Imperial Government see IV. C (iii) (b) 12, vol. iv, p. 227, and V. C (i) (d) 3, in the present volume, pp. 407–9, above. By Galerius's day the Caesar-worship that was then delivering the last desperate counter-attack upon an all but triumphant Christian Church was enlisting allies from every quarter to reinforce its anti-Christian front. It was promoting an archaistic revival of historic pagan worships (see Geffken, J.: *Der Ausgang des Griechisch-römischen Heidentums* (Heidelberg 1920, Winter), pp. 28–30); it was fostering the worship of Sol Invictus; and it was patronizing Iamblichus's Neoplatonic Antichurch (see V. C (i) (d) 6 (δ), pp. 565–6, above, and V. C (i) (d) 8 (δ), vol. vi, p. 88, footnote 3, below).

[4] For Ur-Engur and his work see I. C (i) (b), vol. i, pp. 106 and 109, above.

[5] See Meyer, E.: *Geschichte des Altertums*, vol. i, part (2), 3rd ed. (Stuttgart and Berlin

Dungi changed the Imperial style and title from Ur-Engur's comparatively modest formula 'King of Sumer and Akkad' to the more pretentious formula 'King of the Four Quarters'[1]—that, in calling upon his subjects to worship him as a god, this Sumeric emperor was appealing, as the Roman Caesars appealed, to the gratitude of Mankind towards a being from whose hands they were obtaining the boon of oecumenical unity and peace.[2] At the same time the records of Sumeric history that have been unearthed by the spade of the modern Western archaeologist inform us, fragmentary though they are, that the Sumeric Imperial Cult also resembled its Hellenic parallel in the further point of being a short-lived fair-weather contrivance. Dungi's three direct successors on the throne of 'the Empire of the Four Quarters' at Ur (*imperabant circa* 2222–2180 B.C.) duly claimed and received divine honours in their turns, and Ur-Engur, as the founder of the dynasty, appears to have been given a posthumous apotheosis.[3] But after the collapse of the Third Dynasty of Ur there is only one pretender to dominion over 'the Four Quarters'—Libit-Ishtar of Isin (*imperabat circa* 2096–2086 B.C.)—who is known to have pretended to divinity as well.[4] And, when the equivalent of Diocletian's and Constantine's work was performed for the Sumeric universal state by Hammurabi (*imperabat circa* 1947–1905 B.C.), after the bout of anarchy which had followed the collapse of the Dynasty of Ur and had continued under the ineffective rule of the Dynasty of Isin,[5] we find that this Amorite counterpart of the great Illyrian soldiers

1913, Cotta), pp. 557–8, and Fish, T.: *The Cult of King Dungi during the Third Dynasty of Ur* (Manchester 1927, University Press, reprinted from *The Bulletin of the John Rylands Library*, vol. xi, No. 2, July 1927). The evidence marshalled by Fish shows that Dungi was worshipped as a god at Lagash, Umma, Drehem, and Ur, and possibly also at Nippur; that a temple (locality uncertain) had already been dedicated to him in his lifetime; and that offerings were made to him as a god (though the dated evidence for these offerings is all posterior to Dungi's death).

[1] Meyer, E., op. cit., vol. i, part (2), 3rd ed. (Stuttgart and Berlin 1913, Cotta), p. 557. See also the present Study, V. C (i) (*d*) 7, vol. vi, p. 2, below.

[2] On this point see V. C (i) (*d*) 7, vol. vi, pp. 1–6, below. The conscious association of emperor-worship with the ideal of oecumenical unity is clearly attested in the Sumeric World by the fact that the title 'King of the Four Quarters', which was assumed by Dungi concurrently with his arrogation of divine honours to himself, was not Dungi's own invention but was a revival of the style and title of the Akkadian militarist Naramsin. For Naramsin had also anticipated Dungi in laying claim to divinity, as is indicated by the regular prefixing of the god-determinative to Naramsin's name in his official documents and by the affixing of the visual symbol of divinity—a pair of horns—to the conqueror's helmet on his victory stele (Meyer, op. cit., vol. cit., pp. 516 and 528–9). On the other hand, in the interval between Naramsin's generation and Dungi's, a pretension to divinity was not only asserted but was successfully established by Gudea of Lagash, who was no more than the parochial ruler of a single city-state (ibid., p. 542). In claiming divinity without possessing oecumenical sovereignty Gudea could plead that his reign—coinciding, as it happened to do, with a lull in the Sumeric 'Time of Troubles' between the subsidence of Akkadian militarism and the onset of the Gutaean Völkerwanderung—was at any rate a time of local peace and prosperity.

[3] Ibid., pp. 558–9; Jeremias, C.: *Die Vergöttlichung der Babylonisch-Assyrischen Könige* (Leipzig 1919, Hinrichs), pp. 17–18.

[4] Ibid., pp. 18–21.

[5] See V. C (ii) (*b*), vol. vi, pp. 297–8, below.

who came to the rescue of the Roman Empire adopted, on the
religious issue, a policy which we have seen to have been likewise
the policy of Aurelian and of Constantius Chlorus. Though in
general Hammurabi was deliberately and avowedly restoring the
universal state of Ur-Engur and Dungi,[1] there was one point in
which he broke sharply with Dungi's practice. Instead of ruling
as a god incarnate, like Dungi or Augustus, Hammurabi preferred,
like Constantius or Constantine, to reign as the human servant of
a transcendental divinity who, for this Amorite statesman, took
the shape of the Babylonian double of Enlil: the high god Marduk-
Bel.[2] It will be seen that, in the history of the disintegration of the
Sumeric Society, the deification of human potentates was the
exception, not the rule; and indeed the notion of treating a prince
as a god incarnate seems to have been something distinctly foreign
to the Sumeric temper and outlook.[3]

The Sumeric Emperor Dungi is not the only ruler of a universal
state who has deified himself as the god incarnate of a 'Kingdom
of the Four Quarters'. The self-same title was hit upon—in the
opposite hemisphere and in an age that was divided from Dungi's
by the lapse of more than three millennia—to designate the universal state of the Andean World;[4] and the Sapa Inca ('Unique
Inca')[5] who was the sovereign of this American oecumenical empire was also worshipped, like Dungi, as a god incarnate.[6] How
this Incaic Imperial Cult would have fared if it had been granted
the time to work itself out is a question that can never be answered;
for the Andean universal state had been established for barely a
century when it was overtaken by the Spanish conquest; and this

---

[1] For this see 1. C (i) (b), vol. i, p. 106, footnote 2, above.
[2] Meyer, op. cit., p. 663. For the identification of Marduk of Babylon with Enlil of
Nippur at this stage of Sumeric history see V. C (i) (d) 6 (δ), pp. 529–30, above. In the
Babylonic Society, which was affiliated to the Sumeric, Hammurabi's practice appears
to have prevailed over Dungi's. It is true that the god-determinative was sometimes
prefixed to the names of the barbarian Kassite kings of Karduniash (Meyer, op. cit.,
vol. cit., p. 633; Jeremias, op. cit., pp. 21–2); but this usage was intermittent and
apparently capricious; and there is no reason to suppose that it was intended to be taken
any more seriously than the caliphial style and title which was usurped, after the downfall of the 'Abbasid Caliphate of Baghdad, by its Iranic 'successor-states' (see Arnold,
Sir T. W.: The Caliphate (Oxford 1924, Clarendon Press), chaps. 9–14). Pace Jeremias,
in op. cit., there appears to be no serious evidence for any assumption of divinity by the
kings of Assyria. In the Hittite Society—which, like the Babylonic, was affiliated to the
Sumeric—'le roi n'est pas divinisé de son vivant . . . mais il l'est après sa mort: on ne
dit pas de lui "il est mort", mais bien "il est devenu dieu" [compare the Roman Emperor
Vespasian's expiring sally "puto deus fio"—A.J.T.]. Cette formule, fréquente dans les
textes en langue hittite, n'est pas traduite littéralement dans les textes en akkadien, où
l'on emploie les expressions en usage à Babylone.'—Delaporte, L.: Les Hittites (Paris
1936, Renaissance du Livre), p. 173.
[3] See Meyer, op. cit., vol. ii, part (1), 2nd ed. (Berlin and Stuttgart 1928, Cotta),
p. 512, footnote 1.
[4] See V. C (i) (d) 7, vol. vi, p. 2, below, and Cunow, H.: Geschichte und Kultur des
Inkareiches (Amsterdam 1937, Elsevier), pp. 75–6.
[5] See ibid., p. 74.
[6] See Joyce, T. A.: South American Archaeology (London 1912, Lee Warner), p. 110.

was a storm of such violence that it swept away not only the worship of the Inca Emperor but the Incaic Empire itself, and the
whole Andean culture with it, in one all-engulfing cataclysm.
There are strong grounds, however, for believing that even the
Inca Pachacutec (*imperabat circa* A.D. 1400–48), who may be regarded as the founder of the Andean universal state,[1] did not look
upon the official worship of his own person and office as a cult
which was capable of standing by itself; for it was Pachacutec who
organized a Pan-Andean Pantheon in which the high god was not
the Inca himself but his progenitor and protector the Sun-God of
Corichanca.[2]

In another context[3] we have already noticed the closeness of the
resemblance which the Inca Pachacutec's work of theological and
ecclesiastical organization bears to that of the Pharaoh Thothmes
III; and indeed the divinity of the Pharaohs in its decline, though
not at its apogee in the time of 'the Old Kingdom', seems, like the
divinity of the Incas, to have been regarded and represented as
derivative from that of the human ruler's celestial parent and
patron. If the latter-day Pharaoh was 'the Good God', he enjoyed
this divine status in virtue of being the adoptive son of the Sun-
God Re.[4] Moreover, we have observed that, throughout the long
course of the disintegration of the Egyptiac Civilization from the
time of the Pyramid-Builders onwards, the figure of the Pharaoh
was progressively humanized through being gradually divested
of its divine attributes.[5] And Thothmes' decision to organize
an Egyptiac Pantheon with Amon-Re at its head may perhaps

[1] See II. D (iv), vol. ii, p. 103, footnote 2, above.
[2] See V. C (i) (d) 6 (δ), p. 532, above, and the present Annex, p. 694,
below.
[3] In the first of the two places cited in the preceding footnote.
[4] The Pharaonic title 'Son of Re' is rare in the inscriptions of the Fourth Dynasty
and not much more frequent in those of the Fifth and Sixth Dynasties. It did not
become part of the regular style and title of every Pharaoh until the time of the Heracleo-
polite princes and their successors of the Eleventh Dynasty (Meyer, op. cit., vol. i,
part (2), 3rd ed. (Stuttgart and Berlin 1913, Cotta), p. 204).
'In becoming the son of the Ruler of the Universe the Pharaoh rises in status in
one sense, but in another sense he sinks, through being subordinated to a higher religious idea. Vis-à-vis his father Re the King no longer stands on the footing of equality
on which the living Horus had formerly stood among the gods; he is Re's obedient son
who carries out his father's will. In consequence the Pharaoh of the following age is
no longer "the Great God", as in the time of "the Old Kingdom"; he is now merely
"the Good God" ' (ibid., p. 208).
For 'Adoptionism' in general see further V. C (ii) (a), vol. vi, pp. 271–5, below.
While the living Pharaoh came to be adopted *ex officio* as a son of Re, the living monarchs
of the Hindu overseas dominions of Camboja, Champa, and Java seem to have been
identified with the gods worshipped in temples which these monarchs had founded.
'Thus, when Bhadravarman dedicated a temple to Shiva, the god was styled Bhadrés-
vara. More than this, when a king or any distinguished person died, he was commemorated by a statue which reproduced his features but represented him with the attributes
of his favourite god. . . . Another form of apotheosis was to describe a king by a posthumous title indicating that he had gone to the heaven of his divine patron' (Eliot, Sir Ch.:
Hinduism and Buddhism (London 1921, Arnold, 3 vols.), vol. iii, p. 115).
[5] See IV. C (iii) (c) 2 (β), vol. iv, pp. 408–14, above.

be interpreted as a tacitly yet eloquently conclusive confession, on the Pharaoh's own part, that he himself was not, after all, an incarnation of the high god. Nor, perhaps, would it have lain in Thothmes' power to impose on his subjects any religious system at all—not even this one in which the Pharaoh's person was not the supreme object of worship—if the losing battle which the religion of the Egyptiac dominant minority had been fighting in the preceding age against the rising proletarian-born worship of Osiris had not been unexpectedly suspended to give place to an *union sacrée* against the alien worship of the god of the Hyksos.[1]

Finally, we shall observe that in the Sinic World, as in the Egyptiac and Andean worlds, the human ruler of the universal state exercised his divine authority as a mandatory rather than in his own right. He was merely the Son of Heaven, and not a very god himself;[2] and even for this modest executory role, on which the Emperor's hold upon the loyalty of his subjects mainly depended, he was indebted to the Confucian school of philosophers, who invested the Imperial office with this halo of divinity at second hand as a *quid pro quo* when the Imperial Crown at length came to terms with Confucianism and established it as a philosophy of state. Even in the days of their adversity, before the capitulation of the Han Emperor Wuti,[3] the Confucian scholars had known how to make a hostile empire-builder realize the potential value of their support.

'When the scholar Liu Chia quoted Confucian classics in the presence of the first emperor [of the Han Dynasty], he was cut short by this scolding: "You fool, I have conquered the empire on horseback; what use have I for your classics?" To this, Liu Chia retorted: "Yes, Sire, you have conquered the empire on horseback; but can you govern it on horseback?"[4] The Emperor thought that there was something in that, and told him to write a book on why the Ts'ins [had] lost their empire to *him*. The book was duly written and read to the Emperor chapter by chapter. He was pleased, and gave it the title "The New Book", which is preserved to this day.'[5]

---

[1] See I. C (ii), vol. i, pp. 143–4, above.

[2] See Fitzgerald, C. P.: *China, a Short Cultural History* (London 1935, Cresset Press), pp. 214–15.

[3] For Wuti's conversion to Confucianism, which was one of the momentous events in Sinic history, see Hackmann, H.: *Chinesische Philosophie* (Munich 1927, Reinhardt), p. 173; Forke, A.: *Die Gedankenwelt des Chinesischen Kulturkreises* (Munich and Berlin 1927, Oldenbourg) p. 6; and the present Study, V. C (i) (*d*) 4, pp. 418–9, above, as well as the present Annex, pp. 707–8, below.

[4] This is an exact Sinic equivalent of the modern Western *mot*: 'The one thing that you cannot do with bayonets is to sit on them.'—A.J.T.

[5] Hu Shih: 'The Establishment of Confucianism as a State Religion during the Han Dynasty' in *The Journal of the North China Branch of the Royal Asiatic Society*, vol. lx, 1929, p. 24.

Thereafter Liu Pang's successors on the throne of the Sinic universal state were wise enough to avoid their Ts'in predecessors' fate by coming to terms with the scholars who had inherited—or usurped—Confucius's academic chair;[1] and, as part of this politic *Ausgleich* between the sword and the pen, they were content to accept a status which might fall short of full divinity, but which had the substantial advantage of resting, not upon the arbitrary fiat of the emperors themselves, but upon the moral authority of a school of litterati whose prestige in the sight of the proletariat was rising at this time *pari passu* with the descent of their philosophy towards the proletarian level.[2] It will be seen that the Sinic Son of Heaven stood nearer to Aurelian the servant of Sol Invictus and to Hammurabi the servant of Marduk than he stood to any Divus Julius or Divus Augustus or deified Naramsin or Dungi. And this less than fully divine status into which the emperors of the Sinic universal state settled down in and after the reign of Han Wuti was taken over by the affiliated Far Eastern Civilization when a ghost of the Empire of the Han was conjured up by the Sui and the T'ang and the Sung,[3] and again when, in the course of its disintegration, the main body of the Far Eastern Society was provided with a universal state of its own by the barbarian hands of Mongols and Manchus.[4] It was only in the Japanese offshoot of the Far Eastern Civilization that an effective apotheosis was conferred upon two of the three great militarists through whose cumulative labours a Japanese 'Time of Troubles' was brought to an end by the establishment of a Japanese universal state at the turn of the sixteenth and seventeenth centuries of the Christian Era.[5]

---

[1] 'The Han Emperors entered into the closest possible association with Confucianism; they made its teachings into the foundation of their whole theory of state or (it would hardly be an exaggeration to say) into a hallowed state philosophy.'—Hackmann, H.: *Chinesische Philosophie* (Munich 1927, Reinhardt), pp. 172–3.

[2] For the proletarianization of the Confucian philosophy in the Age of the Han see the passages quoted from Dr. Hu Shih in V. C (i) (d) 6 (δ), pp. 549 and 555–6, above.

[3] This evocation of a ghost of the Sinic universal state in the main body of the affiliated Far Eastern Society has been touched upon in V. C (i) (d) 6 (α), p. 478, above, and is examined further in Part X, below.

[4] See IV. C (ii) (b) 2, vol. iv, p. 87; V. C (i) (c) 1, in the present volume, pp. 53–4; and V. C (i) (c) 4, pp. 348–51, above.

[5] The three founders of the Japanese universal state were, of course, Nobunaga (*dominabatur* A.D. 1568–82), Hideyoshi (*dominabatur* A.D. 1582–98), and Ieyasu (*dominabatur* A.D. 1598–1603; *imperabat* A.D. 1603–16 as a Shogun officially recognized by the Mikado). These three Japanese 'saviours with the sword' are touched upon further in V. C (ii) (a), vol. vi, pp. 186, 188–9, and 191, below. 'All three are now equal in the eyes of the [Japanese] Government, since they are listed as deities of First Class Government Shrines of Special Rank dedicated to those great ones, not of the Imperial House, who have rendered special service to the country' (Professor A. L. Sadler in a letter to the writer of this Study). Whether the posthumous honours originally conferred upon them were likewise equal seems to be a debatable question. According to the same scholar in the same letter, 'the honours received by Hideyoshi and Ieyasu were practically the same when conferred [cf. eundem: *The Maker of Modern Japan*.

The foregoing survey will perhaps have sufficed to demonstrate the congenital feebleness of cults that are propagated by political

The Life of Tokugawa Ieyasu (London 1937, Allen & Unwin), pp. 17, 20, 35, and 327–31]; but the cult of the first was stifled and kept under a bushel very completely all through the Tokugawa Era, whereas that of Ieyasu was naturally elaborated. Nobunaga also received an equivalent deification; but, as his comparatively early death prevented him from becoming master of the whole Empire, as did the other two, he was therefore neglected.' Sir George Sansom appears to concur with Professor Sadler in regard to Hideyoshi and Ieyasu, but to differ from him in regard to Nobunaga, in the following passage from a letter to the writer of this Study: 'Ieyasu and Hideyoshi both received posthumous honours (from the Emperor). Hideyoshi was styled Toyokuni Daimyōjin, and Daimyōjin is a title given to important Shintō deities; whereas Ieyasu was styled Tōshōgū Daigongen, and *gongen* is the word for a manifestation of the Buddha in the form of a Shintō deity. I should say that Ieyasu's posthumous honours were greater. Ieyasu is, or was, spoken of as Gongen Sâma, the divine manifestation *par excellence*. Nobunaga received only the posthumous name Sōgen-in, a Buddhist title which is not a sign of deification. All Buddhists are given such a posthumous name.'

When Ieyasu died, there was a dispute among the experts as to what the dead dictator's posthumous status was to be. An adept in the Zen Mahayanian Buddhism (see V. C (i) (c) 2, pp. 96–103, above), Suden, maintained 'that Ieyasu had told him that he wished to . . . remain or become a Buddha like anyone else, while Tenkai', who was an adept in Shintō, 'quoted his interview of a later date at which he had intimated his intention of becoming a divinity like the late Hideyoshi' (Sadler, *The Maker of Modern Japan*, p. 326). Tenkai's will prevailed; the apotheosis of Ieyasu under a syncretistic Shintō-Mahayanian title was carried out in due form at Nikko in A.D. 1617; and Tenkai devoted the rest of his life to the establishment of the new worship. 'For two hundred and sixty years To-sho-dai-Gongen remained the tutelary deity of the ruling powers, and, through them, of the whole land, until, after the interval of a few decades, his place was taken by the deity of the Meiji Jingu' (Sadler, op. cit., p. 331).

'Ieyasu's successors did not receive the high posthumous rank conferred upon him. The second and third Shoguns had splendid shrines built for them, but did not receive such high posthumous titles as Ieyasu' (Sir George Sansom, in the letter quoted above). Under the present régime in Japan Tokugawa Mitsukuni is, however, included, like the three founders of the Japanese universal state, among the deities of First Class Government Shrines of Special Rank.

The status of the Mikado seems to be ambiguous. Sir George Sansom observes, in the letter quoted above, that 'the reigning members of the Imperial House are not, in my opinion, regarded as living gods, though there is, I believe, a school of thought which endeavours to inculcate this conception. In the earliest Imperial rescripts the reigning emperor describes himself as Aki-tsu-Kami, "a Manifest God", but I do not think that this persisted.' Sir George Sansom's opinion on this point is supported by the fact that, under the present régime in Japan, the authorities aver, when dealing with foreign mission schools, that bowing to a Shinto shrine or to the portrait of the Emperor is *not* an act of worship (on this point see Holtom: *The National Faith of Japan: A Study in Modern Shintō* (London 1938, Kegan Paul), pp. 68–70). On the other hand, Professor Sadler, in the letter quoted above, expresses the opinion that 'the Emperor would seem to be a "*kami*" while living: e.g. the primary school text books published by the Government say: "We love him as a father and we reverence him as a deity" [see the verse quoted in Holtom, p. 79, from one of the national readers for primary schools published by the Department of Education at Tokyo.—A.J.T.]. The word used is the same as of Shintō deities, and the custom of doing reverence before the Palace—much encouraged—is the same also. Of course "*kami*" is not God Almighty by any means. . . . They are not immortal or omnipotent. It seems that Meiji Tenno even had shrines dedicated to him while living.' Sir George Sansom adds that 'the emperors are certainly regarded as of divine descent, and the ritual in the Imperial Palace [see Holtom, p. 173.—A.J.T.] includes worship by the Emperor of his divine ancestors, i.e. the Sun-Goddess, the first Emperor, and the Imperial line in general'. 'But this collective worship of the Imperial House may be correctly regarded as an aspect of the family worship of the Imperial Household' (Holtom, p. 173); and a dead emperor apparently does not, as an individual, become a recipient of divine honours automatically *ex officio*. Out of all the emperors and empresses of the past, historical or mythical, not more than twelve emperors and three empresses are to-day in receipt of public worship at Government shrines (Holtom, pp. 172–3).

The root cause of this ambiguity in the status of both the living and the dead is pointed out by Sir George Sansom in an illuminating *caveat*. 'In a country where ancestor worship is important, it is difficult to draw a line between the worship of a departed great man as a god, his worship as a hero, and his worship as a personal or

potentates from above downwards through the instrumentality of
the propagators' political power. Even when such cults are political
in essence, and religious only in form, and even when they correspond to a popular sentiment that is genuine and spontaneous,
they seem to show little capacity for surviving storms; and they
are at their weakest when they take the shape of a deification of their
human authors. Caesar-worship is apt in course of time either to
be abandoned altogether or else to be bolstered up by being placed
under the aegis of some higher divinity who is not himself just
Caesar masquerading as a god incarnate.

There is another class of cases in which a political potentate
attempts to impose a cult which is not a mere political institution
in a religious guise but is of a genuinely religious character; and
in this field, too, we can point to instances in which the experiment
has been a success. It appears, however, to be a condition of
success in such cases that the religion which is being imposed in
this fashion should already be 'a going concern'—at any rate in
the souls of a minority of its political patron's subjects—and, even
when this condition is fulfilled and when success is attained, the
price that has to be paid turns out to be a prohibitive one; for a
religion which, by an exertion of political authority, is successfully
imposed upon all the souls whose bodies are subject to the ruler
who is imposing it, is apt to gain this fraction of the world at the
price of forfeiting any prospects that it may once have had of
becoming—or remaining—a universal church.

For example, when the Maccabees changed, before the close
of the second century B.C., from being militant champions of the
Jewish religion against a forcible Hellenization[1] into being the
founders and rulers of one of the 'successor-states' of a Seleucid
Empire whose cultural policy they had succeeded in frustrating
by force of arms within their own parochial radius, these violent-
handed opponents of a persecuting Power immediately became
persecutors in their turn. They turned the swords that had first
been drawn in self-defence, in order to save the Jewish religion
from extinction, to the new and sinister use of imposing this self-
same Judaism upon the neighbouring non-Jewish populations—
once subject, like the Jews, to the Seleucidae—whom the Maccabees now succeeded in bringing under their own rule. And this

national ancestor. The act of worship performed by a visitor to, say, the shrine of
Ieyasu does not differ from the act of worship that he would perform before the tablets
of his own ancestors or before the tomb of the Emperor Meiji.'
    [1] For the lapse of Judaism into militancy see I. C (i) (b), vol. i, pp. 90–1; II. D (v),
vol. ii, p. 203; II. D (vi), vol. ii, pp. 234–6; II. D (vii), vol. ii, pp. 285–6 and 374; IV. C
(iii) (b) 12, vol. iv, pp. 224–5; IV. C (iii) (c) 2 (α), vol. iv, p. 263; and V. C (i) (c) 2,
in the present volume, pp. 68–9 and 125–6, above; and V. C (i) (d) 9 (γ), vol. vi, pp.
120–3, below.

Maccabaean policy of religious conversion by political force did avail to extend the domain of the Jewish religion from its native Judaea over Idumaea and over 'Galilee of the Gentiles'[1] and over a narrow Transjordanian Peraea. Even so, however, this triumph of force was narrowly circumscribed; for it failed to overcome either the religious particularism of the Samaritans or the civic pride of the two rows of Hellenic or Hellenized city-states which flanked the Maccabees' dominions on both sides—one row along the Mediterranean coast of Palestine in Philistia and the other along its desert border in the Decapolis. In fact, the extension of the domain of the Jewish religion through the force of Maccabaean arms was inconsiderable; and even the trivial gain of an expansion through persecution within these close-set limits was to cost the Jewish religion the whole of its spiritual future.

It is the supreme irony of Jewish history that the new ground captured for Judaism by the spear of Alexander Jannaeus (*regnabat* 102–76 B.C.) did bring to birth, within a hundred years, a Galilaean Jewish prophet whose message to his fellow men was the consummation of all previous Jewish religious experience, and that this inspired Jewish scion of forcibly converted Galilaean Gentiles was then rejected and done to death by the Judaean leaders of the Jewry of his age.[2] In thus deliberately refusing the opportunity that was offered to it of realizing its manifest destiny of flowering into Christianity by opening its heart to the gospel of its Galilaean step-child, Judaism not only stultified its spiritual past but forfeited its material future into the bargain. In declining to recognize its expected Messiah in Jesus, Judaism was renouncing its birthright in two great enterprises which eventually made the respective fortunes of two different daughters of Judaism by whom these enterprises were duly carried out in the fullness of time. In the first place Judaism was abandoning the fallow and fertile mission-field of the Hellenic universal state to a Christian Church that was to be driven into independence by its eviction from the Jewish fold; and in the second place Judaism was leaving to an Islam whose founder was to be rebuffed by the Jewish Diasporà in his native Hijāz[3] the subsequent political task of reuniting a Syriac World which had been divided against itself as one consequence of the forcible intrusion of Hellenism upon Syriac

---

[1] Matt. iv. 15. For the unexpected and unintended effect of this Maccabaean conquest of Galilee upon the history of Jewry and of the World see II. D (iii), vol. ii, pp. 73–4, above, and V. C (ii) (a), Annex II, vol. vi, pp. 477–8 and 499, below.

[2] On this point see II. D (iii), vol. ii, pp. 73–4, above.

[3] The Prophet Muhammad's decision to found a new religion instead of finding his mission in the conversion of his pagan fellow countrymen to Judaism was expressed symbolically in his substitution of Mecca for Jerusalem as the *qiblah* towards which his followers were to face when they were performing their prayer-drill.

ground.[1] Instead of embracing either of these alternative opportunities for a great career when it had the refusal of both of them, Judaism preferred to fling itself into the forlorn hope of Zealotism—in order to be retrieved as a mere fossil,[2] by the tardy wisdom of Johanan ben Zakkai, from the wantonly incurred cataclysm of A.D. 70.[3]

The same policy of imposing a religious allegiance by the use of political force was adopted, with similar consequences, by the Sasanidae, another dynasty of Syriac anti-Hellenists who succeeded in Iran and 'Irāq in accomplishing once for all that patriotic task of eradicating Hellenism in which the Maccabees were only momentarily successful in their own more exposed position west of the Euphrates.[4] In the much larger domain over which the Sasanidae succeeded in effectively asserting their political authority, they pursued the Maccabaean policy of using their political power as an instrument for imposing their own religious practices and beliefs upon their subjects.[5] In this forcible conversion of the eastern half of the Syriac World to Zoroastrianism the Sasanidae obtained, scale for scale, about the same measure of success as had rewarded the corresponding endeavours of the Maccabees in their miniature *Machtgebiet* in Palestine. The Sasanidae were successful in making Zoroastrianism the prevalent religion within the frontiers of their own empire; but even within these limits they never succeeded in getting rid of every remnant of obstinately non-Zoroastrian religious allegiance; and they were never able to make their forcibly established church secure against raids on the part of Nestorian Christianity and other non-Zoroastrian faiths from beyond the frontiers, or even against outbreaks of heresy—Manichaean, Mazdakite, and so on—within the bosom of the Zoroastrian Church itself. On the other hand, as the price of this partial success in imposing itself, with the aid of the secular arm, upon the subjects of the Sasanian Crown, Zoroastrianism had to make sacrifices which were as heavy as those which were exacted from Judaism by the religious policy of the Maccabees.

[1] For this non-religious function of Islam see I. C (i) (b), vol. i, pp. 73–7, and V. C (i) (c) 2, in the present volume, pp. 127–8, above; and the present Annex, pp. 672–8, below.
[2] For Judaism as a fossil see I. B (iii), vol. i, p. 35; I. C (i) (b), vol. i, pp. 90–2; II. D (vi), vol. ii, p. 235; and II. D (vii), vol. ii, p. 286, above.
[3] See V. C (i) (c) 2, pp. 75–6, above.
[4] For the respective success of the Sasanidae and failure of the Maccabees to achieve an identical aim at different times and in different parts of the Syriac World see II. D (vii), vol. ii, pp. 285–6, and V. C (i) (c) 2, in the present volume, pp. 125–6, above. For the humiliating debt of the Maccabees, for their brief political *floruit*, to the play of the Balance of Power between the rival Seleucid and Roman representatives of a Hellenic dominant minority see the observation quoted from Tacitus (*Histories*, Book V, chap. 8) in V. C (i) (d) 1, p. 390, footnote 3, above.
[5] See Pettazzone, R.: *La Religione di Zarathustra* (Bologna 1920, Zanichelli), pp. 184–7.

In the first place a politically regimented Zoroastrian Church had to abandon the mission-fields at its gates to rival churches which had refrained from selling their birthright of freedom.[1] The Oxus-Jaxartes Basin, with its vast hinterlands in the Eurasian Steppe and on the Steppe's Far Eastern coasts, became a debatable ground between a heretical Manichaean version of Zoroastrianism[2] and a Mahayanian version of Buddhism[3] and a Nestorian version of Christianity,[4] while the orthodox Zoroastrian Church stood aside without taking a hand in the competition for so great a prize.[5] At the same time the militantly Zoroastrian Empire of the Sasanidae failed as signally as the Jewish Zealots had failed in an earlier age to complete by force of arms the achievement of expelling an intrusive Hellenism from the holdings that it still retained on Syriac ground. The official Sasanian dynastic programme of reconstituting the Achaemenian Empire of Darius remained unfulfilled from first to last, notwithstanding the perpetual wars of aggression, with a view to its accomplishment, which were waged against the Roman Empire by the Sasanian Power over a period of four centuries;[6] and the demonic effort of the Sasanian Pādishāh Khusrū Parwīz in the last and most devastating of these Romano-Persian wars (*gerebatur* A.D. 603–28) proved as fatal to the Zoroastrian cause as the forlorn hope of the Jewish Zealots in the greatest of the Romano-Jewish wars (*gerebatur* A.D. 66–70) had proved, in its time, to the cause of Judaism.

The duel between Khusrū Parwīz and his Roman antagonist Heraclius ended in a reversion to the *status quo ante bellum* which left the Zoroastrian aggressor still more seriously enfeebled than his Christian victim. And all that Khusrū achieved was to prepare the way for the swift accomplishment, by an Islam-under-arms, of a war-aim which had never been attained by a Zoroastrianism-under-arms from beginning to end of the Sasanian régime down to Khusrū's own day. On the morrow of Khusrū's deposition from the throne by his own war-weary subjects the Primitive Muslim Arabs duly completed the political reunion of the Syriac World by biting off the Syriac provinces of the Roman Empire and

---

[1] The lifelessness of Zoroastrianism under the Sasanian régime is pointed out by Ameer Ali: *The Spirit of Islam* (revised edition, London 1922, Christophers), pp. xxxv–vi.

[2] For the relation of Manichaeism to Zoroastrianism see V. C (i) (*c*) 2, Annex I, above. For the spread of Manichaeism across Central Asia see II. D (vii), vol. ii, p. 375; II. D (vii), Annex VIII, vol. ii, p. 450; and Part III. A, Annex II, vol. iii, pp. 415 and 451, above.

[3] For the journey of the Mahāyāna from India to the Far East see II. D (vi), Annex, vol. ii, p. 405, footnote 1, and V. C (i) (*c*) 2, in the present volume, pp. 132–46, above.

[4] For the spread of Nestorianism across Central Asia see II. D (vi), vol. ii, pp. 236–8, above.

[5] See V. C (i) (*c*) 3, pp. 249–50, and V. C (i) (*c*) 2, Annex I, pp. 578–9, above.

[6] See V. C (i) (*c*) 3, p. 216, above.

at the same bite swallowing the Sasanian Empire whole; and this preliminary and superficial act of political union was followed up by the gradual spread of Islam, under the aegis of the Arab Caliphate, until it became the uniform faith of a dissolving Syriac Society.[1] By the same token the destiny which was seized upon by Islam was forfeited by Zoroastrianism; and at the end of the story the religion which had allowed itself to be enticed into the false position of depending for its own advancement upon the political power of the Sasanidae had to pay the penalty of being reduced to a fossilized state and being driven forth from its native ground to live a lingering life-in-death as a mere 'Diasporà' among the Gentiles in the alien environment of the western seaboard of India.[2]

The present plight of the Zoroastrian Church would have been inconceivable to the predecessors of our latter-day Parsees in the age when Zoroastrianism—in virtue of having been established as the official religion of the Sasanian Empire, with the whole strength of the Sasanian Government's right arm behind it—was being professed with at any rate an outward show of devotion by all but a small minority of the inhabitants of a vast tract of Asia extending from the Euphrates on the south-west to the Murghab on the north-east. And the extremeness of the change in the fortunes of this once established church of Iran and 'Irāq in the course of the last thirteen centuries raises the question whether another faith—namely, the Imāmī form of Shi'ism—which is prevalent to-day over an area almost co-extensive with the domain of Zoroastrianism in the Sasanian Age,[3] may not perhaps be destined in some future chapter of its history to suffer an equally sensational eclipse, considering that the latest chapter in the history of the Imāmī sect of Shi'ism has borne a singularly close resemblance to the Sasanian chapter in the history of the Zoroastrianism which once enjoyed the same status as the Shī'ah in the same region.

As the now long since ruined material fortunes of Zoroastrianism were made—for a spell of four centuries—at a single stroke when Ardashir, the Sasanian prince of Fars, overthrew his Arsacid overlord and established Zoroastrianism as the official religion of his own new empire early in the third century of the Christian Era, so the present material fortunes of the Imāmī sect of Shi'ism have been made by the career and policy of Shāh Ismā'īl Safawī,[4] who,

---

[1] The reason why Islam escaped the usual nemesis of 'higher religions' that take to politics is discussed on pp. 672–8, below.

[2] For Zoroastrianism as a fossil see I. B (iii), vol. i, p. 35; I. C (i) (b), vol. i, pp. 90–2; and II. D (vi), vol. ii, p. 236, above.

[3] For the present extension of the domain of Imāmī Shi'ism in Iran and 'Irāq see II. D (vi), vol. ii, p. 255, with footnote 3, above.

[4] For Shāh Ismā'īl's momentous career see I. C (i) (b), Annex I, vol. i, pp. 366–88, above.

at the opening of the sixteenth century of the Christian Era, emulated Ardashir's achievements by first overthrowing his Āq Qōyūnlū Türkmen overlord and then carving out a new empire of his own in which he high-handedly imposed his ancestral faith of Imāmī Shi'ism upon the Sunnī majority of the inhabitants of the subjugated territories.[1] Is this forcibly propagated Imāmī Shi'ism destined at some future date to liquidate the sinister debt which it owes to the secular arm of Shāh Ismā'īl and his Safawī successors by paying in full the price which has now long since been paid by Zoroastrianism for its propagation by similar means at the hands of Ardashir and his successors on the throne of the Sasanidae? While the question whether the Imāmī sect of Shi'ism will ever be penalized to the extreme degree of being reduced to the plight of an expatriated 'Diasporà' is manifestly one that can only be answered by the course of future events which the present generation will not live to see, it is a verifiable matter of fact that the first instalment of the price that once had to be paid by Zoroastrianism for the political patronage of the Sasanidae has been paid for the political patronage of the Safawīs by the Imāmī sect of Shi'ism already.

The original note of this variety of Shi'ism—a note which at first distinguished it more sharply than any other feature from the rival Ismā'īlī school—was its adherence to the principle of Non-Violence. The primitive Imāmī Shi'īs, like the *Agudath Israel* in Jewry to-day,[2] held the view that the Millennium which they were awaiting would be inaugurated in God's own time by God's own action; and accordingly they conceived it to be the duty of the true believers to wait passively for the advent of the eagerly desired New Age instead of presumptuously attempting to anticipate this divine event by any human action of theirs.[3] Possibly it was thanks to this disarming tenet that the non-violent Imāmī form of Shi'ism had been allowed to survive in a predominantly Sunnī world in which the intolerably violent Ismā'īlī sect had invited and incurred an almost complete extermination.[4] However that may be, there can be little doubt that the Non-Violence of the Imāmī Shī'ah was one of the attractions that enabled it, in the fifteenth century of the Christian Era, to find a new mission-field, and to win a considerable number of new converts, in a universal

[1] For evidences of the numerical weakness of the Shi'ah in Iran on the eve of Shāh Ismā'īl's forcible conversion of the Sunnī majority of the population see I. C (i) (*b*), Annex I, vol. i, pp. 361-2, above.
[2] For the contrast between the passivism of the *Agudath Israel* and the activism of the Zionists see V. C (i) (*c*) 2, p. 76; V. C (i) (*c*) 2, Annex III, p. 588; and V. C (i) (*d*) 4, Annex, p. 617, footnote 2, above.
[3] For this original Imāmī doctrine see I. C (i) (*b*), Annex I, vol. i, p. 359, with footnote 2, above.
[4] See I. C (i) (*b*), Annex, vol. i, p. 358, above.

state which had recently been established by Ottoman empire-builders in the domain of Orthodox Christendom.[1] The statesmen who were shaping the policy of the Ottoman Empire in that age found no reason to mistrust or oppose the peaceful penetration of their dominions by a religion which was debarred by its own principles from trespassing on the prerogative of the secular power by going into politics on its own account. These fair prospects of the Imāmī Shī'ah in its Anatolian mission-field were compromised, however, when in the middle of the fifteenth century Shaykh Junayd Safawī (*fungebatur* A.D. 1447–60)[2]—the reigning representative of a family of religious adepts in Gīlān which by this time had come to be recognized as entitled to a hereditary spiritual leadership of the Imāmī Shī'ī community—betrayed one of the fundamental tenets of the sect of which he was the head by wantonly shifting the sanction for his authority from a spiritual to a military basis.[3] In the next chapter of the story the Imāmī Shī'ī

[1] For the spread of the Imāmī form of Shi'ism into that region in that age see I. C (i) (*b*), Annex I, vol. i, pp. 365 and 382–3, and V. C (i) (*c*) 2, in the present volume, p. 111, above.

[2] For Shaykh Junayd's career see Hinz, W.: *Irans Aufstieg zum Nationalstaat im Fünfzehnten Jahrhundert* (Berlin and Leipzig 1936, de Gruyter), pp. 22–49, and V. Minorsky's review of Hinz's book in the *Deutsche Literaturzeitung*, 1937, Heft 23, 6th June, pp. 953–7. The pugnacity and aggressiveness of Junayd's character are shown up by the chronicle of his actions and experiences. His patent appetite for temporal power quickly made him suspect to his own sovereign Jahānshāh Qārā Qōyūnlū; and, when he was deposed by this Türkmen war-lord from the headship of the Safawī Order of Ardabīl, the Ottoman Government prudently refused him asylum in Ottoman territory, while those who did show him hospitality were soon given cause to repent of their good nature. In Qāramān he fell into a theological dispute with the head of the dervish *tekke* at Qōnīyah which had received him as its guest, and his method of conducting the controversy was to try to raise a band of wild highlanders against the public authorities! In the dominions of the Mamlūks, to which he then managed to escape, he made himself such a nuisance in the derelict Crusader castle which he rented on the Jabal Arsūs, that the religious authorities at Aleppo complained to the Government at Cairo, with the result that Junayd was ejected from his castle by force of arms. The Ottoman viceroy of Jāniq, whither he next repaired, was glad to see him ride off on a holy war against the Orthodox Christian principality of Trebizond. When this pious enterprise miscarried, the Safawī adventurer settled down for three years at Uzun Hasan Āq Qōyūnlū's court at Diyarbakr, where he received his host's sister in marriage. But even in a bed of roses Junayd was unable to rest. From Diyarbakr he returned to his native Ardabīl, was expelled for the second time, and met his death in an unprovoked invasion of the dominions of the Shirvānshāh.

[3] Shaykh Junayd's momentous new departure from the principles of the Imāmī Shī'ah and from the traditions of his own House has been touched upon in I. C (i) (*b*), Annex I, vol. i, pp. 366–7, above. In that context it has been suggested that Shaykh Junayd was tempted into taking up arms and going into politics by the sudden creation of a political vacuum in Iran and 'Irāq through the collapse of the Timurid Empire upon the death of Shāh Rukh in the very year of Shaykh Junayd's own accession (compare the similar temptation which beset and overcame the Maccabees upon the collapse of the Seleucid Empire in the latter part of the second century B.C.). In this connexion it may be recalled (see I. C (i) (*b*), Annex I, vol. i, p. 364, above) that, although the Safawī House had acquired the leadership of the Imāmī Shī'ī sect, it had not itself originally been of the Imāmī, or even of the Shī'ī, persuasion. The eponym of the House, Shaykh Safiyu'd-Dīn (*vivebat circa* A.D. 1252–1334) appears to have been a Sunnī, and the first head of the House who is known for certain to have been an Imāmī Shī'ī is Shaykh Junayd's grandfather Shaykh Khwāja 'Alī (*pontificali munere fungebatur* A.D. 1392–1427). These non-Imāmī antecedents in the family tradition of Shaykh Junayd perhaps partly account for his lapse from the principles of a faith which his grandfather may have been the first member of the family to embrace.

missionary enterprise in the Ottoman Empire was frustrated altogether when Shaykh Junayd's grandson Shāh Ismāʿīl (*imperabat*
A.D. 1500–24) carried his grandfather's resort to militancy a long
—though not an illogical—stage farther by setting himself the
dual ambition of winning an oecumenical empire by force of arms
and then using a ubiquitous political power as an instrument for
imposing his ancestral faith upon Mankind as a world religion.[1]

In another context[2] we have seen that, in the event, Shāh
Ismāʿīl failed signally to achieve his ambition in either of its two
related aspects. His twenty-five-years-long career of military aggression did not avail either to expand the principality which he
had inherited from his grandfather to the dimensions of a universal
state or to promote the religion which he had inherited from his
great-great-grandfather to the rank of a universal church. All that
he achieved was to found a new empire in the central portion of
the Iranic World and to impose the Imāmī form of Shiʿism by
force upon a majority of the inhabitants of this broad but very
far from world-wide realm.[3] Even on the political plane his
achievement was disappointing; for the extent of the territory
which he was able to bequeath to his descendants was conspicuously narrower than that of the empire which Timur Lenk had
left behind him a hundred years back; and on the religious plane
the results of Shāh Ismāʿīl's career were utterly disastrous for the
religion of which he was the official pontiff and champion.

One consequence—which followed inevitably from Ismāʿīl's
general policy, even if the direct responsibility for it cannot be
brought home to him in the present state of the evidence—was that
the head of the Imāmī mission in the Ottoman dominions, Shāh
Qūlī, took a cue from his Safawī master by taking up arms; and
this resort to militancy was fatal to the cause of the Shīʿah in the
Orthodox Christian World; for the insurrection of the Anatolian
Shīʿīs against the Ottoman Government in A.D. 1511 was answered
by the extermination of this disloyal Shīʿī 'Diasporà' in A.D. 1514
at the command of the Ottoman Pādishāh Selīm the Grim.[4]
Therewith the Imāmī Shīʿah lost its chance of becoming the
universal church of a disintegrating Orthodox Christian Society;
and in our own day, again, this would-be oecumenical religion
has been inhibited, by the lasting effects of its irretrievable error
of going into politics, from entering another new mission-field of
even wider scope and greater promise. The orthodox form of the
Imāmī Shīʿah is not to be found in the company of those 'higher

---

[1] For the evidence for Shāh Ismāʿīl's aims see I. C (i) (*b*), Annex I, vol. i, pp. 367–8,
above.   [2] In I. C (i) (*b*), Annex I, vol. i, pp. 366–400, above.
[3] See I. C (i) (*b*), Annex I, vol. i, p. 392, above.
[4] See I. C (i) (*b*), Annex I, vol. i, pp. 362, 365, 382, and 384, above.

religions' that have latterly begun to compete for the conversion of souls in a Westernized 'Great Society'. On the other hand the list of competitors does include an unofficial and heretical offshoot of the Imāmī established church of the Empire of Iran in the shape of the Bahā'īyah,[1] a free daughter church which has reverted to that principle of Non-Violence which has been abandoned with such disastrous results by its politically compromised mother. The Bahā'īyah sect has been excommunicated by the Imāmī Mujtahids and been evicted from its Iranian homeland; but it is already apparent that these bitter experiences of persecution and expatriation have served this infant religion in good stead; for it has thereby been driven into looking beyond the Mediterranean and the Atlantic for new worlds to conquer in the strength of a principle which is apt to work as an 'open sesame' for any missionary religion that has the faith to embrace it.[2]

The new departure into which the Imāmī sect of the Shī'ah was led by Shaykh Junayd and his grandson Shāh Ismā'īl has an analogue in the Hindu World in the militarization of the religious fraternity of the Sikhs[3] by the sixth and tenth gurus in the Sikh pontifical succession. The sixth guru, Har Govind (*fungebatur* A.D. 1606–45), did for the Sikhs what Shaykh Junayd did for the Imāmī Shī'ah by putting arms into the hands of a community which his predecessors had already transformed from an embryonic church into an embryonic state;[4] and the role of Shāh Ismā'īl, the Imāmī militarist *à outrance*, was played in Sikh history by the tenth guru, Govind Singh (*fungebatur* A.D. 1675–1708).[5] Morally the two militant Sikh gurus were perhaps less blameworthy than

---

[1] For the Bahā'īyah sect and the Bābī movement out of which it sprang see V. C (i) (c) 2, pp. 174–6, above.

[2] It will be seen that the Bahā'īyah stands to the Imāmī Shī'ī established church of Iran as Manichaeism once stood to a Zoroastrian established church of Iran. On this analogy it will further be seen that the successful propagation of the Bahā'īyah, beyond the western bounds of Iran, across 'Irāq and Syria into Europe and America matches the successful propagation of Manichaeism, beyond the north-eastern bounds of Iran, across the Oxus-Jaxartes Basin on to the Eurasian Steppe and into the Far East (see p. 660, above).

[3] For the origins of Sikhism see IV. C (iii) (b) 13, vol. iv, p. 231; V. C (i) (c) 2, in the present volume, p. 106; and V. C (i) (d) 6 (δ), p. 537, footnote 3, above. For the militarization of the Sikhs see Macauliffe, M. A.: 'How the Sikhs became a Militant Race' in *Supplement to the Journal of the United Service Institution of India*, vol. xxxii, July 1903, No. 152, pp. 330–58; eundem: *The Sikh Religion* (Oxford 1909, Clarendon Press, 6 vols.), lives of the sixth and tenth gurus in vols. iv and v respectively.

[4] There seems to have been an intermediate stage in the evolution of the Sikh military machine out of the Sikh religious fraternity which had been founded by Nanak about a hundred years before Har Govind's time. In the last quarter of the sixteenth century of the Christian Era the Sikh community seems to have assumed a form which was already political though it was not yet warlike (see Eliot, Sir Ch.: *Hinduism and Buddhism* (London 1921, Arnold, 3 vols.), vol. ii, p. 268). Guru Angad's advice to a Mughal soldier who had come to ask him for spiritual guidance was that he should do his military duty; and the military virtues were commended by Guru Arjan, who was Har Govind's father and immediate predecessor (Macauliffe, *J.U.S.I.I.*, vol. cit., pp. 331 and 334).

[5] See Eliot, op. cit., vol. ii, p. 270.

the two militant Safawī shaykhs; for, whereas the Safawīs were
tempted into militancy by the sudden collapse of an aggressive
Timurid empire which left the oppressor's former victims in the
presence of a political vacuum,[1] the Sikhs were goaded into
militancy by the tyrannical oppression of an aggressive Timurid
empire which at that time still possessed and exercised both the
will and the power to put its victims to death.[2] Yet, however we
may assess the relative degrees of moral guilt, the penalty for the

[1] See p. 663, footnote 3, above.

[2] The fifth guru, Arjan, who was the father and immediate predecessor of Har
Govind, was summoned to Lahore by Jahangir, obeyed the summons without recalcitrance, and was no sooner in the Mughal Emperor's power than he was commanded
by the tyrant not to maintain any tenets that were incompatible with either Islam or
Hinduism. When the guru refused to obey this Imperial command he was put to
torture, and he died in captivity—enjoining, as his last injunctions, upon his son and
heir Har Govind that he was to bear arms and to maintain an army (Macauliffe, *The
Sikh Religion*, vol. iii, pp. 90–101; *J.U.S.I.I.*, vol. cit., p. 334). Again, the ninth guru,
Tej Bahadur, was a man of peace who fell foul of the Mughal Emperor Awrangzīb
over the latter's misguided policy of trying to impose Islam by force upon his Hindu
subjects. In answer to an appeal for support from the persecuted Brahmans of Kashmir,
Tej Bahadur authorized them to tell Awrangzīb that they were prepared to accept
Islam if the Emperor could first succeed in converting Tej Bahadur himself. Thereupon
Tej Bahadur was summoned by Awrangzīb to Delhi; he obeyed the reigning Mughal
Emperor's summons, as his ancestor and forerunner Arjan had obeyed Jahangir's; and
history repeated itself to the bitter end; for Awrangzīb no sooner had Tej Bahadur in
his power than he put him under arrest, ordered him to embrace Islam, and finally be-
headed him in A.D. 1675 (Macauliffe, *The Sikh Religion*, vol. iv, pp. 377–87; *J.U.S.I.I.*,
vol. cit., pp. 341–3). It will be seen that Har Govind took to the sword under incomparably greater provocation than Junayd, whose father and predecessor Shaykh Ibrāhīm
had died peacefully in his bed, and whose grievance against the world was the purely
personal one of having been himself deposed, in favour of his uncle, from the headship
of the Safawī fraternity, and having then been driven into exile (Hinz, W.: *Irans
Aufstieg zum Nationalstaat im Fünfzehnten Jahrhundert* (Berlin and Leipzig 1936,
de Gruyter), pp. 23–4). It is true that Shāh Ismāʿīl, unlike his grandfather Shaykh
Junayd, was able to find in the mission of avenging his father's death a handsome
pretext for his own persistence in his father's and his grandfather's warlike courses.
Yet Shaykh Haydar Safawī's blood hardly cried aloud for vengeance so imperatively
as Guru Arjan's or Guru Tej Bahadur's. For, whereas these two Sikh gurus were
men of peace who had been inveigled into a tyrant's power and had then been put to
death in cold blood, the Safawī Shaykh Haydar was a hard-bitten militarist who met
his death on the battle-field in a war in which he himself was the aggressor (Hinz,
op. cit., pp. 83–8). Thus a comparison of the respective histories of the militarization
of the Imāmī Shīʿis and the Sikhs seems to show that the Sikh gurus' aberration was
less wanton than that of the Safawī shaykhs.

Both Har Govind and Govind Singh were, no doubt, fully conscious of the new
departure that they were making. Har Govind signalized his accession to the guruship
on the receipt of the news of his father's death in captivity by refusing to be invested
with the hat and cord of a faqīr, which were the Sikh guru's traditional insignia, and
donning, instead, a turban with a royal aigrette and a sword-belt (Macauliffe, *The Sikh
Religion*, vol. iv, p. 2; *J.U.S.I.I.*, vol. cit., pp. 334–6). Govind Singh—consciously
following in his grandfather Har Govind's footsteps—trained his own children to arms,
inculcated militarism in his followers by propaganda, instituted the military initiation
rite of 'Baptism by the Dagger', and boasted 'that he would change his followers from
jackals to tigers, and kill hawks with sparrows' (Macauliffe, *J.U.S.I.I.*, vol. cit., pp.
343–7). Yet neither Har Govind nor Govind Singh was able to carry his policy of
militarization without opposition in his own household. Both gurus were opposed by
the tithe collectors of the fraternity, and Har Govind was also opposed by his counsellor
Bhai Budha and by his mother—the widow of the murdered Guru Arjan (Macauliffe,
The Sikh Religion, vol. iv, p. 3, and vol. v, p. 6; *J.U.S.I.I.*, vol. cit., p. 335). Even
after Har Govind's newly raised army had met and defeated the Mughals on the battle-
field, a Sikh who was noted for his piety exhorted the guru to win security against attack
by detachment from This World—to which Har Govind could only reply that he was
now too deeply implicated in mundane affairs to be able to draw back (Macauliffe,
J.U.S.I.I., vol. cit., p. 337).

social aberration was much the same. As a result of having taken up arms the Sikhs eventually succeeded in taking their revenge upon the descendants of their oppressors Jahangir and Awrangzīb.[1] When the Timurid Mughal empire in India collapsed, in its turn, like Timur's own empire in South-Western Asia three hundred years earlier, the Sikhs were able to make themselves masters of one of the derelict provinces of this alien universal state into which a distracted Hindu World had been momentarily gathered together by the labours of Akbar and his successors; but in the act of achieving this vulgar worldly ambition the Sikhs were at the same time depriving the syncretistic Hindu-Muslim faith which they had inherited from their forefathers of any prospect which it might once have had of becoming the universal church of a Hindu Society in dissolution. On the religious side the Sikhs have even less success to boast of than the Safawīs or Sasanidae or Maccabees. They have not even succeeded in imposing their own religion upon a majority of the inhabitants of those territories in North-Western India in which, for more than a century, the Sikhs themselves were the political masters. In the Panjab to-day the adherents of the Sikh religion account for no more than eleven per cent. of the present population of the province,[2] and in the total present population of the British Indian Empire the fraction represented by the Sikhs is infinitesimally small. Nor has the Sikh religion gained anything from the abrupt extinction of the Sikh 'successor-states' of the Mughal Empire by British arms in the fifth decade of the nineteenth century. A priori it might have been expected that the conversion of Hindu souls to Sikhism—which had received a check when Har Govind transformed the Sikh community from a politico-religious fraternity into a nation-in-arms, and when Govind Singh led his war-band on the war-path[3]—would have

---

[1] Eventually, not immediately. The immediate effect of Govind Singh's plunge into 'totalitarian' militarism was the total defeat and destruction of his army by the combined forces of the Mughal Power and the local Panjābī highland chiefs (compare the total defeat of the Safawī Shaykh Haydar's army by a combination between the forces of the Āq Qōyūnlū war-lord Ya'qub and those of the Shirvānshāh in A.D. 1488). Though Govind Singh (unlike Haydar) escaped alive from the stricken field, his two eldest sons were killed in the rout, and his two youngest sons were betrayed to the Mughals and were put to death after having refused to accept the alternative of apostasy. Govind Singh himself became a fugitive in disguise, with his following reduced to five companions. Though he just outlived his conqueror Awrangzīb, he never recovered his temporal power, and in dying he bequeathed his succession, not to any human guru, but to the Granth (Macauliffe, *J.U.S.I.I.*, vol. cit., pp. 350–5; Farquhar, J. N.: *Modern Religious Movements in India* (New York, 1919, Macmillan), p. 337).

[2] The *Report of the Indian Statutory Commission*, vol. i (London 1930, H.M. Stationery Office), p. 60, estimates the Sikh element in the population of the Panjab at 2¼ million out of a total of 20¼ million.

[3] 'The Khālsā became strong to resist the Mughals, but their organization cut them off from their fellow countrymen, and made them practically a new caste. The transformation of the church into an army produced another evil result: living preaching ceased among the Sikhs, and their religious life began to go down' (Farquhar, J. N., op. cit., pp. 337–8).

begun to make progress again as soon as the Khālsā had been
relieved of the incubus of military and political power through
being forcibly reincorporated into the alien universal state which
re-established itself in India, in the shape of a British instead
of a Mughal Rāj, after the interlude of anarchy which had followed the Mughals' collapse.[1] Yet, so far from having profited
by this salutary divorce from incongruous military and political
activities, the Sikh religion has latterly shown a tendency to
merge itself again into the circumambient Hinduism out of which
it was originally differentiated through being blended with an
Islamic alloy by the syncretistic religious genius of a Kabīr and a
Nanak.[2]

We cannot close this survey of the effects that are apt to follow
from the attempt to impose a religious allegiance by the use of the
secular arm without turning to the ecclesiastical map of the modern
Western World in order to inquire how far the present boundaries
between the respective domains of Catholicism and Protestantism
have been determined by the arms or the diplomacy of the parochial
secular 'successor-states' of a medieval *Respublica Christiana*. No
doubt the influence of external military and political factors upon
the outcome of the religious conflict in Western Christendom in
the sixteenth and seventeenth centuries ought not to be rated too
high; for, to take two extreme cases, it is difficult to imagine that
the action of any secular authority—however potent or however
ruthless—could have availed either to retain the Baltic countries
within the fold of the Catholic Church or to bring the Mediterranean countries over into the Protestant camp. At the same time
there was an intermediate and debatable zone in which the play
of the military and political forces that intervened in the religious
strife of that age was certainly influential and was perhaps decisive;
and this zone embraces such important portions of the modern
Western World as Germany and the Low Countries and France
and England. It was in Germany, in particular, that the classical
formula *Cujus Regio Ejus Religio* was invented and applied;[3] and
we may take it that in Central Europe, at least, the secular princes

---

[1] The episode of Sikh political dominion in the Panjab between the fall of the Mughal
Rāj and the rise of the British Rāj in India presents an analogy with the similar episode
of Maccabaean political dominion in Palestine between the fall of the Seleucid Empire
and the extension of the Roman Empire over the ex-Seleucid territories west of the
Euphrates (see V. C (i) (*d*) 1, p. 390, and the present Annex, p. 659, footnote 4,
above).

[2] For this tendency of Sikhism to relapse into pure Hinduism see Eliot, op. cit., vol. ii,
pp. 272–3. Compare the disappearance, in the Far Eastern World, of the syncretistic
Taoist-Christian religion of the T'aip'ing, which turned militant (see V. C (i) (*c*) 2,
p. 107, above) like the Hindu-Islamic religion of Sikhism, and unlike the Hindu-
Christian Brahmō Samāj.

[3] This formula has been touched upon already, in a different context, in IV. C (iii) (*b*)
11, vol. iv, pp. 221–2, above.

—as well as those shepherds of souls who had gone into politics and had acquired the temporal sovereignty over some of the fragments of a shattered *Respublica Christiana*[1]—did successfully make use of their military and political power in order to force down the throats of their subjects whichever of the two competing forms of Western Christianity the local potentate happened to favour for his own part. In the same glance we can also take the measure of the damage which our Western Christianity, Catholic and Protestant alike, has suffered in the sequel as a penalty for having thus allowed itself to become dependent on political patronage and consequently subservient to *raison d'état*.

One of the first instalments of the price which has been paid for these latter-day political liaisons by the Western Christian churches up to date has been the loss of the Catholic Church's mission-field in Japan; for the seedlings of Catholic Christianity which had been planted in Japan by Jesuit missionaries before the close of the sixteenth century were uprooted before the middle of the seventeenth century by the deliberate action of the rulers of a newly founded Japanese universal state, because these Japanese statesmen had come to the conclusion—after a cool-headed study of the evidence at their command—that the Catholic Church was an insidiously pliant ecclesiastical instrument of the formidable political ambitions of the Spanish Crown.[2] This forfeiture of a large and promising mission-field *in partibus infidelium* must be estimated, however, as a trifling loss by comparison with the spiritual impoverishment which the policy of *Cujus Regio Ejus Religio* was to inflict upon Western Christianity on the home front. For the readiness of all the competing factions of the Western Christian Church in the Age of the Western Wars of Religion to seek a short cut to victory by condoning, and even demanding, the imposition of their own doctrines upon the adherents of rival faiths by the application of political force was a spectacle which sapped the foundations of all belief in the souls for whose allegiance the warring churches were competing.[3]

A Louis XIV might be successful in forcing upon the Protestant minority of his subjects the tyrannical and inhuman choice between renouncing their religious convictions and being driven out of their ancestral homes to find asylum in distant countries out of

[1] For this enormity see IV. C (iii) (b) 11, vol. iv, pp. 220–1, above.
[2] The Western traders in whose wake the Jesuit missionaries had arrived in Japan had been, not Spanish, but Portuguese; but the Portuguese Crown had subsequently come to be associated with the Spanish in a personal union in which Spain was the predominant partner.
[3] The sceptical and cynical spirit of the consequent Enlightenment is touched upon in IV. C (iii) (b) 3, vol. iv, pp. 142–3 and 150; in IV. C (iii) (b) 4, vol. iv, p. 184; in IV. C (iii) (b) 12, vol. iv, pp. 227–8; and in IV. C (iii) (c) 3 (α), Annex, vol. iv, pp. 643–5, above; and in V. C (ii) (b), vol. vi, pp. 316–18, below.

reach of the persecuting arm of the Most Christian King.[1] But
although the tyrant could thus enforce, within the frontiers of his
own dominions, an outward show of conformity with his own
creed and rite, he could neither dragoon his dissenting subjects'
consciences nor prevent his cynically irreligious and childishly
incongruous method of promoting an ecclesiastical cause from
bringing religion of every kind into discredit in the secret places
of the heart to which no spy could penetrate. Louis XIV's methods
of barbarism eradicated Protestantism out of the spiritual soil of
France only to clear the ground for an alternative crop of scepticism; and the spiritual history of France since the latter part of
the seventeenth century is merely one outstanding example of an
experience that has been common to the whole of our Western
Society. In England, for instance, we can see the same sceptical
temper setting in—here in reaction against a militant religiosity
which had fed the flames of the Civil War—at the moment of the
Restoration of A.D. 1660; and we can watch it setting hard after the
Glorious Revolution of A.D. 1688. In fine, the effect of the unholy
mariage de convenance between Religion and Politics was to make
Religion itself anathema; and by the end of the seventeenth
century the Lucretian verdict on Religion—'tantum religio potuit
suadere malorum'[2]—had come to be endorsed by the enlightened
minds of a paganly modern Western World. In the lurid light of
the Religious Wars Religion now appeared in the guise of a sinister
and anti-social frenzy—a veritable Erinys who was as ruthless in
enlisting the secular potentate's sword as she was unscrupulous
in paying her political hirelings in ecclesiastical coin for military
services rendered. Here was a Fury who might have gone on
torturing poor Western Humanity for ever more, if a rescue party
of sharp-sighted philosophers had not made the opportune discovery that this demon had an Achilles' heel. The weak spot of
Religion was its ridiculousness; and any man or woman whose
eyes had been opened to this aspect of the maleficent power was
thereby rendered immune against ever again being goaded into
homicidal mania by the burlesque Fury's scourge. A horror
relieved by ridicule was the defensive posture which had been
assumed towards Religion by enlightened Western minds before
the seventeenth century was over.[3] It was an attitude of mind

---

[1] For the Huguenots' response to the challenge of penalization see II. D (vi), vol. ii,
p. 250, above.
[2] Lucretius: *De Rerum Natura*, Book I, l. 101.
[3] 'It is come, I know not how, to be taken for granted by many persons that Christianity is not so much a subject of inquiry, but that it is now at length discovered to be
fictitious. And accordingly they treat it as if in the present age this were an agreed
point among all people of discernment, and nothing remained but to set it up as a
principal subject of mirth and ridicule, as it were by way of reprisals for its having so

which sterilized Fanaticism at the cost of extinguishing Faith. And this state of mind has lasted from the seventeenth century into the twentieth.

Indeed, in our time this repudiation of a spiritual principle which is no doubt exposed, in human hearts, to the danger of being poisoned or perverted, but which is none the less the breath of human life, has been carried to such lengths in all parts of a Westernized 'Great Society' that it is beginning at last to be recognized for what it is. It is being recognized, that is to say, as the supreme danger to the spiritual health and even to the material existence of the Western body social—a deadlier danger, by far, than any of our hotly canvassed and loudly advertised political and economic maladies. This spiritual evil is now too flagrant to be ignored; but it is easier to diagnose the disease than to prescribe a remedy; for a lost religious faith is not like a standard article of commerce that can be ordered ready-made from a multiple store, nor again is it like an unquestioningly obedient dog that can be driven off at one moment with a kick and summoned back the next moment with a whistle. The spirit bloweth where it listeth, and we cannot expect it to revisit us on call in response to a tardy and casual summons. It will be hard indeed to refill the spiritual vacuum which has been hollowed in our Western hearts by a progressive decay of religious belief that has been going on by this time for some two and a half centuries; and this problem—which is the most formidable and at the same time the most urgent of all the problems that are remorselessly crowding in upon the present generation—has its origin, as we have seen, in a long continuing yet still unexhausted anti-Caesaro-papistical reaction.[1] We are still reacting against a subordination of Religion to Politics which was the crime of our sixteenth-century and seventeenth-century forebears.[2] The policy of *Cujus Regio Ejus Religio* is revenging itself up to the hilt, unto the thirteenth and fourteenth generation, upon the children of fathers who perpetrated and condoned this enormity.

If we take a synoptic view of the several surviving forms of Western Christianity in their present state, and compare them in

---

long interrupted the pleasures of the world.'—Butler, Bishop Joseph: *The Analogy of Religion, Natural and Revealed, to the Constitution and Course of Nature*, advertisement (dated May, 1736) prefixed to the first edition.

[1] For the term 'Caesaro-papism' see IV. C (iii) (*c*) 2 (β), vol. iv, pp. 347 and 352, above.

[2] This still flowing lava-stream of *karma* can be traced back behind the Laodicean Enlightenment and the fanatical Wars of Religion to a medieval fountain-head; for in other contexts we have observed how the secularism and the parochialism which are two of the severest lesions in the social system of our Western Civilization in the Modern Age are due, both alike, to an excessively violent reaction against an excessively autocratic and centralizing tendency to which the Papacy succumbed in the course of its internecine conflict with the Hohenstaufen (see IV. C (iii) (*b*) 11, vol. iv, pp. 214–22, and IV. C (iii) (*c*) 3 (β), vol. iv, pp. 512–84, above).

respect of their relative vitality, we shall find that this varies inversely with the degree to which each of these sects has succumbed
within the last four centuries to secular control. Unquestionably
Catholicism is the form of Western Christianity that is showing
the most vigorous signs of life to-day; and the Catholic Church—
in spite of the lengths to which modern Catholic princes have gone,
in certain countries and at certain times, towards asserting their
own secular control over the life of the Church within their frontiers—has still never lost the inestimable advantage of being united
in an oecumenical communion under the presidency of a single
supreme ecclesiastical authority, while in the meantime 'the Princes
of the Church' have, unwillingly yet auspiciously, been relieved,
by the nineteenth-century encroachments of the secular Powers,
of the fearful incubus of the ecclesiastical principalities.[1] Next to
the Catholic Church in order of present vitality we shall probably
find ourselves placing those 'free churches' of the Protestant persuasion which have extricated themselves from the control of the
secular Governments in whose pockets these marsupial churches
started life.[2] And we shall certainly place at the bottom of the list
the Protestant 'established churches' which still remain tied to the
body politic of this or that modern Western parochial state.[3]

The moral of this odious comparison seems plain. The diversity
in the fortunes of the several fractions of the Western Christian
Church in the Modern Age of our Western history is a piece of
evidence which would appear to complete our empirical proof of
the proposition that a religion stands to lose far more than it can
hope to gain by asking for, or submitting to, the patronage of the
civil power. There is, however, one conspicuous exception to this
apparent rule which will have to be accounted for before the rule
can be allowed to pass muster; and this exception is the case of
Islam; for Islam did succeed in becoming the universal church of
a dissolving Syriac Society[4] in spite of having been politically
compromised at an earlier stage and in an apparently more decisive
way than any of the religions that we have passed under review
in this survey up to this point.

We have seen that Zoroastrianism was compromised by the
action of a dynasty of secular princes in an age when the Zoroas-

---

[1] For the extinction of the temporal power of the Pope and of the Transalpine
Catholic prince-bishops see IV. C (iii) (*b*) 11, vol. iv, pp. 220–1, above. In depriving
these prelates of their political authority the secular Powers of the modern Western World
have perhaps done the same unintentional and unwelcome service to Catholicism as the
British Rāj in India has done to the religion of the Sikhs in extinguishing the temporal
power of the Khālsā (see the present Annex, pp. 667–8, above).

[2] For the free Protestant churches see IV. C (iii) (*b*) 11, vol. iv, p. 222, footnote 2,
above.   [3] See IV. C (iii) (*b*) 11, vol. iv, pp. 221–2, above.

[4] For this achievement of Islam see II. D (vi), vol. ii, p. 235; II. D (vii), vol. ii, pp.
287–8; V. C (i) (*c*) 2, in the present volume, pp. 127–8; and V. C (i) (*c*) 4, pp. 370–1, above.

trian Church had already been in existence for at least three-quarters of a millennium and perhaps for a full thousand years.[1] Judaism was compromised by the action of a family of priests who took up arms against a persecutor at a time when they were not themselves the responsible heads of the Jewish hierarchy. The Sikh community and the Imāmī sect of the Islamic Shī'ah were both of them compromised in a more serious way, because they were both of them launched on a new career of militancy by pontiffs who—unlike the Maccabees—were the responsible heads of their respective churches at the time when they severally committed this flagrant breach of their spiritual trust. The case of the orthodox and original Islam, however, looks at first sight as though it were still more extreme than that of its heretical Imāmī offshoot; for the orthodox Islam was politically compromised within the lifetime of its founder by the action of no less responsible a person than the founder himself.

In another context[2] we have noticed that the public career of the Prophet Muhammad falls into two sharply distinct and seemingly almost contradictory chapters. In the first chapter Muhammad was entirely occupied in the preaching of a religious revelation by methods of evangelization that were purely pacific; in the second chapter he was mainly occupied in building up a political and military power and in using this power in the very way which has turned out, in other cases, to be disastrous for a religion that takes to it.[3] In this Medinese chapter Muhammad used his new-found material power for the purpose of enforcing conformity with at any rate the outward observances of the religion which he had founded in the foregoing chapter of his career, before his momentous withdrawal from Mecca to Medina; and, on this showing, the *Hijrah* ought to mark the date which saw the ruin of Islam, and not the date which saw the making of its fortunes, if we are right in the thesis which we have established inductively as a result of our empirical survey up to this point. How are we to explain the hard fact that a religion which was launched upon the World as the militant faith of a barbarian war-band on the war-path should have succeeded in becoming a universal church in spite of having started under a spiritual handicap that might have been expected, on all analogies, to prove prohibitive?

When we set ourselves this problem in these terms, we shall find

[1] For the wideness of the discrepancy between the dates that have been assigned to the Prophet Zarathustra by different schools of modern Western scholarship see V. C (i) (*c*) 2, p. 121, above.
[2] In III. C (ii) (*b*), vol. iii, pp. 276–8, and III. C (ii) (*b*), Annex II, vol. iii, pp. 466–72, above.
[3] For the political career of Muhammad see III. C (ii) (*b*), vol. iii, pp. 277–8, with III. C (ii) (*b*), Annex II, above.

several partial explanations which, between them, may perhaps amount to a solution.

In the first place we shall be able to discount a tendency which is rife—at least among Christian critics—to over-estimate the extent of the use of force in the propagation of Islam even after the *Hijrah*. For example, in the hour of Muhammad's long-delayed triumph over the men of his own house—those implacable Meccan enemies of his who had rejected his message and had driven him into exile—the now at last victorious prophet-under-arms who had so long been without honour in his own country distinguished himself by the moderation of the terms on which he accepted the capitulation of his obdurate kinsmen the Quraysh; and this example of self-restraint was emulated by the Prophet's successors in the temporal leadership of the Islamic Commonwealth. The show of adherence to the new religion which they exacted by force was limited to the performance of a small number of not very onerous external observances; and the forcible imposition of even this perfunctory conformity upon conquered unbelievers was not attempted beyond the limits of the Arabian no-man's-land in which the new state was filling a political vacuum and in which the new religion was supplanting, for the most part, nothing higher than a primitive paganism.[1] In the former dependencies and dominions of the Roman and Sasanian Governments which now fell into the hands of the Primitive Muslim Arab conquerors, no compulsion to embrace Islam was applied to any of 'the People of the Book'.[2] The choice which was actually offered to the conquered populations outside Arabia itself was not 'Islam or death'; it was 'Islam or a super-tax'.[3] Even the Arab tribes on the Syrian

---

[1] The Jewish and Christian communities in the Yaman and the Jewish communities in the Hijāz were no more than islets in a sea of Arabian paganism. The extermination of the Hijāzī Jews and the forcible conversion of the Yamanī 'People of the Book' are among the worst of the political crimes that have to be laid to the account of the Prophet Muhammad and his immediate successors. These were, however, exceptions and not the rule of primitive Islamic policy.

[2] See IV. C (iii) (b) 12, vol. iv, pp. 225–6, above, and V. C (ii) (a). vol. vi, pp. 204–5, below. Officially 'the People of the Book', who, according to the *Sharī'ah*, were entitled to religious toleration if once they tendered their political submission to the Islamic state, included the Jews and the Christians but not the Zoroastrians. In practice, however, the Zoroastrians were accorded, as a matter of grace, the toleration which the two Biblical sects received as a matter of right. In the Qur'ān the Zoroastrians are only mentioned in the following passage:

'Surely those who believe [i.e. the Muslims] and those who are Jews and the Sabians and the Christians and the Magians and those who associate [others with Allah, i.e. the polytheists]—surely Allah will decide between them on the day of resurrection.' —Surah xxii. 17.

This solitary reference to the Zoroastrians in the Qur'ān leaves their status in doubt. To which of the two sub-groups of non-Muslims is the Prophet consigning them? Is he intending the reader to bracket the Magians with the three sets of 'People of the Book' whose names immediately precede that of the Magians in this catalogue? Or with the polytheists, who are mentioned immediately after? In the event the Prophet's successors humanely and wisely gave the Zoroastrians the benefit of the doubt.

[3] See IV. C (iii) (b) 12, vol. iv, p. 226, footnote 2, and IV. C (iii) (c) 2 (β), Annex III, vol. iv, p. 630, above.

and Mesopotamian and 'Irāqī fringes of the North Arabian Steppe who, before the conquest, had served the Roman and Sasanian Powers as their wardens of the Arabian marches,[1] were allowed by their victorious Muslim Arab kinsmen to remain faithful to Christianity if they chose;[2] and indeed in the first instance all but an inconsiderable minority of the newly elevated imperial people's vast concourse of newly conquered subjects took an honourable advantage of the tolerant choice that was offered them, and opted for paying super-tax in preference to turning renegade. Nor was this option made invidious for the non-Muslim subjects of the Arab Caliphate under the Umayyad régime which came to stay for a century after the brief antecedent dispensation of the four pre-Umayyad Commanders of the Faithful;[3] for the Umayyad Caliphs were Laodiceans to a man,[4] with the exception of 'Umar II (*imperabat* A.D. 717–20).[5]

It was this century of Umayyad tolerance that gave Islam its opportunity to make its fortune by providing a universal church for the Syriac World instead of remaining merely the sectarian religion of a band of barbarian conquerors.[6] It may be true that

---

[1] See I. C (i) (*b*), vol. i, p. 73, footnote 1, and Part III. A, Annex II, vol. iii, p. 398, above.

[2] See, for example, the evidence for the remarkably considerate treatment of the Christian Arab tribe of the Banu Taghlib, which is presented in Arnold, T. W.: *The Preaching of Islam*, 2nd ed. (London 1913, Constable), pp. 49–50. The Banu Taghlib's grazing grounds were in 'Irāq 'Arabī, in the environs of Ctesiphon.

[3] The reigns of the first four Caliphs, taken together, lasted officially from A.D. 632 to A.D. 661, while the Caliphs of the Umayyad Dynasty reigned officially from A.D. 661 to A.D. 750 from first to last. *De facto*, however, the founder of the Umayyad Dynasty, Mu'āwiyah, had been master of Syria for some twenty years before his accession to the Caliphate was officially recognized after the death of the Caliph 'Alī (Wellhausen, J.: *Das Arabische Reich und sein Sturz* (Berlin 1902, Reimer), p. 35). A striking piece of Christian testimony to the popularity of the Umayyad Caliph Yazīd I (*imperabat* A.D. 680–3) has been cited in V. C (i) (*c*) 3, p. 226, above.

[4] The prevailing attitude of the Umayyads towards Islam has been touched upon already in V. C (i) (*c*) 2, p. 128, footnote 5, above. For the scepticism, towards all religions, of the Caliph Mu'āwiyah, who not only founded the Umayyad Dynasty but also set the tone for his successors, see Wellhausen, op. cit., p. 84. The lukewarmness of this dynasty of caliphs towards the established religion of the commonwealth of which they were the secular heads is not at all surprising when it is remembered that the Umayyads were one of the leading families of that Meccan aristocracy which had obstinately opposed the Prophet Muhammad in defence of its vested interest in the local pagan divinities whose worship had made Mecca a goal of pilgrimage before Muhammad had called upon his countrymen to throw this lucrative local paganism away. After the Prophet's final triumph the Umayyads, like the rest of the Quraysh, were quick to see that their cranky fellow tribesman who had eventually succeeded in forcing his own new-fangled religion down their throats had incidentally brought within their reach opportunities of aggrandizement of which they could never have dreamed in 'the Days of Ignorance'. But the skill which was shown by Mu'āwiyah and his descendants in turning the unpalatable results of Muhammad's work to their own advantage, by entering into the fruits of their victorious adversary's material labours, did not imply any enthusiasm on their part for the religion of the prophet on whom they had contrived to take this ironical revenge. (On this point see further pp. 676–7, below.)

[5] See Wellhausen, op. cit., p. 167.

[6] It was in this latter capacity—as the distinctive faith of the trans-frontier barbarians in the Arabian section of the no-man's-la   ' beyond the Syrian *limes* of the Roman Empire—that Islam made its first epiphany (see III. C (ii) (*b*), vol. iii, pp. 276–7; Part III. A, Annex II, vol. iii, pp. 450–1; V. C (i) (*c*) 2, in the present volume, p. 128; and V. C (i) (*c*) 3, in the present volume, p. 230, above).

this service was bound to be performed for that world in that age
by some religion or other; for at that time the Syriac Society was
craving to recover a unity which it had lost as a result of having
been overrun by Hellenism a thousand years back; and, now that
a unitary Syriac universal state had at last been re-established in
the shape of the Arab Caliphate,[1] it was only to be expected that
this reunion on the superficial plane of politics should be extended
to a deeper plane of life through the establishment of a Syriac
universal church within the political framework which the Caliphate had provided. This universal church must be the institutional embodiment of some 'higher religion'; but which of the
religions in the field would now bring this body ecclesiastic to life?
It by no means followed that Islam would succeed in an enterprise
which a number of older religions—Judaism, Zoroastrianism,
Nestorianism, Monophysitism—had already essayed without success.[2] Indeed, a garbled barbarian version of the indigenous Syriac
faiths—and this was what Islam was by origin[3]—might actually
have been expected, *a priori*, to prove less attractive to Syriac souls
than the finer alternatives which they had already discarded. In
these intrinsically adverse circumstances Islam, so far from achieving its historic success, would assuredly have suffered the same
fate as Arianism if the Muslim Umayyads had pursued the intolerant ecclesiastical policy of the Arian Vandals,[4] and had tried to
impose Islam upon their Monophysite and Nestorian and Zoroastrian subjects as the Vandals did try to impose Arianism upon the
Catholic and Donatist communities in the Roman provinces which
Genseric had conquered in North-West Africa. These considerations seem to point to the perhaps unexpected conclusion that the
prospects of an Islam which was not a particularly attractive
religion in itself, and which had been gravely compromised by
its own founder when he withdrew from his spiritual apostolate
at Mecca and plunged into a political career at Medina, were
retrieved by the crypto-pagan Umayyad usurpers of the Meccan
Prophet's political heritage—and this for the paradoxical reason
that the Umayyads were indifferent, or even positively hostile, to
the propagation of the Islamic faith. For the most part, these
worldlings were content to leave the religion of which they were
officially the temporal trustees and champions to shift for itself
while they cynically enjoyed the sweets of the lucrative office which
they were holding on false pretences. And in so far as the progres-

---

[1] For this aspect of the Arab Caliphate see I. C (i) (b), vol. i, pp. 72–7, above.
[2] See II. D (vii), vol. ii, pp. 285–7, and V. C (i) (c) 2, in the present volume, pp. 125–
8, above.
[3] See III. C (ii) (b), vol. iii, p. 277, above.
[4] See V. C (i) (c) 4, p. 358, above, and the present chapter, p. 679, below.

sive conversion of their non-Arab subjects to Islam did attract the
Umayyad Caliphs' attention from time to time, we may suppose
that it exercised—and annoyed—them first and foremost as a
financial problem, since, for the Caliphial treasury, every conversion of a non-Muslim subject of the Caliphial Government to
Islam brought with it a corresponding diminution of super-tax
receipts.

Under these extraordinary conditions Islam had to make its own
way among the non-Arab subjects of the Caliphate very largely on
its own merits—as Zoroastrianism had once had to make its way
among the non-Iranian subjects of the Achaemenidae[1]—and without that fatal assistance from the secular arm which had afterwards
been accepted by Zoroastrianism under the Sasanian régime. In
these circumstances the spread of Islam outside the ranks of the
Arab garrisons of the restored Syriac universal state was slow but
at the same time sure; and, in the hearts of ex-Christians and ex-
Zoroastrians who embraced the new religion in the face of the
indifference, if not actually in the teeth of the displeasure, of their
nominally Muslim Umayyad masters, Islam became a very different faith from what it had formerly been on the sleeves of Arab
warriors who had worn it there as a denominational badge of a
privileged political status. The new non-Arab converts not only
took their adopted religion to heart: they also adapted it to their
own intellectual outlook by doing for Islam what a Clement and
an Origen had done for Christianity at a corresponding stage of
its history.[2] They translated the crude and casual assertions of the
Prophet of the Arabian external proletariat into the more subtle
and more consistent terms of Christian theology and Hellenic
philosophy; and it was in this clothing—in which it was clad by
the spontaneous intellectual labours of non-Arab converts, and not
by the political fiat of Gallionic-minded Arab empire-builders—
that Islam was able to become the unifying religion of a Syriac
World which had been reunited only on the superficial plane of
politics by the sweep of the Arab military conquest.

Within a hundred years of Mu'āwiyah's rise to political power
the non-Arab Muslim subjects of the Caliphate had become strong
enough, even in the military sense, to put down the Laodicean
Umayyads from their seat and to enthrone in their place a dynasty
whose devoutness reflected the religious temper of their supporters. In A.D. 750, when the favour of the non-Arab Muslim
element among the subjects of the Caliphate gave the 'Abbasids
the victory over the Umayyads, it is possible that the numerical

---

[1] For the religious policy of the Achaemenidae see pp. 704–5, below.
[2] See V. C (i) (c) 4, p. 367, and V. C (i) (d) 6 (δ), p. 539, above.

strength of the religious faction which thus turned the scales in the balance of dynastic power was still as small in proportion to the total population of the Arab Empire as were the numbers of the Christians in the Roman Empire at the moment when Constantine overthrew Maxentius.[1] The mass-conversions of the subjects of the Caliphate to Islam probably did not begin before the first collapse of the 'Abbasid Power in the ninth century of the Christian Era, or reach their term until the final dissolution of the 'Abbasid Empire in the thirteenth century, and it can be said of these belated harvests in the Islamic mission-field—with greater assurance than could perhaps be felt in passing the same verdict on the mass-conversions to Christianity during the death-agonies of the Roman Empire in the fourth, fifth, and sixth centuries of the Christian Era—that they were the outcome of a spontaneous movement on the part of the masses themselves and not of political pressure on the part of their rulers. It is true that the 'Abbasids surpassed the Umayyads in their devotion to Islam in the measure in which Constantine surpassed Philippus Arabs in his devotion to Christianity; but it is at the same time true that the earlier 'Abbasids abstained, as conscientiously as Constantine himself, from misusing their political power for the purpose of forcing, upon an unbelieving majority of their subjects, a religion to which they themselves happened personally to be attached; and it is also a fact that the later 'Abbasids for the most part remained faithful to this policy of toleration, in honourable contrast to Constantine's successors. The Islamic counterparts of a Theodosius and a Justinian, who departed from the Constantinian policy and did misuse their political power in order to quench the smoking flax of unbelief, are few and far between[2] in a list of 'Abbasid Caliphs which stretches through five centuries.[3]

If the facts that have now been set forth may be considered to account satisfactorily for the exception which Islam might appear

---

[1] The numerical strength of the Christian element in the population of the Roman Empire in A.D. 312 is estimated at about 10 per cent. by Baynes, N. H.: *Constantine the Great and the Christian Church* (London 1929, Milford), p. 4.

[2] The most flagrant of the exceptions that prove the general rule of 'Abbasid tolerance is the Caliph Mutawakkil (*imperabat* A.D. 847–61) (see V. C (ii) (a), vol. vi, p. 205, footnote 7, below).

[3] This greater constancy which was displayed by the Muslim 'Abbasid Caliphs, in contrast to the Christian Roman Emperors, in abiding by the policy of toleration, is not a matter for surprise; for, whereas the Emperor Constantine's policy of toleration had no sanction behind it except the Emperor's own personal will, the toleration that was practised by the 'Abbasids was founded, not upon a personal or dynastic caprice, but upon one of the standing orders of the religion which the rulers themselves professed. We have noted already (on pp. 674–5, above) that the *Sharī'ah* made it obligatory for the Government of the Islamic Commonwealth to guarantee an effective religious toleration to all politically loyal non-Muslim subjects of the Islamic State who were 'People of the Book'. For the victory of this injunction of the *Sharī'ah* over the blood-thirstiness of the Ottoman Pādishāh Selim the Grim see p. 706, footnote 1, and V. C (ii) (a), vol. vi, p. 204, below.

at first sight to present to our empirically established general rule, then perhaps we can abide by our conclusion that, while it is not impossible for the secular power to obtain some measure of success in forcibly imposing upon its own subjects a religion which is already 'a going concern', the price which the politically compromised religion has to pay, as a rule, for a local enforcement by means of political pressure is the prohibitive price of forfeiting any prospects which that religion may previously have had of attaining —or retaining—universality.

The same prohibitive penalty for the moral offence of attempting to impose a religion by political force may also be incurred when the attempt is unsuccessful even within parochial limits. Indeed, such cases would appear to be at least as numerous as the cases, which we have so far been examining, in which there has been at least some measure of parochial success to be placed on the credit side of the account. Among the more notorious cases in which a religion that has accepted the compromising support of the secular arm has suffered an unmitigated loss—with no grain of even local advantage to set off against it—through the inability of the secular power to impose religious conformity by force even within its own frontiers, we may reckon the failure of the Roman Emperor Justinian to impose his own Catholic Orthodoxy upon his Monophysite subjects beyond the Taurus;[1] the failure of the East Roman Emperors Leo III and Constantine V to impose their own Iconoclasm upon their Iconodule subjects in Greece and Italy;[2] the failure of the Vandal masters of a barbarian 'successor-state' of the Roman Empire in North-West Africa to impose their own Arianism upon the Catholic and Donatist provincials;[3] the failure of the British Crown to impose its own Protestantism upon its Catholic subjects in Ireland;[4] the failure of the Timurid Mughal Emperor Awrangzīb to impose his own Islam upon his Hindu subjects;[5] and finally the failure of the Iranic militarist Nādir Shāh[6] to bring back into the fold of the Sunnah the descendants of a people whose allegiance had been forcibly detached from the

---

[1] See V. C (ii) (*a*), vol. vi, p. 223, below.
[2] See IV. C (iii) (*c*) 2 (β), vol. iv, p. 352, footnote 5, above.
[3] See V. C (i) (*c*) 4, p. 358, and the present chapter, p. 676, above.
[4] See II. D (vii), Annex II, vol. ii, above.
[5] In embarking upon this fatal policy Awrangzīb was not only transgressing the injunctions of the *Sharī'ah* in regard to 'the People of the Book' (a charter of toleration by which the Hindus had at least as good a claim as the Zoroastrians to benefit by analogy): he was also sinning against the light that had been seen by his ancestor Akbar, the enlightened founder of the universal state which Awrangzīb's fanaticism brought to ruin. (For Akbar's religious experience and policy see the present Annex, pp. 699–704, below.)
[6] See I. C (i) (*b*), Annex I, vol. i, p. 399, and V. C (i) (*c*) 1, in the present volume, pp. 44–5, above, as well as Browne, E. G.: *A Literary History of Persia*, vol. iv (Cambridge 1928, University Press), pp. 135–8, and Lockhart, L.: *Nadir Shah* (London 1938, Luzac).

Sunnah and transferred to the Shī'ah, little more than two hundred years before Nādir Shāh's day, by the act of an earlier Iranic militarist, Ismā'īl Shāh Safawī.

These examples show that a signal failure frequently attends the efforts of political potentates to impose upon their subjects a religion of the rulers' choosing, even when this religion is already 'a going concern'; and *a fortiori* it would be difficult to point out a single instance of success in cases in which the system of practices and beliefs which the secular ruler has been attempting to inculcate from above downwards has been not a religion but a philosophy. On the other hand there are two celebrated instances of the failure of an imperial philosopher-missionary. The Roman Emperor Julian failed to establish Neoplatonism as the official philosophy of the Hellenic universal state,[1] and the Maurya Emperor Açoka likewise failed to establish the Hinayanian form of Buddhism as the official philosophy of the universal state into which the Indic World had been gathered up by Açoka's grandfather Chandragupta. This pair of failures is remarkable, considering the strength of the combination of conditions favourable to success under which Açoka and Julian alike embarked upon their respective spiritual missions.

In the first place the philosophies which the two emperors set out to propagate among their respective subjects were not arbitrary systems of the imperial propagandists' own invention, but were 'going concerns' which had been founded and developed by a succession of sages who had not had any political authority at their command but had won a following for their tenets on their intrinsic intellectual and moral merits, long before the birth and accession to power of their latter-day imperial patrons. This is true even of the Neoplatonism that was patronized by the Emperor Julian; for, as we have already observed,[2] the vein of artificiality and crankiness which is so prominent and so feeble a feature in this pagan counterblast to the Christian Church was not introduced into Neoplatonism by the Emperor Julian's personal caprice, but was inherited by the Neoplatonist emperor from the Neoplatonist hierophant Iamblichus.[3]

---

[1] Julian's failure is also touched upon in V. C (i) (c) 2, p. 147; V. C (i) (d) 6 (δ), pp. 565–7; V. C (i) (c) 2, Annex II, p. 584, above; and in V. C (ii) (a), vol. vi, pp. 222–3, below.

[2] See the quotation from Geffken in V. C (i) (d) 6 (δ), p. 565, above.

[3] For an account of the Iamblichan Neoplatonic Antichurch see Bidez, J.: *La Vie de l'Empereur Julien* (Paris 1930, Les Belles Lettres), Iᵉ Partie, chap. xi, 'Chez les Disciples de Jamblique', and chap. xii, 'Théurgie Chaldaïque et Mystères Néoplatoniciennes'; for the Emperor Julian's administrative organization of this Antichurch which he had inherited from the philosopher-hierophant Iamblichus see op. cit., IIIᵉ Partie, chap. ix, 'Théocratie'.

Among the host of non-Christian worships over which the philosopher's mantle of Plotinus and Plato was enthusiastically flung by Iamblichus and his successors—Julian

As for the state of the Hīnayāna in Açoka's day, there is no
trace in it, at that stage, of those elements of decadence which may
partly account for the fiasco of Iamblichus's and Julian's Neoplatonism. The Hīnayāna that was embraced by Açoka was a philosophy that was still in its intellectual and moral prime, like the
Stoicism that was embraced by Marcus Aurelius.[1] In Açoka's
case, at any rate, we cannot trace the failure of his mission to any
inherent weakness in the philosophy of his choice.

Nor, again, can the failure of either Açoka or Julian be traced
to any serious abuse of the enormous power and influence that
were concentrated in the hands of both these emperors in virtue
of their secular office. It is true that, in this matter again, Julian,
with his impulsive and even passionate temperament, has laid
himself open to criticisms against which the mortified monk
Açoka is impregnably proof. Yet even Julian had in him enough
of the true philosopher to restrain him from going very far in
translating into action an animosity against Christianity which he
did not attempt to pluck out of his heart. Julian's first act on
succeeding to the supreme authority in the Roman Empire was to
institute—as far as this could be done by Imperial decree—a

among the rest—the place of honour seems to have been assigned to the rites prescribed
in a work called *The Chaldaean Oracles* from the pen of a Babylonian medicine-man,
practising *in partibus Hellenicis*, who was the namesake of Julian and the contemporary
of Marcus Aurelius.

'Dans la théologie assez touffue de ces oracles, se détachait une figure qui, à elle seule,
était presqu'un panthéon: Hécate-Rhéa, déesse trimorphe, dont les cheveux se dres-
saient comme des flammes, dont les serpents enlacés entouraient les tempes et la cein-
ture, et qui, dans ses flancs, portait du côté droit l'âme du monde, du côté gauche la
fontaine de vertu, et la Nature sous son échine.'

In this professedly Chaldaean divinity we seem to see the Minoan Goddess of the
Snakes and the Helleno-Hittite Artemis of Ephesus with their features and attributes
all exaggerated as they might have been in an Indic caricature; and, indeed, if the
Emperor Julian had succeeded in making the medicine-man Julian's syncretistic
religion prevail over Christianity, we may conjecture that the outcome would have been
something quite as alien from the original philosophy of Plato as the Tantric or
Lamaistic form of Mahayanian Buddhism is from the original philosophy of Siddhārtha Gautama.

Julian's policy was to retort to the Christian Church's tactics of stealing the intellectual
thunder of the Hellenic philosophers by arming his own Neoplatonic Antichurch with
the Christian Church's hierarchical organization and philanthropic activities (see V. C
(i) (*c*) 2, Annex II, p. 584, above). His stumbling-block was the unresponsiveness of
the surviving ministers of the non-Christian religions within the frontiers of the Roman
Empire in Julian's day. The majority of those for whose support he appealed seem to
have failed the Emperor—whether out of laziness or out of timidity or out of a sophisticated self-consciousness which shrank from the prospect of having to make a fool of
itself at Don Quixote's dictation. Whatever the cause of this non-co-operation may have
been, the result was that the Roman Emperor proved unable to emulate the work of the
Pharaoh Thothmes III in 'the New Empire' of Egypt and the work of the Inca Pachacutec in the Andean universal state (for the success of these two non-Hellenic emperors
in consolidating the local worships of their respective worlds into a single hierarchical
organization see V. C (i) (*d*) 6 (δ), pp. 530–31 and 532, and the present Annex, pp. 652–
4, above). If Julian had been able to enlist for his Antichurch the services of a
hereditary corporation or caste of priests like the Magi or the Brahmans (see V. C (i) (*d*)
6 (δ), p. 542, above), then he might have been able to contend with the Christian Church
on less unequal terms than those on which he actually had to fight his losing battle.

[1] For Marcus's notable abstention from any attempt to take advantage of his office in
order to propagate his philosophy see the present Annex, p. 705, below.

régime of complete toleration for all the religions that were current among his subjects, without any official differentiation in favour of Paganism or to the detriment of Christianity.[1] When the pagan mob at Alexandria took the law into its own hands by lynching the late Emperor Constantius's Arian bishop George of Cappadocia— and two Christian civil servants along with him—in reprisal for their victim's vexatious treatment of the local pagan worships during the preceding reign, Julian did at least address a letter of remonstrance to the Alexandrians in which he condemned their crime in strong terms in despite of his own unconcealed sympathy for the cause in the name of which this crime had been perpetrated.[2] Finally, when Julian failed to live up to the ideal of toleration which he himself had proclaimed, the discriminatory measures against the Christians to which he then stooped were at any rate strictly negative. The emperor withheld from all professing Christians, *ex officio religionis*, the official licence without which they could not enter, or even remain in, the teaching profession;[3] and there is some ground for believing that he also went to the further length of excluding the Christians from all branches of the public service: military, administrative, and judicial.[4] Yet all this, taken together, falls far short of that first degree of persecution which is known as 'a dry terror' in the new technical terminology with which our modern Western political vocabulary has been enriched by the march of progress in the fourth decade of the twentieth century of the Christian Era. As for Açoka, he was not only innocent of even the slightest and most indirect recourse to the employment of political pressure for the propagation of the philosophy in which he had put his treasure: he was actually moved to embrace the Hīnayāna by a profound remorse for his own conduct in having once, though once only, resorted to that use of force which is the *ultima ratio regum*. The moral passion which inspired the Emperor Açoka's preaching of the philosophy of Siddhārtha Gautama was the obverse side of his horror at the misery which he himself had caused on that one occasion by waging a victorious war of aggression against the kingdom of Kalinga. After this appalling experience Açoka renounced the use of War as an instrument of his Imperial policy; placed his court on a vegetarian diet; abolished the Imperial Hunt; and made the slaughtering of animals illegal for all his subjects on fifty-six days per annum.[5] So far was Açoka

[1] See Bidez, J.: *La Vie de l'Empereur Julien* (Paris 1930, Les Belles Lettres), pp. 227–9.
[2] Bidez, op. cit., pp. 233–5. The text of the letter will be found in Julian's *Œuvres Complètes*, tome i, 2ᵉ partie: 'Lettres et Fragments', edited and translated by Bidez, J. (Paris 1924, Les Belles Lettres), pp. 69–72.
[3] Bidez, *La Vie de l'Empereur Julien*, pp. 263–6.
[4] Ibid., pp. 295–6.
[5] This last measure was no doubt a rather authoritarian act of interference with the

from inflicting any disabilities upon the majority of his subjects who did not embrace the Emperor's own philosophical tenets that he deprecated an indulgence even in verbal polemics at the expense of any of the diverse religions that were professed in his dominions; and he set a personal example of magnanimity by bestowing benefactions upon at least one non-Buddhist sect of ascetics.[1] Assuredly it would have been impossible for any one in Açoka's position to be more scrupulous than Açoka was in refraining from taking any improper advantage of the formidable secular power which he happened to hold in his hands.

The foregoing evidence suggests that Açoka, at any rate, deserved to succeed in his mission, and that even Julian hardly deserved to fail. Yet Açoka, as well as Julian, did fail conspicuously. The inference would appear to be that the enterprise of attempting to inculcate a philosophy from above downwards into the souls of Mankind in the mass is, for some *a priori* reason, so forlorn a hope that it is doomed to failure even when it is undertaken by an emperor-monk of Açoka's heroic spiritual stature.

With the warning of Açoka's astonishing failure imprinted on our minds, we may feel certain in advance that a political potentate will be found impotent to propagate from above downwards a system of practices and beliefs when this system is not some philosophy that is already 'a going concern', but is a 'fancy religion' that has been imported from abroad, or been manufactured in his own throne-room, by the monarch himself. On this point we shall find our expectations confirmed by a survey of the classical instances.

The most extreme case of the kind that is on record is perhaps that of the Isma'īlī Shī'ī dissident Caliph al-Ḥākim bi'amri'llāh the Fāṭimid (*imperabat* A.D. 996–1020); for, while we are able, from such knowledge as the uninitiated can obtain of the jealously guarded mysteries of Ḥākim's eclectic religion, to trace this and that borrowed element to its source—a source which may prove to be either Jewish or Christian or Zoroastrian or Manichaean or Gnostic or Mandaean or Pythagorean or Neoplatonic or Hindu[2]— 'the basis and distinctive dogma of Druze theology' is to be found, not in any of these crumbs from the tables of richer faiths, but in the deification of Ḥākim himself as the last and most perfect of ten

---

liberty of the subject, but it can hardly be brought within the category of religious persecution.

[1] These facts of Açoka's spiritual experience and political practice are recorded—for the most part on the first-hand evidence of Açoka's own inscriptions—in Smith, V. A.: *The Early History of India*, 3rd ed. (Oxford 1914, Clarendon Press), pp. 156–8 and 176–9.

[2] For an analysis of the sources of the syncretistic element in the religion of Ḥākim see Hitti, P. K.: *The Origins of the Druze People and Religion* (New York 1928, Columbia University Press), especially pp. 4 and 30–54. Hitti's work came into the present writer's hands too late to be mentioned in II. D (vi), vol. ii, p. 258, footnote 1, above.

successive incarnations of God: a divine and immortal Messiah who was to return in triumph to a world from which he had mysteriously withdrawn after a first brief epiphany.[1]

It is true that this cardinal tenet of the Druse religion was not quite so unfamiliar or so shocking to the minds of Ḥākim's contemporaries in Ḥākim's world as might be supposed; for the conception of a god incarnate had been brought within the mental horizon of Islam by the intellectual commerce of Muslim theologians and philosophers with the Christian and Hellenic and Hindu systems of thought; and the Shi'ah, more particularly in the Ismā'īlī branch in which Ḥākim himself had been brought up, had already made the transition from theory to practice by virtually deifying 'Alī and the series of Imāms who were 'Alī's successors.[2] At the same time the worshippers of Ḥākim were careful to propitiate orthodox Muslim opinion by proclaiming themselves to be rigid unitarians;[3] and we have seen already that they had done their best to make their new religion attractive to the surviving adherents or admirers of the older religions and philosophies which Islam had overlaid by decking their central dogma out in a variegated plumage which reflected some of the colours of almost every religion or philosophy under the sun. In fact, the inventors of the Druse religion showed a consummate skill in displaying their bizarre spiritual merchandise to the best possible advantage. And yet, as it turned out, this ingenuity was of little avail. The solitary success of the missionaries of the new faith was the conversion by the apostle Darazī, in A.D. 1016, of one tiny community in the Syrian district of Wādi'l-Taym, at the southern end of the Biqā' and at the foot of Mount Hermon.[4] Not more than fifteen years after this—in A.D. 1031—'the door of the Unitarian Religion was closed' in the sense that the mission of converting the World was deliberately abandoned. Since then the Druse community has neither admitted converts nor tolerated apostates,[5] but has remained a closed hereditary religious corporation whose members bear the name, not of the god incarnate whom they worship, but

[1] Hitti, op. cit., pp. 26, 30, and 31. The concept of the Second Coming has been touched upon in this Study already in III. C (ii) (*b*), Annex I, vol. iii, pp. 462–5, above.

[2] For the precedents to, and parallels with, the deification of Ḥākim see Hitti, op. cit., pp. 27–9. For the worship of 'Alī which has been adopted by the Druses' Syrian neighbours the Nusayrīs, as an accretion to the older elements in the curious religion of this fossilized community, see II. D (ii), vol. ii, p. 56, above. This 'Alī-worship that has thus found its way into the Nusayrī creed and ritual appears to be a travesty of the veneration paid to 'Alī by the Ismā'īlī Shī'īs who forced their way into the Jabal Ansarīyah in the Age of the Crusades (see II. D (vi), vol. ii, p. 258, above).

[3] Hitti, op. cit., p. 33. They actually assumed the name Muwaḥḥidīn, thereby forestalling the puritanical Sunni Berber highlanders from the Atlas who adopted the same name in the twelfth century of the Christian Era with greater justification (see I. C (i) (*b*), Annex I, vol. i, p. 357; II. D (v), vol. ii, p. 204; and V. C (i) (*c*) 3, in the present volume, p. 247, above).

[4] Hitti, op. cit., pp. 18–21.   [5] Ibid., pp. 11–12.

of the missionary who first introduced them to Ḥākim's strange new gospel.[1] Ensconced in the highlands of Hermon and the Lebanon and the *massif* east of the Hawrān which has latterly come to be known as the Jabal-ad-Durūz *par excellence*, the Druse church universal *manquée* has become a perfect example of a 'fossil in a fastness';[2] and, by the same token, Ḥākim's 'fancy religion' has proved a fiasco.[3]

The same fate has overtaken the almost equally presumptuous attempt of the Syrian pervert Varius Avitus Bassianus to install as the high god of the official pantheon of the Roman Empire, not indeed his own person, but his own parochial divinity the Emesan Sun-God Elagabalus, whose hereditary high priest he was, and whose name he continued to bear by choice after a stroke of fortune had placed him on the Roman Imperial Throne under the official appellation of Marcus Aurelius Antoninus.[4]

Elagabalus's endeavour, like Ḥākim's, turns out upon examination to have been somewhat less fantastic than might be supposed; for, in transporting to Rome, and housing on the Palatine, the fetish-stone in which his divine homonym was believed to reside, he could appeal to a notable precedent. In the year 204 B.C., which was a venerably ancient date by the time of Elagabalus's accession to the purple in A.D. 218, the Roman Government of the day had likewise received with official honours, and likewise lodged on the Palatine—in this case, in the Temple of Victory—another fetish-stone which was believed to be charged with the divinity of the Pessinuntine mother-goddess Cybele;[5] and from that day down to Elagabalus's own generation this Anatolian talisman had continued to be honoured in that place with traditional orgiastic rites—performed by eunuch-devotees—which were at least as outlandish in

[1] 'Druse' is a garbled form of the Arabic Durūz, which is the plural of Darazī.

[2] For such 'fossils in fastnesses' see II. D (vi), vol. ii, pp. 255–9, above. Hitti (in op. cit., p. 1) has hit upon the same apt simile for characterizing both the Druses and the Samaritans.

[3] Apropos of the question of the sources of the Druse religion, it is perhaps worth noticing that the district in which it struck root was in the near neighbourhood of two other districts of Syria which had also given birth—simultaneously with one another, though this nearly a thousand years before the day of Ḥākim and Darazī—to two religions each of which likewise preached the divinity of a man as its cardinal doctrine. Christianity arose in the bosom of the Jewish community in Galilee, and the religion in which Simon Magus was worshipped as a god incarnate arose in the bosom of the Samaritan community immediately to the south (for the religion founded by, and centring upon the reputed divinity of, Simon Magus see Meyer, E.: *Ursprung und Anfänge des Christentums*, vol. iii (Stuttgart and Berlin 1923, Cotta), pp. 267–302). The diversity of the respective fates of these three Syrian men-worshipping religions is instructive. The worship of Simon Magus died out in the third century of the Christian Era (Meyer, op. cit., p. 293); the worship of Ḥākim has survived as the peculiar faith of a parochial community in a fastness; the worship of Jesus has become the faith of a universal church.

[4] See V. C (i) (c) 2, p. 82, footnote 4, and the present Annex, p. 649, above.

[5] See II. D (vi), vol. ii, p. 216, and V. C (i) (c) 2, in the present volume, p. 82, above. In the former passage the date of the reception of the Pessinuntine stone at Rome has been erroneously given as 205 B.C. instead of 204 B.C.

Rome as the Syrian worship which the Emperor Elagabalus was seeking to acclimatize there now some four hundred years later. The sense of promiscuity, which had been constantly on the increase in Roman souls during the intervening span of time, might have been expected *a priori* to make Elagabalus's task an easier one than Publius Scipio's.[1] Why was it, then, that the worship of the Pessinuntine fetish which was introduced into Rome in 204 B.C. became a permanent and even an integral element in the Roman religion, whereas the kindred worship of the Emesan fetish which was introduced into Rome in A.D. 218 lasted no longer than the four years which saw out the reign of the emperor who was its patron?

The answer to this question is to be found in the difference in the psychological conditions which respectively attended the successful translation of Cybele to Rome and the abortive translation of Elagabalus.

The Senate's decision to negotiate the transfer of the Cybele-stone from Pessinus to Rome was taken in 205 B.C. at the climax of the Hannibalic War, at a moment when even the sophisticated Roman governing class was overwrought by the strain of the long ordeal to which the Commonwealth had been subjected, while the common people had been reduced by this time to a state of religious emotion which bordered on frenzy. The Senate was acting on precise instructions which had been obtained—or elicited by some shrewd mind—from a consultation of the Sibylline Books, as well as on a hint which was read into an oracle that had lately been received from Delphi; and, when the Government's action duly resulted in the arrival at Rome of the goddess who was to grant the Romans a speedy release from the unrelieved agony of the last fourteen years, the people were enthusiastic. On the day on which the salvation-bringing stone was borne in state from the strand of the Tiber to its new home in the Temple of Victory on the Palatine, 'the whole city poured out into the streets to greet it, while censers, with the incense burning, were placed in front of the doors along the route of the procession'. As the stone was passed from the hands of Scipio, who had received it from its escort on the ship, into the hands of the first ladies of the Commonwealth, who took their turns in carrying it on its way to its resting-place, the goddess was preceded by singers who called upon her 'to enter the city of Rome with good will in her heart and good

---

[1] Publius Cornelius Scipio had been chosen in 204 B.C. for the honour of bringing to land, from the ship in which it was being conveyed to Rome, the Pessinuntine stone-from-heaven. This choice had been made by the direction of the Delphic Oracle, which in the preceding year had instructed the representatives of the Roman Government to choose out the man of best character in Rome for performing this office (see Livy, Book XXIX, chaps. 10, 11, and 14).

fortune in her train'. The day was kept as a feast day; and, when Cybele had been installed in her new shrine, 'the people came in crowds to bring their offerings to her there; a *lectisternium*[1] was celebrated; and games were held which were given the name of *Megalensia* and which became a standing entry in the Roman religious calendar.[2]

It will be seen that, in bringing the Pessinuntine fetish to the Palatine in 205–204 B.C., the Roman Senate was giving satisfaction to a popular demand which was not only spontaneous but was even passionate. On the other hand, in bringing the Emesan fetish to the Palatine in A.D. 218, Elagabalus was abusing his Imperial prerogative in order to gratify a personal whim of his own which found no echo in the hearts of the Roman populace. In other words, it was only in form that the two religious innovations were on a par with one another in point of being introduced from above downwards; for in fact it was Elagabalus's abortive innovation alone that was truly a transaction of this character. In the successful innovation which had been carried out by the Senate four hundred years earlier, a dominant minority had been humouring an internal proletariat by making themselves responsible for a popular act which was so repugnant to their own aristocratic tradition that they might never have brought themselves to perpetrate it if they had had nothing but their personal prejudices to consider.[3] Here is the difference of circumstance which explains

---

[1] A *lectisternium* was a liturgy in which the images of the Gods were displayed in public round a banqueting table which was laid in their honour.—A.J.T.

[2] The passages in inverted commas in this paragraph are quoted from Livy, Book XXIX, chap. 14.

[3] We may add that in all probability the Senate would have ignored even an insistent popular demand for the translation of the Pessinuntine fetish to Rome if this demand had been made in any other psychological circumstances than those prevailing in 205–204 B.C., when the Roman governing class, as well as the common people, was in an abnormal psychological condition. This seems probable when we observe the severity with which another foreign religion—the worship of Dionysus—which was perhaps not less popular than the worship of Cybele, while it was certainly less exotic, was repressed by the Senate less than twenty years later, in 186 B.C., after peace had been restored and the psychological tension of the war-years had been relaxed (see II. D (vi), vol. ii, p. 216, above). The subsequent policy of the Senate towards the worship of Cybele is described as follows by a modern Western scholar who is a master of the subject:

'Quand le Sénat apprit à mieux connaître la divinité que la Sibylle venait de lui imposer, il dut être fort embarrassé du cadeau qu'Attale lui avait fait. L'exaltation enthousiaste, le sombre fanatisme de la dévotion phrygienne contrastaient violemment avec la dignité calme, la réserve honnête de la religion officielle, et ils excitaient dangereusement les esprits.... Les autorités furent balancées entre le respect dû à la puissante déesse, qui avait délivré Rome des Carthaginois, et celui qu'elles éprouvaient pour le *mos maiorum*. Elles se tirèrent d'affaire en isolant complètement le nouveau culte, de façon à se prémunir contre la contagion. Défense fut faite à tout citoyen d'entrer dans le clergé de la déesse exotique ou de prendre part à ses orgies sacrées; les rites barbares, selon lesquels la Grande Mère voulait être adorée, furent accomplis par des prêtres phrygiens et des prêtresses phrygiennes. Quant aux fêtes célébrées en son honneur par le peuple tout entier, les *Megalensia*, elles n'avaient rien d'oriental mais furent organisées conformément aux traditions romaines....

'Mais, malgré la surveillance policière qui l'entourait, malgré les précautions et les préjugés qui l'isolaient, la religion phrygienne vivait. Les esclaves, les affranchis, les

why it was that in 204 B.C. Cybele came to the Palatine to stay, whereas in A.D. 222 Elagabalus was ignominiously ejected from the Palatine as soon as the exercise of the arbitrary political power which had first installed and then maintained him there[1] was suspended by the overthrow and assassination of the intruding Syrian divinity's Imperial namesake and devotee.[2]

While it may not be so surprising to see an Elagabalus and a Ḥākim meet with utter failure in their endeavours to make their public political authority minister to their private religious caprice, we shall perhaps be more deeply impressed with the difficulty of propagating creeds and rites by political action from above downwards when we observe the equally striking ill-success of other

marchands asiatiques allaient se multipliant dans la plèbe, et ces Levantins avaient, pour la grande divinité de leur pays, une dévotion superstitieuse qui s'accordait mal avec les restrictions imposées par l'autorité. Une brèche avait été pratiquée dans la forteresse lézardée des vieux principes romains, et tout l'Orient finit par y passer' (Cumont, F.: *Les Religions Orientales dans le Paganisme Romain*, 4th ed. (Paris 1929, Geuthner), pp. 48–9 and 50).

[1] Elagabalus's arbitrary behaviour in this matter is described as follows in the life of this emperor in the so-called *Historia Augusta* ('Antoninus Heliogabalus', chaps. 3 and 5):

'Ubi primum ingressus est urbem, omissis quae in provincia gerebantur, Heliogabalum in Palatino monte iuxta aedes imperatorias consecravit, eique templum fecit, studens et Matris typum et Vestae ignem et Palladium et Ancilia et omnia Romanis veneranda in illud transferre templum, et id agens ne quis Romae deus nisi Heliogabalus coleretur. Dicebat praeterea Iudaeorum et Samaritanorum religiones et Christianam devotionem illuc transferendam, ut omnium culturarum secretum Heliogabali sacerdotium teneret. . . . Sacra Populi Romani sublatis penetralibus profanavit. Ignem perpetuum exstinguere voluit. Nec Romanas tantum exstinguere voluit religiones, sed per orbem terrae—unum studens ut Heliogabalus deus unus ubique coleretur. Et in penum Vestae, quod solae virgines solique pontifices adeunt, irrupit . . . et penetrale sacrum est auferre conatus. . . . Signum . . . quod Palladium esse credebat abstulit et . . . in sui dei templo locavit. Matris etiam Deum sacra accepit et tauroboliatus est ut typum eriperet et alia sacra quae penitus habentur condita . . . ablatumque sanctum in penetrale dei sui transtulit. . . . Omnes sane deos sui dei ministros esse aiebat, cum alios eius cubicularios appellaret, alios servos, alios diversarum rerum ministros.'

Elagabalus's abuse of his political power in order to commit these insanely provocative acts of sacrilege is reminiscent of the sacrilegious excesses that are attributed to Ḥākim:

'Sunnī Muslim historians . . ., remembering him as the heretic who abolished the Five Pillars of Islam and ordered the names of the early Caliphs [to be] associated with a curse in the public prayer, have portrayed him in terms of a medieval Nero, tyrannical and unbalanced to the point of mental derangement. The Christian historians . . ., associating his memory with the destruction of the Holy Sepulchre in Jerusalem, "leaving not one stone upon another", and the revival of the old regulations . . . which made it incumbent upon all Christians to wear distinctively coloured clothes with heavy wooden crosses dangling from their necks, were equally merciless in his condemnation' (Hitti, op. cit., pp. 26–7).

[2] While the fetish-stone of Pessinus met with better luck at Rome than the fetish-stone of Emesa, there is another fetish-stone at Mecca which has outdone its Pessinuntine as well as its Emesan counterpart by continuing to be an object of adoration from the dawn of Arabian history down to the present day. For this extraordinary survival the Meccan stone is, of course, indebted to the Prophet Muhammad, whose sagacity was as signal as was the folly of the Emperor Elagabalus. Instead of uprooting the Meccan stone and thereby destroying its religious potency, Muhammad preserved this primitive religious force, and harnessed it to the service of his own new religious dispensation, by leaving the Meccan stone *in situ*, without disturbing its traditional association with the worship of a parochial Meccan divinity whom Muhammad had promoted to ubiquity and omnipotence by identifying Allah, the god of the Ka'bah, with the Jewish and Christian God of the Universe (for the Meccan fetish-stone god's success in imparting his own name, on Muslim lips, to the One True God with whom he had thus been equated, see V. C (i) (d) 7, vol. vi, p. 44, below).

rulers who have attempted to take advantage of their political power for the promotion of some religious cause in which they have been interested from more serious and more estimable motives than the sheer desire to gratify a personal whim. There are rulers who have tried and failed to propagate a 'fancy religion' for reasons of state which may have been irrelevant or even irreligious yet at least have not been either personal or disreputable; and there are other rulers who have tried and failed to propagate a 'fancy religion' in which they themselves have devoutly believed, and which they have felt themselves on that account entitled in all good conscience, and perhaps even in duty bound, to communicate by all the means at their command to their suffering fellow men, in order to lighten their darkness and to guide their feet into the way of peace.[1]

The classic example of the cold and calculated manufacture of a new religion for the service of a political end is the invention of the figure and the cult of Serapis by Ptolemy Soter—the founder of the Hellenic 'successor-state' of the Achaemenian Empire in Egypt. In embarking on this Machiavellian religious enterprise the Macedonian statesman was pursuing the politically respectable purpose of seeking to bridge the gulf between his Egyptiac and his Hellenic subjects by bringing the two communities on to a new and virgin plot of religious ground which they were to be invited to cultivate in common;[2] and he enlisted a phalanx of experts whose talents were skilfully selected and co-ordinated for the attainment of the object which their employer had in view. A preliminary plan of religious operations was worked out for Ptolemy by a Helleno-Egyptiac committee of two members, in which the Hellenic side was represented by a scion of the hereditary Eumolpid priesthood of the Eleusinian Mysteries, Timotheus, while the Egyptiac side was represented by one of the rare Philhellenes in the Egyptiac hierarchy in the person of Manetho. A name for the new divinity was coined by combining and Hellenizing the native names of two Egyptiac gods, Usur (Osiris) and Api (Apis); Timotheus contributed a 'Golden Legend' (ἱερὸς λόγος) to lend a supernatural sanction to the newly instituted worship; the Athenian philosopher Demetrius of Phalerum composed a set of paeans in the new god's honour; and the Athenian sculptor Bryaxis carved, for the original and central Serapeum at Alexandria, a statue which endowed Serapis with a distinctive visual shape.

[1] Luke i. 79.
[2] For this Ptolemaic manufacture of the Serapis-cult see Cumont, F.: *Les Religions Orientales dans le Paganisme Romain*, 4th ed. (Paris 1929, Geuthner), pp. 69–94; and Wendland P.: *Die Hellenistisch-Römische Kultur in ihren Beziehungen zu Judentum und Christentum*, 2nd and 3rd ed. (Tübingen 1912, Mohr), pp. 129–30.

Considering the atmosphere of cool professional calculation which surrounded this process of manufacturing a synthetic divinity to a prince's order, we may feel some surprise at the extent of the success that was actually achieved. Even in Egyptiac circles the new worship did not altogether fail to gain a foothold—in spite of the hostility of a Thothmean hierarchy who, though now no longer centralized under the Theban High Priesthood of Amon-Re, were still in no mood to submit to being deprived of a monopoly which, by Ptolemy Soter's day, had been theirs for some twelve hundred years, and which they had successfully maintained, a thousand years back, against the legitimate Egyptiac Pharaoh Ikhnaton's attempt to do for his new version of the Egyptiac Sun-God what the Hellenic usurper was now trying to do for a new version of Osiris.[1] In the Hellenic World the success achieved by the new religion of Ptolemaic manufacture was more extensive— partly, no doubt, because the worship of Serapis had been deliberately accommodated to Hellenic tastes and traditions,[2] and partly thanks to the easy-going êthos of the Olympian Pantheon, whose members could not afford to be 'jealous gods'[3] when they had to rub shoulders with one another either as pullulating creatures of imagination on the narrow summit of Olympus or as thronging statues of stone on the still narrower platform of the Acropolis of Athens. As soon as Bryaxis' chisel had called Serapis into a three-dimensional existence in the Hellenic style of representational art, Zeus and Dionysus and Asklêpios obligingly made room for a new recruit who had duly established an Olympian individuality of his own through a felicitous combination of features borrowed from all three of those older-established recipients of Hellenic worship. In the Hellenic World in the course of the five centuries beginning with Ptolemy Soter's own generation the worship of Serapis made its way on its own merits beyond the limited range of an ephemeral Ptolemaic Empire till it had penetrated to the remotest corners of a Hellenic universal state.[4] It is significant, however, that, in terms of the purpose which had moved the first

---

[1] For the defeat of Ikhnaton by the Thothmean hierarchy see I. C (ii), vol. i, pp. 145-6, and V. C (i) (c) 2, in the present volume, p. 82, footnote 4, above, and the present Annex, pp. 695-6, below.

[2] This Hellenization of Serapis and his worship was not confined to the visual field. While the figure of the new god was adjusted to Hellenic eyes in the statue from the hand of the Hellenic artist Bryaxis, the liturgy was tuned to Hellenic ears by being drafted in the Greek language, and the ritual to Hellenic habits of feeling and thought by being modelled on the Eleusinian pattern.

[3] For the un-Olympian 'jealousy' of the Syriac god Yahweh see V. C (i) (d) 7, vol. vi, pp. 39-40 and 45-7, below.

[4] For the initiation of a trans-frontier barbarian war-lord into the mysteries of Serapis, while he was serving his time as a hostage on the Roman side of the Rhine, about half-way through the fourth century of the Christian Era, see V. C (i) (d) 6 (α), p. 461, footnote 5, above.

of the Ptolemies to build and launch Serapis' bark, the new religion was an utter failure.

While both Hellenes and Egyptians did take up this artificial religion of the Ptolemaic state in their different fashions and to their different degrees, they each went their own way in the worship of Serapis as in everything else, and concurred in nothing but their unanimous avoidance of the common ground on to which Ptolemy Soter had hoped to bring them by enticing both sets of worshippers into his synthetic divinity's precincts. Notwithstanding the skilfully managed inauguration of the worship of Serapis, the political union of Egyptians with Hellenes under the Ptolemaic régime continued to depend entirely upon the brute force of Hellenic arms; and, as soon as this Hellenic military ascendancy began to show signs of weakening, the Egyptiac section of the Hellenic internal proletariat rose in armed revolt.[1] It was not the manufactured worship of Serapis that eventually translated into reality Ptolemy Soter's dream of cementing the compulsory political union between Egyptians and Hellenes by a voluntary union of hearts. The spiritual gulf between the two communities in the dominions of the Ptolemaic Empire was bridged at last by another religion which arose spontaneously out of the bosom of the proletariat in the *ci-devant* Ptolemaic province of Coele Syria a whole generation after the extinction of the last shadow of the Ptolemaic Power,[2] and which made its way from below upwards instead of being propelled from above downwards by the artful hand of a political potentate.

A similar failure attended the religious policy of the Illyrian soldier-emperors who set the Roman Empire on its feet again after its collapse in the middle of the third century of the Christian Era,[3] when they endeavoured to replace—or at least to reinforce— a tottering Caesar-worship by giving the Hellenic universal state a new official religion consisting in the worship of an abstract Sol Invictus.[4] This religious enterprise was taken up successively, yet in the end without success, by Aurelian and Constantius Chlorus and Constantine the Great; and the discomfiture of these forceful personalities is in some ways more striking than the miscarriage of Ptolemy Soter's project; for the Illyrians' inferiority to the Macedonian in the arts of statesmanship was more than offset by their personal sincerity and by the propitiousness of the

---

[1] See V. C (i) (c) 2, p. 68, above.
[2] The remains of the Ptolemaic Empire had been annexed to the Roman Empire by Augustus after the Battle of Actium in 31 B.C.
[3] See V. C (ii) (a), vol. vi, p. 207, below.
[4] For this episode of Hellenic religious history see V. C (i) (c) 2, p. 82, footnote 4, as well as the present Annex, pp. 649–50, above.

atmosphere of the age in which they happened to be living and working. The Sol Invictus in whose divine service the Illyrian soldier-emperors enlisted was not a sheer invention of his Imperial orderlies' minds. They had learned to know him as one of the established gods of the Danubian provinces in which they had been born and bred;[1] and, in their endeavour in later life to raise this god of their boyhood and their homeland to a position of supremacy in Heaven corresponding to the universal dominion which these *novi homines* themselves had won on Earth, we may feel certain that they were not so much actuated by Ptolemaic calculations as they were moved by a spiritual need which they felt in their own hearts and divined in the hearts of their subjects.[2]

[1] This worship of an abstract Sol Invictus, which was already 'a going concern' in the Lower and Middle Danube Basin by the third century of the Christian Era, was presumably a composite product of the radiation of the diverse sun-worships of South-Western Asia, which, at this distance from their respective points of origin, had blended into a single ray with a texture which was more etherial than that of any of the fires from which it had emanated.

[2] We may reflect, however, that, if Sol Invictus had in fact succeeded in gaining the popularity which his Imperial votaries no doubt hoped and expected to see him acquire when they gave their patronage to his cult, he might have undergone a metamorphosis in the hearts and minds of the masses which would have been both surprising and distressing to an Aurelian or a Constantius Chlorus.

In the conception of the Illyrian emperors the Sun-God in whose service they had enlisted was a conservative divinity who presided in Heaven over the work of rescue and reconstruction to which his faithful servants were devoting their energies on Earth; for, although the Illyrian emperors were children of a proletariat who had been borne into power on the wings of the revolutionary upheaval of the third century of the Christian Era, they had made their fortunes and found their mission in salvaging a decadent civilization in which the decay had now gone so far that the children of a dominant minority had ceased to be capable of fending for themselves. This epiphany in a conservative role was not, however, the first appearance of the Sun-God above the Hellenic internal proletariat's horizon; and it is rather surprising that the part which this divinity had played in an earlier chapter of Hellenic history—a part for which the title of Sol Invictus would have been equally apt, though the performance in this previous act had been not conservative but revolutionary—should not have been recalled to proletarian minds, even after four centuries of oblivion, by the dreadful return, in the third century of the Christian Era, of those tribulations which had once evoked the revolutionary proletarian worship of Ἥλιος Ἐλευθέριος in the third and second centuries B.C.

The second and culminating phase of the 'Time of Troubles' which had preceded the foundation of the Hellenic universal state had seen an avatar of the Sun-God which was the very antithesis of Aurelian's idea of him. The proletarian Solar divinity of whom we catch a glimpse in the third-century romance of Iambulus and in the second-century insurrection of Aristonicus (see V. C (i) (c) 2, pp. 69, 70, 82, footnote 4, and 180, and V. C (i) (d) 1, p. 384, above, and V. C (i) (d) 11, vol. vi, Annex I, pp. 350–1, below) was the heavenly patron of an earthly commonwealth which was to be established by the arms of the militant votaries of this Ἥλιος Ἐλευθέριος in the place of the existing Hellenic system of society, in order to reinstate a disinherited internal proletariat in those natural Rights of Man of which they had been brutally and impiously divested by an inhuman dominant minority. The Sun-God of Iambulus and Aristonicus was the just and generous giver who lavished his light upon the poor man who was being oppressed as abundantly as upon the rich man who was this poor man's oppressor; the god's divine gift was the one amenity of life which that dominant minority was powerless to take away from a proletariat which it had succeeded in depriving of every other stake in This World except the procreation of children (see I. B (iv), vol. i, p. 41, footnote 3, above); Helios offered a heavenly city to all who, in the earthly city of destruction, were without a clod of earth to call their own or a night's shelter for a weary head; and it was this divinity's influence that inclined the hearts of slave-owners to emancipate their slaves, in anticipation of a future social state—depicted by Iambulus as already realized in his imaginary 'Islands of the Sun'—in which slavery would be unknown because every one alike would take his turn in performing every fatigue duty and filling every

Yet, in spite—or because—of this spiritual integrity which was so honourable a trait in the characters of the Illyrian Imperial votaries of Sol Invictus, the third and greatest of them was to find from his own experience that the worship of the god whose patronage had been bequeathed to him by his forefathers was not, after all, either sufficient in itself or significant except as a stepping-stone from a dead Caesar-worship to a higher religion which had arisen spontaneously in the bosom of the Hellenic internal proletariat, and had long since become 'a going concern' in despite of steady official disfavour and occasional official persecution. In the vision that resulted in Constantine's conversion to Christianity the votary of Sol Invictus saw that

'athwart the Sun—the earthly representation of the god to whom he owed this inherited allegiance—was cast the cross of light. What else could this mean for Constantine than a revelation of the identity of the god of his worship with the god of the Christians? "Whom therefore ye ignorantly worship, him declare I unto you." The secret of his father's monotheism was disclosed. Apollo—Sol—the pagan panegyrist two years before at Trier had celebrated as "salutifer"; it was true in a sense of which the orator had never dreamt. . . . "Sol Invictus"? What better description for the Victorious Christ?'[1]

If this brilliant reconstruction of the Emperor Constantine's personal religious experience is correct,[2] then we may follow the scholar who has made it in finding in this conscious identification of Sol with Christ the explanation of the continuance of the representation of Sol Invictus upon the coins that issued from Constantine's mint for eleven years after the Emperor's vision on the eve of the Battle of the Milvian Bridge.[3] In any case Sol Invictus did give place to

office (for these traits of the Iambulan and Aristonican Helios see Bidez, J.: *La Cité du Monde et la Cité du Soleil chez les Stoïciens* (Paris 1932, Les Belles Lettres), pp. 34–50, and Tarn, W. W.: *Alexander the Great and the Unity of Mankind* (London 1933, Milford), pp. 9–10).

We may speculate whether this glowing revolutionary avatar of the Sun-God as 'Ηλιος 'Ελευθέριος might not have reasserted itself in the third or fourth century of the Christian Era if the countenance of Constantius Chlorus's Sol Invictus had not been of too pale and sickly a cast to fire the imagination of the *jacquerie* who in Constantius's day were replaying the part of Aristonicus's 'Citizens of the Sun' under the more prosaic names of Bagaudae or Circumcelliones.

[1] Baynes, N. H.: *Constantine the Great and the Christian Church* (London 1929, Milford), pp. 97 and 100.

[2] Professor Baynes' conjecture that Constantine transcended the worship of Sol Invictus by identifying Sol with Christ would appear to be supported by the well-established fact that in the calendar of the Christian Church the celebration of Christmas was deliberately assigned—at some moment in the reign of Constantine's son and immediate successor Constantius II—to the 25th December; for this date had long since been consecrated to the celebration of the *Natalis Invicti*, and its identification with Christmas Day was an act of ecclesiastical policy which directly contradicted and reversed the Church's previous rule of avoiding the celebration of Christmas on any date that was already associated with the worship of a pagan divinity (see Cumont, op. cit., pp. ix and 206–7; Wendland, op. cit., p. 159).

[3] Constantine saw his vision of the Cross athwart the Sun in A.D. 312, whereas his coins bearing the image and superscription of Sol Invictus continued to be struck until A.D. 323 (Baynes, op. cit., p. 95).

Christ in the course of Constantine's reign; and, whether the process took the mental form of identification or that of repudiation, the result was conclusive—as was demonstrated by the failure of Constantine's nephew and ultimate successor the Emperor Julian to undo his uncle's work. It was in vain that Julian sought to rekindle the light of his forefathers' Solar divinity by the unpromising method of robbing him of the soldier-like simplicity which had been the secret of his strength and forcing him into the elaborate system of the Apostate's Neoplatonic Antichurch;[1] this point in Julian's religious policy shared the fate of the rest of his forlorn hope; and the fiasco made it impossible any longer to ignore the truth that, within less than a century of the date at which Aurelian had raised him to a position of oecumenical honour, Sol Invictus either had been transfigured out of all recognition or else was defunct beyond all possibility of being raised from the dead.

> He saw a greater Sun appear
> Then his bright throne or burning axletree could bear.

The abortive attempt to establish Sol Invictus as an oecumenical divinity in the ambit of a Roman Empire which had been salvaged from the débâcle of the third century of the Christian Era has an almost exact Incaic analogue. The founder of the Andean universal state, the Inca Pachacutec, likewise attempted to endow his variegated empire with a single supreme object of worship; and the Cuzcan, like the Illyrian, empire-builder tendered this high god to his subjects in the shape of a local Sun-God who happened to have a hereditary claim upon the emperor's own allegiance.[2] Pachacutec did his utmost to fortify his artificially established religion of state by endowing it—*more Incaico*—with a minutely regulated and strictly centralized ecclesiastical organization of the kind which the Roman Emperor Julian tried in vain to improvise for the benefit of his Neoplatonic Antichurch. Whether this overwhelmingly paternal Incaic official patronage would have helped or hindered the Sun-God of Corichanca, in the long run, in the effort to find his own feet as a high god of the whole Andean World is a question which can never receive its answer, since the experiment was cut short, within a hundred years of its initiation, by Pizarro's destructive conquest of the empire which Pachacutec had founded.[3]

---

[1] For the place assigned to Sol Invictus in Julian's theology see Julian's prose *Hymn to Helios*.

[2] For the Inca Pachacutec's organization of this oecumenical worship of the originally parochial Sun-God whose native seat was Corichanca, the Sun-temple at Cuzco, see V. C (i) (d) 6 (δ), p. 532, and the present Annex, p. 653, above.

[3] If the Andean universal state had been left in peace to live out its natural term, instead of being prematurely shattered, as it was by the impact of an alien civilization

There is yet a third historic case of a Sun-worship being inaugurated and propagated by the ruler of a universal state: namely, Ikhnaton's attempt to substitute for the orthodox Egyptiac Pantheon, under the presidency of Amon-Re, a worship of an etherial and only true God who made his Godhead manifest to human eyes in the Aton or Solar Disk.[1] So far as can be seen, Ikhnaton's attempt to establish this new religion of his was not inspired to any appreciable extent either by Machiavellian considerations of *raison d'état* or by Elagabalus's motive of exerting a despotic power and indulging a personal caprice. If Ikhnaton had been mainly concerned with the political problem of the ecclesiastical unification of the Egyptiac universal state, he would hardly have felt himself called upon to take action, since he would have found his problem practically solved for him already in the syncretistic pantheon and centralized hierarchy which had been effectively established by his predecessor and ancestor Thothmes III; and he would have been under no temptation to try, as he did try, to undo Thothmes' solid work at the cost of tearing a profound schism in the Egyptiac body social.[2] Nor, again, does Ikhnaton's êthos display any striking points of likeness to Hākim's. The demonic spiritual force that drove the Egyptiac emperor-prophet into an uncompromising defiance of the hallowed traditions as well as the vested interests of the society into which he had been born was not an insane egotism: it was a deep religious faith which, like Açoka's philosophical convictions,[3] translated itself into evangelical works. The Imperial convert could not rest until he had communicated to his fellow men a divine revelation which

from the farther side of the Atlantic, we may guess that one of the determining factors in the career of the politically established worship of the Corichancan Sun-God would have been the temper animating the religious policy of the Imperial Government. In some respects the policy was drastic. For example, we have noted already (in V. C (i) (d) 6 (δ), p. 532, footnote 4, above) that the local idols and fetishes were physically removed from their native seats and deposited in the temple of Corichanca. On the other hand fetishes were included in the very short list of articles which were lawful objects of personal property (Joyce, T. A.: *South American Archaeology* (London 1912, Lee Warner), p. 158).

[1] See I. C (ii), vol. i, pp. 145–6, and V. C (i) (c) 2, in the present volume, p. 82, footnote 4, above.

[2] Ikhnaton's new religion did expressly stand for political unity inasmuch as it conceived of the Aton as a universal creator who shone with an equal benevolence upon the Egyptiac masters of 'the New Empire' and upon their non-Egyptiac subjects in Syria and in Nubia (see the passage from Ikhnaton's hymn to the Aton that is quoted in V. C (i) (d) 7, vol. vi, pp. 11–12, below). Yet even this conception of the brotherhood of all Mankind through the common beneficence of God seems to have been foreshadowed in a Hymn to Amon which is a monument of the orthodox Egyptiac religious thought of at least one generation before Ikhnaton's day. (On this point see Erman, A.: *The Literature of the Ancient Egyptians*, English translation (London 1927, Methuen), p. 290, footnote 4.) And there is no reason to suppose that, in transferring this *motif* from the religion of his forefathers to his own new-fangled worship, Ikhnaton was consciously concerned—as Ptolemy Soter assuredly was when he instituted the worship of Serapis—to forge out of a common religious allegiance a political bond between the Egyptiac and the non-Egyptiac section of his subjects.

[3] See pp. 680–3, above.

he was convinced that he had received in order that he might serve as the appointed spokesman of a spiritual truth that had never before been broadcast. The religious motive by which Ikhnaton was inspired was disinterested as well as single-minded; and in its overflow into the secular field it showed itself to be a veritable well-spring of life whose waters possessed the miraculous power of dissolving the classicism of the contemporary Egyptiac litera-ture[1] and the formalism of the contemporary Egyptiac visual art into a new pulsation of creative activity. In fact, Ikhnaton's revelation held out a promise of translating a legendary Egyptiac miracle into a matter of historical fact by evoking new life out of a mummified corpse.[2] It will be seen that on every ground Ikhnaton deserved to succeed in his religious mission, while con-versely the public to which he addressed himself had every reason to accept the emperor-prophet's message with alacrity and grati-tude. And yet Ikhnaton's enterprise ended in a failure that was more extreme than Aurelian's or Ptolemy's, and not less extreme than Elagabalus's or Hākim's. This failure can only be attributed to the one conspicuous weakness in Ikhnaton's noble and beneficent endeavour. It was an attempt on the part of a political potentate to propagate a 'fancy religion' from above downwards; and the penalty which the new revelation had to pay for its Pharaonic origin was the implacable hostility which it aroused in the hearts of all the rest of the Egyptiac dominant minority. In their eyes Ikhnaton was a detestable traitor; and this invincible opposition which the Egyptiac emperor-prophet encountered among his own kind was not counterbalanced by any sympathetic response to his preaching in the hearts of the masses; for in their eyes the new heresy was just as remote and as incomprehensible as the old orthodoxy which it was striving to supersede. Ikhnaton fell between two stools; and this was a fall which all the merits of his character and his gospel were impotent to retrieve.[3]

[1] See V. C (i) (*d*) 6 (γ), p. 496, above.

[2] According to the Osiris-myth, Osiris' son Horus was begotten by his father in an act of sexual union between Osiris and Isis which took place after Osiris had met his death (see Erman, A.: *Die Religion der Ägypter* (Berlin and Leipzig 1934, de Gruyter), pp. 68–9).

[3] 'An instructive parallel [to Ikhnaton's abortive religious reform] is afforded by the Iconoclastic Movement in the Byzantine Empire. There too there was the contradiction between the monotheism of the official doctrine of the Church and the current practice of daily worship led to an attempt to destroy the idolatrous images and forcibly depose the monks who were the head and front of the cult of them; there too there were quite a number of ecclesiastical dignitaries who sided with the Emperor; and there too the enterprise came to grief over a failure to reckon sufficiently with the strength of the religious feelings which the popular form of worship had behind it. The result was that, from that time onwards, the path of progress was closed to the Greek Church', in contrast to the subsequent history of the Western Church.—Meyer, E.: *Geschichte des Altertums*, vol. ii, part (1), 2nd ed. (Stuttgart and Berlin 1928, Cotta), pp. 414–15. For Iconoclasm and its sequel see the present Study, IV. C (iii) (*c*) 2 (β), vol. iv, p. 352, footnote 5, and IV. C (iii) (*c*) 2 (β), Annex II, vol. iv, pp. 594–5, above. For the

A similar congenital defect seems likewise to account for the abortiveness of Orphism. If our reconstruction of its history[1] is correct, this 'higher religion' was called into existence for the purpose of satisfying a spiritual hunger in Hellenic souls; and this hunger was not—like the craving which was answerable for the translation of the fetish-stone of Cybele from Pessinus to Rome in 204 B.C.[2]—a mere passing psychological effect of a temporary social ordeal, but was a deep and enduring demand for that spiritual bread which was not to be found in the social heritage of an adolescent and youthfully ravenous Hellenic Society. This yearning after a 'higher religion' is so strong a passion, and the spiritual vacuum which evoked it in the Hellas of the sixth century B.C. is so grave a malady, that it might have been expected *a priori* that any new religious system which offered even a partial satisfaction for this pressing religious need would enjoy a sensational vogue, unless its prospects were blighted by some inherent weakness. This weakness is not to be found in the provenance of the raw materials out of which Orphism was manufactured; for, although, as we have noticed in another context,[3] these materials were exotic, the craftsmen who worked them up seem to have been careful to mould them into forms which were in harmony with the native Hellenic tradition.[4] When we find that, in spite of this combination of uncommonly skilful workmanship with uncommonly favourable predisposing conditions, Orphism in fact missed fire, the fiasco can only be explained as being an ineluctable nemesis for the interestedness of the motives that were at work and for the disingenuity of the means that were employed in the operations of *entrepreneurs* who had set themselves to supply this spiritual demand for their own material profit. There appears to be ground for believing that the propagation of Orphism received its first impulse from the Athenian despots of the House of Peisistratus,[5] who saw in this 'fancy religion' an apt instrument for their policy of confirming their political hold upon Attica by satisfying the diverse requirements of the formerly unprivileged

petrifaction which overtook not only the Egyptiac religion but the whole of Egyptiac life after Ikhnaton's failure see I. C (ii), vol. i, pp. 144–6, above. It may be noted that Ikhnaton (*imperabat circa* 1370–1352 B.C.) and Leo Syrus (*imperabat* A.D. 717–40) were, philosophically speaking (see I. C (iii) (*c*), in vol. i, above), approximately contemporaries, if we equate the interregnum *circa* 1675–1575 B.C. in Egyptiac history with the interregnum *circa* A.D. 375–675 which was the prelude to the emergence of the Orthodox Christian Civilization.

[1] In V. C (i) (*c*) 2, pp. 84–7, above.
[2] See pp. 685–8, above.
[3] In V. C (i) (*c*) 2, pp. 85–6, above.
[4] For an illustration of this careful process of adaptation see Guthrie, W. K. C.: *Orpheus and Greek Religion* (London 1935, Methuen), pp. 104–7.
[5] See V. C (i) (*c*) 2, p. 87, footnote 2, above. On the other hand Boulanger, A.: *Orphée* (Paris 1925, Rieder), pp. 18–29, argues that the cradle of Orphism is to be looked for, not in Attica, but in Magna Graecia.

classes in the Athenian body politic; and the agent of the Peisistratidae in this religious enterprise (if they are to be credited with it) was almost certainly Onomacritus,[1] an expert in religious lore whose recorded exploits make it highly probable that he approached the task which his political patrons had set him in the same cold-blooded spirit in which, some two hundred years later, Ptolemy Soter's commission to launch the worship of Serapis was executed by a Manetho and a Timotheus and a Demetrius and a Bryaxis.[2] However this may be, the authors of Orphism unquestionably fell between the same two stools as the Pharaonic author of the worship of the Aton.

'Orphism was too philosophical for the masses, too mythological for the intellectual pride of youthful philosophy.'[3]

Such modest success as Orphism did eventually achieve was posterior to the breakdown of the Hellenic Civilization and to the invasion of Hellenic souls by that sense of promiscuity which kept pace with the material expansion of the Hellenic World at the expense of alien societies.[4]

[1] Onomacritus's role is minimized by Boulanger (op. cit., pp. 33–5).

[2] For the evidence which suggests that Onomacritus may have invented the ritual and the mythology of the Orphic Faith and have composed the corpus of poetry which was put into circulation under the name of Orpheus in order to serve as the sacred scriptures of this manufactured church, see Guthrie, W. K. C.: *Orpheus and Greek Religion* (London 1935, Methuen), pp. 13, 58–9, 107–8, 115–16, 217. Onomacritus's standards of honesty are shown up in the following account, from the pen of Herodotus (Book VII, chap. 6), of the circumstances in which—in a later chapter of his career—the Attic theologian came to second his Peisistratid patrons in the house of exile at Susa in their successful efforts to confirm the Achaemenian emperor Xerxes in his project of attempting the conquest of European Greece—a project in which the *ci-devant* despots of Athens, as well as their Aleuad companions in misfortune who had once been the masters of Thessaly, saw a hope of their own restoration to the lordship from which they had been ejected by their former subjects.

'The Peisistratid exiles at Susa . . . used the same arguments with Xerxes as were used by the Aleuadae, and at the same time they tried to get at him in another way by bringing into action their Athenian fellow countryman Onomacritus, who was an expert in oracles and the editor of those of Musaeus. The Peisistratidae were able to command Onomacritus's services on this occasion because they had made up their quarrel with him before repairing to Susa. This quarrel had arisen out of the act of Hipparchus Peisistratus's son in exiling Onomacritus from Attica when he had been caught red-handed by Lasus of Hermione in the offence of interpolating a [spurious] oracle into the corpus of Musaeus's works. . . . For this offence Hipparchus had sent Onomacritus into exile—in a revulsion from the perpetual recourse which the despot had been by way of having to the theologian's services. However, when the Peisistratids took the road to Susa, Onomacritus was one of the party; and, when he had his audience with the Great King, the Peisistratids made such a song about him that he was graciously permitted to recite his oracles. In complying, Onomacritus took care to suppress everything that suggested the likelihood of a Persian reverse, and to pick out all the most auspicious passages.'

If, at an earlier stage of his career, Onomacritus was as unscrupulous as this in the execution of a Peisistratean commission to manufacture the Orphic religion, it is perhaps not to be wondered at if, in the event, Orphism proved no greater a success than the similarly manufactured worship of Serapis.

The parallel between Peisistratus's role in the launching of Orphism and Ptolemy Soter's role in the launching of the worship of Serapis is pointed out by Boulanger (op. cit., pp. 22–3). In Boulanger's belief, however, the expert services which Peisistratus employed for his purpose were not Attic but Italiot.   [3] Guthrie, op. cit., p. 238.

[4] Before the breakdown of the Hellenic Civilization—an event which, in this Study,

Our present survey of abortive attempts to propagate 'fancy religions' by means of political patronage may fittingly close with a glance at the Timurid Mughal Emperor Akbar's abortive Dīn Ilāhī; for, while Akbar's failure was as extreme as the most signal of the comparable fiascos that we have already passed in review, the character and conduct of Akbar himself are so astonishingly Protean that, at one turn or another, they are reminiscent of almost every point that has come to our notice in the several illustrations of our 'law' that we have examined hitherto.[1]

In point of completeness the failure of Akbar's enterprise has only two parallels in the list of failures which we have so far compiled; for, like Ikhnaton's substitution of the worship of the Sun-Disk for that of Amon-Re, and like Elagabalus's installation of the Sun-Fetish whose name he bore in the place of honour in the Roman Pantheon, Akbar's disestablishment of Islam to make way for a 'fancy religion' of his own manufacture did not outlive its Imperial author, but fell to the ground as soon as his death had deprived his religious experiment of the political sanction without which it would never have had the slightest chance of even being

we have equated with the outbreak of the Atheno-Peloponnesian War in 431 B.C.—the Orphics' 'language and a few of their ideas occasionally caught the fancy of philosopher or poet, but in general the gospel which they preached with such enthusiasm and confidence was a cry in the wilderness, because it was a gospel for which the age was not yet ready. . . . It has been said that the rise of mystical cult-societies, or non-social religious groups, seems to coincide with the breaking-up, in the sixth century [B.C.], of the old social units based on the theory or fact of blood-kinship. We see the morality of these old social units subjected to a searching test in Aeschylus. But of the Orphics it may be said with truth that they did not simply reflect and keep step with a social change which was taking place in the Greek World in which they lived (as the statement just quoted might seem to imply), but that they far outstripped that social change in promulgating a religious theory—that of the brotherhood of Mankind—which did not find even philosophical expression until the advent of the Stoics, and for its popular acceptance had to wait until the days of Christianity. . . . There was no place for a religion of this sort in an age when the ties of the family-unit were breaking up only to give place to the equally rigid demands, the new enthusiasms, of the growing city-state. . . . To find a wider response [Orphism] had to wait until the distinctive greatness and distinctive limitations of the Classical Age had broken down' (Guthrie, op. cit., pp. 235 and 238). According to this view the Neo-Orphism of the post-Alexandrine age was not, as Boulanger argues (in op. cit., pp. 58–9), a virtually new religion, but was the authentic Orphism blossoming, at last, in a kindlier social environment.

[1] The quantity of the points of coincidence between Akbar and his compeers will appear the more remarkable when we consider that these similarities were not the product of any conscious policy of imitation on Akbar's part. So far was Akbar from being influenced by the example of any of the other political patrons of 'fancy religions' whom we have mustered in our present review that, in all probability, he was not even aware of the existence of any of them with the possible exception of Hākim (whom he would have heard of only through being taught to reprobate him). Even Açoka, whose dominions had been almost exactly co-extensive with Akbar's own, was presumably unknown to Akbar, since there is no evidence to suggest that Buddhism was one of the several non-Islamic systems of belief with which Akbar found the opportunity to make himself acquainted (on this point see Smith, V. A.: *Akbar the Great Mogul*, 2nd ed. (Oxford 1919, Clarendon Press), p. 162, footnote 1, and p. 338). The only predecessors of Akbar whose example weighed with Akbar on the testimony of Akbar himself were the Prophet Muhammad and the war-lord ʿAlā-ad-Dīn Khilji (*dominabatur* A.D. 1296–1316)—a predecessor with whom Akbar had in common the three points of being a Turk, being a Muslim, and being a militarist who followed his calling in an Indian arena (see Smith, op. cit., pp. 209–11).

given a trial. When we remind ourselves that Hākim's fantastic self-deification is still cherished as the living faith of at any rate one fossilized community of converts, though more than nine hundred years have now elapsed since the death of the capricious founder of the religion of the Druses, and when we further reflect that the Orphic and Serapian churches, which were manufactured in such cold blood at the instance of a Peisistratus and a Ptolemy Soter, not only lived on for centuries after the deaths of their political promoters but also spread far and wide beyond the frontiers of the Peisistratean Principality and the Ptolemaic Empire, we can take the measure of the moral defeat which was suffered by the Dīn Ilāhī when its nominal adherents incontinently abandoned it to the last man upon receipt of the news that their Imperial master was no longer in a position to visit them with his political displeasure if they ceased to humour his religious vagaries.

As for the many-sidedness which is as conspicuous a feature as the ineffectiveness of Akbar's religious interests and activities, it is at best bewildering and at worst inexplicably self-contradictory; and therefore perhaps the least unpromising approach to the formidable task of attempting an analysis of this extraordinary genius will lie in bringing out the points that Akbar has in common with one or other of the Imperial philosophers and theologians and prophets and claimants to divinity whose failures we have already examined.

One vein in Akbar's genius showed itself in a detached intellectual curiosity and a temperate piety that are both of them reminiscent of the Roman Emperor Alexander Severus. It was in this vein that in A.D. 1575 Akbar established his 'Ibādat Khānah ('House of Worship') as a theatre for discussions of religious and philosophical questions between the representatives of different schools of Islamic thought;[1] and from that moment onwards we can watch the range of Akbar's curiosity constantly expanding. In A.D. 1578 he summoned to his court the Zoroastrian theologian Dastūr Meherjī Rānā from Gujerat;[2] in 1579 he invited from Goa the first of the three successive missions of Jesuit fathers that were to visit his court before the close of his reign;[3] in 1582 he sent for the Jain guru Hīravijaya;[4] and, as the Emperor's circle of religious consultants widened by degrees to this, in Muslim eyes, shockingly latitudinarian radius, Akbar seems to have abandoned his exclusively inter-Muslim public disputations in favour of private sessions at which the representatives of all the different religions

---

[1] See Smith, op. cit., pp. 130–4.   [2] Ibid., pp. 162–5.
[3] For this first Jesuit mission see ibid., pp. 169–76.
[4] Ibid., pp. 166–8. Akbar's Jain consultant, like his Zoroastrian consultant, came from Gujerat.

with which he had successively placed himself *en rapport* were
required to meet and debate with one another.[1] The results of
these excursions into the comparative study of religions came to
be reflected in Akbar's daily life in a personal system of private
devotions which departed both from the hours and from the
exercises of the canonical Islamic prayers, and 'consisted . . . in
his latter days . . . largely of acts of reverence to the Sun, fire and
light'.[2]

This intellectual vein, in which Akbar's heart was dominated by
his head, was combined in his person with a mystical vein with
which it might seem incompatible—if the evidence for the existence of both veins in this one personality were not as convincing as
it happens in fact to be. The crucial event in Akbar's religious
experience was a fit of ecstasy which came upon him suddenly and
unawares in the midst of all the bustle and excitement of a *battue*;
and this incident was not an isolated occurrence, for there had been
a premonition of it at a date when Akbar was still in his boyhood,
and the vein that here came to the surface was active underneath at
every stage of Akbar's life.[3] It was a response of this element in
the emperor-mystic's soul to the admonitions of his Svetāmbara
Jain mentor that moved Akbar to pay tribute to the principle of
Ahimsa ('Non-Injury') by imposing on himself and on his subjects
some of the same measures of self-denial which in the same part
of the world, more than eighteen hundred years before, had been
adopted by the Emperor Açoka under the influence of the Hinayanian Buddhism.[4] Like Açoka, Akbar took to a vegetarian diet;[5]
like Açoka, he abolished the Imperial hunt; and, like Açoka, he
established a close time in which the slaughtering of animals was
made illegal.[6]

Though this mystical vein in Akbar's character presents a strong
contrast to the intellectual vein which we have analysed above,
the two veins might both have been expected to contribute—
when it came to the practical enterprise of founding a new religion[7]

[1] Ibid., p. 133.
[2] Ibid., p. 349. Compare the account, that has been quoted above in V. C (i) (d) 6
(δ), p. 549, of the private devotions of Alexander Severus in his eclectically furnished
oratory.
[3] Smith, op. cit., pp. 158–61 and 348–9.
[4] See the present Annex, pp. 682–3, above.   [5] Smith, op. cit., p. 335.
[6] Compare Smith, op. cit., p. 167, with the same author's *The Early History of India*,
3rd ed. (Oxford 1914, Clarendon Press), p. 177. It seems certain that Akbar, and probable
that Açoka, prescribed the death-penalty as a punishment for human beings who in-
fringed these laws for the prevention of cruelty to animals! Açoka, however, did, as we
have seen, apply the principle of *Ahimsa* to his conduct towards human beings as well,
in the capital point of renouncing the use of War as an instrument of his Imperial policy,
whereas Akbar never denied himself the indulgence of extending the range of his empire
by a pursuit of the practice of aggressive warfare.
[7] For the institution of the Dīn Ilāhī see Smith, V. A.: *Akbar the Great Mogul*,
pp. 211–22.

—towards informing this work of Akbar's hands with an etherial and impersonal spirit; and there is one aspect of the Dīn Ilāhī in which this expectation might appear to have been fulfilled; for Akbar's 'fancy religion' was professedly a transcendental monotheism in which an ineffable Godhead was approached in the mind of Akbar—as in the kindred minds of Ikhnaton and Plato and Aurelian and Pachacutec—through an adoration of the Sun in his symbolic role as the Deity's counterpart in the Material Universe.[1] This transcendental aspect of the Dīn Ilāhī was overshadowed, however, by a contrary aspect in which the autocrat's 'fancy religion' can be seen ministering nakedly and unashamedly to its author's overweening egotism.

The promulgation of the new faith in A.D. 1582 was prefaced by two demonstrative assertions of a 'Caesaro-papism' that was as reminiscent of Elagabalus and Hākim as it was profoundly alien from the tradition and the êthos of the orthodox Sunnī Islam in which Akbar had been born and bred.[2] In June 1579 the Emperor insisted on assuming the function of saying the *Khutbah* in the general mosque in his brand-new capital of Fathpur-Sīkrī;[3] and in the September of the same year Shaykh Mubārak—a Sunnī doctor of the Law who pandered to Akbar's clerical ambitions—followed up this first step by promulgating, in the name of the Sunnī *'ulamā* of the Empire, a manifesto[4] conceding to the Emperor the last word in those questions of faith and doctrine which, according to the Sunnah, were soluble exclusively by the consensus of the *'ulamā* themselves and lay entirely beyond the province of the temporal power—even where this was wielded by the Commander of the Faithful himself.[5] Thereafter, when at the beginning of A.D. 1582 Akbar at last took the decisive step of overtly promulgating a new religion, an insistence upon the supreme spiritual authority of its Imperial maker—an authority that was supported by a pretension to a unique spiritual enlightenment— turned out to be the kernel of a so-called Dīn Ilāhī.[6] Converts were called upon to sacrifice Religion, as well as Honour, Life, and Property, upon the demand of the emperor-pontiff; and, if the

---

[1] For Akbar's adoration—under Hindu as well as Zoroastrian influence—of the Sun in particular and of fire and light in general see Smith, op. cit., pp. 164–5 and 349.
[2] For the 'Caesaro-papism' that has been the ruin of the Orthodox Christian Civilization see IV. C (iii) (c) 2 (β), vol. iv, pp. 364–405, and IV. C (iii) (c) 2 (β), Annex II, vol. iv, pp. 593–623, above.
[3] Smith, op. cit., pp. 176–7.   [4] Ibid., pp. 178–80.
[5] For this fundamental rule of the orthodox Sunnī Muslim Faith see the authorities— particularly Arnold, T. W.: *The Caliphate* (Oxford 1924, Clarendon Press)—that are cited in Toynbee, A. J.: *Survey of International Affairs 1925*, vol. i (London 1927, Milford), pp. 25–30. Akbar's outrageous assumption of the authority of an *'ālim* in virtue of being the local *sultān* of the Islamic community in Hindustan seems to have been first mooted by Shaykh Mubārak as early as A.D. 1573 (Smith, op. cit., pp. 213–14).
[6] See ibid., pp. 213–17.

convert was a Muslim, a written declaration of his repudiation of Islam was required of him.   In his special animus against the religion which he himself had deserted, the apostate Sunnī Akbar revealed the apostate Shī'ī Hākim's cloven hoof; and, though he stopped short[1] of attempting to convert his Muslim subjects to the Dīn Ilāhī by force, Akbar did go so far as to sell into slavery beyond the frontiers of his own dominions a number of shaykhs and fakīrs who had been frank enough and bold enough to declare against the Emperor's spiritual pretensions.[2]   There is even reason to believe that Akbar followed Hākim to the length of at any rate playing with the idea of representing himself as an incarnation of the Deity.[3]

The utter failure of this fantastic caprice of an extraordinary genius may perhaps be considered to have completed our demonstration that *Cujus Regio Ejus Religio* is a political programme which is inexorably condemned to miscarry.   And indeed the last word on this vain dream of autocrats intoxicated with *hybris* had already been uttered—and that not only before Akbar's time but also within Akbar's knowledge—by one of the councillors of Akbar's own predecessor and ensample, Sultan 'Alā-ad-Dīn Khiljī, at a privy council meeting at which 'Alā-ad-Dīn had divulged his intention of committing the very act of folly which Akbar did commit three hundred years later.

'Religion and law and creeds', declared the prince's councillor on this occasion, 'ought never to be made subjects of discussion by Your Majesty, for these are the concerns of prophets, not the business of kings.   Religion and law spring from heavenly revelation; they are never established by the plans and designs of Man.   From the days of Adam till now they have been the mission of prophets and apostles, as rule and government have been the duty of kings.   The prophetic office has never appertained to kings—and never will, so long as the World lasts—though some prophets have discharged the functions of royalty.   My advice is that Your Majesty should never talk about these matters.'[4]

The Khiljī prince to whom this counsel was addressed showed himself wiser in his generation than his more enlightened Timurid successor; for 'Alā-ad-Dīn prudently abandoned his foolhardy enterprise in deference to a warning which, in the same social

[1] Ibid., p. 209.   [2] Ibid., p. 221.
[3] See ibid., pp. 177-8, 218, and 351.   This suspicion mainly rests upon the use of the phrase 'Allāhu Akbar' as one of the shibboleths of the new religion; for, while the traditional meaning of this pious ejaculation was 'Allah is without a peer', it was also capable of being interpreted as meaning 'Akbar is identical with Allah'.
[4] Advice given to Sultan 'Alā-ad-Dīn by his councillor 'Alā-al-Mulk, the Kotwāl of Delhi (recorded in Ziyā-ad-Dīn Baranī's Ta'rīkh-i-Fīrūz Shāhī, and quoted by Smith, in op. cit., p. 210, from the English translation given in Elliot, H. M., and Dowson, J.: *The History of India as told by its own Historians* (London 1867-77, Trübner, 8 vols.), vol. iii, p. 170.

environment at the later date, was disregarded by Akbar to that self-willed emperor-pontiff's own exemplary discomfiture.

If the lesson of experience up to date thus proves to be that *Cujus Regio Ejus Religio* is a political programme which spells disappointment for any prince who may be rash enough to make it his own, a study of History will also bring to light a converse principle which is apt to prosper the handiwork of a prince who acts upon it, while even the prince who merely refrains from acting at variance with it may look forward to reaping at least the negative reward of escaping Akbar's and Hākim's fiasco. This counter-principle might be expressed in the antithetical catchword *Religio Regionis Religio Regis*; and we may conclude the present Annex by applying our usual test of an empirical survey to this second formula in its turn—reviewing in the first place the fortunes of those princes who have simply forborne from setting the principle at defiance, and in the second place the fortunes of those who have taken it for their positive rule of conduct.

Our catalogue of rulers who have profited by paying deference to the precept *Religio Regionis Religio Regis* in the merely nega-tive way of keeping on the right side of the law must include the name of the Umayyad dynasty of Caliphs, since the Umayyads did refrain from attempting to force upon their subjects the faith to which they themselves officially subscribed, and did duly reap from this tolerance a reward which can be measured by contrasting the policy and the fortunes of the Umayyads with those of the Maccabees.[1] At the same time we cannot rate even the negative merit of the Umayyads very high, considering that every one of the Caliphs of this dynasty, with the single exception of 'Umar II, was supremely indifferent, if not positively hostile, to the Islam which he officially professed, and was therefore presumably free from any serious temptation to press upon the non-Islamic popu-lations under his rule a religious diet for which their sovereign himself had so little appetite. A greater exercise of self-restraint may be discerned in the similar forbearance of the Achaemenidae, with the single exception of Cambyses in Egypt, from any attempt to indoctrinate their non-Zoroastrian subjects with the Zoroas-trianism which was the domestic religion of the Achaemenian House;[2] for on the one hand the language of their inscriptions suggests that the Achaemenidae were keener converts to Zoroas-

---

[1] For the respective cases of the Umayyads and the Maccabees see the present Annex, pp. 675–7 and 657–9, above. For the case of the Umayyads see also V. C (ii) (*a*), vol. vi, p. 205, below.

[2] Cambyses' outrageous desecration and violent persecution of the Egyptiac religion may perhaps be taken as evidence of a zeal for his own Zoroastrianism—though this Achaemenian fanatic had not time, in Egypt, to progress from the stage of repression to that of propaganda.

trianism than the Umayyads were to Islam,[1] while on the other
hand the Achaemenidae showed themselves so scrupulous in acting
up to their policy of extending toleration to all religions alike[2] as
to have awakened, in the minds of some modern Western scholars,
an uncharitable suspicion that such admirably tolerant princes may
not after all have felt any very deep devotion to the faith which
they personally professed. However that may be, it is at any rate
beyond question that the Achaemenidae served their own interests
better by their tolerance than their Sasanian successors and co-
religionists served theirs by their fanatical efforts to impose their
Zoroastrianism upon their subjects.[3]

Again, we may be sure that Marcus Aurelius never dreamt of
making use of his Imperial prerogative in order to propagate
among his subjects—either by precept, like Açoka, or, *a fortiori*,
by ordinance, like Julian—the philosophy which was the staff of
Marcus's own private life;[4] and this negative service was certainly
the best that Stoicism could have received at the hands of its
Imperial professor. The Incas, too, notwithstanding their deliberate and systematic authoritarianism, had the wisdom to temper
tyranny with discretion in the execution of their religious policy;[5]

---

[1] This is possibly truer of the earlier than it is of the later Achaemenian emperors of
the House of Hystaspes; for a considerable departure from the strict demands of the
Zoroastrian Faith seems to be implied in the public patronage which was extended by
Artaxerxes II (*imperabat* 404–358 B.C.) to the worship of the goddess Anahita—a
divinity who may in form have been incorporated into the Zoroastrian system of
theology, but who was in fact a relic of the pre-Zoroastrian paganism which in all
probability continued, from beginning to end of the Achaemenian Age, to be the everyday religion of a majority of the Great King's Iranian kinsmen inside as well as outside
the frontiers of the Great King's dominions. While the Achaemenidae were thus
inclining to revert from the new 'higher religion' which had been adopted by their
House to an older paganism, the Magi, who, before the advent of the Prophet Zarathustra, had established a position for themselves as the hereditary priesthood of Iran,
and who had therefore at first seen in Zoroastrianism a menace to their own vested
interests, were reversing their original policy of opposition and were setting themselves
to capture a Zoroastrianism which they had found themselves unable to suppress (see
V. C (i) (*d*) 6 (δ), p. 542, above). Thus, in the Achaemenian Age, the Dynasty and the
Magi were already beginning to converge towards the common ground on the religious
plane that was to be the basis of their alliance on the political plane in the Sasanian
Age. The political influence which the Magi were eventually to exercise upon the
Sasanian Government does not, however, seem to have been acquired until after the
fall of the Achaemenian régime (Meyer, E.: *Geschichte des Altertums*, vol. iii (Stuttgart
1901, Cotta), p. 125).

[2] The persecution of the Egyptiac religion by Cambyses is the exception that proves
the rule; for Darius the Great took pains to efface the traces of Cambyses' subversive
work (see Meyer, E.: *Geschichte des Altertums*, vol. iii (Stuttgart 1901, Cotta), p. 163).

[3] See the present Annex, pp. 659–61, above.

[4] In assessing the motives of Marcus's abstention from philosophical propaganda it is
difficult to know how much weight to assign to a scrupulousness of the Achaemenian
kind and how much to the esoteric spirit of the Hellenic philosophers, who were mostly
content to allow their philosophy to remain caviare to the vulgar (see V. C (i) (*d*) 6 (δ),
pp. 559–62, above).

[5] For one piece of evidence see the present Annex, p. 694, footnote 3, above.
For the respect for local customs which was the general policy of the Incas, subject to
the imposition of certain common rules of life in the interest of establishing a framework of social uniformity, see Baudin, L.: *L'Empire Socialiste des Inka* (Paris 1928,
Institut d'Ethnologie), p. 62.

and we may conjecture that, if the Incaic Empire had been allowed to live out its natural term, this touch of latitudinarianism in the religious sphere would have stood the Incas in better stead than a fanaticism of the kind which was subsequently displayed in this same Andean World by the Incas' Spanish conquerors and successors in their efforts to impose their own Catholic Christianity upon the Incas' former subjects; for these Spanish efforts seem to have been as fruitless in reality as they have been successful in appearance. Nor had the 'Osmanli contemporaries of either the Inca Pachacutec (*imperabat circa* A.D. 1400–48) or the Safawī militarist Ismā'īl (*imperabat* A.D. 1500–24) or the Spanish King Philip II (*regnabat* A.D. 1556–98) or the Timurid Mughal Emperor Awrangzīb (*imperabat* A.D. 1659–1707) any cause to regret their own consistently maintained policy of tolerating, in conformity with the *Sheri'ah*, the religious practices and beliefs of the non-Muslim 'People of the Book' who had explicitly submitted to their rule; for the contrast between the long duration of the Ottoman régime and the swift discomfiture of each of those intolerant potentates gives the measure of the reward which the 'Osmanlis obtained for their persistence in resisting all temptations to treat their Christian subjects as the Spanish Crown treated its Muslim subjects and Shāh Ismā'īl his Sunnī subjects and Awrangzīb his Hindus.[1]

Perhaps the most remarkable, as well as the most honourable, examples of this politic forbearance from employing an autocrat's power in order to propagate the autocrat's religion are those in which a dynasty whose domestic faith has been on the point of triumphing by its own efforts over all the rival creeds has still refrained from dealing these defeated opponents their death-blow. In this magnanimous spirit the 'Abbasids refrained from anticipating the victory of Islam over Zoroastrianism and Nestorianism and Monophysitism in the dominions of the Caliphate,[2] while in the Indic World the Guptas similarly refrained from hastening the triumph of the rising Hinduism—which they themselves professed —over a Buddhism which was already declining towards its fall in the society which had brought it to birth. This generosity stands out in auspicious contrast to the implacable fanaticism with which,

---

[1] The exception which proves the rule of Ottoman tolerance is the massacre of the Anatolian Shī'īs in A.D. 1514 (see I. C (i) (*b*), Annex I, vol. i, pp. 302 and 384, above). But this atrocity was committed at a moment of great public danger and under an extreme provocation; and even Sultan Selīm I did not extend his persecution of the Shi'ah to his other non-Sunnī subjects—though there is a story that he did once try to trick his Sheykh-al-Islām into inadvertently sanctioning in advance a project which the Pādishāh had in mind for commanding all his Christian subjects—in utter contravention of the *Sheri'ah*—to embrace Islam under pain of death if they refused (for this story see V. C (ii) (*a*), vol. vi, p. 204, below).

[2] See p. 678, above, and V. C (ii) (*a*), vol. vi, p. 205, below.

in a dissolving Hellenic Society, a Gratian and a Theodosius and a Justinian pressed the pursuit of a retreating Paganism which was so manifestly incapable of rallying that Time could safely have been left to consummate the already assured victory of Christianity without any further aid from the autocrat's arm. In their behaviour in these circumstances it was assuredly the Hindu Guptas and the Muslim 'Abbasids, and not the Christian epigoni of Constantine the Great, who 'fulfilled' that 'which was spoken by Esaias the Prophet':

'Behold my servant, whom I uphold; mine elect, in whom my soul delighteth; I have put my spirit upon him: he shall bring forth judgment to the Gentiles. He shall not cry nor lift up nor cause his voice to be heard in the street. A bruised reed shall he not break, and the smoking flax shall he not quench: he shall bring forth judgment unto truth . . . and the isles shall wait for his law.'[1]

If we now pass from our survey of these rulers who have merely refrained from trying to force their own religion upon their subjects,[2] and proceed to review, in their turn, those other rulers who have gone to the length of embracing their subjects' religion in place of the faith which the ruler-converts have inherited from their own forebears, we may find it illuminating to arrange our examples to the best of our judgement in the descending order of their comparative sincerity.

---

[1] Isa. xlii. 1–4, quoted in Matt. xii. 18–21.
[2] In passing, we may take note of two sets of rulers who have not refrained from trying to force their own religion upon their subjects, but who have nevertheless acknowledged that, in principle, Religion ought not to be inculcated by political coercion, and who have tried to reconcile their liberal theory with their illiberal practice by representing that the rites which they have been constraining their subjects to perform are not really religious rites at all, but are simply civic ceremonies which can be carried out by anybody without giving any legitimate ground for conscientious scruples. This was the attitude taken up by the Roman Imperial authorities towards Christian citizens or subjects of the Empire who professed conscientious objections against performing the ritual of emperor-worship. The same attitude is taken up to-day by the Japanese Imperial authorities in regard to the ritual of State Shinto:
'In the case of a civilized country there must exist freedom of faith. If Shintō is a religion, however, the acceptance or refusal thereof must be left to personal choice. Yet for a Japanese subject to refuse to honour the ancestors of the Emperor is disloyal. Indeed, a Japanese out of his duty as subject must honour the ancestors of the Emperor. This cannot be a matter of choice. It is a duty. Therefore this cannot be regarded as a religion. It is a ritual. It is the ceremony of gratitude to ancestors. In this respect the Government protects the shrines and does not expound doctrines.' (Ariga, Nagao: 'Shintō as a State Religion' in *Tetsugaku Zasshi*, vol. xxv, No. 280 (June 1910), p. 702, quoted by Holtom, D. C.: *The National Faith of Japan: A Study in Modern Shintō* (London 1938, Kegan Paul), pp. 69–70.)
The question whether State Shinto is a religion, which is answered in the negative by the Japanese authority above quoted, is discussed by Holtom in op. cit., pp. 289–316, and is answered by this Western scholar in the affirmative:
'Modern Shrine Shintō is a thorough-going religion. It is the state religion of Japan. In it we discern an extraordinary example of the survival, in the culture of the present day, of a form of national worship which presents interesting parallels with the state religions that dominated the civilizations of Western Asia and the Mediterranean area thousands of years ago' (p. 306).
Holtom's view is shared by Kato, Genchi: *A Study of Shinto, the Religion of the Japanese Nation* (Tokyo 1926, Meiji Japan Society), pp. 2–3.

On this criterion we shall perhaps be inclined to head our list with the Roman Emperor Constantine the Great and with the Sinic Emperor Han Wuti; for, however much Constantine in embracing Christianity, and Wuti in embracing Confucianism,[1] may have gained—and foreseen that he would gain—politically, those modern Western historians who see in the alleged conversion of these two emperors nothing more than a cynically calculated piece of hypocrisy[2] are assuredly guilty of a gross psychological anachronism in attributing to the children of a disintegrating Hellenic and a disintegrating Sinic Society a modern Western behaviour which is manifestly incompatible with the spirit of the time and place in which these alleged hypocrites actually lived. It seems far more probable that, if either Constantine or Wuti had been aware in his own heart that he was not acting in good faith, he would have found himself unable to keep up in the sight of his subjects a pretence with which he had ceased to be able to delude his own understanding. And therefore, when we have to explain to ourselves why Constantine did—after a previous declaration of allegiance to his ancestral tutelary deity Sol Invictus[3]—eventually come to the conclusion that it was his duty as a Roman Emperor 'so far to disavow Rome's past as himself to adopt' a Christianity which was 'professed by perhaps one-tenth of his subjects',[4] we

---

[1] For the Constantinian part which was played by Han Wuti in securing the adoption of Confucianism as the official philosophy of the Sinic universal state see Franke, O.: *Geschichte des Chinesischen Reiches*, vol. i (Berlin and Leipzig 1930, de Gruyter), pp. 295–320, and the present Study, V. C (i) (d) 4, in the present volume, pp. 418–19, and the present Annex, p. 654, above. In this partnership it was not the pliant temporal power but the triumphant philosophy that was the loser. A Confucianism that was already becoming intellectually debased as a result of the social *pammixia* in the Sinic universal state (see V. C (i) (d) 6 (δ), pp. 549 and 555–6, and the present Annex, pp. 654–5, above) was now also spiritually sterilized through being made official (Hackmann, H.: *Chinesische Philosophie* (Munich 1927, Reinhardt), p. 235).

[2] This seems, for example, to be Franke's opinion, to judge by the following passage in op. cit., vol. i, pp. 318–19:
'A remote resemblance may be discerned between the respective positions of the Emperor Constantine and his successors, down to Theodosius the Great, in the Roman Empire in the fourth century, and of Kaoti and his successors, down to Wuti, in the Chinese Empire. Both found themselves confronted by a spiritual movement— Christianity in the one case and Confucianism in the other—with which they were forced to come to a reckoning. Both, in their own hearts, to start with, even if they were not positively inclined to reject this movement, were at any rate without any special penchant towards it: Constantine did not have himself baptized till he was on his death-bed. ... Gratian and Theodosius were the first Roman emperors to confer an exclusive legality and right of protection in the Empire upon the orthodox Christian creed, while we have already seen what the Han emperors' attitude was towards Confucianism. Both, however, were constrained by political circumstances to repress their personal feelings. The Roman Empire became Christian, and the Chinese Confucian.'
This equation of Wuti's attitude towards Confucianism with the fanatical intolerance of Gratian's and Theodosius's devotion to Christianity seems as questionable as the associated equation of Constantine's attitude towards Christianity with the contemptuous hostility which was publicly displayed towards Confucianism by Liu Pang [= Kaoti] according to the evidence that has been cited in this Annex, on p. 654, above, upon the authority of Dr. Hu Shih.

[3] See the present Annex, pp. 650 and 693–4, above.

[4] Baynes, N. H.: *Constantine the Great and the Christian Church* (London 1929, Milford), p. 4.

shall perhaps show ourselves both better psychologists and better historians if we seek an explanation which does not call in question the imperial convert's sincerity. We may make bold to conjecture that the determining consideration that moved Constantine to make a new departure which was apparently hazardous, and was certainly sensational, was the abiding effect of the impression that had been made upon him as a younger man by the experience of witnessing, at close quarters, the indomitable bearing of the Christian Church under the searching ordeal of the Galerian persecution.[1]

The historical sense that warns us against attributing the conversion of a Constantine or a Wuti to motives that are anachronistically cynical will commend an even greater caution in interpreting in terms of an ephemerally and parochially modern Western attitude to life the conversions of barbarian conquerors who have been far less sophisticated than those converted rulers of universal states into whose derelict heritage these barbarians have forced an entry. In other contexts[2] we have observed that the barbarian conquerors who are converted promptly and outright from their primitive paganism to a 'higher religion' that is prevalent among their more civilized subjects are apt to be rewarded by being given a leading part to play in subsequent history; and we have also observed that the maxim 'Better late than never' holds good in this case, since the pagan or heretical barbarian rulers of 'successor-states' who capitulate to the established local orthodoxy at any time down to the eleventh hour are apt at any rate to escape destruction—even if they may have irretrievably forfeited their chances of achieving greatness—whereas the more stiff-necked barbarians who obstinately persist in their ancestral paganism or heresy are apt to pay the prohibitive price of ejection or annihilation. On this showing, a speedy and thorough-going conversion to the faith of his subjects is the barbarian conqueror's best policy from the standpoint of his own material interests; and yet it would be unwarrantable to assume that this has actually been the usual motive in the minds of those barbarians who have in fact undergone conversion before suffering the penalty for recalcitrance. For one thing, not one of these barbarian converts to a 'higher religion' has had the opportunity to acquaint himself with the array of precedents from which the historian's rational induction

[1] Our own contemporary the Chinese 'Christian General' Fêng Yu-hsiang is said to have been converted as a result of having witnessed, as a young man, the martyrdom of Western Christian missionaries during the 'Boxer' insurrection of A.D. 1899–1900.

[2] e.g., in V. C (i) (c) 4, pp. 355–7, above, in general, and also in I. C (i) (b), Annex I, vol. i, pp. 363–4; II. D (vi), vol. ii, p. 145; and III. A, Annex II, vol. iii, pp. 429, 439, and 450, in regard to the particular case of the conversion to Islam of the epigoni of the Mongol conquerors of Dār-al-Islām.

is laboriously extracted; but it is still more pertinent to reflect that, even if these data could be placed at the barbarian's disposal by some extraordinary *tour de force*, he would usually be unable and unwilling to turn them to account because he is both destitute of the training and innocent of the taste for making the cynical calculations of *Realpolitik*.[1]

No doubt there have been individual exceptions to this general rule of barbarian 'mentality' and behaviour. For example, when we observe that the pagan Frankish war-lord Clovis announced his conversion to the Catholic Christianity of the native population of Gaul on the eve of his wars of aggression against the Arian Burgundians and Visigoths who were then still in occupation of the lion's share of the Gallic spoils of the Roman Empire, it is difficult to resist the suspicion that the barbarian mind of the covetous Frankish interloper was making the same Machiavellian calculations as are known to have been made in similar circumstances by the sophisticated minds of an Henri IV and a Napoleon Bonaparte. An exceptional political precocity may be one of those 'sports' that are part of the order of Nature; and our suspicion that Clovis may in fact have been a modern Western statesman born a thousand years before his due Transalpine date[2] is supported by the fact—which we have noticed already in another connexion[3]— that, in spite of the brilliance of his achievements and the importance of their historical effects, the founder of the Frankish power has not become one of the heroes of the Teutonic Epic. It looks as though there was some element in Clovis' character and career which had chilled the imagination and baffled the skill of the minstrels who created the 'heroic' poetry of the barbarian society in which Clovis 'lived and moved'; and this intractable something may have consisted precisely in the fact that this vulgarly successful barbarian 'had his being' in a forbiddingly alien intellectual and moral clime. If, however, this is really Clovis' case, it is probably an exceptional one. For the most part it seems likely that the barbarian converts to the ruling religious orthodoxy of their time and place have been moved far less strongly by conscious calculations of political expediency than by the glamour and prestige

---

[1] The barbarian war-lord may be exonerated from the imputation of being an addict to the vices of Civilization, without being idealized as 'the noble savage'. The sentimental and the 'realistic' portraits of him are equally out of focus, because each, in its way, is an attempt to depict him in modern Western dress. The barbarian who has entered by conquest into a disintegrating civilization's derelict heritage is prone, as we shall find (in Part VIII, below), to lose his *moral*; but the demoralization to which he succumbs is of a kind that is peculiar to the barbarian's own self in these particular circumstances.

[2] In Italy, in contrast to the Transalpine parts of Western Christendom, Clovis' *Realpolitik* would have been a normal phenomenon within eight hundred years of Clovis' actual date.

[3] See V. C (i) (c) 3, Annex III, pp. 610 and 612–14, above.

of a culture which has not lost its power to captivate their imaginations and to daunt their spirits even after they have proved themselves more than a match for it in sheer physical force.[1]

In order to find unquestionably authentic examples of a consciously cynical and deliberately calculating attempt to reap political profit by putting the principle of *Religio Regionis Religio Regis* into practice, we must descend to the Modern Age of a Western or Westernized Society; and in naming Henri IV and Napoleon I we have already recalled two of the outstanding cases in point that are to be found in this modern Western field. It only remains to mention the British practice[2]—which has been current by now for two hundred and fifty years and which is not the outcome of either conscious cynicism or deliberate calculation—of having in the sovereign of the United Kingdom a common member of the Episcopalian Established Church of England and of the Presbyterian Established Church of Scotland, so that, on whichever side of the Border he may happen to be resident at any moment, the King always finds himself at home in matters ecclesiastical as well as in matters secular.[3] This thorough-going application of the principle of *Religio Regionis Religio Regis*[4] has worked as well—at any rate from the political standpoint—for the last two and a half centuries as the previous attempts to regulate the ecclesiastical relations between England and Scotland on the principle of *Cujus Regio Ejus Religio* worked badly during the eighty-six years that intervened between the accession of King James VI of Scotland to the English throne and that of Prince William of Orange to the thrones of both kingdoms. The ecclesiastical status of the Crown that has resulted from the politico-ecclesiastical settlement achieved between A.D. 1688 and A.D. 1707 has indeed been the palladium of the Constitution of the United Kingdom ever since; for the formal equality at law between the respective ecclesiastical establishments of the two kingdoms has been symbolized, in a fashion that can be 'understanded of the people' on both sides of the Border, in the visible fact that, on both sides alike, the King

[1] For example, it was no doubt the spiritual and cultural potency of the Mahāyāna, and not any mental operations of political arithmetic, that led to the conversion of the To Pa barbarian conquerors of one of the northern marches of the Sinic universal state at a moment when, as a matter of statistical fact, the Mahāyāna was already the established religion of some nine-tenths of these barbarian conquerors' native Sinic subjects (for this estimate see Eliot, Sir Ch.: *Hinduism and Buddhism* (London 1921, Arnold, 3 vols.), vol. iii, pp. 249–50).

[2] Touched upon already in V. C (i) (*d*) 6 (δ), pp. 533–4, above.

[3] This has only latterly been a matter of practical importance, since no king or queen ever set foot in Scotland during the first 133 out of the 250 years in question (A.D. 1688–1938).

[4] *Religio Regionis Religio Regis*, but not *Religio Regionis Religio Civis*, since, in both England and Scotland during the period in question, the toleration of dissent has been as much a part of the politico-religious constitution of the country as has been the establishment of the two churches that are severally established in the two kingdoms.

professes a religion which is the officially established (though no longer the exclusively tolerated) religion of the land; and this palpably assured sense of ecclesiastical equality, which is itself the fruit of a spirit of mutual toleration in matters of religion, has provided the psychological foundation for a free and equal political union between two kingdoms which had previously been alienated from one another by a long tradition of hostility and which have never ceased to be differentiated by a wide disparity in area, population, and wealth. The successful negotiation of these formidable obstacles to a union of Scottish and English hearts is a political *tour de force* that is the *chef d'œuvre* of British statesmanship; and by the same token it may be taken as the culminating and decisive proof of our present thesis that *Religio Regionis Religio Regis* is a politically more profitable maxim than *Cujus Regio Ejus Religio* for princes to take as the cue for their ecclesiastical policy.